MOUS
Access 2000
Exam Prep

Lisa Friedrichsen

The Coriolis Group, LLC
14455 N. Hayden Road, Suite 220
Scottsdale, Arizona 85260

480/483-0192
FAX 480/483-0193
http://www.coriolis.com

ISBN: 1-57610-479-6

Library of Congress Card Number: 00-025157

President, CEO
Keith Weiskamp

Publisher
Steve Sayre

Acquisitions Editor
Jeff Kellum

Marketing Manager
Cynthia Caldwell

Product Managers
Sharon Sanchez McCarson
Rebecca VanEsselstine

Production Editors
Kim Eoff
Elena Montillo

Editorial Assistants
Hilary Long
Stacy Parillo

Cover Design
Jesse Dunn

Layout Design
Joseph Lee
April Nielsen

CD-ROM Developer
Robert Clarfield

CORIOLIS™

14455 North Hayden Road • Suite 220 • Scottsdale, Arizona 85260

Coriolis: The Smartest Way To Get Certified™

To help you reach your goals, we've listened to readers like you, and we've designed our entire product line around you and the way you like to study, learn, and master challenging subjects.

In addition to our highly popular *Exam Cram* and *Exam Prep* books, we offer several other products to help you pass certification exams. Our *Practice Tests* and *Flash Cards* are designed to make your studying fun and productive. Our *Audio Reviews* have received rave reviews from our customers— and they're the perfect way to make the most of your drive time!

The newest way to get certified is the *Exam Cram Personal Trainer* —a highly interactive, personalized self-study course based on the best-selling *Exam Cram* series. It's the first certification-specific product to completely link a customizable learning tool, exclusive *Exam Cram* content, and multiple testing techniques so you can study what, how, and when you want.

Exam Cram Insider —a biweekly newsletter containing the latest in certification news, study tips, and announcements from Certification Insider Press—gives you an ongoing look at the hottest certification programs. (To subscribe, send an email to eci@coriolis.com and type "subscribe insider" in the body of the email.) We also sponsor the Certified Crammer Society and the Coriolis Help Center—two other resources that will help you get certified even faster!

Help us continue to provide the very best certification study materials possible. Write us or email us at cipq@coriolis.com and let us know how our books have helped you study. Tell us about new features that you'd like us to add. Send us a story about how we've helped you; if we use it in one of our books, we'll send you an official Coriolis shirt!

Good luck with your certification exam and your career. Thank you for allowing us to help you achieve your goals.

Keith Weiskamp

Keith Weiskamp
President and CEO

Preface

Welcome to *MOUS Access 2000 Exam Prep*. This highly visual book offers users a comprehensive hands-on introduction to Microsoft Access 2000 and also serves as an excellent reference for future use.

▶ Organization and Coverage

This text contains sixteen units that cover basic Access skills. In these units, you learn how to create, format, and use Access databases, including tables, queries, forms, and reports.

▶ About this Approach

What makes this approach so effective at teaching software skills? It's quite simple. Each skill is presented on two facing pages, with the step-by-step instructions on the left page, and large screen illustrations on the right. You can focus on a single skill without having to turn the page. This unique design makes information extremely accessible and easy to absorb, and provides a great reference.

Each unit, or "information display," contains the following elements:

Each 2-page spread focuses on a single skill.

Clear step-by-step directions explain how to complete the specific task. When you follow the numbered steps, you quickly learn how each procedure is performed and what the results will be.

Concise text that introduces the basic principles discussed in the lesson. Procedures are easier to learn when concepts fit into a framework.

Unit A
Access 2000

Viewing the Database Window

When you start Access and open a database, the **database window** displays common Windows elements such as a title bar, menu bar, and toolbar. Clicking the Objects or Groups buttons on the Objects bar alternatively expands and collapses that section of the database window. If all the objects don't display in the expanded section, click the small arrow at the top or bottom of the section to scroll the list. The **Objects** area displays the seven types of objects that can be accessed by clicking the object type you want. The **Groups** area displays other commonly used files and folders, such as the Favorites folder. **Scenario** ➤ John explores the MediaLoft-A database.

Steps

1. Look at each of the Access window elements shown in Figure A-7
   The Objects bar on the left side of the database window displays the seven object types. The other elements of the database window are summarized in Table A-3. Because the Tables object is selected, the buttons you need to create a new table or to work with the existing table are displayed in the MediaLoft-A Database window.

   QuickTip

   Your menu commands may look different depending on which window or object is

2. Click **File** on the menu bar
   The File menu contains commands for opening a new or existing database, saving a database in a variety of formats, and printing. The menu commands vary depending on which window or database object is currently in use.

3. Point to **Edit** on the menu bar, point to **View**, point to **Insert**, point to **Tools**, point to **Window**, point to **Help**, move the pointer off the menu, then press **[Esc]** twice
   All menus close when you press [Esc]. Pressing [Esc] a second time deselects the menu.

4. Point to the **New button** on the Database toolbar
   Pointing to a toolbar button causes a descriptive **ScreenTip** to automatically appear, providing a short description of the button. The buttons on the toolbars represent the most commonly used Access features. Toolbar buttons change just as menu options change depending on which window and database object are currently in use.

5. Point to the **Open button** on the Database toolbar, then point to the **Save button** on the Database toolbar
   Sometimes toolbar buttons or menu options are dimmed which means that they are currently unavailable. For example, the Save button is dimmed because it doesn't make sense to save the MediaLoft-A database right now because you haven't made any changes to it yet.

6. Click **Queries** on the Objects bar
   The query object window provides several ways to create a new query and displays the names of previously created queries, as shown in Figure A-8. There are three previously created query objects displayed within the MediaLoft-A Database window.

7. Click **Forms** on the Objects bar, then click **Reports** on the Objects bar
   The MediaLoft-A database contains the Customers table, three queries, a customer entry form, and three reports.

CLUES TO USE

Viewing objects

You can change the way you view the objects in the database window by clicking the last four buttons on the toolbar. You can view the objects as Large Icons, Small Icons, in a List (this is the default view), and with Details. The Details view shows a longer description of the object, as well as the date the object was last modified and the date it was originally created.

▶ ACCESS A-8 **GETTING STARTED WITH ACCESS 2000**

Hints as well as trouble-shooting advice, right where you need it – next to the step itself.

Clues to Use boxes provide concise information that either expands on one component of the major lesson skill or describes an independent task that is in some way related to the major lesson skill.

Every lesson features large-size, two-color representations of what your screen should look like after completing the numbered steps.

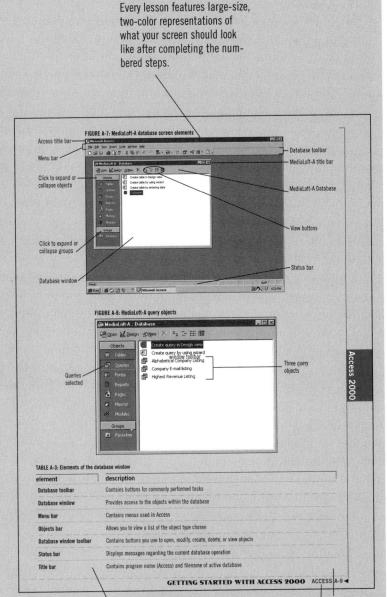

FIGURE A-7: MediaLoft-A database screen elements

Access title bar
Menu bar
Click to expand or collapse objects
Click to expand or collapse groups
Database window

Database toolbar
MediaLoft-A title bar
MediaLoft-A Database
View buttons
Status bar

FIGURE A-8: MediaLoft-A query objects

Queries selected

window toolbar
Three query objects

TABLE A-3: Elements of the database window

element	description
Database toolbar	Contains buttons for commonly performed tasks
Database window	Provides access to the objects within the database
Menu bar	Contains menus used in Access
Objects bar	Allows you to view a list of the object type chosen
Database window toolbar	Contains buttons you use to open, modify, create, delete, or view objects
Status bar	Displays messages regarding the current database operation
Title bar	Contains program name (Access) and filename of active database

GETTING STARTED WITH ACCESS 2000 ACCESS A-9 ◀

Quickly accessible summaries of key terms, toolbar buttons, or keyboard alternatives connected with the lesson material. You can refer easily to this information when working on Your own projects at a later time.

The page numbers are designed like a road map. ACCESS indicates the Access section, A indicates the first unit, and 9 indicates the page within the unit.

Features

The two-page lesson format featured in this book provides the new user with a powerful learning experience. Additionally, this book contains the following features:

▶ **MOUS Certification Coverage**
Each unit opener has a ⌐MOUS⌐ next to it to indicate where Microsoft Office User Specialist (MOUS) skills are covered. The first eight units of this book prepare you for the Access 2000 MOUS Exam, and the complete book covers the skills needed to pass the Access 2000 Expert MOUS exam.

▶ **End of Unit Material**
Each unit concludes with a Concepts Review that tests your understanding of what you learned in the unit. The Concepts Review is followed by a Skills Review, which provides you with additional hands-on practice of the skills. The Visual Workshops that follow the Skills Review helps you develop critical thinking skills. You are shown completed Web pages or screens and are asked to recreate them from scratch.

Access 2000

Contents At A Glance

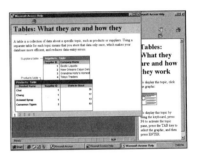

Getting
Started with Access 2000

Objectives

- ▶ **Define database software**
- ▶ **Learn database terminology**
- ▶ **Start Access and open a database**
- ▶ **View the database window**
- ▶ **Navigate records**
- ▶ **Enter records**
- ▶ **Edit records**
- ▶ **Preview and print a datasheet**
- ▶ **Get Help and exit Access**

In this unit, you will learn the purpose, advantages, and terminology of Microsoft Access 2000, a database software. You will also learn how to open a database and how to use the different elements of the Access window. You'll learn how to get help. You'll learn how to navigate through a database, enter and update data, and preview and print data. **Scenario** ▶ John Kim is the director of shipping at MediaLoft, a nationwide chain of bookstore cafés that sells books, music, and videos. Recently, MediaLoft switched to Access from an index card system for storing and maintaining customer information. John will use Access to enter and maintain this critical information for MediaLoft.

Defining Database Software

Microsoft Access 2000 is a database software program that runs on Windows. **Database software** is used to manage data that can be organized into lists of related information, such as customers, products, vendors, employees, projects, or sales. Many small companies record customer, inventory, and sales information in a spreadsheet program such as Microsoft Excel. While this electronic format is more productive than writing information on index cards, Excel still lacks many of the database advantages provided by Access. Refer to Table A-1 for a comparison of the two programs. **Scenario** John reviews the advantages that database software has over a manual index card system.

Data entry is faster and easier

Before inexpensive microcomputers, small businesses used manual paper systems, such as index cards, to record each customer, sale, and inventory item as illustrated in Figure A-1. Using an electronic database such as Access, you can create on-screen data entry forms, which make managing a database easier, more accurate, and more efficient than using index cards.

Information retrieval is faster and easier

Retrieving information on an index card system is tedious because the cards have to be physically handled, sorted, and stored. Also, one error in filing can cause serious retrieval problems later. With Access you can quickly search for, display, and print information on customers, sales, or inventory.

Information can be viewed and sorted in multiple ways

A card system allows you to sort the cards in only one order, unless the cards are duplicated for a second arrangement. Customer and inventory cards were generally sorted alphabetically by name. Sales index cards were usually sorted by date. In this system, complete customer and product information was recorded on each of their individual cards as well as on the corresponding sale cards. This quickly compromises data accuracy. Access allows you to view or sort the information from one or more subjects simultaneously. For example, you might want to know all the customers who purchased a particular product or all the products purchased by a particular customer. A change made to the data in one view of Access is automatically updated in every other view or report.

Information is more secure

Index cards can be torn, misplaced, and stolen. There is no password required to read them, and a disaster, such as a flood or fire, could completely destroy them. You can back up an Access database file on a regular basis and store the file at an offsite location. You can also password protect data so only those users with appropriate security clearances can view or manipulate the data.

Information can be shared among several users

An index card system is limited to those users who can physically reach it. If one user keeps a card for an extended period of time, then others cannot use or update that information. Access databases are inherently multiuser. More than one person can be entering, updating, and using the data at the same time.

Duplicate data entry is minimized

The index card system requires that the user duplicate the customer and product information on each sales card. With Access, you only need to enter each piece of information once. Figure A-2 shows a possible structure for an Access database to record sales.

FIGURE A-1: Using index cards to organize sales data

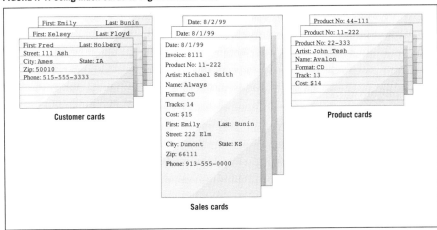

Customer cards

Sales cards

Product cards

FIGURE A-2: Using Access, an electronic relational database, to organize sales data

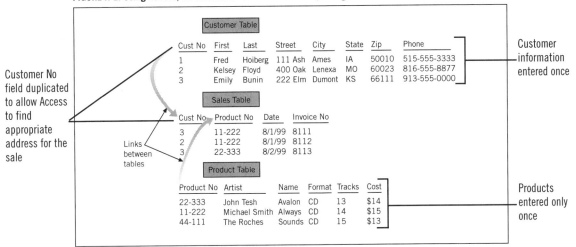

Customer No field duplicated to allow Access to find appropriate address for the sale

Links between tables

Customer information entered once

Products entered only once

TABLE A-1: Comparing Excel to Access

feature	Excel	Access
Layout	Provides a natural tabular layout for easy data entry	Provides a spreadsheet "view" as well as forms which arrange data in a variety of ways
Storage	Limited to approximately 65,000 records per sheet	Able to store any number of records up to 2 gigabytes
Linked tables	Manages single lists of information	Allows links between lists of information to reduce data entry redundancy
Reporting	Limited to a spreadsheet printout	Provides sophisticated reporting features such as multiple headers and footers and calculations on groups of records
Security	Very limited	Each user can be given access to only the records and fields they need
Multiuser capabilities	Does not allow multiple users to simultaneously enter and update data	Allows multiple users to simultaneously enter and update data
Data entry screens	Provides limited data entry screens	Provides the ability to create extensive data entry screens called forms

Learning Database Terminology

To become familiar with Access, you need to understand basic database terminology. Scenario▶ John reviews the terms and concepts that define a database.

Details

 A **database** is a collection of information associated with a topic (for example, sales of products to customers). The smallest piece of information in a database is called a **field**, or category of information, such as the customer's name, city, state, or phone number. A **key field** is a field that contains unique information for each record. A group of related fields, such as all demographic information for one customer, is called a **record**. In Access, a collection of records for a single subject, such as all of the customer records, is called a **table**, as shown in Figure A-3.

 An Access database is a **relational database**, in which more than one table, such as the Customer, Sales, and Product tables, can share information. The term "relational database" comes from the fact that two tables are linked, or related, by a common field.

 Tables, therefore, are the most important **object** in an Access database because they contain all of the data within the database. An Access database may also contain six other objects, which serve to enhance the usability and value of the data. The objects in an Access database are tables, queries, forms, reports, pages, macros, and modules, and they are summarized in Table A-2.

 Data can be entered and edited in four of the objects: tables, queries, forms, and pages. The relationship between tables, queries, forms, and reports is shown in Figure A-4. Regardless of how the data is entered, it is physically stored in a table object. Data can be printed from a table, query, form, page, or report object. The macro and module objects are used to provide additional database productivity and automation features. All of the objects (except for the page objects, which are used to create Web pages) are stored in one database file.

TABLE A-2: Access objects and their purpose

object	purpose
Table	Contains all of the raw data within the database in a spreadsheet-like view; tables can be linked with a common field to share information and therefore minimize data redundancy
Query	Provides a spreadsheet-like view of the data similar to tables, but a query can be designed to provide the user with a subset of fields or records from one or more tables; queries are created when a user has a "question" about the data in the database
Form	Provides an easy-to-use data entry screen, which generally shows only one record at a time
Report	Provides a professional printout of data that may contain enhancements such as headers, footers, and calculations on groups of records
Page	Creates Web pages from Access objects as well as provides Web page connectivity features to an Access database, also called Data Access Page
Macro	Stores a collection of keystrokes or commands, such as printing several reports or displaying a toolbar when a form opens
Module	Stores Visual Basic programming code that extends the functions and automated processes of Access

FIGURE A-3: Tables contain fields and records

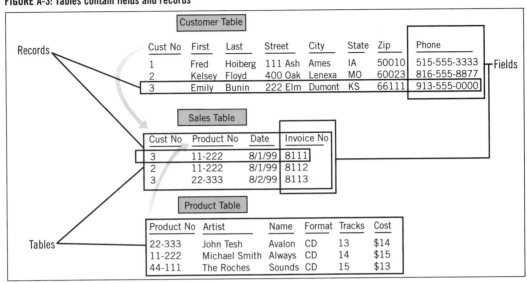

FIGURE A-4: The relationship between Access objects

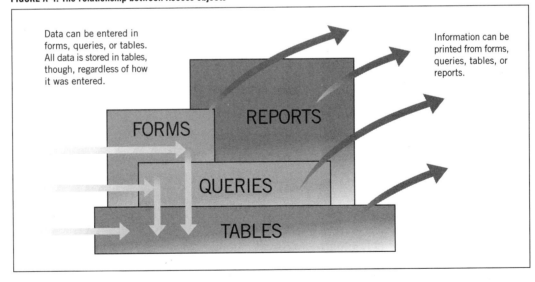

Data can be entered in forms, queries, or tables. All data is stored in tables, though, regardless of how it was entered.

Information can be printed from forms, queries, tables, or reports.

Starting Access and Opening a Database

Access 2000

You can start Access by clicking the Access icon on the Windows desktop or on the Microsoft Office Shortcut Bar. Since not all computers will provide a shortcut icon on the desktop or display the Office Shortcut Bar, you can always find Access by clicking the Start button on the taskbar, pointing to Programs, and then choosing Access from the Programs menu. You can open a database from within Access or by finding the database file on the desktop, in My Computer, or in Windows Explorer, and then opening it. **Scenario** John starts Access and opens the MediaLoft-A database.

1. Click the **Start button** 🏁**Start** on the taskbar

The Start button is in the lower-left corner of the taskbar. You can use the Start menu to start any program on your computer.

Trouble?

If you can't locate Microsoft Access on the Programs menu, point to the Microsoft Office group and look for Access there.

2. Point to **Programs**

Access is generally located on the Programs menu. All the programs, or applications, stored on your computer can be found here.

3. Click **Microsoft Access**

Access opens and displays the Access dialog box, from which you can start a new database or open an existing file.

QuickTip

Make a copy of your Project Disk before you use it.

4. Insert your Project Disk in the appropriate disk drive

To complete the units in this book, you need a Project Disk. See your instructor or technical support person for assistance.

5. Click **More Files**, then click **OK**

The Open dialog box appears, as shown in Figure A-5. Depending on the databases and folders stored on your computer, your dialog box may look slightly different.

Trouble?

These lessons assume your Project Disk is in drive A. If you are using a different drive, substitute that drive for drive A in the steps.

6. Click the **Look in list arrow**, then click **3½ Floppy (A:)**

A list of the files on your Project Disk appears in the Open dialog box.

7. Click the **MediaLoft-A** database file, click **Open**, then click the **Maximize button** on the title bar if the Access window does not fill the screen

The MediaLoft-A database opens as shown in Figure A-6.

Personalized toolbars and menus in Office 2000

Office 2000 toolbars and menus modify themselves to your working style. The toolbars you see when you first start a program include the most frequently used buttons. To locate a button not visible on a toolbar, click the More Buttons button at the end of the toolbar to see the list of additional toolbar buttons. As you work, the program adds the buttons you use to the visible toolbars and moves the buttons you haven't used in a while to the More Buttons list. Similarly, menus adjust to your work habits. Short menus appear when you first click a menu command. To view additional menu commands, point to the double-arrow at the bottom of the menu, leave the pointer on the menu name after you've clicked the menu, or double-click the menu name. If you select a command that's not on the short menu, the program automatically adds it to the short menus. You can return personalized toolbars and menus to their original settings by clicking Tools on the menu bar, then clicking Customize. On the Options tab in the Customize dialog box, click Reset my usage data, click Yes to close the alert box, then close the Customize dialog box. Resetting usage data erases changes made automatically to your menus and toolbars. It does not affect the options you customize.

FIGURE A-5: Open dialog box

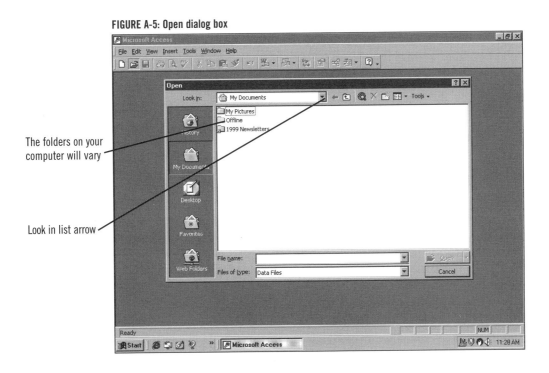

The folders on your computer will vary

Look in list arrow

FIGURE A-6: MediaLoft-A database

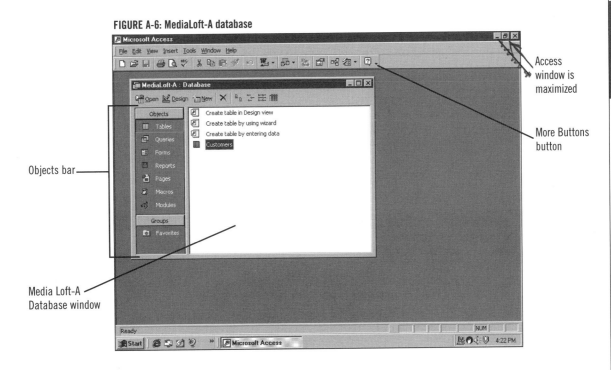

Access window is maximized

More Buttons button

Objects bar

Media Loft-A Database window

Viewing the Database Window

When you start Access and open a database, the **database window** displays common Windows elements such as a title bar, menu bar, and toolbar. Clicking the Objects or Groups buttons on the Objects bar alternatively expands and collapses that section of the database window. If all the objects don't display in the expanded section, click the small arrow at the top or bottom of the section to scroll the list. The **Objects** area displays the seven types of objects that can be accessed by clicking the object type you want. The **Groups** area displays other commonly used files and folders, such as the Favorites folder. **Scenario** John explores the MediaLoft-A database.

Steps

1. **Look at each of the Access window elements shown in Figure A-7**
   The Objects bar on the left side of the database window displays the seven object types. The other elements of the database window are summarized in Table A-3. Because the Tables object is selected, the buttons you need to create a new table or to work with the existing table are displayed in the MediaLoft-A Database window.

2. **Click File on the menu bar**
   The File menu contains commands for opening a new or existing database, saving a database in a variety of formats, and printing. The menu commands vary depending on which window or database object is currently in use.

3. **Point to Edit on the menu bar, point to View, point to Insert, point to Tools, point to Window, point to Help, move the pointer off the menu, then press [Esc] twice**
   All menus close when you press [Esc]. Pressing [Esc] a second time deselects the menu.

4. **Point to the New button ☐ on the Database toolbar**
   Pointing to a toolbar button causes a descriptive **ScreenTip** to automatically appear, providing a short description of the button. The buttons on the toolbars represent the most commonly used Access features. Toolbar buttons change just as menu options change depending on which window and database object are currently in use.

5. **Point to the Open button 🖼 on the Database toolbar, then point to the Save button 🖫 on the Database toolbar**
   Sometimes toolbar buttons or menu options are dimmed which means that they are currently unavailable. For example, the Save button is dimmed because it doesn't make sense to save the MediaLoft-A database right now because you haven't made any changes to it yet.

6. **Click Queries on the Objects bar**
   The query object window provides several ways to create a new query and displays the names of previously created queries, as shown in Figure A-8. There are three previously created query objects displayed within the MediaLoft-A Database window.

7. **Click Forms on the Objects bar, then click Reports on the Objects bar**
   The MediaLoft-A database contains the Customers table, three queries, a customer entry form, and three reports.

Viewing objects

You can change the way you view the objects in the database window by clicking the last four buttons on the toolbar. You can view the objects as Large Icons 🔲, Small Icons 🔳, in a List 🔳 (this is the default view), and with Details 🔳. The Details view shows a longer description of the object, as well as the date the object was last modified and the date it was originally created.

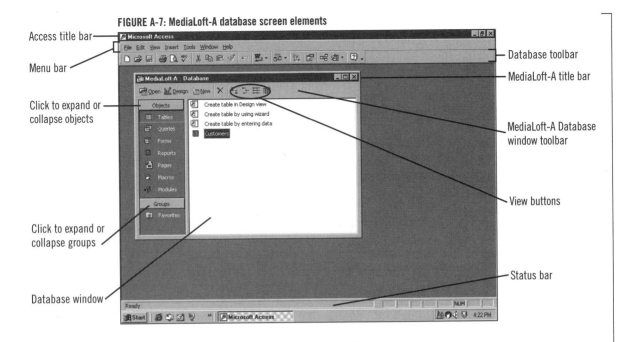

FIGURE A-7: MediaLoft-A database screen elements

Access title bar
Menu bar
Click to expand or collapse objects
Click to expand or collapse groups
Database window

Database toolbar
MediaLoft-A title bar
MediaLoft-A Database window toolbar
View buttons
Status bar

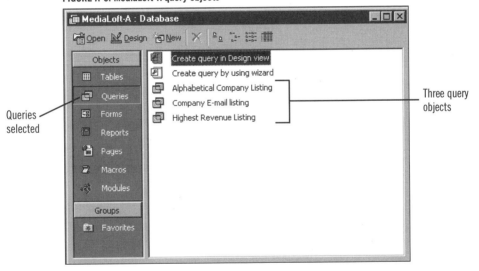

FIGURE A-8: MediaLoft-A query objects

Queries selected

Three query objects

TABLE A-3: Elements of the database window

element	description
Database toolbar	Contains buttons for commonly performed tasks
Database window	Provides access to the objects within the database
Menu bar	Contains menus used in Access
Objects bar	Allows you to view a list of the object type chosen
Database window toolbar	Contains buttons you use to open, modify, create, delete, or view objects
Status bar	Displays messages regarding the current database operation
Title bar	Contains program name (Access) and file name of active database

Navigating Records

Your ability to navigate through the fields and records of a database is key to your productivity and success with the database. You navigate through the information in **Navigation mode** in the table's **datasheet**, a spreadsheet-like grid that displays fields as columns and records as rows. **Scenario** John opens the database and reviews the table containing information about MediaLoft's customers.

QuickTip

You can also double-click an object to open it.

1. **Click Tables on the Objects bar, click Customers, then click the Open button 📖 on the MediaLoft-A Database window toolbar**
   The datasheet for the Customers table opens, as shown in Figure A-9. The datasheet contains 27 customer records with 13 fields of information for each record. **Field names** are listed at the top of each column. The number of the selected record in the datasheet is displayed in the **Specific Record box** at the bottom of the datasheet window. Depending on the size of your monitor and the resolution of your computer system, you may see a different number of fields. If all of the fields don't display, you can scroll to the right to see the rest.

2. **Press [Tab] to move to Sprint**
   Sprint is the entry in the second field, Company, of the first record.

3. **Press [Enter]**
   The data, Aaron, is selected in the third field, First. Pressing either [Tab] or [Enter] moves the focus to the next field. **Focus** refers to which field would be edited if you started typing.

4. **Press [↓]**
   The focus moves to the Kelsey entry in the First field of the second record. The **current record symbol** in the **record selector box** also identifies which record you are navigating. The Next Record and Previous Record **navigation buttons** can also be used to navigate the datasheet.

5. **Press [Ctrl][End]**
   The focus moves to the last field of the last record. You can also use the Last Record navigation button to move to the last record.

6. **Press [Ctrl][Home]**
   The focus moves to the first field of the first record. You can also use the First Record navigation button to move to the first record. A complete listing of navigation keystrokes to move the focus between fields and records is shown in Table A-4.

Changing to Edit mode

If you click a field with the mouse pointer instead of pressing the [Tab] or [Enter] to navigate through the datasheet, you change from Navigation mode to **Edit mode**. In Edit mode, Access assumes that you are trying to edit that particular field, so keystrokes such as [Ctrl][End], [Ctrl][Home], [←], and [→] move the insertion point *within* the field. To return to Navigation mode, press [Tab] or [Enter] which moves the focus to the next field, or press [↑] or [↓] which moves the focus to a different record.

FIGURE A-9: Customers datasheet

Current record symbol

Current focus

Records

Record selector box

Specific Record box

Navigation buttons

Field name

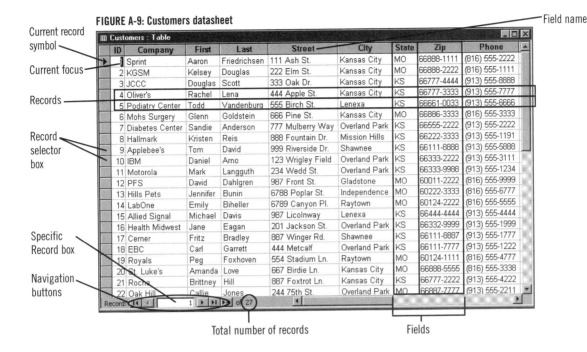

Total number of records

Fields

TABLE A-4: Navigation mode keyboard shortcuts

shortcut key	to move to the
[Tab], [Enter], or [→]	Next field of the current record
[Shift][Tab] or [←]	Previous field of the current record
[Home]	First field of the current record
[End]	Last field of the current record
[Ctrl][Home]	First field of the first record
[Ctrl][End]	Last field of the last record
[↑]	Current field of the previous record
[↓]	Current field of the next record
[Ctrl][↑]	Current field of the first record
[Ctrl][↓]	Current field of the last record
[F5]	Specific record

Access 2000

Entering Records

Adding records to a database is a critical task that is usually performed on a daily basis. You can add a new record by clicking the **New Record button** on the Table Datasheet toolbar or by clicking the New Record navigation button. A new record is always added at the end of the datasheet. You can reorder the records in a datasheet by sorting, which you will learn later. **Scenario** John is ready to add two new records in the Customers table. First he maximizes the datasheet window.

Steps

1. **Click the Maximize button on the Customers Table datasheet window title bar**
   Maximizing both the Access and datasheet windows displays the most information possible on the screen and allows you to see more fields and records.

2. **Click the New Record button ▶* on the Table Datasheet toolbar, then press [Tab] to move through the ID field and into the Company field**
   The ID field is an **AutoNumber** field, which automatically assigns a new number each time you add a record.

3. **Type CIO, press [Tab], type Lisa, press [Tab], type Lang, press [Tab], type 420 Locust St., press [Tab], type Lenexa, press [Tab], type KS, press [Tab], type 66111-8899, press [Tab], type 9135551189, press [Tab], type 9135551889, press [Tab], type 9/6/69, press [Tab], type lang@cio.com, press [Tab], type 5433.22, then press [Enter]**
   The ID for the record for Lisa Lang is 28. AutoNumber fields should not be used as a counter for how many records you have in a table. Think of the AutoNumber field as an arbitrary but unique number for each record. The value in an AutoNumber field increments by one for each new record and cannot be edited or reused even if the entire record is deleted. The purpose of an AutoNumber field is to uniquely identify each new record. It logs how many records have been added to the datasheet since the creation of the datasheet, and not how many records are currently in the datasheet.

Trouble?

The ID number for the new records may be different in your database.

4. **Enter the new record for Rachel Best shown in the table below**

in field:	type:	in field:	type:
ID	29	Zip	65555-4444
Company	RBB Events	Phone	913-555-2289
First	Rachel	Fax	913-555-2889
Last	Best	Birthdate	8/20/68
Street	500 Sunset Blvd.	Email	Best@rbb.com
City	Manhattan	YTDSales	5998.33
State	KS		

Compare your updated datasheet with Figure A-10.

FIGURE A-10: Customers table with two new records

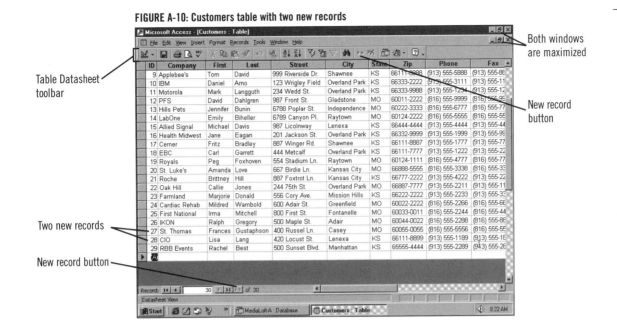

Table Datasheet toolbar

Both windows are maximized

New record button

Two new records

New record button

FIGURE A-11: Moving a field

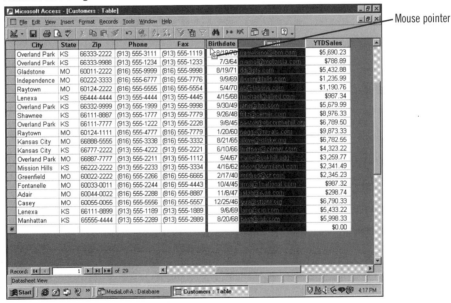

Mouse pointer

Access 2000

Moving datasheet columns

You can reorganize the fields in a datasheet by dragging the field name left or right. Figure A-11 shows how the mouse pointer changes to 🔓 , as the Email field is moved to the left. The black vertical line represents the new location between the Fax and Birthdate fields. Release the mouse button when you have appropriately positioned the field.

Editing Records

Updating information in databases is another important daily task required to keep your database current. To change the contents of an existing record, click the field you'd like to change to switch to Edit mode, then type the new information. You can delete any unwanted data by clicking the field and using the [Backspace] and [Delete] keys to delete text to the left and right of the insertion point. Other data entry keystrokes are summarized in Table A-5. **Scenario** John needs to make some corrections to the datasheet of the Customers table. He starts by correcting an error in the Street field of the first record.

Steps 1234

1. Press **[Ctrl][Home]** to move to the first record, click to the right of **111 Ash St.** in the Street field, press **[Backspace]** three times to delete **St.**, then type **Dr.**
   When you are editing a record, the **edit record symbol**, which looks like a small pencil, appears in the record selector box to the left of the current record, as shown in Figure A-12.

2. Click to the right of **Hallmark** in the Company field in record 8, press **[Spacebar]**, type **Cards**, then press **[↓]** to move to the next record
   You do not need to explicitly save new records or changes to existing records because Access saves the new data as soon as you move to another record or close the data sheet.

3. Click **Shawnee** in the City field for record 17, then press **[Ctrl][']**
   The entry changes from "Shawnee" to "Overland Park." [Ctrl]['] inserts the data from the same field in the previous record.

4. Click to the left of **EBC** in the Company field for record 18, press **[Delete]** to remove the **E**, press **[Tab]** to move to the next field, then type **Doug**
   "Doug" replaces the current entry "Carl" in the First field. Notice the edit record symbol in the record selector box to the left of record 18. Since you are still editing this record, you can undo the changes.

5. Press **[Esc]**
   The Doug entry changes back to Carl. Pressing [Esc] once removes the current field's editing changes.

6. Press **[Esc]** again
   Pressing [Esc] a second time removes all changes made to the record you are currently editing. The company entry is restored to EBC. The ability to use the [Esc] key in edit mode to remove data entry changes is dependent on whether or not you are still editing the record (as evidenced by the edit record symbol to the left of the record). Once you move to another record, the changes are saved, and you return to Navigation mode. In Navigation mode you can no longer use the [Esc] key to remove editing changes, but you can click the **Undo button** 🔄 on the Table Database toolbar to undo the last change you made.

7. Press **[↓]** to move to **Peg** in the First field of record 19, type **Peggy**, then press **[↓]** to move to record 20
   Since you are no longer editing record 19, the [Esc] key has no effect on the last change.

QuickTip

The ScreenTip for the Undo button displays the action you can undo.

8. Click the **Undo button** 🔄 on the Table Datasheet toolbar
   You undo the last edit and Peggy is changed back to Peg. Access only allows you to undo your last action. You can also delete a record directly from the datasheet.

9. Click the **Allied Signal ID 15 Record Selector box**, click the **Delete Record button** ✖ on the Table Datasheet toolbar, then click **Yes** to confirm that you want to delete the record
   You cannot undo a record deletion operation.

FIGURE A-12: Editing records

Edit record symbol

Insertion point

ID	Company	First	Last	Street	City	State	Zip	Phone	Fax
1	Sprint	Aaron	Friedrichsen	111 Ash Dr.	Kansas City	MO	66888-1111	(816) 555-2222	(816) 555-22
2	KGSM	Kelsey	Douglas	222 Elm St.	Kansas City	MO	66888-2222	(816) 555-1111	(816) 555-11
3	JCCC	Douglas	Scott	333 Oak Dr.	Kansas City	KS	66777-4444	(913) 555-8888	(913) 555-88
4	Oliver's	Rachel	Lena	444 Apple St.	Kansas City	KS	66777-3333	(913) 555-7777	(913) 555-77
5	Podiatry Center	Todd	Vandenburg	555 Birch St.	Lenexa	KS	66661-0033	(913) 555-6666	(913) 555-66
6	Mohs Surgery	Glenn	Goldstein	666 Pine St.	Kansas City	MO	66886-3333	(816) 555-3333	(816) 555-22
7	Diabetes Center	Sandie	Anderson	777 Mulberry Way	Overland Park	KS	66555-2222	(913) 555-2222	(913) 555-22
8	Hallmark	Kristen	Reis	888 Fountain Dr.	Mission Hills	KS	66222-3333	(913) 555-1191	(913) 555-11
9	Applebee's	Tom	David	999 Riverside Dr.	Shawnee	KS	66111-8888	(913) 555-5888	(913) 555-88
10	IBM	Daniel	Arno	123 Wrigley Field	Overland Park	KS	66333-2222	(913) 555-3111	(913) 555-11
11	Motorola	Mark	Langguth	234 Wedd St.	Overland Park	KS	66333-9988	(913) 555-1234	(913) 555-12
12	PFS	David	Dahlgren	987 Front St.	Gladstone	MO	60011-2222	(816) 555-9999	(816) 555-99
13	Hills Pets	Jennifer	Bunin	6788 Poplar St.	Independence	MO	60222-3333	(816) 555-6777	(816) 555-77
14	LabOne	Emily	Biheller	6789 Canyon Pl.	Raytown	MO	60124-2222	(816) 555-5555	(816) 555-55
15	Allied Signal	Michael	Davis	987 Licolnway	Lenexa	KS	66444-4444	(913) 555-4444	(913) 555-44
16	Health Midwest	Jane	Eagan	201 Jackson St.	Overland Park	KS	66332-9999	(913) 555-1999	(913) 555-99
17	Cerner	Fritz	Bradley	887 Winger Rd.	Shawnee	KS	66111-8887	(913) 555-1777	(913) 555-77
18	EBC	Carl	Garrett	444 Metcalf	Overland Park	KS	66111-7777	(913) 555-1222	(913) 555-22
19	Royals	Peg	Foxhoven	554 Stadium Ln.	Raytown	MO	60124-1111	(816) 555-4777	(816) 555-77
20	St. Luke's	Amanda	Love	667 Birdie Ln.	Kansas City	MO	66888-5555	(816) 555-3338	(816) 555-33
21	Roche	Brittney	Hill	887 Foxtrot Ln.	Kansas City	KS	66777-2222	(913) 555-4222	(913) 555-22
22	Oak Hill	Callie	Jones	244 75th St.	Overland Park	MO	66887-7777	(913) 555-2211	(913) 555-11
23	Farmland	Marjorie	Donald	556 Cory Ave.	Mission Hills	KS	66222-2222	(913) 555-2233	(913) 555-33
24	Cardiac Rehab	Mildred	Wambold	600 Adair St.	Greenfield	MO	60022-2222	(816) 555-2266	(816) 555-66
25	First National	Irma	Mitchell	800 First St.	Fontanelle	MO	60033-0011	(816) 555-2244	(816) 555-44

Record: ◄ ◄ 1 ► ►I ►* of 29

Datasheet View

TABLE A-5: Edit mode keyboard shortcuts

editing keystroke	action
[Backspace]	Deletes one character to the left of the insertion point
[Delete]	Deletes one character to the right of the insertion point
[F2]	Switches to Edit mode from Navigation mode
[Esc]	Undoes the change to the current field
[Esc][Esc]	Undoes the change to the current record
[F7]	Starts the spell check feature
[Ctrl][']	Inserts the value from the same field in the previous record into the current field
[Ctrl][;]	Inserts the current date in a date field

Resizing datasheet columns

You can resize the width of the field in a datasheet by dragging the thin black line that separates the field names to the left or right. The mouse pointer changes to ◀▶ as you resize the field to make it wider or narrower. Release the mouse button when you have resized the field.

Access 2000

Previewing and Printing a Datasheet

After entering and editing the records in a table, you can print the datasheet to obtain a hard copy of it. Before printing the datasheet, you should preview it to see how it will look when printed. Often you will want to make adjustments to margins and page orientation. **Scenario** John is ready to preview and print the datasheet.

QuickTip

If you need your name on the printed solution, enter your name as a new record in the datasheet.

1. Click the **Print Preview button** 🔍 on the Table Database toolbar

The datasheet appears as a miniature page in the Print Preview window, as shown in Figure A-14. The Print Preview toolbar provides options for printing, viewing more than one page, and sending the information to Word or Excel.

2. Click 🔍 on the top of the miniature datasheet

By magnifying this view of the datasheet, you can see its header, which includes the object name, Customers, in the center of the top of the page and the date on the right.

3. Scroll down to view the bottom of the page

The footer displays a page number centered on the bottom.

4. Click the **Two Pages button** 🔲 on the Print Preview toolbar

You decide to increase the top margin of the printout.

5. Click **File** on the menu bar, then click **Page Setup**

The Page Setup dialog box opens, as shown in Figure A-15. This dialog box provides options for changing margins, removing the headings (the header and footer), and changing page orientation from portrait (default) to landscape on the Page tab.

6. Double-click **1"** in the Top text box, type **2**, then click **OK**

The modified datasheet appears in the window. Satisfied with the layout for the printout, you'll print the datasheet and close the Print Preview window.

7. Click the **Print button** 🖨 on the Print Preview toolbar, then click **Close**

The datasheet appears on the screen.

Hiding fields

Sometimes you don't need all the fields of a datasheet on a printout. To temporarily hide a field from viewing and therefore from a resulting datasheet printout, click the field name, click Format on the menu bar, and then click Hide Columns. To redisplay the column, click Format, then Unhide Columns. The Unhide Columns dialog box, shown in Figure A-13, opens. The empty columns check boxes indicate the columns that are hidden. Clicking the check boxes will bring the columns back into view on the datasheet.

FIGURE A-13: Unhide Columns dialog box

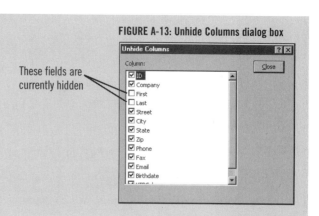

These fields are currently hidden

FIGURE A-14: Datasheet in Print Preview (portrait orientation)

Print
Preview
toolbar

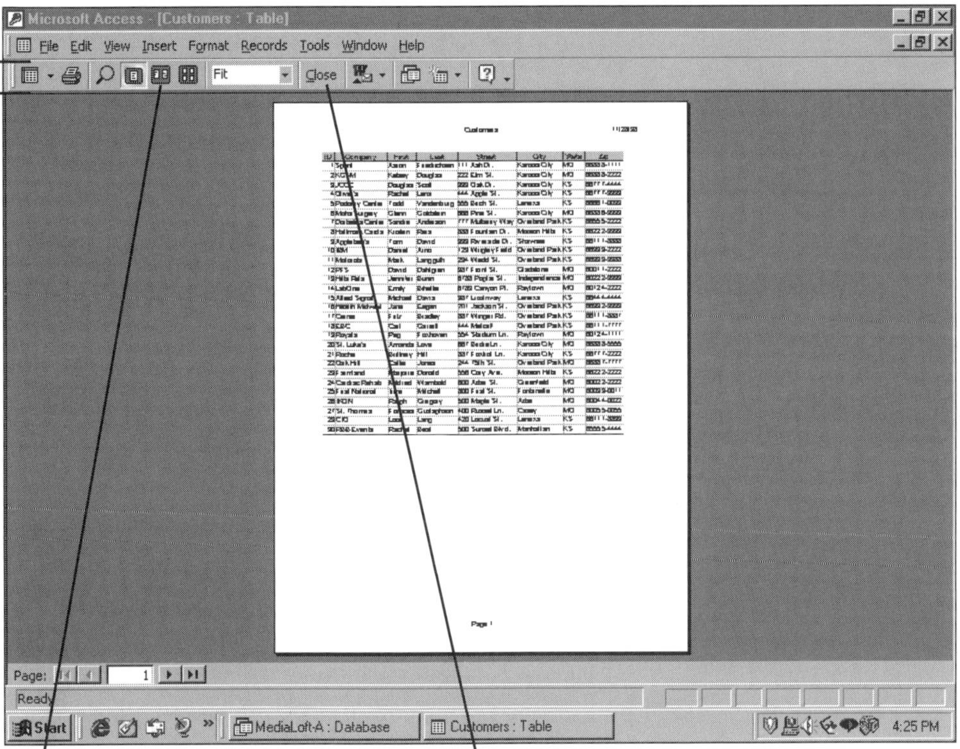

Two pages
button

Click to close the
Print Preview window

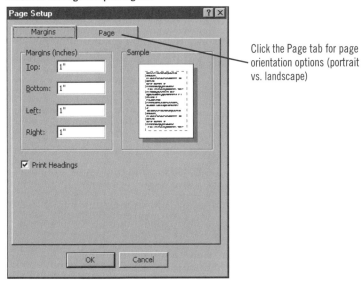

FIGURE A-15: Page Setup dialog box

Click the Page tab for page
orientation options (portrait
vs. landscape)

Getting Help and Exiting Access

Access 2000

When you have finished working in your database, you need to close the object you were working in, such as a table datasheet, and then close the database. To close a table, click Close on the File menu or click the object's Close button located in the upper-right corner of the menu bar. Once you have closed all open objects, you can exit the program. As with most programs, if you try to exit Access and have not yet saved changes to open objects, Access will prompt you to save your changes. You can use the Help system to learn more about the program and get help. **Scenario** John has finished working with Access for now, so he closes the Customers table and MediaLoft-A database. Before exiting, he learns more about the Help system, and then exits Access.

Steps

1. Click the **Close button** for the Customers datasheet
   The MediaLoft-A database window displays. If you make any structural changes to the datasheet such as moving, resizing, or hiding columns, you will be prompted to save those changes.

2. Click the **Close button** for the MediaLoft-A Database, as shown in Figure A-16
   The MediaLoft-A database is closed, but Access is still running so you could open another database or explore the Help system to learn more about Access at this time.

3. Click **Help** on the menu bar, then click **Microsoft Access Help**
   The Office Assistant opens and offers to get the help you need. You can further explore some of the concepts you have learned by finding information in the Access Help system. Table A-6 summarizes the options on the Access Help menu, which provides in-depth information on Access features.

4. Type **What is a table**, click **Search**, click **Tables: what they are and how they work**, then click the **graphic** as shown in Figure A-17

5. Read the information, then click each of the five pages

6. Close the Access Help windows

> **Trouble?**
> Do not remove your Project Disk from drive A until you have exited Access.

7. Click **File** on the menu bar, then click **Exit**
   You have exited Access.

Shutting down your computer

Never shut off a computer before the screen indicates that it is safe to do so. If you shut off a computer during the initial Windows load process (the screen dis-

plays the Windows logo and a cloud background at this time) or before the screen indicates that it is safe to do so, you can corrupt your Windows files.

FIGURE A-16: Closing a database

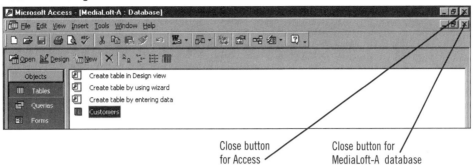

Close button for Access

Close button for MediaLoft-A database

FIGURE A-17: Access Help window

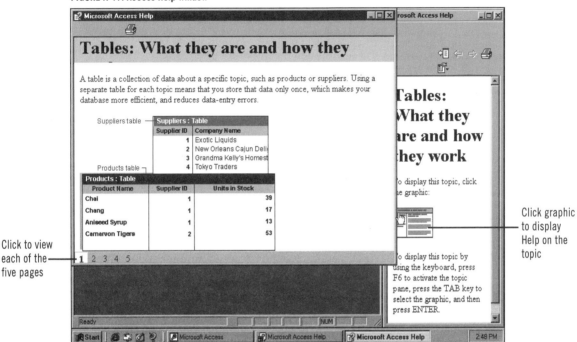

Click to view each of the five pages

Click graphic to display Help on the topic

TABLE A-6: Help menu options

menu option	description
Microsoft Access Help	Opens the Office Assistant; type a question to open the entire Microsoft Access Help manual in a separate window in which you can search for information by the table of contents, index, or keyword
Show the Office Assistant	Presents the Office Assistant, an automated character that provides tips and interactive prompts while you are working
Hide the Office Assistant	Temporarily closes the Office Assistant for the working session
What's This	Changes the mouse pointer to ; this special mouse pointer provides a short explanation of the icon or menu option that you click
Office on the Web	If you are connected to the Web, provides additional Microsoft information and support articles; this Web-based information is updated daily
Detect and Repair	Analyzes a database for possible data corruption and attempts to repair problems
About Microsoft Access	Provides the version and product ID of Access

Practice

► Concepts Review

Label each element of the Access window shown in Figure A-18.

FIGURE A-18

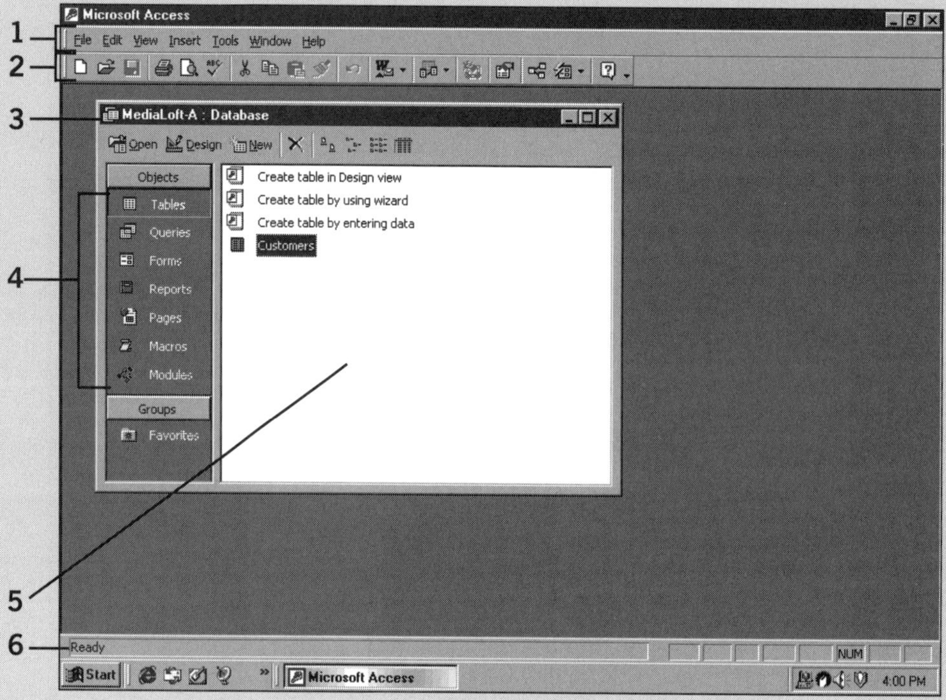

Match each term with the statement that describes it.

7. Objects
8. Table
9. Record
10. Field
11. Datasheet

a. A spreadsheet-like grid that displays fields as columns and records as rows

b. A collection of records for a single subject, such as all the customer records

c. A category of information in a table, such as a customer's name, city, or state

d. A group of related fields, such as all the demographic information for one customer

e. Seven types of these are contained in an Access database and are used to enter, enhance, and use the data within the database

Select the best answer from the list of choices.

12. Which of the following is NOT a typical benefit of relational databases?
    a. Automatic trend analysis
    b. Faster information retrieval
    c. Minimized duplicate data entry
    d. Easier data entry

13. Which of the following is NOT an advantage of managing data with a relational database versus a spreadsheet?
  a. Allows multiple users to enter data simultaneously
  b. Allows links between lists of information
  c. Provides greater security
  d. Doesn't require preplanning before data is entered

14. The object that holds all of the data within an Access database
  a. Report
  b. Table
  c. Form
  d. Query

15. The object that provides an easy-to-use data entry screen
  a. Report
  b. Query
  c. Form
  d. Table

16. This displays messages regarding the current database operation
  a. Object tabs
  b. Title bar
  c. Database toolbar
  d. Status bar

► Skills Review

1. **Define database software.**
  a. Identify five disadvantages of using a paper system, such as index cards, to organize database information. Write down your answers to this and the following questions using complete sentences.
  b. Identify five advantages of managing database information in Access versus using a spreadsheet product like Excel.

2. **Learn database terminology.**
  a. Explain the relationship between a field, a record, a table, and a database.
  b. Identify the seven objects of an Access database, and explain the main purpose of each.
  c. Which object of an Access database is most important? Why?

3. **Start Access and open a database.**
  a. Click the Start button, point to Programs, then click Microsoft Access.
  b. Insert your Project Disk into the appropriate disk drive, click the Open an existing file option button, click More Files, then click OK.
  c. In the Open dialog box, choose the correct drive, then open the Recycle-A database file.
  d. Identify the following items. (*Hint*: To create a printout of this screen, press [Print Screen] to capture an image of the screen to the Windows clipboard, start any word-processing program, then click the Paste button. Print the document that now contains a picture of this screen, and identify the elements on the printout.)
    - Database toolbar
    - Recycle-A database window
    - Menu bar
    - Object buttons
    - Objects bar
    - Status bar

4. **View the database window.**
  a. Maximize both the Access window and the Recycle-A Database window.
  b. Click each of the objects, then write down the object names of each type that exist in the Recycle-A database.
    - Tables
    - Queries
    - Reports
    - Pages
    - Macros
    - Modules
    - Forms

5. **Navigate records.**
  a. Open the Clubs table.
  b. Press [Tab] or [Enter] to move through the fields of the first record.
  c. Press [Ctrl][End] to move to the last field of the last record.
  d. Press [Ctrl][Home] to move to the first field of the first record.
  e. Click the Last Record navigation button to quickly move to the Oak Hill Patriots record.

6. **Enter records.**

   a. In the Clubs table, click the New Record button, then add the following records:

Name	Street	City	State	Zip	Phone	Leader	Club Number
EBC Angels	10100 Metcalf	Overland Park	KS	66001	555-7711	Michael Garrett	8
MOT Friends	111 Holmes	Kansas City	MO	65001	555-8811	Aaron Goldstein	9

   b. Move the Club Number field from the last column of the datasheet to the first column.

7. **Edit records.**

   a. Change the Name field in the first record from "Jaycees" to "JC Club."

   b. Change the Name field in the second record from "Boy Scouts #1" to "Oxford Cub Scouts."

   c. Change the Leader field in the fifth record from "Melanie Perry" to "Melanie Griffiths."

   d. Enter your name and personal information (make up a club name) as a new record, and enter 99 as the Club Number.

   e. Delete the record for Club Number 2.

8. **Preview and print a datasheet.**

   a. Preview the Clubs table datasheet.

   b. Use the Page Setup option on the File menu to change the page orientation from portrait to landscape.

   c. Print the Clubs table datasheet.

9. **Get Help and exit Access.**

   a. Close the Clubs table object, saving the changes.

   b. Close the Recycle-A database.

   c. Use Office Assistant to learn more about creating a database.

   d. Exit Access.

▶ Visual Workshop

Open the Recycle-A database on your Project Disk. Modify the existing Centers table, enter a new record using your name as the contact and Center Number 99, then print the datasheet. The Street field for the first record has changed, the Hazardous field for the first two records has changed, and two new records have been added to the datasheet. See Figure A-19.

FIGURE A-19

	Center Number	Name	Street	City	State	Zip	Phone	Contact	Hazard
	1	Trash 'R Us	989 Main	Lenexa	KS	61111	555-7777	Ben Cartwright	☐
	2	You Deliver	12345 College	Overland Park	KS	63444	555-2222	Jerry Magliano	☐
	3	County Landfill	12444 Pflumm	Lenexa	KS	64222	555-4422	Jerry Lewis	☐
	4	Cans and Stuff	543 Holmes	Kansas City	MO	60011	555-2347	Julee Burton	☑
	5	We Love Trash	589 Switzer	Kansas City	KS	60022	555-3456	Doug Morrison	☑

Record: 1 of 5

Unit B

Using
Tables and Queries

Objectives

- MOUS ► **Plan a database**
- MOUS ► **Create a table**
- MOUS ► **Use Table Design view**
- MOUS ► **Format a datasheet**
- MOUS ► **Understand sorting, filtering, and finding**
- MOUS ► **Sort records and find data**
- MOUS ► **Filter records**
- MOUS ► **Create a query**
- MOUS ► **Use Query Design view**

Now that you are familiar with some of the basic Access terminology and features, you are ready to plan and build your own database. Your first task is to create the tables that store the data. Once the tables are created and the data is entered, you can use several techniques for finding specific information in the database, including sorting, filtering, and building queries. Scenario▶ John Kim wants to build and maintain a database containing information about MediaLoft's products. The information in the database will be useful when John provides information for future sales promotions.

Planning a Database

The first and most important object in a database is the table object because it contains the **raw data**, the individual pieces of information stored in individual fields in the database. When you design a table, you identify the fields of information the table will contain and the type of data to be stored in each field. Some databases contain multiple tables linked together. Scenario> John plans his database containing information about MediaLoft's products.

In planning a database it is important to:

Determine the purpose of the database and give it a meaningful name

The database will store information about MediaLoft's music products. You decide to name the database "MediaLoft," and name the first table "Music Inventory."

Determine what reports you want the database to produce

You want to be able to print inventory reports that list the products by artist, type of product (CD or cassette), quantity in stock, and price. These pieces of information will become the fields in the Music Inventory table.

Collect the raw data that will be stored in the database

The raw data for MediaLoft's products might be stored on index cards, in paper reports, and in other electronic formats, such as word-processed documents and spreadsheets. You can use Access to import data from many other electronic sources, which greatly increases your data entry efficiency.

Sketch the structure of each table, including field names and data types

Using the data you collected, identify the field name and data type for each field in each table as shown in Figure B-1. The **data type** determines what type of information you can enter in a field. For example, a field with a Currency data type does accept text. Properly defining the data type for each field helps you maintain data consistency and accuracy. Table B-1 lists the data types available within Access.

Choosing between the text and number data type

When assigning data types, you should avoid choosing "number" for a telephone or ZIP code field. Although these fields generally contain numbers, they should still be text data types. Consider the following: You may want to enter 1-800-BUY-BOOK in a telephone number field. This would not be possible if the field were designated as a number data type. When you sort the fields, you'll want them to sort alphabetically, like text fields. Consider the following ZIP codes: 60011 and 50011-8888. If the ZIP code field were designated as a number data type, the ZIP codes would be interpreted incorrectly as the values 60,011 and 500,118,888; and sort in that order, too.

FIGURE B-1: Music Inventory table field names and data types

Field Name	Data Type
RecordingID	AutoNumber
RecordingTitle	Text
RecordingArtist	Text
MusicCategory	Text
RecordingLabel	Text
Format	Text
NumberofTracks	Number
PurchasePrice	Currency
RetailPrice	Currency
Notes	Memo

TABLE B-1: Data types

data type	description of data	size
Text	Text information or combinations of text and numbers, such as a street address, name, or phone number	Up to 255 characters
Memo	Lengthy text such as comments or notes	Up to 64,000 characters
Number	Numeric information used in calculations, such as quantities	Several sizes available to store numbers with varying degrees of precision
Date/Time	Dates and times	Size controlled by Access to accommodate dates and times across thousands of years (for example, 1/1/1850 and 1/1/2150 are valid dates)
Currency	Monetary values	Size controlled by Access; accommodates up to 15 digits to the left of the decimal point and 4 digits to the right
AutoNumber	Integers assigned by Access to sequentially order each record added to a table	Size controlled by Access
Yes/No	Only one of two values stored (Yes/No, On/Off, True/False)	Size controlled by Access
OLE Object	Pointers stored that link files created in other programs, such as pictures, sound clips, documents, or spreadsheets	Up to one gigabyte
Hyperlink	Web addresses	Size controlled by Access
Lookup Wizard	Invokes a wizard that helps link the current table to another table (the final data type of the field is determined by choices made in the wizard; a field created with the lookup data type will display data from another table)	Size controlled through the choices made in the Lookup Wizard

Creating a Table

After you plan the structure of the database, your next step is to create the database file itself, which will eventually contain all of the objects such as tables, queries, forms, and reports. When you create a database, first you name it, and then you can build the first table object and enter data. Access offers several methods for creating a table. For example, you can import a table from another data source such as a spreadsheet, or use the Access **Table Wizard**, which provides interactive help to create the field names and data types for each field. **Scenario** John is ready to create the MediaLoft database. He uses the Table Wizard to create the Music Inventory table.

Steps 1 2 3 4

1. Start Access, click the **Blank Access database option button** in the Microsoft Access dialog box, then click **OK**
   The File New Database dialog box opens.

2. Type **MediaLoft** in the File name text box, insert your Project Disk in the appropriate drive, click the **Save in list arrow**, click the **drive**, then click **Create**
   The MediaLoft database file is created and saved on your Project Disk. The Table Wizard offers an efficient way to plan the fields of a new table.

3. If the Office Assistant appears on your screen, click **Help** on the menu bar, click **Hide the Office Assistant**, then double-click **Create table by using wizard** in the MediaLoft Database window
   The Table Wizard dialog box opens, as shown in Figure B-2. The Table Wizard offers 25 business and 20 personal sample tables from which you can select sample fields. The Recordings sample table, which is in the Personal category of tables, most closely matches the fields you want to include in the Music Inventory table.

4. Click the **Personal option button**, scroll down and click **Recordings** in the Sample Tables list box, then click the **Select All Fields button** `>>`
   Your Table Wizard dialog box should look like Figure B-3. At this point, you can change the suggested field names to better match your database.

5. Click **RecordingArtistID** in the Fields in my new table list box, click **Rename Field**, type **RecordingArtist** in the Rename field text box, then click **OK**

6. Click **Next**
   The second Table Wizard dialog box allows you to name the table and determine if Access sets the **primary key field**, a field that contains unique information for each record.

7. Type **Music Inventory**, make sure the **Yes, set a primary key for me option button** is selected, click **Next**, click the **Modify the table design option button**, then click **Finish**
   The table opens in **Design view**, shown in Figure B-4, which allows you to add, delete, or modify the fields in the table. The primary **key field symbol** indicates that the RecordingID field has been designated as the primary key field.

Trouble?

If you don't see all the fields in the table, it is because you have different settings on your monitor. Maximize the window to see all the fields, if necessary.

FIGURE B-2: Table Wizard

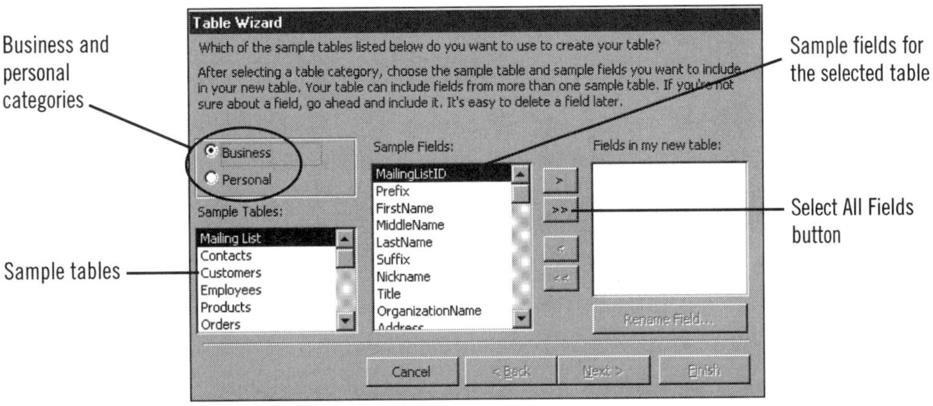

Table Wizard
Business and personal categories
Sample fields for the selected table
Select All Fields button
Sample tables

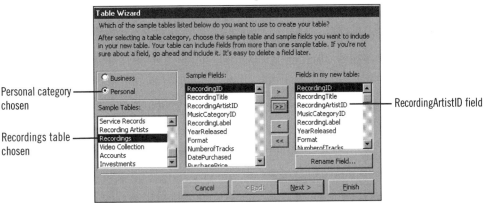

FIGURE B-3: Table Wizard with Recordings table fields

Table Wizard
Personal category chosen
RecordingArtistID field
Recordings table chosen

FIGURE B-4: Music Inventory table in Design view

Microsoft Access
View button
Key field symbol
Field names
Music Inventory : Table

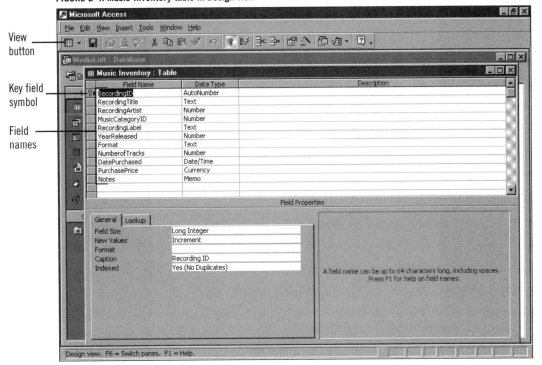

Using Table Design View

Each database object has a **Design view** in which you can modify its structure. The Design view of a table allows you to add or delete fields, add **field descriptions**, or change other field properties. **Field properties** are additional characteristics of a field such as its size or default value. Scenario▶ Using the Table Wizard, John was able to create a Music Inventory table very quickly. Now in Design view he modifies the fields to meet his needs. MediaLoft doesn't track purchase dates or release dates, but it does need to store retail price information in the database.

1. In the Music Inventory table's Design view, click **DatePurchased** in the Field Name column, click the **Delete Rows button** ▣ on the Table Design toolbar, click the **Year Released row selector**, click ▣ to delete the field, click the **Notes** field, then click the **Insert Rows button** ▣

   The Year Released and Date Purchased fields are deleted from the table and a new row appears in which you can add the new field name.

2. Type **RetailPrice**, press **[Tab]**, type **C** (for Currency data type), then press **[Enter]**

   The new field is added to the Music Inventory table, as shown in Figure B-5. The data type of both the RecordingArtist and MusicCategoryID fields should be Text so that descriptive words can be entered in these fields rather than just numbers.

3. Click the **Number** data type in the RecordingArtist field, click the **Data Type list arrow**, click **Text**, click the **Number** data type in the MusicCategoryID field, click the **Data Type list arrow**, then click **Text**

   You must work in the table's Design view to make structural changes to the table.

4. Click to the right of **MusicCategoryID**, press **[Backspace]** twice, then click the **Save button** ▣ on the Table Design toolbar

   A description identifies a field and can list the types of data in that field.

5. Click the **MusicCategory Description cell**, then type **classical, country, folk, gospel, jazz, new age, rap, or rock**

   The **field size property** limits the number of characters allowed for each field.

6. Make sure the **MusicCategory** field is still selected, double-click **50** in the Field Size cell, then type **9**

   The longest entry in the MusicCategory field, "classical," is only nine characters. The finished Music Inventory table Design view should look like Figure B-6.

7. Click the **Datasheet View button** ▣ on the Table Design toolbar, click **Yes** to save the table, then type the following record into the new datasheet:

in field:	type:	in field:	type:
Recording ID	[Tab]	Format	CD
Recording Title	No Words	Number of Tracks	12
RecordingArtist	Brickman, Jim	Purchase Price	$10.00
Music Category ID	New Age	RetailPrice	$13.00
Recording Label	Windham Hill	Notes	

   You are finished working with the MediaLoft database for now.

8. Close the Music Inventory table, then close the MediaLoft database

   Data is saved automatically, so you were not prompted to save the record when you closed the datasheet.

FIGURE B-5: Music Inventory table with new RetailPrice field

YearReleased
field deleted

DatePurchased
field deleted

RetailPrice field
added

RetailPrice field is
selected

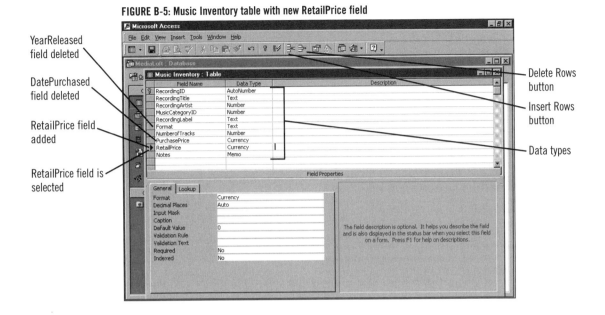

Delete Rows
button

Insert Rows
button

Data types

FIGURE B-6: Description and field size properties for MusicCategory field

Row selector

MusicCategory field
is selected

Field size property
is changed to 9

Field Properties section

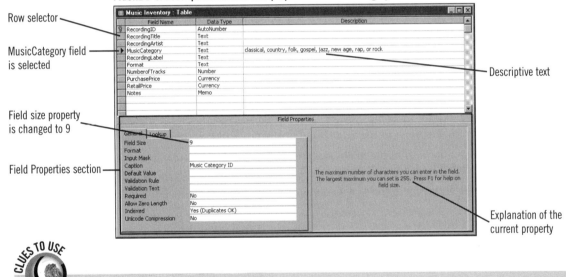

Descriptive text

Explanation of the
current property

CLUES TO USE

Learning about field properties

The properties of a field are the characteristics that define the field. Two properties are required for every field: field name and data type. Many other properties, such as field size, format (the way the field is displayed on the datasheet), caption, and default value, are defined in the Field Properties section of the table's Design view. As you add more property entries, you are generally restricting the amount or type of data that can be entered in the field, which also increases data entry accuracy. For example, you might change the field size property for a State field from the default value of 50 to 2 to eliminate an incorrect entry such as

"NYY." The available field properties change depending on the data type of the selected field. For example, there is no field size property for a Birth Date field, because Access controls the size of fields with a Date/Time data type. Database designers often insist on field names without spaces because they are easier to reference in other Access objects. The **Caption property**, however, can be used to override the technical field name with an easy-to-read caption entry when the field name is displayed on datasheets, forms, and reports. When you create a table using the wizard, many fields have caption properties.

Formatting a Datasheet

Even though the report object is the primary tool to create professional hard copy output from an Access database, you can print a datasheet too. Although you cannot create fancy headings or insert graphic images on a datasheet, you can change the fonts and colors as well as change the gridlines to dramatically change its appearance. **Scenario** John has been busy entering MediaLoft's music information in the Music Inventory table (which is stored in the MediaLoft-B database). He has also simplified many of the field names. Now he will print the Music Inventory datasheet using new fonts and colors.

Steps 1 2 3 4

1. Click the **Open button** 📂 on the Database toolbar, select the **MediaLoft-B** database from your Project Disk, then click **Open**
   The Music Inventory table has data that was entered by John Kim.

QuickTip
You can double-click a table object to open it in Datasheet view.

2. Click **Music Inventory** in the Tables Object window, then click the **Open button** 📄
   Access displays the Music Inventory table, containing 58 records, as shown in Figure B-7. You can change the font and color of the datasheet to enhance its appearance.

3. Click **Format** on the menu bar, click **Font**, click **Comic Sans MS** in the Font list, then click **OK**
   Comic Sans MS is an informal font used for personal correspondence or internal memos. It simulates handwritten text, but is still very readable. You can also change the color and format of the datasheet gridlines.

4. Click **Format** on the menu bar, click **Datasheet**, click the **Gridline Color list arrow**, then click **Red**
   The Sample box in the Datasheet Formatting dialog box displays both the vertical and horizontal gridlines as red.

5. Click the **Border list arrow**, click **Vertical Gridline**, click the **Line Styles list arrow**, click **Transparent Border**, as shown in Figure B-8, then click **OK**
   You removed the vertical gridlines separating the fields. You can also change the left and right margins, and change the page orientation from portrait to landscape to fit all the fields across the page.

6. Click **File** on the menu bar, click **Page Setup**, double-click **1"** in the Top text box, type **0.75**, press **[Tab]**, type **0.75** in the Bottom text box, press **[Tab]**, type **0.75** in the Left text box, press **[Tab]**, type **0.75** in the Right text box, click the **Page tab**, click the **Landscape option button**, then click **OK**
   Print Preview displays your formatted datasheet as it will look when printed.

7. Click the **Print Preview button** 🔍 on the Table Datasheet toolbar to preview the finished product, as shown in Figure B-9
   The red gridlines seem a bit too intense for your printout.

8. Click the **Close button** Close on the Print Preview toolbar, click **Format** on the menu bar, click **Datasheet**, click the **Gridline Color list arrow**, click **Silver**, then click **OK**
   Silver is the default gridline color.

FIGURE B-7: Music Inventory table datasheet

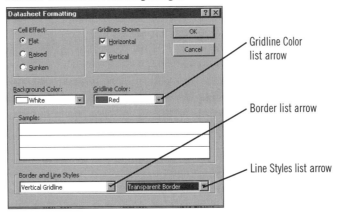

FIGURE B-8: Datasheet Formatting dialog box

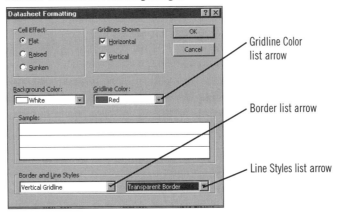

Gridline Color list arrow

Border list arrow

Line Styles list arrow

FIGURE B-9: Previewing the formatted datasheet

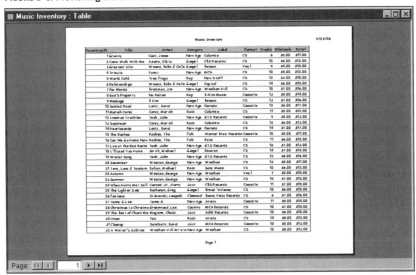

Access 2000

Understanding Sorting, Filtering, and Finding

The records of a datasheet are automatically sorted according to the data in the primary key field. Often, however, you'll want to view or print records in an entirely different sort order. Or you may want to display a subset of the records, such as those within the same music category or those below a certain retail price. Access makes it easy to sort, find data, and filter a datasheet with buttons on the Table Datasheet toolbar, summarized in Table B-2. **Scenario** John studies the sort, find, and filter features to learn how to find and retrieve information in his database.

 Sorting refers to reorganizing the records in either ascending or descending order based on the contents of a field. Text fields sort from A to Z, number fields from the lowest to the highest value, and date/time fields from the oldest date to the date furthest into the future. In Figure B-10 the Music Inventory table has been sorted in ascending order on the Artist field. Notice that numbers sort before letters in an ascending sort order.

 Filtering means temporarily isolating a subset of records, as shown in Figure B-11. This is particularly useful because the subset can be formatted and printed just like the entire datasheet. You can produce a listing of all rock music or a listing based on any category, artist, or field in the datasheet. To remove a filter, click the Remove Filter button to view all the records in the datasheet.

 Finding refers to locating a specific piece of data, such as "Amy" or "500," within a field or an entire datasheet, similar to finding text in a word-processing document. The Find and Replace dialog box is shown in Figure B-12. The options in this dialog box are summarized below.

- **Find What:** Provides a text box for your search criteria. For example, you might want to find the text "Amy", "Beatles", or "Capitol Records" in the datasheet.

- **Look In:** Determines whether Access looks for the search criteria in the current field (in this case the Artist field) or in all fields.

- **Match:** Determines whether the search criteria must match the whole field's contents exactly, any part of the field, or the start of the field.

- **More:** Provides more options to limit your search. For example, it allows you to make your search criteria uppercase- or lowercase-sensitive.

- **Replace tab:** Provides a text box for you to specify "replacement text." In other words, you might want to search for every occurrence of "Compact Disc" and replace it with "CD" by entering "Compact Disc" as your search criteria and "CD" as your replacement text.

TABLE B-2: Sort, Filter, and Find buttons

name	button	purpose
Sort Ascending	↓	Sorts records based on the selected field in ascending order (0 to 9, A to Z)
Sort Descending	↓	Sorts records based on the selected field in descending order (Z to A, 9 to 0)
Filter By Selection		Filters records based on selected data and hides records that do not match
Filter By Form		Filters records based on more than one selection criteria by using the Filter By Form window
Apply Filter or Remove Filter		Applies or removes the filter
Find		Searches for a string of characters in the current field or all fields

FIGURE B-10: Records sorted in ascending order by Artist

Records sorted in ascending order by Artist

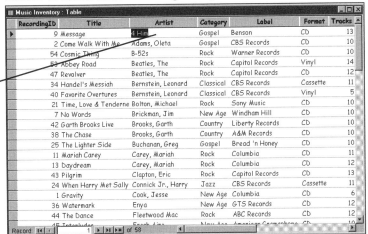

FIGURE B-11: Records filtered by "Rock" category

Sort Ascending button

Sort Descending button

Number of records in filtered subset

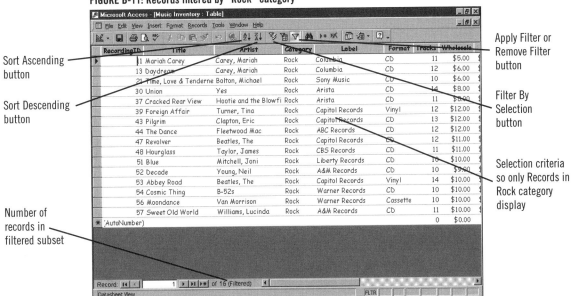

Apply Filter or Remove Filter button

Filter By Selection button

Selection criteria so only Records in Rock category display

FIGURE B-12: Find and Replace dialog box

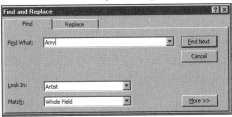

Using wildcards in Find

Wildcards are symbols you can use as substitutes for characters to find information that matches your find criteria. Access uses these wildcards: the asterisk (*) represents any group of characters, the question mark (?) stands for any single character, and the pound sign (#) stands for a single number digit. For example, to find any word beginning with "S," type "s*" in the Find What text box.

Sorting Records and Finding Data

Sorting records and quickly finding information in a database are two powerful tools that help you work more efficiently. Scenario▶ John needs to create several different printouts of the Music Inventory datasheet to satisfy various departments. The Marketing department wants a printout of records sorted by title and artist. The Accounting department wants a printout of records sorted from highest retail price to lowest.

Steps 1234

1. In the Music Inventory datasheet, click **any cell** in the Title field, then click the **Sort Ascending button** ⬆ on the Table Datasheet toolbar
The records are listed in an A-to-Z sequence based on the data in the Title field, as shown in Figure B-13. Next you'll sort the records according to artist.

2. Click **any cell** in the Artist field, then click ⬆
The table is sorted alphabetically in ascending order by Artist. You can preview and print a sorted datasheet at any time.

QuickTip
Scroll to the right if necessary to see this field.

3. Click **any cell** in the Retail field, then click the **Sort Descending button** ⬇ on the Table Datasheet toolbar
The records are sorted in descending order on the value in the Retail field. The CD that sells for the highest retail price, "Skyline Firedance," is listed as the first record. To put the records back in their original order, you can click the key field, RecordingID, and click the Sort Ascending button. Access also lets you find all records based on any search word.

4. Click **any cell** in the Title field, then click the **Find button** 🔍 on the Table Datasheet toolbar
The Find and Replace dialog box opens. You know MediaLoft will want to find the titles that are going to be hot sellers during the Christmas season.

5. Type **Christmas** in the Find What text box, click the **Match list arrow**, then click **Any Part of Field**, as shown in Figure B-14
Access will find all occurrences of the word "Christmas" in the Title field, whether it is the first, middle, or last part of the title. "Christmas" is the search criteria.

6. Click **Find Next**, then if necessary drag the Find and Replace dialog box up and to the right to better view the datasheet
If you started the search at the top of the datasheet, "A Family Christmas" is the first title found. You can look for more occurrences of "Christmas."

7. Click **Find Next** to find the next occurrence of the word "Christmas," then click **Find Next** as many times as it takes to move through all the records
When no more occurrences of the search criteria "Christmas" are found, Access lets you know that no more matching records can be found.

8. Click **OK** when prompted that Access has finished searching the records, then click **Cancel** to close the Find and Replace dialog box

FIGURE B-13: Music Inventory datasheet sorted by Title

RecordingID	Title	Artist	Category	Label	Format	Tracks
55	A Christmas Album	Grant, Amy	Folk	Reunion Records	CD	11
46	A Family Christmas	Tesh, John	New Age	GTS Records	CD	14
32	A Winter's Solstice	Windham Hill Artists	New Age	Windham	CD	10
53	Abbey Road	Beatles, The	Rock	Capitol Records	Vinyl	14
22	Autumn	Winston, George	New Age	Windham	Vinyl	7
51	Blue	Mitchell, Joni	Rock	Liberty Records	CD	10
16	Can We Go Home Now	Roches, The	Folk	Ryko	CD	11
35	Christmas	Mannheim Steamroller	New Age	Sony Music	CD	11
28	Christmas to Christmas	Greenwood, Lee	Country	MCA Records	CD	10
31	Closeup	Sandborn, David	Jazz	MCA Records	Cassette	10
2	Come Walk With Me	Adams, Oleta	Gospel	CBS Records	CD	10
54	Cosmic Thing	B-52s	Rock	Warner Records	CD	10
37	Cracked Rear View	Hootie and the Blowfi	Rock	Arista	CD	11
13	Daydream	Carey, Mariah	Rock	Columbia	CD	12
52	Decade	Young, Neil	Rock	A&M Records	CD	10
20	December	Winston, George	New Age	Windham	CD	12
26	Fantasia	Stokowski, Leopold	Classical	Buena Vista Records	CD	6
40	Favorite Overtures	Bernstein, Leonard	Classical	CBS Records	Vinyl	5
39	Foreign Affair	Turner, Tina	Rock	Capitol Records	Vinyl	12
42	Garth Brooks Live	Brooks, Garth	Country	Liberty Records	CD	10

Record: 1 of 58

Records are sorted in
ascending order by Title

FIGURE B-14: Specify "Christmas" as the search criteria in the Title field

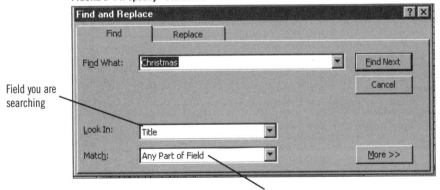

Field you are searching

Tells Access to find the search
criteria anywhere in the selected field

Find and Replace

Find | Replace

Find What: Christmas

Look In: Title

Match: Any Part of Field

Find Next
Cancel
More >>

Access 2000

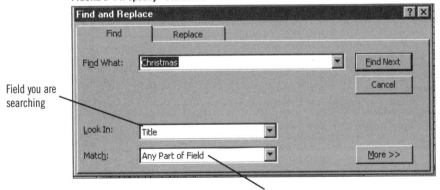

Sorting on more than one field

The telephone book sorts records by last name (**primary sort field**) and when ties occur on the last name (for example, two "Smiths"), it further sorts the records by first name (**secondary sort field**). Access allows you to sort by more than one field using the query object, which you will learn more about later in this unit. Queries allow you to specify more than one sort field in Query Design view, evaluating the sort orders from left to right (the leftmost sort field is the primary sort field).

Filtering Records

Sorting allows you to reorder all the records of a datasheet. Filtering the datasheet displays only those records that match criteria. **Criteria** are rules or limiting conditions you set. For example, you may want to show only those records where the Category field is equal to "Rap," or where the PurchasePrice field is less than $10. Once you have filtered a datasheet to display a subset of records, you can still sort the records and find data just as if you were working with the entire datasheet. To make sure the Filter By Form grid is clear of any previous entries, you should click the Clear Grid button ⊠. Scenario▶ The Accounting department asked John for a printout of cassettes with a retail price of $15 or more. John uses the datasheet's filter buttons to answer this request.

Steps 1 2 3 4

1. In the Music Inventory datasheet, click the **RecordingID** field, click the **Sort Ascending button** ↑↓ on the Table Datasheet toolbar, click any occurrence of **Cassette** in the Format field, then click the **Filter By Selection button** 🔽 on the Table Datasheet toolbar

   Twelve records are selected, as shown in Figure B-15. Filter By Selection is a fast and easy way to filter the records for an exact match (that is, where Format field value is *equal to* Cassette). To filter for comparative data and to specify more complex criteria (for example, where PurchasePrice is *equal to* or *greater than* $15), you must use the Filter By Form feature. See Table B-3 for more information on comparison operators.

QuickTip

If you click the Field List arrow, you can pick an entry from a list of existing entries in that field.

2. Click the **Filter By Form button** 🔲 on the Table Datasheet toolbar, click the **Retail** field, then type **>=15**

   The finished Filter By Form window is shown in Figure B-16. The previous Filter By Selection criteria, "Cassette" in the Format field, is still valid in the grid. Access distinguishes between text and numeric entries by placing quotation marks around text entries. You can widen a column to display the entire criteria. Filter By Form is more powerful than Filter By Selection because it allows you to use comparison operators such as >=. Filter By Form also allows you to enter criteria for more than one field at a time where *both* criteria must be "true" in order for the record to be shown in the resulting datasheet.

3. Click the **Apply Filter button** 🔽 on the Filter/Sort toolbar, then scroll to the right to display the Retail field

   Only two records are true for both criteria, as shown in Figure B-17. The Record Navigation buttons in the lower-left corner of the datasheet display how many records are in the filtered subset. You can remove the current filter to view all the records in the datasheet at any time by clicking the Remove Filter button.

4. Click the **Remove Filter button** 🔽 on the Table Datasheet toolbar

   Be sure to remove existing filters before you apply a new filter or you will end up filtering the existing subset of records versus the entire datasheet. Next find all selections produced under the "A&M Records" recording label.

5. Click **any cell** in the Label field, click ↑↓, **A&M Records** is selected as the Label entry, then click 🔽

   Using both the sort and filter buttons, you quickly found the five records that met the "A&M Records" criteria.

6. Close the datasheet, then click **Yes** if prompted to save the changes to the Music Inventory table

   Any filters applied to a datasheet will be removed the next time you open the datasheet, but the sort order will be saved.

FIGURE B-15: Music Inventory datasheet filtered for "Cassette" records

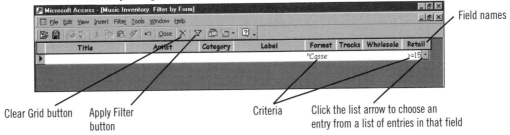

12 records are selected

All records have Cassette in Format field

FIGURE B-16: Filter By Form grid

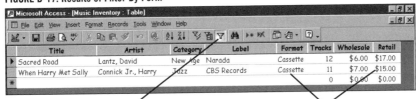

Field names

Clear Grid button Apply Filter button Criteria Click the list arrow to choose an entry from a list of entries in that field

FIGURE B-17: Results of Filter By Form

Filter is applied and the Apply Filter button becomes the Remove Filter button

Both records have Cassette in the Format field and all records have a Retail value >=15

TABLE B-3: Comparison operators

operator	description	expression	meaning
>	Greater than	>500	Numbers greater than 500
>=	Greater than or equal to	>=500	Numbers greater than or equal to 500
<	Less than	<"Bunin"	Names from A through Bunim, but not Bunin
<=	Less than or equal to	<="Calloway"	Names from A through, and including, Calloway
<>	Not equal to	<>"Cyclone"	Any name except for Cyclone

CLUES TO USE

Searching for blank fields

Is Null and **Is Not Null** are two other types of common criteria. Is Null criteria will find all records where no entry has been made in the field.

Is Not Null will find all records where there is any entry in the field, even if the entry is 0. Primary key fields cannot have a null entry.

Creating a Query

A **query** is a database object that creates a datasheet of specified fields and records from one or more tables. It displays the answer to a "question" about the data in your database. You can edit, navigate, sort, find, and filter a query's datasheet just like a table's datasheet. Because a query datasheet is a subset of data, however, it is similar to a filter, but much more powerful. One of the most important differences is that a query is a saved object within the database, which means that it does not need to be recreated each time you want to see that particular subset of data. A **filter** is a temporary view of the data whose criteria is discarded when you remove the filter or close the datasheet. Table B-4 compares the two. **Scenario** John uses a query to correct data in the table and then find all of the music selections in the "country" category.

Steps 1 2 3 4

1. Click **Queries** on the Objects bar, then double-click **Create query by using wizard**
The Simple Query Wizard dialog box opens, allowing you to choose the table or query which contains the fields you want to display in the query. You select the fields in the order you want them to appear on the query datasheet.

QuickTip

You also can double-click a field to move it from the Available Fields list to the Selected Fields list.

2. Click **Category** in the Available Fields list, click the **Select Single Field button** >, click **Title**, click >, click **Artist**, click >, click **Tracks**, then click >
The Simple Query Wizard dialog box should look like Figure B-18.

3. Click **Next**, click **Next** to accept the **Detail option** in the next dialog box, accept the title **Music Inventory Query**, make sure the **Open the query to view information option button** is selected, then click **Finish**
The query's datasheet opens, as shown in Figure B-19, with all 58 records, but with only the four fields that you requested in the query wizard. You can use a query datasheet to edit or add information.

QuickTip

The sort, filter, and find buttons work the same way whether you are working with a query or table datasheet.

4. Double-click **10** in the Tracks cell for record 7, "No Words", then type **11**
This record is now correct in the database.

5. Click the **Design View button** 🔏 on the Query Datasheet toolbar
The **Query Design view** opens, showing you a list of fields in the Music Inventory table in the upper portion of the window, and the fields you have requested for the query in the **query design grid** in the lower portion of the window.

6. Click the **Criteria cell** for the Category field, then type **country**, as shown in Figure B-20
Query Design view is the view in which you add, delete, or change the order of fields, sort the records, or add criteria to limit the number of records shown in the resulting datasheet. Any change made in Query Design view is saved with the query object.

7. Click the **Datasheet View button** 🔳 on the Query Design toolbar
The resulting datasheet has four records that match the criteria "country" in the Category field. You can save a query with a name that accurately describes the resulting datasheet.

QuickTip

The only time you need to save changes in an Access database is when you make structural changes to an object in Design view.

8. Click **File** on the menu bar, click **Save As**, type **Country Music** in the Save Query 'Music Inventory Query' To text box, click **OK**, then close the query datasheet
Both the Music Inventory Query and Country Music queries are saved in this database as objects that you can access in the MediaLoft-B database window.

FIGURE B-18: Simple Query Wizard dialog box

The available fields come from this object

Select Single Field button

Fields for this query

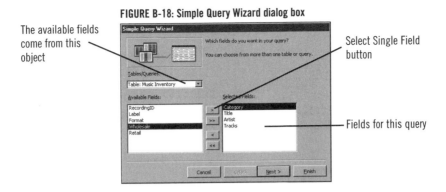

FIGURE B-19: Music Inventory Query datasheet

Design View button

Edit this entry

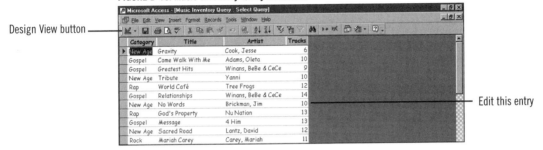

FIGURE B-20: Query Design view

Datasheet View button

Music Inventory field list

Criteria cell for Category field with country criteria

Query design grid

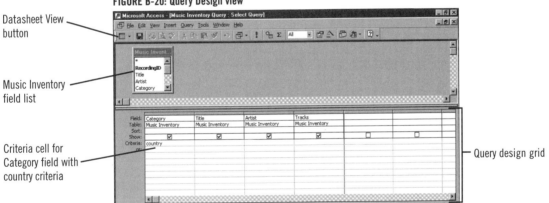

TABLE B-4: Queries vs. filters

characteristics	filters	queries
Are saved as an object in the database	No	Yes
Can be used to select a subset of records in a datasheet	Yes	Yes
Can be used to select a subset of fields in a datasheet	No	Yes
Its resulting datasheet can be used to enter and edit data	Yes	Yes
Its resulting datasheet can be used to sort, filter, and find records	Yes	Yes
Is commonly used as the source of data for a form or report	No	Yes
Can calculate sums, averages, counts, and other types of summary statistics across records	No	Yes
Can be used to create calculated fields	No	Yes

Access 2000

Using Query Design View

Every object in the database has a Design view in which you change the structure of the object. You can build a query by using the Query Design view directly or let the Query Wizard help you. In either case, if you want to add criteria to limit the number of records that you view in the datasheet, or if you want to change the fields you are viewing, you must use the query's Design view. **Scenario** John wants the Country Music query to also display the Retail field. In addition, he wants to add the folk music records and sort all the records according to the recording artist.

Steps 1 2 3 4

1. Click the **Country Music query** in the MediaLoft-B Database window, click the **Design button** in the database window, then click the **Restore button** if necessary
   Query Design view opens, displaying the current fields and criteria for the Country Music query. To add fields to the query, you can drag the fields from the upper field list and place them in any order in the grid.

Trouble?

You may have to scroll through the Music Inventory field list to display the Retail field.

2. Click the **Retail field** in the Music Inventory field list, then drag the **Retail field** to the **Tracks Field cell** in the query design grid
   The Query Design view now looks like Figure B-21. The Retail field is added to the query design grid between the Artist and Tracks fields. When you dropped the Retail field into the fourth column position of the query design grid, the Tracks field moved to the right to make room for the new field. You can also change the order of existing fields in the query design grid.

QuickTip

To remove fields from the query design grid, click the field selector, then press [Delete].

3. In the second column, click **Title**, click the **Title list arrow**, click **Artist**, click **Artist** in the third column, click the **Artist list arrow**, then click **Title**
   You have switched the order of the Title and Artist fields. You can also move fields by dragging them left and right in the query design grid by clicking the field selector, and dragging the field to the new location. The query design grid also displays criteria that limit the number of records in the resulting datasheet.

4. Click the **or: criteria cell** under the "country" criteria of the Category field, then type **folk**
   This additional criteria expression will add the folk selections to the current country selections. You also can enter Or criteria in one cell of the query design grid by entering "country" or "folk," but using two rows of the query design grid inherently joins the criteria in an Or expression.

5. Click the **Sort cell** for the Artist field, click the **Artist Sort list arrow**, then click **Ascending**
   The final Query Design view, as shown in Figure B-22, will find all records that match the Category criteria for "country" or "folk" and sort the records in ascending order by Artist. Notice that text criteria in the query design grid are surrounded by quotation marks (as were filter criteria), but that you did not need to type these characters.

6. Click the **Datasheet view button** on the Query Design toolbar
   Eight records are displayed in both the country and folk music categories, sorted in ascending order by Artist, as shown in Figure B-23.

7. Click **File** on the menu bar, click **Save As**, type **Country and Folk**, click **OK**, then click the **Print button** on the Query Datasheet toolbar

8. Close the query datasheet, close the MediaLoft-B database, then exit Access

Scroll bar
for Music
Inventory
field list

FIGURE B-21: Query Design view with new field, Retail

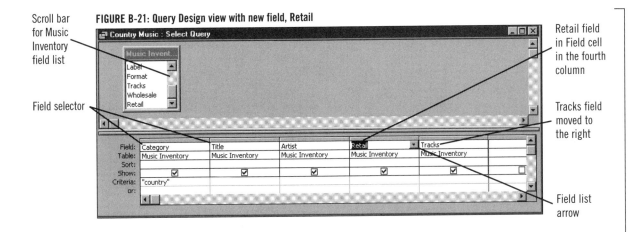

Field selector

Retail field
in Field cell
in the fourth
column

Tracks field
moved to
the right

Field list
arrow

Field order
of Artist and
Title fields
is changed

FIGURE B-22: Adding Or criteria and specifying a sort order

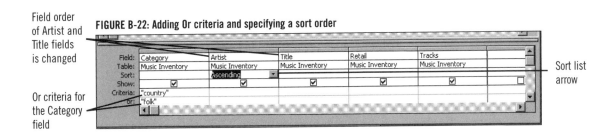

Or criteria for
the Category
field

Sort list
arrow

FIGURE B-23: Final query datasheet

Only Country or Folk
records are displayed

Records are sorted in
ascending order by Artist

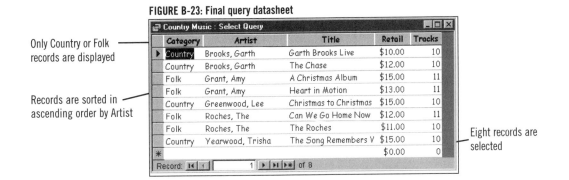

Eight records are
selected

Access 2000

Understanding And and Or criteria

Criteria placed on different rows of the query design grid are considered Or criteria. In other words, a record may be true for *either* row of criteria in order for it to be displayed on the resulting datasheet. Placing additional criteria in the *same* row, however, is considered the And criteria. For example, if "folk" were in the Category Criteria cell and >10 in the Retail Criteria cell, *both* criteria must be true in order for the record to be displayed in the resulting datasheet.

Practice

► Concepts Review

Label each element of the Select Query window shown in Figure B-24.

FIGURE B-24

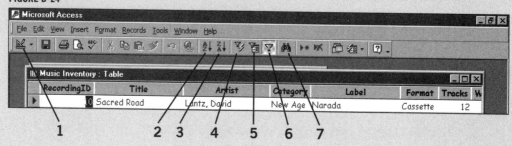

Match each term with the statement that describes it.

8. **Primary key**
9. **Table Wizard**
10. **Filter**
11. **Data type**
12. **Query**

a. Determines what type of data can be stored in each field
b. Provides interactive help to create the field names and data types for each field
c. A database object that creates a datasheet of specified fields and records from one or more tables
d. A field that contains unique information for each record
e. Creates a temporary subset of records

Select the best answer from the list of choices.

13. **Which data type would be best for a field that was going to store birth dates?**
    a. Text
    b. Number
    c. AutoNumber
    d. Date/Time
14. **Which data type would be best for a field that was going to store Web addresses?**
    a. Text
    b. Memo
    c. OLE
    d. Hyperlink
15. **Which data type would be best for a field that was going to store telephone numbers?**
    a. Text
    b. Number
    c. OLE
    d. Hyperlink
16. **Each of the following is true about a filter, *except***
    a. It creates a temporary datasheet of records that match criteria.
    b. The resulting datasheet can be sorted.
    c. The resulting datasheet includes all fields in the table.
    d. A filter is automatically saved as an object in the database.
17. **Sorting refers to**
    a. Reorganizing the records in either ascending or descending order.
    b. Selecting a subset of fields and/or records to view as a datasheet from one or more tables.
    c. Displaying only those records that meet certain criteria.
    d. Using Or and And criteria in the query design grid.

18. **Which criteria would be used in a Category field to find all music except that in the rap category?**
    a. /=/"rap"
    b. <>"rap"
    c. NULL "rap"
    d. IS NULL "rap"

 # Skills Review

1. **Plan a database.**
    a. Plan a database that will contain the names and addresses of physicians. You can use the local yellow pages to gather the information.
    b. On paper, sketch the Table Design view of a table that will hold this information. Write the field names in one column and the data types for each field in the second column.

2. **Create a table.**
    a. Start Access and use the Blank Access database option to create a database. Save the file as "Doctors" on your Project Disk.
    b. Use the Table Wizard to create a new table.
    c. Make sure the Business option button is selected. In the Sample Tables list, click Contacts.
    d. In the Sample Fields list box, choose each of the fields in the following order for your table: ContactID, FirstName, LastName, Address, City, StateOrProvince, PostalCode, Title.
    e. Rename the StateOrProvince field as "State."
    f. Name the table "Addresses," and allow Access to set the primary key field.
    g. Click the Modify the table design option button in the last Table Wizard dialog box, then click Finish.

3. **Use Table Design view.**
    a. In the first available blank row, add a new field called "PhoneNumber" with a Text data type.
    b. Change the Field Size property of the State field from 20 to 2.
    c. Insert a field named "Suite" with a Text data type between the Address and City fields.
    d. Add the description "M.D." or "D.O." to the Title field.
    e. Save and close the Addresses table, then close the Doctors database, but don't exit Access.

4. **Format a datasheet.**
    a. Open the Doctors-B database from your Project Disk. Open the Doctor Addresses table datasheet.
    b. Change the font to Arial Narrow, and the font size to 9.
    c. Change the gridline color to black, and change the vertical gridline to a transparent border.
    d. Change the page orientation to landscape and all of the margins to 0.5". Preview the datasheet (it should fit on one page), then print it.

5. **Understand sorting, filtering, and finding.**
    a. On a sheet of paper, identify three ways that you might want to sort an address list, such as the Doctor Addresses datasheet. Be sure to specify both the field you would sort on and the sort order (ascending or descending).
    b. On a sheet of paper, identify three ways that you might want to filter an address list, such as the Doctor Addresses datasheet. Be sure to specify both the field you would filter on and the criteria that you would use.

6. **Sort records and find data.**
    a. Sort the Doctor Addresses records in ascending order on the Last field, then list the first two doctors on paper.
    b. Sort the Doctor Addresses records in descending order on the Zip field, then list the first two doctors on paper.
    c. Find the records in which the Title field contains "D.O." How many records did you find?
    d. Find the records where the Zip field contains "64012." How many records did you find?

7. Filter records.

a. In the Doctor Addresses datasheet, filter the records for all physicians with the Title "D.O."

b. In the Doctor Addresses datasheet, filter the records for all physicians with the title "M.D." in the "64012" zip code, then print the datasheet.

8. Create a query.

a. Use the Query Wizard to create a new query based on the Doctor Addresses table with the following fields: First, Last, City, State, Zip.

b. Name the query "Doctors in Missouri," then view the datasheet.

c. In Query Design view, add the criteria "MO" to the State field, then view the datasheet.

d. Change Mark Garver's last name to Garvey.

9. Use Query Design view.

a. Modify the Doctors in Missouri query to include only those doctors in Kansas City, Missouri. Be sure that the criteria is in the same row so that both criteria must be true for the record to be displayed.

b. Save the query with the name "Doctors in Kansas City Missouri." Print the query results, then close the query datasheet.

c. Modify the Doctors in Kansas City Missouri query so that the records are sorted in ascending order on the last name, and add "DoctorNumber" as the first field in the datasheet.

d. Print and save the sorted query's datasheet, then close the datasheet.

e. Close the Doctors-B database and exit Access.

► Visual Workshop

Open the MediaLoft-B database and create a query based on the Music Inventory table that displays the datasheet shown in Figure B-25. Notice that only the Jazz category is displayed and that the records are sorted in a descending order on the Retail field. Save the query as "Jazz Selections" in the MediaLoft-B database.

FIGURE B-25

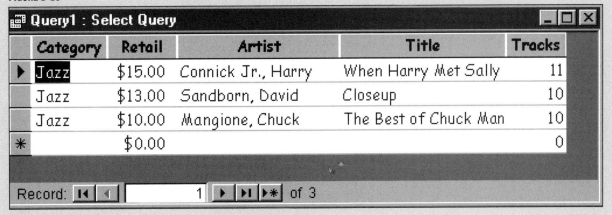

Using
Forms

Objectives

MOUS ► Plan a form
MOUS ► Create a form
MOUS ► Move and resize controls
MOUS ► Modify labels
MOUS ► Modify text boxes
► Modify tab order
MOUS ► Enter and edit records
MOUS ► Insert an image

A **form** is an Access database object that allows you to arrange the fields of a record in any layout. Although the datasheet view of a table or query can be used to navigate, edit, and enter new information, all of the fields for one record are sometimes not visible unless you scroll left or right. A form fixes that problem by using the screen to show the fields of only one record at a time. Forms are often the primary object used to enter, edit, and find data. Scenario► More people are becoming excited about the MediaLoft music inventory database. They have asked John Kim to create a form to make it easier to access, enter, and update this important inventory data.

Planning a Form

Properly organized and well-designed forms make a tremendous difference in the productivity of the end user. Since forms are the primary object used to enter and edit data, time spent planning a form is time well spent. Forms are often built to match a **source document** (for example, an employment application or a medical history form) to facilitate fast and accurate data entry. Now, however, it is becoming more common to type data directly into the database rather than first recording it on paper. Form design considerations, such as clearly labeled fields and appropriate formatting, are important. Other considerations include how the user tabs from field to field, and what type of **control** is used to display the data. See Table C-1 for more information on form controls. **Scenario** John considers the following form design considerations when planning his Music Inventory form.

Determine the overall purpose of the form
Have a good understanding of what information you need to gather through the form. This purpose often becomes the form's title such as "Music Inventory Entry Form."

Determine the underlying record source
The **record source** is either a table or query object, and contains the fields and records that the form will display.

Gather the source documents used to design your form, or sketch the form by hand if a paper form does not exist
When sketching the form, be sure to list all the fields and instructions you want the form to display.

Determine the best type of control to use for each element on the form
Figures C-1 and C-2 show examples of several controls. **Bound controls** display data from the underlying record source and are also used to edit and enter new data. **Unbound controls** do not change from record to record and exist only to clarify or enhance the appearance of the form.

TABLE C-1: Form controls

name	used to	bound or unbound
Label	Provide consistent descriptive text as you navigate from record to record	Unbound
Text box	Display, edit, or enter data for each record from an underlying record source	Bound
List box	Display a list of possible data entries	Bound
Combo box	Display a list of possible data entries for a field, and also provide text box for an entry from the keyboard; a "combination" of the list box and text box controls	Bound
Tab control	Create a three-dimensional aspect to a form so that controls can be organized and displayed by clicking the "tabs"	Unbound
Check box	Display "yes" or "no" answers for a field; if the box is "checked" it displays "yes" information	Bound
Toggle button	Display "yes" or "no" answers for a field; if the button is "pressed," it displays "yes" information	Bound
Option button	Display a limited list of possible choices for field	Bound
Bound image control	Display OLE data, such as a picture	Bound
Unbound image control	Display picture or clip art that doesn't change as you navigate from record to record	Unbound
Line and Rectangle controls	Draw lines and rectangles on the form	Unbound
Command button	Provide an easy way to initiate a command or run a macro	Unbound

FIGURE C-1: Sample form controls

Tab controls

Option group

Labels

List box

Combo box

Text boxes

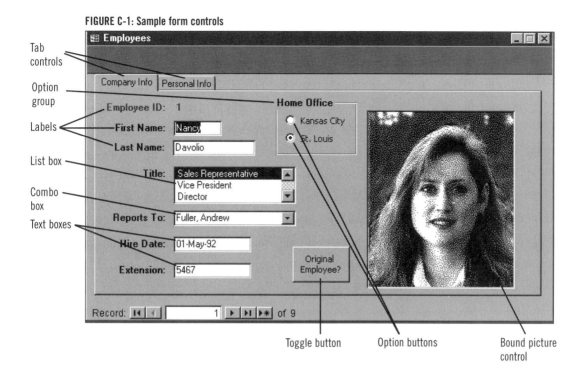

Toggle button   Option buttons   Bound picture control

FIGURE C-2: Sample form controls

Unbound image

Rectangle

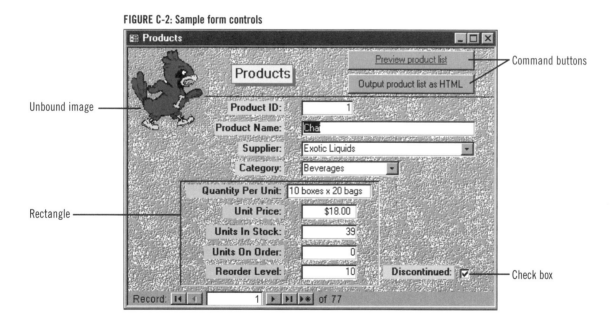

Command buttons

Check box

Creating a Form

You can create a form from scratch using **Form Design view**, or you can use the **Form Wizard** to create an initial form object that can be modified later if needed. The Form Wizard provides options for selecting fields, an overall layout, a style, and a form title. **Scenario▶** John created a sketch and made some notes on how he'd like the final Music Inventory form arranged, shown in Figure C-3. He uses the Form Wizard to get started.

Steps

1. Start Access, click the **Open an existing file option button**, then open the **MediaLoft-C** database from your Project Disk
   This MediaLoft-C database contains an enhanced Music Inventory table. John added more fields and records.

QuickTip
To hide the Office Assistant, click Help on the menu bar, then click Hide Office Assistant.

2. Click **Forms** on the Objects bar in the MediaLoft-C Database window, then double-click **Create form by using wizard**
   The Music Inventory table includes all of the fields required in the Music Inventory form.

3. Click the **Select All Fields button >>**, click **Next**, click the **Columnar layout option button**, click **Next**, click the **Standard** style, click **Next**, then click **Finish** to accept the name **Music Inventory** for the form
   The Music Inventory form opens in **Form view**, as shown in Figure C-4. Descriptive labels appear in the first column, and text boxes that display data from the underlying records appear in the second column. A check box control displays the yes/no data in the PeoplesChoice field. You can enter, edit, find, sort, and filter records using the form.

QuickTip
Sort, filter, and find buttons work the same way in a form as a datasheet, except that a form generally shows only one record at a time.

4. Click the **Artist text box**, click the **Sort Ascending button** on the Form View toolbar, then click the **Next Record button ▶** to move to the second record
   The "Adams, Oleta" record is second when the records are sorted in ascending order by recording artist.

5. Click the **Last Record button ▶I** on the Music Inventory form
   Neil Young's "Decade" is the last record when the records are sorted in ascending order.

6. Click the **Close button** on the Music Inventory form title bar to close the form
   The new Music Inventory form object appears in the Forms section of the MediaLoft-C Database window.

Using AutoForm

You can quickly create a form by clicking a table or query object in the database window, and then clicking the New Object:AutoForm button on the Database toolbar. AutoForm offers no prompts or dialog boxes; it instantly creates a form that displays all the fields in the previously chosen table or query using the same options as those you chose the last time you used the Form Wizard.

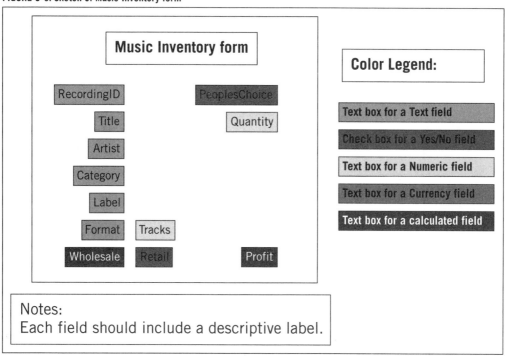

FIGURE C-3: Sketch of Music Inventory form

Music Inventory form

RecordingID   PeoplesChoice

Title   Quantity

Artist

Category

Label

Format   Tracks

Wholesale   Retail   Profit

Color Legend:

Text box for a Text field

Check box for a Yes/No field

Text box for a Numeric field

Text box for a Currency field

Text box for a calculated field

Notes:
Each field should include a descriptive label.

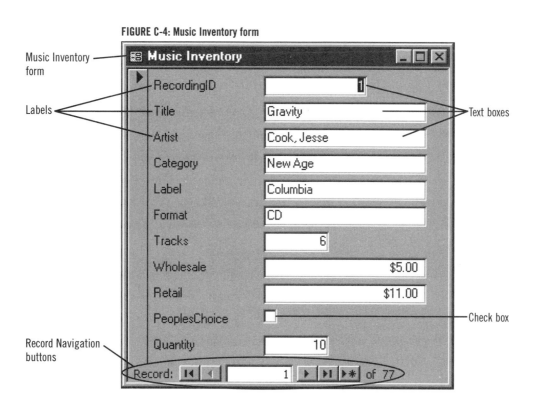

FIGURE C-4: Music Inventory form

Music Inventory form

Labels

Music Inventory

RecordingID	1
Title	Gravity
Artist	Cook, Jesse
Category	New Age
Label	Columbia
Format	CD
Tracks	6
Wholesale	$5.00
Retail	$11.00
PeoplesChoice	☐
Quantity	10

Text boxes

Check box

Record Navigation buttons

Record: 1 of 77

Moving and Resizing Controls

After you create a form, you can modify the size, location, and appearance of existing controls in Form Design view. Form Design view also allows you to add or delete controls. **Scenario** John moves and resizes the controls on the form to better match his original design.

Steps

Trouble?

Be sure you open the Design view of the Music Inventory form and not the Music Inventory table.

1. Click the **Music Inventory form**, click the **Design button** in the MediaLoft-C Database window, then click the **Maximize button** to maximize the Design view of the Music Inventory form

    The Design view of the Music Inventory form opens. The **Toolbox toolbar** contains buttons that allow you to add controls to the form. The **field list** contains the fields in the underlying object. You can toggle both of these screen elements on and off as needed. Widening the form gives you more room to reposition the controls.

2. Click the **Toolbox button** on the Form Design toolbar to toggle it off (if necessary), click the **Field List button** to toggle it off (if necessary), place the pointer on the right edge of the form, then when the pointer changes to ←→, drag the right edge to the **6"** mark on the horizontal ruler

    The form is expanded so that it is 6" wide, as shown in Figure C-5. Before moving, resizing, deleting, or changing a control in any way, you must select it.

3. Click the **PeoplesChoice check box**

    Squares, called **sizing handles**, appear in the corners and on the edges of the selected control. When you work with controls, the mouse pointer shape is very important. Pointer shapes are summarized in Table C-2.

Trouble?

If you make a mistake, immediately click the Undo button and try again.

4. Place the pointer on the **selected control**, when the pointer changes to 🖑, drag the control so that the left edge of the label is at the **4"** mark on the horizontal ruler and the bottom edge is aligned with the **RecordingID text box**

    The text boxes appear as white rectangles in this form. When you move a bound control, such as a text box or check box, the accompanying unbound label control to its left moves with it. The field name for the selected control appears in the Object list box.

QuickTip

You can move controls one pixel at a time by pressing [Ctrl] and an arrow key. You can resize controls one pixel at a time by pressing [Shift] and an arrow key.

5. Select and move the **Quantity** and **Tracks text boxes** using the 🖑 pointer to match their final locations as shown in Figure C-6

    Resizing controls also improves the design of the form.

6. Click the **Retail text box**, then use the ←→ pointer to drag the middle-right edge sizing handle left to the **2"** mark, click the **Wholesale text box**, then drag the middle-right edge sizing handle left to the **2"** mark

    Moving and resizing controls requires great concentration and mouse control. Don't worry if your screen doesn't *precisely* match the next figure, but *do* make sure that you understand how to use the move and resize mouse pointers used in Form Design view. Precision and accuracy are naturally developed with practice, but even experienced form designers regularly rely on the Undo button.

7. Click the **Form View button** on the Form Design toolbar, click the **Artist text box**, click the **Sort Descending button**, then click the **Sort Ascending button** on the Form View toolbar

    Your screen should look like Figure C-7.

FIGURE C-5: Design view of the Music Inventory form

Form View button

Horizontal ruler

Field List button

Labels

Vertical ruler

Text boxes

Toolbox button

6" mark

Right edge of form

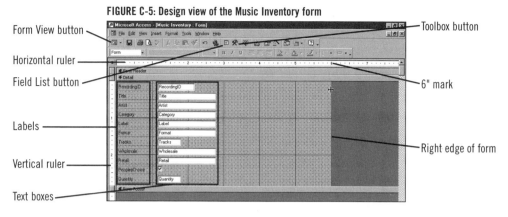

FIGURE C-6: Controls have been moved

Object list box

Text boxes have
been moved

PeoplesChoice label
and check box have
been moved

"Move" mouse
symbol

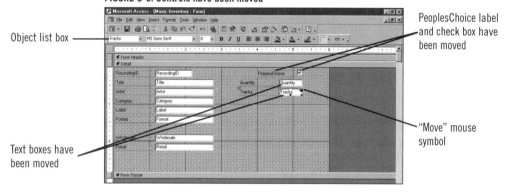

FIGURE C-7: Reorganized Music Inventory form

Check box

Text boxes

Labels

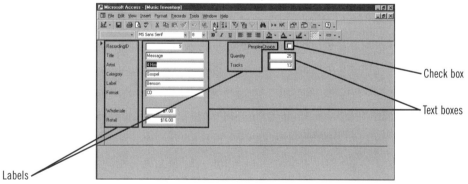

TABLE C-2: Form Design view mouse pointer shapes

shape	when does this shape appear?	action
⬉	When you point to any nonselected control on the form; it is the default mouse pointer	Single-clicking with this mouse pointer *selects* a control
✋	When you point to the edge of a selected control (but not when you are pointing to a sizing handle)	Dragging this mouse pointer moves all selected controls
☝	When you point to the larger sizing handle in the upper-left corner of a selected control	Dragging this mouse pointer *moves only the single control* where pointer is currently positioned, not other controls that may also be selected
↔ ↕ ↖ ↗	When you point to any sizing handle (except the larger one in the upper-left corner)	Dragging this mouse pointer *resizes* the control

Modifying Labels

When you create a form with the Form Wizard, it places a label to the left of each text box with the field's name. Often, you'll want to modify those labels to be more descriptive or user friendly. You can modify a label control by directly editing it in Form Design view, or you can make the change in the label's property sheet. The **property sheet** is a comprehensive listing of all **properties** (characteristics) that have been specified for that control. Scenario▶ John modifies the Music Inventory form's labels to be more descriptive.

Steps

Trouble?

If you double-click a label, you will open its property sheet. Close the property sheet by clicking its Close button, then single-click the label again.

▶ 1. Click the **Design View button** 🖉 on the Form View toolbar, click the **RecordingID label** to select it, click between the **g** and **I** in the RecordingID label, then press **[Spacebar]** to insert a space
   Directly editing labels in Form Design view is tricky because you must select the label and then precisely click where you want to edit it. You can also open the label's property sheet and modify the Caption property to change the displayed text.

2. Click the **Title label**, click the **Properties button** 🖺 on the Form Design toolbar, then click the **Format tab**, as shown in Figure C-8
   The Caption property controls the text displayed by the label control, and the property can be found on either the Format or the All tabs. The All tab is an exhaustive list of all the properties for a control.

Trouble?

Be sure to modify the Title label control and not the Title text box control. Text box controls must reference the *exact* field name in order to display the data within that field.

▶ 3. Click to the left of **Title** in the Caption property text box, type **Recording**, press **[Spacebar]**, then click 🖺 to toggle the property sheet off
   Don't be overwhelmed by the number of properties available for each control on the form. Over time, you may want to learn about most of these properties, but in the beginning, you'll be able to make the vast majority of the property changes through menu and toolbar options rather than by accessing the property sheet itself. Labels can be aligned so that they are closer to their respective text boxes.

4. Click the **Recording ID label**, then click the **Align Right button** 🗏 on the Formatting (Form/Report) toolbar
   The Recording ID label is now much closer to its associated text box. See Table C-3 for a list of techniques to quickly select several controls so that you can apply alignment and formatting changes to many controls simultaneously.

5. Click the **0.5"** mark on the horizontal ruler to select the first column of controls, as shown in Figure C-9, then click 🗏
   All the labels in the first column are right-aligned and next to their text boxes.

6. Click the **Save button** 🖫 on the Form Design toolbar, then click the **Form View button** 🖽 on the Form Design toolbar
   The Music Inventory form is saved, and you can see that the labels are close to the data in the first column.

FIGURE C-8: Looking at a label's property sheet

Recording ID label has been changed

Title label is chosen

Caption property

Properties button

The property sheet title bar tells you what type of control you are working with

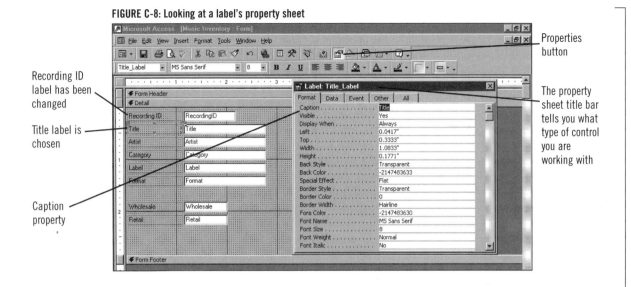

FIGURE C-9: Selecting several labels at the same time

Clicking the 0.5" mark on the ruler

All labels in the first column are selected

Formatting (Form/Report) toolbar

Align Right button

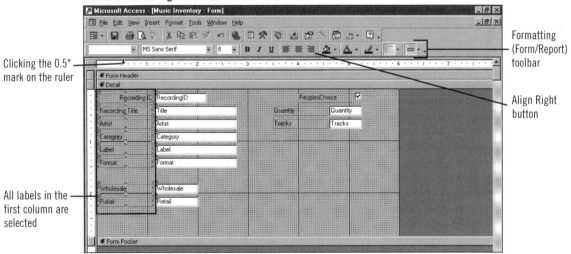

TABLE C-3: Selecting more than one control

technique	description
Click, [Shift]+click	Click a control, then press and hold [Shift] while clicking other controls; each one will be selected
Drag a selection box	If you drag a selection box (an imaginary box you create by dragging the pointer in Form Design view), every control that is in or touched by the edges of the box will be selected
Click in the ruler	If you click in either the horizontal or vertical ruler you will select all controls that intersect the selection line (an imaginary line you create by clicking the ruler)
Drag in the ruler	If you drag through either the horizontal or vertical ruler you will select all controls that intersect the selection line as it is dragged through the ruler

Modifying Text Boxes

Text boxes are generally used to display data from underlying fields and are therefore *bound* to that field. You can also use a text box as a **calculated control** which is not directly bound to a field but rather uses information from a field to calculate an answer. Scenario> John wants the Music Inventory form to calculate the profit for each record. He uses a text box calculated control to find the difference between the Retail and Wholesale fields.

Steps

Trouble?

The Toolbox toolbar may be floating or docked on the edge of your screen. Drag the title bar of a floating toolbar or the top edge of a docked toolbar to move it to a convenient location.

1. Click the **Design View button** 🔽 on the Form View toolbar, click the **Toolbox button** 🛠 on the Form View toolbar, click the **Text Box button** ab on the Toolbox toolbar, the pointer changes to ⁺ab, click just below the Retail text box on the form, then if necessary move the new text box and label control to align with the controls above it
Your screen should look like Figure C-10. Adding a new text box *automatically* added a new label with the default caption "Text22:". You can access the text box's property sheet to bind it to an underlying field or expression, or you can create the calculated expression directly in the text box.

Trouble?

The number in the caption "Text22" varies depending on how many controls you add to the form.

2. Click **Unbound** in the new text box, type **=[Retail]-[Wholesale]**, then press **[Enter]**
When referencing field names within an expression, you *must* use square brackets and type the field name exactly as it appears in the Table Design view. You do not need to worry about uppercase and lowercase letters. The label for any expression should be descriptive.

Trouble?

If your calculated control did not work, return to Design view, click the calculated control, press [Delete], then repeat steps 1 through 4.

3. Click the **Text22: label** to select it, click the **Text22: label** again to edit it, double-click **Text22**, type **Profit** as the new caption, then press **[Enter]**
The calculated text box control and associated label are modified.

4. Click the **Form View button** 🔲 to view your changes, click the **Ascending Sort button** ↑ on the Form View toolbar, then click the **First Record button** ◀
Your screen should look like Figure C-11. The first record is $5 wholesale and sells for $11.00 retail so the profit is calculated as $6. You can use Form Design view to make a few more changes to clarify the form.

5. Click 🔽, click the **Calculated text box**, then click the **Properties button** 🖺 on the Form Design toolbar
By default, the values in text boxes that contain numeric and currency fields are right-aligned. Text boxes that contain fields with other data types or those that start as unbound controls are left-aligned. Monetary values should be right-aligned and display with a dollar sign and cents.

Trouble?

Properties are not listed in alphabetical order so you may have to scroll up or down the property sheet to find the Format and Text Align properties.

6. Click the **Format tab** in the Text Box property sheet, click the **Format property text box**, click the **Format property list arrow**, click **Currency**, click the **Text Align property text box**, click the **Text Align property list arrow**, then click **Right**

7. Click 🖺, switch the position of the Retail and Wholesale text boxes, move and align the Profit label, resize the calculated text box (as shown in Figure C-12), then click 🔲
The calculated profit value should display as $6.00 and be right-aligned within the text box.

FIGURE C-10: Adding a calculated text box

Toolbox button

Text22

New label

New text box

Toolbox toolbar

Click to add a text box control

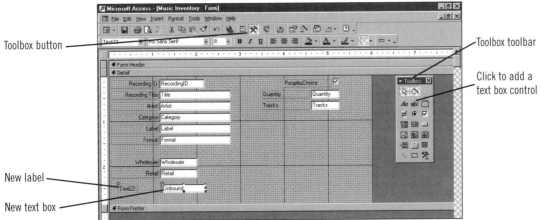

FIGURE C-11: Displaying a calculated text box

New label

New calculated text box control

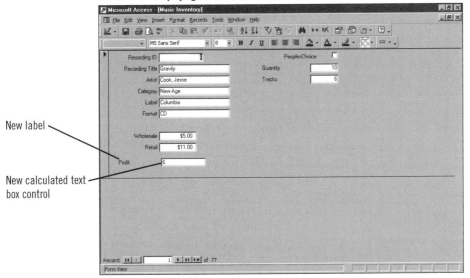

FIGURE C-12: Updated Music Inventory form

Retail and Wholesale fields are switched

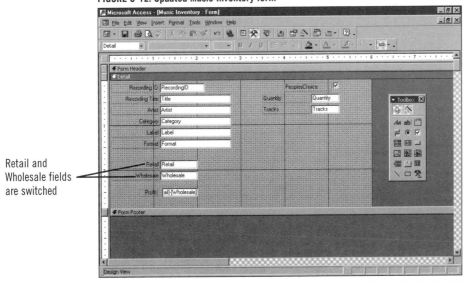

Modifying Tab Order

Once all of the controls have been added, moved, and resized on the form, you'll want to check and probably modify the tab order. The **tab order** is the order in which the **focus** (the active control) moves as you press [Tab] in Form view. Since the form is the primary object by which users will view, edit, and enter data, careful attention to tab order is essential to maintain their productivity and satisfaction with the database. **Scenario** John checks the tab order of the Music Inventory form, then changes the tab order as necessary in Form Design view.

QuickTip

You can also press [Enter] to move the focus from field to field on a form.

1. **Press [Tab]** 11 times watching the focus move through the bound controls of the form
Currently, focus moves back and forth between the left and right columns of controls. For efficient data entry, you want the focus to move down through the first column of text boxes before moving to the second column.

2. **Click the Design View button** 🖊️ **on the Form View toolbar, click View on the menu bar, then click Tab Order**
The Tab Order dialog box opens in which you can drag fields up or down to change their tab sequence. The Tab Order dialog box allows you to change the tab order of controls in three sections: Form Header, Detail, and Form Footer. Right now, all of the controls are positioned in the form's Detail section. See Table C-4 for more information on form sections.

3. **Click the Retail row selector in the Custom Order list, drag it up to position it just below Format, click the Wholesale row selector, drag it under Retail, click the Tracks row selector, then drag it under Quantity as shown in Figure C-13**
With the change made, test the new tab order.

4. **Click OK in the Tab Order dialog box, then click the Form View button** 📧 **on the Form Design toolbar**
Although nothing visibly changes on the form, the tab order is different.

5. **Press [Enter]** 10 times to move through the fields of the form with the new tab order
You should now be moving through all of the text boxes of the first column, with the exception of the calculated field, before you move to the second column.

6. **Click the Save button** 💾 **on the Form View toolbar**

FIGURE C-13: Tab Order dialog box

Tab Order dialog box with Detail section chosen

Form Header section

Detail section

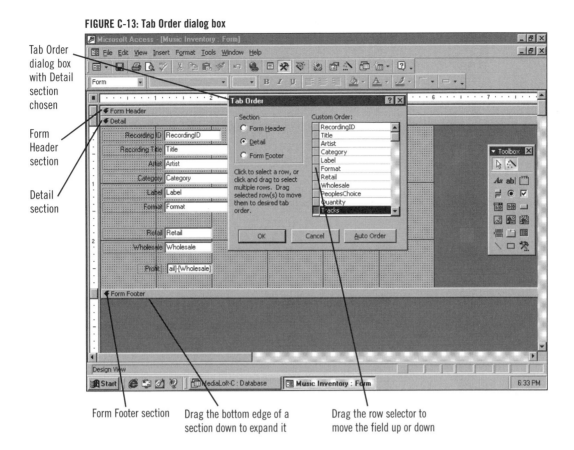

Form Footer section
Drag the bottom edge of a section down to expand it
Drag the row selector to move the field up or down

TABLE C-4: Form sections

section	description
Form Header	Controls placed in the Form Header print only once at the top of the printout; by default, this section is not "opened" in Form Design view, but can be expanded by dragging its bottom edge in Form Design view.
Detail	Controls placed in the Detail section print once for every record in the underlying table or query object; all controls created by the Form Wizard are placed in this section
Form Footer	Controls placed in the Form Footer print only once at the end of the printout; by default, this section is not "opened" in Form Design view, but it can be expanded by dragging its bottom edge down in Form Design view

Entering and Editing Records

The most important reasons for using a form are to find, enter, or edit records to the underlying object. You can also print a form, but you must be careful because printing a form often produces a very long printout because of the vertical orientation of the fields. **Scenario** John uses the Music Inventory form to add a new record to the underlying Music Inventory table. Then he prints the form with the data for only the new record.

1. Click the **New Record button** on the Form View toolbar
A new, blank record is displayed. The text "(AutoNumber)" appears in the Recording ID field, which will automatically increment when you begin to enter data. The Specific Record box indicates the current record number.

2. Press **[Tab]** to move the focus to the **Recording Title text box**, type **The Dance**, then enter the rest of the information shown in Figure C-14
Notice that the Profit text box shows the calculated result of $4.00. The new record is stored as record 78 in the Music Inventory table.

3. Click **File** on the menu bar, click **Print** to open the Print dialog box, click the **Selected Record(s) option button** in the Print Range section, then click **OK**
Forms are also often used to edit existing records in the database.

4. Click the **Recording Title text box**, click the **Find button** on the Form View toolbar to open the Find and Replace dialog box, type **Mermaid Avenue** in the Find What text box, then click **Find Next**
Record 77 appears behind the Find and Replace dialog box, as shown in Figure C-15.

5. Click **Cancel** in the Find and Replace dialog box, press **[Tab]** five times to go to the Retail field, type **20**, then press **[Tab]**
Editing either the Wholesale or Retail fields automatically updates the calculated Profit field. Forms are also a great way to filter the records to a specific subset.

6. Click **Pop** in the Category text box, then click the **Filter By Selection button** on the Form View toolbar
Twelve records were found that matched the "Pop" criteria. Previewing the records helps to determine how many pages the printout would be.

7. Click the **Print Preview button** on the Form View toolbar
Since about three records print on a page, your printout would be four pages long.

8. Click the **Close button** on the Print Preview toolbar, then click the **Remove Filter button** on the Form View toolbar so that all 78 records in the Music Inventory table are available

FIGURE C-14: Entering a new record into a form

Edit record symbol

New Record button

Calculated text box automatically displays the answer

Current record number   New Record button

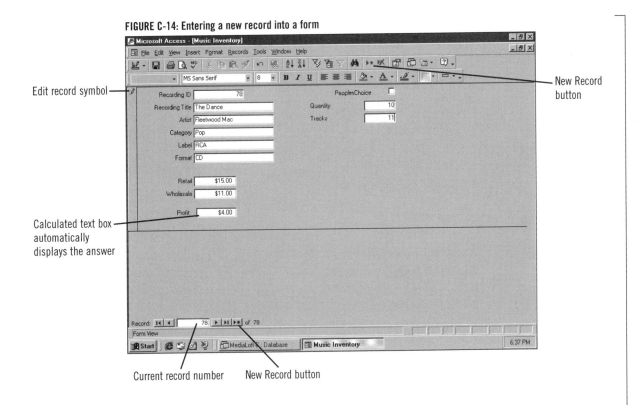

FIGURE C-15: Finding "Mermaid Avenue" using a form

Mermaid Avenue found in Title field

Find button

Record 77

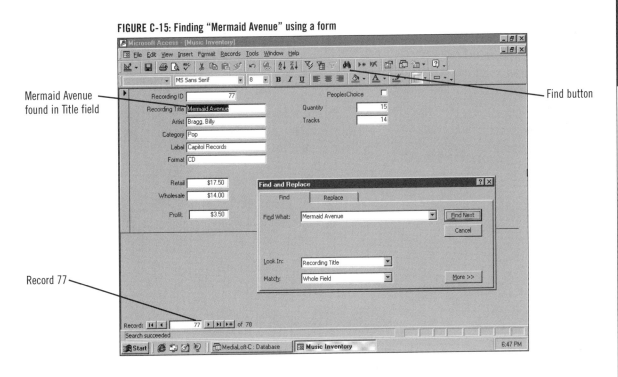

Inserting an Image

Graphic images, such as pictures, a logo, or clip art, can add style and professionalism to a form. If you add a graphic image as an unbound image to the Form Header, the image will appear at the top of the form in Form view and once at the top of the printout when printing records through a form. **Scenario** John adds the MediaLoft logo and a descriptive title to the Form Header section.

Steps 1234

1. Click the **Design View button** 🖾 on the Form View toolbar, place the pointer on the bottom edge of the Form Header, the pointer changes to ✛, then drag the bottom of the Form Header section to the **1"** mark on the vertical ruler
   The Form Header section is open.

2. Click the **Image button** 🖾 on the Toolbox toolbar, the pointer changes to ⁺🖾, then click in the **Form Header section** at the 1" mark on the horizontal ruler
   The Insert Picture dialog box opens. The MediaLoft image file you want to insert in the Form Header is on the Project Disk.

3. Click the **Look in list arrow**, click the drive containing your Project Disk, click **smallmedia**, then click **OK**
   The MediaLoft logo appears in the Form Header, surrounded by handles, as shown in Figure C-16. Form header titles add a finishing touch to a form.

QuickTip

If you need your name on the printed solution, enter your name as a label below the MediaLoft Music label.

4. Click the **Label button** 🗛 on the Toolbox toolbar, the pointer changes to ⁺A, click to the right of the **MediaLoft logo** in the Form Header section, type **MediaLoft Music**, then press **[Enter]**
   Labels can be formatted to enhance the appearance on the form.

5. Click the **Font Size list arrow**, click **24**, point to the **upper-right resizing handle**, then drag the ⤢ pointer so that the label **MediaLoft Music** is completely displayed
   If you double-click a label's sizing handle, the label will automatically adjust to display the entire caption.

6. Click the **Form View button** 🖽 on the Form Design toolbar
   You can go directly to a specific record by typing the record number in the specific record box.

7. Click in the **specific record box** on the Record Navigation buttons, type **11**, then press **[Enter]**
   Compare your form with Figure C-17.

8. Click **File** on the menu bar, click **Print**, click the **Selected Record(s) option button**, then click **OK**

9. Click the **Close button** on the Music Inventory form, then click **Yes** to save any changes if necessary

10. Close the MediaLoft-C database, then exit Access

FIGURE C-16: Adding an image to the Form Header section

1" mark on the ruler

MediaLoft logo

Label button

Image button

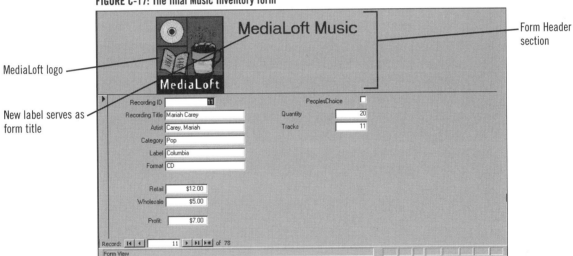

FIGURE C-17: The final Music Inventory form

MediaLoft logo

New label serves as form title

Form Header section

Creating a hyperlink from an image

Once an image is added to a form, you can convert it to a hyperlink by using its property sheet to modify the control's Hyperlink Address property in Form Design view. Depending on what you enter for the Hyperlink Address property, clicking the hyperlinked image in Form view opens another file, Access object, Web address, or e-mail address. For example, C:\Colleges\JCCCDescriptions.doc is the Hyperlink Address property entry to link a Word document at the specified drive and folder location; http://www.jccc.net creates a link between the image and the specified Web address.

Practice

► Concepts Review

Label each element of the Form Design window shown in Figure C-18.

FIGURE C-18

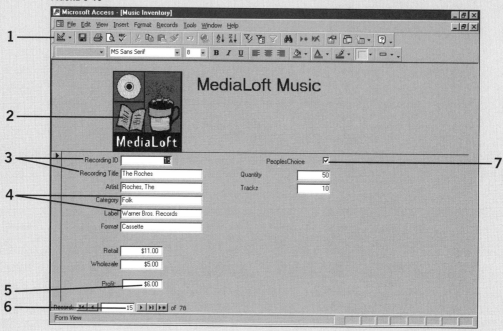

Match each term with the statement that describes it.

8. Sizing handles
9. Detail section
10. Bound control
11. Tab order
12. Form
13. Calculated control

a. The way in which the focus moves from one bound control to the next
b. Displays data from a field in the underlying record source
c. Black squares that appear in the corners and edges of the selected control
d. An Access database object that allows you to arrange the fields of a record in any layout; you use it to enter, edit, and delete records
e. Uses a text box and an expression to display an answer
f. Controls placed here print once for every record in the underlying table or query object

Select the best answer from the list of choices.

14. Every element on a form is called a
    a. Handle.
    b. Control.
    c. Piece.
    d. Property.

15. The pointer used to resize a control is
    a. 👆
    b. ↔
    c. ✋
    d. ✛

16. The most common bound control is the
    a. Check box.
    b. Text box.
    c. Combo box.
    d. Label.

17. The most common unbound control is the
    a. Image.
    b. Text box.
    c. Combo box.
    d. Label.

18. The _____ view is used to modify form controls.
    a. Design
    b. Datasheet
    c. Print Preview
    d. Form

Access 2000

▶ Skills Review

1. Plan a form.
a. Plan a form to use for the data entry of business contacts by looking at several business cards.
b. Write down the organization of the fields on the form. Determine what type of control you will use for each bound field.
c. Identify the labels you would like to display on the form.

2. Create a form.
a. Start Access and open the Membership-C database from your Project Disk.
b. Click the Forms button in the Membership-C Database window, then double-click the Create form by using wizard option.
c. Base the form on the Contacts table, and include all of the fields.
d. Use a Columnar layout, a Standard style, and title the form "Contact Entry Form."
e. Display the form with data.

3. Move and resize controls.
a. Open and maximize the Design View window for the Contact Entry Form.
b. Widen the form so that the right edge is at the 6" mark on the horizontal ruler.
c. Move the LNAME text box and corresponding label to the right of the FNAME text box.
d. Move the DUESOWED and DUESPAID text boxes and corresponding labels to the right of the address controls.
e. Resize the PHONE and ZIP text boxes to be the same size as the CITY text box.
f. Move the PHONE text box and corresponding label between the FNAME and COMPANY controls.

4. Modify labels.
a. Right align all of the labels.
b. Modify the FNAME label to FIRST NAME, the LNAME label to LAST NAME, the DUESOWED label to DUES OWED, and the DUESPAID label to DUES PAID.

5. Modify text boxes.
a. Add a new text box below the DUESPAID text box.
b. Type the expression =[DUESOWED]-[DUESPAID] in the new unbound text box. (*Hint*: Remember that you must use the *exact field names* in a calculated expression.)
c. In the property sheet for the new calculated control, change the Format property to Currency.
d. Right align the new calculated text boxes.
e. Change the calculated text box label from Text20: to BALANCE.
f. Move and resize the new calculated control and label so that it is aligned beneath the DUESOWED and DUES-PAID controls.

6. Modify tab order.
a. Change the Tab order so that pressing [Tab] moves the focus through the text boxes in the following order: FNAME, LNAME, PHONE, COMPANY, STREET, CITY, STATE, ZIP, DUESOWED, DUESPAID, BALANCE text box

7. Enter and edit records.

a. Use the Contact Entry Form to enter the following new records:

	FIRST NAME	LAST NAME	PHONE	COMPANY	STREET
Record 1	Jane	Eagan	555-1166	Cummins Construction	1515 Maple St.
Record 2	Mark	Daniels	555-2277	Motorola	1010 Green St.

	CITY	STATE	ZIP	DUES OWED	DUES PAID
1 con't.	Fontanelle	KS	50033-////	$50.00	$25.00
2 con't.	Bridgewater	KS	50022-////	$50.00	$50.00

b. Print the Mark Daniels record.

c. Find the Lois Goode record, enter IBM in the Company text box, then print that record.

d. Filter for all records with a ZIP entry of 64145. How many records did you find?

e. Sort the filtered 64145 ZIP code records in ascending order by Last Name, then print the first one.

8. Insert an image.

a. In Form Design view, expand the Form Header section to the 1" mark on the vertical ruler.

b. Use the Image control to insert the handin1.bmp file found on your Project Disk in the Form Header.

c. Centered and below the graphic file, add the label MEMBERSHIP INFORMATION in a 24-point font. Be sure to resize the label so that all of the text is visible.

d. Add your name as a label.

e. View the form using the Form view.

f. Print the selected record.

g. Close the form, close the database, then exit Access.

Visual Workshop

Using the Clinic-C database, create the form based on the Demographics table, as shown in Figure C-19. Notice that the label "Patient Form" is 24 points and has been placed in the Form Header section. The clip art, medstaff.bmp, can be found on the Project Disk. The image has been placed on the right side of the Detail section, and many controls had to be resized in order for it to fit. Also notice that the labels are right-aligned. You also need to correct the gender entry for this record.

FIGURE C-19

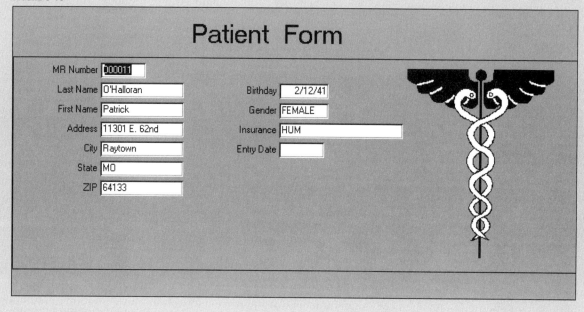

Using

Reports

Unit D

Objectives

- [MOUS] ► **Plan a report**
- [MOUS] ► **Create a report**
- [MOUS] ► **Group records**
- [MOUS] ► **Change the sort order**
- [MOUS] ► **Modify an expression**
- [MOUS] ► **Align controls**
- [MOUS] ► **Format controls**
- ► **Create mailing labels**

A **report** is an Access object used to create printouts. You cannot enter or edit data through a report. Although data displayed in a report can be viewed on the screen, it is usually sent to a printer. Access reports can be based on the fields and records of either a table or a query object, can include extensive formatting embellishments such as clip art and lines, and can include professional headers and footers. Reports can also include meaningful calculations such as subtotals on groups of records. Scenario► John Kim wants to produce reports that he can distribute to MediaLoft employees who do not yet have access to the MediaLoft database.

Planning a Report

Without clear communication, the accuracy and integrity of information being discussed can be questioned, misinterpreted, or obscured. Hard copy reports are often the primary tool used to communicate database information at meetings, with outsiders, and with top executives. Although the **Report Wizard** can help you create an initial report object that you can later modify, the time spent planning your report not only increases your productivity but also ensures that the overall report meets its intended objectives. **Scenario** John has been asked to provide several reports on a regular basis to the MediaLoft executives. He plans his first report that summarizes inventory quantities within each music category.

John uses the following guidelines to plan his report:

Identify a meaningful title for the report

The title should clearly identify the purpose of the report and be meaningful to those who will be reading the report. The title is created with a label control placed in the **Report Header** section. **Sections** are the parts of the report that determine where a control will display on the report. See Table D-1 for more information on report sections. Just like forms, every element on a report is a control.

Determine the information (the fields and records) that the report will show

You can base a report on a table, but usually you create a query to gather the specific fields from the one or more tables upon which to base the report. Of course, using a query also allows you to set criteria to limit the number of records displayed by the report.

Determine how the fields should be laid out on the report

Most reports display fields in a horizontal layout across the page, but you can arrange them in any way you want. Just as in forms, bound text box controls are used on a report to display the data stored in the underlying records. These text boxes are generally placed in the report **Detail** section.

Determine how the records should be sorted and/or grouped within the report

In an Access report, the term **grouping** refers to sorting records *plus* providing a section before the group of records called the **Group Header** section and a section after the group of records called the **Group Footer** section. These sections include additional controls that often contain calculated expressions such as a subtotal for a group of records. The ability to group records is extremely powerful and only available through the report object.

Identify any other descriptive information that should be placed at the end of the report or at the top or bottom of each page

You will use the **Report Footer**, **Page Header**, and **Page Footer** sections for these descriptive controls. John has sketched his first report in Figure D-1.

FIGURE D-1: Sketch of the Quantity Report

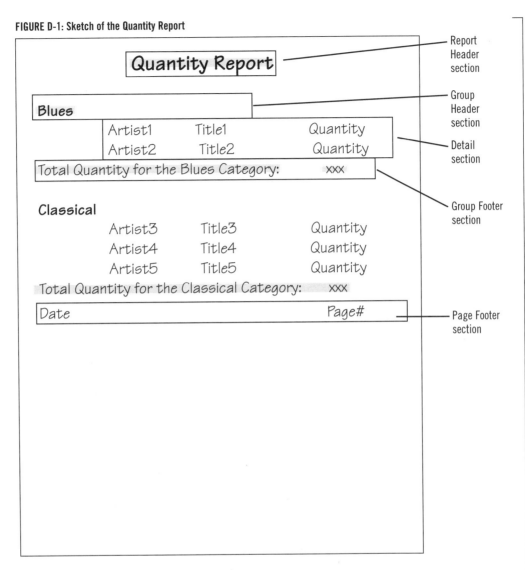

TABLE D-1: Report sections

section	where does this section print?	which controls are most commonly placed there?
Report Header	At the top of the first page of the report	Label controls containing the report title; can also include clip art, a logo image, or a line separating the title from the rest of the report
Page Header	At the top of every page (but below the report header on page one)	Descriptive label controls often acting as column headings for text box controls in the Detail section
Group Header	Before every group of records	Text box control for the field by which the records are grouped
Detail	Once for every record	Text box controls for the rest of the fields
Group Footer	After every group of records	Text box controls containing calculated expressions, such as subtotals or counts, for the records in that group
Page Footer	At the bottom of every page	Text box controls containing page number or date expression
Report Footer	At the end of the entire report	Text box controls containing expressions such as grand totals or counts that calculate an answer for all of the records in the report

Creating a Report

You can create reports in Access in **Report Design view**, or you can use the Report Wizard to help you get started. The Report Wizard asks questions that guide you through the initial development of the report, similar to the Form Wizard. In addition to questions about which object the report is based, which fields you want to view in the report, and the style and layout of the report, the Report Wizard also asks how you want report records to be grouped and sorted. **Scenario** John uses the Report Wizard to create the Quantities Report he planned on paper.

1. Start Access, click the **Open an existing file option button**, then open the **MediaLoft-D** database from your Project Disk
   This database contains an enhanced Music Inventory table and several queries from which you will base your reports.

2. Click **Reports** on the Objects bar in the MediaLoft-D Database window, then double-click **Create report by using wizard**
   The Report Wizard dialog box opens. You'll use the Selection Quantities query for this report. Another way to quickly create a report is by selecting a table or query, clicking the New Object list arrow on the Database toolbar and then selecting AutoReport. AutoReport, however, does not give you a chance to review the options provided by the Report Wizard.

3. Click the **Tables/Queries list arrow**, click **Query: Selection Quantities**, click **Category** in the Available Fields list, click the **Select Single Field button** ⚋, click **Title**, click ⚋, click **Artist**, click ⚋, click **Quantity**, then click ⚋
   The first dialog box of the Report Wizard should look like Figure D-2. The Report Wizard also asks grouping and sorting questions that determine the order and amount of detail provided on the report.

   Trouble?
   You can always click Back to review previous dialog boxes within a wizard.

4. Click **Next**, click **Next** to move past the grouping levels question, click the **first sort order list arrow** in the sort order dialog box, then click **Category**
   At this point you have not specified any grouping fields, but specified that you want the fields sorted by Category. You can use the Report Wizard to specify up to four sort fields in either an ascending or descending sort order for each field.

5. Click **Next**, click **Next** to accept the **Tabular** layout and **Portrait** orientation, click **Corporate** for the style, click **Next**, type **Quantities Report** for the report title, verify that the **Preview the report option button** is selected, then click **Finish**
   The Quantities Report opens in Print Preview, as shown in Figure D-3. It is very similar to the sketch created earlier. Notice that the records are sorted by the Category field.

Why reports should be based on queries

Although you can use the first dialog box of the Report Wizard to select fields from different tables without first creating a query to collect those fields into one object, it is not recommended. If you later decide that you want to add more fields to the report or limit the number of records in the table, you will find it very easy to add fields or criteria to an underlying query object to meet these new needs. To accomplish this same task without using an intermediary query object requires that you change the properties of the report itself, which most users find more difficult.

FIGURE D-2: First Report Wizard dialog box

Base the report on the Selection Quantities query

Select Single Field button

Fields selected for the report

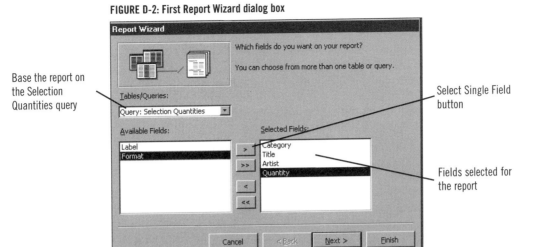

Report Header

Page Header

FIGURE D-3: Quantities Report in Print Preview

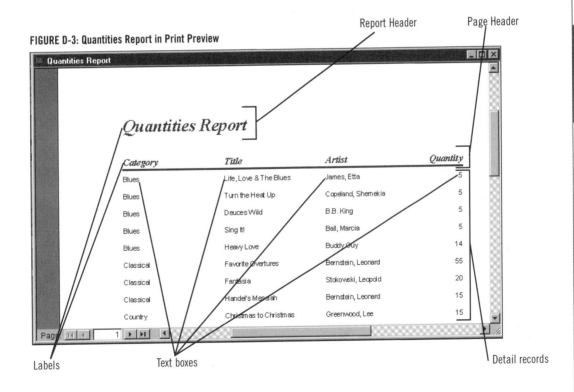

Labels

Text boxes

Detail records

Access 2000

Grouping Records

Grouping refers to sorting records on a report *plus* providing an area above and below the group of records in which additional controls can be placed. These two sections of the report are called the Group Header and Group Footer. You can create groups on a report through the Report Wizard, or you can change an existing report's grouping and sorting fields in Report Design view. Just as with forms, you make all structural changes to a report in the object's Design view. **Scenario** John wants to group the Quantities Report by Category instead of simply sorting it by Category. In addition, he wants to add controls to the Group Header and Group Footer to clarify and summarize information within the report.

Trouble?

If a property has a predetermined set of options, a list arrow will display when you click that property's text box in the property sheet.

1. Click the **Design View button** 📐 on the Print Preview toolbar to switch to Report Design view, as shown in Figure D-4

Report Design view shows you the sections of the report as well as the controls within each section. Labels and text boxes are formatted similarly in Report Design view. You can click a control and then click the Properties button to view the title bar of the property sheet to determine the nature of a control. Report Design view is where you change grouping and sort fields.

2. Click the **Sorting and Grouping button** 📇 on the Report Design toolbar, click the **Group Header text box**, click the **Group Header list arrow**, click **Yes**, click the **Group Footer text box**, click the **Group Footer list arrow**, then click **Yes**

Specifying "Yes" for the Group Header and Group Footer properties opens those sections of the report in Report Design view.

3. Click 📇 to close the dialog box, click the **Category text box** in the Detail section, then drag the **textbox** with the 🖐 pointer directly up into the Category Header section

By placing the Category text box in the Category Header, it will print once for each new group rather than once for each record. You can add calculated subtotal controls for each category of records by placing a text box in the Category Footer section.

QuickTip

The Field list, Toolbox toolbar, and property sheet may or may not be visible, but you can turn them on and off by clicking their respective toggle buttons. You can move them by dragging their title bars.

4. If the Toolbox toolbar is not visible, click the **Toolbox button** 🛠 on the Report Design toolbar, click the **Text Box button** 🔠 on the Toolbox toolbar, then click in the **Category Footer section** directly below the Quantity text box

Your screen should look like Figure D-5. You can use the label and text box controls in the Category Footer section to describe and subtotal the Quantity field respectively.

5. Click the **Text13: label** in the Category Footer section to select it, double-click **Text13**, type **Subtotal**, then press **[Enter]**

Trouble?

If you double-click the edge of a control, you open the control's property sheet.

6. Click the **unbound text box control** in the Category Footer section to select it, click the **unbound text box control** again to edit it, then type **=sum([Quantity])**

The expression that calculates the sum of the Quantity field is now in the unbound text box control. Calculated expressions start with an equal sign. When entering an expression, the field name must be referenced exactly and surrounded by square brackets.

7. Click the **Print Preview button** 🔍 on the Report Design toolbar, then scroll through the report as necessary

The new report that groups and summarizes records by Category appears, as shown in Figure D-6. Since the Category text box was moved to the Category Header section, it prints only once per group of records. Each group of records is trailed by a Group Footer that includes the Subtotal label as well as a calculated field that subtotals the Quantity field.

8. Click **Close** on the Print Preview toolbar, click the **Save button** 💾, then click the **Quantities Report Close button** to close the report

The Quantities Report is now an object in the MediaLoft-D Database window.

FIGURE D-4: Quantities Report Design view

Field List button

Toolbox button

Sorting and Grouping button

Properties button

Sections

Labels

Toolbox toolbar

Text boxes

Field list

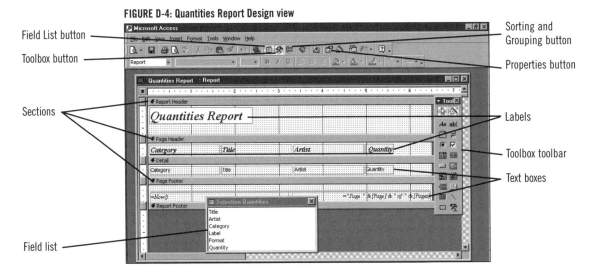

FIGURE D-5: Adding controls to the group footer section

Category Header

Category text box
moved up from
Detail section into
Category Header
section

Category Footer

Text Box button

New text box

New label

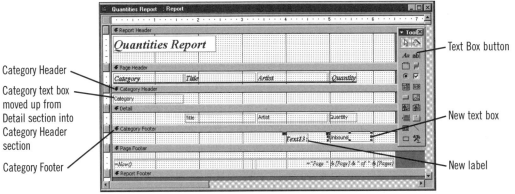

FIGURE D-6: The Quantities Report grouped by Category

Group Header
(Category is the
grouping field)

Report Header

Page Header

Detail

Group Footer
(Category is the
grouping field)

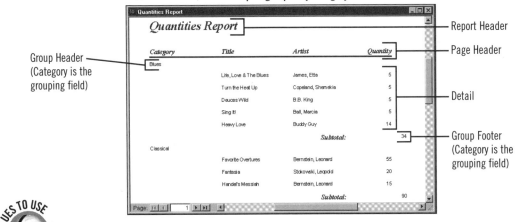

Adding a field to a report

Clicking the Field List button ▣ on the Report Design toolbar toggles the field list of the underlying table or query object. To add a field from this list to the report, simply drag it from the Field list to the appropriate position on the report. This action creates both a label control that displays the field name and a text box control that displays the value of the field from the underlying records.

Changing the Sort Order

Grouping records is really just sorting them with the additional ability to create a Group Header or Group Footer section on the report. The grouping field acts as a primary sort field. You can define further sort fields too. When you further sort records within a group, you order the Detail records according to a particular field. The Report Wizard prompts you for group and sort information at the time you create the report, but you can also group and sort an existing report by using the Sorting and Grouping dialog box in Report Design view. **Scenario** John wants to modify the Quantities Report so that the Detail records are sorted by the Artist field within the Category group.

Steps

1. Click the **Quantities Report** in the MediaLoft-D Database window, then click the **Design button**
   The Quantities Report opens in Report Design view.

2. Click the **Sorting and Grouping button** on the Report Design toolbar, click the **second row Field/Expression text box**, click the **Field/Expression list arrow**, then click **Artist**
   The Sorting and Grouping dialog box looks like Figure D-7. There is no Sorting and Grouping indicator in the Artist row selector. Both the Group Header and Group Footer Group properties are "No" which indicates that the Artist field is providing a sort order only.

3. Click to toggle the Sorting and Grouping dialog box off, then click the **Print Preview button** on the Report Design toolbar
   Part of the report is shown in Print Preview, as shown in Figure D-8. You can use the buttons on the Print Preview toolbar to view more of the report.

4. Click the **One Page button** on the Print Preview toolbar to view one miniature page, click the **Two Pages button** to view two miniature pages, click the **Multiple Pages button** , then drag to **1x4 Pages** in the grid as shown in Figure D-9
   The Print Preview window displays the four pages of the report in miniature. Regardless of the zoom magnification of the pages, however, you can click the **Zoom pointer** to quickly toggle between two zoom magnifications.

5. Point to the **last subtotal** on the last page of the report with the pointer, click to read the number **92**, then click again to return the report to its former four-page magnification level

6. Click the **Close** button on the Print Preview toolbar, then click the **Save button** on the Report Design toolbar

FIGURE D-7: Specifying a sort order

Sorting and Grouping indicator

Grouping sections are turned off for the Artist field

Ascending sort order

Field/Expression list box

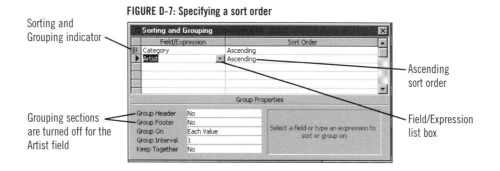

FIGURE D-8: The Quantities Report sorted by Artist

Detail records are now sorted in ascending order by Artist

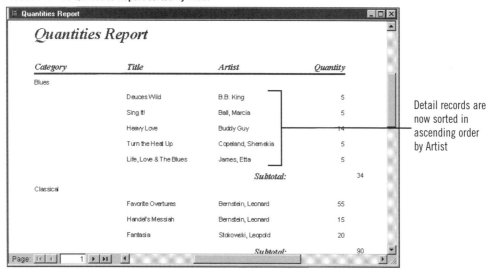

FIGURE D-9: Print Preview

One Page button

Two Pages button

Multiple Pages button

Drag to 1x4 Pages

Currently viewing two pages

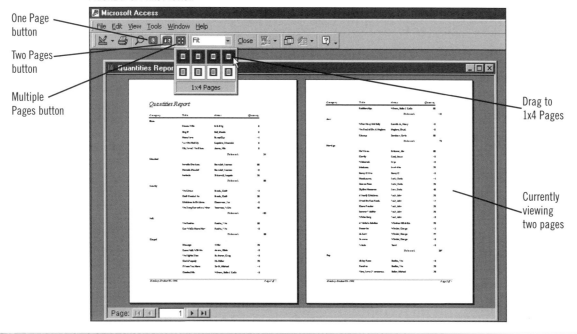

Modifying an Expression

An **expression** is a combination of fields, operators (such as +, -, / and *) and functions that result in a single value. A **function** is a built-in formula provided by Access that helps you quickly create a calculated expression. See Table D-2 for examples of common expressions that use Access functions. Notice that every calculated expression starts with an equal sign, and when it uses a function, the arguments for the function are placed in parentheses. **Arguments** are the pieces of information that the function needs to create the final answer. Calculated expressions are entered in text box controls. **Scenario** John adds a calculated expression to the Quantities Report that uses the Count function to count the number of records within each music category.

Steps

1. Make sure the Quantities Report is in Report Design view, click the **=Sum([Quantity])** **text box** in the Category Footer section, click the **Copy button** on the Report Design toolbar, click in a **blank area** in the left part of the Category Footer section, then click the **Paste button** on the Report Design toolbar
   The text box and accompanying label are copied and pasted, as shown in Figure D-10. Modifying a copy of the existing calculated expression control helps reduce errors and saves on keystrokes.

2. Click the copied **Subtotal label** in the Category Footer section to select it, double-click **Subtotal** to select the text, type **Count**, then press **[Enter]**
   The label is only descriptive text. The text box is the control that actually calculates the count.

3. Click the copy of the **=Sum([Quantity]) text box** to select it, double-click **Sum** to select it, type **count**, then press **[Enter]**
   The expression now counts the number of records in each group.

4. Click the **Print Preview button** on the Report Design toolbar to view the updated report, click the **One Page button** on the Print Preview toolbar, then scroll and zoom as shown in Figure D-11

Using the Office Clipboard

The Office Clipboard works together with the Windows Clipboard to let you copy and paste multiple items within or between the Office applications. The Office Clipboard can hold up to 12 items copied or cut from any Office program. The Clipboard toolbar displays the items stored on the Office Clipboard. The collected items remain on the Clipboard and are available to you until you close all open Office applications.

FIGURE D-10: Copying and pasting a calculated control

Copy button

Paste button

New label control

New text box control

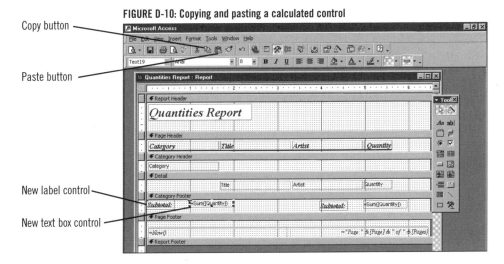

FIGURE D-11: Previewing the Count calculated control

New label control

New text box control

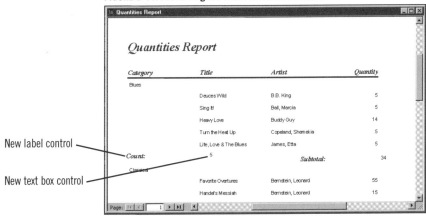

TABLE D-2: Common Access expressions

category	sample expression	description
Arithmetic	=[Price]*1.05	Multiplies the Price field by 1.05 (adds 5% to the Price field)
Arithmetic	=[Subtotal]+[Shipping]	Adds the value of the Subtotal field to the value of the Shipping field
Page Number	=[Page]	Displays the current page number, such as 5, 6, or 10
Page Number	="Page "&[Page]	Displays the word "Page," a space, and the current page number, such as Page 5, Page 6, or Page 10
Text	=[FirstName]&" "&[LastName]	Displays the value of the FirstName and LastName fields in one control separated by a space
Text	=Left([ProductNumber],2)	Uses the **Left** function to display the first two characters in the ProductNumber field
Aggregate	=Avg([Freight])	Uses the **Avg** function to display an average of the values in the Freight field
Aggregate	=Count([FirstName])	Uses the **Count** function to display the number of records that contain an entry in the FirstName field
Aggregate	=Sum([Tracks])	Uses the **Sum** function to display the total value from the Tracks field
Date	=Date()	Uses the **Date** function to display the current date in the form of mm-dd-yy, such as 10-23-00 or 11-14-01

Aligning Controls

Once the information that you want to present has been added to the appropriate section of a report, you may also want to rearrange the data on the report. By aligning controls in columns and rows, you can present your information so it is easier to understand. There are several **alignment** commands that are important to understand. You can left-, right-, or center-align a control *within its own border*, or you can align the edges of controls *with respect to one another*. Scenario▶ John aligns several controls on the Quantities Report to improve the readability and professionalism of the report. His first task is to right-align all of the controls in the Category Footer.

Steps 123 4

1. **Click the Design View button ▨ on the Print Preview toolbar, then click in the vertical ruler to the left of the Count label in the Category Footer section**
   All four controls in the Category Footer section are selected. Text boxes that display numeric fields are right-aligned by default; the labels and text boxes you added in the Category Footer section that display calculated expressions are left-aligned by default. You can use the same techniques for selecting controls in Report Design view as you did in Form Design view.

2. **Click the Align Right button ▤ on the Formatting (Form/Report) toolbar**
   Your screen should look like Figure D-12. Now the information displayed by the control is right-aligned within the control.

3. **With the four controls still selected, click Format on the menu bar, point to Align, then click Bottom**
   The bottom edges of the four controls are now aligned with respect to one another. The Align command on the Format menu refers to aligning controls with respect to one another. The Alignment buttons on the Formatting toolbar refer to aligning controls within their own borders. You can also align the right or left edges of controls in different sections.

4. **Click the Quantity label in the Page Header section, press and hold [Shift], click the Quantity text box in the Detail section, click the =Sum([Quantity]) text box in the Category Footer section, release [Shift], click Format on the menu bar, point to Align, then click Right**
   The right edges of the Quantity label, Quantity text box, and Quantity calculated controls are aligned. With the edges at the same position and the information right-aligned within the controls, the controls form a perfect column on the final report. You can extend the line in the Page Header section to better define the sections on the page.

Trouble?

Don't drag beyond the 6" mark or the printout will be wider than one sheet of paper.

5. **Click the blue line in the Page Header section, press and hold [Shift], point to the right sizing handle, when the pointer changes to ↖↘, drag the handle to the 6" mark, then release [Shift]**
   By pressing [Shift] when you draw or resize a line, the line remains perfectly horizontal as you drag it left or right.

6. **Click the Print Preview button ▣ on the Report Design toolbar, then scroll and zoom**
   Your screen should look like Figure D-13.

FIGURE D-12: Working with the alignment buttons

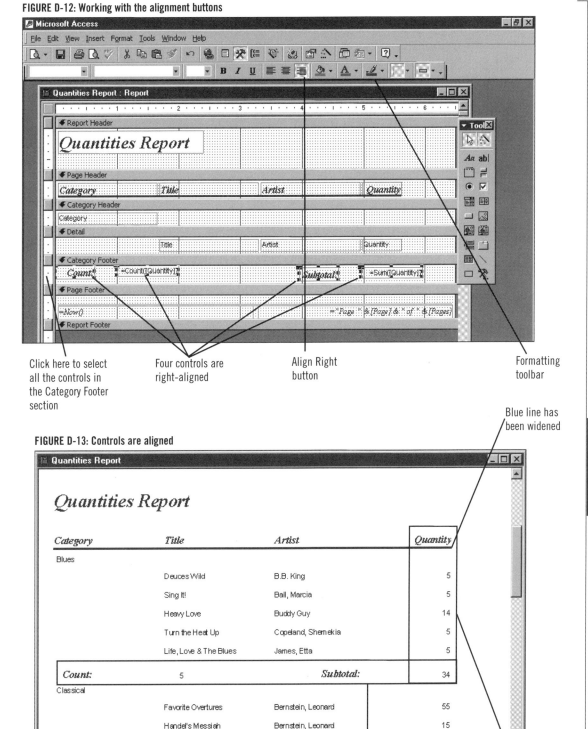

Click here to select all the controls in the Category Footer section

Four controls are right-aligned

Align Right button

Formatting toolbar

Blue line has been widened

FIGURE D-13: Controls are aligned

Bottom edges of controls are aligned

Right edges of controls are aligned

Access 2000

Formatting Controls

Formatting refers to enhancing the appearance of the information. Table D-3 lists several of the most popular formatting commands which can be used with either forms or reports. Although the Report Wizard provides many formatting embellishments on a report, you often want to improve upon the report's appearance to fit your particular needs. Scenario> John doesn't feel that the music category information is prominent on the report, so he wants to format that control to change its appearance.

QuickTip

If you need your name on the printed solution, add a label to the Report Header that displays your name.

1. Click the **Design View button** 📝 on the Print Preview toolbar, click the **Toolbox button** 🔧 to toggle it off, then click the **Category text box** in the Category Header section
   Before you can format any control, it must be selected.

2. Click the **Font size list arrow** on the Formatting (Form/Report) toolbar, click **11**, then click the **Bold button** **B**
   Increasing the font size and applying bold are common ways to make information more visible on a report. You can also change the colors of the control.

Trouble?

If the default color on the Font/Fore Color button is red, click the button.

3. With the Category text box still selected, click the **Font/Fore Color list arrow** 🔺, then click the **Red box** (third row, first column on the left), as shown in Figure D-14
   Many buttons on the Formatting (Form/Report) toolbar include a list arrow that you can click to reveal a list of choices. When you click the color list arrow, a palette of available colors is displayed. You can change the background color of the Category text box using the palette.

4. With the Category text box still selected, click the **Fill/Back Color list arrow** 🎨, then click the **light gray box** (fourth row, first column on the right)
   When you print colors on a black and white printer, they become various shades of gray. So unless you always print to a color printer, be careful about relying too heavily on color formatting, especially background shades that often become solid black boxes when printed on a black and white printer or fax machine. Fortunately, Access allows you to undo your last command if you don't like the change you've made. You must pay close attention, however, because you can only undo your very last command.

5. With the Category text box still selected, click the **Undo button** ↩ on the Report Design toolbar to remove the background color, click the **Line/Border Color list arrow** ✏️, then click the **blue box** (second row, third column from right)

6. Click the **Print Preview button** 🔍 on the Report Design toolbar
   The screen should look like Figure D-15.

7. Click **File** on the menu bar, click **Print**, type **1** in the From text box, type **1** in the To text box, click **OK**, then click **Close** on the Print Preview toolbar
   The first page of the report is printed.

8. Click the **Save button** 💾, then close the Quantities Report

FIGURE D-14: Working with color formats

Bold button

Fill/Back Color button

Font/Fore Color button

Category text box is selected

Line/Border Color button

Blue

Light gray

Red

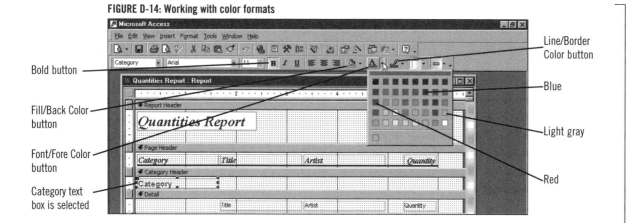

FIGURE D-15: Formatted Quantities Report

Category text box has been formatted

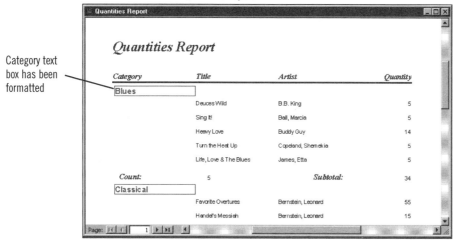

TABLE D-3: Popular formatting commands

button	button name	description
B	Bold	Toggles bold on or off for the selected control(s)
I	Italic	Toggles italics, on or off for the selected control(s)
U	Underline	Toggles underline on or off for the selected control(s)
≣	Align Left	Left-aligns the selected control(s) within its own border
≣	Center	Center-aligns the selected control(s) within its own border
≣	Align Right	Right-aligns the selected control(s) within its own border
🖉 ▾	Fill/Back Color	Changes the background color of the selected control(s)
A ▾	Font/Fore Color	Changes the text color of the selected control(s)
🖉 ▾	Line/Border Color	Changes the border color of the selected control(s)
▾	Line/Border Width	Changes the style of the border of the selected control(s)
▾	Special Effect	Changes the special visual effect of the selected control(s)

Access 2000

Creating Mailing Labels

Mailing Labels are used for many business purposes such as identifying paper folders and providing addresses for mass mailings. Once you enter raw data into your Access database, you can easily create mailing labels from this data using the **Label Wizard**. Scenario John has been asked to create labels for the display cases in the MediaLoft stores with the Artist and Title fields only. The labels are to be printed in alphabetical order by Artist and then by Title. John uses the Label Wizard to get started.

Trouble?
If you don't see Avery, click English units of measure, click the Filter by manufacturer list arrow, then click Avery.

1. Click **Reports** on the Objects bar in the MediaLoft-D Database window, click the **New button** 📄, click **Label Wizard** in the New Report dialog box, click the **Choose the table or query where the object's data comes from list arrow**, click **Music Inventory**, then click **OK**
   The Label Wizard dialog box opens requesting that you specify information about the characteristics of the label, as shown in Figure D-16. Avery 5160 labels are one of the most popular sizes. Avery 5160 label sheets have three columns and ten rows of labels for a total of 30 labels per page.

2. Click **5160**, then click **Next**
   The next wizard dialog box allows you to change the font, font size, and other text attributes. Larger fonts will be easier to read and will fit on this label since there are only two fields of information.

Trouble?
If your system doesn't have the Comic Sans MS font, choose another font appropriate for music labels.

3. Click the **Font size list arrow**, click **11**, click the **Font name list arrow**, scroll and click **Comic Sans MS** (a sample appears in the Sample box), then click **Next**
   The next wizard dialog box, which shows you the prototype label, allows you choose which fields you want to include in each label as well as their placement. Any spaces or punctuation that you want on the label must be entered from the keyboard. Also, if you want to put a field on a new line, you must press [Enter] to move to a new row of the prototype label.

QuickTip
You can double-click the field name in the Available Fields list to move it to the Prototype label list.

4. Click **Artist**, click the **Select Single Field button** ⊳, press **[Enter]**, click **Title**, then click ⊳
   Your screen should look like Figure D-17.

5. Click **Next**
   The next wizard dialog box asks about sorting.

6. Double-click **Artist** for your primary sort field, double-click **Title** for your secondary sort field, then click **Next**
   You should give your labels a descriptive name.

7. Type **Artist-Title Labels** to name the report, click **Finish**, then click the **Zoom pointer** 🔍 to see a full page of labels
   The labels should look like Figure D-18.

8. Click **Close** on the Print Preview toolbar to see the Artist-Title Labels report in Design view, click the **Save button** 💾, then click the **Print button** 🖨

9. Click **File** on the menu bar, then click **Exit** to exit Access

FIGURE D-16: Label Wizard

Avery 5160
label type

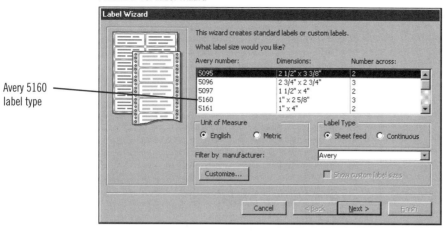

FIGURE D-17: The prototype label

Select Single Field
button

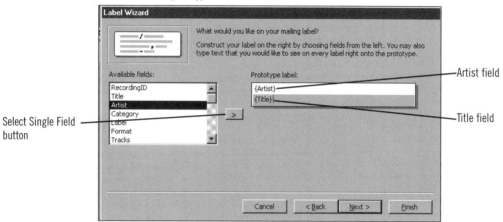

Artist field

Title field

FIGURE D-18: The Artist-Title Labels report

Labels are
3 columns by
10 rows on
each page

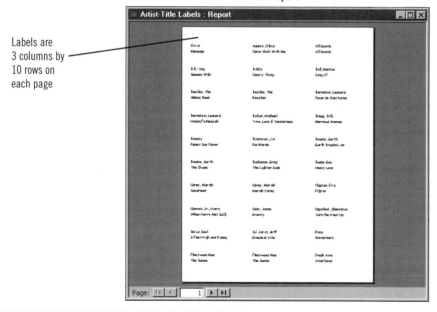

Practice

▶ Concepts Review

Label each element of the Report Design window shown in Figure D-19.

FIGURE D-19

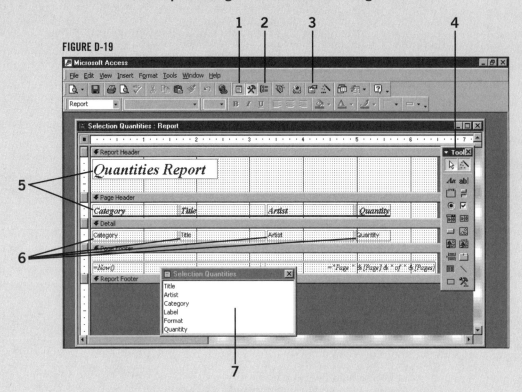

Match each term with the statement that describes it.

8. **Function**   a. Enhancing the appearance of the information
9. **Section**   b. Sorting records *plus* providing a section before and after the group of records
10. **Detail section** c. An Access object used to create paper printouts
11. **Report**   d. Part of the report that determines where a control will display on the report
12. **Formatting**   e. A built-in formula provided by Access that helps you quickly create a calculated expression
13. **Grouping**   f. Prints once for every record

Select the best answer from the list of choices.

14. Press and hold which key to select more than one control in Report Design view?
   a. [Tab]
   b. [Alt]
   c. [Shift]
   d. [Ctrl]

15. Which type of control is most likely found in the Detail section?
   a. List box
   b. Text box
   c. Combo box
   d. Label

16. Which type of control is most likely found in the Page Header section?
   a. Bound image
   b. Combo box
   c. Command button
   d. Label

17. A calculated expression is most often found in which report section?
   a. Group Footer
   b. Detail
   c. Formulas
   d. Report Header

18. Which of the following would be the appropriate expression to count the number of records using the FirstName field?
   a. =Count([FirstName])
   b. =Count[FirstName)
   c. =Count{FirstName}
   d. =Count(FirstName)

19. To align the edges of several controls with respect to one another, you use the alignment commands on the
   a. Format menu.
   b. Standard toolbar.
   c. Print Preview toolbar.
   d. Formatting toolbar.

Access 2000

▶ Skills Review

1. Plan a report.
a. Pretend that you are looking for a job. Plan a report to use for tracking job opportunities. To gather the raw data for your report, find a newspaper with job listings in your area of interest.

b. Identify the Report Header, Group Header, and Detail sections of the report by using sample data based on the following information:
- The title of the report should be "Job Opportunity Report."
- The records should be grouped by job title. For example, if you are interested in working with computers, job titles might be "Computer Operator" or "Computer Analyst." Include at least two job title groupings in your sample report.
- The Detail section should include information on the company, contact, and telephone number for each job opportunity.

2. Create a report.
a. Start Access and open the Club-D database on your Project Disk.

b. Use the Report Wizard to create a report based on the Contacts table.

c. Include the following fields for the report:
STATUS, FNAME, LNAME, DUESOWED, DUESPAID

d. Do not add any grouping or sorting fields.

e. Use the Tabular layout and Portrait orientation.

f. Use a bold style and title the report "Contact Status Report."

g. Preview the first page of the new report.

3. Group records.
a. In Report Design view, open the Sorting and Grouping dialog box, and group the report by the STATUS field in ascending order. Open both the Group Header and Group Footer sections, then close the dialog box.

b. Move the STATUS text box in the Detail section up to the left edge of the STATUS Header section.

c. Preview the first page of the new report.

4. Change the sort order.
a. In Report Design view, open the Sorting and Grouping dialog box, then add LNAME as a sort field in ascending order immediately below the STATUS field.

b. Preview the first page of the new report.

5. Modify an expression.
a. In Report Design view, add a text box control in the STATUS Footer section directly below the DUESOWED text box in the Detail section.

b. Delete the accompanying label to the left of the unbound text box.

c. Add a text box control in the STATUS Footer section directly below the DUESPAID text box in the Detail section.

d. Delete the accompanying label to the left of the unbound text box by clicking the label, then pressing [Delete].

e. Add an unbound label to the report header, and type your name as the label.

f. Modify the text boxes so that they subtotal the DUESOWED and DUESPAID fields respectively. The calculated expressions will be =Sum([DUESOWED]) and =Sum([DUESPAID]).

g. Preview both pages of the report, then print both pages of the report.

6. Align controls.

a. In Report Design view, right-align the new calculated controls in the STATUS Footer section.

b. Select the DUESOWED text box in the Detail section, and the =Sum([DUESOWED]) calculated expression in the STATUS Footer, then right-align the controls with respect to one another.

c. Select the DUESPAID text box in the Detail section, and the =Sum([DUESPAID]) calculated expression in the STATUS Footer, then right-align the controls with respect to one another.

7. Format controls.

a. Select the two calculated controls in the STATUS Footer, click the Properties button, then change the Format property on the Format tab to Currency. Close the property sheet.

b. Select the STATUS text box in the STATUS Header section, change the font size to 12 points, bold and italicize the control, then change the background color to bright yellow.

c. Preview the report, check the new totals, save the report, print it, then close the report.

8. Create mailing labels.

a. Use the Label Wizard and the Contacts table to create mailing labels using Avery 5160 labels.

b. The text should be formatted as Arial, 10 points, Light font weight, black, with no italic or underline attributes.

c. The prototype label should be organized as follows:
FNAME LNAME
COMPANY
STREET
CITY, STATE ZIP

d. Sort the labels by the ZIP field.

e. Name the report "Mailing Labels."

f. Print the first page of the labels, save the report, then close it.

g. Exit Access.

Access 2000

▶ Visual Workshop

Use the Club-D database on your Project Disk to create the report based on the CONTACTS table shown in Figure D-20. The Report Wizard and the Corporate style were used to create this report. Note that the records are grouped by the CITY field and sorted within each group by the LNAME field. A calculated control that counts the number of records is displayed in the Group Footer.

FIGURE D-20

Membership by City

CITY	LNAME	FNAME	PHONE
Bridgewater			
	Daniels	Mark	555-2277
Count: 1			
Fontanelle			
	Eagan	Jane	555-1166
Count: 1			
Industrial Airport			
	Braven	Mary	555-7002
Count: 1			
Kansas City			
	Alman	Jill	555-6931
	Bouchart	Bob	555-3081
	Collins	Christine	555-3602
	Diverman	Barbara	555-0401
	Duman	Mary Jane	555-8844
	Eahle	Andrea	555-0401
	Eckert	Jay	555-7414
	Hammer	Mike	555-0365
	Hubert	Holly	555-6004
	Mackintosh	Helen	555-9414
	Mayberry	Mitch	555-0401
	Olson	Marcie	555-1388
	Parton	Jeanette	555-8773
	Walker	Shirley	555-0403
Count: 14			

Modifying
a Database Structure

Objectives

- ▸ **Examine relational databases**
- ▸ **Plan related tables**
- ▸ **Create related tables**
- ▸ **Define Text field properties**
- ▸ **Define Number and Currency fields**
- ▸ **Define Date/Time and Yes/No fields**
- ▸ **Define field validation properties**
- ▸ **Create one-to-many relationships**

In this unit, you will add new tables to an existing database and link them in one-to-many relationships to create a relational database. You will also modify several field properties such as field formatting and field validation to increase data entry accuracy. **Scenario** David Dumont, director of training at MediaLoft, has created an Access database to track the courses attended by MediaLoft employees. Courses include hands-on computer classes, business seminars, and self-improvement workshops. Because a single-table database will not meet all of his needs, he will use multiple tables of data and link them together to create a relational database.

Examining Relational Databases

A **relational database** is a collection of related tables that share information. The goals of a relational database are to satisfy dynamic information management needs and to eliminate duplicate data entry wherever possible. Scenario▶ MediaLoft employees have tried to track course attendance using a Training database in a single Access table called "Attendance Log," as shown in Figure E-1. Although only four records are shown in this sample, David sees a data redundancy problem because there are multiple occurrences of the same employee and same course information. He knows that data redundancy in one table is a major clue that the database needs to be redesigned. Therefore, David studies the principles of relational database design.

 A relational database is based on multiple tables of data. Each table should be based on only one subject

Right now the Attendance Log table in the Training database contains three subjects: Courses, Attendance, and Employees. Therefore, you have to duplicate several fields of information in this table every time an employee takes a course. Redundant data in one table creates a need for a relational database.

 Each record in a table should be uniquely identified with a key field or key field combination

A **key field** is a field that contains unique information for each record. Typically, an employee table contains an Employee Identification (EmployeeID) field to uniquely identify each employee. Often, the Social Security Number (SSN) field serves this purpose. Although using the employee's last name as the key field might accommodate a small database, it is a poor choice because the user cannot enter two employees with the same last name.

 Tables in the same database should be related, or linked, through a common field in a one-to-many relationship

To tie the information from one table to another, a single field of data must be common to each table. This common field will be the key field in one of the tables, creating the "one" side of the relationship; the field data will be listed "many" times in the other table, creating a **one-to-many relationship**. Table E-1 shows common examples of one-to-many relationships between two database tables.

Attendance Log

Course Description	Prerequisite	Date	Employee
Internet Fundamentals	Computer Fundamentals	2/7/2000	Maria Abbott
Internet Fundamentals	Computer Fundamentals	2/7/2000	Lauren Alber
Introduction to Access	Computer Fundamentals	3/6/2000	Maria Abbott
Introduction to Access	Computer Fundamentals	3/6/2000	Lauren Alber

Redundant data is shaded the same color

Redundant data is shaded the same color

Access 2000

TABLE E-1: One-to-many relationships

table on "one" side of relationship	table on "many" side of relationship	linking field	description
Products	Sales	ProductID	A ProductID field must have a unique entry in a Products table, but will be listed many times in a Sales table as multiple copies of that item are sold
Customers	Sales	CustomerID	A CustomerID field must have a unique entry in a Customers table, but will be listed many times in a Sales table as multiple sales are recorded for the same customer
Employees	Promotions	EmployeeID	An EmployeeID field must have a unique entry in an Employees table, but will be listed many times in a Promotions table as the employee is promoted over time
Vendors	Products	VendorID	A VendorID field must have a unique entry in a Vendors table, but will be listed many times in the Products table if multiple products are purchased from the same vendor

Access 2000

Planning Related Tables

Careful planning is crucial to successful relational database design and creation. Duplicated data is not only error-prone and inefficient to enter, but it also limits the query and reporting capabilities of the overall database. **Scenario** After studying the concepts of solid relational database design, David is ready to apply those concepts and redesign MediaLoft's Training database. He uses the following steps to move from a single table of data to the powerful relational database capabilities provided by Access.

Details

List all of the fields of data that need to be tracked

Typically, these fields are already present in existing tables or paper reports. Still, it is a good idea to document each field in order to examine all fields at the same time. This is the appropriate time to determine if there are additional fields of information that do not currently exist on any report that should be tracked. David lists the fields he wishes to track, including fields about employee information, course information, and attendance information.

Group fields together in subject matter tables

The new MediaLoft training database will track courses attended by employees. It will contain three tables: Courses, Employees, and Attendance. David organizes the fields he listed under their appropriate table name.

Identify key fields that exist in tables

Each table should include a key field or key field combination in order to uniquely identify each record. David will use the SSN field in the Employees table, the CourseID field in the Courses table, and an automatically incrementing (AutoNumber data type) LogID field in the Attendance table to handle this requirement.

Link the tables with a one-to-many relationship via a common field

By adding an SSN field to the Attendance table, David creates a common field in both the Employees and Attendance tables that can serve as the link between them. Similarly, by adding a CourseID field to the Attendance table, David creates a common field in both the Attendance and Courses tables that can serve as the link. For a valid one-to-many relationship, the linking field must be designated as the key field in the "one" side of the one-to-many relationship. The final sketch of David's redesigned relational database is shown in Figure E-2.

FIGURE E-2: One-to-many relationships

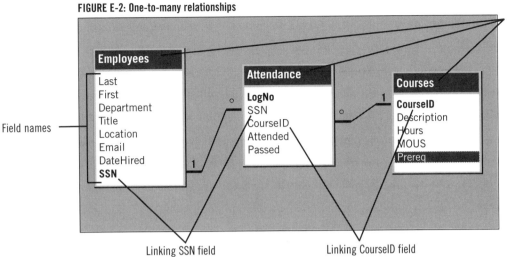

Three tables: Employees, Attendance, Courses

Field names

Linking SSN field

Linking CourseID field

Identifying key field combinations

Identifying a single key field may be difficult in some tables. Examine, for instance, a table that records employee promotions over time that includes three fields: employee number, date, and pay rate. None of the fields individually could serve as a valid key field because none are restricted to unique data. The employee number and date together, however, could serve as a valid **key field combination** because an employee would get promoted only once on any given date; uniquely identifying the record.

Access 2000

Creating Related Tables

Once you have developed a valid relational database design on paper, you are ready to define the tables in Access. All characteristics of a table including field names, data types, field descriptions, field properties, and key fields are defined in the table's **Design view**. In a relational database, it is important to define the length and data type of the linking field the same way in both tables to create a successful link. **Scenario** Using his new database design, David creates the Attendance table.

Steps 1 2 3 4

1. **Start Access and open the Training-E database on your Project Disk**
   The Courses and Employees tables already exist in the database.

2. **Click Tables on the Objects Bar if it is not already selected, then click the New Table button** 📇 **in the Training-E database window**
   You will enter the fields for the Attendance table directly into the table's Design view.

3. **Click Design View in the New Table dialog box, then click OK**
   Field names should be as short as possible, but long enough to be descriptive. The field name entered in a table's Design view is used as the default name for the field in all later queries, forms, and reports.

QuickTip

Press [Enter] or [Tab] to move to the next column in a table's Design view window.

4. **Maximize the Table1: Table window, type LogNo, press [Enter], type a to select the AutoNumber Data Type, then press [Enter] twice to bypass the Description column and move to the second row**
   The LogNo is a unique number used to identify each record in the Attendance table (each occurrence of an employee taking a course). The AutoNumber data type, which automatically sequences each new record with the next available integer, works well for this field. When entering data types, you can type the first letter of the data type; for example, type "T" for Text, "D" for Date/Time, or "C" for Currency. You can also click the Data Type list arrow, then select the data type from the list.

5. **Type the other fields, entering the data types as shown in Table E-2**
   Field descriptions entered in a table's Design view are optional. In Datasheet view, the description of a field appears in the status bar, and therefore provides further clarification about what type of data should be entered in the field. The SSN field will serve as the linking field between the Attendance and Employee tables. The CourseID field will serve as the linking field between the Attendance and Courses tables. You are not required to use the same field name in both tables, but doing so makes it easier to understand the link between the related tables later.

6. **Click LogNo in the Field Name column, then click the Primary Key button** 🔑 **on the Table Design toolbar**
   The LogNo field serves as the primary key field in this table.

7. **Click the Save button** 💾 **on the Table Design toolbar, type Attendance in the Table Name text box in the Save As dialog box, then click OK**
   The completed Table Design view for the Attendance table is shown in Figure E-3.

8. **Click the Attendance: Table Design Close Window button**
   The Attendance table is now displayed as a table object in the Training-E database window.

FIGURE E-3: Design view for the Attendance table

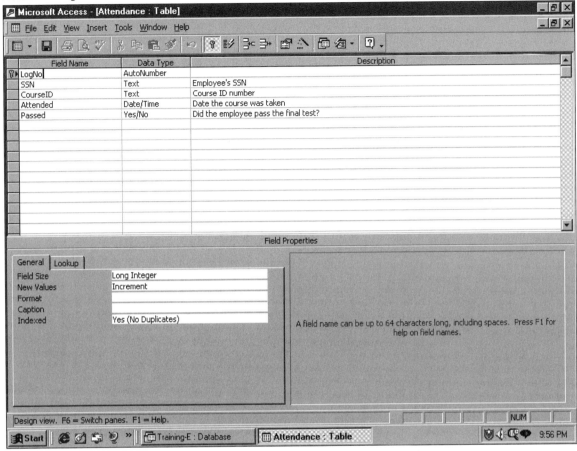

TABLE E-2: Additional fields for the Attendance Table

field name	data type	description
SSN	Text	Employee's SSN
CourseID	Text	Course ID number
Attended	Date/Time	Date the course was taken
Passed	Yes/No	Did the employee pass the final test?

CLUES TO USE

Comparing linked tables to imported tables

A **linked table** is a table created in another database product, or another program such as Excel, that is stored in a file outside the open database. You can add, delete, and edit records in a linked table from within Access, but you can't change its structure. An **imported table** creates a copy of the information from the external file and places it in a new Access table in your database.

Access 2000

Defining Text Field Properties

Field properties are the characteristics that apply to each field in a table, such as field size, default value, or field formats. Modifying these properties helps ensure database accuracy and clarity because they restrict the way data is entered and displayed. You modify field properties in Table Design view. **Scenario** David decides to make field property changes to several text fields in the Employees table. He modifies the size and format properties.

1. Click the **Tables button** on the Objects bar in the database window if it is not already selected, click the **Employees table**, then click the **Design button** ☒ in the Training-E database window

   The Employees table opens in Design view. The Field Properties panel (the lower half of the Table Design view window) changes to display the properties of the selected field, which depend on the field's data type. For example, when a field with a Text data type is selected, the Field Size property is visible. However, when a field with a Date/Time data type is selected, Access controls the Field Size property, so the property is not displayed. Most field properties are optional, but if they require an entry, Access provides a default value.

2. Click the **SSN field name**, look at the Field properties, then click each of the **field names** while viewing the Field Properties panel

QuickTip

Fifty is the default field size for a text field.

3. Click the **Last field name**, double-click **255** in the **Field Size text box** in the Field Properties, then type **30**

   Changing this property to 30 should accommodate even the longest entry for Last Name.

QuickTip

Press [F6] to quickly move between the upper and lower panels of Table Design view.

4. Change the **Field Size property** to **30** for the following Field Names: **First**, **Department**, **Title**, **Location**, and **Email**

   Changing the Field Size property to **30** for each of these text fields in this table should accommodate all the entries. The **Input Mask property** controls both the values that users can enter into a text box control and provides a visual guide for users as they enter data.

Trouble?

Insert the Office 2000 CD to install the Input Mask Wizard if necessary.

5. Click the **SSN field name**, click the **Input Mask text box** in the Field Properties panel, click the **Build button** ▦ to start the Input Mask Wizard, click **Yes** to save the table, then click **Yes** when warned about losing data

QuickTip

You can enter the Input Mask directly in the field properties.

6. Click **Social Security Number** in the Input Mask list, click **Next**, click **Next** to accept 000-00-0000 as the default input mask, click **Next** to accept the option to store the data **without the symbols in the mask**, then click **Finish**

   The Design view of the Employees table should now look like Figure E-4. Notice that the SSN field is chosen, and the Field Properties panel displays the Input Mask property.

7. Click the **Save button** ▦ on the Table Design toolbar, then click the **Datasheet View button** ▦ on the Table Design toolbar

8. Maximize the datasheet, press **[Tab]** seven times to move to the SSN field for the first record, then type **115774444**

   The SSN Input Mask property creates an easy-to-use visual pathway to facilitate accurate data entry. See Table E-3 for more information on Text field properties.

9. Close the Employees table

FIGURE E-4: Changing Text field properties

Employees Table

SSN field is selected

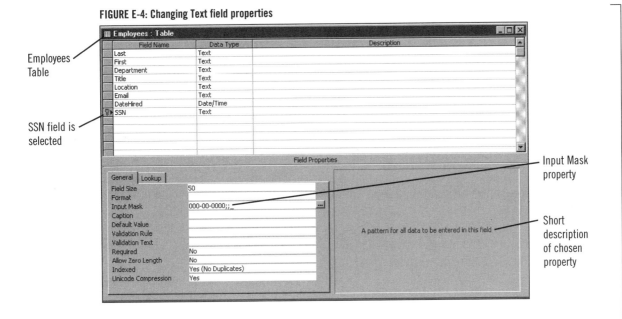

Input Mask property

Short description of chosen property

TABLE E-3: Common Text field properties

property	description	sample field name	sample property entry
Field Size	Controls how many characters can be entered into the field	State	2
Format	Controls how information will be displayed and printed < forces all characters to *display* lowercase even though the data is stored in the same way it was entered > forces all characters to *display* uppercase even though the data is stored in the same way it was entered @ requires that an entry be made & does not require that an entry be made	State	>
Input Mask	Provides a pattern for data to be entered; contains three parts separated by semicolons	Phone	(999)000-0000;1;_
Caption	A label used to describe the field. When a Caption property isn't entered, the field name is used to describe the field	Emp#	Employee Number
Default Value	Value that is automatically entered in the given field for new records	City	Kansas City
Required	Determines if an entry is required for this field	LastName	Yes

CLUES TO USE

Defining input mask property parts

Input mask properties contain three parts. The first part controls what type of data can be entered and how it will be displayed: 9 represents an optional number; 0 represents a required number, ? represents an optional letter; L represented a required letter. The second part determines whether all displayed characters (such as dashes in the SSN field) are stored in the field, or just the entry. The 0 (zero) entry stores all characters. The 1 (one) entry stores only the entered characters. The third part determines which character Access will display for the space where a character is typed in the input mask. Common entries are the asterisk (*), underscore (_), or pound sign (#).

Defining Number and Currency Fields

Even though some of the properties for Number and Currency fields are the same as for Text fields, each field type has its own specific list of valid properties. Numeric and Currency fields have very similar properties because they both contain numbers. One important difference, however, is that a Currency field limits the user's control over the field size. Therefore, you would use a Currency field to prevent rounding off during calculations. A Currency field is accurate to fifteen digits to the left of the decimal point and four digits to the right. **Scenario** The Courses table contains both a Number field (Hours), and a Currency field (Cost). David modifies the properties of these two fields.

Steps

1. Click the **Courses table**, click the **Design button** in the Training-E database window, then click the **Hours field**

   The Field Size property for a Number field defaults to Long Integer. See Table E-4 for more information on common Number field properties.

2. Click the **Field Size text box** in the Field Properties, click the **Field Size list arrow**, then click **Byte**

QuickTip

Choosing Byte and Integer field sizes for numeric fields lowers the storage requirements for that field. Byte allows entries only from 0 to 255.

3. Click the **Cost field**, click the **Decimal Places text box** in the Field Properties, click the **Decimal Places list arrow**, then click **0**

   Your screen should look like Figure E-5. Because all of MediaLoft's courses are priced at a round dollar value, there is no need to display zero cents in each field entry.

4. Click the **Save button** on the Table Design toolbar, then click the **Datasheet View button** on the Table Design toolbar

   Since none of the entries in any of the fields were longer than the new field size entries, you won't lose any data.

5. Press **[Tab]** twice to move to the **Hours** field for the first record, type **1000**, then press **[Tab]**

   Because 1,000 is larger than the Byte field size that the Hours field will allow, you are cautioned with an Access error message indicating that the value isn't valid for this field.

6. Click **OK**, press **[Esc]** to remove the inappropriate entry in the Hours field, then press **[Tab]** three times to move to the **Cost** field

   The Cost field currently displays all data rounded to the nearest dollar.

7. Type **199.75** in the **Cost** field, then press **[↓]**

   Because this field has been formatted to display no cents, remainders are rounded to the nearest dollar and $200 is displayed in the datasheet. Even though remainders of cents are rounded when displayed on the datasheet, 199.75 is the actual value stored in the field. Formatting does not change the actual data, but only the way it is displayed.

8. Close the Courses table

FIGURE E-5: Changing Currency and Number field properties

Courses table

Cost field is chosen

Decimal Places property

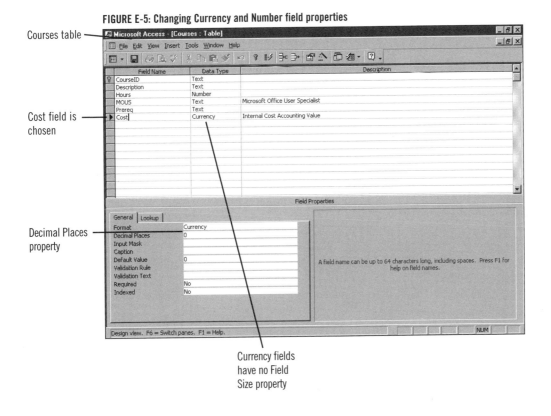

Currency fields have no Field Size property

TABLE E-4: Common numeric and currency field properties

property	description	sample field name	sample property entry
Field size (Number field only)	Determines the largest number that can be entered in the field, as well as the type of data (e.g., integer or fraction) • Byte stores numbers from 0 to 255 (no fractions) Integer stores numbers from −32,768 to 32,767 (no fractions) • Long Integer stores numbers from −2,147,483,648 to 2,147,483,647 (no fractions) • Single stores numbers (including fractions with six digits to the right of the decimal point) times 10 to the −38th to +38th power • Double stores numbers (including fractions with over 10 digits to the right of the decimal point) in the range of 10 to the −324th to +324th power	Quantity	Integer
Decimal Places	The number of digits to the right of the decimal separator	Dues	0

Access 2000

Defining Date/Time and Yes/No Fields

A Date field's Format property is designed specifically to show dates in just about any format such as January 5, 2003; 05-Jan-03; or 1/5/2003. Many of a Date field's other properties such as Input Mask, Caption, and Default Value are very similar to Text and Number field types. Scenario> David wants the database to display all Date fields with four digits for the year, so there is no confusion regarding the century. He will also ensure that the Yes/No field is displayed as a check box versus a text entry of "Yes" or "No."

Steps 1234

1. Click the **Attendance table**, click the **Design button** in the Training-E database window, then click the **Attended field name**

   You want the dates of attendance to display as 01/17/2000 instead of as 1/17/00. You must work with the Attended field's Format property.

2. Click the **Format text box** in the Field Properties, then click the **Format list arrow**

   Although several predefined Date/Time formats are available, none matches the format you want. To define a custom format, enter symbols that represent how you want the date to appear in the Format property text box.

3. Type **mm/dd/yyyy**, then press **[Enter]**

   The updated Format property for the Attended field shown in Figure E-6 forces the date to appear with two digits for the month, two digits for the day, and four digits for the year. The parts of the date will be separated by forward slashes. You want the Passed field to display a check box for this control. The Display Control property is on the Lookup tab.

QuickTip

Click a property, then press [F1] to open the Microsoft Access Help window to the specific page that describes that property.

4. Click the **Passed field name**, click the **Lookup tab** in the Field Properties, click the **Display Control textbox**, then click the **Display Control property's list arrow**

   A Yes/No field may appear as a check box in which "checked" equals "yes" and "unchecked" equals "no," as a text box that displays "yes" or "no," or as a combo box that displays "yes" and "no" in the drop-down list.

5. Click **Check Box** in the Display Control list

   The linking SSN field in the Attendance table must be the same data type and size as it is in the Employees table.

6. Click the **SSN field**, click the **General tab** in the Field Properties, click the **Input Mask text box**, click the **Build button** , click **Yes** to save the table, click **Social Security Number** in the Input Mask Wizard dialog box, click **Next**, click **Next**, click **Finish**, click the **Datasheet View button** on the Table Design, then click **Yes** when prompted

   Entering records tests the property changes.

QuickTip

You can click a check box control or press the spacebar. Click or press the spacebar a second time to clear the check mark.

7. Press **[Tab]** to move to the SSN field, type **115774444**, press **[Tab]**, type **Comp1**, press **[Tab]**, type **1/31/00**, press **[Tab]**, then press **[Spacebar]**

   Your screen should look like Figure E-7. Double-check that the SSN and Attended fields are formatting correctly too.

8. Press **[Enter]**, press **[Tab]** to move through the LogNo field, type **222334444**, press **[Tab]**, type **Comp1**, press **[Tab]**, type **1/31/00**, press **[Tab]**, then press **[Spacebar]**

FIGURE E-6: Changing Date/Time field properties

Attendance table

Attended field is chosen

Custom Format property change is made

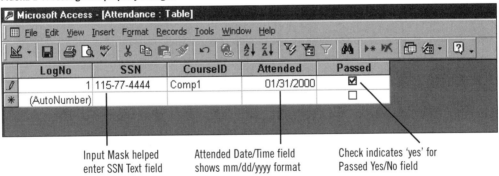

FIGURE E-7: Testing field property changes

Input Mask helped enter SSN Text field

Attended Date/Time field shows mm/dd/yyyy format

Check indicates 'yes' for Passed Yes/No field

Planning for the 21st century

The default Format property (General) for a Date/Time field assumes that dates entered as 1/1/30 to 12/31/99 are twentieth-century dates (1930–1999), and those entered as 1/1/00 to 12/31/29 are twenty-first century dates (2000–2029). If you wish to enter dates outside these ranges, you must enter all four digits of the date.

Defining Field Validation Properties

The **Validation Rule** and **Validation Text** field properties can help you eliminate unreasonable entries by establishing criteria for the entry before it is accepted into the database. For example, the Validation Rule property of a Gender field might be modified to allow only two entries: "male" or "female." The Validation Text property is used to display a message when a user tries to enter data that doesn't pass the Validation Rule property for that field. Without a Validation Rule entry, the Validation Text property is meaningless. **Scenario** MediaLoft started providing in-house courses on January 17, 2000. Therefore, it wouldn't make sense to enter a date before that time. David will modify the validation properties of the Date field in the Attendance table to prevent the entry of incorrect dates.

Steps 1 2 3 4

1. Click the **Design View button** on the Table Datasheet toolbar, click the **Attended field**, click the **Validation Rule text box** in the Field Properties, then type **>=1/17/2000**

   This property forces all course dates to be greater than or equal to 1/17/2000. See Table E-5 for more examples of Validation Rule expressions.

2. Click the **Validation Text text box**, then type **Date must be on or after 1/17/2000**

   The Validation Text property will appear in a dialog box to explain to the user why a field entry that doesn't pass the Validation Rule criteria cannot be accepted. The Design view of the Attendance table should now look like Figure E-8. Access changed the entry in the Validation Rule property to appear as >=#1/17/00#. Pound signs (#) are used to surround date criteria. Access assumes that years entered with two digits in the range 30 and 99 refer to the years 1930 through 1999, whereas digits in the range 00 and 29 refer to the years 2000 through 2029. If you wish to indicate a year outside these ranges, you must enter all four digits of the year.

3. Click the **Save button** on the Table Design toolbar, then click **Yes** when asked to test the existing data

   Because all dates in the Attended field are more recent than 1/17/00, there are no date errors in the current data, and the table is saved. You should test the Validation Rule and Validation Text properties.

4. Click the **Datasheet View button** on the Table Design toolbar, press **[Tab]** three times to move to **Attended field**, type **1/1/99**, press **[Tab]**

   Because you tried to enter a 1999 date in the Attended field of the Attendance datasheet, the Validation rule that you entered appears in a dialog box. See Figure E-9.

5. Click **OK** to close the Validation Rule dialog box

   You know that the Validation Rule and Validation Text properties work properly.

6. Press **[Esc]** to reject the invalid date entry

7. Close the Attendance table

FIGURE E-8: Using the Validation properties

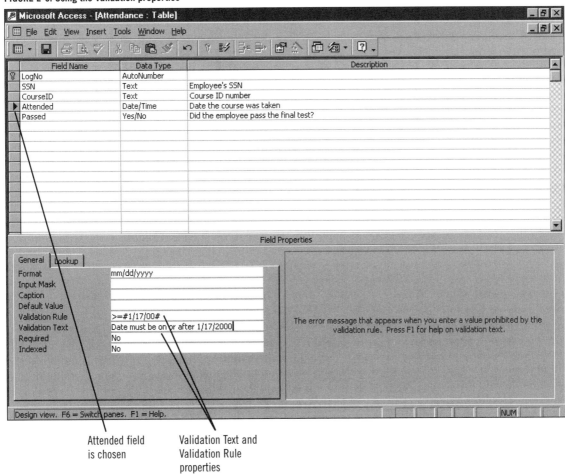

Attended field is chosen

Validation Text and Validation Rule properties

FIGURE E-9: Validation Rule dialog box

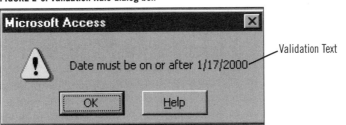

Validation Text

TABLE E-5: Validation Rule expressions

data type	validation rule expression	description
Number or Currency	>0	The number must be positive
Number or Currency	>10 And <100	The number must be between 10 and 100
Number or Currency	10 Or 20 Or 30	The number must be 10, 20, or 30
Text	"IA" Or "NE" Or "MO"	The entry must be IA, NE, or MO
Date/Time	>=#1/1/93#	The date must be on or after 1/1/1993
Date/Time	>#1/1/80# And <#1/1/90#	The date must be between 1/1/1980 and 1/1/1990

Access 2000

Creating One-to-Many Relationships

Once the initial database design and table design phase have been completed, you must link the tables together in appropriate one-to-many relationships. Some field properties that do not affect how the data is stored (such as the Format property), can be changed after the tables are linked, but other properties (such as the Field Size property), cannot be changed once tables are linked. Therefore, it is best to complete all of the table and field design activities before linking the tables. Once the tables are linked, however, you can design queries, reports, and forms with fields from multiple tables.

Scenario David's initial database sketch revealed that the SSN field will link the Employee table to the Attendance table and that the CourseID field will link the Courses table to the Attendance table. David will now define the one-to-many relationships between the tables of the Training-E database.

QuickTip

If the Show Table dialog box is not open, click the Show Table button on the Relationships toolbar.

1. Click the **Relationships button** on the Database toolbar
   The Show Table dialog box opens and lists all three tables in the Training-E database.

2. Click **Employees** on the **Tables tab**, click **Add**, click **Attendance**, click **Add**, click **Courses**, click **Add**, then click **Close**
   All three tables have been added to the Relationships window.

QuickTip

To display all of a table's field names, drag the bottom border of the table window until all fields are visible. Drag the table's title bar to move the field list.

3. Maximize the window, click **SSN** in the **Employees table Field List**, then drag the **SSN field** from the Employees table to the SSN field in the Attendance table
   Dragging a field from one table to another in the Relationships window links the two tables with the chosen field and opens the Edit Relationships dialog box as shown in Figure E-10. **Referential integrity** helps ensure data accuracy.

4. Click the **Enforce Referential Integrity check box** in the Edit Relationships dialog box, then click **Create**
   The **one-to-many line** shows the linkage between the SSN field of the Employees table and the Attendance table. The "one" side of the relationship is the unique SSN for each record in the Employees table. The "many" side of the relationship is identified by an infinity symbol pointing to the SSN field in the Attendance table. The CourseID field will link the Courses table to the Attendance table.

QuickTip

To delete a table or relationship from the Relationships window, click the table or relationship line and press [Delete].

5. Click the **CourseID field** in the Courses table, then drag it from the Courses table to the **CourseID field** in the Attendance table

6. Click the **Enforce Referential Integrity check box**, then click **Create**
   The finished Relationships window should look like Figure E-11. Print the Relationships window to show structural information including table names, field names, key fields, and relationships between tables.

7. Click **File** on the menu bar, click **Print Relationships**, click the **Print button** on the Print Preview toolbar, click the **Close Window button**, click **Yes** to save the report, click **OK** to accep the default report name, click the **Relationships Window Close button**, then click **Yes** to save changes
   When tables are related with one-to-many relationships, their datasheets will show an **expand button**, to the left of the record that can be clicked to show related records in a **sub-datasheet**. When the related records appear, the expand button becomes a **collapse button**, which can be clicked to close the related records window.

8. Double-click the **Courses table**, then click the **Comp1 Expand button**
   Your screen should look like Figure E-12.

9. Close the Training-E database, then exit Access

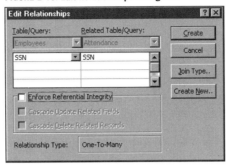

FIGURE E-10: Edit Relationships dialog box

FIGURE E-11: Final Relationships window

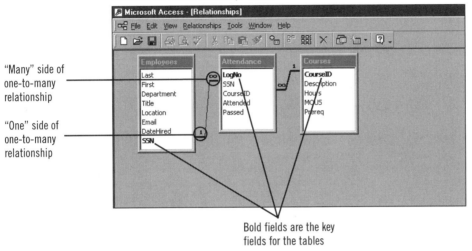

"Many" side of one-to-many relationship

"One" side of one-to-many relationship

Bold fields are the key fields for the tables

FIGURE E-12: A subdatasheet allows you to view related records

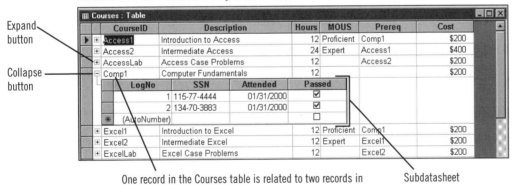

Expand button

Collapse button

One record in the Courses table is related to two records in the Attendance table through the common CourseID field

Subdatasheet

CLUES TO USE

Enforcing referential integrity

Referential integrity ensures that no orphaned records are entered or created in the database. An **orphan record** happens when information in the linking field of the "many" table doesn't have a matching entry in the linking field of the "one" table. For MediaLoft, referential integrity ensures that SSN entries added to the Attendance table are first recorded in the Employees table. Also, referential integrity prevents the user from deleting a record from the Employees table if a matching SSN entry is present in the Attendance table.

Practice

► Concepts Review

Identify each element of the table Design view shown in Figure E-13.

FIGURE E-13

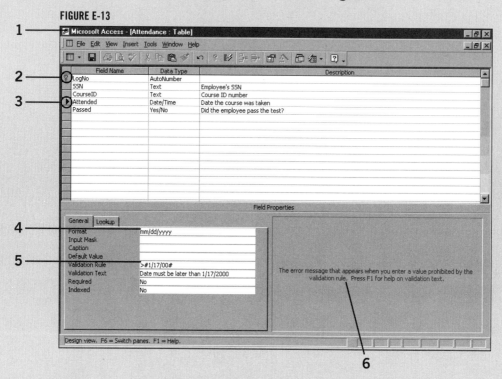

Match each term with the statement that describes its function.

7. **Primary Key**
8. **Field Properties**
9. **Design view**
10. **Validation Rule and Validation Text**
11. **Relational database**

a. Characteristics that apply to each field of a table, such as field size, default values, or field formats

b. A field that holds unique information for each record in the table

c. Where all characteristics of a table, including field names, data types, field descriptions, field properties, and key fields, are defined

d. Several tables linked together in one-to-many relationships

e. Helps you eliminate unreasonable entries by establishing criteria for the entry

Select the best answer from the list of choices.

12. **Which of the following steps would probably help eliminate fields of duplicate data in a table?**
   a. Change the validation properties of the field in which the duplicate data existed.
   b. Redesign the database and add more fields.
   c. Change the formatting properties of the field in which the duplicate data existed.
   d. Redesign the database and add more tables.

13. **Which of the following is NOT defined in the table's Design view?**
    a. Data types
    b. Duplicate data
    c. Field lengths
    d. Key fields

14. **Which of the following is NOT a common data type?**
    a. Date/Time
    b. Alpha
    c. Number
    d. Text

15. **Which feature helps the database designer make sure that one-to-many relationships are preserved?**
    a. Referential integrity
    b. Validation Rule property
    c. Field formatting
    d. Validation Text property

16. **Which character is used to identify dates in a validation expression?**
    a. & (ampersand)
    b. ' (single quote)
    c. # (pound sign)
    d. " (double quote)

17. **Which Format Property Option displays all characters in the field as uppercase?**
    a. @
    b. >
    c. !
    d. <

▶ Skills Review

1. **Examine relational database requirements.**
   a. Examine your address book.
   b. Write down the fields you will need.
   c. Examine which fields contain duplicate entries.

2. **Plan related tables.**
   a. Start Access.
   b. Use the Blank Access Database option button to create a new database file.
   c. Type "Membership-E" as the File name then create the database on your Project Disk.
   d. Click Tables on the Objects bar, then click the New Table button.

3. **Create related tables.**
   a. Use Design view to create the new table using the following field names with the given data types: First, Text; Last, Text; Street, Text; Zip, Text; Birthday, Date/Time; Dues, Currency; MemberNo, Text; CharterMember, Yes/No.
   b. Identify MemberNo as the primary key field.

   c. Save the table as "Names," then close it.

   d. Use Design view to create a new table using the following fields with the given data types: Zip, Text; City, Text; State, Text.

   e. Identify Zip as the primary key field.

   f. Save the table as "Zips," then close it.

   g. Use Design view to create a new table using the following fields with the given data types: MemberNo, Text Activity Date, Date/Time; Hours, Number.

   h. Save the table without a primary key field, name it "Activities," then close it.

4. Define text field properties.

   a. Open the Zips table in Design view.

   b. Change the Field Size property of the State field to 2.

   c. Change the Field Size property of the Zip field to 5.

   d. Save the changes and close the Zips table.

   e. Open the Names table in Design view.

   f. Use the Input Mask Wizard to create the Input Mask property for the Zip field in both the Zips and Names tables. Choose the Zip Code input mask, and use the other default options provided by the Input Mask Wizard.

   g. Change the Field Size property of the First, Last, and Street fields to 30.

   h. Change the Field Size property of the MemberNo field to 5.

   i. Save the changes and close the Names and Zips tables.

   j. Open the Activities table in Design view.

   k. Change the Field Size property of the MemberNo field to 5.

   l. Save the change and close the Activities table.

5. Define number and currency field properties.

   a. Open the Names table in Design view.

   b. Change the Decimal Places property of the Dues field to 0.

   c. Save the change and close the Names table.

   d. Open the Activities table in Design view.

   e. Change the Field Size property of the Hours field to Byte.

   f. Save the change and close the Activities table.

6. Define the Date/Time and Yes/No field properties.

   a. Open the Names table in Design view.

   b. Change the Format property of the Birthday field to m/d/yyyy.

   c. Check to ensure that the Display Control property of the CharterMember field is set to check box.

   d. Save the changes and close the Names table.

   e. Open the Activities table in Design view.

   f. Change the Format property of the ActivityDate field to m/d/yyyy.

   g. Save the change and close the Activities table.

7. Define field validation properties.

   a. Open the Zips table in Design view.

   b. Click the State field name, click the Validation Rule text box, then type ="IA" OR "KS" OR "MO"

   c. Click the Validation Text text box, then type "State must be IA, KS, or MO"

   d. Save the change and close the Zips table.

8. **Create one-to-many relationships.**
   a. Open the Relationships window.
   b. Add all three tables to the Relationships window in this order: Activities, Names, Zips.
   c. Close the Show Table dialog box.
   d. Drag the Zip field from the Zips table to the Zip field in the Names table, creating a one-to-many relationship from the Zips table to the Names table.
   e. Enforce Referential Integrity for the relationship.
   f. Drag the MemberNo field from the Names table to the MemberNo field in the Activities table, creating a one-to-many relationship from the Names table to the Activities table.
   g. Enforce Referential Integrity for the relationship.
   h. Save the changes to the Relationships layout.
   i. Print the Relationships window.
   j. Close the Relationships report, and save it with the given name.
   k. Close the Relationships window.
   l. Close the Memberships-E database.

Visual Workshop

Open the Training-E database, create a new table called "Vendors" using the Table Design view shown in Figure E-14 to determine field names and data types. Additional property changes include changing the Field Size property of the VState field to 2, the VendorID and VPhone fields to 10, and all other text fields to 30. Be sure to specify that the VendorID field is the Primary Key field.

FIGURE E-14

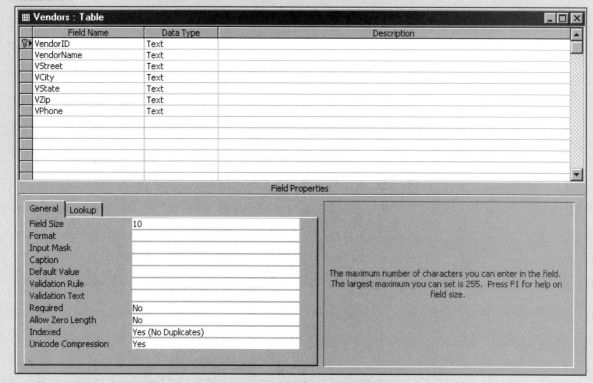

Unit
F

Creating
Multiple Table Queries

Objectives

- [MOUS] ► **Create select queries**
- [MOUS] ► **Sort a query on multiple fields**
- [MOUS] ► **Develop AND queries**
- [MOUS] ► **Develop OR queries**
- [MOUS] ► **Create calculated fields**
- [MOUS] ► **Build summary queries**
- ► **Create crosstab queries**
- ► **Modify crosstab queries**

In this unit, you will create **queries**, which are database objects that answer questions about the data by pulling fields and records that match specific criteria into a single datasheet. A **select query** retrieves data from one or more linked tables and displays the results in a datasheet. Queries can also be used to sort records, develop new calculated fields from existing fields, or develop summary calculations such as the sum or average of the values in a field. **Crosstab queries** present information in a cross-tabular report, similar to pivot tables in other database and spreadsheet products. Scenario David Dumont has spent several days entering information into the Attendance table to record which employees are taking which classes. Now, he can create select queries and crosstab queries to analyze the data in the database.

Creating Select Queries

You develop queries by using the Query Wizard or by directly specifying requested fields and query criteria in **Query Design view**. The resulting query datasheet is not a duplication of the data that resides in the original table's datasheet, but rather a logical view of the data. If you change or enter data in a query's datasheet, the data in the underlying table (and any other logical view) is updated automatically. Queries often are used to present and sort a subset of fields from multiple tables for data entry or update purposes. ▶Scenario◀ David creates a query to answer the question, "Who is taking what course?" He pulls fields from several tables into a single query object to display a single datasheet that answers this question.

Steps

1. Start Access and open the **Training-F** database on your Project Disk

2. Click the **Queries button** 📖 on the Objects bar in the Training-F Database window, then double-click **Create query in Design View**

   The Query1 Select Query Design view window opens and the Show Table dialog box opens listing all the tables in the database. You use the Show Table dialog box to add the tables that contain the fields you need to the Query Design view.

3. Click **Employees**, click **Add**, click **Attendance**, click **Add**, click **Courses**, click **Add**, then click **Close**

   The upper pane of Query Design view displays **field lists** for the three tables. Each table's name is in its field list title bar. You can drag the title bar of the field lists to move them or drag the edge of a field list to resize it. Key fields are bold, and serve as the "one" side of the one-to-many relationship between two tables. Relationships are displayed with **one-to-many join lines** between the linking fields, as shown in Figure F-1. The fields you want displayed in the datasheet must be added to the columns in the lower pane of the Query Design view.

> **Trouble?**
> If you add a table to Query Design view twice by mistake, click the title bar of the extra field list, then press [Delete].

4. Click the **First field** in the Employees table field list, then drag the **First field** to the Field cell in the first column of the query design grid

   The order in which the fields are placed in the query design grid is their order in the datasheet.

> **QuickTip**
> Double-click a field name to place it in the next available column of the query grid.

5. Drag the **Last field** from the Employees table to the Field cell in the second column, drag the **Attended field** from the Attendance table to the third column, drag the **Description field** from the Courses table to the fourth column, then drag the **Hours field** from the Courses table to the fifth column

   Your Query Design view should look like Figure F-2. You may delete a field from the lower pane by clicking the field selector above the field name and pressing [Delete]. Deleting a field from the query design grid removes it from the logical view of this query's datasheet, but does not delete the field from the database. A field is physically defined and the field's contents are physically stored in a table object only.

> **QuickTip**
> If you need to add a field to the query that isn't currently displayed, click the Show Table button 📇 to add the new table.

6. Click the **Hours field selector**, press **[Delete]** to remove the field from the query design grid, then click the **Datasheet View button** 📖 on the query Design toolbar

   The datasheet looks like Figure F-3. The resulting datasheet shows the four fields selected in Query Design view and displays 153 records. The records represent the 153 different times a MediaLoft employee has attended a MediaLoft class. Shayla Colletti appears in eleven records because she has attended eleven classes.

FIGURE F-1: Query Design view with multiple tables

Table names

Fields in the
Employees table

One-to-many
link lines

Query design grid

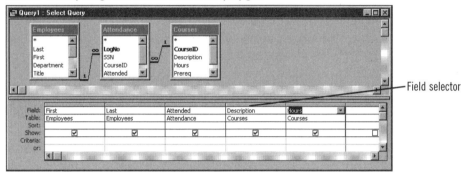

FIGURE F-2: Query Design view with five fields in the query grid

Field selector

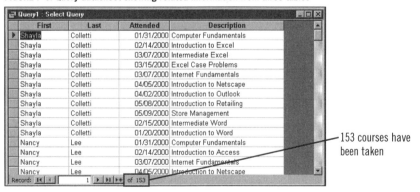

FIGURE F-3: Query datasheet showing related information from three tables

153 courses have
been taken

Resizing Query Design view

Drag the resize bar up or down to provide more room for the upper (field lists) or lower (query design grid) parts of Query Design view. By dragging the resize bar down, you may have enough room to enlarge each field list so that you can see all of the field names in each table, but still have enough room to show all of the information in the query design grid.

Access 2000

Sorting a Query on Multiple Fields

Sorting refers to reorganizing the records in either ascending or descending order based on the contents of a field. Queries allow you to specify more than one sort field in Query Design view, evaluating the sort orders from left to right. The leftmost sort field is the primary sort field. Sort orders defined in Query Design view are saved with the query object. If no sort orders are specified in the query design grid, the records are sorted by the primary key field of the first table that has a field in the query. **Scenario** David wishes to put the records in alphabetical order based on the employee's last name. If more than one record exists for an employee (if the employee has attended more than one class), David wants to further sort the records by the date the course was attended.

Steps

1. Click the **Design View button** on the Query Datasheet toolbar
   To sort the records according to David's plan, the Last field must be the primary sort, and the Attended field the secondary sort field.

QuickTip

You can resize the columns of a datasheet by pointing to the right column border that separates the field names, then dragging ←‖→ left or right to resize as needed. You can double-click ←‖→ to automatically adjust the column width to fit the widest entry.

2. Click the **Sort cell** of the **Last field** in the query design grid, click the **Sort list arrow**, click **Ascending**, click the **Sort cell** of the **Attended field** in the query design grid, click the **Sort list arrow**, then click **Ascending**
   The resulting query design grid should look like Figure F-4.

3. Click the **Datasheet View button** on the Query Design toolbar
   The records of the datasheet are now listed alphabetically by the entry in the Last field, then in chronological order by the entry in the Attended field, as shown in Figure F-5. You notice that Maria Abbott has attended six classes, but that her name has been incorrectly entered in the database as "Marie." Fix this error in the query datasheet.

4. Type **Maria**, then press [↓]
   This update shows that you are using a properly designed relational database because changing any occurrence of an employee's name should cause all other occurrences of that name to be automatically updated. The employee name is physically stored only once in the Employees table, although it is displayed in this datasheet once for every time the employee has attended a course.

QuickTip

If you need to identify your printout, include your name or initials in the query name and it will print in the header of the datasheet.

5. Click the **Close Window button** to close the Select Query, click **Yes** when prompted to save the changes, type **Employee Progress Query** in the Query Name text box, then click **OK**
   The query is now saved and listed as an object in the Queries window in the Training-F database window.

FIGURE F-4: Specifying multiple sort orders in Query Design view

Records will be sorted by Last, then by Attended

Show check box

Resize bar

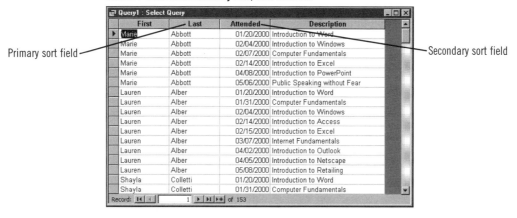

FIGURE F-5: Records sorted by Last, then Attended

Primary sort field

Secondary sort field

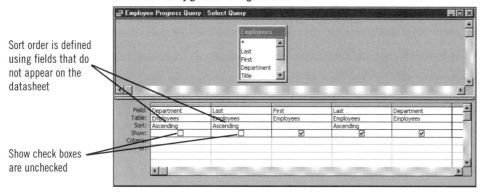

FIGURE F-6: Query grid for sorting out of order

Sort order is defined using fields that do not appear on the datasheet

Show check boxes are unchecked

Specifying a sort order different from the field order in the datasheet

You cannot modify the left-to-right sort order hierarchy in Query Design view. However, if you wish to have the fields in the datasheet appear in a different order than that by which they are sorted, there is a simple solution, as shown in Figure F-6. Suppose you want the fields First, Last, and Department to appear in a datasheet in that order, but want to sort the records by Department, then by Last. The Department and Last fields are the first two fields in the design grid with the appropriate sort order specified, but their Show Check Boxes are unchecked, so these columns do not display in the datasheet. The resulting datasheet would sort the records by Department, then Last, and display the First, Last, and Department fields.

Developing AND Queries

Using Access you can query for specific records that match two or more criteria. **Criteria** are tests, or limiting conditions, for which the record must be true to be selected for a datasheet. To create an **AND query** in which two or more criteria are present, enter the criteria for the fields on the same Criteria row of the query design grid. If two AND criteria are entered for the same field, the AND operator separates the criteria in the Criteria cell for that field. Scenario ▶ David is looking for a person to assist the Access teacher in the classroom. In order to compile a list of potential candidates, he creates an AND query to find all employees who have taken MediaLoft's Access courses and passed the exams.

1. Click the **Employee Progress query**, then click the **Design View button** 📝 on the Query Datasheet toolbar
   Instead of creating a query from scratch, you can modify the Employee Progress query. The only additional field you have to add to the query is the Passed field.

2. Scroll the **Attendance table field list**, then double-click the **Passed field** to move it to the fifth column in the query design grid
   MediaLoft offers several Access courses, so the criteria must specify all the records that contain the word "Access" anywhere in the Description field. You'll use the asterisk (*), a **wildcard character** that represents any combination of characters, to create this criteria.

3. Click the **Description field Criteria cell**, type ***access***, then click the **Datasheet View button** 🔳 on the Query Design toolbar
   The resulting datasheet as shown in Figure F-7, shows thirteen records that match the criteria. The resulting records all contain the word "access" in some part of the Description field, but because of the placement of the asterisks, it didn't matter *where* (beginning, middle, or end) the word was found in the Description field entry. Additional criteria are needed to display a datasheet with only those records where the student passed the final exam.

4. Click the **Design View button** 📝 on the Query Datasheet toolbar, click the **Passed field Criteria cell**, then type **yes**
   The resulting query design grid is shown in Figure F-8. Notice that Access entered double quotation marks around the text criterion in the Description field and added the **Like operator**. See Table F-1 for more information on Access operators.

5. Click **Datasheet View button** 🔳 on the Query Design toolbar to view the resulting records
   Multiple criteria added to the same line of the query design grid (AND criteria) must *each* be true for the record to appear in the resulting datasheet, thereby causing the resulting datasheet to display *fewer* records. Only nine records contain "access" in the Description field and "yes" in the Passed field.

6. Click **File** on the menu bar, click **Save As** to save this query with a new name, type **Potential Access Assistants** in the Save Query 'Employee Progress Query' To: text box, then click **OK**
   The query is saved with the new name, Potential Access Assistants, as a new object in the MediaLoft-F database.

7. Close the Potential Access Assistants datasheet

FIGURE F-7: Datasheet for Access records

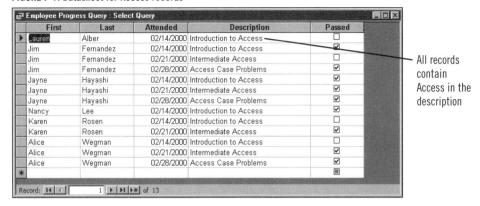

All records contain Access in the description

FIGURE F-8: AND criteria

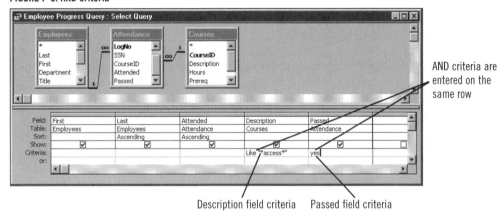

AND criteria are entered on the same row

Description field criteria   Passed field criteria

TABLE F-1: Comparison operators

operator	description	example	result
>	greater than	>50	Value exceeds 50
>=	greater than or equal to	>=50	Value is 50 or greater
<	less than	<50	Value is less than 50
<=	less than or equal to	<=50	Value is 50 or less
<>	not equal to	<>50	Value is any number other than 50
Between...And	finds values between two numbers or dates	Between #2/2/95# And #2/2/98#	Dates between 2/2/95 and 2/2/98, inclusive
In	finds a value that is one of a list	In("IA","KS","NE")	Value equals IA or KS or NE
Null	finds records that are blank	Null	No value has been entered
Is Not Null	finds records that are not blank	Is Not Null	Any value has been entered
Like	finds records that match the criteria	Like "A"	Value equals A
Not	finds records that do not match the criteria	Not 2	Numbers other than 2

Developing OR Queries

AND queries *narrow* the number of records in the resulting datasheet by requiring that a record be true for multiple criteria in one criteria row. **OR queries** *expand* the number of records that will appear in the datasheet because a record needs to be true *for only one* of the criteria rows. OR criteria are entered in the query design grid on different lines (criteria rows). Each criteria row of the query design grid is evaluated separately, adding the records that are true for that row to the resulting datasheet. **Scenario▶** David is looking for an assistant for the Excel courses. He modifies the Potential Access Assistants query to expand the number of records to include those who have passed Excel courses.

Steps 1 2 3 4

1. Click the **Potential Access Assistants** query, then click the **Design button** 📐 in the Training-F database window
   To add OR criteria, you have to enter criteria in the "or" row of the query design grid.

2. Click the **or Description criteria cell** below Like "*access*", then type ***excel***
   As soon as you click elsewhere in the query grid, Access will assist you with criteria **syntax** (rules by which criteria need to be entered) by automatically entering the Like operator when necessary. It also automatically adds double quotes to surround text criteria in Text fields, and pound signs (#) to surround date criteria in Date/Time fields. The criteria in Number, Currency, and Yes/No fields are not surrounded by any characters.

3. Click the **or Passed criteria cell** below Yes, then type **yes**
   If a record matches *either* row of the criteria grid, it is included in the query's datasheet. Each row is evaluated separately, which is why it was necessary to put the Yes criteria for the Passed field in both rows of the grid. Otherwise, the second row would pull all records where "excel" is in the description regardless of whether the test was passed or not. Figure F-9 shows the OR criteria in the query design grid.

4. Click the **Datasheet View button** 🖼 on the Query Design toolbar
   The resulting datasheet displays 28 records, as shown in Figure F-10. All of the records contain course Descriptions that contain the word Access or Excel as well as "Yes" in the Passed field. Also, notice that the sort order (Last, then Attended) is still in effect.

5. Click **File** on the menu bar, click **Save As**, click between **"Access" and "Assistants"**, type **or Excel**, press **[Spacebar]**, then click **OK**
   This query is saved as a separate database object.

6. Close the Potential Access or Excel Assistants query
   The Training-F database displays the three queries you created.

FIGURE F-9: OR criteria

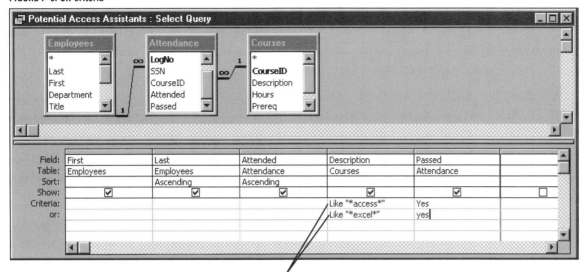

OR criteria are entered on different rows

FIGURE F-10: OR criteria adds more records to the datasheet

First	Last	Attended	Description	Passed
Maria	Abbott	02/14/2000	Introduction to Excel	☑
Lauren	Alber	02/15/2000	Introduction to Excel	☑
Shayla	Colletti	02/14/2000	Introduction to Excel	☑
Shayla	Colletti	03/07/2000	Intermediate Excel	☑
David	Dumont	02/14/2000	Introduction to Excel	☑
Jim	Fernandez	02/14/2000	Introduction to Access	☑
Jim	Fernandez	02/15/2000	Introduction to Excel	☑
Jim	Fernandez	02/28/2000	Access Case Problems	☑
Jayne	Hayashi	02/14/2000	Introduction to Access	☑
Jayne	Hayashi	02/21/2000	Intermediate Access	☑
Jayne	Hayashi	02/28/2000	Access Case Problems	☑
Cynthia	Hayman	02/14/2000	Introduction to Excel	☑
Cynthia	Hayman	03/07/2000	Intermediate Excel	☑
John	Kim	02/14/2000	Introduction to Excel	☑
John	Kim	03/07/2000	Intermediate Excel	☑
John	Kim	03/15/2000	Excel Case Problems	☑
Nancy	Lee	02/14/2000	Introduction to Access	☑

Record: 1 of 28

28 records found

Excel or Access records were found

Passed field is always "Yes"

CLUES TO USE

Using wildcard characters in query criteria

To search for a pattern, use a ? (question mark) to search for any single character and an * (asterisk) to search for any number of characters. Wildcard characters are often used with the Like operator. For example, the criterion Like "10/*/97" would find all dates in October of 1997, and the criterion Like "F*" would find all entries that start with the letter F.

Creating Calculated Fields

Arithmetic operators and functions shown in Table F-2 and F-3, are used to create mathematical calculations within Access. **Functions** are special shortcut formulas that help you calculate common answers such as counts and subtotals on groups of records, a loan payment if working with financial data, or the current date. If you can calculate a new field of information based on existing fields in a database, never define the new piece of data as a separate field in the table's Design view. Rather, use a query object to create the calculated field from the raw data to guarantee that the new field always contains accurate, up-to-date information. **Scenario** David has been asked to report on the "per hour" cost of each course. The data to calculate this answer already exists in the Cost (the cost of the course) and Hours (the number of contact hours per course) fields of the Courses table.

Steps 1234

QuickTip

You can double-click an object in the Show Table dialog box to add it to Query Design view.

1. Click **Queries** on the Objects bar, double-click **Create query in Design view**, click **Courses**, click **Add**, then click **Close** in the Show Table dialog box
   The Courses field list is in the upper pane of the query window.

2. Double-click the **Description field**, double-click the **Hours field**, then double-click the **Cost field**
   A **calculated field** is created by entering a new descriptive field name followed by a colon in the Field cell of the query design grid followed by an expression. An **expression** is a combination of operators such as + (plus), − (minus), * (multiply), or / (divide); raw values (such as numbers or dates); functions; and fields that produce a result. Field names used in an expression are surrounded by square brackets.

QuickTip

If an expression becomes too long to fit completely in a cell of the query design grid, right-click the cell, then click Zoom to use the Zoom dialog box for long entries.

3. Click the blank **Field cell** of the fourth column, type **Hourly Rate:[Cost]/[Hours]**, then drag the ➕ on the right edge of the fourth column selector to the right to display the entire entry
   The query design grid should now look like Figure F-11.

4. Click the **Datasheet View button** ▦ on the Query Design toolbar
   It is not necessary to show the fields used in the calculated expression in the datasheet (in this case, Hours and Cost), but viewing these fields beside the new calculated field helps confirm that your new calculated field is working properly. The Hourly Rate field appears to be accurate, but the data is not formatted well.

5. Click the **Design View button** ▧ on the Query Datasheet toolbar, right-click the calculated **Hourly Rate field** in the query design grid, then click **Properties**
   The Field Properties dialog box opens. This new field represents dollars per hour.

6. Click the **Format text box**, click **Format property list arrow**, click **Currency**, close the property sheet, then click the **Datasheet View button** to display the records
   The data shown in the Hourly Rate field is now rounded to the nearest cent.

7. Press **[Tab]** twice, type **300** in the Introduction to Access Cost field, then press **[Enter]**
   The resulting datasheet is shown in Figure F-12. The Hourly Rate field was updated to the correct value as soon as the Cost field was updated.

Trouble?

If you have already moved to a new record, you must click the Undo button ↺ to undo your last entry.

8. Press **[Esc]** to reverse the Introduction to Access Cost field change, click the **Save button** ▤, type **Hourly Rate** in the Save As dialog box, click **OK**, then close the datasheet

FIGURE F-11: Entering a calculated field in Query Design view

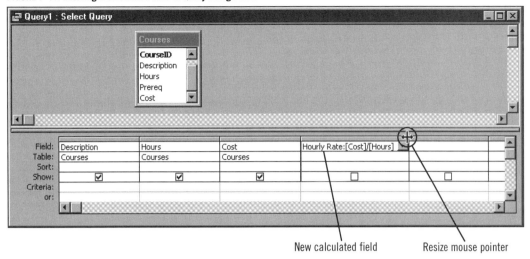

New calculated field   Resize mouse pointer

FIGURE F-12: Formatting and testing the calculated field

Description	Hours	Cost	Hourly Rate
Introduction to Access	12	$300	$25.00
Intermediate Access	24	$400	$16.67
Access Case Problems	12	$200	$16.67
Computer Fundamentals	12	$200	$16.67
Introduction to Excel	12	$200	$16.67
Intermediate Excel	12	$200	$16.67
Excel Case Problems	12	$200	$16.67
Introduction to Internet Explorer	12	$200	$16.67
Intermediate Internet Explorer	12	$200	$16.67
Internet Fundamentals	12	$200	$16.67
Introduction to Netscape	12	$200	$16.67
Intermediate Netscape	12	$200	$16.67
Introduction to Networking	12	$200	$16.67

Record: 1 of 27

Calculated field with Currency format

Updated Cost field

TABLE F-2: Arithmetic operators

operator	description
+	Addition
−	Subtraction
*	Multiplication
/	Division
^	Exponentiation

TABLE F-3: Common functions

function	sample expression and description
DATE	DATE()-[BirthDate] Calculates the number of days between today and the date in the BirthDate field
PMT	PMT([Rate],[Term],[Loan]) Calculates the monthly payment on a loan where the Rate field contains the monthly interest rate, the Term field contains the number of monthly payments, and the Loan field contains the total amount financed
LEFT	LEFT([Lastname],2) Returns the first two characters of the entry in the Lastname field
RIGHT	RIGHT([Partno],3) Returns the last three characters of the entry in the Partno field
LEN	LEN([Description]) Returns the number of characters in the Description field

Building Summary Queries

As your database grows, you will probably be less interested in individual records and more interested in information about groups of records. A **summary query** can be used to calculate information about a group of records by adding appropriate **aggregate functions** to the Total row of the query design grid. Aggregate functions also create calculations, but are special functions in that they calculate information about a *group of records* rather than a new field of information for *each record*. Aggregate functions are summarized in Table F-4. Some aggregate functions such as Sum can be used only on fields with Number or Currency data types, but others such as Min, Max, or Count can be used on Text fields, too. **Scenario** The Accounting Department has asked David for a "cost by department" report that shows how many classes employees of each department have attended as well as the summarized costs for these courses. He builds a summary query to provide this information.

Steps 1 2 3 4

1. Click **Queries** on the Objects bar (if necessary), then double-click **Create query in Design view**

   You need all three tables to develop this query.

2. Click **Courses**, click **Add**, click **Attendance**, click **Add**, click **Employees**, click **Add**, then click **Close** in the Show Table dialog box

3. Double-click the **Department field** in the Employees table, double-click the **Cost field** in the Courses table, then double-click the **Cost field** in the Courses table again

   Even though you don't explicitly use fields from the Attendance table, you need this table in your query to tie the fields from the Courses and Employees tables together. You added the Cost field to the query grid twice because you wish to compute two different summary statistics on the information in this field (a subtotal and a count).

4. Click the **Totals button** Σ on the Query Design toolbar

   The Total row is added to the query grid below the Table row. This is the row that you use to specify how you want the resulting datasheet summarized. You want to group the resulting datasheet by the Department field, but summarize the data in the Cost fields.

5. Click the **Cost field Total cell** in the second column, click the **Group By list arrow**, click **Sum**, click the **Cost field Total cell** in the third column, click the **Group By list arrow**, then click **Count**

   Your Query Design view should look like Figure F-13.

QuickTip

You cannot enter or edit data in a summary query because each record represents the summarization of several records. The resulting datasheet is not updateable.

6. Click the **Datasheet View button** 📖 on the Query Design toolbar

   As you can see from the resulting datasheet, the Accounting Department had $3,500 of internal charges for the 16 classes its employees attended. By counting the Cost field in addition to summing it, you know how many records were combined to reach the total $3,500 figure. You can sort summary queries, too.

7. Click any entry in the **SumOfCost** field, then click the **Sort Descending button** ↓ on the Query Datasheet toolbar

   The resulting datasheet is shown in Figure F-14, listing the in-house training costs in a highest to lowest order for all of the 11 departments at MediaLoft. If you wanted to permanently store this sort order, you would specify it in Query Design view, where it would be stored as part of the query object.

QuickTip

If you need to identify your printout, include your name or initials in the query name.

8. Click the **Save button** 💾, type **Internal Costs**, click **OK**, click the **Print button** 🖨 on the Query Datasheet toolbar, then close the datasheet

FIGURE F-13: Summary Query Design view

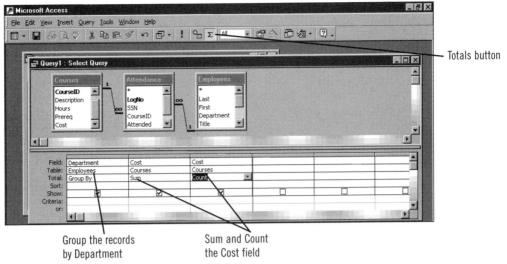

Totals button

Group the records by Department

Sum and Count the Cost field

FIGURE F-14: Summarized records sorted in descending order by SumOfCost

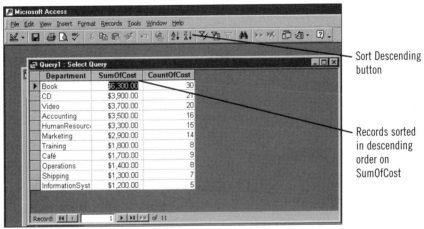

Sort Descending button

Records sorted in descending order on SumOfCost

TABLE F-4: Aggregate Functions

aggregate function	used to find the
Sum	Total of values in a field
Avg	Average of values in a field
Min	Minimum value in the field
Max	Maximum value in the field
Count	Number of values in a field (not counting null values)
StDev	Standard deviation of values in a field
Var	Variance of values in a field
First	Field value from the first record in a table or query
Last	Field value from the last record in a table or query

Creating Crosstab Queries

Crosstab queries provide another method of summarizing data by creating a datasheet in which one or more fields are chosen for the row headings, another field is chosen for the column headings, and a third field, usually a numeric field, is summarized within the datasheet itself. If you wish to base the crosstab query on fields from multiple tables, the first step to creating a crosstab query is to assemble the fields in a single select query. Then you create the final crosstab query based upon the intermediary query object by using the **Crosstab Query Wizard** to identify which fields will be the row and column headings, and which field will be summarized within the grid of the crosstab datasheet itself. ▶Scenario David wishes to expand the information in the Internal Costs query to summarize the total cost for each course within each department. This is a good candidate for a crosstab query because he is summarizing information by two fields, one that will serve as the row heading (Description) and one that will serve as the column heading (Department) for the final crosstab datasheet.

Steps

1. Click **Queries** on the objects bar (if necessary), click **Internal Costs**, then click the **Design View button** 📐 in the Training-F database window
   Instead of creating the intermediate select query from scratch, a couple of modifications to the Internal Costs query will quickly provide the fields you need.

2. Click the **Totals button** Σ on the Query Design toolbar, click the **Cost Field cell** for the third column, click the **Cost list arrow**, then click **Description**
   The intermediary select query should look like Figure F-15. You removed the summary functions (the Total row on the query design grid), then changed the second Cost field to the Description field. It is important to save the query with an appropriate name.

3. Click **File** on the menu bar, click **Save As**, type **Crosstab Fields** in the **Save Query 'Internal Costs' To:** text box, click **OK**, then close the query
   You can build the Crosstab query using the Crosstab Query Wizard.

Trouble?

The Create query by using wizard option from the database window is used only to create a select query, so you must click the New button to use the other query wizards.

4. Click the **New button** 🗋 in the database window, click **Crosstab Query Wizard** in the New Query dialog box, then click **OK**
   The Crosstab Query Wizard dialog box opens. The first question asks you which object contains the fields for the crosstab query.

5. Click the **Queries option button** in the View section, click **Crosstab Fields** in the list of available queries, then click **Next**
   The next questions from the Crosstab Query Wizard will organize how the fields are displayed in the datasheet.

QuickTip

You can click the Back button within any wizard to review previous choices.

6. Click **Description** for the row heading, click the **Select Single Field button** >, click **Next**, click **Department** to specify the column heading, then click **Next**
   The next wizard dialog box asks you to identify the field that is summarized within the body of the crosstab report. Since the Cost field is the only field left, it is automatically chosen, but you still need to specify a function that will determine the way the Cost field is calculated.

7. Click **Sum** in the Functions list
   Your Query Wizard dialog box should look like Figure F-16.

8. Click **Next**, type **Crosstab Query** in the query name text box, then click **Finish**
   The final crosstab query is shown in Figure F-17.

9. Print the resulting datasheet

FIGURE F-15: Select query upon which the crosstab query will be based

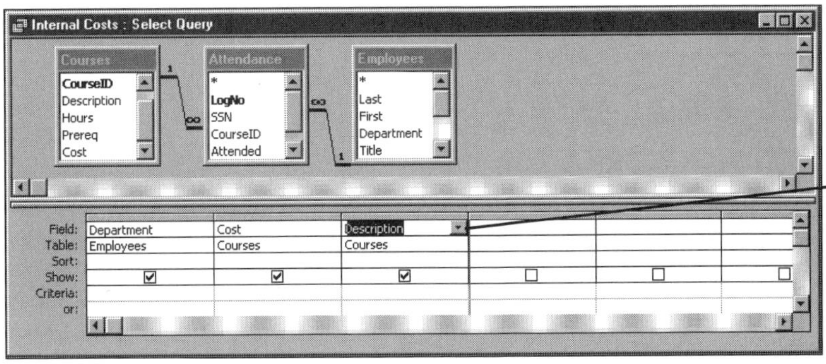

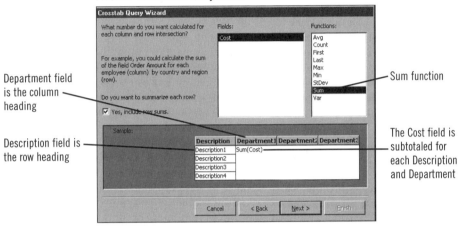

Click this list arrow to choose a different field from the same table

FIGURE F-16: Crosstab Query Wizard

Department field is the column heading

Description field is the row heading

Sum function

The Cost field is subtotaled for each Description and Department

FIGURE F-17: Crosstab Query datasheet

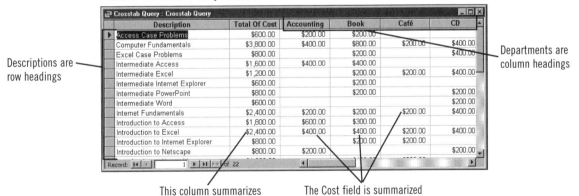

Descriptions are row headings

Departments are column headings

This column summarizes the costs for every row

The Cost field is summarized within the crosstab query

Defining types of Query Wizards

The **Simple Query Wizard** is an alternative way to create a select query, rather than going directly into Query Design view. The **Find Duplicates Query Wizard** is used to determine whether a table contains duplicate values in one or more fields. The **Find Unmatched Query Wizard** is used to find records in one table that don't have related records in another table. To invoke the Find Duplicates, Find Unmatched, or Crosstab Query Wizards, you must click the New button when viewing the query objects within the opening database window.

Modifying Crosstab Queries

Once a crosstab query is created, it can be modified in Query Design view, just like a select query can. Crosstab queries use two additional rows in the query grid: the "Totals" row (similar to a summary query) and a "Crosstab" row that determines the location of the field (column heading, row heading, or summarized value). As with summary queries, crosstab query datasheets cannot be used to update data, because every row represents a summarization of multiple records of data. ▶ Scenario ◀ David will use Query Design view to modify the crosstab query so that he has a count of how many people within each department took each class.

Steps 1 2 3 4

1. Click the **Design View button** 🔎 on the Query Datasheet toolbar
   Query Design view for the Crosstab Query opens, as shown in Figure F-18. The Totals and Crosstab rows are displayed in the query grid. If you had not used the Query Wizard to create this query, you could still display these rows and, therefore, make any existing select query into a crosstab query by selecting the Query Type button and choosing the Crosstab Query from the list.

2. Click **Sum** in the Total row for Cost field, click the **list arrow**, then click **Count**
   This field determines the calculation performed on the field within the body of the crosstab report. Now it will count the number of people within each department that took each class rather than sum the Cost data.

3. Click **Sum** in the Total row for the Total of Cost: Cost field, click the **list arrow**, then click **Count**
   This field determines the second **row heading** and will now count how many courses of each description were taken for all departments.

4. Click the **Datasheet View button** 🖩 on the Query Design toolbar, then click the **Save button** 🖫 on the Query Datasheet toolbar
   The modified crosstab query that counts the number of times each course was taken for employees within each department is shown in Figure F-19.

5. Print the resulting datasheet

6. Close the datasheet, then close the Training-F database

7. Exit Access

FIGURE F-18: Query Design view of a crosstab query

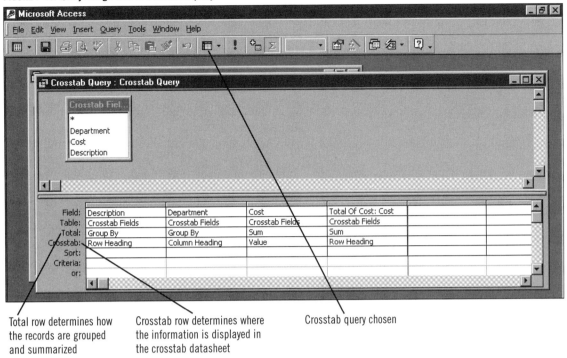

Total row determines how
the records are grouped
and summarized

Crosstab row determines where
the information is displayed in
the crosstab datasheet

Crosstab query chosen

FIGURE F-19: Modified crosstab query that counts courses taken

Description	Total Of Cost	Accounting	Book	Café	CD
Access Case Problems	3	1	1		
Computer Fundamentals	19	2	4	1	
Excel Case Problems	4		1		
Intermediate Access	4	1	1		
Intermediate Excel	6		1	1	
Intermediate Internet Explorer	3		1		
Intermediate PowerPoint	4		1		
Intermediate Word	3				
Internet Fundamentals	12	1	1	1	
Introduction to Access	6	2	1		
Introduction to Excel	12	2	2	1	
Introduction to Internet Explorer	4		1	1	
Introduction to Netscape	4	1			

Record: 1 of 22

A total of 19 Computer
Fundamentals courses
were taken

Accounting Department
employees took 2 Introduction
to Excel courses

Practice

► Concepts Review

Identify each element of the Design view window and Select query window shown in Figure F-20.

FIGURE F-20

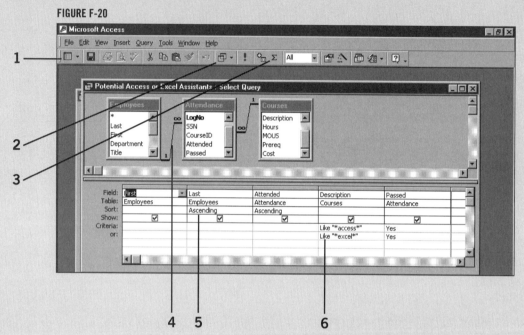

Match each term with the statement that describes its function.

7. Query
8. Arithmetic operators
9. And
10. Sorting
11. Criteria

a. Conditions that select only certain records
b. Used to create mathematical calculations in a query
c. A database object that answers questions about the data
d. Placing the records of a datasheet in a certain order
e. Operator used to combine two expressions

Select the best answer from the list of choices.

12. The query datasheet can best be described as a
   a. Second copy of the data in the underlying tables.
   b. Logical view of the selected data from an underlying table's datasheet.
   c. Separate file of data.
   d. Duplication of the data in the underlying table's datasheet.

13. Queries are often used to:
   a. Present a subset of fields from multiple tables.
   b. Eliminate the need to build multiple tables.
   c. Create option boxes and list boxes from which to choose field values.
   d. Create copies of database files.

14. When you update data in a table that is displayed in a query:
   a. You have the choice whether or not you want to update the data in the query.
   b. You must relink the query to the table.
   c. The data is automatically updated in the query.
   d. You must also update the query.

15. To assemble several fields from different tables, use a(n):
   a. Append Query.
   b. Update Query.
   c. Delete Query.
   d. Select Query.

16. The order in which records are sorted is determined by:
   a. The ascending fields are sorted first in the query design grid, then the descending fields are sorted second.
   b. The alphabetic order of the field names.
   c. The left-to-right position of the fields in the query design grid.
   d. The order in which the fields are defined in the underlying table.

17. Crosstab queries are used to:
   a. Calculate price increases on numeric fields.
   b. Update several records at the same time.
   c. Select fields for a datasheet from multiple tables.
   d. Summarize information based on fields in the column and row headings of the report.

▶ Skills Review

1. Create select queries.
   a. Start Access and open the database Membership-F.
   b. Create a new select query in Design View using both the Names and Zips tables.
   c. Add the following fields to the query design grid in this order:
      First, Last, and Street from the Names table
      City, State, and Zip from the Zips table
   d. Enter your own last name in the Last field of the first record.
   e. Save the query as "Basic Address List", view the datasheet, print the datasheet, then close the query.

2. Sort a query on multiple fields.
   a. Open the Design view for the Basic Address List query. You wish to modify the query so that it is sorted in ascending order by Last, then by First, but you do not want to change the order of the fields in the resulting datasheet.
   b. Drag another First field to the right of the Last field in the query design grid to make the first three fields in the query design grid First, Last, and First.

c. Add the ascending sort criteria to the second column and third column fields, and uncheck the Show check box in the third column.

d. Use Save As to save the query as "Sorted Address List", view the datasheet, print the datasheet, then close the query.

3. Develop AND queries.

a. Return to the Design view for the Basic Address List. You wish to modify the "Basic Address List" query so that only those people from Kansas with a last name that starts with "M" are chosen.

b. Enter M* (the asterisk is a wildcard) in the criteria row for the Last field to choose all people whose last name starts with M. Access assists you with the syntax for this type of criterion and enters "Like M*" in the cell when you click elsewhere in the grid.

c. Enter "KS" as the criterion for the State field. Be sure to enter the criteria on the same line in the query design grid to make the query an AND query. You should have six records in this datasheet.

d. Enter your own hometown in the City field of the first record.

e. Save the query as "Kansas M Names", view, print, then close the datasheet.

4. Develop OR queries.

a. Modify the "Kansas M Names" query so that only those people from KS with a last name that starts with either "M" or "C" are chosen. Do this by entering the OR criterion C* on the or row for the Last field in the query design grid.

b. Be sure to also type the KS criterion on the or row for the State field in the query design grid to make sure that your query doesn't display all names that start with C, but only those who also live in Kansas.

c. Save the query as "Kansas C or M Names", view the datasheet (there should be nine records), print the datasheet, then close the query.

5. Create calculated fields.

a. Create a new select query using Design view using only the Names table. You want to determine the number of days old each person is based on the information in the Birthday field.

b. Add the following fields from the Names table to the query design grid in this order: First, Last, Birthday.

c. Create a calculated field called "Days Old" in the fourth column of the query design grid by entering the expression: Days Old:Date()-[Birthday].

d. Sort the query in descending order on the calculated Days Old field.

e. Select the calculated Days Old field using the column Field selector, open the Property sheet, format the Days Old field with a Standard format, and enter "0" in the Decimal Places property text box.

f. Save the query as "Days Old", view the datasheet, print the datasheet, then close the query.

6. Build summary queries.

a. Create a new select query using Design view, then add the Names and Activities tables.

b. Add the following fields: First and Last from the Names table, Hours from the Activities table.

c. Add the Total row to the query design grid and change the function for the Hours field from Group By to Sum.

d. Sort in descending order by Hours.

e. Save the query as "Total Hours", view the datasheet, print the datasheet, then close the query.

7. Create crosstab queries.

   a. First create a select query with the fields City and State from the Zips table, and Dues from the Names table. Save it as "Crosstab Fields".

   b. Click the New button when viewing query objects, then start the Crosstab Query Wizard, and base the crosstab query on the Crosstab Fields query you just created.

   c. Select City as the row heading and State as the column heading, and sum the Dues field within the crosstab datasheet.

   d. Save and name the query "Crosstab of Dues by City and State".

   e. View, print, then close the datasheet.

8. Modify crosstab queries.

   a. Open the Crosstab of Dues by City and State query in Design view.

   b. Change the Sum function to Count for both the Dues and the Total of Dues: Dues fields.

   c. View, print, then close the datasheet without saving it.

   d. Close the database, then exit Access.

► Visual Workshop

Open the Training-F database and create a new query to display the datasheet as shown in Figure F-21. Notice that the records are sorted alphabetically by the date the course was attended, then by last name. Save the query as "History of Attendance". (*Note:* If you need to identify your work on the printout, add your initials as part of the query name). Print the query.

FIGURE F-21

History of Attendance : Select Query

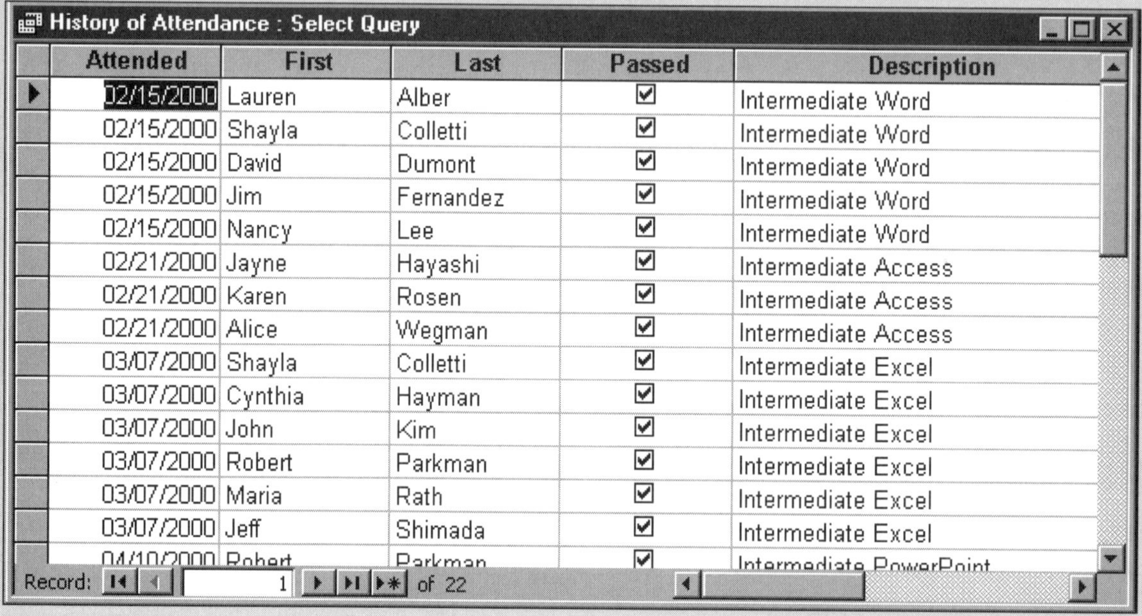

Attended	First	Last	Passed	Description
02/15/2000	Lauren	Alber	☑	Intermediate Word
02/15/2000	Shayla	Colletti	☑	Intermediate Word
02/15/2000	David	Dumont	☑	Intermediate Word
02/15/2000	Jim	Fernandez	☑	Intermediate Word
02/15/2000	Nancy	Lee	☑	Intermediate Word
02/21/2000	Jayne	Hayashi	☑	Intermediate Access
02/21/2000	Karen	Rosen	☑	Intermediate Access
02/21/2000	Alice	Wegman	☑	Intermediate Access
03/07/2000	Shayla	Colletti	☑	Intermediate Excel
03/07/2000	Cynthia	Hayman	☑	Intermediate Excel
03/07/2000	John	Kim	☑	Intermediate Excel
03/07/2000	Robert	Parkman	☑	Intermediate Excel
03/07/2000	Maria	Rath	☑	Intermediate Excel
03/07/2000	Jeff	Shimada	☑	Intermediate Excel
04/10/2000	Robert	Parkman	☑	Intermediate PowerPoint

Record: 1 of 22

Developing
Forms and Subforms

Objectives

▶ **Understand the form/subform relationship**
▶ **Create subforms using the Form Wizard**
[MOUS] ▶ **Create subforms using queries**
[MOUS] ▶ **Modify subforms**
[MOUS] ▶ **Add combo boxes**
[MOUS] ▶ **Add option groups**
[MOUS] ▶ **Add command buttons**
[MOUS] ▶ **Add records with a form/subform**

Viewing, finding, entering, and editing data in a database must be easy and straightforward for all database users. A **form** can be designed to present data in any logical screen arrangement and serve as the primary interface for most database users. Forms contain **controls** such as labels, text boxes, combo boxes, and command buttons to help identify and enter data. Forms with **subform** controls allow you to show a record and its related records from another object (table or query) at the same time. For example, on one screen you may wish to see customer information as well as all of the orders placed by the customer. Well-designed form/subforms will encourage fast, accurate data entry, and will shield the data entry person from the complexity of underlying tables, queries, and datasheets. **Scenario▶** David develops a single form that shows employee information at the top of the form and all of the classes that an employee has attended at the bottom. This requires a subform control. He also upgrades the usability of the forms by adding various controls such as combo boxes, option groups, and command buttons.

Understanding the Form/Subform Relationship

A **subform** control is actually a form within a form. The primary form is called the **main form**, and it contains the subform control. The subform shows related records that are linked to the single record currently displayed in the main form. The relationship between the main form and subform is often called a **parent/child relationship**, because the "parent" record in the main form is linked to many "children" records displayed in the subform. The link between the main form and subform is established through a linking field common to both, the same field that is used to establish the one-to-many relationship between underlying tables in the database. **Scenario** Creating forms with sub-forms requires careful planning, so David studies form/subform planning guidelines before he attempts to create the forms in Access.

 Sketch the layout of the form/subform on paper, identifying which fields belong in the main form and which belong in the subform

David has sketched two forms with subforms that he wants to create. Figure G-1 displays employee information in the main form and attendance information in the subform. Figure G-2 displays course information in the main form and employee information in the subform.

 Determine whether you are going to create separate queries upon which to base the main form and subform, or if you are going to use the Form Wizard to collect fields from multiple tables upon which to create the form and subform objects

This decision may have important consequences later because it determines the form's recordset. The **recordset** is the fields and records that will appear on the form. To modify the recordset of forms created solely through the Form Wizard, you have to modify the form's **Record Source property**, where the recordset is defined. When the form is based on an intermediate query, changing the query object automatically updates the Record Source property for the form, because the query object name *is* the Record Source property entry for that form.

If you use the Form Wizard to create a form with fields from multiple tables without an inter-mediary query object, the Record Source property of the form often displays an **SQL (Structured Query Language) statement**. This SQL statement can be modified to change the recordset, but obviously requires some knowledge of SQL.

 Create the form and subform objects based on the appropriate intermediary queries. If intermediary queries were not created, use the Form Wizard to gather the fields for both the form and subform

David uses the Form Wizard technique as well as the intermediary query technique so that he can compare the two.

FIGURE G-1: Employees Main Form with Attendance Subform

Employees Main Form

| First |
| Last |
| Email |

one person...

1

∞

...can take many courses

Attendance Subform

Attended	Description
Attended	Description
Attended	Description
Attended	Description

FIGURE G-2: Courses Main Form with Employee Subform

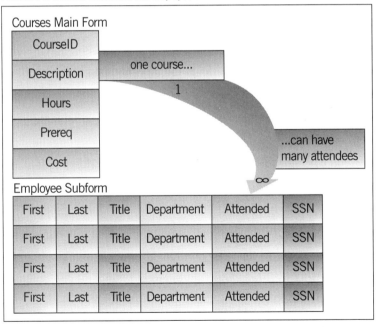

Courses Main Form

| CourseID |
| Description |
| Hours |
| Prereq |
| Cost |

one course...

1

∞

...can have many attendees

Employee Subform

First	Last	Title	Department	Attended	SSN
First	Last	Title	Department	Attended	SSN
First	Last	Title	Department	Attended	SSN
First	Last	Title	Department	Attended	SSN

Creating Forms with Subforms Using the Form Wizard

A form displays the fields of a table or query in an arrangement that you design, based on one of five general **layouts**: Columnar, Tabular, Datasheet, Chart, and PivotTable. **Columnar** is the most popular layout for a main form, and **Datasheet** is the most popular layout for a subform. See Table G-1 for more information on the different form layouts. Once the main form is created, the subform control is added in the main form's Form Design view. If you create the form/subform through the Form Wizard, however, both objects are created in one process. **Scenario** David creates a form and subform showing employee information in the main form and course information in the subform. He creates the form/subform objects without first creating intermediary query objects by using the power of the Form Wizard.

Steps 1234

1. Start Access and open the **Training-G** database

2. Click **Forms** on the Objects bar, then double-click **Create form by using wizard** in the Training-G Database window
   The **Form Wizard** appears and prompts you to select the fields of the form. You need five fields that are stored in three different tables for the final form/subform.

3. Click the **Attended field**, click the **Select Single Field button** ➤, click the **Tables/Queries list arrow**, click **Table: Courses**, click the **Description field**, click ➤, click the **Tables/Queries list arrow**, click **Table: Employees**, click the **First field**, click ➤, click the **Last field**, click ➤, click the **Email field**, then click ➤

   The Form Wizard dialog box should look like Figure G-3. Next, you must decide how to view the data. Arranging the form by Employees places the fields from the Employees table in the main form, and the Attended and Description fields in a subform.

4. Click **Next**, click **by Employees**, click the **Form with subform(s) option button** (if necessary), click **Next**, click the **Datasheet option button** (if necessary) as the layout for the subform, click **Next**, click **Standard** (if necessary) as the style for the main form, click **Next**, then click **Finish** to accept the default form and subform names
   The final Employees main form and Attendance Subform is shown in Figure G-4. Two sets of navigation buttons appear, one for the main form and one for the subform. The navigation buttons show that 19 employees are in the recordset and that the first employee has attended 11 courses. You can resize the form and subform control to display more information.

5. Click the **Design View button** 📐 on the Form View toolbar, click the **Employees Form Maximize button**, click the **subform control** so that sizing handles appear, then drag the subform control bottom middle sizing handle to the horizontal scroll bar at the bottom of the screen using ↕, as shown in Figure G-5
   The controls on the Attendance Subform appear within the subform control, and can be modified, just like controls in the main form.

6. Click the **Form View button** 📧 on the Form Design toolbar to view the resized subform, click the **Save button** 🖫, then close the **Employees** form
   The Employees form and the Attendance Subform appear with other form objects in the Training-G database window.

FIGURE G-3: Form Wizard

Choose Table or Query

Select Single Field button

Fields within the Selected table or query

From Attendance table

From Courses table

From Employees table

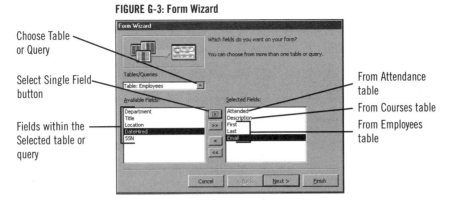

FIGURE G-4: Employees Main Form/Attendance Subform

Employees main form

Attendance Subform

Main form navigation buttons

Subform navigation buttons

Shayla attended 11 classes

19 employees

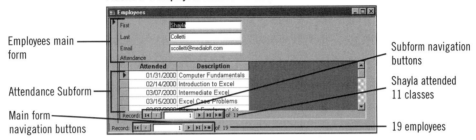

FIGURE G-5: Resizing the Attendance Subform

Attendance Subform is selected object

Subform control

Drag sizing handle down to scroll bar to enlarge the subform

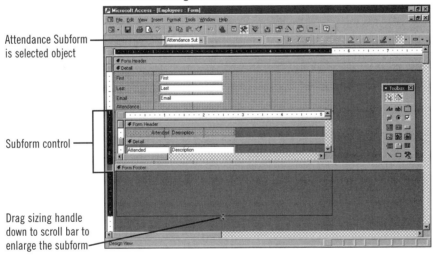

TABLE G-1: Form layouts

layout	description
Columnar	Each field appears on a separate line with a label to its left, one record for each screen
Tabular	Each field appears as a column heading and each record as a row. Multiple records appear just like they do in a datasheet, but you have more design control and flexibility. For example, you can change elements such as colors, fonts, headers, or footers
Datasheet	Each field appears as a column heading and each record as a row. The datasheet layout shows multiple records, but formatting options, except for resizing columns, are limited
Chart	Numeric fields appear in a chart (graph) format
PivotTable	Fields are chosen for column and row headings, and a field is summarized in the intersection of the appropriate column and row in a cross-tabular format

Creating Subforms Using Queries

Another way to create a form with a subform is to create both forms separately, basing them on either table or query objects, then linking the two forms together in a form/subform relationship. Although creating the forms by building them on separate query objects takes more work than building the form/subform using the Form Wizard, the benefit is your ability to quickly change the form's recordset by modifying the underlying query. **Scenario** David creates a form and subform showing course information in the main form and employee information in the subform using query objects that he has already created.

Steps

Trouble?

If the property sheet doesn't show the word "Form" in the title bar, click the Form Selector button.

1. Double-click **Create form in Design View**, click the **Properties button** 🔲 on the Form Design toolbar to display the form's property sheet, click the **Data tab**, click the **Record Source list arrow**, then click **Employee Info**

   The Employee Info query's field list (which supplies the recordset for the form) opens. Another initial property to consider is the **Default View** property, which determines the form's appearance. Datasheet layout is a popular style for subforms because it arranges the fields horizontally.

2. Click the **Format tab**, click the **Default View text box**, click the **Default View list arrow**, click **Datasheet**, then click 🔲 to toggle the property sheet off

   With the Record Source and Default View specified, you are ready to add the fields to the form.

QuickTip

Point to the Field list title bar to display the object name as a ScreenTip.

3. Double-click the **Employee Info field list title bar**, drag the **selected fields** using 📇 to the top of the Detail section at the **1" mark** on the horizontal ruler, as shown in Figure G-6, then click the **Field list button** 🔲 to toggle the field list off

4. Click the **Save button** 🔲 on the Form Design toolbar, the Save As dialog box opens, type **Employee Info Sub** in the Form Name text box, click **OK**, then close the form

   The subform will display the Employees who took each course.

5. Double-click **Create form in Design View**, click 🔲 to display the form's property sheet, click the **Data tab**, click the **Record Source property list arrow**, then click **Courses Info**

   The main form requires all of the fields from the Courses Info query.

Trouble?

If you drag and position the fields incorrectly on the form, click Undo 🔄 and try again.

6. Click 🔲 to close the property sheet, double-click the **Courses Info Field list title bar**, drag the **selected fields** using 📇 to the top of the Detail section at the **1" mark** on the horizontal ruler, click 🔲 to close the Field list, then maximize the form

   The main form is created. Now add the subform to it.

Trouble?

If you get a message box to install the Subform Wizard, insert your Office 2000 CD, then follow the instructions to install the feature.

7. Click the **Toolbox button** 🔧 on the Form Design toolbar to display the Toolbox toolbar (if necessary), be sure the **Control Wizards button** 🔲 is selected, click the **Subform/Subreport button** 🔲 on the Toolbox toolbar, then use ⁺📇 to drag a 6" wide and 2" high rectangle to place the subform just below the Cost controls as shown in Figure G-7

   If you drag a control beyond the edges of an existing form, the form will automatically enlarge to accept the control. The SubForm Wizard appears.

8. Click **Employee Info Sub** as the existing data for the subform, click **Next**, verify that **Show Employee Info for each record in Courses Info using CourseID** is selected, click **Next**, verify the name **Employee Info Sub**, click **Finish**, then click the **Form View button** 🔲

   The final form/subform is shown in Figure G-8. The first of 27 courses, Access1, is displayed in the main form. The six employees who completed that course are displayed in the subform.

FIGURE G-6: Creating the Employee Info Sub

Field list button

1" mark on horizontal ruler

Form Selector button

Drag from the highlighted Field list to the 1" mark

Properties button

Employee Info Field list

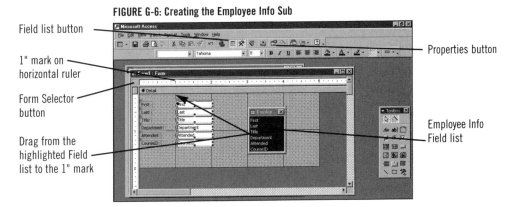

FIGURE G-7: Adding a subform control

Control Wizards button

Subform/Subreport button

Drag a box from the upper-left corner to the lower-right corner of the subform

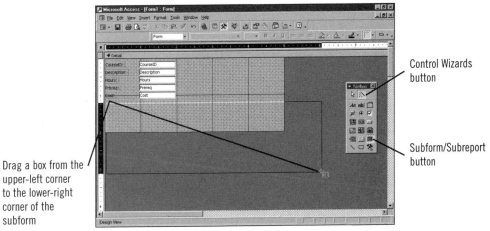

FIGURE G-8: Courses Main Form / Employee Info Subform

Employee Info Sub Subform in Datasheet view

6 employees took this course

27 courses

Subform's horizontal scroll bar

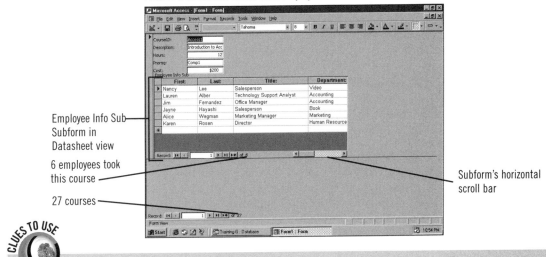

Linking the form and subform

If the form and subform do not appear to be correctly linked, examine the subform's property sheet, paying special attention to the **Link Child Fields** and **Link Master Fields** properties on the Data tab. These properties tell you which field serves as the link between the main form and subform. The field specified for this property should be present in the queries that underlie the main and subforms, and is the same field that creates the one-to-many relationship.

Modifying Subforms

Because the form/subform arrangement packs so much information on one screen, it is important to modify and format the form/subform to present the data clearly. If the subform is displayed in Datasheet view, you can use resize, hide, or move the columns. You can also change the subform's font, grid color, or background color directly in Form view. When viewing the subform control in Design view, you can directly modify the subform's controls just as you can directly modify the main form's controls. Scenario> David likes the form/subform arrangement that displays each course in the main form and each employee who has taken that course in the subform, but he will improve upon the subform's design to display the employee subform information a little more clearly.

Steps

1. Click the **Design View button** ◳ on the Form View toolbar, click the **subform control**, drag the **middle right sizing handle to the 7" mark** on the horizontal ruler, as shown in Figure G-9, then release the mouse button
   Widening the subform control will allow you to display more fields at the same time. Even though the fields of the subform appear to be in a vertical arrangement in the subform control, the "Datasheet" Default View property forces them to display horizontally, like a datasheet. Other options for a form's Default View property are shown in Table G-2.

2. Click the **Form View button** ▦ on the Form Design toolbar to view the widened subform
   The appearance of a horizontal scroll bar on the subform tells you that not all of the fields are visible on the subform's datasheet, but you can resize the columns of the datasheet directly in Form view.

3. Point to the **First and Last field name column separator**, double-click with ↔ to automatically adjust the column to accommodate the widest entry, then double-click each **field name column separator** in the subform
   Your screen should look like Figure G-10. Notice that the horizontal scroll bar disappears when all fields within the subform are visible. Formatting the datasheet makes it more appealing to the user.

4. Click any **field** in the subform, click the **Line/Border color button list arrow** ◢·, click **the Dark Blue box** (first row, second from right), click the **Fill/Back color list arrow** ◭·, then click the **Light Blue box** (last row, fourth from the right)
   You can format the datasheet to best represent the data using line colors, special effects, and fill colors as well as changing the fonts and character formatting.

5. Click the **Save button** 🖫, type **Courses Main Form** in the Form Name text box, click **OK**, then close the form
   You can always sort, filter, and find records directly on a form or subform, but filters are not saved with the form object. By basing form objects on associated queries, however, you can easily modify the form's recordset by modifying the underlying query. MediaLoft's Accounting Department wants to use this form to display only those employees who attended class in January 2000.

6. Click **Queries** on the Objects bar, click **Employee Info**, click the **Design button** ◳ in the database window, click the **Attended field Criteria cell**, then type **1/*/00**, as shown in Figure G-11

7. Click 🖫, close the **Employee Info** query, click **Forms** on the Objects bar, then double-click **Courses Main Form** to open it
   The Employee InfoSub Subform is based on the Employee Info query and does not display any records for the first course, Access1, because no employees attended this course in January of 2000.

8. Press **[Page Down]** three times to move to CourseID Comp1, which is record 4
   The Comp1 course displays 10 records in the subform, indicating that 10 employees took this course in January 2000.

FIGURE G-9: Widening a subform

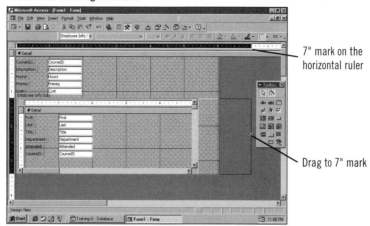

7" mark on the horizontal ruler

Drag to 7" mark

FIGURE G-10: Resizing columns of a subform

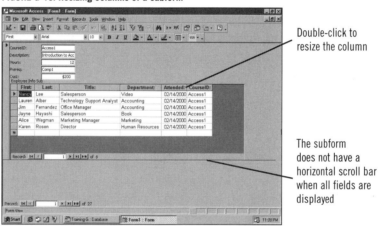

Double-click to resize the column

The subform does not have a horizontal scroll bar when all fields are displayed

FIGURE G-11: Changing the criteria of an underlying query

Employee Info query

Criteria added to include only those employees who attended class in January 2000

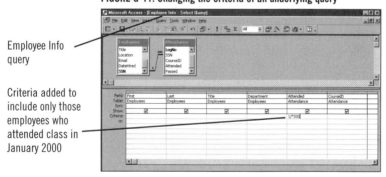

TABLE G-2: Default View property options for forms

default view property	description
Single Form	Displays one record at a time. Gives the user full ability to format the controls placed on the form in Design view and is the most common Default View property entry.
Continuous Form	Displays multiple records at a time, and is often used as the Default View property for subforms. Gives the user the ability to format the controls in Design view.
Datasheet	Displays multiple records at the same time in a datasheet arrangement regardless of how they are formatted in Design view. This is the most common Default View property choice for subforms.

Adding Combo Boxes

By default, fields are added to a form as text boxes, but sometimes other controls such as list boxes, combo boxes, or options buttons would handle the data entry process more easily or quickly for a particular field. Both the **list box** and **combo box** controls provide a list of values from which the user can choose an entry. A combo box also allows the user to make an entry from the keyboard; therefore, it is a "combination" of the list box and text box controls. You can create a combo box by using the Combo Box Wizard to guide your actions, or you can change an existing text box into a combo box control. **Scenario** David changes the Prereq text box (which specifies if a prerequisite course is required in the main form) from a text box into a combo box to allow users to choose from the existing courses offered at MediaLoft.

Steps

1. Click the **Design View button** 🖾 click the **Prereq text box**, then press **[Delete]**
   You can add the Prereq field back to the form as a combo box.

2. Click the **Field List button** 🗐 to toggle it on (if necessary), click the **Toolbox button** 🛠 to toggle it on (if necessary), click the **Control Wizards button** 🖾 to toggle it on (if necessary), click the **Combo Box button** 🖽 on the Toolbox toolbar, click the **Prereq field** in the field list, then drag the **Prereq field** with ⁺🗐 to the space where the Prereq text box was positioned
   The Combo Box Wizard appears. You want the Prereq combo box to display the CourseID and Description information from the Courses table.

3. Click **I want the combo box to look up the values in a table or query** (if necessary), click **Next**, click **Courses**, click **Next**, double-click the **CourseID field**, double-click the **Description field**, click **Next**, double-click ↔ on the right edge of the Description column selector to widen it, click **Next**, click **Next** to accept that the value will be stored in the Prereq field, then click **Finish** to accept the Prereq label
   Your screen will look similar to Figure G-12.

4. Position the **Prereq combo box** between the Hours and Cost fields, click the **Prereq combo box right resizing handle**, drag ↔ to the **3" mark** on the horizontal ruler, click the **Description text box**, then drag the **Description text box right sizing handle** with ↔ to the **3" mark** on the horizontal ruler
   Your screen will look similar to Figure G-13. Your final step will be to change the Cost text box into a combo box as well. MediaLoft has only three internal charges for its classes, $100, $200, and $400, which you want to display in the combo box.

5. Right-click the **Cost text box**, point to **Change To**, then click **Combo Box**
   This action changed the control from a text box to a combo box without the aid of the Combo Box Wizard. Therefore, you need to specify where the combo box will get its values directly in the control's property sheet.

6. Click the **Properties button** 🖾, click the **Data tab** (if necessary), click the **Row Source Type text box**, click the **Row Source Type list arrow**, then click **Value List**
   The combo box will get its values from the list entered in the Row Source property.

7. Click the **Row Source property text box**, type **$100; $200; $400**, click the **Limit to List property list arrow**, click **Yes**, then click 🖾 to close the property sheet
   The entries in the Row Source property list become the values for the combo box's list. By changing the Limit to List property to "Yes," the user cannot enter a new entry from the keyboard.

8. Click the **Save button** 🖾, click the **Form View button** 🖽, click the **Cost combo box list arrow**, then click **$400**
   The updated form with two combo boxes should look like Figure G-14.

FIGURE G-12: Adding the Prereq combo box

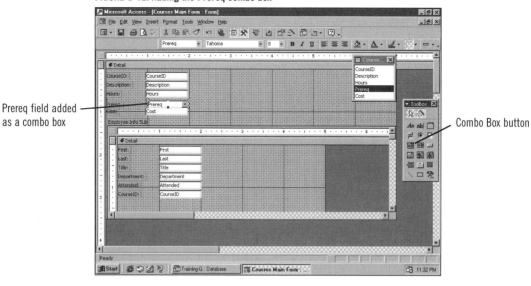

Prereq field added as a combo box

Combo Box button

FIGURE G-13: Moving and resizing controls

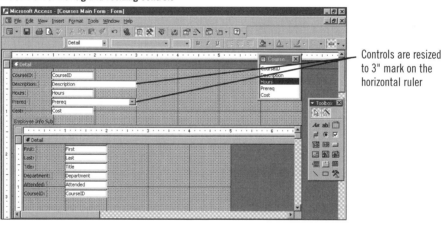

Controls are resized to 3" mark on the horizontal ruler

FIGURE G-14: Adding the Cost combo box

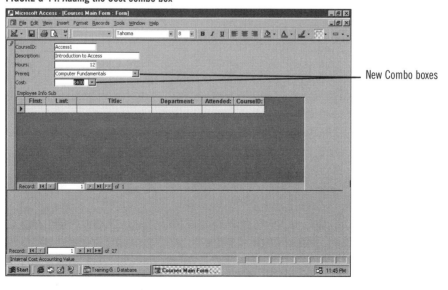

New Combo boxes

Adding Option Groups

An **option group** is a special type of bound control that is often used when a limited number of values are available for a field. The option group control uses **option button** controls (sometimes called radio buttons) to determine the value that is placed in the field. One option button exists for each possible entry. When the user clicks an option button, the numeric value associated with that option button is entered into the field bound to the option group. Option buttons within an option group are mutually exclusive, which means that only one can be chosen at a time. **Scenario** MediaLoft's classes are offered in 6-, 8-, 12-, and 16-hour formats. Because this represents a limited number of options, David uses an option group control for the Hours field to further simplify the Courses Main Form.

Steps 1 2 3 4

1. Click the **Design View button** 🖉, click the **Hours text box**, then press **[Delete]**
   You can add the Hours field back to the form as an option group.

2. Click the **Option Group button** 🖾 on the Toolbox, click the **Hours field** in the field list, then, using ⁺🖾, drag the **Hours field** to the upper-right corner of the form at about the 5" mark on the horizontal ruler
   The Option Group Wizard appears to help guide the process of developing an option group. The first question asks about label names for the option buttons.

3. Type **6 hrs**, press **[Tab]**, type **8 hrs**, press **[Tab]**, type **12 hrs**, press **[Tab]**, type **16 hrs**, click **Next**, choose **No, I don't want a default**, then click **Next**
   The next question prompts you for the actual values associated with each option button.

4. Type **6**, press **[Tab]**, type **8**, press **[Tab]**, type **12**, press **[Tab]**, type **16**, click **Next**, click **Next** to accept **Hours** as the field that the value is stored in, click **Next** to accept **Option button controls** in an **Etched style**, type **Classroom Hours** as the caption, then click **Finish**
   An option group can contain option buttons, check boxes, or toggle button controls. The most common choice, however, are option buttons in an etched style. The **Control Source property** of the option group identifies the field it will update. The **Option Value property** of each option button identifies what value will be placed in the field when that option button is clicked. The new option group and option button controls are shown in Figure G-15.

5. Click the **Form View button** 🖽 to view the form with the new control, then click the **16 hrs option button**
   Your screen should look like Figure G-16. You changed the Access1 course from 12 to 16 hrs. You just found out that MediaLoft is offering 24-hour classes, so you have to add another button to the group.

QuickTip

The option group control will darken when you are adding an option button to it.

6. Click 🖉, click the **Option Button button** ⊙ on the Toolbox toolbar, then click below the **16 hrs option button** in the new option group
   Your screen should look like Figure G-17. This option button in the group will represent 24-hour classes. Change the new option button's label and option value.

Trouble?

The option number may vary.

7. Click the **Option18 label** once to select it, double-click the **Option18 text**, then type **24 hrs**

8. Double-click the new **option button** to open the property sheet, click the **Data tab** (if necessary), double-click **5** in the **Option Value property text box** to select it, type **24**, click the **Properties button** 🖾 to close the property sheet, move the **24 hrs option button control** as necessary to align it with the other option buttons, click the **Save button** 🖫, then click 🖽 to observe the new option button

FIGURE G-15: Adding an Option Group with option buttons

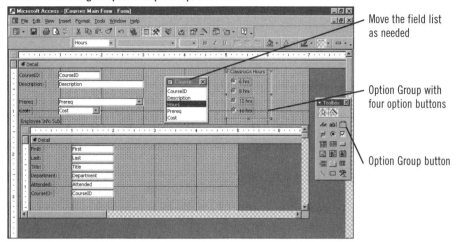

Move the field list
as needed

Option Group with
four option buttons

Option Group button

FIGURE G-16: Using an Option Group

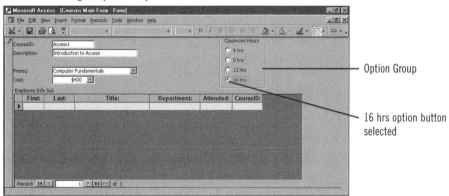

Option Group

16 hrs option button
selected

FIGURE G-17: Adding another option button

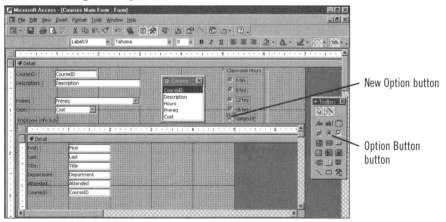

New Option button

Option Button
button

Protecting data

You may not want all the data that appears on a form to be able to be changed by all users who view that form. You can design forms to limit access to certain fields by changing the enabled and locked properties of a control. The Enabled property specifies whether a control can have the focus in Form view. The Locked property specifies whether you can edit data in a control in Form view.

Adding Command Buttons

A **command button** is a powerful unbound control used to initiate a common action such as printing the current record, opening another form, or closing the current form. In Form view, the user clicks a command button to run the specified action. Command buttons are often added to the **form header** or **form footer** sections. **Sections** determine where controls appear and print. See Table G-3 for more information on form sections. Scenario▶ David adds a command button to the Courses Main Form form header section to help the users print the current record.

1. Click the **Design View button** 🔲, click **View** on the menu bar, wait a second or two for the menu to expand (if necessary), then click **Form Header/Footer**
   The form header opens.

2. Click the **Command Button button** 🔲 on the Toolbox toolbar, then click in the **Form Header at the 5" mark** on the horizontal ruler
   The Command Button Wizard opens, listing over 30 of the most popular actions for the command button, organized within six categories.

QuickTip

Resize the Form Header section to make more room for the button, if necessary.

3. Click **Record Operations** in the Categories list, click **Print Record** in the Actions list, click **Next**, click **Next** to accept the choice to display a **Picture of a Printer** on the button, type **Print Current Record** as the button name, then click **Finish**
   Your screen should look like Figure G-18. By default, the Print button 🖶 on the Standard toolbar prints the entire recordset displayed by the form creating a very long printout. Therefore, adding a command button to print only the current record is very useful.

QuickTip

To help identify your printouts, you can add your name as a label to the Detail section of the Courses Main Form.

4. Click the **Form View button** 🔲 to view the new command button, press **[Page Down]** three times to navigate to the fourth record, click the new **Print Record command button**, then save and close the form
   The fourth record for the Computer Fundamentals class contains ten records in the subform that still displays only the January attendees as defined by the Employee Info query. You can adjust the left and right margins so that the printout fits neatly on one page.

5. Click **File** on the menu bar, click **Page Setup**, click the **Margins tab** (if necessary), press **[Tab]** three times to select **1** in the Left text box, type **0.5**, press **[Tab]** once to select **1** in the Right text box, type **0.5**, then click **OK**
   The **Display When** property of the Form Header controls when the controls in that section display and print.

6. Click 🔲, double-click the **Form Header section** to open its property sheet, click the **Format tab** (if necessary), click the **Display When property text box**, click the **Display When list arrow**, click **Screen Only**, then click the **Properties button** 🔲 to close the property sheet
   You don't want the command button on the printouts.

Trouble?

If your printout is still too wide for one sheet of paper, pull the right edge of the form to the left in Form Design view to narrow it.

7. Click the **Save button** 🔲, click 🔲, click the **Next Record button** ▶ several times on the Courses Main Form to navigate to the fourth record (Comp1), then click the **Print Record command button** to print the Comp1 record using the new command button
   Your final Courses Main Form should look like Figure G-19, and your printout should fit on one page, without displaying the form header.

8. Close the **Courses Main Form**

FIGURE G-18: Adding a command button

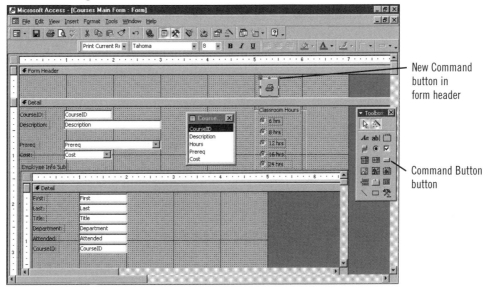

New Command button in form header

Command Button button

FIGURE G-19: The final Courses Main Form

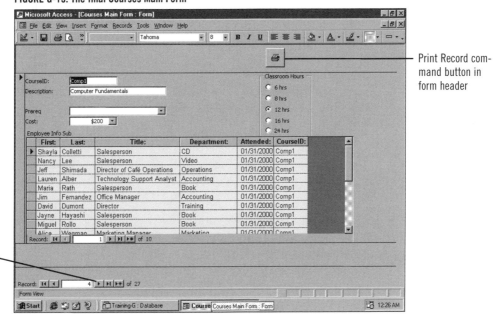

Print Record command button in form header

Next Record navigation button for Courses Main Form

TABLE G-3: Form Sections

section	description
Detail	Appears once for every individual record
Form Header	Appears at the top of the form and often contains command buttons or a label with the form's title
Form Footer	Appears at the bottom of the form and often contains command buttons or a label with instructions on how to use the form
Page Header	Appears at the top of a printed form with information such as page numbers or dates. The Page Header and Page Footer sections can be added to the form by clicking View on the menu bar, then clicking Page Header/Footer
Page Footer	Appears at the bottom of a printed form with information such as page numbers or dates

Adding Records with a Form/Subform

If you want to use the form/subform objects for data entry in addition to finding and viewing data, you must carefully plan the forms to make sure that all of the necessary fields are present that are required to add a record. For example, you cannot add a new employee to a main form unless the SSN field is present in the main form because the SSN is the key field. **Scenario** David built a form/subform for data entry purposes that displays all fields for each employee in the main form. The subform displays fields that reflect which classes that employee has attended. He uses this form/subform to add new employees as well as record new classes that employees have attended.

Steps

1. Double-click the **Employee Details Main Form** in the database window, maximize the form, then press **[Page Down]** once to view the second record for Nancy Lee
   Your screen should look like Figure G-20. Since the SSN field is listed in the main form, this form could be used to add new employees. You can also use the subform to add another class to the list that Nancy has attended.

2. Click the **New Record button** ▶✱ on the subform navigation buttons, press **[Tab]** twice to move through the LogNo and SSN fields, then type **Project1** in the CourseID field
   The LogNo field is an AutoNumber data type, so it will automatically increase to the next available number as determined by the records in the Attendance table. The SSN field is automatically filled in with Nancy Lee's SSN because it serves as the linking field between the main and subforms.

3. Press **[Enter]** to move the focus to the Description field, press **[Enter]**, type **6/1/00** in the Attended field, press **[Enter]**, press **[Spacebar]** to enter a check in the Passed field, then press **[Enter]** to complete the record
   The CourseID entry (when added to the CourseID field of the Attendance table) automatically pulls the associated Description field entry from the Courses table, as shown in Figure G-21. Now enter a new employee into the main form.

   QuickTip

   A pencil icon in the margin of the form indicates the record is being edited.

4. Click ▶✱ on the main form navigation buttons, click in the **First Name text box**, type **Kelsey**, press **[Tab]**, type **Wambold**, press **[Tab]**, type **Video**, press **[Tab]**, type **Salesperson**, press **[Tab]**, type **San Francisco**, press **[Tab]**, type the address **kwambold@medialoft.com**, press **[Tab]**, type **9/1/00**, press **[Tab]**, type **999881111**, then press **[Tab]**
   Kelsey has been added as a new employee in the database. When she starts taking courses, this form will be useful to track her attendance.

5. Close the **Employee Details Main Form**, close the **Training-G** database, then exit **Access**

FIGURE G-20: The Employee Details Main Form and Attendance Update Subform

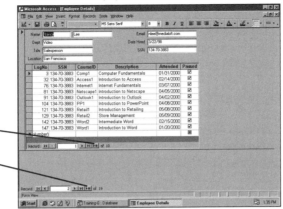

Subform New
Record button

Main form New
Record button

FIGURE G-21: Adding a record to the subform

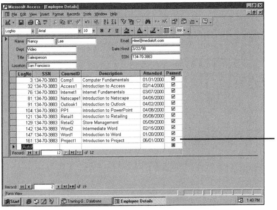

New record added
to subform

FIGURE G-22: The Employee Details Main Form as a Web page

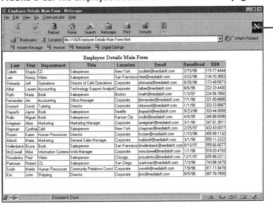

Netscape browser
is displaying this
Web page

CLUES TO USE

Saving a form as a Web page

You can save any form as a Web page in an **HTML** (Hypertext Markup Language, the language used to develop World Wide Web pages) file format. However, unless you create a **Data Access Page**, a database object used to create Web pages that interact with a live Access database, you will not be able to use the Web page to enter or edit data. Use the Export option on the File menu to save a form as an HTML document. You have the option of applying an HTML template that contains formatting instructions. Figure G-22 shows how the fields from the Employee main form would appear when they are exported from Access into an HTML file and are opened in browser software such as Microsoft Internet Explorer or Netscape Navigator.

Practice

► Concepts Review

Identify each element of the form's Design View shown in Figure G-23.

FIGURE G-23

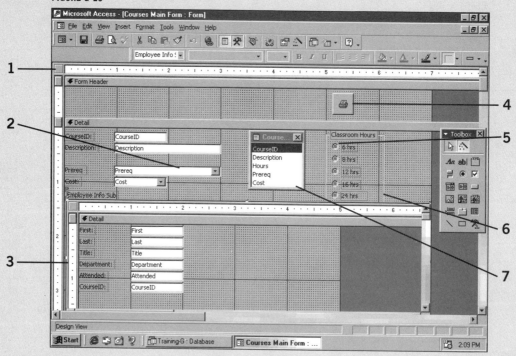

Match each term with the statement that describes its function.

8. Option group
9. Controls
10. Command button
11. Subform
12. Combo box

a. A bound control that is really both a list box and a text box
b. A control that shows records that are related to one record shown in the main form
c. An unbound control that, when clicked, executes an action
d. Elements you add to a form such as labels, text boxes, and list boxes
e. A bound control that displays a few mutually exclusive entries for a field

Select the best answer from the list of choices.

13. **Which control would work best to display two choices for a field?**
    a. Command button
    b. Label
    c. Option group
    d. Text box

14. **Which control would you use to print a form?**
    a. Command button
    b. List box
    c. Text box
    d. Option group

15. **Which control would you use to display a drop-down list of 50 states?**
    a. Combo box
    b. Field label
    c. List box
    d. Check box

16. **To view linked records within a form use a:**
    a. Link control.
    b. List box.
    c. Design template.
    d. Subform.

► Skills Review

1. **Understand the form/subform relationship.**
   a. Start Access and open the Membership-G database.
   b. Click the Relationships button on the Database toolbar.
   c. Click File on the menu bar, wait a second or two for the expanded menu to appear, then click Print Relationships.
   d. The Relationships for Membership-G will appear as a previewed report. Click the Print button on the Print Preview toolbar to print the report, close the preview window without saving the report, and then close the Relationships window. If you need to include your name on the printout, go to Design view and add your name as a label on the report.
   e. Based on the one-to-many relationships defined in the Membership-G database, sketch two form/subform combinations that you might want to create.

2. **Create subforms using the Wizard.**
   a. Click Forms on the Objects bar in the Membership-G database window.
   b. Double-click Create form by using wizard.
   c. Select all of the fields from both the Activities and the Names tables.
   d. View the data by Names.
   e. Accept a datasheet layout for the subform.
   f. Accept a standard style.
   g. Accept the default titles for the forms.
   h. Find the record for Lois Goode (record number 3) and enter your own first and last names in the appropriate text boxes.

i. Resize the columns of the datasheet in the subform so that all of the data is clearly visible.

j. Click File on the menu bar, then click Print. Click the Selected records option button in the Print dialog box to print only the data for your name.

k. Close the Names form.

3. Create subforms using queries.

a. Open the "Zips in IA or MO" query in Design view, and add the criteria to find only those records from IA or MO in the State field.

b. Using either the Form Wizard or Form Design view, build a form based on the "Zips in IA or MO" query using all three fields in the query.

c. Open the Zips in IA or MO form in Design view, and add a subform control about 5" wide by about 3" tall below the three text boxes.

d. Use the Subform Wizard to specify that the subform will use an existing query, then select all of the fields in the Dues query to be part of the subform.

e. Allow the wizard to link the form and subform so that they "Show Dues for each record in Zips in IA or MO using Zip".

f. Accept Dues subform as the subform's name.

g. Maximize the form, expand the size of the subform, move the subform as necessary, and resize the datasheet column widths so that all of the information in the subform is clearly visible. You will know you are done when the horizontal scroll bar does not display in Form view and text from the subform doesn't overlap the main form.

h. Format the datasheet so the First field entry always appears as red text and the Zip field entry always appears as blue text.

i. Find the record for Zip 64105 (the sixth record), enter your last name in the Last field of the first record, and print only that record.

j. Save and close the Zips in IA or MO form.

4. Modify subforms.

a. Click the Queries tab and open the Zips in IA or MO query in Design view.

b. Delete the criteria that specifies that only the records with State values of IA or MO appear in the recordset.

c. Save the modified query as "All Zips".

d. Close the all Zips query.

e. Click the Forms tab and open the Zips in IA or MO form in Design view.

f. Open the property sheet for the form, and change the Record Source property from "Zips in IA or MO" to "All Zips".

g. Save the form and navigate to record number 13, which displays Zip 64145 for Shawnee, Kansas.

h. Change the city to the name of your hometown, then print this record.

i. Close the form, then right-click it and choose Rename.

j. Save the updated form with the name "Zips".

5. Add combo boxes.

a. Open the Names form in Design view and delete the Zip text box.

b. Add the Zip field back to the same location as a combo box, using the Combo Box Wizard.

c. The Combo Box Wizard should look up values from a table or query.

d. Choose the Zips table and the Zip field within the Combo Box Wizard.

e. Store the value in the Zip field, label the Combo Box Zip.

f. Reposition the new Zip label and combo box as necessary, save the form, and display it in Form view.

g. Navigate to the second record, change the address to your own, and change the Zip to 50266 using the new combo box. Print the second record.

6. **Add option groups.**
   a. Open the Names form in Design view, then delete the Dues text box.
   b. Add the Dues field back to the form below the CharterMember check box control using an Option Group control with the Option Group Wizard.
   c. Enter "$25" and "$50" as the label names, and accept $25 as the default choice.
   d. Change the values to "25" and "50" to correspond with the labels.
   e. Store the value in the Dues field, choose option buttons with an etched style, and enter the caption "Annual Dues".
   f. Save the form, display it in Form view, find the record for Jerry Martin (you can use the Find command from the Edit menu), change the first name to your own, and change the Annual Dues to "$50".
   g. Print the updated Martin record.

7. **Add command buttons.**
   a. Open the Names form in Design view.
   b. Open the Form Header to display about 0.5" of space, then add a command button to the upper-right corner using the Command Button Wizard.
   c. Choose the Print Record action from the Record Operations category.
   d. Display the text "Print Current Record" on the button, then name the button "Print".
   e. Save the form and display it in Form view.
   f. Navigate to the record with your own name, change the birth date to your own, and print the record using the new Print Current Record command button.

8. **Add records with a subform.**
   a. Navigate to the first record for Mark Daniels, then click in the subform.
   b. Add two records with the following information:

ActivityDate:	Hours:
3/1/00	4
3/2/00	8

   c. Print the updated record using the Print Current Record command button.
   d. Why is it unnecessary to enter the MemberNo data in the subform? Write a brief answer on your printout.
   e. Use the Export option from the File menu to save the Names form as an HTML document. Do not use an HTML template.
   f. Open the HTML document you created from the Names form in either Netscape or Internet Explorer, whichever browser is available on your system, then print the document.
   g. Close the browser window, return to the Access window, close the Names form, close the Membership-G database, and exit Access.

▶ Visual Workshop

Start Access, then open the Training-G database. Create a new form, as shown in Figure G-24, using the Form Wizard. The First, Last, and Department fields are pulled from the Employees table, the Description field comes from the Courses table, and the Attended and Passed fields come from the Attendance table. Name the form "Employee Basics" and the subform "Test Results." The Department combo box contains the following entries: Accounting, Book, Café, CD, Human Resources, Marketing, Operations, Shipping, Training, and Video. The command buttons in the Form Header print the current record and close the form.

FIGURE G-24

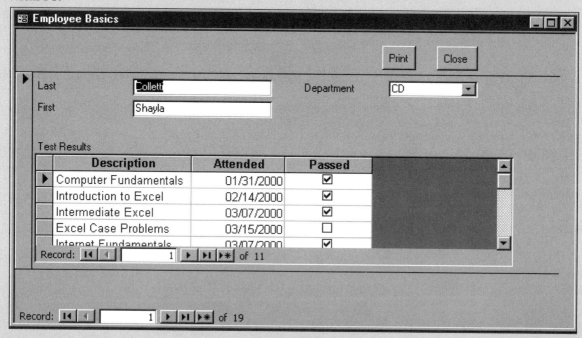

Building

Complex Reports

Objectives

- ▶ Use the Database Wizard
- ▶ Import data
- ▶ Create a report from a parameter query
- ▶ Enhance reports
- ▶ Add lines and rectangles
- ▶ Use the Format Painter and AutoFormats
- ▶ Insert an image
- ▶ Secure the database

Although you can print data in forms and datasheets, **reports** give you more control over how data is printed and greater flexibility in presenting summary information such as subtotals on groups of records. Because a report definition (the report object itself) can be saved, it can be created once and then used many times. Printed reports always reflect the most up-to-date data in a consistent format each time they are printed. As with form designs, report designs allow you to add bound controls such as text boxes and calculated controls, and unbound controls such as lines, graphics, or labels. Scenario▶ Other departments have noted the initial success of David's Training database, and now he is being asked to report the information in new ways. David uses the database to report information electronically, by using the Access import and export features. David also uses database management features such as database compacting to make the database easier to manage. Advanced reporting and formatting features such as parameter prompts, group footer calculations, conditional formatting, images, colors, and lines help David enhance his reports.

Access 2000

Using the Database Wizard

The **Database Wizard** is a powerful Access tool that creates a sample database file for a general purpose such as inventory control, event tracking, or expenses. It also creates objects that you can use or modify. **Scenario** The Accounting Department tracks a training budget to determine how various departments are using MediaLoft's in-house classes. Although David could create a quarterly paper report with this information, he decides to report this information electronically by creating a separate Access database for the Accounting Department into which he can send historical information on course attendance and costs from the Training database.

QuickTip
If Access is started, click the **New button** on the Database toolbar to open the New dialog box.

1. Start Access, click the **Access database wizards, pages, and projects option button** in the Microsoft Access dialog box, click **OK**, then click the **Databases tab**
The Databases tab of the New Dialog box is shown in Figure H-1.

2. Click **Expenses** in the New dialog box, then click **OK**
When you create a new database, you must first name the database file regardless of whether it is created by a wizard or from scratch.

Trouble?
The files for this unit will not fit on one floppy disk. Be sure to save this file to Project Disk 1, which also contains the files DeptCodes.xls and Training.mdb.

3. Click the **Save In: list arrow**, click the **3½ Floppy (A:)** option to save the file on your Project Disk, double-click **expenses1** in the File name text box, type **Accounting**, click **Create**, then click **Next**
The dialog box shown in Figure H-2 opens. The sample database will include four tables and their associated fields.

Trouble?
If the Office Assistant opens, right-click it, then click Hide.

4. Click **Expense report information** in the Tables list, then click **Next**

5. Click **Standard**, click **Next**, click **Corporate**, click **Next**, type **Accounting** as the database title, click **Next**, make sure the **Yes, start the database check box** is checked, then click **Finish**
It takes several seconds for Access to build all of the objects for the Accounting database and then open the Main Switchboard form, as shown in Figure H-3. When you use the Database Wizard, Access creates a **switchboard**, a special Access form that displays command buttons that help make the database easier to use.

Trouble?
The Accounting database window is minimized in the Access Window.

6. Click the **Main Switchboard Close button**, maximize the **Accounting database window**, review the available forms, click **Reports** on the Objects bar, then click the **Tables** on the Objects bar
These objects can be used, modified, or deleted like any user-created object.

7. Click the **Employees table**, click the **Design button**, click the **Insert Rows button** on the Table Design toolbar, type **Department**, press **[Tab]**, click the **Data Type list arrow**, then click **Lookup Wizard**
The Lookup Wizard opens. Use the Lookup Wizard to provide department choices.

8. Click **I will type in the values that I want option button**, click **Next**, press **[Tab]**, then type **Accounting**, press **[Tab]**, type **Book**, press **[Tab]**, type **Cafe**, press **[Tab]**, type **CD**, press **[Tab]**, type **Human Resources**, press **[Tab]**, type **Information Systems**, press **[Tab]**, type **Marketing**, press **[Tab]**, type **Operations**, press **[Tab]**, type **Shipping**, press **[Tab]**, then type **Video**

9. Click **Next**, click **Finish** to accept the Department label, click the **Datasheet View button**, click **Yes** to save the table, then click the **Department field list arrow**
The Lookup Wizard provides the values in the Department list, but you could also type a new value into the Department field if desired.

FIGURE H-1: Database wizards

New dialog box

Database wizards are available on the Databases tab

View buttons

Picture relates to selected Database wizard

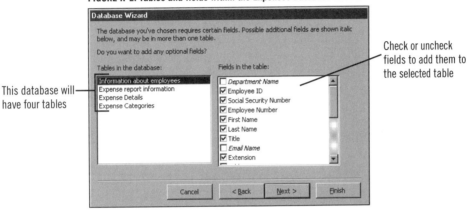

FIGURE H-2: Tables and fields within the Expenses Database Wizard

Check or uncheck fields to add them to the selected table

This database will have four tables

FIGURE H-3: Main Switchboard form for the Accounting database

Main Switchboard Close button

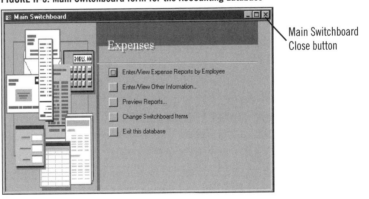

Using the Lookup Wizard

The **Lookup Wizard** is a powerful Access feature that allows a field to "look up" values from a list you type (called a **value list**) or from another table or query. It is not a data type such as Text, Number, or Yes/No. However, the Lookup Wizard helps you determine the final data type for the field based on the values you enter in the list. A lookup field often improves data entry speed, accuracy, and comprehension. A field that has lookup properties will automatically appear as a combo box control when added to a form or viewed on a datasheet. Lookup properties for a specific field can be examined on the Lookup Tab of the field's properties in Table Design view.

Importing Data

Importing is a process to quickly convert data from an external source, such as Excel or another database program, into an Access database. The Access import process copies the data from the original source and pastes the data in the Access database. Therefore, if you update data in either the original source or in the imported copy in Access, the other copy is not updated. See Table H-1 for more information on the types of data that Access can import. **Scenario** Now that the Accounting database has been created, David imports the historical cost and attendance information into it. The integrity of the information will remain intact because the Accounting Department will not be updating or changing the data, but only creating reports.

Steps

Trouble?

You can't import from the Training database if it is opened in another Access window.

1. Click the **Employees table Close button**, click **File** on the menu bar, point to **Get External Data**, click **Import**, click the **Look in list arrow**, locate your **Project Disk**, click **Training**, then click **Import**
   The Import Objects dialog box opens, as shown in Figure H-4. Any object in the Training-H database can be imported into the Accounting database.

2. Click **1QTR-2000**, click **Courses**, click the **Queries tab**, click **Accounting Query**, click the **Reports tab**, click **Accounting Report**, then click **OK**
   The four selected objects are imported into the Accounting database.

3. Click **Tables** on the Objects bar, then click the **Details button** ▦ in the database window
   The Created and Modified dates of both the 1QTR-2000 and the Courses tables should be today's date. If you update these tables in the future, the Modified date will change, but not the Created date.

QuickTip

By default, objects in the database window are sorted by name.

4. Click the **Modified column heading** to sort the Table objects in ascending order on the date they were modified, then click the **Name column heading**

5. Click **Queries** on the Objects bar to make sure that the Accounting Query has been imported, click **Reports** (Your screen should look like Figure H-5.), point to the **Name column heading divider** to display the ↔ pointer, then double-click ↔
   The column expands to accommodate the widest entry in the Name column. This database will also track department codes that are stored in an Excel spreadsheet.

6. Click **File** on the menu bar, point to **Get External Data**, click **Import**, click the **Look in: list arrow**, locate your **Project Disk**, click the **Files of type list arrow**, click **Microsoft Excel**, click **Deptcodes**, then click **Import**
   The Import Spreadsheet Wizard guides you through the rest of the import process.

7. Click **Next**, make sure the **First Row Contains Column Headings** check box is checked, click **Next**, make sure the **In a New Table option button** is selected, click **Next**, click **Next** to accept the default field information, click the **Choose my own primary key option button**, make sure **Code** is displayed in the primary key list box, click **Next**, type **Codes** in the Import to Table text box, click **Finish**, then click **OK**
   The Deptcodes spreadsheet is now a table in the Accounting database.

8. Double-click **Codes** to open it, then review the codes as a datasheet
   The Accounting Department has more work to do before they can use their new database. They must determine if they are going to use the other tables created by the Database Wizard; if they are going to add, modify, or delete any of the existing fields; and most importantly, how they are going to link the tables in one-to-many relationships.

9. Close the codes datasheet, then close the Accounting database

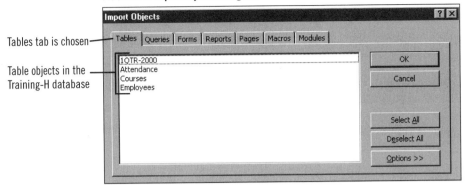

FIGURE H-4: Import Objects dialog box

Tables tab is chosen

Table objects in the Training-H database

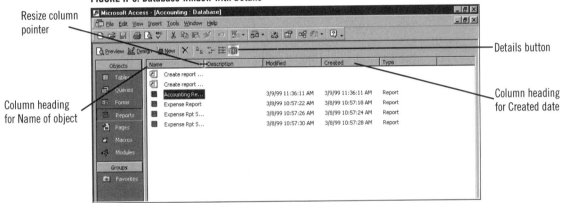

FIGURE H-5: Database window with Details

Resize column pointer

Details button

Column heading for Name of object

Column heading for Created date

TABLE H-1: Data sources Microsoft Access can import

data source	version or format supported
Microsoft Access database	2.0, 7.0/95, 8.0/97, 9.0/2000 (Note: Access version 7.0 is also known as Access version 95. Access version 8.0 is also known as Access 97, and so forth.)
Microsoft Access project	9.0/2000
dBASE	III, III+, IV, and 5
Paradox, Paradox for Windows	3.x, 4.x, and 5.0
Microsoft Excel	3.0, 4.0, 5.0, 7.0/95, 8.0/97, and 9.0/2000
Lotus 1-2-3	.wks, .wk1, .wk3, .wk4
Microsoft Exchange	All versions
Delimited text files	All character sets
Fixed-width text files	All character sets
HTML	1.0 (if a list) 2.0, 3.x (if a table or list)
SQL tables, Microsoft Visual Foxpro, and other data sources that support ODBC protocol	ODBC (Open Database Connectivity) is a protocol for accessing data in SQL (Structured Query Language) database servers.

Access 2000

Creating a Report from a Parameter Query

If you create a report or form by basing it on a **parameter query**, it will display a dialog box prompting you for criteria to customize the **recordset** of the object each time you use it. For example, you might base a report on a parameter query that prompts for date, department, or state criteria so that only those records that are true for that are used for the report. **Scenario** David has been asked by many departments to provide a paper report of which employees have attended which classes. Rather than create a query and corresponding report object for each department, he builds one parameter query that prompts for the Department field criteria and one report object based on this parameter query.

Steps

1. Open the **Training-H** database from your Project Disk, click **Queries** 📇 on the Objects bar, click **Department Query**, then click the **Design button** 📝
   Department Query opens in Design view. It uses fields from all three of the original tables: Courses, Attendance, and Employees.

2. Click the **Department field Criteria cell**, type **[Enter department name:]**, press **[Enter]**, place the pointer on the **right edge of the Department field column selector**, then drag the ↔ pointer to the right to display the entry
   You can see the entire parameter criteria entry, as shown in Figure H-6. Query criteria, including parameter criteria, are not case sensitive.

3. Click the **Datasheet view button** 📇, type **cd** in the Enter department name text box in the Enter Parameter Value dialog box, then click **OK**
   The resulting datasheet shows that the CD department employees attended 21 classes. The parameter criteria entry works.

4. Click the **Save button** 💾, then close the Department Query datasheet
   Use the Report Wizard to quickly create a report based on the Department Query.

5. Click **Reports** 📇 on the Objects bar, double-click **Create report by using wizard**, click the **Tables/Queries list arrow**, click **Query: Department Query**, click the **Select All Fields button** ⏩, click **Next**, then click **by Attendance**
   View choices are actually ways to group the records with multiple fields in the group header.

6. Click **Next**, click **Department**, click the **Select Single Field button** ▶, click **Next**, click the **first sort order list arrow**, click **Last**, click the **second sort order list arrow**, click **First**, click the **third sort order list arrow**, then click **Attended**
   Your Report Wizard sorting and summary dialog box should look like Figure H-7. The rest of the wizard options determine group calculations (summary options), layout, and style information. The Summary Options dialog box allows you to calculate the subtotal, average, or minimum or maximum value for several fields.

7. Click the **Summary Options button**, click the **Hours Sum check box**, click **OK**, click **Next**, click the **Stepped option button**, click the **Portrait option button**, click **Next**, click **Corporate** for the style, click **Next**, type **Department Report** in the title text box, then click **Finish**
   Because the report is based on the Department Query (a parameter query), the entry in the dialog box will determine which department's records will appear on the report.

8. Type **video**, then click **OK**
   The final report should look similar to Figure H-8.

9. Click the **Print button** 🖨 on the Print Preview toolbar

FIGURE H-6: Creating a parameter query

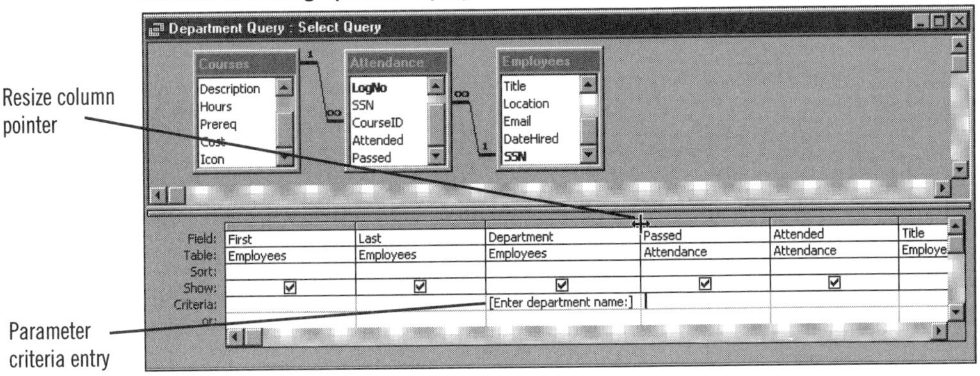

Resize column pointer

Parameter criteria entry

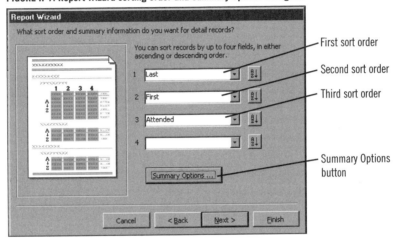

FIGURE H-7: Report Wizard sorting order and Summary Options dialog box

First sort order
Second sort order
Third sort order
Summary Options button

FIGURE H-8: Final Department Report

Records are grouped by Department

Only the Video department is displayed

Records are sorted by Last name

Because there are not two employees with the same last and first names, the records are further sorted by the date in the Attended field

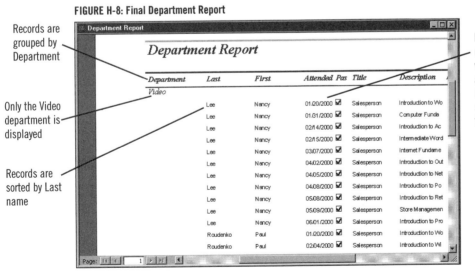

Access 2000

Enhancing Reports

Conditional formatting allows you to change the appearance of a control on a form or report based on criteria you specify. **Grouping controls** is a handy feature that allows you to identify several controls in a group in order to quickly and easily apply the same formatting properties to them. Other report embellishments such as hiding duplicate values and group footer calculations improve the clarity of the report. ▷Scenario David wants to improve the appearance and clarity of the Department Report by using techniques such as hiding duplicate values, grouping controls, and applying conditional formatting.

QuickTip

Clicking a control within a *selected group* selects just that single control.

1. Click the **Design View button** ⬛, click the **Last text box** in the Detail section, press and hold **[Shift]**, click the **First text box** in the Detail section, click the **Title text box**, release **[Shift]**, click **Format** on the menu bar, then click **Group**

   The three text boxes have been grouped and can now be formatted or modified simultaneously. Group selection handles surround the group, so when you click on *any* control in a group, you select *every* control in the group.

QuickTip

The title bar of the Property sheet indicates that multiple controls have been selected.

2. Click the **Properties button** 🖼 on the Report Design toolbar, click the **Format tab** on the Multiple selection property sheet, click the **Hide Duplicates text box**, click the **Hide Duplicates list arrow**, click **Yes**, then click 🖼 to close the property sheet

   With the Hide Duplicates property set to Yes, the First, Last, and Title values will print only once per employee. Because only one department shows on this report, there is no need for the Department Footer because the Report Footer presents the same calculation. To subtotal the number of hours of class attendance for each person, you need a Last Footer section.

3. Click the **Sorting and Grouping button** 🔳, select the **Department field**, click the **Group Footer list arrow**, click **No**, click **Yes** to delete the group section, click the **Last field**, click the **Group Footer list arrow**, click **Yes** to display a footer every time the Last field changes, then click 🔳 to close the Sorting and Grouping dialog box

   The Department Footer section was removed and the Last Footer section was added.

Trouble?

The =Sum([Hours]) text box is not wide enough to display the entire expression, but you can still copy and paste it.

4. Click the **=Sum([Hours]) text box** in the Report Footer, click the **Copy button** 🖹 on the Report Design toolbar, click the **Last Footer section**, then click the **Paste button** 🖺

   Your screen should look like Figure H-9. This calculated control in the Last group footer summarizes the number of hours for each person.

5. Click the **=Sum([Hours]) text box** in the Last Footer section, then use the ✋ pointer to drag the **=Sum([Hours]) text box** to the right edge of the report, directly under the Hours text box in the Detail section

   Both calculated controls will be selected for conditional formatting.

QuickTip

The Font/Fore Color button displays the last color selected.

6. Click the **=Sum([Hours]) text box** in the Last Footer section, press and hold **[Shift]**, click the **=Sum([Hours]) text box** in the Report Footer section, release **[Shift]**, click **Format** on the menu bar, click **Conditional Formatting**, click the **between list arrow** in the Conditional Formatting dialog box, click **greater than**, click the text box, type **100**, click the **Bold button** 🅱, click the **Font/Fore Color list arrow** 🔻, then click the **Red box** on the palette

   Your screen should look like Figure H-10. The conditional formatting will display the subtotaled hours in bold and red if the calculation exceeds 100.

QuickTip

Maximize the report window and scroll to view the entire report.

7. Click **OK** in the Conditional Formatting dialog box, click the **Save button** 🖫, click the **Print Preview button** 🔍, type **book** in the Enter Parameter Value dialog box, then click **OK**

   The Department Report for the Book department should look like Figure H-11.

8. Close the Print Preview window, save the report, then close it

FIGURE H-9: Department Report in Design view

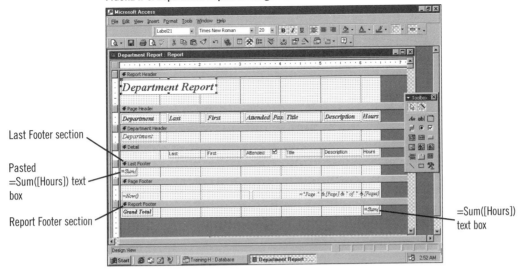

Last Footer section

Pasted
=Sum([Hours]) text
box

Report Footer section

=Sum([Hours])
text box

FIGURE H-10: Conditional Formatting dialog box

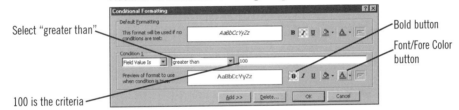

Select "greater than"

100 is the criteria

Bold button

Font/Fore Color
button

FIGURE H-11: Final Department Report for the Book department

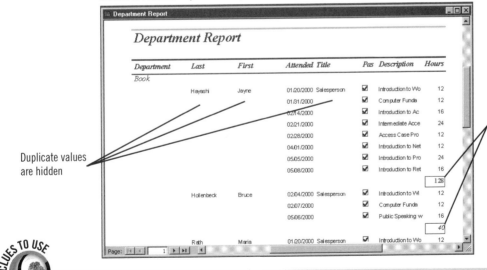

Duplicate values
are hidden

Hours are subtotaled
for each person, and
Conditional Formatting
is applied for values
greater than 100

Applying Conditional Formatting

Conditional Formatting is an excellent tool to highlight important data in a report. For example, you could change the color, background, or style of a text box control, such as a Sales field, if its value exceeds $1,000. Later, if the value of the Sales field becomes less than $1,000, Access would reapply the default formatting for the control.

Adding Lines and Rectangles

Unbound controls such as labels, lines, and rectangles can enhance the clarity of the report. The Report Wizard often creates line controls at the bottom of the Report Header, Page Header, or Group Header sections that visually separate the parts of the report. Lines and boxes can be formatted in many ways. **Scenario** The Personnel Department has asked David to create a report that lists all of the courses and subtotals the courses by hours and costs. David uses line and rectangle controls to enhance the appearance of this report.

Steps

1. Double-click **Create report by using wizard**, click the **Tables/Queries list arrow**, click **Query: Course Summary Query**, click the **Select All Fields button** ⏩, click **Next**, click **by Attendance**, click **Next**, double-click **Department** to add it as a grouping field, then click **Next**

   After determining the grouping field(s), the wizard prompts for the sort fields.

2. Click the **first sort field list arrow**, click **Attended** to sort the detail records by the date the classes were attended, then click the **Summary Options button**

3. Click the **Hours Sum check box**, click the **Cost Sum check box**, click **OK**, click **Next**, click the **Outline 2 Layout option button**, click the **Landscape Orientation option button**, click **Next**, click the **Formal** Style, click **Next**, type **Course Summary Report** as the report title, click **Finish**, then click the **Zoom Out pointer** 🔍 on the report

   Figure H-12 shows several line and rectangle controls. These controls are sometimes very difficult to locate in Design view because they are placed against the edge of the section or the border of other controls. The easiest place to click the line control in the Detail section is between the Passed check box and Description text box controls.

4. Click the **Design View button** 📐, click the **line control** in the Detail section, then press **[Delete]**

   To find the rectangle control in the Department Header section, expand the size of that section.

5. Point to the **top edge of the Detail section** so that the pointer changes to ✛, drag down 0.5", click the **bottom edge of the rectangle control**, click the **Line/Border Color button list arrow** 🖊️ on the Formatting (Form/Report) toolbar, click the **bright blue box** in the second row, click the **Line/Border Width list arrow** ⬛, then click **2** (a measurement of line width)

   Your screen should look like Figure H-13. Short double lines under the calculations in the Report Footer section indicate grand totals.

6. Click the **Line button** ╲ on the Toolbox toolbar, press and hold **[Shift]**, drag a line from the **left edge =Sum([Hours]) text box** to the **right edge of the =Sum([Cost]) text box** in the Report Footer section, then release **[Shift]**

   Copying and pasting lines create an exact duplicate of the line that can be moved to a new location.

7. Click the **Copy button** 📋, click the **Paste button** 📋, press and hold **[Ctrl]**, press **[↑]** five times, then release **[Ctrl]**

   Moving a control with the **[Ctrl]** and arrow key combination moves it one picture element (**pixel**) at a time.

8. Click the **line control** below the Course Summary Report label in the Report Header section, point to the **line** so the pointer changes to ✋, drag the **line** straight down until it rests just above the Page Footer section, click the **Print Preview button** 🔍, then click the **Last Page Navigation button** ▶|

   Your screen should look like Figure H-14.

FIGURE H-12: First page of Course Summary Report

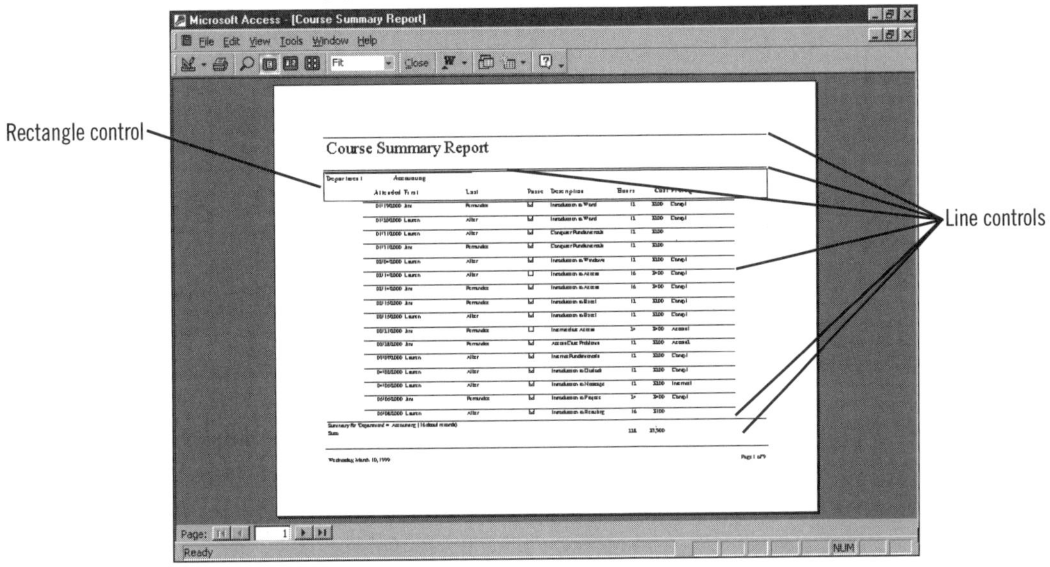

Rectangle control

Line controls

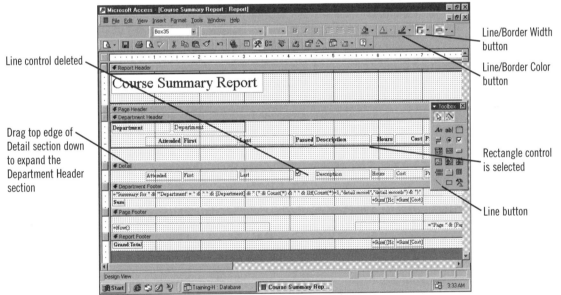

FIGURE H-13: Course Summary Report in Design view

Line/Border Width button

Line/Border Color button

Line control deleted

Drag top edge of Detail section down to expand the Department Header section

Rectangle control is selected

Line button

FIGURE H-14: Last page of modified Course Summary Report

Line was moved from the bottom of the Report Header section to the bottom of the Department Footer section

Lines added to indicate a grand total

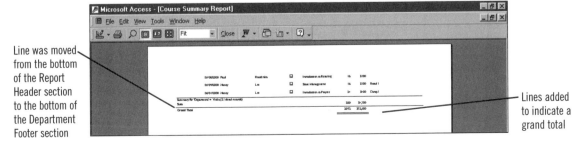

Using Format Painter and AutoFormats

The **Format Painter** is a handy tool used to copy formatting properties from one control to another. **AutoFormats** are predefined formats that you can apply to a form or report and include such items as background pictures, font, color, and alignment choices. Once you have developed a form or report format that you wish to save and apply to other objects, you can add it to the list of AutoFormats provided by Access. ▶Scenario◀ David uses the Format Painter to change the characteristics of other lines on the report, then saves the report's formatting scheme as a new AutoFormat so that he can apply it to other reports he creates.

QuickTip

Double-clicking the Format Painter button will allow you to "paint" more than one control.

1. Click the **Design View button** 📷, click the **blue rectangle control** in the Department Header section, double-click the **Format Painter button** 🖌 on the Formatting (Form/Report) toolbar (the pointer changes to 🗔), click the **line control** in the Report Header section, click the **line control** in the Department Footer section, then click 🖌 to release the paintbrush

Both lines are now bright blue and the same width as the rectangle control.

QuickTip

Press [Esc] to release the Format Painter.

2. Click the **Attended label** in the Department Header section, click the **Font list arrow** [Times New Roman ▼] on the Formatting (Form/Report) toolbar, click **Arial**, click the **Font size list arrow** [10 ▼] click **11**, click the **Align Left button** ≣, double-click 🖌, click the **First**, **Last**, **Passed**, **Description**, **Hours**, **Cost**, and **Prereq labels** in the Department Header section, then click 🖌

The Format Painter copied the font face, font size, and alignment properties from the Attended label in the Department Header section to the other labels, as shown in Figure H-15.

3. Click **Format** on the menu bar, click **AutoFormat**, click the **Customize button** in the AutoFormat dialog box, click the **Create a new AutoFormat based on the Report 'Course Summary Report' option button**, click **OK**, type **Blue Lines-(Your Name)**, then click **OK**

The AutoFormat dialog box should look similar to Figure H-16 (many other AutoFormats may appear). Saving the formatting characteristics of the report as a new AutoFormat will allow you to apply them later to other reports in the Training-H database.

4. Click **OK** to close the AutoFormat dialog box, click **Window** on the menu bar, click **Training-H : Database**, click **Employee Detail Report**, click the 📷, click **Format** on the menu bar, click the **AutoFormat**, click **Blue Lines-[Your Name]** in the Report AutoFormats list, then click **OK**

Your screen should look like Figure H-17. The AutoFormat you applied changed the formatting properties of lines and labels in this report. AutoFormats that you create are available every time you use the Report Wizard (report AutoFormats) and Form Wizard (form AutoFormats).

5. Click the **Save button** 🖫, close the report, then click the **Course Summary Report button** on the taskbar

The Design view of the Course Summary Report appears on your screen.

6. Click **File** on the menu system, click **Save As**, type **Department Summary Report**, then click **OK**

Delete the **Blue Lines-[Your Name]** AutoFormat.

7. Click **Format** on the menu bar, click **AutoFormat**, click **Blue Lines-[Your Name]**, click **Customize**, click the **Delete 'Blue Lines-[Your Name]' option button**, click **OK**, then click **Close**

8. Save and close the Department Summary Report

FIGURE H-15: Using the Format Painter

Font list arrow

Format Painter button

Attended label

Align Left button

Font size list arrow

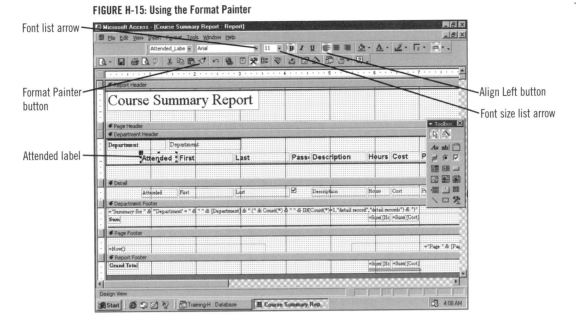

FIGURE H-16: The AutoFormat dialog box

New Report AutoFormat

Customize button

Sample shows the new AutoFormat characteristics

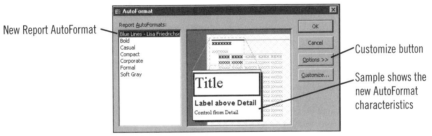

FIGURE H-17: Applying a saved AutoFormat to a different report

Label formatting changed

Line formatting changed

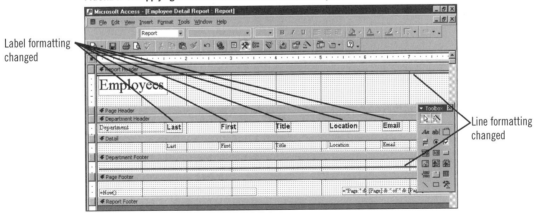

![CLUES TO USE]

Displaying only summary reports

Sometimes you may not want show all the details of a report, but only a portion of it, such as the group summary information that is calculated in the Group Footer section. You can accomplish this by deleting all controls in the Detail section. Calculated controls in a Group Footer section will still calculate properly even if the individual records used within the calculation are not displayed on the report.

Access 2000

Inserting an Image

Multimedia controls those that display picture, sound, motion, or other nontextual information. A control that displays an unbound logo would most likely be placed in the Report Header section, and a control that is bound to a field that contains multimedia information for each record (for example a picture of each employee) would be placed in the Detail section. See Table H-2 for more information on multimedia controls. **Scenario** David added an Icon field to the Courses table that contains a descriptive picture that represents the course's content. He uses the Bound Object Frame control to display this picture for each course in a new report.

1. Double-click **Create report by using wizard**, click the **Tables/Queries list arrow**, click **Query: Microsoft Office Classes**, click the **Select All Fields button** ⧉, click **Next**, click **by Attendance**, then click **Next**

2. Double-click **Description**, click **Next**, click the **first sort order list arrow**, click **Last**, click the **Summary Options button**, click the **Hours Sum check box**, click the **Cost Sum check box**, click **OK**, then click **Next**
   This report groups the records by Description, sorts them by Last (name) within Description (of the course), and summarizes both the Cost and Hours fields.

3. Click the **Outline 1 Layout option button**, click the **Landscape Orientation option button**, click **Next**, click the **Casual** style, click **Next**, type **Microsoft Office Classes** as the report title, click **Finish**, then click the ⧉ on the Print Preview screen
   The first page of the report appears in miniature, as shown in Figure H-18. The wizard created a large control for the picture for each course.

   Trouble?
   Close the Field list if necessary.

4. Click the **Design View button** ⧉, click the large **icon bound image control** in the Detail section, press and hold **[Shift]**, click the **Icon label** in the Description Header section, click the **Description label** in the Description Header section, release **[Shift]**, then press **[Delete]**
   The Icon field can be added to the Description Header section to help announce that the following group of records are all for the same course.

   Trouble?
   Be sure to delete the Description label control on the left and not the Description text box control on the right.

5. Point to the **top edge of the Description Footer section**, drag the ➕ pointer up to the bottom of the controls in the Detail section, click the **Bound Object Frame button** ⧉ on the Toolbox toolbar, click in the **upper-left corner of the Description Header section**, place the pointer on the **Bound Object Frame control lower-right corner sizing handle**, then drag ⬉ up and to the left to the **0.5" mark** on both the horizontal and vertical rulers
   Your screen should look like Figure H-19. Every time you add a control from the Toolbox toolbar, you get an accompanying label. In this case, you do not need the label.

   Trouble?
   The label control is partially behind the new frame.

6. Click the new **label control**, press **[Delete]**, place the pointer on the **top edge of the Detail section**, then drag ➕ up to the bottom of the controls in the Description Header section
   You need to **bind** the frame to the Icon field, which means you change a bound control's **source property** to the associated field name of the field it will represent.

7. Double-click the **Bound Object Frame control** to open its property sheet, click the **Data tab**, click the **Control Source property list arrow**, click **Icon**, click the **Format tab**, click the **Border Style property list arrow**, click **Transparent**, click the **Properties button** ⧉ to close the property sheet, click the **Save button** ⧉, click the **Print Preview button** ⧉, click ⧉ on the screen, then maximize the report window
   Your screen should look like Figure H-20. The icons for both Access and Excel appear in their respective course Description Header sections.

8. Print the report, close the Print Preview window, then close the Microsoft Office Classes report

FIGURE H-18: Microsoft Office Classes report

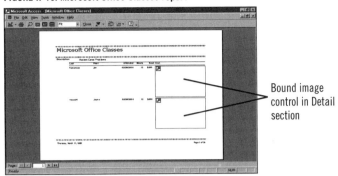

Bound image control in Detail section

FIGURE H-19: Microsoft Office Classes report in Design view

New label

Bound Object Frame

Resized Detail section

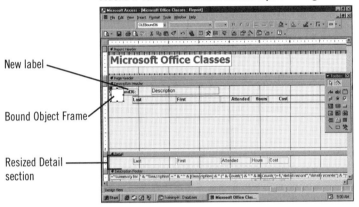

FIGURE H-20: Final Microsoft Office Classes report

Bound Object Control displays the Icon picture in the Description Header section

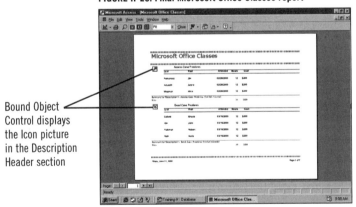

TABLE H-2: Multimedia controls

control name	toolbox icon	bound or unbound	used to display	form/report section where this control is most likely placed	
Image		Unbound	an unbound picture, piece of clip art, or logo	Form Header	Report Header or Page Header
Unbound Object Frame		Unbound	a sound or motion clip a document or spreadsheet	Form Header not often used on a form	Report Footer
Bound Object Frame		Bound	information contained in a field with an OLE data type	Detail	Detail or Group Header

Securing the Database

When you delete data and objects in an Access database, the database can become fragmented and use disk space inefficiently. **Compacting** the database rearranges the data and objects to improve performance by reusing the space formerly occupied by the deleted objects. The compact process also checks to see if the database is damaged and, if so, attempts to repair it. A good time to back up a database is right after it has been compacted. If hardware is stolen or destroyed, a recent backup (most database administrators recommend that databases be backed up each night) can minimize the impact of that loss to the business. Use Windows Explorer to copy individual database files and floppy disks, or use back-up software like Microsoft Backup to create back-up schedules to automate the process. Scenario▶ David needs to secure the Training database. He starts by compacting the database, then backing it up by using Windows Explorer to make a copy.

Steps 1234

1. Click **Tools** on the menu bar, point to **Database Utilities**, click **Compact and Repair Database**
   Access 2000 allows you to compact and repair an open database, but it's a good practice to use the "Compact on Close" feature, which compacts the database every time it is closed.

QuickTip

When working with databases on storage disks of limited size such as floppies, always check the Compact on Close feature.

2. Click **Tools** on the menu bar, click **Options**, click the **General tab** of the Options dialog box, then click the **Compact on Close** check box (if it is not already created)
   The Options dialog box is shown in Figure H-21. **Compact on Close** automatically compacts and repairs the database when you close it if the size can be reduced by at least 256 KB. It is not checked (turned on) by default.

Trouble?

Be sure that your Project Disk is in drive A: and that you have a blank disk ready to complete the step.

3. Click **OK**, close the **Training-H** database, exit **Access**, right-click the **Start button**, then click **Explore**
   You'll use Windows Explorer, as shown in Figure H-22, to make a copy of your Project Disk.

4. Right-click **3½ Floppy (A:)** in the Folders list, then click **Copy Disk**
   The Copy Disk dialog box opens, as shown in Figure H-23. This command allows you to copy an entire floppy disk from one disk to another without first copying the contents to the computer's C: hard drive.

5. Click **Start**
   Windows Explorer will start copying your original Project Disk, the **source disk**, and will prompt you to insert the blank disk, the **destination disk**, where the files will be pasted.

6. When you are prompted to insert the destination disk, do so and click **OK**
   Explorer was able to copy all of the files from the Project Disk to the blank disk with one process. Sometimes you are prompted to reinsert the source disk and then the destination disk because all of the files cannot be copied in one process.

7. Click **Close** in the Copy Disk dialog box, then close **Windows Explorer**

8. Label the disk and place it in a safe place

FIGURE H-21: Options dialog box

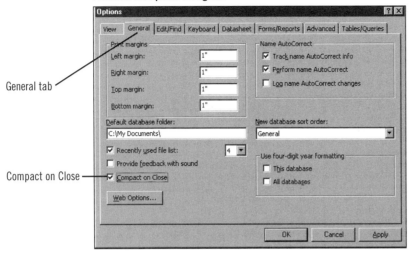

General tab

Compact on Close

FIGURE H-22: Windows Explorer

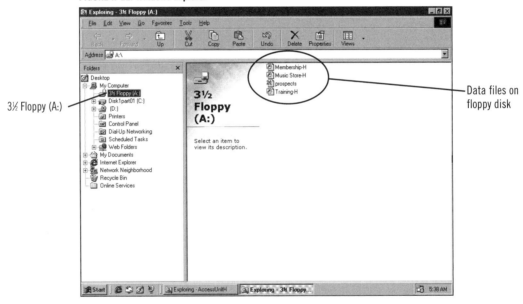

3½ Floppy (A:)

Data files on floppy disk

FIGURE H-23: Copy Disk dialog box

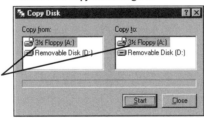

Make sure 3½ Floppy (A:) is chosen in both the Copy from: and Copy to: locations

CLUES TO USE

Compacting a database automatically

Microsoft Access can automatically compact a database file every time you close it. Choose the Options from the Tools menu, then click the General tab. Click the Compact on Close check box, then click OK.

Compacting does not occur when you close the database unless the file size would be reduced by more than 256 KB. It also does not occur if you close the database while another person is using it.

Practice

► Concepts Review

Identify each element of the form's Design view shown in Figure H-24.

FIGURE-H-24

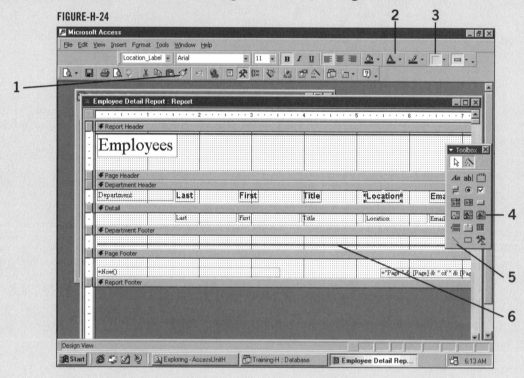

Match each term with the statement that describes its function.

7. **Image control**
8. **Parameter Query**
9. **Bound Object Frame**
10. **Format Painter**
11. **Importing**

a. Used to copy formatting properties from one control to another
b. This displays a dialog box prompting you for criteria each time you open it
c. Used to display information contained in a field with an OLE data type
d. A process to quickly convert data from an external source into an Access database
e. Used to display an unbound picture, clip art item, or logo

Select the best answer from the list of choices.

12. **Which control would work best to present sound clips of each employee's voice stored in a Voice field with an OLE data type?**
    a. Unbound Object Frame
    b. Label
    c. Bound Object Frame
    d. Text box
13. **Which control would you use to separate groups of records on a report?**
    a. Line
    b. Image
    c. Bound Object Frame
    d. Option group
14. **Which wizard would you use to create a database from scratch?**
    a. Lookup Wizard
    b. Table Wizard
    c. Records Wizard
    d. Database Wizard
15. **Which wizard would you use to provide a value list for a field?**
    a. Field Wizard
    b. Lookup Wizard
    c. Value List Wizard
    d. Database Wizard
16. **Which of the following programs or file types cannot serve as a source for data imported into Access?**
    a. HTML
    b. Lotus 1-2-3
    c. Lotus Notes
    d. Excel

▶ Skills Review

1. **Use the Database Wizard.**
   a. Start Access, click the Access database wizards, pages, and projects option button in the Microsoft Access dialog box, then click OK.
   b. Double-click the Contact Management Wizard, and create the new database with the name "Contacts" on a new, blank Project Disk.
   c. Follow the prompts of the Database Wizard and accept all of the default field suggestions. Use the Standard style for screen displays and the Soft Gray style for printed reports.
   d. Accept the name Contact Management as the title of the database.
   e. After all of the objects are created, close the Main Switchboard form, then close the Contacts database.
2. **Import Data.**
   a. Use Windows Explorer to copy the Excel file prospects from Project Disk 2 to the new Project Disk that contains the Contacts database.
   b. Open the Contacts database.
   c. Click File on the menu bar, point to Get External Data, then click Import.
   d. In the Import dialog box, click the Files of type list arrow, click Microsoft Excel, click prospects on your Project Disk, then click the Import button in the Import dialog box.

    e. In the Import Spreadsheet Wizard, make sure that the Show Worksheets option button is selected, click Next, check the First Row Contains Column Headings check box, click Next, click the In an Existing Table list arrow, click Contacts, click Next, then click Finish.

    f. Click OK when prompted that the import was successful, then open the Contacts table in Design view.

    g. Modify the Region field using the Lookup Wizard Data Type by typing the following values. Press [Tab] as you type each value in the column: East, Midwest, North, South, West. Use "Region" for the label.

    h. Save the table, then open it in Datasheet view.

    i. Add your personal information as a new record using "East" as the entry for the Region, regardless of where you live.

    j. Print the datasheet in landscape orientation, then close the datasheet.

3. Create a Report from a Parameter Query.

    a. Start a new query in Design view, then add the Contacts table.

    b. Add the following fields to the Query Design grid in this order: FirstName, LastName, City, StateOrProvince, Region.

    c. Enter the following parameter criteria to the Region field: [Enter Region:].

    d. Save the query, naming it "Customer Regions", then close the query.

    e. Using the Report Wizard, create a new report basing it on the Customer Regions query.

    f. Select all the fields, group the report by Region, sort ascending by LastName, and choose a Block layout, a Portrait orientation, and a bold style.

    g. Accept the name Customer Regions for your report title.

    h. When prompted for the region, enter "East".

    i. Open the report in Design view and add a label to the Report Footer with the text "Created by [Your Name]".

    j. Save, print, and close the report.

    k. Close the Contacts database.

4. Enhance Reports.

    a. Open the Membership-H database.

    b. Using the Report Wizard, create a report on the Query: Member Activity Log using all of the fields in that query.

    c. Group the fields by Last, sort ascending by ActivityDate, and Sum the Hours field.

    d. Use the Outline 2 layout, Portrait orientation, Compact style, and accept the name Member Activity Log as the report title.

    e. Open the report in Design view and select the =Sum([Hours]) calculated field in the Last Footer section.

    f. Use the Conditional Formatting from the Format menu to change Font/Fore color to bold and bright blue if the value is greater than or equal to 10.

    g. Add a label to the Report Footer section, with the text "Created by [Your Name]", then save the report and print the last page.

    h. Open the property sheet for the First text box in the Detail section and set the Hide Duplicates property to Yes.

    i. Group the controls in the Report Footer section, then format the group with a bright blue Font/Fore color.

    j. Save and print the report.

5. Add Lines and Rectangles.

    a. Open the Member Activity Log report in Design view, then delete the following controls:
       Last, First, and Dues labels in the Last Header section
       First and Dues text boxes in the Detail section
       Line in the Detail section (*Hint*: It is between the ActivityDate and Hours text boxes.)
       Line in the Last Header section (*Hint*: It is a short line just above the Last text box.)
       Rectangle in the Last Header section (*Hint*: You will probably have to expand the section to find it.)

b. Move the ActivityDate label in the Last Header section and the ActivityDate text box in the Detail section to the right, so that they are right beside the Hours controls.

c. Move the line control at the top of the Last Footer section to the bottom of the Last Footer section.

d. Draw two short lines under the =Sum([Hours]) control in the Report Footer to indicate a grand total.

e. Use the Save As option from the File menu to save the report as the "Simplified Member Activity Log" and print the first page.

6. Use the Format Painter and AutoFormats.

a. Open the Simplified Member Activity Log in Design view.

b. Format the ActivityDate label in the Last Header section with a bold Tahoma font.

c. Use the Format Painter to copy that format to the Last text box and the Hours label in the Last Header section.

d. Change the color of the lines in the Report Header section to bright red.

e. Create a new AutoFormat named "Red Lines-[Your Name]" based on the Simplified Member Activity Log report.

f. Print the first page of the Simplified Member Activity Log report, then save and close it.

g. Open the Member Activity Log report in Design view, and use the AutoFormat option from the Format menu to apply the Corporate format.

h. Use the Customize button in the AutoFormat dialog box to delete the "Red Lines-[Your Name]" style.

i. Preview, then print the first page of the Member Activity Log report. Save and close the report.

7. Insert an Image.

a. Use the Report Wizard to create a report using all the fields from the Team Members query except for the Team field.

b. Do not group the records, but sort them in ascending order on the Last, then on the First fields.

c. Use a Columnar layout and a Portrait orientation.

d. Apply a Bold style, and accept the name Team Members as the title.

e. In Design view, use the Bound Object Frame control to add a frame to the right of the Last text box in the Detail section. Delete the frame's accompanying label. Be sure to move and resize the frame and right edge of the report so that they do not go beyond the 6.5" mark.

f. On the Data tab of the property sheet for the frame, change the Control Source property to Team.

g. On the Format tab of the property sheet for the frame, change the Size Mode property to Zoom and change the Border Style to Transparent.

h. Put a label control in the Report Header that displays your name, then save, preview, and print the report.

i. Close the Membership-H database and exit Access.

8. Secure the Database.

a. Start Access.

b. Use the Database Utilities option on the Tools menu to Compact and Repair the database.

c. Close the Membership-H database and exit Access.

d. Start Explorer, right-click on the 3½ Floppy (A:) option, then click Copy Disk.

e. Follow the prompts to make a back-up copy of your Project Disk to a new, blank disk.

f. Exit Windows Explorer.

Access 2000

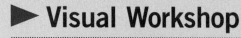

► Visual Workshop

Open the Training-H database and create a new report as shown in Figure H-25 using the Report Wizard. Gather the First, Last, and Department fields from the Employees table and the Description and Hours fields from the Courses table. Sum the Hours, sort in ascending order by the Description, and use the Outline 1, Portrait, and Corporate Wizard options. Enter your name as a label in the Report Header if you need to identify your printout.

FIGURE H-25

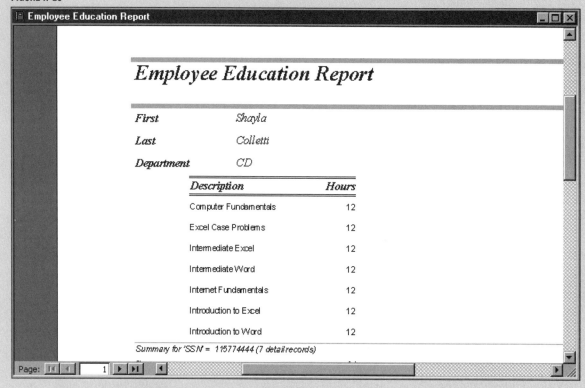

Access 2000

Unit
I

Sharing

Access Information with Other Office Programs

Objectives

- ► **Examine Access objects**
- [MOUS] ► **Examine relationships between tables**
- ► **Importing data from Excel**
- [MOUS] ► **Link data to an Excel worksheet**
- [MOUS] ► **Create hyperlinks**
- [MOUS] ► **Analyze data with Excel**
- ► **Copy records to Word**
- [MOUS] ► **Export data to Excel**

Access is a powerful relational database program that can share data with many other application Microsoft Office 2000 software products. Choosing the right tool for each task is important because you often need to use features from one program and data stored in another type of file. For example, you might want to use financial data in an Excel spreadsheet as part of an Access database. Or, you might want to copy records from an Access query into a Word document that will be published to the Internet. Before you copy or link Access data to another program, however, you should determine if the capability exists within Access. **Scenario** David Dumont, director of training at MediaLoft, has developed an Access database that tracks courses, employees, and course attendance for the internal education provided by MediaLoft. David will share Access data with other software applications to provide each MediaLoft department the data they have requested in a format they can use.

Examining Access Objects

Access 2000

In order to become proficient with Access, it is important for you to understand the capabilities of the seven Access objects. **Scenario** David reviews key Access terminology and the seven Access objects.

Details

A **database** is a collection of data associated with a topic (for example, the training each employee at MediaLoft has received). The smallest piece of information in a database is called a **field**, or category of information such as the employee's name, e-mail address, or department. A **key field** is a field that contains unique information for each record such as an employee's Social Security number. A group of related fields, such as all descriptive information for one employee, is called a **record**. A collection of records for a single subject, such as all of the employee records, is called a **table.** When a table object is opened, the fields and records are displayed as a **datasheet**, as shown in Figure I-1.

Tables are the most important **objects** within an Access database because they contain all of the data within the database. An Access database also may contain six other object types that serve to enhance the usability and value of the data. The objects in an Access database are **tables**, **queries**, **forms**, **reports**, **pages**, **macros**, and **modules**, and are summarized in Table I-1.

Query objects are based on tables; and form, page, and report objects can be based on either tables or queries. Data can be entered and edited in four of the objects—tables, queries, pages, and forms—but is always stored in tables. These relationships are shown in Figure I-2. The macro and module objects are used to provide additional database productivity and automation features such as **GUI** (**graphical user interface**) screens and buttons, which surround and mask the complexity of the underlying objects. All of the objects are stored in one database file.

TABLE I-1: Access objects

object	purpose
Table	Contains all of the raw data within the database in a spreadsheet-like view; can be linked with a common field to share information and therefore minimize data redundancy
Query	Provides a spreadsheet-like view of the data that is similar to tables, but can display a subset of fields and/or records from one or more tables; created when a user has a "question" about the data in the database
Form	Provides an easy-to-use data entry screen that generally shows only one record at a time
Report	Provides a professional printout of data that may contain enhancements such as headers, footers, and calculations on groups of records; mailing labels can also be created from report objects
Page	Creates Web pages from Access objects as well as Web page connectivity features to an Access database
Macro	Stores a collection of keystrokes or commands such as printing several reports in a row or displaying a toolbar when a form opens
Module	Stores Visual Basic programming code that extends the functions and automated processes of Access

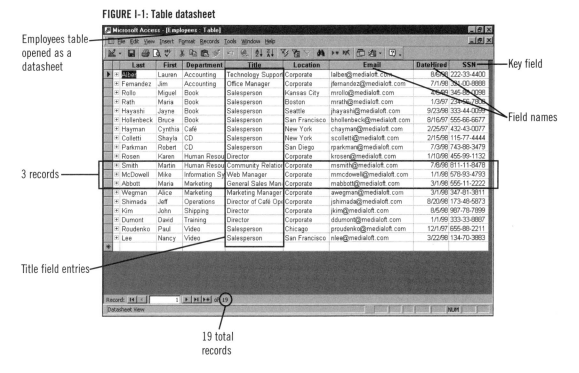

FIGURE I-1: Table datasheet

Employees table opened as a datasheet

3 records

Title field entries

Key field

Field names

19 total records

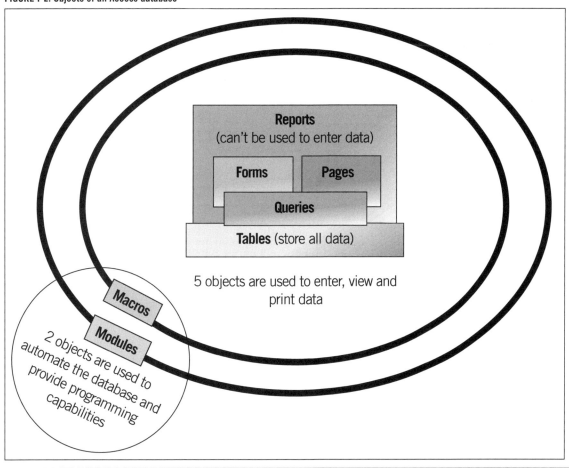

FIGURE I-2: Objects of an Access database

Reports
(can't be used to enter data)

Forms

Pages

Queries

Tables (store all data)

5 objects are used to enter, view and print data

Macros

Modules

2 objects are used to automate the database and provide programming capabilities

Access 2000

Examining Relationships Between Tables

An Access database is a **relational database** in that more than one table can share information, or "relate." The key benefit of organizing your data into a relational database is minimized redundant data. The ability to link separate tables of data improves the accuracy, speed, and flexibility of a relational database. The process of designing a relational database is called **normalization**, and involves determining the appropriate fields, tables, and table relationships. Relationship types are summarized in Table I-2. **Scenario** David develops an Instructors table to store one record for each teacher. He relates the Instructors table to the Courses table so that it participates in the relational database.

QuickTip

The primary key field always acts as the "one" side of a one-to-many relationship.

1. Start Access, open the **Training-I** database on your Project Disk, click **Tables** on the Objects bar, maximize the database window, then double-click the **Instructors table**
   The InstructorID field serves as the **primary key field** so it contains unique data for each record in the Instructors table. The Instructors table should be related to the Courses table with a one-to-many relationship because each instructor teaches many courses.

QuickTip

For clarity, give the primary and foreign key fields of two linking tables the same name.

2. Click the **Instructors Table Close Window button**, click the **Courses table**, then click the **Design button** in the database window
   A matching field, often called the **foreign key field**, must be added to the table on the "many" side of a one-to-many relationship to link with the primary key field of the "one" table.

3. Click the **Field Name cell** in the first blank row, type **InstructorID**, press **[Tab]**, press **N** to select a Number data type, press **[Tab]**, type **Foreign Key** as shown in Figure I-3, click the **Save button**, then close the Courses table Design view window
   The linking field for both tables is created.

4. Click the **Relationships button** on the Database toolbar, click the **Show Table button** on the Relationships toolbar, click **Instructors**, click **Add**, then click **Close**
   The Instructors table appears in the Relationships window without any relationships to other tables. Primary key fields appear in bold.

QuickTip

To display all the fields in a table, drag on a corner of the table until the scroll bars are no longer visible.

5. Drag the **InstructorID field** from the Instructors table to the **InstructorID field** in the Courses table, then click **Create** in the Edit Relationships dialog box
   The link between the Courses and Instructors tables has been established, but the linking line doesn't display the "one" and "many" sides of the relationship.

Trouble?

Double-click the middle part of the linking line to edit the relationship.

6. Double-click the **relationship line** between the Instructors and Courses tables, then click the **Enforce Referential Integrity check box**, see Figure I-4
   The **Enforce Referential Integrity** option does not allow values to be entered in the foreign key field that are not first entered in the primary key field. It also does not allow records to be deleted in the "one" table if related records exist in the "many" table. **Cascade Update Related Fields** automatically updates the data in the foreign key field when the matching primary key field is changed. **Cascade Delete Related Records** automatically deletes all records in the "many" table if the record with the matching key field in the "one" table is deleted.

7. Click **OK** in the Edit Relationships dialog box
   Printing the Relationships window shown in Figure I-5 creates a valuable report that helps you remember what fields are in which tables.

8. Click **File** on the menu bar, click **Print Relationships**, click the **Print button** on the Print Preview toolbar, click **Close**, click, accept the default report name **Relationships for Training-I**, then close the Relationships window

FIGURE I-3: Adding the foreign key field to the Courses table in Design view

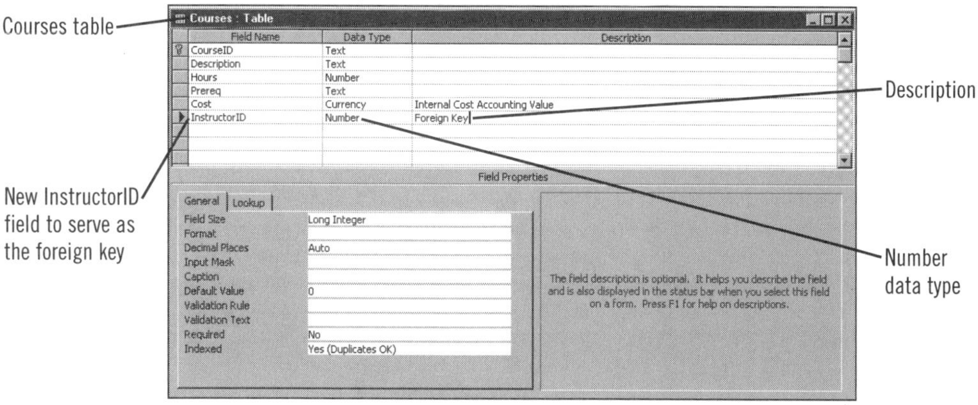

Courses table ——

New InstructorID field to serve as the foreign key

—— Description

—— Number data type

FIGURE I-4: Edit Relationships dialog box

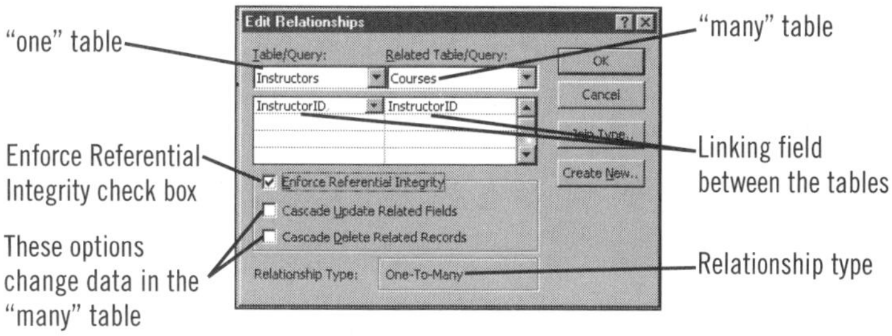

"one" table ——

"many" table

Enforce Referential Integrity check box

Linking field between the tables

These options change data in the "many" table

Relationship type

FIGURE I-5: Relationships window

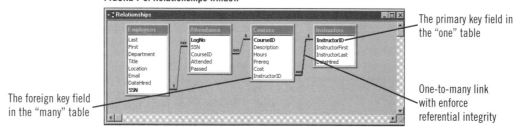

The foreign key field in the "many" table

The primary key field in the "one" table

One-to-many link with enforce referential integrity

TABLE I-2: Relationship types

relationship	description	example	notes
One-to-One	A record in Table X has no more than one matching record in Table Y.	A student table would have no more than one matching record in a graduation table that tracks the student's graduation date and major.	Not common, because all fields related this way could be stored in one table; sometimes used to separate rarely used fields from a table to improve the overall performance of the database
One-to-Many	A single record in Table X has many records in Table Y.	One product can be sold many times, one customer can make many purchases, one teacher can teach many courses, and one student can take many courses.	Most common type of relationship
Many-to-Many	A record in Table X has many records in Table Y, and a record in Table Y has many records in Table X.	One employee can take several courses, and the same course can be taken by several employees. (In the MediaLoft database, the Attendance table serves as the junction table between the Courses and Employees tables.)	It is impossible to directly create many-to-many relationships in Access. Instead, a third table, called a junction table, must be established between the original tables. The junction table contains foreign key fields that link to the primary key fields of each of the original tables and establishes separate one-to-many relationships with them. The junction table serves as the "many" side of each relationship.

Importing Data from Excel

Importing is a process to quickly convert data from an external source into an Access database. You can import data from one Access database to another, or from many other data sources such as Excel, dBase, Paradox, FoxPro, HTML, or delimited text files. A **delimited text file** contains one record on each line, with the fields separated by a common character such as a comma, tab, or dash. Often, external numerical data is stored in an Excel spreadsheet, because many people are comfortable with the easy-to-use spreadsheet structure of Excel. Scenario▶ Karen Rosen, Director of Human Resources, has asked the Training Department to add three new courses to the current offerings. Information about the courses has been entered into an Excel spreadsheet called New Courses.

Steps 123 4

QuickTip

The Files of type list displays the data file formats that can be imported into Access.

1. Click **File** on the menu bar, point to **Get External Data**, click **Import**, click the **Look in: list arrow**, locate your Project Disk, click the **Files of Type list arrow**, click **Microsoft Excel**, then double-click **New Courses**
   The Import Spreadsheet Wizard dialog box opens, as shown in Figure I-6.

2. Click **Next**, then verify that the **First Row Contains Column Headings check box** is checked
   The second dialog box of the Import Spreadsheet Wizard, shown in Figure I-7, is extremely important. In order to successfully import data from an Excel spreadsheet to an existing table, the spreadsheet fields (columns) must be consistent with the fields of the Access table.

3. Click **Next**, click the **In an Existing Table list arrow**, click **Courses**, click **Next**, click **Finish**, then click **OK**
   The three records from the New Courses spreadsheet were successfully imported into the Courses table of the Training-I database.

4. Double-click the **Courses** table to open its datasheet
   The Courses datasheet, with the three new records, is displayed in Figure I-8. By default, the records in the Courses table sort by the primary key field, CourseID. Note that the new records do not have any values in the Prereq field, but they do have entries in the InstructorID field. Even if the field is **null** (contains nothing), the number and type of fields in the Excel spreadsheet must be consistent with the Access table to successfully import the Excel data. If you import an Excel spreadsheet into a new table, Access will choose an appropriate data type and field name for each field in the new table.

5. Close the **Courses** datasheet
   Now that the Excel data has been imported into the Access Training-I database, it can link to many other tables of data to create valuable queries, forms, and reports, and therefore it can serve the varied needs of simultaneous users.

FIGURE I-6: Import Spreadsheet Wizard's first dialog box

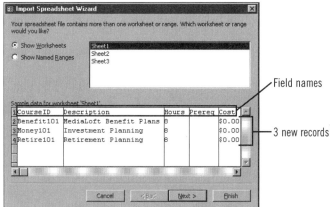

Field names

3 new records

FIGURE I-7: Import Spreadsheet Wizard's second dialog box

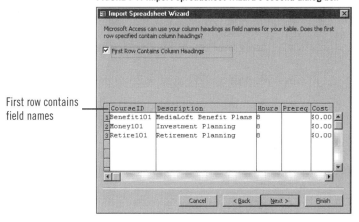

First row contains
field names

FIGURE I-8: Courses table with three new imported records

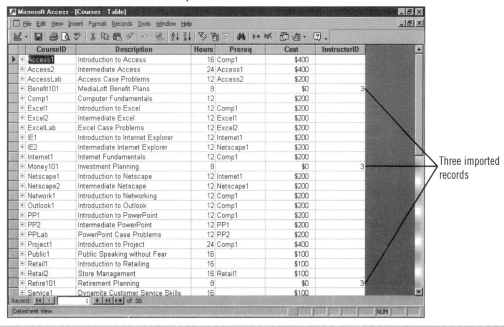

Three imported
records

Linking Data with Excel

Linking connects an Access database to data in an external file such as another Access, dBase, or Paradox database; an Excel or Lotus 1-2-3 spreadsheet; a text file; an HTML file; and other data sources that support **ODBC** (**Open Database Connectivity**) standards. If you link, data can be entered or edited in either the original file or the Access database even though the data is only stored in the original file. Changes to data in either location are automatically made in the other. **Importing**, in contrast, makes a duplicate copy of the data in the Access database, so changes to either the original data source or the imported Access copy have no effect on the other. ▶Scenario◀ David asked the new instructors to make a list of all of their class materials. They created this list in an Excel spreadsheet, and wish to maintain it there. David creates a link to this data from within the Training database.

1. Click **File** on the menu bar, point to **Get External Data**, then click **Link Tables**
   The Link dialog box opens, listing Access files in the current folder.

▶ **Trouble?**

If your Project Disk files do not display in the Link dialog box, click the Look in: list arrow to locate your Project Disk.

2. Click the **Files of Type list arrow**, click **Microsoft Excel**, click **Course Materials** in the files list, then click **Link**
   The Link Spreadsheet Wizard appears, as shown in Figure I-9. Data can be linked from different parts of the Excel spreadsheet. The data you want is on Sheet 1.

3. Click **Next**, click the **First Row Contains Column Headings check box** to specify **CourseID**, **Materials**, and **Type** as field names, click **Next**, type **Course Supplies** as the Linked Table Name, click **Finish**, then click **OK**
   The Course Supplies table appears in the database window with a linking Excel icon, as shown in Figure I-10. A linked table can and must participate in a one-to-many relationship with another table if it is to share data with the rest of the tables of the database.

4. Click the **Relationships button** 🖧 on the Database toolbar, click the **Show Table button** 📇, double-click **Course Supplies**, then click **Close**
   Rearranging the tables in the Relationships window can improve the clarity of the relationships.

▶ **QuickTip**

If you update data in a linked table, it will update the original source.

5. Drag the **Course Supplies table title bar** to a position under the Attendance table, drag the **CourseID field** in the Courses table to the **CourseID field** in the Course Supplies table, then click **Create** in the Edit Relationships dialog box
   A one-to-many relationship is established between the Courses and Course Supplies tables. You cannot establish referential integrity when one of the tables is a linked table, but the table can now participate in queries, forms, pages, and reports that use fields from multiple tables. Your screen should look like Figure I-11.

6. Click the **Save button** 🖫, close the **Relationships window**, double-click the **Course Supplies table** to open it, click the **New Record button** ▶* on the Table Datasheet toolbar, type **Access1**, press **[Tab]**, type **MediaLoft.mdb**, press **[Tab]**, then type **File**
   You added a new record. When first creating a linked table, you should check the original data source, the Course Materials Excel file, to make sure that the data was automatically updated there.

7. Close the **Course Supplies table**, right-click the **Start button** in the taskbar, click **Explore**, locate your Project Disk, double-click the **Course Materials Excel file** to open it in Excel, then press **[Page Down]**
   The new Access1 record should be visible in row 40 of the Excel spreadsheet.

8. Click **File** on the menu bar, click **Exit** to close the worksheet and exit Excel, then close Explorer

FIGURE I-9: Link Spreadsheet Wizard dialog box

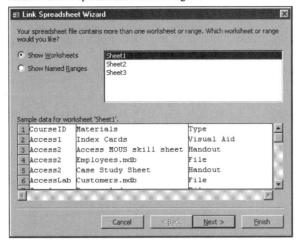

FIGURE I-10: Course Supplies table is linked from Excel

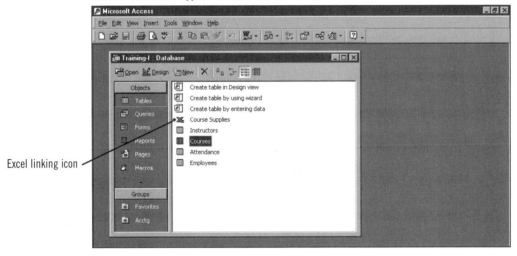

Excel linking icon

FIGURE I-11: Relationships window with Course Supplies table

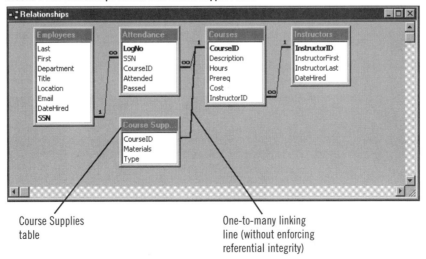

Course Supplies
table

One-to-many linking
line (without enforcing
referential integrity)

Creating Hyperlinks

A **hyperlink** is a label, button, or image that when clicked automatically opens another object, document or graphic file, e-mail message, or World Wide Web page. Hyperlinks can be added as labels, pictures, or buttons on a form. A field with a **hyperlink data type** can be defined in a table's Design view so that the datasheet displays and stores different hyperlink information for each record. **Scenario** David created a Word document called "Directions to MediaLoft Corporate" that gives detailed directions to the San Francisco training facility. Within the Word document he created two **bookmarks**, specific locations within the document marked by a bookmark code, called "fromTheNorth" and "fromTheSouth" that identify the beginning of the paragraph that describes each route. Because employees often ask for detailed directions to the training facility when they sign up for a course, David will create hyperlinks to these instructions from the Courses form.

Steps

1. Click **Forms** on the Objects bar, then double-click the **Courses form** to open it in Form view
   The Courses form displays course information in the main form, whereas the subform logs the SSN, date attended, and other information about each employee signed up for each course. Create hyperlinks from the Courses form to the Directions document.

2. Click the **Design View button** 🖾, click the **Toolbox button** ✕, click the **Label button** 𝐴𝑎 on the Toolbox, click ⁺A in the **Detail section** of the form at the 5" mark, then type **Directions from the north**
   Any label on a form can become a hyperlink if the hyperlink properties are entered.

3. Click the **Properties button** 🖾 to open the label property sheet, click the **Format tab** (if necessary), click the **Hyperlink Address text box**, then click the **Build button** ⬚
   The Insert Hyperlink dialog box appears, as shown in Figure I-12. This dialog box helps you link to a file, Web page, database object, or e-mail address.

4. Click **File**
   The Link to File dialog box opens.

5. Locate your Project Disk, then double-click **Directions to MediaLoft Corporate**
   The file name appears in the Type the file or Web page name text box.

6. Click **OK**
   The entry for the Hyperlink Address property appears in the label's property sheet. Use the Hyperlink SubAddress property to specify the bookmark name within the Directions document to link to a specific paragraph within the document.

7. Click the **Hyperlink SubAddress text box**, type **FromTheNorth**, click 🖾 to close the property sheet, then click the **Form View button** 🖾 on the Form Design toolbar to view the updated Courses form
   Your screen should look like Figure I-13. By default, a hyperlink label appears in blue and is underlined. This style is similar to the way hyperlinks usually appear on Web pages.

8. Click the **Directions from the north hyperlink**
   The Directions document appears in Word, as shown in Figure I-14. A hyperlink that has been clicked changes from blue to purple, similar to Web hyperlinks. You can copy, paste, and modify the hyperlink to create a link to the directions from the south bookmark within the Directions document.

9. Close the Word window, then save and close the Courses form

FIGURE I-12: Insert Hyperlink dialog box

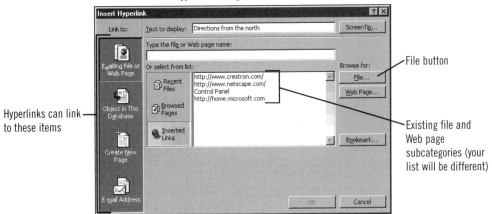

Hyperlinks can link
to these items

File button

Existing file and
Web page
subcategories (your
list will be different)

FIGURE I-13: Hyperlink label displayed in Form view

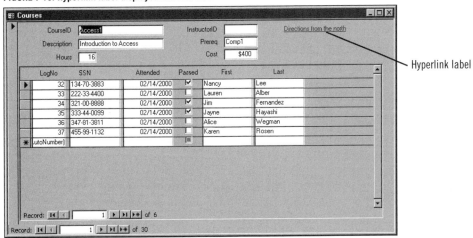

Hyperlink label

FIGURE I-14: Directions to the Media Loft Corporate Word document with bookmark highlighted

Directions to
MediaLoft Corporate
Word document

Back button

FromTheNorth
bookmark

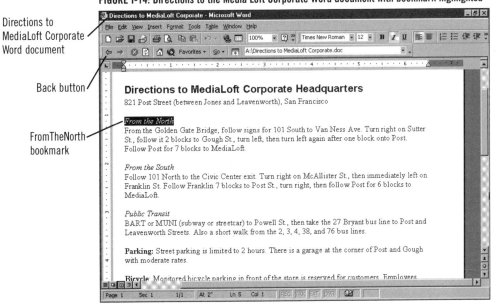

Analyzing Data with Excel

Excel, the spreadsheet software program within the Microsoft Office Suite, is an excellent tool for projecting numeric trends into the future. For example, you may wish to analyze the impact of a price increase on budget or income projections by applying several different numbers. This reiterative analysis is sometimes called "what-if" analysis. **What-if analysis** allows a user to apply assumptions interactively to a set of numbers and watch the resulting calculated formulas update instantly. This is a very popular use for Excel. You can use the **Analyze It with MS Excel** feature to quickly copy Access data to Excel. **Scenario** David has been asked by the Accounting Department to provide some Access data in an Excel spreadsheet so they can analyze how various percentage increases in the cost of the Access classes would affect each of the departments. He has gathered the raw data into a report, called Access Courses Report, and will use the power of Excel to analyze the impact of increased costs.

Steps

1. Click **Reports** on the Objects bar, click the **Access Courses Report**, click the **OfficeLinks button list arrow** on the Database toolbar, then click **Analyze It with MS Excel**
   The data within the report was automatically exported into an Excel spreadsheet, as shown in Figure I-15. When you use the Analyze It with MS Excel or Publish It with MS Word buttons, the spreadsheet or document you create has the same name as the Access object, and it is usually automatically saved in the My Documents folder of your C: drive. You can send the **recordset** (the fields and records) of a table, query, form, or report object to Excel using the Analyze It with MS Excel button.

2. Click cell **G1** (column G, row 1), type **Increase**, click cell **A16**, type **Increase %**, click cell **A17** (column A, row 17), type **10%**, then press **[Enter]**
   Cell G2 will contain a formula that calculates the additional increase in cost (in column E) for the Access classes. Cell A17 stores an "assumption" that will be used in the formula, the 10% growth factor.

3. Click cell **G2**, type **=E2*A17**, then press **[Enter]**
   Your screen should look like Figure I-16. All formulas in Excel begin with an equal sign. This formula multiplies the cost value in cell E3 by 10% to calculate the $20.00 increase for the Introduction to Access class. The Accounting Department completed this Excel spreadsheet analysis in another spreadsheet file.

4. Click **File** on the Excel menu bar, click **Close** to close the **Attendance Log Report file**, click **No** if prompted to save changes, click the **Open button**, locate your Project Disk, then double-click the **Final Attendance Log Report**
   The Final Attendance Log Report has subtotaled and graphed the increased cost for Access classes for each department, as shown in Figure I-17. The 10% cost increase assumption in cell A22 is shaded bright yellow.

5. Click cell **A22**, type **12%**, then press **[Enter]**
   By changing assumption values, Excel automatically updates all dependent formulas and graphs. You can enter any number in cell A22 to see "what if" the percentage increased by different amounts.

6. Click **File** on the Excel menu bar, click Exit to close **Final Attendance Log Report**, then click **Yes** if prompted to save the changes

FIGURE I-15: Attendance Log Report spreadsheet

Access Courses
Report data in an
Excel spreadsheet

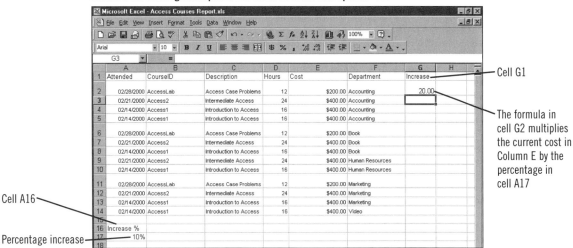

FIGURE I-16: Entering assumptions and formulas in an Excel spreadsheet

Cell G1

The formula in
cell G2 multiplies
the current cost in
Column E by the
percentage in
cell A17

Cell A16

Percentage increase

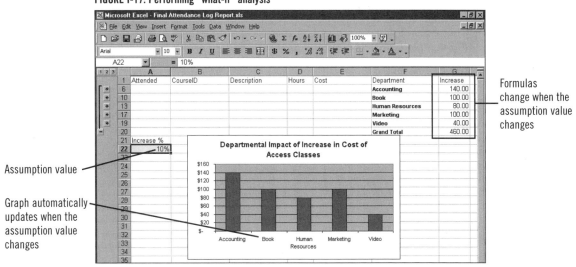

FIGURE I-17: Performing "what-if" analysis

Formulas
change when the
assumption value
changes

Assumption value

Graph automatically
updates when the
assumption value
changes

Copying Data to Word

Word, the word processing program within the Microsoft Office Suite, is a premier tool for entering, editing, and formatting large paragraphs of text. You may wish to copy the recordset from an Access table, query, form, or report into a Word document in order to integrate the Access data with a larger word-processed document. You can use the **Publish it with MS Word** feature to quickly copy Access data to Word. You can send the **recordset** (the fields and records) of a table, query, form, or report object to Word using the Publish It with MS Word button. Table I-3 lists a variety of other techniques for copying Access data to Word. Scenario> David has been asked to comment on the Access courses his department has provided. He will use the Office Links buttons to send the Access Courses Report to Word, then summarize his thoughts about the classes in a paragraph of text in the Word document.

Steps

Trouble?

If a dialog box appears indicating that the file already exists, click Yes to replace the existing file.

1. Click **Access Courses Report**, click the **OfficeLinks button list arrow** 🗔▾ on the Database toolbar, then click **Publish It with MS Word** 📄

   The records from the Access Courses Report object appear in a Word document with an **RTF (rich text format)** file format, as shown in Figure I-18. The RTF format does not support all advanced Word features, but it does support basic formatting embellishments such as multiple fonts, colors, and font sizes. The RTF file format is commonly used when two different word processing programs need to use the same file. You can send the **recordset** (the fields and records) of a table, query, form, or report object to Word using the Publish It with MS Word button.

2. Press **[Enter]** three times to increase the space between the top of the document and the Access information, press **[Ctrl][Home]** to position the insertion point at the top of the document, then type the following:

   To: Management Committee
   From: [*type your name*]
   Re: Analysis of Access Courses
   Date: [*type the current date*]

   The following information shows the recent demand for Access training. The information is sorted by department, and shows that the Accounting Department has had the greatest demand for Access courses. Since Access databases are currently being developed in many MediaLoft areas, I predict that the demand for Access training will increase in the near future.

3. Proofread your document, which should now look like Figure I-19, then click the **Print button** 🖨

4. Click **File** on the menu bar, click **Exit**, then click **No** to close the Access Courses Report document without saving it

FIGURE I-18: Publishing an Access report to Word

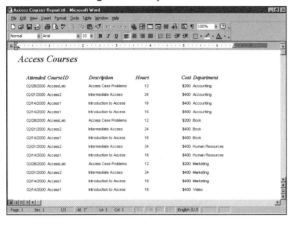

FIGURE I-19: Using Word to enter text

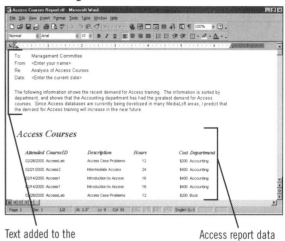

Text added to the
Word document

Access report data

TABLE I-3: Techniques to copy Access data to other applications

technique	button or menu option	description
OfficeLinks buttons		Sends selected data to Excel or Word
	Analyze It with MS Excel	Sends a selected table, query, form, or report object's records to Excel
	Publish It with MS Word	Sends a selected table, query, form, or report object's records to Word
	Merge It with MS Word	Helps merge the selected table or query recordset with a Word document
Office Clipboard	Copy and Paste	Copies selected fields and records in a datasheet or a record in a form to the Clipboard. Open a Word document or Excel spreadsheet, click where you want to paste the data, then click the Paste button. The copied data remains on the Office Clipboard until you close all open Office applications in case you want to paste it again.
Exporting	File on the menu bar, then Export	Copies information from an Access object into a different file format
Drag and drop	Right-click an empty space on the taskbar, then choose the Tile Windows Horizontally or Tile Windows Vertically option	With the windows tiled, drag the Access table, query, form, or report object icon from the Access window to the target (Excel or Word) window. You cannot drag an object icon from one window to the next if the windows are maximized.

Creating form letters with Merge It to MS Word

You can merge the information in a table or query with a Word document to create form letters by clicking the object, then clicking the Merge It to MS Word button. Word will start and load a blank document that will serve as the form letter. Type the standard text into the document, then use the Insert Merge Field button on the Mail Merge toolbar to position the table or query fields in the appropriate positions in the letter. Merge the Access data into the form letter by clicking the Merge to New Document button also on the Mail Merge toolbar within Word.

Exporting Data

Exporting is a way to send Access information to another database, spreadsheet, or file format. Exporting is the opposite of importing. Importing is a process to copy and paste information *into* an Access database, whereas exporting is a process used to copy and paste data *out of* the database. Unlike linking, importing and exporting retain no connection between the original source of data. Therefore, when exporting data, changes in either the original Access database or the exported copy do not affect the other. Table I-4 shows the data formats that Microsoft Access can export data to. **Scenario** Jim Fernandez, Office Manager of the MediaLoft Accounting Department, has requested that David export the first six months of training activity into an Excel spreadsheet. Jim wants to use his Excel skills to further analyze the historical training activity data using Excel formulas and graphing tools. David gathered the fields that Jim requested into a query called Accounting Data. David also will provide Jim with a list of the courses offered by the MediaLoft Training Department. David never misses an opportunity to take advantage of the power of Access.

Steps

QuickTip
You can also right-click an object in the database window and click Export from the shortcut menu.

1. Click **Queries** on the Objects bar, click **Accounting Data**, click **File** on the menu bar, then click **Export**
   The Export Query 'Accounting Data' To… dialog box opens, requesting information on the location and format for the exported information.

2. Locate your Project Disk, click the **Save as type list arrow**, click **Microsoft Excel 97-2000**, then click **Save**
   The fields and records in the Accounting Data query have been exported to an Excel file.

3. Right-click the **Start button** in the taskbar, click **Explore**, locate your Project Disk, then double-click the **Accounting Data** Excel file to open it, right-click the **Exploring button** on the task bar, then click **Close**
   Your screen should look like Figure I-20. Each field became a column and each record a row of data within Excel. A common reason to export Access information to Excel is to use Excel's extensive graphing (charting) capabilities. Yet another way to export Access information to Excel is the **drag-and-drop** method.

4. Click **File** on the menu bar, click **Close** to close the **Accounting Data** file (but leave Excel open), click the **New button** 🗋 on the Excel Standard toolbar to open a new workbook, right-click an empty space on the **taskbar**, then click **Tile Windows Vertically**
   Depending upon how many programs you have open, you may have several windows tiled on the screen. If they are too small to work with, close or minimize the windows you do not need and retile the windows. Your screens should look like figure I-21.

5. Click **Tables** on the Objects bar in the Access window, click **Courses** in the Training-I Database window, then drag the **Courses table icon** to cell **A1** in the Excel window
   Your screen should look like Figure I-22. You can drag any table or query object from an Access database window to an Excel window. This action copies the recordset from the Access object to the Excel spreadsheet just as export or copy and paste does.

6. Close the Excel window without saving the changes, then close the **Training-I** database

7. Exit Access

FIGURE I-20: Excel Accounting Data file

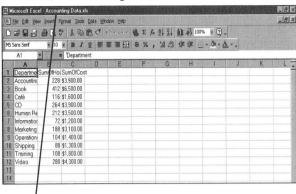

Excel Accounting
Data file

FIGURE I-21: Tiling Windows

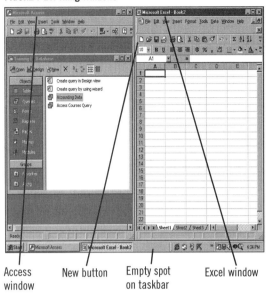

Access   New button   Empty spot   Excel window
window   on taskbar

FIGURE I-22: Drag-and-Drop to Excel

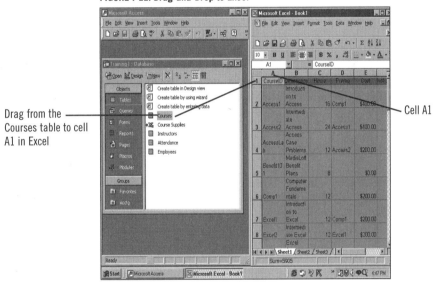

Drag from the
Courses table to cell
A1 in Excel

Cell A1

TABLE I-4: Data formats Microsoft Access can export

application	version or format supported	application	version or format supported
Microsoft Access database	2.0, 7.0/95, 8.0/97, 9.0/2000	Lotus 1-2-3	.wk1 and .wk3
Microsoft Access project	9.0/2000	Delimited text files	All character sets
dBASE	III, III+, IV, and 5	Fixed-width text files	All character sets
Paradox, Paradox for Windows	3.x, 4.x, and 5.0	HTML	1.0 (if a list) 2.0, 3.x (if a table or list)
Microsoft Excel	3.0, 4.0, 5.0, 7.0/95, 8.0/97, 9.0/2000	SQL tables, Microsoft Visual FoxPro, and other data sources that support ODBC protocol	Visual FoxPro 3.0, 5.0, and 6.x

Practice

► Concepts Review

Identify each element of the form's Design view shown in Figure I-23.

FIGURE I-23

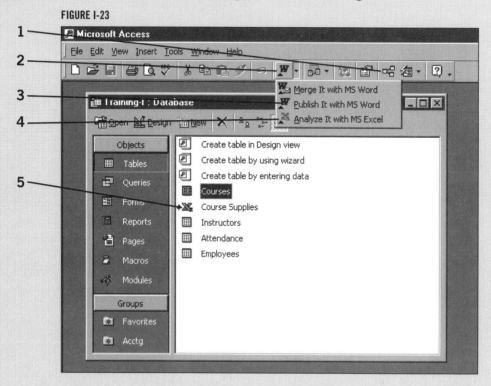

1
2
3
4
5

Match each term with the statement that describes its function.

6. hyperlink
7. junction table
8. linking
9. what-if analysis
10. key field
11. normalization

a. The process of determining the appropriate fields, records, and tables when designing a relational database
b. Testing different assumptions in a spreadsheet
c. Contains foreign key fields that link to the primary key fields of each of two other tables
d. A field that contains unique information for each record
e. A way to connect to data in an external source without copying it
f. A label, button, or image placed on a form that when clicked automatically opens another object, file, e-mail message, or Web address

Select the best answer from the list of choices.

12. **Which of the following is NOT an Access object?**
    a. Query
    b. Report
    c. Table
    d. Spreadsheet

13. **Which of the following is NOT part of the normalization process?**
    a. Creating database hyperlinks
    b. Identifying the correct number of tables within the database
    c. Establishing table relationships
    d. Determining the appropriate fields for the database

14. **Which of the following is NOT true about linking?**
    a. Linking is the same thing as copying and pasting
    b. Changes to linked data will be updated in the original data source
    c. Changes to the original data source will be displayed in the linked data
    d. Linking does not duplicate data

15. **Which of the following software products would most likely be used to analyze and graph the effect of several potential price increases?**
    a. PowerPoint
    b. Excel
    c. Access
    d. Word

16. **Which of the following is NOT an OfficeLinks button?**
    a. Merge it with MS Word
    b. Publish it with MS Word
    c. Present it with MS PowerPoint
    d. Analyze it with MS Excel

▶ Skills Review

1. **Examine Access Objects.**
   a. Start Access, then open the Machinery-I database from your Project Disk.
   b. On a separate piece of paper, list the seven Access objects and the number of each type that exist in the Machinery-I database.
   c. List each Access table name, then use the table's Datasheet and Design views to write down the number of records and fields within each table.

2. **Examine Relationships.**
   a. Click the Relationships button on the Database toolbar.
   b. Drag the ProductID field from the Products table to the ProductID field of the Inventory Transactions table to create a one-to-many relationship between those tables.
   c. Click Enforce Referential Integrity in the Edit Relationships dialog box, then click Create.

d. Drag the PurchaseOrderID field from the Purchase Orders table to the PurchaseOrderID field of the Inventory Transactions table to create a one-to-many relationship between those tables.

e. Click Enforce Referential Integrity in the Edit Relationships dialog box, then click Create.

f. Print the Relationships, then save and close the Relationships window.

3. Importing Data from Excel.

a. Click File on the menu bar, point to the Get External Data option, then click Import.

b. In the Import dialog box, change the Files of type list to Microsoft Excel, then import the Machinery Employees Excel file on your Project Disk.

c. In the Import Spreadsheet Wizard, be sure to specify that the first row contains column headings and that five data records are imported in a new table.

d. Do not make any changes to fields you are importing, and be sure to select the EmpNo field as the table's primary key.

e. Name the new table "Employees".

f. Click the Relationships button on the Database toolbar.

g. Drag the EmpNo field from the Employees table to the EmployeeID field of the Purchase Orders table.

h. Click Enforce Referential Integrity in the Edit Relationships dialog box, then click Create.

i. Save and close the Relationships window.

4. Link Data to Excel.

a. Click File on the menu bar, point to the Get External Data option, then click Link Tables.

b. In the Link dialog box, change the Files of type list to Microsoft Excel, then link to the Machinery Vendors Excel file on your Project Disk.

c. In the Link Spreadsheet Wizard, be sure to specify that the first row contains column headings and that five data records are linked.

d. Name the new table "Vendors".

e. Open the Relationships window.

f. Click the Show Table button on the Relationship toolbar.

g. Double-click the Vendors table in the Show Table dialog box to add it to the Relationships window, then close the Show Table dialog box.

h. Drag the VendorNo field from the Vendors table to the SupplierID field of the Purchase Orders table.

i. Drag the title bars of the field lists in the Relationships window to more clearly present the relationships between the tables.

j. Save and close the Relationships window.

5. Create Hyperlinks.

a. Open the Product Entry Form in Design view.

b. Add a label with the caption "Product Contacts" to the right side of the form.

c. In the Hyperlink Address property of the Product Contacts label, click the Build button, then browse for the Product Contacts file (it is a Word document) on your Project Disk.

d. Close the new label's property sheet, and display the Product Entry Form in Form view.

e. Click the Product Contacts hyperlink, which will open the Product Contacts Word document, then print and close the Product Contacts Word document.

f. Save and then close the Product Entry Form.

6. Analyze Data with Excel.

    a. Click the Reports button on the Object bar, click the Every Product We Lease report, click the Office Links List arrow, then click the Analyze It with MS Excel button to send the information to Excel.

    b. Press [Tab] seven times to move to column H, type "Tax" in cell H1, then press [Enter] to move to cell H2.

    c. In cell H2, type =6%*D2, the formula to calculate tax that is 6% of the Unit Price, then press [Enter].

    d. Print the Excel spreadsheet, then close the Every Product We Lease spreadsheet without saving the changes. Don't exit Excel.

7. Copy Data to Word.

    a. Click the Machinery-I Database button on the taskbar to open the window on your screen.

    b. Click the Reports button on the Objects bar, click the Every Product We Lease report, click the Office Links list arrow, then click the Publish It with MS Word button to send the information to Word.

    c. Click to the right of the "We" in the title and type "Lease".

    d. Press [Ctrl][Home] to go to the top of the document, press the [Enter] key twice, then press [Ctrl][Home] to return to the top of the document.

    e. Type the following at the top of the document:

    INTERNAL MEMO

    From: [Your Name]

    To: Sales Staff

    Date: [Today's Date]

    When quoting prices to customers over the phone, do not forget to mention the long lead times on the Back Hoe and Thatcher products. We usually do not keep these expensive items in stock.

    f. Proofread the document, then print it.

    g. Close the document without saving changes, then exit Word.

8. Export Data.

    a. Right-click an empty space on the taskbar, then choose Tile Windows Vertically.

    b. Click Tables on the Objects bar in the Access window, click the New button on the Excel standard toolbar, then drag the Products table icon to cell A1 in the Excel window.

    c. Maximize the Excel window, click cell A9, and type your name.

    d. Print the Excel spreadsheet, then close the Excel window without saving the Excel spreadsheet.

    e. Maximize the Access window, then click the Employees table.

    f. Choose File from the menu bar, then Export.

    g. Locate your Project Disk, choose Microsoft Excel 97-2000 as the option in the Save as type list, and save the spreadsheet with the name "Employees".

    h. Close the Machinery-I database and exit Access.

► Visual Workshop

Use any technique you wish (drag-and-drop, export, Analyze It with MS Excel, or copy and paste) to copy the Field Goal Stats query to an Excel spreadsheet shown in Figure I-24. Enter the formula =B2/C2 in cell D2 to determine the field goal percentage. Enter your name in cell F2, then print the first page of the spreadsheet.

FIGURE I-24

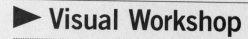

Access 2000

Creating
Data Access Pages

Objectives

The Internet has an enormous wealth of information, unlimited potential for business opportunity, and ability for instant global communication. A tremendous amount of energy is being focused on how to connect **World Wide Web pages**, which are hyperlinked documents that make the Internet easy to navigate, directly to underlying databases. Linked pages enable employees, customers, or vendors to view, find, enter, edit, analyze, and order products via an Internet connection rather than having direct access to the database file. Access 2000 provides a connection between Web pages and an Access database through the **page** object. Scenario MediaLoft employees are located throughout the United States, and David Dumont would like to give them the ability to access the Training-J database via the Internet.

Understanding the World Wide Web

Creating Web pages that dynamically interact with an Access database is an exciting process that involves many underlying technologies. Understanding how the Internet, the World Wide Web, and Web pages interact is extremely important in order to successfully connect a Web page to an underlying Access database. **Scenario** David reviews some of the history and key terminology of the Internet and World Wide Web to better prepare himself for the task of connecting a Web page to an Access database.

Details

The **Internet** is a worldwide network of computer networks that sends and receives information through a common **protocol** (set of rules) called **TCP/IP** (Transmission Control Protocol/Internet Protocol).

The Internet supports many services including:

- **E-Mail:** electronic mail
- **File Transfer:** uploading and downloading files
- **Newsgroups:** similar to e-mail, but messages are posted in a "public mailbox" that is available to any subscriber rather than sent to one individual
- **World Wide Web (WWW):** a vast number of linked documents stored on thousands of different Web servers

The Internet has experienced tremendous growth in the past decade partly because of the following three major factors:

- In the early 1990s, the U.S. government lifted restrictions on commercial Internet traffic, causing explosive growth in electronic commerce activities.
- Technological innovations resulted in breakthroughs in hardware such as faster computer processors and storage devices, and in networking media such as fiber-optics and satellite transmission.
- Less expensive and easier-to-use Internet systems and program software were developed for both **clients** (your computer) and **servers** (the computer that "serves" the information to you from the Internet).

Behind all of these innovations are many amazing people. Of special note is the scientist who saw the need to easily share real-time information with colleagues. This scientific initiative grew into today's World Wide Web. Table J-1 introduces more Internet and World Wide Web terminology. Figure J-1 shows how hyperlinks work on a Web page.

FIGURE J-1: Hyperlinks on a Web page

URL

Hyperlinks can be pictures, clip art, or text.

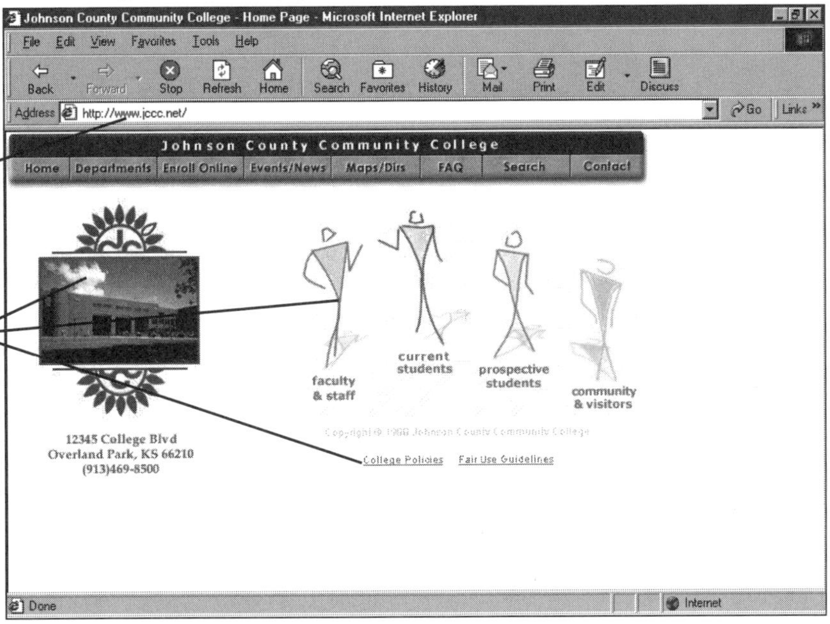

TABLE J-1: Internet and World Wide Web terminology

term	definition
Web page	A special type of file created with HTML code that contains hyperlinks to other files
Web server	A computer that stores Web pages
Hyperlink	Text (usually underlined), an image, or an icon on a Web page that when clicked, presents another Web page. Hyperlinks can jump to another part of the same Web page, a different page on the same Web server, or to a different Web server in another part of the world.
HTML	Hypertext Markup Language. HTML is a special programming language used to create Web pages. An HTML programmer writes HTML code to create a Web page. Nonprogrammers create HTML Web pages using FrontPage or by converting files such as Word, Excel, and PowerPoint files into HTML Web pages using menu options within those programs.
Browser	Software such as Microsoft's Internet Explorer (IE) or Netscape Navigator used to find and display Web pages. HTML files created through the Access Page object are best displayed with IE version 5 or later.
ISP	Internet Service Provider. To access the Internet from a home computer, your computer first must dial an ISP that connects your computer with the Internet. National ISPs include America Online, The Microsoft Network, and Sprint's Earthlink Internet. Hundreds of regional and local ISPs exist as well.
Modem	Short for *modulate-demodulate*. A modem is hardware (usually located inside the computer) that converts digital computer signals to analog telephone signals to allow a computer to send and receive information across ordinary telephone lines.
URL	Uniform Resource Locator. Each resource on the Internet (including Web pages) has an address so that other computers can accurately and consistently locate and view it. http://www.course.com/products/ is the URL for the Web page that displays information about Course Technology, Inc. (the publisher of this textbook.) There is never a space in a URL.
Domain name	The middle part of a URL, such as www.course.com. The middle part of the domain name is often either the company's name or words that describe the information you will find at that site. The last part of the domain name indicates the type of site, such as commercial (com), educational (edu), military (mil), organizational (org), or governmental (gov).
Home page	The first page displayed on a Web server.

Using Hyperlink Fields

A **Hyperlink field** is a field defined with the Hyperlink data type in Table Design view. The entry in a hyperlink field can be a **Universal Naming Convention (UNC) path** or a **Uniform Resource Locator (URL) address**. Table J-2 gives more information about networks. URLs may also specify an Internet e-mail address, a newsgroup address, an intranet Web page address, or a file on a local area network. **Scenario** Many MediaLoft employees have requested more information about the internal classes. To accommodate these requests, David creates a Hyperlink field called Online Resources to store the URL for a World Wide Web page that contains up-to-date information on the subject of the class.

Steps

1. Start **Access**, open the **Training-J** database from your Project Disk, click **Tables** on the Objects bar, click the **Courses table**, click the **Design button** in the Database window, then maximize both the database and the table windows (if not already maximized)
   The Courses table opens in Design view, where you can add fields and specify their properties.

2. Click the first empty **Field Name cell** below InstructorID, type **Online Resources**, press **[Tab]**, press **h**, click the **Save button**, then click the **Datasheet View button**
   The Courses table with the new Online Resources field opens in datasheet view.

> **QuickTip**
> The first part of an Internet Web address (http://) can be omitted when entering a URL into a hyperlink field.

3. Press **[Tab]** six times to move to the new Online Resources field, type **www.microsoft.com/access**, press **[↓]** point to the right edge of the **Online Resources field name**, double-click **↔**, then click
   Your screen should look like Figure J-2. The column is widened to display all of the data in the Online Resources field. Note that hyperlinks appear underlined in bright blue just like text hyperlinks on Web pages.

> **QuickTip**
> [Ctrl]['] copies the entry in the field of the previous record to the same field of the current record.

4. Press **[Ctrl][']**, then press **[↓]**

5. Point to **www.microsoft.com/access** in either record so that the pointer changes to 👆, then click **www.microsoft.com/access**
   If you are currently connected to the Internet and have Microsoft Internet Explorer browser software loaded on your computer, your screen should look similar to Figure J-3. Netscape Communicator is another popular browser program that will also open and display HTML files. Web pages are continually updated as new information is announced, so the content of the Web page itself may vary. If you are not already connected to the Internet, your **dialer** (software that helps you dial and connect to your ISP) may appear. Once connected to your ISP, the Microsoft Access Web page should appear.

> **QuickTip**
> Visited links will change to the color purple.

6. Click the **Courses: Table button** in the taskbar, click the **Online Resources field** for record **5** (Introduction to Excel), type **www.microsoft.com/excel**, click the **Online Resources field** for record **11** (Introduction to Netscape), type **www.netscape.com**, then press **[Enter]**
   Hyperlink entries can point to a different Web page on the same Web server or to an entirely different Web server.

7. Click **www.netscape.com**
   The Netscape Netcenter Web page appears on your screen.

8. Right-click the **Courses: Table button** on the taskbar, click **Close**, click **Yes** to save the changes to the layout of the table, then close any open browser windows

FIGURE J-2: A hyperlink entry

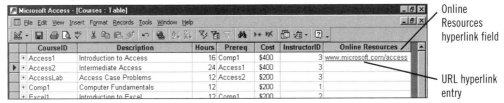

Online Resources hyperlink field

URL hyperlink entry

FIGURE J-3: www.microsoft.com/access Web page

Microsoft Internet Explorer (browser software)

URL

Web page

TABLE J-2: Types of networks

type of network	description
LAN (local area network)	Connects local resources such as file servers, user computers, and printers by a direct cable. LANs do not cross a public thoroughfare such as a street because of distance and legal restrictions on how far and where cables can be pulled.
WAN (wide area network)	Created when a LAN is connected to an existing telecommunications network, such as the phone system, to reach resources across public thoroughfares such as streets and rivers
Internet	Largest WAN in the world, spanning the entire globe and connecting many diverse computer architectures
Intranet	WANs that support the same services as the Internet (i.e., e-mail, Web pages, and file transfer) and are built with the same technologies (e.g., TCP/IP communications protocol, HTML Web pages, and browser software), but are designed and secured for the internal purposes of a business. To secure intranet information and resources from outsiders, passwords and data encryption techniques are used.

CLUES TO USE

Understanding the Universal Naming Convention (UNC)

Universal Naming Convention (UNC) is another naming convention (in addition to URL) to locate a file on a network. The structure of a UNC is \\server\sharedfoldername\filename. UNCs are used for local resources, such as a file stored on a local area network. URL addresses are used for Web pages on the Internet or a company intranet.

Creating Pages for Interactive Reporting

The **page** object, also called the **data access page (DAP),** is a special Access object used to create Web pages designed for viewing, editing, and entering data stored in a Microsoft Access database. Data access pages may also include data from other sources such as Microsoft Excel or a Microsoft SQL Server database. You create data access page objects in Access, but the Web pages they create are separate HTML files stored outside the Access database file. DAPs appear when you click Pages on the Objects bar. Table J-3 describes three major purposes for a DAP.

Scenario David uses the page object to publish interactive reports from the Training-J database that can be viewed using Internet Explorer.

Steps

1. Click **Pages** on the Objects bar, then double-click **Create data access page by using wizard**

   You can create a page object using a wizard or develop it from scratch in Design view.

2. Click the **Tables/Queries list arrow,** click **Query: Attendance Details,** click the **Select All Fields button** `>>`, click **Next,** click **Department** as the grouping level, click the **Select Field button** `>`, then click **Next**

   The Page Wizard prompts for sorting fields as well as a page title.

Trouble?

Click the Page View button if you are viewing Page Design view instead of Page view.

3. Click the **first sort list arrow,** click **Last,** click **Next,** type **Department Training Information,** click the **Open the page option button,** then click **Finish**

   Your screen should look like Figure J-4. The **Expand button** indicates that detail records grouped within the Accounting Department can be viewed by clicking that button. The **navigation buttons** are similar to those for a datasheet or form. The **filter** and **sort buttons** appear on the right side of the navigation buttons of a page object and provide filtering and sorting capabilities to the person who is viewing this information as a Web page when the data access page is posted to an Internet or intranet Web server.

Trouble?

If your page doesn't display correctly, click the Page Design View button, then click the Page View button.

4. Click the **Expand button** `⊕`, click **1/31/00** in the Attended text box, then click the **Sort Ascending button** `↑↓` on the Attendance Details 1 of 16 navigation bar

   Your screen should look like Figure J-5. The Expand button has become the **Collapse button.** When clicked, the Collapse button collapses the detail records within that group.

Trouble?

When you click a text box on a data access page used for interactive reporting, you may not see the blinking insertion point inside the text box.

5. Click the **Last Record button** `▶|` on the Attendance Details Department 1 of 11 navigation buttons to display the Video group, click `⊕`, click **Lee** in the Last field, then click the **Filter by Selection button** `🔽` on the Attendance Detail 1 of 21 navigation buttons

   Your screen should look like Figure J-6.

6. Click the **Remove Filter button** `🔽` on the Attendance Details 1 of 11 toolbar to view all 21 detail records within the Video department, click the **Save button** `💾` on the Page View toolbar, locate your Project disk, type **Department Training** in the File name text box, then click **Save**

   You do not need to save the HTML file with the same name as the corresponding DAP, but it helps keep them organized if they have similar names. An HTML file named Department Training has been saved to your Project Disk. Internet Explorer opens HTML files as Web pages.

7. Close the Department Training Information page object window

FIGURE J-4: Department Training Information data access page

Page Design View button

Expand button

Department Navigation buttons

Filter and Sort buttons

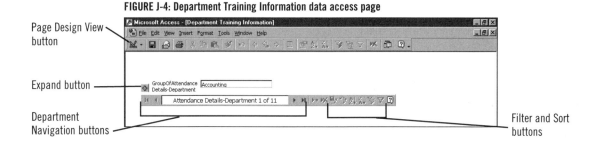

FIGURE J-5: Expanded and sorted data access page

Last field is listed at the top because that's how the detail records are sorted

Attended field

Accounting employees took 16 classes

Detail record for the Accounting Department

Sort Ascending button

11 different departments

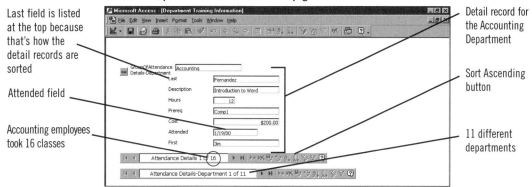

FIGURE J-6: Filtered data access page

Within the video department, Nancy Lee attended 11 classes

"Lee" entry in Last text box

Filter by Selection button

Department Last Record button

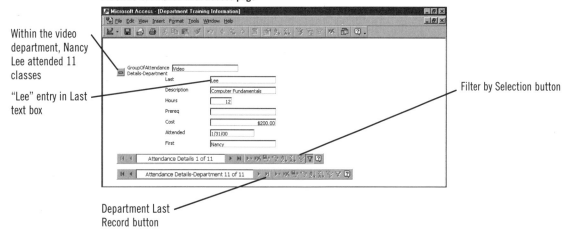

TABLE J-3: Purposes for data access pages

purpose	description
Interactive reporting	To publish summaries of information using sorting, grouping, and filtering techniques
Data entry	To view, add, and edit records
Data analysis	To analyze the data using pivot tables and charts

Creating Pages for Data Entry

Using a data access page for data entry is similar to using an Access form except that the data access page also creates a Web page to be viewed through Microsoft Internet Explorer. Within the data access page you can view, enter, edit, and delete data, just like in a form. ▶Scenario◀ The Human Resources department has offered to help David find, enter, and update information on instructors. David creates a data access page based on the Instructors table within the Training-J database to give the HR department the ability to also view and update this data using Internet Explorer.

Steps

1. Double-click the **Create data access page by using wizard**, click the **Tables/Queries list arrow**, click **Table: Instructors**, click the **Select All Fields button** >> , click **Next**, then click **Finish** to accept the rest of the defaults
   The data access page opens in **Page Design view**, as shown in Figure J-7. The Toolbox and the Alignment and Sizing toolbars may be open. The Field list, which organizes fields and objects much like Internet Explorer organizes files and folders, is open. Page objects contain controls just as reports and forms do.

2. Click the **Page View button** 🖽 on the Page Design toolbar to view the data access page, click the **Save button** 🖫 on the Page View toolbar, locate your Project Disk, type **Instructor Updates** in the File name text box, then click **Save**
   The Instructors data access page shows the three records that are currently in the Instructors table. You *could* use this page object within Access to enter or edit data, but the purpose of a data access page isn't for data entry (forms are much more powerful data entry tools if you have direct access to the database file). The real power of the data access page object is its ability to create dynamic HTML files (Web pages) that can be used to enter and update data by people who *do not* have direct access to the database, but who *do* have Internet Explorer browser software.

3. Close the **Instructor Updates** data access page
   Use Microsoft Internet Explorer to open the Instructor Updates HTML file to make changes to the Training-J database *even though you are not directly using the Training-J database file.*

Trouble?

You do not need to be connected to the Internet to load Web pages stored in your Project Disk.

4. Click **Start** on the taskbar, point to **Programs**, click **Internet Explorer** (IE), click **File** on the IE menu bar, click **Open**, click **Browse** in the Open dialog box, locate your Project Disk, click **Instructor Updates.htm**, click **Open,** then click **OK**
   The Instructor Updates.htm file opens in Internet Explorer, as shown in Figure J-8.

Trouble?

You cannot press [Page Up] and [Page Down] to move from record to record when viewing records through an HTML file.

5. Click the **New Record button** ▶ on the navigation bar, type **Sarah**, press **[Tab]**, type **Chalupa**, press **[Tab]**, type **9/1/00**, click the **Previous Record button** ◄ , then click the **Next Record button** ▶
   You verify that the record for Sarah Chalupa was entered successfully.

6. Close **Internet Explorer**, click the **Training-J database button** on the taskbar, click **Tables** on the Objects bar, then double-click the **Instructors table** to open it in Datasheet view
   Your screen should look like Figure J-9. The new record appears in the table. You used an HTML Web page opened in Internet Explorer to dynamically update an underlying Access database. If you had been using the Internet or a company intranet, the Instructor Updates.htm file would have to have been stored on a Web server rather than your Project Disk. To open the Instructor Updates.htm file on a Web server, you have to enter the URL or UNC address for the file.

7. Close the **Instructors** datasheet

FIGURE J-7: Page Design view

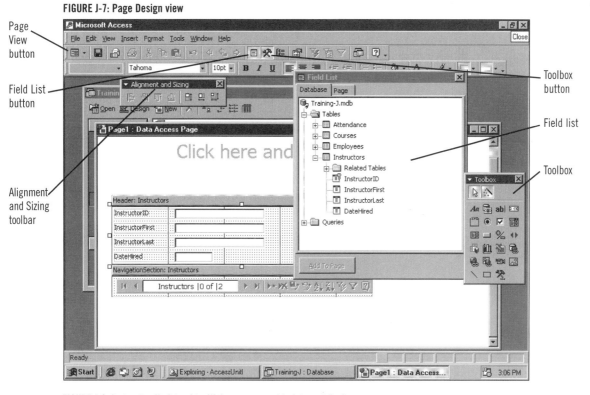

Page View button

Field List button

Alignment and Sizing toolbar

Toolbox button

Field list

Toolbox

FIGURE J-8: Instructor Updates.htm Web page opened in Internet Explorer

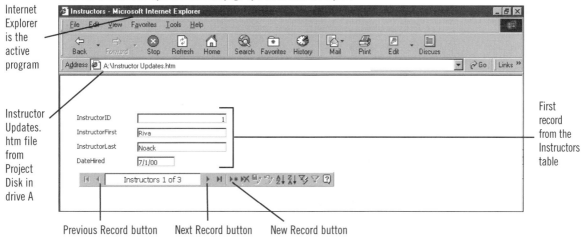

Internet Explorer is the active program

Instructor Updates. htm file from Project Disk in drive A

First record from the Instructors table

Previous Record button   Next Record button   New Record button

FIGURE J-9: Updated Instructors table

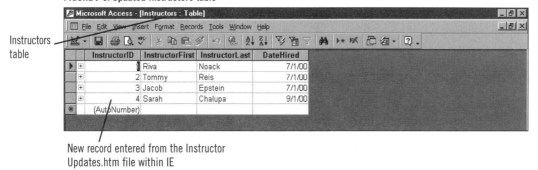

Instructors table

New record entered from the Instructor Updates.htm file within IE

Access 2000

Creating Pages for Data Analysis

A **PivotTable list** is a bound control created in Design view of a data access page. It helps you analyze data by allowing you to organize data in many different ways. In a pivot table, one field is used for the column heading, one field is used for the row heading, and one field is summarized for each column and row. The PivotTable list control presents information in a data access page in a way that is similar to how a Crosstab query presents data in a query. You cannot use the PivotTable List control to edit, delete, or add new data. In this respect, DAPs created for data analysis using the PivotTable List control are similar to those created for interactive reporting. Neither can be used to update data. **Scenario** David creates a data access page using the PivotTable list control so that information about course attendance can be viewed in many different ways.

QuickTip

You can move the Alignment and Spacing toolbar, the Field list, and the Toolbox by dragging their title bars.

1. Click **Pages** on the Objects bar, double-click **Create data access page in Design view**, then maximize the Design View window
   The Design view of a page, as shown in Figure J-10, is very similar to that of a form or report. Table J-4 summarizes some of the key terminology used in Design view.

Trouble?

Click the Field List button 📄 to toggle it on (if necessary), click the Toolbox toolbar button 🛠 to toggle it on (if necessary).

2. Click the **Office PivotTable button** 📊 on the Toolbox, click the **Queries Expand button** ➕ in the Field list, then drag the **Department Charges** query into the upper-left area of the **Section: Unbound**
   The Layout Wizard helps guide you through the rest of the process.

3. Click the **PivotTable List option button**, click **OK**, then click 📄 to toggle the Field list off
   Your screen should look like Figure J-11. The four fields within the Department Charges query are the column headings in the PivotTable List control.

4. Point to the **middle sizing handle** on the right edge of the PivotTable List control, drag ↔ to the right edge of the section to view the Cost field, then click the **Page View button** 📄 on the Page Design toolbar
   The data access page appears within Access, and the fields display interactive list arrows.

5. Click the **Department list arrow**, click the **(Show All) check box** to clear all of the check marks, scroll and click the **Video checkbox**, then click **OK**
   Only the records with "Video" in the Department field appear. Choices made within these lists are temporary and are not saved with the page object, so every time you open the page, all of the records are visible.

Trouble?

The PivotTable List control must be selected before you can move the fields within it. The PivotTable List control will have a hashed border when selected.

6. Click the **Design View button** 📄, **click the PivotTable List control**, right-click the **Description field name**, click **Move to Row Area**, then click 📄
   Your screen should look like Figure J-12. The Description field entries are now organized as row headings, and the other fields from the Department Charges query still appear as column headings. The PivotTable List control's major benefit is its ability to quickly rearrange data in many different ways.

QuickTip

Saving an HTML file saves both the HTML file and the corresponding DAP with the same name.

7. Click the **Save button** 💾 on the Page View toolbar, locate your Project Disk, type **Department Pivot**, click **Save**, then close to access page
   The new Department Pivot data access page object is stored within the Training-J database window and the Department Pivot HTML file is stored on your Project Disk. The PivotTable List control looks and behaves the same way whether you access it as a DAP within Access or view the corresponding HTML file as a Web page within IE.

FIGURE J-10: Design view of a Page

Section: Unbound control

Queries Expand button in Field list

Office PivotTable button

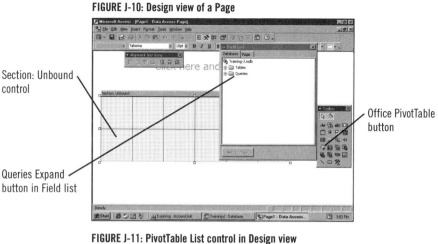

FIGURE J-11: PivotTable List control in Design view

Description field within the PivotTable List control

Sizing handle

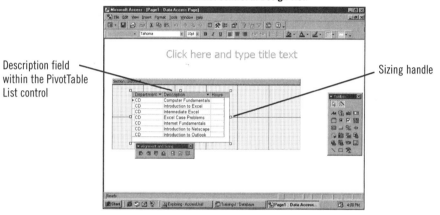

FIGURE J-12: Modified PivotTable List control in Page view

Row heading

Collapse buttons

Column headings

Scroll to view more course descriptions

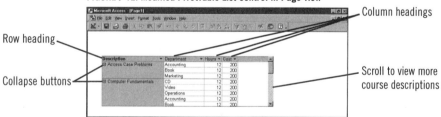

TABLE J-4: Design view terminology

term	definition
Field list	List that contains all of the field names that can be added to an object in Design view
Toolbox toolbar	Toolbar that contains all of the bound and unbound controls that can be added to the object in Design view
Control	Each individual element that can be added, deleted, or modified in an object's Design view
Bound controls	Controls that display data from an underlying recordset. Common bound controls are text boxes, list boxes, and pivot table lists
Unbound controls	Controls that do not display data from an underlying recordset. Common unbound controls for a page are labels, lines, and toolbars
Sections	Areas of the object that contain controls. Sections determine where and how often a control will appear or print
Properties	Characteristics that further describe the selected object, section, or control

Working in Page Design View

Like every other object within Access, page objects have a Design view that you use to modify the object's structure. Page Design view closely resembles that of Form and Report Design view, but there are some key differences, as identified in Table J-5. **Scenario** David works in Page Design view to add a caption and some formatting enhancements to the Department Training Page object.

Steps 1 2 3 4

1. Click the **Department Training page**, click the **Design button** in the Database window, then click the **Sorting and Grouping button** on the Page Design toolbar
   The Sorting and Grouping dialog box opens, as shown in Figure J-13. Several options are available, including the ability to display a caption section and record navigation section.

2. Click the **Caption Section property text box**, click the **Caption section property list arrow**, click **Yes**, then click
   The Sorting and Grouping dialog box closes. The Caption section is often used for descriptive labels.

3. Click the **GroupOfAttendance Details-Department label** in the Header: Attendance Details-Department section, press **[Delete]**, click the **Label button** on the Toolbox, click on the **left side of the Caption section**, then type **DEPARTMENTS**
   Your screen should look similar to Figure J-14. Many of the moving and resizing skills you learned in Form and Report Design view work exactly the same way in Page Design view, so you can move and resize controls if necessary.

4. Click **Click here and type title text** at the top of the page, then type **Attendance Records Grouped by Department**
   The body of the page is not a part of any section, but rather is the title text for the HTML Web page that this DAP creates.

5. Click the **Save button** on the Page Design toolbar, then click the **Page View button**
   The changes you made to the Department Training page are displayed in the Page view.

6. Close the Department Training page object
   The Department Training page looks and behaves the same whether you are viewing it in Page view through Access or as a Web page opened in Internet Explorer.

7. Start **Internet Explorer**, click **File** on the menu bar, click **Open**, click **Browse**, locate your Project Disk, double-click **Department Training**, then click **OK**
   After a few moments, the Department Training HTML file opens within Internet Explorer, as shown in Figure J-15.

8. Close **Internet Explorer**

FIGURE J-13: Sorting and Grouping dialog box for the Data Access page

Caption Section
property text box

Record Navigation
Section property
text box

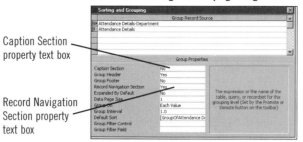

FIGURE J-14: Adding label controls

New label in
Caption section

Label button

Label was deleted

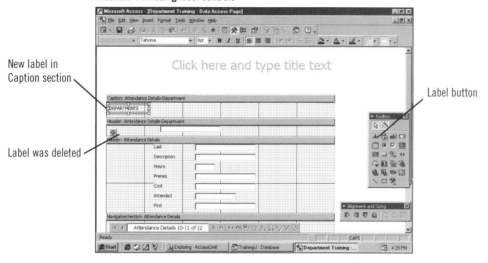

FIGURE J-15: Viewing the updated Web page in Internet Explorer

New label added
to the body

New label in
Caption section

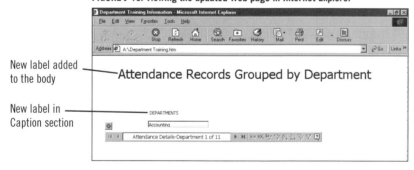

TABLE J-5: New Features within Page Design view

item	description
Body	Basic design surface of the data access page that displays text, controls, and sections. When viewed in Page view or in Internet Explorer, the content in the body automatically adjusts itself to fit the size of the browser
Sections	New sections within a page object include the record navigation section used to display the navigation toolbar and the caption section used to display text. Neither of these two new sections can contain bound controls
Positioning	By default, the position of text, sections, and other elements in the body of a page are relative to one another (determined by the preceding content on the page)
Toolbox	Several new controls are displayed in the Toolbox toolbar that are specific to page objects, including the Office PivotTable, Expand, and Record Navigation controls
Field list	The Field List window displays *all* Tables, Queries, and associated fields within them. The Page tab of the Field list displays the bound controls and grouping choices within the Details section

Inserting Hyperlinks to Other Pages

Once the Access page objects are finished, you may wish to connect them using hyperlinks. Hyperlinks allow the user to access one Web page from another with a single click, just like World Wide Web pages reference other Web pages throughout the Internet. You add hyperlinks to pages in Page Design view. Then, when you browse through the pages, you can jump between them by clicking the hyperlinks. **Scenario** David wants to create a hyperlink between the Department Training and Department Pivot data access pages so that one page can be accessed from the other. He uses Page Design view to add the hyperlinks to both pages.

Steps 123⁴

1. Click the **Training-J** database button in the taskbar (if necessary), click **Pages** on the Objects bar, click **Department Pivot**, then click the **Design button** ◤ in the database window
   Hyperlink controls are added to page objects by using the Hyperlink control.

2. Click the **Hyperlink button** 🖳 on the Toolbox, then click the hyperlink pointer ⬚ in the page body above the left edge of the Section: Unbound control
   The Insert Hyperlink dialog box opens, as shown in Figure J-16. You may choose links from existing files, Web pages, pages in this database, new pages, or e-mail addresses.

3. Click **Page in This Database**, click **Department Training** from the Select a page in this database list, click **OK**, then click the **Page View button** 🔲 on the Page Design toolbar
   The Department Pivot page displays the new hyperlink. Pointing to a hyperlink on a page displays information about the hyperlink.

Trouble?
If Netscape opens the Web page, you may want to change file type associations within Explorer so that IE is used to open HTML files.

4. Place the pointer over **Department Training** so that the pointer changes to 🖑, observe the ScreenTip, then click the **Department Training hyperlink** to test the link
   The Department Training Web page with records grouped by department should be displayed within an IE window. Now add a hyperlink to go from the Department Training Web page back to the Department Pivot Web page.

5. Click the **Department Pivot button** in the taskbar to return to Access, save and close the **Department Pivot** page, click **Department Training** page object in the Training-J database window, then click ◤

6. Click 🖳 on the Toolbox, then click ⬚ on the **page body** above the left edge of the Caption: Attendance Details-Department section

7. Click **Page in This Database** in the Insert Hyperlink dialog box, click the **Department Pivot** page, click **OK**, then click 🔲

Trouble?
To make sure that IE is displaying the latest version of a Web page, click the Refresh button 🔃 on the IE Standard Buttons toolbar.

8. Click the **Department Pivot hyperlink**, then click the **Print button** on the IE Standard Buttons toolbar
   The Department Pivot Web page should open in IE, as shown in Figure J-17. Now you can move between the two pages by clicking their hyperlinks.

9. Close IE, then close the Training-J database, saving any changes.

FIGURE J-16: Insert Hyperlink dialog box

Existing file or Web Page button is currently chosen

Click to view Page in This Database

Inserted Links is chosen

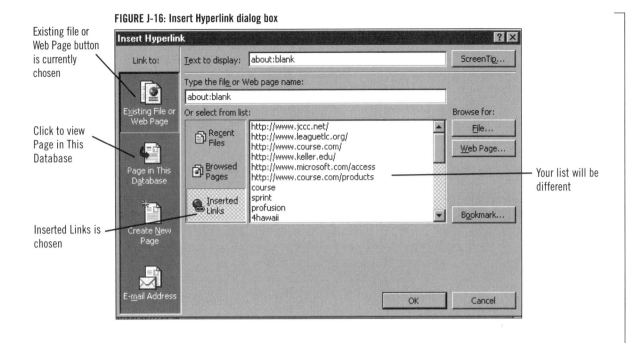

Your list will be different

FIGURE J-17: Department Pivot Web page viewed through IE

Refresh button

Hyperlink

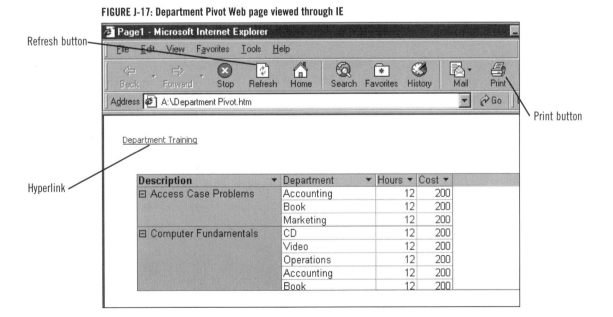

Print button

Publishing Web Pages to Web Servers

Access 2000

Making Web pages available over the Internet or a company intranet requires publishing your Web pages to a **Web server**, a computer devoted to storing and downloading Web pages. Web servers contain **Web folders**, which are special folders dedicated to storing and organizing Web pages. Once your Web page files are stored appropriately, **clients**, computers with appropriate browser and communication software that have access to the Web folder, may download and use those files. Scenario David reviews the steps necessary to publish the Instructor Updates Web page for use over MediaLoft's intranet.

 Store the Access database in a shared network folder on the Web server

On a network, most folders are not available to everyone, so you must be sure to put the Access database in a folder that the appropriate people have permission to use (**shared network folder**). Access databases are inherently **multi-user**, so that many people can enter and update information at the same time, provided they are given permission to use the files inside that folder. Two people cannot, however, update the same record at the same time (**record locking**). Also, it doesn't matter whether the individuals are accessing the Access database through the database file itself (for example, two people updating the same database using forms or datasheets) or whether they are using Web pages created by DAPs.

 Use the Access database to create DAPs, which in turn create dynamic HTML Web pages

 Save the HTML Web page files in the same shared network folder as the Access database

It is not required that the database and HTML files be in the same folder, but this helps keep them organized.

 Give the users the URL or UNC address to access the Web pages using IE

URLs are used to access Internet Web pages. UNCs can be used when the file is located on the same local area network as the client computer. As users access the Web pages, the underlying Access database will be updated automatically.

 Use professional networking resources as necessary

Publishing a Web page to a Web Folder on a Web Server is very similar to saving an existing file with a new name in a new location, but the existing networking infrastructure (including connectivity between the Web server and your computer), along with appropriate security clearances, needs to be in place before you can save Web pages to any location on a company intranet or on the Internet. This requires the knowledge and skills of professionals dedicated to the field of computer networking. People who build networking infrastructures are often called **network administrators**. Those who work with Web Servers, Web Folders, and supporting Internet technologies are often called **Webmasters**. Table J-6 provides more tips and information about working with Web pages and Access. Figure J-18 illustrates the infrastructure involved with publishing a Web page to a Web server.

FIGURE J-18: Publishing to a Web server

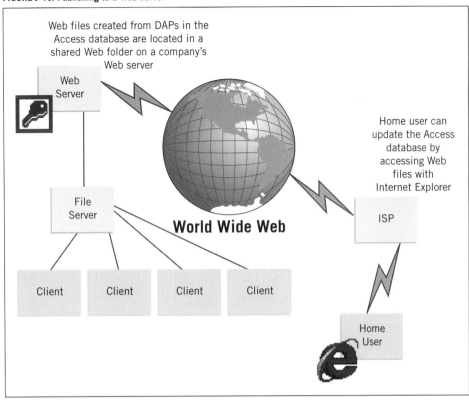

TABLE J-6: Tips for Working with Web pages and Access

to:	do this:
Open dynamic HTML files created by Access in a browser other than IE—dynamic files display live data from the underlying Access database	Use the Export option on the File menu to create server-generated HTML files from tables, queries, and forms. (Save as file type ASP for Microsoft Active Server Pages or IDC/HTX Microsoft IIS 1-2 file types.) Server-generated HTML files pages are dynamic, and therefore show current data, but are read-only.
Open static HTML files created by Access in a browser other than IE—static files display data that is current only as of the moment that the Web page was created	Use the Export option on the File menu to create static HTML files from tables, queries, forms, and reports. The files display a snapshot of the data at the time the static HTML file was created.
Open an HTML file created by another program in Access	Right-click the file in the Open dialog box, then click Open in Microsoft Access on the pop-up menu.

Practice

► Concepts Review

Identify each element of the form's Design View shown in Figure J-19.

FIGURE J-19

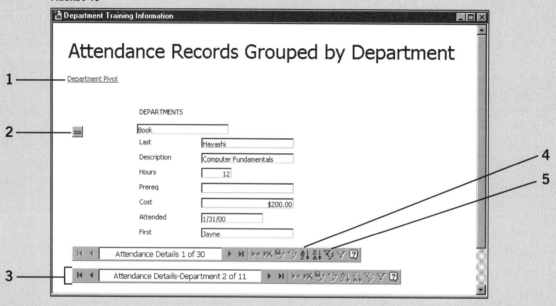

Match each term with the statement that describes its function.

6. **data access page**
7. **URL**
8. **HTML**
9. **World Wide Web pages**
10. **browser**
11. **World Wide network of computer networks**

a. Internet
b. Software loaded on a microcomputer and used to find and display Web pages
c. Access 2000 object that provides a connection between Web pages and an Access database
d. Programming language used to create Web pages
e. Web page address
f. Hyperlinked documents that make the Internet easy to navigate

12. **The communications protocol for the Internet is**
    a. ISP.
    b. HTML.
    c. URL.
    d. TCP/IP.
13. **To connect to the Internet through your home computer, you must first call a(n):**
    a. Webmaster
    b. ISP
    c. Home page
    d. URL
14. **Which of the following is NOT a service provided by the Internet?**
    a. Cable TV
    b. File transfer
    c. World Wide Web
    d. E-mail
15. **Which of the following is browser software?**
    a. Microsoft Excel
    b. Internet Explorer
    c. Microsoft Access
    d. Windows NT
16. **Which of the following is a special type of Web page designed for viewing, editing, and entering data stored in a Microsoft Access database?**
    a. Pivot table
    b. Home page
    c. Data access page
    d. Browser
17. **Making Web pages created through Access available to other users is called**
    a. Rendering.
    b. Uploading.
    c. Transferring.
    d. Publishing.

 # Skills Review

1. **Understanding the World Wide Web.**
   a. Interview five people and ask them if they have recently used the World Wide Web for the following purposes. If the answer is "Yes," ask them to also identify the URL for the Web page.

   - To sell or purchase a product or service
   - For entertainment
   - To index or reference other Internet resources (search engines)
   - To gather information
   - To take a class

   b. Ask five people who access the Internet from home who they use as their ISP, then write down the names.

2. **Using Hyperlink Fields.**

   a. Open the Machinery-J database, then open the Products table in Design view.

   b. Add a new field named "HomePage" with a Hyperlink Data Type.

   c. Save the Products table, open it in Datasheet view, then enter the following home page URLs into the new field for the first six records:

      1) www.toro.com
      2) www.caseih.com
      3) www.snapper.com
      4) www.deere.com
      5) www.troybilt.com
      6) www.stihl.com

   d. Click the link for www.deere.com and print the first page. If you are not already connected to the Internet, your dialer may appear, prompting you to connect with your chosen ISP. Once connected to your ISP, the John Deere home page should appear.

3. **Creating Pages for Interactive Reporting.**

   a. Click Pages on the Objects bar and double-click Create data access page by using wizard.

   b. Select the ProductName and the ReorderLevel fields from the Products table, then select the TransactionDate and UnitPrice fields from the Inventory Transactions table.

   c. Group the fields by ProductName, and sort in ascending order by TransactionDate.

   d. Type "Product Activity" for the page title, then open the new page in Page view.

   e. Open the Design view, maximize the Design view window, click in the title text area of the body of the Page and type the title "*Your Name's* Garden Shop Orders".

   f. Click the Page View button, click the Product Name text box, sort the ProductName in descending order, expand the ProductName group, then navigate to the 7/1/99 TransactionDate record within the Weed Wacker ProductName and print the page.

   g. Save the HTML file as "Garden Orders" on your Project Disk, then close the page.

4. **Creating Pages for Data Entry.**

   a. Click Pages on the Objects bar, then double-click Create data access page by using the wizard.

   b. Select all of the fields in the Products table.

   c. Do not add any grouping levels, but sort the records in ascending order on ProductName.

   d. Title the page "Product Update Page".

   e. In Design view, click in the title text area of the body of the page and type the title "Your Name's Products".

   f. Save the HTML file as "Products" on your Project Disk, then open Products.htm within Internet Explorer.

   g. Find and change the price of the "Mulcher" from $69.50 to $79.50 by changing the 6 to a 7, then print the Web page within Internet Explorer in which you made this change.

   h. Navigate to the next record within IE, then back to the Mulcher record to make sure that the price change was saved. Close IE.

   i. Open the Products table in the Machinery-J database, and make sure the Mulcher record now displays $79.50 as the Unit Price.

   j. Close the Products table within the Machinery-J database and the Products Web page within IE.

5. **Creating Pages for Data Analysis.**

   a. Click Pages on the Objects bar, then double-click Create data access page in Design view.

   b. Open the Field list window if necessary, then click the Expand button to the left of the Queries folder.

   c. Drag the Products Query to the upper-left corner of the Section: Unbound control, click the PivotTable List option button, then click OK.

   d. Click the PivotTable control to select it, right-click the ProductName field in the PivotTable control, then choose Move to Row Area.

   e. Resize the control so that all three columns are clearly visible.

   f. Click in the title text area of the body of the page and type the title "*Your Name's* Units Ordered Page", then display the page in Page view.

   g. Use the TransactionDate list arrow to select only the 7/1/99 dates, then print the page.

   h. Save the HTML file as Units Ordered to your Project Disk.

6. Working in Page Design view.

   a. Open the Products page in Design view, then modify all of the labels in the first column so that a space exists between the descriptive words (e.g., change "ProductName" to "Product Name"). (*Hint*: Change these labels by clicking them once to select them, then clicking them again to edit them, just as you would the label control of any form or report.)

   b. Click and drag across "*Your Name's* Products" in the body. Format the text to a bright blue, Britannic Bold font. (*Hint*: Use the Formatting (Page) toolbar just as you would when you format a control for any form or report.)

   c. Save the changes.

7. Inserting Hyperlinks to other Pages.

   a. Open the Products page in Design view, use the Hyperlink button on the toolbox to add a hyperlink control named "Units ordered" above the upper-left corner of the Header: Products section. Create the hyperlink so that it opens the Units Ordered page.

   b. Save the Products page and close it.

   c. Open the Units Ordered page in Design view, then add a hyperlink control named "Products" that opens the Products page above the upper-left corner of the Section: Unbound control.

   d. Save the Units Ordered page and close it.

   e. Open the Units Ordered Web page in IE, then click the Products hyperlink to make sure it works.

   f. From the opened Products Web page, click the Units Ordered hyperlink to make sure it works.

   g. Print the Units Ordered Web page within IE, close IE, and close the Machinery-J database.

8. Publishing Web Pages to Web Servers.

   a. Call your ISP and ask for information about the requirements to publish Web pages to their Web server. (If you are not currently connected to the Internet from home, research any ISP of your choice.)

   b. If your ISP does not allow members to publish Web pages, continue researching ISPs until you find one that allows members to publish Web pages.

   c. Print the documentation on how to publish Web pages to the ISP's Web server.

   d. Open IE and type "www.geocities.com" in the Address list box. Follow the links on the Web page to determine how to create your own Web page at the geocities Web site, then print the documentation.

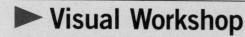

▶ Visual Workshop

As the manager of a college women's basketball team, you wish to enhance the Basketball-J database by developing a Web page to display player scoring information as a pivot table. Figure J-20 shows the data access page, called ISU Scoring, that you need to create. Develop the page in Design view, use the Scoring query as a pivot table control. You will have to move the Home-Away field and the Last field to the Row Area. Include your initials in the title text area. Save the HTML file with the name "Scoring" to your Project Disk. View and print the page in IE. Close all open applications.

FIGURE J-20

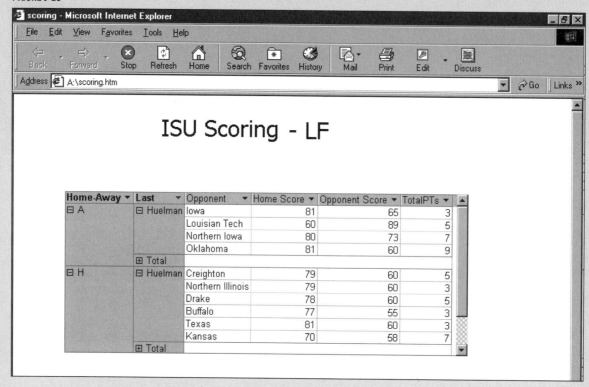

Creating
Advanced Queries

Objectives

- ▶ **Query for Top Values**
- ▶ **Create an advanced parameter query**
- ▶ **Modify query properties**
- ▶ **Create an update query**
- ▶ **Create a make-table query**
- ▶ **Create an append query**
- ▶ **Create a delete query**
- ▶ **Specify join properties**

Queries are database objects that answer questions about the data. The most common query is the **select query**, which displays fields and records that match specific criteria into a single datasheet. Other types of queries, such as top value, parameter, and action queries, are powerful tools for displaying, analyzing, and updating data. An **action query** is one that makes changes to the data. There are four types of action queries: delete, update, append, and make-table. Scenario▶ David Dumont, director of training at MediaLoft, has become very familiar with the capabilities of Access. Users come to David with extensive data-analysis and data-update requests, confident that he can provide the information they need. David uses powerful query features and new query types to handle these requirements.

Querying for Top Values

Once a large number of records are entered into a table of a database, it is less common to query for all of the records, and more common to list only the most significant records by choosing a subset of the highest or lowest values from a sorted query. The **Top Values** feature within the Query Design view allows you to respond to these types of requests. **Scenario** Employee attendance at MediaLoft classes has grown. To help plan future classes, David wants to print a datasheet listing the names of the top five classes, sorted by number of students per class. David creates a summarized select query to find the total number of attendees for each class, then uses the Top Values feature to find the five most attended classes.

Steps 1 2 3 4

1. Start Access, open the **Training-K** database, click **Queries** on the Objects bar, click the **New button** in the database window, click **Design View**, then click **OK**
   You need fields from both the Attendance and Courses tables.

2. Double-click **Attendance**, double-click **Courses**, then click **Close** in the Show Table dialog box
   Query Design view now displays two related tables in the upper portion of the screen.

3. Double-click **LogNo** in the Attendance table, then double-click **Description** in the Courses table
   You want to count the LogNo entries for each course Description.

QuickTip

Click the Datasheet View button at any time during the query design development process to view the resulting datasheet.

4. Click the **Totals button** Σ on the Query Design toolbar, click **Group By** for the LogNo field, click the **Group By list arrow**, then click **Count**
   You identified the fields and summarized the records by counting the LogNo entries for each Description. Your screen should look like Figure K-1. Sorting determines which records will be on "top."

5. Click the **LogNo field Sort cell**, click the **LogNo field Sort list arrow**, then click **Descending**
   A descending order will put the courses most attended by MediaLoft employees, those with the highest count, at the top.

6. Click the **Top Values list arrow** All on the Query Design toolbar
   The Top Values feature is used to display a subset of the records. You can select a number or percentage from the list or enter a specific value or percentage. See Table K-1 for more information on how to use the Top Values feature.

7. Click **5**, then click the **Datasheet View button** on the Query Design toolbar
   Your screen should look like Figure K-2. The Introduction to Access course and the Computer Fundamentals course both had 19 attendees. If more than one course had 14 attendees (a summarized value of 14 in the CountOfLogNo field), then all courses that "tied" for fifth place would have been displayed too.

8. Click the **Save button** on the Query Datasheet toolbar, type **Top 5 Courses**, click **OK**, then close the datasheet
   The Top 5 Courses query appears as a query object in the database window.

FIGURE K-1: Designing a summary query for top values

Count LogNo

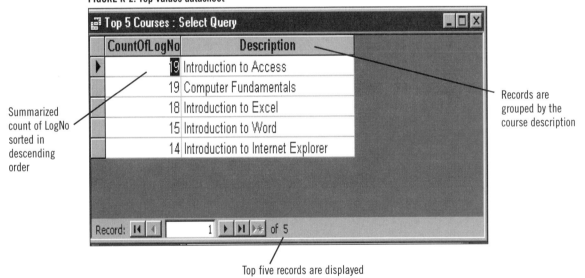

Top Values list arrow

Totals button

Sort cell for LogNo

Group By Description entries

FIGURE K-2: Top Values datasheet

CountOfLogNo	Description
19	Introduction to Access
19	Computer Fundamentals
18	Introduction to Excel
15	Introduction to Word
14	Introduction to Internet Explorer

Top 5 Courses : Select Query

Record: 1 of 5

Summarized count of LogNo sorted in descending order

Records are grouped by the course description

Top five records are displayed

TABLE K-1: Top Values options

action	to display
Click 5, or 25, or 100 from the Top Values list	Top 5, 25, or 100 records
Enter a number such as 10 in the Top Values text box	Top 10 (in this case) records
Click 5% or 25% from the Top Values list	Top 5 or 25 percent of records
Enter a percentage, such as 10%, in the Top Values text box	Top 10 percent (in this case) of records

Creating an Advanced Parameter Query

A **parameter query** displays a dialog box prompting you for information to enter as limiting criteria each time the query runs. You can build a form or report based on a parameter query, too. When you open the form or report, the parameter prompt appears. The entry in the prompt determines which records to include in the query, which in turn, determines which records to display in the form or report. **Scenario** David wants to enhance the Top 5 Courses query to display the top five courses within a specific date range. He adds parameter prompts to the Top 5 Courses query so that the resulting datasheet only shows the top five courses for the dates he specifies.

1. Click the **Top 5 Courses query**, click the **Design button** ☒ in the database window, then double-click the **Attended field** in the Attendance table
   The Attended field contains the date that the course was taken.

2. Click the **Attended field Criteria cell**, type **Between [Enter start date:] And [Enter end date:]**, then click the **Datasheet View button** ▦
   Your screen should look like Figure K-3. Parameter criteria must be entered within [square brackets]. The **Between ... And** operator will help you find all records on or between two dates. Using greater than or equal to, >=, and less than or equal to, <=, operators works in the same way.

3. Type **1/1/00** in the Enter start date text box, press **[Enter]**, type **6/30/00** in the Enter end date text box, then press **[Enter]**
   Your screen should look like Figure K-4. The datasheet displays the top five courses attended between 1/1/00 and 6/30/00. Because three courses tied for fifth place, seven records are displayed instead of five. You can enter as many parameter criteria entries in as many fields as you wish. Access displays the parameter prompts one at a time, and uses the entries you've made to determine which records belong in the final datasheet.

4. Click **File** on the menu bar, click **Save As**, click to the left of the word **"Courses"** in the text box, type **– Parameter – Your Initials**, then click **OK**
   Because the object name always appears in the header of a datasheet printout, descriptive query names can help identify the information or creator of the information.

5. Click the **Print button**, then close the Top 5 Courses – Parameter – Your Initials query
   The Top 5 Courses – Parameter – Your Initials query appears as an object in the database window.

FIGURE K-3: A parameter prompt

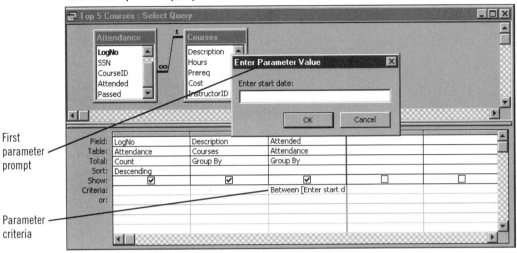

First parameter prompt

Parameter criteria

FIGURE K-4: Top 5 Courses – Parameter query

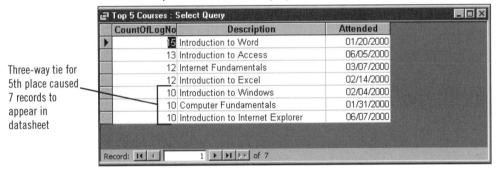

Three-way tie for 5th place caused 7 records to appear in datasheet

Access 2000

CLUES TO USE

Concatenating a parameter prompt to a wildcard character

You can concatenate parameter prompts with a wildcard character such as the asterisk (*) to create more flexible queries. For example, the entry: **LIKE [Enter the first character of the company name:] & "*"** placed in the Criteria cell of the Company field searches for companies that begin with a specified letter. The entry: **LIKE "*" & [Enter any character(s) to search by:] & "*"** placed in the Criteria cell of the Company field searches for words that contain the specified characters anywhere in the field. The **ampersand** (&) is used to concatenate items in an expression and double quotation marks (" ") are used to surround text criteria.

Modifying Query Properties

Properties are characteristics that define the appearance and behavior of the database itself; objects, fields, sections, and controls. You set properties by using the **property sheet** for that item. The property sheet can be displayed in many ways, such as right-clicking the item you wish to examine or modify, and then clicking Properties. The title bar of the property sheet always indicates which properties are being displayed. If you change a field's properties within Query Design view, they are modified for that query only. If you change a field's properties within Table Design view, they are modified for the entire database. **Scenario** David uses the query and field properties of the Department Charges query to improve the datasheet's appearance.

Steps 1234

1. Right-click the Department Charges query, then click Properties
The Department Charges Properties dialog box opens, providing information about the query and also allowing you to enter a description for the query.

QuickTip

Click the column headings to sort the objects in ascending or descending order.

2. Type Lists the department, description, hours, and cost, click OK, click the Details button 🔲 in the Training-K database window, then maximize the database window
Five columns of information about each query object appear, as shown in Figure K-5. The Description property entry appears in the Description column.

3. Click the Design button 🖾 on the database toolbar, right-click to the right of the Employees table, click Properties, click the Recordset Type text box, click the Recordset Type list arrow, then click Snapshot
Your screen should look like Figure K-6. Viewing the query property sheet from within Query Design view gives a complete list of the query's properties. The Snapshot property makes the Recordset not updateable.

Trouble?

Separate the new field name from the calculated expression with a colon (:) and be sure to surround field names in [square brackets].

4. Close the Query Properties dialog box, click the blank Field cell in the fifth column, type PerHour:[Cost]/[Hours], then click the Datasheet View button 🔲
The datasheet appears with the cost per hour calculated in the fifth column, but the calculated values are hard to read because they are unformatted.

Trouble?

The title bar of the property sheet should say "Field Properties." If it doesn't, close the dialog box and try again.

5. Click the Design View button 🖾, right-click the PerHour field, then click Properties
The Field Properties dialog box allows you to change field properties within this query. When you start making an entry in a property, a short description of the property appears in the status bar.

6. Click Format text box, click the Format list arrow, click Currency, click the Decimal Places text box, click the Decimal Places list arrow, click 2, click the Caption property text box, then type Cost Per Hour
Your screen should look like Figure K-7.

7. Close the property sheet, click the 🔲 on the Query Design toolbar, type Video in the Department field for the first record to view the message in the status bar
The message "This recordset is not updateable" appears because the query Recordset Type property was set to "Snapshot," which allows you to view the records but not update them. The caption and formatting properties of the calculated field clarify the information.

8. Save and close the Department Charges query

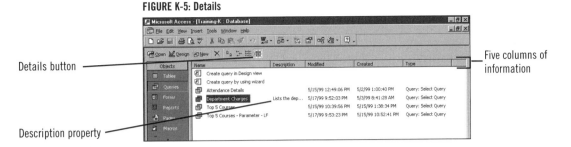

FIGURE K-5: Details

Details button

Description property

Five columns of information

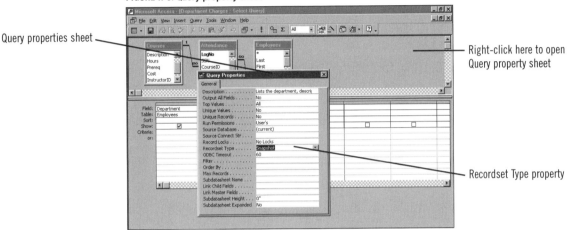

FIGURE K-6: Query property sheet

Query properties sheet

Right-click here to open Query property sheet

Recordset Type property

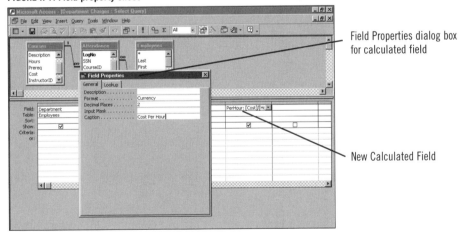

FIGURE K-7: Field property sheet

Field Properties dialog box for calculated field

New Calculated Field

CLUES TO USE

Optimizing queries using indexes and SQL

Indexes are used to speed up queries that are often sorted or grouped. For example, if you commonly sort by a LastName field, setting the **Indexed property** to Yes would improve the performance of any query that also sorted or grouped by the LastName field. You can only set the Indexed property of a field in Table Design view, but if you know **SQL** (Structured Query Language) you can create an index on a field within a

query. SQL is a national standard database language for querying a wide range of relational database products. If you want to query an Access database in a manner that is beyond the capabilities of the Query Design view, knowledge of SQL is required. To access the SQL statements for any query, click the Datasheet View list arrow ▦ ▾ and choose SQL View. To add an index, use the SQL CREATE INDEX statement.

Creating an Update Query

An **action query** makes changes to the data of many records. There are four types of action queries: delete, update, append, and make-table. See Table K-2 for more information on action queries. An **update query** is a type of action query that makes a change to the data of the tables. For example, you may wish to increase the price of a product in a particular category by 5% or change an area code with one operation. **Scenario** The Training Department upgraded their equipment on June 1, and David has been given approval to increase by 5% the internal cost of all courses provided after that date to cover the upgrade expense. He creates an update query to change the data in the tables to reflect the cost increase.

Steps

1. Click the **New button** on the database window, click **Design View** in the New Query dialog box, click **OK**, double-click **Attendance** in the Show Table dialog box, then click **Close** in the Show Table dialog box

2. Double-click **CourseID**, double-click **Attended**, and double-click **Cost**
   The three fields are added to the query design grid. You have to change only those courses offered on or after June 1.

3. Click the **Attended Criteria cell**, type **>=6/1/00**, then click the **Datasheet View button** on the Query Design toolbar
   Every action query starts as a select query. Always look at the datasheet of the select query before initiating any action that will change data to make sure which records will be affected.

4. Click the **Design View button** on the Query Datasheet toolbar, click the **Query Type button list arrow** on the Query Design toolbar, then click **Update Query**
   The Query Type button displays the Update Query icon and the Update To: row appears in the query design grid, as shown in Figure K-8. All action query icons include an exclamation point that indicates data will be changed when you click the Run button on the Query Design toolbar.

5. Click the **Cost field Update To cell**, type **[Cost]*1.05**, click the **Run button** on the Query Design toolbar, then click **Yes** to indicate that you want to update 41 rows
   Any time you run an action query, Access prompts you with an "Are you sure?" message before actually updating the data. The Undo button will not undo changes made by action queries.

6. Click on the Query Design toolbar
   Your screen should look like Figure K-9. The datasheet of an update query shows only the updated field.

7. Close the update query without saving the changes
   You rarely need to save an update query, because once the data has been updated, you don't need the query object anymore. Also, if you double-click an action query of any type from the database window, you run the query. Therefore, don't save any queries that you won't need again, especially action queries.

FIGURE K-8: Creating an update query

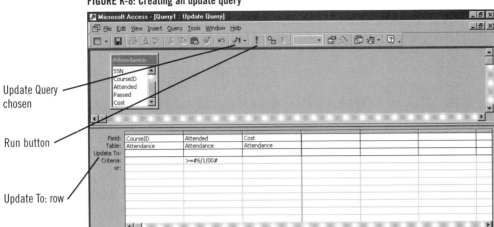

Update Query chosen

Run button

Update To: row

FIGURE K-9: Updated cost fields

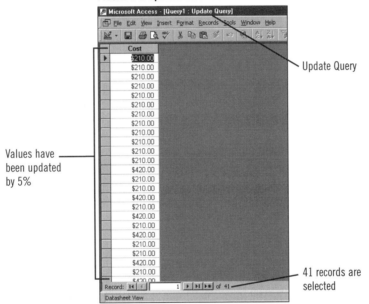

Update Query

Values have been updated by 5%

41 records are selected

TABLE K-2: Action queries

type of action query	query icon	description	example
Delete	✕!	Deletes a group of records from one or more tables	Remove products that are discontinued or for which there are no orders
Update	✐!	Makes global changes to a group of records in one or more tables	Raise prices by 10 percent for all products
Append	✦!	Adds a group of records from one or more tables to the end of a table	Merge the product table from a business you just acquired to the existing product table for the company
Make-Table	▦!	Creates a new table from all or part of the data in one or more tables	Export records to another Access database, make a backup copy of a table, or create reports that display data from a specified point in time

Access 2000

Creating a Make-Table Query

A **make-table query** creates a new table in either the current or in another Access database. When using the make-table query feature to make a table in another Access database, it works like an export feature. Sometimes the make-table query is used to create a backup copy of a table or a backup copy of a subset of records for a certain date range. In the latter case, date criteria used in the query design grid determine which records are exported to the new table. **Scenario** David uses a make-table query to archive the records in the Attendance table for the first quarter of 2000.

1. Click the **New button** 🔲 on the database window, click **OK** to accept Design View in the New Query dialog box, double-click **Attendance** in the Show Table dialog box, then click **Close** in the Show Table dialog box

2. Double-click the * **(asterisk)** at the top of the Attendance table's field list
   Putting the asterisk in the query design grid puts all of the fields in that table in the grid. Later, if fields are added to this table, they also will be automatically added to this query because of the asterisk.

3. Double-click the **Attended field** to add it to the second column of the query grid, click the **Attended field Criteria cell**, type **<4/1/00**, then click the **Attended field Show check box** to uncheck it
   Your screen should look like Figure K-10. Before changing this select query into a make-table query, it is always a good idea to view the datasheet.

QuickTip

The sort and filter buttons work on a query datasheet in exactly the same way that they work in a table datasheet or form.

4. Click the **Datasheet View button** 🔲 on the Query Design toolbar, click any entry in the **Attended field**, then click the **Sort Descending button** 🔤 on the Query Datasheet toolbar
   The descending sort on the Attended field allows you to check that no records on or after 4/1/00 are present in the datasheet. (*Note*: None of the cost values for these records were updated because the previous update query affected courses on or after 6/1/00.)

5. Click the **Design View button** 🔲, click the **Query Type list arrow** 🔲, click the **Make-Table Query button** 🔲, type **First Quarter 2000 Attendance Log** in the Table Name text box, then click **OK**
   Your screen should look like Figure K-11. The Query Type button displays the Make Table icon. The make-table query is ready to be run, but the new table has not yet been created. Action queries do not delete, update, append, or make data until you click the Run button.

6. Click the **Run button** 🔲 on the Query Design toolbar, click **Yes** when prompted that you are about to paste 102 records, then close but do not save the query
   Make-table queries are rarely saved unless you intend to use them again.

7. Click **Tables** on the Objects bar, then double-click **First Quarter 2000 Attendance Log** to view the new table's datasheet
   All 102 records were pasted into the new table, as shown in Figure K-12. Field properties such as the input mask for the SSN field and the check box display for the Passed field were not duplicated, but you could modify the Design view of this table to change the appearance of the fields just like you could for any other table. (*Note*: -1 is sometimes used to designate "yes" and 0 is used to designate "no" in a Yes/No field).

8. Close the First Quarter 2000 Attendance Log table

FIGURE K-10: Using the asterisk in a query grid

Asterisk in the field list

Asterisk in the query grid

Date criteria

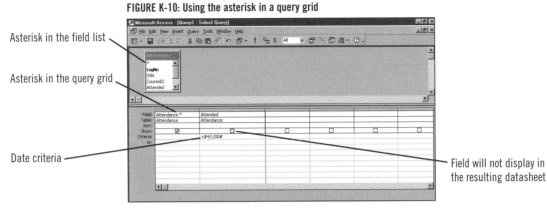

Field will not display in the resulting datasheet

FIGURE K-11: Creating a make-table query

Make-Table Query chosen

Run button

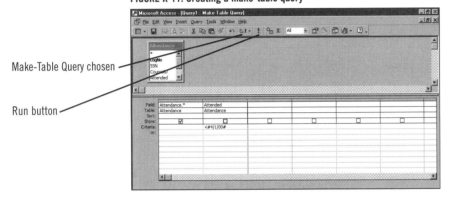

FIGURE K-12: First Half 2000 Attendance Log datasheet

New table

102 records

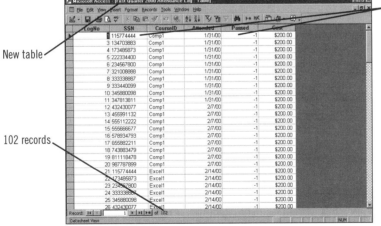

Field properties were not duplicated

Resolving Year 2000 Issues

If you type only two digits of a date, Access assumes that the digits 00 through 29 are for the years 2000 through 2029. If you type 30 through 99, Access assumes the years refer to 1930 through 1999. If you want years outside these ranges, you must type all four digits of the year or customize the way two-digit date entries are interpreted by using the Microsoft Office 2000 Resource Kit. If you want Access to display all dates with four digits, regardless of how they are entered, click the "Use four-digit year formatting" check box found on the General tab of the Options dialog box. Click the Tools menu item, then click Options to open the Options dialog box.

Creating an Append Query

An **append query** adds a group of records to an existing table in either the current or in another Access database. The most difficult thing about an append query is making sure that all of the fields you have selected within the append query match fields in the target table where you wish to append (paste) them. If the target table has more fields than the append query, the append query will append the data in the matching fields and ignore the other fields. If the target table is lacking a field that the append query contains, an error message will appear indicating that there is an unknown field name that will cancel the action. Scenario▶ David would like to append April's records to the First Quarter 2000 Attendance Log table. He uses an append query to do this, then he renames the table to accurately reflect its contents.

1. Click **Queries** 🖼 on the Objects bar, click the **New button** 🖼 on the database window, click **OK** to accept Design view in the New Query dialog box, double-click **Attendance** in the Show Table dialog box, then click **Close** in the Show Table dialog box

2. Double-click the **Attendance table's field list title bar**, then drag the **highlighted fields** to the first column of the query design grid
   Double-clicking the title bar of the field list highlights all of the fields, so you were able to add all the fields to the query grid quickly. An append query does not allow the same field to be referenced twice, even if the show check box is cleared for one occurrence of the field.

3. Click the **Attended field Criteria cell**, type **>=4/1/00 and <=4/30/00**, then click the **Datasheet View button** 🖼 on the Query Design toolbar
   There should be 29 records with an April date in the Attended field.

4. Click the **Design View button** 🖼 on the Query Datasheet toolbar, click the **Query Type button list arrow** 🖼▾ on the Query Design toolbar, click **Append Query** 🖼, click the **Table Name list arrow** in the Append dialog box, click **First Quarter 2000 Attendance Log**, then click **OK**
   Your screen should look like Figure K-13. The Query Type button displays the Append Query icon, and the Append To row was added to the query design grid. You would use the Append To row to choose fields in the target table if they were different than the query fields. The append action is ready to be initiated by clicking the Run button.

5. Click the **Run button** 🖼 on the Query Design toolbar, click **Yes** to indicate that you want to append 29 rows, then close the query without saving the changes

6. Click **Tables** on the Objects bar, double-click the **First Quarter 2000 Attendance Log**, click any entry in the Attended field, then click the **Sort Descending button** 🖼 on the Table Datasheet toolbar
   The April records were appended to the table for a total of 131 records, as shown in Figure K-14.

7. Close the First Quarter 2000 Attendance Log without saving changes, right-click **First Quarter 2000 Attendance Log** in the database window, click **Rename**, type **Jan-April 2000 Log**, then press **[Enter]**
   The backup table with attendance records from January through April 2000 has been renamed.

FIGURE K-13: Creating an append query

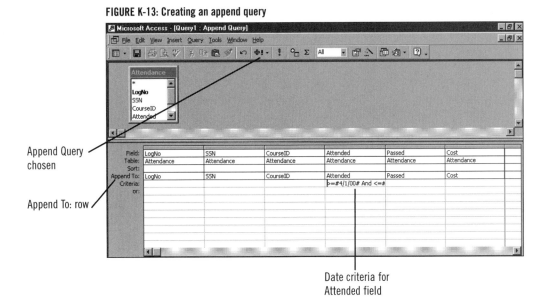

Append Query chosen

Append To: row

Date criteria for Attended field

FIGURE K-14: Updated table with appended records

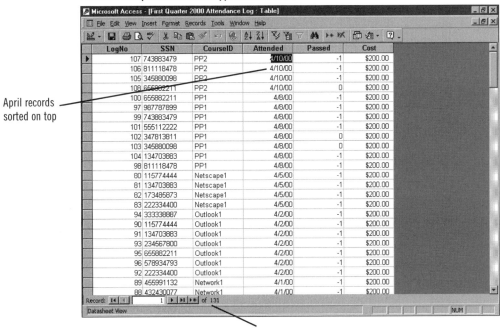

April records sorted on top

131 records

Creating a Delete Query

A **delete query** deletes a group of records from one or more tables as defined by a query. Delete queries always delete entire records, and not just selected fields within records, so they should be used carefully. Since the delete query destroys records without the ability to undo the action, it is wise to always have a current backup of the database before running any action query, especially the delete query. **Scenario** Now that David has the first four months of attendance records archived in the Jan-April 2000 Log table, he wishes to delete them from the Attendance table. He uses a delete query to accomplish this task.

Steps 1234

1. Click **Queries** on the Objects bar, click the **New button** on the database window, click **OK** to accept Design view in the New Query dialog box, double-click **Attendance** in the Show Table dialog box, then click **Close** in the Show Table dialog box

2. Double-click the * **(asterisk)** at the top of the Attendance table's field list, then double-click the **Attended** field
   All the fields from the Attendance table are added to the first column of the query design grid, and the Attended field is added to the second column of the query design grid.

3. Click the **Attended field Criteria cell**, type **<=4/30/00**, then press **[Enter]**
   It is important to check the datasheet to make sure that you have selected the same 131 records that are in the Jan-April 2000 Log table.

4. Click the **Datasheet View button** on the Query Design toolbar to confirm that there are 131 records in the datasheet, click the **Design View button** on the Query Datasheet toolbar, click the **Query Type button list arrow**, then click **Delete Query**
   Your screen should look like Figure K-15. The Query Type button displays the Delete Query icon, and the Delete row was added to the query design grid. The delete action is ready to be initiated by clicking the Run button.

5. Click the **Run button** on the Query Design toolbar, click **Yes** to confirm that you want to delete 131 rows, then close the query without saving the changes.

6. Click **Tables** on the Objects bar, double-click **Attendance**, click **any entry in the Attended field**, then click the **Sort Ascending button** on the Table Datasheet toolbar
   The oldest records should start in the month of May, as shown in Figure K-16. All prior records were deleted by the delete query.

7. Save and close the Attendance table datasheet

FIGURE K-15: Creating a delete query

Delete Query chosen

Delete: row

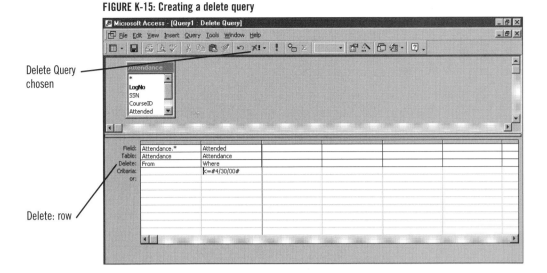

FIGURE K-16: Attendance table without January-April records

Attendance table

Field sorted in ascending order

65 records remain

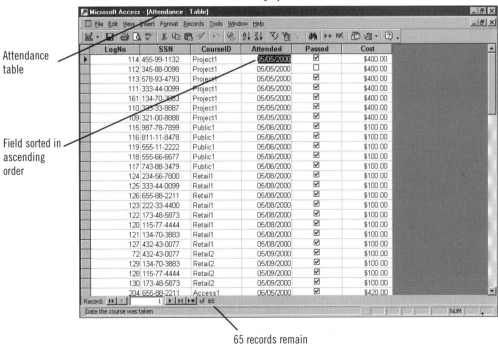

Specifying Join Properties

When more than one table's field list is used in a query, the tables are joined as defined in the Relationships window. If referential integrity was enforced, a "1" appears next to the table whose field serves as the "one" side of the one-to-many relationship, and an infinity sign (∞) appears next to the table whose field serves as the "many" side. If no relationships have been established, Access automatically creates join lines if the tables have a field with the same name and comparable data type, and if the field is a primary key in one of the tables. The "one" and "many" symbols do not appear, however, because referential integrity is not enforced. You can edit this relationship by double-clicking the join line. **Scenario** David would like to create a query to find out which courses have never been attended. He modifies the join properties between the Attendance and Courses table to get this answer.

Steps

1. Click **Queries** on the Object bar, click the **New button**, click **OK** to accept Design view, double-click **Courses**, double-click **Attendance**, then click **Close**
   Because the Courses and Attendance tables already have a one-to-many relationship with referential integrity enforced in the Relationships window, the join line appears, linking the two tables using the CourseID field common to both.

2. Double-click the **one-to-many join line** between the field lists
   The Join Properties dialog box opens, as shown in Figure K-17, showing which tables and fields participate in the join. The lower half of the dialog box shows that, by default, option 1 is chosen, which specifies that the query will display only records where joined fields from *both* tables are equal. That means that if any courses exist in which there was no matching attendance record, those courses would not appear in the resulting datasheet.

3. Click the option **2 option button**
   By choosing option 2, you are specifying that you wish to see all of the records in the Courses table, regardless of whether there are any matching records in the Attendance table. Because referential integrity is enforced, option 3 would be the same as option 1, because referential integrity makes it impossible to enter records in the Attendance table that do not have a corresponding record in the Courses table.

4. Click **OK**
   The join line's appearance changes as shown in Figure K-18.

5. Double-click **CourseID** from the Courses field list, double-click **Description** from the Courses field list, double-click **Attended** from the Attendance field list, double-click **Cost** from the Attendance field list, then click the **Datasheet View button**
   All courses are listed in the datasheet. The ones with corresponding attendance records have an entry in the Attended and Cost fields. By using a filter, you can quickly display those with no entry in the Attended field to determine exactly which courses have not been attended.

6. Click the **Access2 Attended field** (it is null), then click the **Filter by Selection button** on the Query Datasheet toolbar
   The 18 filtered records represent those courses as shown in Figure K-19.

7. Click the **Save button** on the Query Datasheet toolbar, type **No Attendance Since 5/1/00 – *Your Initials*** in the Query Name text box, click **OK**, click the **Access2 Attended field**, click (to refilter for null values), then click the **Print button**

8. Close the datasheet, then exit Access

FIGURE K-17: Join Properties dialog box

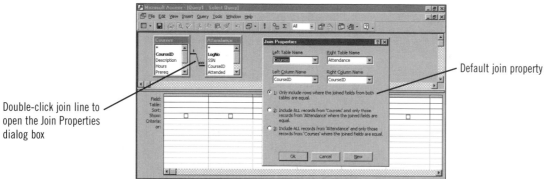

Double-click join line to open the Join Properties dialog box

Default join property

FIGURE K-18: The join line's appearance changes when its properties are changed

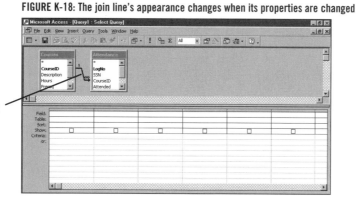

Join line's appearance shows that *all* records from the Courses table will be included in the datasheet

FIGURE K-19: Filtering for courses with no attendance records

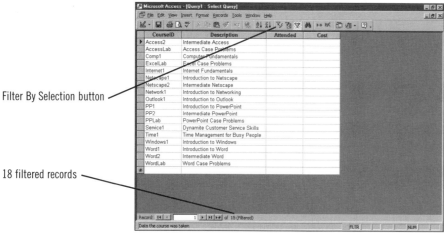

Filter By Selection button

18 filtered records

CLUES TO USE

Reviewing referential integrity

Referential integrity between two tables may be established when tables are joined in the Relationships window, and it ensures that no orphaned records are entered or created in the database. An **orphan record** happens when information in the linking field of the "many" table doesn't have a matching entry in the linking field of the "one" table. For the Training-K database, for example, referential integrity ensures that CourseNo entries added to the Attendance table are first recorded in the Courses table. Also, referential integrity prevents the user from deleting a record from the Courses table if matching CourseNo entries are present in the Attendance table.

Practice

▶ Concepts Review

Identify each element of the form's Design view shown in Figure K-20.

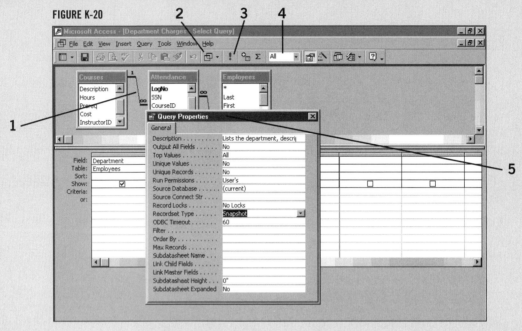

FIGURE K-20

Match each term with the statement that describes its function.

6. **Top values query**
7. **Select query**
8. **Action query**
9. **Properties**
10. **Snapshot**
11. **Parameter query**

a. Displays fields and records that match specific criteria into a single datasheet
b. Makes changes to the data
c. Displays only the highest or lowest values from a sorted query
d. Displays a dialog box prompting you for information to enter as criteria
e. Makes the Recordset not updateable
f. Characteristics that define the appearance and behavior of almost everything within the database

Select the best answer from the list of choices.

12. The entry for the Recordset Type query property that does not allow you to modify any of the data is
  a. Dynaset (No Nulls).
  b. Snapshot.
  c. Referential Integrity.
  d. No Updates.

13. Which of the following shows the proper way to enter parameter criteria in the query design grid?
  a. >=Type minimum value here:
  b. >=Type minimum value here: }
  c. >=[Type minimum value here:]
  d. >=(Type minimum value here:)

14. You cannot use the Top Values feature to:
  a. Show the bottom 10 percent of records.
  b. Show the top 30 records.
  c. Update the top 10 records.
  d. Display a subset of records.

15. Which of the following is not an action query?
  a. Append query
  b. Delete query
  c. Make-table query
  d. Union query

16. Which of the following precautions should you take before running a delete query?
  a. Understand the relationships between the records you are about to delete in the database.
  b. Have a current backup of the database.
  c. Check the resulting datasheet to make sure the query selects the right records.
  d. All of the above

17. When querying tables in a one-to-many relationship with referential integrity enforced, which records will appear (by default) on the resulting datasheet?
  a. All records from both tables will appear at all times
  b. All records from the "one" table, and only those with matching values from the "many" side
  c. All records from the "many" table, and only those with nonmatching values from the "one" side
  d. Only those with matching values in both tables

▶ Skills Review

1. Query for Top Values.
  a. Start Access then open the Seminar-K database.
  b. Create a select query with the EventName field from the Events table and the RegistrationFee field from the Registration table.
  c. Add the RegistrationFee field a second time, then click the Totals button. In the Total row of the query grid, Group By the EventName field, Sum the first RegistrationFee field, and count the second Registration Fee field.
  d. Sort in descending order by the Summed RegistrationFee field.
  e. Enter 2 in the Top Values list box to display the top two seminars in the datasheet.
  f. Save the query as "Top 2 Seminars – Your Initials", view the resulting datasheet, print the datasheet, then close the datasheet.

2. Create an Advanced Parameter Query.

  a. Create a select query with the AttendeeLastName field from the Attendees table, and the EventName and Date fields from the Events table. (*Hint*: You'll need to add the Registration table to this query as well as join the Attendees and Events tables.)

  b. Add the parameter criteria "Between [Enter Start Date:] And [Enter End Date:]" in the Date field.

  c. Specify an ascending sort order on the Date field.

  d. Click the Datasheet View button, then enter "5/1/00" as the start date and "6/30/00" as the end date in order to find everyone who has attended a seminar in May or June of the year 2000. You should view 22 records.

  e. Save the query as "May and June Seminar Attendance – Your Initials", then print the datasheet.

3. Modify Query Properties.

  a. Open the "May and June Seminar Attendance – Your Initials" query in Design view, open the property sheet for the query, change the Recordset Type property to Snapshot, then close the query property sheet.

  b. Right-click the Date field, and click Properties from the shortcut menu to open the Field Properties dialog box. Enter "Date of Seminar" as the Caption property, change the Format property to Medium Date, then close the property sheet.

  c. Display the records for the months of May and June of 2000, and print the datasheet.

  d. Save and close the query.

4. Create an Update Query.

  a. Create a select query and select all the fields from the Registration table.

  b. Add criteria to find those records in which the RegistrationDate is on or after 5/1/00. View the datasheet, and observe and note the values in the RegistrationFee field. There should be six records. Expand the columns to view all of the data.

  c. In Design view, change the query to an update query, then enter "[RegistrationFee]+5" in the RegistrationFee field Update To cell in order to increase each value in that field by $5.

  d. Run the query to update the six records.

  e. Change the query back to a select query, then view the datasheet to make sure that the RegistrationFee fields were updated properly.

  f. Close the query without saving the changes.

5. Create a Make-Table Query.

  a. Create a select query and select all the fields from the Registration table.

  b. Add criteria to find those records in which the RegistrationDate is on or before 3/31/00.

  c. View the datasheet. There should be 15 records.

  d. In Design view, change the query into a make-table query that creates a new table in the current database with the Table Name "1Qtr2000 – Your Initials".

  e. Run the query to paste 15 rows into the 1Qtr2000 – Your Initials table.

  f. Close the query without saving it, click Tables on the Objects bar, open the 1Qtr2000 – Your Initials table, view the 15 records, print the datasheet, then close it.

6. Create an Append Query.

  a. Create a select query and select all the fields from the Registration table.

  b. Add criteria to find those records in which the RegistrationDate occurred on any day during April 2000. (*Hint*: Use the criteria >=4/1/00 and <=4/30/00.)

  c. View the datasheet. There should be one record.

  d. Change the query to an append query that appends to the 1Qtr2000 – Your Initials table.

  e. Run the query to append the row into the 1Qtr2000 – Your Initials table.

f. Close the query without saving it.

g. Rename the 1Qtr2000 – Your Initials table to "Jan-Apr2000 – Your Initials", open the datasheet (there should be 16 records), print it, then close it.

7. Create a Delete Query.

a. Create a select query and select all the fields from the Registration table.

b. Add criteria to find those records in which the RegistrationDate occurred before May 1, 2000.

c. View the datasheet. There should be 16 records.

d. Change the query into a delete query.

e. Run the query that deletes 16 records from the Registration table.

f. Close the query without saving it.

g. Open the Registration table in datasheet view to confirm that there are only six records, then close it.

8. Specify Join Properties.

a. Create a select query with the following fields: AttendeeFirstName and AttendeeLastName from the Attendees table, and RegistrationFee from the Registration table.

b. Double-click the link between the Attendees and Registration tables to open the Join Properties dialog box. Click the option button to include *all* records from Attendees and only those records from Registration where the joined fields are equal. Click OK to close the dialog box.

c. View the datasheet, and add your own first and last name as the last record, but do not enter anything in the RegistrationFee field for your record.

d. Print the datasheet, save the query with the name "Current Attendees", then close the datasheet.

e. Close the Seminar-K database and exit Access.

▶ Visual Workshop

As the manager of a college women's basketball team, you wish to create a query from the Basketball-K database with the fields shown. The query is a parameter query that prompts the user for a start and end date. Figure K-21 shows the datasheet where the start date of 12/1/00 and end date of 12/31/00 are used. Save and name the query "Offense – Your Initials", then print the datasheet.

FIGURE K-21

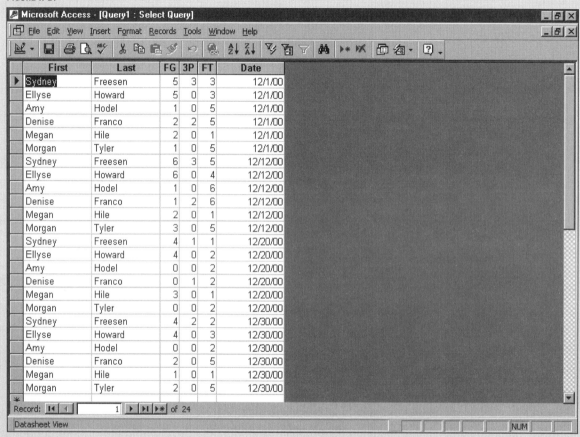

Access 2000

Unit L

Creating
Advanced Forms and Reports

Objectives

- ► **Add check boxes and toggle buttons**
- ► **Use Conditional Formatting**
- ► **Create custom Help**
- ► **Add tab controls**
- ► **Add charts**
- ► **Modify charts**
- ► **Add subreport controls**
- ► **Modify section properties**

Advanced controls such as tab controls, charts, and subreports are powerful communication tools. Conditional formatting allows you to highlight exceptional information within a form or report to more clearly present key information. Knowing how to use these advanced features to enhance forms and reports will improve the value of your database to every user. David Dumont wants to enhance existing forms and reports to more professionally and clearly present the information. David will use powerful form and report controls and features such as check boxes, conditional formatting, tab controls, charts, and subreports to improve the training database's forms and reports.

Access 2000

Adding Check Boxes and Toggle Buttons

A **check box** is a control that is often used to display Yes/No fields on a form because it can appear in only one of two ways: checked or unchecked. The checked state intuitively means on, yes, or true, and the unchecked state means off, no, or false. It is much easier for a user to answer questions on a form by using the mouse to click a check box control than to type the word "True" or "Yes" in a text box control. By default, Access represents any field with a Yes/No data type as a check box control on a form, regardless of whether the field was added to the form through the Form Wizard, AutoForm options, or in Form Design view. **Scenario** David would like to improve the visual appeal of the Employee Course Attendance form and Attendance Subform. He changes the properties of the Attendance Subform and a Yes/No field.

1. Open the **Training-L** database, click **Forms** on the Objects bar, then double-click the **Employee Course Attendance form**
   The form opens in Form view and the Attendance Subform appears as a datasheet within it.

Trouble?

If the subform appears as a white rectangle, click the Form View button, then click the Design View button to refresh the screen.

2. Click the **Design View button** on the Form View toolbar, then maximize the **Employee Course Attendance form** window
   Your screen should look like Figure L-1. In order to change the appearance of the controls on the subform, the Default View property for the form has to be changed from Datasheet (which allows no special formatting) to Continuous Forms.

3. Double-click the **subform's Select form button**, click the **Format tab** (if necessary) on the property sheet, click the **Default View text box**, click the **Default View list arrow**, click **Continuous Forms**, then click the **Form View button**
   Your screen should look like Figure L-2. The property sheet for the currently selected control, the Last text box, appears because Access allows you to change the properties of some bound controls in Form view. Some modifications can be made only in Design view, however, such as adding, deleting, moving, or resizing a control, or modifying an unbound control such as a label.

4. Close the **property sheet**
   Because of the change to the subform's Default View property, the subform now displays the records in exactly the same way that they appear formatted in Design view, and not as a datasheet.

5. Click on the Form View toolbar, click the **Passed check box** to select it, right-click the **Passed check box**, point to **Change To**, then click **Toggle Button**
   Changing a control into a different control can be accomplished only in Design view. See Table L-1 for more information on which controls are interchangeable by using the "Change To" shortcut menu option.

6. Point to the **middle-right resize handle** on the toggle button, drag ↔ to the right edge of the form, click the **toggle button**, type **Click if Yes**, then click
   Your screen should look similar to Figure L-3. Notice that when the value is "yes," the toggle button appears indented or "pushed in." The text displayed on the button can be changed using the Caption property on the Format tab in the toggle button's property sheet.

7. Click the **Save button** on the Form View toolbar
   The changes are saved to the Employee Course Attendance form and the Attendance Subform.

8. Close the Employee Course Attendance form

FIGURE L-1: Form and subform in Design view

Subform's select form button

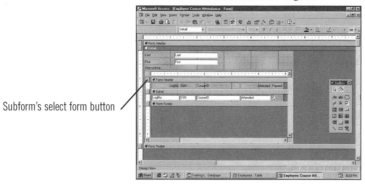

FIGURE L-2: Form view displaying the property sheet

Text box is selected

Property sheet for last text box

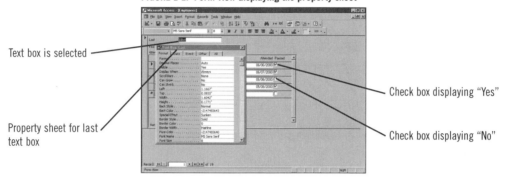

Check box displaying "Yes"

Check box displaying "No"

FIGURE L-3: Command buttons displaying "yes" and "no" values

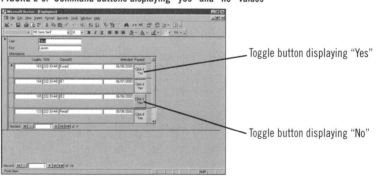

Toggle button displaying "Yes"

Toggle button displaying "No"

TABLE L-1: Interchangeable bound controls

control	can be interchanged with	used most commonly when the field has
Text box	List box, combo box	An unlimited number of choices such as a Price, LastName, or Street field
List box	Text box, combo box	A limited number of predefined values such as Manager, Department, or State fields
Combo box	Text box, list box	A limited number of common values, yet you still need the ability to enter a new value from the keyboard, such as the City field
Check box	Toggle button, option button	Only two values, "yes" or "no," such as a Veteran field
Option button	Check box, toggle button	A limited number of values, such as "female" or "male" for a Gender field. The option button is most commonly used in conjunction with an option group that can contain several option buttons, each representing a possible value for the field
Toggle button	Check box, option button	Only two values, "yes" or "no," and you want the appearance of the field to look like a button rather than a check box

Using Conditional Formatting

Conditional Formatting can be used to determine the appearance of a field on a form or report based on its value, a value in another field, or when the field has the focus. **Focus** is the ability to receive user input through the keyboard or mouse. Conditional formatting provides a way to alert the user to exceptional situations as data is being entered or reported. Format changes include changing the text color, background color, or style of the control. If you conditionally format a control based on a value in another field, you must use an **expression**, a combination of field names, operators, and values that calculate an answer. ▶Scenario▶ The users of the Courses form (which includes the Course-Employee Subform) would like David to modify the form so that they can quickly identify those course attendees with a title of "Salesperson." Additionally, David uses conditional formatting to more clearly show which text box has the focus.

Steps

Trouble?

If the subform appears as a white rectangle, click the Form View button, then click the Design View button to refresh the screen.

1. Double-click the **Courses form**, view the overall layout of the form and subform, then click the **Design View button** 🔲 on the Form View toolbar
   The subform represents each person who attended the course, and the main form provides four fields of information about the course.

2. Click the **subform horizontal ruler** to select the subform, click the **subform vertical ruler** to the left of the **Last text box** in the subform to select all four text boxes in the Detail section of the subform, click **Format** on the menu bar, then click **Conditional Formatting**
   The Conditional Formatting dialog box opens. The first condition will highlight the field with the focus.

3. Click the **Condition 1 list arrow**, click **Field Has Focus**, click the **Condition 1 Fill/Back Color list arrow** 🎨▾, then click **bright yellow** (fourth row, third box from the left)
   The second condition will highlight which attendees have the title of "Salesperson."

QuickTip

You can include up to three conditions in the Conditional Formatting dialog box.

4. Click **Add** in the Conditional Formatting dialog box, click the **Condition 2 list arrow**, click **Expression is**, press **[Tab]**, type **[Title]="Salesperson"**, click the **Condition 2 Bold button** 🅱, click the **Condition 2 Font/Fore Color list arrow** 🅰▾, then click **bright red** (third row, first box from the left)
   Your screen should look like Figure L-4. When an expression is used in the Conditional Formatting dialog box, the expression must evaluate to be either "true," which turns the formatting on, or "false," which turns the formatting off.

5. Click **OK**, click the **Form View button** 🔲 on the Form Design toolbar, then click **Colletti** (the first field value in the first record) in the subform
   Your screen should look like Figure L-5.

6. Press **[Tab]** three times to move the focus to the Salesperson entry for the first record, press **[Delete]**, then press **[Tab]**
   Your screen should look like Figure L-6, in which the first record in the subform is no longer red and boldface. Conditional formatting reverts to default formatting if the condition is no longer true.

QuickTip

You can also click the Undo button 🔄 on the Form View toolbar to undo the last action.

7. Click **Edit** on the menu bar, then click the **Undo Saved Record button** 🔄
   The Title Salesperson is restored for the first record and it is in red boldface text.

8. Save then close the Courses form

FIGURE L-4: Conditional Formatting dialog box

Field Has Focus

Expression

Expression Is

Back/Fill Color button

Bold button

Font/Fore Color button

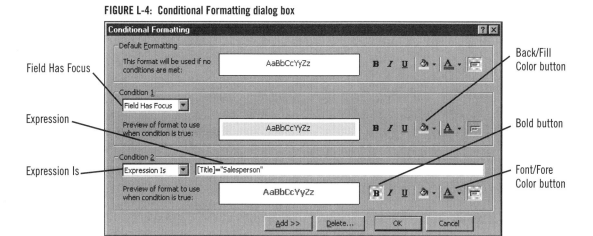

FIGURE L-5: The control with the focus is bright yellow

This control has the focus

Conditional formatting for [Title]= "Salesperson"

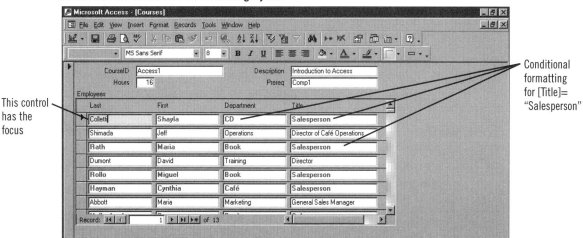

FIGURE L-6: Conditional formats change as data is edited

Title value is no longer "Salesperson"

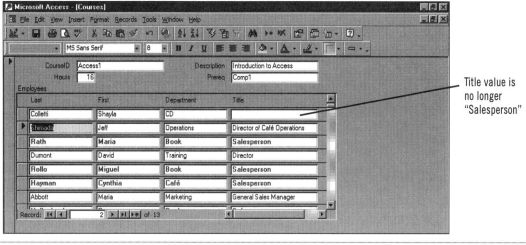

Creating Custom Help

You can create several types of custom Help for a form or a control on a form. If you want to display a textual tip that pops up over a control when you point to it, use the **ControlTip Text** property for that control. Or, use the **Status Bar Text** property to display helpful information about a form or control in the status bar. **Scenario** David wants to allow other users to enter new course records as those courses become available. He quickly creates a new form based on the Courses table, then adds custom help to guide the new users as they enter the data.

Steps

1. Click the **New button** in the database window, click **AutoForm: Columnar**, click the **Choose the table or query where the object's data comes from list arrow**, click **Courses**, then click **OK**

    A Courses form is created. You can modify the ControlTip Text and Status Bar Text properties for text boxes and other bound controls from Form view.

2. Click **View** on the menu, click **Properties**, click the **Other tab** in the CourseID text box property sheet, click the **ControlTip Text property text box**, type **Use a 1 suffix for an introductory course**, press **[Enter]**, then point to the **CourseID text box**

    A control tip pops up, as shown in Figure L-7. You can view and enter a long entry using the Zoom dialog box.

> **QuickTip**
>
> Click a property, then press [Shift][F2] to open the Zoom dialog box for that property.

3. Right-click the **ControlTip Text property**, click **Zoom**, click to the right of the word "**course**" in the Zoom dialog box, press **[Spacebar]**, then type **and a 2 suffix for an intermediate course**

    The Zoom dialog box should look like Figure L-8.

4. Click **OK**, then click the **Prereq text box**

    The property sheet now shows the properties for the Prereq text box.

> **QuickTip**
>
> Click a property, then press [F1] to open the Microsoft Access Help window for the specific explanation of that property.

5. Click the **Status Bar Text text box** in the Text Box Prereq property sheet

    When the property sheet is open, a short description of the selected property appears in the status bar.

6. Right-click the **Status Bar Text text box**, click **Zoom**, type **Comp1 can be waived by achieving an 80% score on the Computers 101 test**, click **OK**, then close the property sheet

7. Click **File** on the menu bar, click **Save As**, type **Courses Entry Form** in the Save From Form 1 To text box, click **OK**, then close the property sheet and the form

8. Double-click **Courses Entry Form** in the database window, then click the **Prereq text box**

    Your screen should look like Figure L-9. The status bar displays the entry in the Status Bar Text property for this control. Unbound properties such as labels do not have a Status Bar Text property because they cannot have the focus. A label can have a ControlTip Text property that displays text when you point to the label. A label's ControlTip Text property can be modified only in Form Design view, because that's the only place you can select an unbound control in order to access its property sheet.

9. Close the Courses Entry form

FIGURE L-7: Using the ControlTip Text property

ControlTip Text

CourseID text box property sheet

Other tab

ControlTip Text property

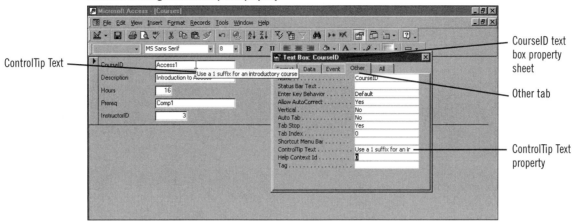

FIGURE L-8: Zoom dialog box

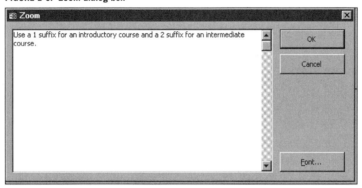

FIGURE L-9: Using the Status Bar Text property

Status Bar Text

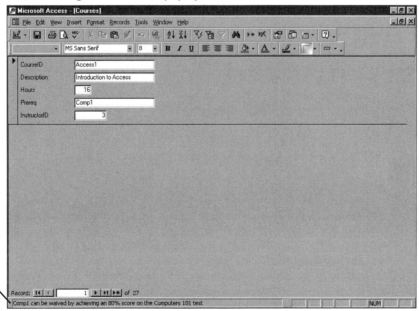

Access 2000

Adding Tab Controls

The **tab control** is a powerful unbound control used to organize a form and give it a three-dimensional look by presenting several "pages" on a single form. When you want to show a lot of information on a form at one time, the tab control is an excellent tool to logically organize many fields. You are already familiar with using tab controls because they are used in many Access dialog boxes such as the property sheet. The property sheet also uses tabs to organize properties identified by their category name in the tab (Format, Data, Event, Other, and All). **Scenario** David has started to develop an Employee Update Form, but wants to use the tab control to organize and present employee information in an easy-to-use way.

Steps

1. Click the **Employee Update Form**, click the **Design View button** 🔳 in the database window, click the **Toolbox button** 🛠 to toggle the Toolbox on (if necessary), click the **Tab Control button** 🔲 on the Toolbox toolbar, then click just below the **First label** in the Detail section of the form
   Your screen should look like Figure L-10. The tab control appears with two "pages," with the default names of Page17 and Page18, on the respective tabs.

2. Double-click **Page17** to open its property sheet, click the **Other tab**, verify Page17 is selected in the Name text box, type **Personnel Info**, click the **Page18 tab** on the form, double-click **Page18** in the Name text box of the property sheet, type **Course Attendance**, then close the property sheet
   The tabs now describe the information they will contain.

   QuickTip
   The page will become dark gray when you are successfully placing a control on that page.

3. Click the **Personnel Info tab**, click the **Field List button** 🔳 on the Form Design toolbar to toggle it on (if necessary), click **Department** in the field list, press and hold **[Shift]**, click **SSN** in the field list (you may have to scroll) to select all fields between the Department and SSN, release **[Shift]**, then drag the **highlighted fields** to the middle of the Personnel Info page
   Your screen should look like Figure L-11. The six fields are added to the Personnel Info page on the tab control. You can add any control, even a subform control, to a page.

   Trouble?
   The Control Wizards button must be selected prior to clicking the Subform/Subreport button on the Toolbox to activate the Subform Wizard.

4. Click the **Course Attendance tab**, click the **Subform/Subreport button** 🔳 on the Toolbox, click the **upper-left corner of the Course Attendance page**, click the **Use existing Tables and Queries** option button in the SubForm Wizard dialog box, click **Next**, click the **Select All Fields button** 🔳, click **Next**, click **Show Attendance for each record in Employees using SSN**, click **Next**, type **Attendance Info**, then click **Finish**
   The tab control as well as the entire form has been automatically widened to better accommodate the wide subform control.

5. Click the **Form View button** 🔳, click the **Course Attendance tab**, then maximize the Employee Update Form window
   Your screen should look similar to Figure L-12.

   Trouble?
   Your page control number may be different than 27.

6. Click 🔳, right-click the **Course Attendance tab**, click **Insert Page**, double-click **Page27** to open the property sheet, click the **Other tab** (if necessary), double-click **Page27**, type **Course Feedback**, close the property sheet, click 🔳, then click all three tabs
   You probably want to move and resize several of the controls on this form before using it, but for now the Course Feedback tab is prepared and ready for you to add controls to it in Design view to hold information for a future time.

7. Save and close the Employee Update Form

FIGURE L-10: Adding a tab control

New tab control

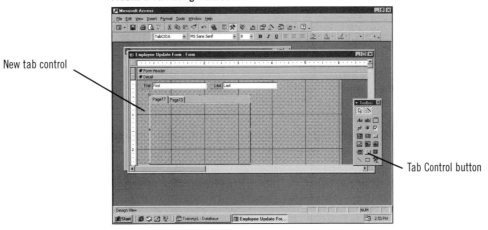

Tab Control button

FIGURE L-11: Adding fields to a tab control

Field List button

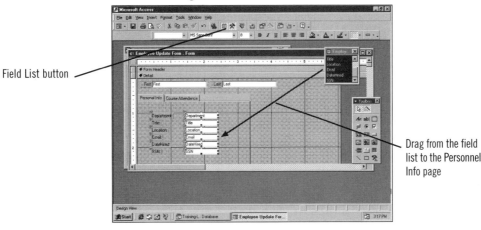

Drag from the field list to the Personnel Info page

FIGURE L-12: The tab control in Form View

Course Attendance tab

Attendance Info subform

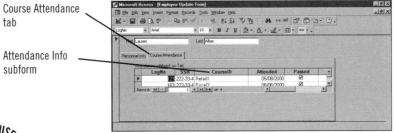

CLUES TO USE

Referencing controls with Text## and Page##

Access sequentially numbers each control on a form and uses that number in the Name property for the control. The label and tab control that display the name property as part of the control, you see the sequential number in the name of the control. For example, when adding a tab control to the form, the word "Page" plus the sequential number of that control are used as the default entry for the Name property

and appear on the tab itself. If you add a control and then delete it, that sequential number is not used over. Since users build their forms in different ways, adding and deleting controls as necessary, it is common to reference the new label or tab controls as "Text##" or "Page##" because the exact number represented by ## will be different from user to user.

Access 2000

Adding Charts

Charts, sometimes called graphs, are visual representations of numeric data that help users see comparisons, patterns, and trends in data. Charts can be inserted on a form, report, or data access page object. Access provides a **Chart Wizard** that steps you through the process of creating charts within forms and reports. Before using the Chart Wizard, however, you must determine what data you want the graph to show. Often you'll use an intermediate query to gather the specific fields that you wish to graph into one object before using the Chart Wizard to create the graph, especially if the data comes from multiple tables or if you wish to graph a subset of records. Scenario David created a Department Summary query with two fields: Attended from the Attendance table and Department from the Employees table. Instead of reporting this information as a datasheet of summarized numbers, he uses the report object's Chart Wizard to visually display a total count of attendance by department.

Steps

1. Click **Reports** on the Objects bar, click the **New button** in the database window, click **Chart Wizard**, click the **Choose the table or query where the object's data comes from list arrow**, click **Department Summary**, then click **OK**

   The Chart Wizard starts and presents the fields in the Department Summary query.

2. Click **the Select All Fields button** , then click **Next**

   The next Chart Wizard dialog box, shown in Figure L-13, determines the type of chart that will be created. See Table L-2 for more information on common chart types. Column Chart, the button in the first row, first column on the left, is the default chart type.

   > **QuickTip**
   >
   > Click any chart button to read a description of that chart in the lower-right corner of the Chart Wizard dialog box.

3. Click **Next**

   The next dialog box determines which fields will be used for the x-axis, bar, and series (legend) areas of the chart. For this chart, you want the bars to represent a count of the Attended field. The Department field should be used as x-axis labels.

4. Drag the **Attended field button** from the field buttons on the right to the **Data** area, then drag the **Attended by month button** from the Series area out of the chart area, as shown in Figure L-14

   Since the Attended field holds date data, bars should count the number of entries.

   > **QuickTip**
   >
   > If you drag a numeric field into the Data area, you can double-click the button to change the way it is summarized to Sum, Avg, Min, or Max value of the field.

5. Click **Next**, type **Total Attendance by Department** in the title for your chart text box, then click **Finish**

   Your chart should look similar to Figure L-15. The chart is difficult to read as it currently appears, but Access provides charting tools to improve the appearance of charts.

FIGURE L-13: Chart types

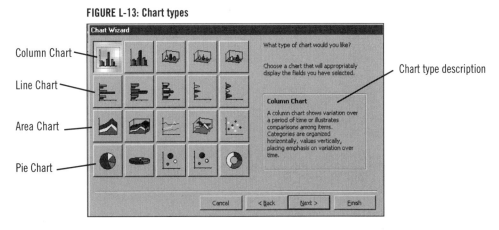

Column Chart

Line Chart

Area Chart

Pie Chart

Chart type description

FIGURE L-14: Determining chart layout

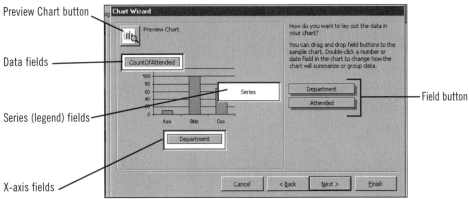

Preview Chart button

Data fields

Series (legend) fields

X-axis fields

Field button

FIGURE L-15: Total Attendance by Department chart

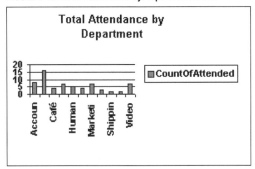

TABLE L-2: Common chart types

chart type	chart icon	most commonly used to show	example
Column		Comparisons of values	Each bar represents the annual sales for a different product for the year 2000
Line		Trends over time	Each point on the line represents monthly sales for one product for the year 2000
Pie		Parts of a whole	Each slice represents total quarterly sales for a company for the year 2000
Area		Cumulative totals	Each section represents monthly sales by representative, stacked to show the cumulative total sales effort for the year 2000

Modifying Charts

All charts are modified in Design View of the form or report where the chart exists. Modifying a chart is challenging because Design View doesn't show you the actual chart values and elements, but rather shows you a chart placeholder that represents the embedded chart object. Scenario▶ David sees that the chart would be clearer if he removes the legend and resizes the chart to better display the values on the axes. He makes all modifications to the existing chart in Report Design view.

Steps

QuickTip

The hashed border of the chart placeholder control indicates that the chart is in edit mode.

1. Click the **Design View button** 📐, maximize the Report Design View window, then double-click the **chart** to edit it

   The chart is now ready to be edited, as shown in Figure L-16. You can delete, move, or resize the chart object without double-clicking it, but if you want to modify any of the chart elements, you must double-click the chart placeholder to open the chart menu bar and toolbar. If you double-click the edge of the chart placeholder, you will open its property sheet. All chart editing and formatting is done in Report Design view, but the actual chart data displays only in Print Preview.

Trouble?

You may have to click the More Buttons button 📊 on the Chart toolbar to locate the Legend button.

2. Click the **Legend button** 📧 on the Chart toolbar to toggle off the legend, click **outside the chart** to exit chart editing mode, click the **Print Preview button** 🔍 on the Chart toolbar, then click the chart

   Your chart should look similar to Figure L-17. Because the chart has only one series of bars, a clear title (rather than a legend) can be used to describe the series. Most of the elements, including the y-axis labels and bars, are still too small to clearly display the information.

Trouble?

Be sure you work within the vertical ruler in the Detail section.

3. Click 📐 on the Print Preview toolbar, click the **chart placeholder** to select the control, then drag the **lower-right sizing handle** down and to the right to the **5"** mark on the horizontal ruler and the **3.5"** mark on the vertical ruler

   With the chart placeholder resized, you can expand the size of the chart within it.

Trouble?

Click the View Datasheet button 📧 on the Standard toolbar to close the chart's datasheet if it opens.

4. Double-click the **chart placeholder**, then drag the lower-right corner sizing handle of the fuzzy border of the chart to just within the border of the chart placeholder, as shown in Figure L-18

   You can modify any element such as the labels on the x-axis or y-axis, but you must select them before you change or format them.

QuickTip

The Category Axis is the x-axis, and the Value Axis is the y-axis.

5. Click the **East label** to select the Category Axis, click the **Font Size list arrow** 10 ▾, click **8**, click the **Total Attendance by Department Chart Title**, click 12 ▾, click **10**, click outside the chart to exit chart edit mode, click 🔍 on the Report Design toolbar, then click the chart

   The final chart is shown in Figure L-19. It clearly shows that the Book Department has far more attendees at MediaLoft's internal training courses than any other department.

6. Click **File** on the menu bar, click **Save As**, type **Department Graph-*Your Initials***, then click **OK**

7. Click the **Print button** 🖨, then close the Department Graph-Your Initials report

FIGURE L-16: Editing a chart in Design view

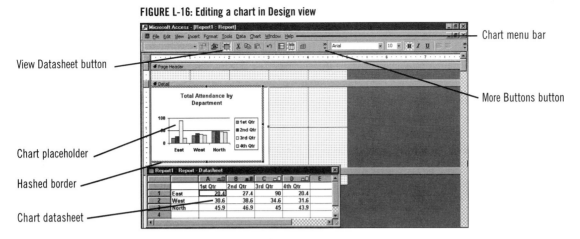

Chart menu bar

View Datasheet button

More Buttons button

Chart placeholder

Hashed border

Chart datasheet

FIGURE L-17: Chart still needs improvement

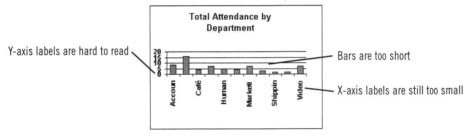

Y-axis labels are hard to read

Bars are too short

X-axis labels are still too small

FIGURE L-18: Increasing the chart size

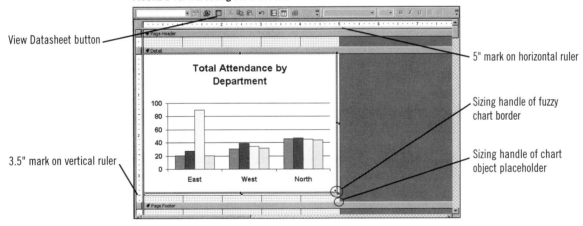

View Datasheet button

5" mark on horizontal ruler

Sizing handle of fuzzy chart border

3.5" mark on vertical ruler

Sizing handle of chart object placeholder

FIGURE L-19: Final chart

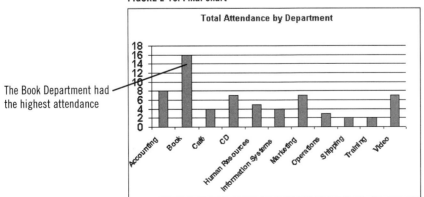

The Book Department had the highest attendance

Adding Subreport Controls

A **subreport control** displays a report within another report. The **main report** contains the subreport control. You use the subreport control when you want to link two reports together to automate printing. You also can use a subreport control when you want to change the order in which information normally prints. If you want report totals (generally found in the Report Footer section, which prints on the last page) to print on the first page, you could use a subreport control that calculates report grand totals in the subreport's Report Footer section and place it in the main report's Report Header section. **Scenario** Now that David has created the Department Graph report, he wishes to add it as a subreport to the bottom of the Report Footer section of the Department Enrollment report so that it is viewed and printed at the same time.

Steps 1234

1. Click the **Department Enrollment** report, click the **Design button** 🔏 in the database window, scroll to the bottom of the report, then use the ✛ pointer to drag the bottom edge of the report down **1"**
   You've expanded the size of the Report Footer section to make room for the subreport control.

2. Click the **Toolbox button** 🛠 on the Report Design toolbar to toggle it on (if necessary), click the **Subform/Subreport button** 🖿 on the Toolbox, then click below the **Grand Total label** in the Report Footer section
   The SubReport Wizard opens, as shown in Figure L-20.

3. Click the **Use an existing report or form option button**, click **Department Graph Report-***Your Initials***, click **Next**, click **Finish** to accept the name **Department Graph-***Your Initials*** for the subreport, maximize the Report Design view window (if necessary), then scroll down to view the Report Footer section
   The subreport control appears in Report Design view, as shown in Figure L-21, and expands the size of the report to accommodate the large control. You can modify a subreport's controls directly within the main report just as you can modify a subform's controls within a main form.

4. Click the **Print Preview button** 🔍 on the Report Design toolbar, then click the **Last page button** ▶I on the navigation buttons
   Your screen should look like Figure L-22. The Report Footer section contains the subreport and, therefore, displays the graph on the last page.

5. Close the Department Enrollment report, then save the changes when prompted

FIGURE L-20: SubReport Wizard

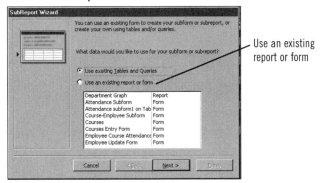

Use an existing report or form

FIGURE L-21: Subreport in Report Design view

Report Footer section

Grand Total label

Subform/Subreport button

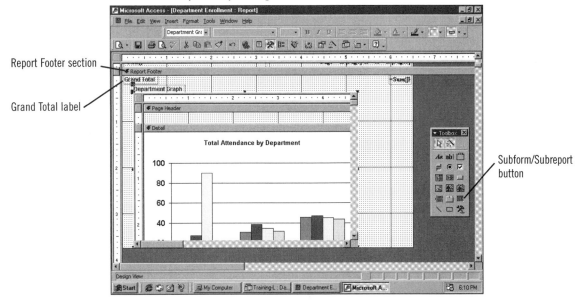

FIGURE L-22: Department graph displayed as a subreport

Page Header controls

Report Footer controls

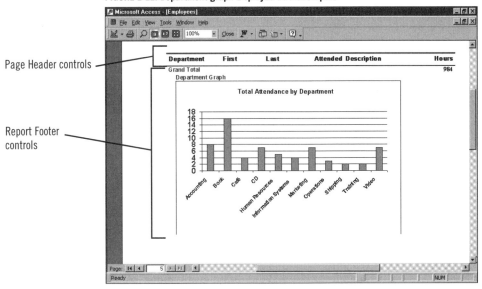

Modifying Section Properties

Report **section properties** can be modified to help determine how the sections of the report print. For example, you might want each group's header section to always print at the top of a new page. Other report section properties control formatting issues such as the section's back color property. See Table L-3 for more information on common section properties. **Scenario** David doesn't want the Detail records (the courses each employee has attended) of the Department Enrollment report to span two pages. In addition, he'd like the records for each new department to start at the top of a new page. He makes these section property changes in Report Design view.

Steps

1. Click the **Department Enrollment report**, click the **Design button** in the database window, double-click the **Department Footer section** to open its property sheet, then click the **Format tab** in the property sheet
   The property sheet for the Department Header section opens, as shown in Figure L-23.

2. Click the **Force New Page list arrow**, then click **After Section**
   This property change will force the report to continue at the top of the next page after the Group Footer prints.

3. Click the **Back Color text box**, click the **Back Color Build button**, click the **light yellow box** (second column on the top row), then click **OK**
   Now the entire section will appear with a light yellow background color in print preview, and on the printout if a color printer is used.

4. Click the **Department Header section**, click the **Back Color text box** in the property sheet, click, click the **light yellow box**, click **OK**, close the property sheet, click the **Print Preview button**, then Zoom Out
   Your screen should look like Figure L-24. By modifying section properties, you have clarified where the group starts and stops by shading those sections, and have forced a page break at the end of each Group Footer.

5. Click, click the **Label button** on the Toolbox toolbar, click to the right of the **Department Enrollment label** in the Report Header section, type **Your Name**, click the **Save button**, then click

6. Click **File** on the menu bar, click **Print**, click the **Pages option button** in the Print Range section, type **1** in the From text box, click the **To text box**, type **1**, then click **OK**
   The first page of the Department Enrollment report showing the section shading is sent to the printer.

7. Close the **Department Enrollment** report, close **MediaLoft-L database**, then exit **Access**

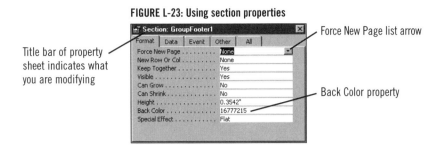

FIGURE L-23: Using section properties

Title bar of property sheet indicates what you are modifying

Force New Page list arrow

Back Color property

FIGURE L-24: Using section colors

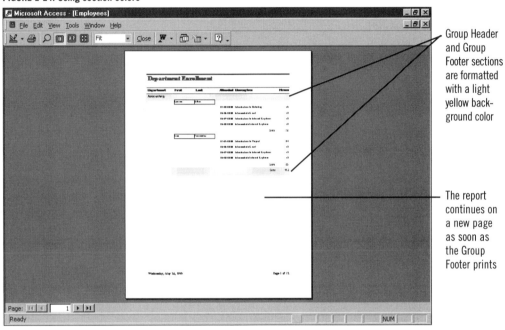

Group Header and Group Footer sections are formatted with a light yellow background color

The report continues on a new page as soon as the Group Footer prints

TABLE L-3: Common report section properties

property	options	description
Force New Page	None (default) Before Section After Section Before and After	Determines whether a section starts on the current page or a new page, or whether a new page starts after the section
New Row or Col	None (default) Before Section After Section Before and After	Often used to specify that a Group Header prints at the top of a new column in a multiple-column report
Visible	Yes (default) No	Determines whether the section is visible in Print Preview
Keep Together	Yes (default) No	Determines whether the records in that section must print on the same page or whether they can span multiple pages
Back Color	Number that corresponds to a color	Controls the color of the background of that section

Practice

▶ Concepts Review

Identify each element of a form's Design view shown in Figure L-25.

FIGURE L-25

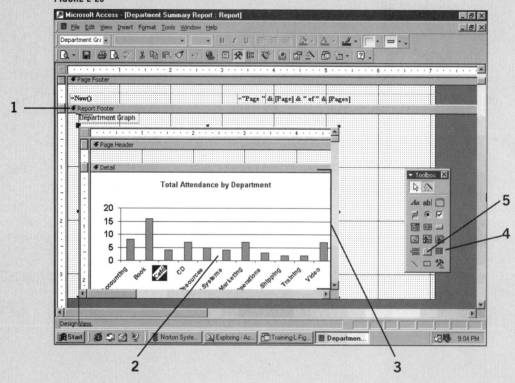

Match each term with the statement that describes its function.

6. **Focus**
7. **Tab control**
8. **Sections**
9. **Conditional formatting**
10. **Charts**
11. **Check box**

a. Determine where and how controls print on a report
b. Visual representations of numeric data
c. The ability to receive user input through the keyboard or mouse
d. Allows you to change the appearance of a control on a form or report based on criteria you specify
e. A control that is often used to display Yes/No fields on a form
f. An unbound control used to organize a form and give it a three-dimensional look

Select the best answer from the list of choices.

12. **Which controls are NOT interchangeable?**
    a. Check box and option group
    b. Combo box and list box
    c. Check box and toggle button
    d. Text box and combo box

13. **When would you most likely use a toggle button control?**
    a. In place of an unbound label
    b. For a field with only two choices: Yes or No
    c. In place of a command button
    d. For a field with a limited set of choices

14. **You would most likely use which control for a City field?**
    a. Command button
    b. Combo box
    c. Check box
    d. List box

15. **To display text that pops up over a control when you point to it, you would modify which control property?**
    a. Help Text
    b. Status Bar Text
    c. Popup Text
    d. ControlTip Text

16. **Which type of chart would you most likely use to show an upward sales trend over several months?**
    a. Line
    b. Column
    c. Scatter
    d. Pie

17. **Which type of control would you use to display report totals as the first page of a report?**
    a. Main Report
    b. Subreport
    c. Calculated Properties
    d. Report Footer

▶ ## Skills Review

1. **Adding Check Boxes and Toggle Buttons.**
   a. Start Access and open the Seminar-L database from your Project Disk.
   b. Open the Attendees form in Form view, and check the EarlyBirdDiscount check box for the first record in the subform of the first person, Phuong Pham.
   c. Open Design view of the Attendees form. If the subform doesn't display the controls (but rather a white box), click the Form View button, then click Design view a second time in order to see the controls in the subform.

d. Change the Default View property of the subform to Continuous Forms. (*Hint*: Open the property sheet for the form in the subform control.)

e. Change the EarlyBirdDiscount check box into a toggle button.

f. Expand the subform's height about one inch, then expand the size of the EarlyBirdDiscount toggle button to the width of the subform.

g. Add the text "Click for Early Bird Discount" to the toggle button (either by typing directly on the button or by modifying the toggle button's Caption property).

h. Close the property sheet, then view the form in Form view. Expand the size of the subform control using Design View to clearly display three records in the subform when viewed in Form view.

i. Open the form in Form view, and click the toggle button to enter "Yes" in the EarlyBirdDiscount field for the second record in the subform for Phuong Pham.

j. Enter your own last name in place of "Pham" and print only this record.

k. Save and close the form.

2. **Using Conditional Formatting.**

a. Open the Attendees form in Design view.

b. Click the RegistrationDate text box, then press and hold [Shift] while clicking the RegistrationFee text box to select both controls in the Detail section of the subform. If you see a white box for the subform control, click the Form View button, then the Design View button to refresh the screen.

c. Click Format on the menu bar, click Conditional Formatting, set Condition 1 to Expression Is, then set the criteria to [RegistrationFee]>10

d. Format the Condition 1 for this expression so any values meeting the criteria display as bold, with a bright blue Font/Fore Color. Close the Conditional Formatting dialog box.

e. Save the changes.

f. Still in Design view, select both the AttendeeFirstName and AttendeeLastName text box controls in the Detail section of the main form.

g. Click Format on the menu bar, click Conditional Formatting, then set Condition 1 to Field Has Focus.

h. The Condition 1 format should be black text against a light blue Fill/Back color.

i. Display the form in Form view, then enter your own first name in place of "Phuong."

j. Change the Registration Fee to $11 for the first record in the subform, then tab through the record to make sure that both the RegistrationDate and RegistrationFee text boxes are conditionally formatted.

k. Save the form, print the first record, then close the form.

3. **Creating Custom Help.**

a. Open the Attendees form in Design view.

b. Open the property sheet for the EarlyBirdDiscount toggle button, then select the Other tab.

c. Enter the following as the ControlTip Text property: "To qualify, registration must be one month before the event." Use the Zoom dialog box if you wish.

d. Use the Zoom dialog box to enter the following as the Status Bar Text property: "Discounts can also be given for group registrations."

e. Close the property sheet, save the form, then open the form in Form view.

f. Point to the button for the third record in the subform to make sure that the ControlTip Text property works.

g. Point to, then click the command button for the third record in the subform to make sure that the Status Bar Text property works.

h. Close the Attendees form.

4. Adding Tab Controls.

   a. Open the Events form in Design view.

   b. Add a tab control under the Event Name label.

   c. Modify the Page5 Name property of the first tab to be "Event Info".

   d. Modify the Page6 Name property of the second tab to be "Participants".

   e. Open the Field List, then add the Location, Date, and AvailableSpaces fields from the Field List to the middle of the Event Info page.

   f. Add a subform to the Participants page, using the Subform Wizard to guide your actions. Click the Existing tables or queries option button. Select the RegistrationDate field from the Registration table, and the AttendeeFirstName and AttendeeLastName fields from the Attendees table.

   g. Link the main form to the subform by using the "Show Registration for each record in Events using EventID" option.

   h. Name the subform "Registration".

   i. Expand the height of the subform control to fill the page, then view the form in Form view.

   j. Click the Participants tab to make sure both tabs work correctly, then print the first record twice, once with the Event Info tab displayed and once with the Participants tab displayed.

   k. Save and close the Events form.

5. Adding Charts.

   a. Click Reports on the Objects bar, then click the New button in the database window.

   b. Click the Chart Wizard, choose Registration as the table or query where the object's data comes from, then click OK.

   c. Choose the EventID and RegistrationFee as the fields for the Chart.

   d. Choose a Column Chart type.

   e. Sum the RegistrationFee field in the Data area, and use the EventID field as the x-axis. (*Hint*: These should be the defaults, but click the Preview Chart button to make sure.)

   f. Title the chart "Registration Fee Totals-Your Initials".

   g. Print the chart, then save the report as "Registration Fee Totals".

6. Modifying Charts.

   a. Open Registration Fee Totals in Design view.

   b. Double-click the chart to edit it.

   c. Remove the legend, and increase the size of both the control and the chart within it to as large as will comfortably fit on your screen.

   d. Click any value in the y-axis to select it, choose Format on the menu bar, then click the Number option.

   e. Click the Number tab in the Format Axis dialog box, click the Currency category, change the Decimal places text box to 0, then click OK in the Format Axis dialog box.

   f. Click outside the chart object to return to Report Design view, preview the report with the chart, print it, save the changes, then close the Registration Fee Totals report.

7. Adding Subreport Controls.

   a. Use the Report Wizard to create a report on all of the fields in the Events table.

   b. Do not add any grouping levels, but sort the records in ascending order by EventID.

   c. Use a Tabular layout, a Portrait orientation, and a Casual style.

   d. Title the report "Event Information".

   e. Open Event Information in Design view.

   f. Increase the size of the Report Footer section by about one inch.

   g. Add a subreport control to the upper-left part of the Report Footer section.

h. Use the SubReport Wizard to guide your actions in creating the subreport. Click the Registration Fee Totals report in the first dialog box, and accept the name "Registration Fee Totals" as the subreport's name in the second.

i. Preview the report, print it, then save and close the Event Information Report.

8. Modifying Section Properties.

a. Use the Report Wizard to create a report on all of the fields in the Registration table, and the EventName field in the Events table.

b. View the data by Events, but do not add any grouping levels or sorting fields.

c. Use an Outline 2 layout, a Landscape orientation, and a Compact style.

d. Title the report "Event Details".

e. Open Event Details in Design view, then open the property sheet for the Events_EventID Header section.

f. Change the Force New Page property on the Format tab to Before Section. Change the Back Color property to light blue. (*Hint*: Use the Build button to locate the color on the palette.)

g. Close the property sheet, add your name as a label in the Report Header section, preview the report, then print the first two pages.

h. Save and close the Event Details report.

i. Close Seminar-L and exit Access.

► Visual Workshop

As the manager of a college women's basketball team, you wish to create a form that highlights outstanding statistics if either their scoring or their rebounding totals are equal to or greater than 10 for an individual game effort. Start Access and open the Basketball-L database. Open the Players form in Design view, and use the conditional formatting feature to format the FG (field goals), 3P (three-point shots), and FT (free throws) text boxes in the Stats Subform1 to have a bright yellow background if the following expression that totals their scoring for that game is true: 2*[FG]+3*[3P]+[FT]>=10. Conditionally format the Reb-O (offensive rebounds) and Reb-D (defensive rebounds) text boxes to be have a light blue background if the following expression that totals rebounds is true: [Reb-O]+[Reb-D]>=10. Display the second record for Ellyse Howard, which should look like Figure L-26. Print the form.

FIGURE L-26

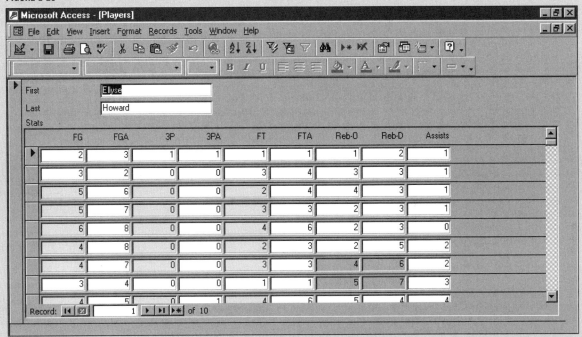

Managing
Database Objects

Objectives

- ▶ **Work with objects**
- ⌐MOUS⌐ ▶ **Use the Documenter**
- ▶ **Group objects**
- ▶ **Modify groups**
- ▶ **Create a dialog box**
- ▶ **Create a pop-up form**
- ⌐MOUS⌐ ▶ **Create a switchboard**
- ▶ **Modify a switchboard**

As your database grows in size and functionality, the number of objects (especially queries and reports) will grow as well. Your ability to find, rename, delete, and document objects as well as your proficiency to present objects in an organized way to other database users through groups and switchboards will become important skills. Scenario▶ Kristen Fontanelle is the network administrator at MediaLoft headquarters. She has developed a working database to document MediaLoft computer equipment in use throughout the company. The large quantity of objects within the database makes it increasingly difficult to find and organize information. Kristen will use powerful Access documentation, object grouping, and switchboard features to manage the growing database.

Access 2000

Working with Objects

Working with Access objects is very similar to working with files in Windows Explorer. For example, the **View buttons** (Large Icons, Small Icons, List, and Details) on the database window toolbar can be used to arrange the objects in four different ways just as files can be arranged within Explorer. Similarly, you right-click an object within Access to open, copy, delete, or rename it just as you would right-click a file within Explorer. Scenario▶ Kristen wants to work with several objects to improve the database window interface. She deletes, renames, sorts, and adds descriptions to several objects.

Steps

1. Start Access, open the **Technology-M database** on your Project Disk, maximize the database window, click **Queries** on the Objects bar, then click the **Details button** on the database window toolbar

   Your screen should look like Figure M-1, with five columns of information for each object: Name, Description, Modified (date the object was last changed), Created (date the object was originally created), and Type. By default, objects are sorted in ascending order by name, and the Description column is blank.

QuickTip

Point to the line between column headings, then drag ✛ left or right to resize that column.

2. Click the **Modified column heading** to sort the objects in ascending order on the date they were last modified, click **Modified column heading** again to sort the objects in descending order on the date they were last modified, then click the **Name column heading**

   The query objects are now sorted in ascending order by name. The Description column is a special object property that is used to further describe the object.

3. Right-click the **Equipment Specs query**, then click **Properties**

   The Equipment Specs Properties dialog box opens, as shown in Figure M-2.

4. Type **Includes RAM, hard drive, and processor information for PCs**, then click **OK**

   Part of the description appears in the database window and helps describe the object. If an object is no longer needed, you should delete it to free up disk space and keep the database window organized.

5. Right-click the **Employees Query**, click **Delete**, then click **Yes** when prompted

   Even though object names can be 64 characters long and can include any combination of letters, numbers, spaces, and special characters except a period (.), exclamation point (!), accent (`), or brackets ([]), they should be kept short yet descriptive. Short names make them easier to reference in other places in the database such as in the Record Source property for a report.

6. Right-click the **Human Resources query**, click **Rename**, type **HR**, press **[Enter]**, right-click the **Information Systems query**, click **Rename**, type **IS**, then press **[Enter]**

   Your final screen should look like Figure M-3. With shorter query names, all of the object names are visible in the database window without resizing the columns.

FIGURE M-1: Viewing object details

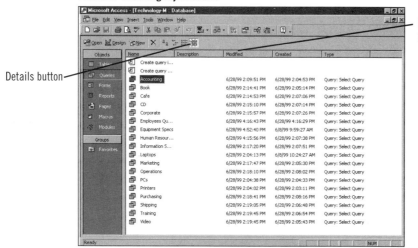

Details button

Modified column heading

FIGURE M-2: Equipment Specs Properties dialog box

FIGURE M-3: Final Query object window

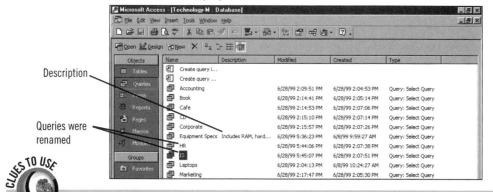

Description

Queries were renamed

CLUES TO USE

Updating names with Name AutoCorrect

Name AutoCorrect fixes discrepancies between references to field names, controls, and objects when you rename them. For example, if a report is based on a query named "Department Income," and the query name is changed to "Dept Inc," the Name AutoCorrect feature will automatically update the Record Source property for the report to "Dept Inc." Similarly, if a query includes a field name of "LastName" that changes to "LName" in the Design view of the original table, the Name AutoCorrect feature will update the field name reference within the query as well. Name AutoCorrect will not repair references in Visual Basic code, replicated databases, linked tables, or a number of other database situations. Click Tools on the menu bar in the database window, click Options, and then click the General tab to view the Name AutoCorrect options. By default, the first two of the three Name AutoCorrect options should be checked.

Using the Documenter

As your Access database becomes more successful, users will naturally find new ways to use the data. Your ability to modify an existing database will revolve largely around your understanding of existing database objects. Access provides an analysis feature called the **Documenter** that creates reports on the properties and relationships between the objects in your database. This documentation is especially helpful to those who need to use the database but did not design the original tables. **Scenario** Kristen uses the Documenter to start creating the paper documentation that will support the Technology-M database for other MediaLoft employees.

Steps

1. Click **Tools** on the menu bar, point to **Analyze**, click **Documenter**, then click the **Tables tab**
   The Documenter dialog box opens, displaying tabs for the object types.

2. Click **Options** in the Documenter dialog box
   The Print Table Definition dialog box, shown in Figure M-4, opens. This dialog box gives you some control over what type of documentation you wish to print for the table. The documentation for each object type varies slightly. For example, the documentation on forms and reports would include information on controls and sections.

3. Click **Cancel** in the Print Table Definition dialog box
   You work through the Documenter dialog box, deciding which objects and options you want to document. Clicking the Select All button is a fast way to select all of the objects on that tab. You can also select or deselect individual objects by clicking the check box beside their name.

QuickTip

Information about the progress of Documenter will appear in the status bar.

4. Click **Select All**, click the **Forms tab**, click **Select All**, then click **OK**
   Documenter is now creating a report about all of the table and form objects in the Technology-M database, and will display it as an Access report. This can be a lengthy process (several minutes) depending on the speed of your computer and the number of objects that Documenter is examining. When completed, your screen will look like Figure M-5, which shows a report that displays information about the first table, Assignments, on the first page.

5. Click the **Last Page button** ▶| in the navigation buttons, click the **Previous Page button** ◄, then scroll down so that your screen looks like Figure M-6
   The report contains about three pages of documentation for each table, and about six pages per form. The properties for each control on the form are listed in two columns. Because most form controls have approximately 50 properties, you can quickly see why the documentation that lists each control and section property can become so large. You can print or send the report to a Word document using the OfficeLinks buttons, but you cannot work in the report's Design view or save the report as an object within the database window.

6. Click the **Close button** on the Print Preview toolbar

FIGURE M-4: Print Table Definition dialog box

Tools menu

Tables tab in Documenter dialog box

Print Table Definition dialog box

Click to open Print Table Definition dialog box

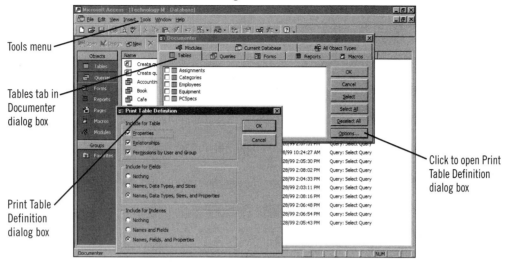

FIGURE M-5: First page of documentation

Table name

Date report is created

Table properties

Field properties for SerialNumber

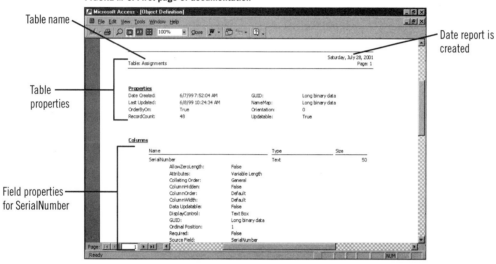

FIGURE M-6: Second to last page of documentation

Design View button is not available

Label control

Two columns of the label control's properties

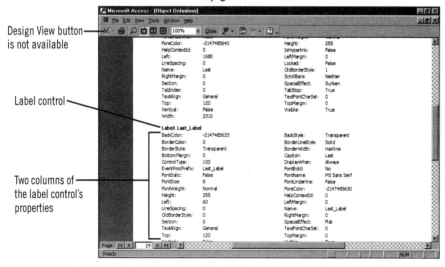

Grouping Objects

Viewing every object in the database window can be cumbersome when your database contains many objects. Objects can be placed in **groups** to help you easily organize or classify objects. For example, you might create a group for each department that uses the database so that the forms and reports used by each department are presented as a set. A group consists of **shortcuts** (pointers) to the database objects that belong to the group and does not affect the object's original location. To work with groups, click the **Groups bar** below the Objects bar in the Database window. **Scenario** Kristen organizes the objects in the Technology-M database by creating groups for the objects used by two different departments: Human Resources (HR) and Accounting.

Steps

1. **Right-click Favorites on the Groups bar, click New Group, type HR, click OK, then click HR on the Groups bar**
   Your screen should look like Figure M-7. Since the HR group was just created, there are no objects referenced in that group. The Favorites group is provided for every new Access database and is similar in function to the Favorites folder used in other Microsoft applications. Within an Access database, the Favorites group organizes *objects* rather than files because it is an Access group (rather than a folder).

2. **Right-click Favorites on the Groups bar, click New Group, type Accounting, then click OK**
   With the two new groups in place, you are ready to organize objects according to these groups.

3. **Click Queries on the Objects bar, drag the Accounting query into the Accounting group, drag the Equipment Specs query into the Accounting group, then drag the HR query into the HR group**
   Shortcuts to these three queries have been placed in their respective groups; the original objects do not move.

4. **Click Reports on the Objects bar, drag the Accounting report into the Accounting group, drag the Human Resources report into the HR group, then click Accounting on the Groups bar**
   Your screen should look like Figure M-8, with three shortcut icons representing two queries and one report in the Accounting group. Because both an original query and a report object were named "Accounting," Access added a "1" to the second "Accounting" shortcut icon. These shortcuts are just pointers to the original objects and, therefore, do not change the name of the original object. You can open or design an object by clicking its shortcut icon. You also can drag an object to more than one group, thereby creating more than one shortcut to it.

5. **Click Groups on the Groups bar**
   Clicking Groups expands the Groups bar and collapses the Objects bar, as shown in Figure M-9.

6. **Click Groups on the Groups bar**
   Clicking Groups when it is expanded collapses the Groups bar. The Objects bar works in the same way.

7. **Place the pointer on the top edge of Groups, and drag up with the ↕ mouse pointer to just below Modules on the Objects bar**
   Displaying all of the Objects and all of the Groups is a good way to arrange the Objects and Groups bars when you start a new Access database.

FIGURE M-7: Creating groups

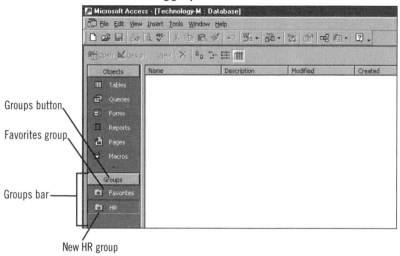

Groups button

Favorites group

Groups bar

New HR group

FIGURE M-8: Dragging objects to groups

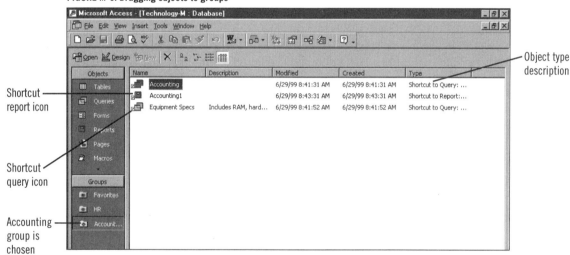

Shortcut report icon

Shortcut query icon

Accounting group is chosen

Object type description

FIGURE M-9: Expanding groups

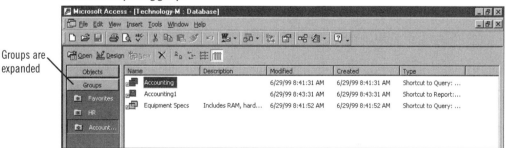

Groups are expanded

Modifying Groups

Once groups are created and object shortcuts are added to them, you modify the shortcuts in each group similarly to how you work with the actual objects themselves. For example, you can delete, rename, copy, or print a shortcut by right-clicking it and choosing the appropriate command from the short-cut menu. The biggest difference between working with shortcuts and actual objects is that if you delete a shortcut, you do not permanently delete the object. Groups also can be renamed and deleted. **Scenario** Kristen modifies both the groups and the shortcuts within them to clarify the Technology-M database.

Steps

1. Right-click the **Accounting1 shortcut** in the Accounting group, click **Rename**, type **Accounting Report Sorted by Name**, press **[Enter]**, point to the **right edge of the Name column** so that the pointer changes to ↔, then double-click the column separator

   The Name column resizes to display the full shortcut name. A shortcut name does not have to have the same name as the object that it points to, but, it is important that the shortcuts be clearly named. The shortcut icon to the left of the shortcut indicates the type of object it represents. See Tables M-1 and M-2 for information about a popular object and field type naming convention developed by the Kwery Corporation, called the Leszynski Naming Convention.

2. Right-click **Accounting** on the Groups bar, click **Rename Group**, type **Acctg**, then press **[Enter]**

   The Groups bar should look like Figure M-10.

3. Right-click **Acctg**, click **New Group**, type **IS** in the New Group dialog box, then press **[Enter]**

4. Drag the **Equipment Specs shortcut** from the Acctg group to the IS group

   Shortcuts to the same object can be found in multiple groups. They can have the same or different names within each group.

5. Click **IS** on the Groups bar, double-click the **Equipment Specs shortcut** in the IS group to open the query's datasheet, double-click **32** in the Memory field for the second record (SerialNo RT55XLQ5), type **64**, then close the datasheet

   Edits and entries made to data in this query's datasheet (whether you opened the datasheet from the original query object or from a shortcut) are stored in the original table object.

6. Click **Tables** on the Objects bar, double-click the **PCSpecs table** to open its datasheet, then click the **Sort Descending button** on the Table Datasheet toolbar

   The records are sorted in descending order on SerialNo, as shown in Figure M-11. Note that the entry for the Memory field for SerialNo RT55XLQ5 is 64.

7. Close the PCSpecs datasheet without saving changes

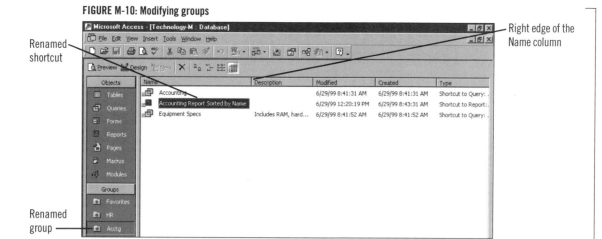

FIGURE M-10: Modifying groups

Renamed shortcut

Renamed group

Right edge of the Name column

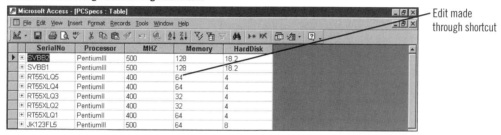

FIGURE M-11: A change made through a shortcut

Edit made through shortcut

TABLE M-1: Leszynski Naming Convention for objects

object	tag	example
Table	tbl	TblEmployees
Form	frm	FrmEmployeeEntry
Query	qry	qryIncome2000
Report	rpt	rptAccount1Qtr
Macro	mcr	McrHRToolbar

TABLE M-2: Leszynski Naming Convention for data types

field data type	tag	example
Currency	cur	CurRetail
Date/Time	dtm	DtmSaleDate
Number (Integer)	int	IntDistrictNo
Number (Double)	dbl	DblMicrons
Number (Single)	sng	SngMillimeters
Memo	mem	MemComments
OLE Object	ole	OlePicture
Text	str	StrFName
Yes/No	ysn	YsnGoldClub

Creating a Dialog Box

A **dialog box** is a special form that is used to display information or to prompt a user for a choice. For example, you might create a dialog box to prompt the user to select a report to print. Dialog boxes are used to simplify the Access interface rather than forms used in their traditional role (to support easy, accurate data entry). Special form properties such as **Border Style** and **Auto Center** make a form appear like a dialog box. Scenario▶ Kristen would like to create a dialog box that gives access to the three reports that the Accounting Department regularly prints. Then she'll add a shortcut to the dialog box in the Accounting group to simplify the printing process.

Steps

1. Click **Forms** on the Objects bar, click the **New button** 📇, then click **OK**
   A dialog box is not bound to an underlying table or query and doesn't use the form's Record Source property. A dialog box often contains command buttons to automate tasks.

2. Click the **Toolbox button** 🛠 on the Form Design toolbar (if necessary), verify that the **Control Wizards button** 🔨 is selected on the Toolbox, click the **Command Button button** ▭ on the Toolbox, then click ⁺▭ in the upper-left corner of the form
   The **Command Button Wizard** dialog box opens.

3. Click **Report Operations** in the Categories list, click **Preview Report** in the Actions list, click **Next**, click **Accounting** as the report choice, click **Next**, click the **Text option button**, press **[Tab]**, type **Sorted by Name**, click **Next**, type **Name** in the button name text box, then click **Finish**
   The command button appears in Form Design view, as shown in Figure M-12. The dialog box will contain two more buttons to preview the other two Accounting reports.

4. Click ▭, click ⁺▭ below the first command button, click **Report Operations** in the Categories list, click **Preview Report** in the Actions list, click **Next**, click **Accounting Manufacturer**, click **Next**, click the **Text option button**, press **[Tab]**, type **Sorted by Manufacturer**, click **Next**, type **Mfg**, then click **Finish**

5. Click ▭, click ⁺▭ below the second command button, click **Report Operations** in the Categories list, click **Preview Report** in the Actions list, click **Next**, click **Accounting MHz**, click **Next**, click the **Text option button**, press **[Tab]**, type **Sorted by Speed**, click **Next**, type **Speed**, then click **Finish**
   The Design view of the form should look like Figure M-13.

Trouble?
Every command button must be given a unique name that is referenced in underlying Visual Basic code. Deleting a command button from Design view does not delete the underlying code, so each new button name must be different, even if the button has been deleted.

6. Double-click the **Form Selector button** to open the form's property sheet, click the **Format tab**, click the **Border Style text box**, click the **Border Style list arrow**, then click **Dialog**
   The **Dialog** option for the Border Style property indicates that the form will have a thick border and can include only a title bar, a close button, and a control menu button. The form cannot be maximized, minimized, or resized.

7. Click the **Navigation Buttons text box**, click the **Navigation Buttons list arrow**, click **No**, click the **Record Selectors text box**, click the **Record Selectors list arrow**, then click **No**

8. Close the property sheet, restore the form, resize the form to 3" wide by 3" tall, save the form as **Accounting Reports**, then click the **Form View button** 📧
   Restoring and resizing the form best displays the property changes you made to the Border Style, Navigation Buttons, and Record Selectors properties as shown in Figure M-14.

9. Click the **Sorted by Speed command button**
   The report sorts the PCs in the Accounting Department in descending order by MHz (megahertz).

10. Close the **Accounting MHz report**, then close the **Accounting Reports form**

FIGURE M-12: Adding a command button

Command button's name

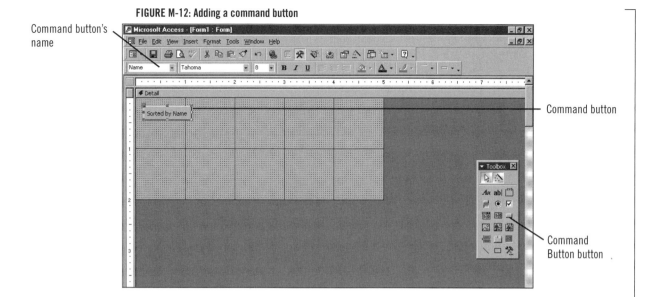

Command button

Command Button button

FIGURE M-13: The final dialog box in Form Design view

Form Selector button

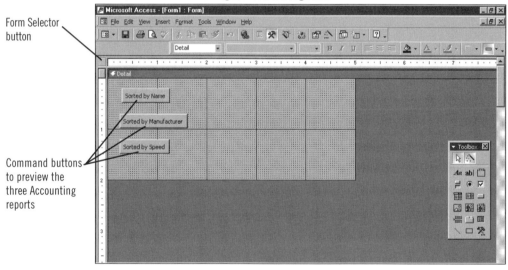

Command buttons to preview the three Accounting reports

FIGURE M-14: The final dialog box in Form view

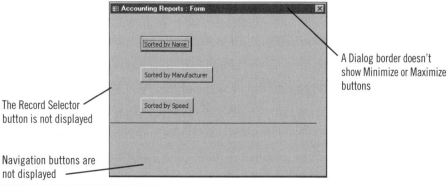

A Dialog border doesn't show Minimize or Maximize buttons

The Record Selector button is not displayed

Navigation buttons are not displayed

Access 2000

Creating a Pop-up Form

A **pop-up form** is another special type of form that stays on top of other open forms, even when another form is active. For example, you might want to create a pop-up form to give the user detailed information about an employee that isn't always visible on the main form. A command button is usually used to open the pop-up form. **Scenario** Kristen creates a pop-up form to access employee e-mail information, and adds a command button on the Employees form to open the pop-up form.

Steps

1. Click **Forms** on the Objects bar, click the **New button** in the database window, click **Form Wizard**, click the **Choose the table or query where the object's data comes from list arrow**, click **Employees**, then click **OK**
   You need only three fields of information in the pop-up form.

2. Double-click **Last**, double-click **First**, double-click **Email**, click **Next**, click **Tabular** for the layout, click **Next**, click **Standard** for the style, click **Next**, type **Email Info** for the title of the form, then click **Finish**
   The Email Info form opens in Form view, as shown in Figure M-15. You can modify the form so that it behaves as a pop-up form in Form Design view.

3. Click the **Design View button**, double-click the **Form Selector button**, click the **Other tab** in the form's property sheet, click the **Pop Up list arrow**, click **Yes**, close the property sheet, save the form, then close the form
   With the Email Info pop-up form created, you are ready to connect it via a command button to the Employees form.

4. Double-click the **Employees form** to open it in Form view, then maximize the Employees form
   The Employees form contains four bound fields: Last, First, Department, and Title, as well as a subform that displays the equipment assigned to that employee.

5. Click on the Form view toolbar, place the pointer on the **right edge of the form**, then drag to the **6.5"** mark on the horizontal ruler
   The command button will be placed in the upper-right corner of the form.

6. Click the **Command Button button** on the Toolbox, click to the right of the Title text box, click **Form Operations** in the Categories list, click **Open Form** in the Actions list, click **Next**, click the **Email Info** form, click **Next**, click the **Open the form and show all the records option button**, click **Next**, click the **Text option button**, press **[Tab]**, type **Email Addresses**, click **Next**, type **Email** as the name of the button, then click **Finish**
   Your screen should look similar to Figure M-16.

7. Click the **Form View button**, click the **Email Addresses command button**, then drag the **Email Info title bar** so that your screen looks like Figure M-17
   The power of pop-up forms is that they stay on top of all other forms and can be turned on and off as needed by the user.

8. Click in the **Last text box** in the Employees form, click the **Sort Ascending button**, double-click **Maria** in the First text box of the Employees form, type **Mary**, then press **[Tab]**
   "Maria" also changed to "Mary" in the pop-up form because both forms are tied to the underlying Employee table.

9. Close the **Email Info** pop-up form, close the **Employees** form and save the changes when prompted

FIGURE M-15: Creating the Email Info pop-up form

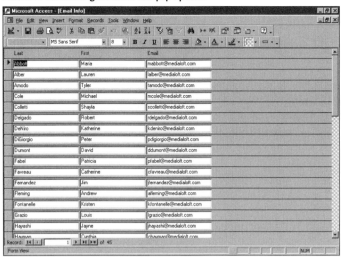

FIGURE M-16: Adding a command button to the Employees form

Command button's name

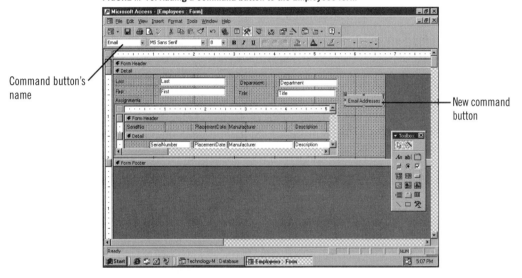

New command button

FIGURE M-17: The final form and pop-up form

Employees form

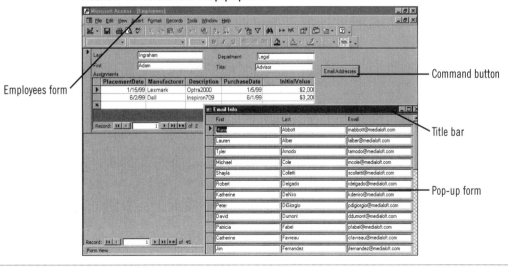

Command button

Title bar

Pop-up form

Access 2000

Creating a Switchboard

A **switchboard** is a special type of Access form that uses command buttons to simplify and secure the database. Switchboards are created and modified by using the **Switchboard Manager**. Using the Switchboard Manager requires very little knowledge of form design techniques, control types, or property settings. The Switchboard Manager is an Access **Add-In**, an extra feature that is not a part of the core Access program. A typical Access installation will include the Switchboard Manager as well as a few other Microsoft-supplied Add-Ins. More Add-Ins that extend the capabilities of Access are available through third-party vendors, and many can be downloaded from the Microsoft Web site. Scenario▶ Kristen creates a switchboard form to make the database extremely easy to navigate.

1. Click **Tools** on the menu, point to **Database Utilities**, click **Switchboard Manager**, then click **Yes** when prompted to create a switchboard
   The Switchboard Manager dialog box opens, displaying one switchboard with the name of "Main Switchboard (Default)." One switchboard is always identified as the default switchboard, a designation that can be used to automatically open the switchboard form when the database opens.

2. Click **Edit** in the Switchboard Manager dialog box
   The Edit Switchboard Page dialog box opens. There are no items currently on the switchboard form.

3. Click **New**
   The Edit Switchboard Item dialog box opens, asking for three important items: Text (a label on the switchboard form that identifies the corresponding command button), Command (which corresponds to a database action that will be chosen), and Switchboard (which further defines the command button action). The Switchboard option changes depending on the action chosen in the Command list.

4. Type **Open Employees Form** in the Text text box, click the **Command list arrow**, click **Open Form in Edit Mode**, click the **Form list arrow**, then click **Employees**
   The Edit Switchboard Item dialog box should look like Figure M-18.

5. Click **OK** to add the first command button to the switchboard, click **New**, type **Accounting Reports** in the Text text box, click the **Command list arrow**, click **Open Form in Edit Mode**, click the **Form list arrow**, click **Accounting Reports**, then click **OK**
   The Edit Switchboard Page dialog box should look like Figure M-19. Each entry in this dialog box represents a command button that will appear on the final switchboard. Recall that the object "Accounting Reports" is a form with three command buttons that allow the user to preview three different reports.

6. Close the Edit Switchboard Page dialog box, then close the Switchboard Manager dialog box

7. Click **Forms** on the Objects bar, double-click the **Switchboard form**, then click the **Switchboard Restore Window button** (if it is maximized)
   The finished switchboard opens in Form view, as shown in Figure M-20.

8. Click the **Open Employees Form command button** on the Switchboard, click the **Email Addresses command button** on the Employees form, close the **Email info form**, close the **Employees form**, click the **Accounting Reports command button**, click the **Sorted by Name command button** in the Accounting Reports dialog box, maximize the report window, then close the report window and the Accounting Reports dialog box
   You have successfully tested the Switchboard, which should be on the screen. Most users consider Switchboard forms to be the easiest way to navigate through the objects of a large database.

FIGURE M-18: Edit Switchboard Item dialog box

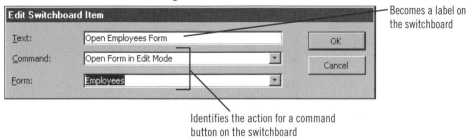

Becomes a label on
the switchboard

Identifies the action for a command
button on the switchboard

FIGURE M-19: Edit Switchboard Page dialog box

FIGURE M-20: Finished Switchboard

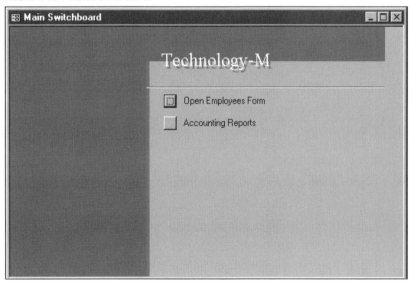

Access 2000

Modifying a Switchboard

Although switchboard forms don't *appear* to be very complex, in reality they are probably much more technically involved than any other form in the database. The Switchboard Manager hides that complexity by providing a series of dialog boxes you can use to add, delete, move, and edit the command buttons displayed on the switchboard. Cosmetic changes to a switchboard form, such as changing the label that serves as the title of the form, or changing form colors, can be accomplished in the form's Design view, but *always* use the Switchboard Manager to make changes to the command buttons and associated labels. Scenario ➤ Kristen is happy with the initial switchboard form she created, but she would like to improve it by changing the title, colors, and order of the command buttons. She uses Form Design view to make the formatting changes and the Switchboard Manager to change the order of the buttons.

QuickTip

If you need to uniquely identify your switchboard, add a label to the upper-right corner with your name.

Trouble?

The Switchboard Manager creates a table called Switchboard Items that stores a record of information for each item in each switchboard. Deleting this table deletes all switchboards created within the database.

1. Click the **Design View button** 🖳 on the Form View toolbar, then click the **dark green rectangle** on the left of the Detail section
   The Switchboard form is in Design view. The dark green colors on the left and top portion of the switchboard are actually just clip art, added to provide color to the form.

2. Click the **Fill/Back Color button list arrow** 🌢▾ on the Formatting (Form/Report) toolbar, click **bright yellow**, click the **dark green rectangle** on the top of the Detail section, click 🌢▾, then click **bright red**

3. Click the **white Technology-M label**, drag the **white Technology-M label** using 🖐 up into the red rectangle, click the **gray Technology-M** label, then press **[Delete]**
   Your screen should look like Figure M-21. Other than changing colors, the title label, and adding or deleting clip art, there isn't much more you should modify in Form Design view when you are working with a switchboard. The Switchboard Manager gives you all the power you need to make changes to the command buttons.

4. Save and close the switchboard, click **Tools** on the menu, point to **Database Utilities**, click **Switchboard Manager**, then click **Edit**
   You can create more than one switchboard form, and chain them together through command buttons. In this case, you have only one switchboard.

5. Click **Accounting Reports**, click **Edit**, click to the left of the **A** in the Text text box, type **Preview**, press **[Spacebar]**, then click **OK**
   In addition to changing the labels connected to each command button on a switchboard, you can add, delete, move, or edit them from the Edit Switchboard Page dialog box.

6. Click **Move Up** to make Preview Accounting Reports the first item in the switchboard, click **Close**, then click **Close**

7. Double-click the **Switchboard** form to open it in Form view
   The modified switchboard should look like Figure M-22.

8. Print and close the switchboard, then exit Access

FIGURE M-21: Switchboard in Design view

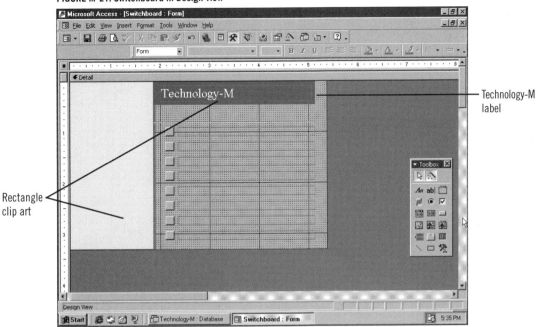

Technology-M label

Rectangle clip art

FIGURE M-22: Modified Switchboard

Command button label was modified using the Switchboard Manager

Order has been changed using the Switchboard Manager

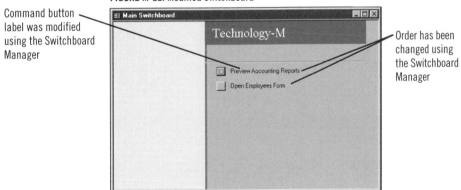

Illustrating Access features with Sample Databases

Microsoft provides four sample databases with Access 2000 that illustrate many different ways to use Access objects and features. All four databases are installed on first use in a default installation (or can be installed to your hard drive directly from the Microsoft Office 2000 CD from the Microsoft Access for Windows; Sample Databases installation category). The Northwind database, in particular, provides several examples of exciting switchboards and dialog boxes.

Practice

► Concepts Review

Identify each element of the database window shown in Figure M-23.

FIGURE M-23

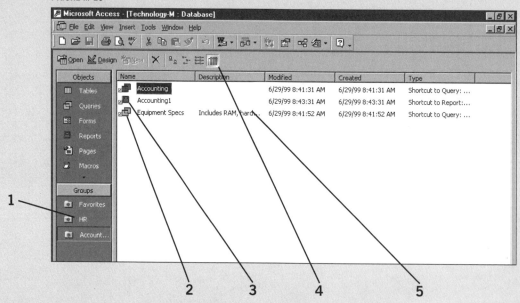

Match each term with the statement that describes its function.

6. **Group**
7. **Pop-up form**
8. **Shortcut**
9. **Add-In**
10. **Documenter**
11. **Switchboard**

a. Special type of Access form that uses command buttons to simplify and secure access to database objects
b. Pointer to database objects
c. Special type of form that stays on top of other open forms, even when another form is active
d. Creates reports on the properties and relationships between the objects in your database
e. Extra feature that is not a part of the core Access program
f. Helps you easily organize and classify objects

Select the best answer from the list of choices.

12. **Which View button do you use to see the date that the object was created?**
    a. Details
    b. Small Icons
    c. Date
    d. List

13. **Which feature fixes discrepancies between references to field names, controls, and objects when you rename them?**
    a. Switchboard Manager
    b. Renamer
    c. Name AutoCorrect
    d. Documenter

14. **If you wanted to add another command button to a switchboard, which technique would you use?**
    a. Use the Switchboard Analyzer.
    b. Modify the switchboard in Report Design view.
    c. Use the Switchboard Manager.
    d. Modify the switchboard in Form Design view.

15. **Which technique would NOT provide much help to organize the Access objects that the Human Resources (HR) Department most often uses?**
    a. Create an HR group and add shortcuts to the objects the HR Department most commonly uses.
    b. Create a switchboard that provides command buttons to the appropriate HR objects.
    c. Create a dialog box with command buttons that reference the most commonly used HR reports.
    d. Create a report that lists all HR employees.

16. **Northwind is the name of a sample**
    a. Dialog box.
    b. Database.
    c. Pop-up form.
    d. Switchboard form.

17. **A dialog box is really a _____ with special property settings.**
    a. Report
    b. Form
    c. Macro
    d. Table

▶ Skills Review

1. **Working with Objects.**
   a. Open the Basketball-M database.
   b. Click the Details button to view the details, click Reports on the Objects bar, then resize the Name column so that the entire report name is visible in the database window.
   c. Right-click the Player Field Goal Stats report, click Properties, type "Forwards and Guards" as the Description, then click OK.

  d. Click Queries on the Objects bar, right-click the Games query, click Rename, then type "Score Delta" as the new query name.

  e. Open the Games Summary Report in Design view, open the report property sheet, then check the Record Source property on the Data tab. Because the Games Summary Report was based on the former Games Query object, the new query name should appear in the Record Source property. (*Hint*: If the query name, Score Delta, doesn't appear in the Record Source property, click the Record Source property list arrow, then click Score Delta. Check the AutoCorrect options. From the database window, click Tools on the menu bar, click Options, click the General tab, then check the Name AutoCorrect options. By default, the first two of the three Name AutoCorrect options should be checked. Close the Options dialog box by clicking OK.)

  f. Close the property sheet, then save and close the report.

2. Using the Documenter.

  a. Click Tools on the menu bar, point to Analyze, then click Documenter.

  b. Click the Tables tab, click Select All, click the Reports tab, click the Games Summary Report check box, then click OK

  c. Watch the status bar to track the Documenter's progress.

  d. The final report is 20 pages long. Click File on the menu bar, click Print, click the Pages option button, type "1" in the From text box, type "1" in the To text box, then click OK to print the first page.

  e. Click File on the menu bar, click Print, click the Pages option button, type "20" in the From and To text boxes, then click OK to print page 20.

  f. Close the report created by Documenter.

3. Grouping Objects.

  a. Right-click Favorites on the Groups bar, click New Group, then type Forwards to create a new group named "Forwards".

  b. Drag the Forward Field Goals query to the Forwards group, then drag the Forward Field Goal Stats report to the Forwards group. Verify that the shortcuts are on the Forwards group.

  c. Create a new group named "Guards", then add shortcuts for the Guard Field Goals query and Guard Field Goal Stats report objects to it. Verify that the shortcuts are on the Guards group.

4. Modifying Groups.

  a. Click Forwards on the Groups bar, right-click the Forward Field Goals query shortcut, then rename the shortcut as "Forward FG Query".

  b. Rename the Forward Field Goal Stats report as "Forward FG Report".

  c. Click Guards on the Groups bar. Rename the Guard Field Goals query shortcut as "Guard FG Query".

  d. Rename the Guard Field Goal Stats report shortcut to "Guard FG Report".

  e. Click Forwards on the Groups bar, double-click the Forward FG Query shortcut, then enter your own name to replace Amy Hodel on any record her name currently occupies. As soon as you move off the record you are editing, the change will be made to the underlying Players table, which will update every record in this datasheet.

  f. Print the datasheet, then close it.

5. Creating a Dialog Box.

  a. Start a new form in Design view. Do not select any underlying tables or queries.

  b. Using the Toolbox, add a command button to the upper-left corner of the form using the Command Button Wizard. Select Report operations from the Categories list, then select Preview Report from the actions list since this is a form to preview the Games Summary Report.

  c. The Text for the button should be "Preview Games Summary Report" and the name of the button should be "Games".

  d. Using the Toolbox and the Command Button Wizard, create a second command button below the first to preview the Player Field Goal Stats report.

  e. The Text for the button should be "Preview Player FG Stats" and the name of the button should be "Players".

f. Below the two buttons, add a label to the form with your name in it.

g. Open the Form's property sheet, click the Format tab, change the form's Border Style property to Dialog, change the form's Record Selectors property to No, then change the form's Navigation Buttons property to No.

h. Close the property sheet, restore the form (if it is maximized), resize it to approximately 3" wide by 3" tall, save the form as "Team Reports", click the Form View button, test the buttons, then print the form.

6. Creating a Pop-up Form.

a. Using the Form Wizard, create a form with the following fields from the Players table: First, Last, and PlayerNo.

b. Use a Tabular layout, a Standard style, and title the form "Player Pop-up".

c. In Design view of the Player Pop-up form, resize the First and Last labels and text boxes to about half of their current width.

d. Move the Last and PlayerNo labels and text boxes close to the First label and text box so that the entire form can be narrowed to no larger than 3" wide. Resize the form to 3" wide.

e. Open the Forms property sheet, change the Pop Up property on the form's Other tab to Yes. Close the property sheet.

f. Save and close the Player Pop-up form.

g. In the Design view of the Team Reports form, use the Toolbox and Command Button Wizard to create a command button on the right side of the form that opens the Player Pop-up form and shows all of the records.

h. The Text for the new button should be "Open Player Pop-up" and the name of the button should be "Player Pop-up".

i. Save and view the Team Reports form in Form view, then click the Open Player Pop-up command button to test it. Test the other buttons as well. The Player Pop-up form should stay on top of all other forms and reports unless you close it.

j. Save and close all open forms and reports.

7. Creating a Switchboard.

a. Click Tools, point to Database Utilities, click Switchboard Manager, then click Yes to create a new switchboard.

b. Click Edit to edit the Main Switchboard, then click New to add the first item to it.

c. The Text for the first item should be "Choose a Team Report", the Command should be Open Form in Add Mode, and the Form should be Team Reports.

d. Click New to add a second item to the switchboard. The Text for the second item should be "Open Player Entry Form", the Command should be Open Form in Add Mode, and the form should be Player Entry Form.

e. Close the Edit Switchboard manager dialog box, close the Switchboard Manager dialog box. Open the Switchboard form and click both command buttons to make sure they work. Notice that when you open a form in "Add Mode" (rather than using the Open Form in Edit Mode action within the Switchboard Manager), the navigation buttons indicate that you can only add a new record, and not edit an existing one.

f. Close all open forms including the Switchboard form.

8. Modifying a Switchboard.

a. Click Tools, point to Database Utilities, click Switchboard Manager, then click Edit to edit the Main Switchboard.

b. Click Open Player Entry Form, then click Edit.

c. Change the Command to Open Form in Edit Mode, choose the Player Entry Form in the Form list, then click OK.

d. Move the Open Player Entry Form item above the Choose a Team Report item, then close the Switchboard Manager.

e. In Design view of the Switchboard Manager, delete both the white and gray Basketball-M labels, add a label with your team's name, then add a label with your own name. Place the two new labels at the top of the Switchboard form, and be sure to format them with a color that is visible in Form view.

f. Save, print, and close the Switchboard form.

g. Close the Basketball-M database.

h. Exit Access.

▶ Visual Workshop

As the manager of a doctor's clinic, you have created an Access database called Patients-M to track insurance claim reimbursements that are fixed (paid at a predetermined fixed rate), or denied (not paid by the insurance company). Create a switchboard form to give the users an easy interface, as shown in Figure M-24. Both command buttons on the switchboard open forms in edit mode. Add and modify the two labels in the switchboard's Design view, and be sure to add your own name as the manager.

FIGURE M-24

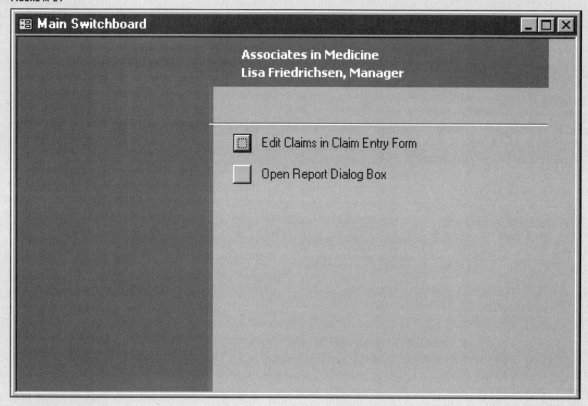

Creating
Macros

Objectives

- ► **Understand macros**
- ► **Create a macro**
- ► **Modify actions and arguments**
- ► **Create a macro group**
- ► **Set conditional expressions**
- ► **Assign a macro to an event**
- ► **Customize toolbars with macros**
- ► **Troubleshoot macros**

A **macro** is a database object that stores Access actions. When you run a macro, you execute the stored set of actions. Almost any repetitive Access task such as printing a report, opening a form, or exporting data is a good candidate for a macro. Automating routine and complex tasks as stored actions in a macro builds efficiency, accuracy, and flexibility into your database. **Scenario** Kristen noticed that several tasks are repeated on a regular basis and could be automated with macros. Although she hasn't worked with macros before, Kristen recognizes the benefits and is excited to get started.

Understanding Macros

A macro may contain one or more **actions**, the tasks that you want Access to perform. When you **run** a macro, the actions execute in the order in which they are listed in the **Macro window**. Each action has a specified set of **arguments** that provide additional information on how to carry out the action. For example, if the action were OpenForm, the arguments would include specifying the Form Name, the view (Form or Design) that the form should open to, and whether you want to apply any filters when you open the form. Scenario▶ Kristen studies the major benefits of using macros, the key terminology she needs to know when developing macros, and the components of the Access Macro window before she builds her first macro.

 The major benefits of using macros:

- Save time by automating routine tasks.

- Increase accuracy by ensuring that tasks are executed consistently.

- Make forms and reports work together by providing command buttons bound to macros that enable users to quickly and easily move between the objects.

- Make the database easier to use by providing command buttons bound to macros to filter and find records automatically.

- Ensure data accuracy in forms by responding to errors in data entry with different messages developed in macros.

- Automate data transfers such as exporting data to an Excel workbook.

- Create your own customized environment by customizing toolbars and the menu system.

 Key macro terminology:

- **macro**: An Access object that stores a series of actions to perform one or more tasks.

- **action**: Each task that you want the macro to perform. Each macro action occupies a single row in the macro window.

- **macro window**: The window in which you create a macro, as shown in Figure N-1. See Table N-1 for a description of the macro window components.

- **arguments**: Properties of an action that provide additional information on how the action should execute.

- **macro group**: An Access macro object that stores more than one macro. The macros in a macro group run independently of one another, but are grouped together to organize multiple macros that have similar characteristics. For example, you may wish to put all of the macros that print reports in one macro group.

- **expression**: A combination of values, identifiers (such as the value in a field), and operators that result in a value.

- **conditional expression**: An expression that results in either a "true" or "false" answer that determines if a macro action will execute or not. For example, if the field Country contained a null value, you may wish for the macro to execute an action that sends the user a message.

- **event**: Something that happens on a form, window, toolbar, or datasheet—such as the click of a command button or an entry in a field—that can be used to initiate the execution of a macro.

FIGURE N-1: Macro window of a macro group

Macro Names button

Macro names

Close macro is selected

Conditions evaluate to "true" or "false"

Suppliers macro group

Conditions button

Optional comments

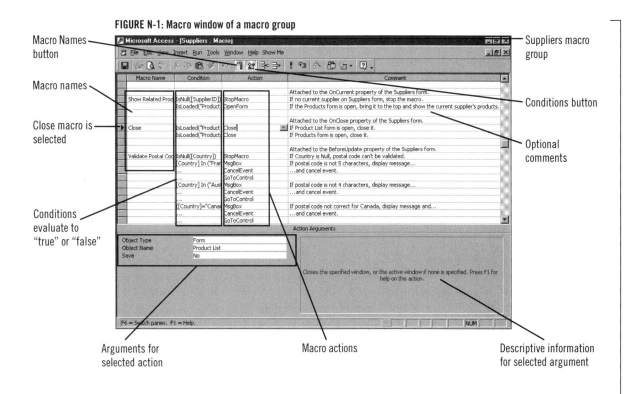

Arguments for selected action

Macro actions

Descriptive information for selected argument

TABLE N-1: Macro window components

component	description
Macro Name column	Contains the names of individual macros within a macro group. If the macro object contains only one macro, it isn't necessary to use this column because you can run the macro by referring to the macro object's name. View this column by clicking the Macro Names button
Condition column	Contains conditional expressions that are evaluated either "true" or "false." If "true," the macro action on that row is executed. If "false," the macro action on that row is skipped. View this column by clicking the Conditions button
Action column	Contains the actions (steps, instructions, or commands) that the macro executes when it runs.
Comment column	Contains optional explanatory text for each macro action.
Close macro	Is only two actions long. Both actions are "close" actions and will be executed only if the conditional expression in the corresponding row is "true."
Action arguments	Displays action characteristics and values that further define the selected macro action. In Figure N-1, the Close action has three arguments. Action Arguments change based on the action.

Creating a Macro

In some software programs, you can create a macro by having a "macro recorder" monitor and save your keystrokes and mouse clicks while you perform a task. In Access, you create a macro by specifying a series of actions in the Macro window. Because the Macro window is where a macro is designed, it is analogous to the Design view of other Access objects. There are more than 50 macro actions, and many of the common ones are listed in Table N-2. Scenario ▶ Kristen observed that the users of the Technology database waste time closing the Employees form to open and print the All Equipment report several times a week, so she decides to create a macro to automate this task.

Steps 1234

1. **Start Access, open the Technology-N database from your Project Disk, click Macros on the Objects bar, then click the New button in the database window**
   The Macro1 Macro window opens, ready to accept your first action statement. The Macro Name and Condition columns are not visible by default, but could be toggled on by clicking their respective buttons on the Macro Design toolbar.

2. **Click the Action list arrow, scroll the Action list, then click OpenReport**
   The OpenReport action is added as the first line of the Macro window, and the arguments that further define the action appear in the Action Arguments panel. The Open Report action has two required arguments: the name of the report that you want to open and the view in which you want to open the report. The Filter Name and Where Condition arguments are optional.

3. **Click the Report Name text box in the Action Arguments panel, click the Report Name List arrow, then click All Equipment**
   All of the report objects in the Technology-N database display in the Report Name list when you choose the OpenReport action.

4. **Click the View text box in the Action Arguments panel, click the View list arrow, then click Print**
   Your screen should look like Figure N-2. Macro actions can contain conditional expressions that execute only if the result of the conditional expression is true. Macros can be one or many actions long. In this case, the macro is only one action long and there are no conditional expressions.

5. **Click the Save button on the Macro Design toolbar, type Print All Equipment Report in the Macro Name text box, click OK, then close the Macro window**
   The Technology-N database window shows the Print All Equipment Report object as a Macro object.

6. **Click the Run button in the Technology-N Database window**
   The All Equipment report prints.

QuickTip
Add a label with your name to the All Equipment report if you need to uniquely identify your printout.

FIGURE N-2: Macro window with OpenReport action

OpenReport action

Report Name
argument value

View argument
value

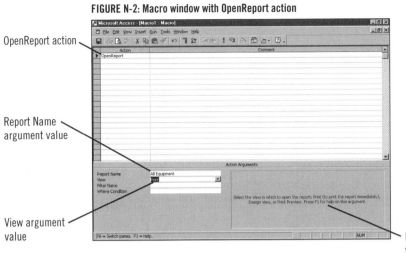

Information about
the View Argument

TABLE N-2: Common macro actions

subject area	macro action	description
Handling data in forms	ApplyFilter	Restricts the number of records that appear in the resulting form or report by applying limiting criteria
	FindRecord	Finds the first record that meets the criteria
	GoToControl	Moves the focus (where you are currently typing or clicking) to a specific field or control
	GoToRecord	Makes a specified record the current record
Executing menu options	RunCode	Calls a Visual Basic function (a series of programming statements that do a calculation or comparison and return a value)
	RunCommand	Carries out a specified menu command
	RunMacro	Runs a macro or attaches a macro to a custom menu command
	StopMacro	Stops the currently running macro
Importing/Exporting data	TransferDatabase TransferSpreadsheet TransferText	Imports, links, or exports data between the current Microsoft Access database and another database, spreadsheet, or text file
Manipulating objects	Close	Closes a window
	Maximize	Enlarges the active window to fill the Access window
	OpenForm	Opens a form in Form view, Design view, Print Preview, or Datasheet view
	OpenQuery	Opens a select or crosstab query in Datasheet view, Design view, or Print Preview; runs an action query
	OpenReport	Opens a report in Design view or Print Preview, or prints the report
	OpenTable	Opens a table in Datasheet view, Design view, or Print Preview
	PrintOut	Prints the active object, such as a datasheet, report, form, or module, in the open database
	SetValue	Sets the value of a field, control, or property
Miscellaneous	Beep	Sounds a beep tone through the computer's speaker
	MsgBox	Displays a message box containing a warning or an informational message
	SendKeys	Sends keystrokes directly to Microsoft Access or to an active Windows-based application

Modifying Actions and Arguments

Macros can contain as many actions as necessary to complete the process that you want to automate. Each action is evaluated in the order in which it appears in the Macro window, starting at the top. While some macro actions manipulate data or objects, others are used only to make the database easier to use. **MsgBox** is a particularly useful macro action because it displays an informational message. **Scenario** Kristen decides to add an action to the Print All Equipment Report macro to clarify what is happening when the macro runs. She adds a MsgBox action to the macro to display a descriptive message for the user.

QuickTip

Press [F1] to display Help text for the action and argument currently selected.

1. Click the **Design button** 📝 in the database window
   The Print All Equipment Report macro opens in Design view.

2. Click the **Action cell** just below the OpenReport action, click the **Action list arrow**, scroll the **Action list**, then click **MsgBox**
   Each action has its own arguments that further clarify what the action will accomplish.

3. Click the **Message text box** in the Action Arguments panel, then type **The All Equipment Report has just been sent to the printer**
   The Message argument determines what text appears in the message box. By default, the Beep argument is set to "Yes" and the Type argument is set to "None."

4. Click the **Type text box** in the Action Arguments panel, read the description in the lower-right corner of the Macro window, click the **Type list arrow**, then click **Information**
   The Type argument determines which icon will appear in the dialog box that is created by the MsgBox action.

5. Click the **Title text box** in the Action Arguments panel, then type **Important Information!**
   Your screen should look like Figure N-3. The Title argument specifies what text will display in the title bar of the resulting dialog box. If you leave the Title argument empty, the title bar of the resulting dialog box will display "Microsoft Access."

6. Click the **Save button** 💾 on the Macro Design toolbar, then click the **Run button** ❗ on the Macro Design toolbar
   If your speakers are turned on, you should hear a beep, then the message box should appear, as shown in Figure N-4. The report prints a second time.

7. Click **OK** in the dialog box, then close the Print All Equipment Report Macro window
   The modified Print All Equipment Report macro is saved.

FIGURE N-3: Print All Equipment Report macro with additional MsgBox action

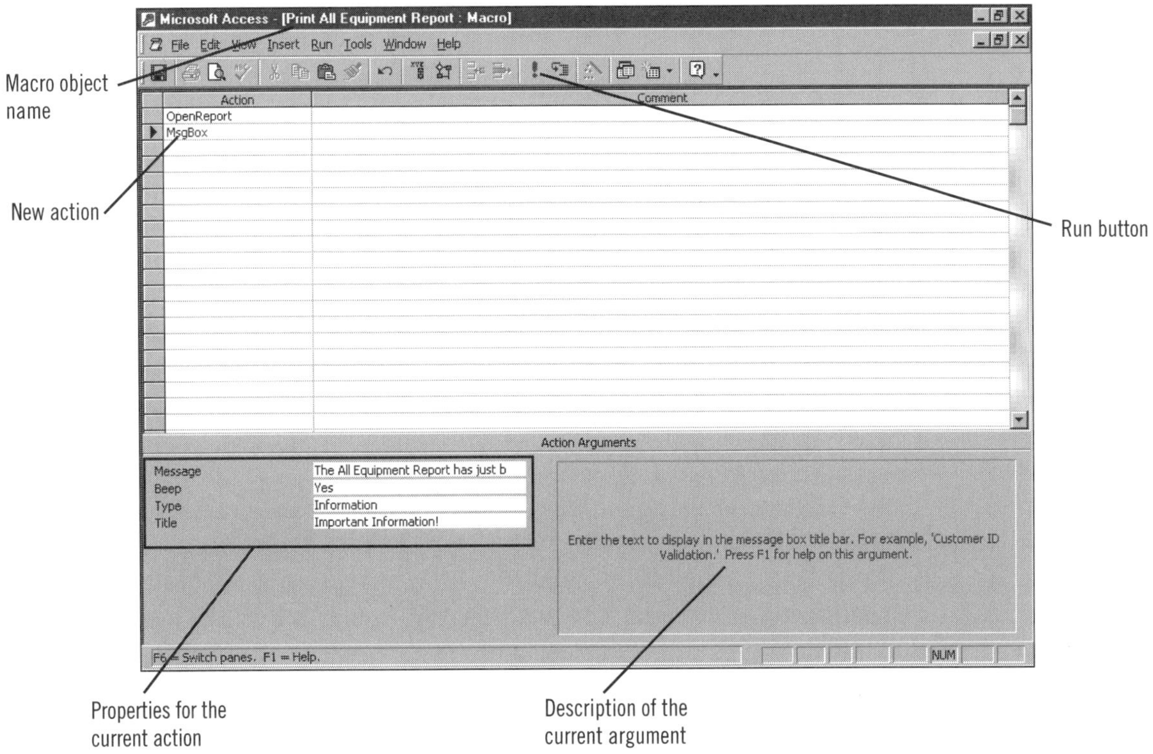

Macro object name

New action

Run button

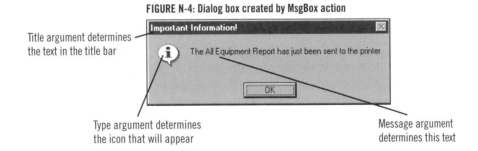

Properties for the current action

Description of the current argument

FIGURE N-4: Dialog box created by MsgBox action

Title argument determines the text in the title bar

Type argument determines the icon that will appear

Message argument determines this text

Creating a Macro Group

A **macro group** is a macro object that stores several macros together. Macro groups are used to organize multiple macros that have similar characteristics, such as all the macros that print reports or all the macros that are attached to the same form through command buttons. When you put several macros in the same macro object to create a macro group, you must enter a unique name for each macro in the Macro Name column (in the same row as the first macro action) to identify where each macro starts. **Scenario** Kristen adds a macro that prints the Accounting Report to the Print All Equipment Report macro object. By adding this new macro and any additional macros that print reports in one object, she creates a macro object.

Steps 1234

1. Right-click the **Print All Equipment Report macro**, click **Rename**, type **Print Reports Macro Group**, then press **[Enter]**
   The object name should explain the contents of the object as clearly as possible. The name should reflect the fact that the macro object contains more than one macro.

2. Click the **Design button** 🔛 in the database window, click the **Macro Names button** 🔡 on the Macro Design toolbar, type **Print All Equipment** in the Macro Name column, then press **[Enter]**
   An individual macro is given the name of the macro object *unless* a macro name is entered in the Macro Name column. If several macros are stored as a macro group in one object, it is imperative that each be given a unique name so that each can be clearly referenced later.

3. Click in the **Macro Name cell** in the third row, type **Print Accounting Report**, then press **[Enter]**
   A new macro starts when a new name is entered in the Macro Name column.

QuickTip

Some macro developers leave a blank row between macros to further clarify where a new macro starts.

4. Click the **Action list arrow**, scroll and click **OpenReport**, click in the **Report Name text box** in the Action Arguments panel, click the **Report Name list arrow**, then click **Accounting Report**
   Your screen should look like Figure N-5. The other two arguments associated with the OpenReport action are already correctly specified.

5. Click the **row selector of the MsgBox action of the Print All Equipment macro**, click the **Copy button** 🖺 on the Macro Design toolbar, click the **fourth row selector**, then click the **Paste button** 🖺 on the Macro Design toolbar
   Being able to copy and paste actions in a Macro window is another benefit of using macro groups. Action argument values are copied and pasted along with the action, so they don't need to be reentered. Sometimes, however, the arguments need to be edited.

QuickTip

Add a label with your name to the Accounting Report if you need to uniquely identify your printout.

6. Delete **All Equipment** in the Message text box in the Action Arguments panel, type **Accounting**, then click the **Save button** 🖫 on the Macro Design toolbar
   To run a specific macro from within a macro group's window, you must use the menu.

7. Click **Tools** on the menu bar, point to **Macro**, click **Run Macro**, click the **Macro Name list arrow** in the Run Macro dialog box, click **Print Reports Macro Group.Print Accounting Report**, then click **OK**
   Your screen should look like Figure N-6. Referring to a specific macro within a macro group by separating them with a period is called **dot notation**. Dot notation syntax is also used when developing modules with Visual Basic programming code.

8. Click **OK**, then close the Macro window
   The Print Reports Macro Group object containing two macros is shown in the database window.

FIGURE N-5: Creating a macro group

Paste button

Macro name

Row selector

Macro Names button

Copy button

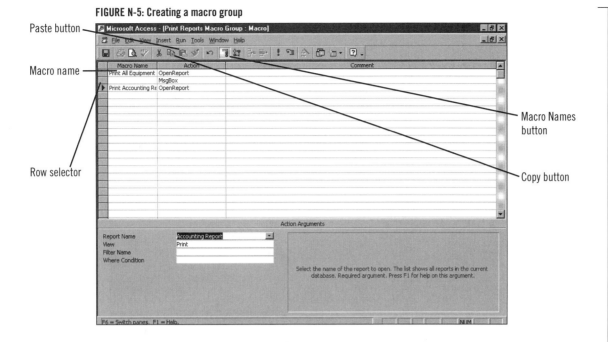

FIGURE N-6: Running the Print Accounting Report macro

MsgBox action was pasted

Message argument was edited

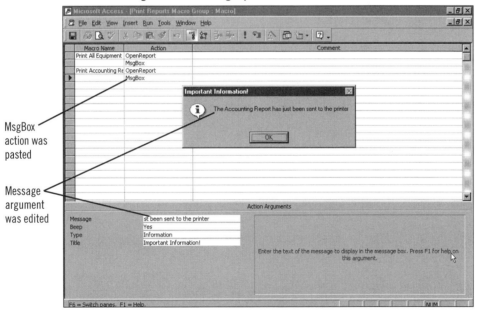

Assigning a macro to a key combination

You can assign macros to a key combination (such as Ctrl+L) by creating a macro group object called **AutoKeys**. In the Macro Names column of the AutoKeys Macro window, enter the key combination

to press when you want to run the macro. Any key combination assignments you make in the AutoKeys macro override those that Access has already specified (for example, Ctrl+C is the key combination for copy).

Setting Conditional Expressions

Access 2000

Conditional expressions are entered in the Condition column of the Macro window. They result in a true or false value. If the condition evaluates true, the action is executed: if false, the macro skips that row. When building a conditional expression, to refer to a value of a control on a form in a macro, use the following syntax: [Forms]![*formname*]![*controlname*]. To refer to a value of a control on a report, the syntax is [Reports]![*reportname*]![*controlname*]. Separating object types from object names from control names by using square brackets [] and exclamation points is called **bang notation**. Scenario At MediaLoft, everyone who has been with the company longer than five years is eligible to take their old PC equipment home as soon as it has been replaced. Kristen uses a conditional macro to highlight this information in a form.

QuickTip

The columns of the Macro window can be resized using the ◆▶ mouse pointer.

1. Click the **New button** 🗊 in the database window, click the **Conditions button** 🖅 on the Macro Design toolbar, right-click the **first Condition cell**, click **Zoom**, then type **[Forms]![Employees]![DateHired]<Date()-(5*365)** in the Zoom dialog box
   The Zoom dialog box should look like Figure N-7. This conditional expression says "Check the value in the DateHired field of the Employees form to see if it is earlier than five years before today's date."

2. Click **OK** to close the Zoom dialog box, click the **Action cell** for the first row, click the **Action list arrow**, scroll, then click **SetValue**
   The SetValue macro action has two arguments.

3. Click the **Item text box** in the Action Arguments panel, type **[Forms]![Employees]![PCProgram]**, click the **Expression text box** in the Action Arguments panel, then type **yes**
   Your screen should look like Figure N-8.

4. Click the **Save button** 🖫 on the Macro Design toolbar, type **5PC** in the Macro Name text box, click **OK**, then close the 5PC macro
   Test the macro using the Employees form.

5. Click **Forms on the Objects bar**, double-click the **Employees form**, maximize the Employees form, click the **Date Hired text box**, then click the **Sort Ascending button** 🛂 on the Form View toolbar
   The record for Evelyn Storey, hired 1/1/92, appears. Because she has five years of service with MediaLoft, she is eligible for the PC program.

6. Click **Tools** on the menu bar, point to **Macro**, click **Run Macro**, click the **Macro Name list arrow**, click **5PC**, then click **OK**
   After evaluating the date of this record and determining that this employee has been working at MediaLoft longer than five years, the PC Program check box was automatically checked (set to "Yes"), as shown in Figure N-9.

7. Click the **Last Record button** 🖳 on the Main Form Navigation buttons, click **Tools** on the menu bar, point to **Macro**, click **Run Macro**, verify that **5PC** is in the **Macro Name text box**, then click **OK**
   Because Kristen Fontanelle was hired recently, the PC Program check box was not checked (set to "yes") by running the macro.

8. Close the Employees form

FIGURE N-7: Zoom dialog box

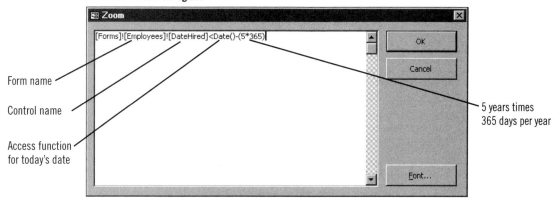

Form name

Control name

Access function
for today's date

5 years times
365 days per year

FIGURE N-8: Creating a conditional expression

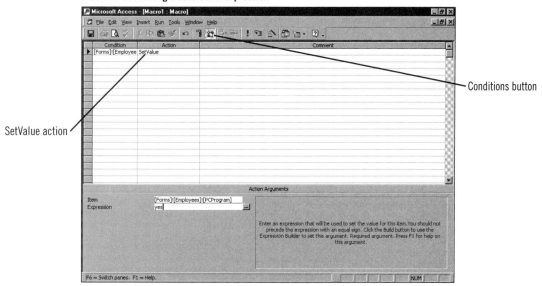

Conditions button

SetValue action

FIGURE N-9: Running the 5PC macro

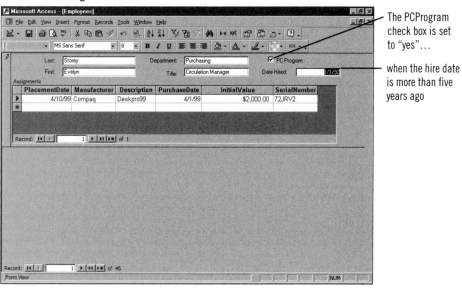

The PCProgram
check box is set
to "yes"...

when the hire date
is more than five
years ago

Assigning a Macro to an Event

An **event** is a specific action that occurs within the database such as clicking a command button, changing the data, or opening or closing a form. Events are usually the result of user action. By assigning a macro to an event, you can customize the response to an event that occurs on a form, report, or control, and therefore further automate and enhance your database. Scenario▶ Now that Kristen has developed the 5PC macro, she will attach it to an event on the Employees form so that she doesn't have to run the macro for each record.

Steps

QuickTip

Click any event property text box, then press [F1] for more help on that property.

▶ **1.** Click **Forms** on the Objects bar, click **Employees**, click the **Design button** 🔍 in the database window, double-click the **Detail section**, then click the **Event tab** in the Detail section property sheet

All objects, sections, and controls have a variety of events to which macros can be attached. Most event names are self-explanatory, such as the On Click event for the Detail section. Any macro attached to this event would run when the Detail section of the form is clicked.

Trouble?

Close the Toolbox and Field list and move the property sheet to better view the form.

▶ **2.** Click the **Last text box** in the Detail section of the Employees form

There are 15 different events for a text box, many of which are very similar. Knowing which to use is a matter of experience. The Help manual provides more information on the subtle differences between the events.

3. Click the **On Got Focus text box** on the Event tab, click the **On Got Focus list arrow**, then click **5PC**

Your screen should look like Figure N-10.

4. Click the **Properties button** 🗐 on the Form Design toolbar to close the property sheet, click the **Form View button** 🖼 on the Form View toolbar

As you move through the records of the form, the Last text box will automatically have the focus because it is listed first in the form's tab order, and the 5PC macro will automatically run.

5. Click the **Next Record button** ▶ in the main form navigation buttons ten times while observing the PC Program check box

For every Date Hired value that is more than five years earlier than today's date, the PC Program check box should be checked automatically (set to "yes").

6. Save and close the Employees form

FIGURE N-10: Assigning a macro to a text box event

Last text box is selected

5PC macro assigned
to On Got Focus event

Properties button

CLUES TO USE

Assigning a macro to a command button

You can add a command button on a form to run a macro. One way to accomplish this is to build the command button using the Command Button Wizard. Use the wizard to specify the Run Macro action found in the Miscellaneous category. Another way to assign a macro to a command button is to open the command button's property sheet and enter the macro name in the appropriate event property. The most common event property for a command button is the **On Click** event, which triggers as soon as you click the command button in Form view.

Customizing Toolbars with Macros

There are many ways to run a macro: by clicking the Run button in the Macro window, by going through the Tools menu, by assigning the macro to an event on a control, or by assigning it to a button on a toolbar, menu, or shortcut menu. The benefit of assigning a macro to a toolbar button over assigning it to a command button on a specific form is that the toolbar can be made available to the user at all times, whereas a command button on a form is available only when that specific form is open. Macros that are run from multiple forms are great candidates for custom toolbars. **Scenario** Kristen decides to create a new toolbar for the print macros.

1. Click **Macros** on the Objects bar, click the **Print Reports Macro Group**, click **Tools** on the menu, point to **Macro**, then click **Create Toolbar from Macro**

   The Print Reports Macro Group toolbar appears on your screen. All of the macros in that group are automatically added to the toolbar.

Trouble?

If the new toolbar docks in an undesirable location, point to the left edge of the toolbar so that your mouse pointer changes to ✛, then drag it to the desired location.

2. Drag the **Print Reports Macro Group toolbar title bar** to dock it just below the Database toolbar, as shown in Figure N-11

   Because this toolbar contains buttons for only two macros (the two found in the Print Reports Macro Group), the entire name of the macro fits comfortably on the toolbar. If you add several more macros to the toolbar, however, you will quickly run out of room.

3. Right-click the **Print Reports Macro Group toolbar**, click **Customize** to open the Customize dialog box, right-click the **Print All Equipment macro button** on the Print Reports Macro Group toolbar, then point to **Change Button Image**

   Your screen should look like Figure N-12. The shortcut menu that allows you to modify toolbar button images and text is available only when the Customize dialog box is open.

4. Click the **Shoes icon** 👟 on the icon palette, right-click the **Print All Equipment macro button** again, then click **Default Style**

   The Default Style for a button displays only the button image, not the text.

5. Right-click the **Print Accounting Report macro button** on the Print Reports Macro Group toolbar, point to **Change Button Image**, click the **Scales icon** ⚖ on the icon palette, right-click the **Print Accounting Report macro button**, then click **Default Style**

   The image on a toolbar button can be edited.

6. Right-click ⚖, then click **Edit Button Image**

   The Button Editor dialog box opens, which allows you change the appearance of the picture pixel by pixel.

7. Click the **bright green color box** on the Colors palette, then click all 11 squares in the **left scale**, as shown in Figure N-13

   With enough time and patience, you could create any number of unique button images. Once created, the images can be copied and pasted from one button to another.

8. Click **OK**, then click **Close** to close the Customize dialog box

   The Print Reports Macro Group toolbar can be turned on or off from anywhere within the database. As with buttons on other toolbars, these buttons can be deleted and modified, and new ones can be added later.

9. Point to the ⚖, then point to the 👟 on the Print Reports Macro Group toolbar

   Each button on the new Print Reports Macro Group toolbar has a ScreenTip and functions like the buttons on other toolbars.

FIGURE N-11: Print Reports Macro Group toolbar

New toolbar with two macro buttons

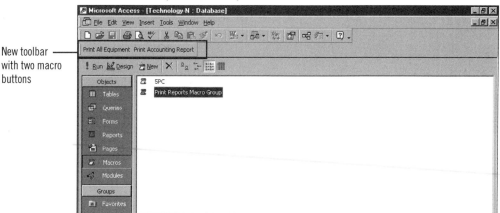

FIGURE N-12: Customizing a button image

Shoes

Scale

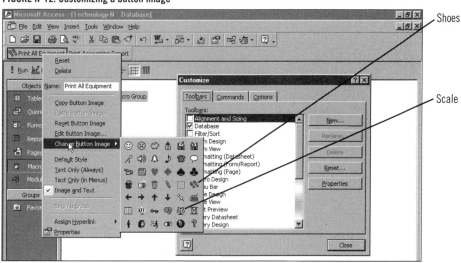

FIGURE N-13: Button Editor dialog box

Bright green

Left scale

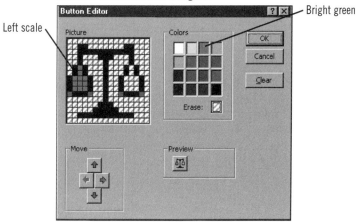

Troubleshooting Macros

Access 2000

When macros don't execute properly, Access supplies several techniques to debug them. **Debugging** means to determine why the macro doesn't run properly. **Single stepping** runs the macro one line at a time, so you can observe the effect of each macro action in the Macro Single Step dialog box while it executes. Another option is to disable a macro action by entering "False" in the Condition cell in the row of the action that you wish to temporarily skip. **Scenario** Before building more sophisticated macros, Kristen uses the Print Reports Macro Group to learn debugging techniques.

Steps

1. Click **Print Reports Macro Group**, click the **Design button**, click the **Single Step button** on the Macro Design toolbar, then click the **Run button** on the Macro Design toolbar

   The screen should look like Figure N-14, with the Macro Single Step dialog box open. This dialog box displays information including the macro's name, whether the current action's condition is true, the action's name, and the action arguments. From the Macro Single Step dialog box you can step into the next macro action, halt execution of the macro, or continue running the macro without single stepping.

2. Click **Step** in the Macro Single Step dialog box

   Stepping into the second action allows the first action to execute. The Macro Single Step dialog box now displays information about the second action.

3. Click **Step**

   The second action, the MsgBox action, executes, displaying the message box.

4. Click **OK**

   You can use the Condition column to temporarily ignore an action while you are debugging a macro.

5. Click the **Conditions button** on the Macro Design toolbar, click the **Condition cell** for the first row, then type **False**

   Your screen should look like Figure N-15.

6. Click the **Save button** on the Macro Design toolbar, then click

   The Macro Single Step dialog box still displays description information about the action, but because the Condition value is False, the OpenReport action will not execute, so the All Equipment report will not be sent to the printer.

7. Click **Halt** in the Macro Single Step dialog box, double-click **False** in the Condition cell, then press **[Delete]**

8. Click the **Single Step button** on the Macro Design toolbar to turn it off

   You could leave the Single Step feature on for future work, but you should turn it off now so that the next time you open a database and run a macro it will not be on.

9. Save and close the Print Reports Macro Group, close the Technology–N database, then exit Access

FIGURE N-14: Single stepping through a macro

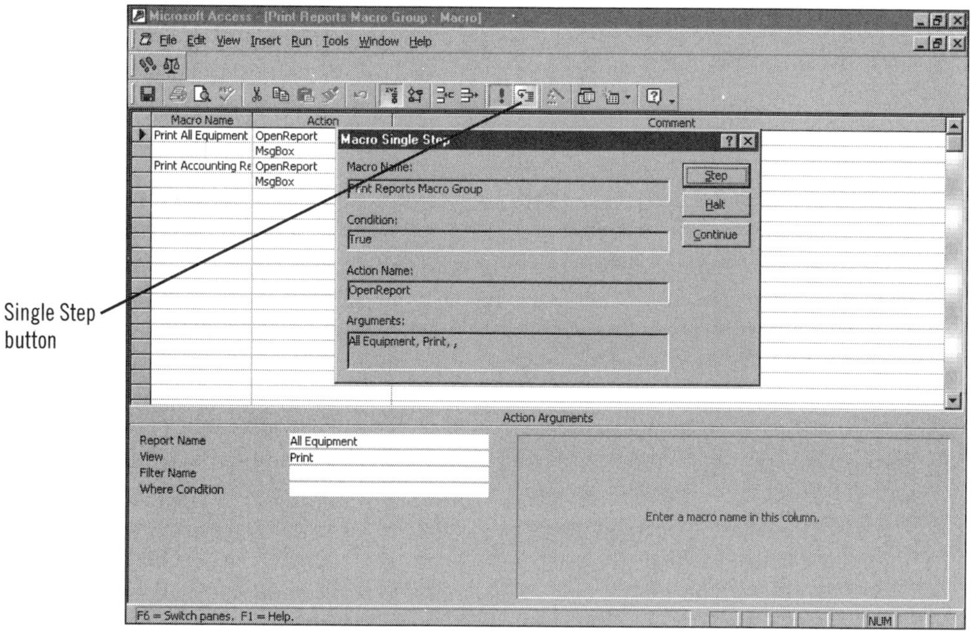

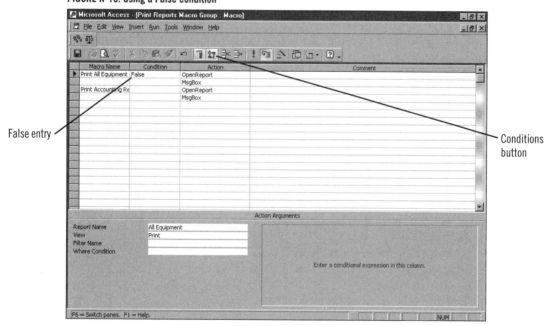

Single Step
button

FIGURE N-15: Using a False condition

False entry

Conditions
button

Practice

► Concepts Review

Identify each element of the macro window shown in Figure N-16.

FIGURE N-16

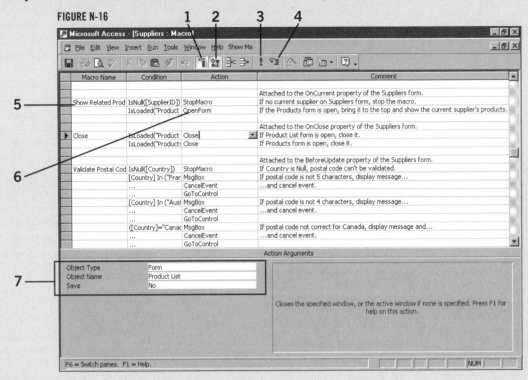

Match each term with the statement that describes its function.

8. Macro
9. Conditional expression
10. Arguments
11. Debugging
12. Actions
13. Event

a. Determining why a macro doesn't run properly
b. Individual tasks that you want the Access macro to perform
c. Access object that stores a series of actions that perform a series of tasks
d. Specific action that occurs within the database such as a mouse click, a change in data, or a form opening or closing
e. Provide additional information to define how an Access action will perform
f. Evaluates as either true or false, which determines whether Access will execute a macro action or not

Select the best answer from the list of choices.

14. Which of the following is *not* a major benefit of using a macro?
    a. To redesign the relationships among the tables of the database
    b. To ensure consistency in executing routine or complex tasks
    c. To make the database more flexible by adding macro command buttons to forms
    d. To save time by automating routine tasks

15. Which of the following *best* describes the process of creating an Access macro?
    a. Open the Macro window and add actions, arguments, and conditions to accomplish the desired task
    b. Use the single-step recorder feature to record clicks and keystrokes as you complete a task
    c. Use the Macro Wizard to determine which tasks are done most frequently
    d. Use the macro recorder to record clicks and keystrokes as you complete a task

16. Which of the following does *not* run a macro?
    a. Add the macro as an entry on the title bar
    b. Assign the macro to an event of a control on a form
    c. Add the macro to a toolbar
    d. Click the macro name in the Database window, then click Run

17. Which is *not* a reason to run a macro in single-step mode?
    a. You want to run only a few of the actions of a macro
    b. You want to observe the effect of each macro action individually
    c. You want to debug a macro that isn't working properly
    d. You want to change the arguments of a macro while it runs

18. Which is *not* a reason to use conditional expressions in a macro?
    a. Conditional expressions give the macro more power and flexibility
    b. Conditional expressions allow you to skip over actions when the expression evaluates to false
    c. You can enter "False" in the Conditions column of the Macro window to skip that action
    d. More macro actions are available when you are also using conditional expressions

19. Which example illustrates the proper syntax to refer to a specific control on a form?
    a. [Forms]![*formname*]![*controlname*]
    b. (Forms)!(*formname*)!(*controlname*)
    c. Forms!*formname.controlname*
    d. {Forms}!{*formname*}!{*controlname*}

▶ Skills Review

1. **Understanding Macros.**
    a. Start Access and open the Basketball-N database from your Project Disk.
    b. Open the Macro Design window of the Print Macro Group and record your answers to the following questions on a sheet of paper:
    * How many macros are in this macro group?
    * What are the names of the macros in this macro group?

- What actions does the first macro in this macro group contain?
- What arguments does the first action contain? What values were chosen for those arguments?

   c. Close the Macro window for the Print Macro Group object.

2. Creating a Macro.

   a. Open a new Macro window.

   b. Add the OpenQuery action to the first row of the Macro window.

   c. Select Score Delta as the value for the Query Name argument of the OpenQuery action.

   d. Select Datasheet for the View argument of the OpenQuery action.

   e. Select Edit for the Data Mode argument for the OpenQuery action.

   f. Save the macro object with the name "Score Delta".

   g. Run the macro to make sure it works, then close Score Delta query and the Score Delta Macro window.

3. Modifying Actions and Arguments.

   a. Open the Score Delta macro in Macro Design view.

   b. Add a MsgBox action in the second row of the Macro window.

   c. Type "We had a great season!" for the Message argument in the Action Arguments panes of the MsgBox action.

   d. Select Yes for the Beep argument of the MsgBox action.

   e. Select Warning! for the Type argument of the MsgBox action.

   f. Type "Iowa State Cyclones" for the Title argument of the MsgBox action.

   g. Save the macro, then run it to make sure the MsgBox action works as intended.

   h. Click OK in the dialog box created by the MsgBox action, then close the Score Delta query and close the Macro window.

4. Creating a Macro Group.

   a. Rename the Score Delta macro with the name "Query Macro Group".

   b. Open the Query Macro Group's Macro Design window.

   c. Open the Macro Name column and type the name "Score Delta Macro" on the first line for the first macro.

   d. Create another macro and name it "Forward FG Macro".

   e. Add an OpenQuery action for the first action of the Forward FG Macro.

   f. Select Forward Field Goals for the Query Name argument of the OpenQuery action and use the default entries for the other two arguments.

   g. Add a MsgBox action for the second action of the Forward FG Macro.

   h. Type "Forward Field Goals" as the Message argument for the MsgBox action.

   i. Select Yes for the Beep argument of the MsgBox action.

   j. Select Critical for the Type argument of the MsgBox action.

   k. Type "2000-2001 Season" for the Title argument of the MsgBox action.

   l. Save the macro.

   m. Click Tools on the menu bar, point to Macro, click Run macro, then run the Forward FG Macro.

   n. Click OK in the 2000-2001 Season dialog box created by the MsgBox action, then close the query datasheet and close the Macro window.

5. Setting Conditional Expressions.

    a. Open a new Macro window.

    b. Click the Conditions button to open the Condition column.

    c. Type the following condition in the condition cell of the first row: [Forms]![Game Summary Form]![Home Score]>[Opponent Score] (*Hint*: Use the Zoom dialog box or widen the column to more clearly view the entry.)

    d. Add the SetValue action to the first row.

    e. Type the following entry in the Item argument value for the SetValue action: [Forms]![Game Summary Form]![Victory]

    f. Type "Yes" for the Expression argument for the SetValue action.

    g. Save the macro as "Victory Calculator" and close the Macro window.

6. Assigning a Macro to an Event.

    a. Open the Game Summary Form in Design view.

    b. Open the Property sheet for the Detail section.

    c. Assign the Victory Calculator macro to the On Click event of the Detail section.

    d. Close the property sheet, save the form, then open it in Form view.

    e. Navigate through the first four records, while single clicking each record in the Detail section (click to the right of the text box controls). The Victory checkbox should be marked for the first three records, but not the fourth.

    f. Close the Game Summary form.

7. Customizing Toolbars with Macros.

    a. Click Macros on the Objects bar, click the Print Macro Group, click Tools on the menu bar, point to Macro, then click Create Toolbar from Macro.

    b. Dock the toolbar with the three text buttons just below the Database toolbar in the database window.

    c. Right-click the new toolbar, then click Customize to open the Customize dialog box.

    d. Change the button image for each of the three macros to the question mark icon and a default style (image only).

    e. Edit the button images so that the second macro question mark button is bright red (instead of yellow) and the third is bright blue (instead of yellow).

    f. Close the Customize dialog box and point to each icon to make sure that the ScreenTip relates to the three macro names in the Print Macro Group.

8. Troubleshooting Macros.

    a. Open the Print Macro Group's Macro window.

    b. Click the Single Step button on the Macro Design toolbar, then click the Run button.

    c. Click Step twice to step through the two actions of this macro, then click OK on the resulting message box.

    d. Open the Condition column by clicking the Conditions button on the Macro Design toolbar (if it's not already opened).

    e. Add the value "False" as a condition to the first row, the OpenReport action of the Games Summary macro.

    f. Save the macro, then click the Run button.

    g. Click the Step button twice to move through the actions of the macro. This time the Games Summary report should *not* be printed. Click OK when prompted.

    h. Delete the False condition in the first row, save the macro, then close the Macro window.

    i. Turn off the Single Step button.

    j. Close the Basketball-N database.

    k. Exit Access.

Access 2000

► Visual Workshop

As the manager of a doctor's clinic, you have created an Access database called Patients-N to track insurance claim reimbursements. Develop the macro group called Query Group with the actions and argument values shown in Table N-3 and Figure N-17 . Run both macros to test them. Debug them if necessary.

TABLE N-3: Macro actions and arguments for the Query Group

macro name	action	argument	argument value
Denied	OpenQuery	Query Name	Monthly Query – Denied
		View	Datasheet
		Data Mode	Edit
	Maximize		
	MsgBox	Message	These claims were denied
		Beep	Yes
		Type	Information
		Title	Denied
Fixed	OpenQuery	Query Name	Monthly Query – Fixed
		View	Datasheet
		Data Mode	Edit
	Maximize		
	MsgBox	Message	These claims were fixed
		Beep	Yes
		Type	Information
		Title	Fixed

FIGURE N-17

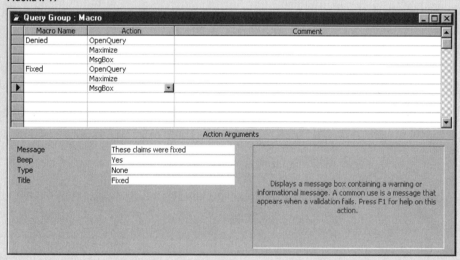

Creating
Modules

Objectives

- ► Understand modules
- ► Compare macros and modules
- ► Create a function procedure
- ► Use If statements
- ► Document a procedure
- ► Examine class modules
- ► Create a sub procedure
- ► Troubleshoot modules

Access is an extremely robust and easy-to-use relational database program. Reports and screens that took hours to create using complex programming code are now created using wizards, graphical tools, and property sheets. Macros that formerly took hours to debug can now be written, tested, and attached to a command button or control event in minutes. Because Access provides so many user-friendly tools to accomplish tasks, many Access database administrators don't need to work with the Access programming language, **Visual Basic for Applications** (**VBA**), to meet the needs of the users. When programming is required, however, the Visual Basic code is stored in a database object called a **module**. Scenario ► Kristen learns about and creates some small Access modules to enhance the capabilities of the Technology database.

Access 2000

Understanding Modules

A **module** is an Access object that contains Visual Basic for Applications programming code, and it is written in the **Visual Basic Editor Code window** (**Code window**), shown in Figure O-1. The components and text colors of the Code window are described in Table O-1. Programming code contained within the module can be executed by clicking a command button or in response to an event. A database has two kinds of modules: **class modules**, which are used only with a particular form or report and are, therefore, stored as a part of the form or report object; and **standard modules**, which can be executed from anywhere in the database and are displayed as module objects in the database window. Scenario▶ Kristen wants to learn more about VBA modules, so she studies several key questions that explain the purpose and terminology of modules.

Details

What does a module contain?

A module contains VBA programming code organized in units called **procedures**. A procedure may be a few or several lines (**statements**) long. Modules also contain **comment lines** to help document and explain the code. Comment lines in Visual Basic are preceded by an apostrophe.

What is a procedure?

A **procedure** is a series of VBA programming statements that perform an operation or calculate an answer. There are two types of procedures: Functions and Subs. **Declaration statements** precede procedure statements and help set rules for how the statements in the module are processed.

What is a function?

A **function** is a procedure that returns a value. Access supplies many built-in statistical, financial, and date functions, such as Sum, Pmt, and Now, that can be used in an expression in a query, form, or report to calculate a value. Using VBA, you could create a new function called StockOptions, for example, which calculates the date an employee is eligible for the corporate stock options, and use the unique method of calculating that date specified by your company.

What is a sub?

A **sub** (or **sub procedure**) performs a series of VBA statements, but does not return a value and cannot be used in an expression. You use subs to manipulate controls and objects. For example, you might create a sub called SetSchoolNameFocus that moves the focus on a form to a text box bound to a SchoolName field when the user marks a check box that indicates he or she is a college graduate.

What are arguments?

Arguments are constants, variables, or expressions passed to a procedure (function or sub) that are required for it to execute. For example, the full syntax for the Sum function is Sum(*expr*), where *expr* represents the argument for the Sum function. Arguments are specified immediately after a procedure's name and are enclosed in parentheses. When there are multiple arguments, they are separated by commas.

What is a method?

A **method** is an action that an object can perform. For example, the GoToPage method moves the focus to the first control on a specified page in the active form. Procedures are often written to invoke methods (database actions) in response to user actions. For example, you may wish to invoke the GoToPage method when the user clicks a command button.

FIGURE O-1: Visual Basic Editor Code window for a standard module

Object box

Declaration statements

New Function named IsLoaded is defined

Procedure View button

Full Module View button

Name of module

Procedure box

Comment line

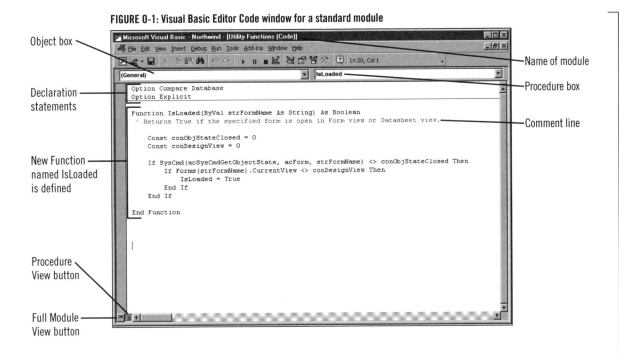

TABLE O-1: Components and text colors of the Code window

component or color	description
Procedure View button	Shows the statements that belong only to the current procedure
Full Module View button	Shows all the lines of VBA (all of the procedures) in the module
Declaration statements	Contains statements that apply to every procedure in the module such as declarations for variables, constants, user-defined data types, and external procedures in a dynamic link library
Object box	In a class module, lists the objects associated with the form or report (in VBA, "**objects**" are the form or report's controls, sections, the form or report itself, and subs already defined)
Procedure box	In a standard module, lists the procedures in that module. In a class module, lists the events (such as Click or Dblclick) that the item selected in the Object box can use
Comment line	Descriptive text that serves as explanatory documentation; comment lines start with an apostrophe
Blue	Keyword text—blue words are reserved by VBA and are already assigned specific meanings
Black	Normal text—black words are the unique VBA code developed by the user
Red	Syntax error text—a line of code in red indicates that it will not execute correctly because there is a syntax error (perhaps a missing parenthesis or a spelling error)
Green	Comment text—any text after an apostrophe is considered documentation, and is therefore ignored in the execution of the procedure

Comparing Macros and Modules

Both macros and modules help run your database more efficiently (faster) and effectively (with fewer errors). To create either requires some understanding of programming concepts, an ability to follow a process through its steps, and patience. Some tasks can be accomplished using either an Access macro or a module, but there are some guidelines and rules that will help guide your choice of which object is best for the task. Scenario▶ Kristen learns how macros and modules compare by studying several key questions.

Details

For what types of tasks are macros best suited?

Macros are an easy way to handle repetitive, simple details such as opening and closing forms, showing and hiding toolbars, and printing reports.

Which is easier to create, a macro or a module, and why?

To create a module, you must know the correct syntax for each line of code, and write the statement yourself. Modules consist of VBA programming code, a robust programming language with endless possibilities. Macros are generally easier to create because you don't have to know about programming syntax. With a macro, you choose actions (a limited list of about 50) from a list. Once the action is chosen, the arguments associated with that action are displayed automatically in the Action Arguments panel.

Is there ever a situation when I must use a macro?

You must use macros to make global shortcut key assignments. You can also use an automatic macro that carries out a series of actions that are beyond the capabilities of the startup options when the database first opens.

When should I use a module?

There are at least five reasons to use a module rather than a macro:

- Class modules, like the one shown in Figure O-2, are stored as part of the form or report object in which they are created. Therefore, if you develop forms and reports in one database and copy them to another, class modules are copied with the object.

- You must use modules to create unique function procedures. For instance, you might want to create a function called COMMISSION that calculates the appropriate commission on a sale using your company's unique commission formula.

- Modules can contain procedures used to mask error messages. Access error messages can be confusing to the user. But using VBA procedures, you can detect the error when it occurs and display your own message or take some action.

- You can't use a macro to accomplish many tasks outside Access, but VBA code stored in modules works with other products in the Microsoft Office suite to pass information back and forth between the programs.

- VBA code can contain nested If statements, Case statements, and other programming code, which makes it more powerful and flexible than macros. Some of the most common VBA keywords are shown in Table O-2. Because each is a reserved VBA keyword, each appears in blue in the Code window.

FIGURE O-2: Code window for a class module

The Form object is selected

Sub named Form_Close() is defined

Sub named Form_Current() is defined

The Current event is selected

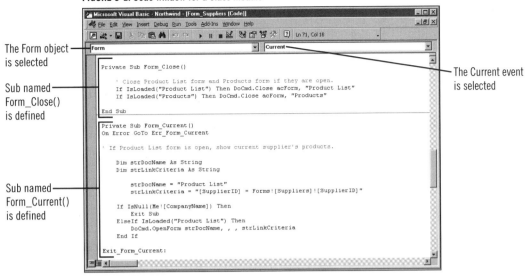

TABLE O-2: Common VBA keywords

statement	explanation
Function	Declares the name and arguments that create a new function procedure.
End Function	When defining a new function, the End Function statement is required as the last statement to mark the end of the VBA code that defines the function.
Sub	Declares the name, arguments, and code that create a new sub procedure. **Private Sub** indicates that the sub procedure is accessible only to other procedures in the module where it is declared.
End Sub	When defining a new sub, the End Sub statement is required as the last statement to mark the end of the VBA code that defines the sub.
If **Then**	Used to execute code (code that follows the Then statement) if the value of the expression is true (the expression follows the If statement). The If…Then statement has additional optional parts including Then, and ElseIf statements.
End If	When creating an If…Then statement, the End If statement is required as the last statement.
Const	Declares the name and value of a **constant**, an item that retains a constant value throughout the execution of the code.
Option Compare Database	A declaration statement that determines the way string values (text) will be sorted.
Option Explicit	A declaration statement that specifies that you must explicitly declare all variables used in all procedures. If you attempt to use an undeclared variable name, an error occurs at **compile time**, the period during which source code is translated to executable code.
Dim	Declares a **variable**, a named storage location that contains data that can be modified during program execution.
On Error GoTo	Upon error in the execution of a procedure, the On Error GoTo statement specifies the location (the statement) where the procedure should continue. If you don't use an On Error statement, any run-time error that occurs is fatal; that is, an error message is displayed and execution stops.
Select Case	Executes one of several groups of statements, depending on the value of an expression. Each group of statements is a new **Case**. Use the Select Case statement as an alternative to using **ElseIf** in **If…Then…Else** statements when comparing one expression to several different values.
End Select	When defining a new Select Case group of statements, the End Select statement is required as the last statement to mark the end of the VBA code.

Access 2000

Creating a Function Procedure

While there are hundreds of Access-supplied functions, there may be times when you want to create a unique function to accomplish a specific task. You can create a Function procedure in a standard module so that it can be used in any query, form, or report in the database. **Scenario** MediaLoft has implemented a program that allows employees to purchase corporate equipment when it is replaced. Equipment that is less than a year old will be sold to employees at 75% of its initial value, and equipment that is more than a year old will be sold at 50% of its initial value. Kristen defines a new function called StreetValue that will determine the employee purchase price of equipment that MediaLoft replaces.

Steps

Trouble?

If the Projects or Properties windows are open as small windows on the left side of the screen, click their Close buttons to close them.

1. Start Access, open the **Technology-O** database, click **Modules** on the Objects bar, click the **New button** in the database window, then maximize the Code window
   The Code window opens, and Access automatically inserts the Option Compare Database declaration statement. The Technology-O database window minimizes on the taskbar.

2. Type **Function StreetValue(corpvalue)**, then press **[Enter]**
   This statement declares a new function name, StreetValue, which contains one argument, corpvalue. VBA automatically adds the End Function statement because it is required to mark the end of the code that defines the new function. Because both Function and End Function are VBA keywords, they are colored blue. The insertion point is positioned between the statements so that you can further define how the new StreetValue function will calculate.

3. Press **[Tab]**, type **StreetValue = corpvalue * 0.5**, then press **[Enter]**
   Your screen should look like Figure O-3. This statement explains how StreetValue will calculate. StreetValue will be equal to the corpvalue argument times 0.5. It is not necessary to indent statements, but many programmers indent code between matching Function/End Function, Sub/End Sub, or If/End If statements to enhance the program's readability.

4. Click the **Save button** on the Standard toolbar, type **Functions** in the Save As dialog box, then click **OK**
   Now that the function is created, it can be used in a query, form, or report. You need to close the Visual Basic window and return to Access.

5. Click **File** on the menu bar, then click **Close and Return to Microsoft Access**
   The Visual Basic window closes, and the Microsoft Access window and the Technology-O database window are open on your screen.

6. Click **Queries** on the Objects bar, click **Employee Pricing**, then click the **Design button** in the database window
   The Employee Pricing query opens in Design view. You can create calculated expressions in a query using either Access functions or the ones you define in modules.

QuickTip

Right-click the blank Field cell, then click Zoom to enter the calculated expression in a Zoom dialog box.

7. Maximize the Query Design window, click the **blank Field cell** to the right of the InitialValue field, type **EmployeePrice:StreetValue([InitialValue])**, then click the **Datasheet View button** on the Query Design toolbar
   Your screen should look like Figure O-4. In this query you created a new field called EmployeePrice that used the StreetValue function that contains one argument (called corpvalue in the module). The value in the InitialValue field (stored in the Equipment table) was entered as the corpvalue argument. The StreetValue function multiplied the InitialValue field by 0.5 to determine the EmployeePrice field. By creating the StreetValue function in a module, you can add powerful logic to it that calculates different StreetValues depending on the age of the equipment and use it over and over again.

8. Save the Employee Pricing query, then close the datasheet

FIGURE O-3: Creating the StreetValue function

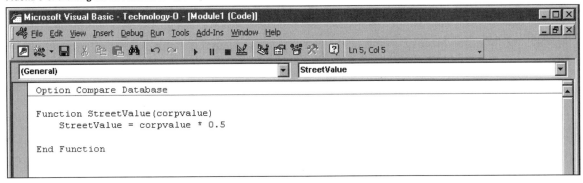

```
Microsoft Visual Basic - Technology-O - [Module1 (Code)]

File  Edit  View  Insert  Debug  Run  Tools  Add-Ins  Window  Help

(General)                                              StreetValue

Option Compare Database

Function StreetValue(corpvalue)
    StreetValue = corpvalue * 0.5

End Function
```

FIGURE O-4: Creating the EmployeePrice field using the StreetValue function

SerialNo	Manufacturer	Description	PurchaseDate	InitialValue	EmployeePrice
242XG1	Micron	Transtrek3000	7/1/99	$2,000.00	1000
242XG2	Micron	Transtrek3000	7/1/99	$2,000.00	1000
295XT4	Micron	Prosignet303	7/15/99	$1,800.00	900
295XT5	Micron	Prosignet303	7/15/99	$1,800.00	900
295XT6	Micron	Prosignet303	7/15/99	$1,800.00	900
295XT7	Micron	Prosignet303	7/15/99	$1,800.00	900
300RZ1	Micron	Prosignet303	8/1/99	$1,700.00	850
300RZ2	Micron	Prosignet303	8/1/99	$1,700.00	850
300RZ3	Micron	Prosignet303	8/1/99	$1,700.00	850
330RZ4	Micron	Prosignet303	8/1/99	$1,700.00	850
388MQS1	Compaq	Centuria8088	6/1/99	$1,500.00	750
388MQS2	Compaq	Centuria8088	6/1/99	$1,500.00	750
388MQS3	Compaq	Centuria8088	6/1/99	$1,500.00	750
388MQS4	Compaq	Centuria8088	6/1/99	$1,500.00	750
4848XH1	Micron	Transtrek3000	7/15/99	$1,900.00	950
4848XH2	Micron	Transtrek3000	7/15/99	$1,900.00	950
4848XJ3	Micron	Transtrek3000	8/1/99	$1,800.00	900
4848XJ4	Micron	Transtrek3000	8/1/99	$1,800.00	900
4848XK5	Micron	Transtrek3000	8/15/99	$1,750.00	875
511984CDE1	Lexmark	Optra2000	1/5/99	$2,000.00	1000
511984CDE2	Lexmark	Optra2000	1/5/99	$2,000.00	1000
72JRV1	Compaq	Deskpro99	4/1/99	$2,000.00	1000
72JRV2	Compaq	Deskpro99	4/1/99	$2,000.00	1000
72JRV3	Compaq	Deskpro99	4/1/99	$2,000.00	1000
72JRV4	Compaq	Deskpro99	4/1/99	$2,000.00	1000

Record: 1 of 53

Datasheet View

Calculated
EmployeePrice field

Access 2000

Steps

Using If Statements

The **If...Then...Else** statement allows you to test a logical condition and execute commands only if the condition is true. The If...Then...Else statement can be one or several lines of code, depending on how many conditions you want to test and how many answers the result can be. **Scenario** Kristen needs to add logic to the StreetValue function. As originally designed, the calculation is *always* at 50%. If the equipment is less than one year old, the function should calculate the answer at 75% of the original value. She uses an If statement in the StreetValue function to determine the correct value based on age.

1. Click **Modules** on the Objects bar, click **Functions**, then click the **Design button** 🔲
The Functions Code window with the StreetValue function opens. To determine the age of the equipment, which in turn determines whether 50% or 75% should be used in the calculation, the StreetValue function needs to evaluate another argument, which represents the purchase date.

> **Trouble?**
> Be sure to type the arguments exactly as specified to avoid getting errors later.

2. Click between the **e** in **corpvalue** and the **right parenthesis** in the Function statement, type **,** (a comma), press **[Spacebar]**, then type **corppurchasedate**
Now that another argument has been established, the argument can be used in the function.

3. Click to the right of the **right parenthesis** in the Function statement, press **[Enter]**, then type **If (Now( ) – corppurchasedate) >365 Then**
This expression evaluates whether today's date (represented by the Access function Now) minus the value represented by the corppurchasedate argument is greater than 365 days. If true, this would indicate that the equipment is older than one year old and the StreetValue should be recalculated at 50%.

4. Type the **Else** and **End If** statements precisely as shown in Figure O-5
The Else statement will be executed only if the expression is false (if the equipment is less than 365 days old). The End If statement is needed to mark the end of the If block of code.

5. Click the **Save button** 🔲 on the Visual Basic Standard toolbar, click **File** on the menu bar, click **Close and Return to Microsoft Access**, click **Queries** on the Objects bar, click **Employee Pricing**, then click 🔲 in the database window
Because you modified the StreetValue function to include two arguments, you have to change the expression in the query to include two arguments for the StreetValue function as well.

6. Right-click the **EmployeePrice field** in the query design grid, click **Zoom**, click to the right of the **right square bracket**, then type **,[PurchaseDate]**
Your Zoom dialog box should look like Figure O-6. Both of the arguments used to calculate the StreetValue function are field names, so they must be typed exactly as shown and surrounded by square brackets. Commas separate multiple arguments in the function.

> **Trouble?**
> If you get a compile or syntax error, open the query design grid, check your function against Figure O-6, and correct any errors.

7. Click **OK** in the Zoom dialog box, then click the **Datasheet View button** 🔲 on the Query Design toolbar

8. Click any entry in the **PurchaseDate field**, then click the **Sort Ascending button** 🔼
The StreetValue function now calculates two ways, depending on the age of the equipment determined by the date in the PurchaseDate field, as shown in Figure O-7. The EmployeePrice will calculate based on the current date on your computer, so your results may vary. Check to make sure that all records with PurchaseDate values more recently than one year ago calculate the EmployeePrice field at 75% of the InitialValue field.

9. Save and close the Employee Pricing query

FIGURE O-5: If...Then...Else statements

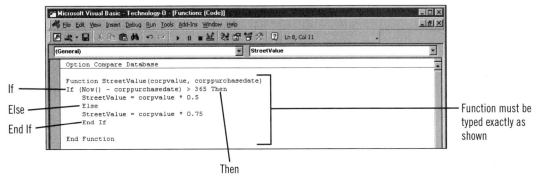

If —
Else —
End If —

Function must be typed exactly as shown

Then

FIGURE O-6: Modifying the expression

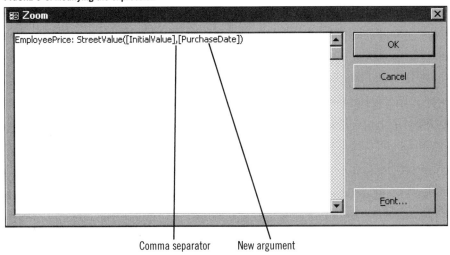

Comma separator   New argument

FIGURE O-7: Final EmployeePrice field is calculated using the StreetValue function

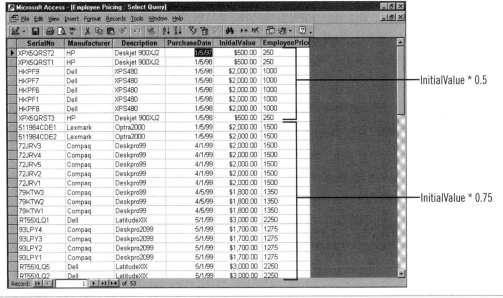

InitialValue * 0.5

InitialValue * 0.75

Documenting a Procedure

A good programmer documents code with frequent explanatory statements or comment lines. **Comment lines** are text in the code that do not affect the running of the program and are used simply to document the code. At any future time, when you want to modify the code, you'll be able to write the modifications much more quickly if the existing statements are properly documented. If you expect someone else to be able to maintain or modify the code, comment lines are a must. **Scenario** Kristen documents the StreetValue function in the Functions module with descriptive comments so she can easily follow the purpose and logic of the function.

Steps 1 2 3 4

1. Click **Modules** on the Objects bar, click **Functions**, then click the **Design button** in the database window
   The Code window for the Functions module opens.

2. Click to the left of the **Function statement**, press **[Enter]**, press **[Up arrow]**, type **'This function is called StreetValue and has two arguments**, then press **[Enter]**
   Comments always start with an apostrophe and are green in the Code window.

Trouble?

Be sure to use an ' (apostrophe) and not a " (quotation mark) to begin the comment line.

3. Type **'Created by Your Name on Today's Date**, then press **[Enter]**
   Your screen should look like Figure O-8. Comments also can be placed at the end of an existing line. Either way, however, they always start with an apostrophe.

4. Click to the right of **Then** at the end of the If statement, press **[Spacebar]**, then type **'Now( ) is today's date**
   This comment explains that the Now() function is today's date. All comments are green, regardless of whether they are on their own line or at the end of an existing line.

5. Click to the right of **0.5**, press **[Spacebar]**, then type **'If > 365 days, value is 50%**

6. Click to the right of **0.75**, press **[Spacebar]**, then type **'If < 365 days, value is 75%**
   Your screen should look like Figure O-9. Table O-3 provides more information about the Standard toolbar buttons in the Code window.

7. Click the **Save button** on the Standard toolbar, click **File** on the menu bar, click **Print**, then click **OK**

8. Click **File** on the menu bar, then click **Close and Return to Microsoft Access**

FIGURE O-8: Adding comments to the Code window

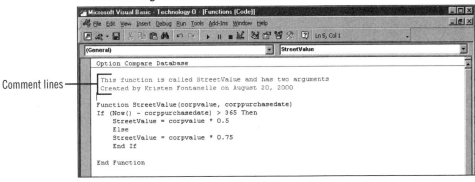

Comment lines

FIGURE O-9: Adding comments at the end of a statement

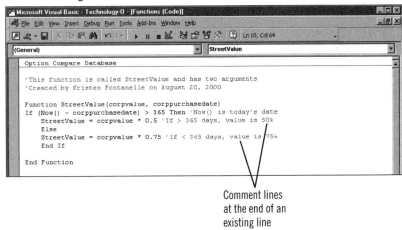

Comment lines
at the end of an
existing line

TABLE O-3: Standard toolbar buttons in the Code window

button name	button	description
View Microsoft Access		Toggles between the host application and the active Visual Basic document
Insert		Opens a new module or class module code window, or inserts a new procedure in the current code window
Run Sub/UserForm		Runs the current procedure if the insertion point is in a procedure or runs the UserForm if it is active
Break		Stops execution of a program while it's running and switches to **break mode**, the temporary suspension of program execution in which you can examine, debug, reset, step through, or continue program execution
Reset		Resets the procedure
Project Explorer		Displays the **Project Explorer**, which displays a hierarchical list of the currently open **projects**, (set of modules) and their contents
Object Browser		Displays the **Object Browser**, which lists the defined modules and procedures as well as available methods, properties, events, constants, and other items that you can use in the code

Examining Class Modules

Class modules are contained and executed within specific forms and reports. Class modules most commonly contain sub procedures and execute in response to an event such as the click of a command button. You do not always have to know VBA code to create class modules. The Command Button Wizard, for example, creates sub procedures. You can examine them to see how sub procedures work and how they are associated to specific events. **Scenario** Kristen used the Command Button Wizard to create four command buttons on the Equipment Entry Form. She examines the sub procedures in this form in order to understand class modules.

Steps 1234

1. Click **Forms** on the Objects bar, click the **Equipment Entry Form**, then click the **Design button** in the database window
   The Equipment Entry Form opens in Design view. The form has four command buttons: three to manipulate records and one to close the form.

QuickTip

The Command Button Wizard prompts you for the command button's name as its last question.

2. Maximize the form, click the **Add New Record command button**, view the **Object list** on the Formatting (Form/Report) toolbar, then click each command button while viewing the Object list
   Your screen should look like Figure O-10. The Object list identifies the name of the selected control as determined by the control's Name property. In this case, the word "object" is used as a VBA programmer would use it, and does not refer to the seven basic object types (tables, queries, forms, pages, reports, macros, and modules) of an Access database.

Trouble?

If the Immediate Window is open below the code window, close it.

3. Click the **Code button** on the Form Design toolbar, then maximize the Form_Equipment Entry Form (Code) window
   The Code window for the VBA code stored in the Equipment Entry Form class module appears, as shown in Figure O-11. This code was created by using the Command Button Wizard. The names of the two subs displayed at the top of the code window correspond with the first two command buttons on the form, the AddNewRecordButton and the DeleteThisRecordButton. The _Click() suffix on the sub names identifies the event that will cause this sub to execute.

4. Click **File** on the menu bar, click **Close and Return to Microsoft Access**, double-click the **AddNewRecord command button** to open its property sheet, click the **Event tab**, click the **On Click text box**, then click the **Build button**
   The class module is opened in the specific location where the AddNewRecordButton_Click() sub is stored. If you wanted to create another sub that was executed from another event associated with that command button (for example, to display a message box when the command button gets the focus) you could use the property sheet to help you with the syntax of correctly defining the sub's name.

5. Click **File** on the menu bar, click **Close and Return to Microsoft Access**, click the **On Got Focus text box** on the Command Button AddNewRecordButton property sheet, click , click **Code Builder** in the Choose Builder dialog box, then click **OK**
   The class module Code window opens, as shown in Figure O-12. Because you entered the Code window through a specific event (On Got Focus) of a specific control (AddNewRecordButton), VBA knew what to name the sub and to automatically supply the last line of the procedure, the End Sub statement. The rest of the sub's statements, however, require individual programming, because you are not using a wizard to create the code.

6. Select all of the statements from **Private Sub AddNewRecordButton_GotFocus()** through the **End Sub** statement, press **[Delete]**, click the **Save button** on the Microsoft Visual Basic Standard toolbar, click **File** on the menu bar, click **Close and Return to Microsoft Access**, close the property sheet, then close the Equipment Entry Form

FIGURE O-10: Four command buttons in Form Design view

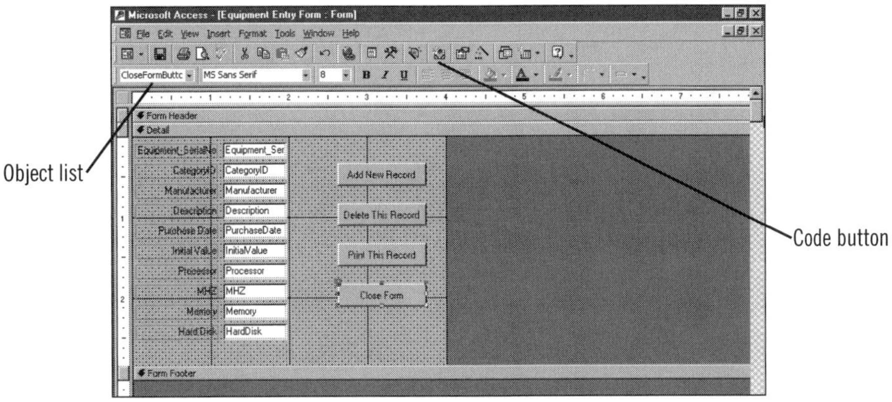

Object list

Code button

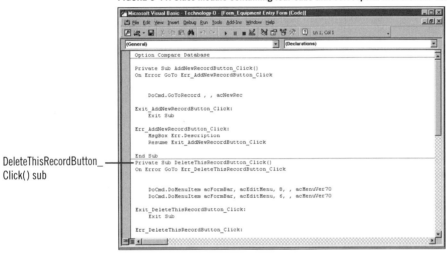

FIGURE O-11: Class module containing four subs that correspond with the four command buttons

DeleteThisRecordButton_
Click() sub

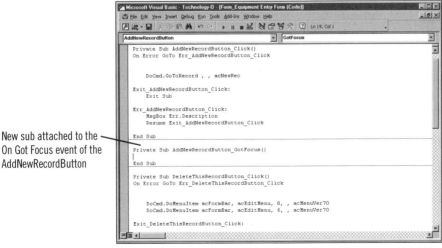

FIGURE O-12: Examining a new sub for a command button

New sub attached to the
On Got Focus event of the
AddNewRecordButton

Creating a Sub Procedure

While it is easiest to create class module sub procedures using wizards, not all subs can be created this way. The Command Button Wizard, for example, always attaches its code to the Click event of a command button. You might want to create a sub that executes based on another action, such as double-click, or one that is assigned to a control (called objects in VBA) other than a command button. **Scenario** Kristen would like to create all of the Technology forms with built-in documentation that the user can access by clicking the form. To accomplish this, she writes a sub procedure in the form's class module.

Steps

1. Click the **Equipment Entry Form**, click the **Design button** in the database window, then click the **Properties button** to open the form's property sheet

2. Click the **Event tab**, click the **On Click text box**, click the **Build button**, click **Code Builder** in the Choose Builder dialog box, then click **OK**
   The class module opens with two new statements to identify the new sub, which is called Form_Click( ). The name of the new sub references both the specific object and event you were examining through the property sheet. You can use the Object and Procedure lists within the Code window to find specific statements.

3. Click the **Object list arrow** below the Standard toolbar, click **FormFooter**, then scroll up so that your screen is similar to Figure O-13
   A new sub, named FormFooter_Click( ), was created.

4. Click the **Procedure list arrow** below the Standard toolbar, then click **DblClick**
   A new sub, named FormFooter_DblClick( ), was created. You do not wish to keep the FormFooter subs.

5. Click the **Undo button** twice, type **MsgBox ("Created by Your Name on Today's Date")** as the single statement of the Form_Click() sub, then click the **Save button** on the Standard toolbar
   Your screen should look like Figure O-14.

6. Click **File** on the menu bar, click **Close and Return to Microsoft Access**, close the property sheet, click the **Form View button** on the Form Design toolbar, then click the **record selector box** to the left of the record
   The MsgBox statement in the Form_Click() sub created the dialog box, as shown in Figure O-15.

7. Click **OK** in the message box, then close the form
   Visual Basic for Applications programming code is as robust and powerful as the Access application itself. It takes years of experience to appreciate the vast number of objects, events, methods, and properties that are available. With only modest programming skills, however, you can create basic modules as well as edit those that do not work as intended.

FIGURE O-13: Using the Object and Procedure lists

Undo button

Procedure list arrow

Form_Click( ) sub

FormFooter_Click( ) sub

Object list arrow

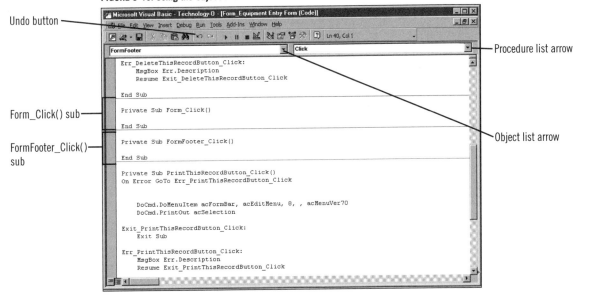

FIGURE O-14: Creating a sub procedure

MsgBox statement

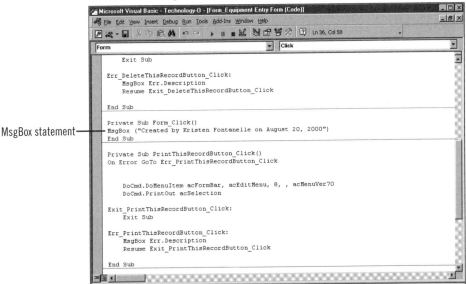

FIGURE O-15: The MsgBox action

Record selector box

Dialog box created by Msgbox

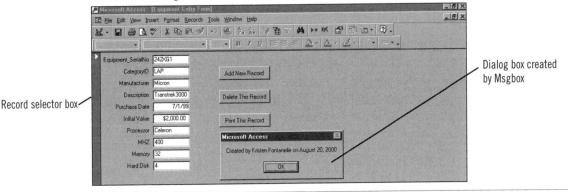

Access 2000

Troubleshooting Modules

There are three types of errors you may encounter as your code runs, and Access provides several techniques to help you **debug** (find and resolve errors) them. **Compile-time errors** occur as a result of incorrectly constructed code. For example, you may have forgotten to write an End If statement following an If clause, or you may have a **syntax error**, such as a missing parenthesis. These are easiest to find because your code will turn red as soon as it detects a syntax error. **Run-time errors** occur after the code starts to run and include attempting an illegal operation such as dividing by zero or moving focus to a control that doesn't exist. When you encounter a run-time error, VBA will stop the execution of your procedure at the line in which the error occurred so you can examine it. **Logic errors** are more difficult to troubleshoot because they occur when the code runs without problems, but the procedure still doesn't produce the expected results. **Scenario** Kristen studies debugging techniques using the Functions module.

Steps 1 2 3 4

1. Click **Modules** on the Objects bar, click **Functions**, click the **Design button** ▣ in the database window, click to the left of the **Option Compare Database** statement, type **Your Name**, then press the **[Down arrow key]**

   The Functions module opens in the Code window, and when you attempt to move out of that line of code, VBA notices the syntax error and displays the statement in bright red.

QuickTip

Click the gray bar to the left of the VBA statement to toggle breakpoints on and off.

2. Click **OK** in the Compile error message box, delete **Your Name**, then click in another statement

   The Option Compare Database statement changes to blue (because it uses reserved VBA keywords) as soon as you successfully delete your name and click elsewhere in the code window. One debugging technique is to set a **breakpoint**, a bookmark that suspends execution of the procedure at that point in time to allow the user to examine what is happening.

3. Click anywhere in the **If** statement, click **Debug** on the menu bar, then click **Toggle Breakpoint**

   Your screen should look like Figure O-16.

QuickTip

If you suspend the execution of a procedure by using a breakpoint, pointing to an argument in the Code window will display a pop-up with the argument's current value.

4. Click the **View Microsoft Access button** ▣ on the Standard toolbar, click **Queries** on the Objects bar, then double-click **Employee Pricing**

   When the Employee Pricing query opens, it immediately runs the StreetValue function. Because you set a breakpoint at the If statement, that statement is highlighted, as shown in Figure O-17, indicating that the code has been suspended at that point.

5. Click **View** on the menu bar, click **Immediate Window**, type **? corppurchasedate**, then press **[Enter]**

   Your screen should look like Figure O-18. The **Immediate Window** is a scratch pad window in which statements are evaluated immediately, so you can determine the value of any argument at any point in the procedure. There are many other debugging tools available in the Code window when you are working with more complex code.

6. Click **Debug** on the menu bar, click **Clear All Breakpoints**, click the **Continue button** ▶ on the Standard toolbar to execute the rest of the function, close the **Immediate Window**, click **File** on the menu bar, then click **Close and return to Microsoft Access**

   The Employee Pricing query's datasheet should be visible.

7. Close the Employee Pricing datasheet, close the Technology-O database, save the changes to Functions, then exit Access

FIGURE O-16: Setting a breakpoint

Debug menu

Toggle breakpoint

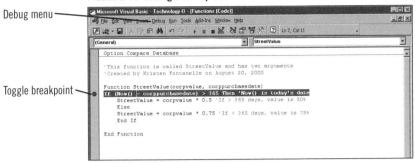

FIGURE O-17: Stopping execution at a breakpoint

Breakpoint
highlighted

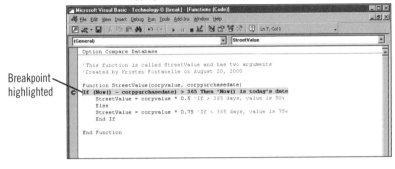

FIGURE O-18: Using the Immediate window

Continue
button

Immediate
window

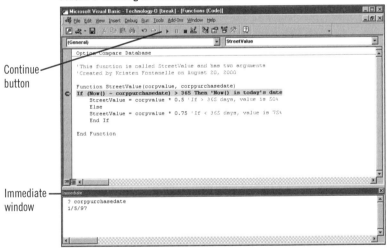

CLUES TO USE

Interpreting Visual Basic syntax

When you enter a Visual Basic keyword such as MsgBox, shown in Figure O-19, Visual Basic prompts appear to help you complete the statement. In the MsgBox function syntax, the bold italic words are **named arguments** of the function. **Arguments** enclosed in brackets are optional. (Do not type the brackets in your Visual Basic code.) For the MsgBox function, the only argument you must provide is the text for the prompt.

FIGURE O-19: MsgBox function

```
MsgBox |
MsgBox(Prompt, [Buttons As VbMsgBoxStyle = vbOKOnly], [Title], [HelpFile], [Context])
As VbMsgBoxResult
```

Practice

▶ Concepts Review

Identify each element of the code window shown in Figure O-20.

FIGURE O-20

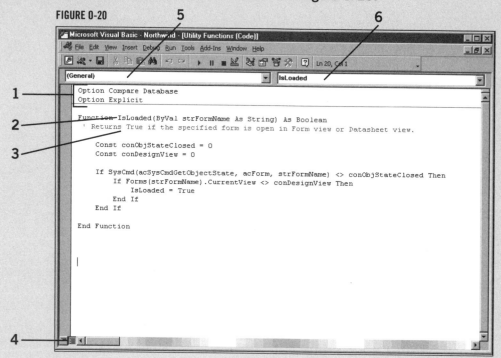

Match each term with the statement that describes its function.

7. Procedure
8. If...Then...Else statement
9. Debugging
10. Class modules
11. Visual Basic for Applications
12. Function
13. Arguments
14. Breakpoint
15. Module

a. A procedure that returns a value
b. The programming language used in Access modules
c. A line of code that automatically suspends execution of the procedure
d. Allows you to test a logical condition and execute commands only if the condition is true
e. Constants, variables, or expressions passed to a procedure to further define how it should execute
f. Stored as part of the form or report object in which they are created
g. The Access object where VBA code is stored
h. A series of VBA statements that perform an operation or calculate a value
i. A process to find and resolve programming errors

Select the best answer from the list of choices.

16. A module contains VBA programming code organized in units called:
    a. Procedures.   **c.** Breakpoints.
    b. Arguments.   **d.** Macros.

17. Which type of procedure does NOT return a value?
    a. Macro   **c.** Module
    b. Function   **d.** Sub

18. Which of the following is NOT a reason to use modules rather than macros?
    a. Modules are usually easier to write than macros.
    b. Modules contain code that can work with other Microsoft Office software programs.
    c. Modules can contain procedures that mask error messages.
    d. Modules are used to create unique functions.

19. Which of the following is NOT a type of VBA error?
    a. Class action   **c.** Logic
    b. Run time   **d.** Compile time

Skills Review

1. **Understanding Modules.**
    a. Start Access and open the Basketball-O database.
    b. Click Modules on the Objects bar, click the Shot Statistics module, then click the Design button.
    c. Record your answers to the following questions on a sheet of paper.

    - What is the name of the function defined in this module?
    - What are the names of the arguments defined in this module?
    - In your own words, what is the purpose of the If statement?
    - What is the purpose of the End Function statement?
    - Why is the End Function statement in blue?
    - Why are some of the lines indented?

2. **Comparing Macros and Modules.**
    a. If not already opened, open the Code window for the Shot Statistics module.
    b. Record your answers to the following questions on a sheet of paper.

    - Why was a module rather than a macro used to create this function?
    - Why is code written in the Shot Statistics code window generally more difficult to create than a macro?
    - Identify each of the keywords or keyword phrases, and explain the purpose for each.

3. **Creating a Function Procedure.**
    a. If not already opened, open the Code window for the Shot Statistics module.
    b. Create a function called "Contribution" below the End Function statement of the TotalShotPercentage function by typing the following VBA statements: (*Hint*: Type the function exactly as written below.)
    Function Contribution(fg, threept, ft, offreb, defreb, assists)
            Contribution = (fg * 2 + threept * 3 + ft + offreb * 2 + defreb + assists * 2)
    End Function

    c. Click the Save button to save the Shot Statistics code

    d. Close the Visual Basic Code window and return to Access.

    e. Use Query Design view to create a new query using the First and Last fields from the Players table and all of the fields from the Stats table.

    f. Create a calculated field called Rank in the first available column by carefully typing the Contribution function as follows:
Rank: Contribution([FG],[3P], [FT], [Reb-O], [Reb-D], [Assists])

    g. View the query datasheet

    h. Change PlayerNo 21 to your first and last name, then print the first page of the datasheet in landscape orientation.

    i. Save the query as "Rankings" and close the datasheet.

4. Using If Statements.

    a. Click Modules on the Objects bar, open the Shot Statistics Code Design window, click to the right of the Function Contribution statement, press [Enter], then type the following If statements:
(*Hint:* You can use copy and paste to copy repeating statements, then edit for the differences.)

        If fg+threept+ft = 0 Then
        Contribution = (fg * 2 + threept * 3 + ft + offreb * 2 + defreb + assists * 2)/2
        ElseIf offreb+defreb = 0 Then
        Contribution = (fg * 2 + threept * 3 + ft + offreb * 2 + defreb + assists * 2)/3
        Else
        Contribution = (fg * 2 + threept * 3 + ft + offreb * 2 + defreb + assists * 2)
        End If
    End Function

    b. Save and close the Shot Statistics Code window and return to Access.

    c. Open the Rankings query, then print the first pages of the datasheet in landscape orientation. You should see the calculated Ranking field change for PlayerNo 21 for Games 1, 2, and 3 in which the player had either zero offense or zero rebounds.

    d. Close the datasheet.

5. Documenting a Procedure.

    a. Click Modules on the Objects bar, open the Shot Statistics Code design window, and edit the Contribution function to include the following five comment statements:
Function Contribution(fg, threept, ft, offreb, defreb, assists)
'If no field goals, 3 pointers, or free throws were made
        If fg + threept + ft = 0 Then
'Then the Contribution statistic should be divided by 2
        Contribution = (fg * 2 + threept * 3 + ft + offreb * 2 + defreb + assists * 2) / 2
'If no offensive or defensive rebounds were grabbed
        ElseIf offreb + defreb = 0 Then
'Then the Contribution statistic should be divided by 3
        Contribution = (fg * 2 + threept * 3 + ft + offreb * 2 + defreb + assists * 2) / 3
        Else
        Contribution = (fg * 2 + threept * 3 + ft + offreb * 2 + defreb + assists * 2)
        End If
    End Function
'This function was created by **Your Name** on **Today's Date**

Practice

b. Save the changes to the Contribution function and Shot Statistics module, print and close the Code window, then return to Access.

6. Examining a Class Module.
a. Open the Player Entry Form in Design view.
b. Select the Command Button on the right side of the form that does the Print Record Action. It has the picture of a printer on the button and is named PrintCurrentRecord.
c. Open the property sheet for the button, click the Event tab, click the On Click property, then click the Build button to open the class module.
d. Edit the comment on the last line to document your name and the current date; save, print, then close the Code window.

7. Creating a Sub Procedure.
a. Open the Player Entry Form in Design view, if not already opened.
b. Open the property sheet for the form, click the Event tab, click the On Mouse Move text box, click the Build button, click Code Builder, then click OK.
c. Enter the following statement between the Private Sub and End Sub statements:
[First].ForeColor = 255
d. Enter a comment below this statement as follows:
'When the mouse moves, the First control will become bright red
e. Save and close the Code window. Return to Access.
f. Close the property sheet, then open the Player Entry Form in Form view.
g. Move the mouse beyond the edge of the Detail section of the form. The color of the First text box should turn bright red.
h. Save and close the Player Entry Form.

8. Troubleshooting a Module.
a. Open the Code window for the Shot Statistics module.
b. Click anywhere in the If fg + threept + ft = 0 statement in the Contribution function.
c. Click Debug on the menu bar, then click the Toggle Breakpoint option to set a breakpoint at the If fg + threept + ft = 0 statement in the Contribution function.
d. Save and close the Code window and return to Microsoft Access.
e. Click Queries on the Objects bar, then double-click the Rankings query. This action should call the Contribution function, which will stop and highlight the statement where you set a breakpoint.
f. Click View on the menu bar, click Immediate Window, type "?fg", then press [Enter].
g. Type ?offreb, then press [Enter].
h. View the results in the Immediate window, close the Immediate window, click Debug on the menu bar, click Clear All Breakpoints, click the Continue button on the Standard toolbar, then close the Code window and return to Access.
i. Close the Rankings query, close the Basketball-O database, then exit Access.

▶ Visual Workshop

As the manager of a college basketball team, you are helping the coach build meaningful statistics to compare the relative value of the players in each game. The coach has stated that one offensive rebound is worth as much to the team as two defensive rebounds, and would like you to use this rule to develop a "rebounding impact statistic" for each game. Open the Basketball-O database and use Figure O-21 to develop a function called ReboundImpact in a module called Rebound Statistic to calculate this statistic. Be sure to put your own name and date as a comment in the last row. Print the function.

FIGURE O-21

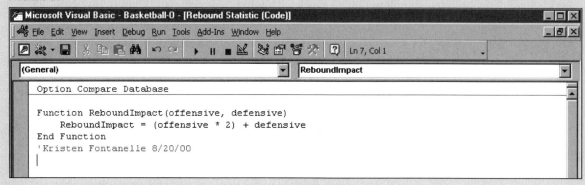

Access 2000

Unit P

Managing
the Database

Objectives

- ▶ **Convert databases**
- ▶ **Set passwords**
- ▶ **Change Startup options**
- ▶ **Encrypt and decrypt a database**
- ▶ **Analyze performance**
- ▶ **Split a database**
- ▶ **Replicate using the Briefcase**
- ▶ **Synchronize using the Briefcase**

After you have invested months of effort into developing an Access database, spending a few hours protecting the database, analyzing its use, and improving its performance is a practical and wise investment. As more and more users become dependent on the database, any effort you take to make the database faster, easier, and more secure will provide tremendous benefits. Proper administration of a database is an important responsibility. **Scenario** Kristen examines several administrative issues such as setting passwords, changing startup options, and analyzing database performance to protect, improve, and enhance the Technology database.

Converting databases

When you **convert** a database you change the file into one that can be opened in another version of Access. For example, it would be necessary to convert an Access 97 database to an Access 2000 database if your company upgraded from the Office 97 suite to the Office 2000 suite of Microsoft software. In Access 2000, you can convert an Access 2000 database to an Access 97 database with only a few conversion exceptions (links to data access pages are lost, for example). Access 2000 is the first Access database version that has supported this downward conversion capability. ▧Scenario▷ Kristen has been asked by the Training Department to convert the Technology-P database to a version that can be opened and used in Access 97 for use in their training classes. She uses the conversion capability of Access 2000 to accomplish this.

Steps 1 2 3 4

1. Start Access, then open the **Technology-P database** on your Project Disk
   To convert a database, you must make sure that no other users have it open. Because you are the sole user of this database, you can start the conversion process.

2. Click **Tools** on the menu bar, point to **Database Utilities**, point to **Convert Database**, then click **To Prior Access Database Version**
   The Convert Database Into dialog box opens, prompting you for the name of the database.

3. Make sure the Save In list references your Project Disk, then type **Technology97** in the File name text box
   Your screen should look like Figure P-1. Because both Access 2000 and Access 97 databases have the same **.mdb** file extension, it is helpful to identify the version of Access in the file name if you are going to be working with both file types on the same computer.

4. Click **Save** in the Convert Database Into dialog box
   Access starts the conversion process; you can follow the progress on the status bar. Access creates a database file Technology97 in an Access 97 format on your Project Disk. There are no prompts indicating that the process is finished. Rather, you are returned to your original Access 2000 file, Technology-P.

Trouble?
You may need to click expand buttons (they appear as plus signs) in the Folders list to view all of the folders on the Project Disk.

5. Right-click the **Start button** on the taskbar, click **Explore**, locate your Project Disk, then view the contents on your Project Disk

6. Click the **Views button list arrow** 〔▦▾〕 on the Explorer Standard Buttons toolbar, then click **Details**
   Your screen should look similar to Figure P-2. You can see a column of information for file types. Notice that the list includes Technology97, the database that was just created by converting the Technology-P Access 2000 database to an Access 97 version database. The filename Technology-P appears twice, as an .mdb and .ldb file. The **.ldb** file is a temporary file that keeps track of record-locking information when the database is open. It helps coordinate the multiuser capabilities of an Access database so that several people can read and update the same database at the same time. If you had Access 97 on your computer, you could open the Technology97 database into that application window without any conversion or error messages.

7. Click **File** on the menu bar, then click **Close**
   The Technology-P database window appears on your screen.

FIGURE P-1: Convert Database Into dialog box

Save the file to your Project Disk

New file name

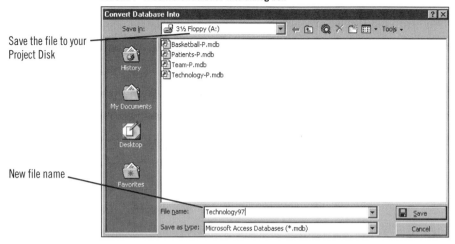

FIGURE P-2: Exploring the Project Disk

Views button

Technology97.mdb is an Access 97 database

Project Disk in drive A

Expand buttons

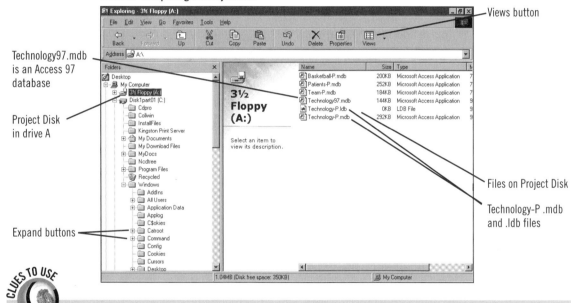

Files on Project Disk

Technology-P .mdb and .ldb files

CLUES TO USE

Converting from Access 97 to Access 2000

If you open an Access 97 database file in Access 2000, the dialog box shown in Figure P-3 will appear, enabling you to convert the database to an Access 2000 version as you open it or to just open it without converting it. If you open it without converting it, you will be able to view all objects and change data, but you will not be able to modify any of the objects in Access 2000. In this way, both Access 97 and Access 2000 users can share the same database.

FIGURE P-3: Convert/Open Database dialog box

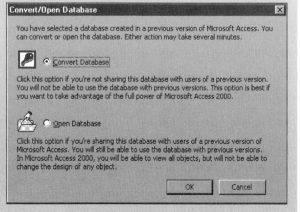

Access 2000

Setting Passwords

There are three types of passwords that can be set on an Access database: database, security account, and Visual Basic for Applications (VBA) passwords. If you set a **database password**, all users must enter that password before they are allowed to open the database, but they then have full access to the database. **Security account passwords** are applied to **workgroups**, files that determine the users, objects, and permissions to which the users are granted (such as read, delete, or edit) for specific objects in the database. **VBA passwords** prevent unauthorized users from modifying VBA code. Scenario▶ The Technology database contains sensitive information about MediaLoft assets that Kristen wants to protect. She uses a database password to further secure the information.

QuickTip

It's always a good idea to back up a database on another disk before creating a database password.

1. Click **File** on the menu bar, then click **Close**

The Technology-P database closes, and the Access window remains open.

2. Click the **Open button** 🖾 on the Database toolbar, navigate to your Project Disk, click **Technology-P** in the database window, click the **Open list arrow** in the Open dialog box, then click **Open Exclusive**

To set a database password, you must open it in exclusive mode. **Exclusive mode** means that you are the only person who has the database open, and others will not be able to open the file during this time.

3. Click **Tools** on the menu bar, point to **Security**, then click **Set Database Password**

The Set Database Password dialog box opens, as shown in Figure P-4. Passwords are case sensitive, and if you lose or forget your password, it can't be recovered. For security reasons, your password will not appear as you type; for each keystroke, an asterisk will appear. Therefore, you must enter the exact same password in both the Password and Verify text boxes to make sure that you didn't make a typing error.

QuickTip

Check to make sure the Caps Lock light is not on if your password is lowercase letters.

4. Type **cyclone** in the Password text box, press **[Tab]**, type **cyclone** in the Verify text box, then click **OK**

Passwords should be easy enough to remember, but not obvious—such as your name, the word "password," the name of the database, or the name of the company.

5. Click **File** on the menu bar, then click **Close**

You closed the Technology-P database, but left the Access window open. An important part of database administration is testing a new database password.

6. Click 🖾 on the Database toolbar, navigate to your Project Disk, then double-click **Technology-P** in the database window

The Password Required dialog box opens, as shown in Figure P-5.

7. Type **cyclone**, then click **OK**

The Technology-P database opens, giving you full access to all of the objects. You must exclusively open a database to remove a database password, as was required to set a database password.

8. Click **File** on the menu bar, click **Close**, click 🖾 on the Database toolbar, navigate to your Project Disk, click **Technology-P** in the database window, click the **Open list arrow** in the Open dialog box, click **Open Exclusive**, type **cyclone** in the Password Required dialog box, then click **OK**

9. Click **Tools** on the menu bar, point to **Security**, click **Unset Database Password**, type **cyclone**, then click **OK**

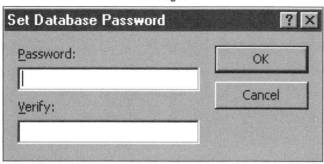

FIGURE P-4: Set Database Password dialog box

FIGURE P-5: Password Required dialog box

 Creating workgroups

To create workgroups that define the specific users and object permissions to which the users have access, use a program called **Workgroup Administrator**. Workgroup Administrator is started by double-clicking the Wrkgadm.exe file found in the C:\Program Files\Microsoft Office\Office folder of a typical installation. If you lose or forget any of the entries you make to workgroup information files, however, there is no way to recover them. Also, all entries in the workgroup information files are case sensitive, just like the database password.

Access 2000

Changing Startup Options

Startup options are a series of commands that execute when the database is opened. Many common startup options can be defined through the Startup dialog box, such as which form and menu bar to display when the database opens. Other startup options require that a **command-line option**, a special series of characters that starts with a forward slash added to the end of the path to the file (for example, C:\My Documents\MediaLoft.mdb /excl), execute a command when the file is opened. See Table P-1 for more information on several startup command-line options. Scenario▶ Because she knows that most users immediately open the Employees form as soon as they open the Technology-P database, Kristen uses the Startup dialog box to specify that the Employees form opens as soon as the Technology-P database opens.

1. Click **Tools** on the menu bar, then click **Startup**
   The Startup dialog box opens, as shown in Figure P-6.

2. Click the **Display Form/Page list arrow**, then click **Employees**
   In addition to specifying which form will open when the Technology-P database opens, the Startup dialog box provides several other options as well.

3. Click in the **Application Title text box**, type **MediaLoft Computer Assets**, click the **Allow Toolbar/Menu Changes check box** to clear the check box, then click **OK**
   Clearing the Allow Toolbar/Menu Changes check box will not allow users to customize or change the view of toolbars or menus in any way. Provided the correct toolbars appear on each screen, not allowing the users to change them can simplify and improve the usability of the database. The text entered in the Application Title text box appears in the Access window title bar.

4. Close the Technology-P database, click the **Open button** 🖼 on the Database toolbar, navigate to your Project Disk, then double-click **Technology-P** in the database window
   The Technology-P database, followed by the Employees form, opens, as shown in Figure P-7. You can press and hold [Shift] while opening a database to bypass the startup options. If the database is also password protected, you would have to remove the password before you could bypass the startup options.

5. Close the Employees form, then click **View** on the menu bar
   The Toolbars option is no longer available because you disabled toolbar changes in the Startup dialog box.

6. Right-click the **database toolbar**
   There are no shortcut menus available from any toolbars because you disabled toolbar changes in the Startup dialog box.

FIGURE P-6: Startup dialog box

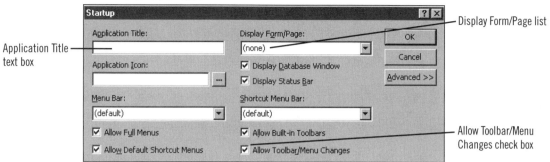

Application Title text box

Display Form/Page list

Allow Toolbar/Menu Changes check box

FIGURE P-7: Employees form automatically opens

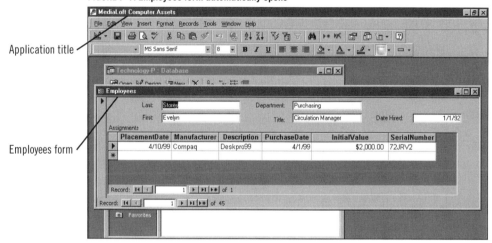

Application title

Employees form

TABLE P-1: Startup command-line options

option	effect
/excl	Opens the database for exclusive access
/ro	Opens the database for read-only access
/pwd *password*	Opens the database using the specified *password*
/repair	Repairs the database (In Access 2000, compacting the database also repairs it. So if the Compact on Close feature is chosen, the /repair option is not needed.)
/convert *target database*	Converts a previous version of a database to an Access 2000 database with the *target database* name
/x *macro*	Starts Access and runs specified *macro*
/nostartup	Starts Access without displaying the startup dialog box
/wrkgrp *workgroup information file*	Starts Access using the specified *workgroup information file*

Encrypting and Decrypting a Database

Encrypting means to make the database objects and data itself indecipherable to other programs. **Decrypting** reverses the encryption. If you are concerned that your Access database file might be stolen and the data stripped from it by another program (such as another database program, a word processor, or a utility program), encryption may be warranted. Other potential threats to the security of your database are described in Table P-2. ▶Scenario MediaLoft has recently connected their corporate file servers to the Internet, so Kristen is more concerned about securing corporate data than ever before. She uses Access encryption and decryption to learn how to secure the data within the Technology-P database.

QuickTip

It's always a good idea to back up a database on another disk before encrypting it.

1. Click **File** on the menu bar, click **Close**
   The Technology-P database window closes, but the Access window is still open. You cannot encrypt an open database.

2. Click **Tools** on the menu bar, point to **Security**, then click **Encrypt/Decrypt Database**
   The Encrypt/Decrypt Database dialog box opens, as shown in Figure P-8.

3. Click the **Look in list arrow**, navigate to your Project Disk, double-click **Technology-P**
   The Encrypt Database As dialog box appears, as shown in Figure P-9.

4. Type **Technology-P** in the File name text box, click **Save** in the Encrypt Database As dialog box, then click **Yes** to replace the existing file
   You can encrypt a database file to the same file name or to a new file name. In either case, a back-up copy of the database on a separate disk protects your file should the encryption be unsuccessful (unlikely but possible) or the equipment malfunctions during the encryption process. An encrypted database works in exactly the same way as the original file to users authorized to open the file. Encryption helps protect the data as it is being sent over network connections. You decrypt a database using the same steps.

5. Click **Tools** on the menu bar, point to **Security**, then click **Encrypt/Decrypt Database**

6. Click the **Look in: list arrow**, navigate to your Project Disk, then double-click **Technology-P**
   The Decrypt Database As dialog box opens, because Technology-P is currently encrypted. For now, decrypt the database back to its original state.

7. Double-click **Technology-P** in the Decrypt Database As dialog box, then click **Yes** when prompted to replace the existing file

FIGURE P-8: Encrypt/Decrypt Database dialog box

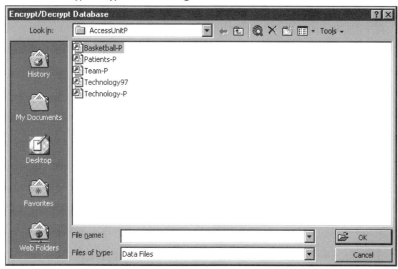

FIGURE P-9: Encrypt Database As dialog box

TABLE P-2: Database threats

incident	what can happen	appropriate action
Virus	Viruses can cause a vast number of damaging actions, ranging from profane messages to destruction of files.	Purchase the leading virus-checking software for each machine, and regularly update it.
Power outage	Power problems such as **brown-outs** (dips in power often causing lights to dim) and **spikes** (surges in power) can cause damage to the hardware, which may render the computer useless.	Purchase a **UPS** (Uninterruptible Power Supply) to maintain constant power to the file server (if networked); purchase a **surge protector** (power strip with surge protection) for each end user.
Theft or intentional damage	Computer thieves or other scoundrels steal or vandalize computer equipment.	Place the file server in a room that can be locked after hours; use network drives for end user data files that are backed up on a daily basis; use off-site storage for backups; set database passwords and encryption so that files that are stolen cannot be used; use computer locks for equipment that is at risk, especially laptops.

Analyzing Performance

Access provides a powerful tool called the **Performance Analyzer** that studies the structure and size of your database and makes a variety of recommendations on how you could improve its performance. Usually, the decision whether to fix a database that runs too slowly boils down to two choices: time and money. With adequate time and knowledge of Access, you can alleviate many performance bottlenecks by using software tools and additional programming techniques. With extra money, however, you can purchase faster processors and more memory to accomplish the same thing. See Table P-3 for more tips on optimizing the performance of your computer. Scenario▶ Kristen uses the Performance Analyzer to see whether Access has any easy recommendations on how to maintain peak performance of the Technology-P database.

1. Open the **Technology-P database** on your Project Disk, then close the **Employees form** that automatically opens

2. Click **Tools** on the menu bar, point to **Analyze**, then click **Performance**
The Performance Analyzer dialog box opens, as shown in Figure P-10. You can choose to analyze selected objects or the entire database.

3. Click the **All Object Types tab**, click **Select All**, then click **OK**
The Performance Analyzer examines each object and presents the results in a dialog box as shown in Figure P-11. The key shows that the analyzer gives four levels of advice regarding performance: recommendations, suggestions, ideas, and items that were fixed.

4. Click the **Table 'Assignments': Change data type of field 'SSN' from 'Text' to 'Long Integer'** in the Analysis Results list
The icon tells you that this is an idea. The Analysis Notes section of the Performance Analyzer dialog box gives you additional information regarding that specific item. In this case, the idea is to change the data type of the field SSN from Text to Number (with a Long Integer field size). While this might not be an appropriate action for an SSN field, the three fields in the PCSpecs table—Memory, HardDisk, and MHz—all represent numeric values that could be changed from Text to Number with the suggested field size. All of the Performance Analyzer's ideas should be considered, but they are not as important as recommendations and suggestions.

5. Click **Close** to close the Performance Analyzer dialog box

FIGURE P-10: Performance Analyzer dialog box

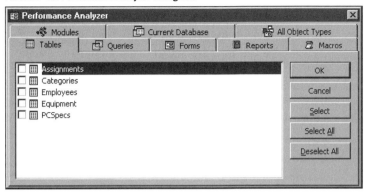

FIGURE P-11: Performance Analyzer results

Selected idea

Explains icons

Additional explanation for the selected item

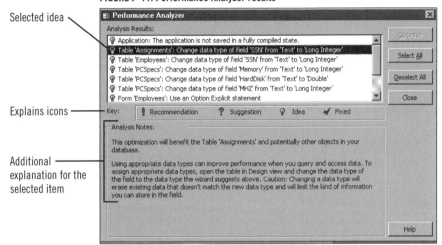

TABLE P-3: Tips for optimizing performance

degree of difficulty	tip
Easy	Close all applications that you don't currently need to free up memory and other computer resources.
Easy	Eliminate memory-resident programs such as complex screen savers, e-mail alert programs, and virus checkers if they can be run safely on an "as-needed" basis.
Easy	If you are the only person using a database, open it in exclusive mode.
Easy	Use the Compact on Close feature to regularly compact and repair your database.
Moderate	Add more memory to your computer; once the database is open, memory is the single most important determinant of overall performance.
Moderate	If others don't need to share the database, load it on your local hard drive instead of the network's file server (but be sure to back up local drives regularly, too).
Moderate	**Split** the database so that the data is stored on the file server, but other database objects are stored on your local, faster hard drive.
moderate to difficult	If using disk compression software, stop doing so or move the database to an uncompressed drive.
moderate to difficult	Run Performance Analyzer on a regular basis, examining and appropriately acting on each recommendation, suggestion, and idea.
moderate to difficult	Make sure that all PCs are running the latest versions of Windows and Access; this may involve purchasing more software or upgrading hardware to properly support these robust software products.

Access 2000

Splitting a Database

A successful database grows in many new ways and creates the need for higher levels of database connectivity. **Local area networks** (**LANs**) are installed to link multiple PCs together so they can share hardware and software resources. Once a LAN is installed, a shared database will often be moved to a **file server**, a centrally located computer in which every user can access the database through the network. The more users that share the same database, however, the slower it will respond. The **Database Splitter** feature improves the performance of a database shared among several users by allowing you to split the database into two files: the **back-end database**, which contains the actual table objects, and the **front-end database**, which contains the other database objects as well as links to the back-end database tables. The back-end database is stored on the file server. The front-end database is stored on user PCs. **Scenario** Kristen uses the Database Splitter to split the Technology-P database into two databases in preparation for the new LAN being installed in the Information Systems Department.

QuickTip

It's always a good idea to back up a database on another disk before splitting it.

1. Click **Tools** on the menu, point to **Database Utilities**, then click **Database Splitter**
   The Database Splitter dialog box opens, and provides additional information on the process and benefits of splitting a database, as shown in Figure P-12.

Trouble?

Verify that the file's path is to your Project Disk.

2. Click **Split Database**
   The Create Back-end Database dialog box opens, prompting you for a name of the back-end database, the one that will hold the table objects. The suggested name Technology-P_be.mdb is acceptable.

3. Click **Split**
   As the Database Splitter is working on your database, the status bar indicates that tables are being exported. The Database Splitter dialog box prompts you that the database is successfully split.

4. Click **OK**
   The Technology-P database has become the front-end database, with all database objects intact except for the table objects. Technology-P no longer contains any table objects, but rather links to the Technology-P_be database that stores the actual data. See Figure P-13.

5. Click **File** on the menu bar, then click **Exit**
   You closed the Technology-P database and exited Access. In a LAN environment, splitting a database then storing the back-end on the file server and the front-end on the **client** (the user's PC) dramatically improves performance when compared to using a database that is completely stored on the file server. On a split database, the only traffic that travels through the network is the actual data. All of the other objects that users need are stored on their local hard drives. (As many copies of the front-end database can be made as are needed so that each user has a copy of the front-end database on his or her own machine.) Storing the actual tables in the back-end database on the file server maintains data integrity because all users update the same database file.

FIGURE P-12: Database Splitter dialog box

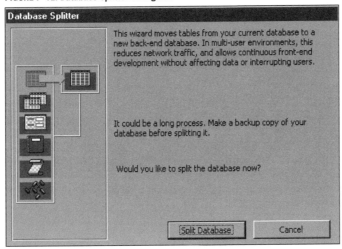

FIGURE P-13: Tables are linked in the front-end database

Front-end database

Link icon

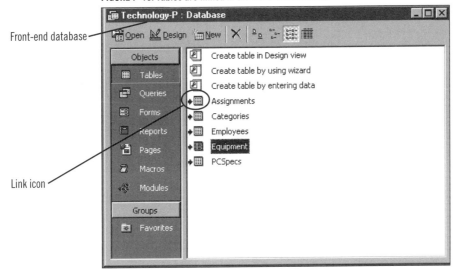

Defining client/server computing

Splitting a database into a front-end and back-end database that work together is an excellent example of client/server computing. **Client/server computing** can be defined as two or more information systems cooperatively processing to solve a problem. In most implementations, the **client** is defined as the user's PC and the server is defined as the shared file server, mini-, or mainframe computer. The **server** usually handles corporate-wide computing activities such as data storage and management, security, and connectivity to other networks. Within Access, client computers generally handle those tasks specific to each user such as storing all of the objects (other than table objects) used by that particular user. Effectively managing a vast client/server network in which many front-end databases link to a single back-end database is a tremendous task, but the performance and security benefits are worth the effort.

Access 2000

Replicating Using the Briefcase

If you want to copy a database to another computer, such as a home or laptop computer that you use on the road, the Windows Briefcase feature can help you. The **Briefcase** makes a special copy of the original database (called a **replica**) and keeps track of changes made in either the original database (called the **master**) or the replica so that they can be resynchronized at a later date. The master database and all replica database files created from the master are called the **replica set**. The process of making the copy is called **replication**, and the process of reconciling and updating changes between the replica and the master is called **synchronization**. Scenario Kristen is heading to a conference and wants to take the Technology-P_be database with her so that she can enter and update information in the Employee table. She uses the Briefcase program to keep the original database and the copy she will put on her laptop synchronized.

QuickTip

It's always a good idea to back up a database on another disk before replicating it.

1. Right-click the **Start button**, click **Explore**, locate your Project Disk in the Folders list, click **Technology-P_be** in the list of files, click the **Copy button** 📋 on the Standard Buttons toolbar, then close Explorer
   You placed the Technology-P_be.mdb file on the Windows Clipboard.

2. Minimize all open windows, right-click the **Desktop**, then click **Paste**
   You copy the master database to the desktop because you can't create a replica set with a master and replica both stored on floppy disks.

Trouble?

To install Briefcase: open Control Panel, double-click Add/Remove Programs, click Windows Setup tab, double-click Accessories, click Briefcase check box, click OK.

3. Right-click the **Technology-P_be** file on the desktop, click **Copy**, double-click **My Briefcase** 💼, click **Edit** on the menu bar, click **Paste**, click **Yes** to continue, click **No** to not backup your database, click **OK** to accept the Original copy as the database that will allow design changes, click **View** on the menu bar, then click **Details**
   Your screen should look like Figure P-14.

Trouble?

The My Briefcase window may look different due to the Windows 98 settings on your computer.

4. Close the My Briefcase window, remove any existing disks from **drive A**, insert a blank formatted disk into **drive A**, right-click 💼 on the Desktop, point to **Send To**, then click **3½ Floppy (A)**
   For this lesson, you will update the replica on the floppy disk using your existing machine.

Trouble?

If the My Briefcase wizard is open on the desk top, click Finish to continue.

5. Double-click the **My Computer icon** 🖥️, double-click **3½ Floppy (A)** 💾, double-click 💼 in the 3½ Floppy (A:) window, double-click **Technology-P_be** in the My Briefcase window, then double-click the **Employees table**
   The Replicated Employees table opens. You can add a new record to the table.

6. Click the **New Record button** ▶*, then add yourself as a new record using the following information:

last	first	Department	title	location	e-mail	DateHired	SSN
Your Last Name	Your First Name	Information Systems	CIO	Corporate	yourname@ medialoft.com	1/1/00	444-33-2222

7. Close the Employees table datasheet
   Your screen should look like Figure P-15. Both the title bar of the database and the table icons indicate that you are working with a replica. The replica contains the record you just added, but the master does not.

8. Click **File** on the menu bar, then click **Exit**

FIGURE P-14: My Briefcase

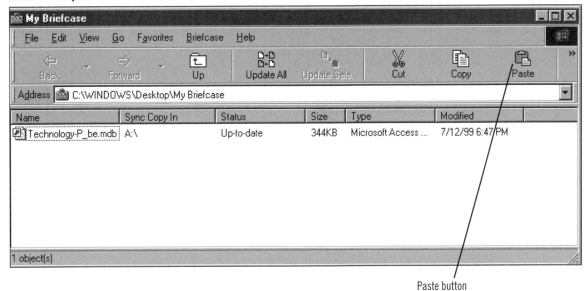

Paste button

FIGURE P-15: Replica database

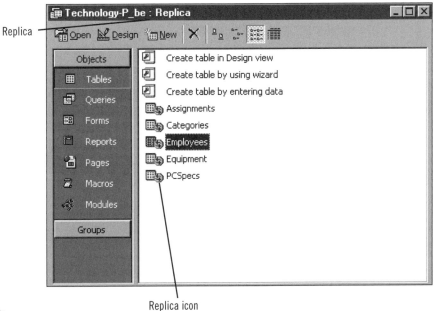

Replica

Replica icon

Creating a Briefcase folder

By default, the desktop displays a single Briefcase icon called "My Briefcase." Briefcase icons are actually a special type of folder designed to help users with two computers keep the files that are used on both computers updated. If you open the My Briefcase folder and find other files in it, or if there is no Briefcase on the desktop, you can easily create as many new Briefcase folders as you need. You create, delete, copy, and move a Briefcase folder in exactly the same manner as with a regular folder in Windows Explorer. For example, if you want to create a new Briefcase folder on the Desktop, you can right-click the Desktop, point to New, then click Briefcase.

Access 2000

Synchronizing Using the Briefcase

Access 2000

The Briefcase controls synchronization of the master and replica databases. If the Briefcase folder that contains the replica is stored on a floppy disk (which has been used in a secondary computer), the floppy disk would have to be inserted into the computer on which the master is stored before synchronization could occur. Synchronization updates all records and objects in each member of the replica set. The Briefcase reports on any synchronization discrepancies that it cannot resolve. **Scenario** Now that Kristen has created a replica of the Technology-P_be database and added a record to it, she is anxious to synchronize it with the master to see how the Briefcase keeps the replica set up-to-date.

Steps

Trouble?

If the A:/My Briefcase window is not open on the desktop, double-click the My Computer icon, double-click 3½ Floppy (A:) , then double-click My Briefcase in the 3½ Floppy (A:) window

1. **Click the Update All button** 🔀 **on the My Briefcase Standard Buttons toolbar**

   Your screen should look like Figure P-16. The Briefcase program read both database files and determined that the replica had been updated but the master had not. Therefore, it recommended the replace action. If there had been many files in the Briefcase, each one would be listed with a suggested action (replace, skip, merge).

2. **Click Update**

   The Briefcase replaces the master file on your desktop with the replica file on your floppy and displays the My Briefcase window with an "Up-to-date" Status message for the Technology-P_be.mdb file, as shown in Figure P-17. Had you made changes to both the master and the replica, the Briefcase window would have recommended a more complex action (merge), as shown in Figure P-18. The **merge** action evaluates the changes in each object and applies them to the other. For example, the merge action will resynchronize the two databases if you edit or add records in both the master and replica. You also can add new objects to both. You can make design changes only to existing objects, however, in the master database.

3. **Close the My Briefcase window**

4. **Close the 3½ Floppy (A:) window, then close the My Computer window**

Trouble?

If you created a new Briefcase folder for this unit, delete it.

5. **Delete the Technology-P_be Design Master from the desktop**

Using the Briefcase with a laptop computer

A common scenario in which Briefcase folders have tremendous value is when a master database is stored on a file server and the replica is stored on the hard drive of a laptop computer. When you are in the office, your laptop computer is connected to the network through a docking station so you can use the master database just like all of the other users. When you are in the field, however, your laptop computer is disconnected from the corporate database and you work on the replica stored in a Briefcase folder on the laptop's hard drive. When you return to the office, you use the Briefcase update features to resynchronize the two copies.

FIGURE P-16: Update My Briefcase window—Replace action

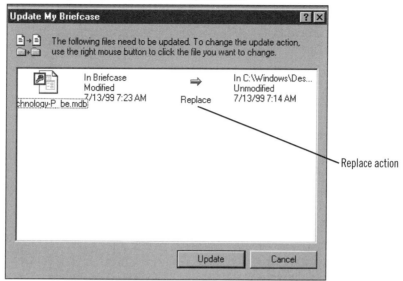

Replace action

FIGURE P-17: My Briefcase window showing an up-to-date file

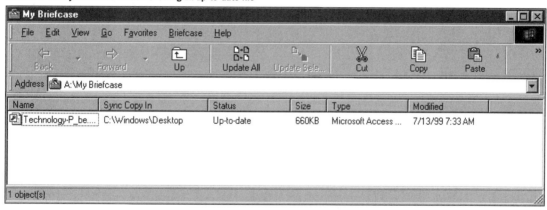

FIGURE P-18: Update My Briefcase window—Merge action

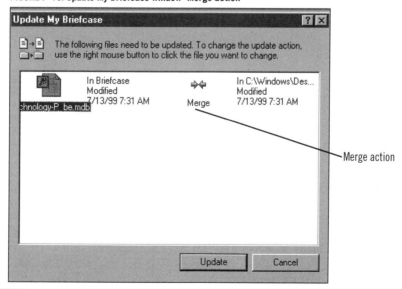

Merge action

Practice

► Concepts Review

Identify each element of the Explorer window shown in Figure P-19.

FIGURE P-19

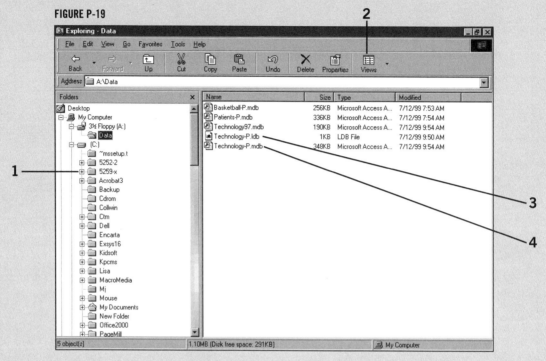

Match each term with the statement that describes its function.

5. **Exclusive mode**
6. **Database Splitter**
7. **Encrypting**
8. **Performance Analyzer**
9. **Synchronization**

a. Scrambles a database so that it is indecipherable when opened by another program.

b. Breaks the database into two files to improve performance. One database contains the table objects and the other contains the rest of the objects with links to the table objects.

c. Updates the files in a replica set so that they all have the same information.

d. Studies the structure and size of your database and makes a variety of recommendations on how you can improve its speed.

e. Means that no other users will have access to the database file while it's open.

Select the best answer from the list of choices.

10. Changing a database file into one that can be opened in another version of Access is called
- **a.** Encrypting.
- **b.** Analyzing.
- **c.** Converting.
- **d.** Splitting.

11. Which is NOT a type of password that can be set on an Access database?
- **a.** Visual Basic for Applications
- **b.** Security account
- **c.** Object
- **d.** Database

12. Which of the following determines the users, objects, and permissions to which the users are granted?
- **a.** Briefcase names
- **b.** Workgroups
- **c.** Permission logs
- **d.** Passwords

13. Which character precedes a command-line option?
- **a.** ^
- **b.** @
- **c.** /
- **d.** !

14. Which of the following is NOT an advantage of splitting the database using the Database Splitter?
- **a.** It creates replica sets that can be used to synchronize files on laptops.
- **b.** It gives the users local control over form and report objects.
- **c.** It helps increase the overall performance of a LAN.
- **d.** It keeps the data centralized in the back-end database for all users to access.

15. Startup command line options are:
- **a.** Special objects that execute first when the database is opened.
- **b.** Entered in the Startup dialog box.
- **c.** Used to automate the synchronization of a replica set.
- **d.** A special series of characters added to the end of the path to the file that start with a forward slash.

16. Client/server computing can be defined as:
- **a.** A way to study the structure and size of your database to make a variety of recommendations on how you could improve its performance.
- **b.** A process to resynchronize a replica set.
- **c.** A LAN, WAN, or the Internet.
- **d.** Two or more information systems cooperatively processing to solve a problem.

17. If you want to copy a database to another computer, such as a home or laptop computer you'll use on the road, which of the following features would keep the databases up-to-date?
- **a.** Briefcase
- **b.** Performance Analyzer
- **c.** Startup Options
- **d.** Database Splitter

▶ Skills Review

1. Converting databases.
   a. Start Access and open the Basketball-P database.
   b. Click Tools on the menu bar, point to Database Utilities, point to Convert Database, then click To Prior Access Version.
   c. Navigate to your Project Disk in the Convert Database Into dialog box, type "Basketball97" as the file name, then click Save.
   d. Open Windows Explorer, open your Project Disk, and check to make sure that both the Basketball-P and Basketball97 databases are stored on the Project Disk. You also will see a Basketball-P.ldb file, because Basketball-P.mdb is currently open.
   e. Close Explorer.

2. Setting Passwords.
   a. Close Basketball-P, but leave Access open.
   b. Click the Open button on the Database toolbar, navigate to your Project Disk, then click Basketball-P.
   c. Click the Open list arrow, then click Open Exclusive.
   d. Click Tools on the menu bar, point to Security, then click Set Database Password.
   e. Check to make sure the Caps Lock light is not on, type the word "colonial" in the Password text box, tab, type "colonial" in the Verify text box, then click OK. (Remember that passwords are case sensitive.)
   f. Close the Basketball-P database, but leave Access open.
   g. Open the Basketball-P database, type "colonial" in the Password Required dialog box, then click OK.
   h. Close the database, then open the Basketball-P database in Exclusive mode.
   i. Click Tools on the menu bar, point to Security, click Unset Database Password, type "colonial", then click OK.

3. Changing Startup Options.
   a. Click Tools on the menu bar, then click Startup to open the Startup dialog box.
   b. Type "SUNY Binghamton Women" in the Application Title text box, click the Display Form/Page list arrow, click the Player Entry Form, clear the Allow Toolbar/Menu Changes check box, then click OK. Notice the change in the title bar.
   c. Close the Basketball-P database, but leave Access open.
   d. Open the Basketball-P database.
   e. Close the Player Entry Form that automatically opened when the database was opened.
   f. Check the Access title bar to make sure it displays "SUNY Binghamton Women."
   g. Right-click the Database toolbar to make sure that you are unable to change or modify any of the toolbars.
   h. On a piece of paper, identify one reason for changing each of the three startup options modified in steps b, c, and d.
   i. Close the Basketball-P database, but leave Access open.

4. Encrypting and Decrypting a Database.
   a. To encrypt the database, click Tools on the menu bar, point to Security, then click Encrypt/Decrypt Database.
   b. Navigate to your Project Disk, click Basketball-P, then click OK.
   c. In the Encrypt Database As dialog box, click Basketball-P, then click Save.
   d. Click Yes when asked to replace the existing Basketball-P file.
   e. To decrypt the database, click Tools on the menu bar, point to Security, then click Encrypt/Decrypt Database.
   f. In the Decrypt Database dialog box, click Basketball-P, then click OK.

g. In the Decrypt Database As dialog box, click Basketball-P, click Save, then click Yes.

h. On a piece of paper, identify two database threats for which encryption could be used to protect the database.

5. Analyzing Performance.

a. Open Basketball-P, then close the Player Entry Form.

b. Click Tools on the menu bar, point to Analyze, then click Performance.

c. Click the All Object Types tab, click Select All, then click OK.

d. Click each of the Analysis Results and read the Analysis notes.

e. On a piece of paper, record the analysis results (there should be three entries), and identify whether they are recommendations, suggestions, ideas, or items that were fixed.

f. Close the Performance Analyzer dialog box.

6. Splitting a Database.

a. Click Tools on the menu, point to Database Utilities, then click Database Splitter.

b. Click Split Database, make sure that the Save in: list points to your Project Disk, then click Split to accept the default name of Basketball-P_be as the file name.

c. Click OK when prompted that the database was successfully split.

d. On a sheet of paper, identify two reasons for splitting a database.

e. On the paper, identify the back-end and front-end database file names, and explain what these databases contain.

f. On the paper, explain what the table icons in the front-end database look like and what they represent.

g. Close the Basketball-P database.

7. Replicating Using the Briefcase.

a. Copy the Team-P database from your Project Disk, then paste it to the Desktop of your computer.

b. Copy the Team-P database from your Desktop, then paste it to an empty Briefcase folder. Click Yes when asked to continue, click No when asked to make a back-up copy, then click OK to choose the Original File.

c. Double-click the Team-P database in the New Briefcase window, double-click the Players table, then modify the record for PlayerNo 21 with your own First and Last names, HomeTown, and HomeState. (*Hint*: If no empty Briefcase window exists on your Desktop, create one by right-clicking the Desktop, pointing to New, then clicking Briefcase.)

d. Close the Players table, then close the Team-P Replica database and exit Access. Close the Briefcase window.

e. Open the Team-P Design Master database from your Desktop, then open the Players table. PlayerNo 21 will not be modified.

f. Change PlayerNo 22 so that a friend's First and Last names, HomeTown, and HomeState are entered.

g. Close the Players table, then close the Team-P Design Master database and Access window.

8. Synchronizing Using the Briefcase.

a. Open the Briefcase on the Desktop where the replicated Team-P database exists, click the Update All button, then click the Update button to merge the databases.

b. Double-click the Team-P entry in the Briefcase window to open the replica database, double-click the Players table, then print the Players datasheet. Both PlayerNo 21 and 22 should show the changes you made.

c. Close the Players datasheet, close the Team-P Replica, and close the Briefcase window.

d. Delete any files you created in the desktop.

▶ Visual Workshop

As the manager of a doctor's clinic, you have created an Access database called Patients-P to track insurance claims. Use the Performance Analyzer to generate the results shown in Figure P-20 by analyzing all object types.

FIGURE P-20

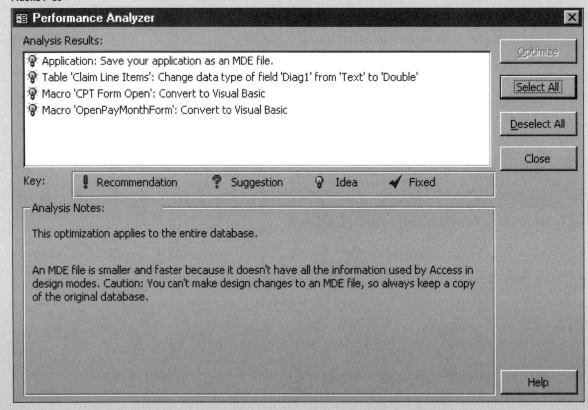

Glossary

.ldb The file extension for a temporary file that exists when an Access database is open that keeps track of record locking information when the database is opened.

.mdb The file extension for Access databases.

Action A task that you want a macro to perform. Each macro action occupies a single row in the macro window.

Action query A query that makes changes to underlying data. There are four types of action queries: delete, update, append, and make-table.

Add-In An extra Access feature that extends the functionality of Access but is not part of the core program. Some add-ins are available through Microsoft and some by third parties. They are "added in" when the user chooses to install them.

Aggregate functions Special functions used in a summary query that calculate information about a group of records rather than a new field of information about each record.

Ampersand (&) The character used to concatenate items in an expression.

Analyze It with MS Excel An Access feature that quickly copies Access data to a blank Excel workbook.

And criteria Criteria placed in the same row of the query design grid. All criteria on the same row must be true in order for a record to appear on the resulting datasheet.

AND query A query which contains AND criteria (two or more criteria present on the same row of the query design grid. Both criteria must be true for the record to appear on the resulting datasheet).

Append query An action query that appends records to another table.

Argument For a macro, arguments are additional information for each action of a macro that further clarifies how the action is to execute. For a module, arguments are constants, variables, or expressions that are passed to a procedure and are required for it to execute.

Arguments The pieces of information a function needs to create the final answer. In an expression, multiple arguments are separated by commas. All of the arguments are surrounded by a single set of parentheses.

Arithmetic operators Plus (+), minus (-), multiply (*), divide (/), and exponentiation (^) characters used in a mathematical calculation.

Ascending order A sequence in which information is placed in alphabetical order or from smallest to largest. For a text field, numbers sort first, then letters.

Text ascending order: 123, 3H, 455, 98, 98B, animal, Iowa, New Jersey
Date ascending order: 1/1/57, 1/1/61, 12/25/61, 5/5/98, 8/20/98, 8/20/99
Number ascending order: 1, 10, 15, 120, 140, 500, 1200, 1500

AutoFormats Predefined formats provided by Access that contain background pictures and font, color, and alignment choices that can quickly be applied to an existing form or report.

AutoKeys A special name reserved for the macro group object that contains key combinations (such as Ctrl+L) that are used to run associated macros.

AutoNumber A data type in which Access enters a sequential integer for each record added into the datasheet. Numbers cannot be reused even if the record is deleted.

Back-end database When a database has been split using the Database Splitter, a back-end database is created which contains all of the data and is stored on a computer that is accessible by all users (which is usually the file server in a LAN).

Bang notation Syntax used to separate parts of an object (the parts are separated by an exclamation point, hence "bang") in the Visual Basic programming language.

Between . . . And operator Used when specifying limiting criteria between two values in a query; it is equivalent to >= (greater than or equal to) and <= (less than or equal to).

Body The basic design surface of the data access page that displays text, controls, and sections.

Bookmark A specific location within a Word document marked by an invisible code. Hyperlinks within Access can be created to open a Word document and display the text at a particular bookmark.

Bound control A control used in either a form or report to display data from the underlying record source; also used to edit and enter new data in a form.

Bound image control A bound control used to show OLE data such as a picture on a form or report.

Break mode Temporary suspension of program execution in which you can examine, debug, reset, step-through, or continue program execution.

Breakpoint A bookmark set in VBA code that temporarily suspends execution of the procedure at that point in time so that the user can examine what is happening.

Briefcase A Windows program used to help synchronize two computers that regularly use the same files.

Brown-out Dip in the level of electrical current causing the lights to dim or "brown-out."

Browser Software loaded on a microcomputer such as Microsoft's Internet Explorer (IE) or Netscape Navigator used to find and display Web pages.

Calculated control A control that uses information from existing controls to calculate new data such as subtotals, dates, or page numbers; used in either a form or report.

Calculated field A field created in Query Design view that results from an expression of existing fields, Access functions, and arithmetic operators. For example the entry Profit: [RetailPrice]-[WholesalePrice] in the field cell of the query design grid creates a calculated field called Profit that is the difference between the RetailPrice and WholesalePrice fields.

Caption property A field property used to override the technical field name with an easy-to-read caption entry when the field name appears on datasheets, forms, and reports.

Caption section A section available in the Design view of a page object used to display text.

Cascade Delete Related Records An option available when enforce referential integrity is applied that automatically deletes all records in the "many" table if the record with the matching key field in the "one" table is deleted.

Cascade Update Related Fields An option available when enforce referential integrity is applied that automatically updates the data in the foreign key field if the matching key field is changed.

Chart Graph: Visual representation of numeric data that helps a user see comparisons, patterns, and trends in data.

Chart placeholder A picture of a chart that represents the chart control within Report Design view. You must double-click the chart placeholder to edit the chart.

Chart Wizard Access Wizard that steps you through the process of creating charts within forms and reports.

Check box Bound control used to display "yes" or "no" answers for a field. If the box is "checked" it indicates "yes" information in a form or report.

Class modules Modules used only within a particular form or report object and therefore stored within the form or report object.

Client In client-server computer architectures, the client computer is generally the user's computer.

Client/server computing Two or more information systems cooperatively processing to solve a problem. In Access, a back-end and front-end database participate in client/server computing, each assigned to the tasks to which it is best suited.

Clipboard The temporary location that can store up to 12 items that are copied. When you paste, you paste information that is stored on the Clipboard.

Clipboard toolbar A toolbar that shows the contents of the Office Clipboard; contains buttons for copying and pasting items to and from the Office Clipboard.

Code window See *Visual Basic Code window*.

Collapse button A "minus sign" to the left of a record displayed in a datasheet that when clicked on, collapses the subdatasheet that is displayed. When you click a Collapse button on a page, less detail about the item being collapsed will appear.

Combo box A bound control used to display a list of possible entries for a field in which you can also type an entry from the keyboard. It is a "combination" of the list box and text box controls.

Command button An unbound control used to provide an easy way to initiate an action or run a macro.

Command Button Wizard A Wizard that steps you through the process of creating a command button.

Command-line option A special series of characters added to the end of the path to the database file that start with a forward slash and modify the way that the database is opened.

Comment line A VBA statement that does not execute any actions but is used to clarify or document other statements. Comment lines appear in green in the Code window and start with a single apostrophe.

Compacting Rearranging the data and objects on the storage medium so that space formerly occupied by deleted objects is eliminated. Compacting a database doesn't change the data, but it generally reduces the overall size of the database.

Compile time The period during which source code is translated to executable code.

Compile time error A VBA error that occurs because of incorrectly constructed VBA code.

Conditional expression An expression that results in either a "true" or "false" answer that determines whether a macro action will execute or not.

Conditional formatting Formatting applied to a control on a form or report that changes depending upon a value in a field, an expression, or on which field has the focus. For example, a text box may be conditionally formatted to display its value in red if the value is a negative number.

Constant In VBA, a constant is an item that retains a constant value throughout the execution of the code.

Control Any element on a form or report such as a label, text box, line, or combo box. Controls can be bound, unbound, or calculated.

Control Source property The most important property of a bound control on a form or report because it etermines which field the bound control will display.

ControlTip Text property Property of a control that determines what text displays in tip that pops up when you point to that control with the mouse.

Converting Changing a database file into one that can be opened by an earlier version of Access.

Criteria The entry that determines which records are displayed when finding or filtering records in a datasheet or form, or when building a query.

Crosstab query A query that presents data in a cross-tabular layout (fields are used for both column and row headings), similar to pivot tables in other database and spreadsheet products.

Crosstab Query Wizard A wizard used to create crosstab queries that helps identify which fields will be used for row and column headings, and which fields will be summarized within the datasheet.

Currency A data type used for monetary values.

Current record symbol A black triangle symbol that appears in the record select box to the left of the record that has the focus in either a datasheet or a form.

Data The unique entries of information that you enter into the fields of the records.

Data Access Page See *Page*.

Data type A required property for each field that defines the type of data that can be entered in each field. Valid data types include AutoNumber, Text, Number, Currency, Date/Time, OLE Object, Memo, Yes/No, and Hyperlink.

Database A collection of data associated with a topic (for example, sales of products to customers).

Database password A password that is required to open a database.

Database software Software used to manage data that can be organized into lists of things such as customers, products, vendors, employees, projects, or sales.

Database Splitter An Access feature that improves the performance of a shared database by allowing you to split it into multiple files.

Database window The window that includes common elements such as the Access title bar, menu bar, and toolbar. It also contains an Objects bar to quickly work with the seven different types of objects within the database by clicking the appropriate object button.

Database Wizard A powerful Access wizard that creates a sample database file for a general purpose such as inventory control, event tracking, or expenses. The objects created by the Database Wizard can be used and modified.

Datasheet A spreadsheet-like grid that shows fields as columns and records as rows.

Datasheet view A view that lists the records of the object in a datasheet. Table, query, and most form objects have a Datasheet view.

Date/Time A data type used for date and time fields.

Debug To determine why a macro doesn't run properly.

Declaration statements VBA statements that precede procedure statements and help set rules for how the statements in the module are processed.

Decrypt To reverse the encryption process.

Delete query An action query that deletes records based on an expression.

Delimited text file A file that contains one record on each line with the fields separated by a common character such as a comma, tab, or dash.

Descending order A sequence in which information is placed in reverse alphabetical order or from largest to smallest. For a text field, letters sort first, then numbers.

Text descending order: Zebra, Victory, Langguth, Bunin, 99A, 9854, 77, 740, 29, 270, 23500, 1

Date descending order: 1/1/99, 1/1/98, 12/25/97, 5/5/97, 8/20/61, 8/20/57

Number descending order: 1500, 1400, 1200, 140, 120, 15, 10, 1

Design view A view in which the structure of the object can be manipulated. Every Access object has a Design view.

Detail section The section of the form or report that contains the controls that are printed for each record in the underlying query or table.

Dialer Software that helps you dial-up to connect you to your ISP.

Dialog box A special form that is used to display information or to prompt a user for a choice.

Documenter An Access feature that creates reports on the properties and relationships between the objects in your database.

Domain Name The middle part of a URL such as www.course.com where "course" is the domain name.

Dot notation Syntax used to separate parts of an object (the parts are separated by a period, hence "dot") in the Visual Basic programming language.

Drag and drop A process which involves dragging an Access icon from the database window to another application window (the target window) in order to quickly copy and paste information. The target window is usually a Word document or Excel workbook window.

Dynamic HTML file An HTML file (Web page) that is tied to an underlying database and therefore displays current information and data.

Dynaset A type of recordset displayed within a query's datasheet that allows you to update all fields except for those on the "one" side of a one-to-many relationship.

Dynaset (inconsistent updates) A type of recordset displayed within a query's datasheet that allows you to update all fields.

E-mail Electronic mail sent and received without printed paper by using computers.

Edit mode The mode in which Access assumes you are trying to edit that particular field, so keystrokes such as [Ctrl][End], [Ctrl][Home], [←]and [→] move the insertion point within the field.

Edit record symbol A pencil-like symbol that appears in the record selector box to the left of the record that is currently being edited in either a datasheet or a form.

Embedded Refers to the relationship between a chart created within Access and the database itself. Although the chart is created through the MS Chart program, it is embedded and stored within the Access database. Sometimes embedded is compared to linked data. Linked data is physically stored outside the Access database file. Embedded data is stored within the file.

Encrypt To make the database objects and data within the database indecipherable to other programs.

Enforce referential integrity An option applied to a one-to-many relationship between two tables that does not allow a value to be entered into the foreign key field that is not first entered into the primary key field. It also does not allow records to be deleted in the "one" table if related records exist in the "many" table.

Event Something that happens within a database (such as the click of a command button or the entry of a field) that can be used to initiate the execution of a macro. Events are associated with toolbars, objects, and controls, and can be viewed by examining that item's property sheet.

Excel The spreadsheet software application within the Microsoft Office Suite.

Exclusive mode If you open an Access database in exclusive mode, others cannot open the file. You must open a database in exclusive mode before you can set a database password.

Expand button A "plus sign" to the left of a record that is displayed in datasheet view that when clicked, will show related records in a sub-datasheet. When you click an Expand button, more detail about the item being expanded will appear.

Explorer A Windows program used to manage files, folders, and disk drives.

Exporting A process that copies data from Access into a different Access database or file format.

Expression A combination of values, functions, and operators that calculates to a single value. Access expressions start with an equal sign and are placed in a text box in either Form or Report Design view.

Field The smallest piece or category of information in a database such as the customer's name, city, state, or phone number.

Field list A list of the available fields in the table or query that it represents.

Field names The names given each field in Table Design or Table Datasheet view. Field names can be up to 64 characters long.

Field Property See *Properties*.

File server A centrally-located computer to which every user has access on the network. The function of the file server is to store and serve application and data files to the individual client computers on the LAN.

File transfer Uploading and downloading of files through computing networks.

Filter A temporary view of a subset of records. A filter can be saved as a query object if you wish to apply the same filter later without recreating it.

Filter window A window that appears when you click the Filter by Form button when viewing data in a datasheet or in a form window. The Filter window allows you to define the filter criteria.

Find Duplicates Query Wizard A wizard used to create a query that determines whether a table contains duplicate values in one or more fields.

Find Unmatched Query Wizard A wizard used to create a query that finds records in one table that doesn't have related records in another table.

Focus The property that refers to which field would be edited if you started typing.

Footer Information that prints at the bottom of every printed page (or section when using forms and reports).

Foreign key field The field added to the "many" table involved in a one-to-many relationship.

Form An Access object that provides an easy-to-use data entry screen that generally shows only one record at a time.

Form Design toolbar The toolbar that appears when working in Form Design View with buttons that help you modify a form's controls.

Form Footer A section that appears at the bottom of screen in Form View for each record, but prints only once at the end of all records when the form is printed.

Form Header A section that appears at the top of the screen in Form View for each record, but prints only once at the top of all records when the form is printed.

Form View toolbar The toolbar that appears when working in Form View with buttons that help you print, edit, find, filter, and edit records.

Format Painter A tool used within Form and Report Design view to copy formatting characteristic from one control, and paint them on another.

Formatting Enhancing the appearance of the information in a form, report or datasheet.

Front-end database When a database has been split using the Database Splitter, a front-end database is created which contains links back to the data stored in the back-end database as well as any objects needed by the user. The front-end database is stored on the user's computer, which is also called the client computer.

Function Special, predefined formula such as Sum, Count, Date, Left, and Avg that are part of an expression and perform a specific calculation that returns a value. Access supplies many built-in functions. VBA allows you to create your own unique functions as well.

Functions A special, predefined formula that provides a shortcut for a commonly used calculation, for example, SUM

Graphic See *Image*.

Group Footer section The section of the report that contains controls that print once at the end of each group of records.

Group Header section The section of the report that contains controls that print once at the beginning of each group of records.

Grouping controls Specifying that several controls in the Design view of a form or report are in a "group" so that you can more productively format, move, and change them.

Grouping records In a report, grouping records means to sort them based on the contents of a field, plus provide a group header section that precedes the group of records as well as a group footer section that follows the group of records.

Groups bar Located just below the Objects bar in the database window, the Groups bar displays the Favorites and any user-created groups, which in turn contain shortcuts to objects. Groups are used to organize the database objects into logical sets.

GUI (Graphical User Interface) A characteristic of the design of the screens of a computer program. If GUI, the user interacts with the computer program using point-and-click, click-and-drag, and double-click techniques as well as graphical symbols such as icons, command buttons, and list arrows. Non-GUI screens use text-based menu options or command lines to prompt for user input.

Handles See *Sizing handles*.

Header Information that prints at the top of every printed page (or section when using forms and reports).

Help system Pages of documentation and examples that are available through the Help menu option, the Microsoft Access Help button on the Database toolbar, or the Office Assistant.

Home page The first page displayed on a Web server.

HTML (Hypertext Markup Language) A programming language used to create Web pages.

Hyperlink A data type that stores World Wide Web addresses.

If . . . Then . . . Else A series of VBA statements that allow you to test for a logical condition and execute one set of commands if the condition is true and another if the condition is false.

Image A nontextual piece of information such as a picture, piece of clip art, drawn object, or graph. Because images are graphical (not numbers or letters), they are sometimes referred to as graphical images.

Imported table A table created in another database product or application such as Excel, that is copied and pasted within the Access database through the import process.

Importing A process to quickly convert data from an external source, such as Excel or another database application, into an Access database

Index A field property used to speed up queries that are often sorted or grouped by that field.

Input mask A field property that controls both the values that the users can enter into a text box, as well as provides a visual guide for users as they enter data.

Input mask wizard A wizard that helps you determine the three parts of the input mask property.

Internet A worldwide network of computer networks that send and receive information through a common protocol called TCP/IP.

Intranet A WAN that is built with the same technologies as those used to support the Internet, yet is secured for the internal purposes of a business.

ISP (Internet Service Provider) A company that provides Internet access. To access the Internet from a home computer, your computer must first dial an ISP that in turn connects your computer with the Internet.

Junction table A table that links two other tables with a many-to-many relationship. The junction table holds two foreign key fields that create separate links to the original tables in separate one-to-many relationships.

Key field A field that contains unique information for each record. Also known as *Primary key field*. A key field cannot contain a null entry.

Key field combination Two or more fields that as a group, contain unique information for each record.

Key field symbol In a table's Design view, the symbol that appears as a miniature key in the field indicator box to the left of the field name. It identifies the field that contains unique information for each record.

Label An unbound control that displays static text on forms and reports.

LAN (Local Area Network) A computer network of local resources connected by a direct cable. LANs do not cross public thoroughfares such as streets or rivers.

Layout The general arrangement in which a form will display the fields in the underlying recordset. Layout types include Columnar, Tabular, Datasheet, Chart, and PivotTable. Columnar is most popular for a form, and Datasheet is most popular for a subform.

Leszynski Naming Convention A naming convention in which each object or field is preceded by a three-character tag to help identify it. For example, tables are named starting with the tag "tbl" as in "tblEmployees."

Line control An unbound control used to draw lines on a form or report that divide it into logical groupings.

Link Childs field A subform property that determines which field will serve as the "many" link between the subform and main form.

Link Masters fields A subform property that determines which field will serve as the "one" link between the main form and the subform.

Linked table A table created in another database product or application such as Excel, that is stored outside of the open database, but which can still be used within Access to modify and use its data.

Linking A way to connect data in an external source to an Access database in a way that does not copy or move the original data yet allows it to be manipulated within the Access database.

List box A bound control that displays a list of possible choices from which the user can choose. Used mainly on forms.

Logic error A VBA error that occurs because the code runs without problems, but the procedure still doesn't produce the desired results.

Lookup Wizard A wizard used in Table Design view that allows one field to "lookup" values from another table or query. For example, you might use the Lookup Wizard to specify that the CustomerNumber field in the Sales table display the CustomerName field entry from the Customers table.

Macro An Access object that stores a collection of keystrokes or commands such as printing several reports in a row or providing a toolbar when a form opens.

Macro group An Access macro object that contains more than one macro.

Macro window The Design View of a macro in which you specify which actions and the order in which they will run.

Main form A form that contains a subform control.

Main report A report that contains a subreport control is called the main report.

Make-table query An action query that creates a new table.

Many-to-many relationship The relationship between two tables in an Access database in which one field value in each table can have more than one matching record in the other. You cannot directly create a many-to-many relationship between two tables in an Access database. A junction table is used to connect two tables with this relationship.

Master The original Access database file that is copied to the Briefcase.

Memo A data type used for lengthy text such as comments or notes. It can hold up to 64,000 characters of information.

Merge An action that may occur during the synchronization of a replica and master database in which changes in each database are analyzed and applied to the other.

Merge It with MS Word An Access feature that begins the process of connecting Access data to a Word document for the purpose of creating merged letters, envelopes, or labels.

Method An action that an object can perform.

Microsoft Office Premium Edition The Microsoft software products of Word, Excel, Access, PowerPoint, and Outlook that are sold as an integrated set.

Modem Short for modulate-demodulate; hardware that converts digital computer signals to analog telephone signals to allow a computer to send and receive information across ordinary telephone lines.

Module An Access object that stores Visual Basic programming code that extends the functions and automated processes of Access.

MsgBox A macro action that displays an informational message.

Multimedia controls Non-textual controls such as those that display picture, sound, or motion information.

Multi-user The characteristic that allows multiple people to use the same file or resource at the same time.

My Computer A icon on the Windows desktop that gives the user access to the drives, folders, and files within the computer.

Name AutoCorrect An Access feature that fixes discrepancies between references to field names, controls, and objects when you rename them.

Navigation buttons Buttons in the lower-left corner of a datasheet or form that allow you to quickly navigate between the records in the underlying object as well as add a new record.

Navigation mode A mode in which Access assumes that you are trying to move between the fields and records of the datasheet (rather than edit a specific field's contents), so keystrokes such as [Ctrl][Home] and [Ctrl][End] move you to the first and last field of the datasheet, respectively.

Network administrator A person who builds or manages a networking infrastructure.

New Record button A button that, when clicked, presents a new record for data entry. It is found on both the Form View and Datasheet toolbars as well as part of the Navigation buttons.

Newsgroups Groups with a common interest that provide public mailboxes (accessible only by computers) in which members can send and read messages. Messages posted to a newsgroup are intended for anyone who cares to read the messages in that newsgroup.

Normalization The process of designing a relational database, which involves determining the appropriate fields, tables, and table relationships.

Null The term that refers to a state of "nothingness" in a field. Any entry such as 0 in a numeric field or an invisible space in a text field is *not* null. It is common to search for empty fields by using the criteria "Is Null" in a filter or query. "Is Not Null" criteria finds all records where there is an entry of any kind.

Number A data type used for numeric information used in calculations, such as quantities.

Object A table, query, form, report, page, macro, or module.

Object Browser A window that lists the defined modules and procedures as well as available methods, properties, events, constants, and other items that you can use in the code.

Objects bar In the opening database window, the toolbar that presents the seven Access objects. When you click an object button on the Objects bar, options and wizards to create an object of that type as well as existing objects of that type appear in the main portion of the database window.

ODBC (Open Database Connectivity) A protocol for accessing data in SQL database servers.

Office Assistant An animated character that appears to offer tips, answer questions, and provide access to the program's Help system.

Office Clipboard A temporary storage area shared by all Office programs that can be used to cut, copy and paste multiple items within and between Office programs. The Office Clipboard can hold up to 12 items collected from any Office program. See also *Clipboard* and *Clipboard toolbar*.

OfficeLinks buttons The set of three buttons on the Database toolbar that are used to quickly copy Access data to the Word or Excel programs.

OLE Object A data type that stores pointers that tie files created in other programs to a record such as pictures, sound clips, word-processing documents, or spreadsheets.

One-to-many line The line that appears in the Relationships window that shows which field is duplicated between two tables to serve as the linking field. The one-to-many line displays a "1" next to the field that serves as the "one" side of the relationship and an infinity symbol next to the field that serves as the "many" side of the relationship when referential integrity is specified for the relationship. Also called one-to-many join line.

One-to-many relationship The relationship between two tables in an Access database in which a common field links the tables together The field is a key field in the "one" table of the relationship, but can be listed "many" times in the "many" table of the relationship.

One-to-one relationship The relationship between two tables in an Access database in which a common field links the tables together. The same field value can be entered only one time in each of the tables. One-to-one relationships are rare, and tables linked in this way can be combined into one table.

Option Button A bound control used to display a limited list of mutually exclusive choices for a field such as "female" or "male" for a gender field in a form or report. Also called a radio button.

Option Group A bound control placed on a form that is used to group together several option buttons that provide a limited number of values for a field.

Or criteria Criteria placed on different rows of the query design grid. A record will appear in the resulting datasheet if it is true for any single row.

OR query A query that contains OR criteria (two or more criteria present on different rows in the query design grid. A record will appear on the resulting datasheet if it is true for either criteria.)

Orphan record A record in the "many" table of a one-to-many relationship between two tables that has no matching record in the "one" table. If referential integrity is enforced, it is not possible to create orphan records.

Page An Access object that creates Web pages from Access objects as well as provides Web page connectivity features to an Access database. Also called Data Access Page.

Page Design view The window in which you develop page objects by adding, moving, and manipulating controls.

Page Footer section The section of the form or report that contains controls that print once at the bottom of each page.

Page Header section The section of the form or report that contains controls that print once at the top of each page. On the first page of the report, the Page Header section prints below the Report Header section.

Parameter query A query that displays a dialog box prompting you for criteria each time you run it.

Parent/Child relationship The relationship between the main form and subform. The main form acts as the parent, displaying the information about the "one" side of a one-to-many relationship between the forms. The subform acts as the "child" displaying as many records as exist in the "many" side of the one-to-many relationship.

Password A combination of characters required to gain access to the user's computer or files. See also *Database password, Security account password,* and *VBA password.*

Performance Analyzer An Access feature that studies the size and structure of your database and makes a variety of recommendations on how you could improve its performance.

PivotTable list A bound control used with the page object that helps you reorganize data into summarized columns and rows similar to a crosstabular datasheet.

Pop-up form A special type of form that stays on top of other open forms, even when another form is active.

Positioning The relative space between the text, sections, and other elements on the body of a data access page.

Primary key field See *Key field.*

Primary sort field In a query grid, the left-most field that includes sort criteria. It determines the order in which the records will appear and can be specified "ascending" or "descending."

Print Preview A window that displays how the physical printout will appear if the current object is printed.

Procedure A series of VBA programming statements that perform an operation or calculate an answer. There are two types of procedures: functions and subs.

Properties Characteristics that further define the field (if field properties), control (if control properties), section (if section properties), or object (if object properties).

Property sheet A window that displays an exhaustive list of properties for the chosen control, section, or object within the form or report Design view.

Protocol A set of rules.

Publish It with MS Word An Access feature that quickly copies Access data to a blank Word document.

Publishing Sending (uploading) Web page files to a Web server.

Query An Access object which provides a spreadsheet-like view of the data similar to tables. It may provide the user with a subset of fields and/or records from one or more tables. Queries are created when the user has a "question" about the data in the database.

Query design grid The bottom pane of the Query Design view window in which you specify the fields, sort order, and limiting criteria for the query.

Query Design view The window in which you develop queries by specifying the fields, sort order, and limiting criteria that determine which fields and records are displayed in the resulting datasheet.

Raw data The individual pieces of information stored in the database in individual fields.

Record A group of related fields, such as all demographic information for one customer.

Record locking An Access feature that prevents two people from changing the same record at the same time.

Record Navigation section A section available in the Design view of a page object used to display the navigation toolbar.

Record selector box The small square to left of a record in a datasheet that marks the current record or edit record symbol when the record has focus or is being edited. Clicking the record selector box selects the entire record. In Form view, the record selector box expands to the entire height of the form because only one record is viewed at a time.

Record source In a form or report, either a table or query object that contains the fields and records that the form will display. It is the most important property of the form or report object. A bound control on a form or report also has a record source property. In this case, the record source property identifies the field to which the control is bound.

Record source property The most important property of a form or report because it determines the recordset that the form or report will display.

Recordset The fields and records that are displayed by the object.

Rectangle control An unbound control used to draw rectangles on the form that divide the other form controls into logical groupings.

Referential integrity Ensures that no orphaned records are entered or created in the database by making sure that the "one" side of a linking relationship (CustomerNumber in a Customer table) is entered before that same value can be entered in the "many" side of the relationship (CustomerNumber in a Sales table).

Relational database A database in which more than one table, such as the customer, sales, and inventory tables, can share information. The term "relational database" comes from the fact that the tables are linked or "related" with a common field of information. An Access database is relational.

Replica The copy of the Access database file that is stored in the Briefcase.

Replica set Both the original (master) and replicated (replica) database file. There may be more than one replica in a replica set, but there is only one master.

Replication The process of making replicas of a master database file using the Briefcase.

Report An Access object that creates a professional printout of data that may contain such enhancements as headers, footers, and calculations on groups of records

Report Footer section On a report, a section that contains controls that print once at the end of the last page of the report.

Report Header section On a report, a section that contains controls that print once at the top of the first page of the report.

Row selector The small square to the left of a field in Table Design view.

RTF (Rich Text Format) A document file format that retains many basic formatting embellishments such as fonts and colors but does not support advanced features such as bookmarks and clip art. The RTF format is commonly used when more than one word processing program needs to share a file, because an RTF file can be opened in most of the leading word processing software packages.

Run Executing actions. For example, you run an action query to change data and you run a macro to execute the actions contained therein.

Run-time error A VBA error which occurs because you are attempting an illegal or impossible operation; such as dividing by zero or moving focus to a control that doesn't exist.

ScreenTip A pop-up label that appears when you point to a button. It provides descriptive information about the button.

Secondary sort field In a query grid, the second field from the left that includes sort criteria. It determines the order in which the records will appear if there is a "tie" on the primary sort field. (For example, the primary sort field might be the State field. If two records both contained the data "IA" in that field, the secondary sort field, which might be the City field, would determine the order of the IA records in the resulting datasheet.)

Section A location of a form or report that contains controls. The section in which a control is placed determines where and how often the control prints.

Section properties Properties associated with form, report, or page sections that control how the sections will display and print.

Security account password A password applied to workgroups used to determine which objects each workgroup has access to and at what level.

Select query The most common type of query that retrieves data from one or more linked tables and displays the results in a datasheet.

Server In client-server computer architectures, the server computer is generally the one that serves files.

Server-generated HTML files Web pages created by the Web server. They are dynamic, and therefore show current data, but are read-only.

Shared network folder A folder on a computer network to which multiple people have access.

Shortcuts Pointers to objects placed in the Favorites or user-created groups in the Groups bar.

Show Check Box A check box in Query Design View that determines whether the chosen field will be displayed on the datasheet or not.

Simple Query Wizard A wizard used to create a select query.

Single stepping Running a macro one line at a time, and observing the effect of each line as it is executed.

Sizing handles Small squares at each corner of a selected control. Dragging a handle resizes the control. Also known as *handles*.

Snapshot A type of recordset displayed within a query's datasheet that does not allow you to update any field.

Sort To place records in an order (ascending or descending) based on the values of a particular field.

Source document The original paper document that records raw data such as an employment application. In some databases, there is no source document because raw data is entered directly into the computer.

Specific record box Part of the Navigation buttons that indicates the current record number. You can also click in the specific record box and type a record number to quickly move to that record.

Spike A surge in electricity that can cause damage to a computer.

SQL (structured query language) statement, A standard programming language for selecting and manipulating data stored in a relational database.

Standard modules Modules stored as objects within the database window. Standard modules can be executed from anywhere within the database.

Startup options A series of commands that execute when a database is opened.

Statement A line of VBA code.

Static HTML file An HTML file (Web page) that is current only as of the moment that the Web page was created. It is not linked to an underlying Access database.

Status bar The bar at the bottom of the Access window that provides informational messages and other status information (such as whether the Num Lock is active or not).

Status Bar Text property Property of a control that determines what text displays in the status bar when that control has the focus.

Sub A procedure that performs a series of VBA statements but does not return a value nor can it be used in an expression. You create subs to manipulate controls and objects.

Sub procedure See *Sub*.

Subdatasheet A datasheet that shows related records. It appears when the user clicks a record's expand button.

Subform A form placed within a form that shows related records from another table or query. A subform generally displays many records at a time in a datasheet arrangement.

Subreport A report placed as a control within another report.

Summary query A query used to calculate and display information about records grouped together.

Surge protector Equipment that protects computers in the event of surges or spikes in electricity.

Switchboard A special type of form that uses command buttons to simplify and secure access to database objects.

Switchboard Manager An Access feature that simplifies the creation and maintenance of switchboard forms.

Synchronization The process of reconciling and updating changes between the master and replicas of a replica set.

Syntax error A VBA error which occurs because of a typing error or misspelling. Syntax errors are highlighted in the Code window in red.

Tab control An unbound control used to create a three-dimensional aspect to a form so that other controls can be organized and shown in Form view by clicking the "tabs."

Access 2000

Tab order The sequence in which the controls on the form receive the focus when pressing [Tab] or [Enter] in Form view.

Table An Access object which is a collection of records for a single subject, such as all of the customer records. Tables can be linked with a common field to share information and therefore minimize data redundancy.

Table Datasheet toolbar The toolbar that appears when you are viewing a table's datasheet.

TCP/IP (Transmission Control Protocol/Internet Protocol) The communications protocol by which the Internet routes messages and Web pages through the Internet network.

Text A data type that allows text information or combinations of text and numbers such as a street address. By default, it is 50 characters but can be changed to 50 characters. The maximum length of a text field is 255 characters.

Text box A common control used on forms and reports to display data bound to an underlying field. A text box can also show calculated controls such as subtotals and dates.

Toggle button A bound control used to indicate "yes" or "no" answers for a field. If the button is "pressed" it displays "yes" information.

Toolbox toolbar The toolbar that has common controls that you can add to a report or form when working in the report or form's Design view.

Top Values feature A feature within Query Design view that allows you to limit the number of records in the resulting datasheet to a value or percentage of the total.

Unbound controls Controls that do not change from record to record and exist only to clarify or enhance the appearance of the form, such as labels, lines, and clip art.

Unbound image control An unbound control used to display clip art that doesn't change as you navigate from record to record on a form or report.

UNC (Universal Naming Convention) A convention used to locate a file on a network. The structure of a UNC is \\server\sharedfolder-name\filename and it is commonly used to locate files stored on a local area network.

Update query An action query that updates data based on an expression.

UPS (Uninterruptible Power Supply) Equipment that maintains constant electricity to a computer over a period of time in the event of brownouts, power surges, or power outages.

URL (Uniform Resource Locator) Each resource on the Internet (including Web pages) has an address so that other computers can accurately and consistently locate and view them.

Validation rule A field property that establishes criteria for an entry to be accepted into the database.

Validation text A field property that determines what message will appear if a user attempts to make a field entry that does not pass the validation rule for that field.

Variable A named storage location that can contain data that can be modified during program execution.

VBA (Visual Basic for Applications) The Access programming language that is very similar to Visual Basic and which is stored within module objects.

VBA password A password that prevents unauthorized users from modifying VBA code.

View buttons Four buttons in the database window that determines how the object icons are displayed (as Large Icons, Small Icons, List, and Details).

Visual Basic Code window The Design View of a module in which you write Visual Basic for Applications programming code.

Visual Basic for Applications See *VBA*.

WAN (Wide Area Network) A computer network that connects computers and LANs across public thoroughfares. WANs must use existing telecommunications networks (usually telephone lines) to accomplish this.

Web folder Special folders dedicated to storing and organizing Web pages on a Web server.

Web page A special type of file created with HTML code that contains hyperlinks to other files.

Web server A file server (large microcomputer) that stores, downloads, and routes Web pages.

Webmaster A person who works with Web servers, Web folders, and supporting Internet technologies.

What if analysis A process in which a user interactively applies assumptions to a set of numbers in an Excel spreadsheet to watch the resulting formulas recalculate automatically.

Wildcard characters Special characters used in criteria to find, filter, and query data. The asterisk (*) stands for any group of characters. For example, the criteria I* in a State field criteria cell would find all records where the state entry was IA, ID, IL, IN, or Iowa. The question mark (?) wildcard stands for only one character. The pound sign (#) can only be used as a wildcard in a numeric field and stands for a single number.

Wizard An interactive set of dialog boxes that guides you through an Access process such as creating a query, form, or report.

Word The word processing application within the Microsoft Office Suite.

Workgroup A description of users, objects, and permissions to which those users have access to the objects stored as a file.

Workgroup administrator A program used to create workgroups.

World Wide Web See *WWW*.

World Wide Web page A hyperlinked document that makes the Internet easy to navigate.

WWW (World Wide Web) A vast number of linked documents stored on thousands of different Web servers.

Yes/No A data type that stores only one of two values (Yes/No, On/Off, True/False).

Zoom dialog box A dialog box that allows you to enter and view a large expression in a query or property text box.

Index

Index

Index

Index

Index

creating forms/subforms with, ACCESS G-2, ACCESS G-6–7
crosstab, ACCESS F-1, ACCESS F-14–15, ACCESS F-14–17
defined, ACCESS A-4, ACCESS B-16, ACCESS F-1, ACCESS I-2
delete, ACCESS K-9, ACCESS K-14–15
filters *vs.*, ACCESS B-17
indexes for, ACCESS K-7
make-table, ACCESS K-10–11
modifying properties of, ACCESS K-6–7
multiple-table, ACCESS F-1–17
OR, ACCESS F-8–9
parameter, ACCESS H-6–7
removing fields from, ACCESS B-18
reports based on, ACCESS D-4
select, ACCESS F-1, ACCESS F-2–3, ACCESS K-8
sorting, ACCESS F-4–5, ACCESS F-12–13
specifying multiple sort fields in, ACCESS B-13
SQL for, ACCESS K-7
summary, ACCESS F-12–13
for top values, ACCESS K-2–3
update, ACCESS K-8–9, ACCESS K-9
using wildcard characters in, ACCESS F-9
Queries button, ACCESS F-2
Query Datasheet toolbar, ACCESS F-6, ACCESS K-8
Query design grid, ACCESS B-18
for sorting out of order, ACCESS F-5
Query Design toolbar, ACCESS K-6, ACCESS K-8
Query Design view, ACCESS B-13, ACCESS B-16–17
creating Crosstab queries in, ACCESS F-14
creating Select queries in, ACCESS F-2–3
creating top values queries in, ACCESS K-2–3
modifying Crosstab queries in, ACCESS F-16–17
opening, ACCESS B-18
resizing, ACCESS F-3
sorting records in, ACCESS F-4–5
summary queries in, ACCESS F-12–13
using, ACCESS B-18–19
query objects, ACCESS B-16
query object window, ACCESS A-8, ACCESS A-9
Query Wizards, ACCESS B-18–19
types of, ACCESS F-15
question mark (?) wildcard, ACCESS B-11, ACCESS F-9

►R

radio buttons, ACCESS G-12–13
raw data
collecting, ACCESS B-2
defined, ACCESS B-2
record locking, ACCESS J-16
Record Navigation buttons, ACCESS B-14, ACCESS C-5
records
adding with forms/subforms, ACCESS G-16–17
defined, ACCESS A-4, ACCESS A-5, ACCESS I-2
deleting, ACCESS A-14
editing, ACCESS A-14–15, ACCESS C-14–15
entering, ACCESS A-12–13, ACCESS C-14–15
entering with forms, ACCESS C-14–15
filtering, ACCESS B-10–11, ACCESS B-14–15
finding, ACCESS B-10–11, ACCESS B-12–13

finding with forms, ACCESS C-14–15
grouping in reports, ACCESS D-2, ACCESS D-6–7
navigating, ACCESS A-10–11
number of, displayed on datasheet, ACCESS A-10
orphan, ACCESS E-17, ACCESS K-17
in reports, ACCESS D-2
sorting, ACCESS B-10–11, ACCESS B-12–13
sorting on multiple fields, ACCESS B-13
uniquely identifying, ACCESS E-2
record selector box, ACCESS A-10
recordsets
analyzing, ACCESS I-12
copying to Word, ACCESS I-14–15
customizing, ACCESS H-6
defined, ACCESS G-2
record source, ACCESS C-2
Record Source property, ACCESS G-2
updating, ACCESS M-3
rectangle controls, ACCESS C-2, ACCESS C-3
rectangles
adding to reports, ACCESS H-10–11
red text
in Code window, ACCESS O-3
referential integrity, ACCESS E-16, ACCESS E-17, ACCESS K-16–17
relational database
defined, ACCESS I-4–5
relational databases, ACCESS A-4. *See also* databases
creating one-to-many relationships, ACCESS E-16–17
creating related tables, ACCESS E-6–7
data redundancy in, ACCESS E-2
defined, ACCESS E-2
defining date/time fields, ACCESS E-12–13
defining field validation properties, ACCESS E-14–15
defining number and currency fields, ACCESS E-10–11
defining text field properties, ACCESS E-8–9
defining yes/no fields, ACCESS E-12–13
features of, ACCESS E-2–3
planning related tables, ACCESS E-4–5
relationships, ACCESS E-2–3
defined, ACCESS I-4
many-to-many, ACCESS I-5
one-to-many, ACCESS E-2–3, ACCESS E-4, ACCESS E-5, ACCESS E-16–17, ACCESS I-5, ACCESS K-16–17
one-to-one, ACCESS I-5
types of, ACCESS I-5
Relationships button, ACCESS E-16, ACCESS I-4
Relationships window, ACCESS E-16–17
Remove Filter button, ACCESS B-14, ACCESS C-14
replicas
defined, ACCESS P-14
on laptop computers, ACCESS P-16
replicating
using Briefcase, ACCESS P-14–15
report definitions, ACCESS H-1
Report Design view
creating groups in, ACCESS D-6–7
creating reports in, ACCESS D-4
Report Footer section, ACCESS D-2, ACCESS D-3, ACCESS L-14
Report Header section, ACCESS D-2, ACCESS D-3, ACCESS L-14
reports, ACCESS H-1–17

adding fields to, ACCESS D-7
adding lines and rectangles to, ACCESS H-10–11
aligning controls in, ACCESS D-12–13
based on queries, ACCESS D-4
benefits of, ACCESS H-1
changing sort order in, ACCESS D-8–9
creating, ACCESS D-4–5
creating from parameter queries, ACCESS H-6–7
Database Wizard and, ACCESS H-2–3
defined, ACCESS D-1, ACCESS I-2
Detail section, ACCESS D-2, ACCESS D-3
enhancing, ACCESS H-8–9
fields in, ACCESS D-2
formatting controls in, ACCESS D-14–15
Group Footer section, ACCESS D-2, ACCESS D-3, ACCESS D-6–7, ACCESS D-8
Group Header section, ACCESS D-2, ACCESS D-3, ACCESS D-6, ACCESS D-8
grouping records in, ACCESS D-2, ACCESS D-6–7
importing data for, ACCESS H-4–5
inserting images into, ACCESS H-14–15
landscape orientation, ACCESS H-10
layout of, ACCESS H-10
mailing labels, ACCESS D-16–17
modifying expressions in, ACCESS D-10–11
modifying section properties, ACCESS L-16–17
Page Footer section, ACCESS D-2, ACCESS D-3
Page Header section, ACCESS D-2, ACCESS D-3
planning, ACCESS D-2–3
records in, ACCESS D-2
Report Footer section, ACCESS D-2, ACCESS D-3
Report Header section, ACCESS D-2, ACCESS D-3
sections in, ACCESS D-2
securing the database, ACCESS H-16–17
summary, ACCESS H-13
titles for, ACCESS D-2
using AutoFormats, ACCESS H-12–13
using Format Painter, ACCESS H-12–13
report totals, ACCESS L-14
Report Wizard, ACCESS D-2
adding lines and rectangles to reports with, ACCESS H-10–11
creating groups with, ACCESS D-6
creating reports in, ACCESS D-4–5
formatting reports with, ACCESS D-14
Report Wizard dialog box, ACCESS D-4–5
Required property
for text fields, ACCESS E-9
Reset button
on Standard toolbar, ACCESS O-11
resizing
controls, ACCESS C-6–7
datasheet columns, ACCESS A-15
labels, ACCESS C-16
RIGHT function, ACCESS F-11
row headings, ACCESS F-16
rows
inserting, ACCESS B-6
Row Source property, ACCESS G-10
RTF (rich text format), ACCESS I-14
RunCode macro action, ACCESS N-5
RunCommand macro action, ACCESS N-5
RunMacro macro action, ACCESS N-5, ACCESS N-13
Run Sub/User Form button

Index

What's On The CD-ROM

The **MOUS Access 2000 Exam Prep**'s companion CD-ROM contains elements specifically selected to enhance the usefulness of this book, including:

► Projects designed to reinforce concepts learned from the book

► Solutions for the Concepts Review questions found at the end of each chapter in the book

System Requirements
Software:

► Your operating system must be Windows 95, 98, NT4, or higher.

► Microsoft Access 2000 is needed to complete the projects included in this book. (The software is not provided on this CD-ROM.)

Hardware:

► An Intel (or equivalent) Pentium 100MHz processor is the minimum platform required.

► 32MB of RAM is the minimum requirement.

Textbook of Dermatologic Surgery

Textbook of Dermatologic Surgery

Editor-in-Chief

John Louis Ratz, M.D., F.A.C.P.

Clinical Associate Professor of Dermatology
Louisiana State University School of Medicine
New Orleans, Louisiana
Tulane University School of Medicine
Metairie, Louisiana

Associate Editors

Roy G. Geronemus, M.D.

Clinical Associate Professor of Dermatology
New York University Medical Center
Laser and Skin Surgery Center of New York
New York, New York

Mitchel P. Goldman, M.D.

Associate Clinical Professor of Dermatology/Medicine
University of California, San Diego
La Jolla, California

Mary E. Maloney, M.D.

Professor of Dermatology
M.S. Hershey Medical Center
Pennsylvania State University College of Medicine
Hershey, Pennsylvania

R. Steven Padilla, M.D., Exc. M.B.A.

Professor of Dermatology
University of New Mexico School of Medicine
Albuquerque, New Mexico

Lippincott - Raven
P U B L I S H E R S

Philadelphia • New York

Acquisitions Editor: Richard Winters
Developmental Editor: Delois Patterson
Manufacturing Manager: Dennis Teston
Production Manager: Maxine Langweil
Production Editor: Mary Ann McLaughlin
Cover Designer: Karen Quigley
Indexer: Ann Cassar
Compositor: Maryland Composition
Printer: Courier Westford

Printed in the United States of America

9 8 7 6 5 4 3 2 1

Library of Congress Cataloging-in-Publication Data
Textbook of dermatologic surgery / editor-in-chief, John L. Ratz ;
    associate editors, Roy G. Geronemus . . . [et al.] ; with
    contributors.
        p.   cm.
    Includes bibliographical references and index.
    ISBN 0-397-51495-6 (hard cover)
    1. Skin—Surgery.   I. Ratz, John L. (John Louis)
    [DNLM: 1. Skin Diseases—surgery.   2. Surgery, Operative—methods.
3. Laser Surgery.   WR 650 T355   1997]
    RD520.T49   1997
    617.4′77—dc21   97-41386
                                                                    CIP

Care has been taken to confirm the accuracy of the information presented and to describe generally accepted practices. However, the authors, editors, and publisher are not responsible for errors or omissions or for any consequences from application of the information in this book and make no warranty, express or implied, with respect to the contents of the publication.

The authors, editors, and publisher have exerted every effort to ensure that drug selection and dosage set forth in this text are in accordance with current recommendations and practice at the time of publication. However, in view of ongoing research, changes in government regulations, and the constant flow of information relating to drug therapy and drug reactions, the reader is urged to check the package insert for each drug for any change in indications and dosage and for added warnings and precautions. This is particularly important when the recommended agent is a new or infrequently employed drug.

Some drugs and medical devices presented in this publication have Food and Drug Administration (FDA) clearance for limited use in restricted research settings. It is the responsibility of health care providers to ascertain the FDA status of each drug or device planned for use in their clinical practice.

There is no way in the world that this book could have ever been completed if it had not been for the love and understanding of my wonderful family. I would be truly remiss without acknowledging their contribution. And so, with all my love, I dedicate this book to:

My wife, Shirley
My daughters, Kristi and Stacie
My son, and buddy, T.J.

Contents

Section 1: Perioperative Considerations (Mary E. Maloney)

Section 2: Scalpel Surgery (R. Steven Padilla)

Contributing Authors

Thomas H. Alt, M.D.
Associate Clinical Professor
Department of Dermatology
University of Minnesota
Alt Cosmetic Surgery Center
4920 Lincoln Drive
Minneapolis, Minnesota 55436

Marc Avram, M.D.
Director, Cosmetic Surgery Unit
Department of Dermatology
Cornell University
927 5th Avenue
New York, New York 10021

Mark R. Balle, M.D.
Director of Mohs Surgery
Department of Dermatology
Henry Ford Hospital
6777 West Maple Road
West Bloomfield, Michigan 48322

Elizabeth M. Billingsley, M.D.
Department of Medicine
Division of Dermatology
M.S. Hershey Medical Center
Pennsylvania State University College of
  Medicine
Hershey, Pennsylvania 17033

David Brodland, M.D.
Department of Dermatology
University of Pittsburgh Medical Center
Shadyside Hospital
5200 Centre Avenue
Pittsburgh, Pennsylvania 15232

David P. Clark, M.D.
Associate Professor and Chief of Cutaneous
  Micrographic Surgery
University of Missouri at Columbia
University Hospital
1 Hospital Drive
M-173
Columbia, Missouri 65212

William P. Coleman, III, M.D.
Clinical Professor of Dermatology
Department of Dermatology
Tulane University School of Medicine
4425 Conlin Street
Metairie, Louisiana 70006

Paul S. Collins, M.D.
Guest Lecturer
Department of Dermatology
Stanford University Medical School
84 Santa Rosa St.
San Luis Obispo, California 93405

Laurence M. David, M.D.
Institute of Laser Cosmetic Surgery
415 Pier Avenue
Hermosa Beach, California 90254

Lynn Dimino-Emme, M.D., F.R.C.P.C.
Coastline Dermatology and Laser Center
275 Victoria Street
1H Costa Mesa
Costa Mesa, California 92627

Jeffrey Steven Dover, M.D., F.R.C.P.C.
Associate Chairman
Department of Dermatology
Beth Israel Deaconess Medical Center
Associate Professor of Clinical Dermatology
Harvard Medical School
Beth Israel Deaconess Medical Center
110 Francis Street
Suite 7H
Boston, Massachusetts 02215

Raymond G. Dufresne, Jr., M.D.
Associate Professor
Department of Dermatology
Brown University School of Medicine
A.P.C. 10
Rhode Island Hospital
593 Eddy Street
Providence, Rhode Island 02903

Michael J. Fazio, M.D.
Assistant Professor
Department of Dermatology
University of California at Davis
Skin Cancer Surgery Center
2805 J Street
Suite 100
Sacramento, California 95816

Eric M. Finley, M.D.
Dermatologic Surgery, Department of
 Dermatology
Keesler Medical Center
Keesler Air Force Base
Mississippi 39534

Frederick Fish, M.D., F.A.C.P.
Associate Clinical Professor
University of Minnesota
Director of Department of Dermatology and
 Cutaneous Surgery
Regions Hospital

Richard E. Fitzpatrick, M.D.
Associate Clinical Professor
Departments of Dermatology and Medicine
University of California, San Diego
850 Prospect Street
La Jolla, California 92037

Alina A.M. Fratila, M.D.
Facharztin fur Haut - und
 Geschlechtskrankheiten
Friedrichstrasse 57-53111 Bonn
Germany

Roy G. Geronemus, M.D.
Clinical Associate Professor of Dermatology
New York University Medical Center
Director
Laser and Skin Surgery Center of New York
317 East 34th Street
Suite 11 North
New York, New York 10016

Mitchel P. Goldman, M.D.
Associate Clinical Professor of Dermatology/
 Medicine
University of California, San Diego
Dermatology Associates of San Diego County,
 Inc.
850 Prospect Street
La Jolla, California 92037

Gloria F. Graham, M.D.
Clinical Professor of Dermatology
University of North Carolina
Chapel Hill, North Carolina
P.O. Box 2804
106 Cypress Drive
Atlantic Beach, North Carolina 28512-2804

Joop M. Grevelink, M.D., Ph.D.
Assistant Professor of Dermatology
Harvard University
Massachusetts General Hospital
Professional Office Building 503
275 Cambridge Street
Boston, Massachusetts 02114-3108

Christine M. Hayes, M.D.
Director of Dermatologic Surgery
Department of Medicine and Surgical
 Dermatology
Tufts New England Medical Center
750 Washington Street
Boston, Massachusetts 02111

Julio Hernandez, M.D.
All One Skin Cancer & Dermatology
6525 West Sack Drive, Suite 302
Glendale, Arizona 85308

George J. Hruza, M.D.
Associate Professor
Department of Medicine (Dermatology), Surgery,
 Otolaryngology
Washington University School of Medicine
Director of Cutaneous Surgery
Barnes Hospital
1 Barnes Hospital Plaza
Suite 16411
St. Louis, Missouri 63110

Brooke A. Jackson, M.D.
Instructor
Department of Dermatology
Harvard Medical School
Mohs Surgery Fellow
DermSurgery Associates
7515 Main St., Suite 240
Houston, Texas 77030

Francisco J. Jimenez, M.D.
Fellow in Hair Restoration Surgery
Department of Dermatology
The Stough Clinic
Suite 304
1 Mercy Lane
Hot Springs, Arkansas 71913

Timothy M. Johnson, M.D.
Assistant Professor
Department of Dermatology
University of Michigan
University of Michigan Hospital
Department of Dermatology
1910 Taubman Center
Ann Arbor, Michigan 48109

Arielle N.B. Kauvar, M.D.
Clinical Assistant Professor of Dermatology
New York University Medical Center
Laser and Skin Surgery Center of New York
317 East 34th Street
New York, New York 10016

Suzanne Linsmeier Kilmer, M.D.
Assistant Clinical Professor
Department of Dermatology
University of California, Davis,
School of Medicine
Director
Laser and Skin Surgery Center of Northern
* California*
87 Scripps Drive
Suite 202
Sacramento, California 95825

Mary E. Maloney, M.D.
Professor of Dermatology
M.S. Hershey Medical Center
Pennsylvania State University College of
* Medicine*
500 University Drive
Hershey, Pennsylvania 17033

Deborah F. MacFarlane, M.D.
Department of Dermatology
Oklahoma University Health Sciences
Oklahoma University
619 Northeast 13th Street
Oklahoma City, Oklahoma 73104

Elizabeth I. McBurney, M.D.
Clinical Professor
Louisiana State University Medical School
1452 Tulane Avenue
New Orleans, Louisiana 70112
Tulane Medical School
1430 Tulane Avenue
New Orleans, Louisiana 70112

David H. McDaniel, M.D.
Assistant Professor of Clinical Dermatology
Department of Dermatology and Plastic Surgery
Eastern Virginia Medical School
Hofheimer Hall
825 Fairfax Avenue, Suite 646
Norfolk, Virginia 23507

Gary D. Monheit, M.D.
Department of Dermatology
University of Alabama at Birmingham
2100 16th Avenue South
Suite 202
Birmingham, Alabama 35205

Rhoda S. Narins, M.D.
Clinical Associate Professor of Dermatology
Department of Dermatology
New York University Medical Center
550 Fifth Avenue
New York, New York 10016

Marcy Neuburg, M.D.
Associate Professor of Dermatology and Surgery
Department of Dermatology and Surgery (Plastic
* and Reconstructive)*
Chief, Section of Dermatologic Surgery
Medical College of Wisconsin Clinic at
* Froedtert-West*
Froedtert Memorial Lutheran Hospital
9200 West Wisconsin Avenue
Milwaukee, Wisconsin 53226

Rebecca B. O'Sullivan, M.D.
Instructor in Dermatology
Harvard Medical School
Dermatology and Dermatologic Surgery
West Roxbury/Brockton Veterans Affairs Medical
* Center*
1400 V.F.W. Parkway
West Roxbury, Massachusetts 02132

R. Steven Padilla, M.D., Exc. M.B.A.
Professor and Chairman
Department of Dermatology
University of New Mexico School of Medicine
4775 Indian School Road N.E., Suite 100
Albuquerque, New Mexico 87110

Isaac Perez, M.D.
Fellow, Mohs Micrographic Surgery
200 West Esplanade, Suite 106
Kenner, Louisiana 70119

Désirée Ratner, M.D.
Assistant Clinical Professor of Dermatology
Department of Dermatology
Columbia-Presbyterian Medical Center
161 Fort Washington Avenue
Suite 750
New York, New York 10032

John Louis Ratz, M.D., F.A.C.P.
Clinical Associate Professor of Dermatology
Louisiana State University School of Medicine
New Orleans, Louisiana 70112
Tulane University School of Medicine
Metairie, Louisiana

Mark G. Rubin, M.D.
Assistant Clinical Professor
Department of Dermatology
University of California, San Diego
The Lasky Clinic
201 South Lasky Drive
Beverly Hills, California 90212

Richard K. Scher, M.D., F.A.C.P.
Professor of Clinical Dermatology
Columbia University
25 Sutton Place South
New York, New York 10022

Jack E. Sebben, M.D.
Associate Clinical Professor
Department of Dermatology
University of California, Davis
1605 Alhambra Boulevard, #2300
Sacramento, California 95816

William Slue, M.D.
Clinical Instructor
Department of Dermatology
New York University Medical Center
550 First Avenue
New York, New York 10016

Dow B. Stough, M.D.
Clinical Assistant Professor of Dermatology
University of Arkansas for Medical Sciences
The Stough Clinic
One Mercy Lane
Suite 304
Hot Springs, Arkansas 71913

Nia K. Terezakis, M.D.
Clinical Professor
Tulane University
Department of Dermatology
Clinical Associate Professor
Louisiana State University School of Medicine
Department of Dermatology
2633 Napoleon Avenue, Suite 905
New Orleans, Louisiana 70115-6382

Nhu-Linh T. Tran, M.D.
Clinical Assistant Professor
Department of Dermatology
Emory University
3193 Howell Mill Road
Suite 220
Atlanta, Georgia 30327

Walter P. Unger, M.D., F.R.C.P.(C.)
Associate Professor of Medicine
Department of Dermatology
University of Toronto
111 Avenue Road
Suite 800
Toronto, Ontario M5R3J8
Canada

Heidi A. Waldorf, M.D.
Assistant Clinical Professor
Department of Dermatology
Mount Sinai Medical Center
New York, New York 10029
Surgical Director
Waldorf Dermatology and Laser Associates
57 North Middletown Road
Nanuet, New York 10954

Carl V. Washington, Jr., M.D.
Assistant Professor
Department of Dermatology
Emory University School of Medicine
5001 Woodruff Memorial Building
1639 Pierce Drive
Atlanta, Georgia 30322
Co-Director, Dermatologic Surgery Unit
The Emory Clinic
1365 Clifton Road N.E.
Suite A-1400
Atlanta, Georgia 30322

Robert A. Weiss, M.D.
Assistant Professor
Department of Dermatology
Johns Hopkins University School of Medicine
54 Scott Adam Road
Hunt Valley, Maryland 21030

John M. Yarborough, Jr., M.D.
Clinical Professor
Department of Dermatology
Tulane University Medical School
2820 Napoleon Avenue
Suite 990
New Orleans, Louisiana 70115

Brian D. Zelickson, M.D.
Assistant Professor
Department of Dermatology
University of Minnesota
Skin Specialists, Ltd.
7373 France Avenue South
Suite 510
Edina, Minnesota 55435

John A. Zitelli, M.D.
Private Practice
University of Pittsburgh Medical Center—
* Shadyside*
5200 Centre Avenue
Suite 303
Pittsburgh, Pennsylvania 15232

Foreword

One does not have to be a student of the history of medicine to go back to the time at which dermatologic surgery really became a recognized discipline or subspecialty. By the mid-1960s there was a small, but enthusiastic, nucleus of dermatologists in both academia and private practice who were devoting their time and energy into incorporating more surgical procedures into their therapeutic armamentarium. Some were literally self-taught, others had the good fortune to have a mentor in one of the traditional surgical disciplines, such as general surgery, otolaryngology, or plastic surgery. A few had received their dermatologic training in programs where there was an already established procedural/surgical presence.

Fortunately, medicine is a field that promotes and thrives on the open interchange of ideas. Within a relatively few years, several forums for such scientific interchange were established. In 1967, the American College of Chemosurgery (now the American College of Mohs Micrographic Surgery and Cutaneous Oncology) was founded by Dr. Frederic Mohs and a handful of colleagues. Three years later, the American Society for Dermatologic Surgery was born. In 1975, Dr. Perry Robins created the *Journal of Dermatologic Surgery and Oncology* (now *Dermatologic Surgery*). By 1978, this evolution of what had once been a purely medical discipline had joined together colleagues from numerous countries, leading to the creation of the International Society for Dermatologic Surgery.

Despite the presence of skeptics both within dermatology and in the surgical specialties, more and more dermatologists eagerly embraced surgery as a challenging and exciting new extension of their profession. Moreover, with dermatology as the single specialty in medicine in which practitioners are comprehensively educated in the biology, anatomy, and pathophysiology of the skin, it made ultimate sense for practicing dermatologists to be able to offer their patients surgical therapies as well as medical ones. The historical reality that dermatologists had traditionally provided radiation therapy and cryotherapy for their patients made the addition of numerous surgical procedures evolutionary rather than revolutionary.

Further legitimacy was bestowed on this evolution during the 1980s by the addition of very specific surgical requirements to the residency training requirements for dermatology by the Residency Review Committee under the ACGME. Likewise, the American Board of Dermatology began to incorporate more surgical content into its certifying examinations. Ultimately, it became mandatory for every residency program to have a designated director of dermatologic surgery training in order to retain accreditation.

The American Academy of Dermatology also responded quickly and contributed greatly to the growing presence of surgery as part of the specialty. Many surgical programs were added to the Academy's annual meeting format, and sponsored courses were established around the country. This provided a mechanism to enable dermatologists who had trained in residencies prior to the ''surgical era'' to gain education and skills. The ASDS has also been instrumental in this continuing education effort.

As a natural result of these events, several textbooks on the subject of dermatologic surgery have appeared over the past decade. Some have been highly focused on a limited aspect of the field, while others have been more comprehensive in scope. Some have been manuals concentrating on the ''how to'' aspects of surgical procedures; others have been lengthy volumes replete with historical reviews and lengthy bibliographies.

This textbook promises to be of great value not because it covers topics previously unreported or because it presents more exhaustive references. Rather its value comes from the fact that it represents the practical distillation of the knowledge and expertise of many of the specialty's new generation of practitioner/educators. Many of the authors are current directors of surgical training in prominent residency programs. Others are directors of surgical fellowship programs. All are recognized for the quality and honesty of their work and their dedication to excellence in patient care.

The editor-in-chief of this text, Dr. John Louis Ratz, has undertaken this volume as a labor of love. I have had the pleasure and privilege of knowing and working with him over many years—first as my resident and surgical fellow, later as my colleague at the Cleveland Clinic. John has experienced the practice of dermatologic surgery in both academic institutions and in private practice. He has trained residents, fellows, and practitioners in various aspects of dermatologic surgery, and he has authored numerous papers, chapters, and textbooks. His commitments to education, to quality care of the surgical patient, and to innovation and clinical research run very deep. This book reflects those commitments and a desire to raise the level of dermatologic surgery even higher.

Philip L. Bailin, M.D., F.A.C.P.

Preface

When Richard Winters of Lippincott–Raven first approached me several years ago about assuming the role of editor-in-chief of a proposed textbook in dermatologic surgery, my first inclination was to ask if another textbook in dermatologic surgery was really needed. After all, several texts had already been published, and, as time went on, several more were to follow. However, his concept was of a *comprehensive* text in dermatologic surgery that would be conformed in an "how to do it" format of about 1,000 pages in length, supplemented by some 2,000 illustrations. These illustrations would include both intraoperative photographs as well as complementary, detailed artistic renderings for clarification.

The idea was somewhat unique, but doubts still lingered in my own mind.

I felt the task was too great an undertaking for one person, and I requested the aid of at least four associate editors. What followed was one of the most difficult, but most rewarding, projects of my career. Fortified by an exceptionally strong editorial staff, a singularly talented medical illustrator, and a remarkable show of support from the publisher, I began the project.

The first task was to assemble a company of authors, particularly for the procedural chapters, who were simply the best of the best. The list of authors was compiled after several meetings of the editorial staff, and, to the surprise of all, virtually all first choices were recruited to contribute to their respective areas of excellence.

Although deadlines were difficult to meet, the majority of chapters were submitted on schedule, and we worked hard to achieve a certain uniformity of style. Supplemental illustrations have been created to amplify procedures and are the product of a single and extremely talented medical illustrator. The final product is one that conforms as well as humanly possible to the originally proposed format. Although there may seem to be some duplication (as in the two sections on hair transplantation), such duplication is purposeful, in that two slightly different, but significant, approaches are presented for completeness.

The wish of both the publishing and editorial staffs is to have a product of unsurpassed excellence and clarity which will be of significant aid to both novice and experienced dermatologic surgeon alike. It is also our hope that this work will be both supplemented and complemented by additions and revisions in CD-ROM format in the very near future.

The reader should remember that textbooks and articles describing various procedures are no substitute for hands-on experience. For this purpose, courses, preceptorships, and fellowships are highly recommended. Nevertheless, for all those involved in the production of this work, I sincerely hope that, as a text, this book meets or surpasses all of your expectations.

Acknowledgments

A book of this type and magnitude is never the result of one person. It has been my great privilege to have been surrounded by the finest of staffs, both publication and editorial. I would like to single out Richard Winters of Lippincott–Raven Publishers as the person whose brainchild this was, and to credit him with the fortitude to see it through. I would also like to acknowledge Delois Patterson of Lippincott–Raven for taking the responsibility of doing all the legwork necessary to put something like this together—that includes ensuring that every chapter conformed as much as possible in style, and that all chapters were submitted as close to deadline as possible.

I would also like to thank my editorial staff for their endeavors in recruiting and ''hounding'' some of the finest talents in our field. And so, a heartfelt thank you to Steve Padilla, Roy Geronemus, and Mitch Goldman. In addition, I would like to extend my deepest appreciation and gratitude to Mary Maloney, whose efforts in her section were truly and undeniably outstanding.

A very special commendation goes to Jaye Slesinger, our medical illustrator. Jaye is a truly gifted artist whose fine work has given the illustrations in this book a uniformity of style and excellence. Her medical knowledge runs much deeper than I had ever anticipated and, combined with her excellent artistic ability, made it a pleasure to work with her in developing the artwork for this book.

I would like to thank all contributing authors for their fine work in completing their respective chapters, and for bearing with us for what seemed like an endless number of revisions.

Additionally, on behalf of the authors, editors, and publishers of this book, I would like to recognize all of those responsible for our experiences. Any one person is really only the product of his or her experiences, derived from real life situations involving family, friends, patients, nurses, students, residents, fellows, colleagues, and especially teachers. For me, personally, I would like to thank all of those who have helped foster and mold my career, including those persons at Case Western Reserve University School of Medicine, the Cleveland Clinic, the University of Cincinnati, and the Ochsner Clinic.

Finally, I would like to thank you, the reader, for taking the effort to learn from this volume and to encourage you to do your best in all that you attempt to do.

Textbook of Dermatologic Surgery

SECTION I

Perioperative Considerations

Textbook of Dermatologic Surgery, edited by John L. Ratz.
Lippincott–Raven Publishers, Philadelphia © 1998.

CHAPTER 1

Preoperative Evaluation

Marcy Neuburg

Psychological Profile
Medical and Surgical History
  Patient Demographics
  Physical Examination
  Allergies and Medications
  Tobacco and Alcohol
  Medical History

Bleeding Tendency
  Normal Hemostasis
  Abnormal Hemostasis
  Preoperative Screening
  Laboratory Tests
  Management
Suggested Reading List

The preoperative evaluation is often the initial contact between the operating physician and the patient. As such, this encounter represents a critical point in establishing the nature and the quality of the ensuing physician-patient relationship. This chapter is intended as a review of those activities which, in combination, are referred to as the preoperative evaluation. This evaluation is really an overall assessment of the patient's suitability as a candidate for the surgical procedure that is being planned. In achieving this end, the preoperative evaluation must include an assessment of the psychological, physical, and medical profile of the patient. Proper preoperative identification of patients at risk for intraoperative or postoperative problems allows the physician the best opportunity to prevent surgical complications and optimize surgical outcomes.

PSYCHOLOGICAL PROFILE

Individuals vary greatly in their response to the idea of undergoing surgery. Most cutaneous surgery does not fall into the life-threatening or emergent category, so dermatologic surgeons are not regularly faced with patients who are additionally stressed by these issues. However, this fact must not detract from the importance to the surgeon of accurately assessing the psychological status of his or her patients. Who best carries out the psychological assessment of the patient varies between practitioners. In some practices, the direct, one-on-one, nonsurgical patient activities are dele-

gated to allied health care personnel. The information and impressions thus gathered are then communicated to the doctor in a setting separate from the patient. There is much important unspoken information to be gained from patients when talking with them face to face, rather than through an intermediary. Although less efficient than the delegation method, this interaction provides the surgeon with an opportunity to get to know the patients and, perhaps more important, the patients to know and gain trust in their surgeon. Other practitioners choose to perform an initial assessment (including psychological) and then delegate data gathering and patient education activities to ancillary personnel. Whatever style of practice is chosen, it is imperative that patients perceive that they have an opportunity to voice their concerns to an informed, responsive, and empathetic listener.

The psychological profile of the patient is developed from a variety of verbal and nonverbal cues, most of which can be obtained informally during the initial patient interview. The main elements of the psychological profile are outlined in detail by Goin and Goin. They include appearance, orientation, mood, affect, thought processing, and judgment and insight (Table 1-1). The appropriateness of the patient's appearance can usually be discerned by simple observation. The clothing should be appropriate to both the patient and the occasion of the office visit. Extremes of neatness, disheveledness, or odor should be noted. Nonverbal cues such as excessive sweating, tremulousness, or wringing of the hands may alert the physician to increased anxiety in an otherwise calm individual. Orientation is usually self-evident. In the population of patients seen by the dermatologic surgeon, lack of orientation to person, time, and place is probably

Marcy Neuburg: Medical College of Wisconsin, Milwaukee, WI 53226.

TABLE 1-1. *Elements of the psychological profile*

Appearance
Affect
Mood
Orientation
Thought processing
Judgment and insight

most common in elderly individuals. Open-ended questions in the context of the patient history usually uncover this problem. Mood can usually be ascertained by the physician on the lookout for certain clues. Patients who are difficult to engage in terms of both conversation and eye contact may be suffering from depression. These same patients tend to give monosyllabic answers in a monotonous voice. Conversely, the manic or hypomanic patient talks excessively and may display an elevated mood inappropriate to the setting. The patient's affect may be similarly revealing. The patient's thought processing, as well as judgment and insight, is best revealed through open-ended questions posed during the patient interview. The tangential thinker is difficult to keep on track and may have reduced insight regarding the situation under discussion. Similarly, patients with so-called ''flight of ideas,'' who unconsciously move from one unrelated subject to the next, may be unable to give informed consent. Given the opportunity, most patients reveal intact thought processes and sound judgment based on good insight within the context of the initial patient interview.

Although not strictly a part of the patient's psychological profile, patient education is a very important part of the preoperative visit. The experienced clinician soon learns that the amount of educational information that is appropriate for one patient is not necessarily appropriate for another patient who is scheduled to undergo the same procedure. Some patients find comfort in knowing the precise details of the surgery ahead of time. Others find such information threatening or anxiety provoking and are more comfortable not knowing the details. Only by talking to the patient face to face can the surgeon accurately assess what level of education will best serve the needs of that individual patient. The use of patient handouts is helpful but should not be relied on exclusively for this important preoperative activity.

The attitudes of patients are often influenced by factors beyond the control of the dermatologic surgeon. Patients may approach the initial interaction with preconceived ideas. For instance, a patient may have had an unfavorable experience with a physician that will be projected onto your relationship, or the patient may have a relative or close friend who underwent similar surgery and had a less than favorable experience or outcome. When confronted with these concerns, it is important not only to allow the patient to be heard, but also to let the patient know that you are listening to his or her concerns. Addressing such issues early in the physician-patient relationship can go far to put the patient at ease and

establish a basis for optimal communication. At the same time, the surgeon should be leery of patients who have been seen by multiple physicians for the same problem. If a list of esteemed colleagues has failed to satisfy the expectations of this patient, perhaps you should give serious thought to whether you can realistically expect to succeed where others have failed.

The subject of the patient psychological profile is of special importance in the area of cosmetic surgery. Specifically, patients with unrealistic expectations concerning just what will be accomplished by undergoing cosmetic surgery must be identified and appropriately counseled before the planned procedure. A patient may attribute a problem such as poor self-esteem or marital strife to acne scarring or patterned hair loss. A patient with a clinical eating disorder may seek liposuction. A patient with self-inflicted disease resulting in extensive scarring is not likely to benefit from a simple scar revision procedure. In the case of cosmetic surgery, it is critical that the patient and physician have shared expectations concerning the outcome of the planned procedure in terms of both what it will look like and how the patient's specific needs will be met. Patients who will benefit from preoperative counseling or counseling rather than surgery are best identified early in the physician-patient interaction.

MEDICAL AND SURGICAL HISTORY

An accurate and thorough medical and surgical history allows the physician to identify patients who represent increased intraoperative and postoperative risk of complications. This can be accomplished with preoperative questionnaires that are filled out by the patient and reviewed by the physician. As an alternative, this information can be gathered during a preoperative visit or interview performed by the physician or allied health care personnel (Fig. 1). Such preoperative identification of risk allows the surgeon to appropriately alter the surgical plan to minimize risks and subsequent complications.

Patient Demographics

An important place to begin is documenting the names of the referring physician (where appropriate) and the patient's medical doctor. This gives easy access to the names of caregivers who will receive copies of the assessment, questions regarding concurrent medical issues, photographs, and/or copies of the operative record.

Physical Examination

The previously described information is followed by a written description characterizing the objective findings on physical examination. Where appropriate, lesion size and

Preoperative Evaluation

Name:_____ DOB:_____ Hospital #_____

Address:_____ Phone #_____

Referring M.D._____ Primary Care M.D._____

Location:_____
Size:_____
Biopsy result:_____
Previous therapy:_____

Allergies:_____
Medications:_____
_____
Aspirin:_____
Tobacco:_____ Ethanol:_____
HIV risk factors (blood transfusion, past contact, bisexual or
homosexual activities), is yes, HIV status:_____
Hepatic disease (hepatitis, jaundice):_____
CNS disease (TIA, stroke, seizure):_____
Renal disease:_____
Respiratory disease:_____
Cardiac disease (MI, angina, arrhythmia, murmur, pacemaker):___
_____
Prosthesis:_____ Diabetes:_____ Glaucoma:_____
Hypertension:_____ Bleeding:_____ Poor healing:_____
Scarring:_____
Previous surgeries:_____
Other:_____
Last medical check up __/__

Pre-op photo:_____ Pre-op instructions:_____
Consult appointment:_____
Medical clearance required?_____
        if so, by whom?_____ reason?_____

NOTES:

_____M.D.

_____date

FIG. 1. Preoperative evaluation form.

location, pertinent biopsy results, and associated abnormalities such as lymphadenopathy or nerve deficits are included. An accompanying diagram or drawing is very helpful. In the case of cutaneous malignancies, a list of previous treatments and the dates of those treatments is important. Similarly, a history of antecedent radiation therapy may alter wound healing and/or predispose the patient to the development of subsequent primary tumors. Photographic documentation is extremely helpful and often more accurate than written descriptions, particularly for cosmetic procedures. In today's medical climate the importance of complete and ac-

curate documentation cannot be stressed enough. This area of the record should clearly document what the patient has and how this condition justifies the proposed procedure. The adage "If you didn't write it, you didn't do it" is worth keeping in mind.

Allergies and Medications

An allergy history is essential. It is important to specifically ask about allergies to medications. If the patient denies allergies, it is still helpful to ask about penicillin allergy by name, since it is the most prevalent drug allergy and use of penicillin and its derivatives in the perioperative period is very common.

A review of the patient's medication history must include prescription as well as nonprescription drugs. The three classes of nonprescription drugs of particular importance are aspirin, nonsteroidal anti-inflammatory drugs (NSAIDs), and sedative antihistamines. Aspirin and NSAIDs are important because of their potential to interfere with normal platelet function, thus potentiating bleeding complications. Both are discussed in detail at the end of this chapter. Sedative antihistamines are contained in many over-the-counter preparations. Patients receiving sedation during surgery should avoid taking sedating nonprescription or prescription medications before surgery. A patient taking a cold remedy that contains a sedative antihistamine might require a reduced dose of diazepam for intraoperative sedation.

Prescription medications should be listed by name and dosage. Potential adverse drug interactions with planned anesthesia should be identified and addressed. Special attention must be given to medications that have the potential to increase intraoperative or postoperative bleeding (see later discussion), including certain β-lactam antibiotics and warfarin. NSAIDs, aspirin, and sedatives are also common ingredients of prescription medications. Systemic steroids, although not a contraindication to skin surgery, may act to delay healing or make patients more susceptible to postoperative infection.

Tobacco and Alcohol

All patients should be asked about their use of alcohol and tobacco. People who smoke are more likely to have slower or complicated wound healing. Smokers should be warned that their smoking may interfere with optimal healing. The viability of flaps and grafts may be adversely affected by tissue hypoxemia associated with smoking. Patients who drink excessive quantities of alcohol have the potential for increased intraoperative bleeding as a result of direct platelet effects of alcohol (acute) or hepatic insufficiency related to chronic alcohol consumption. For patients requiring intraoperative sedation, heavy drinkers are more likely to require larger doses to achieve adequate sedation compared with nondrinkers.

Medical History

The medical history should be detailed enough to accurately identify patients who are potential operative risks. Clearly, the complexity of the planned procedure, the possible complications, and their implications may be reflected in the extent of the medical history one may choose to elicit from the patient. An entire medical history may add very little to the excision of a simple cyst, whereas it might be quite appropriate when considering an extensive micro-

graphic excision of a multiply recurrent basal cell carcinoma followed by skin grafting. On completion, the physician should have a clear profile of the patient's current and past medical problems.

The most organized approach to the medical history and review of systems is in terms of organ systems. The exact order is quite arbitrary, but the content is relatively constant.

Central Nervous System

Is there a history of stroke, seizure, or transient ischemic attack (TIA)? If the patient has had a recent stroke, it is helpful to know the extent and results of the medical evaluation and whether the patient is receiving warfarin, dipyridamole, or aspirin. If a patient is taking an anticoagulant for a recent TIA or stroke, it should probably not be discontinued before surgery. Preoperative medical clearance by the treating physician should be considered. Elderly patients with vertebrobasilar insufficiency may have problems with head positioning during surgery on the face. A brief phone call to the patient's neurologist may avert a serious complication. In patients with seizure disorders requiring medication, it is helpful to know that their blood level is in the therapeutic range. Most patients receiving short- or long-term antiepileptic medication are monitored by drug levels on a regular basis by the physician who prescribes the medication. If the patient cannot verify this, the surgeon should consider checking a blood level preoperatively. It is also useful to know the frequency and nature of the seizures.

Liver

A history of liver disease (infectious, alcoholic, or other types) may have implications in terms of bleeding complications. In addition, safe use of certain anesthetic agents that depend on hepatic metabolism may require altered dosage. In the era of universal precautions, the potentially infectious nature of patients' body fluids no longer dictates special procedures or special handling.

Kidney

Diminished renal function is a problem only in its advanced stages. Uremia interferes with the normal clotting mechanisms and may be associated with increased intraoperative bleeding. Uremic patients also do not clear many drugs or their metabolites at the normal rate.

Pulmonary Condition

Acute respiratory disease uncovered during the medical history is usually a reason to delay surgery. Examples include pneumonia or heart failure. If a nasal-tip, full-thickness skin graft is planned, a simple "cold" or upper respiratory tract syndrome with rhinorrhea may interfere with optimal healing. More commonly, one encounters patients with chronic pulmonary conditions that may limit their ability to lie flat for prolonged periods or to generally tolerate the surgery. Most patients requiring supplemental oxygen are able to be without the oxygen for brief periods. Extreme caution should be exercised with the use of electrocautery in the presence of supplemental oxygen. In patients who are poorly compensated from the standpoint of their pulmonary disease, it may be appropriate to question whether they will tolerate a surgical procedure or whether an alternative mode of treatment should be considered.

Cardiac History

Patients should be queried quite specifically regarding heart disease in terms that are clearly understandable. Patients should be asked whether they have ever been told that they had a heart attack, angina or chest pain, irregular heart beat, heart failure, heart murmur, or mitral valve prolapse, and also whether they have ever been told that they should take antibiotics before dental work because of a heart problem. For patients who have angina, the surgeon should know what pattern is typical (what sort of activity brings it on and how often does this happen?), how long they have had this pattern and if it is changing (escalating). You need to know whether their pain abates with sublingual nitroglycerin and how often they take it. A patient with an escalating pattern of angina that is brought on with minimal activity or occurs at rest who takes nitroglycerin frequently represents a significant cardiac risk for any procedure. Consideration should be given to delaying the procedure until the patient is medically cleared by a cardiologist or cancelling the procedure in favor of an alternate mode of therapy. If a patient has had a recent myocardial infarction, elective surgery should be delayed 3 to 6 months.

The need for prophylactic antibiotics before skin surgery in patients with heart murmurs, prosthetic heart valves, mitral valve prolapse, or pacemakers is controversial. There are no large, controlled studies of skin surgery as a source for bacterial endocarditis. Prophylactic antibiotics should be given to patients undergoing prolonged surgical procedures (>30 minutes) according to current American Heart Association guidelines. This includes ''high-risk'' patients with prosthetic heart valves, previous bacterial endocarditis, congenital cardiac malformations, rheumatic or other acquired valvular dysfunctions, hypertrophic cardiomyopathy, and mitral valve prolapse with valvular regurgitation. Surgery through infected skin is also an indication for the use of preoperative antibiotics in at-risk patients. Outside these patient groups, the use of antibiotic prophylaxis is controversial. This subject is comprehensively reviewed in chapter 3.

Prostheses

As with cardiac indications for prophylactic antibiotics, there exist no good data supporting the use of prophylactic antibiotics in patients with orthopedic prosthetic devices. Patients should be questioned about the presence of artificial joints, metal screws, pins, or plates. Some orthopedic surgeons specifically instruct their patients to take prophylactic antibiotics before all dental or surgical procedures. Others make no mention of this. For more extensive skin surgeries, it is best to contact the patient's orthopedic surgeon, describe the planned procedure, and ask about their preference regarding the use of prophylactic antibiotics.

Diabetes

Patients with diabetes are more prone to surgical infections and delayed healing. Preoperative identification of patients at increased risk for such complications may lead to alterations in surgical planning such as choice of repair (e.g., flap vs. graft) or the empiric use of postoperative systemic antibiotics.

Hypertension

When the stress of undergoing surgery is combined with uncontrolled hypertension, patients are at increased risk for cardiovascular events such as myocardial infarction or stroke. The use of sublingual nifedipine or diazepam may acutely reduce diastolic hypertension. Care should be exercised in treatment of the elderly hypertensive individual with systolic hypertension. Acute reduction of systolic pressure may lead to hypoperfusion.

Scarring

Patients who have had problems with scarring include those with broad scars, hypertrophic scars, or keloid scars. Patients with a history of abnormal scarring should be considered at risk for future abnormal scarring. Occasionally, formation of broad scars is a sign of an underlying collagen vascular disease. Patients should be questioned carefully about the presence of scars, including scars that are not from a surgical procedure. Frequently, patients say that they scar abnormally when in fact they have a spread scar in a location such as the back, where scars tend to spread, or they may have a scar from a full-thickness injury that was not sutured. In any case, all scars should be examined, even if they are located away from the region of the planned surgery. Previous scarring is a good predictor of future scarring.

Other Medical Problems

For completeness, it is helpful to ask patients if they are under the care of a physician for any other medical problems. This should further reveal patients with clinically significant medical problems that might affect surgical planning. Caution should be exercised in interpreting the entirely negative history and review of systems. Not infrequently, the clinician encounters patients who report perfect health. It is important to ask such patients when they last saw a doctor or had a medical checkup. Sometimes patients report lack of medical problems or history because they simply have never seen a physician. In these patients, particularly if they are elderly or if a major procedure is planned, a preoperative examination by an internist or family physician should be considered.

Previous Surgeries

Patients should be carefully questioned regarding previous surgeries, major and minor. As a surgeon, you want to know whether there were complications and, if so, what the nature of the complication(s) was. Patients who have had complications such as infection, slow healing, or bleeding are more likely to have these complications with subsequent surgery.

HIV Risk Factors

It is important to both the patient and the surgical team to know if any HIV risk factors are present in the patient's past history, so that appropriate precautions and pre- and postoperative care be altered for the mutual protection of both the patient and the staff. Although this is a delicate subject, it can be approached very reasonably by asking the patient if he or she is aware of the presence of any HIV risk factors, which include previous history of blood transfusion, known contact with HIV contaminated materials or HIV positive person, and past history of bisexual or homosexual activity. If the patient answers in the affirmative, he or she should be asked about his or her HIV status. If this is unknown, the test can be completed with reasonable confidentiality. To ignore any query about HIV status, is to ignore a complete and pertinent history, and to compromise the well-being of both the patient and the surgical team.

BLEEDING TENDENCY

As previously stated, the intent of the preoperative evaluation, in general, is to identify patients at increased risk for perioperative complications and to alter planned procedures to avoid those complications. One problem of great concern to the dermatologic surgeon is bleeding. Bleeding during or after dermatologic surgery can be the initiating event in what Stegman referred to as the "terrible tetrad" of hematoma, infection, dehiscence, and necrosis. This complication is to a large extent avoidable with proper preoperative screening. In the remainder of this chapter the preoperative evaluation is discussed in terms of predicting patients who are at risk for excessive bleeding.

Normal Hemostasis

Normal hemostasis is a complicated interplay between platelets, circulating clotting factors, vascular endothelium, and tissue-derived factors. Maintenance of the fluid phase of blood depends on adequate blood flow and an intact endothelial surface protecting circulating clotting factors and platelets from contact with the underlying collagen and intercellular matrix. Greatly diminished blood flow or, as in surgery, disruption of the endothelial surface initiates a series of events leading to hemostasis. Normal hemostasis depends on what are referred to as primary and secondary mechanisms. Primary hemostasis refers to the role of platelets. Secondary hemostasis refers to the role of the coagulation cascade, or circulating clotting factors. In surgery, when bleeding occurs from disrupted blood vessels, initial hemostasis occurs via localized platelet aggregation (primary hemostasis). This is followed by stabilization of the platelet plug via extensive cross-linking of fibrin, an activity driven by the intrinsic arm of the clotting cascade (secondary hemostasis).

Abnormal Hemostasis

Disordered hemostasis is also categorized into primary and secondary events. Abnormalities of primary hemostasis include both qualitative and quantitative problems with platelets. Of these, the qualitative type are much more common and account for most bleeding complications encountered by the surgeon. Such disorders of platelet function are most commonly acquired and are caused by drugs (Table 1-2). Aspirin or aspirin-like preparations are by far the most likely offenders. Less common causes of qualitative platelet abnormalities are diseases in which there is abnormal platelet function as a secondary phenomenon (as in uremic states or dysproteinemias) or diseases characterized by the production of abnormal platelets, as in Wiskott–Aldrich syndrome (Table 1-3).

TABLE 1-2. *Drugs associated with abnormal bleeding time and clinical bleeding*

Nonsteroidal anti-inflammatory drugs
Aspirin
Diclofenac
β-Lactam antibiotics
Carbenicillin
Mezlocillin
Piperacillin
Ticarcillin
Nafcillin
Cefotaxime
Moxalactam
Cardiovascular drug
Quinidine

Modified from George and Shattil.

TABLE 1-3. *Causes of abnormal platelet function*

Inherited
Wiskott–Aldrich syndrome
Storage pool disease
von Willebrand's disease
Acquired
Drugs
Renal failure
Hepatic failure
Paraproteinemias
   Myeloproliferative disorders
Acquired von Willebrand's disease

Quantitative platelet defects are characterized by disorders of insufficiency or excess, the former being the more common of the two. Thrombocytopenia can be caused by drugs, increased destruction or sequestration (mechanical heart valves, hypersplenism), or diseases associated with decreased production. Thrombocytosis is usually the result of a reactive process or a primary myeloproliferative disorder in which platelet function may be affected, causing bleeding.

The perioperative management of drugs associated with clinical bleeding is discussed later in this chapter. Although the dermatologic surgeon should certainly be aware of platelet-related problems in patients, questions of treatment involving more than discontinuing a drug given on an elective basis should be referred to a specialist. The use of long-term platelet transfusions in individual patients can result in the formation of platelet alloantibodies, making the patient's underlying condition refractory to platelet therapy. Ideally, the platelet count should be 50,000 cells/μL before surgery and even higher (90,000 cells/μL) when the implications of a bleeding complication are more ominous, as in surgery of the eye.

Clinically significant abnormalities of secondary hemostasis can result from a deficiency or an absence of any of the coagulation factors except factor XII. Such abnormalities are usually the result of an underlying disease state in which the clotting defect is secondary, as in liver disease or vitamin K deficiency attributable to recent use of β-lactam antibiotics or starvation. Rarely, defective secondary hemostasis is due to a primary factor deficiency, as in hemophilia or von Willebrand's disease. For completeness, it should also be mentioned that disordered secondary hemostasis can also result in a hypercoagulable state in which there is inappropriate activation of the clotting cascade. This leads to the formation of thrombin that manifests as thrombosis and pathologic plugging of vessels. An example of this phenomenon is disseminated intravascular coagulation.

Disruptions of primary and secondary hemostasis have different clinical manifestations. In abnormal primary hemostasis there is no platelet plug formed at the site of endothelial injury. This typically leads to continued oozing in the operative field and bleeding around needle puncture sites. Thus a patient who gives a history of excessive *intraopera-*tive bleeding should be evaluated for a *primary* hemostatic defect. In disordered secondary hemostasis there is good initial hemostasis because of the presence of the platelet plug. However, absence of secondary clot stabilization via fibrin cross-linking leads to subsequent bleeding that may occur hours later. Patients with abnormal secondary hemostasis typically give a history of bleeding problems occurring hours after surgery.

Preoperative Screening

The preoperative evaluation of surgical patients with regard to bleeding tendency can be divided into three parts: the patient history, the physical examination, and the screening laboratory tests. Of these three areas, the patient history is by far the most important in terms of accurately predicting the bleeding tendency in a given patient. In this setting the patient history must include medical and surgical history, as well as medication and family history.

Clearly, a history of major medical problems may make a patient a poor candidate for surgery for reasons unrelated to bleeding. However, certain medical problems, while not specifically contraindicating surgery, may predispose the patient to excessive bleeding. Examples include liver disease in which abnormal function may affect production of clotting cascade elements. In chronic renal failure with uremia there is a direct effect on platelets interfering with primary hemostatic mechanisms. The presence of a connective tissue disease may lead to easy bruising resulting from vessel wall abnormalities. Patients with underlying hematologic disorders may have abnormal platelet function or platelet counts. Specific questions regarding jaundice, hepatitis, alcohol consumption, broad scars, easy bruising, poor healing, nose bleeds, and gingival bleeding may aid in identifying patients at risk for abnormal hemostasis.

Next, a complete history of previous surgical procedures with specific attention to bleeding complications is essential. A history of previous bleeding is the single best predictor of future bleeding. In addition, a complete surgical history answers the important question of whether the patient's hemostatic system has been sufficiently stressed (by previous surgery) in such a way that the clinician can decide whether a negative bleeding history is in fact reliable. Put another way, one wants to know whether the patient's bleeding history is negative because the hemostatic system is normal or because it has not been subjected to sufficient stress to give evidence of an underlying abnormality. For this reason it is very important to include minor procedures in a surgical history. Many patients do not consider dental extraction as surgery. The same is true of childbirth. However, in many otherwise healthy individuals, such a history may be the only valid test of hemostatic function. Unless specifically questioned, most patients do not volunteer minor procedures as part of their surgical history. Patients who have undergone surgery involving the mucous membranes without excessive bleeding are less likely to have occult von Willebrand's disease. Similarly, childbirth that is not complicated by untoward bleeding is unlikely in the setting of a clinically significant factor deficiency or platelet defect.

Occasionally, the patient's family history provides clues regarding the presence of an occult bleeding disorder. Factor deficiencies, many of which are inherited, can be subtle; hemostasis may appear to be normal in the absence of sufficient stresses. A positive family history of blood transfusions or postsurgical bleeding may be helpful in this setting.

The preoperative evaluation of bleeding tendency must include a detailed and complete review of the patient's medications. Although most patients readily admit to prescribed medications taken on a daily basis, they may not include prescription drugs taken on an as-needed basis or over-the-counter medications. Often, carefully directed questions are necessary to elicit an accurate medication history. Patients should be asked specifically (by name) about over-the-counter analgesics. These preparations, as mentioned previously, are the single most common cause of qualitative platelet defects. As such, they are an important cause of increased intraoperative bleeding.

The physical examination is probably the least helpful part of the preoperative evaluation for identifying patients at risk for bleeding and is included here only for completeness. Typically, one would embark on this examination only in the presence of a history suggestive of a frank bleeding diathesis, which in itself requires referral to a hematologist. The list of physical findings is relatively short. One searches for evidence of bleeding including purpura and petechiae. The findings of hepatomegaly or splenomegaly may be indicative of underlying diseases, many of which may adversely affect primary or secondary hemostasis. Telangiectasias, while usually the result of photoaging, may be seen in the setting of occult or advanced liver disease, connective tissue diseases, or acquired immunodeficiency syndrome. Broad scars are a sign of abnormal wound healing and may signal the presence of a connective tissue abnormality. Guaiac-positive stools may be due to abnormal hemostasis but more frequently indicate an unrelated problem.

Laboratory Tests

The widespread use of preoperative laboratory testing is becoming increasingly unpopular for outpatient surgery as attention is focused on cost containment and outcomes. When deciding whether to obtain preoperative studies, it is helpful to understand just what the tests are testing for. Like hemostasis, these tests can be divided into tests of primary and secondary hemostasis. Tests of primary hemostasis include the platelet count and the bleeding time. While the platelet count gives a quantitative assessment, the bleeding time reflects platelet function or the ability of the platelets to form a platelet plug in the absence of secondary stabilization. Secondary hemostasis is evaluated using the prothrombin

time (PT) or the partial thromboplastin time (PTT). The PT measures the activity of the extrinsic pathway of the clotting cascade, and the PTT measures the intrinsic pathway. Together, these tests (PT and PTT) assess the function of all elements of secondary hemostasis with the exception of factor XIII.

Preoperative laboratory testing for abnormalities of hemostasis represents, for the most part, *in vitro* screening. As such, these tests should not be relied on exclusively for the evaluation of patients. That being said, there are certainly situations in which preoperative blood tests are indicated. A helpful approach to identify such situations is to categorize patients into one of three groups. In the first group, the patient's history and physical examination reveal no suggestion of defective hemostasis and the patient has been subjected to sufficient stress in the past to determine that hemostatic function is normal. Such stresses include any prior surgery, tooth extractions, or childbirth. The vast majority of patients fall into this category. In this group the bleeding risk is considered minimal, and no screening tests are indicated. Patients in the second group have similar findings on history and physical examination but an absence of prior stresses (surgery) on their hemostatic system precludes making an accurate assessment of their hemostatic function. In such patients, if the development of intraoperative or postoperative bleeding would represent a serious complication, a general screen including PTT and platelet count is indicated, to establish that the patient has an adequate number of platelets and a functioning intrinsic pathway. The normal bleeding history and physical examination make an occult disorder of platelet function highly unlikely. In the third category the patient's history or physical examination, or both, suggests the presence of defective hemostasis. These patients should have a platelet count, and tests of PTT and bleeding time before any surgery in which a bleeding complication might have serious implications or consequences. Most non–drug-related and/or unexplained abnormalities on screening laboratory tests are best handled by referral to a hematologist.

Management

Drugs have been mentioned as a common and important cause of acquired bleeding tendency. A brief review of the mechanism by which certain commonly encountered drugs influence hemostatic function will aid in the development of guidelines for the preoperative management of drugs that are frequently problematic in the generally older patient population of dermatologic surgery. Specifically, aspirin, NSAIDs, and warfarin are discussed. The management discussed here represents recommendations pertaining to elective skin surgery, but the discussion is not meant to suggest that all surgery is contraindicated in patients taking these drugs.

Aspirin irreversibly acetylates platelet cyclooxygenase. The end result is defective platelet aggregation. Megakaryocytes are similarly affected, so megakaryocyte release from the bone marrow is necessary to restore normal function. Unlike most drugs whose effect is cleared after a period corresponding to five half-lives, clearance of the aspirin effect on platelets depends on the half-life of the irreversibly altered platelet. Therefore the effect of aspirin on platelet function is not dose-dependent. That is, it does not matter whether the patient takes a daily ''baby'' aspirin for cardiac prophylaxis or full therapeutic doses for osteoarthritis; the platelet effect is the same. After 4 days of withholding aspirin, 40% of normal function is restored. Ideally, aspirin-containing products should be withheld for 2 weeks before surgery. For reasons that are not entirely clear, ingestion of alcohol appears to potentiate the effect of aspirin on platelet function.

NSAIDs affect platelet function via a mechanism similar to aspirin, but the binding is reversible and not as strong. For this reason the effect is dose-dependent. Further, the antiplatelet effects of this class of drugs is quite variable. Ibuprofen is the main NSAID of clinical importance, since it is commonly used and is a recognized cause of platelet dysfunction. Naproxen also causes platelet dysfunction but is less commonly used. Indomethacin, a third common NSAID, has been shown to cause platelet dysfunction *in vitro* but appears to have no clinical effect. When possible, NSAIDs should be discontinued 24 hours before surgery.

Warfarin is a structural analog of vitamin K. As such, this drug, which is given for both elective and nonelective indications, inhibits the production of the vitamin K–dependent clotting factors VII, IX, and X and prothrombin. The half-life of warfarin is 24 hours; thus the PT normalizes when the drug is witheld for 5 days. When warfarin is given electively, as in atrial fibrillation or deep vein thrombosis below the knee, it can be safely discontinued before surgery. Nonelective warfarin can be stopped before surgery when it is given for aortic valve replacement. In this setting, the high-flow state across the artificial valve in the aortic position leaves the patient relatively well protected during the surgery. In contrast, patients with mechanical mitral valves are at higher risk for thrombosis as a result of the relatively low-flow state across the mitral position. These patients should have their anticoagulation adjusted from 1.5 to 2 times control values down to 1.2 to 1.4 times control values with medical consultation. Intraoperative heparin is sometimes recommended in this setting.

SUGGESTED READING LIST

1. George JN, Shattil SJ. The clinical importance of acquired abnormalities of platelet function. N Engl J Med 1991;324(1):27.
2. Goin JM, Goin MK. Changing the body: psychological effects of plastic surgery. Baltimore: Williams & Wilkins, 1981.
3. Patrono C. Aspirin as an antiplatelet drug. N Engl J Med 1994;330(18): 1287.
4. Rapaport SI. Preoperative hemostatic evaluation: which test, if any? Blood 1983;61(2):229.

Textbook of Dermatologic Surgery, edited by John L. Ratz.
Lippincott–Raven Publishers, Philadelphia © 1998.

CHAPTER 2

Preparation of the Surgical Site

Christine M. Hayes

Increasingly, the trend is toward more outpatient-based surgery rather than surgery performed in the traditional hospital operating room. Such an outpatient setting may be located in an outpatient surgical center at a hospital, a freestanding ambulatory surgery center, or a surgical suite in a doctor's office. For years, dermatologists have performed surgical procedures in their offices. This practice is more efficient, less expensive, and convenient for both patients and doctors. When all standards of care are met, these sites provide equal quality and safety of care for the patients.

As office-based surgery has become routine, standards and regulations have been developed by a number of organizations. The Joint Commission on Accreditation of Healthcare Organizations (JCAHO), the Accreditation Association for Ambulatory Health Care (AAAHC), and the American Association for Accreditation of Ambulatory Plastic Surgery Facilities (AAAAPSF) address the issues of standards in office- and hospital-based surgery. The JCAHO rules apply to operating suites based at a medical center. The other groups are involved in the standards and voluntary accreditation of office and ambulatory surgery centers that are separate from medical centers. Accreditation by these latter organizations can be useful in setting and maintaining standards of care.

SURGICAL SUITE

The design of a surgical suite is important for all concerned. The surgeon and staff spend much time there, and patients must be comfortable and reassured. The space required is variable and depends on the square footage available, the number of surgical rooms desired, the chosen layout, and the available finances.

Layout

There are many options for the layout of the surgical suite. The manufacturers of surgical office equipment have sample office designs from which ideas can be gathered. As an alternative, architects and interior designers with an architectural background can be helpful, although more expensive. However, little is published in the medical literature assisting with design. Visiting established dermatologic surgeons to determine what ideas are applicable to your office space may be most helpful.

Clustering the surgical rooms in a less-trafficked area of the clinic is ideal. If a surgical laboratory is needed, it should be placed near the operating rooms. The plans can include a nearby changing area for the patients and personnel and a separate waiting area for surgery patients and their families. The number of surgical rooms required depends on the volume of cases expected, overall patient flow, and the other activities to be conducted in this space. In a mainly surgical practice, at least two rooms are needed, but three or more

Christine M. Hayes: Dermatology Department, Tufts New England Medical Center, 750 Washington Street, Box 114, Boston, MA 02111 may be ideal. Also, an additional room with a surgical table that could be used as a clinic room is often useful.

The surgical room dimensions should be a minimum of 8 × 10 feet, although 10 × 12 feet is more comfortable; even larger spaces allow the flexibility to add new techniques and equipment. Placement of the surgical table in the center of the room gives the surgeon easy access to different sites on the patient. Mobile waste containers, suction, cautery, and Mayo stand allow movement to the appropriate position. There should be only one door to the room, which should be closed as much as possible to minimize entry of possible contaminants, such as dust and bacteria.

The walls should be light colored, fresh in appearance, and washable. The floor should be vinyl or tiled, easily washable, and resistant to stains. Carpeting should not be used. A deep sink for hand washing should be present in each room, with hand and optional foot controls. Adequate cabinet space along the walls is essential for the storage of surgical preparation solutions, gloves, instruments, specimen containers, bandaging supplies, and so forth. Countertop space can be useful for placing in sterile fashion equipment that does not fit on the Mayo surgical stand and for bandaging supplies.

Electrical outlets should be easily accessible and plentiful. Outlets should be supplied by an electrical system with an emergency power supply that will be operational in the event of loss of electricity to the standard outlets.

Equipment

Tables

The choice of a surgical table is important. The table must be comfortable, able to maintain several positions, washable, and sturdy. A wider table may be more comfortable for a large patient, although a narrower table allows the surgeon easier access to the patient (Fig. 1). It is important to lie on

FIG. 1. DMI 230 power surgical table. This table has a narrow head region for improved access. (Courtesy of DMI Division, West Valley City, UT.)

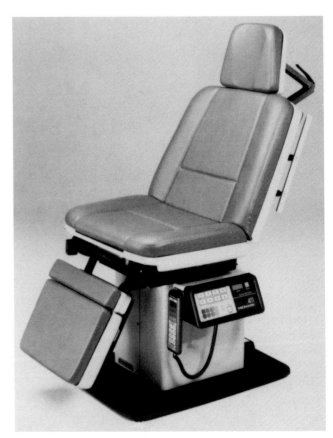

FIG. 2. Midmark 411 surgical table with hand and foot controls. (Courtesy of Midmark Corporation, Versailles, OH.)

the table for at least 10 minutes to assess the comfort level, since the patient will be on the table for a much longer period. The table position should be controlled by foot controls. Some models have hand controls also (Fig. 2), which are useful for preoperative positioning but are not helpful with position changes during the procedure.

Models that can attain a number of positions allow comfortable positioning of the patient, regardless of the surgical site. The ability to raise or lower the head and feet and tilt the table is imperative. All tables *must* be able to attain the Trendelenburg position. The overall table height should be adjustable to allow the surgeon to sit or stand (Fig. 3). Surgical table accessories include headrests, armboards, footboards, and stirrups.

Lighting

Lighting contributes significantly to the ease of any procedure. The intensity of the light output is usually expressed in footcandles, which is related to the type of bulb and filters. Field size and focus depth are important factors that are related to the reflective dish diameter and shape of the light. Some lights have a reflective area around the bulb, which disperses the light and provides a greater field size (Fig. 4). The reflective light also minimizes shadow and produces

FIG. 3. Dexta Mark 52X surgical table can be fitted with armboards and is foot controlled. (Courtesy of Dexta Corporation, Napa, CA.)

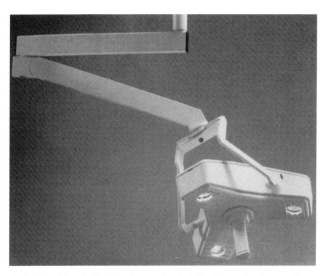

FIG. 5. Boyd S-11400 surgical light in a single, ceiling-mounted style. (Courtesy of Boyd Industries, Largo, FL.)

less heat on the surgical field. Lights can be mounted on the ceiling, wall, or floor (Fig. 5). Ceiling lights are superior, since they move easily, take up no floor space, and transmit less heat to the patient because of the distance from the patient. They can be mounted singly or in tandem and ideally track mounted to increase their range. It is helpful to have two lights to approach the site from different angles or to illuminate separate sites. Dual lights eliminate shadows and provide light in recessed surgical sites such as the conchal bowl. A single light with multiple light sources accomplishes the same goal (Fig. 6). Wall units have limited maneuverability, do not provide easy access to the patient, and are not recommended. Floor lights take up floor space and may topple if top heavy, are inconvenient, and are not recommended.

Some lights have a focusing handle, which sharpens the intensity of focus. This can be very useful. Sterilizable or disposable light-handle covers are available to allow easy positioning during a procedure. It is prudent to invest in the best possible lighting available and/or affordable.

Electrosurgical Equipment

A complete discussion of electrosurgery of the skin is beyond the scope of this chapter. Please review the Suggested Reading List for a thorough treatment of the topic. In general, electrosurgical equipment varies in the type of oscillating current used, the generated outputs, and the resultant capabilities of the unit.

Electrocautery is the use of electrically heated metal to transfer energy directly to tissue by contact, which results in tissue desiccation and necrosis. Examples of electrocautery units include the Geiger unit and the Shaw hemostatic scalpel. A battery-powered, pen-shaped, disposable unit is avail-

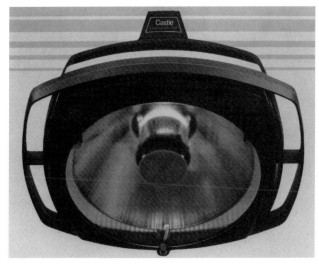

FIG. 4. Castle examination light with a concave reflector surface. (Courtesy of MDT Diagnostic Company, North Charleston, SC.)

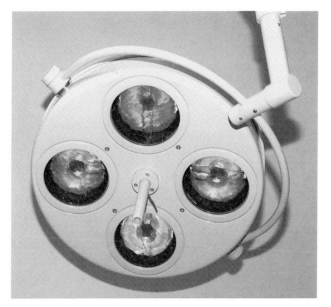

FIG. 6. A single light with multiple light sources provides good light and eliminates shadow. (Hanaulux Oslo light, photo courtesy of Mark Jones, MD.)

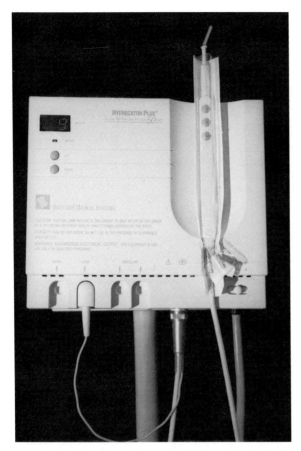

FIG. 7. Birtcher hyfrecator is a widely used, effective coagulator. (Courtesy Mark Jones, MD.)

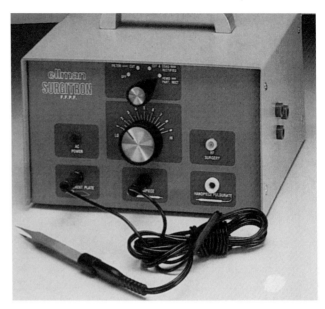

FIG. 8. Ellman Surgitron with bipolar forceps. (Courtesy of Ellman International, Inc., Hewlett, NY.)

able and is useful for biopsies and hospital consults but is inadequate for surgery. Electrocautery units can be used safely in patients with pacemakers, since there is no current involved.

The Birtcher hyfrecator, a widely used instrument in the dermatologist's office, is an effective coagulator (Fig. 7). However, it does not have enough power to be used in a surgical case with extensive bleeding and does not have a cutting current.

Many electrosurgical instruments have both coagulation and cutting currents. The Bovie is a well-known, reliable instrument and comes in two models. The 400CT model has more power and better serves the dermatologic surgeon. The Ellman Surgitron (Fig. 8) uses a radiowave frequency and requires a brief warm-up period. Elmed Incorporated, Cameron-Miller (Fig. 9), and Valley Laboratory Corporation also make excellent units.

Many accessories, such as spatulated tips and loop electrodes, are available. Sterility of the needle tips and handles is important. Needle tips are of two types: reusable, autoclavable tips or single-use, disposable tips. Reusable tips are less expensive, but disposable tips are more convenient. Handles (with cords) for the electrosurgical instruments can also be repackaged and gas sterilized between uses or disposed of

after a single use. The handle and cord can also be inserted into a sterile sleeve and only the sleeve discarded after use.

Suction

Suction is often helpful in cutaneous surgery, especially in extensive cases or scalp surgery. Wall suction is often not practical, since it is immobile and may not reach the surgical site. Portable suction units offer the dual benefits of versatility and small size. Many good units are available. Gomco has an extensive line of suction devices and canisters (Fig. 10). The Vacu-Aide by DeVilbiss is an alternative portable suction device. Tubing is available from surgical supply stores and is presterilized and easily attached. Both reusable and disposable suction tips are available. However, many of the commercially available, handheld tips are too large for

FIG. 9. Cameron-Miller electrosurgical unit has both cutting and coagulation current. (Courtesy of Cameron-Miller, Inc., Chicago, IL.)

FIG. 10. Gomco portable surgical aspirator. (Courtesy of Gomco Division, Allied Health Care Products, Inc., St. Louis, MO.)

cutaneous surgery. A sterile eye dropper may be very useful (Fig. 11).

Mayo Stand

The Mayo surgical stand is an important piece of equipment for the surgical suite (Fig. 12). It allows easy access to the instruments and is mobile. Instruments can be set up on the removable tray and then sterilized. There are two different styles: a four-wheel, easily movable version and a two-wheel model with a leaning edge, which must be raised to move the stand. The four-wheel version rolls most easily; the two-wheeled model will not inadvertently roll away.

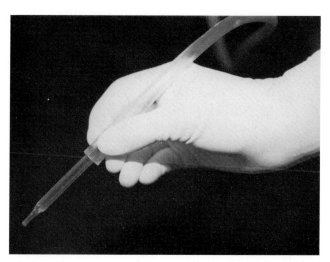

FIG. 11. A sterile eyedropper can be used as a suction tip. (Courtesy of Mark Jones, MD.)

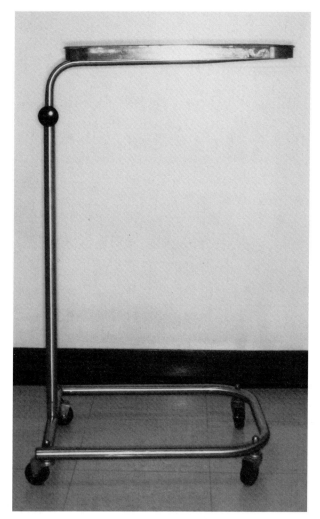

FIG. 12. Mayo surgical stand with four wheels.

They vary in size and mechanism used to alter the tray height.

Waste Receptacle

The waste containers should be open to allow easy access. The kick bucket on wheels is the most versatile (Fig. 13), but a medium to large receptacle with a hospital waste bag will suffice. Each room should have at least one waste container.

Emergency Equipment

Emergency equipment is a necessity in any surgical suite. If a hospital cart is not readily accessible, suitable equipment must be available and should include a stethoscope and blood pressure cuff, intravenous (IV) access equipment, IV fluids, oxygen, and emergency medications. Other important equipment include oropharyngeal airways, endotracheal tubes, ambu-bags, and a cardiac monitor with defibrillator. A cart

FIG. 13. Kick bucket is the most versatile waste receptacle because of its mobility.

and the required equipment can be purchased separately. Prepackaged emergency equipment kits are also available from a number of companies (Fig. 14).

Accessibility is not enough. The physician and ancillary staff should be familiar with and trained in the use of the emergency medications and equipment and know their location. The cart should be inspected on a regular basis to replace expired medications.

If the office does not adjoin a medical center, the physicians (and ancillary staff if possible) should be certified in Advanced Cardiac Life Support.

Laboratory

An on-site laboratory is necessary in a surgical suite in which Mohs' surgery will be performed. This requires space, personnel, and equipment. Equipment needs include a cryostat, staining equipment, a ventilation hood, storage space for chemicals, and a fireproof cabinet for storage of flammable chemicals. A second cryostat is often valuable as a backup in the event of malfunction of the primary unit. These laboratories are under the direction of the Clinical Laboratory Improvement Act (CLIA) of 1988 and must meet its requirements.

Patient Positioning

Considerations for patient positioning include patient comfort, physician access to the surgical site and instrumentation, and surgeon comfort.

Table Position

The surgeon can operate from a seated or standing position. This is usually based on individual preference. Table height depends on the position of the surgeon. The patient should be supine for any surgical procedure on the face, chest, abdomen, or extensor surface of the legs. Adjustments can be made for the patient who is unable to lie flat. The supine position is beneficial for access and hemostasis, and in an anxious patient it decreases the likelihood of a vasovagal response. The Trendelenburg position is also quickly attained from a supine position. The prone position is preferable for surgery on the posterior scalp, back, buttocks, or flexor surface of the legs, although lateral positioning can be used. For patient comfort a pillow under the chest or chin may help. The seated position for the surgeon may be optimal when operating on the arm, leg, hand, foot, finger, or toe. The patient may be supine on the table, or the head of the bed may be raised.

Aids

Most surgical tables have optional accessories. These include alternative headrests, armboards, footboards, and stirrups. The headrest and armboard are very useful, the foot-

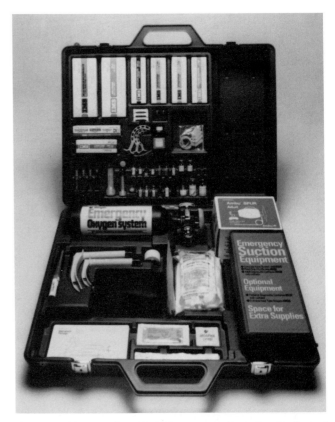

FIG. 14. Banyon Stat Kit 800, a prepackaged collection of emergency medications and equipment. (Courtesy of Banyon International Corp., Abilene, TX.)

board less so, and the stirrups the least useful. There are a variety of available headrests. A small headrest is helpful for head and neck surgery, since it stabilizes the head of the patient and allows close proximity to the site. An extra pillow to cushion the head may be more comfortable for the patient.

Armboards are available in several lengths and may attach to the table or rest on the floor. They are very helpful for arm, hand, or finger surgery and allow excellent access to most areas. The style that attaches to the table is the most stable.

On some surgical tables the "foot" end of the table can be placed at a 90-degree angle to the table and used as a footboard. This footboard is useful when operating on the foot or toes. Placing the patient supine with raised knees so that the foot is flat on the table is another helpful position for toenail surgery. Stirrups can be used to provide access to the posterior aspect of the leg or arm in a patient who is unable to maintain a prone position. As an alternative, if there are multiple sites on a patient and one is located on the flexor aspect of the leg, stirrups can be used to provide access to the site while the patient is supine. When using stirrups, it is important to avoid restricting blood flow at any point. Cushioning of the limb and prompt removal of the limb from the stirrups at the end of the procedure help to increase patient comfort.

SURGICAL SITE PREPARATION

Preparation of the surgical site is a standard component of every operation. Its purpose is to reduce the incidence of surgical wound infections.

Surgical wounds are classified into the following categories: clean, clean-contaminated, contaminated, and dirty. Clean wounds are incisions intentionally made under ideal operating room conditions. No inflammation is evident, and no entry is made into the oropharyngeal cavity or the respiratory, alimentary, or genitourinary tract. There are no breaks in sterile technique. Clean-contaminated wounds are wounds that may enter the oropharyngeal cavity or the respiratory, alimentary, or genitourinary tracts with little spillage. There may be minor breaks in sterile technique. Contaminated wounds are wounds that enter the oropharyngeal cavity or the respiratory, alimentary, or genitourinary tract with significant spillage or fresh wounds of traumatic origin. There may be major breaks in sterile technique. Dirty wounds include old traumatic wounds, clinically infected tissue, and wounds that involve devitalized tissue or a perforated viscus.

Cutaneous surgical wounds are usually clean or clean-contaminated wounds. The anticipated wound infection rate for these procedures is very low. The appropriate preparation of the surgical site assists in minimizing the frequency of surgical wound infections.

Surgical Scrub

The skin harbors a number of resident bacterial flora. The goal of the surgical preparation is to reduce the number of bacteria, although it is impossible to reduce the number to zero. A shower the night before surgery using an antibacterial soap has been shown to decrease the number of bacteria on the skin. Washing closer to the time of surgery is not as beneficial. Showers are not commonly used before dermatologic surgery.

Preparation on the day of surgery includes paying adequate attention to hair in a hair-bearing site, cleansing the area with a skin preparatory solution, and draping the area.

The removal of hair from the surgical site is less commonplace today. Frequently it can be affixed from the immediate surgical area, minimizing hair loss. Nonetheless, in the scalp, beard, or groin area hair removal may be necessary before surgery. It has been shown that the optimal method of hair removal before surgery is to trim with scissors. Shaving the area leads to small breaks in the skin, which cause some loss of the barrier function of the skin and a higher rate of wound infection. Trimming removes the hair without trauma or injury to the skin and has been shown to result in no increase in wound infection rate. The trimming should occur immediately before application of the preparatory solution. The use of a depilatory is another option that does not increase the infection rate, but it may cause skin irritation.

Scrubbing of the skin with a skin preparatory solution has been shown to be more beneficial in reducing the number of organisms than simply wiping the skin with the solution. Therefore it is recommended to first scrub the site with a scrub solution before wiping the skin with a preparatory solution. When operating on the face, it is worthwhile to prepare the entire face to decrease the potential of suture or instruments coming into contact with an unprepared area.

Surgical Preparatory Solutions

There are a variety of surgical preparatory solutions (Table 2-1). The preparatory solution decreases the amount of bacterial flora residing on the skin, although it is not possible to eliminate all organisms. The ideal solution would have a rapid onset, prolonged action, a wide spectrum of antibacterial activity, low irritancy, low cost, and ready availability. The standard skin preparatory solutions include alcohol, povidone-iodine (Betadine), chlorhexidine (Hibiclens), benzalkonium chloride (Zephiran), and hexachlorophene (pHisoHex). Currently the most commonly used skin preparatory solutions include povidone-iodine and chlorhexidine solutions.

Both ethyl and isopropyl alcohol in 70% to 90% concentration can be used as a preoperative skin disinfectant. Alcohol has activity against gram-positive and gram-negative bacteria. It has a rapid onset of action but no prolonged activity and must be allowed to dry to be bactericidal. Alcohol is flammable when wet and the laser or electrosurgical devices should not be used until the area is completely dry. It is probably underutilized as a surgical preparatory agent.

Iodine and iodophors such as povidone-iodine are widely

TABLE 2-1. *Antiseptic surgical scrub and skin preparation solutions*

Group	Available preparations	Onset activity	Sustained activity
Alcohol	Ethanol, isopropanol	Fast	None
Iodine	Iodine tincture, Lugol's solution, iodine topical solution	Fast	None
Iodophor	Betadine	Moderate	Yes
	Isodine, Preptodyne, Septodyne	Fast	Up to 1 hour
Hexachlorophene	pHisoHex	Slow	Yes (hours)
Chlorhexidine	Hibiclens, Hibistat, Hibitane	Fast	Yes (hours)
Benzalkonium chloride	Zephiran	Slow	No

used as skin antiseptics. Iodine is poorly water soluble. To increase solubility, it is complexed with polyvinyl pyrrolidine and becomes an iodophor. Free iodine is released slowly from iodophor, giving it a long duration of activity, as long as it is not removed from the site. Iodine and iodophors are effective against both gram-positive and gram-negative bacteria. They must be on the skin for a few minutes to exert the antiseptic effect and must remain on the skin to have residual sustained antimicrobial activity. Iodine and tincture of iodine can cause an irritant contact dermatitis, whereas povidone-iodine may cause allergic contact dermatitis. All these agents are toxic to cells and should not be used on open wounds. Chlorhexidine is a commonly used skin disinfectant. It is effective against both gram-positive and gram-negative bacteria. Chlorhexidine is fast acting and has a very long duration of activity because of its ability to bind to the skin. Activity persists even if the skin is wiped. The use of chlorhexidine is recommended in patients with an iodine allergy. It is to be used with caution around the eyes, because of irritation; around the ears, because of ototoxicity; and on tendons or tendon sheaths, because of scar formation.

Benzalkonium chloride is a quaternary ammonium cationic detergent. It is used as a skin antiseptic and for the disinfection of surgical instruments. It is more easily contaminated than other disinfectants and therefore is used less commonly than povidone-iodine and chlorhexidine. It is a rare cause of allergic contact dermatitis.

Hexachlorophene, a halogenated phenol, is bacteriostatic against gram-positive organisms and is absorbed through the skin. Teratogenic effects have been reported in fetuses from expectant mothers who used it for hand washing. The application of talc with hexachlorophene to the buttocks of hospitalized infants has resulted in toxic brain damage. This once widely used antiseptic is no longer recommended.

All antiseptic agents can become contaminated with bacteria. The single-use applicator prevents this potential complication but is more costly. In a busy surgical setting, there may be rapid use of preparatory solution and therefore less opportunity for contamination. In a practice where surgery is an occasional event, the use of the single applicators may be advantageous to avoid this bacterial contamination of multiuse solution containers.

The choice of agent depends on the surgical site, sensitivities of the patient, and proposed length of the procedure. Several options should be available for any situation.

Surgeon's Surgical Scrub

The surgeon's surgical scrub has evolved over the years. Regular hand washing during clinical practice and after bathroom use is adequate to remove recently acquired bacterial organisms. Before surgery, the surgeon should scrub hands and arms to elbows before donning gloves. The duration of the scrub is debated and has decreased over the years. The first scrub of the day should be 2 to 5 minutes long, and repeat scrubbing may be for 1 to 2 minutes. Many scrub solutions are available including parachlorometaxylenol (PCMX), povidone-iodine, chlorhexidine, and benzalkonium chloride. The long duration of chlorhexidine may provide some benefit over the other solutions.

The nails harbor bacteria and should be vigorously cleansed with a nail brush when scrubbing. Nails should be clean and short, without nail polish. Jewelry can harbor organisms; therefore both rings and watches should be removed before the surgical scrub.

Drapes

Proper draping of the surgical site allows the surgeon access to the site, encloses the prepared area, and provides a sterile area for the placement of gauze, instruments, and suture. Drapes are available in cotton cloth, paper, and plastic. Cotton cloth drapes are washable, reusable, and inexpensive. Such cloth drapes demonstrate a significant wicking action when wet and *may* draw bacteria through the fabric, causing contamination of the surgical site. This may be of concern in long or bloody cases. If cloth drapes become saturated with blood, they should be removed and replaced. The wicking action was demonstrated in the laboratory, but a clear correlation to wound infection has been difficult to establish. The discovery of the wick phenomenon, a potential mechanism in the development of a wound infection, led to efforts to improve the barrier qualities of cotton gowns and drapes by increasing the density of the threads. The increased density may decrease wicking and improve their barrier function.

Paper drapes are an excellent alternative and were developed in an attempt to improve the barrier to bacterial contamination during surgery. They are woven out of spun-bonded olefin, disposable, and relatively inexpensive. No wicking action has been demonstrated with paper drapes. The main disadvantage of paper drapes is their tendency to slip from the surgical site. Paper gowns can be worn over surgical scrub attire to further decrease the potential contamination from the surgeon and assistants.

Plastic drapes are disposable and convenient, although more expensive than cloth and paper drapes. Some patients find the plastic adherent drapes claustrophobic or uncomfortable. Both paper and plastic drapes have adhesive edges that inhibit but may not completely prevent drape migration from the site.

Other preparation may include use of a surgical cap on the patient's scalp to provide coverage of the hair, sebum, and scale. This also aids in keeping hair off the surgical field. A drape can be placed over the cap. Coverage of the foot or hand with a drape when operating on the leg or arm is helpful. This can be accomplished with a stockinglike wrap over the foot. A sterile glove can be used when operating on a digit. Simply prepare the finger for surgery, cut the appropriate finger off the glove, and place the sterile glove on the hand with the affected digit exposed through the removed portion (Fig. 15).

Gloves

Surgical gloves provide a barrier against bacterial contamination from the surgeon and patient. They also protect the surgeon from blood-borne organisms such as the hepatitis and human immunodeficiency viruses.

During surgery, bacteria increase in number on the gloved hand. The longer the surgical procedure, the higher the bacte-

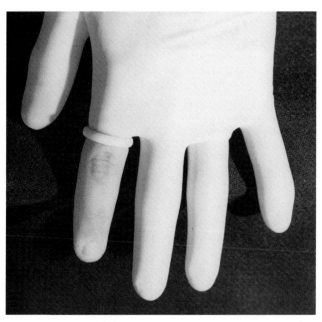

FIG. 15. A sterile glove may be used as a "drape" for the finger. The appropriate finger is cut from the glove, leaving the rest of the glove to cover the other digits in sterile fashion.

rial count. Glove punctures occur frequently. Some gloves may be perforated before use, in the act of gloving, or during the procedure. The incidence of glove perforation also increases with the duration of surgery. In the event of a glove puncture, the gloves should be replaced to prevent bacterial contamination of the site.

The type of glove chosen depends on the performance of the surgeon. Latex, hypoallergenic, vinyl, powdered, or powder-free gloves are some of the options. The type of gloves does not have an impact on the surgical procedure.

SURGICAL ATTIRE

Surgical attire varies but should be appropriate for the operating room. Surgical scrub suits made from open-weave cotton are standard attire but do not provide a dense barrier to shed skin and bacteria. Sterile paper gowns, on the other hand, have a tighter weave and provide a stronger impediment to shed skin and bacteria from the operating room personnel. They can be worn over scrubs or street clothes. In cutaneous surgery no clear advantage, in terms of infection rates, is associated with the use of paper or cloth gowns. Therefore cotton surgical scrub suits are acceptable. Street clothes are unsatisfactory, since they may carry bacteria and dust into the operating room.

Masks are used to decrease potential wound contamination from the oropharynx of the operating room personnel. They also protect the mouth and nose from any splash of blood or anesthetic. Laser masks are necessary when using a laser, to provide protection from possible viral particles in the smoke plume.

Eyewear is important for all operating room personnel. Protecting the eyes from any splash of blood or anesthetic is critical, since the external ocular surface is highly sensitive to fluid and chemical exposure. Wrap-around goggles or glasses with side pieces are indicated for all members of the operating team when performing surgery.

OPERATING ROOM PRACTICES

Standard operating room practices exist to provide the best care of the patient and staff. Each surgeon is responsible for upholding these standards within the context of his or her operating arena. The preparation of the patient, personnel, and surgeon should be a well-established and adhered-to routine. The basics include obtaining a history of allergies including allergies to antiseptic agents. Adequate exposure of the surgical site, preparation of a large area with a skin disinfectant before draping, and draping the area to allow sufficient exposure for undermining and possible tissue movement are all important. All members of the surgery team should be properly dressed before entering the room, where they can scrub and don gloves. Any saturated towel or perforated glove should be replaced, and care taken to avoid contaminating the surgical field. The surgical tray and field should be kept clear of used gauze, swabs, and other debris. After the surgery the drapes, needles, and other materials must be disposed of properly, and the room should be cleaned.

CONCLUSION

The preparation of the operating suite and the surgical site are critical components of successful cutaneous surgery. Careful attention to detail and adherence to protocol are important for the maintenance of high standards in the surgical suite.

SUGGESTED READING LIST

1. Bennett RG. Fundamentals of cutaneous surgery. St. Louis: CV Mosby, 1988.
2. Buchberg H, Amstutz H, Wright J, Lodwig R. Evaluation and optimum use of directed horizontal filtered air flow for surgeries. Clin Orthop 1975;11:151.
3. Cohen L, Fekety F, Cluff L. Studies of the epidemiology of staphylococcal infection: infections in the surgical patient. Ann Surg 1964;159:321.
4. Cruse P. The epidemiology of wound infection: a 10-year prospective study of 62,939 wounds. Surg Clin North Am 1980;60:27.
5. Davis J. The need to redefine levels of surgical care. JAMA 1980;51:2527.
6. Elliott RA, Hoehn JG. The office surgery suite: the physical plant and equipment. Clin Plast Surg 1983;10:225.
7. Fee W. Use of the Shaw scalpel in head and neck surgery. Otolaryngol Head Neck Surg 1981;89:515.
8. Fisher A. Contact dermatitis. Philadelphia: Lea & Febiger, 1986:178.
9. Hass AF, Grekin RC. Antibiotic prophylaxis in dermatologic surgery. J Am Acad Dermatol 1995;32:155.
10. Hill GJ. Outpatient surgery: what are the indications for it? Surgery 1975;77:333.
11. Hill GJ, ed. Outpatient surgery. Philadelphia: WB Saunders, 1980.
12. Lynch WS. Surgical equipment and instrumentation. In: Wheeland R, ed. Cutaneous surgery. Philadelphia: WB Saunders, 1994:91.
13. Maloney ME. Infection control. In: Lask G, Moy R, eds. Principles and Techniques of Cutaneous Surgery. New York: McGraw-Hill, 1996, 57.
14. Maloney ME. The dermatologic suite: design and materials. New York: Churchill Livingstone, 1991.
15. Moylan J, Kennedy B. The importance of gown and drape barriers in the prevention of wound infection. Surg Gynecol Obstet 1980;151:465.
16. Natof H. Complications associated with ambulatory surgery. JAMA 1980;5:1116.
17. Polk H, Simpson C, Simons B, Alexander J. Guidelines for prevention of surgical wound infection. Arch Surg 1983;118:1213.
18. Pollack SV. Electrosurgery of the skin. New York: Churchill Livingstone, 1991.
19. Price P. The bacteriology of normal skin: a new quantitative test applied to a study of the bacterial flora and the disinfectant action of mechanical cleansing. J Infect Dis 1938;63:301.
20. Prince H, Nonemaker W, Norgard R, Prince D. Drug resistance studies with topical antiseptics. J Pharm Sci 1978;67:1629.
21. Sandusky WR. Use of prophylactic antibiotics in surgical patients. Surg Clin North Am 1980;60:83.
22. Simons R. The office surgical suite: pros and cons. Otolaryngol Clin N Am 1980;13:391.

Textbook of Dermatologic Surgery, edited by John L. Ratz.
Lippincott–Raven Publishers, Philadelphia © 1998.

CHAPTER 3

The Role of Antibiotics in Dermatologic Surgery

Elizabeth M. Billingsley

Bacterial Flora
Antibiotic Prophylaxis for Wound Infections
Endocarditis Prophylaxis

Orthopedic Procedures
Suggested Reading List

The role of prophylactic antibiotics has been a controversial area with few definitive guidelines available for those performing cutaneous surgery. Such prophylactic antibiotics may be helpful in dermatologic surgery in preventing wound infection and decreasing the incidence of bacterial endocarditis. This is a confusing area, not only for dermatologists but also for dentists, surgeons, and internists.

Indications for use of prophylactic antibiotics, which antimicrobial is appropriate, and duration of therapy are not clearly defined for cutaneous procedures. There are guidelines available addressing endocarditis prophylaxis for dental and gastrointestinal tract procedures, but these may not be applicable in the dermatology setting. Dermatologists are frequently presented with the dilemma of a patient with an artificial cardiac valve who needs a surgical procedure, and the question of the need for antibiotic prophylaxis arises. The question may also arise in patients with other cardiac abnormalities, pacemakers, or prosthetic joints.

Prophylactic antibiotics are also considered in certain patients to prevent wound infection. Although it is not difficult to administer antimicrobials, they certainly are not indicated in all situations. Unnecessary prophylaxis can be time-consuming and expensive, and increases the risk of drug toxicity.

A recent study regarding antibiotic prophylaxis by dermatologists revealed that almost all dermatologists surveyed used antibiotic prophylaxis for their patients in certain situations. However, the survey also revealed that 7% to 10% of dermatologists do not use prophylaxis for incision and drainage of an abscess in a patient with a prosthetic heart valve. In addition, the survey results indicated that antibiotics were often used inappropriately—excessive duration of treatment, improper dosing and administration, choice of the wrong antibiotic, and prophylaxis with little or no indication. The need for appropriate guidelines and education regarding appropriate antibiotic prophylaxis to avoid unnecessary complications is evident.

BACTERIAL FLORA

A knowledge of skin flora is necessary to understand the role of antibiotic prophylaxis in dermatologic surgery. Resident flora are organisms on the skin that are relatively stable in number and composition. They live on the surface of the stratum corneum and within the outermost layers of the epidermis (Table 3-1). Transient flora lie free on the skin surface, are derived from exogenous sources, and vary widely in number and type. Coagulase-negative staphylococci are the most frequently found organisms of the normal skin flora. *Staphylococcus epidermidis,* which is coagulase-negative, is abundant on the upper body and accounts for more than 50% of resident staphylococci. It is often the cause of bacterial endocarditis after a transient bacteremia because of its inherent ability to adhere to synthetic surfaces and is infrequently found in wound infections. *Staphylococcus aureus,* which is coagulase-positive, is not normally a member of the resident flora but can be found in intertriginous

Elizabeth M. Billingsley: Department of Medicine, Division of Dermatology, Pennsylvania State University College of Medicine, The Milton S. Hershey Medical Center, Hershey, PA 17033.

TABLE 3-1. *Resident skin flora*

Organism(s)	Common Site(s)
Micrococcaceae (gram-positive Cocci)	
Staphylococcus spp.	Most common organisms of normal flora
Coagulation (−)	
S epidermidis	
S hominis	
(In some patients) Coagulation (+)	Intertriginous areas; occasional nasal carriage; ↑ in some skin
S aureus	disease
Micrococcus spp.	
Peptococcus spp.	
Coryneform organisms (gram-positive rods) (diphtheroids)	
Corynebacterium spp.	Lipophilic, especially in intertriginous areas
Group JK organisms	Intertriginous areas; resistant to most antibiotics except vancomycin
Brevibacterium spp.	Intertriginous areas, especially toe webs
Propionibacterium acnes (anaerobic, gram-positive rod)	Sebaceous areas, present in almost 100% of adults
Acinetobacter sp. (gram-negative rod)	Moist intertriginous areas, mucosa; ↑ number with perspiration
Pityrosporum spp. (lipophilic yeast)	Sebaceous areas
Candida spp.	Mucous membranes, rarely on skin; ↑ colonization in immunosuppressed patients diabetics, atopics, psoriatics

areas such as the perineum and can also be harbored in the nose. Certain skin diseases, such as psoriasis and atopic dermatitis, may be associated with high counts of *S aureus*, and this organism can account for up to 80% of normal flora in these individuals. *S aureus* is frequently isolated in wound infections and can occasionally cause endocarditis.

The composition of skin flora varies significantly with body locations. The head, neck, and upper trunk have many sebaceous glands and therefore a greater number of lipophilic organisms (especially *Propionibacterium* spp.). The face, neck, and hands are exposed areas and have higher total numbers of bacteria, in particular, higher numbers of transient bacteria, such as group A streptococci. The axilla, perineum, and toe webs are warm, moist areas because of occlusion and are more heavily colonized, especially with gram-negative rods, coryneforms, and in some cases, *S aureus* (Table 3-2).

Many other factors such as age, sex, race, occupation, exposure to soaps and disinfectants, medications, and exposure to ultraviolet light can modify the types and number of bacteria present on the skin. In general, men have higher total bacterial counts than women. Young children and infants have higher levels of bacteria such as micrococci, cory-

neforms, and gram-negative organisms, whereas levels of *Pityrosporum* and *Propionibacterium* spp. are much lower before puberty and in elderly patients. Climate affects resident bacteria, since increases in both temperature and humidity together increase bacterial counts. Although adequate surgical preparation may eliminate transient flora and reduce resident flora to a minimum, it is important to realize that, despite vigorous attempts in preparing surgical sites, it is impossible to sterilize the skin completely. It is estimated that approximately 20% of resident flora remain in the pilosebaceous units after scrubbing with antiseptics.

ANTIBIOTIC PROPHYLAXIS FOR WOUND INFECTIONS

Antibiotics are given in some situations to prevent wound infection. These antibiotics are given before an organism has the opportunity to proliferate in tissue and produce an infection, and the choice of antibiotic is based on knowledge of which microbes would be the most likely to be involved. Most of the literature regarding antibiotic prophylaxis for wound infection is in the general surgery literature. It is

TABLE 3-2. *Effect of anatomic location on bacterial flora*

Location	Effects
Face, neck, hands (exposed areas)	↑ Total number of bacteria
	↑ Number of transient bacteria (Group A streptococci)
Head, upper trunk (sebaceous areas)	↑ Lipophilic organisms (*Propionibacterium*)
	↑ *Staphylococcus epidermidis*
Axilla, perineum, toe webs (partially occluded areas)	↑ Number of bacteria, especially gram-negative rods, coryneforms, and *Staphylococcus aureus* in some
Arms, legs (dry areas)	↓ Total number of bacteria

difficult to apply these data to cutaneous surgery because of the differences in types of procedures performed: many general surgery procedures invade body cavities, most general surgery patients have preoperative hospitalization, the procedures are usually performed in an operating room, and the patients have recovery while in the hospital with increased exposure to nosocomial factors. However, wound classification, certain patient characteristics, procedure types, and anatomic location may warrant antibiotic prophylaxis in some dermatologic surgery patients because of an increased risk of bacterial infection.

Wounds are generally categorized into the following classes:

1. Class I (clean wounds): Wounds created in noncontaminated skin with sterile surgical technique. Infection rate should be less than 5%.
2. Class II (clean-contaminated wounds): Wounds in contaminated areas such as the oral cavity, respiratory tract, axilla, or perineum *or* procedures with minor breaks in aseptic technique. Infection rate is approximately 10%.
3. Class III (contaminated wounds): Wounds caused by trauma, with major breaks in sterile technique, or wounds with acute nonpurulent inflammation. Infection risk is approximately 20% to 30%.
4. Class IV (infected wounds): Wounds that are grossly contaminated with foreign bodies, or devitalized tissue. Infection risk is 30% to 40%.

Because of the very low risk of infection with class I wounds, there is little indication for antibiotic prophylaxis to prevent wound infection in these types of procedures. Antibiotics are almost always used in classes III and IV wounds, and the use is considered therapeutic, not prophylactic. Most dermatologic procedures fall into class II wounds because of nonintact skin or small breaks in aseptic technique, and the need for antibiotics is often unclear. Prophylaxis in these cases is aimed at decreasing the flora of bacteria typically involved in postoperative infections.

Certain patient characteristics may increase the likelihood of wound infection. These include malnutrition, anergy, chronic renal failure, obesity, age, chronic immunosuppression, and diabetes. Also, body site, type of procedure, and length of procedure can affect risk of infection. Infection rate almost doubles with each hour of operation. The risk of wound infection is higher when hair in the surgical site is shaved rather than clipped, or not trimmed at all. Unknown factors such as nasal carriage of S aureus by the patient or the surgical team can also play a role in postoperative wound infection.

A recent study of wound infections following Mohs' surgery revealed that certain anatomic sites such as the ear, as well as large surgical defects (mean area ≥5.75 cm^2), had an increased incidence of infection. When the cartilage of the ear was exposed, the rate of wound infection was significantly higher. Prophylactic antibiotics should be considered in these situations. Particularly lengthy procedures are con-

TABLE 3-3. *Criteria for consideration of antibiotic prophylaxis against wound infection*

Grossly infected wounds
Contaminated locations (axilla, perineum, toe webs)
Patient health problems (diabetes, renal failure, immunosuppression)
Other dermatologic conditions (psoriasis, atopic dermatitis)
Large defects and/or lengthy procedures
Location on ear (especially if cartilage is exposed)

sidered an indication for antibiotic prophylaxis by some dermatologic surgeons.

Overall, because rates of infection for surgical procedures on noninfected skin are low, prophylaxis against wound infection does not need to be performed unless the area is grossly infected or highly contaminated or the patient is considered to be at risk because of immunosuppression or other health problems. Although not warranted in all patients with health problems, prophylaxis for higher-risk patients should be considered for procedures performed on nonintact skin, in heavily colonized areas, and if associated with dermatologic conditions, such as psoriasis or dermatitis, in which skin is frequently colonized with potentially virulent organisms. Large defect size, location on the ear, and lengthy procedures, as mentioned earlier, also are considerations for prophylaxis in all patients (Table 3-3). Haas and Grekin comment that curettage wounds, biopsy sites, and wounds healing by second intention do not benefit from prophylaxis unless they meet the preceding criteria. The authors recommend a single preoperative dose of antibiotics for such wounds in contaminated body areas. It is difficult for systemic antibiotics given postoperatively to penetrate the fibrin base of granulating wounds. In addition, the importance of preoperative surgical site cleansing, as well as hand scrubs, gloves, and drapes, cannot be overemphasized.

The selection of the appropriate antimicrobial to use for wound infection prophylaxis depends on the most likely infecting bacteria. First-generation cephalosporins are active against most gram-positive cocci, *Escherichia coli,* and *Klebsiella* organisms, but not against enterococci, *Pseudomonas* spp., some *S epidermidis,* or methicillin-resistant *S aureus* (MRSA) (a low incidence in the outpatient setting). These are 90% to 95% effective against *S aureus.* Dicloxacillin is 90% to 95% active against *S aureus* but does not cover *S epidermidis* as well. If penicillin allergy is a problem and there is concern about cross-sensitivity to cephalosporins, clindamycin can be considered, since it is 90% effective against *S aureus.* The association with pseudomembranous colitis is of note but thought not to be a problem with the short course used for prophylaxis. Erythromycin, although effective against streptococci, is 65% to 75% effective against *S aureus* and has minimal gram-negative coverage. Various preparations of erythromycin are available, and recommended dosing regimens vary depending on the form of erythromycin prescribed. Vancomycin is the drug of choice

TABLE 3-4. *Antimicrobial agent for prophylaxis*

Antibiotics	Comments
Dicloxacillin	Good gram-positive coverage, including *Staphylococcus aureus*; some coverage against *Staphylococcus epidermidis*
Cephalosporins	Broad gram-positive and gram-negative coverage, including *S aureus*, and some coverage against *S epidermidis* 5% to 10% incidence of PCN cross-sensitivity
Erythromycin	Coverage of many gram-positive, some gram-negative organisms; some *S aureus* resistance; dose depends on preparation
Clindamycin	Aerobic gram-negative (+) cocci, gram-positive and gram negative anaerobes; usually active against *S aureus* and *S epidermidis*
Vancomycin	Good coverage for gram-positive organisms, including *S epidermidis*, MRSA and diphtheroids; must be given intravenously over 1-hour period

MRSA, methacillin-resistant staph-aureus.

for coverage when *S epidermidis* and MRSA are of major concern. Vancomycin must be given intravenously slowly over an hour to minimize the hypotensive effect, and the dose must be adjusted for renal impairment (Tables 3-4–3-6).

Antibiotics given to prevent wound infection should be given preoperatively. High levels of antibiotics are needed in the bloodstream and tissue in the minutes after the incision to prevent bacterial residence in the operative wound. Ideally the antibiotic should be given 1 to 2 hours before surgery. Giving the antibiotic more than 2 hours before surgery increases the chance of developing resistant organisms. If the antibiotic is given more than 3 hours after the start of the procedure, the coagulum that forms in the wound may pre-vent the antibiotic from reaching the trapped bacteria. Studies have also shown that agents given for prophylaxis should not be prescribed for longer than 48 hours following the procedure. Extended coverage increases the chance of drug toxicity and also can contribute to development of resistant organisms. Some authors believe that a single preoperative dose of antibiotic is sufficient, whereas others continue coverage for up to 24 hours after the procedure.

ENDOCARDITIS PROPHYLAXIS

Bacterial endocarditis is a disease of significant morbidity and potential mortality. The risk of development of endocarditis from a dermatologic procedure depends on the patient's underlying cardiac abnormality, degree of bacteremia accompanying a procedure, and the specific type of bacteria involved. Endocarditis following a cutaneous surgical procedure is very rare, especially considering the tremendous number of biopsies, excisions, and other procedures performed daily in the dermatology setting. Very few cases of endocarditis in the literature have been suggested to be related to dermatologic procedures. Two cases occurred after skin biopsies, one case after an excision, and one case possibly was associated with cryosurgery.

Endocarditis is caused by blood-borne bacteria lodging on a damaged, abnormal, or artificial heart valve or on the endocardium. Surgical and dental procedures involving mucosal surfaces or contaminated tissue commonly cause transient bacteremias. Although these bacteremias rarely last more than 15 minutes, in some cases these transient episodes lead to endocarditis. It is estimated that only approximately 15% of cases of bacterial endocarditis can be associated with a previous surgical, dental, or medical procedure. It is known that certain dental procedures are associated with a 85% incidence of bacteremias, but also that bacteremias occur on a daily basis as a result of eating, oral hygiene, and other normal activities. Spontaneous bacteremias can occur in pa-

TABLE 3-5. *Suggested prophylaxis regimens for dermatologic surgery*

	1 hour before surgery	6 hours later
High-risk patients		
First-generation cephalosporin	1 g po	500 mg po
Erythromycin	See Table 3-6	
Dicloxacillin	1 g po	500 mg po
Contaminated skin		
First-generation cephalosporin	1 g po	500 mg po
Dicloxacillin	2 g po	500 mg po
Clindamycin	300 mg po	150 mg po
MRSA/*Staphylococcus epidermidis*		
Vancomycin	500 mg IV	250 mg IV
Oral mucosa		
Amoxicillin	3 g po	1.5 g po
Erythromycin	See Table 3-6	
Clindamycin	300 mg po	150 mg po

po, by mouth; IV, intravenously; MRSA, methacillin-resistant staph-aureus.

TABLE 3-6. *Erythromycin regimens based on preparation*

	Before surgery	6 hours later
Erythromycin base	1 g, 2–3 hours (empty stomach)	500 mg
Enteric-coated base (PCE, E-mycin, Ery-tab)	1 g, 3 4 hours (empty stomach)	500 mg
Erythromycin stearate	1 g, 2–3 hours (empty stomach)	500 mg
Erythromycin estolate	1 g, 1½–2 hours	500 mg
Erythromycin ethylsuccinate	1.6 g, 1½–2 hours	800 mg

tients with lung and skin infections and in patients with severe periodontal diseases. It may be that very few of the cases of endocarditis are preventable, and there is no definite proof that antibiotic prophylaxis decreases the risk of endocarditis. However, we should be vigilant with appropriate indications for prophylaxis when there is a significant risk of bacteremia and subsequent risk of endocarditis. The incidence of bacteremia related to cutaneous surgery is not known. Sabetta and Zitelli concluded that the incidence of transient bacteremia following surgery on eroded but not clinically infected skin is less than 8.4%. Other studies have shown that manipulation of clinically infected skin is associated with a 35% incidence of bacteremia with organisms known to be associated with bacterial endocarditis. A well-designed study by Halpern et al. looked at blood cultures of 45 patients undergoing cutaneous surgery of the head and neck. Three patients (7%) had bacteria in their blood cultures: two had *Propionibacterium acnes,* and one had *Staphylococcus hominis.* Neither organism commonly causes endocarditis.

In native valve endocarditis, 60% to 80% of affected patients have a predisposing cardiac lesion, most commonly, mitral valve prolapse. The risk of endocarditis in a patient with mitral valve prolapse is significantly higher if a systolic murmur is present. Congenital heart disease is the underlying abnormality in 10% to 20% of patients who develop endocarditis. Degenerative heart disease, including calcific aortic stenosis, can be a risk factor for endocarditis in elderly individuals. Streptococci account for 50% to 70% of the cases of native valve endocarditis and are usually *Streptococcus viridans* from the oropharynx. Enterococci from the gastrointestinal tract and anterior urethra account for 10% of the cases. Coagulase-positive staphylococci, accounting for 23% of cases, attack normal or damaged valves and cause a fulminant endocarditis, whereas coagulase-negative staphylococci, accounting for 2% of cases, cause an indolent infection of abnormal valves. The bacteria adhere to thrombi that are formed when platelets and fibrin are deposited on any of these cardiac lesions. The most commonly affected valve is the mitral valve, followed by the aortic valve. In native valve endocarditis in non–drug abusers, men are affected more frequently (male:female ratio, 3:1).

Prosthetic valve endocarditis (PVE) is associated with significant morbidity and mortality and accounts for 10% to 20% of all cases of endocarditis. The aortic prosthetic valve is most commonly affected. If infection occurs within 60 days of valve replacement, it is considered "early," and the pathogen is often hospital acquired through wound inoculation or procedures (Table 3-7). The mortality rate is estimated to be 60% to 70%. The bacteria most commonly isolated in early PVE is *S epidermidis.* Late PVE occurs after the valves have been endothelialized and more closely resembles native valve endocarditis. It is frequently caused by streptococci, but *S epidermidis* still accounts for approximately 25% of the cases (Table 3-8).

The American Heart Association (AHA) recommends antibiotic prophylaxis for patients with specific cardiac lesions when undergoing dental or surgical procedures (Table 3-9). The only cutaneous procedure listed in the recommendations is incision and drainage of infected tissue. Prophylaxis in not recommended for cardiac catheterization or cesarean section, procedures that both involve incisions in the skin (Table 3-10). Organisms encountered during dental and other surgical procedures are different from those encountered during cutaneous surgery, and the AHA-recommended antibiotic regimens may not adequately cover potentially pathogenic skin flora.

Recommendations by Haas and Grekin regarding endocarditis prophylaxis are to direct coverage against staphylococci and streptococci. Because of the very low risk when performing surgery on intact, uninfected skin, prophylaxis is usually not indicated, even in patients with high-risk cardiac lesions. However, judgment is necessary, since prophylaxis may be considered, even on intact skin, in these patients if the procedure is lengthy or the wound is especially large or located in a contaminated area. Prophylaxis should be used in high-risk patients, especially patients with a prosthetic valve, when surgery is being performed on eroded, noninfected skin or infected tissues, since there is a significantly higher risk of bacteremia in these cases.

Antibiotics should be given 1 to 2 hours before surgery so that tissue levels are adequate at the time of surgery. A

TABLE 3-7. *Causes of native valve endocarditis*

Organism	Percentage
Streptococci	50% to 70%
Staphylococci	25%
S. aureus	(23%)
S. epidermidis	(2%)
Enterococci	10%
Culture negative	5% to 10%
Others (fungi, diphtheroids, gram-negative miscellaneous)	5% to 10%

TABLE 3-8. *Causes of prosthetic valve endocarditis*

Organism	Early (<60 days before placement)	Late (>60 days after placement)
Staphylococci	45% to 50%	30% to 40%
S. aureus	(15% to 20%)	(10% to 12%)
S. epidermidis	(25% to 30%)	(23% to 28%)
Streptococci	5% to 10%	25% to 30%
Enterococci	<1%	5% to 10%
Gram-negative bacilli	20%	10% to 12%
Culture negative	5% to 10%	5% to 10%
Others (fungi, diphtheroids, miscellaneous)	15% to 25%	10% to 18%

first-generation cephalosporin or dicloxacillin (1 to 2 g 1 hour before surgery and 500 mg every 6 hours for one or two doses) has been recommended by some authors. In patients who are allergic to penicillin, clindamycin or erythromycin can be used; however, some strains of staphylococci may be resistant to erythromycin. This prophylactic regimen should be used in high-risk patients, whether the procedure is a punch biopsy, shave biopsy, curettage, or excision. To prevent endocarditis in patients with recently implanted cardiac valves (less than 60 days), intravenous vancomycin is recommended for coverage against *S epidermidis* and diphtheroids. These are recommendations for head and neck surgery; however, coverage would be different for surgery in the groin, axilla, or foot. These recommendations do not fully cover all the potential infecting organisms. The incidence of endocarditis caused by organisms such as gram-negative bacilli and fungi has been increasing, and these organisms are not affected by the current regimens.

TABLE 3-9. *Cardiac conditions**

Endocarditis prophylaxis recommended
Prosthetic cardiac valves, including bioprosthetic and homograft valves
Previous bacterial endocarditis, even in the absence of heart disease
Most congenital cardiac malformations
Rheumatic and other acquired valvular dysfunction, even after valvular surgery
Hypertrophic cardiomyopathy
Mitral valve prolapse with valvular regurgitation
Endocarditis prophylaxis not recommended
Isolated secundum atrial septal defect
Surgical repair without residua beyond 6 months of secundum atrial septal defect, ventricular septal defect, or patent ductus arteriosus
Previous coronary artery bypass graft surgery
Mitral valve prolapse without valvular regurgitation†
Physiologic, functional, or innocent heart murmurs
Previous Kawasaki's disease without valvular dysfunction
Previous rheumatic fever without valvular dysfunction
Cardiac pacemakers and implanted defibrillators

* List of selected conditions is not meant to be all-inclusive.
† Individuals who have a mitral valve prolapse associated with thickening and/or redundancy of the valve leaflets may be at increased risk for bacterial endocarditis, particularly men who are 45 years of age or older.

Table used with permission from JAMA, 1990, vol 264; no. 22: p. 2919–2921. Copyright 1990, American Medical Association.

TABLE 3-10. *Dental or surgical procedures**

Endocarditis prophylaxis recommended
Dental procedures known to induce gingival or mucosal bleeding, including professional cleaning
Tonsillectomy and/or adenoidectomy
Surgical operations that involve intestinal or respiratory mucosa
Bronchoscopy with a rigid bronchoscope
Sclerotherapy for esophageal varices
Esophageal dilatation
Gallbladder surgery
Cystoscopy
Urethral dilatation
Urethral catheterization if urinary tract infection is present†
Urinary tract surgery if urinary tract infection is present†
Prostatic surgery
Incision and drainage of infected tissue†
Vaginal hysterectomy
Vaginal delivery in the presence of infection†
Endocarditis prophylaxis not recommended‡
Dental procedures not likely to induce gingival bleeding, such as simple adjustment of orthodontic appliances or fillings above the gum line
Injection of local intraoral anesthetic (except intraligamentary injections)
Shedding of primary teeth
Tympanostomy tube insertion
Endotracheal intubation
Bronchoscopy with a flexible bronchoscope, with or without biopsy
Cardiac catheterization
Endoscopy with or without gastrointestinal tract biopsy
Cardiac catheterization
Endoscopy with or without gastrointestinal tract biopsy
Cesarean section
In the absence of infection for urethral catheterization, dilation and curettage, uncomplicated vaginal delivery, therapeutic abortion, sterilization procedures, or insertion or removal of intrauterine devices

* List of selected procedures is not meant to be all-inclusive.
† In addition to prophylactic regimen for genitourinary tract procedures, antibiotic therapy should be directed against the most likely bacterial pathogen.
‡ In patients who have prosthetic heart valves, a previous history of endocarditis, or surgically constructed systemic-pulmonary shunts or conduits, physicians may choose to administer prophylactic antibiotics even for low-risk procedures that involve the lower respiratory, genitourinary, or gastrointestinal tracts.

Table used with permission from JAMA, 1990, vol 264; no. 22: p. 2919–2921. Copyright 1990, American Medical Association.

The AHA guidelines do not include pacemakers in the list of cardiac conditions at risk for infection. Infections of pacemakers usually occur from wound contamination at the time of placement; otherwise, patients with pacemakers are not thought to be at high risk for infection from a surgical procedure.

ORTHOPEDIC PROCEDURES

The question arises about use of prophylactic antibiotics in patients with prosthetic joints. There are no established guidelines regarding the need for antibiotic prophylaxis in these patients when undergoing cutaneous surgery. Infections of prosthetic joints are often caused by organisms found on the skin, such as *S aureus* and *S epidermidis*, but rarely by streptococci. In reported cases, when infection of the prosthesis has been caused by hematogenous dissemination, the site of origin was an established infection and not related to a cutaneous procedure. In a study of 1000 patients with a total joint replacement, 224 patients subsequently underwent 128 dental and 147 surgical procedures without antibiotic prophylaxis. No patient developed an infection of the arthroplasty. The procedures performed included abdominal, genitourinary tract, endoscopic, and orthopedic operations. The American College of Oral Medicine has not recommended prophylaxis in patients with prosthetic joints when undergoing dental procedures (known to have a higher incidence of bacteremia than the skin procedures). There does not seem to be enough data to justify prophylactic use of antibiotics for these patients who undergo manipulation of the skin unless infected tissues are encountered. However, some physicians do believe that antibiotic prophylaxis is required in these patients before any procedure that is likely to induce transient bacteremia. With any concern, the patients orthopedic surgeon should be consulted about the need for and choice of antibiotic.

The goal in any of the situations with antibiotic prophylaxis is the prevention of infection that would be potentially disastrous. The need for clear guidelines for dermatologic surgery is obvious. Widespread use of antibiotics when not indicated is impractical and costly and would lead to complications associated with their use. Also of concern is the development of resistant strains of bacteria with widespread exposure to antimicrobials.

SUGGESTED READING LIST

1. Ainscow DAP, Denham RA. The risk of haematogenous infection in total joint replacements. J Bone Joint Surg 1984;66B:580.
2. Bencini PL, Galimberti M, Signorini M, Crosti C. Antibiotic prophylaxis of wound infections in skin surgery. Arch Dermatol 1991;127:1357.
3. Browning DK, Martin ME. Erythromycin preparations: which one should be prescribed for SBE chemoprophylaxis? Gen Dentistry 1990;38(3):216–217.
4. Crose PJE, Foord R. A five-year prospective study of 23,649 surgical wounds. Arch Dermatol 1973;107:206.
5. Dajani AS, Bisno AL, Chung KJ, et al. Prevention of bacterial endocarditis: recommendations by the American Heart Association. JAMA 1990;264:2919.
6. Futoryan T, Grande D. Postoperative wound infection rates in dermatologic surgery. Dermatol Surg 1995;21:509.
7. George PM. Dermatologists and antibiotic prophylaxis: a survey. J Am Acad Dermatol 1995;33:418.
8. Haas AF, Grekin RC. Antibiotic prophylaxis in dermatologic surgery. J Am Acad Dermatol 1995;32:155.
9. Halpern AC, Leyden JJ, Dzubow LM, McGinley KJ. The incidence of bacteremia in skin surgery of the head and neck. J Am Acad Dermatol 1988;19:112.
10. Korzeniowski OM, Kaye D. Endocarditis. In: Gorbach SL, Bartlett JA, Blacklow NR, eds. Infectious diseases. Philadelphia: WB Saunders, 1992:548.
11. Richards JH. Bacteremia following irritation of foci of infection. JAMA 1983;99:1496.
12. Roth RR, James WD. Microbiology of the skin: resident flora, ecology, infection. J Am Acad Dermatol 1989;20:367.
13. Sabetta JR, Zitelli JA. The incidence of bacteremia during skin surgery. Arch Dermatol 1987;123:213.
14. Sebben JE. Prophylactic antibiotics in cutaneous surgery. J Dermatol Surg 1985;11:901.
15. Spelman DW, Weinmann A, Spicer WJ. Endocarditis following skin procedures. J Infection 1993;26:185–189.

Textbook of Dermatologic Surgery, edited by John L. Ratz.
Lippincott–Raven Publishers, Philadelphia © 1998.

CHAPTER 4

Anesthesia

David P. Clark

Control of pain is an essential first step in surgery. Cutaneous surgery usually requires anesthesia. Each type of anesthesia adds to the cumulative morbidity of a particular operation. In this chapter the essential physiology, biochemistry, and side effects of anesthetic agents used in cutaneous surgery are discussed.

LOCAL ANESTHETICS

Local anesthetics result in the temporary loss of sensation. Because the effect is rapid, localized, and relatively free of side effects, this technique is ideal for cutaneous surgery. All local anesthetics act by slowing or stopping nerve conduction. Both peripheral motor and sensory nerves can be affected by these anesthetic agents. However, the central nervous system function is left intact.

History

Local anesthetics were first introduced into medical practice in 1884. Reports of South American natives using the coca plant to "numb" had prompted attempts to use this plant for patient comfort. Cocaine was first extracted from the coca plant in 1860, but it was not until 1884 that Kollar and Freud successfully used the purified compound as a topical agent. Halsted and Hall infused cocaine into the brachial vein in late 1884 to achieve regional anesthesia. Procaine was synthesized in 1905, and lidocaine in the mid-1940s.

Local anesthetic agents are functionally divided into two groups: amino amide agents and amino ester groups (Table 4-1). All agents have similar chemical structures containing three components: an amine portion, an intermediate chain, and an aromatic ring portion. Lipid solubility is a function of the aromatic ring, and the amine portion is hydrophilic and assists with water solubility. The intermediate chain contains the ester or amide linkage that serves to classify these anesthetics. (Fig. 1).

Neural membranes are dominated by lipid and represent the site of action for anesthetic agents. Modifications in the aromatic ring affect the ability of agents to diffuse through nerve membranes. However, water solubility is a key feature for compounding, storing, and administering any anesthetic. Modifications of the amine portion of the compound affect the amount of active agent present in the milieu surrounding the nerve. Amides are stable agents

David P. Clark: 1 Hospital Drive, M-175, Columbia MO 65212

TABLE 4-1. *Commonly used anesthetic agents*

Generic name	Trade name	Type
Cocaine	None	Ester
Procaine	Novocain	Ester
Tetracaine	Pontocaine	Ester
Lidocaine	Xylocaine	Amide
Bupivacaine	Marcaine	Amide
Mepivacaine	Carbocaine	Amide
Prilocaine	Citanest	Amide
Etidocaine	Duranest	Amide

TABLE 4-2. *Physiology of common anesthetic agents*

Generic name	Metabolism	Onset	Duration (MIN) No EPI	Duration (MIN) w/EPI
Cocaine	Plasma	Rapid	45	No Data
Procaine	Plasma	Rapid	15–30	30–90
Tetracaine	Plasma	Slow	120–240	240–480
Lidocaine	Hepatic	Rapid	30–130	60–400
Bupivacaine	Hepatic	Slow	120–240	240–480
Mepivacaine	Hepatic	Slow	30–120	60–400
Prilocaine	Hepatic	Slow	30–120	60–400
Etidocaine	Hepatic	Slow	200	300

and can be stored for long periods. Amino esters are degraded in the plasma by cholinesterase enzymes. The para-aminobenzoic acid metabolite produces the allergic reactions reported with ester anesthetics.

Pharmacology

Anesthetic agents differ in their intrinsic potency, onset, and duration of action. Traditional pharmacology suggests that the profile of individual agents is determined by their unique physicochemical characteristics. However, it is the interaction of these compounds with the organic tissue that determines effect. Human tissue has its own unique physical chemical and biologic activity. Indeed, it is this complex interaction that produces pain relief. For the clinician, isolated chemical data regarding anesthetic agents acquire new meaning when considered in a specific tissue or tissues (see Table 4-2).

Mechanism of Action

Impermeability of the nerve cell membrane to sodium ions in the outside milieu and potassium ion inside the cell pro-

duces a stable electrical potential difference between the intracellular and extracellular fluid. Depolarization of the nerve cell causes sodium channels within the membrane to open and abolishes the resting potential. Depolarization of the nerve membrane is propagated along the nerve, producing impulse conduction. Blockade of the nerve impulse by local anesthetics is mediated in part by direct action on specific receptors in the sodium channel inhibiting sodium flux.

Anesthetic Potency

Lipid solubility appears to mediate isolated anesthetic potency. Wildsmith et al. defined a precise relationship between lipid solubility and concentrations of anesthetic required to block nerve conduction. The effects noted between anesthetics in isolated nerve functions may not be so apparent *in vivo*. Lidocaine is often reported to have high potency. While experiments using isolated nerve data support this assertion, the strong vasodilator qualities of lidocaine in human tissue cause rapid vascular absorption, and less drug is available for nerve blockade. Etidocaine is highly lipid soluble and in isolated nerves produces profound blockade. However, because this agent is sequestered in adipose tissue, again, relatively few molecules are available for anesthesia.

Latency of Conduction Blockade

In isolated nerve preparations onset of anesthetic action is correlated with the agent's negative logarithm of the acid ionization constant (pK_a). The degree of ionization of the individual agents determines the rate of diffusion for local anesthetics across nerve membranes. In general, neutral bases pass through the nerve membranes faster than the cationic forms. All local anesthetics have a pK_a greater than physiologic pH. Agents with a low pKa have more active drug in the ionized form and therefore exhibit a rapid onset. Onset of anesthetic action in the human may also be somewhat concentration-dependent (Fig. 2).

Duration of Action

Duration of local anesthetic action is related to the degree of protein binding. This binding action to a specific receptor

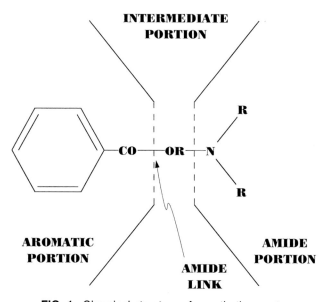

FIG. 1. Chemical structure of anesthetic agents.

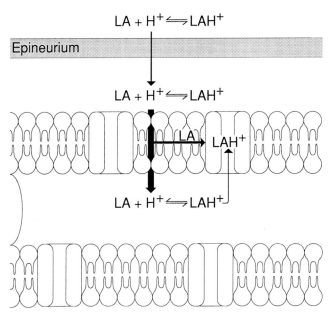

$$LA + H^+ \rightleftharpoons LAH^+$$

Epineurium

$$LA + H^+ \rightleftharpoons LAH^+$$

$$LA + H^+ \rightleftharpoons LAH^+$$

FIG. 2. Movement of anesthetic agents across membranes.

mediates sodium channel blockade and therefore anesthesia. Perhaps of equal importance in determining actual anesthetic duration is the effect of a given agent on local blood vessels. Some agents (cocaine and ropivacaine) cause vasoconstriction and therefore longer anesthetic activity. The addition of epinephrine prolongs the action of all anesthetic agents.

Metabolism

The ester group of local anesthetics is hydrolyzed in the plasma by pseudocholinesterase. The rare patient with a deficiency of pseudocholinesterase may have an increased risk of drug toxicity. Amides are metabolized in the liver. Patients with liver disease may be at greater risk of toxicity for lidocaine and other related drugs.

Dosage

Actual drug performance and peak serum levels represent a delicate balance. Concentration of injected anesthetic, vascularity of the site, duration of injection, and the host's ability to metabolize drugs all play an important role in determining *in vivo* drug function.

Anesthetics and Pregnancy

Lidocaine is considered a nonteratogenic drug and can be used with safety during pregnancy. No evidence currently exists linking exposure to local anesthetics during the first 4 months of pregnancy and the subsequent development of fetal deformities. Lidocaine is significantly metabolized dur-

ing the first pass through the maternal liver. However, lidocaine does cross the placental membrane, and the fetus will be exposed to the drug.

Use of lidocaine is considered safe in children. Parabens, if used for stabilization of the anesthetic, are selectively bound to albumin. This raises the possibility of displacement of bilirubin if lidocaine is used in the jaundiced newborn. Paraben-free solutions should be used in all newborns.

Mixtures of Anesthetics

Combining different local anesthetics may use to advantage the useful properties of each drug. Most commonly, a long-acting anesthetic is combined with a short-acting drug. For example, bupivacaine has a prolonged onset but lasts 2 to 4 hours and is combined with lidocaine, taking advantage of this drug's quick onset. At least one study suggests that these combinations do not meet expectations. However, many surgeons often use a short-acting amide anesthetic followed sequentially with a long-acting agent. Because the activity, onset, and length of action in part depend on the pH of the treatment site, two different agents will have somewhat different activities than could be predicted by *in vitro* activity.

Additions to Local Anesthetics

Substances are often added to local anesthetics to improve effect. These additives are important to understand. By modifying the local anesthetic, the drug-tissue interaction is manipulated. Often these modifications produce a superior milieu for surgery but must be balanced by possible drug toxicity or adverse reactions.

Vasoconstrictors

All local anesthetics with the exception of cocaine are direct vasodilators. By relaxation of vascular smooth muscle, anesthetics cause increased bleeding at the operative site. Vasoconstrictors added to the anesthetic have been helpful in reducing operative bleeding. In addition, vasoconstrictors decrease the absorption of anesthetics and allow a greater total amount of drug to be used safely.

Epinephrine is the most common vasoconstrictor used in conjunction with a local anesthetic. Proprietary companies often supply premixed combinations of lidocaine with epinephrine in a concentration of 1:100,000.

Epinephrine is a strong β-agonist. β-Adrenergic stimulation causes restlessness, increased heart rate, and palpitations. These drug-related symptoms may be a minor problem in patients with an adequate cardiac reserve; however, in individuals with impaired cardiac function the increased cardiac work may have disastrous effects.

Epinephrine undergoes oxidation with exposure to air.

Without the addition of preservatives lidocaine-epinephrine combinations contain less than 2% of the original epinephrine concentration after 2 weeks. The preservatives placed in the commonly available lidocaine-epinephrine mixtures produce a very acidic solution. In addition to increased pain with injection, the lowered pH of the solution also alters the amount of drug absorbed at the tissue-nerve interface. Although these preservatives decrease the oxidation of the vasoconstrictor, over weeks the effective epinephrine concentration does decrease.

Epinephrine added to lidocaine does provide excellent vasoconstriction. The onset of vasoconstriction ranges from 5 to 15 minutes after injection. The skin pallor produced by the vasoconstriction is short-lived, usually resolving within 30 to 45 minutes. However, an occasional patient has prolonged pallor and/or a subsequent cyanosis. The elimination of minute oozing in the operative site is a welcome event, but the artificial hemostasis caused by the drug may be the source of delayed postoperative bleeding. In addition, the use of epinephrine on digits is to be discouraged. Case reports of skin necrosis and even gangrene have been reported in patients with impaired vasculature (e.g., diabetes). Although some authorities suggest the deletion of vasoconstrictors when operating on the nose and ears, few data support any additional risk.

A potential interaction between epinephrine and β-blockers has been reported. The peripheral vascular β$_2$-receptors are blocked by the β-blocker, allowing epinephrine's unopposed α-receptor stimulation to produce marked hypertension and subsequent reflex bradycardia. In a 1986 study, Dzubow showed that this interaction is extremely rare. Selective β-blockers such as atenolol are thought to cause this uncontrolled hypertensive response to a much lesser degree than "unselective" β-blockers such as propranolol.

The use of vasoconstrictors with lidocaine decreases the absorption of the anesthetic agent. Smaller amounts of drug can produce a longer duration of action when vasoconstrictors are used. Because of the more tightly tissue-bound characteristics of the long-acting anesthetics (i.e., bupivacaine and etidocaine), vasoconstrictors have less effect.

The most effective concentration of vasoconstrictor produces the maximal effect with the least morbidity. Winton suggested that concentrations stronger than 1:200,000 produce no greater hemostasis or prolonged anesthesia but do increase adverse drug effects. This requires a mixing of the commercially available concentration of 1:100,000 with the same anesthetic without epinephrine to achieve the more dilute concentrations of 1:200,000 or 1:300,000.

Sodium Bicarbonate

Lidocaine and most other local anesthetics have an alkaline or neutral pH. As mentioned earlier, epinephrine is quite labile in an alkaline pH. To prevent this degradation of epinephrine, most commercial preparations are buffered to an acidic pH. Lidocaine at an acidic pH results in considerably more pain to the patient than an injection with a similar compound at neutral pH. Sodium bicarbonate added to the lidocaine:epinephrine mixture produces less pain with injection. Adding 1 ml of 8.4% sodium bicarbonate to each 10 ml of 1% lidocaine with epinephrine produces a neutral solution. Neutralized solutions with epinephrine degrade at a rate of 25% per week. In addition, many concerns have been raised concerning the effectiveness of buffered lidocaine. Although this dilution does not affect the concentration of lidocaine, the basic pH may result in a shorter duration of effective anesthesia.

Allergy to Local Anesthetics

Allergic reactions to the commonly used local anesthetics are rare, accounting for less than 1% of reported adverse reactions. Most reports of allergic responses involve the use of agents from the ester category. The prototype esther anesthetic, procaine, can cause either a type 1 anaphylactic or type 4 delayed hypersensitivity allergic response. Although no cross-reactivity between ester anesthetics and amide anesthetics has been documented, procaine can cross-react with other ester anesthetics, compounds containing paraben preservatives, and procaine penicillin preparations. Additive agents, especially preservatives, have been implicated as the cause of many immediate type 1 allergic reactions initially thought to be due to the anesthetic agent.

Type 1 reactions to amide anesthetics are unusual. Immunoglobulin E (IgE)-mediated responses include hives, rhinorrhea, bronchospasm, and angioedema. For patients with a history of allergy to "caine" local anesthetics, skin testing and incremental challenge may be appropriate. Patients who tolerate pinprick testing and subcutaneous challenge are at no greater risk for an anaphylactic reaction than the general public.

An alternate strategy to provide local pain relief for minor skin procedures is the use of 1% diphenhydramine injected subcutaneously. Because diphenhydramine causes vasodilation, epinephrine at a 1:100,000 concentration is often added. Sedation is possible but rarely a practical problem when small amounts are used. More worrisome is a report of digital gangrene following use of diphenhydramine as a local anesthetic in a finger. Studies have validated the use of 1% diphenhydramine for minor skin procedures with less discomfort than lidocaine. In addition, no clinically important complications were noted in 24 patients, including digits, who received treatment with diphenhydramine.

Sodium chloride has been used for local anesthesia. While some pain relief is possible, procedures of any magnitude require additional measures.

Contact hypersensitivity to anesthetic agents has been reported. Benzocaine, a synthetic ester anesthetic, is a potent sensitizer. Topical lidocaine in concentrations ranging from 2.5% to 30% has produced true contact allergy reproducible with patch testing.

REGIONAL ANESTHESIA

Injection of anesthetic agents (Figs. 3–10) in close proximity to a sensory nerve is an effective, efficient method of obtaining anesthesia. A specific nerve block provides pain relief without the local distortion sometimes seen with local infiltration at a surgical site. In addition, use of topical mucosal anesthesia before intraoral nerve block injections may allow far more patient comfort than local infiltration methods alone. Specific blockade of peripheral nerves is especially useful for local procedures involving the head, neck, and upper extremities.

Field block anesthesia involves infiltration of local anesthetic proximal to a surgical site. By encircling an operative site with anesthetic, pain control is obtained without distorting the surgical site. Proper technique allows infusion of anesthetic in the same fascial compartment as the relevant nerve to be blocked. Direct injection into the nerve is to be carefully avoided, since permanent nerve injury may result.

The central face lends itself to use of field block anesthesia. The multiple foramina provide direct access to the innervating nerve trunks (Figs. 3–5,10). The infraorbital nerve exits the infraorbital foramen and innervates a majority of the medial cheek and nose. The mental nerve, exiting the body at the mental foramen, supplies sensation to the lower

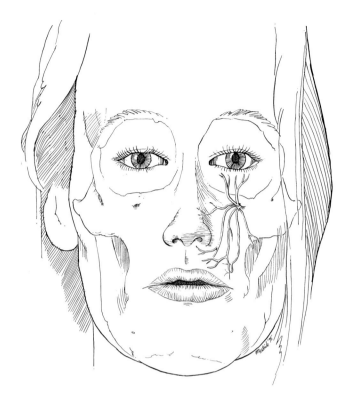

FIG. 4. Infraorbital nerve distribution.

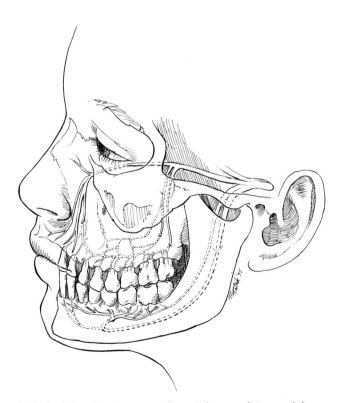

FIG. 3. Infraorbital nerve and mental nerve: intercranial portion.

lip and chin. The forehead can be anesthetized with a field block of the supraorbital nerve foramen as located on a line drawn vertically through the pupil in the neutral position.

Field anesthesia of the infraorbital and mental nerves can be achieved by a cuticular or an intraoral approach. The intraoral approach may actually involve less pain, since the mucosal surfaces can be effectively rendered painless with topical anesthesia.

To produce a block of the infraorbital nerve, the needle is introduced just lateral to the palpated foramen (Fig. 6). The needle is then directed inferomedially using the distal portion of the nasal ala as a landmark and passes through the fat into the appropriate fascial plane. Always ensure a nonintravascular location, with simple aspiration before injection of anesthesia. Occasionally, immediate parasthesias of the upper lip or oral mucosa signal close proximity to the nerve trunk. When using the intraoral method, the needle enters the mucosa at the level of the canine incisor (Fig. 7). With the needle directed toward the foramen the nerve trunk is approached in an inferosuperior direction.

Due to the complex innervation of the central face, blockade of the infraorbital nerve often must be supplemented with a small amount of local anesthesia. The addition of local anesthetic with epinephrine is frequently welcome for both comfort and hemostasis. Bilateral infraorbital blockade is the anesthetic method of choice for resurfacing upper-lip rhytides. Dermabrasion or high-energy CO_2 laser surgery is not well served by the distortion of injected local infiltration.

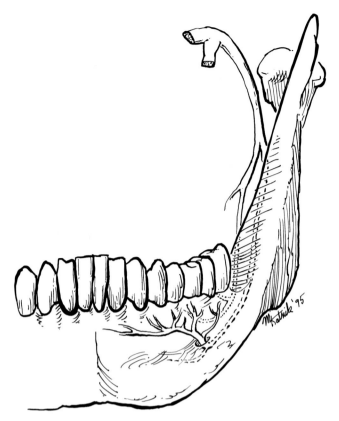

FIG. 5. Mental nerve: intermandible course.

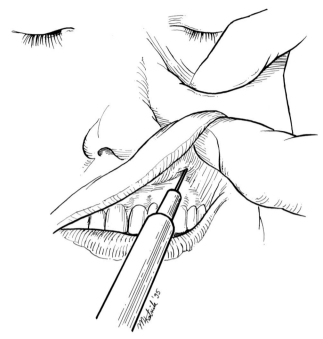

FIG. 7. Injection technique for infraorbital field block (intraoral approach).

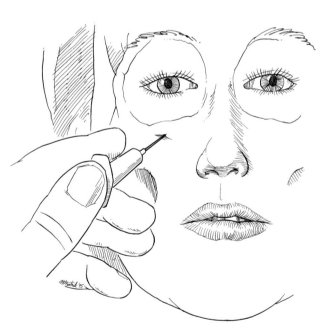

FIG. 6. Technique for infraorbital nerve field block (cutaneous approach).

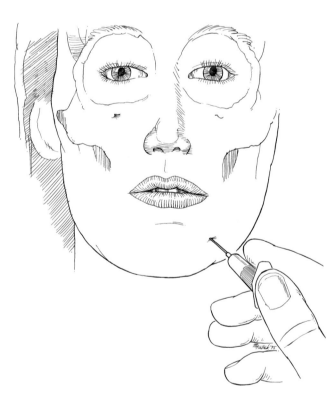

FIG. 8. Technique for mental nerve field block (cutaneous approach).

Submental nerve blockade is very useful for achieving anesthesia of the lower lip and chin. The nerve exits the mandible approximately 2.0 to 2.5 cm from the facial midline. The nerve can be approached from the skin, introducing the needle slightly medially to the palpated foramen and injecting anesthetic in a mediolateral fashion (Fig. 8). The oral approach is often more satisfactory. Locate the first bicuspid, and advance the needle through the inferior labial sulcus in a inferolateral direction (Fig. 9).

Local Anesthesia of Fingers and Toes

Digital nerve block of fingers is a commonly used form of regional anesthesia. Each finger is supplied with two superior and two inferior digital nerves. To effectively anesthetize the digit, one of two methods can be used. The needle is introduced through the skin on the side of the finger just distal to the metacarpophalangeal joint. By directing the needle inferiorly and then superiorly, both inferior and superior digital nerves can be anesthetized. Occasionally, another injection site at the base of the digit is used. The more sensitive palmar skin is entered at the base of the digit in the midline. The needle is placed just proximal to the digital-palmar crease and is directed laterally and distally. Care must be taken to anesthetize an adequate length of each nerve in order to achieve complete pain relief. Usually 2 ml of 2% plain lidocaine is adequate. Large volumes (greater than 6 to 8 ml) may result in circulatory compromise.

Wrist Blocks

Median Nerve

The median nerve resides in the carpal tunnel between the palmaris longus tendon and the flexor carpi radialis. Dorsiflex the wrist to emphasize the tendons in question, then insert the needle at the proximal crease of the wrist. Injecting the wrist in a proximal to distal fashion provides nerve blockade.

Ulnar Nerve

The ulnar nerve is located medial and slightly deep to the easily located ulnar artery. Inject subcutaneously from the proximal wrist crease over the flexor carpi ulnaris tendon to approximately the midpoint of the dorsal wrist.

Radial Nerve

Although radial nerve block is possible, often the sensory nerves of the radial nerve are difficult to completely treat. Just lateral to the radial artery at the proximal wrist crease, infiltrate the subcutaneous space to the midpoint of the dorsal wrist.

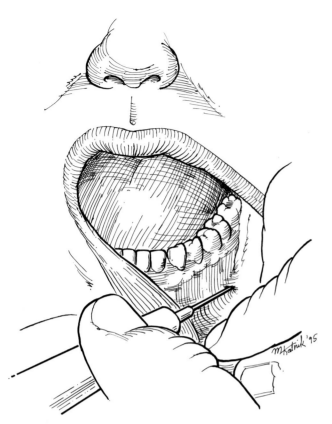

FIG. 9. Injection technique for a mental nerve field block (intraoral approach).

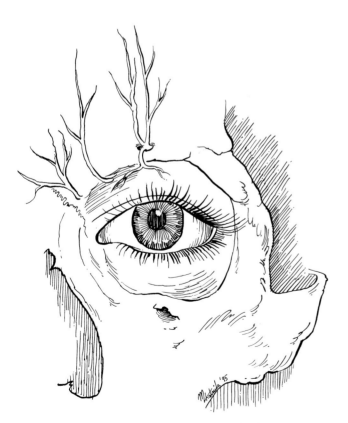

FIG. 10. Supraorbital nerve distribution.

Ankle and Foot Nerve Block

Sural Nerve

The sural nerve is a combination of branches from the tibial nerve and the peroneal nerve. The volar surface of the foot and heel has sensory innervation from the sural nerve. This nerve is superficial and hence available to be blocked posterolateral to the lateral malleolus. At the level of the midpoint of the lateral malleolus, between the lateral edge of the Achilles tendon and the malleolus, the needle is introduced and the subcutaneous space injected with 2 to 4 ml 2% lidocaine.

Penile Nerve Block

The penis is innervated by two dorsal nerves. Effective sensory blockade is carried out with an injection in the sub-pubic space near the posterior inferior aspect of the symphysis. The infusion is then carried laterally in a "ring" fashion at the base of the penis. Care must be taken not to infuse so much anesthesia as to impair the vascular supply.

TUMESCENT TECHNIQUES

Jeffery Klein introduced low-concentration lidocaine anesthesia (tumescent technique) for cutaneous surgery in the late 1980s. Defined as direct infiltration of dilute lidocaine (<1 mg/L), epinephrine (<1 mg/L), and sodium bicarbonate (10 mEq/L), tumescent anesthesia provides excellent pain control with minimal morbidity. Initially used for liposuction, this method of local anesthesia has been successfully used in hair transplantation, removal of skin tumors, localized phlebectomy, laser surgery, and dermabrasion.

Klein noted that although the literature firmly stated the individual safe maximal dosage of lidocaine with epinephrine to be 7 mg/kg body weight, no data existed to support this assertion. In fact, lidocaine's initial release in 1943 was predicated on lidocaine having a similar pharmacologic profile to procaine. Almost all the current toxicity and dosage guidelines have been derived from studies concerning intravenous infusion of lidocaine.

Systemic lidocaine toxicity depends on the peak plasma concentration of drug. In nonintravenous infusion methods of lidocaine use, the peak plasm concentration varies with the rate of lidocaine absorption from distant tissues. Klein, in a landmark study published in 1990, infused 35 mg/kg of lidocaine with 1 mg/L of epinephrine into subcutaneous fat with complete safety. Peak lidocaine levels were quite low, and a maximum level was reached between 12 and 24 hours after anesthesia administration. Pain control and hemostasis were prolonged and associated with few side effects. Studies by Lillis et al. confirmed this finding and expanded the "safe" infusion limits to 50 mg/kg and higher without achieving toxic peak plasma lidocaine levels.

Klein found an interesting relationship between peak plasma levels and lidocaine concentration. Traditional teaching suggested that in an intramuscular lidocaine injection absorption rates were independent of lidocaine concentration (1% to 10%). During tumescent lidocaine infusion into subcutaneous fat, dilute lidocaine concentrations are absorbed at a much slower rate than standard 1% to 2% concentrations. In addition, the data confirmed that slow infusion rates result in slower systemic absorption of lidocaine than do rapid infusion rates.

The site of infusion matters. As could be anticipated, the absorption kinetics of lidocaine from the peripheral compartment to the vascular compartment depends on the vascularity of the distant compartment. This observation is confirmed by the finding that tumescent infusion of the face for facelift surgery results in peak plasma levels 4 to 5 hours after infusion (lidocaine concentration, 0.18% with 1:563,500 epinephrine).

INFUSION TECHNIQUES

Subcutaneous infiltration is started with a small (25 to 30 gauge) needle. A 20-gauge spinal needle is then used to complete the infiltration of subcutaneous fat. Use of an infusion pump often speeds the process. The deepest planes of the fat should be infiltrated first, and a careful "fanning" of the tracts is necessary to achieve complete anesthesia. Often the surgeon must wait 15 to 20 minutes after completing the infusion to ensure sufficient vasoconstriction and anesthesia.

Initially the tumescent technique used lidocaine concentrations of 0.1% lidocaine. With experience, diminished concentrations of 0.025% lidocaine have been used effectively. However, some areas, notably the abdomen, require the higher concentrations for effective pain relief.

TOPICAL ANESTHETICS

The epidermis is an effective barrier to the effective use of most topical anesthetics. The physical chemistry of most anesthetics precludes their passage into the dermis in any clinically relevant manner. Mucous membranes, without a stratified epidermis, are much more amenable to topical anesthetics.

Cocaine

The well-known agent of cocaine has been an effective topical anesthetic for many years. Cocaine, a potent vasoconstrictor, has been most effective in minor procedures on mucous membranes and the upper airway. Most frequently supplied as a 1% to 4% topical solution, effective anesthesia is accomplished in approximately 5 minutes after application and last 20 to 30 minutes. Toxicity can occur with doses as low as 20 mg. Tachycardia and hypertension are the usual early findings of drug toxicity. The large scope of illegal cocaine use has made this drug much more difficult to obtain and retain in a busy clinic.

Benzocaine

Benzocaine is a synthetically produced ester anesthetic that is primarily used for topical anesthesia. Available commercially as a 20% gel or a 2.5% to 20% solution, benzocaine is most effective for rapid superficial mucous membrane anesthesia. The onset of activity is within minutes but is short-lived.

Topical Lidocaine

Topical lidocaine in concentrations up to 30% has been used on keratinized skin. Anesthesia is variable and requires 45 to 120 minutes to achieve its full effect after application. The use of occlusion or dermal patch delivery system has made the process more efficient. As might be expected, techniques to strip the epidermis before application of the topical anesthetic improve penetration.

Mucous membranes are effectively treated with 2% viscous jelly or a 4% topical solution. Onset of anesthesia is short, with a duration of 15 to 45 minutes. Lidocaine in spray form has been used effectively on genital mucosa for minor laser surgery. Total dose provided effective analgesia in 3 to 5 minutes and had a duration of 20 to 30 minutes.

Recently 2.5% lidocaine has been combined with 2.5% prilocaine and marketed as Eutectic Mixture of Local Anesthetics (EMLA). EMLA is supplied in a cream base and is applied under an occlusive dressing. Onset of anesthesia is variable but often requires at least 45 minutes. This preparation has been most helpful in pediatric oncology and cutaneous laser surgery. Often a combination of topical EMLA followed by injectable lidocaine (full-strength or tumescent anesthesia) allows safe, comfortable outpatient surgical procedures in children that would have required general anesthesia in the past. EMLA is not usually adequate anesthesia for resurfacing procedures, dermabrasion, or CO_2 laser because the level of effective pain control is not deep enough.

Iontophoresis of lidocaine has been successfully used for superficial surgical procedures. Four percent lidocaine is delivered using a galvanic generator and a polymer gel-medication electrode. Currently the technique is limited by the maximal size of the treatment electrode (2×4 cm) and the prolonged times needed for obtaining anesthesia (20 to 90 minutes). However, this method has much potential for outpatient minor surgery.

Tetracaine

Tetracaine is a long-acting ester anesthetic. The primary use for this agent is as a topical agent in ophthalmology. A 0.5% solution is used in small amounts. Comparative studies suggest that in these small amounts tetracaine is safe and effective.

SUGGESTED READING LIST

1. Aldrete JA, O'Higgins JW. Evaluation of patients with history of allergy to local anesthetic drugs. South Med J 1971;64:1118.
2. Alper MH. Agents in obstetrics: mother, fetus, and newborn. In Smith NT, Miller RD, Corgascio AN, eds. Drug interactions in anesthesia. Philadelphia: Lea & Febiger, 1981.
3. Barer MR, McAllen MK. Hypersensitivity to local anesthetics: a direct challenge test with lidocaine for definitive diagnosis. Br Med J 1982; 284:1229.
4. Brown DT, Beamish D, Wildsmith JAW. Allergic reaction to amide local anaesthetic. Br J Anaesth 1981;53:435.
5. Covino BG. Pharmacology of local anesthetic agents. Br J Anaesth 1986;58:701.
6. Courtney KR. Mechanism of frequency-dependent inhibition of sodium currents in frog myelinated nerve by the lidocaine derivative GEA-968. J Pharmacol Exp Ther 1975;195:225.
7. deJong RH. Toxic effects of local anesthetics. JAMA 1978;239:1166.
8. Dzubow LM. The interaction between propranolol and epinephrine as observed in patients undergoing Mohs surgery. J Am Acad Dermatol 1986;15:71.
9. Ernst AA, Marvez-Valls E, Mall G, et al. 1% lidocaine verses 0.5% diphenhydramine for local anesthesia in minor laceration repair. Ann Emerg Med 1994;23(6):1328.
10. Feinstein MB. Reaction of local anesthetics with phospholipids: a possible chemical basis for anesthesia. J Gen Physiol 1964;48:357.
11. Feldman HS, Covino BG. Comparative motor-blocking effects of bupivacaine and ropivacaine, a new amino amide local anesthetic, in the rat and dog. Anesth Analg 1988;69:1047.
12. Foster CA, Aston SJ. Propranolol-epinephrine interaction: a potential disaster. Plast Reconstr Surg 1983;72:74.
13. Galindo A, Benavides O, Ortega de Munos, et al. Comparison of anesthetic solutions used in lumbar and caudal epidural anesthesia. Anesth Analg 1978;57:175.
14. Galindo A, Witcher T. Mixtures of local anesthetics: bupivacaine-chloroprocaine. Anesth Analg 1980;59:683.
14a. Garrison FH. An introduction to the history of medicine. Philadelphia: W.B. Saunders Company, 1926.
15. Glinert RJ, Zachary CB. Local anesthetic allergy: its recognition and avoidance. J Dermatol Surg Oncol 1991;17:491.
16. Gormley DE. Cutaneous surgery and the pregnant patient. J Am Acad Dermatol 1990;23:248.
17. Grant RL, Acosta D. Comparative toxicity of tetracaine, proparacaine and cocaine evaluated with primary cultures of rabbit corneal epithelial cells. Exp Eye Res 1994;58(4):469.
18. Green SM, Rothrock SG, Gorchynski J. Validation of diphenhydramine as a dermal local anesthetic. Ann Emerg Med 1994;23(6):1284.
19. Grekin RC, Auletta MJ. Local anesthesia in dermaotlogic surgery. J Am Acad Dermatol 1988;19:599.
20. Hansten PD. Beta-adrenergic blockers and epinephrine. Drug Interact Newslett 1983;3:41.
21. Heinonen OP, Slone D, Shapiro S. Birth defects and drugs in pregnancy. Littleton, MA: Publishing Sciences Group, 1977:357–365.
22. Hille B. Local anaesthetics: hydrophilic and hydrophobic pathways for the drug-receptor reaction. J Gen Physiol 1977;60:497.
23. Hutton KP, Podolsky A, Roenigk RK, Wood MB. Regional anesthesia of the hand for dermatologic surgery. J Dermatol Surg Oncol 1991; 17:881.
24. Incaudo G, Schatz M, Patterson R, et al. Administration of local anesthetics to patients with a history of prior adverse reaction. J Allergy Clin Immunol 1978;61:339.
25. Kano T, Nakamura M, Hashiguchi A, et al. Skin pretreatments for shortening onset of dermal patch anesthesia with 3% GA MHPh 2Na–10% lidocaine gel mixture. Anesth Analg 1992;75(4):555.
26. Kennard CD, Whitaker DC. Iontophoresis of lidocaine for anesthesia during pulsed dye laser treatment of port-wine stains. J Dermatol Surg Oncol 1992;18:287.
27. Kitamoto Y, Kana T, Mishima M, et al. Dermal patch anesthesia: pain-free puncture of blood access in hemodialysis patients. Am J Kidney Dis 1992;20(5):489.
27a. Klein JA. Anesthesia for liposuction in dermatologic surgery. J Dermatol Surg and Oncol 1988;14:1124.
27b. Klein JA. Tumescent technique for regional anesthesia permits lido-

caine doses of 35mg/kg for liposuction. J Dermatol Surg Onc 1990; 16(3):248–63.

28. Kollar C. On the use of cocaine for producing anesthesia on the eye. Lancet 1884;2:990.

29. Kuhnert BR, Knapp DR, Kuhnert PM, et al. Maternal fetal and neonatal metabolism of lidocaine. Clin Pharmacol Ther 1976;26:213.

29a. Lillis PJ. The tumescent technique for liposuction surgery. Dermatologic Clinics. 1990;8(3)439–50.

30. Maloney JM, Bezzant JL, Stephen RL, Petelenz TJ. Iontophoretic administration of lidocaine anesthesia in office practice: an appraisal. J Dermato Surg Oncol 1992;18(11):937.

31. Nagel JE, Fuscaldo JT, Fireman P. Paraben allergy. JAMA 1977;237:1594.

32. Ramsdell WM. Severe reaction to diphenhydramine. J Am Acad Dermatol 21:1318 (letter to the editor).

33. Rasmussen LF, Ahlfors CE, Wennberg RP. The effect of paraben preservatives on albumin blinding of bilirubin. J Pediatr 1976;89:475.

34. Roberts EW, Loveless H. The utilization of diphenhydramine for production of local anesthesia: report of a case. Texas Dent J 1979;97:13.

35. Sperling LC, Weber CB, Rodman OG. Toward less painful anesthesia: water, saline, and lidocaine. J Dermatol Surg Oncol 1981;7:730.

36. Sweet PT, Magee DA, Holland AJC. Duration of intradermal anesthesia with mixtures of bupivacaine and lidocaine. Can Anaesth Soc J 1982; 29(5):481.

37. Wagner RF, Flores CA, Argo LF. A double-blind placebo-controlled study of a 5% lidocaine/prilocaine cream (EMLA) for topical anesthesia during thermolysis. J Dermatol Surg Oncol 1994;20:148.

38. Wiener SG: Injectable sodium chloride as a local anesthetic for skin surgery. Cutis 1979;23:342.

39. Winton GB. Anesthesia for dermatologic surgery. J Dermatol Surg Oncol 1988;14:41.

40. van der Burght M, Schonemann NK, Laursen JK, Arendt-Nielsen L, Bjerring P. Onset and duration of hypoalgesia following applicaiton of lidocaine spray on genital mucosa. Acta Obstet Gynecol Scand 1994; 73(10):809.

41. v.d. Berg GM, Lillieborg S, Stolz E. Lidocaine/prilocaine cream (EMLA[R]) versus infiltration anaesthesia: a comparison of the analgesic efficacy for punch biopsy and electrocoagulation of genital warts in men. Genitourin Med 1992;68(3):162.

42. Verlander JM, Johns ME. The clinical use of cocaine. Otolaryngol Clin North Am 1981;14:521.

42a. Wildsmith JA, Gissen AJ, Takman B, Covino BG. Differential nerve blockade: esters v. amides and the influence of pKA. British Journal of Anaesthesia 1987;59(3):379–84.

Textbook of Dermatologic Surgery, edited by John L. Ratz.
Lippincott–Raven Publishers, Philadelphia © 1998.

CHAPTER 5

Conscious Sedation and General and Pediatric Anesthesia

Julio Hernandez and Isaac Perez

ANESTHESIA IN DERMATOLOGIC SURGERY

In the past decade dermatologic surgery has undergone many changes. Traditionally, local anesthesia has been sufficient for most dermatologic surgery procedures. As dermatologists become more sophisticated and proficient in more complex procedures, and with the current surge in dermatologic cosmetic surgery, the need for deeper levels of anesthesia has increased. These include regional anesthesia, conscious sedation, and general anesthesia. In the outpatient surgery setting intravenous (IV) sedation as a supplement to local anesthesia is now commonplace. This requires a more thorough knowledge of the appropriate use of IV and local anesthetic agents, potential drug interactions, and advanced cardiac life support techniques.

Dermatologic surgery anesthesia has the goal of slow absorption with moderate sedation. As a result, rather than a bolus of IV infusion of narcotics or other anesthetic agents, the sublingual, subcutaneous, intramuscular (IM), and slow IV infusion methods of administration of these agents are preferably used.

The appropriate management of patients undergoing regional anesthesia, conscious sedation, or general anesthesia begins with proper patient selection and preparation. These include a thorough medical and drug history, including use of illicit substances and alcohol. When the administration

of large volumes and doses of medications are contemplated, history may include the following:

Allergies: Including previous reaction to local anesthetics
Back and neck: Patient with recurrent back or neck pain might not tolerate a lengthy procedure under local anesthesia
Cardiac: Congestive heart failure, myocardial infarction, angina, hypertension, arrhythmias, rheumatic fever
Central nervous system: Fainting, seizures, localized weakness
Dental status: Loose teeth, bridges, and dentures pose a potential for airway obstruction
Gastrointestinal tract: Liver disease; hiatal hernia or peptic ulcer disease might be exacerbated by surgery
Infectious diseases: Acquired immunodeficiency syndrome (AIDS), positive human immunodeficiency virus (HIV) test result; positive hepatitis-B antigen; herpes labialis
Medications: Including but not limited to acetylsalicylic acid and other nonsteroidal antiinflammatory drugs, monoamine oxidase (MAO) inhibitors, phenothiazines, tricyclic antidepressants, βtoblockers
Pregnancy
Pseudocholinesterase deficiency
Pulmonary: Bronchitis, asthma, emphysema, smoking
Renal
Thyroid: Epinephrine reaction could trigger thyroid storm

A general physical examination should be performed, and, if indicated, clearance for anesthesia by the primary care physician should be obtained if risk factors are involved. This examination should include baseline vital signs, includ-

Julio Hernandez: Mohs Micrographic Surgery, PO Box 6599, Glendale AZ 85312

Isaac Perez: Mohs Micrographic Surgery, 200 West Esplanade, Suite 106, Kenner, LA 70065

ing height, weight, and age. This information allows the physician to assess the physical status of the patient and assign the patient a category, following the American Society of Anesthesiologist Physical Status Classification (Table 5-1). Patients who fall into classes 1 and 2 are suitable candidates for ambulatory surgery.

Class 3 patients have been approved for outpatient surgery but only under supervision of an anesthesiologist. In addition, it would be prudent to assess the patient's emotional state, communication ability, and perceptions regarding the procedure and sedation.

The safety and well-being of the patient are primary considerations. To achieve these, proper intraoperative monitoring is required. The following equipment should be present and ready for use in the room where IV conscious sedation is administered:

Oxygen
Suction
Bag and mask devices
Oral and nasopharyngeal airways and endotracheal tubes in various sizes
Sphygmomanometer or noninvasive blood pressure monitor
Electrocardiograph
Pulse oximeter

Monitoring parameters should include the following:

Respiratory rate
Oxygen saturation
Blood pressure
Cardiac rate and rhythm
Level of consciousness
Skin condition

The degree of monitoring varies with the degree of anesthesia. For instance, full monitoring is not needed if only local, regional, or tumescent anesthesia is to be used. In these situations, the surgeon could be in charge of the surgery and the monitoring. On the other hand, if deeper levels of anesthesia are required, the surgeon would be better served having a nurse anesthetist or an anesthesiologist in charge of the monitoring. In this manner, the physician can dedicate

TABLE 5-1. *American Society of Anesthesiologists Physical Status Classification*

Class	Description
1	A healthy patient
2	A patient with mild systemic disease
3	A patient with severe systemic disease that is not incapacitating
4	Life-threatening systemic disturbance
5	Moribund patient with little chance of survival
E + class no.	Any patient in one of the above classes who is operated on as an emergency

TABLE 5-2. *Discharge criteria*

1. A responsible adult escort is present.
2. Vital signs are stable for at least 1 hour.
3. No respiratory depression is noted.
4. Patient is oriented to person, place, and time.
5. Patient is able to dress and walk unassisted.
6. Patient is able to take fluids and void.
7. No nausea or vomiting is present.
8. There is absence of excessive pain.
9. No bleeding is observed.
10. Either patient or escort is able to understand and carry out postoperative care.

his or her concentration to the surgery, rather than being split in attention to two demanding roles.

The appropriate management of patients undergoing regional anesthesia, conscious sedation, or general anesthesia should include the adherence to strict discharge criteria (Table 5-2). Obviously, not all of these criteria would apply if the procedure required only local or regional anesthesia.

CONSCIOUS SEDATION

Definition: Conscious sedation is a medically controlled, minimally depressed level of consciousness that provides sedation, amnesia, and analgesia, while retaining the patient's ability to maintain a patent airway independently and continuously, maintain protective reflexes, and respond appropriately to physical stimulation and verbal command.

The medically controlled aspect of the definition is the key to conscious sedation. This state is dose-dependent and may end in general anesthesia. The most important aspect of this type of anesthesia is that the cardiac, respiratory, or reflex functions are altered to the extent of requiring external life support devices.

Conscious sedation enjoys a low rate of potential complications, as long as the following general principles are observed:

Proper patient selection and preparation
Slow titration of small drug increments allowing sufficient time between doses to assess clinical response
Adequate local anesthesia to help minimize the total dose of IV agents
Intraoperative monitoring
Addition of a nurse anesthetist as part of the operating team
Adherence to strict discharge criteria

In general, the advantages and disadvantages of conscious sedation can be summarized as follows:

Advantages

Alleviates stress and anxiety
Minimizes dosage of local anesthetic
Safer than general anesthesia
Endotracheial intubation not needed
Partial amnesia of surgery

Disadvantages

Risk of respiratory depression
Narcotics can cause postoperative nausea
Pulse oximeter monitor preferred
Anesthetist usually preferred
Requires fasting preoperatively

Agents Used in Conscious Sedation

Agents used for conscious sedation include sedative hypnotics, opioids, and narcotic agonists/antagonists (Table 5-3). These agents have a high clearance rate and short elimination half-life, which allow for blood concentration and clinical responses to be altered quickly, minimizing the problem of drug accumulation during surgery, which in turn minimizes prolonged postoperative recovery.

The most commonly used combination is a benzodiazepine and an opiod analgesic. Analgesics result in significant improvement in patient cooperation and more profound sedation intraoperatively. Benzodiazepines provide amnesia and anxiolysis.

Benzodiazepines

Diazepam (Valium) and midazolam (Versed) are the two most commonly used benzodiazepines in dermatologic surgery. Diazepam has excellent anxiolytic and amnesic properties of short duration. As a result of the use of propylene glycol as a solvent, it causes pain on IM or IV injection and

TABLE 5-3. *Agents used in conscious sedation*

Sedative-hypnotic
Benzodiazepines
  Diazepam (Valium)
  Midazolam (Versed)
Barbiturates
  Thiopental
  Thiamylal
  Methohexital
Propofol (Diprivan)
Antihistamines
Promethazine (Phenergan)
Dissociative analgesics
Ketamine (Ketalar)
Narcotic analgesics
Meperidine (Demerol)
Morphine sulfate
Fentanyl (Sublimaze)
Alfentanil (Alfenta)
Sufentanil (Sufenta)
Narcotic agonists/antagonists
Butorphanol (Stadol)
Nalbuphine (Nubain)
Inhalants
Nitrous oxide

has a high incidence of thrombophlebitis. It also forms active metabolites that peak at 48 hours after IV administration, and may lead to prolonged sedation. Adminstration of diazepam can be sublingual, IM, or IV at a dose of 2 to 10 mg.

Midazolam is the agent of choice because of faster onset of action, more profound sedation and antegrade amnesia (both IM and IV), lack of vein irritation, and shorter half-life when compared with diazepam. It has relatively short duration of action and provides a rapid recovery. In prolonged dermatologic procedures, repeated doses may be needed.

For short procedures, a single dose of 0.07 mg/kg (about 2.5 to 5 mg) produces sedation within 5 to 10 minutes. An IM dose of 0.12 mg/kg usually produces somnolence. For longer procedures, the IV route is usually better tolerated than repeated IM injections. Midazolam is more potent than diazepam and able to cause significant respiratory depression at IV doses a low as 2 mg. It can be given in small, incremental doses of 0.035 mg/kg until slurred speech occurs, and titrated up to a total dose of 5 mg. The onset of sedative and anxiolytic effects of midazolam occurs within 1 to 2 minutes after an IV bolus dose, and the maximal effect is evident within 4 to 5 minutes. By carefully repeating small (1 mg) doses of IV midazolam every 5 minutes, the risks of dangerous respiratory depression can be minimized.

Precaution should be taken when administering midazolam in elderly individuals and in patients with chronic obstructive pulmonary disease (COPD) or hepatic or renal dysfunction. Midazolam is metabolized in the liver by microsomal oxidation and has a rapid first-pass hepatic extraction. Its effect can be prolonged and increased in patients with hepatic disease. Respiratory depression can occur more readily in elderly individuals or patients with COPD. In addition, patients receiving anxiolytics, guanabenz, monoamine oxidase (MAO) inhibitors, or tranquilizers should be monitored carefully for central nervous system and respiratory depression. Because very small doses of fentanyl-like narcotic analgesics potentiate the hypnotic effect of midazolam, smaller doses should be given when these drugs are used concomitantly. Midazolam can not be reliably reversed by either naloxone or physostigmine. Flumazenil (RomaziconR) is an imidazobenzodiazepine that blocks the benzodiazepine receptor and acts as a highly specific antagonist to the actions of midazolam and other benzodiazepines. The initial dose is 0.2 mg, titrated in 0.2-mg increments every minute until a total dosage of 1.0 mg is given or until the sedation is adequately reversed. The half-life of flumazenil, however, is shorter than that of midazolam, and resedation is a potential problem in the ambulatory setting.

Barbiturates

The thiobarbiturates sodium thiopental and thiamylal are the gold standards for IV induction of anesthesia because of their predictable ability to induce anesthesia in one arm–brain circulation time. The pharmacokinetic profile of these two drugs makes them undesirable for brief ambulatory anesthesia and conscious sedation. Awakening time after a small, single dose of thiopental is rapid. Thiopental is metabolized and eliminated very slowly (elimination half-life, 10 to 12 hours) and the metabolic products of thiobarbiturates have significant sedative properties. Studies have shown residual psychomotor impairment 8 hours after a single dose of a thiobarbiturate. Another disadvantage of the thiobarbiturates is their transient cardiovascular and respiratory depression.

Methohexital (Brevital), a methyloxybarbiturate, has a shorter elimination half-life and therefore is cleared more quickly from the body, providing a slight advantage over thiopental. Other side effects like myoclonus, coughing, and hiccuping during anesthesia make it less satisfactory for ambulatory anesthesia. Cardiovascular and respiratory depression also occur after methohexital.

Propofol

Propofol, a new alkyltophenol IV sedative hypnotic agent, is currently the most common induction agent for adult ambulatory anesthesia. It is extremely rapid in onset with a smooth induction and brief duration attributable to extensive redistribution and rapid elimination. This allows for easy titration of clinical effects. Its rapid hepatic metabolism into inactive products, and resultant high clearance rate, results in a ''clearheaded'' arousal with a nominal hangover effect. Psychomotor function also returns to baseline quickly. Another advantage is its antiemetic property. The complications observed with propofol use are pain on injection (in particular, if a small vein is used), hypotension, and depressed myocardial contractility. No thrombophlebitis is observed. Propofol is given as a bolus 20 to 40 mg per 10 minutes or as a continuous infusion at 0.1 to 0.2 µg/kg per minute. Transient respiratory and cardiac side effects can be eliminated by lowering the total dose to 1 mg/kg.

Promethazine

Promethazine, a phenothiazine derivative, possesses antihistaminic, sedative, anti–motion-sickness, antiemetic, and anticholinergic effects. It is useful in the prevention and control of nausea and vomiting associated with anesthesia and as an adjunct to anesthesia and analgesia, most commonly used with meperidine. The central nervous system–depressant effects of narcotics and barbiturates are additive with promethazine. The preferred route of administration is IM, at a dose of 25 to 50 mg for adults and 0.5 mg/pound (1.1 mg/kg) in children. The IV route can be used but carries the hazard of gangrene of the affected extremity if it is inadvertently injected intraarterialy. If IV administration is used, the dose should be no greater than 25 mg/ml at a rate not to exceed 25 mg/min. In addition, subcutaneous injection is contraindicated, since it may result in tissue necrosis.

Ketamine

Ketamine is a rapidly acting phencyclidine derivative. It produces a state of dissociative analgesia characterized by catalepsy, catatonia, amnesia, and analgesia. Ketamine produces excellent analgesia of the skin. Cutaneous analgesia is usually achieved at doses well below those required to produce loss of consciousness. In the dissociative state the corneal reflex is intact and pupils react to light, and the protective reflexes of the pharynx and larynx, such as coughing and swallowing, are not depressed. Ketamine causes an increase in heart rate, cardiac output, and blood pressure. It can cause a slight degree of transient respiratory depression immediately after IV injection. This effect is potentiated by premedication with narcotics or sedatives. This transient effect is followed by respiratory stimulation and bronchodilation. Other side effects can include nightmares and extensive salivation. In moderate to high doses, prolonged sedation and a significant number of emergent reactions and hallucinations can limit its use. Ketamine may interact with metrizamide and theophylline to produce seizures. If cocaine or epinephrine is used in conjunction with ketamine, cardiac arrhythmias may occur as a result of decreased uptake of catecholamines induced by ketamine.

IV doses are usually in the range of 1.0 to 2.0 mg/kg. A low-dose IV ketamine (0.5 mg/kg), given in conjunction with a low-dose IV midazolam (0.05 mg/kg in divided doses), provides excellent analgesia, sedation, and amnesia.

Morphine Sulfate and Meperidine

Morphine and meperidine, the slow- and long-acting µ-receptor agonist narcotic analgesics, are rarely used for ambulatory anesthesia. Meperidine is used more often for postoperative pain relief. It can be used for anesthesia, usually given IM or IV, in doses ranging from 25 to 100 mg. It is frequently given with promethazine to decrease the postoperative nausea. Intravenous use increases the risks of side effects, including cardiorespiratory depression, orthostatic hypotension, and muscle rigidity. Meperidine can induce seizure activity at only five times its therapeutic dose. The incidence of opiod-induced side effects, especially postoperative nausea, drowsiness, dizziness, and constipation, is much higher with these agents than with their more potent, short-acting counterparts, such as fentanyl derivatives.

Fentanyl

Fentanyl is a synthetic narcotic analgesic related to the phenypiperidines, the prototype being meperidine. Fentanyl has 100 times the potency of morphine. Some physicians consider it the narcotic of choice for outpatient anesthesia. The onset of analgesia is extremely rapid (1 to 3 minutes) following IV administration. Because 98% of the dose is cleared in 60 minutes, the duration of effect of fentanyl is short.

For ambulatory surgical procedures, the usual dose of fentanyl is 2 μg/kg, either IV or IM. The dose range for outpatient surgery is 1 to 5 μg/kg, although rarely is a dose of more than 3 μg/kg needed. Doses of 5 μg/kg to 50 μg/kg at 1-to 2-minute intervals can be used but usually require artificial ventilation.

Caution is needed when administering fentanyl to patients receiving tranquilizers, other narcotics, benzodiazapines, barbiturates, and guanabenz to avoid additive central nervous system depression. Severe hypotension may occur when fentanyl is combined with calcium channel blockers, β-blockers, benzodiazepines, and tranquilizers.

Alfentanil

Alfentanil is a less potent fentanyl derivative (about one-fifth the potency of fentanyl) with a faster onset and shorter duration of action. The major disadvantages of alfentanil are a higher incidence of postoperative nausea and vomiting and an analgesic effect that does not always extend into the immediate postoperative period (because of its short duration of action). It also produces more hypotension, sedation, and muscular rigidity than fentanyl. It is best used by continuous infusion at 0.5 mg/kg following a loading dose of 5 μg/kg because its rapid onset and equilibrium allow for easy titration of clinical effects.

Sufentanil

Sufentanil is a structural analog of fentanyl and is about 7 to 10 times more potent than fentanyl. Its onset of action is faster, and it has a shorter duration of action than an equivalent dose of fentanyl. Patients who receive sufentanil rather than fentanyl appear to be more alert, less drowsy, and less nauseated immediately after the operation.

Sufentanil at a dose of 0.25 to 0.5 μg/kg may be sufficient for a short ambulatory procedure. If infusion is desired, an infusion rate of 0.2 to 0.5 μg/kg per hour is appropriate after a loading dose of 0.2 to 0.5 μ/kg. Some physicians consider sufentanil too potent for outpatient use.

Butorphanol

Butorphanol and its major metabolites are agonists at μ-opiod receptors and mixed agonist-antagonists at μ-opiod receptors. In addition to analgesia, central nervous system effects include depression of spontaneous respiratory activity and cough, stimulation of the emetic center, miosis, and sedation. Effects possibly mediated by non–central nervous

system mechanisms include alteration in cardiovascular resistance and capacitance, bronchomotor tone, vascular resistance, gastrointestinal tract secretory and motor activity and bladder sphincter activity.

Sedation is commonly noted at doses of 0.5 mg or more. Narcosis is produced by 10- to 12-mg doses administered over 10 to 15 minutes IV. Nausea and/or vomiting may be produced by doses of 1 mg or more administered by any route. Onset of analgesia is within a few minutes for IV administration, within 10 to 15 minutes for IM route, and within 15 minutes for the nasal spray doses. Peak analgesic activity occurs within 30 to 60 minutes following IV and IM administration and within 1 to 2 hours following the nasal spray administration. Butorphanol has a half-life of 4.5 hours except in the elderly, where it can be as long as 6 hours. As a preoperative medication, the usual adult dose is 2 mg IM, administered 60 to 90 minutes before surgery. This is approximately equivalent in sedative effect to 10 mg of morphine or 80 mg of meperidine. For anesthesia use, the usual dose is 2 mg IV shortly before induction and/or 0.5 to 1.0 mg IV in increments during anesthesia.

The long duration of sedation is a drawback in outpatient surgery.

Nalbuphine

Nalbuphine is a synthetic narcotic agonist-antagonist analgesic of the phenanthrene series. Its analgesic potency is essentially equivalent to that of morphine on a milligram basis. Its onset of action occurs within 2 to 3 minutes after IV administration and in less than 15 minutes following subcutaneous or IM injection. The plasma half-life is 5 hours, and the analgesic activity ranges from 3 to 6 hours.

Induction doses of nalbuphine range from 0.3 mg/kg to 3.0 μg/kg IV to be administered over a 10- to 15-minute period with maintenance doses of 0.25 to 0.50 mg/kg in single IV administrations as required.

The long duration of sedation is a drawback in outpatient surgery.

Nitrous Oxide

Nitrous oxide is one of the most commonly used inhalational agents and produces hypnosis, amnesia, and analgesia when administered in concentrations of 50% to 70%. It has a benign effect on the cardiovascular and respiratory systems, is nonirritating and odorless, has no significant organ toxicity, especially after short-term usage, and has a low cost. When used in conjunction with IV anesthetics like propofol, fentanyl, or ketamine, nitrous oxide reduces the chance of awareness without prolonging the recovery time. The addition of nitrous oxide reduces the requirement for other, more potent anesthetic agents. Recovery from nitrous oxide is very rapid.

GENERAL ANESTHESIA

Balanced anesthesia is the most common form of general anesthesia for ambulatory surgery. After induction of anesthesia with an IV agent, anesthesia is maintained with a combination of a variety of agents to achieve the anesthetic state that provides hypnosis, amnesia, analgesia, muscle relaxation, and hemodynamic stability. The agents and principles of IV general anesthesia are the same as those for conscious sedation. The difference is in the dosage or the frequency of administration. The reader is referred to that section. These agents are reviewed only briefly in this section. The inhalation anesthetics are the mainstay of general anesthesia.

Inhaled Anesthetics in Balanced Anesthesia

Halothane, Enflurane, and Isoflurane

At present, isoflurane, with its low blood-gas solubility and minimal potential for metabolism and organ toxicity, remains the most common volatile anesthetic agent for ambulatory anesthesia. Enflurane, with a blood-gas solubility of 1.8, is preferred by some anesthesiologists because it appears to cause less tachycardia intraoperatively and less respiratory irritability such as coughing, salivation, and laryngospasm at emergence. Halothane is rarely used in adults for maintenance of anesthesia because of concerns about hepatotoxicity, a higher incidence of ventricular arrhythmias, and its relatively high blood-gas solubility. These characteristics make recovery from halothane anesthesia slower, especially in obese patients.

Desflurane

A fluorinated methyl-ethyl ether, desflurane has a low blood-gas solubility (0.420, which is even less than that of nitrous oxide [0.47]). This characteristic of desflurane makes the onset and offset of anesthesia extremely fast and also allows quick intraoperative alteration of the depth of anesthesia. Desflurane also has a low potential for organ toxicity. The drawback is its pungent smell, and it produces severe irritation of the respiratory tract (leading to coughing, salivation, and laryngospasm) during inhalation induction. In addition, it has a low boiling point (23°C) and a high saturated vapor pressure (669 mm Hg), which make storage and dispensing complicated. A special, heated vaporizer is required for the drug to be dispensed. Storage in hot climates can be difficult. Other problems include an increased incidence of postoperative nausea and vomiting compared with propofol, especially when used with nitrous oxide; transient tachycardia, when used in high concentrations or when the inspired concentration is quickly increased; and its relatively low potency, which makes it less cost-effective.

Sevoflurane

A fluorinated methyl-isopropyl ether, sevoflurane has a low blood-gas partition coefficient, so its onset and early recovery are likely to be fast. However, it is not pungent and causes minimal airway irritation during induction and emergence. Sevoflurane is not as stable as desflurane, with significant biodegradation in the body.

Nitrous Oxide

Nitrous oxide is the most common inhalation anesthetic for general anesthesia. It has very low blood-gas solubility, is amnestic and has analgesic effects, has a benign effect on the cardiovascular and respiratory systems, is relatively inert with no significant organ toxicity, and has a low cost. When used in conjunction with IV anesthetics like propofol, nitrous oxide reduces the change of awareness without prolonging the recovery time. It appears that in certain circumstances, particularly when used with narcotics, nitrous oxide can increase the incidence of postoperative nausea and vomiting.

Intravenous General Anesthesia

The introduction of propofol and the simultaneous availability of simple, practical syringe pumps have made IV maintenance anesthesia for ambulatory surgery easier and more practical.

Propofol Infusion

Propofol is a fast-acting anesthetic with a short elimination half-life and a very high clearance rate (noncumulative), making it an ideal agent for continuous infusion. A loading dose of 1.5 to 2.5 mg/kg is used, followed by an initial infusion rate of 200 μg/kg per minute, reduced 10 to 15 minutes later to 150 μg/kg per minute, and subsequently reduced to a maintenance dose of 100 μg/kg per minute. As an alternative, the loading dose can be given with the same syringe pump at a rate of approximately 600 μg/kg per minute until the patient goes to sleep; then the rate is lowered to 100 to 200 μg/kg per minute. Giving the initial loading dose slowly via the syringe pump avoids the hypotension and apnea associated with rapid bolus injections. An option to the continuous infusion technique is to give propofol in small (20 to 40 mg), incremental boluses. This method is cumbersome and more likely to produce peaks and valleys in plasma and brain concentrations, resulting in a greater chance of operative awareness. To avoid the possibility of awareness and reduce the amount of intraoperative opiod usage, unless contraindicated, nitrous oxide should be routinely added at a concentration of 50% to 70% in the inspired mixture while using infusion of propofol for maintenance anesthesia.

Other Intravenous Anesthetics

Midazolam 0.25 to 1.5 μg/kg per minute along with an infusion of a short-acting narcotic provides good anesthetic condition. It has no real advantage over propofol infusion. A midazolam/narcotic mixture is likely to prolong recovery time. The effect of midazolam and μ-narcotics can be reversed by the use of flumazenil and naloxone, respectively, but the regimen could be expensive.

Ketamine has been used because of its analgesic and dissociative effects at a low-dose infusion (10 to 20 μg/kg per minute as an adjunct to other anesthetics like propofol or midazolam.

In addition, opiod agonists like *fentanyl, alfentanil, and sufentanil* and hypnotics like methohexital can be used for maintenance anesthesia. For more details on these agents, see the section on conscious sedation.

The infusion schemes for anesthesia, sedation, and analgesia are summarized in Table 5-4.

PEDIATRIC ANESTHESIA

The approach to anesthesia in the pediatric patient is similar to that in the adult. A major difference is the route of administration of the different anesthetic agents. Pediatric patients may be anxious during ambulatory surgery because of the unfamiliar environment. Controversy exists on the use of premedication in pediatric patients who will undergo general anesthesia. Some authorities believe that induction of anesthesia can be safely completed in most unpremedicated children without undue emotional distress and that premedication may be reserved for the child who is extremely apprehensive or emotionally disturbed.

Premedication is perhaps more important in pediatric surgery than in adult surgery. In small outpatient and short surgical procedures, premedication might be all that is needed. Conscious sedation can also be used in lengthier procedures.

Premedication

Oral Administration

Midazolam has proved to be the most popular of all premedications. Oral midazolam 0.5 to 0.75 mg/kg, offered 30 minutes before the procedure or induction of anesthesia, is an effective premedication that does not prolong recovery time after procedures lasting 1.5 to 2.0 hours. Oral ketamine 6 mg/kg has also been found to be predictable and acceptable premedication when given with a cola-flavored soft drink 20 to 30 minutes before the procedure or induction of anesthesia. Oral transmucosal fentanyl citrate 15 to 20 μg/kg is readily accepted, safe, and effective; however, the incidence of postoperative emesis was found to be 37% compared with 18% in children who received no premedication.

Intramuscular Injection

Morphine sulfate is an effective premedication, but children who have received it are significantly more drowsy and have a higher incidence of postoperative vomiting that results in prolonged stay in the surgical facility. Ketamine 2 to 3 mg/kg IM provides sedation within 2 to 3 minutes. Intramuscular ketamine 3 mg/kg is three times as effective as meperidine 1 mg/kg for sedating a child under 2 years of age. There is no prolongation of recovery time, and the emotional state following anesthesia is not different among patients receiving ketamine and meperidine. Since the introduction of oral midazolam, IM premedication has been used less frequently.

Induction and Sedation

In general, the presence of an anesthesiologist or nurse anesthetist is wise or essential in the induction and sedation of pediatric patients. Some agents require continuous monitoring, and the patient and the surgeon are better served by having a dedicated person in charge of the monitoring.

TABLE 5-4. *Infusion schmes for anesthesia, sedation, or analgesia*

Drug	Anesthesia loading dose (μg/kg)	Anesthesia maintenance infusion (μg/kg/min)	Sedation or analgesia loading dose (μg/kg)	Sedation or analgesia maintenance infusion (μg/kg/min)
Analgesics				
Alfentanil	50–150	0.5–3.0	10–25	0.25–1.0
Fentanyl	5–15	0.03–0.1	1–3	0.01–0.03
Sufentanil	1–3	0.01–0.05	—	—
Hypnotics				
Ketamine	1500–2500	25–75	500–1000	10–20
Propofol	1000–2500	50–150	250–1000	10–50
Midazolam	50–150	0.25–1.5	25–100	0.25–1.0
Methohexital	1500–2500	50–150	250–1000	10–50

Intranasal Route

Intranasal midazolam 0.2 mg/kg and sufentanil 2.0 μg/kg, administered nasally from a syringe, provides sedation within 10 minutes. Intranasal midazolam is a more reliable sedative compared with intranasal sufentanil and provides greater analgesia but requires close monitoring of oxygenation. Intranasal fentanyl is being studied for sedation in outpatient procedures and relief of migraine headaches in the outpatient setting.

Rectal Route

Rectal methohexital is most effective in children between 1 and 4 years of age. Hiccuping and defecation may occur. Airway resuscitation equipment, including oxygen, must be immediately available. The usual dose is 25 mg/kg of methothexital in a 2% or 10% solution. The patient should be watched for signs of airway obstruction and respiratory depression. An anesthesiologist must be available to detect and treat any such complications. The major disadvantages of rectal administration of drugs are unpredictable absorption, long duration of action, and possible irritation of rectal mucosa.

Intramuscular and Intravenous Routes

The IV route is preferred in the induction and sedation of the pediatric patient. Ketamine 3 to 5 mg/kg IM or 2% methohexital 6 mg/kg IM is useful.

A number of agents, including barbiturates and ketamine, have been successfully used to sedate children. Midazolam, propofol, and fentanyl are current favorites. Midazolam, administered as a continuous infusion at a rate of 0.25 3.0 μg/kg per minute after a bolus does, provides sedation without endotracheal intubation for as long as 11 hours. Propofol 25 to 100 μg/kg per minute has also been successfully used. Fentanyl at a dose of 2 to 3 μg/kg can be used for induction and maintenance of anesthesia in children 2 to 12 years of age.

SUGGESTED READING LIST

1. American Academy of Dermatology Guidelines/Outcomes Committee. Guidelines of care for local and regional anesthesia in cutaneous surgery. J Am Acad Dermatol 1995;33:504.
2. Amrein R, Leighman B, Bentzinger C, et al. Flumazenil in benzodiazepine antagonism: actions and clinical use in intoxications and anesthesiology. Med Toxicol 1987;2:411.
3. Brown C. Drug interaction in dermatologic surgery. J Dermatol Surg Oncol 1992;18:512.
4. Chisman BB, Watson MA. Outpatient anesthesia. J Dermatol Surg Oncol 1988;14:939.
5. Cooke JE. Drug interaction in anesthesia. Clin Plast Surg 1985;12:83.
6. Cooper JB, Newbower RS, Kitz RJ. An analysis of major errors and equipment failures in anesthesia management: considerations for prevention and detection. Anesthesiology 1984;60:34.
7. Corssen G. Intravenous anesthesia and analgesia. Philadelphia: Lea & Febiger, 1988.
8. Drake LA et al. Guidelines of care for office surgical facilities. Part I. J Am Acad Dermatol 1992;26:763.
9. Drake LA et al. Guidelines of care for office surgical facilities. Part II. Self-assessment checklist. J Am Acad Dermatol 1995;33:265.
10. Feld LH, Negus JJB, White PF. Oral midazolam preanesthetic medication in pediatric outpatients. Anesthesiology 1990;73:831.
11. Fragen RD, ed. Drug infusions in anesthesiology. New York: Raven, 1991.
12. Joint Commission protocol for conscious sedation. Same Day Surgery 1995;10:125.
13. Kissin I, Vinik HR, Bradley El Jr. Alfentanil potentiates midazolam-induced unconsciousness in subanalgesic doses. Anesth Analg 1990;71:65.
14. Klein JA. Anesthesia for liposuction in dermatologic surgery. J Dermatol Surg Oncol 1988;14:1124.
15. Kwik RSH, Cullen BF. Adverse drug interactions. Semin Anesth 1990;9:32.
16. McConn K. Characteristic of propofol in outpatient oral and maxillofacial surgery. Oral Surg Oral Med Oral Pathol 1994;78(6):705.
17. McDowall RH. Total IV anesthesia for children undergoing brief diagnostic or therapeutic procedures. J Clin Anesth 1995;7(4):273.
18. Mueller RA, Lundberg DBA. Manual of drug interactions for anesthesiology. New York: Churchill Livingstone, 1988.
19. Murphy M. Sedation. Ann Emerg Med 1996;4:461.
20. Phillips M. Drugs for anesthesia in day surgery. Can Operating Room Nurs J 1994;12(4):5.
21. Raybould D, Bradshaw EG. Premedication for day case surgery: a study of oral midazolam. Anaesthesia 1987;42:591.
22. Roeizen MF, Kaplan EB, Schreider BD, et al. The relative roles of the history and physical examination and laboratory testing in the preoperative evaluation for outpatient surgery: the Starling curve of preoperative laboratory testing. Anesth Clin North Am 1987;5:15.
23. Sadove AM, Eppley B. Pediatric plastic surgery. Clin Plast Surg 1996;23(1):139.
24. Seymour G. Medical assessment of the elderly surgical patient. Rockville, MD: Aspen Systems, 1987.
25. Shaw C. Conscious sedation: a multidisciplinary team approach. J Postanesth Nurs 1996;11(1):13.
26. Smith I. The role of sevoflurane in outpatient anesthesia. Anesth Analg 1995;81(suppl 6):67.
27. Wetchler BV. Anesthesia for ambulatory surgery. Philadelphia: J.B. Lippincott, 1991.
28. White P. Ambulatory anesthesia: past, present and future. Int Anesthesiol Clin 1994;32(3):1.
29. White P. Outpatient anesthesia. 2nd ed. New York: Churchill Livingstone, 1990.
30. Winton GB. Anesthesia for dermatologic surgery. J Dermatol Surg Oncol 1988;14:41
31. Young ML, Conahan TJ. Complications of outpatient anesthesia. Semin Anesth 1990;9:62.

Textbook of Dermatologic Surgery, edited by John L. Ratz.
Lippincott–Raven Publishers, Philadelphia © 1998.

CHAPTER 6

Monitoring

Mark R. Balle

In the last several years there has been a dramatic increase in the number of surgeries formerly performed in the operating room that are now performed in an outpatient setting. Along with this increase in number has come an increase in sophistication not only in the nature of the procedures performed by dermatologic surgeons and others, but also in the requirements for anesthesia for these patients. Whereas in the past simple surgeries were performed with local anesthetics, now a wide range of surgical procedures are performed using all types of anesthetics. As nonanesthesia practitioners become more directly involved in overseeing the sedation management of their patients, a thorough understanding of and adherence to monitoring standards, guidelines, and practices are paramount.

EQUIPMENT

The primary purpose of monitoring anesthetized patients is to afford the greatest margin of safety possible by giving the earliest warning of any adverse change or trend, thus allowing for prompt intervention before irreversible damage occurs. Monitoring encompasses many activities. The fundamental basis of all monitoring is the continuously vigilant clinician through whose eyes, ears, tactile sense, and sense of judgment some of the most important data are gathered. Inspection, palpation, and auscultation can reveal much about the patient being anesthetized. Through advances of modern equipment, the practitioner's ability to ascertain objective data has been greatly enhanced. As equipment has

Mark R. Balle, Department of Dermatology, Henry Ford Hospital, 6777 W. Maple Rd., West Bloomfield, MI 48322.

improved, so has the ability to detect changes before some clinical signs become evident. As this new technology has evolved, so have the standards for the use of this equipment.

Routine Monitors

Common monitoring equipment includes a blood pressure monitor, a stethoscope, an electrocardiogram (ECG) monitor, and a pulse oximeter. These devices are used in monitoring virtually all patients undergoing anesthesia and may also be used for high-risk patients undergoing procedures under regional or local anesthesia.

Noninvasive Blood Pressure Monitoring

Blood pressure can be measured noninvasively using the familiar blood pressure cuff with an inflatable bladder by palpation and auscultation of Korotkoff sounds. The width of the cuff should ideally be 40% of the extremity circumference to minimize false readings.

Oscillometry is the automated technology that has become the standard for noninvasive blood pressure measuring devices, such as the Dinamap (Fig. 1). It operates by sensing oscillations produced by the arterial pulsations transmitted from a deflating blood pressure cuff. An algorithm is then used to derive a blood pressure estimation. These monitors have given the practitioner the freedom to perform other tasks while having the advantage of monitoring blood pressure at preset, regular intervals. They automatically measure systolic pressure, diastolic pressure, mean arterial pressure, and heart rate. A problem not commonly encountered can be edema of the extremity distal to the cuff, which can be

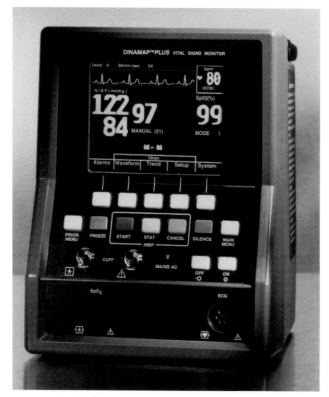

FIG. 1. Vital signs monitor. (Courtesy of Johnson and Johnson Medical, Inc., Tampa, FL.)

minimized by avoiding cycling frequencies that are too short.

Stethoscopes

The stethoscope is an indispensable instrument for continually monitoring breath sounds and heart sounds. A weighted precordial stethoscope is a modified scope that is placed over the suprasternal notch or heart before anesthesia induction. The esophageal stethoscope is placed after tracheal intubation. Its closeness to the heart allows for clearly audible heart sounds and breath sounds, permitting early detection of changes in cardiac rhythm, heart rate, development of increased airway resistance, and failure of ventilation of the lungs. It is especially important in pediatric care, since it can detect loss of breath sounds from a mechanical disconnection or endobronchial intubation well before an alarm sounds.

Electrocardiogram Monitor

The ECG monitor is essential for anesthesia patients. It detects cardiac arrythmias, can help detect myocardial ischemia, and can signal changes in potassium balance. Each QRS complex triggers an audible indicator. Because lead II parallels the P wave vector, it shows the maximum P-wave

amplitude and is ideal for detection of cardiac arrythmias. It can also show inferior wall ischemia by ST-segment depression. Anterior and lateral wall ischemia, which is more common than inferior wall ischemia, is best shown by precordial lead V_5. Therefore a V_5 lead is most often used when the concern is monitoring for ischemia. It is important to keep in mind that the ECG measures cardiac electrical activity, not heart function.

Pulse Oximetry

The pulse oximeter has become a standard monitor for patients undergoing anesthesia. It provides noninvasive, continuous monitoring of arterial oxygen saturation. This can give early warning of hypoxemia. It can also give an early warning of a loss of pulse (Fig. 2).

Early work in the development of oximetry began in Germany in the 1930s. Spectrophotometric principles employing the kinetics of tissue oxygenation and the Beer–Lambert law formed the basis for the first oximeters. Pulse oximeters were first originated in the 1970s by Aoyagi and developed in Japan. Reinvention and development by Wilbur, New, and Lloyd led to the development of today's pulse oximeter.

The pulse oximeter, whose operation is based on detecting differences in absorption of particular wavelengths of light by oxygenated and reduced hemoglobin, has a sensor that is clipped or taped to the patient's finger. Contained in the sensor are two photodiodes and a photodetector. The photodiodes generate light at 660 nm and at 900 to 940 nm. A microprocessor switches the photodiodes on and off many times each second as the photodetector records the change in the amount of red and infrared light absorbed. A calculation based on the pulsatile and nonpulsatile components for both wavelengths is analyzed by the microprocessor, which digitalizes the information, and is then processed by a computer to give an estimate of the oxygen saturation of hemoglobin.

Today's pulse oximeters are accurate to within 3% when oxygen saturation ranges from 70% to 100%. Below 70% there is a great deal of variation in accuracy among the different units.

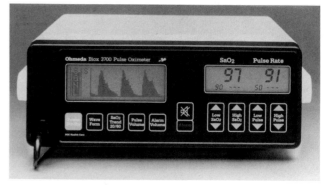

FIG. 2. Pulse oximeter. (Compliments of Ohmeda, Liberty Corner, NJ.)

The pulse oximeter has limitations. The most common cause of failure is motion of the finger or probe, which can lead to inaccurate readings. Anything that significantly reduces vascular pulsation can lead to a decreased ability to calculate oxygen saturation, including hypothermia, a patient with a constricted vascular system attributable to an extremely cold room, a blood pressure cuff being inflated on the same arm as the pulse oximeter, hypotension with a systolic pressure less that 50 mm Hg, vasoconstrictive drug administration, or severe peripheral vascular disease. Pulse oximetry does not detect carbon monoxide. Methemoglobin gives erroneous readings, whereas fetal hemoglobin is read correctly. Accuracy is also affected by intravascular dyes such as methylene blue. Electrosurgery occasionally interferes with readings. Ambient light can cause false readings; however, newer technology has lessened this problem significantly. Pulse oximetry does not reflect carbon dioxide retention during anesthesia, especially when supplemental oxygen is administered. Thus it does not reflect ventilation, which may be a more desirable goal for prevention of hypoxemic injury in some patients.

Other Common Monitors

There are many other types of devices that may be useful for patient monitoring. Many of these devices are important in surgicenters or operative sessions using general anesthesia. They may not be useful or feasible in the outpatient or office surgical setting. These devices should be managed by the anesthetist, not the surgeon.

Capnography

Capnography has become an important monitor. It is the continuous monitoring of a patient's capnogram, which is the four-phased continuous-time display of the end-tidal CO_2 concentration sampled at the patient's airway during ventilation. It provides information reflecting alveolar ventilation distribution of blood flow and metabolic activity. Capnography has significantly reduced the potential for unrecognized accidental esophageal intubation. Decreased end-tidal CO_2 concentrations can occur with a cardiac arrest, pulmonary embolism, decreased pulmonary blood flow from hypotension, or a partial leak in the anesthesia delivery system. Increased end-tidal CO_2 concentrations can occur because of hypoventilation, sepsis, malignant hyperthermia, and rebreathing.

Mass Spectrometry

Mass spectrometry can provide breath-by-breath analysis of respiratory and anesthetic gases. It gives an indication of the integrity of the anesthesia delivery system. For example, a sudden rise in the nitrogen concentration in exhaled gas can indicate the introduction of air from a leak in the anesthesia delivery system or a venous air embolism.

Oxygen Analyzers

An oxygen analyzer is routinely used to ensure that the anesthesia machine is delivering adequate concentrations of oxygen. An alarm is set to sound when the oxygen concentration decreases below the threshold level of 25% to 30%. It is mandatory for low-flow or closed-circuit administration of air mixtures containing nitrous oxide. Although the sensor may be placed on the inspiratory or expiratory side, it is more commonly placed in the inspiratory limb distal to the one-way valve. There are three types: paramagnetic, polorographic, and galvanic cell monitors.

Ventimeter

A ventimeter or respirometer in the exhalation limb measures the tidal volume and permits calculation of minute ventilation (rate of breathing multiplied by tidal volume).

Airway Pressure Gauge

Airway pressure is measured by a gauge on the anesthesia machine. When the maximal inspiratory pressure does not reach a predetermined level, an alarm sounds, which indicates a large leak or disconnection. Excessive airway pressure reflects low pulmonary compliance or an obstruction in the anesthetic breathing system.

Clinical Monitoring of Breathing

The pattern of spontaneous respirations, including rate, depth, and regularity, should be continuously monitored during general anesthesia. This is accomplished by visual and tactile (hand on the bag) monitoring of the movements of the reservoir bag on the anesthetic breathing system, by observing chest movement, and by auscultation of the chest via a precordial or esophageal stethoscope. Noting the character of the respiratory movements helps in assessing depth of anesthesia.

Temperature Monitoring

Common sites for measuring core temperature include the esophagus, nasopharynx, rectum, bladder, and tympanic membrane. For every patient, the appropriate equipment should be available for measuring body temperature when necessary. Decreases in body temperature resulting from exposure to cold operating rooms may delay postoperative awakening. Shivering can significantly increase oxygen demand, cardiac output, and minute ventilation, which may pose a special problem in patients who are anemic or have coronary artery disease. Small children are very susceptible to rapid heat loss because of their high ratio of surface area to body mass. Monitoring temperature is important in cases involving infants.

Malignant hyperthermia (MH), a group of inherited disorders, is characterized by a hypermetabolic state that can be triggered by inhalation anesthetics and muscle relaxants, especially succinylcholine. In addition to tachycardia and hypercapnia, MH is often characterized by a rapid rise in temperature. If a patient is suspected to have MH by family history, temperature monitoring should be a strong consideration, even though a rise in temperature usually follows later than hypercapnia. The death rate with MH is high if the condition is not diagnosed and promptly treated.

Renal Function Monitoring

Monitoring urine output is helpful in certain patients for whom knowledge of fluid and volume status is important.

Invasive Monitors

During complex or prolonged operations or in patients with significant systemic diseases, invasive monitoring of the cardiovascular system may be indicated. Invasive monitoring is associated with increased risk. This, however, must be balanced with the benefits in each situation. Common examples of invasive monitors are intraarterial, central venous, and pulmonary artery catheters.

Neurologic Monitors

The electroencephalogram (EEG) can show early evidence of cerebral ischemia during carotid endarterectomy or cardiopulmonary bypass. It also has been advocated to monitor depth of anesthesia. The EEG can be difficult to evaluate accurately in the operating room setting.

Evoked potentials are the electrophysiologic responses of the nervous system to visual, auditory, or somatic sensory stimulation. They allow evaluation of neural pathway integrity during anesthesia for some surgeries, although they do have limitations.

Other Equipment

In addition to monitors, other equipment is necessary when providing sedation or anesthesia. An oxygen delivery system is essential, with appropriate bag and mask sizes depending on the circumstances. A suction device with appropriate catheter sizes is needed. An emergency cart should be readily available with laryngoscopes and endotracheal tubes. All equipment must be maintained and checked on a regular basis, with the proper documentation.

Electrical Hazards

Monitoring equipment can be a source for leakage of current that can be conducted to the patient, causing burns or cardiac arrhythmias. Care must be taken to eliminate extraneous voltage sources and to use equipment that has been properly designed to conduct leakage currents to the ground, not the patient.

MONITORING STANDARDS AND GUIDELINES

As the usage of sedatives and anesthetics in physician offices, subspecialty procedure suites, ambulatory surgery centers, and other settings has increased, so has the need for awareness, education, and adherence to patient monitoring standards and guidelines for all personnel involved in the care of these patients.

Harvard Minimal Monitoring Standards

The first set of standards for patient monitoring during anesthesia was adopted by the Department of Anaesthesiology at Harvard Medical School in 1985. The standards came about as a result of a risk management/quality assurance effort. Harvard's own medical malpractice insurance company was concerned about the number of incidents and claims related to anesthesia care. A committee was formed to study the problem and to make recommendations. As they examined the data, they concluded that a large number of the cases that involved significant morbidity or death were probably preventable. The most common problem leading to patient death or severe injury caused directly by anesthesia care was the failure to adequately ventilate the patient's lungs. In an effort to improve patient care and reduce the number of adverse outcomes related to anesthesia accidents, the committee formulated a set of patient monitoring standards. These were considered to be minimum standards that could and would be routinely exceeded. The essence of the Harvard Standards is continuous monitoring of ventilation and circulation. Characteristics deemed important to the nature of these standards were that they had to be realistic and attainable, be technically achievable, and place emphasis on behavior and attitude rather than on technology (Table 6-1).

American Society of Anesthesiologists Monitoring Standards

The American Society of Anesthesiologists (ASA) Standards for Basic Intraoperative Monitoring were adopted in 1986. They called for continual evaluation of oxygenation, ventilation, circulation, and temperature, with an emphasis on a combination of behavior and technology. In the 1990 amendment to these standards pulse oximetry was made a formal standard of care (Table 6-2).

TABLE 6-1. *Harvard Minimal Monitoring Standards*

These standards apply for any administration of anesthesia involving Department of Anaesthesia personnel and are specifically referrable to preplanned anesthetics administered in designated anesthetizing locations (specific exclusion: administration of epidural analgesia for labor or pain management). In emergency circumstances in any location, immediate life support measures of whatever appropriate nature come first with attention turning to the measures described in these standards as soon as possible and practical. These are minimal standards that may be exceeded at any time based on the judgment of the involved anesthesia personnel. These standards encourage high-quality patient care, but observing them cannot guarantee any specific patient outcome. These standards are subject to revision from time to time, as warranted by the evolution of technology and practice.

Anesthesiologist's or nurse anesthetist's presence in operating room
For all anesthetics initiated by or involving a member of the Department of Anaesthesia, an attending or resident anesthesiologist or nurse anesthetist shall be present in the room throughout the conduct of all general anesthetics, regional anesthetics, and monitored intravenous anesthetics. An exception is made when there is a direct known hazard (e.g., radiation) to the anesthesiologist or nurse anesthetist, in which case some provision for monitoring the patient must be made.

Blood pressure and heart rate
Every patient receiving general anesthesia, regional anesthesia, or managed intravenous anesthesia shall have arterial blood pressure and heart rate measured at least every 5 minutes, where not clinically impractical.*

Electrocardiogram
Every patient shall have the electrocardiogram continuously displayed from the induction or institution of anesthesia until preparing to leave the anesthetizing location, where not clinically impractical.*

Continuous monitoring
During every administration of general anesthesia, the anesthetist shall employ methods of continuously monitoring the patient's ventilation and circulation. The methods shall include, for ventilation and circulation each, at least one of the following or the equivalent†:

  For ventilation: Palpation or observation of the reservoir breathing bag, auscultation of breath sounds, monitoring of respiratory gases such as end-tidal carbon dioxide, or monitoring of expiratory gas flow. Monitoring end-tidal carbon dioxide is an emerging standard and is strongly preferred.
  For circulation: Palpation of a pulse, auscultation of heart sounds, monitoring of a tracing of intraarterial pressure, pulse plethysmography/oximetry, or ultrasound peripheral pulse monitoring.
It is recognized that brief interruptions of the continuous monitoring may be unavoidable.

Breathing system disconnection monitoring
When ventilation is controlled by an automatic mechanical ventilator there shall be in continuous use a device that is capable of detecting disconnection of any component of the breathing system. The device must give an audible signal when its alarm threshold is exceeded. (It is recognized that there are certain rare or unusual circumstances in which such a device may fail to detect a disconnection.)

Oxygen analyzer
During every administration of general anesthesia using an anesthesia machine, the concentration of oxygen in the patient's breathing system will be measured by a functioning oxygen analyzer with a low concentration limit alarm in use. This device must conform to the American National Standards Institute No. Z.79.10 standard.*

Ability to measure temperature
During every administration of general anesthesia, there shall be readily available a means to measure the patient's temperature. Rationale: A means of temperature measurement must be available as a potential aid in the diagnosis and treatment of suspected or actual intraoperative hypothermia and malignant hyperthermia. The measurement/monitoring of temperature during every general anesthetic is not specifically mandated because of the potential risks of such monitoring and because of the likelihood of other physical signs giving earlier indication of the development of malignant hyperthermia.

---

* Under extenuating circumstances, the attending anesthesiologist may waive this requirement after so stating (including the reasons) in a note in the patient's chart.
† Equivalence is to be defined by the chief of the individual hospital department after submission to and review by the department heads, Department of Anaesthesia, Harvard Medical School, Boston.
From the Department of Anaesthesia, Harvard Medical School; adopted March 25, 1985; revised July 3, 1985.

Guidelines for Sedation

As nonanesthesiologists are increasingly involved in taking care of patients who undergo sedation in non–operating room settings, the impetus for monitoring recommendations has become more important. As specific minimal monitoring standards are a relatively recent development (1985 and 1986), the guidelines for sedation outside of the traditional settings are even more recent and are still being modified and updated.

Before detailing guidelines, it is important for nonanesthe-siologists to be aware of several aspects of sedation that have been well known to anesthesiologists. First, the level of consciousness of a patient who is being sedated is a continuum, and despite the intended level of sedation or route of administration, a patient may lose protective reflexes and move easily from a light level of sedation to obtundation. The distinction between conscious and deep sedation is made for the purpose of appropriate levels of monitoring. Deep sedation and general anesthesia are virtually inseparable for the purposes of monitoring. Therefore the evaluation, planning, monitoring, and ongoing care of *all* sedated patients

TABLE 6-2. *American Society of Anesthesiologists—Standards for basic intraoperative monitoring*

These standards apply to all anesthesia care although, in emergency circumstances, appropriate life support measures take precedence. These standards may be exceeded at any time based on the judgment of the responsible anesthesiologist. They are intended to encourage high-quality patient care, but observing them cannot guarantee any specific patient outcome. They are subject to revision from time to time, as warranted by the evolution of technology and practice. This set of standards addresses only the issue of basic intraoperative monitoring, which is one component of anesthesia care. In certain rare or unusual circumstances, (1) some of these methods of monitoring may be clinically impractical, and (2) appropriate use of the described monitoring methods may fail to detect untoward clinical developments. Brief interruptions of continual† monitoring may be unavoidable. Under extenuating circumstances, the responsible anesthesiologist may waive the requirements marked with an asterisk (*); it is recommended that when this is done, it should be so stated (including the reasons) in a note in the patient's medical record. These standards are not intended for application to the care of the obstetric patient in labor or in the conduct of pain management.

Standard I

Qualified anesthesia personnel shall be present in the room throughout the conduct of all general anesthetics, regional anesthetics, and monitored anesthesia care.

Objective

Because of the rapid changes in patient status during anesthesia, qualified anesthesia personnel shall be continuously present to monitor the patient and provide anesthesia care. In the event there is a direct known hazard (e.g., radiation) to the anesthesia personnel that might require intermittent remote observation of the patient, some provision for monitoring the patient must be made. In the event that an emergency requires the temporary absence of the person primarily responsible for the anesthetic, the best judgment of the anesthesiologist will be exercised in comparing the emergency with the anesthetized patient's condition and in the selection of the person left responsible for the anesthetic during the temporary absence.

Standard II

During all anesthetics, the patient's oxygenation, ventilation, circulation, and temperature shall be continuously evaluated.

Oxygenation

Objective

To ensure adequate oxygen concentration in the inspired gas and the blood during all anesthetics.

Methods

1. Inspired gas: During every administration of general anesthesia using an anesthesia machine, the concentration of oxygen in the patient's breathing system shall be measured by an oxygen analyzer with a low oxygen concentration limit alarm in use.*
2. Blood oxygenation: During all anesthetics, a quantitative method of assessing oxygenation, such as pulse oximetry, shall be employed.* Adequate illumination and exposure of the patient is necessary to assess color.*

Ventilation

Objective

To ensure adequate ventilation of the patient during all anesthetics.

Methods

1. Every patient receiving general anesthesia shall have the adequacy of ventilation continually evaluated. While qualitative clinical signs such as chest excursion, observation of the reservoir breathing bag and auscultation of breath sounds may be adequate, quantitative monitoring of the CO_2 content and/or volume of expired gas is encouraged.
2. When an endotracheal tube is inserted, its correct positioning in the trachea must be verified. Clinical assessment is essential and end-tidal CO_2 analysis, in use from the time of endotracheal tube placement, is encouraged.
3. When ventilation is controlled by a mechanical ventilator, there shall be in continuous use a device that is capable of detecting disconnection of components of the breathing system. The device must give an audible signal when its alarm threshold is exceeded.
4. During regional anesthesia and monitored anesthesia care, the adequacy of ventilation shall be evaluated, at least, by continual observation of qualitative clinical signs.

Circulation

Objective

To ensure the adequacy of the patient's circulatory function during all anesthetics.

Methods

1. Every patient receiving anesthesia shall have the electrocardiogram continuously displayed from the beginning of anesthesia until preparing to leave the anesthetizing location.*
2. Every patient receiving anesthesia shall have arterial blood pressure and heart rate determined and evaluated at least every 5 minutes.*
3. Every patient receiving general anesthesia shall have, in addition to the above, circulatory function continually evaluated by at least one of the following: palpation of a pulse, auscultation of heart sounds, monitoring of tracing of intraarterial pressure, ultrasound peripheral pulse monitoring, or pulse plethysmography or oximetry.

Body temperature

Objective

To aid in the maintenance of appropriate body temperature during all anesthetics.

Methods

There shall be readily available a means to continuously measure the patient's temperature. When changes in body temperature are intended, anticipated, or suspected, the temperature shall be measured.

---

† Note that "continual" is defined as "repeated regularly and frequently in steady rapid succession," whereas "continuous" means "prolonged without any interruption at any time."

From The American Society of Anesthesiologists; adopted October 6, 1986; effective January 1, 1990.

should be at a level consistent with the potential for general anesthesia, since the level of depressed consciousness and depressed reflexes, ventilation, and blood pressure can change with time even though a patient may initially appear minimally depressed as a result of a given drug regimen.

Second, monitoring a patient who is undergoing sedation during a given procedure requires a person specifically trained and exclusively dedicated to this task. Not only does this free the surgeon or operator to devote full attention to the procedure, but, most important, it allows for increased vigilance in early detection of any change in the patient's status, thus increasing the opportunity to make adjustments before small problems become disasters. It is only through a rational, consistent approach to sedation and monitoring that an overall increase in the safety margin can occur.

Third, it is important that a meticulous, accurate anesthesia record be maintained. It should be a time-based record that includes vital signs and response to drugs given. This allows for accurate review and audit so that guidelines may be reviewed and revised. It also provides a monitoring mechanism so that patient responses can be analyzed and appropriate action taken.

Definitions

As discussed earlier, the definitions of levels of consciousness are somewhat artificial, since they represent a continuum. Nonetheless, for purposes of understanding guidelines the following are presented:

Conscious sedation: A minimally depressed level of consciousness that retains the patient's ability to maintain protective reflexes, to maintain a patent airway independently and continuously, and to respond appropriately to physical stimulation and verbal commands. There is no intent to produce a loss of consciousness by the drugs, doses, and techniques used.

Deep sedation: A controlled state of depressed consciousness or unconsciousness from which the patient is not easily aroused and is unable to respond purposefully to physical stimulation or verbal command. This may be accompanied by a partial or complete loss of protective reflexes and an inability to maintain a patent airway independently.

General anesthesia: A controlled state of unconsciousness accompanied by a loss of protective reflexes, including the ability to maintain a patent airway independently or to respond purposefully to physical stimulation or verbal command.

Local anesthesia: The introduction of a local anesthetic drug by injection in subcutaneous tissue, in proximity to a nerve, or by topical application in such a fashion as to avoid intravascular injection. At blood levels considered toxic, all local anesthetics possess both excitatory (seizure) and depressant (loss of consciousness) central nervous system effects and may, in addition, have profound cardiovascular depressant effects. There may also be inter-active effects between local anesthetic drugs and sedative medications.

American Society of Anesthesiologists Physical Status Classification

Table 6-3 presents the ASA Physical Status Classification. It is used as a tool to help categorize a patient's risk and tolerance for a particular proposed anesthesia plan.

There exists a relative paucity of published guidelines for sedation. Two key sources are among the most complete to date. The first is "Guidelines for Sedation by Nonanesthesiologists During Diagnostic and Therapeutic Procedures," adopted in 1992 by the Department of Anaesthesia of Harvard Medical School and published in 1994. The second is "Guidelines for Monitoring and Management of Pediatric Patients During and After Sedation for Diagnostic and Therapeutic Procedures," published in 1992 by the American Academy of Pediatrics Committee on Drugs. This publication represents a significant revision of that committee's 1985 guidelines. Both sets of guidelines parallel each other quite closely and are intended to serve as minimal guidelines that can be exceeded at any time when judged necessary. As a general rule, patients who are ASA class I or II are frequently considered appropriate candidates for sedation. Patients in ASA class III or IV present special problems such that they must be considered on an individual basis. The following guidelines are from the Department of Anaesthesia at Harvard Medical School.

Guidelines and Recommendations

Personnel and Training

The practitioner responsible for the treatment of the patient and/or the administration of drugs for sedation shall be appropriately trained.

1. The minimum number of available personnel shall be two—the operator (who performs the surgical or diagnostic procedure) and the monitor (an assistant trained to monitor appropriate physiologic variables and to assist in any support or resuscitation measures required), each assigned to their

TABLE 6-3. *Physical Status Classification of the American Society of Anesthesiologists*

Status*	Description
1	Healthy patient
2	Mild systemic disease
3	Severe systemic disease, not incapacitating
4	Severe systemic disease that is a constant threat to life
5	Moribund, not expected to live 24 hours, irrespective of operation

* An E is added to the status number to designate an emergency operation.

specific roles in patient care for the purpose of the planned procedure. Such personnel will be available to the patient from the time of administration of the sedative medication until recovery is judged adequate or the care of the patient is transferred to personnel performing recovery care.

2. The director of the care unit or service performing the procedure shall certify that all physicians administering sedative medications are trained in airway management and trained in the safe use of these drugs. (a) ''Trained in airway management'' shall mean that their training is consistent with the airway management goals and procedures used for advanced cardiac life support, including positioning of the airway, the use of oropharyngeal and nasopharyngeal airways, and the application of positive-pressure ventilation by bag and mask. (b) ''Trained in the safe use of these drugs'' shall be achievable through suitable educational programs, which may include training with members of the department of anesthesia, as described below.

3. The department of anesthesia will participate in the organization of a hospital-wide educational program to inform practitioners of guidelines for the use of sedating drugs and monitoring modalities. It would be appropriate for such a program to be accredited for continuing education in risk management.

4. The means for notifying additional support services such as respiratory therapy, practitioners skilled in tracheal intubation (e.g., an anesthesiologist), and activating ''code'' pages should be clearly identified and posted in procedure/ sedation areas.

Equipment and Maintenance

1. A self-inflating positive-pressure oxygen (O_2) delivery system capable of delivering at least 90% O_2 at a 15-L/min flow rate for at least 60 minutes must be available. Various bag and mask sizes must be available in those circumstances where appropriate (e.g., for pediatric patients.)

2. A source of suction (portable or wall) must be available, with a vacuum capability of 18 to 24 inches of mercury or a flow capability of 100 L/min with an orifice size of 14 mm.

3. An emergency cart or kit must be readily available and should include the necessary drugs and equipment to resuscitate an apneic and unconscious patient and provide continuous support while that patient is being transported to another area. Standardized hospital resuscitation carts can generally be used for this purpose.

4. Equipment appropriate to the technique being used should be available in good working order immediately before, during, and after the procedure. This shall include means for providing supplemental O_2 delivered via nasal prongs and nonrebreathing or rebreathing O_2 masks.

5. When inhalation sedation is provided with nitrous oxide (N_2O), it must be delivered with equipment that (a) cannot provide a concentration of N_2O in excess of 50% inspired; (b) will provide a maximum of 100% and never less than 21% O_2 concentration; (c) is outfitted with an O_2

analyzer to monitor the accuracy of delivered gases; and (d) is checked and calibrated annually, or according to a maintenance schedule established in conjunction with the hospital's biomedical engineering department. Inhalation sedation also must be delivered with a care plan that excludes or limits the prior administration of other sedative or opioid medications.

6. A pulse oximeter for noninvasive monitoring of O_2 must be continuously in use during conscious or deep sedation.

7. All equipment shall be inventoried and maintained on a regularly scheduled basis, in conjunction with policies established by the hospital's biomedical engineering department.

Consent

The patient or guardian must be informed about the risks of and alternatives to sedation as a component of the planned procedure. Documentation of consent should be placed in the medical record before the procedure.

Monitoring

Whenever drugs for conscious or deep sedation are administered, a trained individual should monitor the patient. A conscious-sedation patient shall be frequently observed by a trained person. A deep-sedation patient shall always, without interruption, continuously be observed by a trained person.

1. Heart and respiratory rates should be recorded at specific intervals. A stethoscope for monitoring heart rate (HR), respiratory rate (RR), and adequacy of tidal volume is considered to be the minimum monitoring equipment needed. Continuous ECG monitoring for arrhythmias and in patients with preexisting cardiac disease is recommended

2. Skin color (e.g., nail beds, mucosae) shall be visually monitored whenever possible and recorded every 5 minutes. If a restraining device is used and covers the patient, a hand or foot should be left exposed whenever possible.

3. Head position should be checked frequently and adjusted if necessary to ensure a patent airway.

4. Oxygen saturation shall be monitored noninvasively on a continuous basis by pulse oximeter.

Documentation

There shall be written documentation of all aspects of care rendered to the patient. A standard document as part of the medical record would be useful for all sedation locations within the institution, as it could be reviewed for purposes of quality assurance and improvement of general patient care.
Before Procedure.

1. Baseline health evaluation shall include a brief health

history reflecting (a) allergies and previous adverse drug reactions, (b) current medications, (c) diseases, disorders, and abnormalities, (d) prior hospitalizations, (e) pertinent family history of disease or disorders, and (f) review of systems. It also should include a physical examination reflecting (g) height and weight, (h) vital signs, (i) airway assessment, and (j) pulmonary and cardiac examination, as well as a risk assessment including the ASA Physical Status Classification.

2. Recent and last food intake time must be assessed, and dietary precautions (fasting history) consistent within the institution must be followed.

3. Rationale for sedation.

4. The sedation plan.

5. Patient's physician and telephone number.

During Procedure. The designated monitor shall record the following:

1. Vital signs, including HR, blood pressure (BP), RR, and patient responsiveness every 5 minutes.

2. Oxygenation: Patient's color (nail beds, mucosae) when feasible; oxygen saturation by pulse oximetry every 5 minutes.

3. Medications given (route, site, time, drug, and dose), including O_2 therapy in liters per minute and means delivered (e.g., nasal prongs, rebreathing mask).

After Procedure.

1. The time of discharge and patient condition.

2. Discharge plan (name of responsible party, patient location).

3. Patient instructions, including an explanation of potential or anticipated postsedation effects and limitations on activities and behavior, such as dietary precautions. A 24-hour emergency contact telephone number should be provided to all patients.

Provisions for Patient Care Following the Procedure and Discharge Planning

When the procedure has been completed and the patient is being readied for discharge or transfer, the vital signs and patient responsiveness shall be monitored by skilled nursing practitioners in a properly equipped area with (a) functioning suction apparatus; (b) the capability of delivering more than 90% O_2 with positive-pressure ventilation (bag and mask); (c) a means of obtaining and recording vital signs at specific intervals; and (d) pulse oximetry monitoring until the patient returns to the preprocedure state.

Release to a less well-monitored level of care should be permitted only when the patient has returned to presedation status with regard to (a) airway, breathing, and circulation; (b) level of consciousness; (c) ability to sit unaided; (d) ability to walk with assistance; and (e) state of hydration.

If patients are to be discharged home, they must be under the care of a competent adult.

If patients are to be transferred to further care within the institution, standard criteria shall be applied for transfer of care between skilled nursing practitioners.

CONCLUSION

As an increasing number of nonanesthesiologists have become involved in the sedation management of their patients, knowledge of safety monitoring guidelines and their development has become essential. With the appropriate use of monitoring equipment and a consistent, rational approach to sedation, including assigning a person dedicated to the monitoring task, patient safety can be greatly enhanced.

SUGGESTED READING LIST

1. American Academy of Pediatrics Committee on Drugs. Guidelines for monitoring and management of pediatric patients during and after sedation for diagnostic and therapeutic procedures. Pediatrics 1992;89:1110.
2. Barash PG, Cullen BF, Stoelting RF. Evaluation of the patient and preoperative preparation. In: Barash PG, Cullen BF, Stoelting RF, eds. Handbook of clinical anesthesia. Philadelphia: J.B. Lippincott, 1993:3.
3. Barash PG, Cullen BF, Stoelting RK. Monitoring the anesthetized patient. In: Bavash PG, Cullen BF, Stoelting RK, eds. Handbook of clinical anesthesia. Philadelphia: J.B. Lippincott, 1993:63.
4. Barker SJ, Tremper KK. Pulse oximetry: applications and limitations. Int Anesthesiol Clin 1987;67:551.
5. Cook DR. Pediatric anesthesia. In: Barash PG, Cullen BF, Stoelting RK, eds. Clinical anesthesia. Philadelphia: J.B. Lippincott, 1992:1335.
6. Council of Scientific Affairs, American Medical Association. The use of pulse oximetry during conscious sedation. JAMA 1993;270:1473.
7. Eichhorn JH. Contemporary anesthesia practice and quality assurance. In: Barash PG, Cullen BF, Stoelting RK, eds. Clinical anesthesia. Philadelphia: J.B. Lippincott, 1992:35.
8. Eichhorn JH. Effect of monitoring standards on anesthesia outcome. Int Anesthesiol Clin 1993;31(3):181.
9. Eichhorn JH. Pulse oximetry as standard of practice in anesthesia. Anesthesiology 1993;78:423.
10. Eichhorn JH. Standards for patient monitoring. In: Rogers MC, Tinker JH, Covino BG, Longnecker DE, eds. Principles and practice of anesthesiology. St. Louis, MO: Mosby–Year Book, 1993:745.
11. Eichhorn JH, Cooper JB, Cullen DJ, Maier WR, Philip JH, Seeman RG. Standards for patient monitoring during anesthesia at Harvard Medical School. JAMA 1986;256:1017.
12. Gomez MN. Planning for monitoring in healthy patients. In: Rogers MC, Tinker JH, Covino BG, Longnecker DE, eds. Principles and practice of anesthesiology. St. Louis, MO: Mosby–Year Book, 1993:74.
13. Hall SC. Pediatric sedation: guidelines and ASA. American Society of Anesthesiologists Newsletter 1995;59:13.
14. Holzman RS, Cullen DJ, Eichhorn JH, Philip JH. Guidelines for sedation by nonanesthesiologists during diagnostic and therapeutic procedures. J Clin Anesth 1994;6:265.
15. McPherson RW. Intraoperative neurologic monitoring. In: Rogers MC, Tinker JH, Covino BG, Longnecker DE, eds. Principles and practice of anesthesiology. St. Louis, MO: Mosby–Year Book, 1993:803.
16. Petersdorf RG. Alterations in body temperature. In: Peterdorf, Adams, Braunwald, Isselbacher, Martin, Wilson, eds. Harrison's principles of internal medicine. New York: McGraw-Hill, 1983:50.
17. Severinghaus JW, Naifeh KIT. Accuracy of response of six pulse oximeters to profound hypoxia. Anesthesiology 1987;67:551.
18. Singer R, Thomas PE. Pulse oximeter in the ambulatory aesthetic surgical facility. Plast Reconstr Surg 1988;82:111.
19. Stoelting RF, Miller Rd. Monitoring. In: Stoelting RF, Miller RD, eds. Basics of anesthesia. New York: Churchill Livingstone, 1989:211.
20. Yaster M. Anesthesia for surgical emergencies in newborns. In: Rogers MC, Tinker JH, Covino BG, Longnecker DE, eds. Principles and practice of anesthesiology. St. Louis, MO: Mosby–Year Book, 1993:2137.

Textbook of Dermatologic Surgery, edited by John L. Ratz.
Lippincott–Raven Publishers, Philadelphia © 1998.

CHAPTER **7**

Surgical Complication: Prevention, Recognition, and Treatment

Raymond G. Dufresne, Jr.

Surgical complications are an expected outcome of surgery for a small percentage of patients. With dermatologic surgery, complications can range from serious problems such as infections and tissue necrosis to minor problems such as milia (Table 7-1). A minor surgical complication can compound and result in other, potentially more serious complications. For example, poor hemostasis can result in a hematoma, which places the wound at risk of a hematoma, frequently resulting in a hypertrophic scar.

An understanding of the complications of any procedure is required. In most instances, one can screen for the risk factors for complications and institute prophylactic measures. Prudent recognition of a potential complication allows adequate treatment. Patient education of the potential risks and identification of early signs of complications can have a major impact on the patient's perception of the surgical outcome. Thus familiarity with surgical complications increases success in dermatologic surgery.

Raymond G. Dufresne, Jr.: Department of Dermatology, Brown University School of Medicine; Rhode Island Hospital, University Dermatology, 593 Eddy Street, Providence, RI 02903.

BLEEDING AND HEMATOMA

Minor bleeding occurs during cutaneous surgery, but severe bleeding can have a negative impact on the final outcome of wound healing. The causes of a bleeding complication are myriad (Table 7-2): defects in coagulation or platelet abnormality, mechanical problems such as hypertension (>150/100 mm Hg), or failure of adequate surgical hemostasis.

In the evaluation for bleeding risk, the history of prior bleeding may be one of the most cost-effective and high-yielding approaches to the identification of a patient at risk. One should inquire about problems with past surgery, dental procedures, or excessive menstrual bleeding. A family history of bleeding should be discovered. The medical history should be reviewed for medicines and diseases that increase the risk for bleeding. Further progression to laboratory evaluation is not necessary if no problems are identified in the history. In larger procedures or if the history suggests a problem, a screening evaluation can be performed with a prothrombin time (PT), partial thromboplastin time (PTT), com-

TABLE 7-1. *Surgical complications: A partial list*

Ecchymosis
Bleeding
Hematoma
Seroma
Tissue necrosis
Dehiscence

Wound infection
Cellulitis
Chondritis
Osteomyelitis
Tendon rupture
Toxic shock
Infection of implants
Infection of cardiac malformation

Scar
Scar contracture
Hypertrophic scar
Keloid

Patient dissatisfaction
Pain
Edema
Foreign body reactions: Suture, talc, starch
Pruritus
Telangiectasia
Pyoderma gangrenosa
Milia
Hypopigmentation
Hyperpigmentation
Erythema
Koebnerization
Contact dermatitis

Anaphylactic reactions
Medication toxicity
Seizures
Cardiac arrhythmia
Cardiac arrest
Respiratory depression

plete blood cell count (CBC) with platelets, and a bleeding time. The PT tests for an intrinsic cascade defect (factors II, V, VII, and X); the PTT detects an extrinsic cascade defect (factors VIII, IX, XI, and XII). A platelet count measures the number of platelets but not their functional activity. A bleeding time can be used to further evaluate platelet function. In most cases of cutaneous surgery, screening laboratory tests are not necessary.

Obviously, medications such as heparin, warfarin (Coumadin), and aspirin can have major effect on operative bleeding. Heparin, with a half-life of about 1 hour (intravenous [IV]), can be reversed perioperatively by discontinuation for a brief period. If needed, protamine sulfate IV can be used to block the effects of heparin. Thrombocytopenia can occur as a complication of heparin therapy, and a platelet count should be obtained.

Warfarin is a commonly encountered medication in the

office setting. However, for most procedures in which complex reconstruction is not involved, the final outcome does not appear to be affected by the use of warfarin. If a complex closure is anticipated, the warfarin can usually be discontinued. The primary care physician should be involved to help weigh the risk of temporary discontinuation (e.g., low risk [thrombosis prophylaxis] or high risk [anticoagulation for an artificial valve]). If warfarin must be discontinued in a patient who requires anticoagulation, subcutaneous heparin can be used during the perioperative period.

If excessive bleeding occurs in a patient receiving warfarin, vitamin K (oral, IV, or intramuscular [IM]) can be used to reverse the warfarin effects. If the situation is urgent, fresh-frozen plasma or cryoprecipitate of plasma can be used to restore the needed coagulation proteins.

Aspirin irreversibly inactivates platelets and can have a significant effect on bleeding complications, especially in skin grafting and other complex reconstructions (Fig. 1). This common drug may not be recognized by the patient as an ingredient in many over-the-counter medications. Patients can be given an extensive list of products that contain aspirin.

In common coagulation defects, such as von Willebrand's disease (VIII), hemophilia A, and hemophilia B, taking ε-aminocaproic acid before and after minor procedures decreases bleeding complications. Consultation with the responsible hematologist is obviously important.

During the operative procedure, if excessive bleeding is observed, a review of the risks such as alcohol and aspirin should be made and the blood pressure determined. Medications can be reviewed again. More careful attention to he-

TABLE 7-2. *Hemostasis*

Physical problems
Hypertension
Vessel retraction
Failure of suture ligation
Transient vasoconstriction
  Epinephrine
  Traumatic vessel response
Platelet problems
Abnormal number
  Bone marrow failure
  Disseminated intravascular coagulation
  Idiopathic thrombocytopenia
  Thrombocytosis
Platelet dysfunction
  Drugs: Aspirin and nonsteroidal anti-inflammatory drugs; dipyridamole, phenothiazine, furosemide, vitamin E
  Disease states: Uremia, liver failure, von Willebrand's disease
Coagulation cascade defects
Hemophilia A/(factor VIII)
Hemophilia B/(factor IX)
von Willebrand's disease
Coumadin
Heparin
Liver disease
Vitamin K deficiency
Lupus anticoagulant

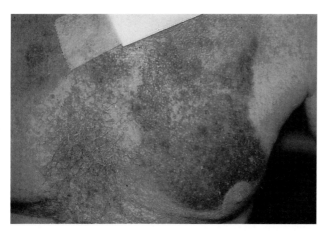

FIG. 1. Postoperative ecchymosis of the chest attributable to aspirin use. (See Color Plate 1.)

mostasis with electrocautery and suture ligation of larger vessels may result in significant improvement. A pressure dressing should be implemented followed by examination of the wound the next day. A drain (Penrose or suction drain) can also be used for 24 hours to avoid the development of a hematoma. To minimize the risk of infection, the drain should be removed as soon as possible, usually within 24 hours.

If postoperative bleeding continues or is significant intraoperatively, further hematologic evaluation for an underlying coagulopathy should be pursued. An immediate CBC with platelet count, PT, and PTT can be obtained to identify any underlying problem. A bleeding time may help identify a platelet functional problem such as aspirin use. This will allow a specific approach in reversing the underlying condition.

Mild ecchymosis around the wound is not uncommon. Minor bleeding under the surface gives the classic ecchymosis, usually associated with edema. This resolves in a few weeks after progressing through a yellow-brown resorption phase. Certain sites, such as the periorbital area, are more prone to ecchymosis. Ecchymosis can be striking in certain patients, especially in patients with an underlying coagulapathy or incipient aspirin use. Ice packs may aid the edema, but the "treatment" is evaluation to rule out a hematoma and reassurance to the patient.

A hematoma can arise from slippage of ligation, inapparent bleeding that was masked by the vasoconstriction of local anesthetics, or a coagulopathy. A dead space is an invitation to hematoma development. If a hematoma does develop, this can be addressed by trying to remove the somewhat gelatinous hematoma that is present in the first few days. The wound is partially opened, and the hematoma can be massaged and removed with a mosquito forceps or similar appliance. This wound should be observed closely to ensure that the bleeding process has, indeed, resolved. The wound can be resutured. Later in the progression of a hematoma (7

to 10 days), there is breakdown to a more fluidlike material. This fluid may be expressed via a large-bore needle or a small incision. With time, complete resolution of minor hematoma occurs. Mild firmness may be persistent for several weeks to months until the hematoma has been fully reorganized and absorbed.

A hematoma under tension, resulting from a significant arterial bleeding or sustained excessive oozing, presents more of a concern. This tension can result in significant tissue necrosis in a relatively short period. Pain is the first and constant clue to a tension hematoma. In such a tension lesion the sutures should be removed and the identifying arterial bleeding ligated.

Hematomas can be more dangerous in certain locations. Excessively tense hematomas in the neck attributable to rhytidectomy have compromised breathing. Retrobulbar hematoma can result in blindness, a well-described complication of blepharoplasty. In an extremity, bleeding can result in a significant loss of blood and in extreme situations result in a compartment compression syndrome.

SEROMA

Seromas result from the transudation of serum into the wound. Generally, a seroma is a less significant problem than a hematoma. Many seromas can be simply drained by means of a large-bore needle and syringe or be focally opened and drained. Small seromas resolve spontaneously.

Seromas may interfere with the adhesion of a skin graft. Classically, tie-down dressings for skin grafting have been used to minimize the development of seroma. Machine meshings can be used to allow seromas and hematomas to drain. Fibrin glues have been used as a new approach to avoid a seroma in a head and neck surgery animal model and have been employed in skin grafts. Fibrin types of glue may prove to have a wider role in dermatologic surgery.

TISSUE NECROSIS

Tissue necrosis is usually a result of interference of the circulatory supply to a flap or skin edges. Tension on the wound is a common cause of tissue necrosis; excess tension may result from poor or limited design options or from a complication such as infection or a large hematoma. Poor tissue handling with crush injury can also play a role. Excessive edema also increases the tension. The use of ice packs and elevation may be helpful in the initial 24 hours. Hematoma may cause necrosis by tension, especially a tension hematoma, but hematoma-associated necrosis is also associated with free radicals that may play a role in tissue necrosis.

In a flap, blood supply can also be compromised by multiple factors: poor design with a compromised pedicle, excessive edema, venous congestion, hematoma, or infection. Smoking is a significant risk; smoking more than one pack

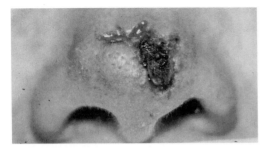

FIG. 2. Necrotic flap in a patient who smoked cigarettes.

of cigarettes a day increases the risk of necrosis of a flap or skin graft threefold (Fig. 2). In a skin graft, tissue necrosis can occur as a result of lack of appropriate attachment to the base (e.g., movement, hematoma, or seroma), poor vascular supply at the base of the graft (e.g., cartilage/bone) (Fig. 3), or infection. Traditionally, a tie-down dressing has been an attempt to minimize this, although the tie-down dressing may not be as essential as it was considered to be in the past. As an alternative, the graft can be quilted (basting sutures) to the deep margin to achieve the same goal. Fibrin glues may increase survival of infected skin grafts.

When tissue necrosis occurs in a skin graft or a flap, initially there will be erythema or violatious changes around the wound, followed by development of a black tissue eschar (Fig. 2). Over the ensuing week or so, there will be further demarcation of the necrotic tissue. The initial inclination toward aggressive debridement should be limited until the demarcation is quite obvious. The dead tissue then can be removed with the scalpel or sharp scissors. Frequently there may be only a superficial loss at the end of demarcation, and a larger than expected amount of the skin graft or flap remains intact. In many cases, further revision is not necessary, since the defect can heal with second intention with excellent cosmetic results.

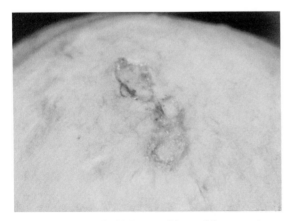

FIG. 3. Failure of split-thickness skin graft in a poorly vascularized site.

DEHISCENCE

Dehiscence of a wound is an unfortunate outcome. Dehiscence may be associated with delayed healing, excessive tension, premature removal of sutures, or complications such as infection or hematoma. Age (>65 years), pulmonary disease, obesity , uremia, systemic steroid use, malnutrition, and cytotoxic drugs among other factors have been identified as risks for dehiscence (Table 7-3). Trauma from poor technique may compromise the closure. Excessive electrocautery and electrosurgery are associated with a decrease of tensile strength. Extrasecure closures (e.g., long-lasting materials such as polygloconate) can be used in wounds at risk of dehiscence. The added support from a stretching suture such as polybuster (Novafil) may be beneficial in dehiscence avoidance.

Tension is a major factor in a dehiscence. Simply stated, tension can mechanically separate the wound. In addition, tension may operate in a more pathophysiologic manner causing increased neutrophils, which leads to decreased wound strength. However, patients may not realize that the wound strength is weak in the first few weeks of healing. Wound strength is about 5% of normal tissue strength at 2 weeks, increasing to 35% at 1 month. With trauma and excessive movement the wound may simply open. The use of taping, adhesive strips, or polyurethane adhesive dress-

TABLE 7-3. *Risk of dehiscence*

Systemic
Obesity
Uremia
Systemic steroids
Cushing's disease
Thyroid disease
Liver disease
Congestive heart failure
Pulmonary
Hypertension
Ascites
Hyperalimentation
Systemic infection
Malignancy
Hypoproteinemia
Surgical complications
Crush trauma
Electrosurgery
Hematoma
Infection
Tension
Medications
Anticoagulants
Aspirin
Colchicine
Systemic corticosteroids
Penicillamine
Cyclosporine
Metronidazole
β-Aminopropionitrile
Cytotoxic/medications/chemotherapeutics

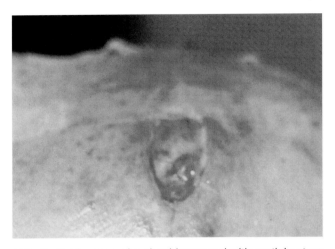

FIG. 4. Dehiscence of a shoulder wound with partial suture closure and supported with taping.

ings can be an effective reminder to limit activities, even if these devices do not offer significant strength to the closure. A sling can be used to decrease movement and support the extremities.

Despite the best technique and postoperative care, however, a dehiscence may still occur. In the uncomplicated dehiscence, the defect frequently can be resutured within the first 24 hours. Opinions differ on the need to prophylactically treat for an infection in a simple dehiscence.

Traditional wisdom prohibits the resuturing of dehiscence caused by an infected wound. The wound should be open to allow ample drainage of the infected site. In larger, deeper wounds, packing such as Iodoform gauze can be placed and removed gradually as the wound heals. The use of routine

antibiotics is not defined. If frank purulent drainage is present or the dehiscence is associated with cellulitis, Gram's stain and culture, if possible, and appropriate antibiotics would be prudent.

In larger dehiscence, there is growing support for the secondary closure of dehiscence wounds in the surgical literature. A delayed closure without wide resection is effective and safe. The wounds are debrided if needed and allowed to develop early granulation tissue. If there is no clinical organism of infection or with low bacterial counts (less than 100,000/g per gram tissue), the wound is safely reapproximated. Such reclosure is not routine in dermatologic surgery, but near-complete partial closures with polyglyconate can be performed and should be further evaluated (Fig. 4). A short course of perioperative antibiotics may be wise in this situation, although the use of perioperative antibiotics is debated in the general surgery and gynecology literature.

WOUND INFECTIONS

Wound infections are an uncommon complication of clean wound surgery—about 0.7% percent in skin surgery, significantly less than the 1.8% risk of infection in clean general surgery procedures. However, postoperative wound infection is a serious complication leading to dehiscence, necrosis, and cellulitis (Fig. 5).

The patient should be evaluated for risks of infection such as a history of wound infections, abnormal skin that may be colonized with bacteria, poor overall health, and debilitation. Routine treatments with preoperative antibiotics have been advocated by some authors. However, this is not the standard of care in clean skin surgery. The low incidence of postoper-

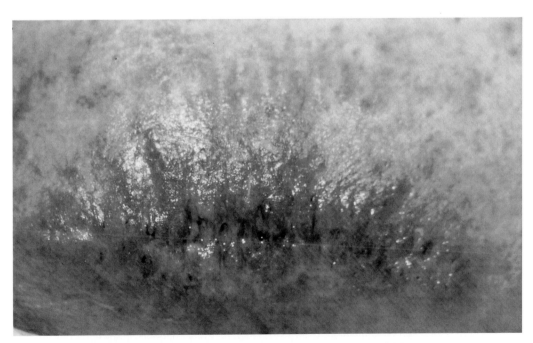

FIG. 5. Cellulitis and wound infection with partial early dehiscence.

TABLE 7-4. *Factors that increase the risk of infection*

Malnutrition
Renal failure
Immunosuppression
   Corticosteroids
   Cytotoxic medications
   Myeloproliferative disorders
Obesity
Poorly regulated diabetes
Advanced age
Surgical drains
Alcohol abuse
Myeloproliferative disease

ative wound infections in clean and clean-contaminated wounds makes systemic treatment of routine cutaneous surgery both unnecessary and potentially dangerous.

In addition, during the consultations, medical conditions such as cardiac valves replacement, congenital or rheumatic valvular disease, and mitral valve prolapse with regurgitation must be detected so that the patient can be provided prophylactic antibiotics. Patients with joint replacements, new arterial grafts, and cerebral spinal shunt can be considered for prophylactic therapy; recommendation from the responsible physician is essential. There are no clear guidelines for prophylaxis of endocarditis or artificial implants in cutaneous surgery. Bacteremia has been demonstrated in contaminated wounds and occasionally in clean but ulcerated skin cancers. Prudent care would thus suggest prophylaxis. Prophylaxis usually consists of dicloxicillin or a cephalosporin 1 to 2 g hour preoperatively with 500 mg 6 hours postoperatively. Clindamycin, vancomycin, and erythromycin are alternatives in the penicillin-allergic patient. Patients with pacemakers and hemodialysis shunts probably do not merit routine prophylaxis. See Chapter 3 for a full discussion of antibiotic treatment.

Grossly contaminated wounds or surgery in contaminated fields (e.g., mucosal surfaces, axillae or groin) can be considered for prophylactic antibiotic therapy. Judgment can be used in circumstances that are associated with increased infection rates (Table 7-4). In the prophylactic avoidance of wound infections, antibiotic administration 1-2 hrs before the surgery is the most important aspect of therapy. The use of antibiotics for days before or after the surgery is not any more effective and offers higher risks than a preoperative and postoperative dose.

The physician and staff must follow standard methods of infection control. These include hand washing, surgical preparation, sterile drapes and instruments, sterile intraoperative technique, and application of sterile dressings. Masks and gowns should be standard to protect the patient and staff alike. Should a series of infections be detected, the office may harbor a staphloccocus carrier, or supplies (such as ink, disinfectants) or even the air can be contaminated.

The initial treatment of a skin infection depends on the anticipated organisms based on clinical parameters. Gram's stain (and, later, a culture) may help in the selection of antibiotics. *Staphylococcus aureus* is the principal serious organism in wound infections. Other gram-positive organisms such as β-hemolytic streptococci or *Staphylococcus epidermidis* can cause wound infections. In intertriginous sites gram-negative organisms such as *Escherichia coli* and *Proteus* or *Pseudomonas* species must be considered. *Pseudomonas* organisms can be a particular problem in the external ear.

Unusual exposures of the wound may result in unusual infection. *Pseudomonas* wound infection resulting from a whirlpool infection or contaminated surgical preparations has been described. Rarely, wounds can be contaminated with *Mycobacterium* or *Aspergillus* organisms. Wounds that are not responding well to the usual antibiotics and are demonstrating no growth on standard bacterial culturing should have an expanded differential diagnosis of infection. This is especially important in patients who are immune compromised. Unusual complications can occur, such as toxic shock, osteomyelitis, and tendon rupture, especially in large or deep wounds.

In most cases of cutaneous wound infections, a penicillinase-resistant penicillin, or first-generation cephalosporin is sufficient. Time-honored opening and draining of purulent material and packing of the wound must be employed. In the rare serious infection, debridement and IV antibiotics may be needed.

Chondritis of the ear is a potentially serious infection. Mild chondritis is common in ear surgery (Fig. 6). Antidotal use of tetracycline or erythromycin as a prophylactic mea-

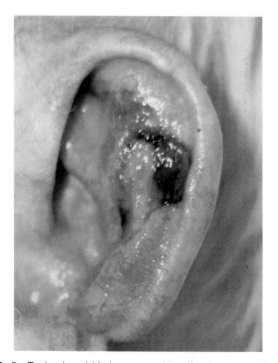

FIG. 6. Early chondritis in a wound healing by second intention.

sure has been suggested. Acetic acid soaks (.25%) may help prevent pseudomonas infection and are soothing. Nonsteroidal agents and cool compresses may give some relief. Skin grafting has been advocated by some authors as a prophylactic measure to prevent infection.

In chondritis, pain is a prominent symptom, along with erythema and warmth. *Pseudomonas* and *Staphylococcus* organisms are the two most common pathogens. However, severe infections can result in malignant external otitis. This infection is characterized by progressive chondritis, an infiltrating infection of the ear, spreading into the adjacent bony tissues with a poor response to systemic antibiotics alone. *Pseudomonas* organism is usually the responsible agent, although rarely, other organisms such as *Aspergillus* species may be pathogenic for malignant otitis. This destructive process requires aggressive treatment including gross debridement, hospitalization, and intravenous antibiotics.

Candidal infection is probably an underrecognized secondary infection. It can easily occur in the popular moist, occluded approach to wound care. Candidal infection can occur in wounds healing by second intention, sutured wounds, and dermabrasion. There may be erythema and possibly focal crusting, and occasionally pustules may be evident in the area. Removal of the occlusive dressing and the use of topical anticandidal therapy quickly resolve this complication.

Herpetic activation by a surgical procedure must be considered before a procedure. Certain risks for viral activation can be identified based on a history of herpetic disease in the proposed surgical site or in sites such as the perioral area, which are at high risk of herpetic involvement. In these situations prophylactic treatment would be wise. The optimal dosage for prophylaxis is not known. One gram of acyclovir in divided doses before surgery, followed by 200 mg three times daily until the wound is healed has been an effective schedule. If activated, these lesions spread along the surgical site and can be extensive in wounds such as those caused by dermabrasion. Usually these infected wounds heal without sequelae, but scarring can occur.

SCARRING

Simple Scarring

Scarring is intrinsic to the healing process after injury as new collagen is deposited and remodeled, but never exactly replicating the original. Scar avoidance is impossible. Proper design to minimize tension and cosmetic scar placement are basic to cutaneous surgery.

Early dermabrasion has been found to be of benefit in the treatment of scars. Yarborough's report of wire-brush dermabrasion of traumatic scarring suggested that early dermabrasion was possible and offered superior results to late dermabrasion. The effectiveness of early scar abrasion was confirmed in facial and nonfacial excision scars using a diamond fraise. The optimal response to dermabrasion of scar was at 8 weeks. These studies confirmed and quantified the earlier reports on the usage of dermabrasion of scars.

Widening of Scars

Scar widening is a particularly vexing problem, especially on the trunk and proximal extremities. The patient must be forewarned that this is the usual, expected result in these sites. These truncal sites are slow to heal and are subject to the high stress of strong large-muscle movement. Reducing stress on the areas by lessening mobility and supporting of the extremities such as with an arm sling may be helpful. However, the patient usually returns to activity in a few weeks, long before the final scar maturation has occurred, a process that requires a year.

The literature is replete with attempts to minimize the expansion of scar. Tension across the wound is a defined factor in this development (Fig. 7). With tension, collagen deposition is aligned to the wound, allowing widening to occur with stress. The widening of scars appears to be progressive and linear, so any approach that delays the initial component of stretching decreases scar width.

Running, buried, nonabsorbable sutures such as prolene or nylon can be left in place for 3 weeks or more. Suture removal can be difficult if sutures are left in place for a longer period. Slow-absorbing sutures such as Maxon or polydioxanone suture (PDS) can be used in a similar manner. The use of these absorbable materials with prolonged tensile strength is associated with improved scar outcomes when compared with materials that quickly lose their strength. The use of catgut and Dexon have no effect in limiting wound widening.

In facial scars, widening occurs less frequently but is more of a concern to the patient and the physician. The develop-

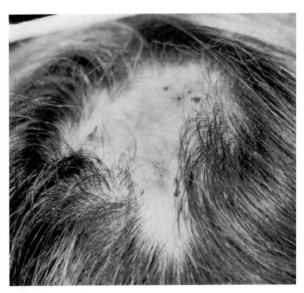

FIG. 7. Widening of scalp scar closed under tension.

ment of unusually high tension usually leads to this complication. This tension may occur because of limited closure options. Proper design of the closure may be the best preventive measure. Wide undermining and intraoperative tissue expansion can decrease the wound closure tension. In the event that this widening occurs and is a cosmetic or functional problem, the scar can be excised later, after tissue relaxation has occurred. The surgeon can consider options such as tissue expansion, local flaps, or Z- or W-plasty to redistribute the tension.

Rarely, striae have been reported as a complication of excisional surgery. This complication has been reported in three Japanese women on the buttocks and postaxillary region. No clear treatment for striae distensae has been demonstrated. Use of tretinoin (Retin-A), CO_2 laser abrasion, and pulsed dye laser have been discussed as possible modes of therapy for striae.

Scar Contracture

Healthy wounds heal with contracture. In second-intention healing a myofibroblast may be responsible for the initial contraction. This is usually to the patient's benefit, resulting in a decreased size of the final defect. Occasionally, this contraction can present a problem, pulling on an important structure, especially along a free edge. Skin grafting, especially full-thickness skin grafting, may significantly decrease wound contracture and deformity at a free edge.

Scar contracture also occurs in linear closures. Sommerland reported a 15% rate of scar contracture at 3 months, but this is usually of little medical significance. However, contracture on a free edge such as the lower lip, eyelid, nose, or ears in the previously well-executed closure may result in functional or cosmetic problems.

Prevention of scar contracture at free edges begins with the design. M-Plasty can be used to avoid the unnecessary extension of a defect toward the free edge. Z-Plasty can be used for prophylaxis. If a contraction occurs, massage of the wound and intralesional therapy with steroids such as triamcinolone may help solve the problem. However, a scar revision may be necessary. Classically, Z-plasty can be used to extend the scar and redistribute tension.

Hypertrophic Scars and Keloid

Hypertrophic scars and keloid can occur in many locations but are more common on the trunk and extremities than on the face. Certain individuals demonstrate a familial tendency, a historical fact that is highly important to elicit during a preoperative evaluation. Electrodesiccation and CO_2 laser can cause hypertrophic scars, especially in nonfacial locations. Wound healing complications such as excessive tension, infection, or hematoma are frequently followed by hypertrophic scar.

In a patient at risk for hypertrophic scars the prophylactic

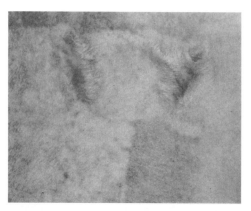

FIG. 8. Hypertrophic scar of neck after argon laser therapy of port wine stain.

use of potent topical steroids has been advocated by some authorities. Silicone sheeting is a safe, effective approach. If a hypertrophic scar develops, intervention with intralesional steroids (possibly adjunctively with class I topical steroids) or silicone gel sheeting usually results in good resolution. At times, hypertrophic scars may improve without any intervention. The telangiectatic nature of a hypertrophic scar responds to the pulsed dye laser.

Hypertrophic scarring can be a particular problem in advanced procedures. Certain procedures and locations are associated with hypertrophic scarring. The argon or KTP laser is well described in association with hypertrophic scarring, especially on the neck (Fig. 8) and the extremity. In dermabrasion and deep chemical peelings, scarring on the malar or mandibular rim is a defined risk. Patients who have had previous treatment with oral retinoids are a particular problem. Early recognition of scarring in these patients with persistent erythema should be addressed immediately with potent topical steroids and if needed, intralesional therapy with corticosteroids to stop the progression and aid in the resolution of these scars (Figs. 9 and 10).

Keloids do not tend to spontaneously improve. The prophylactic treatment or intervention with silicone sheet gel, applied at least 12 hours daily to the site, should be initiated in the patient at risk. Numerous traditional therapies are in use to control keloid formation. Potent intralesional steroids (e.g., 20 to 40 mg% triamcinolone) may control the problem. Close, long-term follow-up is important to avoid the "escape" of the growth. Compression appliances that the patient can wear or compression earrings or splints have been used as an adjunct to intralesional therapy. Pulsed dye lasers may also improve the appearance of keloids. At times, adjunctive radiation therapy can be used to decrease recurrence of a particularly difficult keloid. Details on treatment of keloids are available elsewhere in this text.

Trap Door Deformity

Trap door deformity is a well-recognized complication of flap reconstruction (Fig. 11) or larger circular closures.

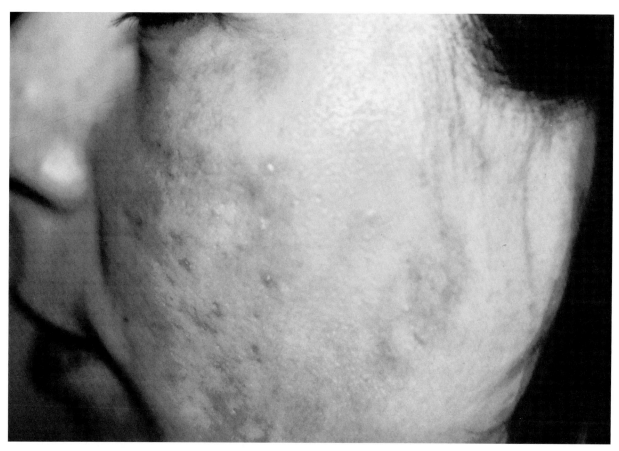

FIG. 9. Postdermabrasion: milia, hyperpigmentation,and persistent erythema.

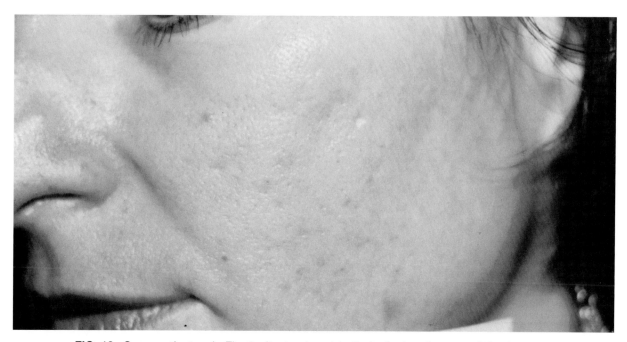

FIG. 10. Same patient as in Fig. 9 after treatment tretinoin, hydroquinone, and Cordran tape.

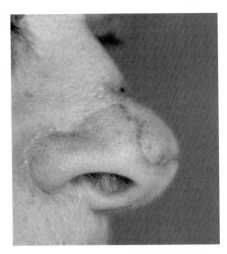

FIG. 11. Trap door deformity of nasal tip.

These "trap doors" may be associated with excess subcutaneous tissue and/or the overdevelopment of fibrous bands causing a ringlike constriction around the flap. The scar contraction may be minimized by initial wide undermining of the adjacent tissue before the suturing of the flap. At times, scar revision such as the Z- or W-plasty can be considered and at times can be considered prophylactically in larger circular closures.

The excess subcutaneous tissue may simply improve with time. A conservative approach with intralesional steroid therapy can also be initiated, but frequently the flap must be partially reexcised to remove this excess subcutaneous tissue and release the contraction. In small flaps, postoperative dermabrasion may help decrease the central thickening and blend the flap into the adjacent tissues (Fig. 12).

SUTURE REACTIONS

Suture Extrusion and Stitch Abscess

Buried, absorbable sutures are routine in any skin closure of significance. However, the sutures may at times be resistant to absorption, and they exude themselves towards the surface. The patient usually notes a papular, pustular, or crusted lesion along the closure 2 weeks to 2 months after the surgery. Removal results in prompt healing.

Risk factors for extrusion include suture placement close to the surface, superficial knot placement, and the size of suture material. Certain materials are more prone to inflammation. The older chromated "catgut" initiates inflammation via degradation by proteolytic enzymes. New synthetic materials, such as Maxon or PDS, are broken down by hydrolysis but have more time to work their way to the surface. In addition, a personal observation has been made that some patients are more prone to this reaction and may exude all the sutures eventually.

Treatment is to remove the offending agent. A No.11

blade can nick the suture just under the surface and be removed with the forceps. The irritation usually responds very quickly when the offending agent is removed.

Suture Tracks

The use of sutures for the superficial aspect of the closure can result in "railroad tracking." Certain patients appear to be more prone to this tendency, and it may be more obvious in some fair-skinned patients.

Tension plays an important role in these marks. Tension may be inherently due to the closure tension, but frequently the sutures are tied too tightly, regardless of the wound tension. Immediately after surgery the wound becomes edematous, increasing the tension. Novafil, a somewhat elastic synthetic suture, "gives" with the postoperative tension and is an aid to decrease the risk of suture tracks. However, proper timing of suture removal is essential in minimizing suture tracks. Complex schemes such as serial placement of sutures have been suggested to avoid suture marks.

The treatment of suture tracks is limited. Early postoperative dermabrasion may be the best option. Suture tracks may lead to other healing problems such as keloid formation and, rarely, pyoderma gangrenosum.

Suture Allergy

True suture allergy is uncommon, especially with the use of newer synthetic materials. However, allergic reactions to materials such as silk and especially catgut are well described in the older surgical literature. Frequently these reactions are misdiagnosed as a complication of infection or dehiscence; thus the underlying process is missed. Reactions to both chromated and plain gut have been reported.

HYPOPIGMENTATION

Hypopigmentation can be a complication of several types of cutaneous surgery, including standard excision, dermabrasion, chemical peeling, laser therapy, electrodesiccation and

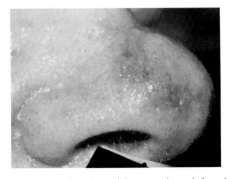

FIG. 12. Spot dermabrasion of the trap door deformity blends the flap into adjacent tissue.

curettage, and cryosurgery. In these circumstances, the melanocytes are damaged and apparently are unable to reestablish themselves fully in the site. Cryosurgery and cryoanesthesia are especially associated with the development of hypopigmentation, possibly as a result of the well-known damage to pigment cells by relatively minor temperature depression (approximately 4°C). Hypopigmentation may persist, but there may be improvement with time. Hypopigmentation can also occur from intralesional or potent topical steroids. This is usually self-limited. Treatment options for hypopigmentation of other origins are relatively limited. Use of camouflage cosmetics can be initiated to cover the discoloration.

HYPERPIGMENTATION

Hyperpigmentation after a surgical procedure can be due to several different factors. These factors are quite variable and include traumatic tattooing from such material as Monsel's solution, deposition of iron from blood (with the dye in Q-switch lasers or sclerotherapy), or stimulation of normal pigment cells in the skin in secondary postinflammatory hyperpigmentation.

A reactionary type of postinflammatory hyperpigmentation can occur as a sequela of any type of surgical procedure on the skin. Certain skin types are more prone to this, and this is more obvious with the middle to darker skin types. The tendency to hyperpigmentation is exacerbated by sun exposure during and after the immediate postoperative period and hormonal therapy, such as estrogen, or pregnancy during or soon after the healing phase. Certain elective procedures such as dermabrasion and chemical peelings should be postponed during heavy sun exposure or during pregnancy. The use of broad-spectrum sunscreens before and for months after the procedure is highly recommended. The use of tretinoin with hydroquinones before the procedure can be considered in a patient at risk for hyperpigmentation.

Postinflammatory hyperpigmentation may improve with sun protection and time. Tretinoin in combination with bleaching creams such as a hydroquinone and corticosteroid is a classic treatment, since Klingman's initial tretinoin (Retin-A) 0.1%/5% hydroquinone/dexamethasone combination was reported (Fig. 10). Hydroquinones have been used in combination with 10% hydroxy acids with a similar intent. The treatment of such hyperpigmentation with physical destructive techniques, including new technology such as lasers, has been variable in response. Camouflage cosmetics may offer some improvement; sometimes the covering of dark areas can be surprisingly difficult. The use of a white underface to totally block the irregular pigmentation, followed by an overlaying of further cosmetics, may be a more effective approach for many of these patients.

Hyperpigmentation can occur in a skin graft, probably as a result of an increase in melanin production. This may improve with time. If not, a superficial destructive method such as superficial dermabrasion is helpful to blend the graft.

Hyperpigmentation has also been described in the use of lasers, such as the pulsed dye laser, which results in an immediate ecchymotic response. The brownish discoloration, attributable to heme deposition, usually resolves in several weeks to a few months without sequela. Heme deposition of iron is also responsible for the linear hyperpigmentation that occurs after sclerotherapy. On the legs, this resolution is much slower than on the face, may persist for months to years, and occasionally may not totally resolve. Because of its nature, one would not expect a good response to bleaching creams or treatment with superficial destruction such as liquid nitrogen, which have been attempted in the past. Partial success has been reported in the treatment of this postsclerotherapy hyperpigmentation with the copper vapor or pulsed dye (510 nm) laser.

In addition, the patient can be tattooed as a result of such material as Monsel's solution (ferric subsulfate) or silver nitrate. This reaction is an unusual occurrence, especially with light application. The use of Monsel's solution on a fair-skinned person with flawless coloration should be avoided.

REACTIONS TO TOPICAL AGENTS

Contact Dermatitis

Irritation in the operative site can be due to tapes, antiseptics, or dressings that are used. However, true contact dermatitis can develop in the postoperative period. Adhesives such as the benzoin or the tape, surgical scrubs (povidone-iodine, rarely chlorhexidine), and local anesthetics can all cause a delayed hypersensitivity reaction. However, topical antibiotics are the most common allergens.

Contact sensitization to topical antibiotics is a relatively common problem, occurring in up to 4.2% of procedures. (Fig. 13). Neomycin is the most common sensitizer, although polymyxin and bacitracin are well described as causative agents of contact sensitization. Contact sensitization can also result from other topical antibiotics such as erythromycin, garamicin (Garamycin) ointment, silver sulfadiazine (Silvadene), or mafenide (Sulfamylon).

Contact sensitization to local anesthetics is more common with the ester type of drugs such as procaine and tetracaine; contact allergy is rarely reported with lidocaine or other amide-based anesthetics.

Treatments for these reactions are not unique: topical steroids and systemic steroids in severe cases. The final outcome is usually not affected by the contact dermatitis.

Anaphylactic Reactions

Topically applied preparations can rarely cause a systemic anaphylactic reaction. Examples in the literature include case reports of bacitracin and chlorhexidine. This emergency situ-

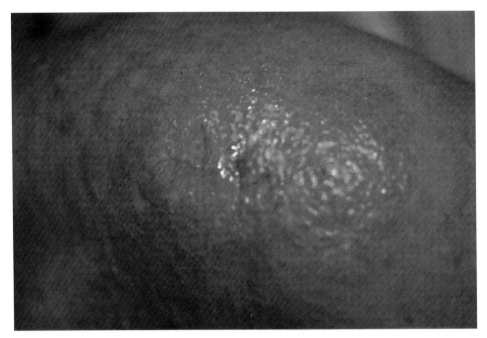

FIG. 13. Contact dermatitis from topical antibiotic. (See Color Plate 1.)

ation should be considered in the patient with acute decompensation.

NERVE DAMAGE

Cutaneous surgeons should be fully familiar with the anatomy of the significant sensory and motor branches of the facial nerve, spinal accessory nerve, and the peroneal nerve. Sensory or motor nerve damage can occur from transient local anesthesia effects or the inadvertent pressure or tension on a nerve in surgery (neuropraxia), or as a transection of the nerve. The local anesthesia effect will clear in a day, whereas neuropraxia may persist for months. A review of the excised material, looking for nerve bundles, and testing such as electromyelogram can be helpful to differentiate neuropraxia from transection.

Transection of the supraorbital or supratrochlear nerves results in numbness superior to their origin into the scalp. The numbness resolves over a few months. The infraorbital nerve can also be transected in facial surgery in deeper resections such as in aggressive skin cancers, resulting in significant numbness on the cheek and nose. Disturbance of the mental nerve can present an even greater functional problem with subsequent numbness on the lip.

The transection of facial motor nerves has even greater morbidity because of the associated loss of function. Damage to the temporal branch of the facial nerve can occur as it traverses temporal fossa. In many people there is very little fat protecting the nerve that is lying superficially on the muscle. This is especially true in elderly patients. Knowledge of the anatomy and careful dissection and separation of tissue planes are essential. The use of high-volume tumescent anesthesia can be helpful in this dissection. If nerve damage has occurred, brow lift and/or eyelid surgery may be needed. The facial nerve can also be injured in deep surgery on the cheek after it leaves the protection of the parotid gland, which presents a significant problem for movement of the cheek and upper lip. Because of excellent anastomosis in this area, this loss of movement may resolve with time.

The main trunk of the facial nerve is at risk for damage in the resection of deep tumor with origination in the posteroinferior auricular/mastoid region. A team approach in the resection of deep tumors in this location is recommended. Identification of the facial nerve with attempts at preservation is optimal. Anastomosis or nerve transplantation techniques are available and can frequently restore function to the facial nerve if a section of the nerve must be sacrificed.

MILIA

A milium is a ''microepidermal cyst'' that can occur primarily or secondarily as a complication of skin surgery. Milia have been described as a result of destructive procedures such as cryosurgery or in excisional surgery, forming along the suture lines. Milia are also a common complication of dermabrasion. In dermabrasion, implantation of the epidermal debris is believed to be responsible for the development of milia. Scrubbing the dermabraded skin with saline immediately after surgery decreases milia formation. The use of tretinoin before and after dermabrasion is also associated with a decreased development of milia.

Milia are easily treated with simple expression of the cyst, which can be accomplished with a needle or a No. 11 blade. The use of a comedo extractor or forceps may be helpful to remove the cyst. Hot cautery, quickly applied to the top of the lesion in a fast, effective manner, may be used. In more extensive cases an initial trial of exfoliation with tretinoin, with or without a glycolic acid, or light abrasion with a buff puff can be tried before initiating extensive expression of multiple lesions.

TELANGIECTASIA

Telangiectasia is a sequela of cutaneous surgery, both basic excisional and advanced procedures, such as chemical peeling. The origin is unknown. Wound tension is frequently associated with the development of telangiectasias. This tension may be due to limitations in closure design or complications such as hematoma or infection. Many of these patients demonstrate telangiectasias at other nonoperative sites, suggestive of an underlying tendency to form telangiectasias.

Frequently the telangiectasias spontaneously resolve during a course of observation for 6 or 12 months. However, multiple modalities are available for the treatment of telangiectasias. Treatment by electrosurgery with a fine needle, as well as continuous-wave lasers such as argon, KTP, or yellow light lasers, can be used to trace out individual telangiectasias. Frequently the persistent telangiectasias are in a matted network, making the pulsed dye vascular laser ideal to treat the entire area. In the past, and still in selective cases, the CO_2 laser ''abrasion'' or dermabrasion has been used to treat extensive lesions. These destructive methods may be most worthwhile, especially as part of an overall scar abrasion.

ERYTHEMA

Erythema is part of the healing process and is usually present in most healing wounds, whether a result of standard excision, chemical peel, or dermabrasion. However, with dermabrasion or laser-abrasion diffuse erythema and sensitivity of the skin can sometimes occur and may persist for a longer period, which causes great concern to the patient. A mild, topical cortisone cream and antihistamines may have a modulating effect. Sun protection may also be helpful in these sensitive patients. Frequently the use of camouflage cosmetic techniques, such as inclusion of a green-tinted foundation, may be helpful in handling this unusual complication.

Patchy erythema, arising immediately after dermabrasion, is a tip-off to the impending development of a scar, especially if developing in high-risk sites or situations for scarring such as along the mandibular rim or malar prominence or in a patient previously treated with isotretinoin (Accutane). Early intervention with Cordran tape and, at times, intralesional steroids if the scar advances further, may have a substantial inhibitory effect on the further development of scar and also hasten resolution.

PRURITUS

Pruritus is normally associated with wound healing. In hypertrophic scars and keloids, histamine may be increased. Histamine plays a role in the overall fibroblast growth as part of the wound healing process.

In general, a wound with pruritus can be treated with assurance. However, potent topical steroids or intralesional steroids (triamcinolone, 5 to 40 mg/cc) may give some relief. This is especially effective if pruritus is part of an early hypertrophic scar.

At times, pruritus may be related to simple reestablishment of sensory nerves in an area that has been traumatized. Bennett noted that a crawling sensation may at times be a symptom of a recurrent tumor. Perineural involvement of tumor is usually asymptomatic but may become evident with pain or dysethesia.

HYPERGRANULATION

Overexuberant growth of the fibroblasts and endothelial cells in a wound results in hypergranulation. This beefy, friable tissue bleeds with minor trauma. Hypergranulation tissue has been shown to be inhibitory to fibroblast, substantiating the observation that hypergranulation delays wound healing. In addition to delaying healing, the granulation tissue is a major burden to the patient because of the easily friable bleeding. Curettage, electrocautery, or silver nitrate sticks can be used to treat the hypergranulation. One must be aware that silver nitrate has the potential of tattooing the tissues. EMLA can be an adjunct for improved tolerance of treatment.

CONCLUSION

The frequency of complications can be decreased by the recognition and avoidance of surgical risk factors. Early intervention may minimize the extent of a complication. However, even in the best of circumstances, complications may occur. With appropriate measures most unfortunate situations improve with time. The patient-physician relationship is tested when a suboptimal outcome results. A compassionate, confident approach is more effective in alleviating the situation than withdrawal or other defensive posturing.

ACKNOWLEDGMENTS

Thanks to my wife, Laura Riddick Dufresne, and Ann Burlage, MD, for review of this document.

SUGGESTED READING LIST

Reviews Articles

Hayes CM, Whitaker DC. Complications of cutaneous surgery. Adv Dermatol 1974;9:161–176.

Salasche SJ. Acute surgical complications: cause, prevention and treatment. J Am Acad Dermatol 1986;15:1163–1185.

Hematoma, Seroma, and Dehiscence

Dahistrom K, Weis-Fogh US, Medgyesi S, et al. The use of autologous fibrin adhesive in skin transplantation. Plast Reconstr Surg 1992;89:968–972.

Davenport M, Daly J, Harvey I, Griffiths RW. The bolus tie-over ''pressure'' dressing in the management of full-thickness skin grafts: is it necessary? Br J Plast Surg 1988;41:28–32.

Davidson PM, Batchelor AG, Lewis-Smith PA. The properties and uses of nonexpanded machine meshed skin grafts. Br J Plast Surg 1986;39:462–468.

Goldsmith SM, Leshin B, Owen J. Management of patient's taking anticoagulants and platelet inhibitors prior to dermatologic surgery. J Dermatol Surg Oncol 1993;19:578–581.

Hicks PD, Stromberg BV. Hemostasis in plastic surgery patients. Clin Plast Surg 1985;12:17–23.

Koyama H, Isshiki N, Noda R, Nishimura R. Long-term survival of a split-thickness skin graft on a large seroma. Plast Reconstr Surg 1987;79:110–113.

Kram HB, Nathan RC, Stafford FJ, Fleming AW, Shoemaker WC. Fibrin glue achieves hemostasis in patients with coagulation disorders. Arch Surg 1989;124:385–387.

Lindsey WH, Masterson TM, Llaneras M, Spotnitz WD, Wanebo HJ, Morgan RF. Seroma prevention using fibrin glue during modified radical neck dissection in a rat model. Am J Surg 1988;156:310–313.

Mahaffey PJ, Wallace AF. Blindness following cosmetic blepharoplasty: a review. Br J Plast Surg 1986;39:213–221.

Malviya VK, Deppe G. Control of intraoperative hemorrhage in gynecology with the use of fibrin glue. Obstet Gynecol 1989;73:284–286.

Rees TD, Lee YC, Coburn RJ. Expanding hematoma after rhytidectomy. Plast Reconstr Surg 1973;51:149–153.

Straith RE, Raju DR, Hipps CJ. The study of hematoma in 500 consecutive face lifts. Plast Reconstr Surg 1977;59:694–698.

Tissue Necrosis and Dehiscence

Angel MF, Narayanan, Swaaartz WM, et al. The etiology of free radicals in hematoma-induced flap necrosis. Plastic Reconstr Surg 1986;77:795–803.

Arprey CJ, O'Donnell MJ, Whitaker DC. Surgical pearl: alternative to adhesive strips after suture removal. J Am Acad Dermatol 1994;31:264–265.

Diaz DD, Freeman SB, Wilson JF, Parker GS. Hematoma-induced flap necrosis and free radical scavengers. Arch Otolaryngol Head Neck Surg 1992;118:516–518.

Dodson MK, Magann EF, Meeks GR. A randomized comparison of secondary intention in patients with superficial wound dehiscence. Obstet Gynecol 1992;80:321–324.

Goldminz D, Bennett RG. Cigarette smoking and flap necrosis and full-thickness graft necrosis. Arch Dermatol 1991;127:1012–1015.

Harris DR. Healing of the surgical wound. Part I. The basics considerations. J Am Acad Dermatol 1979;1:197–207.

Hogstrom H, Haglund U, Zederfelldt B. Tension leads to increased neutrophil accumulation and decreased laparotomy wound strength. Surgery 1990;107:215–219.

Lawrence WT, Murphy RC, Robson MC, et al. The detrimental effect of cigarette smoking on the skin flap survival: an experimental study in the rat. Br J Plast Surg 1984;37:216–219.

Rappaport WD, Hunter GC, Allen R, et al. Effect of electrocautery on wound healing in midline laparotomy incisions. Am J Surg 1991;160:618–620.

Riou JP, Cohen JR, Johnson H. Factors influencing wound dehiscence. Am J Surg 1992;163:324–330.

Robson MC, Shaw RC, Heggers JP. The reclosure of postoperative incisional abscesses based on bacterial quantification of the wound. Ann Surg 1970;171:279–282.

Rodeheaver GT, Nesbit WS, Edlich RF. Novafil A dynamic suture for wound closure. Ann Surg 1986;204:193–199.

Urschel JD. Laparotomy closure reinforced with buried polyglyconate retention sutures. Am J Surg 1991;161:687–689.

Wound Infection

Bencini PL, Galimberti M, Signorini M, Crosti C. Antibiotic prophylaxis of wound infections in skin surgery. Arch Dermatol 1991;127:1357–1360.

Cunnningham M, Yu VL, Turner J, Curtin H. Necrotizing otitis externa due to aspergillus in an immunocompetent patient. Arch Otolaryngol Head Neck Surg 1988;114:5554–5556.

Cruse PJE, Foord R. A 5-year prospective study of 23,649 surgical wounds. Arch Surg 1973;107:206–210.

Dzubow LM. Scarring following herpes simplex infection of postsurgical cutaneous sites. J Dermatol Surg Oncol 1989;15:655–670.

Giandoni MB, Grabski WJ. Candidiasis as a cause of delayed surgical wound healing. J Am Acad Dermatol 1994;30:981–984.

Haas AF, Grekin RC. Antibiotic prophylaxis in dermatologic surgery. J Am Acad Dermatol 1995;32:1555–1576.

Huntley AC, Tanabe JC. Toxic shock syndrome as a complication of dermatologic surgery. J Am Acad Dermatol 1987;16:227–229.

Lai CS, Lin SD, Chou CK, Lin HJ. Aspergilillosis complicating the graft skin and free muscle flap in a diabetic. Plast Reconstr Surg 1993;92:532–536.

Larson PO, Ragi G, Mohs FE, Snow SN. Excision of exposed cartilage for management of Mohs defects of the ear. J Dermatol Surg Oncol 1991;17:749–752.

Safranek TJ, Jarvis WR, Carson LA, et al. *Mycobacterium chlonae* wound infections after plastic surgery employing contaminated gentian violet skin marking solution. N Engl J Med 1987;317:197–201.

Schelech WF, Sinonsen N, Sumarah R, Martin RS. Nosocomial infections of *Pseudomonas aeruginosa* folliculitis associated with a physiotherapy pool. Can Med J 1986;134:909–913.

Sebben JE. Sterile technique and prevention of wound infection in office surgery. Part I. J Dermatol Surg Oncol 1988;14:1364–1371.

Sebben JE. Sterile technique and prevention of wound infection in office surgery. Part II. J Dermatol Surg Oncol 1989;15:38–48.

Siegle RJ, Chiaramonti A, Knox DW, Pollack SV. Cutaneous candidosis as a complication of facial dermabrasion. J Dermatol Surg Oncol 1984;10:891–900.

Whitaker DC, Grane DJ, Johnson SC. Wound infection rate in dermatologic surgery. J Dermatol Surg Oncol 1988;14:525–528.

Scarring

Ahn ST, Monafo WM, Mustoe TA. Topical silicone gel for the prevention and treatment of hypertrophic scar. Arch Surg 1991;126:499–504.

Burgess LPA, Morin GV, Rand M, et al. Wound healing: relationship of wound closure tension to scar width in rats. Arch Otolaryngol Head Neck Surg 1990;116:798–802.

Chantarasak ND, Milner RH. A comparison of scar quality in wounds closed under tension with PGA (Dexon) and polydioxanone (PDS). Br J Plast Surg 1989;42:687–691.

Collins PS, Farber GA. Postsurgical dermabrasion of the nose. J Dermatol Surg Oncol 1984;10:476–477.

Elliot D, Mahaffey PJ. The stretched scar: the benefit of prolonged dermal support. Br J Plast Surg 1989;42:74–78.

Gabbiani G, Hirschel BJ, Ryan GB, et al. Granulation tissue as a contractile organ. J Exp Med 1972;135:719–734.

Gahhos FN, Simmons RI. Immediate Z-plasty for semicircular wounds. Plast Reconstr Surg 1987;80:416–419.

Hochman M, Branham G, Thomas JR. Relative effects of intraoperative tissue expansion and undermining on wound closure tension. Arch Otolaryngol Head Neck Surg 1992;118:1185–1187.

Katz BE, Gioconda MA, Oca S. A controlled study of the effectiveness of spot dermabrasion (scar abrasion) on the appearance of surgical scar. J Am Acad Dermatol 1991;24:462–466.

Kaufman AJ, Kiene KL, Moy RL. Role of tissue undermining in the trap door effect of transposition flap. J Dermatol Surg Oncol 1993;19:128–132.

Koranda FC, Webster RC. Trap door effect in nasolabial flaps. Arch Otolaryngol Head Neck Surg 1985;11:421–424.

Maackay DR, Saggers GC, Kotwal N, Manders EK. Stretching skin: undermining is more important than intraoperative expansion. Plast Reconstr Surg 1990;86:722–730.

Murry JC, Pollack SV, Pinell SR. Keloids: a review. J Am Acad Dermatol 1981;4:461–470.

Ono T, Matsunaga W, Yoshimura K. Striae distensae after tension requiring skin suture. J Dermatol 1991;18:47–51.

Pierce HE. Postsurgical acrylic ear splints for keloids. J Dermatol Surg Oncol 1986;12:583–585.

Sommerlad BC, Creasy JM. The stretched scar: a clinical and histologic study. Br J Plast Surg 1978;31:34–35.

Spoat JE, Dalcin A, Weietauer N, Roberts RS. Hypertrophic sternal scars: silicone gel sheet versus Kenalog injection treatment. Plast Reconstr Surg 1992;90:988–992.

Yarborough JM. Ablation of facial scars by programmed dermabrasion. J Dermatol Surg Oncol 1988;14:292–294.

Zachariae H. Delayed wound healing and keloid formation following argon laser treatment or dermabrasion during isotretinoin treatment. Br J Dermatol 1988;118:703–706.

Miscellaneous Topics

Suture Reactions

Crikelair GF. Skin suture marks. Am J Surg 1958;96:631–639.

Engler RJM, Weber CB, Turnicky R. Hypersensivity to chromated catgut sutures: a case report and review of the literature. Ann Allergy 1986; 56:317–320.

Long CC, Jessop J, Young M, Holt PJA. Minimizing the risk of postoperative pyoderma gangrenosum. Br J Dermatol 1992;127:45–48.

Moy RL, Waldman B, Hein DW. A review of sutures and suturing techniques. J Dermatol Surg Oncol 1992;18:785–795.

Van Rijssel EJC, Brand R, Admiraal C, et al. Tissue reaction and surgical knots: the effect of size, knot configuration, and knot volume. Obstet Gynecol 1989;74:64–68.

Wolf R. Serial placement of sutures for preventing suture marks. J Dermatol Surg Oncol 1993;19:1131.

Pigmentation Complications

Farooqui Jz, Auclair BW, Robb E, et al. Histologic, biochemical and ultrastructural studies on hyperpigmented human xenografts. Pigment Cell Res 1993;6:226–233.

Georgiev M. Postsclerotherapy hyperpigmenation: a 1-year follow-up. J Dermatol Surg Oncol 1990;16:608–610.

Goldman MP. Postsclerotherapy hyperpigmentation: treatment with a flashlamp excited pulsed dye laser. J Dermatol Surg Oncol 1992;18: 417–422.

Klingman AM, Willis I. A new formula for depigmenting the human skin. Arch Dermatol 1975;111:40–48.

Thibault P, Wiodarczk J. Postsclerotherapy hyperpigmentation: the role of serum ferritin levels and the effectiveness of treatment with the copper vapor laser. J Dermatol Surg Oncol 1992;18:47–52.

Reactions to Topical Agents

Elsner P, Pevny I, Burg G. Anaphylaxis induced by topically applied bacitracin. Am J Contact Dermatol 1990;1:162–164.

Gette MT, Marks JG, Maloney ME. Frequency of postoperative allergic contact dermatitis to topical antibiotics. Arch Dermatol 1992;128: 365–367.

Klein CE, Gall H. Type IV allergy to amide-type local anesthetics. Contact Dermatitis 1991;25:45–48.

Okano M, Nomura M, Hata S, et al. Anaphylactic symptoms due to chlorhexidine gluconate. Arch Dermatol 1989;125:50–52.

Schechter JF, Wilkinson RD, DelCarpio J. Anaphylaxis following the use of bacitracin ointment. Arch Dermatol 1984;120:909–911.

Other Readings

Cohen BH. Prevention of postdermabrasion milia. J Dermatol Surg Oncol 1988;14:1301–1302.

Cottel WI. Perineural invasion by squamous cell carcinoma. J Dermatol Surg Oncol 1982;8:589–600.

Goldman MP, Weiss RA, Brody HJ, Coleman WP, Fitzpatrick RE. Treatment of facial telangeactasia with sclerotherapy, laser surgery and/or electrodesiccation. J Dermatol Surg Oncol 1993;19:899–908.

Grabski WJ, Salasche SJ. Management of temporal nerve injuries. J Dermatol Surg Oncol 1985;11:145–151.

Mandy SH. Tretinoin in the preoperative management of dermabrasion. J Am Acad Dermatol 1986;15:878–880.

Mcgrath J, Schofield O. Treatment of excessive granulation tissue with EMLA cream and 95% silver nitrate pencils. Clin Exp Dermatol 1990; 15:468.

Shakespeare V, Shakespeare P. Effects of granulating tissue conditioned medium on the growth of human keratinocytes in vitro. Br J Plast Surg 1991;44:219–223.

Terris DJ, Fee WE. Current issues in nerve repair. Arch Otolaryngol Head Neck Surg 1993;119:725–731.

Textbook of Dermatologic Surgery, edited by John L. Ratz.
Lippincott–Raven Publishers, Philadelphia © 1998.

CHAPTER 8

Photography

William Slue

Equipment	**Labeling and Storage**
Photographic Consent	**Suggested Reading List**
Documenting Surgical Cases	

Dermatologic photography has become an increasingly important way of documenting both diseases of the skin and surgical procedures. As in most other areas of medicine, the purpose of photography is threefold: medical/legal documentation, teaching, and patient follow-up. As one looks through the dermatologic literature, photographs of variable standards can be seen. The purpose of this chapter is to help the dermatologist in his or her quest for excellent clinical dermatologic photography before, during, and after surgical procedures. Most of us would like to be able to take a camera and just push a button to achieve good pictures without much thought. Obviously, if this were possible, there would be no need for photographic instruction such as this chapter.

It is important to identify the field image that will document the finding of importance. As an example of clinical photographs, Fig. 1 is a poor clinical picture of a case of ichthyiosis. Not only is the clinical information difficult to see, but even more prominent is the needless and distracting information concerning the patient's footwear, underwear, and standing or sitting position, as well as information about the room in which the patient is located. In the much improved clinical photograph in Fig. 2 there is an immediate difference in the clinical information presented as compared with Fig. 1.

The word "snapshot" is often used in taking clinical photographs. Webster's *Ninth New Collegiate Dictionary* defines a snapshot as a "casual photograph made typically by an amateur with a small handheld camera and without regard to technique." With this definition in mind, it is obvious that the clinician should try not to take snapshots, but rather to take medical photographs. It becomes quite clear that Fig. 1 can be identified as a snapshot, not the medical photograph seen in Fig. 2.

A medical photograph has been defined as a photograph that accurately maximizes clinical information presented and at the same time minimizes irrelevant data. With these thoughts in mind, it is important to define exactly what is going to be the focus of the image before photographs are taken. If it is not the desire to take a snapshot, such distracting elements as jewelry, clothing, hair ribbons, background furniture, or extraneous objects should not be a part of the clinical photographs. If the objective is to take a medical photograph, you must define what medical information you are about to capture and set out to maximize this information so that the finished photograph will accurately depict the facts about to be captured.

When a good photograph is seen, whether in the clinical setting or not, the question often asked is, "What kind of camera was used?" This question implies that the photograph is taken by the camera, and that the person taking the photograph is almost superfluous. However, to achieve good-quality clinical photographs, it is important that the photographer take control of actually producing the clinical images.

It is also important that the taking of such medical photographs be simple and easy for the dermatologist or his or her staff. Since it is not the goal of this chapter to make the reader a medical photographer, much emphasis is placed on simplicity and an easy way to accomplish the goal of taking good clinical photographs.

Emphasis also is placed on the most important ability to take consistent photographs in a reproducable manner. If "before-and-after" photographs are going to be taken, it is important that both images fully represent what was actually seen. Not infrequently, photographs purporting to be before-and-after images are not truly representative of what was seen in the patient. These are called (with tongue in cheek) photographic cures. Figure 3 shows what is clinically pre-

William Slue: Department of Dermatology, New York University, 550 First Avenue, New York, NY 10016.

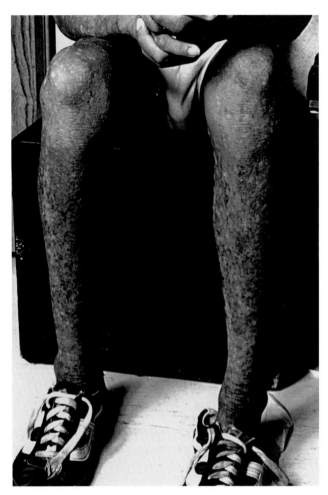

FIG. 1. A poor clinical presentation of ichythyiosis with many distracting elements.

sented as before-and-after pictures of hair growth that seem to indicate good clinical results. These photographs are deceiving. Figure 4 shows what appears to be good results in a patient being treated for photoaging. This also is deceptive. Both Fig. 3 and Fig. 4 were taken within a few minutes of each other. Photographic cures are often seen when before-and-after pictures are not taken with the same film or film emulsion; when there is a change in focal length; or when one photograph is taken from a different distance than that from which the second photograph was taken. Photographic cures can also be achieved when there is a change in lighting or when there is a difference in exposure between one photograph and the next. In Fig. 3 the before-and-after photographs were taken only 1 minute apart; the only difference is that one photograph is lighter than the other. The darker photograph represents the apparently improved hair growth, while the lighter photograph represents the ''before'' clinical presentation. In Fig. 4, one sees the effect of a difference in the angle of lighting. The first photograph is made with side lighting to accentuate the photoaging, while the second photograph is made with flat lighting (the light is directly across from the patient) to diminish the photoaging. Accurate pho-

todocumentation must be used to show the true results or treatment of dermatologic disorders. To maintain accuracy, control of the variables, as previously described, that compose the makeup of the final documentation is essential (Fig. 5). It is the goal of this chapter to help the dermatologist accomplish this.

When the camera is put to the eye, the first question should be, ''What am I photographing?'' If the answer to that question differs from what is seen, an adjustment must be made. In Fig. 6 one sees a clinical representation of a keloid. However, when looking through the camera lens, there is extraneous clutter that does not relate to the clinical presentation of keloids. An adjustment should be made (Fig. 7). If irrelevant items such as background clothing and jewelry are seen, they must be eliminated from the viewing field. If one answers the question, ''What am I photographing?'' one will clearly isolate the clinical features to be documented and proceed with the medical photograph.

Details of diagnosis such as translucency, lichenification, induration, wrinkling, atrophy, scaling, follicular accentuation or plugging and telangiectasia, as well as anatomic locations, are the highly significant features that must be evident

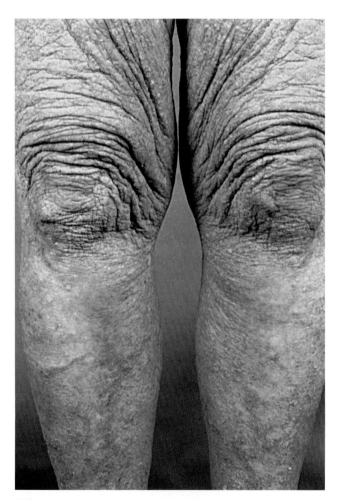

FIG. 2. A better clinical presentation of ichythyiosis without distracting elements.

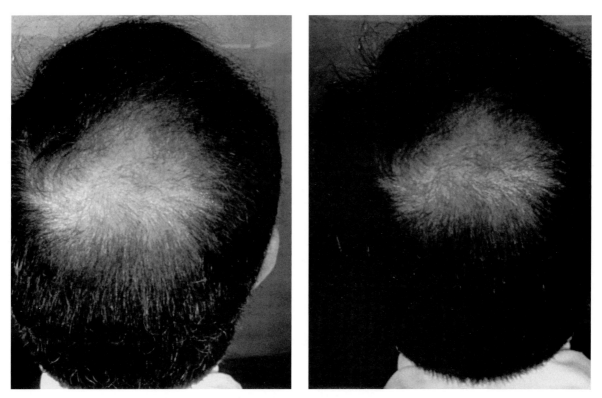

FIG. 3. A deceptive set of photographs showing hair growth.

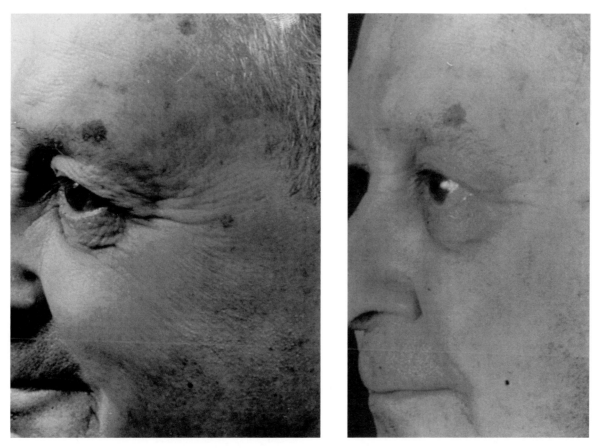

FIG. 4. Improvement before and after photoaging treatments that is presented in a deceptive manner.

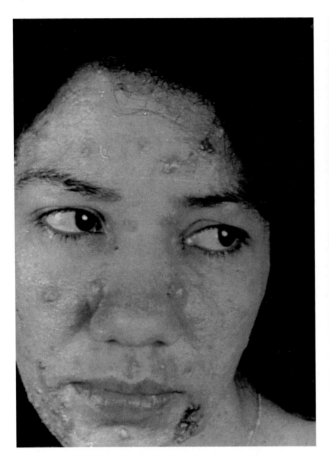 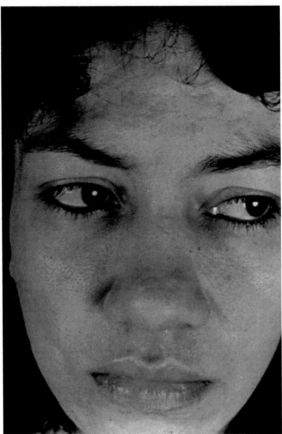

FIG. 5. Treatment in an acne patient. These photographs are made in an accurate, consistent way.

in photodocuments. Figure 8A illustrates this in a patient with dermatomyositis. The photograph shows the anatomic locations and some clinical features of this disease. Although the image is not blurred and is clinically suggestive, the specific morphologic qualities that enable the clinician to diagnose dermatomyositis confidently are not effectively highlighted in this photograph. Figure 8B clearly depicts the cuticular telangiectases that are significant in diagnosing this connective tissue disease. Figure 8C emphasizes not only the anatomic location, but also the morphologic features of incipient Grotton's papules that are so valuable in diagnosing and documenting dermatomyositis. The conclusion to be drawn here is to highlight that which makes a diagnosis unique, as well as provide photographic documentation of lesions and procedures.

EQUIPMENT

The choices of photographic equipment are many and varied. However, with certain principles in mind, it is not difficult to decide which equipment to purchase. Although there are cameras of different formats, the format of choice is the 35-mm. The 35-mm slide is universally used for teaching, and one can produce prints from this format. This format is also much easier to use than the larger-format cameras that

may be used by a medical photographer. Of major importance is the ability to easily do close-up photography using this format. A variety of lenses and other accessories are available for the 35-mm format. In addition to the camera, a lens is needed that allows close-up photography as well as documentation of anatomic sites and the distribution of skin lesions. In addition, an electronic flash is needed that simulates the production of daylight in conjunction with daylight film that will be used. With the 35-mm camera, lens, and flash, you are now equipped to tackle the task of taking good dermatologic photographs.

The first issue is the camera itself. There seems to be a correlation between use of camera equipment and the cost of the equipment. If the camera will be used intensively, it is important to buy a camera that will be more durable. The average camera meant for the individual who uses it three or four times each year for celebrations or vacation is not suitable for medical photographs. For the nonprofessional, that camera will last a number of years, but for the practicing dermatologist taking many photographs each week or month, there is need to purchase a 35-mm camera that will withstand the repeated act of picture taking. The 35-mm camera should be a single-lens reflex as opposed to a 33-mm range-finder camera. The single-lens reflex camera allows the photographer to see through the same lens that will be taking the photographs. In contrast, the range-finder camera is designed so that viewing and picture taking occur through two different lenses. This can allow mistakes to occur, such as inadvertently photograghing a finger over the lens and thus losing an important photograph. In clinical photography, I have been using Nikon equipment for the last 25 years. The infrequency of repair has been impressive with this brand of equipment. Other manufacturers may also have excellent service records.

The other decision-making factor in purchasing a 35-mm camera is the ability to purchase a range of lenses to allow sharply focused photographs. There are manufacturers of cameras who do not make suitable close-up or macro lenses or other accessories. For example, an eyeglass wearer may opt to purchase equipment for which diopters can be purchased for the viewfinder, to minimize the use of eyeglasses during photography. The photographer must ascertain his or her true needs before making purchasing decisions. It is also important to assess the availability of compatible accessories for the camera body.

The choice of photographic lens for the camera is an important decision. A telephoto macro lens, which, in fact, is a combination of two lenses, is an excellent choice for use

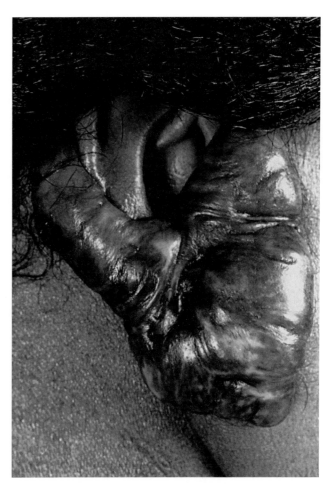

FIG. 7. A medical photograph that shows a large keloid and is free of clutter.

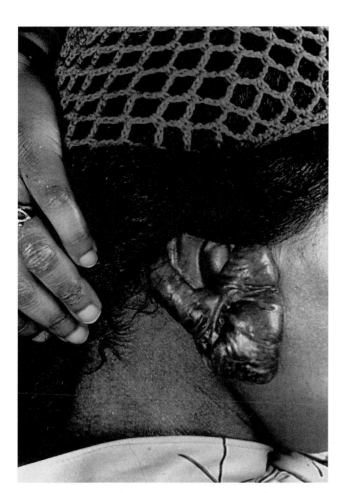

FIG. 6. A snapshot showing much clutter and extraneous information.

in dermatologic photography. The telephoto lens brings the viewing field "close" while allowing the photographer to be far enough away from the skin surface. A macro lens allows photographs that show both the distribution and location of skin lesions, and also allows the capture of a close-up photograph showing details of the lesion. The combination of these lenses produces what is known as a telephoto macro lens. Many manufacturers including Nikon, Cannon, Olympus, and Minolta make these types of lenses that will fit on their cameras. A lens that has a focal length of 90 to 135 mm adequately allows accomplishment of this goal. The other advantage of using such a lens is that when you place an electronic flash on the camera, you will be far enough away from the skin lesion to get even light exposure across the skin.

The light source to be used in medical photography is an electronic flash. There are many kinds of electronic flashes, ranging from flashes used in the studio setting to simple flashes on a camera. The flash appropriate for dermatology is the flash that is attached to the camera (Fig. 9). Flashes are placed on the camera directly or on a bracket that allows the flash to be held either above or on either side of the

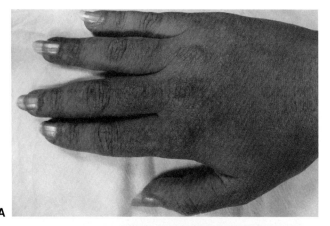

A

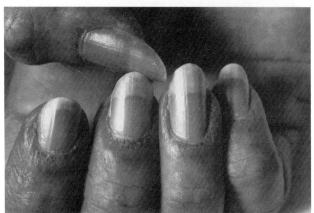

B

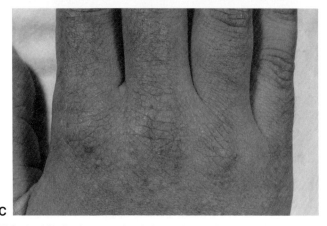

C

FIG. 8. (A) A photograph of the patient's hand (body part), as opposed to a medical photograph of the disease **(B and C)**. Medical photographs that show the location of the disease as well as its morphologic findings.

when the flash on the camera produces harsh lighting. Use of a diffusion disk on the flash may be necessary to soften the flash effect on the skin surface in such instances. The ring flash is useful with intraoral photographs and photographs of very flat surfaces. However, this light source produces very flat images, losing the third dimension of depth and elevation. Many photographers opt for a combination of both ring flash and a flash on the camera, depending on what is being photographed. I have created a system for dermatologists, which seems to work well, so that the correct combination of camera flash and lens, when put together in its appropriate manner, yields excellent dermatologic photographs. This system is discussed at the end of this chapter.

The next ingredient for good dermatologic photographs is the choice of film. A film that will bring realism and detail as accurately as possible should be chosen. Although there are many films on the market today, the choice of film is determined by the intended use of the image. Many photographers choose to use print film such as Kodacolor or Ektacolor if only prints are desired. Price and production present a set of problems that are beyond the photographer's control. Believable color in medical photography can be achieved only if the film is good (i.e., not expired), the light source

FIG. 9. A typical setup with a flash mounted on the side of the camera.

camera. There are occasions when flashes are placed in the front of the camera lens (called ring flashes; Fig. 10). There are advantages and disadvantages to all types of flash units. The flash that is placed on the camera usually casts a shadow that can sometimes be distracting and other times can add the third dimension of depth to your photography. Any flash that is placed too close to the camera, such as the flash in instamatic cameras, often creates the "red-eye syndrome" that is frequently seen in family snapshots. There are times

FIG. 10. A ring flash mounted on a camera.

is appropriate (using an electronic flash), and the color processing is accurate. If all these criteria are met, the color seen in the image will be natural. On the other hand, when negative rather than print film is used to achieve prints, a color printer with its various filter controls will be setting the standards. These standards may differ from the true colors seen at the time of the clinical photographs. For this and many other reasons, the use of print film is not recommended and is not emphasized in this chapter.

There are other ways to obtain prints for the patient's chart. Vivatar makes a slide printer that allows you to generate Polaroid prints from slides. The emphasis in this chapter is on the use of slide films in dermatologic photography.

There are two major families of slide film that are often used by biomedical photographers, as well as by dermatologists. The first family includes Ektachrome, Fujichrome, and Akfachrome. These films can be processed by local photographic laboratories. The other family of film, which has been quite popular for years, includes the Kodachromes, which require special processing by either Kodalux or other specially equipped laboratories. For many years the differences between Kodachrome (preferred by the professionals) and Ektachrome were quite noticeable. Over the past few years, with the advance of the Ektachrome images, little difference is seen.

Slide films are made with speeds (film sensitivity) from ISO 25 to ISO 1600. The lower the number, the less grainy the slide films will be. Since it is important that the images be very sharp with a minimal amount of grain from the film, the choice is limited to films that are 100 ASA or lower. This limits film choice to Kodachrome, which comes in either ASA 25 or ASA 64, or Ektachrome 100.

With camera, flash, lens, and film, the physician is now ready to take photographs. The first step involves holding the camera. Hold the camera in such a way as to provide support for the lens, which tends to weigh the camera down in a forward motion (Fig. 11). When the camera is held incorrectly without lens support (Fig. 12), there is a tendency for the weight of the lens to bring the entire camera on a downward tilt as the shutter is pressed. This accounts for photographs in which heads have been accidentally "chopped off." The correct way of holding the camera during photography is to provide the support (Fig. 13) that ensures minimum movement of the camera during the exposure.

The way the photographer stands during picture taking is also very important. Often, the photographer uses "body focusing," which means that the camera lens is set at a fixed distance from the patient as indicated on the barrel of the

FIG. 11. Holding the camera in the correct manner so that the lens is supported during picture taking.

lens. Then the camera is moved into position, where the lesion is brought into sharp focus. To do this, move the body back and forward until the image is correctly focused. Place one foot in front of the other, thereby facilitating the movement of both camera and body into position for sharply focused images. The value of body focusing is essential in realizing the importance of photographing patients in a repeatable manner.

It is very important that the film plane (camera back) be parallel to the skin being photographed. This allows for a greater depth of field (area in sharp focus) and better prospective view of the image. In surgical photography it may be necessary to use a step stool in order to be above the image and have the camera parallel to it.

Before starting any photographic sessions, it is important to check the camera to ensure that the film is loaded correctly and that there are enough exposures left to complete the photographic session. This is especially true in surgical photography, where reloading the camera during a surgical procedure will be awkward or difficult. The next item to check is the state of the batteries in the electronic flash. Weak batteries account for slow recycling time and slow down the picture-taking process. There are manufacturers, including

Nikon and Quantum, that sell battery kits which enhance the performance of the flash by speeding up the recycling time. These manufacturers also sell their units with rechargeable batteries so that a quick recharge is all it takes to get ready.

PHOTOGRAPHIC CONSENT

Taking clinical photographs without signed consent is not recommended. Most medical journals request written consent for any published photographs. If the photographs are to be used in a lecture, consent should be obtained, since there is little difference between the use of these photographs in publication or in a public setting. A third reason for obtaining a signed consent form is legal protection for physicians who may lend their photographs to colleagues. These photographs may be duplicated and used in settings different from that originally planned. They may appear in poster sessions or in teaching cassettes provided by drug companies. Since it is difficult to control what happens with photographs that are duplicated, it is best to obtain photographic consent from the patient initially.

Consent should be obtained permitting the taking of photographs during diagnostic treatment sessions, operations, or surgical medical procedures. The patient should waive all

FIG. 12. The incorrect way to hold the camera.

FIG. 13. The camera is held correctly, and the feet positioned so that body focusing can be achieved.

rights to payment and royalties from the photograph. Such waivers should apply to whatever the eventual use of the photographs might be. Consent should release the physician and the medical facility from any liability in connection with the use of the photograph. A consent form used at New York University Department of Dermatology is shown in Fig. 14.

In the actual picture-taking session there are three basic views that are often taken. To facilitate the technical aspect of dermatologic photography, a "dermatologic formula" is referred to for taking these photographs. This formula can easily be remembered by using the mneumonic LSD: *loca*tion, *s*can, and *d*etail.

The location of the photograph is important because skin diseases are characteristic of certain locations, and it is important for the physician to show that location. The photograph should make clear where the disease is located by showing the site relative to a recognizable body part such as wrist, knee, or ear; that is, it should be obvious that the lesions are on the chest, not the shoulder blade, or on the leg, not the arm. It may also be important to document the location in case the site must be identified later. This makes the location photograph clinically informative (Fig. 15A).

The scan photograph should show how widespread a dis-

ease is. This is best done with a series of sectional photographs (Fig. 15B). When the entire body is involved, avoid taking a head-to-toe photograph for the following reasons. First, photographs taken at such a distance eliminate much of the detail you may want to show. Second, head-to-toe photographs violate your patients' privacy and dignity (avoid showing genitals and face together). Third, the photographs include the genital areas, which may not be appropriate for some audiences. Fourth, when patients insist on or are given the choice of wearing their underwear, sectional scan photographs help you to avoid photographing this distracting element. Fifth, a head-to-toe photograph brings the rest of the room into your photograph, thereby giving you the unprofessional, snapshot look.

The detail part of the mneumonic, that is, to show all the varied characteristics of the disorder, is probably the most important. Detail should show such important aspects as translucency, wrinkling, different hues and colors, borders, telangiectases, hair follicles, skin markings, and scales (Fig. 15C).

Using the single-lens reflex 35-mm camera; an on-camera electronic flash; and a telephoto macro lens such as the 105 macro lens the photographer can begin to establish fixed positions on the lens for each of the three views (location, scan, and detail) (Fig. 13). On the lens are numbers that tell how far the camera is from the subject or the ratio of image size to the actual size of the subject. These numbers are used to get fixed positions on the lens for the location, scan, and detail views. For example, the "location photo" could use a ratio of 1:8 (image to actual size), the "scan photo" a 1:12 ratio, and the "detail photo" a 1:2 ratio. This means that if the ratio is 1:8, the image on the slide is exactly one-eighth of life size. Figure 15A shows a typical location photograph. Figure 15B shows a scan photograph, and Fig. 15C shows a detailed photograph of the same patient. Focusing is in the manual mode and accomplished by predetermining the position on the lens. Once location, scan, and detail have been decided, photographs can be made repeatedly. For example, if the face is photographed in the L (location) position every time a patient is followed up, the photographs will be exactly the same each time. To take the photograph, hold the camera in the correct manner and move the camera into the spot where the image is in sharp focus. This technique, as described earlier, is referred to as body focusing. The only variable now is to determine the correct exposure for each of the three positions to be used in the dermatologic formula.

A test roll of film should be shot to determine the correct lens opening. The test is made using manual settings on both the flash and the camera because this imparts the best detail and quality of photographs. Exposure setting or "F stop" controls the amount of light coming through the lens. The lower the F number, the more light that enters. Given sufficient light, the higher the F number, the better the detail. Avoid overexposure and underexposure, both of which distort the photograph and lose details. The correct exposure

Patient Name_____   Chart #_____
                                     Photo #_____

                    NEW YORK UNIVERSITY MEDICAL CENTER
                          UNIVERSITY HOSPITAL
                          SKIN AND CANCER UNIT

                    CONSENT FOR MEDICAL PHOTOGRAPHS

        I, the undersigned, consent to the taking of
photographs of me during diagnostic and/or treatment
sessions, operations and/or other surgical or medical
procedures.

        I authorize the Skin & Cancer Unit to allow
photography personnel and their equipment in the areas
of the institutions (UH, Bellevue, VA) where photography
will take place.

        I waive all rights that I may have to payment or
royalties and the right to inspect or approve the
finished photographs, or printed material that may be
used in conjunction therewith or to the eventual use
that it might be applied.

        I release New York University Hospital physicians,
hospital employees and consultants from any liability in
connection with the use of such materials.

Date:_____

Signed:_____
        (patient or person authorized to give consent)

Witness:_____

FIG. 14. A typical consent form.

setting can be determined by running a simple test. At the focusing position for the detailed photograph, take shots at F 22, F 16, and F 11. (Remember to use the manual settings on both the flash and the lens.) Location photographs might be shot at F 16, F 11, and F 8, and the scan photographs at F 11, F 8, and F 5 or F 6. Write down the exposure setting in the order that the exposures are made because slides usually come back numbered in the same sequence in which they were taken. Pick out the best slides (in terms of color and detail) for each of the location, scan, and detail views, and refer to the notes to find their respective exposure settings. Record these settings on the electronic flash unit (Fig. 15D) so that you will have them for future reference while taking photographs.

This is a relatively foolproof system for producing good-quality photographs consistently with little or no loss of motion because the exposure and the image size will be consis-

tent every time, thereby eliminating "photographic cures" and other misleading clinical photographs. All that is required is to determine which type of photographs (location, scan, or detail) are needed for each patient. Once this is all completed, the system takes over and can be repeated by anyone using the camera. Use a simple light box to illuminate the slides. It should be in the area where the photography is done so that the image and patient position are consistent in before-and-after photographs.

It must be decided whether to hold the camera in a vertical or a horizontal format. Keeping in mind that the purpose of taking the photograph is to maximize clinical information, determine whether the vertical or the horizontal format maximizes that information. For example, if photographing the lower legs, presenting this in the horizontal format would not maximize the clinical information that is being presented and would include too much of the surrounding background.

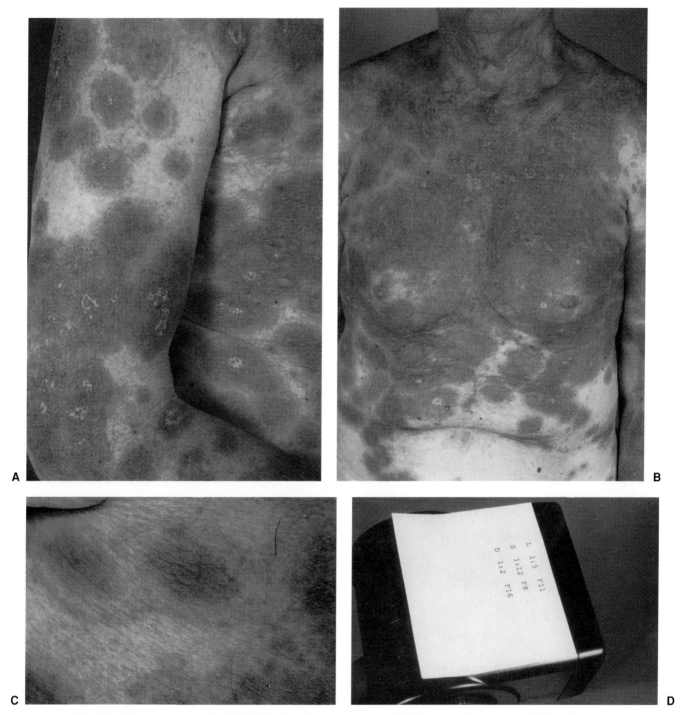

FIG. 15. ''Three-views method.'' **(A)** The location photograph. **(B)** The scan photograph. **(C)** The detail photograph. **(D)** The proper ratio and F stop setting for the three-views method is recorded and placed on top of the flash.

A

B

FIG. 16. (A) This photograph shows "the centering syndrome." **(B)** A better photograph that maximizes the information about this person.

The vertical format would give you a greater view of the lower leg while simultaneously eliminating irrelevant data. Another factor that works along with determining horizontal versus vertical format is the factor of "the centering syndrome." The centering syndrome is the habit of placing what is apparently the most important aspect in the center of the photograph, as opposed to maximizing all the clinical information to be presented. This habit is often seen in home pictures, as illustrated in Fig. 16A. Whether using the horizontal or vertical format, the head is usually right in the middle of the frame, often including irrelevant information. Figure 16B shows a photograph of the same person in which the information about the individual is maximized by not placing the head in the center of the photograph, thereby improving the photograph. This principle of avoiding the centering syndrome should be applied in clinical photographs. It prevents giving the "snapshot" appearance, especially when the location photograph is taken to include a recognizable site.

The background is an important part of the photographic presentation. The background should not distract from the clinical information to be presented. Such things as the furnishings in the room, the floor, the baseboard, the switch on the wall, and the shelves in the office should be avoided.

Figure 17A is a clinical presentation of parapsoriasis. What is seen is a patient standing on the floor in a room with his shoe behind him, his pants hanging on the door, a cloth on the floor, and the kind of boxer shorts that he is wearing, together with the site of the biopsy. If it is the intention to present the disease of parapsoriasis, the photograph has clouded the issue with detail that has nothing to do with the clinical presentation. Figure 17B is another presentation of parapsoriasis showing a scanned photograph that fills the frame with as much information as possible, and this is supplemented with a detailed photograph showing the clinical manifestation of this disease (Fig. 17C).

Figure 18A is a photograph labeled erythema nodosum. Here again, there is much information to be seen that does not relate to the clinical presentation. All of the criticisms that were made of the previous photograph can be made of this one as well. In contrast, Figure 18B shows the same disease, and the location is supplemented by a close-up (Fig. 18C). A distracting background is also evident in Fig. 19A, in which the clinical presentation of keratoacanthoma is being shown. Instead of concentration on the skin manifestation of this disease, the nostrils, as well as the eyeglasses, are distracting. In contrast, Fig. 19B shows this disease on both wrists, but without the distraction.

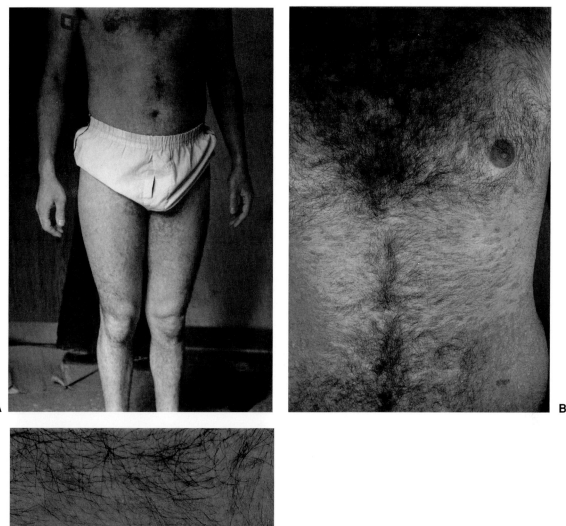

FIG. 17. (A) A snapshot of parapsoriasis. **(B)** The scanning view of parapsoriasis in the three-views method. **(C)** The detail view in the three-views method.

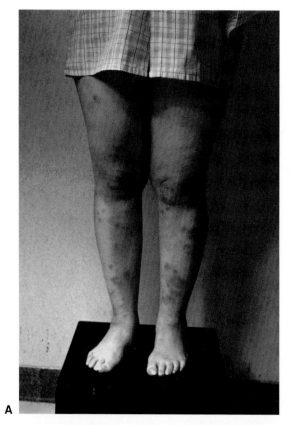

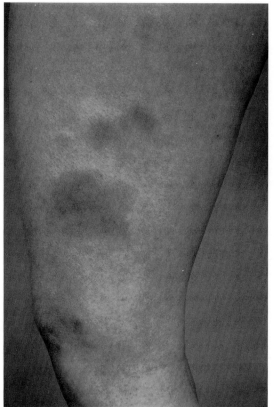

FIG. 18. (A) A snapshot of erythema nodosum. **(B)** A location photograph of erythema nodosum. **(C)** A detail photograph of erythema nodosum.

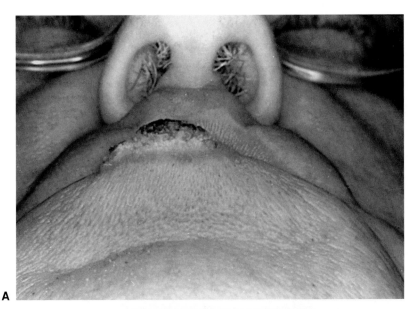

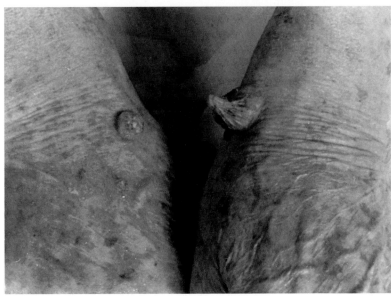

FIG. 19. **(A)** A distracting photograph of keratoacanthoma. **(B)** Medical photograph without the distracting keratoacanthoma elements.

Background color is one of preference. My personal preference for a background is light blue. A light blue background appears in photographs much darker than it really is, since the settings are for the patient, not the background. A light blue, when underexposed, appears as royal blue, which is the color most universally accepted as less disturbing to the eye when seen for a long time.

DOCUMENTING SURGICAL CASES

This chapter has discussed much about dermatologic photography as it relates to general dermatology. However, those who specialize in surgery must understand that it is important to master general dermatologic photography; once this is accomplished, it is quite easy to apply the principles to surgical dermatology. All the principles that have previously been discussed apply to surgical photography. The series of photographs in Fig. 20 shows a simple surgical procedure being performed. The series is obtained by choosing a setting; then each step of the procedure is documented by body focusing the shot and being certain there is an adequate background. The photographs made in sequence tell the entire story of the procedure.

Liposuction is a procedure that many dermatologists perform. Documenting the subtle contour changes seen in this procedure becomes very important for both patients and physicians. This can only be accomplished effectively if a system of standardization, as previously discussed, is established. Once established, the slight changes, as seen in liposuction in Fig. 21, become quite apparent. Without accurate documentation it is especially difficult for the patient to discern the changes.

In an effort to make photodocumentation simple and easy

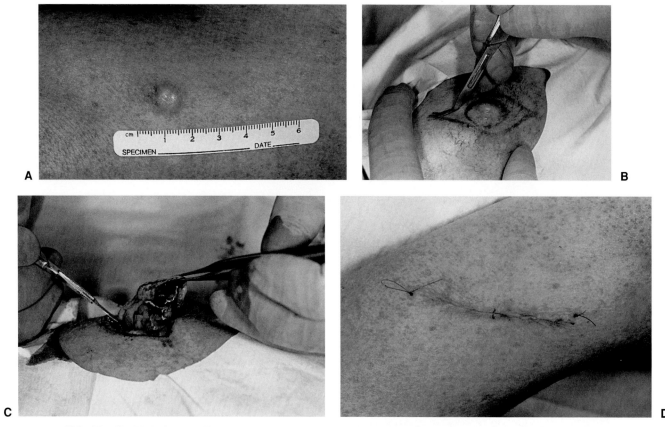

FIG. 20. (A–D) A dermatofibrosarcoma protuberans being documented during excision.

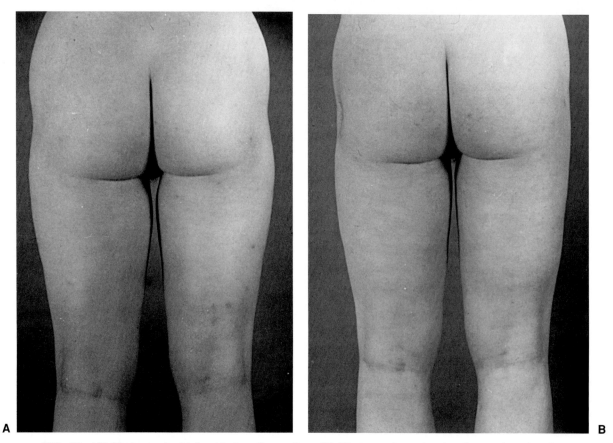

FIG. 21. (A) Photograph obtained before liposuction. **(B)** Photograph made after liposuction showing the subtle changes.

A

B

C

FIG. 22. **(A)** The photographic system for dermatologists. **(B and C)** The color coding makes it easy to determine which views to take. (See Color Plate 2.)

for the dermatologist, a system has been created. The system consists of a Nikon 35-mm camera, a macro lens, and a flash connected in such a way that the three-view method is used (Fig. 22A). As seen in Fig. 22B and C, the three views are color coded so that it is quite easy to determine by colors which view is being obtained. All that is now necessary is the lining up of the colors so that the three views can be maintained. Once the colors are lined up, simply by body focusing, the clinical photographs are made in a consistent, repeatable manner. Figure 23 is a classic example of photodocumentation of basal cell carcinoma that has been treated with radiation therapy in which the before-and-after photographs are taken in an identical manner. The advantage of this system is that it can be used for both regular clinical and surgical photography. Once it has been established

which views need be obtained, the physician or an assistant can easily learn the method of body focusing by using the three views. The other advantage of this system is that it simplifies the entire process of taking clinical photographs.[*]

As stated earlier, placing the previously taken slides on the light box before taking follow-up photographs helps in positioning the patient in a similar manner and allows the framing of the photograph in a fashion similar to the previous photographs. In Fig. 21 the photographs made before and after liposuction show the need to properly frame and position the patient each time the clinical photographs are taken, to demonstrate the efficacy of the procedure.

---

[*]The company that manufactures and distributes this system is Canfield Scientific, Inc., 218 Little Falls Road, Cedar Grove, NJ 07009-1231.

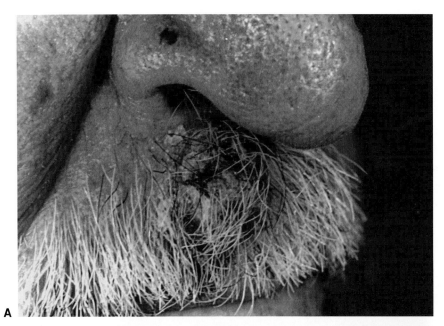

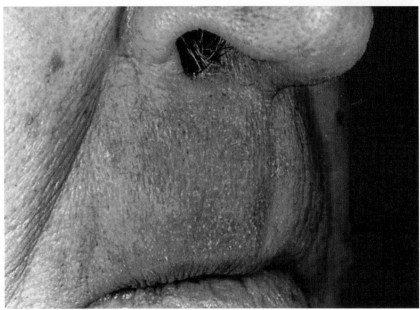

FIG. 23. (A) BCC before treatment. **(B)** Surgical site after treatment. Note the reproducible view and exposure produced by using the system as detailed in the text.

When photographing pigmented lesions or any lesion for which it is important to demonstrate the size, place a ruler next to the lesion so that the size of the lesion is easily determined when the photograph is reviewed. Some physicians have used rulers given to them by drug companies. This practice should not be encouraged, since it is a form of advertising. In addition, these rulers do not always meet the necessary specifications in a medical photograph. The ruler must be nonreflective and must also have room to make notations such as patient's initials (or other means of identification), date of the photograph, and other relevant information. Rulers can be purchased for this specific purpose (Fig. 24). Another practice to be discouraged is the use of ink on patients when it is not necessary. Sometimes, when flap design or the surgical procedures must be documented, this is

acceptable. However, circling the lesion, putting arrows next to the lesion, or making other random markings is not professional. In photographs with ink marks, not only are they distracting, but the photographs takes on the appearance of "snapshots." The photographer and surgeon must be careful not to photograph poor surgical technique, such as performing procedures without protective gloves.

LABELING AND STORAGE

The photographs must be labeled when they are returned from processing and then stored in a manageable filing system, which allows the retrieval of these photographs as needed. The initial step is identifying the photographs when they are returned from processing. A few systems are used to identify the photographs that are taken. Many physicians photograph the patient's initials on a piece of paper before taking the set of clinical photographs, and since the photographs are numbered when they are returned, it is easy to follow each patient's photographs in sequence. Another method of identifying the photograph is by creating a log book. The patient's name and site are recorded, and all photographic sessions on that roll of film are recorded on one page sequentially. At the end of the roll, that page number is photographed so that when the film is returned, there is a log of each patient's photographs in consecutive order. By these two methods, the patient's anonymity is maintained and mix-ups are avoided.

The system of storage depends mainly on how the slides will be used. Some slides can be used for patient records, as well as for teaching. Based on usage, a system of filing and storage is designed to facilitate retrieval. Slides used chiefly as a patient record can be stored in flat polyethylene slide pages and kept in the patient's record. It is usually easy to recognize a good teaching case as the photographs are being taken; a few extra shots can then to be stored in a separate teaching collection that can be filed in alphabetical order by skin diseases or surgical procedures.

For slides used chiefly for teaching, the most effective way of filing and retrieving would be by using a computer-based retrieval system. The system comprises two basic components: the hardware, which is the computer itself, and

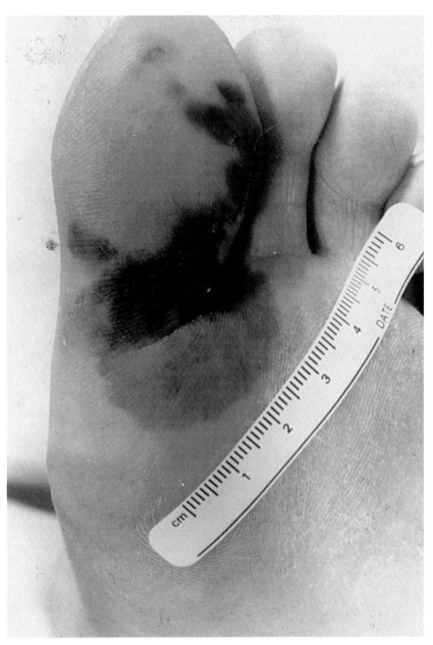

FIG. 24. Using a ruler to help demonstrate the size of the lesions.

the software, which is the program that enables the computer to carry out the design task. Either IBM or Macintosh machines are adequate in accomplishing this task, and the software is a database or data-based management system. The software enables you to enter, sort, or search for the data and have a printout of such information. This database is divided into files, records, and fields. With this system, enter the patient's record, which will include the patient name or an assigned code number; the date the patient was photographed; the disease or surgical procedure; areas of the body that were photographed; and other relevant information, such as whether a biopsy was performed and how many slides were taken, wanted during the search. Once the system has been structured and the data have been entered, it is easy to search for and to find the slides based on all the parameters entered. For example, if slides of a particular disease are needed, it is quite easy to print out all the photographs made of patients with this disease. If slides of a particular surgical procedure based on areas of the body, or of a particular area of the body, are needed, these are easily found with a database program. The ability to make a quick, detailed search of a large amount of information is the main reason why the computer is such an important tool in data management. The process of searching involves simply asking the computer to find records based on data that have been entered; once the database has been established, it is quite easy for a person with only the basic computer skills to use it to retrieve the slides. Some systems even create labels so that, once the information has been entered into the database system, the computer can generate labels to put on the slides. An additional feature that can be placed in the database system is what is called a loan program. You may find that photo-graphs are of such high quality that colleagues will be borrowing them. In the database system a record of slides lent to colleagues can be created, establishing a time for their return and printing out a record of all delinquent borrowers so that the slides can be retrieved and refiled in the slide storage system.

The picture quality of the Kodachromes last longer when stored in a dark, cool environment of low humidity. When purchasing storage containers for the slides, remember that as the slide collection grows, the storage system must be able to expand to accommodate such growth. There are many suppliers of products used to store slides, including the following manufacturers:

1. Light Empressions Incorporated, 439 Monroe Ave., Rochester, NY 14607.
2. Process Materials Corporation, 7 Caesar Place, Moona-chie, NJ 07074.
3. Hollinger Corporation, 3810 South Four Mile Run Drive, P.O. Box 6185, Arlington, VA 22206.
4. Carr McLean and Company, 461 Horner Ave., Toronto, Ontario, M8W4X2, Canada.

SUGGESTED READING LIST

1. Slue WE: Photographic cures for dermatologic disorders. Arch Dermatol 1989;125:160.
2. Slue WE: Unmasking the Lone Ranger. N Engl J Med 1989;321:550.
3. Slue WE: Picture imperfect. Dermatol Digest 1990;1:1.
4. Slue WE: Snapshot versus medical photographs. Cutis 1993;51:345.
5. Slue WE: Better dermatologic office photography: getting started. Cutis 1994;54:177.
6. Slue WE: Better dermatologic office photography: taking the photograph. Cutis 1994;54:271.
7. Vetter JP. Biomedical photography. Butterworth-Heinemann. Stoneham, MA 1992:201–299.

SECTION II

Scalpel Surgery

Textbook of Dermatologic Surgery, edited by John L. Ratz.
Lippincott–Raven Publishers, Philadelphia © 1998.

CHAPTER 9

Surgical Instrumentation and Wound Closure Materials

Lynn Dimino-Emme, Carl V. Washington, Jr., and Nhu-Linh T. Tran

Dermatologic surgery requires dexterity and skill. Although the surgeon's training is critical, equally important are the tools of the trade. A thorough knowledge of surgical instrumentation and wound closure materials can help cutaneous surgeons master their craft. The basic armamentarium of the dermatologist has become more sophisticated as the specialty has evolved. Although personal preference will always dictate the instruments and sutures a surgeon chooses, a general understanding of the instruments and materials available will aid in this decision-making process. In this chapter we review basic instrumentation and wound closure materials for the dermatologic surgeon.

SURGICAL INSTRUMENTATION

Scalpel Handles and Blades

A variety of scalpel handles and blades is available to the cutaneous surgeon. The most commonly used scalpel handle

Lynn Dimino-Emme: Coastline Dermatology, and Laser Center 275 Victoria Street, Suite 1H, Costa Mesa, CA 92627.

Carl V. Washington, Jr.: Department of Dermatology, Emory University School of Medicine, 5001 Woodruff Memorial Building, 1639 Pierce Drive, Atlanta, GA. 30322

Nhu-Linh T. Tran: Atlanta Dermatologic Surgery Consultants, PC, 3193 Howell Mill Road, Suite 220, Atlanta, GA. 30327.

in dermatologic surgery is a No. 3, which is usually paired with a No. 15 blade (Fig. 1). This handle is available with or without a centimeter scale and can be purchased in regular or long sizes. Other handles are available that vary in shape (flat, round, and octagonal) and weight distribution. Although octagonal handles are not commonly used, some surgeons prefer them for fingertip control. Most scalpel handles accept all standard blade sizes except the Beaver system, which has its own specialized handle (see later discussion).

The scalpel blade may also vary in size and shape. It is commonly made of stainless steel or carbon steel. Although carbon steel is sharper, stainless steel blades tend to remain sharper longer. The most commonly used scalpel blades in dermatologic surgery include the Nos. 10, 11, 15, and 15c blades (Fig. 2).

The No. 10 blade is wide and convexly curved and has a very sharp belly, which makes it advantageous for large excisional surgeries and thicker tissues (e.g., the back). The No. 11 blade has a pointed, very sharp tip and is most suited for incision and drainage, suture removal, and incising sharp angles on flaps. The No. 15 blade is the standard most versatile blade used in cutaneous surgery. It is similar in shape to, but smaller than, the No. 10 blade, and it is the most frequently used blade for excisional surgery. The No. 15c blade is similar in shape to the No. 15 blade, but is one-third narrower and tapers more acutely at the tip. It resembles

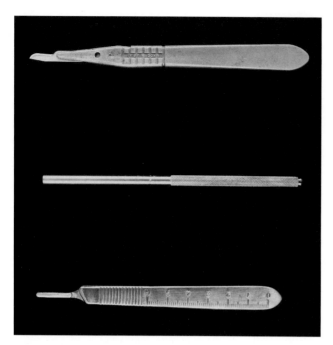

FIG. 1. (Top to bottom) disposable handle and blade, Beaver scalpel handle, and Scalpel handle No. 3.

the Beaver No. 67 blade (see later discussion) but can be attached to the standard No. 3 scalpel handle. The No. 15c blade is most useful for small lesions and when operating on thin skin.

Disposable scalpel blades on plastic handles are also available (Fig. 1). These are lighter instruments that are weighted differently than the standard handle is and generally are less desirable for fine excisional work.

The Beaver blade system is specifically designed for delicate work (Fig. 1). In this system the handle is narrow and pencil-like. It may be hexagonal or round and comes in a variety of different lengths and diameters. Although Beaver blades are sharper and smaller than standard scalpel blades, they lose their sharpness more rapidly than the standard system blades. The most commonly used Beaver blades are the Nos. 67 (a smaller, sharper-tipped equivalent to the No. 15), (Fig. 2) and 65 (the Beaver equivalent of the No. 11 blade). The No. 64 blade with round tip can be a useful addition for precise work. The Beaver system is especially advantageous for delicate work around the eyes and ears and for small excisions.

Another type of scalpel system is the Shaw hemostatic scalpel. This instrument uses a Teflon-coated, surgical steel blade that is connected to a separate electronic controller. The heat is provided by intricate microcircuitry that is conducted from the blade. The temperature is operator-activated and can be adjusted between 110°C and 270°C. This instrument is useful to seal off tiny blood vessels and is particularly useful when hemostasis may be a problem or in patients with coagulopathies or thrombocytopenias.

Also useful, especially for shave biopsies, is the Gillette

Super Blue blade (Fig. 2). This double-edged razor blade is sharp, flexible, economical, and disposable with a 1-inch cutting edge. The blade is broken in half longitudinally before use, and the Castroviejo blade breaker and holder are useful for this purpose. Once broken, this razor blade is relatively easy and safe to use without a holder. These blades are available unsterile, but they can be autoclaved without a significant decrease in their sharpness. The Derma Blade (dispensed by Personna Medical) is a new, modified version of the Gillette Blue blade. All but one cutting edge of the blade is encased in flexible plastic. This design allows for a firmer grip, more flexibility, and increased safety.

Scissors

Although scissors selection is mainly a matter of personal preference, certain principles are universal. Short-handled

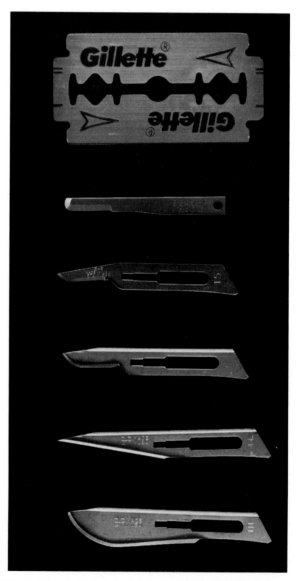

FIG. 2. (Top to bottom) Gillette Super Blue blade, Beaver No. 67, and Scalpel blades Nos. 15c, 15, 11, and 10.

scissors work best for delicate superficial work, whereas long-handled scissors are best used to reach under tissue at a distance. Straight blades are better for cutting tough tissue, scar, or nail plates and are helpful for trimming grafts and flaps. Curved blades, in general, are better suited for fine dissections, as in cyst excision. Curved blades have 30% to 40% more mobility than straight blades and are usually better to help visualize the surgical field. Sharp-tipped scissors dissect nicely, whereas blunt-tipped scissors cause less trauma to neurovascular structures and are best for undermining. Scissors are available with smooth (plain) blades or one smooth and one serrated blade. The one serrated blade helps grip the tissue while cutting, and this feature is helpful in cutting thin skin with little subcutaneous tissue.

Four major groups of scissors are commonly used in dermatologic surgery. These include tissue-cutting, undermining, suture removal, and bandage scissors. These categories are not exclusive, and many scissors can be used for more than one purpose.

Tissue-cutting scissors are used to excise tissue and are available with straight or curved blades, sharp or blunt tips, long or short shanks, and with serrated or diamond-cut edges. Sharpness is imperative. In general, most dermatologic surgeons prefer small scissors ($3\frac{1}{2}$ to 5 inches long), which are better suited for delicate work. The most popular tissue-cutting scissors include the Gradle, Gibbs-Gradle, Stevens tenotomy, and Iris scissors. The Westcott, Castroviejo, LaGrange, and Mayo scissors also have very useful purposes.

The Gradle scissors, compared with the Stevens tenotomy and Iris scissors, have the most fulcrum power because they have the shortest screw-to-tip distance (Fig. 3). The Gradle scissors have very sharp, fine, slightly curved tips and short handles, and the blades have a short arc. These features all combine to produce excellent cutting scissors for delicate work and fine dissections. This is an excellent choice for cutting fine, delicate tissue. The Gibbs-Gradle scissors are 1 mm shorter and have a slighter curve than the original Gradle but otherwise serve a similar function.

The Stevens tenotomy scissors resemble the Gradle scissors, except that the tips are straighter and slightly larger and are not quite as sharp, which some surgeons believe make them more versatile than the Gradle scissors. The Stevens tenotomy scissors have slightly less fulcrum power than the Gradle and are available in blunt or sharp and curved or straight models.

The Iris scissors are slightly heavier than the Gradle or Stevens scissors and have a much longer screw-to-tip distance; thus cutting-tissue fulcrum power is decreased. Iris scissors have short shanks and sharp tips and are available in curved or straight models (Fig. 3). Serrated Iris scissors can also be purchased, and these are useful to prevent tissue slippage, particularly when cutting lax or mobile skin such as the eyelid. Iris scissors have many uses in cutaneous surgery, including snipping acrochordons, fine dissections, and cutting.

Westcott and Castroviejo scissors are spring-tipped scissors with very sharp, fine points that are both excellent for extremely delicate dissection, as in the periorbital area. The LaGrange scissors have intermediate-length shanks and reverse, curved, sharp tips. Because of their unique curvature, they are advantageous in removing hair transplant plugs from donor sites.

Mayo scissors have a 1 : 1 handle-to-blade ratio, so the blades pass through a long arc as they cut, making them ideal for cutting through thick tissue and suture. Although Mayo scissors are more commonly used by general surgeons, they are useful as "heavy-duty" scissors in dermatologic surgery.

The ideal undermining scissors have blunt, broad tips and a longer handle, to minimize trauma to neural and vascular structures and provide access to subcutaneous tissue. Strabismus, Stevens tenotomy, and Metzenbaum scissors are all advantageous for undermining. Strabismus scissors are

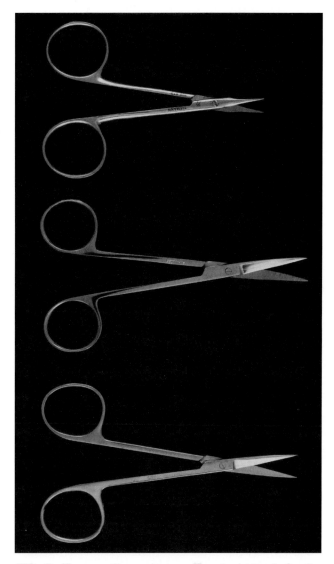

FIG. 3. Tissue-cutting scissors: (Top to bottom) Gradle, curved, and straight Iris scissors.

tapered, spreading ends with no cutting edges, so they preserve blood vessels as they dissect. They are also particularly useful for scalp reductions.

Although any scissors can cut suture, the fine, sharp Gradle, Iris, and Stevens scissors dull quickly if used for this purpose. Therefore specific suture scissors have been designed.

Spencer, Shortbent, Northbent, and Littauer are all popular stitch scissors (Fig. 5). All have a hooked tip that helps catch the suture as it is cut. The Spencer stitch scissors are 3½- or 4½-inch straight scissors. The Shortbent scissors are identical to the Spencer but are curved. The Northbent scissors are similar in shape but larger than the Shortbent and are a good all-purpose suture scissors. The Littauer scissors strongly resemble the Spencer type but are larger. O'Brien scissors are similar in size to the Spencer, but the tips are

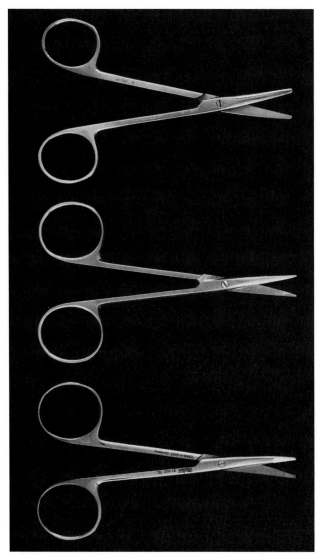

FIG. 4. Undermining scissors: (Top to bottom) "Baby" Metzenbaum, strabismus, and blepharoplasty scissors.

about 4 inches long and are available in straight or curved versions (Fig. 4). The curved strabismus scissors are our choice for most undermining. The Stevens tenotomy scissors, in addition to being good tissue-cutting scissors, are excellent for undermining, particularly in delicate areas. The curved variety is particularly helpful in keeping the plane of undermining more parallel to the cutaneous surface. The Metzenbaum (Lahey) scissors are useful for more extensive, wide undermining and thicker tissues. The baby Metzenbaum is a smaller version of the original and is more appropriate for delicate work (Fig. 4). Blepharoplasty scissors are also known as Kaye scissors, which usually include serrations along one cutting edge for stability and a sharp outer edge of the scissors blade to facilitate undermining (Fig. 4).

The iconoclast or blunt dissector of Luikart is an instrument designed for more forceful spreading of relative adherent tissue from deeper structures. These scissors have long,

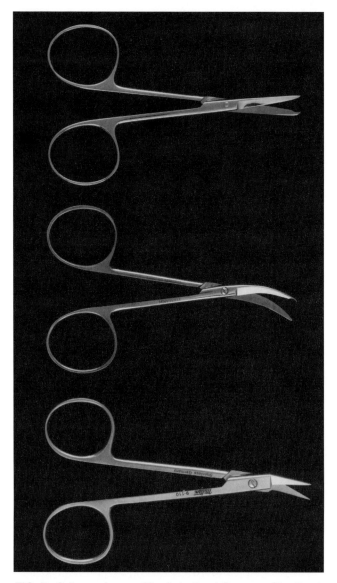

FIG. 5. Suture scissors: (Top to bottom) Spencer, Shortbent, and O'Brien scissors.

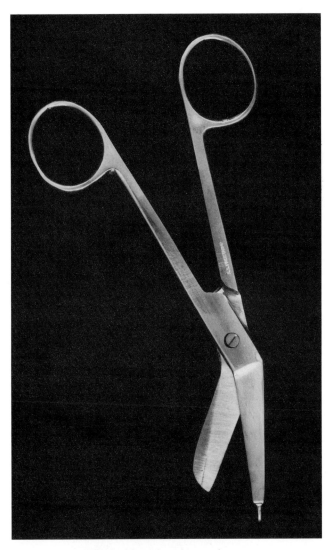

FIG. 6. Lister bandage scissors.

angled and sharp (Fig. 5). Because dermatologic surgery often involves delicate work with fine sutures, we prefer the 3½-inch, small Spencer scissors.

The bandage scissors are another important instrument in dermatologic surgery. The Lister type is the most popular in this category. Lister scissors have one large, blunted tip and thick, angled blades that fit comfortably between dressings and the skin (Fig. 6). They come in a variety of sizes and cut gauze easily. The universal bandage scissors are the second main type of bandage scissors. They have large, thick, plastic handles and a serrated blade edge. These are heavy duty scissors that maintain their sharpness better than the Lister type.

Forceps

Gentle handling of skin edges and tissue is essential in dermatologic surgery, and a variety of forceps or pickups is available for this purpose. In general, pickups are available

in smooth, serrated, or toothed models. Function and tissue type determine the type of forceps selected. For most dermatologic surgery the smooth-tipped pickups do not adequately grasp tissue. Finely serrated forceps are commonly known as dressing forceps. They are more likely to cause crush injury to tissue. Toothed forceps with one to three teeth manipulate tissue much more gently than the serrated models. Pickups can be broadly categorized into dressing and tissue forceps and splinter, fixation, and epilating forceps. Dressing and tissue forceps include Adson, Semken, Iris, Bishop-Harman, and Foerster models.

Adson forceps are the most commonly used and most versatile forceps in cutaneous surgery (Fig. 7). They have a long, tapered tip and a broader handle. The serrated models come with 1-mm or delicate (0.6 mm) tips. The toothed variety is available with 1 × 2 or 2 × 3 teeth and 0.6-, 1-, or 1.8-mm tips. The Semken pickup has a narrower handle and a more gradual taper than the Adson model. Semken dressing forceps are available with serrated heavy (4½-inch) or delicate jaws (5 inches). The tissue forceps are available as straight or curved models in heavy 1 × 2 teeth (4½ inches), delicate 1 × 2 teeth (5 inches), or delicate 2 × 3 teeth (5 inches) models. They serve a similar purpose as the Adson forceps. Another variety of forceps is the Frankel-Adson forceps, which are actually a modification of a tissue Adson forceps with a hook placed on one arm. This type of forceps is a combination of a skin hook and tissue forceps. Advocates of this instrument believe it saves time by decreasing the need to change instruments when suturing. Although some surgeons prefer it, it takes time to successfully master the technique. Iris tissue forceps are useful for more delicate work (Figs. 7 and 8). They are shaped similarly to the Semken pickup and are available in standard (0.8-mm-wide tip) and extra-delicate (0.5-mm-wide tip) versions. These are 4-inch tissue forceps with 1 × 2 teeth and are available in straight, half-curved, or full-curved models.

Bishop-Harman forceps are also used for delicate surgery, as on thin eyelid skin (Fig. 7). These are light-weight instru-

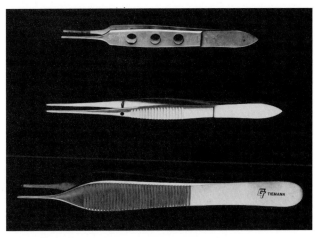

FIG. 7. Tissue forceps: (Top to bottom) Bishop-Harman, Iris, and Adson.

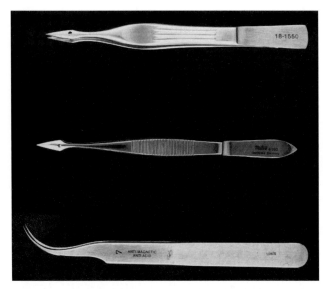

FIG. 8. Splinter forceps: (Top to bottom) Walter forceps, Carmalt and Jeweler's forceps with superfine, curved tip.

ments with fine tips. Each handle has three holes for a secure hold and easier handling. These forceps are 3⅜ inches long and are available with serrated, 0.6-mm tips or with 1 × 2 teeth with 0.3-, 0.4-, or 0.6-mm tips. Foerster forceps are another ideal pickup for delicate work. The handle has a tapered tip and a central, octagonal hole that facilitates a firm grasp. They are available with serrated, 0.6-mm tips or with 1 × 2 teeth with 0.6-mm tips in a straight or curved style.

Splinter forceps are another category of pickups that are useful in dermatology. They are available with fine, extrafine, or superfine tips. They are useful for placing minigrafts during hair transplantation, removal of sutures, and grasping small blood vessels for pinpoint electrocoagulation. Because of their fine tips, they are less suitable for stabilizing tissue because the tips bend easily. Popular models of splinter forceps are the jeweler's, Carmalt, and plain types.

The jeweler's forceps are available in fine, narrow fine, or superfine (4⅜-inch, 4½-inch, or 4¾-inch) types (Fig. 9). They are available with straight or curved tips. The straight-tip models are ideal for spot electrocoagulation and suture removal, whereas the curved variety is perfectly suited to place minigrafts during hair transplantation surgery. The Carmalt splinter forceps have sharp, pointed tips with a triangular configuration (Fig. 9). The serrated jaws are separated by a pin at the widest point. This design permits excellent grasping of even the finest suture. Carmalt splinter forceps are available in curved or straight versions. They are ideal for removing sutures and placing Steri-Strips, and for pinpoint electrocoagulation. Walter splinter forceps are similar to the Carmalt type but have sturdier handles (Fig. 9). The plain splinter forceps are similar to the straight jeweler's forceps except that they have a narrow, serrated tip. These forceps have serrations on the outer handle for a more secure grasp.

Fixation forceps are the third major type of pickups. They are specialized to stabilize and firmly grasp tissue. Three common varieties of fixation forceps are Brown-Adson, Graefe, and Dejardin forceps.

The Brown-Adson model is similar in configuration to the Adson pickup but has seven or eight teeth, instead of two or three, to secure a firmer grasp on difficult-to-grip tissue such as cartilage (Fig. 8). The Graefe fixation forceps are another type of pickup with a similar function to the Brown-Adson variety. They have slightly flared tips with fine teeth. They are 4¼ inches long and are available with straight or curved jaws with or without a catch-locking system. DeJardin forceps are similar to the Graefe pickup with wide jaws and teeth.

Epilating forceps are also occasionally used in dermatology. Originally designed to extract hair, some surgeons prefer them for suture removal. Most have a wide, flat tip that permits firm, even pressure. The Barraquer forceps and Bergh epilating forceps are examples in this category. The Barraquer forceps come in a 4- or 4½-inch, straight or curved model with a smooth, rounded tip platform. The Bergh pickup serves a similar purpose as the Barraquer model but has a wider, putty knife–shaped tip.

Another useful type of forceps is the Allis forceps (Fig. 8). The handle resembles hemostatic forceps, but only the curved tips of the instrument meet. This pickup is available in the regular, 6-inch model with 5 × 6 teeth; the delicate, 5-inch type with 4 × 5 teeth; and the extra-delicate, 4¾-

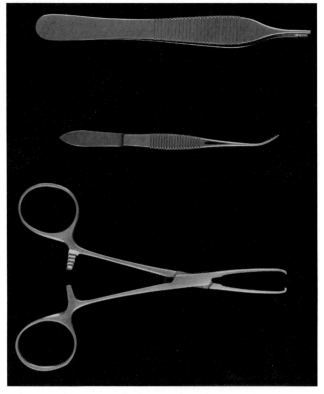

FIG. 9. (Top to bottom) Brown-Adson, curved Iris, and Allis forceps.

inch version with 4 × 5 teeth. The Allis forceps are excellent to obtain a good grasp on cysts and lipomas to facilitate their extraction.

Hemostats

Although most hemostasis in dermatologic surgery can be obtained with electrocoagulation, occasionally the presence of arterial and arteriolar bleeding necessitate the clamping and tying off of blood vessels. Hemostatic forceps are designed just for this purpose. Hemostats provide a dry, surgical field that holds the vessels securely to facilitate suture ligation. They can also be used in conjunction with electrocoagulation to control smaller arterioles. Hemostats can also be used to help anchor cysts and lipomas during their dissection and to help remove the nail plate in nail surgery. Although a variety of hemostats are available, most models used in dermatologic surgery are delicate instruments with fine tips. Curved or straight hemostats are available.

The Halsted mosquito and Hartmann hemostats work well in cutaneous surgery. The mosquito hemostat is available in regular, delicate, or angled 5-inch models. The Hartmann clamp resembles the Halsted type but is a shorter, 3½-inch instrument. It is also available in regular or delicate models. Both the Halsted and Hartmann hemostats have tips that are serrated throughout their entire length. The Jacobson micro-mosquito forceps (5 inches) has a narrower tip than the Halstead or Hartmann variety and is useful for clamping delicate, small arterioles and arteries.

For the clamping of large vessels, the Kelly, Providence, Crile, and Lahey clamps are all useful. The Kelly clamp (5½ inches) has a broader, longer tip than the previously mentioned models. Unlike the Halsted or Hartmann clamps, the tip is serrated only on its distal half. The Providence hospital forceps also have serrations only on the distal half of its tip. The Crile clamp comes in 5½- and 6¼-inch models and is serrated over its entire tip. The "baby" Crile model is the delicate version of the heavier original. The Lahey hemostat resembles the Crile model with serrations over its entire jaw. Much care must be taken when using these heavier hemostats in dermatologic surgery because they tend to crush tissue easily.

Skin Hooks

Skin hooks and retractors are essential instruments for the dermatologic surgeon. Many surgeons consider them indispensible for true atraumatic handling of tissue. Even the finest forceps injure tissue more than skin hooks. This is an important consideration, especially when cosmesis is critical and any amount of tissue trauma is undesirable. They are used to gently move tissue during suturing, or to help manipulate flaps or approximate tissue protrusions.

The tips of the skin hooks may be sharp or blunt and are available with one, two, or three prongs. The instruments

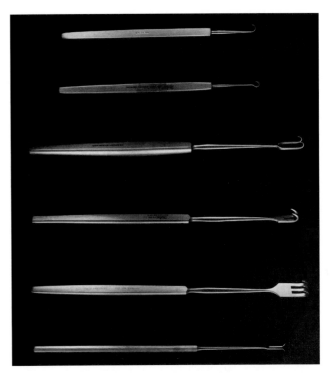

FIG. 10. (Top to bottom) Frazier, Frazier-Shepherd, and double-pronged Guthrie skin hooks; double- and triple-pronged rakes; and dura twist hook.

also come with flexible or inflexible heads. Skin hooks are actually a type of small retractor, and hooks with more than two prongs are classified as rakes. Although double-pronged hooks provide a better grasp and visualization of the wound, the single-pronged models are the most commonly used types in dermatologic surgery. Sharp tips are generally preferred to blunt tips because, although they pose more risk to the operator, they provide a better grasp of tissue. Commonly used skin hooks include the Frazier, Tyrell, Joseph, and Guthrie models. Frequently used retractors include the Alm self-retaining retractor and the Senn retractor.

The Frazier hook is a single-pronged skin hook that is available with a 3.5-mm hook radius and with a more curved Shepherd's hook; the former is more popular (Fig. 10). The Tyrell hook is similar in shape to the Frazier-Shepherd hook model but is smaller and more delicate. It is also available with sharp or blunt tips and is ideal for very delicate tissues such as the eyelids. The Joseph skin hook comes in a single-pronged model that resembles the 3.5-mm-radius Frazier hook or in a variety of double-pronged versions. The double-pronged variety is available in two-pronged separations of 2, 5, 7, 10, or 12 mm. The more narrowed, double-pronged versions are appropriate for dermatologic surgery and provide good visualization of wound depth. The Guthrie skin hook is similar to the fine, double-pronged Joseph hook and is the most popular double-pronged skin hook. It is a delicate instrument with two fine, sharp prongs and is available with 2- or 3-mm-wide separations. The dura twist hook, a neurosurgical instrument, can be helpful in grasping the galea or periosteum during scalp surgery (Fig. 10).

Rakes are small retractors that resemble skin hooks but are heavier instruments with broader prongs (Fig. 10). Their main purpose is to retract skin edges to better visualize wound cavities. The Senn retractor is a useful instrument for retraction during large dematologic surgical cases. It has three prongs on one end and a right-angle scoop on the other end. The Alm self-retaining retractor, although not commonly used in dermatologic surgery, can be a great asset when assistance is not available. It has two arms with spikes that are connected by an adjustable, screw-hinge mechanism. The retractor can be purchased in small ($2\frac{3}{4}$-inch) or large (4-inch) models.

Needle Holders

Needle holders are an essential tool in the dermatologic surgeon's armamentarium. They are available in a variety of sizes and models. In general, small needles and fine sutures work well with small needle holders, whereas larger needle holders are better suited for bigger needles and thicker sutures. The different models are available with smooth or finely serrated jaws. The smooth-jawed variety is the most popular type in cutaneous surgery because it is less damaging to delicate suture material. The striated or serrated type may provide a more secure grasp on the needle or suture but may actually fray or cut fine suture. Needle holders are also available with hardened, alloy inserts. The tungsten carbide needle holders such as Diamond-Jaw and Carb-N-Sert purport to hold the needle more securely and to undergo less instrument wear. They usually come with gold-plated handles and are significantly more expensive than the nonalloy-coated models.

The smooth-jawed Webster needle holder ($4\frac{1}{2}$ inches) is the most commonly used model in dermatologic surgery (Fig. 11). It has a tapered tip and small handles and is ideal for 6-0 or finer suture, although it is also often used with heavier suture. Its shape makes it advantageous for working in small, deep areas. The Neuro-smooth needle holder is about 6 inches long and has narrowed jaws. It is best suited for fine suture; 5-0, 6-0, or 7-0 sutures; and small needles. The fine, smooth-jawed Halsey needle holder is also useful for handling fine needles and delicate sutures (Fig. 11).

For extremely delicate work or for suturing under magnification the Castroviejo needle holder is a very useful tool (Fig. 11). It has very small tips that will not damage fine needles, and it works via a spring type of action, which is advantageous when placing many tiny sutures. This instrument fits very comfortably in small hands and is ideal for periocular work.

For larger needles and thicker sutures the Crile-Wood, heavy Halsey, Collier, and Baumgartner needle holders all work well. The Crile-Wood model (6 inches) has tapered, blunt, serrated tips and is ideal for 3-0, 4-0, or 5-0 suture

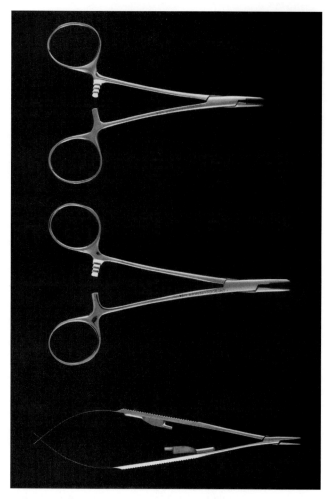

FIG. 11. (Top to bottom) Webster, Halsey, and Castroviejo needle holders with tungsten carbide inserts.

and larger needles. It is also useful for suturing thicker skin such as on the back. The heavy Halsey needle holder with smooth jaws is 5 inches long with a thicker tip but a similar configuration to the fine Halsey model (Fig. 12). It provides excellent control with larger needles. Similarly, the Baumgartner ($5\frac{1}{4}$- or $5\frac{1}{2}$-inch) with horizontal serrations and Collier with cross-serrations also work well with thicker sutures and needles (Fig. 12).

Needle holders are also available with a cutting option. The Gillies, Foster and Olsen-Hegar needle holders are all examples of models that incorporate scissors into their design. The Gillies needle holder resembles scissors but instead of a sharp tip, it has needle-holder jaws. The newer versions have slim, slightly curved, pointed jaws, and the cutting edge lies between the joint and the jaw to allow easy cutting of the suture. The Foster model resembles the Gillies needle holder but is smaller and more suitable for delicate sutures and needles. The Olsen-Hegar is another type of needle holder with a scissor modification (Fig. 12). It is available in $5\frac{1}{2}$- or $4\frac{3}{4}$-inch models and with serrated or smooth jaws. Although these combination needle holder/scissors can save time by not requiring an assistant to cut suture, they can also be a nuisance when a stitch is inadvertently cut while suturing.

Punches

Skin punches (trephines) are a basic tool in dermatology. The Keyes punch was the original model (Fig. 13). It has a heavy handle with slanted sides and a rounded or beveled, sharp cutting edge. Because of this design, it cuts pieces of tissue with more epidermis than dermis. It is available in sizes ranging from 1 to 10 mm. The Loo punch is another variety of trephine that has a thinner, less beveled wall than the Keyes model. This type is useful when a perpendicular incision is needed, such as when removing depressed scars.

Specialized cutaneous punches have been designed for use in hair transplantations. The Orentreich model has a straight

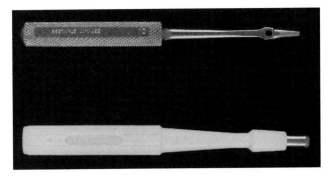

FIG. 13. (Top to bottom) Keyes and disposable skin punches.

inner wall and beveled outer sides. The Australian punch has a beveled inner surface and a straight outer side. Both models are available as a manual or power type. Because the previously mentioned permanent punches must be sterilized, they lose their sharpness after frequent use. Disposable punches, on the other hand, have the advantage of always initially being sharp (Fig. 13). They are available in 2.0-, 3.0-, 3.5-, 4.0-, and 6.0-mm sizes through Accuderm and Baker-Cummings. The 3- and 4-mm punches are the most frequently used types. We do not advocate the use of punches greater than 4 mm in size because of the resulting tissue protrusions.

Curettes

The cutaneous curette is a versatile, scooplike instrument. It is useful in the removal of benign and malignant lesions and can also help delineate the borders of basal cell or squamous cell carcinomas before excision. Curettes are available in a variety of sizes and shapes with straight or angled handles.

The Fox curette has a round cutting edge and a slender, straight, or angled handle (Fig. 14). It is available in sizes ranging from 1 to 8 mm. The Fox oval curette differs in that it has an elongated, oval cutting edge and a heavier handle and is only available in small, medium, and large sizes. The Piffard model resembles the Fox oval curette with its broad, heavy handle but has a less elongated, oval head (Fig. 14). The Cannon curette has an oval, slightly angled head and a thin handle. The Reu curette has a round or oval head and is available in a variety of sizes. It has a narrow handle with appropriately placed indentations to help ensure a secure grasp. In most dermatologic surgery procedures curettes with heads of 3 or 4 mm in diameter are the most useful.

The tiny Skeele, Heath, and Meyhofer curettes are advantageous for working in small cystic cavities or for delineating small tumor pockets. These were all originally designed to treat chalazions. The Skeele model has a small (1.0 to 2.5 mm), cup-shaped head with serrated edges, which aid in removing small cyst walls (Fig. 14). It has a very small aperture. The Heath curette is a smaller version of the Fox model (sizes 0.5 to 3.0 mm) with a barrel-shaped head but

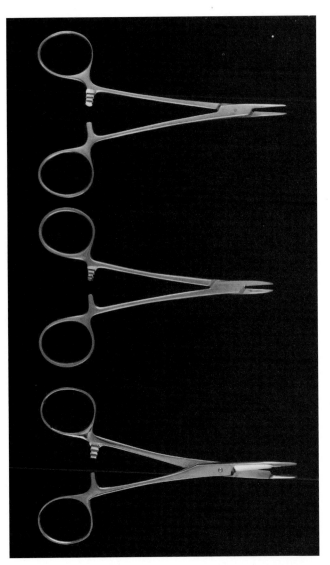

FIG. 12. (Top to bottom) Heavy Halsey, Collier, and Olsen-Hegar needle holders.

FIG. 14. (Top to bottom) Fox round and oval, Piffard, Skeele, Meyhofer, and disposable curettes.

a wide aperture to allow tissue to pass through it. The third type of delicate curette, the Meyhofer (Fig. 14), has a cupped head like the Skeele model but lacks serrations. It is available in several sizes ranging from 0.5 to 3.5 mm.

Disposable curettes are also now available in a variety of sizes (Fig. 14). They tend to be very sharp, do not always easily distinguish between normal and abnormal tissue, and may cause inadvertent damage to normal skin.

Comedo Expressors

Comedo expressors are instruments used during acne surgery (Fig. 15). Although many models are available, the Schamberg expressor is probably the most commonly used. Each end is slightly curved with an elongated opening for passage of comedone contents. There is also a ribbed, central portion to help ensure a secure grasp. The Unna expressor

has slightly angled ends and an elongated cup shape, with a smaller aperture than the Schamberg type. The Walton model has one cup-shaped end with a small opening and one tailored with a lancet that helps to remove the top of the comedone before expression of its contents. The Saalfeld model is similar in function. The Zimmerman-Walton expressor is a modification of the Walton model with a similar cupped end, but with a tapered tail end that is able to fit a disposable 30-gauge needle hub. The Heilen model is designed for less delicate work.

Miscellaneous Instruments

The chalazion clamp is a very useful instrument in dermatologic surgery. Although originally designed for chalazion surgery, these clamps are also particularly useful when working on the eyelids or lips. They immobilize the tissue and provide a tourniquet effect to minimize blood loss. They also provide a firm surface for excisions. The chalazion clamp is particularly advantageous for immobilizing mucous membranes, which are freely mobile and difficult to grasp. For working in the orbital area, the chalazion clamp also helps to protect the globe. The Desmarres clamp is the prototype for the chalazion clamp (Fig. 16). This instrument has an oval opening on one side and a solid surface on the other with a central thumb screw that, when tightened, brings these two surfaces together, immobilizing any tissue between them. This model is available in small (20 mm), medium (26 mm), and large (31 mm) sizes. The Hirsch mucosal clamp has a longer handle that is better suited for oral surgery (Fig. 16). The sizes available are the same as for the Desmarres clamp. Similarly, the Serrefine clamp can be useful for hemostasis and stabilizing the lip margins during surgery (Fig. 16).

Other useful instruments, particularly for Mohs' surgery, are periosteal elevators and bone chisels (Fig. 17). Periosteal elevators help gently lift periosteum off the bone and are useful when tumors invade this tissue. Likewise, bone chisels help the cutaneous surgeon sample bone that may have been invaded by carcinoma.

Towel clamps are also helpful in dermatologic surgery

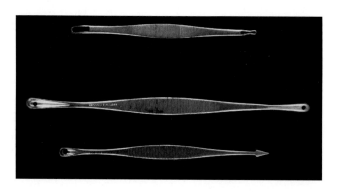

FIG. 15. (Top to bottom) Schamberg, Unna, and Saalfeld expressors.

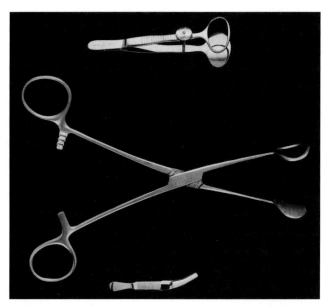

FIG. 16. (Top to bottom) Desmarres, Hirsch, and Serrefine clamps.

(Fig. 17). They anchor sterile drapes or hold the electrocautery handle in place during surgery. We also find that this instrument facilitates closure of large wounds intraoperatively.

Nail surgery is an aspect of dermatologic surgery that requires its own basic instruments. The nail elevator and splitter are especially useful in nail surgery. The nail elevator or spatula helps lift the nail plate off the nail bed, which is necessary before matrix or nail bed biopsies or for onychocryptosis surgery. Nail elevators are available in flexible or rigid models with narrow or wide spatula ends (Fig. 18). Periosteal elevators can also be used interchangeably with nail elevators during nail surgery (Fig. 18). The nail splitter has one cutting, flat, tapered edge, which fits comfortably under the nail without injury to the bed, and one thick, curved

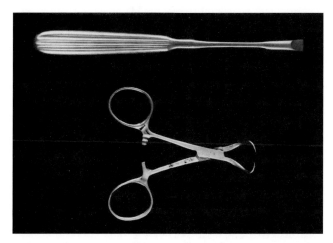

FIG. 17. (Top to bottom) Periosteal elevator and towel clamp.

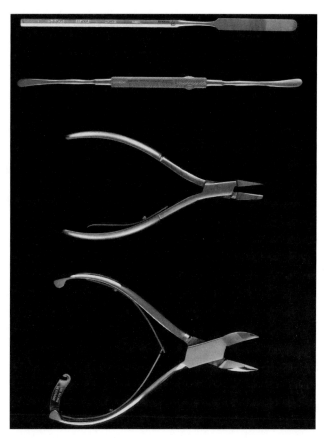

FIG. 18. (Top to bottom) Nail elevator, Freer septum elevator, nail splitter, and nail nipper with double spring and concave jaws.

edge (Fig. 18). It has a spring action system that provides great force in cutting through even the thickest nails, and it greatly facilitates clipping and removing nails. The nail nipper is helpful in trimming and paring extremely thickened nails (Fig. 18). The double- or barrel-spring models provide more power for heavy-duty work than the single-spring variety. The nippers are available with straight, concave, or angled jaws.

WOUND CLOSURE MATERIALS

Sutures

A thorough understanding of suture material is essential in cutaneous surgery. The choice of a particular suture varies depending on the biologic properties of the wound, anatomic location, and the intended purpose of the suture material. The ideal suture should have excellent tensile strength, handle easily, have good knot security, cause minimal tissue reaction, and not promote infection. It should be inexpensive and should be able to accommodate wound swelling and contraction. Currently there is no ideal suture for all circumstances, so important compromises in suture selection must be made.

Important in this selection process is an understanding of certain standardized terms used to describe suture material. These descriptive terms include tensile strength, knot strength, physical configuration, capillarity, elasticity, and tissue reactivity. Tensile strength is calculated by dividing the amount of weight necessary to break a suture by its cross-sectional area. In general, tensile strength increases with larger suture diameters. The U.S. Pharmocopeia provides a digit-zero system for defining tensile strength, in which the higher digits correspond to smaller suture diameters (i.e., 4-0 nylon suture has greater diameter and tensile strength than 6-0 nylon suture). However, this system does not define an exact diameter, so 4-0 sutures of various types have slightly different diameters. For example, 4-0 nylon suture is slightly smaller than 4-0 catgut or 4-0 Vicryl suture.

Knot strength is defined as the force required to cause knot slippage and therefore depends on the coefficient of friction for the suture. The slicker the suture material, the more likely it is that the knot will slip. A suture's physical configuration refers to whether it is monofilamentous (single stranded) or multifilamentous (multiple strands). Multifilamented sutures can be braided, which increases the sutures' handling and tying capability but also increases the likelihood of wound infection. The capillarity of a suture depends on the physical configuration of that suture. It refers to the ability of fluid to travel along the suture from the immersed wet portion to the dry, nonimmersed portion. Sutures with high capillarity have a greater tendency to promote wound infection. Braided multifilament sutures have greater capillarity than monofilamentous sutures and, correspondingly, a greater ability to take up bacteria.

Elasticity is defined as a suture's ability to regain its original form and length after being stretched. This is in contrast to plasticity, which is the property of suture to retain its new length after being stretched. Most sutures have elasticity, but few (e.g., polypropylene) also have plasticity. Elasticity is beneficial because it allows the suture to stretch as tissue edema occurs and then contract as the swelling resolves to ensure good wound approximation. Plasticity helps prevent the suture from cutting into the tissue, but as the edema subsides, the suture retains its larger size and may no longer adequately approximate the wound.

Memory depicts the stiffness of a suture and is related to both elasticity and plasticity. It refers to the inherent tendency of a suture to return to its original shape on deformation, such as tying. High-memory sutures are stiff sutures that are difficult to handle and have an increased tendency to untie once knotted. Therefore for additional knot security it is important to tie more throws into a knot when using suture with high memory.

Tissue reactivity refers to the ability of a suture to generate an inflammatory response in the wound. Because all suture material is foreign material, some tissue reaction will occur. Tissue reactivity peaks within 2 to 7 days and depends on the type, as well as quantity, of suture. Monofilamentous sutures are less tissue-reactive than multifilamentous sutures. Natural fibers in general cause more tissue reaction than synthetic sutures. The more suture material present in the wound, the greater the tissue reaction. Therefore the cutaneous surgeon should be careful to use no more than the necessary amount and the finest-diameter suture that is appropriate for the wound.

Sutures are generally classified as absorbable or nonabsorbable. An absorbable suture is defined as one that loses the majority of its tensile strength within 60 days after implantation subepidermally. This does not imply complete absorption, and in fact, catgut may persist for years in tissue. Absorption takes place by either enzymatic digestion or tissue hydrolysis.

Absorbable Sutures

Most absorbable sutures are used as buried sutures to help close the dermis and decrease tension on epidermal wound edges. Therefore the ideal characteristics of absorbable sutures are high tensile strength, delayed absorption time, low tissue reactivity, and good knot security. Absorbable sutures can be divided into natural and synthetic types. Natural absorbable sutures include surgical gut (plain or catgut), and chromic gut. Examples of synthetic absorbable sutures are found in Table 9-1 and include polyglycolic acid (Dexon), polyglactin 910 (Vicryl), polydioxanone (PDS), and glycolic acid (Maxon).

Surgical gut (plain gut or catgut) is derived from the submucosal layer of sheep intestine or from the intestinal serosa of cattle. It is twisted strands of highly purified, processed collagen. Plain catgut is digested by lysosomal proteolytic enzymes from neutrophils in 60 to 70 days. It loses most of its tensile strength within only 7 to 10 days. It also elicits a significant inflammatory reaction within the wound and has poor knot-holding ability in the presence of body fluids. Considering these characteristics, plain catgut is less often used in cutaneous surgery. It is occasionally useful to tie off superficial blood vessels or to provide immediate hemostasis in wounds under minimal tension, such as punch biopsy sites. Unlike other sutures, surgical gut comes wet, packaged in alcohol, because breakage will occur if it dries out.

Fast-absorbing surgical gut is a type of plain gut that is heat treated twice to facilitate absorption. It is absorbed completely within 2 to 4 weeks. This can be a useful percutaneous suture in split-thickness skin grafts and facial wounds under minimal tension, or in the closure of children's wounds where suture removal can be challenging. Chromic catgut is catgut treated with chromium salts. This process delays absorption and decreases tissue reactivity. Although chromic catgut loses most of its tensile strength in 10 to 14 days, it is not completely absorbed for approximately 80 days. In general, catgut has unpredictable absorption, and different batches vary somewhat in tensile strength. Chromic

TABLE 9-1. *Absorbable sutures*

Suture	Raw material	Configuration	Absorption time	Degradation	Tensile strength	Tissue reactivity	Knot security	Knot tying	Memory	Recommended uses
Surgical gut (plain)	Animal collagen	Twisted	Unpredictable, 60–70 days	Proteolytic	Poor; 0% at 2–3 weeks	Moderate to high	Poor	Fair	Low	Subcutaneous closure, small vessel ligation
Surgical gut (fast-absorbing)	As above, but heat treated twice	Twisted	Unpredictable, 2–4 weeks	Proteolytic	Poor, 50% at 3–5 days	Low	Poor	Fair	Low	Percutaneous suture in wounds under no tension, STSG, punch biopsies
Surgical gut (chromic)	As above, treated with chromic salts	Twisted	Unpredictable, 80 days	Proteolytic	Poor, 0% at 2–3 weeks	Moderate to high (less than plain gut)	Poor	Poor	Low	Subcutaneous closure
Polyglactin-910 (coated vicryl)	Copolymer of lactide and glycolide coated with chromium stearate and polyglactin-370	Braided	Predictable, 60–120 days (average, 80 days)	Hydrolytic	Good, 60% at 14 days, 30% at 21 days	Low	Fair	Good	Low	Subcutaneous closure, vessel ligation
Polyglycolic acid (Dexon)	Homopolymer of glycolic acid	Braided	Predictable, 60–120 days (average, 90 days)	Hydrolytic	Good, 50% at 21 days	Low	Good	Good	Low	Subcutaneous closure, vessel ligation
Polydioxanone (PDS)	Polyester polymer	Monofilament	Predictable, 180 days	Hydrolytic	Good, 70% at 14 days, 50% at 30 days, 25% at 42 days	Low	Poor	Poor	High	Subcutaneous closure of high-tension wounds, vessel ligation
Glycolic acid, polglyconate (Maxon)	Glycolic acid and trimethylene carbonate	Monofilament	Predictable, 180–210 days	Hydrolytic	Good, 70% at 14 days, 55% at 21 days	Low	Good	Fair	Moderate	Subcutaneous closure of high-tension wounds, vessel ligation

catgut can also be used as ligature for small blood vessels in wounds left open to heal by second intention. In this instance the suture may actually stimulate the granulation process. In general, however, all forms of catgut are less often used in dermatologic surgery because more suitable synthetic sutures are available.

The four most commonly used synthetic, absorbable sutures today are polyglycolic acid, polyglactin 910, polydioxanone, and glycolic acid.

Polyglycolic acid is a high-molecular-weight polymer of glycolic acid. Introduced in 1970, it was the first synthetic absorbable suture. It is braided for easier handling and tying. Unlike catgut, which is digested by enzyme proteolysis, polyglycolic acid is degraded mainly by hydrolysis into carbon dioxide and water. Because polyglycolic acid is not a naturally occurring substance, it produces less tissue inflammation than catgut. Dexon has good tensile strength and retains 50% of it at 21 days. It is predictably absorbed within 60 to 120 days (average, 90 days). The original uncoated Dexon (Dexon-S) suture often catches on itself, making knot tying and suturing more difficult. Coated Dexon (Dexon Plus) is now available, which has better handling characteristics. Polyglycolic acid is useful as a completely buried suture to help provide wound apposition and decrease the likelihood of wound dehiscence, especially after percutaneous sutures are removed. Because of its braided configuration, this suture should be avoided in contaminated wounds where bacteria can become trapped in the interstices. In addition, Dexon should be reserved for subcutaneous rather than percutaneous sutures because its absorption rate is unpredictable when it is not buried. As a percutaneous suture, Dexon increases the chance of wound infection by serving as a "wick" to draw bacteria into the wound. Polyglycolic acid is available as an undyed (clear) or green suture.

Polyglactin 910 is a braided synthetic absorbable suture similar to Dexon. It is a copolymer of a mixture of lactide and glycolide and is coated with polyglactin 370 and calcium stearate for easier handling. Like Dexon, it is also degraded mainly by hydrolysis, so minimal tissue reaction occurs. Vicryl has a tensile strength almost as high as that of Dexon, and it retains 60% of that strength at 14 days and 30% at 21 days. Vicryl is absorbed at a slightly faster rate than Dexon. Although the absorption rate for both Dexon and Vicryl is between 60 and 120 days, Vicryl is usually absorbed by 80 days. This slightly faster absorption rate diminishes Vicryl's tissue reactivity when compared with Dexon.

Vicryl sutures have a slightly larger diameter than Dexon and a smaller diameter than catgut. Suture is available as clear or violet, but the violet type should be avoided in thin skin, where it may be transepidermally visible. Vicryl functions similarly to Dexon as a suture for subcutaneous closure. Because of its high tensile strength, Vicryl, like Dexon, can cut through tissue, and if buried too superficially, may be transepidermally eliminated (spit) before it is absorbed.

Polydioxanone is a new absorbable synthetic suture made from a polyester polymer (*p*-dioxanone). Unlike Dexon and Vicryl, PDS is a monofilamentous, absorbable suture. It is also degraded by hydrolysis, but at a much slower rate, taking approximately 180 days to completely absorb. It retains higher tensile strength than Vicryl or Dexon with 70% remaining at 14 days, 50% at 30 days, and 25% at 42 days. Because of its monofilamentous structure, PDS causes less tissue reactivity, so it is especially useful for suturing cartilage where inflammation of the perichondrium may cause significant discomfort. It may be a better choice in contaminated wounds because it lacks the interstices of braided suture that trap bacteria. Polydioxanone is much stiffer and thus more difficult to handle and tie than the braided synthetic sutures. It is also more expensive than the braided synthetic sutures.

Glycolic acid or polyglyconate is a newer synthetic absorbable suture. It is a monofilament suture composed of glycolic acid and trimethylene carbonate. Like PDS, it is slowly degraded by hydrolysis, taking 180 to 210 days to completely absorb. It has a high tensile strength, retaining 70% at 14 days and 55% of its original tensile strength at 21 days. It serves a similar function to PDS, but Maxon was designed to combine the high tensile strength of PDS with the manageability of the synthetic braided sutures. Maxon has 60% less rigidity than PDS with good knot security with its first throw. Like PDS, it is more expensive than Dexon or Vicryl.

Nonabsorbable Sutures

Nonabsorbable suture is defined as a material that resists degradation by hydrolysis and digestion by proteolysis, so it retains most of its tensile strength after 60 days within a wound. Except for polyester (Dacron), polypropylene (Prolene), and stainless steel, nonabsorbable sutures, with time, will eventually be degraded and absorbed. The nonabsorbable sutures most often used in cutaneous surgery are listed in Table 9-2 and include silk, nylon, polypropylene, polyester, polybutester, and stainless steel.

Silk suture is a naturally occurring protein fiber extruded by the larvae of silkworms as they build cocoons. Silk is a braided suture with excellent handling, tying, and knotting characteristics. It is classified as a nonabsorbable suture but is eventually degraded by phagocytosis and enzymatic action after several years. Silk has a relatively low tensile strength compared with the synthetic nonabsorbable sutures, with 0% to 50% tensile strength at 365 days. As a natural fiber, silk provokes significant tissue inflammation, which is only slightly less than with catgut.

Because of its braided configuration, silk suture also has a high degree of capillarity, which allows bacteria to be absorbed, increasing the potential for wound infection. The interstices of the braid also have a tendency to develop crusts, which can make suture removal difficult. Silk is a very soft suture that is unlikely to tear tissue. These qualities make it an excellent choice for suturing the oral or genital

TABLE 9-2. *Nonabsorbable sutures*

Suture	Configuration	Tensile strength	Handling	Knot security	Memory	Tissue reactivity	Recommended uses
Silk	Braided	0%–50% at 365 days	Good	Good	Poor	High	Epithelial closure of mucosal surfaces
Nylon							
Ethilon	Monfilament	High	Poor	Poor	High	Low	Percutaneous suture, vessel ligation
Dermalon	Monofilament	High	Poor	Poor	High	Low	Percutaneous suture, vessel ligation
Surgilon	Braided	High	Fair	Fair	Fair	Low to moderate	Percutaneous suture
Nurolon	Braided	High	Good	Fair to good	Fair	Low to moderate	Percutaneous suture
Polypropylene							
Prolene	Monofilament	Fair	Poor	Poor	High	Minimal to low	Skin closure (subcuticular running suture)
Surgilene	Monofilament	Fair	Poor	Poor	High	Minimal to low	Skin closure (subcuticular running suture)
Polyester							
Mersilene	Braided	High	Good	Good	Fair	Moderate	Epithelial closure of mucosal surface, skin closure
Ethibond	Braided	High	Good	Good	Fair	Minimal to moderate	Epithelial closure of mucosal surface, skin closure
Dacron	Braided	High	Good	Good	Fair	Minimal to moderate	Epithelial closure of mucosal surface, skin closure
Polybutester (Novafil)	Monofilament	High	Good to fair	Poor	Low	Low	Percutaneous closure
Stainless steel	Monofilament or multistranded twisted or braided	High	Poor	Good	Poor	Extremely low	Respiratory tract closure, tendon repair

mucosa, lips, conjunctiva, or intertriginous areas, and as a temporary suture for tissue retraction during surgery. The diameter of silk is slightly smaller than comparable U.S. Pharmacopeia–sized catgut and larger than nylon or polyglycolic acid.

Nylon suture, an inert synthetic polyamide polymer, is the most popular nonabsorbable suture in cutaneous surgery. It is manufactured in black, green, or clear colors, and in monofilamentous (Ethilon, Dermalon) or multifilamentous (Nurolon and Surgilon) configurations. Although it is classified as a nonabsorbable suture, if buried, it loses approximately 20% of its tensile strength annually via hydrolysis. Nylon has high tensile strength and excellent elastic properties and causes minimal tissue reaction. It has high memory and is somewhat stiff, so knots are less secure unless additional loops are placed. It may also easily cut through thin skin. Monofilamentous nylon sutures are ideal as percutaneous sutures and for ligating large vessels. Braided nylon sutures are more expensive than monofilamentous varieties and are less often used in dermatologic surgery. Nonetheless, multifilamentous nylon sutures have better handling characteristics than monofilament nylon.

Polypropylene (Prolene, Surgilene) is a new synthetic, plastic, monofilamentous suture composed of linear hydrocarbon polymers. It has good tensile strength and is not digested by tissue enzymes, so it remains in tissue for an extended period. It is extremely inert and does not promote bacterial growth. It has a smooth, slippery surface (low coefficient of friction), so it pulls easily through tissue with minimal drag. The amount of work necessary to pull polypropylene suture through tissue is about one-third to two-thirds that of nylon and one-fourth to one-half that of silk. This characteristic makes polypropylene ideal for subcuticular running closures, but it is also appropriate as a percutaneous suture. This low coefficient of friction also contributes to its poor knot-holding ability, so additional loops are necessary to secure a knot. Polypropylene is also known for its plasticity. As wound edema occurs, this suture stretches to accommodate it, but as swelling resolves, the suture remains loosened. This may lead to poor wound approximation. Polypropylene has a high memory, contributing to its poor handling characteristics.

Polyester (Mersilene, Ethibond, and Dacron) is composed of braided, multifilamentous strands of polyester or polyethylene terephthalate. This suture has high tensile strength and is retained *in vivo* indefinitely. Only metal suture is stronger than polyester. It is available uncoated (as Mersilene and Dacron) or coated with polybutilate (as Ethibond). The uncoated types have significant tissue drag compared with the coated variety. The uncoated polyester causes minimal tissue reactivity. Although other coatings in the past provoked a significant inflammatory reaction by shedding into the wound, polybutilate does not elicit significant tissue reactivity. Polyester suture tends to combine the high tensile strength and low tissue reactivity of nylon with better manageability and improved knot security. Although polyester is a braided suture, it has considerably less propensity for wound infection than the natural braided sutures. Because of its braided configuration, polyester is a soft suture, ideal as a replacement for silk in the closure of oral or genital mucosal wounds and in intertriginous areas. Polyester suture, however, is more expensive than silk. These sutures are available in green or white.

Polybutester (Novofil) is a newer polyester suture composed of polyglycol terephthate and polybutylene terephthate. It is a monofilamentous suture that induces minimal tissue reaction and has extended tensile strength within tissue. Polybutester has the good handling and tying characteristics of polyester sutures, but with the plasticity and low coefficient of friction of polypropylene.

Stainless steel sutures are only rarely used in cutaneous surgery. They are available in monofilament or multifilament strands. Steel has extremely high tensile strength and maintains this strength indefinitely. It is quite inert and thus causes little tissue reactivity. Stainless steel sutures, however, are more difficult to tie without breaking and have a tendency to cut through tissue. These sutures are not popular in dermatologic surgery.

Needles

A thorough knowledge of suture is not complete without a good understanding of surgical needles. The proper selection and use of needles is essential for producing good cosmetic results. They are designed to carry suture material through tissue in as atraumatic a fashion as possible. They are generally made of high-quality stainless steel.

Many varieties of needles are available (Fig. 19), and their selection should be determined by the tissue to be sutured, anatomic location, accessibility, and suture size. It is important to match the needle thickness with the suture diameter so that fine needles are paired with delicate sutures and thicker needles with larger sutures. Although needles are available in curved or straight models, only the curved needles are routinely used in cutaneous surgery. The curvature is expressed as a percentage of a circle. As the radius increases, the needle size increases. Although there are a variety of needle curvatures available, the $\frac{3}{8}$-circle and the $\frac{1}{2}$-circle needles are most commonly used in dermatologic surgery. The $\frac{3}{8}$-circle needle is the most popular for work in large or superficial wounds. In small, deep, or confined spaces, the $\frac{1}{2}$-circle needle is easier to manipulate.

All surgical needles can be anatomically divided into three components: the eye or shank, body, and point. The eye or shank of the needles routinely used in dermatology is swaged or eyeless. Rather than the suture being threaded through a hole in the needle, the suture is firmly crimped to the end of the needle. This swaged needle is a control-release needle, although the needle should not release while suturing the wound. A quick tug on the shank causes release of the suture. In a swaged needle the suture and needle are the same diameter; thus less tissue trauma occurs with suture placement. The diameter of the swaged component is the thickest part of the needle and thus determines the size of the suture tract. Because of the crimping process, the shank is the weakest part of the needle, and if the needle is grasped here, it may break or bend.

The body of the needle is the portion of the needle grasped by the needle holder. The correct placement of the needle holder is between $\frac{1}{4}$ and $\frac{1}{2}$ of the distance from the swaged portion to the point. The cross-sectional shape of the body

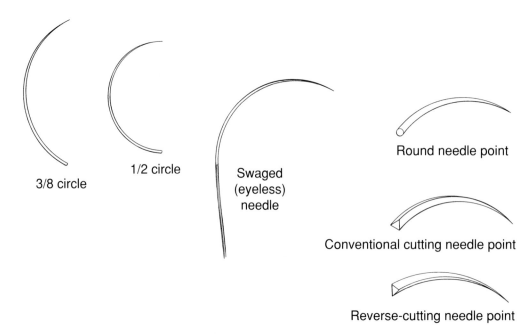

3/8 circle

1/2 circle

Swaged (eyeless) needle

Round needle point

Conventional cutting needle point

Reverse-cutting needle point

FIG. 19. Needle varieties.

may be round, oval, triangular, flattened, or trapezoid. Some needles have ribs along the convexed surface to help secure the needle in the needle holder. The round bodies taper to a point. The triangular bodies found with the for skin (FS), cutting $\frac{3}{8}$-circle (CE), plastic reverse $\frac{3}{8}$-circle (PRE), and slim blade $\frac{3}{8}$-circle (SBE) needle series have three cutting edges. The ovoid bodies have rounded sides and a flat top and bottom and are found in precision point (P) and plastic skin (PS) needles. The precision cosmetic (PC) needle body is flattened on its side, producing a trapezoid configuration.

The needle point (Fig 19), specifically its cross-sectional shape, is the portion of the needle determining its major class. Based on cross-sectional shape, there are three general types of needle points: round, conventional-cutting, or reverse-cutting. The round needle point, like the body, has a tapered point. This needle point has no cutting edges, so it is less likely to tear tissue than the other types and is ideal for suturing fascia, muscle, and aponeuroses. This type of needle, however, is rarely used in dermatologic surgery.

The conventional-cutting needle point has a triangular tip in cross-section. It has three cutting edges—two opposing cutting edges and a third cutting edge that is directed along the inner surface of the needle. The apex of the needle point (triangle) points toward the wound. This design allows for the cutting surfaces to face the wound edge and the flat surface to face away from the wound. Because of this configuration, this needle has a tendency to tear tissue. One new variation of the conventional cutting needle is the Precision PC series by Ethicon. It has a long, thin, extremely sharp tip that actually decreases the tendency of the needle to tear tissue. This needle point is advantageous for fine suturing of the wound.

The reverse-cutting needle tip is the most commonly used needle in cutaneous surgery. This tip is also triangular in cross-section, with two opposing cutting edges and a third cutting edge on the outer rather than inner curvature. The apex of this needle tip (triangle) points away from the wound. This configuration allows the flat surface to face the wound, which makes it less likely to cut through the wound edges. Most needles designed for cutaneous surgery are reverse-cutting, including the CE, FS, P, PS, and PRE needle series.

The degree of tip sharpness also varies among needles. In general, needles that are hand honed or more carefully machine-sharpened are sharper than conventionally machine-honed needles. These very sharp needle tips pass smoothly through tissues with less trauma and are ideal for fine cosmetic work. The general-use needle, by comparison, is relatively dull but may be adequate for the scalp, trunk, and extremities.

The nomenclature for the sizing and identification of needles is confusing because there is no standard, and there are several different series of needles by different manufacturers. Ethicon and Davison-Geck are the two major needle manufacturers. Ethicon needles for cutaneous surgery include the FS, PS, P, conventional plastic surgery (CPS), and PC types.

The FS is the least expensive and sharp of the cutaneous needles. It is designed for the placement of buried absorbable sutures and for epidermal closure of thick skin wounds when fine cosmesis is not critical. The FS $\frac{3}{8}$-circle needles, in order of increasing curvature, are the FS-3, FS-2, FS-1, FS, FSL, and FSLX.

The PS is another reverse-cutting needle but is sharper than the FS series and is good for cosmetic procedures. The P series needle also has a reverse-cutting tip that is sharper and smaller than the PS series, and is designed for delicate work. The P and PS series are honed approximately 24 more times than the FS needles, which accounts for their increased sharpness. The P-3 has a slightly larger curvature than the P-1, and both are available as $\frac{3}{8}$-circle needles. Unlike the P-1 and P-3 needles, the P-2 is a $\frac{1}{2}$-circle needle and is smaller in size and curvature than the P-3 or P-1 needles. The $\frac{3}{8}$-circle, precision point needles, in order of increasing curvature, are P-6, P-1, P-3, PS-3, PS-2, and PS-1. The $\frac{1}{2}$-circle, precision point needles, in order of increasing curvature, are P-2, PS-6, PS-5, and PS-4.

The CPS needle differs from the FS, P, and PS series in that its triangular cutting edge occupies only $\frac{1}{3}$ of the needle's arc. It has a flattened body that helps eliminate needle twisting and allows a secure grasp while suturing. It is a higher-quality needle than the FS, PS, or P needle series. The PC is made of stronger stainless steel than are the other series, and it is the top-of-the-line cutaneous surgery needle. Unlike the other needle types, the PC has a conventional-cutting, very sharp, thin tip and square-to-trapezoid body that causes less tissue trauma with suturing. In order of increasing curvature, the types of PC $\frac{3}{8}$-circle needles are PC-1, PC-3, and PC-5. The cross-sectional diameter of the PC-1 is smaller than that of the P-3, contributing to the former's finer suturing capability. The Davison-Geck Company manufactures comparable needles to the Ethicon series. Popular cutaneous needles include the PRE, CE, diamond point (DP), skin closure (SC), and SBE types. All but the SC needle are reverse-cutting needles. In this series the ''E'' indicates a $\frac{3}{8}$-circle needle. The CE is a relatively inexpensive needle, comparable to the Ethicon FS series. The DP needle has a diamond-point, more precise tip. The SC needle has a conventional-cutting tip. The PRE needle is a superior-quality needle that is extremely sharp and ideal for thin skin and fine cosmetic surgery. It is smaller and sharper than the CE series and is comparable to the Ethicon P series. The SBE is another premium Davison-Geck needle with a very thin body.

Staples

A method of skin closure that is becoming increasingly popular in dermatologic surgery is the use of skin staples. Staples are particularly advantageous for large truncal and extremity excisions and scalp reductions and for securing split-thickness skin grafts. There are several advantages to the use of surgical staples under the correct circumstances. The main advantage of staples is that they permit rapid wound closure. A long wound can be stapled in 25% to 50% less time than it can be sutured. Staples can also reduce tissue trauma if correctly placed.

The staple should be placed so that it rides high. This correct placement prevents tissue strangulation as swelling occurs and avoids cross-hatching. Although study results differ, some reports have shown that with potentially contaminated wounds, staples may decrease the chance of an infection compared with sutures. Unlike percutaneous sutures, staples do not form one continuous tract from the skin surface into the wound, and they close only 60% to 80% of the amount of tissue that sutures surround. In addition, staples are very strong and are useful for closing wounds under significant tension. Staples also provide excellent wound eversion and are relatively painless to remove, especially in hair-bearing areas such as the scalp. Staples may be left in the wound for weeks with little tissue reaction because they are made of inert stainless steel. Nonetheless, staples are not ideal for all wound closures. They may be uncomfortable in intertriginous locations. Although for most wounds they provide adequate cosmesis, they may be less appropriate for fine cosmetic closures on the face.

Over the past 15 years a variety of staplers has become available. They are all designed to form an incomplete rectangular staple consisting of three parts: a top, exposed portion that lies parallel to the wound, two legs that are the height of the staple and extend into the skin, and two pointed tips that are bent inward and lie beneath the wound. The final staple is formed by squeezing the stapler handle, which causes a plunging action that places the staple. The depth of staple placement is determined by the pressure on the staple gun. The angle of insertion of the staple is important because as wound swelling occurs, a rectangular staple rotate to a 90-degree angle, perpendicular to the skin. The smaller the angle of insertion, the greater the staple rotation. Thus, with an insertion angle of 45 degrees, as the rotation reaches 90 degrees, there is more space between the top of the staple and the skin to accommodate wound swelling than with a staple placed at a 90-degree angle of insertion. This space helps prevent cross-hatching of the skin.

Staples are available in both disposable and permanent varieties. In general, the disposable models are more commonly used in dermatologic surgery. The more popular stapler models include the Premium, Proximate, Auto Suture SFS, and Precise staplers.

The Premium stapler by the United States Surgical Corporation (USSC) is a sterile, disposable stapler that is preloaded with staples in regular or wide size. The regular-width staples are 4 mm wide × 3.4 mm high and are most versatile in cutaneous surgery for closing wounds in thin or normal skin. The wide staples are 6.5 mm wide × 4.7 mm high and are particularly useful for closing scalp reductions or large wounds in thicker skin such as the back. Staples are available in packages of 12, 25, or 35. Of all models, the Premium allows the surgeon the best visualization of staple insertion. It dispenses its staple at a 60-degree angle of insertion. The Premium also offers a precock mechanism that allows more accurate staple placement. It has a swivel tip, so the nose rotates 360 degrees to help gain better access to the wound. An ejector-spring release is also available that allows easy disengagement of the staple. The Premium also allows good visual access to the amount of sutures being used.

The Proximate staplers by Ethicon are available in several models. The Proximate II stapler is a favorite among many dermatologic surgeons. Staples are available in regular (5.7 mm wide × 3.9 mm high) and wide (6.9 mm wide × 3.9 mm high) sizes. The unit functions similarly to a desk stapler. The Proximate II stapler has a short nose for good visibility of the staple during placement. There is no precock mechanism on this unit; with any discontinuous pressure on the handle, the staple may slip off the stapler. The angle of insertion is 90 degrees; if significant pressure is applied to the handle, the staple may be placed immediately against the skin with no space to allow for tissue edema. Cross-hatching may then result. The Proximate II stapler also lacks an ejector-spring release option; to disengage the staple, the stapler must be moved posteriorly. It is also difficult with this model to visualize the staple count. The Proximate III model is similar to the Proximate II version, but it has a staple-remaining indicator and a finger notch on the handle for a better grip. The Proximate III model is designed for precise staple placement. Staples are available in regular and wide sizes, in packages of 15, 25, or 35. There is also a Proximate RH stapler that has a rotating head for easier access to the wound. Staples for this instrument are also available in several sizes.

The Auto Suture SFS is also a USSC stapler. It functions similarly to the Premium model but is nondisposable and can be resterilized. Presterilized staple packets are also available for this stapler in packages of 12, 25, and 35 staples.

The Precise stapler by 3M is another popular stapler on the market. The staples for this unit are available in regular (5 mm wide × 3.5 mm high) and wide (7.5 mm × 4.2 mm high) sizes, in packages of 2 to 35 staples. This instrument, unlike the other staples, has handles on both sides of the unit and is held like forceps. The Precise model, unlike the Premium, has a precock mechanism for more accurate suture placement. It has an angle of insertion of 45 degrees, which allows for ample tissue swelling without strangulation. This stapler does not have an ejector-spring release; to disengage the staple, the stapler must be moved anteriorly.

To remove staples, specially designed staple extractors are available. They are similar in shape to suture removal scissors but have broader tips. Ethicon makes a popular staple extractor.

CONCLUSION

A thorough knowledge of dermatologic surgical instruments and sutures is essential to achieve excellence in cutaneous surgery. Each surgeon must learn what tools work best in his or her hands to ensure the finest surgical results. Although personal preference is a strong factor in the choice of surgical instruments and suture materials, the selection process must also involve sound scientific knowledge, to provide patients with the best surgical results attainable.

SUGGESTED READING LIST

1. Arista Surgical Instruments. New York, NY: Arista Surgical Supply Co., Inc., 1994:1.
2. Aston SJ. The choice of suture material for skin closure. J Dermatol Surg 1976;2:1:57.
3. Bartlett RE. Use of the Desmarres clamp in major eyelid surgery. Ann Ophthalmol 1977;9:360.
4. Bennett RG. Instruments and their care. In: Klein E, ed. Fundamentals of cutaneous surgery. St. Louis: CV Mosby, 1988:240.
5. Bennett RG. Materials for wound closure. In: Klein E, ed. Fundamentals of cutaneous surgery. St. Louis: CV Mosby, 1988:274.
6. Bennett RG. Selection of wound closure materials. J Am Acad Dermatol 1988; 18:4:619.
7. Bernstein G. The 15c scalpel blade. J Dermatol Surg Oncol 1987;13:9:969.
8. Bernstein G. Needle basics. J Dermatol Surg Oncol 1985;11(12):1177.
9. Vorges AF. Basic techniques. In: Harahap M, ed. Skin surgery. St. Louis: Warren H. Green, 1985:85.
10. Brooks-Tighe SM. Plastic set. In: Coon NL, ed. Instrumentation for the operating room. 3rd ed. St. Louis: CV Mosby, 1989:27.
11. Campbell JP, Swanson NE. The use of staples in dermatologic surgery. J Dermatol Surg Oncol 1982;8:680.
12. Ceiley RI. Scissor surgery. In: Roenigk RK, Roenigk HH Jr, eds. Dermatologic surgery. New York: Marcel Decker, 1989:171.
13. Dermal Instrument Catalog. New York: George Tiemann and Co., 1995:1.
14. Fish FS, Perez M, Greenway HT. The Carmalt straight splinter forceps: a versatile economical instrument. J Dermatol Surg Oncol 1991;17:428.
15. Frankel DH. The use of a combination skin hook and tissue forceps: a new instrument for dermatologic surgery (Frankel-Adson forceps). J Dermatol Surg Oncol 1988;14(5):497.
16. Garrett AB. Wound closure materials. In: Wheeland, RG, ed. Cutaneous surgery. Philadelphia: WB Saunders, 1994:199.
17. Grabski WJ, Salasche SJ, Mulvaney MJ. Razor blade surgery. J Dermatol Surg Oncol 1990;16:1121.
18. Grande DJ, Neuberg M. Instrumentation for the dermatologic surgeon. J Dermatol Surg Oncol 1989;15(3):288.
19. Holt GR, Holt JE. Suture materials and techniques. Ear Nose Throat J 1981;60:23.
20. Koranda FC, Luckasen JR. Instruments and tips for dermatologic surgery. J Dermatol Surg Oncol 1982;8(6):451.
21. Lerner SP. The modified skin hook: a new instrument in cutaneous surgery. J Dermatol Surg Oncol 1985;11(6):586.
22. Lober CW, Fenske NE. Suture materials. In: Roenigk RK, Roenigk HH Jr, eds. Dermatologic surgery. New York: Marcel Decker, 1989:85.
23. Lynch WS. Surgical equipment and instrumentation. In: Wheeland RG, ed. Cutaneous surgery. Philadelphia: WB Saunders, 1994:91.
24. Meyer RD, Antonini CJ. A review of suture materials. Part I. Compend Cont Educ Dent 1989;10(5):260.
25. Meyer RD, Antonini CJ. A review of suture materials. Part II. Compend Cont Educ Dent 1989;10(6):360.
26. Miltex Surgical Instruments. New York: Miltex Instrument Co., Inc., 1995:12.
27. Moy RL, Lee A, Zalka A. Commonly used suture materials in skin surgery. American Family Physician 1991;44:2123.
28. Salyer KE. Use of a new hemostatic scalpel in plastic surgery. Ann Plast Surg 1984;13:532.
29. Smith MF, Stehn JL. Basic surgical instrumentation. Philadelphia: WB Saunders, 1993.
30. Stonek JJ. Surgical diagnostic and therapeutic instruments. Oxford, England: Blackwell Scientific, 1986.
31. Trier WC. Considerations in the choice of surgical needles. Surg Gynecol Obstet 1979;149:84.
32. Webster RC, Pedroza L, Pedroza F, Pedroza LV, Hall B, Hopping SB, Smith RC, Smith KF. The Iconoclast as an aide in blunt dissection of flaps of the scalp and forehead. J Dermatol Surg Oncol 1982;8(9):793.

Textbook of Dermatologic Surgery, edited by John L. Ratz.
Lippincott–Raven Publishers, Philadelphia © 1998.

CHAPTER 10

Wound Closure and Suture Technique

Gary D. Monheit

The purpose of suturing is wound closure. Ideally suturing should approximate the wound edges so that the tissues can reestablish closure with a final scar that is functional and aesthetic. The method and techniques of suturing, as well as materials used, are determinants in the final outcome. The surgeon must also have a full understanding of wound healing, tensile strength, and wound closure to perform skin approximation. Ideally the wound should be approximated with little tension and the skin edges handled gently. It is the fine attention the surgeon gives to handling skin edges and the techniques of approximation that create the optimal aesthetic scar line. This chapter reviews the techniques and materials available for suturing wound closure.

HISTORY

The history of dermatologic surgery begins in the ancient world, where, in the EdwinSmith papyrus, evidence of surgical wound closure is found relating methods of suturing and dressings. The document describes a deep facial wound that was closed with silk sutures and covered with linen dressings and ointments. Wound closure was also noted in ancient Indian Sanskrit texts describing suture material made of animal sinews, bark, leather straps, and even ant pincers.

The importance of cosmesis in wound closure was noted by the Greek and Roman writers with the first description of layered closures, local flaps, and pedicles. Galen referred to the usage of catgut and silk suture material for closures and as vessel ligature. Lister's principles of antiseptics later

enabled wound closure to progress to use in the modern era for fine cosmetic dermatologic surgery.

SUTURE TECHNIQUE

Effective closure of surgical wounds requires preoperative planning in evaluating depth and tension on the proposed repair. These factors will help determine the simple or complex nature of that repair. A simple closure is the use of direct, interrupted nonabsorbable skin sutures to close the wound (Fig. 1E). A layered closure entails buried absorbable sutures and interrupted permanent skin sutures. A complex closure involves the essentials of layered closures along with methods to reduce skin tension such as undermining and tissue transfer. The surgeon must evaluate the excision and the defect for the anatomic site and the nature of skin tensions for the appropriate closure. Each of these is reviewed in the discussion of general concepts of wound closure. Interrupted suture closure is the simplest and easiest method to close uncomplicated wound defects. To use interrupted suture as the primary mechanism of closure, the defect must (1) be a skin defect extending to subcutaneous tissue but without dead space or a deep tissue defect and (2) have little or no skin tension on the wound edges.

Place an interrupted suture through opposite wound edges at full thickness through the skin to bring the wound edges together. Accomplish the technique as follows:

1. Grasp the needle with the needle holder three fourths of the length along the body of the needle, and point the needle tip perpendicular to the skin surface. It is

Gary D. Monheit: Department of Dermatology, University of Alabama at Birmingham, Birmingham, AL 35294.

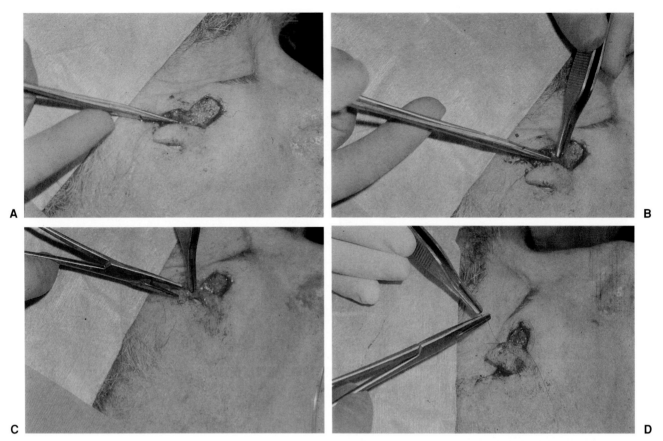

FIG. 1. Suture closure of a local flap. **(A)** Subdermal absorbable suture is placed through the donor area of the transposition flap. **(B)** The needle is grabbed with needle forceps. **(C)** The needle is lifted, and a surgical instrument tie is made to place the knot in the subcutaneous tissue. **(D)** The donor area is closed, and the suture is clipped at the knot. **(E)** Interrupted sutures are placed along the incision line. **(F)** The incision line is approximated with No. 6-0 mild chromic suture in a running suture line. **(G)** Final flap closure.

usually inserted 1 to 2 mm from the wound edge, and the point pierces through epidermis and dermis. Accomplish this with a rotational thrust beginning perpendicular and extending in an arc outward to subcutaneous tissue. At this point, the surgeon feels a pop of the needle through the dermis as it advances into subcutaneous tissue (Fig. 2).

2. Continue the arc of the half circle through subcutaneous tissue below the deepest point of the defect, advancing to the dermis of the opposite side perpendicular to the plane of the skin surface, and emerging the same distance from the skin edge as the entrance point—1 to 2 mm. As the needle tip emerges through the skin surface, an assistant grasps it with needle forceps and pulls it through the surface. It is important that the needle be pulled through either by an assistant or by the surgeon (with the opposite hand) so that it does not fall back into subcutaneous tissue when tension is released.

3. The surgeon then pulls the needle through the surface, advancing the suture through the wound so that 1 to 2 cm of suture remains on the opposite side. Grasp the end of the suture with a pair of forceps and the opposite side with a needle holder, then test the closure tension along the skin edge. Ideal closure tension should advance the skin margins together but not crush tissue within the suture. Test the point of pressure before tying the surgeon's knot.

4. Accomplish the surgeon's knot as a double square knot. The square knot is the fundamental knot used; when placed properly, it lies flat on the skin surface and maintains its position without slipping. To tie the knot, pull the long end of the suture across the skin edge; bring the needle holder across the wound edge and loop the long end of the suture twice along the end of the needle holder. The needle holder grasps the suture end, and the two loops are brought into approximation. Place a single loop over the double loop tie, and place securely over the double loop. Place an additional single loop in the opposite direction over the second single loop, to make a square knot. As the last loop is tightened, the knot is approximated so that further pressure does not put any further tension on the wound edge.

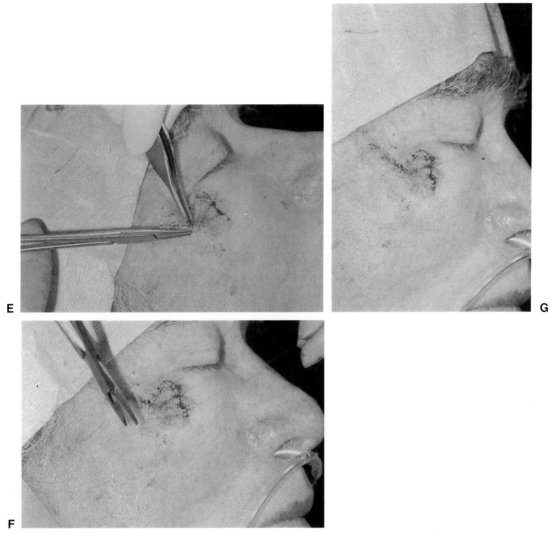

FIG. 1. *Continued*

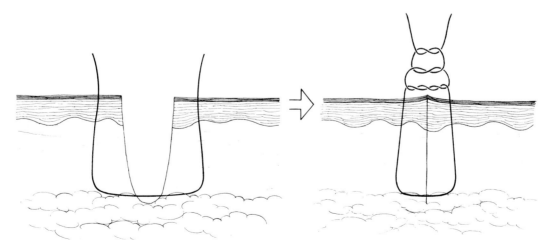

FIG. 2. Interrupted suture. The needle traverses through the skin, beveling outward to subcutaneous tissue and to opposing skin edge. The wound is gently approximated with a surgeon's knot.

SIMPLE CLOSURES

The advantages of interrupted sutures for a simple closure is the ease and simplicity of the procedure. The risks are small and the interrupted suture provides stability for the wound edges during healing. Disadvantages include inversion of the suture line if the suture is placed too superficially. That is, if the tension pull across the suture line is too superficial, it pulls the scar line downward, creating a trough. Another disadvantage is the "railroad tracking" or scar tunnels that are left by the suture if it is kept in place for the 5 to 7 days necessary for wound healing.

Vertical Mattress Sutures

Use the vertical mattress suture to accentuate eversion when there is significant skin tension and to close dead space in deeper tissue defects (Fig. 3). Vertical mattress sutures can be placed in conjunction with interrupted sutures to ensure sufficient wound closure tension and skin edge evertion. Between these, place interrupted sutures. Begin the vertical mattress suture 0.5 to 1 cm from the wound edge with the needle pointed vertically to the depth of the wound, then through the base of the wound and back out along opposing sides equidistant from the wound edge. Then reverse the direction of the needle; penetrate the skin again on the same side but closer to the wound edge. At this point, the needle and suture pass superficially through dermis to the opposite side, exiting the same distance from the wound margin, 1 to 3 mm from the wound edge. Pull the sutures together, bringing the wound edges together and at the same time obliterating dead space and everting the wound edge. Care must be taken to place the right amount of tension on the suture edge to close the defect without crushing tissue and skin caught within the suture. Excessive pressure at the depth of the wound can cause ischemic necrosis from strangulation, so it is important to minimize wound tension before tying the knots. The vertical mattress suture is a strangulating suture with significant tension on the scar line. Thus it is rarely used on the face because it does produce scarring. Other methods of reducing tension, such as

buried suture with fine approximating sutures, are reserved for facial closures.

Horizontal Mattress Sutures

Use horizontal mattress sutures for minimizing wound tension, closing dead space, and further exaggerating wound edge eversion. In areas with significant wound tension such as the back, the chest, and the scalp a horizontal mattress suture may be needed to ensure that tension is reduced during healing. On wound closure, one or two horizontal mattress sutures may be used in conjunction with interrupted sutures to approximate a wound edge properly. With a horizontal mattress suture the needle penetrates the skin 0.5 to 1 cm from the wound edge and passes vertically to the depth of the defect, across the depth of the defect, then back out along the opposing side the same distance from the wound edge. It reenters at the same distance from the wound edge and passes vertically to the depth of the wound and back out along an equidistant space on the opposing side (Fig. 4). Use the double square knot to tie this off, being careful that tension approximates the skin edges and is not too great. This is a strangulating suture, similar to the vertical mattress suture, and can crush the tissue with tension. A bolster may be used with the horizontal suture.

LAYERED CLOSURES

Use layered closure for buried absorbable sutures in fascia, subcutaneous tissue, and deep dermis, combined with the use of buried absorbable suture in deeper skin and tissue. It removes the tension from the skin edge and provides stable reduction of closure tension during healing. To perform a layered closure correctly, prepare the wound. This includes undermining the skin a minimum of 2 mm and at times up to 1 cm beyond the wound edge to reduce skin tension and to ensure the accurate placement of the buried absorbable suture. Accomplish meticulous hemostasis before suture placement. The type of buried suture that is used depends on the thickness of the defect, the tension on the wound, and the amount of dead space.

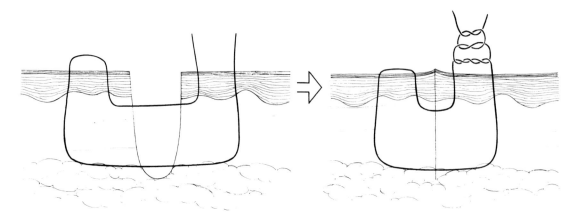

FIG. 3. Vertical mattress suture. Double suture is used to accentuate skin edge eversion when there is significant tension on the wound edge. Care must be taken not to crush the skin edge.

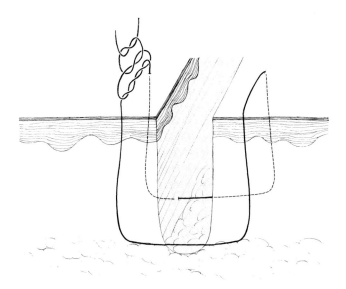

FIG. 4. Horizontal mattress suture can be used to further minimize tension in areas of the back, chest, and scalp.

The buried subcutaneous suture or the dermal subdermal stitch is begun, first, to the deep side of one of the undermined edges of the defect (Fig. 5). Accomplish this by lifting the wound edge with a skin hook and advancing the needle tip 1 or 2 mm from the wound edge on the undersurface of the skin (Fig. 6). This allows the suture pathway to proceed upward through subcutaneous tissue, entering into mid dermis. Then it passes through the wound margin at mid dermis and reenters the opposite wound side through mid dermis, proceeding in an arc downward to the opposing subcutaneous tissue and exiting 2 or 3 mm from the wound edge. Tie the suture lines with the knot pulled along the long axis of the defect. This allows the knot to slide to the base of the defect in the subcutaneous tissue, burying the knot. Pulling the suture line perpendicular to the scar line traps the suture upward, creating an inadequate closure and a knot that is placed too high. Place multiple buried subcutaneous sutures along the defect, reducing tension along the skin edge at critical points. This allows the placement of single interrupted sutures with no tension on the skin edge, minimizing scarring. This also stabilizes wound closure so that the interrupted suture may be removed in less than 7 days, producing

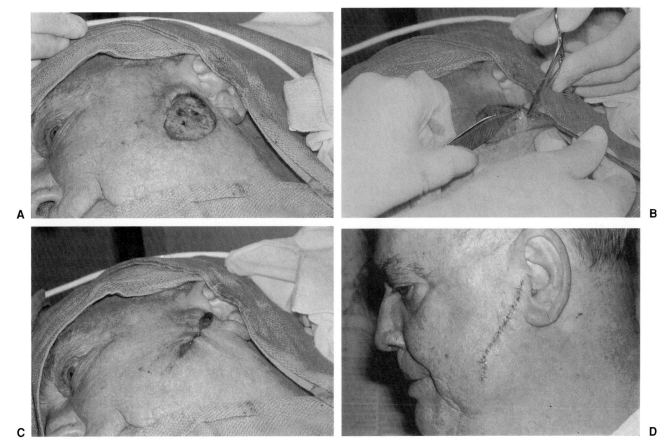

FIG. 5. (A) Cheek defect for closure. **(B)** Buried subcutaneous suture placed to remove tension from skin edge. **(C)** Tension relieved with No. 4-0 chromic subdermal sutures. **(D)** Final skin closure with No. 5-0 polypropylene (Prolene) and No. 6-0 mild chromic suture.

a better cosmetic result. This also lessens the risk of surgical dehiscence when the interrupted sutures are removed. The buried absorbable suture maintains closure tension during healing. Layered closure using buried sutures is a useful technique for skin closures and can be used in most areas of the skin surface. Dangers with buried sutures include foreign body reaction, strangulation of deep tissue with necrosis, local infection, and prolonged inflammation.

Chromic suture has the highest potential for inflammation and secondary infection. This potential increases if the suture is placed high in the surface or the knot strangulates deep tissue, causing necrosis. If the knot is placed superficially in a wound resulting in a significant amount of inflammation, a nodule can occur that may last for months. Tissue inflammation leading to suppuration and necrosis may cause extravasation or ''spitting'' of the suture through the surface. This can induce scar tissue that creates a persistent nodular deformity. Techniques to prevent these complications include the following:

1. Choose the appropriate suture material (both size and type).
2. Avoid absorbable buried suture in closure of a wound that has the potential for infection or is bacterially contaminated.
3. Place the knot deep in the subcutaneous tissue to avoid scar that leads to persistent nodules.
4. Keep the knot small and slide it to the base, avoiding strangulation or necrosis.

If the buried suture has been placed correctly, wound edge tension will be eliminated from the skin margin. At this point, the skin surface can be draped together and approximated with interrupted sutures. These can be removed in 4 to 6 days because there is no tension on the skin margin. Thus it is possible to avoid stitch marks along the scar line by removing the sutures early.

INTERMEDIATE AND COMPLEX CLOSURES

Complex and intermediate closures usually involve more extensive undermining and local skin movement. Both closure techniques involve a combination of suture techniques in the deeper dermis and on the skin surface. Each of these closure techniques is reviewed in the context of the clinical situation in which it is most likely to be used. These techniques depend on reducing skin tension with buried deep sutures. Accomplished this with fascial sutures, buried subcutaneous sutures, and interrupted dermal sutures to take the tension off the skin edge. Only then can the variety of running suture, running locking suture, tip stitch, and running subcuticular sutures be used for skin margin approximation.

Tip Stitch

The tip stitch is a modification of the horizontal mattress suture in which half the suture is buried. Use it to secure and close acute angles of closure with tips of skin that would be damaged by interrupted suture. In this way, the suture travels through the dermis of the tip and advances the tip with interrupted sutures on either sides. Thus use it to secure the tip of skin flaps without compressing the epidermal tissue, avoiding ischemic necrosis. Mechanically pass the needle through the skin on one side of the V-shaped area, exit (mid dermis) and penetrate the tip at the same level and back out along the opposite side in the mid dermis. As the suture is pulled, the tip advances into the V-shaped area with enough pressure for good closure (Fig. 7). Tie the suture with a double square knot. The tip stitch is useful in the closure of M-plasties (Fig. 8), angles along transposition flaps, geometric broken-line closures, and Z-plasties.

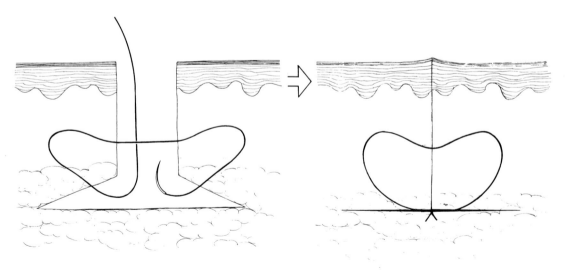

FIG. 6. Buried absorbable subcutaneous suture removes tension from the skin edge. As a complex layered closure with interrupted sutures, it produces a fine cosmetic result.

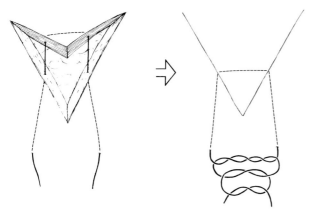

FIG. 7. Tip stitch is a half-buried mattress suture that is used to close acute angles as part of a complex closure.

Running Suture

Use the running suture to close skin edges in wounds in which tension has been reduced fully. It is an approximating suture that can simply and easily close a long scar line. Using permanent suture, it is useful on body surface areas such as the retroauricular sulcus, upper eyelids, and supraclavicular neck where skin grafts are harvested. Use it also for closures of body skin in which tension has been reduced with interrupted subcutaneous sutures. In facial closures use a running suture of No. 6-0 mild chromatized sorbable gut in conjunction with buried subcutaneous sutures to reduce tension. The mild chromatized gut suture is absorbed in 4 to 6 days. This prevents suture marks or cross-hatch scars and alleviates the need for suture removal.

Initiate the running suture by placing a simple interrupted suture at one end of the wound that is tied but not cut. Place simple suture passes down the length of the wound as a "baseball suture" until the end of the suture line is reached (Fig. 9). At this point, tie off suture material with a simple knot created by the last loop of suture. Running suture reduces and shares tension along the entire closure line, creating an even scar line. It is an easy, rapid method of closing wounds; when used correctly, it creates a cosmetically superior scar line. Performed incorrectly, it can cause tissue to bunch and pucker and, if placed too deeply, may create uneven edges. It can strangulate the epidermal edge if pulled too tight and create an uneven, cross-hatched scar.

Running Locked Suture

Locking each running suture as the wound is closed is a modification that counteracts some degree of tension on the skin edge. Perform the running suture as a locked suture for each pass when needed for areas of tension along the excision line. In addition, it may help prevent inversion of the wound edge, which can account for an uneven thickness (Fig. 10). This suture technique is best performed with an assistant who can grab the needle with each pass and place it back in the surgeon's needle holder. Thus it can be used efficiently for both running and running locked suture lines. The major disadvantage of this technique is that it may strangulate the skin edges, thereby creating excessive scarring. Scar is minimized by taking small bites and keeping minimal tension on the suture line.

Running Subcuticular Suture

The running subcuticular suture uses a permanent monofilament suture placed as a horizontal running intradermal suture (Fig. 11). The successful use of this suture depends on reduction of tension below the skin surface with buried subcutaneous sutures. When skin tension is removed, the two skin edges can be draped together and approximated with a running subcuticular suture. Begin the running subcuticular suture by placing the needle through one wound edge and entering the needle into the defect. Hold the opposite edge firmly with a skin hook as the needle is passed in a horizontal plane through the mid dermis. The needle exits at 0.5-cm intervals, and is approximate to the opposite wound side. A similar stitch is placed at the same level in the opposite wound edge. Repeat this on alternate sides of the wound as the suture is advanced down the wound edge. Terminate at the skin surface; then pull the monofilament back and forth to adjust the tension correctly. Because the suture is entirely below the skin surface, permanent monofilament suture may be left in place for 2 or even 3 weeks without risk of skin marks. At that time, remove the suture promptly by pulling it out along the long axis of the scar line. Braided or silk suture should not be used as a subcuticular stitch, since this type of suture cannot be removed after 2 weeks. Use the subcuticular suture primarily to enhance the cosmetic results with defects in wounds where tension has been fully reduced and the skin edges are of relatively equal thickness.

Combined Closure Techniques

A preferred approach to facial defects in which maximal cosmetic results are necessary is to use as a complex closure of both buried absorbable suture and permanent suture. Perform closure in a layered fashion with buried dissolvable suture in fascial layers of subcutaneous tissue and buried dissolvable suture placed in the skin. Use chromic suture or polyglactin 910 (Vicryl) suture No. 4-0 or 5-0 depending on the thickness of the skin and the location of the excision. Reduce tension from the skin with buried sutures so that the permanent skin sutures placed for final approximation do not have any tension or pull. This reduces the incidence of suture lines and cross-hatches or a spread scar line. For further approximation of an elliptic closure, use No. 5-0 polypropylene (Prolene) suture where tension still exists on the skin edge. Repair "dog-ears" or skin redundancy at the tips

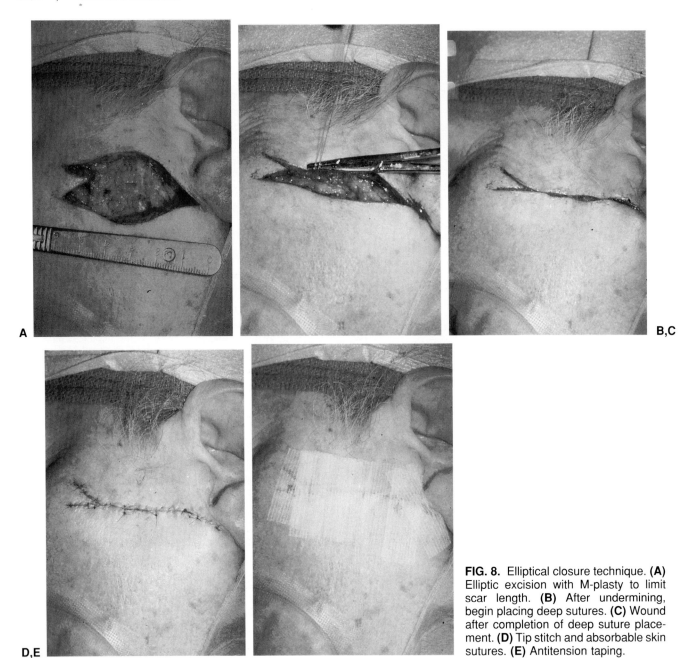

A

B,C

D,E

FIG. 8. Elliptical closure technique. **(A)** Elliptic excision with M-plasty to limit scar length. **(B)** After undermining, begin placing deep sutures. **(C)** Wound after completion of deep suture placement. **(D)** Tip stitch and absorbable skin sutures. **(E)** Antitension taping.

FIG. 9. Running suture is used to close skin edges in wounds in which tension has been reduced with buried interrupted suture.

at the time of closure, and close geometric points with appropriate tip stitches. Place a final skin layer of No. 6-0 mild dissolvable chromic suture in the facial skin to further coapt the skin edges and level the sides equally. Place a running baseball suture with no tension and tied at the ends. Cover the mild chromic suture or fast-dissolving suture with Steri-Strips. Since this suture dissolves within 5 days, there will be no epithelial channels created in the skin that leads to cross-hatching or suture marks when the dressing is removed in 7 to 10 days. Being able to leave the wound dressing in place for this longer time period enhances the stability of the scar and lessens the incidence of dehiscence.

Antitension tape stripping is important for both wound occlusion and to take tension off skin edges. These strips,

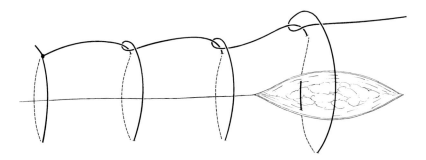

FIG. 10. Running locked suture is a modification of the running suture that is used to counteract tension on the skin edge.

which are covered with narrow, half-inch, flesh-colored paper tape, create a stable wound bandage that may be left in place for up to a week. This technique also protects the wound and improves the cosmetic result.

CONCLUSION

Techniques of suture and wound closure are essential for good dermatologic surgery. Although many of the techniques appear basic, a thorough understanding of these techniques is essential for the dermatologic surgeon to close wounds correctly.

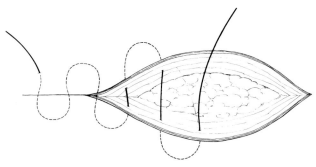

FIG. 11. Running subcuticular suture uses a permanent monofilament suture that is placed as a running intradermal suture.

SUGGESTED READING LIST

1. Aston SJ. The choice of suture material for skin closures. J Dermatol Surg 1976;2:57.
2. Bennett RG. Fundamentals of cutaneous surgery. St. Louis: CV Mosby, 1988.
3. Blumstedt B, Jacobssen S. Experience with polyglactin 910 (Vicryl) in general surgery. Acta Chir Scand 1977;143:259.
4. Borges AF. Techniques of wound suture. In: Elective incisions and scar revision. Boston: Little Brown, 1973:65.
5. Chu CC. Mechanical properties of suture materials: an important characterization. Ann Surg 1981;193:365.
6. Davidson TM. Subcutaneous suture placement. Laryngoscope 1987; 97:501.
7. Edstrom LE. Clinical experience with polydioxanane monofilament absorbable suture in plastic surgery. Plast Reconstr Surg 1983;72:221.
8. Ethicon, Inc. Suture use: wound closure manual. Summerville, NJ: Ethicon, Inc., 1985:8.
9. Ftaiha Z, Snow SM. The buried running dermal subcutaneous suture technique. J Dermatol Surg Oncol 1989;15:264.
10. Garrett Algin. Suture materials. In: Roenigk RK, Roenigk HH Jr, eds. Dermatologic surgery. New York: Marcel Dekker, 1989:1178.
11. Lober CV. Suturing techniques. In: Roenigk RK, Roenigk HH Jr, eds. Dermatologic surgery. New York: Marcel Dekker, 1989:205.
12. McCarthy JG. Introduction to plastic surgery. In: McCarthy JG, ed. Plastic surgery. Philadelphia: WB Saunders, 1990:1.
13. Noe JM. Where should the knot be placed? Ann Plast Surg 1980;5: 145.
14. Stegman SJ, Tromovitch TA, Glogau RG. Suture material. In Stegman SJ, Tromovitch TA, Glogau RG, eds. Basics of dermatologic surgery. Chicago: Yearbook Medical, 1982:36.
15. Swanson MA. Basic techniques. In: Atlas of cutaneous surgery. Boston: Little, Brown, 1987:26.
16. Weber SJ, Dzubow LM. Suture tension. J Dermatol Surg Oncol 1990; 16:535.

Textbook of Dermatologic Surgery, edited by John L. Ratz.
Lippincott–Raven Publishers, Philadelphia © 1998.

CHAPTER 11

Incisional Surgery

Frederick Fish

HISTORY

The origins of incisional surgery are the origins of the practice of surgery itself. The earliest descriptions of the practice of surgery date back to 1800 BC in the Ebers Papyrus and the Edwin Smith Papyrus describing the Egyptian practices of medicine and surgery. Through the ages of the practice of medicine and surgery innumerable techniques have evolved. In this chapter, the technique of surgery in one of its most basic forms, and probably one of the most commonly performed, is reviewed in detail.

Incisional surgery is a useful surgical technique for the removal of benign subcutaneous neoplasms. Lipomas and epidermal cysts are commonly removed using this technique, and treatment of abscesses is frequently accomplished by this method.

PREOPERATIVE PLANNING

Most lipomas can be easily removed with incisional surgery. However, some lipomas require special consideration. Lipomas are common benign tumors that represent a proliferation of histologically normal-appearing adipose tissue. They may be solitary or multiple and may occur anywhere in the subcutaneous tissues of the skin or deeper organ systems. They are most commonly found in the subcutaneous tissue of the neck, shoulders, or back, followed in frequency of occurrence by the forearms, thighs, buttocks, face, and scalp.

It is important to remember that lipomas vary in depth

Frederick Fish: Dept. of Dermatology and Cutaneous Surgery, Ramsey Hospital, St. Paul, MN 55101.
Dept. of Dermatology University of Minnesota, Minneapolis, MN.

depending on their anatomic location. Lipomas on the forehead and scalp frequently lie in the deeper subcutaneous tissue and often are found within or just below the muscle. These lipomas appear protuberant on clinical examination, as though they could be easily removed. Their appearance is deceiving; often a great deal of time and effort is required to dissect them free from the underlying fascia and muscle. Lipomas on the upper extremities commonly infiltrate along fascial planes and can extend beneath muscle bundles. On the trunk and distal extremities, lipomas usually lie within the fat layer and are surrounded by a loose connective tissue capsule, which separates them from the surrounding fatty tissue. These lipomas tend to be superficial and are usually removed easily.

TECHNIQUE

Lipoma

Preoperative planning ensures optimal results when removing lipomas with incisional surgery. First, palpate the perimeter of the lipoma carefully (Fig. 1). Mark the margins of the lipoma using a marking pen. Then infiltrate the area with local anesthesia, using ample quantities of anesthetic in and around the lipoma. The anesthetic helps separate the lipoma from surrounding normal fat. The addition of a small amount of epinephrine to the anesthetic agent helps with hemostasis during the procedure. Once the area has been adequately anesthetized, make a small incision over the tumor (Fig. 2). Center the incision over the lipoma, and place it parallel to the relaxed skin tension lines. The length of the incision should initially be approximately one-third to one-half the diameter of the lipoma down to the tumor. Making the incision as small as possible allows for a better final

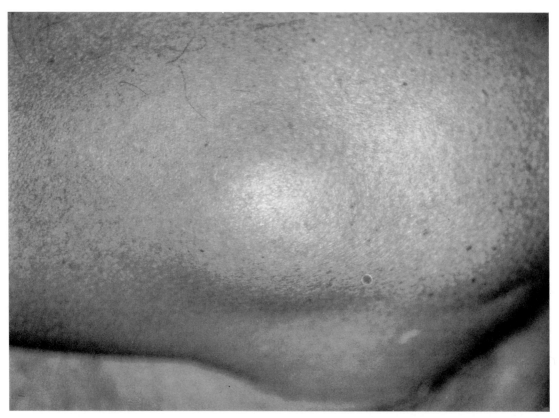

FIG. 1. Protuberant lipoma on the back of the upper arm with well-defined clinical margins.

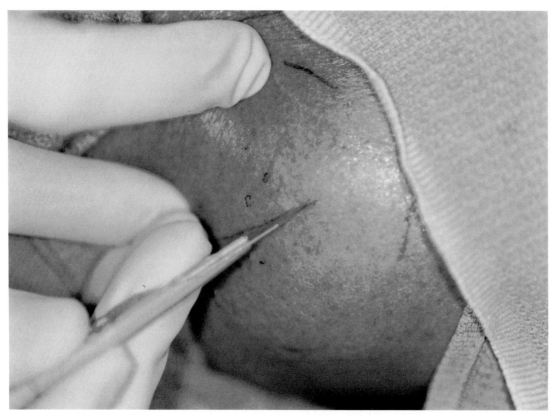

FIG. 2. In the center of the lipoma, make an incision that runs parallel to relaxed skin tension lines and is approximately one-third to one-half the diameter of the lipoma.

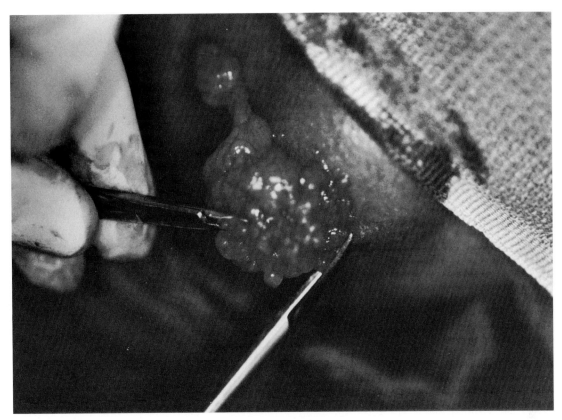

FIG. 3. Dissection of the lipoma free from the surrounding subcutaneous tissue. With the hemostat grasp and stabilize the tumor while performing the dissection with scissors.

cosmetic result. After making the incision, dissect the tumor free from the surrounding subcutaneous fat using dissecting scissors such as Metzenbaum or Ragnell scissors (Fig. 3). Dissection can be assisted by using a blunt hemostat. Grasp the lipoma in the hemostat, and use it to move the lipoma to expose all of its edges as they are being dissected free. After the lipoma has been dissected out, it can be easily removed. If the incision is too small to allow for easy removal, lengthen it to the needed size. Carefully palpate the wound site after removal to determine whether there is residual tumor that feels firm on palpation. In removing larger lipomas, it is not uncommon for a portion of the lipoma to break away as it is being removed. If there are residual fat lobules in the wound, remove them as well. After removal of the lipoma, obtain hemostasis with electrocautery. Once the lipoma has been removed, close the incision with careful attention to dead-space closure (Fig. 4). With larger lipomas a layered closure works best. This closure prevents healing with a depressed scar. Wound closure is accomplished by approximating the subcutaneous tissue with an absorbable suture material, and the skin edge with either an absorbable or a nonabsorbable suture material. For example, use 4-0 or 5-0 Vicryl suture to close the subcutaneous tissue, and make a running subcuticular closure using 4-0 Prolene suture to achieve skin edge approximation. In addition, in cases involving larger wounds, several 6-0 Chromic simple, interrupted sutures can be used to reinforce the skin edge (Fig.

5). Place a pressure dressing over the wound, and have the patient leave it in place for 24 to 48 hours. Instruct the patient regarding activity restriction to avoid hematoma formation. When removing larger lipomas, have the patient cool the area postoperatively with an ice pack to help prevent excess bruising and hematoma formation. This is especially useful in the first 24 hours after surgery.

In removing small lipomas, use the same steps with regard to palpation, surgical marking, and anesthesia. Plan the incision placement in a similar manner, parallel to resting skin tension lines. Make the incision one-fourth to one-third the diameter of the lipoma. After making the incision, dissect the lipoma free using a small hemostat or blunt-nosed scissors such as Ragnell or Metzenbaum scissors. Grasp the lipoma between the thumb and forefinger, and with a firm, squeezing motion extrude the lipoma from the incision (Fig. 6). If the lipoma does not extrude easily, dissect it free from the surrounding stroma. In most cases the incision can be closed using absorbable or nonabsorbable suture material (**see Chapter 9**). In some cases, a layered closure may be preferable. Again, instruct the patient regarding activity restriction and apply a pressure dressing to prevent hematoma formation.

A variation of the preceding technique is performed using a 2-mm curette to free the lipoma from surrounding subcutaneous tissue. The fragmented adipose tissue is then removed through a small (2 to 3 mm) stab incision. The problem

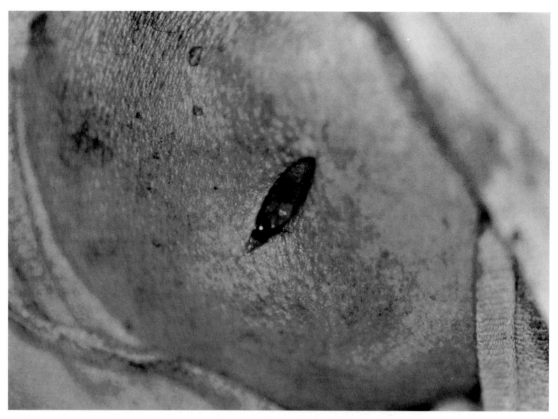

FIG. 4. Incision site after removing the lipoma, showing slight depression. A layered closure works best in this situation.

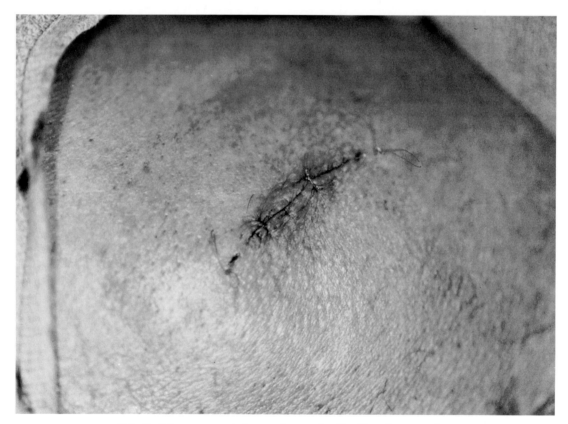

FIG. 5. Primary wound closure (layered) with skin edge eversion.

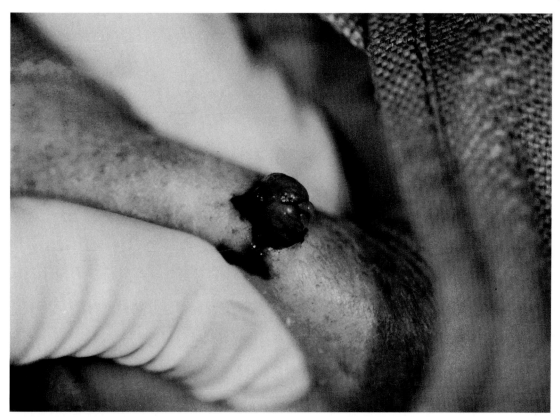

FIG. 6. Extrusion of a lipoma on the forearm through a small incision using a firm, squeezing motion with the thumb and forefinger.

with this technique is that small portions of the lipoma are frequently left behind. This technique works well if it is not necessary to remove the entire lipoma.

Epidermal Cyst

Epidermal cysts can be removed by incisional surgery. Epidermal cysts are the most frequently occurring cutaneous epithelial cysts and account for about 80% of all cysts. They were formerly erroneously called ''sebaceous cysts.'' As the pathogenesis of epidermal cysts has become better understood, this term has fallen into disuse. Epidermal cysts are usually solitary and occur most often in middle-aged individuals, but can occur at any age. They usually become evident with a history of a slowly growing nodule of 1 to 5 cm, but occasionally can be larger. They occur commonly on the head, neck, and trunk, but have been reported in unusual sites such as the palms and soles.

Removal begins, first, by careful inspection of the tumor and its location. Preoperative inspection often reveals a dilated central pore (Fig. 7). Note the orientation of the relaxed skin tension lines overlying the cyst. Plan the incision parallel to the relaxed skin tension lines with the incision passing through the central pore. The local anesthetic agent should contain a dilute amount of epinephrine to help achieve hemostasis. Infiltrate the anesthetic along the edge of the cyst to help dissect it free from the surrounding subcutaneous tissue (Fig. 8). After adequate anesthesia and vasoconstriction have been obtained, make an incision centrally over the cyst, parallel to the relaxed skin tension lines, and through the central pore. The incision should be one-third to one-half the diameter of the cyst. (Fig. 9). Carry the incision down to expose the cyst wall. Dissect the cyst wall free from the surrounding skin and subcutaneous tissue using a skin hook and small dissecting scissors such as Stevens Tenotomy or Gibbs-Gradle scissors (Fig. 10). If the cyst is too large to easily remove through the incision, decompress it. Do this by making a small incision in the cyst wall. Grasp the cyst between two fingers and apply firm pressure to extrude its contents (Fig. 11). After decompression, remove the remaining cyst wall and contents (Fig. 12). Irrigate the cyst cavity using a cotton-tipped applicator and sterile saline to remove residual keratin (Fig. 13). If the incision is small, perform a simple closure using absorbable or nonabsorbable suture (see Chapter 9). For slightly larger cysts, use a layered closure for a better cosmetic result. Close the subcutaneous tissue with an absorbable suture, and the skin edge with an absorbable or a nonabsorbable suture (Fig. 14). Simple

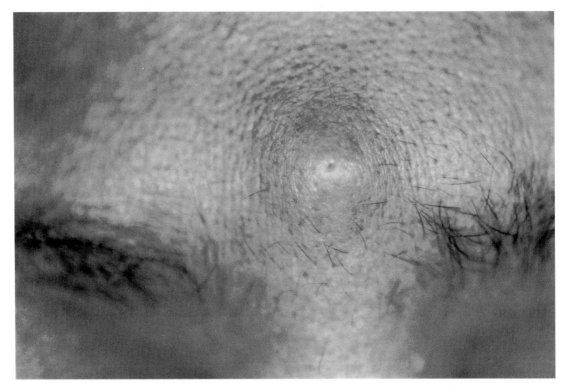

FIG. 7. Glabellar cyst showing protrusion and a central dilated pore.

interrupted 5-0 Vicryl sutures can be used to close the subcutaneous tissue, and 6-0 Chromic simple interrupted sutures to achieve skin edge approximation. This combination consistently gives excellent cosmetic results (Fig. 15).

After surgery apply a light pressure dressing over the wound to help prevent hematoma formation. Steri-Strips are useful to maintain wound edge apposition in cosmetically important areas. Depending on the location and size of the wound, instruct the patient regarding activity restriction. When there is inflammation in and around the cyst or there is concern about infection, consider a short course of oral antibiotics.

Small epidermal cysts can frequently be removed intact. The method for removal is the same as for larger cysts, but the cyst is removed intact, without the decompression step. The incision usually needs to be larger than one-half the diameter of the cyst, to remove the cyst intact (Fig. 16).

Larger epidermal cysts that have been present for a significant period frequently stretch the skin. When removing these cysts with incisional surgery, remove the excess skin, which causes the wound to pucker and makes closure difficult. In these cases, excisional surgery with removal of the excess skin along with the cyst is preferable.

Incision and Drainage

Incisional surgery can be used to drain an infected or inflamed cyst or an abscess pocket. First, inspect the inflamed area, and palpate it for fluctuance to determine whether

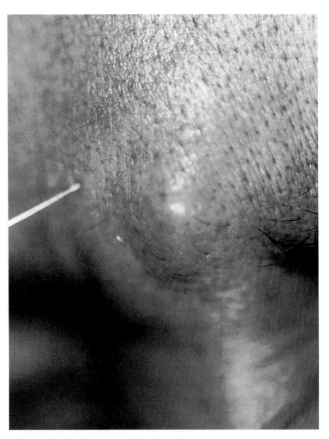

FIG. 8. Inject local anesthetic around the cyst to help separate it from the surrounding subcutaneous tissue and achieve local anesthesia.

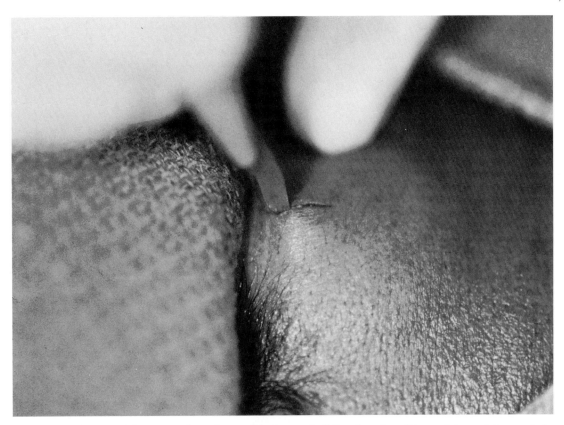

FIG. 9. Make an incision approximately one-third to one-half the diameter of the cyst through the central pore and parallel to relaxed skin tension lines.

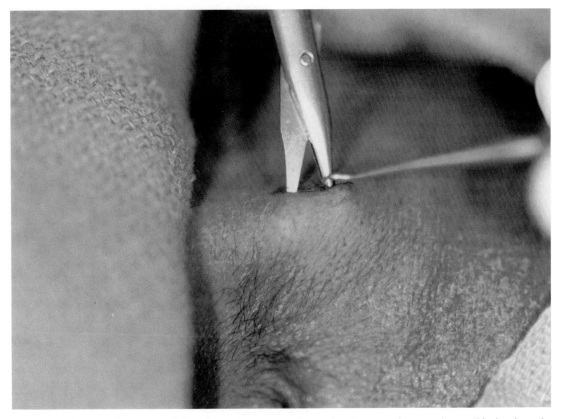

FIG. 10. Dissect the cyst wall free from the surrounding subcutaneous tissue using a skin hook and Gibbs-Gradle scissors.

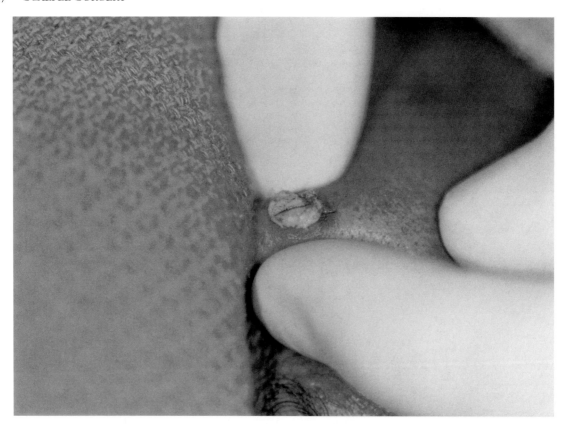

FIG. 11. Cyst decompression: Make a small incision in the cyst wall and squeeze out the cyst contents.

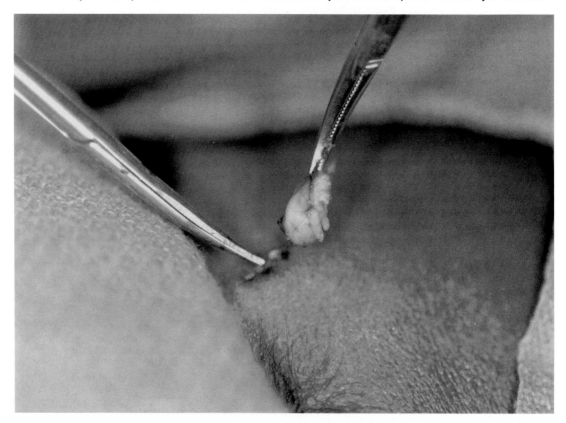

FIG. 12. Remove the cyst wall and remaining cyst contents.

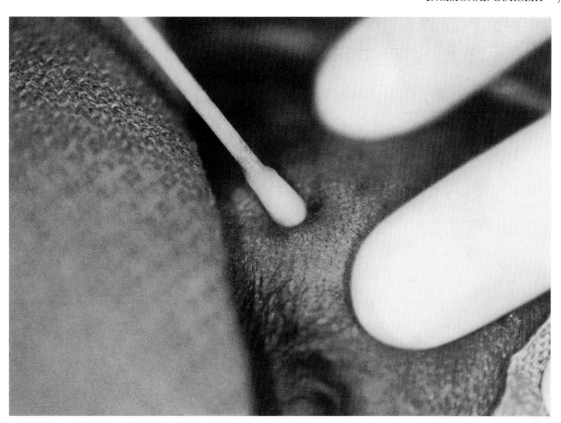

FIG. 13. Irrigate the cyst cavity using cotton-tipped applicators and sterile saline to remove any residual keratin.

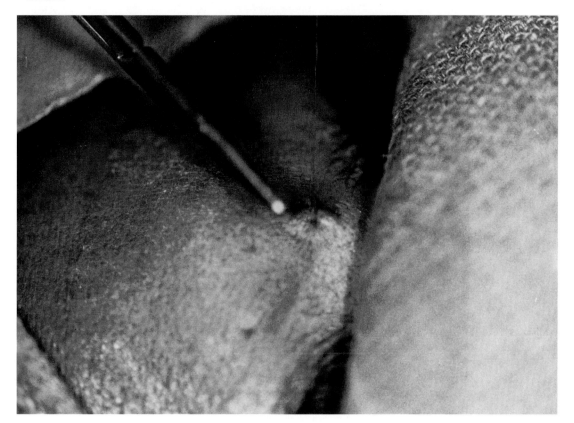

FIG. 14. Close the incision with a layered closure using 5-0 Vicryl to approximate the subcutaneous tissue and 6-0 Chromic simple interrupted sutures to approximate the skin edge.

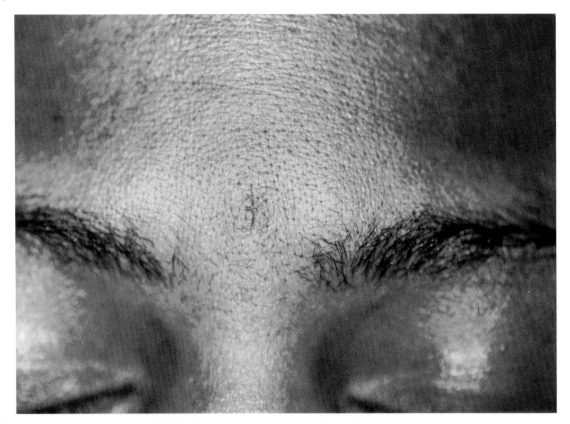

FIG. 15. Surgical wound 2 weeks after surgery.

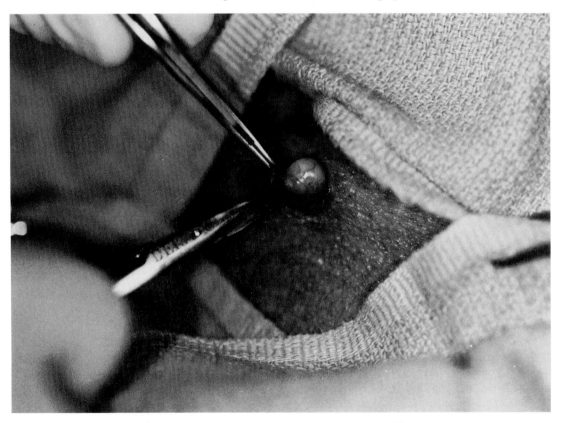

FIG. 16. Dissection of a small cyst and its removal intact.

drainage is necessary. Once a decision is made to proceed with incision and drainage, local anesthesia must be achieved. The inflamed area is often exquisitely tender, and one of the best ways to achieve local anesthesia is to initially use a spray refrigerant. The skin refrigerant decreases the pain of the local anesthetic injection. The subsequent injection of 2% lidocaine without epinephrine is less painful than injecting epinephrine containing local anesthetics. Once the area has been anesthetized, make a small stab incision in the area of maximum fluctuance with a No.11 blade. Wear protective eyewear and a mask when performing this procedure, since the abscess can be under significant pressure, which causes its contents to spray upward through the incision. Once the pocket of inflammation or infection has been entered, insert a hemostat into the cavity and spread it apart to open up a channel for evacuation of the purulent material. When free flow is established, apply gentle pressure along the edges of the inflamed area to assist in drainage. After the cavity has been drained, if packing or a drain is necessary, this can be accomplished with plain or Iodoform gauze. Pack the wound completely with the packing material. This can be achieved simply with a forceps or hemostat to advance the packing material. The gauze helps with drainage. Over the next several days, gradually retract the gauze with each dressing change until it is completely removed. If there is concern about infection, place the patient on a course of oral antibiotics. In such cases, it is best to allow the wound to heal by second intention.

ADVERSE SEQUELAE AND COMPLICATIONS

Adverse events associated with incisional surgery are primarily deformities associated with healing. Most can be avoided by meticulous attention to surgical technique and orientation of the surgical incision. Placing the incision parallel with or in a relaxed skin tension line often hides the surgical scar. Careful attention to the multilayered suturing technique to avoid dead space and achieve comparable tissue apposition prevents a depressed or puckered wound.

Incisional surgery may be complicated by infection. Although uncommon, this is not unexpected. A skin infection in a surgical wound can lead to an unsightly scar. As discussed in the section on incision and drainage of abscesses, necessary precaution to prevent the spread of infection by administering the appropriate antibiotic is always warranted. In patients who are at high risk for infection, the use of broad-spectrum antibiotics should be considered.

SUGGESTED READING LIST

1. Arizpe SR, Candiani J. Giant epidermoid cyst: clinical aspect and surgical management. J Dermatol Surg Oncol 1986;12(7):734.
2. Breasted JH. The Edwin Smith Surgical Papyrus. Chicago: University of Chicago Press, 1930;1.
3. Greer KE. Epidermal inclusion cyst of the sole. Arch Dermatol 1974; 109:251.
4. Hardened FF. A simple technique for removing lipomas. J Dermatol Surg Oncol 1982;8:316.
5. Kligman AM. The myth of the sebaceous cyst. Arch Dermatol 1964; 89:253.
6. Love WR, Montgomery H. Epithelial cysts. Arch Dermatol Syph 1943; 47:185.
7. McGavran MH, Binnington B. Keratinous cysts of the skin. Arch Dermatol 1966;94:499.
8. Moore C, Greer DM Jr. Sebaceous cyst extraction through mini-incisions. Br J Plast Surg 1975; Vol 28(4):307–309.
9. Rhydholm A, Berg NO. Size, site, and clinical insights of lipoma. Acta Orthop Scand 1983;54:929.
10. Salasche SJ, McCollough ML, et al. Frontalis-associated lipoma of the forehead. J Am Acad Dermatol 1989;20:462.
11. Stegman SJ, Tromovitch TA. Lipomas. In: Stegman SJ, Tromovitch TA, eds. Cosmetic dermatologic surgery. Chicago: Yearbook Medical Pub., 1984;23.
12. Truhan AP, Garden JM, Caro WA, et al. Facial and scalp lipomas: case reports and study of prevalence. J Dermatol Surg Oncol 1985;11: 91.

Textbook of Dermatologic Surgery, edited by John L. Ratz.
Lippincott–Raven Publishers, Philadelphia © 1998.

CHAPTER 12

Tangential and Shave Excision: Horizontal Surgery for Epidermal Resurfacing

Nia K. Terezakis

HISTORY OF TANGENTIAL SURGERY

Techniques for epidermal surgery were described and popularized 40 years ago by Dr. Walter Shelley. The term ''epidermal surgery'' was coined by Shelly in 1976 and described as:

> ... the high art of precise and specific removal of lesions which are strictly epidermal in depth and extent.... There is a branch of dermatologic surgery that is poorly defined, disparaged by those who cut and stitch, and often is unacknowledged by its practitioners.... Surgery on the epidermis calls for sophistication in spatial perception as well as lesion recognition.... *Epidermal surgery* is the *surgery* of the *horizontal*. It is practiced best by those who not only have confidence in their recognition of the epidermal lesion, but who will forego the scalpel and use the instruments better suited for surgery on the unique avascular cellular sheath of the skin that is epidermis.

TANGENTIAL SHAVE BIOPSIES AND EXCISIONS

Many clinicians regard the skin biopsy as an elementary procedure, but the information it yields with proper selection of technique can be critical to a diagnosis. Most dermatologists excel in selecting appropriate biopsy techniques, whether the procedure be a ''punch'' excision, a deep scalpel excision, or a horizontal epidermal excision. The experi-

enced clinician selects a method based on the information to be gained.

The shave (tangential) biopsy, or excision, is a horizontal rather than a vertical procedure and yields a larger specimen than is possible with most cutaneous punch procedures. The razor blade, as an instrument for both diagnostic biopsy information and tangential shave excision, has many advantages over other techniques for papular and exophytic skin lesions. It is also useful for skin lesions anatomically situated within the epidermis and within the superficial dermis, but it is of no use for disease suspected to be in the deep dermis or the underlying fat (Fig. 1).

The razor blade is very inexpensive, always sharp, requires no maintenance, and is always easy to obtain. The techniques for using razor blades are quite simple to master and require no exceptional training.

Appropriate lesions for biopsy, as well as size of the lesion, depth of specimen, and method of obtaining the tissue, are not only directly proportional to the technician's knowledge of cutaneous pathology, microanatomy, and cutaneous surgical principles, but also directly proportional to the technician's experience and clinical judgment. Since skin uniquely mirrors most internal disease, simple skin biopsy techniques can yield significant diagnostic and therapeutic information.

The experienced clinician does not use a shave excision to remove suspected melanomas or other worrisome skin lesions.

A tangential shave procedure can be performed quickly

Nia K. Terezakis: 2633 Napoleon Avenue, Suite 905, New Orleans, LA 70118.

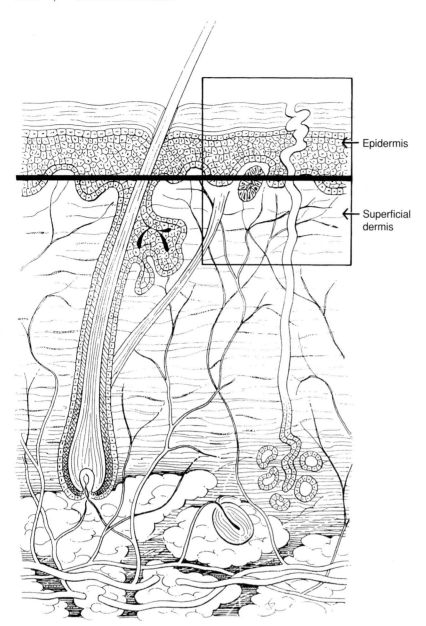

→ Epidermis

→ Superficial dermis

FIG. 1. Epidermis. Diagram shows approximate depth of tangential excision for pinch graft (see bold line).

in an office setting or at the hospital bedside if necessary, with a minimal amount of discomfort, and the site usually heals without significant disfigurement. The relative superficial nature of the skin excision allows for prompt healing, and depending on the ultimate information or result desired, incisional or excisional specimens can be obtained and submitted for histopathologic interpretation. The shave technique leaves the lower levels of the dermis intact, should further procedures (e.g., electrodesiccation, cryosurgery, curetage) be necessary.

Tangential techniques are also ideal procedures for biopsy of the lower extremities, which can be difficult to heal at any age. The resulting morbidity and scar are usually minimal when compared with those which can result from deeper biopsy and excision techniques.

Agents and modalities commonly used by dermatologists

for hemostasis (e.g., aluminum chloride, Monsel's solution, gel foam, and electrodesiccation) make horizontal shave excisions an ideal method of obtaining skin tissue from some patients with coagulation defects who would never be good candidates for most other surgical procedures.

PREOPERATIVE PLANNING

Primary Uses for Horizontal Shave Techniques

The horizontal shave technique is used for biopsy or excision of papular and exophytic skin lesions (i.e., nevi, seborrheic keratoses, basal cell carcinoma, and other skin appendage tumors situated in the epidermis or upper dermis) (Figs. 2–4).

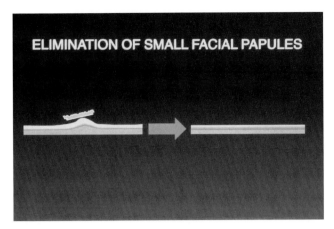

FIG. 2. Small papules can be tangentially excised by stretching the skin between thumb and forefinger using a sawing motion.

Warts, callouses, and corns can be pared, although a less sharp instrument than the carbon steel blade may be the most efficient tool for thick, calloused lesions, as well as the safest implement in most hands. Use the horizontal shave technique to obtain a biopsy specimen of "epidermal skin diseases" (i.e., bullous dermatoses) where lesional and perilesional tissue can be submitted intact along with the superficial dermis. This procedure can also be used to obtain epidermal specimen to examine for fungal hyphae, keratinocytes, or fibroblasts for tissue culture techniques and epidermal "pinch grafts" for grafting leg ulcers (see Epidermal Resurfacing). Large, exuberant keloids can be removed before intralesional injections of steroids or before using silicone gel sheets (see Structural Redefinition).

Methods and Materials

One of the sharpest razor edges can be found on the safety razor blades. The carbon steel blade has a cutting edge that is 1 millionth of an inch thick and is coated with a bacteriostatic and anticorrosive agent(zinc naphthenate) and with a fluorocarbon telomer (Vydex) to enhance its cutting capabilities (Fig. 5).

The carbon steel blade has been placed on bacterial culture media on numerous occasions, and bacteria have never grown on cultures when the blades were taken directly from the packaging.

Single-edge blades are not recommended for horizontal cutaneous surgery, since they cannot be used to achieve appropriate or precise depth of removal, nor can they be bent to conform to every skin surface contour. Although the shave technique with a scalpel blade may be more appropriate for a few isolated anatomic sites (i.e., inner canthus) and for paring callouses and corns, it is not as sharp, flexible, versatile, or precise an instrument as the carbon steel blade.

Preparing Blades for Use

Carbon steel blades may be purchased individually wrapped directly from the manufacturer, from surgical instrument companies, from dermatologic supply companies, or from some pharmacies that still supply individual packages of safety razor blades.

A double-edge razor blade is easily broken by longitudinal bending of the blade while still in its paper packaging. By breaking the blade lengthwise while it is still packaged, there should never be any possibility of accidental injury, and the

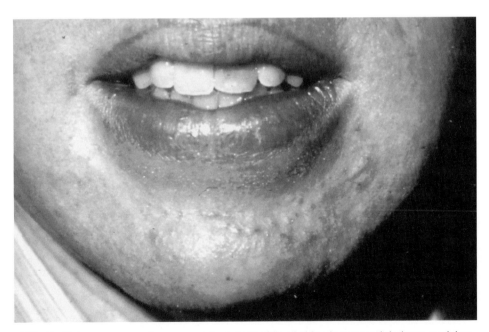

FIG. 3. Sebaceous papules removed on right side of chin via tangential shave excision.

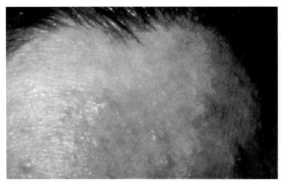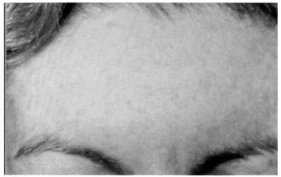

FIG. 4. (A) Multiple sebaceous papules and nodules on forehead. **(B)** Forehead after tangential excision of sebaceous papules. Individual lesions were removed over months.

blade remains sterile until it is removed from the package. The single-edge blades can be placed between sterile gauze and then placed on the surgical tray for use. They can be easily and safely used with one hand, although some surgeons may prefer special adaptors for handling. The blades should then be discarded and never reused (Fig. 6).

TECHNIQUE

Epidermal Surgery with a Razor Blade

First, properly cleanse the skin. Mark the edges of the site to be excised; otherwise, vasoconstriction of tissue caused by the epinepherine in the lidocaine (Xylocaine), as well as the pressure of the injected solution within the skin, may obliterate the site to be removed. Use a local anesthetic such as lidocaine with epinepherine for most anatomic sites. Grasp the blade between the thumb and forefinger (Fig. 7).

The opposing ends of the blade are not sharp, and there should never be any traumatic injury to the fingers when the blade is handled appropriately. While holding the skin taunt with the opposing hand, use a back-and-forth sawing motion to excise the anesthetized site. Try to hold the blade at a horizontal angle over the skin. Curve the blade slightly if necessary; however, if the blade is curved excessively, a

concave scar may be produced (Fig. 7). Control of bleeding is easily achieved with aluminum chloride or Monsel's solution. The use of electrocautery or electrodesiccation for hemostasis may result in significantly more scarring and depigmentation of the site. Use a very small needle (30-gauge)

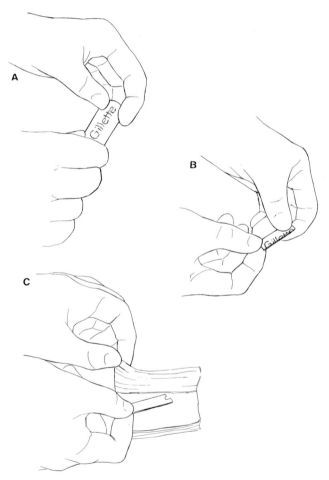

FIG. 6. (A) Proper handling of the carbon steel blade. **(B)** Simple, safe method of breaking the carbon steel blade in half. **(C)** Blades can be placed within sterile gauze pads before placement on the surgical tray.

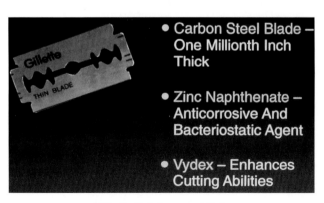

- Carbon Steel Blade – One Millionth Inch Thick

- Zinc Naphthenate – Anticorrosive And Bacteriostatic Agent

- Vydex – Enhances Cutting Abilities

FIG. 5. Safety razor blade.

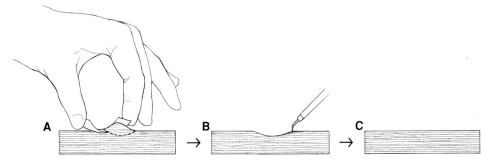

FIG. 7. Appropriate technique in razor surgery. **(A)** A concave defect may occur if blades are held with a deep curve. **(B)** The edges of a concave defect can be made less noticeable by feathering the edge with very light electrodesiccation using a 30-gauge needle as an electrode and a very low current. **(C)** Ideally, there should be no defect with horizontal excision.

as an electrode on the electrodesiccator to ''feather'' the epidermal edge of the site for better cosmesis. If an extremely low setting of electrocurrent is selected, and the tip of a 30-gauge needle is to be used as an electrode for refining the edges of the site, excessive depigmentation should rarely occur with this method. Cover the shallow wound with a dressing or bandage for a few hours or overnight. Subsequently leave the wound open to heal by epithelialization or by epidermization, depending on the depth of the excision.

Structural Redefinition

Skin surface recontouring is accomplished when the razor blade is used to ''sculpt'' an involved area of the face, nose, or ears so that it resumes an appearance as close to normal as possible. The horizontal excision of skin surface papules, nodules, and scars with a razor blade need not always be performed at one sitting but can be staged as multiple minor excisions over a period of weeks or months, depending on the individual circumstances of each patient. Accordingly, further procedures are easily terminated if initial results are not entirely satisfactory.

The face and nose of many mature adults are quite rich with sebaceous glands, and indeed it is the patient with exuberant sebaceous hyperplasia who is the ideal candidate for skin structural redefinition and recontouring with a razor

blade. For these patients, the aggressive use of topical tretinoin shortly before and especially after tangential procedures for recontouring greatly enhances the ultimate cosmetic potential (Figs. 8 and 9).

Patients with severely hyperplastic rosacea and rhinophyma continue to benefit cosmetically from the long-term use of topical tretinoin after any tangential recontouring procedure (Fig.10).

When facial skin is dermabraded or the rhinophymatous nose is recontoured by various methods, take care not to remove tissue below the plane of the sebaceous glands or below the upper dermis because it is primarily from the pilosebaceous follicles that the epidermis is resurfaced. Dermabrasion or tangential procedures on the trunk and extremities are not successful because of the paucity of rich sebaceous follicles. Other adnexal structures and the epidermal edges also contribute to the healing process. Rigidly follow the identical approach with razor blade recontouring if scarring is to be minimized.

When tangential surgical procedures are used to remove exuberant keloidal scars for the recontouring of a skin surface or skin appendage (i.e., the ear), the concomitant use of intralesional steroids both during the procedure and within a very few weeks after the procedure on a regular basis cannot be stressed enough. The timing of intralesional steroids is critical if a larger, recurrent keloid is to be avoided

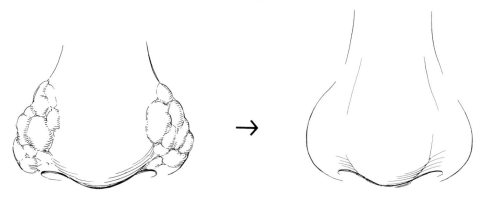

FIG. 8. Shave excision of multiple papular nodules.

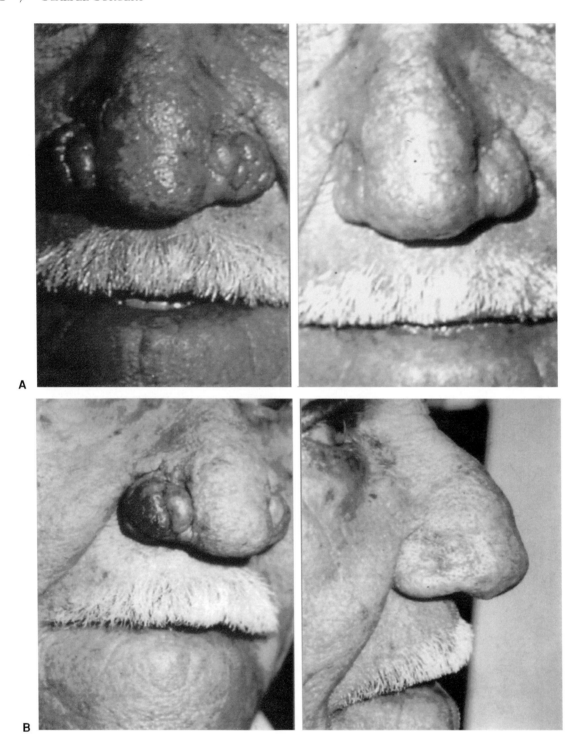

FIG. 9. Repair of rhinophymas were performed as a series of staged procedures over several months, since the patients were not good candidates for a major procedure. **(A–F)** Rhinophyma before and after tangential excision of nodules. *(Continued)*

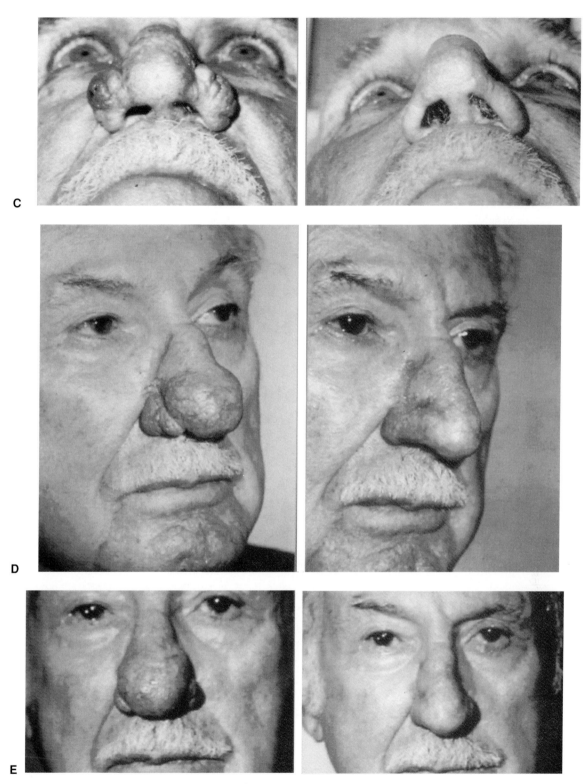

FIG. 9. *Continued.*

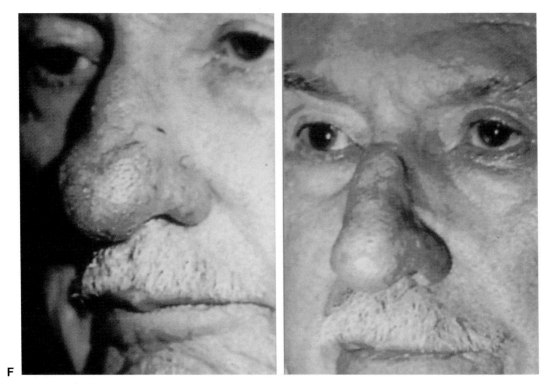

F

FIG. 9. *Continued.*

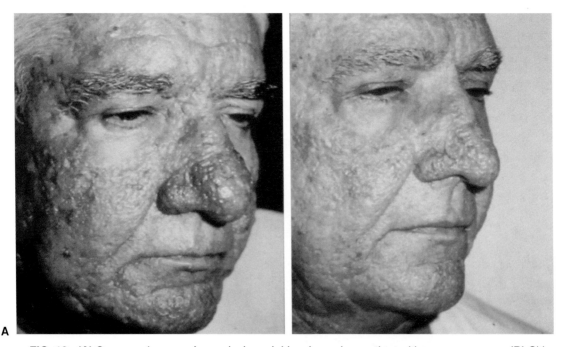

A

B

FIG. 10. **(A)** Severe sebaceous hyperplasia and rhinophyma in a patient with severe rosacea. **(B)** Skin surface recontouring and reduction of rhinophyma was accomplished gradually over 1 year. Patient was also using tretinoin aggressively.

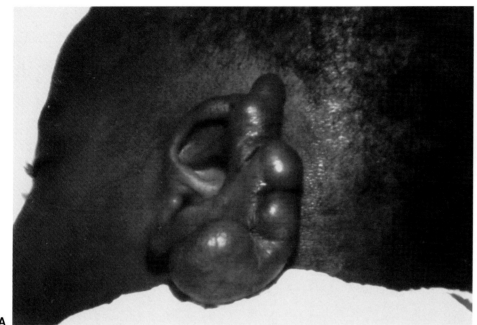

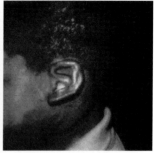

FIG. 11. Large, exuberant keloids in thermal burn scars that were removed via tangential razor excision. Triamcinolone (20 to 30 μg/u) was injected at 3- to 6-week intervals until the skin remained flat. **(A)** Patient before excision. **(B)** Patient after excision.

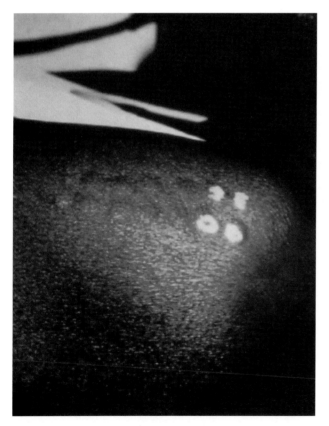

FIG. 12. Intradermal placement of lidocaine to facilitate removal of small, thin grafts.

(Fig. 11). Silicone gel sheets and rigid pressure dressings are frequently used to prevent keloids on some surface areas, but these are not always practical for active, small, and growing children; the noncompliant patient; and some anatomic locations.

The correct use of appropriate intralesional steroids for large and recurrent keloids does not seem to either hinder the healing process or predispose the patient to infection, although their use in some premenopausal women may cause menstrual irregularities.

Some facial skins and certain facial deformities are more amenable to surface recontouring than others, but, with everyday use of razor surgery techniques for biopsy and removal of nevi, considerable expertise is developed with the daily and continued implementation of the shave excision procedures. Judgment in selecting appropriate candidates becomes easy for the observant technician who has become skilled by repetitive use of the modality.

Epidermal Resurfacing

Leg ulcers are often recalcitrant to many treatments. Epidermal resurfacing of ulcers with small pinch grafts are easily and successfully performed as an outpatient procedure on patients who must remain ambulatory. The grafting can be done gradually with only a few grafts placed at a sitting to ensure an adequate "take."

Thin pinch grafts can be taken from almost any donor site (arm or abdomen) via a tangential shave excision with a razor blade after raising the skin surface by injecting the lidocaine very superficially, as if performing an intradermal skin test (Fig. 11-12).

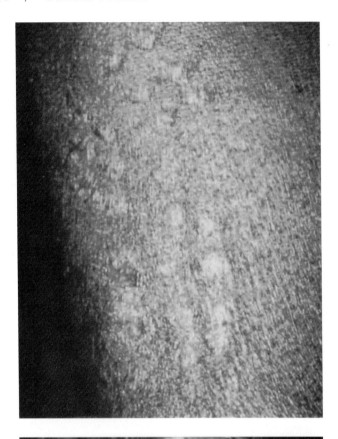

FIG. 13. Donor site has healed with repigmentation of skin and minimal scarring.

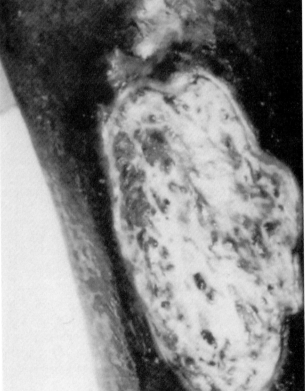

FIG. 14. Large ulcer in a patient with pyoderma gangrenosa. "Nubbins" of granulation tissue are ideal "receptor sites" for placement of grafts.

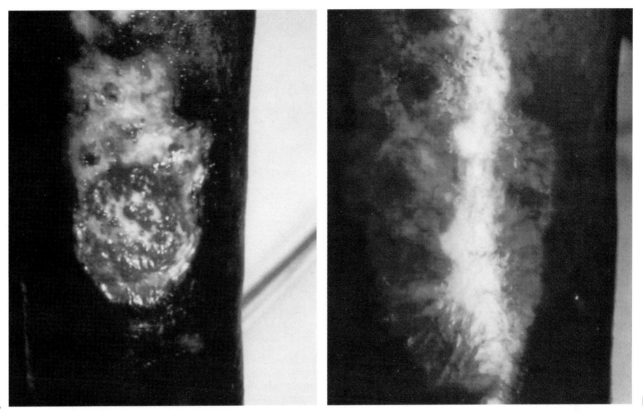

A   B

FIG. 15. (A) Partially resurfaced ulcer. Note extension of grafted cells much beyond original size of graft. **(B)** Healed ulcer resurfaced entirely as an outpatient procedure with pinch grafts. Procedure was staged and performed at three different times.

When the grafts are removed in a very thin layer, as a split-thickness tissue, both the donor and recipient sites will probably repigment normally as melanocytes will be present on both the graft and the rete pegs of the donor site (Figs. 1 and 13).

The grafts should be placed directly on the ulcer surface from the blade. Select sites on the ulcer bed that demonstrate "nubbins" of granulation tissue (Fig. 14). The grafts will start to generate new cells beyond their placement site as if in a tissue culture (Fig. 15). The entire ulcer need not be resurfaced in one sitting, but grafts can be done gradually over a period of weeks, depending on the individual circumstances of the patient and the expertise of the physician.

COMPLICATIONS

Complications for horizontal surgical procedures are usually uncommon but parallel those for most surgeries and include infection, scar or keloid formation, depigmentation, postinflammatory erythema and postinflammatory hyperpigmentation. Achievement of the ultimate result may be prolonged with staged procedures.

CONCLUSION

There are several advantages of using the horizontal epidermal shave procedure. Exophytic lesions are easily removed (i.e., nevi and seborrheic keratoses), those lesions confined to the epidermis. The resulting skin defect usually heals with less scarring, than those resulting from a deeper tangential procedure. Flat or non raised lesions can also be removed, whether they are small or broad (e.g., lentigenes and flat nevi). Biopsy of some depressed or flat lesions is usually accomplished with a saucerization technique. Leg ulcers, both small and large, can be resurfaced with thin "pinch grafts" on an outpatient basis. Deep, pitting scars

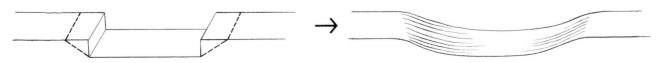

FIG. 16. Diagram demonstrates graphically the recontouring of punched-out or "ice-pick" scars.

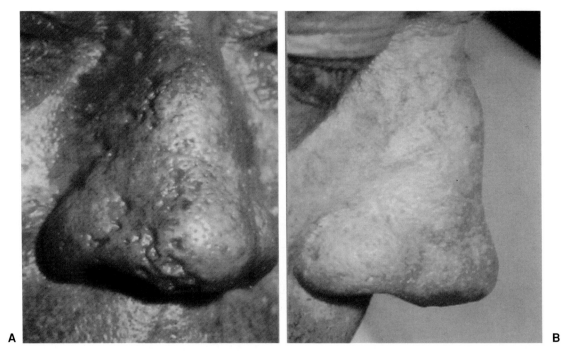

FIG. 17. Patient has deep, punched-out scars on the nose after infection with herpes zoster. Scars are carved almost individually and recontoured over several months. More exacting control of final result was achieved with razor recontouring than with a wire brush dermabrasion, since *depth* of each scar varied considerably. **(A)** Before surgery and **(B)** after surgery.

and small, localized scars can be more precisely excised and revised without using a wire brush.

Repigmentation of areas of vitiligo can be accomplished with epidermal grafts. The recipient surface should first be dermabraded to remove the surface epithelium before applying the small or large pinch grafts. Small scars may be more easily revised than by using a dermabrasion procedure (Fig. 18) or easily combined with several other modalities such as excision (see earlier discussion), dermabrasion (see Chapter 28) and chemical peeling (see Chapter 29).

"Staged" procedures are easily accomplished (i.e., resurfacing leg ulcers or areas of vitiligo with pinch grafts or the gradual excision of rhinophyma in a patient who is receiving aspirin or anticoagulant drugs and who is not a good candidate for a major surgical procedure). There is usually minimal morbidity for the patient.

Mastery of the technique discussed in this chapter is simple and easily perfected with daily implementation for biopsy and shave excision procedures, and it requires no exceptional training or certification.

Medical expenses for the procedure should be considerably less for the patient and the practitioner. The double edge razor blade is the most "cost-effective" instrument for epidermal surgery in the United States and is especially useful and available in undeveloped countries.

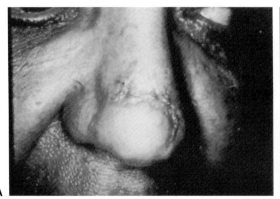
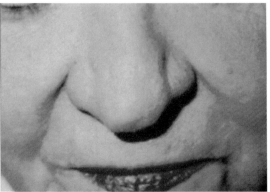

FIG. 18. Scars from traumatic injury both **(A)** before and **(B)** after repairs with razor blade surgery.

SUGGESTED READING LIST

1. Ackerman AB. Biopsy: why, where, when, how. J Dermatol Surg 1975; 1:21.
2. Ackerman AB. Shave biopsies: the good and right, the bad and wrong. Am J Dermatopathol 1983;5:21 (editorial).
3. Agrawal K, Agrawal A. Vitiligo: repigmentation with dermabrasion and thin split-thickness skin graft. Dermatol Surg 1995;21:292.
4. Albom MJ. Scalpel and scissors surgery. In: Epstein's techniques in skin surgery. Philadelphia: Lea & Febiger, 1979;56.
5. Arndt KA. Operative procedure. In: Manual of dermatologic therapeutics with essentials of diagnosis. 4th ed. Boston: Little, Brown, 1991; 171.
6. Arthur R, Shelly WB. The epidermal biopsy: its indications and techniques. Arch Dermatol 1959;80:133.
7. Bennett RG. Fundamentals of cutaneous surgery. St. Louis: CV Mosby, 1988.
8. Biopsy of skin: an underutilized laboratory "test." N Engl J Med 1967; 277:49 (editorial).
9. Braum M. Surgical gem: the razor curet. J Dermatol Surg Oncol 1982; 8:10.
10. Caro MR. Skin biopsy technique. Arch Dermatol 1957;76:9.
11. Epstein LI. Obtaining razor blades suitable for use in plastic surgery. Plast Reconstr Surg 1977;59:740.
12. Harvey DT, Fenske NA. The razor blade biopsy technique. Dermatol Surg 1995;21:345.
13. Kahn AM, Cohen MJ, Kaplan L, Highton A. Vitiligo: treatment by dermabrasion and epithelial sheet grafting: a preliminary report. J Am Dermatol 1993;28:733.
14. Kopf AW, Popkin GL. Shave biopsies for cutaneous lesions. Arch Dermatol 1974;110:637.
15. Levy S. Pinch grafting. Cutis 1976;17:402 (letter).
16. O'Donnell BP, Mulvaney MJ, McMarlin SL. Thin tangential excision of tattoos. Dermatol Surg 1995;21:601.
17. Sachs W, Sachs PM, Atkinson SC. Peripheral, or five-point, method of skin biopsy. JAMA 1950;142:902.
18. Shelley WB. Epidermal surgery. J Dermatol Surg 1976;2:125.
19. Shelley WB. The razor blade in dermatologic practice. Cutis 1975;16: 843.
20. Sox HC, Ginsburg JA, Scott HD. Physician assistants and nurse practitioners. Ann Intern Med 1994;121:714.
21. Winkelmann RK. Skin biopsy. In: Epstein's techniques in skin surgery. Philadelphia: Lea & Febiger, 1979.

Textbook of Dermatologic Surgery, edited by John L. Ratz.
Lippincott–Raven Publishers, Philadelphia © 1998.

CHAPTER 13

Excision

Rebecca B. O'Sullivan and R. Steven Padilla

HISTORY

Historical evidence of surgery has been found in many countries and cultures documenting the evolution of current medical and surgical practices. The earliest record of surgery is found in an Egyptian pictorial representation dating from as early as 2750 to −2626 BC. This Egyptian treatise on healing, the "Smith Medical Papyrus," documents early surgical practices and principles that are supported by subsequent studies on mummies. Like many cultures, in India for centuries Vedic priests intermingled practical therapeutic treatment with the exorcism of evil and the practice of various forms of magic.

Specific descriptions of excisional surgery are hard to find until about 600 BC, when Sushruta, a priest and disciple of the Hindu god of healing, wrote the "Samhita," a collection of writings describing the art of Ayurveda or healing. The

Samhita classified "ills and fevers" as natural or supernatural, included nearly a thousand medicinal plants, placed emphasis on cleanliness of instruments and surroundings, and described surgical operations. This meticulous document described 121 different surgical instruments including scalpels, scissors, needles, probes, forceps, and syringes. Sushruta divided the surgical art into eight categories: scarification, incision, excision, aspiration, probing, extraction of foreign bodies, extraction of foreign fluids, and suturing. Thus the "Samhita" of Sushruta may be the earliest record of excisional surgery.

In primitive times mutilation was a common form of punishment in India as well as other countries and cultures. Plastic surgical techniques were developed to repair the resultant deformities. Hindu surgeons were reputed to have excelled in reconstructive techniques; in the fourth century AD, when Alexander the Great invaded India, reports of reconstructive surgery were brought back to Europe. Great contributions were made by Greek and Roman surgeons in the first and second centuries of the Roman Empire, including Celsus, who based his writings on the works of Hippocrates; Heliodorus, who described the technique of tying blood vessels; and Rufus, who examined anatomy. However, in the Dark and Middle Ages the influence of the Church

Rebecca B. O'Sullivan: West Roxbury/Brockton Veterans Affairs Medical Center, 1400 V.F.W. Parkway, West Roxbury, MA 02132.
R. Steven Padilla: Department of Dermatology, University of New Mexico School of Medicine, 4775 Indian School Road NE, Suite 100, Albuquerque, New Mexico 87110.

halted progress, since surgery was not condoned by the pope. The emergence of barber-surgeons followed, and surgery was held in low esteem except in times of battle. As late as the 16th century, plastic surgery was still held in disfavor, since it was "an interference with the hand of God." In the Age of Enlightenment, the Renaissance period, and the centuries that followed, the surgical art evolved greatly as techniques were developed by clinicians while scholars compiled and documented the theoretical considerations. The greatest advances were made by those such as Paré and Clowes, who followed armies, wrote of their experiences, and disapproved of quackery. In reference to the surgeons of the sixteenth century, Benton and Hewlett wrote, in *Surgery Through the Ages* (1944), that "quacks . . . constituted even in that comparatively advanced day, the majority of surgeons. Since the quack has not yet been entirely eliminated from the healing field this is hardly a subject of surprise."

Today, as surgery continues to evolve and excisional techniques are perfected, despite many new developments, we may appreciate how some principles and practices remain unchanged, and how often patterns, observations, controversies, and sentiments repeat themselves through history.

GENERAL CONSIDERATIONS

Throughout the ages, surgery has been interwoven with medicine, drawing upon knowledge and appreciation of general principles as applied to organ systems and complexities of disease processes. The integumentary system is the largest in the body, and its respective pathologic processes range from simple to complex. Mastery of excisional surgery involves the application of general surgical principles to cutaneous processes. This requires knowledge and appreciation of dermatopathology, the science of wound healing, and regional anatomic variation.

Proficiency in excisional surgery is achieved with training and practice; judgment and technique are enhanced with experience. When planning an excision, the surgeon must appreciate the intrinsic properties of skin and how movement of underlying musculature creates overlying skin lines. With skill and attention to these principles, the postoperative results reflect the art of excisional surgery.

The realm of excisional surgery encompasses numerous procedures, which vary in technique and application. Multiple approaches to the same clinical situation can lead to acceptable results; the method selected is determined by the judgment of the dermatologic surgeon. Factors that influence the choice of procedure and technique may be related to anatomic considerations, the nature of the diagnosis (benign vs. malignant neoplasm), patient characteristics, and the skill and training of the surgeon.

The properties of skin vary from patient to patient. These factors are not within the surgeon's control, and influence not only the selection of procedure, but also the degree of difficulty of each procedure. For example, the resilience of skin and properties of elasticity (tensile strength provided by underlying collagen, ability to stretch and recoil) and turgor may be influenced by factors such as nutrition, hydration, age of the patient, dermatoheliosis, scars or sequelae of prior treatments, and underlying metabolic aberrations (i.e., amyloidosis, scleroderma, Ehlers-Danlos syndrome). Other underlying medical conditions may also influence the immunologic integrity of the skin, such as diabetes, systemic lupus erythematosus, thermal burns, and human immunodeficiency virus (HIV) disease. Establish this information preoperatively, since these conditions have the potential to complicate wound healing.

EXCISIONS

This chapter discusses various techniques used for excisions of benign and malignant tumors of the skin. These include procedures that range from biopsies to definitive treatment techniques, each of which may be indicated in specific clinical situations. These are individually addressed.

For our purposes, dermatologic excisional surgery is divided into two basic categories: biopsies and definitive excisions. A biopsy provides tissue for analysis that can lead to a diagnosis. An excision is a definitive treatment that results in the complete surgical removal of a benign or malignant tumor. Both allow histologic confirmation of a clinical impression from within a proposed differential diagnosis, which may form the basis for important clinical decisions.

Biopsy techniques are categorized as follows: shave biopsy, punch biopsy, incisional biopsy, and excisional biopsy. An excision may be carried out in many ways, and we refer to the varying excision methods based on the following configurations: circumferential (circular), fusiform (elliptical), and wedge shaped. In specific clinical situations the punch and shave biopsy techniques may be used for definitive excisions as well.

BIOPSIES

When performing a biopsy, the surgeon must choose the best technique and site to gain the most information with the smallest piece of tissue. To accomplish this, one must consider what information is desired in relation to what can be gained from each biopsy technique. This type of decision is based on knowledge of clinical dermatology and appreciation of histopathology. For example, only a small amount of tissue may be necessary to confirm the diagnosis of basal cell carcinoma, yet a full-thickness biopsy specimen including fat may be needed to make a diagnosis of morphea or panniculitis. A full-thickness biopsy specimen is necessary for the diagnosis of most neoplasms, including malignant melanoma or when distinguishing keratoacanthoma from squamous cell carcinoma.

Recognition of varied clinical signs of disease or lesion morphology often dictates the preferred site for a biopsy.

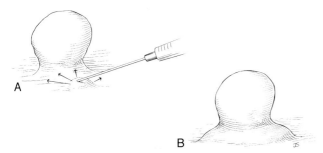

FIG. 1. (A) Carefully infiltrate the local anesthetic into the base of a polypoid or pedunculated tumor. **(B)** Infiltration with the local anesthetic produces a wheal that may distort the natural skin markings.

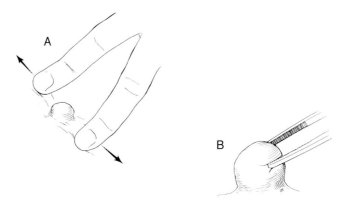

FIG. 2. Stabilize the skin by applying lateral traction or by grasping the tumor with forceps.

For a generalized process, a representative lesion should be chosen. For a solitary plaque or large tumor, diagnostic information may be found in the thickest or most unusual region. Underlying disease activity in an annular or expanding plaque is usually found in the leading edge. In a bullous process it is important that the biopsy specimen include not only the blister but, most important, the blister edge and adjacent normal skin, where pathologic changes may be diagnostic.

Shave Technique

The shave technique may be used for either a biopsy or an excision. Please refer to Chapter 12 for detailed discussion.

Indications

The shave technique is primarily indicated for epidermal processes and some superficial tumors, when removal of a portion of the mass or process is sufficient for a diagnosis. However, it is difficult to adequately sample the dermis with the shave technique; thus use of the punch, incision, or excision technique provides more tissue for diagnosis in dermal processes and in most cases when a skin malignancy is suspected.

Preoperative Considerations and Technique

Create the sterile field by preparing and draping the skin. Infiltrate the local anesthetic around the biopsy region (Fig. 1). For polypoid or pedunculated growths, a small amount infiltrated carefully into the base of the lesion should provide adequate anesthesia. When lidocaine with epinephrine is used, adequate anesthesia is usually achieved once vasoconstriction is apparent (seen as relative blanching of the skin).

Keep in mind that tissue infiltration often leads to loss of the natural skin markings and vasoconstriction, which may obscure the tumor margin and underlying anatomic structures such as the vermillion border of the lip. Therefore the

area for biopsy or important landmarks should be outlined with a surgical marking pen before infiltration of the anesthetic.

Stabilize the skin by applying lateral traction or by grasping the tissue with forceps in the case of a polypoid or pedunculated lesion (Fig. 2). Using a No. 11 or 15 scalpel blade held parallel to the skin surface, make the incision on a plane that is even with the skin surface. With forceps, elevate the specimen as the incision is made (Fig. 3).

Obtain hemostasis after the shave is completed by applying pressure or by the topical application of 20% aluminum chloride or Monsel's solution. Apply these with a cotton-tipped applicator using a gentle, rolling motion over the defect (Fig. 4). It is usually not necessary to use electrocautery. Apply a small amount of antibiotic ointment to the wound, and cover it with a Band-Aid or simple dressing.

Always be careful to avoid crushing the specimen by inadvertently pinching or squeezing with the forceps. "Crush artifact" is a common occurrence with indelicately handled specimens and compromises the histologic evaluation, thereby detracting from the value of the biopsy.

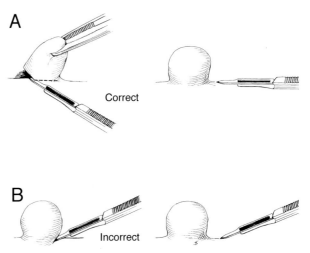

Correct

Incorrect

FIG. 3. Make the incision on a plane that is even with the skin surface.

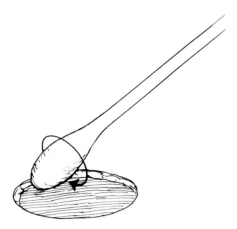

FIG. 4. Obtain hemostasis after the shave is completed by applying a chemical styptic such as aluminum chloride or Monsel's solution.

Variations

Some practitioners advocate the deep shave technique using a flexible blade for biopsy of an inflammatory process or for removal of certain benign tumors (Fig. 5). However, considerable practice and skill are needed to ensure adequate depth of the biopsy. Therefore most practitioners prefer to use other biopsy methods to ensure consistently reliable and uniformly deep biopsy specimens (i.e., punch or incision).

Risks, Complications, and Contraindications

The risks and complications associated with the shave technique include bleeding, infection, and scarring. A small, proportional scar may result and may be atrophic or, rarely, hypertrophic. When the biopsy includes the basal layer, a hypopigmented scar may result. If the technique is performed carefully, it usually yields a smooth postoperative defect and a minimal scar that is flush with the adjacent skin.

Punch Technique

Indications

The punch is an expedient method used most often for routine diagnostic biopsies. It provides a full-thickness spec-

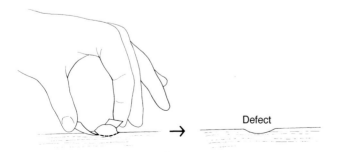

FIG. 5. Excision using the deep shave technique.

imen when a small amount of tissue is sufficient for histopathologic analysis. Thus it is ideal for taking a sample of a large plaque or tumor, or to obtain a sample of a diffuse disease process from a representative lesion. Occasionally, the punch technique may be used for complete excision and may be considered for a small papule or condition such as a dilated pore of Winer.

The punch technique is usually employed to obtain specimens for light microscopic study. It also provides adequate material for special studies such as immunofluorescence, electron microscopy, or cell culture or for cellular and molecular biologic studies. This technique may also be used when tissue is needed for microbiologic culture to confirm bacterial or fungal infection in an immunocompromised patient.

General Principles and Preoperative Considerations

The punch technique uses a trephine or cylindrical blade which, when rotated under gentle pressure, creates a circular specimen and corresponding defect. The trephines range in diameter from 1.5 to 8 mm. The size selected is influenced by anatomic location, skin laxity, size of the pathologic process, and quantity of tissue needed for diagnosis. In most clinical settings a 3-mm punch is adequate. However, if microbial culture is necessary in addition to histopathologic study, use a 4- or 6-mm punch instrument, to minimize the number of biopsy specimens; then the specimen can be divided.

After the location for biopsy is selected, examine the natural skin lines in the area to facilitate selection of the proper orientation for the biopsy. The ideal orientation allows closure parallel to or within the skin lines. Orient the biopsy specimen by applying countertraction (perpendicular to the relaxation plane) to the adjacent skin before and during the biopsy. When the skin is released, the circular defect is usually passively converted into an oval defect. The resultant oval defect is thereby oriented within skin lines and, consequently, closes easily and with less tension upon wound closure.

Techniques

Prepare and drape the area. Skin preparation is accomplished using alcohol, povidone-iodine (Betadine), pHisohex, or Hibiclens solution, among others. Superficially infiltrate 1 ml of local anesthetic into the biopsy region. The local anesthetic used most often is 1% lidocaine with epinephrine (1:100,000); however, plain lidocaine may be preferable in some circumstances, such as patients with tachyarrhythmias or coronary artery disease or patients taking beta-blocking medications; in certain anatomic locations use of epinephrine may be contraindicated (i.e., in biopsy of the fingers, toes, and penis).

Using one hand, stabilize the biopsy site by stretching the

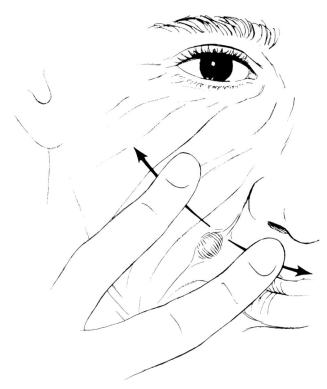

FIG. 6. Apply countertraction to stabilize the biopsy region. Stretch the skin in opposing directions on a plane that is perpendicular to the skin lines.

skin in opposing directions, in the plane that is perpendicular to the skin lines (Fig. 6). While applying gentle, downward pressure, rotate the punch instrument continuously until the punch blade penetrates through the skin into the subcutaneous layer (Fig. 7). This is usually achieved when the hub, or blade handle, meets the skin. Exceptions to this rule include anatomic regions where the skin is very thin with little sub-

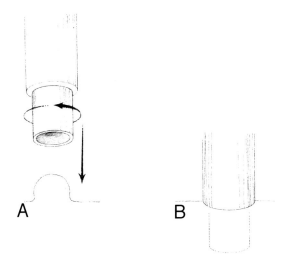

FIG. 7. While applying gentle pressure, rotate the punch instrument as the blade penetrates through the dermis to the subcutis.

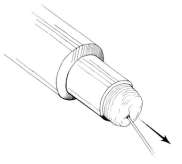

FIG. 8. If the specimen remains in the trephine, it may be extracted with the tip of the hypodermic needle, forceps, or a skin hook.

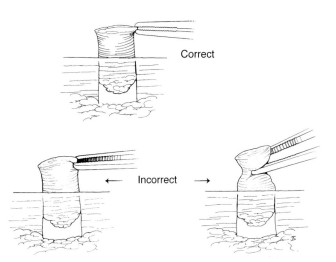

FIG. 9. Gently grasp the edge of the specimen, to avoid crushing the tissue.

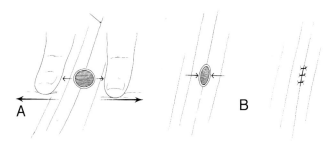

FIG. 10. (A) Apply tension in opposing directions, on the plane that is perpendicular to the skin lines. **(B)** When the traction on the skin is released, the skin edges fall into an oblong defect oriented within the skin lines, which is closed more easily.

cutaneous fat or where vessels are close to the surface, such as the eyelids or dorsal aspect of the hands or feet.

Remove the punch instrument carefully, since the specimen often remains attached to the subcutaneous tissue. Occasionally, the specimen may detach and the plug of skin remains inside the tubular blade. If this occurs, the specimen may be extracted using a forceps, a skin hook, or the tip of the hypodermic needle (Fig. 8). Gently grasp the edge of the specimen, to avoid crushing the tissue, and pull the specimen out to cut its base free with scissors (Fig. 9).

When the traction on the skin is released after the tissue is removed, the skin edges fall into an oval defect oriented within the skin lines (Fig. 10). The exception to this is when the biopsy site is within a tumor mass, in which case the density of the tumor may prevent relaxation of the defect or obliterate any natural skin lines.

Hemostasis is achieved with pressure and suturing. The defect can be closed with interrupted sutures. The choice of suture material may vary with anatomic location of the biopsy. For example, nylon is preferred on the trunk and extremities, whereas on mucous membranes it is common to use an absorbable suture material. However, use of nonabsorbable suture, such as nylon, on the mucous membranes may have advantages in some circumstances, since it produces less tissue reaction and allows the surgeon more control over the time to suture removal. The diameter of the suture is determined by wound tension and by anatomic considerations. Generally, 5-0 or 6-0 suture material is used on the face or neck, where there is less tension and rapid healing, whereas 4-0 or 5-0 suture is preferred on the extremities and trunk, where there is more tension and sutures are left in place longer. Similarly, the size of the needle used varies according to the anatomic location and associated considerations. On the face, where the skin is delicate and repairs are detailed, smaller needles such as P-3 and P-1 are indicated. In contrast, when operating on the trunk, where the dermis is thick and more fibrous, a larger, thicker needle facilitates accuracy and is less likely to bend under pressure. When a biopsy specimen is taken from within a large tumor, usually no suturing is required.

As an alternative, the punch defect may be allowed to heal secondarily by granulation. This is acceptable, but keep in mind that suturing the defect has the advantages of facilitating hemostasis, leading to optimal cosmesis, and minimizing healing time.

Postoperative Considerations

Wash the operative site with saline after 24 hours. After washing, apply topical antibiotic ointment to the wound, followed by a simple dressing. Repeat this each day until suture removal. The time until suture removal may vary according to the anatomic site of the biopsy. Subtle anatomic differences in vascularity and motion influence the rate of healing; sutures on the face may be removed in 4 to 5 days, those on the extremities in 10 to 14 days, and those on the back in 2 to 3 weeks.

Adverse Sequelae and Complications

Possible complications of a punch biopsy or an excision include bleeding, infection, and a small scar. If the wound is large, or if the wound is under tension, closure of a circular defect has the inherent risk of central tension and the formation of dog-ears at the ends.

Incisional Biopsy

Indications and General Principles

An incisional biopsy removes part of a lesion. An incisional biopsy is indicated when a full-thickness specimen (including subcutis) is necessary for diagnosis but the tumor or nodule is so large that, if excised, it would present a potential reconstructive challenge, or when diagnosis for tumor staging is necessary. Often, treatment options for certain malignancies vary greatly based on diagnosis and classification schema.

Examples of clinical situations in which an incisional biopsy is indicated include inflammatory processes, vasculitis, infections caused by atypical mycobacteria or deep fungal infections, lupus vulgaris, and some neoplasms including cutaneous T-cell leukemia and leukemia cutis. The location that yields the most information should be selected carefully (i.e., a representative lesion in a generalized process, the region containing the edge of a bulla, or the most atypical segment of a pigmented plaque).

Incisional biopsy may also be advantageous in a setting in which multiple pieces of tissue are needed for histopathologic study or culture. For example, rather than performing multiple biopsies in a febrile neutropenic patient with suspected plaques, the tissue from an incisional biopsy may subsequently be divided for bacterial and fungal cultures, in addition to pathologic study.

The main problem with an incisional biopsy is the potential to miss the diagnostic portion of a pathologic process. This is the strongest argument against use of this technique, particularly when malignant melanoma is the suspected diagnosis. In the case of malignant melanoma, a full-thickness biopsy specimen is imperative, but controversy exists regarding the merits versus the disadvantages of incisional vs. excisional biopsy.

Techniques

After sterile preparation is completed, administer local anesthetic in the manner described previously. Stabilize the skin using outstretched fingers, a forceps, or a skin hook. Using a scalpel, make a full-thickness incision through the

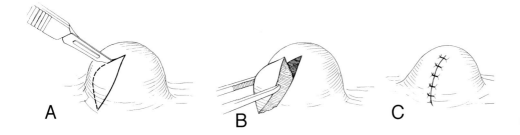

FIG. 11. Wedge technique.

tissue process. The scalpel should be held perpendicular to the skin surface during the incision so that the wound margins are at 90-degree angles and to a uniform depth. Make the incision in the shape of a wedge or an ellipse. Remove the specimen delicately with forceps, with care not to crush the tissue; then cut it free at the base with scissors or scalpel. After removing the specimen, achieve hemostasis with direct pressure, topical hemostatic agents, or electrocautery. Once hemostasis is adequate, sew the tissue closed with simple interrupted sutures (Fig. 11). Apply antibiotic ointment and a simple dressing.

Postoperative Management

Wound care includes daily cleansing of the biopsy site with saline, application of topical antibiotic ointment, and daily dressing changes until sutures are removed.

Adverse Sequelae and Complications

The risks and complications include those which apply to any surgical procedure, namely, bleeding and infection. If the incisional biopsy is made into a malignant growth, wound healing may be delayed.

Excisional Biopsy

Indications

An excisional biopsy may be considered for a suspected lesion of relatively small size, in cases when the treatment will not be altered (i.e., excision is desired, regardless of diagnosis), or in a clinical setting in which it is advantageous to minimize the number of procedures performed. The most controversial, yet potentially serious, indication for an excisional biopsy is when a pigmented nevus has clinically atypical features suspicious for malignant melanoma. One argument in favor of an excisional biopsy is that the most histologically atypical focus could be missed with an incisional biopsy; thus, unless the size or anatomic location are prohibitive, complete excision is indicated.

DEFINITIVE EXCISIONS

Surgical excisions may be carried out in many ways and with techniques that may vary with each surgeon. Different approaches to excisions usually are a function of the pathologic process and the clinical setting. The surgeon's ability to achieve excellent results is directly related to technique and appreciation of basic surgical principles. Factors that exemplify this principle include atraumatic technique, accurate apposition of the wound margins, and placement of scars within the direction of the skin lines. Conditions that cannot be controlled include anatomic location, age of the patient, and preexisting disease or conditions which have the potential to complicate wound healing.

In the following sections examples provide general principles of excision techniques for selected pathologic processes to illustrate the spectrum encountered in clinical practice. These examples may be applied and modified to solve each clinical problem encountered.

Preoperative Considerations

A differential diagnosis is formulated before surgery based on history and physical findings; then the diagnosis is confirmed by biopsy. Whether a lesion is benign or malignant may influence the planning and execution of an excision. If a lesion is expected to be benign (i.e., an intradermal nevus), make every effort to minimize removal of normal tissue at the periphery of the tissue process. Usually, it is wise to carry out an excision with margins that are only 1 to 2 mm beyond the clinically apparent margin. Certainly, for a benign tumor the postoperative result should be less conspicuous than the lesion itself.

If a malignancy is suspected or has been previously confirmed, a wider excision margin is indicated. The recommended excision margins may vary with diagnosis. If a preoperative diagnosis is not available, it will be possible to go back later for more definitive treatment after histopathologic evaluation is made. In the case of a basal cell carcinoma a 3-mm margin is usually recommended, but occasionally as much as 5-mm may be necessary. For squamous cell carcinomas wider margins are indicated (i.e., 4 to 5 mm). For a dermatofibrosarcoma protuberans or malignant melanoma the treatment is based on accepted guidelines for excision of the tumor with margins of normal tissue. These considerations, coupled with anatomic factors and tumor size, often contribute to the creation of a greater reconstructive challenge.

Techniques

Many methods for excision are used, and these may be carried out in varying configurations. Common excision techniques, grouped according to their shape, include elliptical, wedge shaped, and circular. Anatomic considerations and the size of the growth dictate the best approach.

Circular Excision

A circular or circumferential excision is carried out just outside the perimeter of the lesion. This technique may be chosen when the region involved overlies cartilage (i.e., nasal tip or ear rim) or when the best repair orientation or approach is not apparent before the excision.

Before executing a circular excision, using a surgical marking pen or suitable ink, identify the perimeter of the tumor and draw a line 1 to 2 mm outside the clinically apparent tumor margin following the entire circumference (Fig. 12). This should be drawn with the skin relaxed and before infiltration of local anesthetic, to best visualize the tumor margin. Then stabilize the skin by applying traction on the tissue that surrounds the tumor, to administer the local anesthetic. When the skin is properly anesthetized, make the incision following the drawn lines. With the scalpel held at a 90-degree angle to the skin, incise in a continuous motion around the tumor circumference down through the dermis to the subcutaneous tissue. Using blunt dissection, while lifting the tumor mass with forceps from one edge, gently dissect the specimen free from the fatty subcutaneous tissue

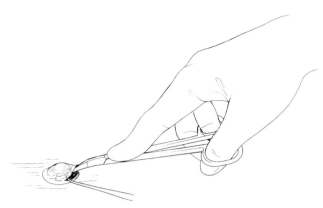

FIG. 13. While lifting the specimen from one edge, gently undermine using blunt dissection.

(Fig. 13). Achieve hemostasis once the tissue specimen is removed.

After the circular excision is completed, often, the circular defect becomes elongated with its long axis oriented according to local skin tensions. Examine the defect carefully to take advantage of this phenomenon, if possible, when designing the repair.

Based on the anatomic region, size of a defect, and intrinsic properties of the involved skin, the design for repair of a circular defect should allow closure in the most anatomically functional and cosmetically advantageous manner. In some cases repair options may be limited to grafts or rotation flaps. Often, the circular defect can be converted into an ellipse, which is oriented within the skin lines or in the long axis of the defect created by adjacent skin tension. In the appropriate circumstances bilateral advancement flaps can be created that arise from within the ellipse drawn as described earlier. The triangular subcutaneous flaps, which remain attached to their blood supply, are advanced to fill the defect when they are sutured to each other.

Wedge

The wedge excision technique creates a V-shaped resection defect; two incisions are made that begin on each side of a tumor and meet at a point below the tumor (Fig. 14A–C). This technique is most often used for removal of tumors arising on the perimeter of rounded anatomic structures (i.e., the auricle, the lip, the nasal alar rim, and, occasionally, the eyelid). Approach, technique, and repair vary depending on the anatomic site at which a wedge excision is executed.

Ellipse

In dermatologic surgery most excisions are designed to be fusiform (i.e., in the shape of an ellipse). In contrast to a true geometric ellipse, the apices of the surgeon's ellipse are not rounded but come to a point as in a convex lens.

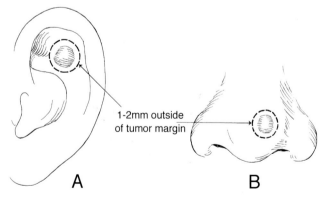

1-2mm outside of tumor margin

A   B

FIG. 12. Before executing a circular excision, using a surgical marking pen or suitable ink, the perimeter of the tumor should be identified and a line drawn outside the clinically apparent tumor margin following the entire circumference.

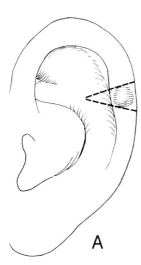

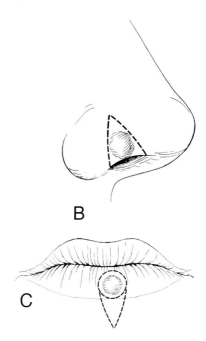

FIG. 14. The wedge excision technique is used most often for removal of tumors arising on the perimeter of rounded anatomic structures such as the auricle, the lip, the nasal alar rim, and, occasionally, the eyelid.

Thus under ideal circumstances an elliptic excision yields a lenticular defect. The angles formed at the apices of an elliptic excision are a function of the length-to-width ratio of the ellipse, which is more acute as the sides of the ellipse become longer. Optimally, the angle at each apex should be less than or equal to 30 degrees. To achieve this, ideally, the sides of the ellipse should be of equal length and the length should be three to four times that of the width (Fig. 15). In most cases the sides of an elliptical excision are slightly rounded. Bennett has described a design method, which he refers to as ''tangent-to-circle excision,'' that maximizes the ability to achieve an acute angle at the apices of a surgeon's ellipse by using straight sides. In general, regardless of the method used, the goal is to create a defect that, when closed, creates little distortion of tissue and is under minimal tension across its entire length, thus avoiding the formation of a dog-ear.

An advantage of the lenticular defect is that it can be oriented with its long axis within or parallel to skin lines and wrinkles (Fig. 16). With the ideal fusiform morphologic features and by the placement of multiple sutures in close proximity to one another in a layered fashion, the wound edge tension is distributed across the length of the incision, and the resultant scar has a tendency to lie flat and to remain thin, while maintaining a natural contour with respect to underlying anatomic structures.

Variations

An ellipse is versatile because it may be modified in various clinical situations and in difficult anatomic locations. Morphologic variations of an ideal ellipse include the M-plasty, the ''lazy S'' (S-plasty), and the crescentic variation. These may be helpful in specific circumstances. For example, use an M-plasty to shorten an ellipse when in proximity to a vital structure such as an eye or the nasal ala. Convert the ellipse into a lazy S (S-plasty) to take advantage of natural creases or anatomic curvature. Use a crescentic variation over convex surfaces such as the forearm, where one side is longer than the other. However, if these alternatives are not ideal or feasible, other excision designs must be considered (Figs. 17–20).

When the design of an ellipse is modified in the aforementioned manner, because the sides of the resultant defect are not of equal length, asymmetry leads to tissue distortion, uneven tension, and the formation of a dog-ear upon suturing (Fig. 21). When this type of defect results after wound clo-

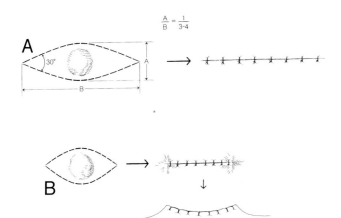

$$\frac{A}{B} = \frac{1}{3\text{-}4}$$

FIG. 15. The ideal surgeon's ellipse is lenticular or fusiform. Optimally, the apical angles should be less than or equal to 30 degrees and the length-to-width ratio should be 3 or 4 : 1.

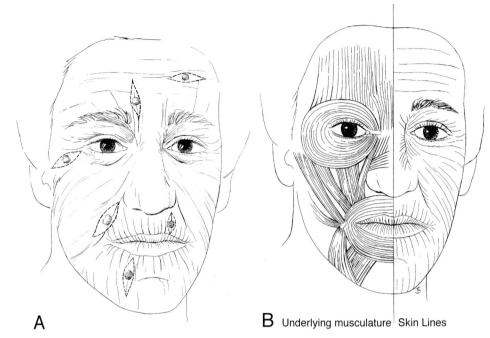

A

B Underlying musculature | Skin Lines

FIG. 16. (A) The fusiform ellipse should be oriented within skin lines and wrinkles. **(B)** The skin lines and wrinkles that are formed arise perpendicular to the underlying muscles.

sure, it is important to repair the dog-ear abnormality. If the asymmetry of the wound margins is not significant, one manner in which to prevent dog-ear formation is to close the wound following the rule of halves. Correction of asymmetry by both of these methods is discussed later.

Ellipse Excision Technique

Before beginning the excision, prepare and drape the region in the usual manner. Before infiltration of anesthetic, design the incision or outline the perimeter of the tumor with a surgical marking pen. Infiltration of the local anesthetic leads to swelling and blanching (epinephrine effect), which distorts and disguises the skin markings and border. Infiltrate the local anesthetic around the perimeter of the lesion and then deep below the base of the lesion, taking care not to puncture or infiltrate the lesion. Usually less than 1 ml of local anesthetic is necessary for papules or plaques smaller than 1 cm in diameter.

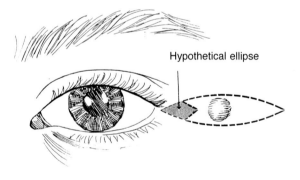

Hypothetical ellipse

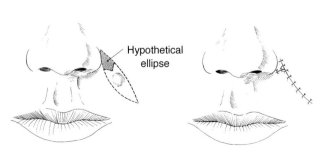

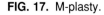

Hypothetical ellipse

FIG. 17. M-plasty.

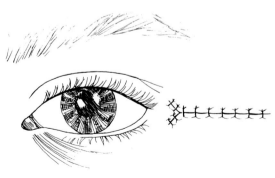

FIG. 18. M-plasty.

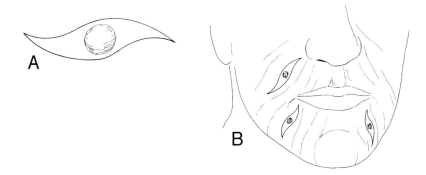

FIG. 19. S-plasty ("lazy S").

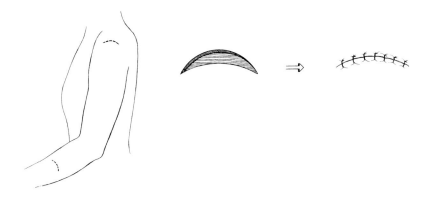

FIG. 20. Crescentic ellipse variation.

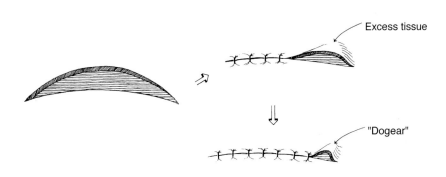

Excess tissue

"Dogear"

FIG. 21. Because the sides of the defect are of unequal length, the asymmetry may result in the formation of a dog-ear on suturing.

90°

FIG. 22. Hold the scalpel perpendicular to the skin surface, and incise to a uniform depth in the subcutis.

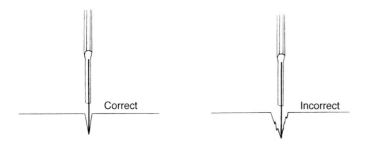

FIG. 23. To avoid an irregular or jagged wound margin, the incision should be smooth and continuous and the minimal number of passes should be made with the scalpel.

Once the sterile preparation and anesthesia are complete, make the incision along the previously drawn lines in the following manner. Stabilize the skin with lateral tension to allow for precision and control (Fig. 22). Hold the scalpel perpendicular to the skin surface, incising to a uniform depth within the subcutaneous layer. The motion should be smooth and continuous to avoid an irregular or jagged wound margin (sawing motion should never be used) (Fig. 23).

The techniques and preferences for beginning the execution of an elliptical excision may vary with each surgeon. Some surgeons advocate beginning the incision at one apex of the drawn ellipse and incising in a single motion toward the other apex. It is also possible to begin in the center and incise toward each apex in separate motions. It is possible to begin at each apex with separate incisions that meet in the center (Fig. 24).

What matters is that the incisions do not overlap to yield jagged edges on the sides of the ellipse, and that the incisions do not overlap to form cross-hatches at the apices (Fig. 25). To avoid these errors, it is advisable to use careful, deliberate, continuous motions of the scalpel and to minimize the number of incisions made. If any irregularities are apparent after the incision is made, it is advisable to trim the margins delicately with either scissors or the scalpel before wound closure. This ensures smooth, vertical wound margins for good tissue apposition (Fig. 26).

After the incision is made through the dermis and to the subcutis along the entire perimeter of the specimen, following the drawn lines, blot the area dry to aid visualization. Then grasp the tissue specimen delicately with fine-toothed forceps, taking care not to crush it, and cut the tissue free at its base with scissors or a scalpel. Ideally, blunt dissection carried out with Iris scissors allows separation of a uniformly thick specimen in the subdermal layer with minimal injury to microvasculature and nerves (Fig. 27). Be careful to ensure uniform thickness around the entire specimen (Fig. 28). Depending on the size of the defect and anatomic location, some undermining may be necessary to achieve a primary closure with minimal tension. Undermine carefully using blunt dissection within the plane that separates most easily and, if possible, where undermining is least likely to cause injury to vessels and nerves. The most appropriate or ideal level in which to undermine varies with anatomic location. Be careful to undermine at the same level all the way around the perimeter of a defect and to do so only as far as is neces-

sary to provide mobility of the tissue as a consequence of separating fibrous subcutaneous attachments.

The ideal technique for undermining is as follows. Using a forceps or skin hook, gently raise one lateral edge of the defect. Using the other hand, insert unopened, blunt-tipped scissors into the subcutaneous tissue at the chosen level, then gently open the scissors and pull back on the instrument. When repeated around the circumference of the defect, this motion gently separates the tissues, pulls fibrous attachments apart, and results in mobility of the overlying skin with mini-

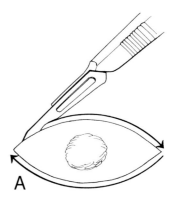

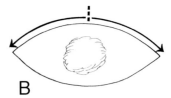

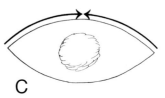

FIG. 24. The execution of an elliptic excision may be carried out in several manners.

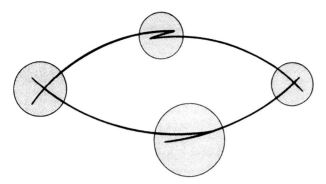

FIG. 25. When incising an ellipse, it is important to avoid overlapping or jagged edges and to avoid cross-hatches at the apices.

FIG. 27. Blunt dissection allows separation of the specimen in the subdermal layer with minimal injury to microvasculature and nerves.

mal injury to subcutaneous nerve fibers and blood vessels. It is advisable to avoid using the scalpel or scissors to cut the tissues free, since a sharp dissection significantly increases the probability of injuring nerves and cutting vessels. It may be difficult to avoid inadvertent injury to nervous tissue and or vessels; thus undermining should always be performed delicately and the plane for undermining should be chosen carefully. The amount of undermining necessary and appropriate varies with each case and is influenced by the anatomic location, the size of the defect, and intrinsic properties of the skin. For example, on the scalp the ideal plane for undermining is in the subgaleal space, which is relatively avascular and the level at which injury to hair follicles is least likely. On the face, undermine within the subcutaneous tissue considering the underlying nervous innervation (i.e., undermine superficially on the cheeks and temple, but deeper on the forehead). On the trunk and extremities the level for undermining may vary but should be above the underlying muscle fascia.

After undermining is completed, examine the defect to determine the degree of tension. Decide whether a simple or a layered closure will achieve ideal apposition of the wound margins by considering anatomic features, location, and size of the defect. In most cases a layered closure is preferable

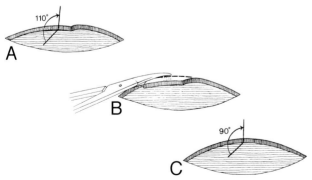

FIG. 26. If the wound edges are beveled or irregular after an ellipse is excised, it is advisable to delicately trim the margins to ensure ideal tissue apposition.

to a simple closure. Exceptions include a defect that is small, one under minimal tension, or one that is located on the eyelid.

Decide which size and type of suture to use based on the evident degree of tension and anatomic location. (Please refer to Chapter 9 for suture material selection.)

Obliterate any dead space at this time. If dead space is apparent, create subcutaneous tissue flaps, which may then be advanced toward one another and sutured together with 4-0 absorbable sutures before the placement of the subcutaneous-dermal sutures. In some cases horizontal mattress sutures may be required to achieve sufficient purchase in the relatively fragile subcutaneous tissue. Buried knots are not required at this deep level.

Although horizontal mattress sutures are occasionally used, they are generally contraindicated because of the vertical orientation of the dermal microvasculature and the consequent potential to strangulate the dermal plexus with horizontally oriented sutures . For this reason, vertically oriented subcutaneous sutures are preferable most of the time.

To approximate the subcutaneous dermal layer, place inverted sutures (with the knots buried) of absorbable material (i.e., monocryl or plain or chromic gut). Gently raise the lateral edge of the incision with a skin hook or fine-toothed forceps (e.g., Bishops) to provide visualization and allow accurate placement of the suture. Place the suture deep at the subcutaneous-dermal junction, and insert it so that it exits in the low to middle dermis. Then place the needle in the same site, at the same level, on the contralateral side, which corresponds to the opposing lateral edge of the incision. The suture material completes a loop when the needle is pulled out at the opposing subcutaneous-dermal junction. The two free ends of the loop should be deep, and as they are tied into a knot, the subcutaneous-dermal layers will be symmetrically approximated by the inverted suture (Fig. 29).

When placed carefully along the wound margin, the inverted subcutaneous-dermal sutures diminish the degree of tension on the epidermis, facilitate epidermal approximation, help create ideal circumstances for wound healing, and subsequently lead to a fine, thin scar.

Under ideal circumstances, after the deep sutures are placed the epidermis should be well approximated. Thus the minimal number of skin sutures may be placed. Choose the

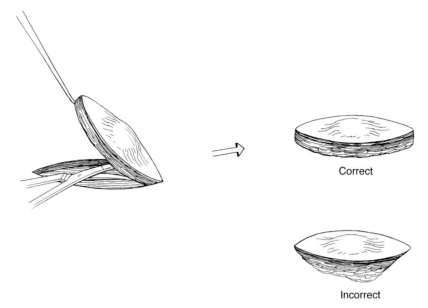

Correct

Incorrect

FIG. 28. After careful dissection, the specimen should be of uniform thickness when removed.

technique with which to suture the skin by considering multiple factors that include the size and nature of the defect, the tension on the wound, the anatomic site, aesthetic principles, and intrinsic properties of the skin. Once the ideal technique for wound closure is selected, the epidermis is sewn closed.

SUTURING TECHNIQUES FOR SKIN CLOSURE

Wound closure techniques are discussed below in some detail but are discussed in more detail in Chapters 10 and 14.

The most important goals in wound closure are to ensure approximation of the subcutaneous tissues and thus to obliterate any dead space, to achieve minimal tension on the epidermis, and to skillfully place the sutures so that accurate, symmetric apposition of the wound edges results.

Make decisions regarding technique for wound closure considering factors such as tension on the wound margins, anatomic location, and size of the incision. Close small incisions with simple interrupted and vertical mattress sutures. Other options include using a running continuous ''over-and-over'' suture or a running subcuticular stitch.

The number of sutures necessary to close an incision is influenced by the tension on the wound margins. Ideally the minimal number of stitches necessary to close a wound should be used. If there is no tension on the epidermis as a result of effective approximation of the tissues by deep sutures, fewer sutures may be necessary. If tension is evident at the wound margins, it is often advantageous to use more sutures in close proximity to each other (i.e., 1 to 3 mm apart and 1 to 2 mm from the wound margin), to distribute the tension (Lilliputian principle) (O'Sullivan, personal communication). This is in contrast to using fewer sutures or larger sutures of greater distance from the wound margins, in which case it is more likely that suture marks will result.

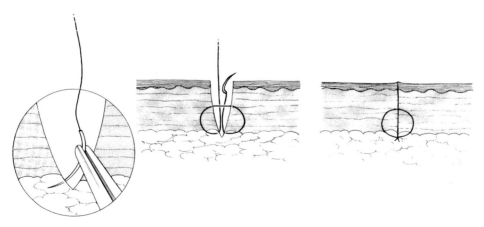

FIG. 29. Inverted subcutaneous-dermal suture.

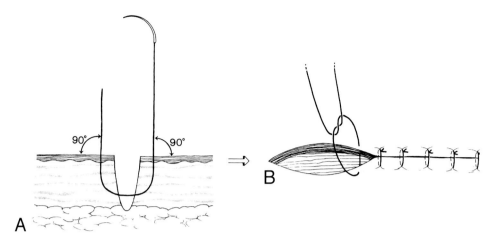

FIG. 30. Simple interrupted suture.

Simple Interrupted Suture

Simple interrupted sutures are used to close wounds of all types. They are sufficient for most biopsies and in all circumstances when the subcutaneous tissue layers are adequately approximated, or when there is no tendency for inversion of the wound margins. It is necessary to pay attention to the symmetry of placement and angle of needle entry and exit from the skin when placing a simple suture. Bilateral symmetry and perpendicular needle entry and exit are important to create an arc that will achieve ideal wound approximation with some degree of wound edge eversion. Simple interrupted sutures may also be used in combination with other types of stitch technique. For example, a simple interrupted suture may be used to supplement a running subcuticular stitch as a buttress, or in an alternating fashion with vertical mattress sutures, if tension is noted along the wound margin.

To place a simple interrupted suture, insert the needle into the skin at a 90-degree angle. Push it through the dermis where an arc is created in the subdermal space so that the needle reenters the dermis on the opposite side of the defect at a point equidistant from the opposing wound edge. The needle should exit the epidermis on the opposite side at a 90-degree angle, to then complete the arc upon tying a surgeon's knot. It is important that the insertion and exit points are equally spaced from the wound edges, but not too far from the wound edge. Be sure to place the suture at the same depth bilaterally so that on closure the skin edges will be accurately approximated. If sufficient depth is achieved into the subcutaneous tissue by the arc of suture material, when the suture is closed, the wound will be slightly everted. This wound eversion is ideal for wound healing and flattens after suture removal. In the process of tying the surgeon's knot, be careful to tie the knot in such a way that the tissue is gently approximated. If the suture is too tight, there is a risk of creating ischemia at the wound margin (Fig. 30A and B).

When the wound edge skin is of unequal thickness or the two sides of the defect differ in property, inaccurately opposed skin edges may result when the suture is placed in the manner described above. In these circumstances the bites of tissue taken by the needle on each side of the defect may need to be of unequal depths to compensate and to reestablish accurate apposition of the dermis and epidermis (Fig. 31A). For example, a deeper bite of tissue is recommended on the thinner side and a more superficial bite on the thicker side so that the wound edges are accurately approximated when the suture is closed. As an alternative, a vertical mattress suture could be used. When the sutures are placed carefully, accurate skin apposition with slight wound edge eversion results and yields a flat scar (Fig. 31B and C).

Running Continuous Suture

Wound closure may be achieved quickly with a running continuous suture. This has also been referred to as a continuous over-and-over stitch. To begin, the needle is placed and carried through the tissue as in a simple interrupted stitch. However, when the surgeon's knot is tied, the suture is not cut free. Instead, the needle is inserted in the next point where a suture is deemed necessary along the wound margin, the loop is completed, and this motion is repeated sequentially for the entire length of the defect (Fig. 32A). Once the incision is sutured closed, when the final loop is completed, a surgeon's knot is tied to secure the running stitch. While placing each loop in a continuous stitch, be careful that each is placed in a symmetric manner with equal bilateral depth penetration to ensure accuracy of wound edge approximation and to avoid wound edge inversion (Fig. 32B).

Running Subcuticular Suture

The running subcuticular suture may also be referred to as an intradermal continuous suture. Use of a running subcuticular stitch has the advantage that it lacks the risk of "track" or "suture marks." Consider using a running subcuticular stitch either when the incision is under minimal tension and located in a prominent location (of cosmetic

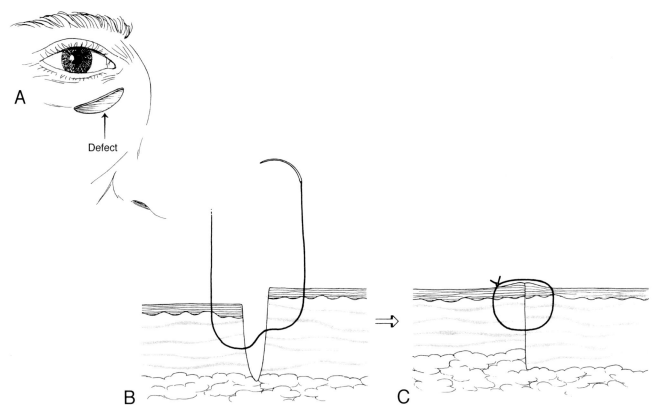

FIG. 31. When the wound edges are of uneven thickness, the bites of tissue taken should be of unequal depth to compensate and thereby to establish accurate wound edge apposition on closure.

concern to the patient) or when the defect is in a region of tension, where it would be beneficial to leave the sutures in place for a longer period.

To place a running subcuticular stitch, begin by securing the end of the suture material. To do this, insert the needle into the skin at one end of the incision and bring the needle out through the defect. Pull the suture through almost completely; then grasp it with a hemostat, where a knot is tied in the distal of the suture material. With one hand, gently retract the suture material, while the needle is carefully inserted into the subcuticular dermis at the proximal end of the incision. Take a bite of tissue so that the needle is brought through the dermis horizontally to exit several millimeters distal to the point of entry, at the same depth. Pull the suture material through; then place a similar bite into the opposite wound margin. Try to stagger the bites as they are placed

alternately on one side and then the other. When the end of the incision is reached, bring the needle from the inside of the incision out through the cutaneous surface, where another knot is tied to secure the suture (Fig. 33).

When placing a running subcuticular stitch, be careful to place the suture at the same level within the dermis on both sides, to ensure that the opposing edges of the wound are symmetrically aligned when approximated.

One disadvantage is that wounds closed with a running subcuticular stitch tend to lack tensile strength; therefore the suture should stay in place longer before removal (i.e., 3 weeks instead of 2). In areas of stress (e.g., the back or extremities), if necessary, reinforce the running subcuticular stitch with interrupted sutures of 5-0 nylon, or 6-0 on the face. The additional layer of nylon skin buttress sutures may be removed early to obviate suture marks. Leaving the run-

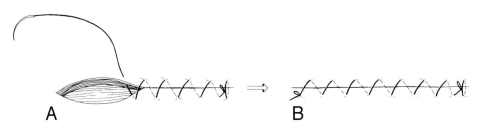

FIG. 32. Running continuous suture.

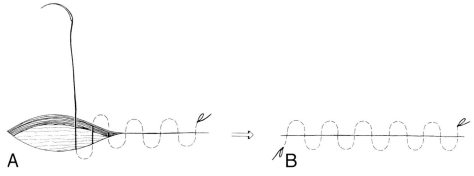

FIG. 33. Running subcuticular suture.

ning suture in place for a longer period may diminish the tendency for the scar to widen in the months following suture removal.

Vertical Mattress Suture

Vertical mattress sutures are indicated where there is potential for wound edge inversion or when the defect is in a region under tension. When placed carefully, vertical mattress sutures create a degree of wound edge eversion while ensuring accurate wound margin apposition. In some circumstances, vertical mattress sutures may be alternated with simple interrupted sutures.

The technique for placement of a vertical mattress suture is as follows. Place the needle into the skin at a 90-degree angle, and insert it through the subcutaneous tissue in an arc so that the needle exits at a point equidistant from the opposite wound margin, also at an angle of 90 degrees. Insert the needle back into the same side, entering between the exit site and the wound margin and emerging superficially (high up in the dermis, below the epidermis) into the center of the wound. Complete the stitch by inserting the needle into the opposite wound margin at the same level so that it exits between the wound edge and the original insertion site. Tie the suture material into a surgeon's knot (Fig. 34A–D).

Half-Buried Horizontal Mattress Suture

Half-buried horizontal mattress sutures are very useful in specific circumstances. Usually this stitch technique is used for securing the tip of a flap or at the corner of a geometric or V-shaped incision. This stitch provides tensile strength in approximating a portion of a wound margin while minimizing the number of skin sutures necessary.

To place a half-buried horizontal mattress suture, the needle is inserted into the skin and exits in the middermis into the center of the wound. The needle is then inserted horizontally into the point of the flap or tip of the V of the opposite tissue edge, at the same level. Push the needle through horizontally so that it exits at the same level at a point which is symmetrically opposed to the entry point on the other side of the tissue flap. Insert the needle back into the dermis of the original wound margin at the same level, and push it through to exit a few millimeters away from the original entrance point. Tie a surgeon's knot to complete the stitch (Fig. 35).

Horizontal Mattress Suture

Horizontal mattress sutures are used infrequently but are most useful in wounds under tension. The horizontal orientation of the stitch has the potential to create a degree of local ischemia upon wound closure as a result of the vertical orientation of the dermal microvasculature.

Other methods of closing wounds without suturing include the use of staples, skin tape, and adhesive materials.

COMPLICATIONS

The risks associated with an excision are those faced with any surgical procedure: infection, bleeding, and scar formation. These are minimized with the use of sterile technique, an adequate occlusive dressing to obviate hematoma and minimize swelling, and conscientious postoperative wound care.

ADVERSE SEQUELAE

If the sides of a defect are of unequal length, or if an ellipse is too short with respect to its width, puckering of excess tissue at one or both ends may occur when the sides are approximated to close the wound. As a result, the skin will not lie flat. Skin elasticity and anatomic concavity, convexity, or curvature contribute to this problem. Various terms are used to refer to the resultant undesirable defect, including dog-ear, tissue protrusion, pucker, tricone, and standing cutaneous cone (Fig. 36).

Do not underestimate the benefit of taking a few moments to correct this type of deformity. If the dog-ear is allowed to remain, the deformity and the scar become more noticeable as a result of the elevations at the ends of the wound.

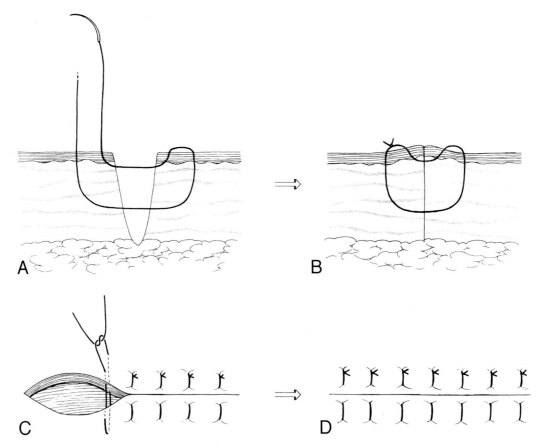

FIG. 34. Vertical mattress suture.

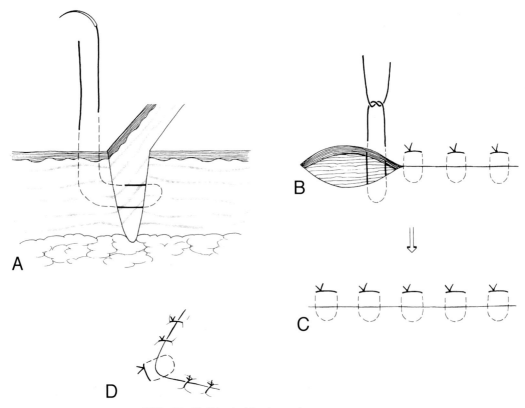

FIG. 35. Half-buried horizontal mattress suture.

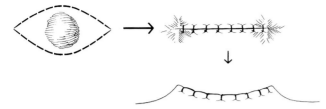

FIG. 36. (See Fig. 15B and C diagrams.) If the sides of an ellipse are of unequal length or if an ellipse is too short relative to its width, puckering of excess tissue at one or both ends may result.

These elevations are particularly conspicuous when a shadow is cast (i.e., in indirect lighting). If tension is evident, when the length is too short relative to the width, extension of the ellipse distributes the tension more effectively, while simultaneously correcting the dog-ear. Uncorrected, when tension is a component, compensatory widening of the scar may result. Rarely, the dog-ear may flatten with time.

Dog-Ear Repair

Techniques to correct a dog-ear involve extending the wound followed by removal of a triangle of excess tissue. Ideally, if this is indicated, extension of the incision should be placed within relaxed skin tension lines and conform to nearby anatomic structures. Several approaches have been described, all of which are based on the same principle and essentially differ in the angle created with extension of the incision for the repair. Some of the terms used by other authors include hockey-stick, curved, and L-shaped repair.

One approach to repairing a tissue protrusion is to simply extend the original ellipse in a bilaterally symmetric manner, which leads to a linear extension of the incision. Use this technique if the length of the ellipse is too short with respect to its width (Fig. 37).

If the standing cone of skin is resulting from asymmetry in the ellipse or asymmetry secondary to anatomic factors (i.e., curvature such as that seen overlying the shoulder or on the distal aspect of an extremity), correct the dog-ear by extending the incision on one side at an angle that is determined to best align with nearby skin lines. This asymmetric manner of extending the incision corrects the tissue deformity and leads to a flat scar that becomes camouflaged within the anatomic contours and skin lines (Fig. 38).

The method to correct the tissue protrusion is as follows. To plan the repair, gently lift the standing cone of skin with a forceps or skin hook and examine the deformity. Make a short, right-angled or curved incision at the end of the existing incision (i.e., extend the defect). If possible, extend the incision into the adjacent skin lines, or turn the scissors so that the curvature of the instrument follows the tissue's natural anatomic curvature. Elevate the tissue with a skin hook or forceps, gently pull the excess tissue over the opposing wound edge, and delicately trim off the overlapping triangle

of skin with curved, fine scissors. This extends the ellipse a few millimeters while eliminating the dog-ear, but without sacrificing excess tissue. When the new wound margins are pulled together and closed with sutures, the incision lies flat, yielding a more cosmetically acceptable scar. This technique may be varied to accommodate different clinical situations. Each surgeon eventually develops his or her own techniques, which may be modified to fit each clinical setting.

Rule of Halves

When the sides of a defect are unequal in length, it is useful to close the defect following the rule of halves. The rule of halves is a guide to suture placement that leads to even distribution of tissue on opposing sides of a defect and thereby prevents dog-ear formation.

To close a wound following the rule of halves, begin each stitch by inserting the needle at the midpoint of one side of the defect. Then guide the needle through the subcutaneous tissue and epidermis so that it exits at the midpoint of the opposing side of the defect. Using the suture material, carefully approximate the two margins so that the two midpoints are coincident. Then tie a surgeon's knot. In a sequential

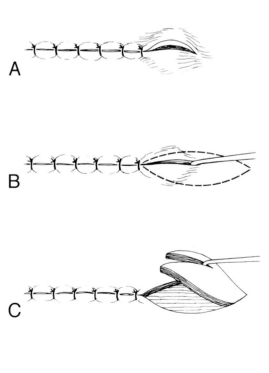

FIG. 37. One approach to repair a tissue protrusion is to extend the original ellipse in a bilaterally symmetric manner, which extends the incision linearly.

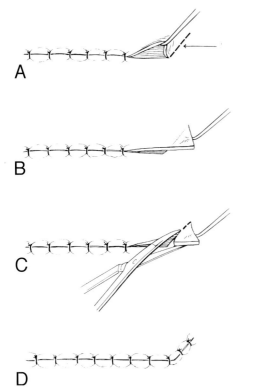

FIG. 38. If the dog-ear results from asymmetry in the ellipse, extend the incision into the adjacent skin lines. Make a right-angled or curved incision, the angle of which varies with each case; then the excess tissue is removed as a triangle.

fashion, repeat this procedure at the center of each remaining free edge, to progressively approximate the margins of the defect (Fig. 39).

EXAMPLES OF EXCISION TECHNIQUES FOR SELECTED PATHOLOGIC PROCESSES

Excision of Nevi and Other Benign Tumors

Indications and General Principles

Most melanocytic nevi are benign tumors that can be excised with a narrow margin. Benign nevi are classified based on histologic criteria (i.e., the location of nevus nests in the skin: intradermal, compound, or junctional). However, it is difficult to know clinically where the true histologic margins lie. Therefore all nevi should be examined carefully (i.e., note size, pigmentary pattern, blurring or irregularities of margins) before determining margins for excision.

Certain clinical features including size and irregularities in shape, border, or pigmentary pattern may correlate with underlying histologic features of architectural and or cellular atypia. Although any of these features may be found in benign nevi, when irregularities in size, shape, and pigment are all observed simultaneously, these nevi are referred to as clinically atypical or dysplastic nevi. Histologic examination is essential to confirm a diagnosis based on clinical grounds for dysplastic nevi. The importance of the diagnosis is the potential of these atypical pigmented melanocytic nevi

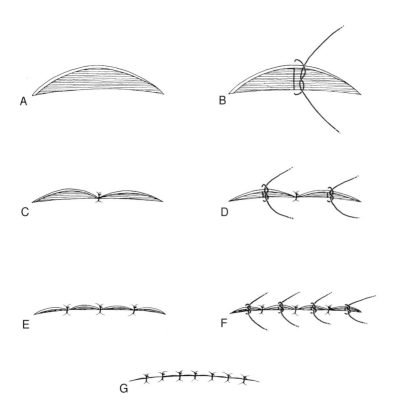

FIG. 39. The rule of halves.

to be either precursors of or markers for malignant melanoma. Thus these atypical nevi may require a wider margin for excision (or subsequent reexcision) based on the degree of histologic cellular or architectural atypia.

The guidelines for reexcision of atypical nevi and melanoma are based on clear histologic margins and principles of immunology. After histologic atypia is confirmed in a pigmented melanocytic nevus, or if a pigmented lesion is found to be a malignant melanoma, standard guidelines are available for recommended surgical reexcision margins taken from the edge of the scar. It is prudent to establish the diagnosis before treatment; for this reason, initially all nevi should be excised with a narrow margin. It is not advisable to excise a suspected pigmented lesion with a wide margin at the time of the biopsy in attempt to avoid a later reexcision.

Much controversy exists with regard to diagnosis and treatment of atypical melanocytic proliferations. Thus this is not discussed further in this text beyond the recommendation that currently accepted guidelines should be followed for proper treatment.

Reexcision of a melanocytic nevus is usually carried out by drawing an appropriate margin on each side of the scar, then designing an ellipse which, when excised, includes the entire scar and extends to a uniform depth in the subcutis. Some surgeons prefer to recreate the original defect, before executing the reexcision; that is, the sutures are removed and the wound is reopened to establish the orientation with respect to subcutaneous tissue. If the wound has already healed, an incision is made along the scar. Then the appropriate excision margins are drawn, and the reexcision is carried out.

Most nevi are excised in an elliptical fashion. The approach may vary based on the anatomic site. It is not uncommon for a nevus to show elongated growth in an orientation that lies within the skin lines. Similarly, after a nevus is excised, if the longest axis of the defect is not oriented favorably, convert the ellipse into the skin lines before closure to achieve optimal results.

Techniques and Variations

The region should be prepared, draped, and anesthetized. Using a surgical marking pen, design the incision (Fig. 40A). Stabilize the surrounding skin with one hand. Incise the skin down to the subcutis in one smooth, continuous motion. Be careful to hold the scalpel perpendicular to the skin surface to avoid a bevel. Take care to avoid cross-hatching the incision at the points of the ellipse. To facilitate this, start at each end of the ellipse, moving the scalpel toward the center. After the incision is complete, using the tips of Iris scissors, bluntly dissect the specimen free from the underlying subcutis; then gently lift it from one pole and cut it free. Leave a pad of uniformly thick subcutaneous tissue on the base of the specimen (Fig. 40B). The thickness of this may vary based on anatomic location and should be influenced by

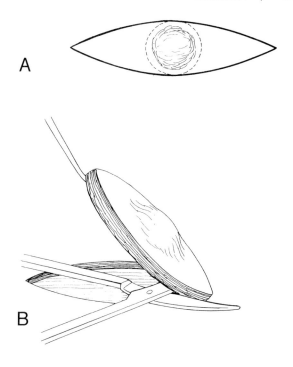

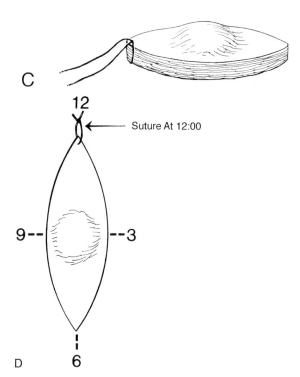

FIG. 40. **(A–C)** Excision of a nevus or benign neoplasm. **(D)** Use suture or make a diagram for orientation of the specimen.

preoperative diagnosis; that is, a thin layer should be adequate in the case of a benign lesion, whereas full-thickness subcutaneous tissue may need to be resected with the tissue specimen for malignant tumors. In the case of malignant melanoma, the excision should be carried out down to but not including the underlying fascia.

Once the specimen is removed, make a diagram and use suture to identify the orientation of the specimen for the pathologist's or Mohs technician's orientation, (e.g., a suture may be placed at the 12 o'clock position) (Fig. 40 C and D). Examine the defect to determine whether undermining is necessary. If there is little tension or if the anatomic site is one with lax tissue, undermining may not be needed. However, on sites where tension is apparent, such as the upper back, it is advisable to bluntly undermine at the fatty subcutaneous tissue layer. Undermining divides the fibrous tissue attachments and creates local flaps to advance toward one another to approximate the wound margins without tension.

Hemostasis should be achieved at this time. If the defect is small, pressure may suffice; however, electrocautery may be needed. Keep in mind that thermal injury to the wound margins may slow or complicate wound healing; therefore it is important to avoid any such injury to the wound edges.

The beneficial effect of a layered closure on wound healing justifies its use in most circumstances. A layered closure is indicated when a defect is large, under tension, or located in a region of motion such as the shoulder or back.

Using forceps, taking care not to crush the skin edges, gently lift back the skin edge to facilitate placement of deep subcutaneous sutures, if necessary, followed by a more superficial closure in the subcutaneous-dermal layer. Using absorbable suture material such as 5-0 or 4-0 monocryl, place inverted sutures with the knots buried. Careful placement should effectively approximate the dermis, ideally diminishing tension from the epidermal margins. This allows wound healing under minimal tension. The absorbable subcutaneous sutures continue to add tensile strength to the newly formed collagen network of the dermis for weeks after the skin sutures are removed.

Base the decision for choice of suture material and its size on evident degree of tension and anatomic location. In general, use 6-0 suture material on the face, 5-0 on the trunk where minimal tension is observed, and 4-0 or 5-0 suture on the extremities and overlying joints or in regions of motion.

Postoperative Management

Conscientious postoperative wound care is imperative. Ideally, the incisions should be covered by a layer of topical antibiotic ointment, followed by an occlusive dressing (gauze) for the first 24 hours. After the initial dressing is removed, wound care should consist of frequent or daily cleansing with saline followed by antibiotic ointment and a clean dressing until suture removal. In locations such as on the face or anterior chest, wound care regimens using saline compresses and daily occlusive dressings may be beneficial for wound healing. Elsewhere, wound care regimens may be more simple.

Adverse Sequelae and Complications

The potential adverse sequelae, as previously described, include bleeding, infection, and scar formation. Scar formation is influenced by several aforementioned individual factors and minimized by proper orientation of the surgical incision and accurate wound apposition. Bleeding, hematoma, or seroma formation is unlikely if an adequate pressure dressing is applied in the first 24 to 48 hours. The risk of infection is reduced by frequent dressing changes, which are carried out daily until suture removal. Many practitioners have preferred techniques and methods of postoperative wound care. One popular approach is to use a dressing that is left in place for 1 to 2 weeks without changing. Although this is convenient, the risk of wound infection is increased, which may result in dehiscence of the wound at the time of suture removal; therefore this type of dressing is not recommended. Daily dressing changes, although time-consuming, minimize postoperative infections and facilitate early intervention in the event of any complication.

Cysts

Indications and Preoperative Considerations

The most commonly excised benign cysts are usually epidermal or pilar (trichilemmal) cysts. In most cases these are asymptomatic. However, some cysts may become large, ruptured, or secondarily infected, which can lead to painful recurrent infections. Some individuals are susceptible to the development of numerous cysts. Surgical excision may be considered electively in these aforementioned circumstances.

The most important principle of cyst excision is that the entire cyst wall, in addition to its punctum (in an epidermal cyst), must be removed to prevent recurrence. However, this may be a challenging process, depending on the size of the cyst and its anatomic location, and further complicated by rupture or infection. Prior infections can lead to fibrosis, which may make excision technically more difficult. Before proceeding with surgical excision, if there is a history or any ongoing sign of infection, a preoperative course of oral antibiotics is recommended, until all signs of inflammation have subsided.

Techniques and Variations

When planning the excision, it is advisable to determine whether the cyst is freely movable; usually this is determined by palpation. If possible, identify the punctum (Fig. 41A).

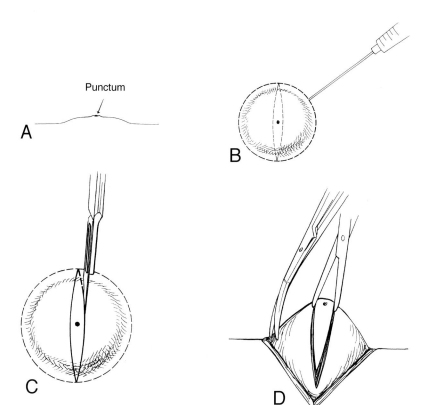

Punctum

A

B

C

D

FIG. 41. Cyst excision technique. **(A)** Identify the punctum, then draw a narrow ellipse that overlies the cyst and includes the punctum. **(B)** Infiltrate superficially outside the palpated margins of the cyst wall, then deep, in a circumferential manner. **(C)** Make the incision delicately so that the scalpel does not penetrate the underlying cyst wall. **(D)** Hold on with gentle traction to the thin ellipse of skin to allow elevation of the cyst while gently dissecting the cyst wall free from the adjacent tissues.

Guided by palpation, mark the perimeter of the cyst with a surgical marking pen before infiltration of the local anesthetic. A narrow ellipse is drawn that overlies the cyst and includes the punctum.

Block anesthesia is used. Stabilize the skin with one hand while infiltrating the local anesthetic into the skin. Often the skin overlying the cyst is so thinned that infiltration of local anesthetic directly over the cyst is not possible. Infiltrate superficially outside the palpated margins of the cyst wall, then deep, in a circumferential manner (Fig. 41B). Be careful not to infiltrate into the cyst, since this could lead to puncture of the cyst wall or may cause distention and possible rupture of the cyst. Once adequate anesthesia is achieved, it may be difficult to discern the cyst margins.

Make the incision delicately so that the scalpel penetrates only the epidermis and partially into the dermis, without incising the cyst wall (Fig. 41C). During the incision, apply gentle, lateral traction to facilitate separation of the overlying skin, in order to visualize the cyst wall as soon as it is reached. The cyst wall usually appears to be glistening white, in contrast to the dull hue of the dermis. When the cyst wall is identified, carefully extend the entire incision to that depth. At this point, using curved Iris scissors, divide the fibrous and fibrinous adhesions between the cyst wall and the adjacent tissues, delicately dissecting the cyst free from the surrounding dermis and subcutaneous tissue. Using forceps or a hemostat, if possible, hold on with gentle traction to the thin ellipse of skin that contains the punctum, to allow elevation of the cyst without the risk of rupturing the cyst

wall. Be gentle so that the skin does not separate from the cyst wall. When the cyst is stabilized in this manner, visualization and dissection of the cyst wall from its bed are facilitated. If significant fibrosis is evident, it may be difficult to dissect the cyst free without inadvertent rupture of the cyst wall. Make every attempt to keep the cyst intact or to minimize extravasation of the cyst contents.

If the cyst has been infected and ruptured with resultant fibrosis in the surrounding subcutaneous tissue, the cyst is less likely to be freely mobile. In this instance it is advisable to excise the entire cyst along with the fibrotic tissue, so as to avoid leaving any cyst wall fragments behind. Before excision, draw an ellipse overlying the cyst that is wide enough to allow complete removal, and proceed to excise the ellipse in the manner discussed above (Fig. 42).

Obtain hemostasis with pressure or electrocautery after the cyst wall has been completely removed. Examine the defect to identify any residual cyst wall fragments, all of which should be removed. Obliteration of the dead space is an essential consideration at this point. If there is residual dead space, it becomes a potential site for accumulation of blood or serous fluid, and this dead space may eventually lead to a depressed defect. To obliterate the dead space, undermine peripherally in the subcutaneous tissue plane, thus creating subcutaneous tissue flaps, which are advanced toward one another. Approximate these flaps with horizontal mattress sutures of monocryl, Vicryl, or other absorbable suture material. The subcutaneous dermal layer is closed with inverted absorbable monocryl sutures. Close the skin

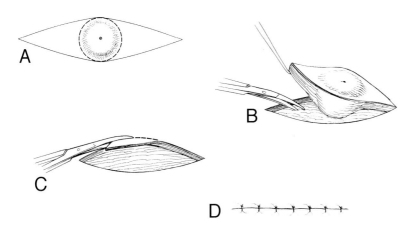

FIG. 42. In some circumstances the entire cyst is excised in an ellipse that includes the overlying skin and the surrounding fibrotic tissue.

edges with interrupted sutures of nonabsorbable suture material. If a cyst is large, the overlying skin is often thinned. Once the deep tissues have been approximated, redundant epidermis may be evident, which may be trimmed before suturing. Sometimes the thinned epidermis must be sacrificed to achieve satisfactory wound closure. In either case, trimming may necessitate lengthening of the wound to achieve a smooth, contoured closure. As an alternative, the thinned skin may be included in the ellipse that is sacrificed in the design of the cyst excision.

The techniques used for removal of a pilar cyst differ slightly from those for excision of an epidermal cyst. Trichilemmal (pilar) cysts are primarily located on the scalp. This anatomic site is highly vascular; thus hemostasis may be more challenging. Pilar cysts do not have an apparent punctum and are not attached to the overlying scalp epithelium. It is not always necessary to excise an ellipse of skin when removing a pilar cyst.

After preparing the affected region, plan the excision based on the location and size of the cyst. It is unnecessary to shave the overlying area when removing a pilar cyst. Although some surgeons prefer to shave the area to aid visualization, it has been shown that preoperative shaving of the region may lead to an increased risk of secondary infection. Either draw an ellipse that overlies the cyst or make a linear incision directly over the cyst. Pull open the incision with lateral traction to expose the cyst, which is then dissected free and easily extracted intact, since the cyst wall is quite firm. Another accepted method of removing a pilar cyst involves a linear incision directly overlying the cyst, which is then extended into the cyst. The area is then vigorously massaged to express the cyst contents first, followed by extraction of the cyst wall. This incisional method of cyst removal is discussed in Chapter 11.

Hemostasis is achieved with pressure and approximation of the defect. Subcutaneous sutures are not required after removal of a pilar cyst. The epidermis is sewn closed using interrupted sutures. Colored suture material such as 4-0 or 5-0 Prolene is recommended because it is easily visualized and differentiated from scalp hair at the time of suture removal.

Postoperative Management

Postoperative management differs minimally from other procedures. Cover the incision with a topical antibiotic ointment and a pressure dressing for the first 24 hours. Cleanse the wound daily with saline, then apply a fresh layer of antibiotic ointment and a gauze dressing. On the scalp and hair-bearing regions it may be difficult to achieve adherence of a bandage, so after the first 24 hours it may be possible to cover the incision with antibiotic ointment alone. It is advisable to shampoo daily, followed by cleansing the incision with saline and then applying antibiotic ointment.

Adverse Sequelae and Complications

If any portion of the cyst wall is left in place, a recurrence is inevitable. If the cyst wall ruptures leading to extravasation of cyst contents, this may lead to inflammation. This may be obviated by profuse irrigation with saline or antibiotic solution before wound closure. A depressed defect results when dead space is not obliterated. This is noticeable, since it tends to cast a shadow in indirect lighting.

The complications associated with cyst removal include bleeding, infection, and scar. In the case of epidermal cysts, if the dead space is inadequately obliterated, the risk of hematoma or seroma formation is increased. Even though the use of subcutaneous advancement flaps obliterates the dead space intraoperatively, it is essential to place a large pressure dressing to prevent the formation of a hematoma or a seroma after surgery.

Lipomas

Indications and Preoperative Considerations

Lipomas and angiolipomas are generally benign tumors. These soft, mobile subcutaneous nodules are well circumscribed and encapsulated. Malignant tumors of fat derivation are encountered but are relatively rare. Surgical excision of fatty tumors is indicated if there is any evidence of increasing

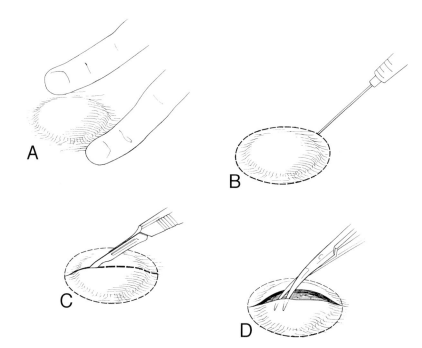

FIG. 43. Excision of a lipoma or subcutaneous mass. **(A)** Identify the margins of the subcutaneous mass by palpation. **(B)** Infiltrate the local anesthetic in a circumferential manner beginning superficially around the perimeter of the mass, then deep under the lipoma. **(C)** Make a linear incision and extend it to a uniform depth. **(D)** While delicately pulling the edges apart, dissect down to the mass to free it from the surrounding tissues.

size, tenderness, or pain. Excision may also be considered if a mechanical problem is associated with a tumor because of its large size or critical position (e.g., location on a finger). When many tumors are present, when they are recurrently traumatized or painful, it may be prudent to excise one or more for histopathologic examination, to confirm benignity.

Technique

Before surgery, identify the margins of the subcutaneous mass by palpation (Fig. 43A). Infiltrate the local anesthetic in a circumferential manner beginning superficially around the perimeter of the mass, then deep under the lipoma (Fig. 43B). Again, be careful not to infiltrate directly into the tumor. After anesthesia is complete, plan the excision by drawing an ellipse over the subcutaneous mass that is slightly narrower than the palpated margins and oriented in the skin lines directly over the tumor. Make a linear incision following the drawn markings, and extend it to a uniform depth in the subcutis (Fig. 43C). While delicately pulling the skin edges apart, dissect, using Iris scissors, through the subcutaneous tissue to the lipoma; then gently dissect it free from the surrounding tissues (Fig. 43D). Lipomas usually have an almost imperceptible, transparent glistening capsule, and are fairly easily differentiated from the normal surrounding fatty subcutaneous tissue by the difference in lobulation, color, and consistency. Because of these features, they are usually easily extricated from the surrounding tissue, and occasionally they may be popped out of the wound with external manipulation. An alternative technique involves making a solitary linear incision directly above the mass, through the skin, but not extending into the underlying tumor. After making the incision, dissect the tumor free in

the aforementioned manner. Consider this approach when the tumor or lipoma is small or when the anatomic location is not ideal for excision of a skin ellipse with the subcutaneous mass.

Using pressure and electrocautery, if necessary, obtain hemostasis. At this point, every effort should be made to obliterate the dead space. Subcutaneous flaps may be necessary and may be created at this time. Using inverted subcutaneous dermal sutures, approximate the dermis, then sew the epidermis closed. If excision of a large lipoma results in dead space that cannot be adequately obliterated, or if it is difficult to obtain adequate hemostasis within the peripheral vascular network, a drain is required. Place a drain so that it originates in a deep or dependent position within the dead space; then extend it through the overlying tissue to exit in the overlying epidermis, where it is sewn in place. Use of a Penrose drain is often sufficient and requires less care than a Jackson Pratt drain.

Postoperative Management

Topical antibiotic ointment should be applied to the incision after surgery. A pressure dressing is placed for the first 24 hours. Daily thereafter, the incision should be cleaned with saline and covered with antibiotic ointment and a clean dressing, until sutures are removed. If a drain is in place, dressings may have to be changed more frequently. The drain is removed once the amount of drainage diminishes, usually 3 to 7 days after surgery.

Adverse Sequelae and Complications

The adverse sequelae associated with lipoma removal are usually associated with residual dead space (i.e., hematoma

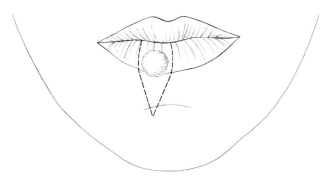

FIG. 44. The wedge excision technique is indicated in many cases. Significant defects may be created after resection of infiltrative tumors. When planning the lip wedge excision, mark the landmarks before surgery.

or seroma formation). If this occurs, it usually occurs within the first 24 hours and goes on to form a depressed defect or scar. The risk of infection is increased if a hematoma forms. The scar is usually minimal, since it corresponds to the linear incision made in the skin lines. A drain site incision scar is usually relatively small once contracture takes place.

Tumors of the Lip

Indications and General Principles

When excision of a tumor of the lip is planned, the surgeon must know the anatomy of the region and appreciate the aesthetic and functional properties of the lips to achieve optimal function and cosmesis on reconstruction. The laxity and intrinsic properties of the lips allow removal of as much as one third of the lower lip and one fourth of the upper lip without compromising function. Significant defects may be created upon resection of infiltrative tumors such as squamous cell carcinoma. In anticipation of reconstruction of such a defect, design the excision using the wedge technique, which is useful and indicated in many cases (Fig. 44). However, if a tumor occupies more than one third or one fourth of the involved upper or lower lip, respectively, resection with primary closure may lead to loss of function (i.e., compromised phonation or ability to open the mouth). Thus in the case of particularly large tumors it may be necessary to consider other, more complex approaches to reconstruction to optimize the cosmetic and functional result. Complex repairs for defects following excision of large tumors are not discussed here but may include the use of flaps, a pentagonal incision, an inferiorly based M-plasty, or a ''lip-switch.'' Decisions regarding the optimal reconstructive method should be based on the size of the defect, its location, surrounding anatomic features, and the surgeon's skill and experience.

The mucosal surface of the lip is separated from the external or cutaneous surface by the vermillion border. Surrounding anatomic contours separate what are often referred to as cosmetic units. Make every effort to respect and preserve these contours, which include the philtrum, the nasolabial lines, the labiomental crease, and the lateral commissures. Take advantage of these contours and natural skin lines by orienting scars within them. If an incision is made on the lip that cannot be oriented within the abovementioned anatomic units or contour lines, make sure to always orient the incision perpendicular to the underlying orbicularis muscle; this ensures scar orientation within the skin lines.

When reconstructing the lip after excision of a tumor, the most important goal is to preserve the vermillion border. Infiltration of local anesthetic into the lip creates swelling and blanching of the vermillion border, which may complicate the reconstruction. Therefore it is wise to mark these landmarks preoperatively with ink or a suture to facilitate reapproximation of the vermillion border. For best results, use block anesthesia when removing tumors from the lips.

Techniques and Variations

When planning the wedge excision, consider a point under the tumor at which the two lateral incisions will meet. (Imagine forming an isosceles triangle with the vermillion as the hypotenuse.) Draw the plan for excision, and begin planning reconstruction as much as is possible.

Stabilize the lip bilaterally by gripping it firmly; this simultaneously aids hemostasis by applying pressure to the inferior or superior labial artery. Consider holding the tissue with a piece of gauze to minimize slipping. Insert a dental roll or gauze between the lip and mandible to help keep the field dry and to facilitate exposure. Suction may be necessary. Make the incision, as planned, through the lip with a scalpel blade (No. 10 or 15) from the mucosa to the skin surface (Fig. 45). If a defect has already been created, as in the case of circumferential excision with frozen section control or Mohs' micrographic surgery, this step may be unnecessary. If the labial artery can be identified, it should be cauterized or clamped with a hemostat and ligated as soon

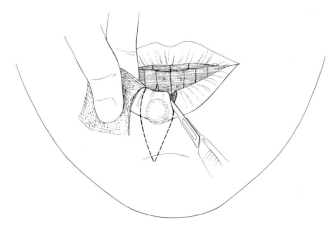

FIG. 45. Stabilize the lip by gripping it firmly; then make the incision as planned.

as possible using absorbable suture material (i.e., 5-0 polydioxanone [PDS] or Vicryl).

Once expeditious hemostasis is achieved, examine the defect for features of symmetry. The first step is to place a submucosal, buried inverted suture of absorbable material (i.e., monocryl) through the muscle to approximate the tissue and alleviate the tension. Approximate the vermillion border at this point using vertical mattress sutures of 6-0 nylon to ensure perfect alignment. If the width of the vermillion differs on either side, correction can be accomplished by removing a triangular piece of mucosa from the wider side to create a smooth vermillion border and avoid notching. Establishing symmetry is essential and can be challenging if the defect is off-center.

Once the vermillion border is reconstructed, the remainder of the reconstruction should follow. A layered closure is imperative. Begin with approximation of the muscularis using a strong absorbable suture such as 5-0 monocryl. Close the cutaneous surface of the lip with interrupted vertical mattress sutures of nonabsorbable material. If approximation of the defect results in tension or deformity, extend the incision inferiorly to alleviate and distribute the tension. Continue to extend the incision until the tissue lies flat when sutured closed. Undermining may be necessary. Another option to consider at this point is to use an M-plasty (Fig. 46).

The mucosal surface of the lip is closed last. Any excess tissue or asymmetry may be corrected by excising triangles of tissue on the mucosal side of the lip. Many dermatologic surgeons close the mucosal epithelium with buried interrupted sutures of absorbable suture material. Consider, also, the use of nylon or other nonabsorbable suture material for suturing the mucosal surface closed. The advantages of using nonabsorbable suture on mucosa include that it is less reactive and that it allows the surgeon to have more control over the time to suture removal (i.e., absorbable suture material does not effectively support the tissues if it is absorbed too quickly), which may be important if the wound is under tension. Preferences regarding this issue are usually based on each surgeon's experience.

Postoperative Care and Considerations

After the wound is gently cleansed with saline, apply a layer of an antibiotic ointment before the placement of a pressure dressing. Remove the sutures in 1 week (i.e., usually in 5 to 7 days on the cutaneous surface of the lip and in 7 to 10 days on the mucosal surface. The wound care involves daily cleansing with saline solution, followed by application of antibiotic ointment and a clean saline dressing (wet to dry).

Tumors of the Ear

Indications and General Principles

When malignant tumors arise on the ear, it is important to determine whether cartilage is involved before or at the time of surgery. If a tumor is superficial and involves only overlying skin, simple excision is executed, ideally with fro-

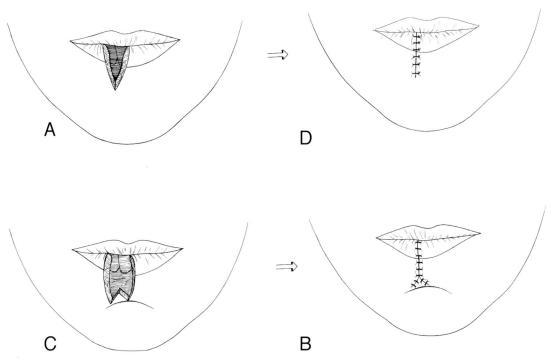

FIG. 46. Extend the incision until the tissue lies flat when sutured closed. To shorten the wedge or to preserve anatomic contours, an M-plasty may be used.

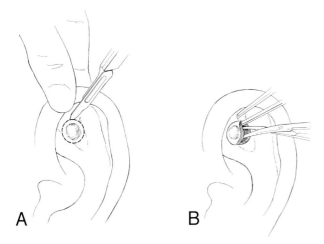

FIG. 47. (A) Circumferential excision of an ear tumor is carried out with a margin of tissue around the tumor perimeter. While providing support from behind the ear, make the incision down to perichondrium. **(B)** Gently undermine superficial to the perichondrium with the tips of delicate scissors.

zen section control of the margins. In most cases a circular or circumferential excision is carried out, excising the tumor with a 2- to 3-mm margin of tissue around the tumor perimeter and down to perichondrium. When a circular excision is performed in a concave region (i.e., the concha), it is possible to allow the wound to heal by granulation; however, in other locations and in general, second-intention healing does not lead to optimal cosmetic and functional results. In most circumstances, full-thickness skin grafts are necessary to repair defects that are overlying cartilage. The use of other advancement flaps may be indicated as well.

If cartilage is known to be involved before surgery or found to be involved during surgery, it will be necessary to sacrifice the involved cartilage, which usually leads to a more challenging reconstruction or unavoidable deformity. If the tumor is arising on or near the ear rim, often the best

results will be obtained with a wedge resection followed by primary closure. Use this technique when one fourth or less of the ear circumference is involved, to ensure maximal preservation of anatomic landmarks. If a wedge is not feasible or the involved tumor is very large, the use of a composite graft may be indicated.

Techniques and Variations

The size and location of a tumor on the ear determine the preferred method for excision. If a tumor is located on the helical rim or the earlobe, often the wedge technique is indicated. When a tumor arises in most other regions of the ear, such as the concha, the fossae, or on the antihelix, it is advisable to initially excise the tumor in a circumferential manner. Once the margins are clear of tumor, examine the defect to determine the optimal method for reconstruction. In some instances it may be advantageous to convert a circular excision defect into a wedge before reconstruction. These challenging and complex repairs are discussed in detail in the following chapters.

A circular excision on the ear is performed in a manner similar to use of this technique in other anatomic locations. The area is prepped and draped in the usual sterile manner. Before infiltration of the local anesthetic, plan the excision by first marking the perimeter of the tumor with a surgical marking pen. Make the incision gently yet deliberatively, holding the scalpel perpendicular to the skin surface, while providing support from under the ear with the nondominant hand or that of an assistant (Fig. 47A). The incision should extend to the perichondrium. After the circumference is incised, using a forceps, gently raise an edge of the tissue with one hand to facilitate removal of the specimen. Then gently undermine superficial to the perichondrium with the tips of curved Iris or other delicate scissors (Fig. 47B). Once the specimen is bluntly dissected free, hemostasis should be achieved; however, take caution, since extensive cauterization may lead to cartilage necrosis. Once the margins are

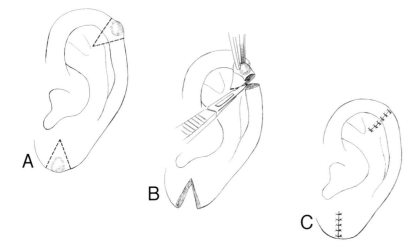

FIG. 48. If a tumor is on the helical rim or earlobe, a wedge resection may be executed. The V-shaped incision extends medially.

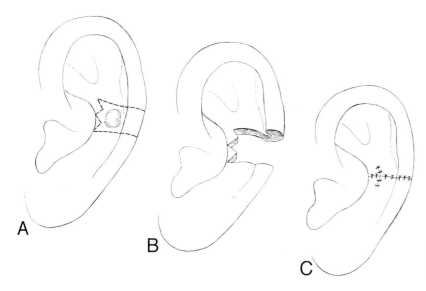

FIG. 49. Shorten the length of the wedge by converting the apex into a W or stellate shape to preserve the ear architecture.

determined to be free of tumor, decisions regarding reconstruction can be made.

Wedge excisions on the ear are usually executed with a V-shaped incision, which encompasses the involved tissue or tumor on the rim or helix and extends medially (Fig. 48). Ideally the angle at the apex should not exceed 30 degrees. If the length of the long axis of the incision is so long as to threaten preservation of the architecture of the helix, it is advisable to modify the wedge morphology. Manners in which a wedge may be modified include changing the angle so that it courses superiorly along the medial aspect of the helical rim (thus preserving the helix) or shortening the length of the wedge by converting the apex into a W shape (similar principle to an M-plasty) or into a stellate shape as described by Lask. These morphologic modifications, when designed well, take advantage of anatomic features and structural variations, which differ in each patient. Upon closure of these defects, it is hoped that maximal structural symmetry can be preserved, thereby achieving optimal cosmetic results (Fig. 49).

Postoperative Care and Considerations

After surgery, cleanse the incision with saline solution and apply a topical antibiotic ointment. A postoperative pressure dressing is important, as is the case in other anatomic locations; however, its placement is considerably more challenging on the ear. Some surgeons advocate the use of an adhesive such as mastisol and tape to secure a gauze bandage; others recommend applying generous amounts of gauze behind and around the entire ear, over which a cling bandage may be wrapped circumferentially around the head. The latter dressing style is considerably more bulky but also protects the surgical site and is less likely to become dislodged. Dressing changes should be performed daily, and the incision cleansed with saline each time. Each surgeon develops his or her preferences with experience.

Complications and Adverse Sequelae

Complications encountered when operating on the ears include infectious perichondritis or otitis externa, cartilage necrosis, and hematoma formation. Prophylactic oral antibiotics may be considered and are prescribed routinely by some surgeons in this anatomic location, to obviate the risk of *Pseudomonas* species infections, usually becoming evident as otitis externa or perichondritis. The risk of these infectious complications may be diminished by carefully cleaning the ear before surgery to diminish transient and resident bacterial flora. In addition, careful technique with gentle tissue handling, cautious hemostasis, and an effective occlusive dressing all aid in minimizing the chance of these adverse sequelae.

After a wedge resection, varying degrees of ear deformity may result, ranging from a notch in the helical rim to significant alteration in the shape or circumference of the ear. Since most ears are bilaterally asymmetric to begin with, if the patient has been warned preoperatively, adjustment to subtle alterations in size is possible. However, with large defects, alternative considerations such as the use of prostheses may be more acceptable to the patient.

SUMMARY

Excisional surgery involves the integration of surgical principles, cutaneous pathology, and technical skills. When an excision is executed with careful planning, attention to detail, appreciation of anatomy, and technical expertise, the postoperative result reflects the art of excisional surgery.

SUGGESTED READING LIST

1. Bennett RG. Fundamentals of cutaneous surgery. St. Louis: CV Mosby, 1988.

2. Davis TS, Graham WP III, Miller SH. The circular excision. Ann Plast Surg 1980;4:21.
3. Epstein E, Epstein E Jr. Techniques in skin surgery. Philadelphia: Lea & Febiger, 1979.
4. Hiller LA, Benton P, Hewlett JH. Surgery through the ages. New York: Hastings House, 1944.
5. Kneissel CJ. The selection of appropriate lines for elective surgical incisions. Plast Reconstr Surg 1951;8:1.
6. Moschella SL, Hurley HJ. Dermatology. 3rd ed. Phildadelphia: WB Saunders, 1992 (vol 2).
7. O'Sullivan, RB. Personal communication.
8. Ridge MD, Wright V. The directional effects of skin. J Invest Dermatol 1965;46:4.
9. Rook. Textbook of dermatology. 5th ed. Oxford: London: Blackwell Scientific, 1992.
10. Salasche SJ, Bernstein G, Senkarik M. Surgical anatomy of the skin. East Norwalk, CT: Appleton & Lange, 1988.
11. Salasche SJ, Roberts LC. Dog-ear correction by M-plasty. J Dermatol Surg Oncol 1984;10:6.
12. Schwartz SI, Shires GT, Spencer FC. Principles of surgery. 6th ed. New York: McGraw-Hill, 1994.
13. Smith JW, Aston SJ. Grabb and Smith's plastic surgery. 4th ed. Boston: Little, Brown, 1991.
14. Stegman SJ. Suturing techniques for dermatologic surgery. J Dermatol Surg Oncol 1978;4:1.
15. Stegman SJ. Planning closure of a surgical wound. J Dermatol Surg Oncol 1978;4:5.
16. Webster RC, Smith RC. Cosmetic principles in surgery on the face. J Dermatol Surg Oncol 1978;4:5.
17. Wheeland R. Cutaneous surgery. Philadelphia: WB Saunders, 1994.

Textbook of Dermatologic Surgery, edited by John L. Ratz.
Lippincott–Raven Publishers, Philadelphia © 1998.

CHAPTER 14

Complex Closures

David Brodland

Z-PLASTY

History

The Z-plasty is one of the oldest and most basic of skin flaps. The classic Z-plasty as we know it today evolved from the transposition flap. Although the typical image that is conjured by the term *Z-plasty* consists of two equal angles with a common middle limb that are mutually interpositioned, it should be recognized that there are many variations on this theme. In fact, when one looks closely, the essence of a Z-plasty can be found in some transposition flaps (Fig. 1).

Preoperative Plan

Z-plasties can be used to accomplish a number of goals in scar revision and wound closure, but the single most important effect of a Z-plasty is the lengthening of the skin in the direction of the middle limb of the Z-plasty. Whether a Z-plasty is used to repair an eclabion, eyelid retraction, or

David Brodland: Suite 303, 5200 Centre Ave., Pittsburgh, PA; University of Pittsburgh Medical Center, Shadyside Hospital, Pittsburgh, PA 15232.

incorporated in a flap or used as a flap, its most useful quality is the net gain of tissue in the required direction (Fig. 2). It also may be used as a technique to achieve a broken-line closure. Broken-line closures are useful to help camouflage long, visible scars by breaking up the continuity of the scar line and making it less easy to visualize. Z-plasties are also an effective way to redirect scars that are in an undesirable direction in relation to the relaxed skin tension lines. The Z-plasty may be the closure of choice when both lengthening of tissue in a certain direction and a broken-line closure or redirection of a scar are desirable.

Technique

The classic Z-plasty consists of three separate, equal limbs that form two adjacent, equal angles which, when interposed, redirect the middle limb (Fig. 3). The effect of this interposition of two angles is a net gain of length in the original direction of the middle limb. The theoretical gain of length from a Z-plasty is predictable in equal-angle Z-plasties (Table 14-1). A simple rule of thumb is that for every increase of 15 degrees there is a 25% theoretical gain in length.

One variation on the Z-plasty is Z-plasty closures of unequal angles. Combinations of unequal angles bring limitless

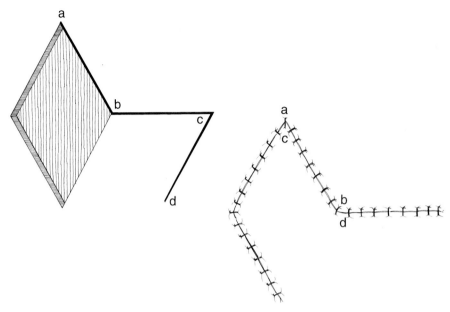

FIG. 1. Rhombic flap with highlighted Z-plasty inherent in the design (line abcd). Angles *b* and *c* will be interposed upon transposition of the flap.

alternatives to an individual planning a Z-plasty. These unequal-angled Z-plasty closures enable the surgeon to tailor the limbs of the incision as best suits the need. Indeed, when an acute angle is combined with a more obtuse angle, the result is a geometric figure that resembles a transposition flap (Fig. 4). The differences are that in a standard transposition flap there is a defect to be filled, and only the acute angle is undermined and mobilized entirely.

Z-plasties can be designed in a series along a common line or as a multiple-flap Z-plasty. Z-plasties in series can be used as a method of breaking up a conspicuous scar line, as well as

lengthening the tissue in the direction of the scar. This can be advantageous in the revision of a scar running counter to the relaxed skin tension lines and on a depressed, contracted scar line on a convex surface (Fig. 5). A multiple-flap Z-plasty is one in which obtuse angles of a classic Z-plasty are bisected and interposed between one another (Fig. 6).

Not surprisingly, the principle of directional tissue lengthening is useful in flap closure. In fact, it is this fundamental that makes transposition flaps so useful in wound reconstruction. The other basic forms of wound closure—rotation and advancement—rely almost entirely on the laxity of the donor

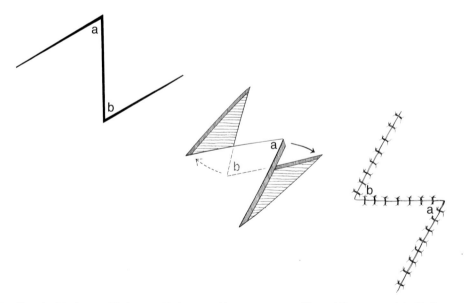

FIG. 2. Classic 60-degree Z-plasty with interposition or transposition of flaps *a* and *b*. Notice net gain in length in the vertical direction along line from *a* to *b*.

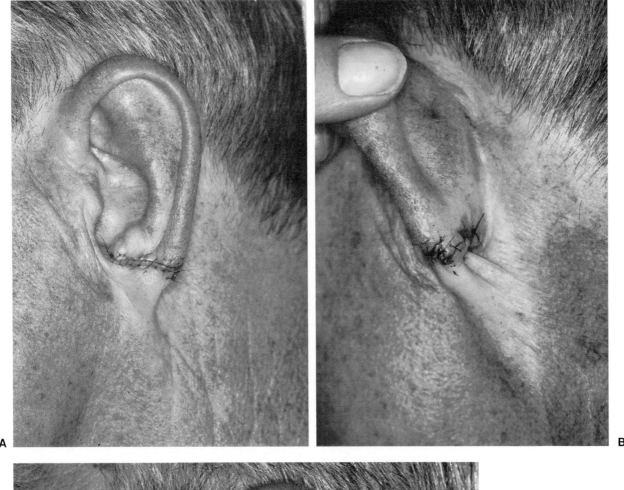

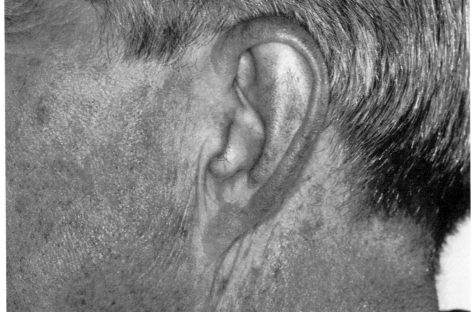

FIG. 3. (A) Wide excision of large A-V tumor of the ear lobe. **(B)** Z-plasty placed at margin of lobule to avoid notch. **(C)** Six-month follow-up.

TABLE 14-1. *Predicted net tissue gain with Z-plasty*

Z-plasty angle (degrees)	Tissue gain (%)
30	25
45	50
60	75
90	125

skin or the inherent elasticity of the flap skin. Z-plasty flaps do depend to some degree on rotation and advancement, but their unique feature can be thought of as a reorientation or redistribution of length. In all transposition flaps some form of Z-plasty can be found. The two angles of the Z-plasty are what are usually thought of as the transposing lobe of the flap and the peninsula of skin intervening between the flap and the defect (Fig. 1). Just as in a classic Z-plasty, these two angles are transposed. Many reconstructive surgeons recognize that wide undermining including that intervening peninsula of skin over which the flap will be transposed results in improved tissue dynamics. This fact is not surprising, since undermining both angles of tissue simply allows the principles of tissue gain in Z-plasties to be completely manifest. Even variations on a classic transposition flap such as the bilobed flap can be viewed as a Z-plasty–augmented closure (Fig. 7). Since the first lobe of the bilobe is often rounded, this flap is technically an S-plasty in series with a Z-plasty.

A Z-plasty is a unique closure technique that makes use of geometric principles to accomplish three things for the surgeon. First and most important, it adds a predictable amount of length in a predictable direction. Second, it can be used to realign unfavorably placed scars into better concordance with the relaxed skin tension lines. Third, it can be used as a camouflaging technique taking advantage of the aesthetic principle that short, broken lines are less visible to the casual observer than long, straight, unbroken lines.

W-PLASTY

History

To the individual who is unfamiliar with complex closures, the W-plasty may seem similar to Z-plasties. How-

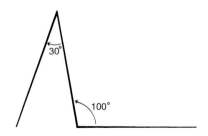

FIG. 4. Z-plasty of unequal angles. Note similarity of this Z-plasty and a transposition flap.

ever, other than multiple angles along the line of closure, they are very dissimilar with entirely different design processes, tissue dynamics, and purposes.

Preoperative Plan and Technique

A W-plasty is a simple excision in which the edges being approximated are characterized by multiple angles that result in a sawtooth-like appearance of the skin edge. In designing and incising this flap, the two opposing edges are cut in a complementary fashion so that the angles of the wound edge interdigitate. The wound edges fit together much like a puzzle and result in a zigzag incision line (Fig. 8). This is in contrast to the Z-plasty, which is actually made of triangular flaps that are interposed. The major advantage of the Z-plasty is the net tissue gain in a given direction. The main utility of a W-plasty, in contrast, is that it is a broken-line closure which, because of its very short, angular lines, gives the illusion that the incision is shorter or may make the scar less perceptible to the causal observer. Another advantage of the W-plasty is that if it is being used for a scar that is in variance to the relaxed skin tension line (RSTL), it can be designed so that a large portion of that line is placed in the direction of the RSTL and therefore would be less perceptible. In this regard, a W-plasty is the closure of choice to aesthetically improve a scar at great variance to the RSTL.

Although a W-plasty does not provide tissue gain in a particular direction, it does result in a more elastic scar than a straight, linear scar. A single straight line is rigid, since all tension vectors inherent in that scar are directed in the same plane. With a W-plasty, the tension vectors are directed in many different planes corresponding with the directions of the individual incisions. Therefore any long, straight-line scar extending across convex surfaces will be more conspicuous because of a greater tendency to be depressed. This depressed scar is most noticeable when not parallel to the RSTL or across convex surfaces because as the scar contracts, the line shortens and results in a linear depression in the skin. A W-plasty, with its inherent accordion-like elasticity and multidirectional contraction tension vectors, diminishes this effect (Fig. 9).

A W-plasty is simply an excision in which the advancing wound edges are cut in complementary, stair-step–like angles in which every other incised angle is placed in the direction of the RSTL. Generally the wound edges should fit together precisely, much like a puzzle. This necessitates meticulous preoperative planning and precise intraoperative incisions. One of the most challenging portions of the W-plasty is at each end of the incision. A technique that simplifies execution of this portion of incision is to draw an equilateral 30-degree triangle whose base is 90 degrees to the direction of the scar (Fig. 10). From the ends of the equilateral limbs of the triangle, begin a parallel, zigzagging incision along the scars.

One of the prime indications for a W-plasty is a scar that

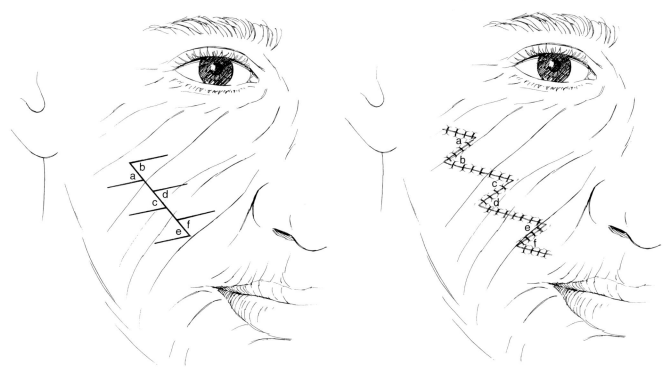

FIG. 5. Series of Z-plasties along a scar that is long and oriented against the relaxed skin tension line (RSTL).

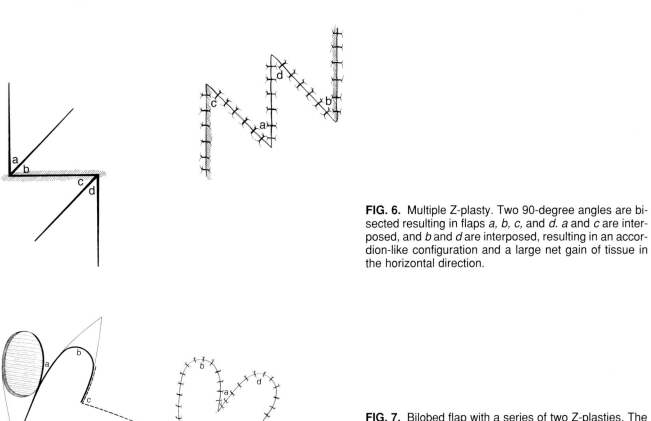

FIG. 6. Multiple Z-plasty. Two 90-degree angles are bisected resulting in flaps *a, b, c,* and *d. a* and *c* are interposed, and *b* and *d* are interposed, resulting in an accordion-like configuration and a large net gain of tissue in the horizontal direction.

FIG. 7. Bilobed flap with a series of two Z-plasties. The first is indicated by the darkened lines and results in interposition of angle *a* and flap *b*. The second is indicated by the hashed lines and is the interposition of flaps *c* and *d.*

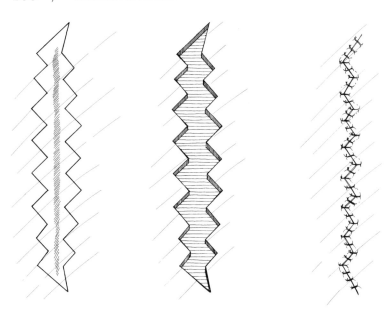

FIG. 8. W-plasty designed to form a zigzag line in which half of the lines are oriented in the RSTLs.

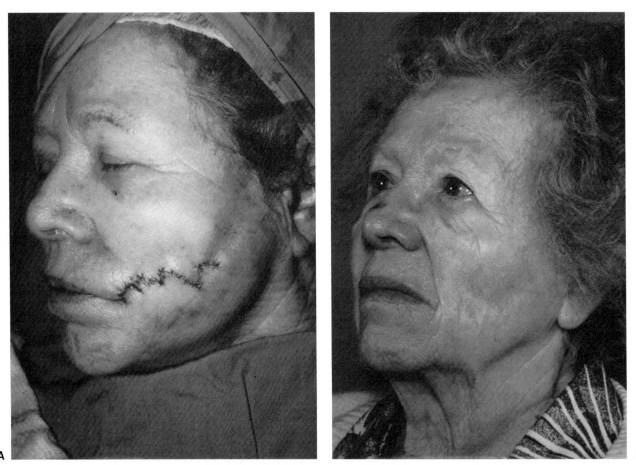

A   B

FIG. 9. (A) W-plasty in scar perpendicular to RSTL. Scar is composed of multiple short lines, some in the RSTL, that result in accordion-like elasticity of the scar. **(B)** Postoperative result 4 years later.

does not fall in the direction of the RSTLs. The greater the variance from the RSTLs, the greater the potential for improvement with a W-plasty. However, to achieve this desirable outcome, the preoperative planning should be designed such that one of the limbs of the W-plasty angle is placed precisely in the direction of the RSTL. This effectively changes a unidirectional scar that is entirely at variance to the RSTL into a series of connected, very short scars, 50% of which fall into the RSTL and thus are less conspicuous.

W-plasties can be useful in revision of curvilinear scars as well as linear scars (Fig. 11). When a curvilinear W-plasty is being planned, planning is done in the same fashion as for straight-line W-plasties with the exception that the angles to be cut on the skin edge to the inside of the arc are more narrow than the corresponding, complementary angles of the outer wound edge. This is necessary because the wound edges would be of unequal length and the larger angles on the outer wound edge compensate for this inequality.

Perhaps more crucial to the W-plasty than any other complex closure technique is the suturing technique. For a zigzag scar to blend in nicely and to become as inconspicuous as possible, meticulous care in approximating the wound edges is of paramount importance. The skin edges must be sutured so that the opposing sides are level, accurately placed, and

FIG. 11. W-plasty revision of curvilinear scar. The angles of the inner incision are slightly more acute but the length of the sides of the angles are approximately the same as in the outer incision.

everted. Six to 8 weeks after surgery a dermabrasive procedure may be beneficial to blend the scar into the surrounding skin.

V- TO Y-PLASTY

History

The use of the V- to Y-type repair or V- to Y-plasty preceded the popularization of the island pedicle flap. However, the basic principles are the same for these two closure techniques. They both advance a triangular flap in the direction of its base. Closure of the resulting defect is accomplished by simply recruiting skin lateral to the donor site to form a side-to-side approximation (Fig. 12). The triangular flap is advanced in the desired direction to correct a defect. In the case of an island pedicle flap the defect is in the form of a wound or loss of tissue that it will directly replace.

Preoperative Plan

A V- to Y-plasty is used when there is intact tissue that is retracted, malpositioned, or displaced, most commonly as a result of the traction from a scar. Therefore a V- to Y-plasty is used most often to revise an unsightly scar (Fig. 13).

Preoperative planning of this repair is crucial, and meticulous precision ensures the desired outcome.

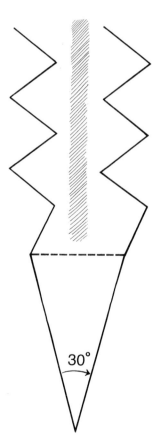

FIG. 10. A simplified method to plan the terminal portion of a W-plasty. The base of the 30-degree equilateral triangle serves as the starting point for the complementary parallel lines.

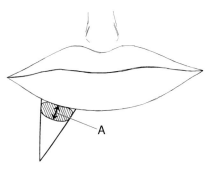
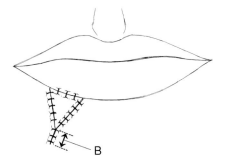

FIG. 12. V to Y flap. The extent of the defect is measured preoperatively **(A)** and should be the same as the advancement of the apex of the flap. The "stem" of the "Y" **(B)** should equal the height of the tissue defect being corrected.

Technique

Determine and measure the extent of the defect before injection of the anesthetic. Record this measurement and use it as the basis for planning the degree of tissue advancement. Next, determine the width of the defect. This width should be precisely the width of the base of the triangle that will be advanced.

A helpful variation on the classic design of the V- to Y-plasty flap is to design the flap as a pentagon with the height of two parallel sides being equal to the extent of the retraction. This diminishes distortion of the delicate tissues normally associated with free margins such as the lips, palpebral margins, and alar rim. Then make the incision with the apex of the pentagon being a 30-degree angle. Since disruption of blood vessels at the base of the flap is undesirable, do

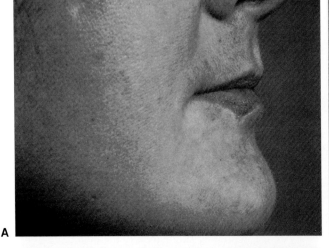

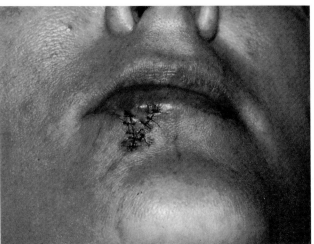

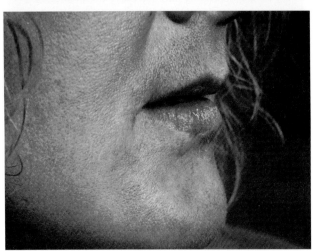

FIG. 13. (A) Eclabion of right-side lower lip. **(B)** V to Y advancement flap repositions vermilion border. **(C)** Six months after surgery.

not undermine the island flap at its base. In addition, undermine the surrounding skin edges. The flap is then ready to be advanced or pushed in the desired direction. The best way to be certain that there is adequate advancement of tissue is to suture the apex of the flap at a distance from the apex of the donor site that is exactly the same as the preoperative measurements of the defect being corrected. Suture these skin edges with aesthetic technique, and the donor site is closed side to side.

If performed with precision, the results of this revisionary technique can be very gratifying to both patient and physician.

S-SHAPED CLOSURE

History

The S-shaped closure is a simple but useful technique that is sometimes referred to as the lazy-S closure. The utility of this variation on a simple side-to-side closure is in defects situated over convex surfaces. The term *S-plasty* is sometimes used for this technique and is a misnomer. An S-plasty is a variant of a Z-plasty that interposes two lobes rather than two triangular flaps.

Preoperative Plan and Technique

The S-shaped closure is simple to design, especially on convex surfaces (Fig.14A and B). Complementary, converging curvilinear lines are incised at each end. On an extremity, the direction of the curve is generally toward the proximal limb at the proximal pole of the incision and distally at the distal aspect of the incision. The wound edges are undermined, and the wound edges can be approximated using the rule of halves.

The S shape of this closure is advantageous on convex surfaces such as the cheek and extremities, not only because the RSTLs are often S-shaped, but, more importantly, be-

cause this curved line has inherent flexibility in it, unlike the more rigid straight line. With the tension of wound closure there is often a ''bow-stringing'' effect resulting in a straight, linear depression across convex surfaces. By using an S-shaped closure, there is distensibility of the scar in the plane of the skin, which lessens the tendency toward a depressed scar (Fig. 15).

M-PLASTY

History

An M-plasty is a modification of a simple ellipse. This modification in effect shortens the length of the standard fusiform excision. As such, the M-plasty is tissue sparing. It is most easily characterized as a bifid fusiform closure. By dividing the tapering and converging lines of a fusiform excision into two portions, the total length of the scar can be shortened while maintaining angles acute enough to ensure an esthetic closure.

Preoperative Plan

The utility of the M-plasty modification is in any situation where a standard ellipse is too long and results in impingement on an important landmark, for example, a simple primary closure that would extend onto a highly visible portion of the face or impinge on vital cosmetic or functional structures, such as the eyelids, lips, ears, or nose (Fig. 16). When a fusiform closure would impinge on these structures, an M-plasty can be used and the final length of the closure would be shortened. In the case of the vermilion border, an M-plasty can be used to avoid violating this delicate cosmetic structure. Similarly, excisions near the eyelids need not extend through the palpebral margin of the eyelid. Another beneficial use of the M-plasty is when the fusiform incision would end immediately adjacent to a delicate cosmetic structure such as the lip or eyelid. Even acute-angled,

Proximal extremity

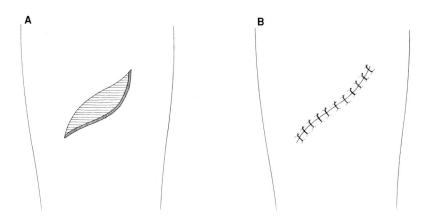

A   B

FIG. 14. (A and B) Curvilinear closure, also known as the "lazy-S closure."

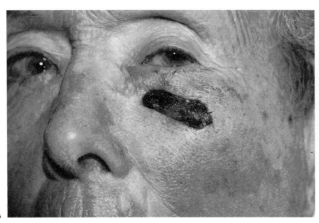

A

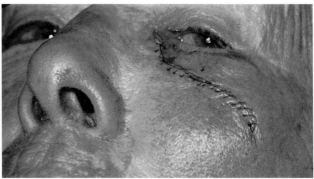

B

FIG. 15. **(A and B)** Curvilinear, S-shaped closure on the convex surface of the cheek.

well-designed, fusiform excisions have a tendency to form standing vertical cones (''dog-ears''), even though constructing a fusiform closure with acute angles only lessens this tendency. If an incision ends near the vermilion border or an eyelid margin, there is a ''push'' of tissue at the ends of the fusiform closure (Fig. 17). This occurs because all fusiform incisions create arcs of wound edges that are then sutured in a straight line. The length of the arcs is greater than the length of the straight line between the apices of the fusiform closure; therefore approximation creates a push of tissue at its apices. When the fusiform incision ends close to a delicate structure such as a vermilion border or palpebral margin, this normally insignificant tissue excess is magnified and may distort these structures. The M-plasty is effective at lessening this effect by distributing the excess tissue over two apices and in effect distributes the distortion over these two points (Fig. 17). This fact, in addition to ending the incisions at a point farther away from the distortable structures, leads to an improved aesthetic outcome.

A single M-plasty reduces the length of an incision by approximately 10%. Therefore, if M-plasties are performed on each end of a fusiform incision, the overall length of the incision is reduced by a total of 20%. On the other hand, scars with converging angles such as those produced by an M-plasty are difficult to maintain in the RSTLs, and such convergence is unnatural-looking in most areas. Therefore, it is not recommended that M-plasties be performed for the sake of shortening incision lines unless there is a specific reason as described earlier. For example, the advantage of reducing a 10-cm scar to an 8-cm scar by placing an M-plasty at each end of the fusiform closure does not justify the more noticeable Y-shaped scar.

Technique

The simplest way to plan an M-plasty is to plan the excision as a simple fusiform excision (Fig. 18). Once those lines are drawn, identify the point on the defect or proposed tumor excision margin that is equidistant from the lines of the fusiform excision and draw two lines that converge at 30-degree angles to the fusiform excision (Fig. 18). The result will be two 30-degree angles that, when approximated, will not leave noticeable standing vertical cones (dog-ears).

At the time of suturing the wound, care must be taken to position the triangular peninsula of skin properly in relation to the skin lateral to the incision. Malpositioning this triangle can lead to unwanted aesthetic consequences after healing. Likewise, care must be taken when suturing this area that

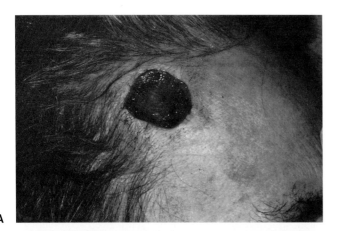

A

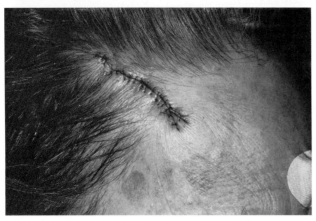

B

FIG. 16. **(A)** Large defect of the forehead. **(B)** Repair with M-plasty at inferior portion of scar to shorten wound and reduce its extension onto the visible portion of the forehead.

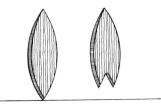

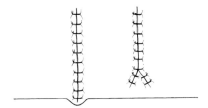

FIG. 17. Simple fusiform closure and closure with M-plasty . Approximation of the two arcs results in a straight line that is longer and results in a "push" of the free margin. M-plasty distributes the push over a larger segment of the free margin, resulting in less distortion.

the margins of skin are sutured at the same level. Otherwise, the final result will be either a protrudant or depressed triangle in the skin.

M-plasties are excellent modifications to a standard fusiform excision when shortening the length of the incision by 10% or 20% has significant advantages. On the other hand, the increased noticeability of an M-plasty scar compared with a simple straight-line scar of a fusiform excision would suggest that M-plasty should not be overused for the sake

of shortening the total length of a scar. As with any modification of closures, good aesthetic judgment is imperative.

GEOMETRIC BROKEN-LINE CLOSURE

History

The geometric broken-line closure (GBLC) technique attempts to take advantage of the basic principle that a series of short, unpatterned lines is more difficult for the casual observer to perceive. The easiest line for the human eye to perceive is a long, straight line. Typically any line longer than 2 cm becomes increasingly more noticeable. A W-plasty makes use of numerous short, straight lines in a series to keep the individual lines as inconspicuous as possible. However, the repetitive pattern inherent in a W-plasty makes this closure more likely to be noticed than a more irregular scar. The GBLC capitalizes on the irregularization of a series of short, broken lines for a greater degree of imperceptibility. Geometric broken-line closure is a series of geometric shapes with the complementary or mirror-image pattern on the opposite wound edge (Fig. 19). In apposition, these wound edges fit together like a puzzle or key and lock.

Preoperative Plan and Technique

Geometric broken-line closure requires very careful, meticulous planning and precise incisions. These types of closures are most commonly used in revision of linear and/or depressed scars that are in variance to the RSTLs. Since this type of closure requires excision of both scar and some normal skin, it is a consideration only when there is ample laxity lateral to the incision. Besides being time-consuming

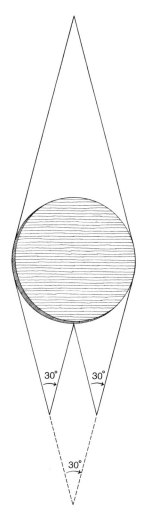

FIG. 18. M-plasty design. Plan two 30-degree Burow's triangles within a standard 30-degree Burow's triangle.

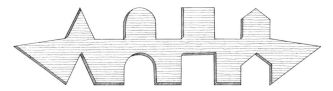

FIG. 19. Geometric broken-line closure. Lock-in-key design maximizes irregularity of design to minimize perceptibility of scar.

during the planning stage, the suturing of GBLC is also very time-consuming.

When designing the GBLC, the geometric figures that can be used include triangles, squares, rectangles, semicircles, and any variation or combination of these. The individual geometric components should be no longer or wider than 3 to 5 mm. Larger components begin to become more visible to the casual observer. Incisions can be made with a No. 11 blade that can be maneuvered around and through these very small, sharp corners. Care should be taken to ensure that the incisions are made at a 90-degree angle to the skin. Closure of the wound edges requires meticulous attention to precise approximation to avoid nonlevel or inverted skin edges. Suturing of a GBLC typically takes a great deal longer than suturing of other incision lines of equal length. However, the final result depends on precise approximation of the wound edges.

As with all closures in which cosmesis is of the ultimate importance, dermabrasion should be considered 6 to 8 weeks after closure. Dermabrasion can blend the scar into the surrounding skin to the point of being nearly imperceptible. This is especially true if, despite meticulous suturing technique, some of the wound edges were not perfectly level with the surrounding skin.

O- TO Z-PLASTY, O TO Z FLAPS, AND O TO T FLAPS

History

Unlike the previously described complex closures, the O to T and O to Z flaps are simply multiple flap closures. An O- to Z-plasty is similar to a Z-plasty in that the defect to be repaired, the ''O,'' is the middle limb and the arms of the ''Z'' become arcs (Fig. 20).

Preoperative Plan and Technique

Devising an O- to Z-plasty is quite similar to designing a standard Z-plasty. A curvilinear or straight tangential incision is made from contralateral sides of the defect. These flaps are then raised and interposed exactly as the flaps of a Z-plasty are. The main difference is that there will be not only rotational movement, but also advancement of the skin at the base of the flaps. This may result in significant tension on the tips of the flap, and vascular compromise attributable to the tension on the base of the flaps can be a problem. Therefore, tension-relieving sutures may be necessary before transposing and suturing the flaps.

An O- to Z-plasty is useful when there is ample skin laxity in one direction and a need for net tissue gain in another. Such situations include closure of an oval wound near a free margin that, if closed by a simple fusiform closure, would create ectropion or eclabion. The O- to Z-plasty could be used to close the defect and redirect tension vectors to a horizontal position to the eyelid or lip (Fig. 21). Another situation might be on a convex surface such as an extremity where an O- to Z-plasty could be used to close an oval or circular defect while minimizing the flattening of the convex surface through redistribution of length in the direction of the convexity. The O- to Z-plasty closure may also be useful in closure of circular wounds in which there is no predominant direction of tissue laxity. The tissue movement dynamics of this flap are such that tissue laxity is consumed from several directions (Fig. 20). A related flap is the S-plasty. It is essentially the same as the O- to Z-plasty except that there is no defect intervening between the two lobed flaps (Fig. 22). Two rounded lobes are interposed, in contrast to the angular flaps that are interposed in a standard Z-plasty.

An A to T flap is simply symmetric, single-tangent advancement flaps. A single-tangent advancement flap or Burow's wedge advancement flap is created by incising in a

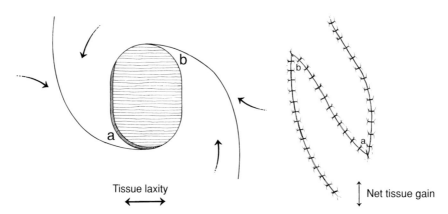

FIG. 20. O- to Z-plasty with transposition of two rotational flaps. There is a net gain of tissue in the vertical direction and a net loss in the horizontal direction.

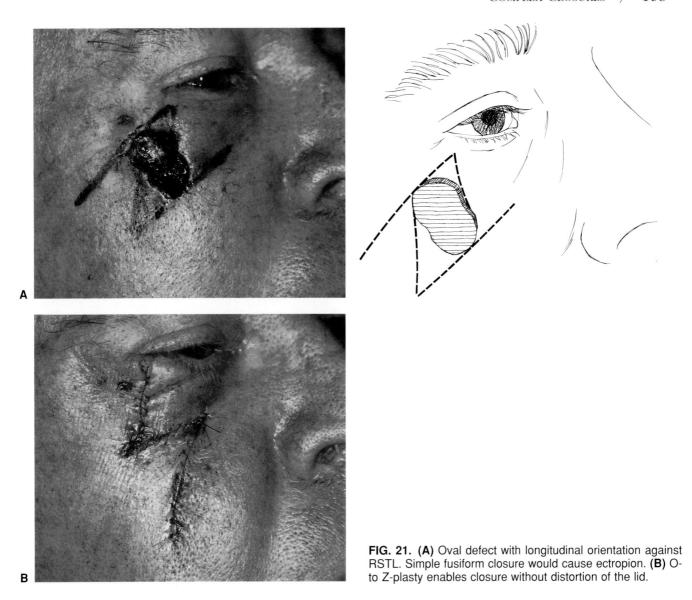

FIG. 21. (A) Oval defect with longitudinal orientation against RSTL. Simple fusiform closure would cause ectropion. **(B)** O-to Z-plasty enables closure without distortion of the lid.

straight line tangentially from a defect (Fig. 23). A Burow's triangle is taken at some point along this tangential line to correct for the wound edges of unequal length as the flap is advanced into the defect. The other Burow's triangle is taken in the same manner as if the defect were being closed by a simple fusiform closure. An A to T flap is similar except that symmetric tangents in opposite directions are incised, creating two flaps (Fig. 24).

An O to Z flap is simply two rotational flaps that are created by two arciform incisions that extend tangentially from a defect in opposite directions (Fig. 25). Both the A to T and the O to Z flaps are useful for closure of a moderately large defect that for one reason or another cannot be closed by simple fusiform closure or in wounds in which it is advantageous to design a flap with the tangential incisions as described. Typical areas for the use of O to Z flaps would

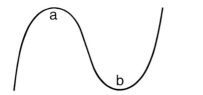
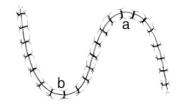

FIG. 22. S-plasty is the transposition of two curvilinear, lobed flaps.

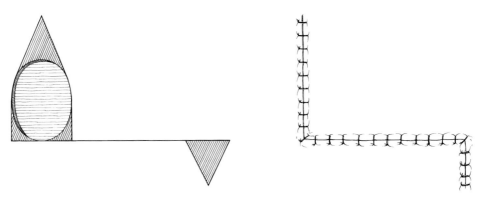

FIG. 23. Single-tangent advancement flap, also known as Burow's wedge advancement flap.

be the forehead, scalp, trunk, and extremities (Fig. 26). An A to T flap is especially useful on the forehead, to avoid distortion of the eyebrows (Fig. 27).

When planning these flaps, care must be taken to ensure that the incisions are placed in optimal position to take advantage of any expression line or other aesthetic landmarks that can improve camouflage of the scar. The Burow's triangles can be planned anywhere along the tangential incision and should be placed in the least conspicuous and least functionally and aesthetically disruptive position.

Once the incisions are made, the flaps should be raised by dissecting in the subcutaneous plane and the remaining bordering skin undermined to facilitate tissue movement. After careful hemostasis, the flaps should be rotated or advanced and sutured with dermal or subcutaneous sutures as well as epidermal sutures using good suturing technique to ensure wound edge eversion. It is sometimes beneficial to wait to excise the Burow's triangles until after the first deep suture is placed to tack the flaps in place. One should avoid the temptation of removing too small of a Burow's triangle to conserve tissue, since this risks perceptible redundancy of the wound edge adjacent to the flap.

Since these are broad-based flaps, necrosis of the tip of the flaps is unusual. However, when there is a great deal of wound tension at the time of closure, assuming the wound

edges have been adequately undermined, other tension-relieving techniques must be used. For example, a suspension stitch that tacks the deep dermis and suspends it from an underlying structure such as the periosteum or deep fascia can help alleviate the tension that may otherwise be placed directly on the tips of the flap. Other tension-reducing techniques include the intentional redistribution of tension by suturing along the entire length of the tangential excision.

In summary, these multiple flap closures can be helpful in reconstructing large defects adjacent to vital structures. Although their names would imply similarity to Z-plasty and W-plasty closure, the similarities end with their names.

POSTOPERATIVE MANAGEMENT, ADVERSE SEQUELAE, AND COMPLICATIONS OF COMPLEX CLOSURES

Postoperative management following complex closure is not appreciably different from routine closures. Any difference would be related to the larger size of a complex closure. Routine care for the immediate postoperative period includes cleansing of the sutured skin, application of a liquid tape adhesive to the skin surrounding the wound, and application of a thin film of antibiotic ointment in petrolatum base di-

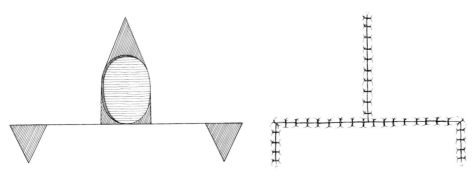

FIG. 24. A to T flap is a bilateral single-tangent advancement flap.

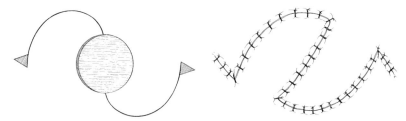

FIG. 25. O to Z flap is a double-rotation flap in which the two flaps rotate into the defect from opposite directions.

rectly over the sutured wound. Lay nonstick gauze padding over the sutures, and cut it to fit the wound. Then apply a small amount of fluffed absorbent gauze over the entire area; use this as a pressure dressing by tightly taping it to the skin, which creates a downward pressure over the entire undermined wound bed. Flesh-colored tape can be used to make the bandage less conspicuous. Leave this bandage in place for up to a week or, if preferred, have the patient change it daily or twice daily 1 day after surgery. Bandage changes consist of bandage removal and cleansing of the wound with peroxide. A thin coat of antibiotic ointment is applied to the sutured skin, and a nonstick gauze pad is again taped over the wound. If the patient is at high risk for postoperative bleeding attributable to anticoagulation, anti-

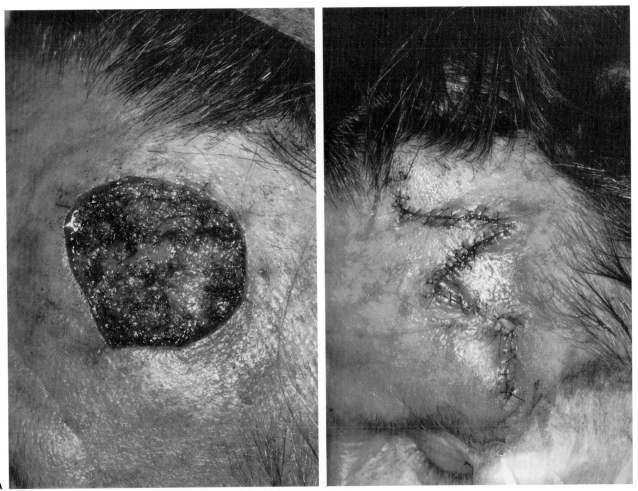

A **B**

FIG. 26. (A) Large defect of the upper forehead. **(B)** O to Z flap with two rotation flaps. The superior flap was rotated in from the superomedial area of forehead. The lower flap is from the inferolateral area of forehead.

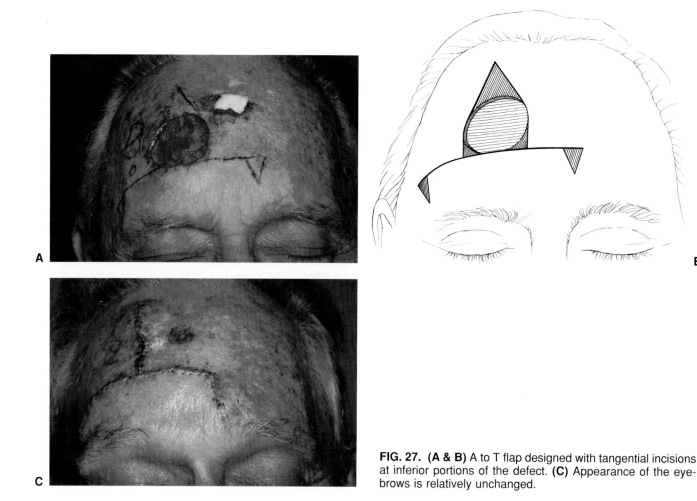

FIG. 27. (A & B) A to T flap designed with tangential incisions at inferior portions of the defect. **(C)** Appearance of the eyebrows is relatively unchanged.

platelet therapy, or coagulopathy, you may suture a pressure bandage into place prophylactically. Likewise, if the wound is in an appropriate location such as the forehead, lateral or posterior scalp, or extremity, an elastic bandage can be applied circumferentially around the head or extremity. Elastic wraps are routinely employed for lower-extremity wounds in elderly individuals, especially if they have a propensity toward pedal edema. These prevent unwanted swelling of the leg that may lead to increased wound tension, vascular compromise, and congestion. Remove the sutures as early as safety permits. They can be removed quite early in wounds that are adequately supported by dermal sutures.

Adverse sequelae after complex closure may include an uneven or depressed scar, hypertrophic or keloidal scar, pigmentary changes around the wound, reactive erythema, and persistent telangiectasia in association with the scar. Occasional adverse sequelae that may be avoided by careful preoperative planning include misorientation of facial or scalp hair, alteration of important facial landmarks, and undercorrection or overcorrection of the defect for which the complex closure was intended.

Irregularities of contour in the scar can be corrected in a number of ways, usually in the form of a resurfacing procedure. These resurfacing techniques include dermabrasion, laserbrasion, and dermal planing. Timing these procedures 6 to 8 weeks after the procedure optimizes the clinical benefits from the resurfacing procedure, but they can be performed at any time after approximately 4 weeks. Hypertrophic scarring can be improved by measures as simple as vigorous massaging and kneading of the scar by the patient beginning 1 month after the surgery. Application of Silastic sheets has been reported to be of benefit as well. Intralesional injections with steroids can also expedite the reduction of hypertrophic scar tissue. Sometimes, reassuring the patient that the scar contraction is maximal 6 to 8 weeks after the procedure and that this firmness will gradually resolve over the coming year is therapy enough. Keloidal scarring following surgery can be a serious and difficult management problem and is beyond the scope of this chapter.

Pigmentary change commonly resolves within a year after the surgery. If it is due to hypermelanization of the epidermis, it may benefit from a course of topical 4% hydroquinone cream. Occasionally, treatment with a pigmented lesion laser can expedite the resolution of hyperpigmentation. Reduction of melanocyte stimulation by ultraviolet light with sunscreens is also helpful and occasionally prophylactic in a patient who may be predisposed to postinflammatory hyperpigmentation.

Occasionally, hyperemia or telangiectasia will develop in the skin adjacent to the wound. This often improves with time, but occasionally, permanent neovascularization occurs. If the erythema does persist and the patient desires therapy, this condition can be nicely improved by means of vascular lasers.

Complications in complex closures are similar to those in any other skin surgery. Complications are not entirely unavoidable and occur to anyone performing cutaneous surgery. However, they can be minimized with attention to good surgical technique, recognition and avoidance of risk factors, comprehensive preoperative planning, and good postoperative care. One of the most common complications is hematoma. The management of hematomas depends on the clinical setting, the postoperative timing in which the hematoma comes to the attention of the physician, and whether the hematoma is stable or expanding. Many hematomas are venous in origin and come to the attention of the physician 24 or more hours after the procedure. These tend to be self-limited, and tamponade occurs, stabilizing the hematoma. The options in management of these range from no treatment because of their tendency to resorb over several months to reopening the wound, evacuating the hematoma, and obtaining hemostasis. The course of action depends on the judgment of the physician and may depend on factors such as the size of the hematoma, location, age of hematoma, aesthetic considerations, and host factors.

An actively expanding hematoma, in contrast to the stable variety, must be addressed. These individuals frequently come to medical attention within 6 to 12 hours of the surgery with complaints of acute pain and an expanding mass in the closure site. This clinical scenario usually heralds an active arterial source of bleeding. Typically the sutured wound must be opened, the hematoma evacuated, and the active bleeding sites eliminated. Often, a small to medium-size artery is found that is responsible for the hematoma. Once hemostasis is achieved, the wound bed is irrigated with sterile saline and the wound edges are resutured.

Obviously, prevention of a hematoma begins with meticulous intraoperative hemostasis. On occasion, despite excellent technique that includes visualization of all of the wound bed surfaces including the undermined skin, a significant vessel can be missed, either because of the vasoconstrictive effect of epinephrine or because of a location that is difficult to visualize. Other possible causes of bleeding after closure include an action by the patient such as Valsalva's maneuver or an accidental bump of the site. Ineffective or defective clotting mechanisms can also lead to postoperative bleeding. Thorough postoperative instruction that restricts activity for at least 48 hours and describes application of pressure dressings postoperatively should be given; in the case of anticipated bleeding tendencies in a patient who is receiving anticoagulation or antiplatelet therapy or has a known coagulopathy, a bolster dressing can be sutured over the wound and produces a stable, effective compression bandage. It is wise to strongly consider antibiotic prophylaxis in any patient who develops a hematoma, whether or not the hematoma is evacuated. An unevacuated hematoma can serve as culture media for bacterial infections. Likewise, the evacuation of a hematoma results in the introduction of bacteria in the enclosed space of the wound.

Wound infection is another relatively common complication and most typically becomes evident clinically 3 to 7 days postoperatively. The most common clinical manifestations are erythema, warmth, and pain that may be associated with a purulent exudate. Sterile operative technique is the most obvious preventive measure for infections, but there are other factors that can predispose the individual to infection. The presence of a hematoma, seroma, or devitalized tissue predisposes the individual to infections. Excessive wound tension and host factors that reduce the effectiveness of the immune system are also predisposing factors.

When an infection is suspected, a culture should be obtained, and antimicrobial susceptibility assays should be requested. Empiric antibiotic therapy should be initiated before the confirmation of susceptibility. An argument can be made for prophylactic antibiotic therapy if the patient is considered at risk for infection because of immunosuppression, prolonged procedure time, excessive devitalized tissue within the wound, a contaminated wound, excessive wound tension, and so forth.

Wound edge necrosis may be more common in complex closures than other closures, since many of these have sharply angulated flaps and may be used to close high-tension wounds. For example, the Z-plasty is occasionally used for high-tension closures and the vascular supply to these angulated flaps can be compromised. Perhaps the most important factor in avoiding this complication is the gentle handling of the wound edges during closure. Care should be taken to avoid crushing the tissue or otherwise devitalizing it in the process of wound closure. In the event that flap necrosis does occur, the management is that of second-intention wound healing. Gentle debridement may be necessary, but care should be taken to avoid further injury to viable tissue.

Dehiscence is often a secondary complication related to a prior complication such as infection or flap necrosis. If wound dehiscence does occur, there is no uniform approach to management. If dehiscence is within 48 hours of the surgery, some practitioners resuture the wound. Otherwise, healing by second intention should be allowed to occur, and an assessment of the functional and cosmetic outcome performed later. If the wound is clinically infected, culture and appropriate antibiotics are indicated.

While postoperative care, adverse sequelae, and complications in complex closure are similar in any form of cutaneous closure, unique features arise from the complexity of the closures. Nonetheless, thorough, insightful preoperative planning and excellent surgical technique diminish the frequency of complications and enhance the ultimate aesthetic and functional outcome of the closure.

SUGGESTED READING LIST

1. Borges AF. Linear scar revision technique: Z-plasty and W-plasty. In: Borges AF, ed. Elective incisions and scar revision. Boston: Little, Brown, 1973:45.

2. Borges AF. Surgical incisions of choice. In Borges AF, ed. Elective incisions and scar revision. Boston: Little, Brown, 1973:91.

3. Borges AF. W-plasty. In: Thomas JR, Holt GR, eds. Facial scars: incision, revision, and camouflage. St. Louis: CV Mosby, 1989:150.

4. Davis WE, Renner GJ. Z-plasty and scar revision. In: Thomas JR, Holt GR, eds. Facial scars: incision, revision, and camouflage. St. Louis, MO: CV Mosby, 1989:137.

5. Frodel JL, Wang TD. Z-plasty. In: Baker SR, Swanson NA, ed. Local flaps in facial reconstruction. St. Louis: CV Mosby, 1995:131.

6. McCarthy JG. Introduction to plastic surgery. In: McCarthy JG, ed. Plastic surgery. Philadelphia: WB Saunders, 1990:1.

7. Thomas JR. Geometric broken-line closure. In: Thomas JR, Holt GR, eds. Facial scars: incision, revision, and camouflage. St. Louis, MO: CV Mosby, 1989:160.

8. Wheeland RG. Random pattern flaps. In: Roenigk RK, Roenigk HH Jr, eds. Dermatologic surgery: principles and practice. New York: Marcel Dekker, 1989:265.

Textbook of Dermatologic Surgery, edited by John L. Ratz.
Lippincott–Raven Publishers, Philadelphia © 1998.

CHAPTER 15

Skin Grafts

Timothy M. Johnson and Désirée Ratner

HISTORY

The origin of skin grafting can be traced to the Hindu Tilemaker Caste over 2,500 to 3,000 years ago. Grafts were used for nasal reconstruction following nasal amputation that was performed as punishment for theft and infidelity. The Western world was introduced to skin grafting in the 19th century following several reports of successful free full-thickness skin grafting using the ancient Indian method. Education and interest in skin grafting increased in Europe and the West in the latter half of the 19th century following published reports of pinch grafting by Reverdin in 1889; split-thickness skin grafting by Ollier and Thiersch in 1872 and 1886, respectively; and full-thickness skin grafting by Wolfe and Krause in 1875 and 1893. More than 100 years later, the techniques and instrumentation used for skin grafting procedures have been modified and refined. Today soft tissue reconstruction with various types of skin grafts is routinely used by reconstructive surgeons.

Free skin grafts are obtained by complete surgical removal of a piece or pieces of skin from their local vascular supply with subsequent transfer to another location and vascular bed. In this chapter skin grafts are classified into three basic types: full-thickness skin grafts (FTSGs), split-thickness

Timothy M. Johnson: Department of Dermatology, University of Michigan, Ann Arbor, MI 48109-0001.

Désirée Ratner: Department of Dermatology, Columbia-Presbyterian Medical Ctr., 161 Fort Washington Ave., New York, NY 10032.

skin grafts (STSGs), and composite grafts. Full-thickness skin grafts include the epidermis and full thickness of dermis, including hair follicles, sweat glands, and other adnexal structures. Split-thickness skin grafts include the epidermis and partial-thickness dermis. Split-thickness skin grafts can be further subdivided into thin, medium, and thick depending on the thickness of dermis included in the graft (Fig. 1). Composite grafts are composed of two different tissue types—full-thickness skin and cartilage—for the purposes of our discussion.

FULL-THICKNESS SKIN GRAFTS

Preoperative Planning

Indications

The best reconstructive effort is usually accomplished by approaching each patient and defect individually and assessing all reconstructive options via a systematic mental exercise. The morbidity, cost, risks, and potential complications of each option should be considered for each patient and defect. Often, more than one reconstructive technique will result in a good cosmetic and functional outcome. If healing by second intention (granulation), primary closure, or flap repair is not a favorable option, use of a skin graft should be considered. Full-thickness skin grafts may result in good to excellent cosmetic and functional outcomes, most commonly for defects on the face, particularly of the nasal tip,

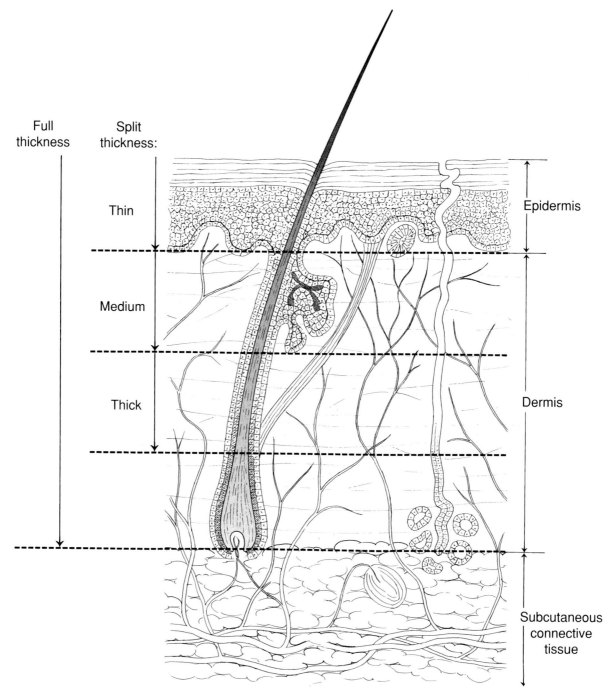

Full
thickness

Split
thickness:

Thin

Medium

Thick

Epidermis

Dermis

Subcutaneous
connective
tissue

FIG. 1. Full-thickness skin grafts include the epidermis and full thickness of dermis, including the adnexal structures. Split-thickness skin grafts include the epidermis and partial-thickness dermis. Split-thickness skin grafts can be further subdivided into thin, medium, and thick depending on the amount of dermis included in the graft.

dorsum, bridge, ala, lateral nasal sidewall, eyelid, and ear. Full-thickness skin grafts may be used to cover defects on any anatomic site as long as there is a suitable recipient bed.

The suitability of the recipient bed primarily depends on the vascular supply for capillary regrowth to and from the graft and fibroblasts to produce collagen for graft adherence. All skin grafts described in this chapter are completely sepa-

rated from their original vascular bed and therefore are entirely dependent on the development of a new blood supply from the recipient bed for their survival. The thicker the graft, the greater the need for a good vascular bed for survival. In general, exposed bone, cartilage, and tendon devoid of periosteum, perichondrium, and peritenon are often unable to support FTSGs. Small, exposed areas, however, may

TABLE 15-1. *Feature comparison of various graft types*

	Recipient bed vascularity	Infection risk	Tissue match	Graft contraction risk	Durability	Skill
Full-thickness skin graft	High	Low	Good	Low	Good	Moderate
Split-thickness skin graft	Low	Low	Fair to poor (good for auricle)	High	Fair to good	Moderate
Composite graft	Very high	Moderate to high	Good	Low	Good	High

support FTSGs as a result of the bridging phenomenon. Full-thickness skin grafts can provide good matches for color, consistency, and thickness in properly selected facial defects. Wound contraction is often minimal, and dermal adnexal structures are intact. The two most important points in preoperative planning are recipient site vascularity and donor tissue match with respect to color, texture, adnexal quality, and tissue thickness.

Donor Site Planning

The skin on the head and neck varies in thickness from approximately 0.75 to 2.5 mm. The skin of women is generally thinner than that of men. Selection of the best donor site for FTSGs depends primarily on the tissue qualities (color, texture, adnexal qualities) exhibited in the skin that is removed to create the defect and the thickness and size of the defect. The size of the skin graft harvested is limited only by the ability to close the donor site.

All available donor sites should be examined carefully for tissue quality match, thickness, and size. This approach facilitates choosing the best donor site selection for each individual patient defect. The thinnest FTSGs are usually obtained from the upper eyelid and postauricular regions. Thicker grafts are usually harvested from the preauricular, cervical, nasolabial crease, and supraclavicular locations. Relatively large grafts may be obtained from the supraclavicular and upper inner arm locations. Donor site thickness varies from patient to patient.

A regional approach to donor site selection may also be used to obtain the best possible tissue match for a given surgical defect. Redundant upper-eyelid skin may be used as an FTSG to repair lower-eyelid defects. A good tissue match is provided from this site, in addition to creating a well-hidden donor site scar. Full-thickness skin grafts used to repair lower-eyelid defects should be oversized by 100% to 200% to prevent an ectropion caused by graft contraction. Usually the thinner the graft, the more it contracts. Postauricular skin is most useful as an FTSG for auricular, eyelid, and thin nasal defects. Postauricular skin is relatively sun protected and may not provide as good a color or other tissue quality match for facial defects in areas of chronic sun exposure. The ease of hiding the donor site scar in the postauricular sulcus, however, makes this a common donor area for FTSGs. Preauricular, cervical, and nasolabial skin is often highly desirable as a donor site because of the frequently

excellent tissue quality match. Care must be taken not to harvest terminal hair-bearing skin in grafts taken from these areas. The inclusion of terminal follicular units results in the undesirable outcome of hair growth within the graft at the recipient site. The donor site scar in these regions is usually easily camouflaged. Supraclavicular and lateral neck skin areas may provide larger grafts of sun-exposed skin for larger defects. Larger grafts may also be obtained from the upper, inner arm; forearm; and inguinal region, although the tissue match is often suboptimal.

Technique

Numerous variations in technique for FTSGs exist. In this chapter a commonly used technique is described. After selection of the donor site with the best tissue match, make a template of the defect by placing a flexible material such as paper, foil, gauze, or Telfa into the recipient wound. Mark the recipient border site with a marking pen, and press Telfa against the recipient wound. The resulting outline from the inked margin then serves as a guide for cutting the template that corresponds to the exact wound size and shape. Place the template over the donor site, and ink the margin. The graft should be 5% to 15% larger than the template, to account for contraction and shrinkage following excision of the graft. As stated earlier, eyelid grafts should be oversized by 100% to 200% to avoid ectropion. Mark the donor site before administration of local anesthesia to prevent incorrect sizing after tissue swelling that is due to infiltration of local anesthesia. Achieve local anesthesia at the donor and recipient sites. Epinephrine may be used at the donor site. However, harvest the graft before maximum vasoconstriction. Reports of increased graft failure have been noted with maximum vasoconstriction at the donor site. Prepare and drape the donor and recipient sites in the usual sterile manner.

Excise the donor graft with a scalpel to the level of the adipose tissue. Harvest the graft and place it in sterile saline solution in a sterile Petri dish. Trim the graft of all fat and close the donor site in layered fashion. If necessary, a local skin flap may be used to close the donor defect. Defatting the graft to the dermis is an essential, important step (Fig. 2) because adipose tissue is a poor tissue for neovascularization to and from the graft. Defat the graft by placing it on the fingers or palm, fat side up. Trim all fat with sharp scissors to the level of the dermis. Then place the graft in the recipient site and trim its edges if necessary for a perfect fit. For a

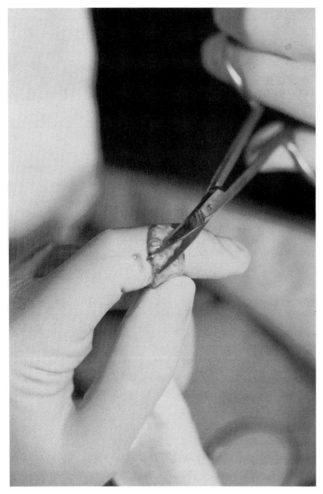

FIG. 2. After removing the donor graft, trim the fat to the level of the dermis with sharp scissors.

FTSG on the auricle, remove exposed cartilage that is not needed for structural support to enhance vascularity of the recipient bed and increase the graft survival.

Secure the graft to the recipient bed by a combination of perimeter sutures, basting sutures, and a pyramid pressure dressing. If basting sutures are used, place them before placing the perimeter sutures, since bleeding may result from placement of the basting suture. Basting sutures of 5-0 absorbable suture may be particularly useful for large grafts to provide additional support, to prevent graft movement and, for concave surfaces, to ensure graft-bed contact and prevent tenting. Basting sutures should be snug but not strangulating.

If a tie-over bolster dressing is planned, first place perimeter sutures with interrupted 4-0 or 5-0 nonabsorbable (polypropylene [Prolene], nylon) sutures at opposite edges of the graft (i.e., at 12, 3, 6, and 9 o'clock positions). Cut the end of each interrupted suture long enough to tie with the contralateral suture over the pyramid bolster dressing. To maximize graft-bed contact and graft stabilization, place a simple running suture around the perimeter of the graft with rapidly absorbing 5-0 or 6-0 chromic gut. Place this suture in epicu-

ticular fashion, passing the needle through the graft slightly higher in the dermis on the graft side and slightly deeper in the dermis on the recipient-bed side to prevent tenting of the graft edge and maximize graft-bed contact.

A wide variety of pyramid pressure dressings may be employed to immobilize the graft and prevent hematoma and seroma formation. One type of commonly used pyramid dressing involves first applying a layer of N-terface gauze over the graft to prevent trauma when removing the dressing. After doing this, apply a layer of Xeroform or antibiotic-petrolatum–impregnated gauze followed by small pieces of sterile cotton. Tie the long, nonabsorbable perimeter sutures over the pyramid dressing as a bow would be tied over a package (Fig. 3). As an alternative, secure a layer of Hypafix with Mastisol and place it over the pyramid dressing to provide immobilization and slight pressure (Fig. 4). For large grafts or wounds at higher risk of hematoma, make small scalpel slits or stabs to mesh the graft and to allow for drainage of accumulated blood or serum that might inhibit graft-bed contact (Figs. 5–8).

Postoperative Management

Remove the donor site dressing in 24 hours, cleanse it once or twice daily with hydrogen peroxide, and apply antibiotic ointment. Leave the graft dressing undisturbed for 1 week following the procedure. At 1 week, remove the graft dressing. The ideal graft is white to light pink but may range from dark pink to blue to purple. Patients may be alarmed at the patchlike appearance and the color changes that usually occur during the evolutionary phases of early wound healing. They are much less alarmed if informed of these descriptions before placement of the graft and during removal of the dressing. A black graft is a sign of necrosis and failure. The entire epidermis may necrose and blacken without necrosis of the graft dermis and appendages (Fig. 9). For this reason, do not debride eschar; instead, leave it in place to act as a biologic dressing for second-intention healing in the event of graft death or to protect viable graft dermis and promote reepithelialization with partial graft necrosis.

Following suture removal, cleanse the graft gently with hydrogen peroxide on a cotton-tip swab stick to remove loose debris and crusts, and follow this by applying a thin layer of ointment. Counsel patients that the new vascular support to the graft may remain fragile for weeks. Therefore they should avoid factors associated with trauma and swelling, such as direct shower spray and moderate exercise, for several weeks.

Adverse Sequelae

The adverse sequelae associated with FTSGs may be divided into the short-term problem of graft failure and the long-term problem of poor functional and cosmetic outcome. Uninterrupted direct contact between the graft and recipient bed is key to neovascularization and graft survival. The most

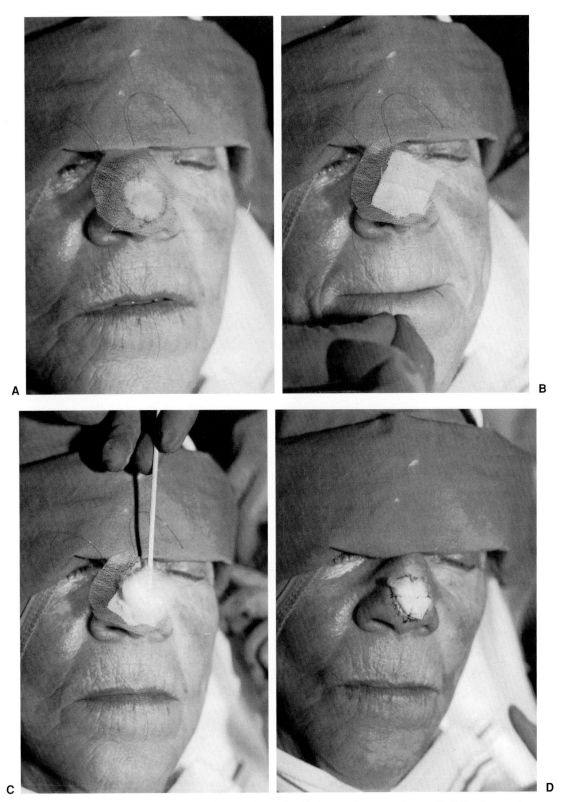

FIG. 3. (A) Tie-over bolster dressing. Secure the graft with four perimeter sutures with 5-0 polypropylene suture at four quadrants, and cut the suture long enough to tie over to the contralateral suture over the pyramid dressing. Place a running perimeter suture around the entire perimeter of the graft with rapidly absorbing 6-0 chromic gut. Apply a layer of N-terface gauze over the graft to prevent trauma when the dressing is removed. **(B)** Next, apply a layer of Xeroform gauze over the N-terface gauze. **(C)** Place sterile cotton over the Xeroform gauze for stabilization and slight pressure. **(D)** Tie the polypropylene sutures over the perimeter dressing as if tying a bow over a package.

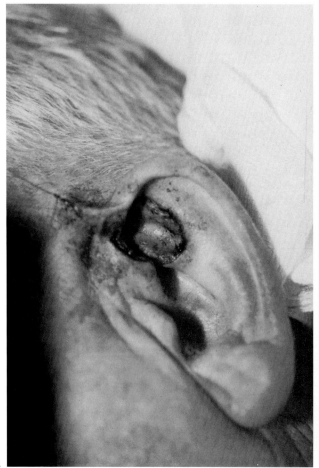

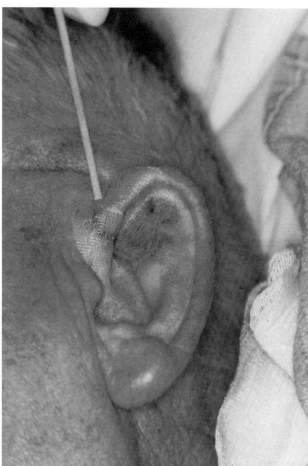

A

B

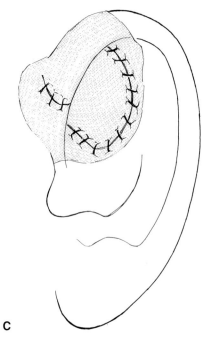

C

FIG. 4. **(A)** Hypafix bolster dressing. Full-thickness defect with perichondrium intact, located in the triangular fossa of the ear following Mohs' excision of a basal cell carcinoma. Make an incision in the crus of the helix, and reflect the crus of the helix to improve exposure and ease placement of the graft. **(B and C)** Secure the graft with a running, rapidly absorbing 6-0 chromic gut suture. Reapproximate the crus of the helix with 6-0 polypropylene sutures. Again, first apply a layer of N-terface gauze over the graft. *(continued)*

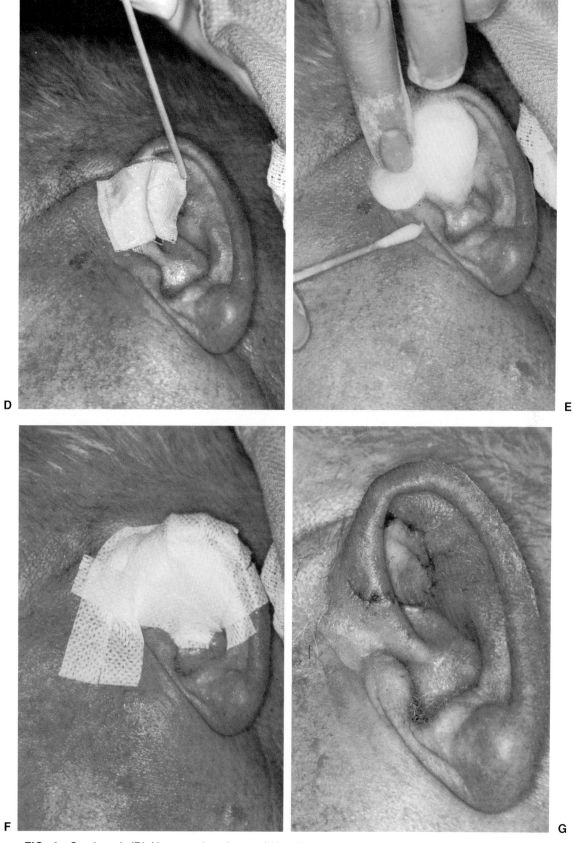

FIG. 4. *Continued.* **(D)** Next, apply a layer of Xeroform gauze over the N-terface gauze. **(E)** Apply sterile cotton balls over the Xeroform gauze. Apply a layer of Mastisol around the perimeter of the dressing. **(F)** Apply a layer of Hypafix to provide immobilization and slight pressure. **(G)** Remove the dressing at 1 week. The N-terface allows atraumatic removal of the dressing. The ideal graft is pink to white.

207

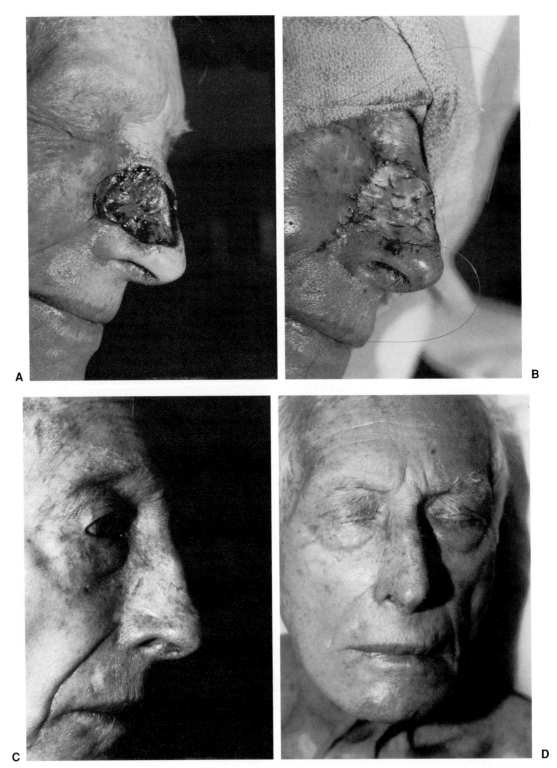

FIG. 5. (A) A 3.5 × 3.8 cm Mohs' surgical defect is present following removal of a basal cell carcinoma with Mohs' surgery. Assess all donor areas for size, tissue match, and thickness. The supraclavicular skin provides the best donor match with adequate size in this patient. **(B)** Make an incision in the nasal facial sulcus, and advance the cheek to the nasal facial sulcus to repair the cheek defect using the concept of maintaining cosmetic units and junctions. Secure the cheek flap to the underlying periosteum with 4-0 absorbable suture. Secure the graft in the usual fashion. Place small scalpel slits to mesh the graft and allow drainage that might inhibit graft-bed contact because of the size of the graft. Apply several interrupted bolster sutures in the center of the graft with 5-0 chromic suture. **(C)** Eight-month postoperative result (side view). **(D)** Eight-month postoperative result (front view). (Reprinted with permission from Mosby−Year Book, Inc., *Journal of American Academy of Dermatology* 27:151−165, 1992.)

208

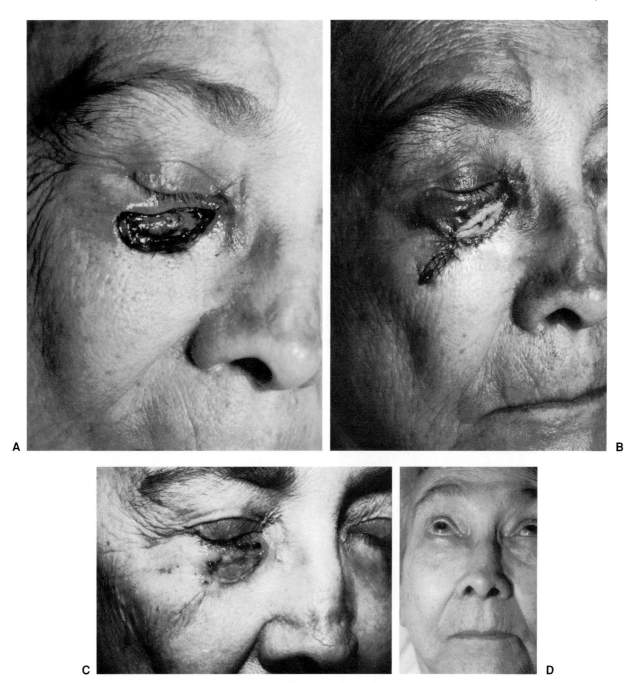

FIG. 6. **(A)** A full-thickness eyelid defect is present following removal of basal cell carcinoma with Mohs' surgery. **(B)** Close the lateral aspect of the defect primarily to decrease the size of the primary defect that requires a full-thickness skin graft. Assess all available donor sites for tissue match. The postauricular skin provided the best tissue match in this case. Oversize the graft by 100% to 200% for eyelid defects. Secure the graft in the usual fashion, as described previously. **(C)** Remove the dressing at 1 week. The ideal graft is light pink to white. **(D)** Six-month postoperative result.

common causes of graft failure are infection, hematoma and seroma, and nicotine. Infection after grafting of facial defects is uncommon and usually occurs in wounds in which local defense mechanisms are overwhelmed by large amounts of bacteria or by increased bacterial virulence. Gentle intraoperative handling of tissue and minimization of devitalized tissue by electrocautery are important to decrease the risk

of infection. Preoperative and/or perioperative antibiotics for staphylococcal and streptococcal organisms may decrease the risk of infection in select situations, particularly in patients with poor general health, systemic problems with vascular compromise, immunosuppression, diabetes mellitus, and/or prolonged intraoperative time. Additional antibiotic coverage for pseudomonal infection may also be necessary

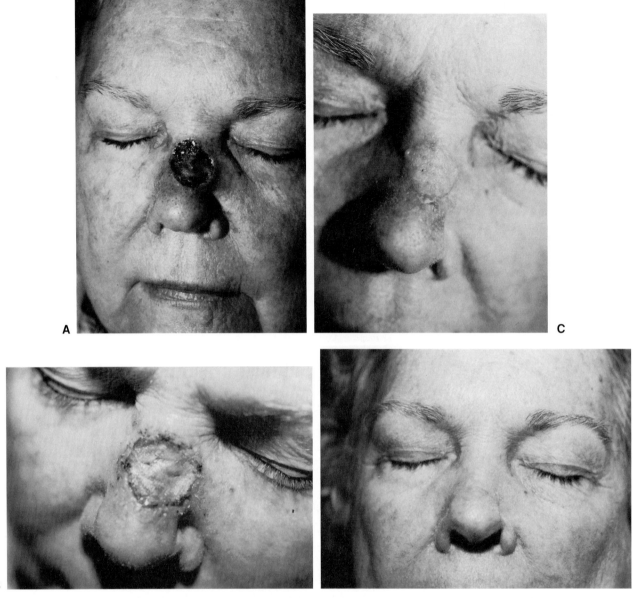

FIG. 7. (A) Full-thickness defect is present on the nasal bridge following removal of basal cell carcinoma with Mohs' surgery. A rich muscular bed is present. Assess all donor options for tissue match. Preauricular skin provided the best tissue match in this patient. **(B)** Remove the dressing in 1 week. Gently cleanse the peripheral crusting with hydrogen peroxide and a cotton swab. The peripheral crusting is due to the rapidly absorbing chromic gut suture. **(C)** Six-week postoperative result. Slight irregularities are evident at the periphery of the graft. Spot dermabrasion minimizes the irregularities. In addition, incorporating the entire cosmetic unit with the dermabrasion prevents the patchlike appearance of the graft. Perform a spot dermabrasion incorporating the graft into the entire cosmetic unit of the nasal bridge. **(D)** Four-month postoperative result following spot dermabrasion.

for auricular grafts. The sequelae of hematoma/seroma are minimized by meticulous intraoperative hemostasis; pressure dressings; preoperative avoidance of aspirin, nonsteroidal antiinflammatory agents, and warfarin; and postoperative avoidance of moderate activity, bending, and lifting. Because nicotine-induced vasoconstriction is associated with increased risk of graft failure, patients are encouraged to decrease the number of cigarettes smoked to the greatest degree possible for several days before and after surgery.

The long-term adverse sequelae consist of poor functional and cosmetic outcomes. Full-thickness skin grafts usually require 6 months to heal before the final appearance can be ascertained. Comprehensive preoperative counseling helps to alleviate the patient's fear during the first months of healing. Makeup can generally be applied 2 to 4 weeks after the grafting procedure. Contour abnormalities can sometimes be avoided by allowing the wound to granulate for several weeks before graft placement. Spot dermabrasion of the graft

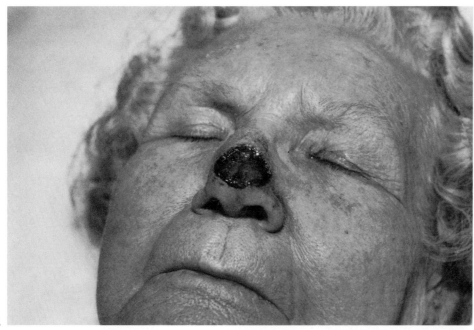

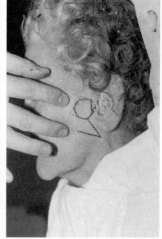

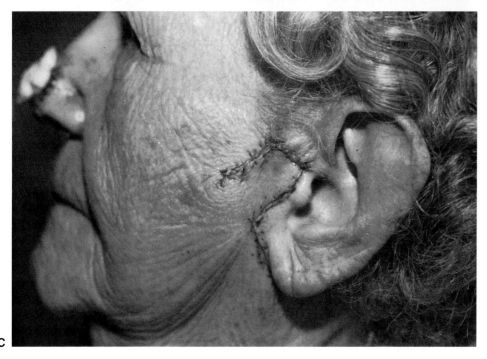

FIG. 8. **(A)** A full-thickness nasal tip defect exists following Mohs' surgery for a basal cell carcinoma. **(B)** The best tissue match for this defect was found in the preauricular region. A rhombic transposition flap was designed to take advantage of the loose adjacent tissue located inferiorly to the donor site. This will allow closure of the donor site without affecting fit of the patient's hearing aid. Most preauricular sites can be closed primarily. **(C)** Closed donor site with a rhombic transposition flap. No distortion of the tragus is created. This is advantageous in this patient because of bilateral hearing aids. *(continued)*

and the surrounding complete cosmetic unit usually improves color, consistency, and elevation abnormalities significantly. The dermabrasion can be performed at any time but is best performed 6 to 8 weeks following the grafting procedure. Functional complications generally occur as a result of graft contraction. Graft contraction usually increases as the thickness of the graft decreases. Therefore grafts placed in defects with lax free margins such as the eyelid, lip, or nasal ala should be oversized initially to account for graft contraction. If poor functional outcomes result, revisional surgery is needed.

SPLIT-THICKNESS SKIN GRAFTS

Preoperative Planning

Indications

Split-thickness skin grafts consist of epidermis and a variable portion of the underlying dermis. Split-thickness skin grafts vary in thickness from approximately 0.008 to 0.030 of an inch and are classified as thin (0.008 to 0.012 of an inch), medium (0.012 to 0.018 of an inch), and thick (0.018

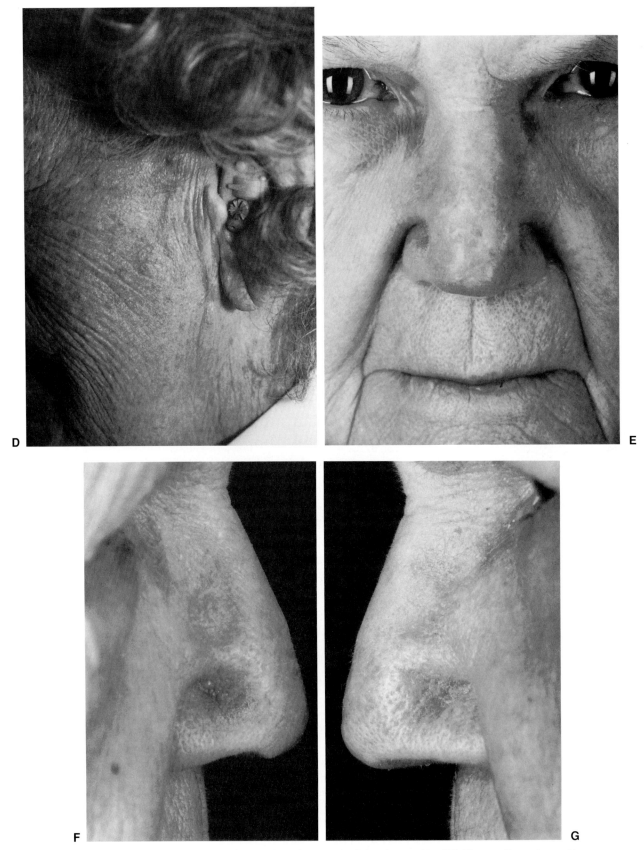

FIG. 8. *Continued.* **(D)** Six-month postoperative result of the donor site. **(E)** Six-month postoperative result of recipient site. **(F and G)** Six-month postoperative result of recipient site.

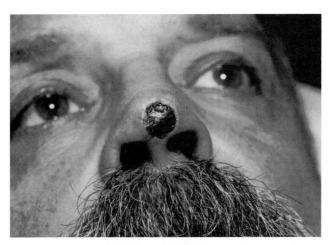

FIG. 9. After removal of the dressing at 1 week, a necrotic graft is evident. Do not remove the eschar, since part of the dermal component of the graft containing the adnexal structures may still be viable. The potentially viable dermal component will be removed if an attempt to remove the eschar is made. Reepithelialization from the dermal component of the graft facilitates granulation. This eschar may take 4 to 6 weeks to naturally resolve. A second revisional procedure will probably be necessary.

to 0.030 of an inch). The most common STSGs used in cutaneous surgery are of medium thickness. Split-thickness skin grafts have greater potential for survival than FTSGs because of the greater capillary network exposed on the deep portion of the graft and the decreased total tissue requiring

revascularization for survival. These factors improve the chance of STSG success for wounds with some degree of vascular compromise. Split-thickness skin grafts may be placed over periosteum, perichondrium, and peritenon. Split-thickness skin grafts are also useful for covering large defects that cannot be covered as easily with a skin flap or would heal slowly by granulation. Most important, STSGs are ideal for reconstruction of surgical defects at higher risk of local tumor recurrence. In this way, STSGs serve as a window to monitor for deep tumor recurrence that grows through the STSG and is easily visible (Fig. 10). After an appropriate time interval (approximately 2 years for squamous cell carcinoma, 5 to 10 years for basal cell carcinoma) the STSG can be excised and a definitive cosmetic and functional reconstruction can be performed, sometimes with the use of tissue expansion.

The main disadvantages of STSGs are poor cosmetic outcome, the presence of a granulating donor site, greater graft contraction, and special instrumentation and equipment required to harvest the graft. Poor color and texture match is to be expected with STSGs. Split-thickness skin grafts are usually white, smooth, and hairless with impaired sweating properties. The contrast between the STSG and the surrounding skin usually creates a ''tire-patch'' appearance in most locations except the ear, where acceptable cosmetic and functional outcomes may be routinely achieved.

Ideal donor sites for STSGs are located where there is a relatively broad area of tissue that can be harvested and still remain hidden under clothing, such as the upper thigh; upper,

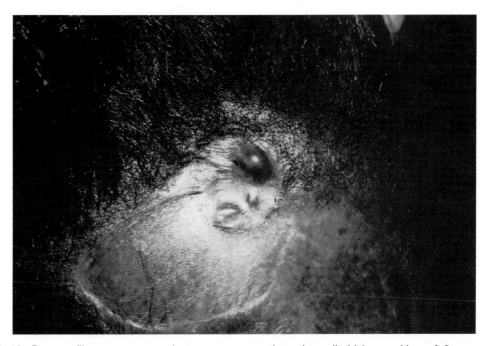

FIG. 10. Dermatofibrosarcoma protuberans recurrence through a split-thickness skin graft 8 years after primary excision. The tumor grows through the split-thickness graft; in this way the graft serves as a window to monitor for deep tumor recurrence. Closure of this defect with a skin flap would have masked recurrence of tumor, delaying recurrence detection. Split-thickness skin grafts are ideal for reconstruction of surgical defects at higher risk of local tumor recurrence.

inner arm; and buttocks-hip region. The anteromedial thigh is our preferred donor site because harvesting and wound care are convenient.

Techniques

A wide variety of instruments ranging from freehand to electric dermatomes may be used to harvest an STSG. Examples of freehand dermatomes include scalpel blades, razor blades, and specialty knives such as the Weck, Humby, or Blair knives. Considerable technical experience is required to harvest a graft of even size, thickness, and edges using a freehand dermatome. Nevertheless, freehand STSGs are ideal for small defects such as pinch grafts that are used for coverage of chronic recalcitrant ulcers.

Electric dermatomes, such as the Brown, Padgett, and Zimmer, are the most common and widely used instruments for STSG reconstruction. The Zimmer dermatome offers the advantage of its consistent capability to harvest grafts of predetermined width and uniform thickness. The Zimmer dermatome can be powered by electricity or nitrogen. The Zimmer air dermatome is easily maneuvered in the operating room. The Zimmer dermatome has the advantage of providing vibration-free power. Four predetermined-width plates measuring 1, 2, 3, and 4 inches may be selected and inserted in the dermatome to obtain the desired STSG width. The width plates are easily fastened and removed with an attached screwdriver. The thickness of the graft ranges from 0.008 to 0.030 of an inch and is easily set by adjusting the thickness lever. A disposable sterile blade is used for each procedure.

Obtain local anesthesia at the donor and recipient sites, usually with lidocaine with epinephrine. Prepare and drape both sites in the usual sterile manner. Lubricate the donor site with mineral oil or another lubricant to facilitate a gliding travel of the dermatome over the skin. Place the dermatome handpiece on the donor site at a 30- to 45-degree angle. Have your surgical assistant(s) apply firm pressure to the surrounding area by pulling the skin away from the donor site to create a flat, even donor surface. Press the throttle control on the handpiece and guide the dermatome forward with downward pressure across the donor site. Use a sterile tongue depressor to press firmly against the skin in front of the advancing dermatome; this creates a flat, even surface over which the dermatome can glide.

As the dermatome proceeds over the donor area, the STSG emerges in a pocket area of the dermatome. Have your assistants carefully lift the graft away from the dermatome with tissue forceps or hemostats. Once the desired graft size is harvested, pull the dermatome away from the donor site and place the STSG in sterile saline before transfer to the recipient site. While the graft is secured into the defect, the donor site can be dressed (Fig. 11).

Split-thickness skin grafts are secured to the recipient site in a fashion similar to the FTSG described earlier so that infection, hematoma, seroma, and mechanical shearing forces are minimized or prevented during the time of neovascularization of the graft. The perimeter and the base of the graft must be secured to maximize graft survival. The graft edge may be approximated in a less exact fashion than with FTSGs because the portion that overlaps the skin will slough without affecting the final cosmetic outcome. Secure the graft perimeter with suture or staples, or a combination of these. Staples are particularly timesaving for larger grafts. Because of the size of these grafts, meshing of the graft is usually performed with a scalpel to allow for drainage of accumulated blood or serum that may otherwise impede direct graft-bed contact that is necessary for its survival. Meshing is also used to expand the surface area of an STSG. The use of a meshing machine may expand the graft surface area by a ratio ranging from 3:1 to 9:1, thereby providing coverage of larger wounds with smaller donor grafts. Once the graft is secured, apply a pyramid pressure dressing as previously discussed (Figs. 12 and 13).

Postoperative Management

The STSG dressing should remain in place for 1 week. Postoperative management is similar to that for FTSGs described previously. Harvesting STSGs, unlike FTSGs, creates a second donor partial-thickness defect that heals by second intention. Numerous dressings and postoperative wound care methods have been employed for the donor defect, including simple granulating-wound care instructions and application of hydrogen peroxide and antibiotic ointment once or twice daily. The advent of vapor-permeable dressings such as Opsite has greatly increased comfort and ease of care.

Immediately after harvesting the STSG, clean and dry the donor area. Apply a thin coat of Mastisol to the skin around the perimeter of the donor site and allow it to dry. Place an Opsite dressing over the wound. Secure the Opsite with paper tape, followed by a pressure gauze dressing and an ace bandage. A donor site on the leg can be dressed by one team while the graft is secured to the recipient defect by the surgeon.

During the first postoperative day a considerable amount of serosanguineous fluid may accumulate beneath the dressing. The fluid may be drained with needle and syringe, or the dressing removed and a new one applied. The dressing can be left in place until healing is complete, or routine wound care can be performed if the Opsite dressing is difficult to change. The donor site usually has complete reepithelialization in 1 to 3 weeks, and the scar progresses from pink to white over 6 to 12 months

Adverse Sequelae

The adverse sequelae associated with STSGs are similar to those described for FTSGs. The most important and pre-

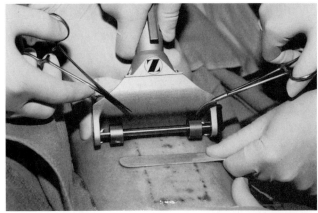

A

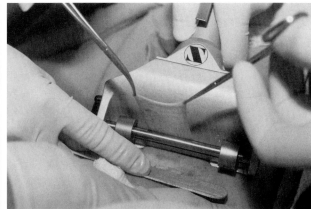

B

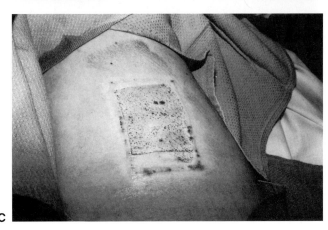

C

FIG. 11. **(A)** Prepare and drape the donor site (thigh in this case) in the usual sterile fashion. Apply firm, pulling pressure to the skin directed away from the donor site to create a flat, even donor surface. Lubricate the donor site with mineral oil to facilitate a gliding travel of the dermatome over the skin. Place a tongue depressor blade to lead the dermatome, again to create a flat even, surface. **(B)** Place the dermatome handpiece over the donor site at a 30- to 45-degree angle. As the dermatome glides over the donor site, secure the graft with hemostats as it emerges from the dermatome pocket. Continue travel of the dermatome until the desired graft is obtained. **(C)** Transfer the graft to the recipient site and begin the closure. While the graft is secured, dress the donor site as described in the text.

dictable difference is poor color and texture match, which is routinely seen with STSGs. As a result, STSGs are not routinely employed for cosmetic purposes. Acceptable cosmetic outcomes usually can be obtained with STSGs on the auricle and digits. Functional adverse outcomes are of particular concern. An STSG contracts more than an FTSG and may result in joint contractures when placed over or near joints. Physical therapy may be necessary to minimize this sequela. A scar may occur at the donor site and may require intralesional steroids for control. Because of possible significant contraction, STSGs are not routinely used in areas with lax free margins such as the eyelid, nasal ala, and lip. Most important, STSGs are fragile and may break down and ulcerate in sites of trauma or areas of little soft tissue support as a result of the smaller amount of protective dermis in the graft.

COMPOSITE GRAFTS

Preoperative Planning

Composite grafts contain two different types of tissue layers, namely, skin and cartilage (for the purposes of this chapter.) Composite grafts are most useful for nasal defects with loss of supportive fibrofatty tissue on the nasal ala, full-thick-

ness alar rim defects, and full-thickness defects located in the soft triangle of the nose. Composite grafts require a rich vascular bed for rapid revascularization and increased nutritional and vascular support. Numerous donor sites of skin and cartilage are located on the ear. Similar to FTSGs, the preferred donor site is based on the amount and shape of cartilage desired and the tissue match of the overlying skin.

Technique

The technique for harvesting composite grafts from the ear is similar to that described previously for FTSGs. Unlike FTSGs, composite grafts require harvesting of cartilage and skin. Donor site repair may require a layered closure or a local flap or may be allowed to heal by granulation. For full-thickness alar rim defects, secure the graft in two layers. First secure the mucosal layer that replaces the internal lining of the nose with 5-0 or 6-0 absorbable suture. Then secure the skin surface by closing with 5-0 or 6-0 nonabsorbable suture. Place the sutures with minimal trauma using small bites to minimize vessel strangulation and maximize the number of potential vessels available for reanastamosis. The cartilage is usually not secured for this type of full-thickness alar rim defect. Use a minimal-pressure dressing, and have

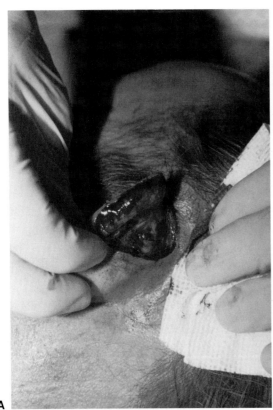

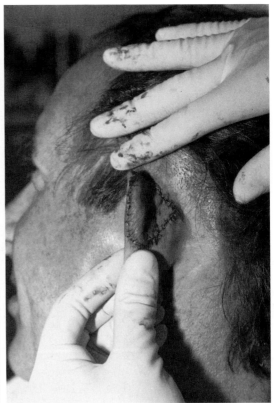

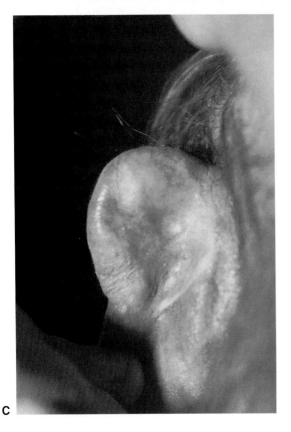

FIG. 12. (A) A 4 × 4.2 cm Mohs' surgical defect is located on the posterior aspect of the ear with preservation of the perichondrium. Plan a split-thickness skin graft that will result in rapid healing and easier monitoring for local recurrence. **(B)** Secure the split-thickness skin graft with a rapidly absorbing 6-0 chromic gut with several simple, interrupted 5-0 polypropylene sutures. Apply a pyramid bolster dressing, and leave in place for 1 week. **(C)** Six-month postoperative result. Both the donor and recipient site were completely healed at 2 to 3 weeks in this case. (Reprinted with permission from Mosby–Year Book, Inc., *Journal of American Academy of Dermatology* 27:151–165, 1992.)

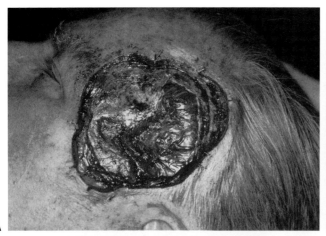

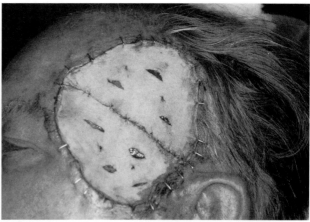

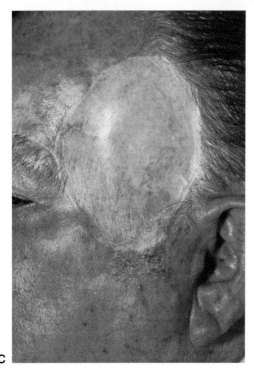

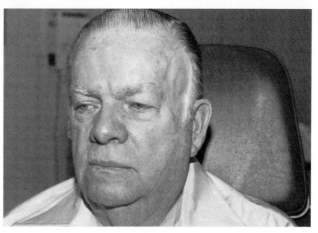

FIG. 13. **(A)** A 7 × 9 cm Mohs' surgical defect is present following removal of a previously irradiated, multiply recurrent, aggressive growth pattern basal cell carcinoma of the left temple. A split-thickness skin graft is ideal to monitor for local recurrence of this high-risk tumor. In addition, the wound will be healed in 2 to 4 weeks with a split-thickness skin graft. **(B)** Secure the split-thickness skin graft with several bolster sutures. Secure the perimeter of the graft with staples. Place the staples in a fashion to maximize graft-bed contact. Mesh the graft using a scalpel, to expand the surface area and prevent hematoma and seroma formation under the graft. Apply a pyramid bolster dressing as described previously. **(C)** Patient remains tumor free 7 years after surgery. A patchlike appearance is evident, which is to be expected with a split-thickness skin graft. **(D)** Long-term result; patchlike appearance and contour deformity are evident. The contour deformity can be minimized by allowing the wound to heal by granulation several weeks before placement of the split-thickness skin graft, if desired. A brow lift was performed because of ablation of the superficial temporal branch of the facial nerve. The graft could be removed with reconstruction using tissue expansion if desired following an appropriate time interval to monitor for recurrence. For a high-risk basal cell carcinoma as in this case, an appropriate interval to monitor for recurrence ranges from 5 to 10 years. (Reprinted with permission from Mosby–Year Book, Inc., *Journal of American Academy of Dermatology* 27:151–165, 1992.)

the patient apply ice packs often for several days. Remove sutures at 1 week.

For partial-thickness alar rim and other nasal defects, the composite graft is secured in the following manner. Secure the cartilage graft in place to the underlying recipient bed with 5-0 or 6-0 monofilament absorbable suture. Then secure the skin in the usual fashion for an FTSG, and place a bolster over the wound. Remove the dressing in 7 days, and instruct the patient in postoperative management, which is the same as for FTSG management as previously described (Fig. 14).

Administer oral antibiotics to reduce staphylococcal overgrowth that can occur in composite grafts placed around the nose because of common bacterial colonization that can result in a higher risk of failure.

Adverse Sequelae

Composite grafts require a rich vascular bed, and the risk of graft failure is significantly higher than for FTSGs or STSGs. Partial-graft necrosis and wound contraction often

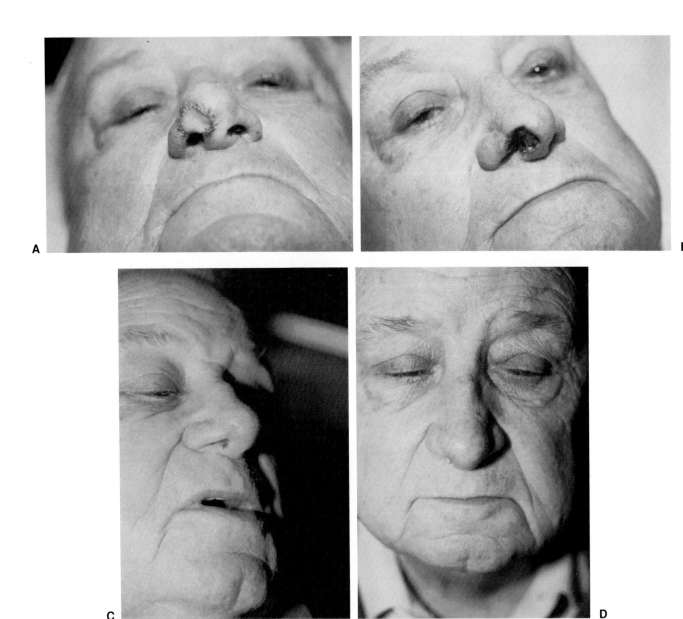

FIG. 14. (A) Full-thickness defect located in the soft triangle of the nose. Obtain a composite graft from the crus of the helix of the ear to recreate the soft triangle of the nose. **(B)** Secure the composite graft to the primary defect using a running, rapidly absorbing 6-0 chromic gut suture and several interrupted 6-0 polypropylene sutures. Secure the internal lining of the graft before securing the external component. Place a minimal-pressure dressing for 1 week, and give oral antibiotics to cover staphylococcal and streptococcal infection. **(C and D)** Six-month postoperative result. A spot dermabrasion was performed at 8 weeks to improve cosmesis and suture line irregularities.

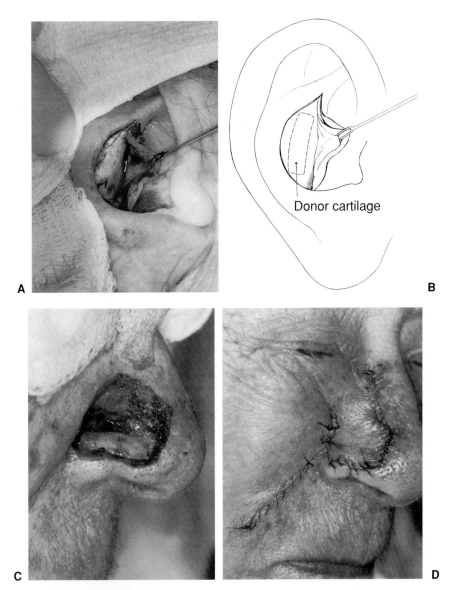

A

B

Donor cartilage

C

D

E

FIG. 15. (A) Clinical and **(B)** schematic nasal defect with loss of fibrofatty alar tissue. Obtain a free cartilage graft from the concha of the ear with appropriate size and contour of the alar rim. Make an incision at the junction of the concha and antihelix. Reflect the conchal skin to expose the donor cartilage. Excise the free cartilage graft with perichondrium attached. Replace the conchal skin into the primary defect and secure using a running 5-0 or 6-0 nonabsorbable suture. Place a bolster suture to remove dead space following removal of the free cartilage graft. **(C)** Secure the free cartilage graft to provide structural support and contour to the lobule. Secure the graft with multiple absorbable monofilament 5-0 or 6-0 suture. **(D)** Proceed with a superiorly based nasolabial transposition flap. Undermine widely, use a periosteal tackdown suture in the nasofacial sulcus, and aggressively thin the flap for contour. Thin cautiously in patients with a smoking history. **(E)** Four-month postoperative result with good contour and total functional support of the alar rim.

TABLE 15-2. *Causes of graft necrosis or failure*

Poor recipient bed vascularity
Inadequate vascular bed
Exposed cartilage, bone, tendon
Nicotine-induced vasoconstriction
Poor graft-bed contact
Hematoma
Seroma
Poor immobilizing pressure dressing
Perioperative physical activiy, bending, lifting
Infection
Staphylococcus species
Streptococcus species
Pseudomonas species (especially ear)
Host factors
Poor general health
Immunosuppression
Diabetes mellitus
Systemic conditions with vascular compromise (connective tissue disease, others)
Technique
Rough handling of tissue
Excessive devitalization of tissue via electrocautery
Inadequate graft size: Increased tension
Inadequate meticulous hemostasis
Inadequate adipose trimming

require secondary revisional surgery. Because of the location and higher risk of necrosis, infection rates are potentially higher with composite grafts. Therefore perioperative oral antibiotics are often used.

FREE CARTILAGE GRAFTS

Free cartilage grafts from the ear to the nose are useful for alar rim defects with loss of supportive structural alar rim fibrofatty tissue with preservation of mucosa. These free cartilage grafts are placed before flap reconstruction to provide alar rim support that cannot be provided by soft tissue from the flap. Harvest the cartilage graft with the perichondrium intact from the antihelix or concha of the ear. Suture the overlying skin back into place following removal of the cartilage at the ear donor area. Place the cartilage graft into the alar rim defect and secure it using 5-0 or 6-0 monofilament absorbable suture. Once the alar rim structural support is regained by placing the free cartilage graft, a skin flap can be placed above it to provide soft tissue coverage of the defect. The most common flaps used in combination with this procedure are the nasolabial transposition flap, forehead flap, and the staged cheek-to-nose interpolation flap. Free cartilage grafts placed anywhere on the nose or ear are highly successful and provide excellent structural support before flap closure (Fig. 15).

SUGGESTED READING LIST

1. Beare RLB, Bennett JP. The nasolabial full-thickness graft. Br J Plast Surg 1972;25:315.
2. Breach NM. Preauricular full-thickness skin grafts. Br J Plast Surg 1978;1:124.
3. Brown JB, McDowell F. Skin grafting. Philadelphia: JB Lippincott, 1958:70-8, 92-5, 124-30, 346-7.
4. Ceilley RL, Bumsted RM, Panje WR. Delayed skin grafting. J Dermatol Surg Oncol 1983;9:288.
5. Corwin TR, Klein AW, Habal MB. The aesthetics of the preauricular graft in facial reconstruction. Ann Plastic Surg 1982;9:312.
6. Davis JS, Kitlowski EA. The immediate contraction of cutaneous grafts and its cause. Arch Surg 1931;23:954.
7. Field LM. Nasal alar rim reconstruction utilizing the crus of the helix, with several alternatives for donor site closure. J Dermatol Surg Oncol 1986;12:253.
8. Glogau RG, Stegman SJ, Tromovitch TA. Refinements in split-thickness skin grafting technique. J Dermatol Surg Oncol 1987;13:853.
9. Goldminz D, Bennett RG. Cigarette smoking and flap and full-thickness graft necrosis. Arch Dermatol 1982;127:1012.
10. Higton DIR, James DW. The force of contraction of full-thickness wounds of rabbit skin. Br J Surg 1964;51:462.
11. Hill TG. Contouring of donor skin in full-thickness skin grafting. J Dermatol Surg Oncol 1987;13:883.
12. Hill TG. Enhancing the survival of full-thickness grafts. J Dermatol Surg Oncol 1984;10:639.
13. Hill TG. Reconstruction of nasal defects using full-thickness skin grafts: a personal reappraisal. J Dermatol Surg Oncol 1983;9:995.
14. James JH, Watson ACH. The use of Opsite, a vapour permeable dressing, on skin graft donor sites. Br J Plast Surg 1975;28:107.
15. Jewell ML. Staples to secure skin grafts. Plast Reconstr Surg 1988; 82(1):204 (letter to the editor).
16. Johnson TM, Ratner D, Nelson BR: Soft tissue reconstruction with skin grafting. J Am Acad Dermatol 1992;27:151.
17. Kaplan HY. A quick stapler tie-over fixation for skin grafts. Plastic Reconstr Surg 1989;22(2):203.
18. Larson PO. Foam-rubber stents for skin grafts. J Dermatol Surg Oncol 1990;16:851.
19. Maves MD, Yessenow RS. The use of composite auricular grafts in nasal reconstruction. J Dermatol Surg Oncol 1988;14(9):994.
20. McLaughlin CR. Composite ear grafts and their blood supply. Br J Plast Surg 1954;7:274.
21. Mellette JR, Swinehart JM. Cartilage removal prior to skin grafting in the triangular fossa, antihelix, and concha of the ear. J Dermatol Surg Oncol 1990;16:1102.
22. Niranjan RS. A modified tie-over dressing for skin grafts. Br J Plast Surg 1985;38:415.
23. Noe HM, Kalish S. The problem of adherence in dressed wounds. Surg Gynecol Obstet 1978;147:185.
24. Peled IJ, Wexler MR. Designing and dressing of skin grafts by means of patterns on sponges of polyurethane. J Dermatol Surg Oncol 1981; 7:664.
25. Rigg BM. Importance of donor site selection in skin grafting. CMA J 1977;117:1028.
26. Roenigk RK, Roenigk HH. Dermatologic Surgery: Principles and practice. New York: Marcel Dekker, 1989:324.
27. Ruch MK. Utilization of composite free grafts. J Int Coll Surg 1958; 30:274.
28. Rudolph R, Fisher JC, Ninneman JL. Skin Grafting. Boston: Little, Brown, 1987:27.
29. Rudolph R. The effect of skin graft preparation. Surg Gynecol Obstet 1976;142:49.
30. Salasche SJ, Feldman BD. Skin grafting: perioperative technique and management. J Dermatol Surg Oncol 1987;13:863.
31. Salasche SJ, Winton GB. Clinical evaluation of a nonadhering wound dressing. J Dermatol Surg Oncol 1986;12:1220.
32. Salasche SJ. Acute surgical complications: cause, prevention, and treatment. J Am Acad Dermatol 1986;15:1163.
33. Silverskiold KL. A new pressure device for securing skin grafts. Br J Plast Surg 1986;39:567.
34. Skouge JW. Skin grafting. New York: Churchill Livingstone, 1991:2-45, 52-63, 65-71.
35. Skouge JW. Techniques for split-thickness skin grafting. J Dermatol Surg Oncol 1987;13:841.
36. Swanson NA. Atlas of Cutaneous Surgery. Boston: Little, Brown, 1987: 136.
37. Symonds FC, Crikelair GF. Auricular composite grafts in nasal reconstruction: a report of 36 cases. Plast Reconstr Surg 1966;37:433.

38. Thomas JR, Mechlin DC, Templer J. Skin grafts. Arch Otolaryngol 1982;108:437.

39. Tipton JB. Priority in using staples to secure skin grafts. Plast Reconstr Surg 1989;83(1):194 (letter to the editor).

40. Tromovitch TA, Stegman SJ, Glogau RG. Flaps and grafts in dermatologic surgery. Chicago, Year-Book Medical, 1989:49-54, 65-7.

41. Vecchione TR. Reconstruction of the ala and nostril sill using proximate composite grafts. Ann Plast Surg 1980;5:148.

42. Wheeland RG. The technique and current status of pinch grafting. J Dermatol Surg Oncol 1987;13:873.

43. Whitaker DC, Grande DJ, Koranda FC, et al. Rapid application of split-thickness skin grafts. J Dermatol Surg Oncol 1982;8:499.

Textbook of Dermatologic Surgery, edited by John L. Ratz.
Lippincott–Raven Publishers, Philadelphia © 1998.

CHAPTER 16

Flaps

Michael J. Fazio and John A. Zitelli

HISTORY

The history of flap reconstruction is filled with "trial-and-error" approaches to wound repair and anecdotal reports. The first reports of suturing wounds was found in early Egyptian literature, around 1800 BC. Elaborate descriptions of nasal reconstruction using cheek and forehead flaps were documented around 700 BC by a group of specialists known as the Koomas. Since nasal amputation was a common punishment for criminal acts in ancient India, nasal reconstruction was often performed by the Koomas. In early Roman history Celsus and Galen made many advances with respect to facial flap reconstructive surgery. Several of these observations and techniques remain applicable today (e.g., layered closures and ideal placement of incisions).

In later years interest in facial reconstruction became apparent in both the European and American literature. The Tagliacozzi method of nasal tip and ear repairs was described in 1597; this innovative technique consisted of delayed skin flaps. In 1814 Carpue described and illustrated a staged procedure for nasal reconstruction; this procedure is commonly performed today and is known as the forehead flap. In 1893 Dunham described a method for reconstruction of facial defects created by resection of skin cancers; this technique was a pedicled flap based on the temporal artery and has several useful applications.

Michael J. Fazio: Department of Dermatology, University of California at Davis, Skin Cancer Surgery Center, 2805 J Street, Suite 100, Sacramento, CA 95816.

John A. Zitelli: University of Pittsburgh Medical Center—Shadyside, 5200 Centre Avenue, Suite 303, Pittsburgh, PA 15232.

Local anesthesia was not discovered for surgical procedures until the late 19th century. Therefore, reconstructive surgery was usually reserved for extensive, disfiguring defects with patients who had a strong will and desire for corrective procedures. The advent of local anesthesia has greatly enhanced the progress of reconstructive techniques to allow for development of a wide range of facial flap procedures with minimal patient discomfort.

The sophistication of flap biomechanics and physiology today has been built on the work of the early pioneers of reconstructive surgery. The literature is replete with different flaps that may be applicable to almost any type of defect. Therefore it is incumbent upon the surgeon to understand not only the indications of a particular flap, but also the limitations.

PREOPERATIVE PLANNING

Reconstruction of cutaneous wounds resulting from removal of cancerous or benign lesions requires technical skills and application of basic surgical principles. Knowledge of basic surgical principles can be acquired through literature and textbook review, but technical skills are best learned through hands-on experience in a proctored situation such as residency, fellowship, or reconstructive surgery courses. Although many of the reconstructive techniques described in this chapter may appear simple in principle, implementation of these flaps in a clinical setting requires a certain level of surgical expertise; otherwise, complications are inevitable. The insightful Dr. Ian Jackson pointed out that "the greatest drawback to the use of skin flaps is that they require planning and experience.'' Careless or inappropriate planning or poor execution can have devastating consequences and defeat the purpose of flap reconstruction.

Often there can be several reconstructive surgery options that will work for a specific wound, but usually there is one option that will give the highest likelihood of a successful outcome and minimize complications. In this chapter an approach to facial flap surgery is presented. A general guideline for choosing the appropriate flap and flap design is emphasized. The reconstructive modality of choice is often predictable, and the results are reproducible based on the location of the wound (i.e., the island pedicle flap for lateral cutaneous upper lip and bilobed flap for lower third of the nose). Therefore it is not the intent to present every possible closure for a particular wound, but instead to share experiences and present closures that most often produce optimal functional and cosmetic outcome.

General Principles

Preoperative considerations require an expansive knowledge of surgical anatomy including ''danger zones,'' cosmetic boundaries, favorable lines of closure, vascular supply, motor and sensory innervation, areas of tissue availability, and effects of tissue movement. The same basic surgical techniques that are used in excisional surgery and primary closure are also applied to complex flap reconstructive surgery. The outlining of cosmetic units and favorable lines of closure and preoperative planning should be accomplished before infiltrating local anesthetic, which commonly distorts the normal anatomy. Optimal aesthetic results are usually obtained if incision lines can be placed along or parallel to junction lines that separate cosmetic units (e.g., melolabial fold, nasofacial sulcus, vermilion, preauricular crease). If the location of the wound precludes use of junction lines, the flaps should be designed so that incisional lines are within the favorable lines of closure (relaxed skin tension lines) (Fig. 1).

The level of tissue undermining varies depending on the location of the wound. Common site-specific areas of tissue dissection include cheeks and temple (subcutaneous fat), scalp and forehead (subgaleal), nose and ears (submuscular or perichondrial) and lips and chin (supramuscular). Blunt dissection by spreading and teasing tissue planes apart with an opening motion of scissors may be useful in loose tissue planes involving the fascia (i.e., galea or perichondrial), but in other locations undermining is usually best performed by careful and meticulous sharp dissection. This leads to less tissue trauma and a more even, flat undermining plane. Again, it is imperative for the surgeon to have a thorough understanding of the surgical anatomy. Wide undermining of the defect, flap, and donor site and thinning of the subcutaneous fat from the flap will minimize ''pincushioning'' (''trapdoor'' deformity).

The same suturing techniques that apply to excisional sur-

FIG. 1. Favorable lines of closure on the face. Note the forehead lines extend vertically from the orbicularis muscles.

gery and primary closure also apply to the more advanced reconstructive procedures. The use of the buried vertical mattress stitch is difficult to master, but has several advantages over the standard subcutaneous stitch. The buried vertical mattress stitch is based on the same principle and effect as the cutaneous vertical mattress suture, and it likewise achieves good wound-edge eversion, but the effect is prolonged, thus preventing scar depression. In addition, the buried vertical mattress suture provides support and thus prevents wound dehiscence. Also, it approximates the skin edge, thus relieving tension on the more superficial cutaneous sutures, which are necessary for epidermal approximation. Thus the facial cutaneous sutures can be removed five days after surgery, thereby eliminating ''railroad track'' scars as well as fear of dehiscence or scar inversion. When suturing wound edges, it is important to remember the effects of skin elasticity. After incision and undermining, the deepest part of the flap contracts more than the superficial portion (Fig. 2). Therefore, the surgeon must make a conscious effort to reach beneath the flap and include the retracted subdermis within the buried sutures to prevent inversion of the scar.

Once the flap and wound edges have been approximated with buried vertical mattress subcutaneous sutures, the skin edges can be meticulously reapproximated with a running nylon suture. Vicryl (No. 5-0 or 6-0, PS-6 needle) and Ethilon (No. 6-0, P-1 needle) are commonly used for facial flaps. The combination of the buried vertical mattress and running cutaneous sutures is the standard layered closure that is used for all primary closures and flap reconstruction.

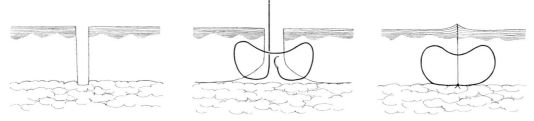

FIG. 2. After undermining the flap, the deep tissue retracts more than the superficial tissue. Therefore, when placing the buried vertical mattress suture for wound edge eversion, the surgeon must make a special effort to include a portion of the retracted subcutaneous tissue.

The periosteal suspension suture is a useful technique to minimize cutaneous tension at the wound edge. This suture is based on the principle that routine side-to-side closure shares tension and motion with both sides of the wound, while the periosteal suture achieves closure with tension and motion limited to one side of the wound because the opposite side of suture attachment is to the tissues over immobile periosteum. This stitch is placed through a small portion of the dermis of the flap and suspended to the periosteum or deep fascia. A properly placed periosteal suture can also be used to close dead space (i.e., alar crease, inner canthus), redefine cosmetic boundaries or landmarks (i.e., nasofacial sulcus or melolabial fold), or prevent excessive tension on a free tissue margins (i.e., lip or eyelid) and thus minimize functional disturbance. The most common applications of periosteal sutures in facial reconstructive surgery include cheek advancement flaps (to recontour the melolabial fold), large cheek rotation flaps (to relieve flap tension and prevent lower eyelid ectropion formation) and nasolabial flaps (to prevent tenting at the nasofacial sulcus).

Flap Classification

There are several classification schemes for flaps, but they are most commonly categorized with respect to the properties of the primary tissue movement, that is, advancement, rotation, or transposition. Other classifications are based on the location of the tissue recruitment (local vs. distant flaps) or the pattern of blood supply for the flap (axial vs. random). Most facial flaps (advancement, rotation, or transposition) are categorized as local, random pattern flaps, which means that the tissue adjacent to the defect is used and the blood supply is derived from the subcutaneous and dermal plexus. A paramedian forehead flap, which is used in nasal reconstruction, is based on the supratrochlear artery and is classified as a distant, axial pattern flap.

In general, most advancement, rotation, and transposition flaps used in facial reconstructive surgery have unique tissue dynamics but share similar basic principles. Burow's triangles are often displaced to less conspicuous locations to facilitate recruitment of adjacent tissue laxity, thereby minimizing wound tension and facial distortion. Although this categorization is an oversimplification of flap mechanics and

tissue movement, a review of basic flap design is presented to facilitate an understanding of more complex flap procedures.

SURGICAL TECHNIQUE

Advancement Flap

Advancement flaps are the simplest extension of a primary closure. Wide undermining of tissue around the defect often allows primary advancement of the tissue without the need for releasing incisions or displaced Burow's triangles. But if anatomic considerations preclude removal of primary Burow's triangles directly above or below the wound (i.e., the lip), releasing incisions are often required to allow removal of Burow's triangles distant from the wound (i.e., melolabial fold). Make releasing incisions perpendicular to the line of closure, displace the Burow's triangles at variable length away from the wound, and place the triangles base parallel to the primary line of closure. Adequate undermining of the flap and surrounding tissue facilitates sliding of the advancement flap in a linear fashion into the defect (Fig. 3). As a general rule, the length of the flap should not be more than three times the width of the base of the flap.

Large defects on the cutaneous portion of the lips can often be reconstructed with a complex advancement flap (Fig. 4). Complex advancement flaps require extensive un-

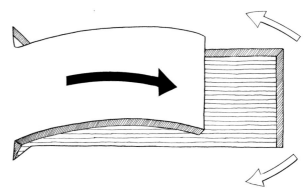

FIG. 3. Classic advancement flap, showing primary movement *(solid arrow)* and secondary movement *(open arrow)*.

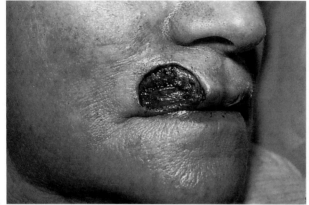
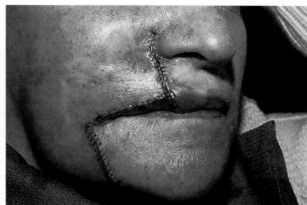
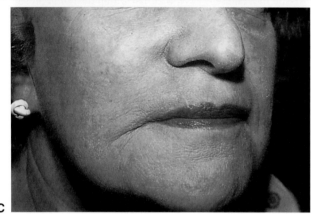

FIG. 4. (A) Large defect involving the upper lip. **(B)** Complex advancement flap. Note a periosteal suture attaching the base of the flap to the pyriform aperture of the maxilla was used to re-create the melolabial fold and minimize trapdoor deformity. **(C)** Results eight weeks postoperatively.

dermining to release the redundant tissue of the lateral lip and cheek. Like the fusiform closure, tissue movement is in the horizontal direction; however, the superior and inferior Burow's triangles are displaced laterally into the melolabial fold. Make a releasing incision lateral to the defect extending along the vermilion-cutaneous junction. This incision should extend lateral to the oral commissure. A crescent-shaped Burow's triangle should then be removed in the perialar region superior to the defect. A similar crescent-shaped Burow's triangle should be removed infralateral to the defect extending along the melolabial fold. The flap and wound edges should be undermined in a supramuscular plane. The level of undermining should be consistent even when crossing the melolabial fold into the subcutaneous fat of the cheek. Advancement of the wedge-shaped flap medially tends to displace the vermilion border inferiorly; thus it may be necessary to trim the inferior edge of the flap for proper alignment of the vermilion. A common complication of any flap crossing the melolabial line is blunting of the melolabial fold. Therefore, place the first stitch to connect the periosteum of the pyriform aperture of the maxilla to the dermis of the flap. A properly placed periosteal suture should restore the natural crevice of the superior portion of the melolabial fold. The periosteal suture also approximates the wound edges so that tension and distortion of the lip are minimal. Once the periosteal suture has been placed, the advancement flap can be sutured using a standard layered closure.

Although the CO_2 laser is commonly used for vermilionectomy of the actinically damaged lower lip, epidermal-mucosal advancement flaps may be useful for deeper wounds (Fig. 5). Wide wounds of the lower lip may lead to significant deformity if repaired primarily by wedge resection. In these circumstances mucosal advancement flaps can be used to minimize functional and cosmetic distortion. Furthermore, most patients with squamous cell carcinoma of the lower lip have widespread actinic cheilitis, which is also treated by vermilionectomy and epidermal-mucosal advancement. Make an incision along the vermilion cutaneous junction and the red line of the vermilion border to remove a Burow's triangle from both lateral aspects of the wound. Undermine the vermilion tissue anteriorly in a supramuscular plane. Undermine the mucosal tissue to the gingival sulcus. Advance the mucosal tissue over the remaining orbicularis muscle, and suture the mucosal flap using a standard layered closure.

Helical rim defects often involve a portion of the underlying auricular cartilage and commonly result in a significant and conspicuous indention if left to heal by second intention or repaired with a skin graft. Wedge resection leads to shrinkage and cupping of the ear, and the results are often unsatisfactory. Helical rim advancement preserves the auricular cartilage and minimizes shrinkage of the ear (Fig. 6). The repair is useful for defects up to 2.5 cm along the helical rim. Make an incision along the anterior crease of the helical

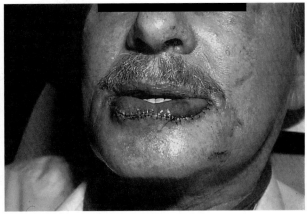

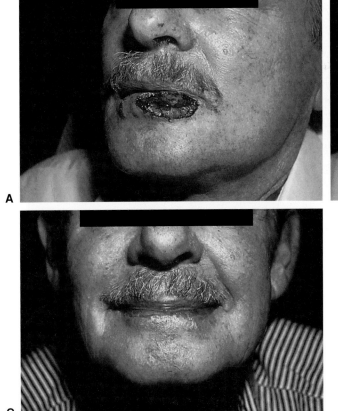

FIG. 5. (A) Wide defect of the lower lip involving a portion of the orbicularis muscle. **(B)** Reconstruction by complete vermilionectomy and epidermal-mucosal advancement. **(C)** Results five months postoperatively.

rim, and extend the incision through the cartilage but not through the posterior auricular skin. Widely undermine the postauricular skin in a perichondrial plane. To prevent bunching of the postauricular skin, remove a Burow's triangle from the helical rim to the postauricular crease. To facilitate maximal advancement of the helical rim tissue, remove a Burow's triangle form the inferior aspect of the inferior releasing incision at the level of the earlobe. The flaps are then advanced and approximated using a standard closure.

Because of the tissue laxity of the cheek and preauricular skin, even complicated wounds can often be repaired with a primary advancement flap along the normal relaxed skin tension lines (Fig. 7). Medial cheek lesions are often designed in a lazy-S fashion to conform to the normal, relaxed skin tension lines from the inner canthus to the oral commissure, parallel to the nasofacial sulcus and the melolabial fold. Make incisions inferior to the defect extending parallel to the melolabial fold to remove a crescent-shaped Burow's triangle. The smaller Burow's triangle should then be removed superior to the defect toward the inner canthus, extending along the nasofacial sulcus. Widely undermine the skin edges in a supramuscular plane along the lower eyelid, the nasal sidewall, and the upper lip. Similar-undermining should be carried out lateral to the defect extending along the subcutaneous tissue of the cheek (approximately 2 to 3 cm). Advance the flap so that the tension of closure is hori-

zontal and parallel to the lower eyelid, and suture the wound in the standard layered fashion.

Island Pedicle Flap

The island flap is based on the underlying subcutaneous or muscular vascular supply. Because of the generous blood supply, the flap can be dissected to a small central vascular pedicle with little likelihood of ischemic complications. Since a triangular wedge of tissue is being advanced into the defect, the tension of closure is almost entirely redistributed to the donor site (Fig. 8).

The island pedicle flap has several useful applications for repair of wounds in the perioral tissue. Defects of the upper lateral lip are ideally located for wound closure with an island pedicle flap (Fig. 9). Make a triangular-shaped incision infralateral to the defect extending deeply into the subcutaneous tissue. Carefully dissect the triangular flap to a small central vascular pedicle. Because of the abundant vascularity in the perioral tissue, a relatively small central subcutaneous pedicle provides adequate blood supply and allows for maximal mobility of the flap. After the subcutaneous pedicle has been meticulously dissected, superficially undermine the defect, flap, and donor skin (approximately 2.0 mm) to facilitate wound-edge eversion during closure. To minimize pin-

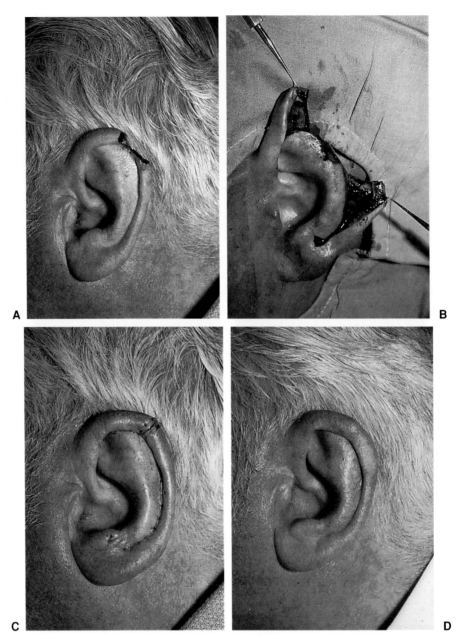

FIG. 6. (A) Defect of the helical rim. **(B)** Intraoperative dissection of a helical rim advancement flap. **(C)** Suturing of the flaps. **(D)** Results six months postoperatively.

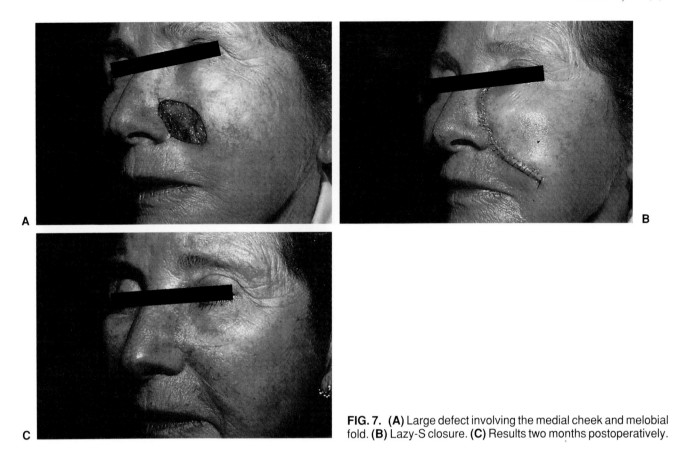

FIG. 7. (A) Large defect involving the medial cheek and melobial fold. **(B)** Lazy-S closure. **(C)** Results two months postoperatively.

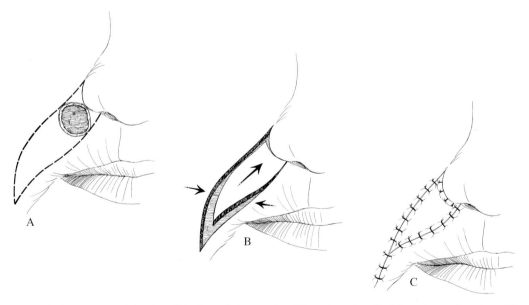

FIG. 8. Subcutaneous island pedicle flap. Sutures should be placed so that the closure tension of the donor site is horizontal to avoid lip elevation.

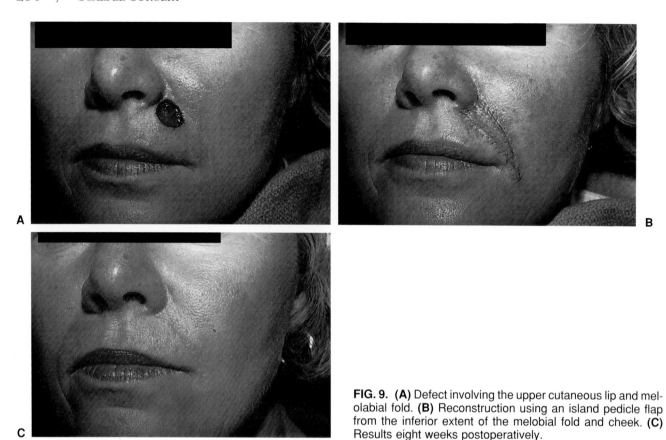

FIG. 9. (A) Defect involving the upper cutaneous lip and melolabial fold. **(B)** Reconstruction using an island pedicle flap from the inferior extent of the melobial fold and cheek. **(C)** Results eight weeks postoperatively.

cushioning of the flap, square off the circular defect before advancement of the triangular-shaped island pedicle flap. Advance the flap into the defect, and suture the flap and secondary defect in a standard layered fashion.

Rotation Flap

Rotation flaps are capable of recruiting large amounts of tissue from local or distant sites. A large, arclike releasing incision is commonly made along the superior aspect of the wound. The length of the incisional arc is directly proportional to the size of the wound. The length of the arc should be approximately three to four times the size of the defect. In general, lengthening the incisional arc disperses the closure tension over a greater surface area and results in less tension and distortion at the primary wound site. To facilitate rotation of the flap, a variable-sized Burow's triangle must be removed at the pivot point of the flap, which is commonly at the inferior aspect of the defect. A Burow's triangle must be removed at the tail end of the releasing incision. This last Burow's triangle is most commonly removed from the lateral aspect of the releasing incision (Fig. 10A). If greater mobility is necessary to facilitate flap closure, the last Burow's triangle can be removed from the medial aspect of the arc in a back-cut fashion (Fig. 10B). Carry out the back-cut with a great deal of caution, since this removes a portion of the

vascular base of the flap and may lead to vascular insufficiency.

Rotation flaps are ideally suited for large defects involving the medial area of the cheek (Fig. 11). Remove a Burow's triangle inferior to the defect, similar to a primary closure. Because of insufficient tissue availability superior to the defect; make a large releasing incision lateral to the superior edge of the defect in a wide, arclike fashion that extends parallel to and above the zygomatic arch. At the lateral canthus the releasing incision should be directed superior to the lateral canthus to minimize downward tension and the potential for an ectropion formation. Continue the arc of the releasing incision to the sideburn and down the preauricular crease. A Burow's triangle should be excised from the infra-auricular region. Undermine the defect, the donor site, and the entire flap widely to facilitate rotation of the flap under minimal tension and distortion. The flap should be able to rotate into the defect with minimal tension. Use No. 4-0 Vicryl suture to connect the periosteum of the lateral orbital rim to the undersurface of the flap to minimize pull down of the lower eyelid. This will help prevent ectropion formation. Then suture the flap in a standard layered fashion.

When dealing with large wounds that involve the lateral area of forehead and suprabrow region, a rotation flap may be useful to recruit the adjacent tissue from the upper cheek and lateral temple region (Fig. 12). Make a releasing incision at the infralateral aspect of the defect, and extend it along

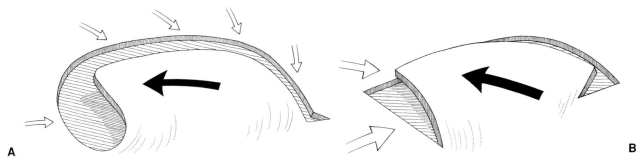

FIG. 10. (A) Rotation flap, showing shared tension around primary and secondary defects. **(B)** Rotation flap with back cut. This provides additional tissue movement by rotation and advancement. (Primary movement: *solid arrows;* secondary movement: *open arrows.*)

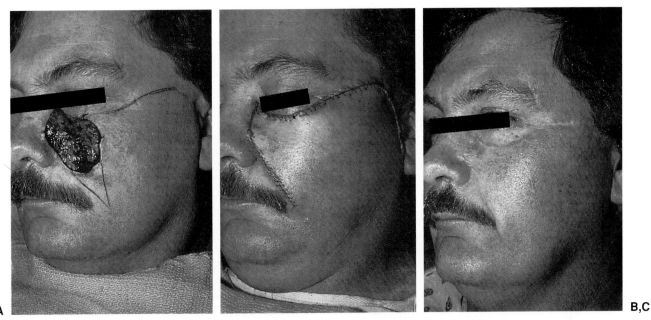

FIG. 11. (A) Large defect of cheek and nasofacial sulcus. **(B)** Reconstruction with a cheek rotation flap. **(C)** Results six months postoperatively.

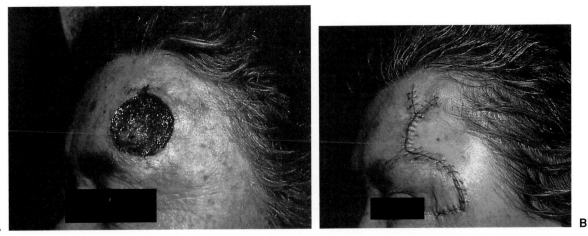

FIG. 12. (A) Large defect involving the lateral forehead. **(B)** Reconstruction using a rotation flap and M-plasty.

the superior aspect of the eyebrow. The releasing incision should be carried in an arclike fashion inferior to the lateral canthus. A large Burow's triangle should be removed in the area of the lateral canthus to facilitate maximal movement of the rotation flap while minimizing distortion of the eyebrow and eyelids. The superior Burow's triangle can be taken out primarily or converted to an M-plasty (as in Figure 12) to minimize tissue tension. Then undermine carefully in a superficial fascial plane to avoid damage to the temporal branch of the facial nerve. The flap can then be rotated into the defect and closed in the usual layered manner.

Extensive defects involving the upper or lower lip may require recruitment of a large amount of local tissue via a Karapandzic flap (Fig. 13). This is essentially a bilateral rotation flap. Make an incision on both lateral aspects of the defect extending along the nasal sill and lateral but parallel to the melolabial fold in an arclike fashion. The incision should be carried to the level of the commissure. Remove Burow's triangles from the infralateral aspects of the releasing incisions. Next undermine the flaps widely in the supramuscular plane in the perioral region and the superifical subcutaneous tissue along the cheek and preauricular region. Carefully dissect the flaps to a central neurovascular pedicle at the level of the modiolus. Rotate the flaps into the defect, and close the wound in a multilayered fashion using No. 5-0 Vicryl for the submucosal, muscular, and subcutaneous

tissue. The epidermal edges are then carefully approximated using No. 6-0 Ethilon.

Transposition Flap

The transposition flap is the workhorse for facial reconstructive surgery. This flap is extremely versatile and able to mobilize local tissue from any adjacent tissue source. Depending on tissue laxity and location of the cosmetic boundaries, the angle of transposition is usually between 30 and 60 degrees (Fig. 14). The classic rhombic transposition flap was first described by Limberg in 1963. Several clinically important modifications of the Limberg flap have been described by Dufourmental, Webster, and Becker. The rhombic flap can be designed to redistribute wound tension and minimize distortion of free tissue margins (i.e., nose, eyelids, lips). Therefore this flap has a wide range of applications in almost every aspect of facial reconstructive surgery.

A superiorly based transposition flap is extremely useful in repairing defects of the lateral cutaneous upper lip (Fig. 15). Make an incision at the junction of the wound and the melolabial fold, and extend this inferior to the oral commissure. The width of the flap should approximate the width of the wound. A perialar crescentic Burow's triangle is then removed along the lateral alar crease. The flap, donor site, and the wound edges are then widely undermined in supra-

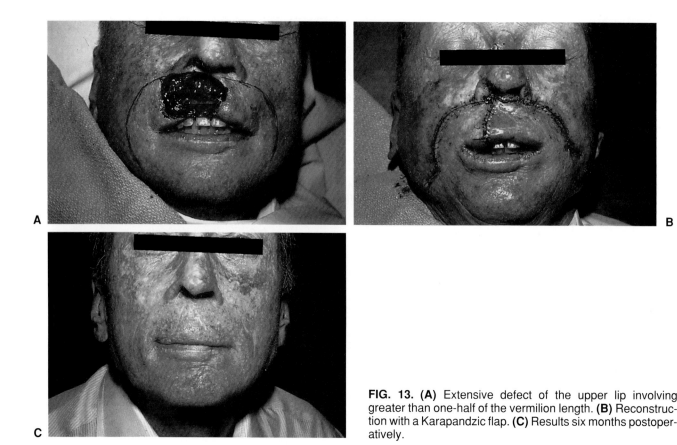

FIG. 13. (A) Extensive defect of the upper lip involving greater than one-half of the vermilion length. **(B)** Reconstruction with a Karapandzic flap. **(C)** Results six months postoperatively.

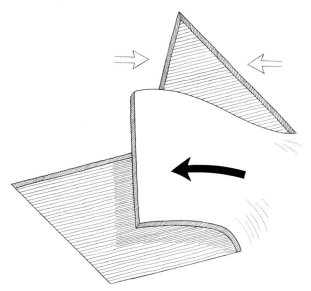

FIG. 14. Classic rhombic transposition flap. Note that most secondary movement (*open arrows*) results from tension created by closure of the secondary defect. (Primary movement: *solid arrows*).

muscular and superficial subcutaneous planes. The rhombic flap is transposed into the defect under minimal tension and distortion. A periosteal suture is placed at the base of the flap to recreate the crevice of the melolabial fold (see previous description in Advancement Flap). Trim the tip of the flap

to conform to the size and shape of the defect, and suture the flap into place in a standard layered fashion.

Defects of the chin can often be repaired with a transposition flap to recruit tissue laxity from the submental region and minimize inferior pull of the lower lip (Fig. 16). Convert the defect to a rhombic-shaped wound. Make an incision medial to the defect extending along the mentum parallel of the mental crease. The width of the transposition flap should approximate the size of the defect. Widely undermine the flap and wound edges in a supramuscular plane. Transpose the flap into the defect, and close the wound in a standard layered fashion. A small dog-ear may be created at the pivot point of the transposition flap; therefore a triangular incision may be necessary to flatten the surrounding tissue.

The rhombic transposition flap is especially useful to repair defects involving the upper two thirds of the nose (Fig. 17). Incise a rhombic transposition flap superior to the defect extending along the nasal dorsum and onto the nasal root. The width of the flap should approximate the size of the defect. The flap and defect are widely undermined in a supramuscular plane. Trim the tip of the flap to conform to the rounded configuration of the defect. Transpose the flap into the defect, and suture the flap in the normal layered fashion. A small dog-ear may be created along the pivot point of the flap at the sidewall of the nose; therefore a triangular incision may be necessary to flatten the surrounding tissue.

Transposition flaps are capable of recruitment of large

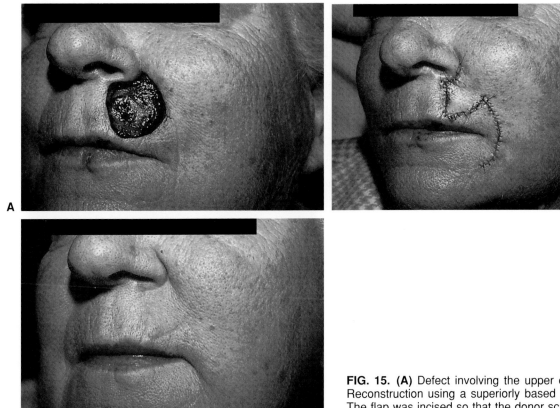

FIG. 15. (A) Defect involving the upper cutaneous lip. **(B)** Reconstruction using a superiorly based transposition flap. The flap was incised so that the donor scar would match to the existing melolabial fold.

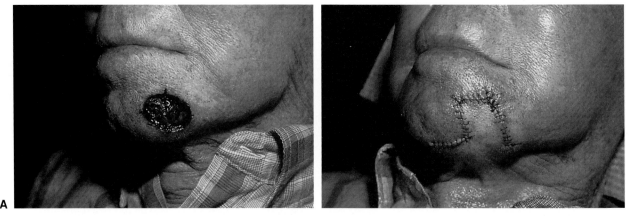

FIG. 16. (A) Defect of the chin. **(B)** Reconstruction using a transportation flap. The flap was designed to recruit the abundant tissue laxity from the submental region and thus minimize tension and pull on the lower lip.

amounts of tissue laxity to redirect wound tension away from free tissue margins such as the eyelids (Fig. 18). Make an incision superior to the defect and extending parallel to the normal, relaxed skin tension lines. The width of the rhombic flap should be similar to the size of the defect. Widely undermine the flap and wound edges in the superficial subcutaneous plane. Trim the tip of the flap to conform to the rounded configuration of the defect. Transpose the flap into the defect, and suture it in a standard layered fashion. If a dog-ear

is created at the pivot point of the transposition flap, make a small triangular incision to flatten the surrounding tissue.

The single-stage melolabial (nasolabial) transposition flap is a variation of the classic rhombic flap and can be used to repair defects of the nasal sidewall or large alar defects (Fig. 19). Make an incision from the lateral aspect of the defect and extend this inferior and parallel to the melolabial fold. The width of the nasolabial flap should approximate the width of the defect. The angle of transposition is approxi-

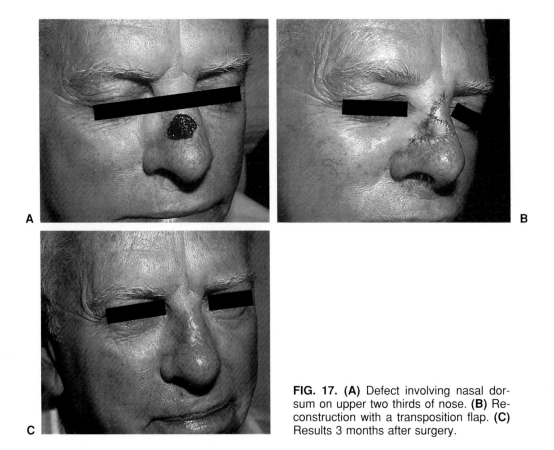

FIG. 17. (A) Defect involving nasal dorsum on upper two thirds of nose. **(B)** Reconstruction with a transposition flap. **(C)** Results 3 months after surgery.

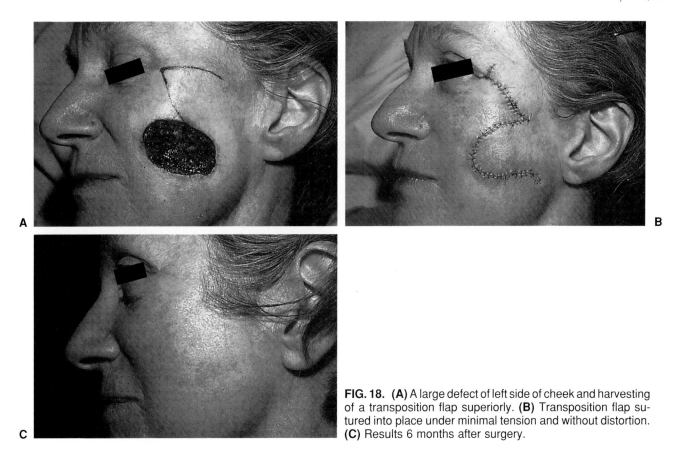

FIG. 18. **(A)** A large defect of left side of cheek and harvesting of a transposition flap superiorly. **(B)** Transposition flap sutured into place under minimal tension and without distortion. **(C)** Results 6 months after surgery.

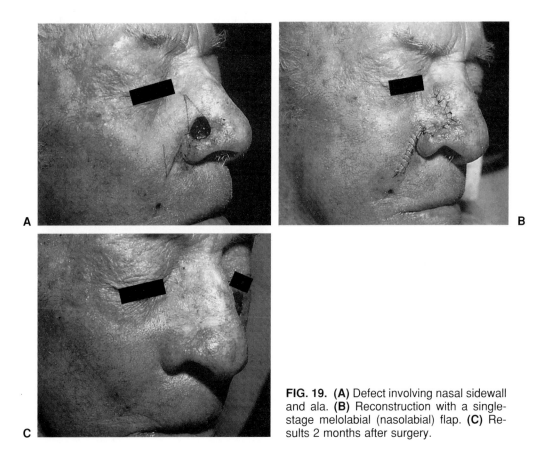

FIG. 19. **(A)** Defect involving nasal sidewall and ala. **(B)** Reconstruction with a single-stage melolabial (nasolabial) flap. **(C)** Results 2 months after surgery.

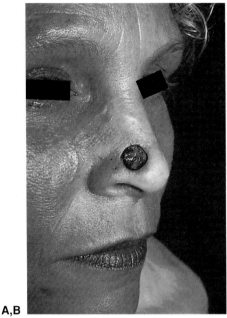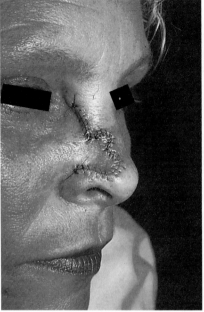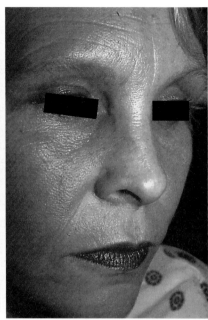

A,B   C

FIG. 20. (A) Defect involving nasal supratip and distal nasal dorsum. **(B)** Reconstruction using a bilobed transposition flap. **(C)** Results 6 months after surgery.

mately 30 degrees. To facilitate transposition of the flap with minimal tension of the ala and nasal tip, remove a large Burow's triangle along the nasal sidewall. Undermine the flap and the skin edges widely in a supramuscular plane along the nose and in a superficial subcutaneous plane under the flap and donor cheek. Carefully trim the fat globules from the undersurface of the nasolabial flap. The thickness of the flap should be slightly less than the thickness of the defect. This allows for proper insetting of the flap and minimizes trapdoor formation. Use No. 4-0 Vicryl suture to approximate the periosteum of the nasal sidewall to the base of the flap, to minimize tension and distortion of the ala. Place a second suture, connecting the base of the flap to the deep portion of the alar crease, to recreate the alar crease. Trim the excess portion of the flap to conform to the rounded configuration of the defect. Close the flap and donor site in the standard layered fashion.

The bilobed flap is one of the most useful flaps for nasal reconstruction; it is simply a double transposition flap (Fig. 20). The bilobed flap was first described by Esser in 1918. Ziminy later expanded the use of this flap for a variety of truncal and extremity wounds. In 1989 Zitelli described modifications of the flap to improve the aesthetic outcome for nasal repair. This is the repair of choice for defects of 0.5 to 1.5 cm involving the distal and lateral aspect of the nose. The initial lobe should be the same size as the defect. The secondary lobe may be slightly smaller to allow for donor site closure with minimal distortion. The angle of transposition is approximately 45 to 50 degrees for each lobe. An adequate Burow's triangle must be removed from the pivot point to eliminate bunching of the dog-ear formation. Incise the previously outlined bilobed transposition flap

over the nasal dorsum. Remove a small Burow's triangle from the lateral aspect of the wound. Widely undermine the skin edges in a supramuscular plane lateral to the nasofacial sulcus and medially over the supratip of the nose and nasal dorsum. Transpose the bilobed flap into the defect and donor site under minimal tension and distortion. Trim the excess portion of the second lobe of the flap to conform to the rounded configuration of the defect. Suture the primary flap, secondary flap, and donor sites into place in the standard layered fashion.

Pedicled Flaps

Pedicled flaps were first noted in the writings of Sushruta in 800 BC; he described nasal reconstruction performed by the Koomas. Dunham and Monks later refined the surgery of ancient India, and further developed the use of pedicled flaps in reconstructive surgery. Today there is a wide variety of pedicled flaps for all aspects of facial reconstruction.

The forehead flap is the most versatile pedicle flap for nasal reconstruction. This is a complex staged procedure which, when properly designed and executed, can provide excellent functional and aesthetic results even with extensive nasal wounds (Fig. 21). This is an axial flap based on the supratrochlear artery; therefore vascular insufficiency is an extremely uncommon event. The essential principles of a forehead flap are described below.

Freshen the edges of the defect, and remove any bevel. The flap will be less conspicuous if the entire cosmetic subunit is replaced. Therefore remove the remaining portion of the cosmetic subunit before proceeding with reconstruction. Make a foil template of the defect, and use this to outline

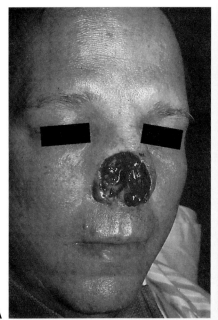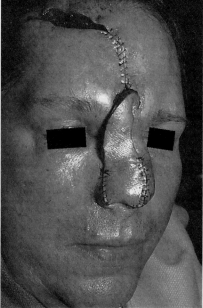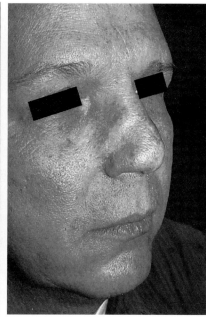

A   B,C

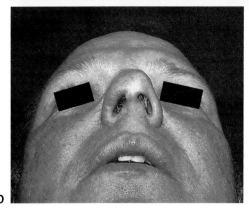

D

FIG. 21. (A) Extensive full-thickness defect involving the nose. **(B)** Reconstruction with a combination paramedian forehead flap, cartilage grafting, and sliding-bucket mucosal flap for nasal lining. **(C and D)** Results 6 months after surgery.

the distal aspect of the forehead flap, which is usually just inferior to the hairline. Use 4 × 4-inch gauze to estimate the length of the pedicle necessary to allow the forehead flap to reach the defect with minimal tension of the pedicle. The supratrochlear artery is consistently found approximately 1.0 cm lateral to the midline in the glabellar crease line; this is the pivot point for the gauze when estimating the flap length. Once the appropriate length of the pedicle and the distal template of the flap have been decided, clearly mark this on the forehead. The base of the flap must be approximately 1.5 cm in width. Incise the forehead flap at the previously outlined areas. The depth of the incision should extend to the subcutaneous fat at the distal aspect; the more proximal portion of the pedicle should extend to the galea. Meticulous dissection is necessary at the most proximal portion of the flap so that the supratrochlear vessels are not interrupted. Undermine the forehead wound in a subgaleal plane, and close the donor defect in a standard layered fashion. The distal portion of the donor site may not close primarily and often heals best by second intention. Meticulously thin and trim the flap to match the thickness and dimensions

of the nasal defect. Suture the flap into the defect in a standard layered fashion.

The second stage of the forehead flap is performed approximately 3 weeks after surgery. Release the proximal portion of the flap approximately 2.0 mm distal to the turndown crease, and convert the base of the pedicle into an upside down V shape. Make a mirror incision in the glabella superior to the proximal stump. Defat the trunk of the pedicle flap, inset this into the glabellar region, and suture this area in a standard layered fashion. Transect the distal aspect of the forehead flap at the area that corresponds to the nasal defect. Meticulously trim and defat this portion of the forehead flap, inset this into the nasal defect, and suture this area in the standard layered fashion.

The reverse melolabial (nasolabial) pedicled flap may be useful if the surgical wound involves the alar base and destroys the attachment of the ala to the cheek and lip (Fig. 22). The reverse melolabial pedicled flap is outlined and planned in a manner similar to the previously described single-staged melolabial flap. When performing the reverse melolabial flap, it is important to carefully dissect to a vascu-

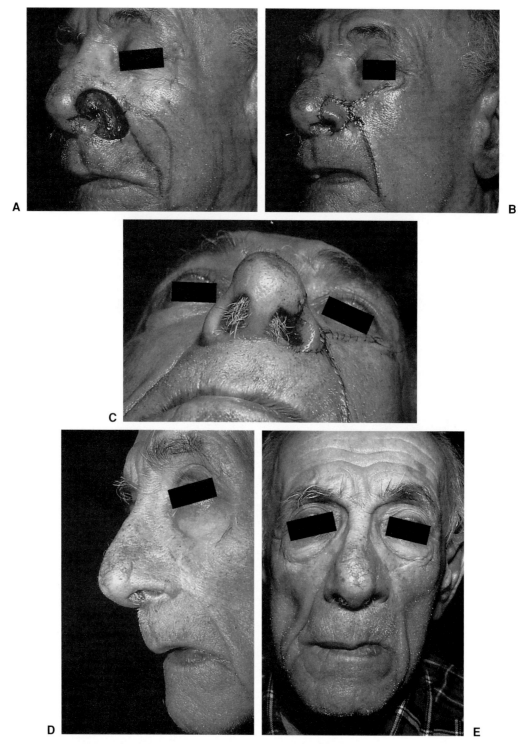

FIG. 22. **(A)** Large defect of the ala involving the alar base. **(B)** Reconstruction with a turnover melolabial (nasalolabial) subcutaneous pedicle flap. **(C)** Inferior view of the turnover flap. **(D and E)** Results 6 months after surgery.

lar-rich muscular pedicle approximately 2.0 mm lateral to the alar defect. The flap is meticulously trimmed, and the excess fat globules are removed. The flap is turned on its vascular pedicle to form the lateral alar crease and inner nasal lining. Suture the nasal mucosa to the cutaneous surface of the flap using No. 5-0 chromic gut. Once the lining has been secured, turn the flap upon itself to reform the alar rim. The cutaneous portion of the flap should be sutured to the cutaneous portion of the defect in a standard layered fashion. The donor site is closed in a standard layered fashion. If a dog-ear is created along the superior portion of the nasal wound, make a triangular incision in this area to flatten the surrounding tissue; this dog-ear repair should also be closed in a standard layered fashion.

A two-staged melolabial (nasolabial) interpolation flap is used for repair of large defects involving the ala, especially wounds too large or too deep or wounds involving the rim, where skin grafts are less useful (Fig. 23). Make a foil template of the contralateral ala. As previously discussed with the forehead flap, the entire cosmetic subunit of the ala should be excised to allow for reconstruction of a complete subunit region of the nose. The template should be turned over to represent the ipsilateral ala and transferred to the medial donor site of the cheek along the melolabial fold. Incise the flap along the melolabial fold, and carefully dissect the flap to a vascular-rich muscular pedicle at the superior portion of the melolabial fold. Trim the distal portion of the flap so that the previously outlined template exactly

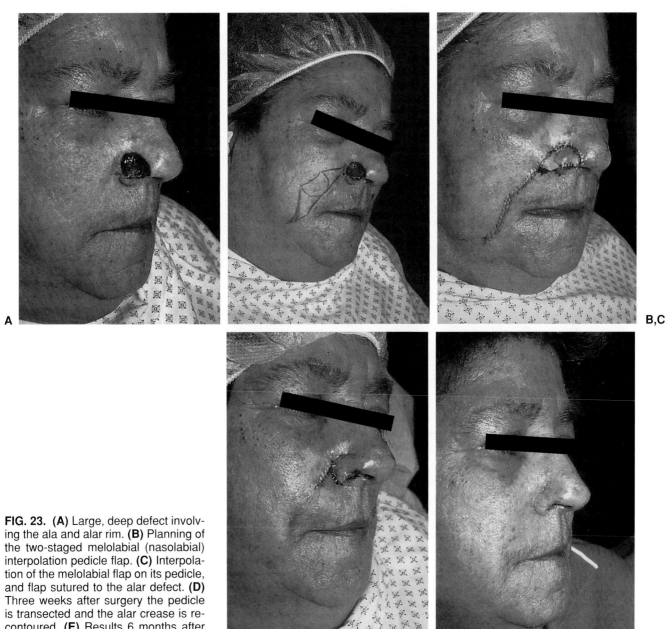

FIG. 23. (A) Large, deep defect involving the ala and alar rim. **(B)** Planning of the two-staged melolabial (nasolabial) interpolation pedicle flap. **(C)** Interpolation of the melolabial flap on its pedicle, and flap sutured to the alar defect. **(D)** Three weeks after surgery the pedicle is transected and the alar crease is recontoured. **(E)** Results 6 months after surgery.

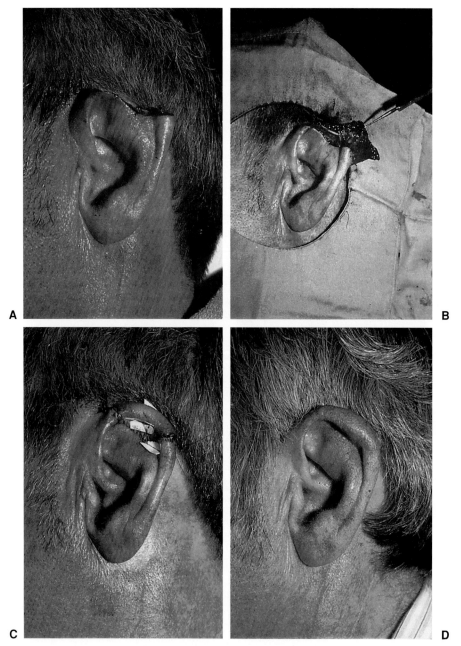

FIG. 24. (A) Large, full-thickness defect of auricle. **(B)** Dissection of the postauricular skin. **(C)** Postauricular pedicle flap and cartilage grafting. **(D)** Results 6 months after surgery.

matches the size of the defect. Suture the pedicle flap onto the alar wound in a standard layered fashion. The donor site should also be closed in a standard layered fashion. Three weeks after surgery, detach the vascular pedicle and thin the base of the pedicle to reform the normal cervice of the lateral alar crease and melolabial fold.

The staged postauricular pedicle flap is very useful for large full-thickness defects of the auricle, especially those with loss of cartilage (Fig. 24). Depending on the size of the defect, cartilage grafting may also be combined with this procedure to optimize the aesthetic outcome. Make a foil template of the defect, and use this to harvest cartilage from

the concha. The cartilage is secured to the defect with No. 5-0 chromic gut suture. The donor site heals well by second intention. Once the cartilage is secured, use the template to mark the size of the flap needed in the postauricular sulcus. Incise the newly marked flap, and extend the incisions laterally to the hairline. Elevate the flap in a subcutaneous plane, and meticulously trim and defat the fat globules to fit the contours and thickness of the defect. Secure the flap over the anterior portion of the wound using a standard layered closure. Secure a bolster dressing using through-and-through No. 4-0 Vicryl sutures to recreate the helical rim. Approximately 3 weeks after surgery the patient should return for the second stage of the procedure. Divide the flap at the base of the pedicle, and fold the base of the pedicle to cover the posterior portion of the wound. This portion of the flap should be carefully thinned to approximate the thickness of the skin of the ear. The donor site can be left to heal by second intention or repaired with a skin graft.

POSTOPERATIVE MANAGEMENT

Even in perfectly designed and executed reconstructive surgery, appropriate postoperative care and follow-up are necessary to optimize the final outcome. In general, postoperative management of all flap reconstructive surgery is handled in a similar manner. It is best to educate patients that the normal healing process may take 6 weeks to 6 months before the final outcome can be evaluated. If a staged procedure is necessary, review with the patient the timing of subsequent surgery. It may also be useful to point out the potential need for blending procedures such as dermabrasion or surgical scar revision to optimize the outcome. Give the patient typed wound care instructions that outline expected changes during the healing process. This reinforces verbal instructions, which are often misunderstood or forgotten once the patient leaves the office.

After wound reconstruction, an antibiotic ointment is applied to the wound, which is covered with a Telfa pad followed by a simple pressure dressing. The patient is asked to leave the dressing in place for 24 to 48 hours after surgery. After 1 to 2 days the patient can remove the pressure dressing and begin daily application of antibiotic ointment. Cutaneous sutures are usually removed 5 to 7 days after surgery. Steri-Strips are commonly applied, and they are covered by skin-colored paper tape. The patient can remove the Steri-Strips approximately 72 hours later. The patient is usually instructed to return 4 to 6 weeks after surgery to be evaluated for evidence of hypertrophic scarring or stitch reaction. If there is any uncertainty concerning the normal progression of wound healing, the patients may be asked to come back approximately 3 months after surgery. Surgical revision is usually not performed until approximately 6 months after surgery, after the scar has completely matured.

To minimize bleeding complications, all patients should take no aspirin, ibuprofen, or alcohol. If the patient is taking warfarin (Coumadin), the medication is commonly stopped 2 days before surgery and restarted 1 day after surgery. If the reconstructive surgery is extensive, patients may be without warfarin for an extended period. This should always be cleared and coordinated with the primary care physician to prevent more serious complications.

Flap viability is strongly dependent on vascularity and oxygenation. Since smoking has been well documented to cause vasoconstriction and lower the oxygen saturation of blood, it has obvious significant and profound deleterious effects on flap reconstructive surgery. Therefore it is extremely important to inform the patient that the ultimate aesthetic outcome of the reconstructive surgery directly depends on their ability to refrain from smoking. Ideally, it would be best to have the patients stop smoking 10 days before the reconstructive procedure and continue not to smoke for 2 weeks after surgery. However, many patients continue to smoke even if educated about the potential complications.

COMPLICATIONS AND ADVERSE SEQUELAE

Perhaps the best indicator of a surgeon's experience and expertise is how well he or she manages postoperative complications. Anyone who performs reconstructive procedures invariably encounters a suboptimal outcome. The complication may be physician or patient related or may be idiosyncratic but often requires some form of intervention to limit the complexity of the problem. Poorly managed complications can have devastating effects and may potentially have medicolegal ramifications.

As with most medical problems, the best way to manage complications is to prevent them. *Physician-related complications* can be minimized by adhering to a strict surgical protocol. Instruments should be sterilized, and the procedure performed with good sterile technique. Diligent hemostasis can eliminate many postoperative complications resulting from hematomas, such as "trapdooring" and excess wound contraction. Avoiding tissue injury with crushing forceps and choice of suture material have a significant impact on the surgical outcome.

Patient-related complications are often multifactorial but can usually be avoided by careful, thorough patient evaluation and education. An in-depth preoperative evaluation rules out potential intrinsic problems (e.g., bleeding diathesis, poor immune status) or extrinsic problems (medications, alcohol, smoking). Also, a careful explanation, both verbal and written, regarding postoperative wound care should be given to the patient and potential caregivers who will be participating in the wound management. Explaining to the patient before surgery the potential for complications lessens the burden on the physician when complications do occur. The patient is usually more accepting of a complication if he or she perceives this as an inherent risk of the flap surgery and not necessarily a result of surgeon error or mistake.

Bleeding-related complications are fairly common after surgery. Making sure the patient is not taking any blood-thinning medications (aspirin, nonsteroidal drugs, warfarin), meticulous vessel ligation and pinpoint electrodesiccation, proper placement of postoperative pressure dressing, and careful wound management markedly reduce bleeding-related problems. Postoperative bruising and swelling are most commonly seen in vascular, thin-tissue areas such as perioral and periorbital skin. Although this may be quite alarming to the patient and family members, the bruising is usually

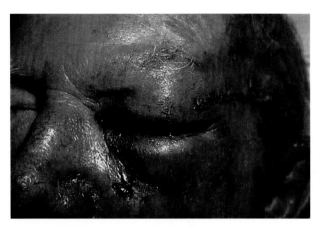

FIG. 25. Significant postoperative periorbital bruising in a patient who is taking warfarin (Coumadin).

self-limiting; therefore intervention is not commonly needed (Fig. 25).

On the other hand, postoperative swelling accompanied by crescendo pain should alert the surgeon to the potential of an expanding hematoma. Acute hematomas require emergent intervention to minimize flap necrosis. Generally, all sutures should be removed and the hematoma should be evacuated as soon as possible. When exploring a wound for bleeding complications, it is best to use lidocaine without epinephrine for local anesthesia so that bleeding vessels can be more easily identified. Once the hematoma has been evacuated, the wound is irrigated with sterile saline and diligent hemostasis is obtained with electrodessication. Once hemostasis has been achieved, it is a good idea to maneuver and stretch the tissue to determine whether this will initiate further bleeding. The open wound should be observed for 5 to 10 minutes for further evidence of bleed before resuturing the flap. Most hematomas are small and inconsequential. Intervention is not often necessary, since most hematomas are self-limiting and resorb spontaneously over several months.

Wound infections occur very infrequently in clean surgical defects performed in the outpatient office. However, the consequence of wound infections on a flap can be catastrophic. Early signs such as redness, swelling, and tenderness may be obscured by normal postoperative wound healing. As with hematomas, crescendo pain should be a red flag for urgent evaluation. If there is abscess formation, this should be evacuated and cultured. Similarly, if there is gross purulent drainage, this should be cultured. Commonly, exquisite tenderness, erythema, and swelling without purulent drainage are present. In these circumstances, empiric treatment with a first-generation cephalosporin is usually curative. In most cases, there are no long-term sequelae of the wound infection. Occasionally, there may be flap necrosis or wound dehiscence, which should be allowed to heal by second intention. If the ultimate scar is not satisfactory, a revision can be performed 6 months after the initial surgery.

Flap necrosis can be related to poor flap design or surgical

technique or associated with other complications such as infections or hematomas. Flap necrosis is most often associated with heavy smokers. Once flap necrosis is clinically apparent, it is best to carefully debride the fibrinous, necrotic tissue to facilitate healing by second intention. Scar revision may be necessary 6 months after surgery. Smokers should be educated that the outcome of the surgery directly depends on their ability to refrain from or minimize smoking. A short course of oral diazepam (Valium) is often given to assist patients in overcoming anxiety and symptoms experienced after cessation of smoking.

Dehiscence of a flap is very rare. All flaps are sutured in a layered fashion so that there is no tension on the cutaneous sutures. Therefore, the cutaneous sutures can be removed 4 to 7 days after surgery without fear of wound separation. Dehiscence is most commonly related to other complications such as infection, hematoma, necrosis or trauma. If dehiscence results from trauma, a common practice is to freshen the edges and resuture the flap. If other factors are involved, the wound is managed as outlined above (Fig. 26).

Hypertrophic scars can occur even under ideal surgical conditions and often lead to unsatisfactory outcomes. A myriad of growth factors, cytokines, and proteases form an intricate web that heals the wound. When the checks and balances of this system go awry, the wound "overheals" itself, which results in a hypertrophic scar. Proper flap design and careful handling of tissue minimize this problem, but occasionally, even in the most expert hands, hypertrophic scars appear. They usually become evident 4 to 6 weeks after surgery as exaggerated induration along the scar line of the flap and donor site. Triamcinolone at concentrations of 5 to 10 mg/ml is injected into the hypertrophic scar at 4- to 6-week intervals. Atrophogenic concentrations of triamcinolone (40 mg/ml) may be necessary for significant hypertrophic scars or keloids. The patient is advised to massage the scar several times a day. If conservative management fails, surgical revision in the form of multiple Z-plasties or a running W-plasty may be useful several months after surgery.

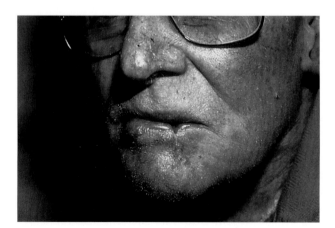

FIG. 26. Wound dehiscence of a wedge closure involving the lower lip.

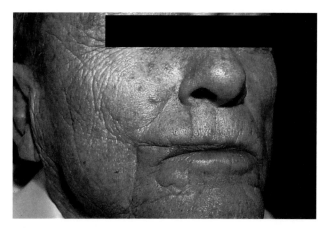

FIG. 27. Trapdoor deformity of a flap crossing the melolabial fold on the right side of the upper lip.

Deformity that is due to flap contraction may have a similar origin to hypertrophic scars, and the treatment follows a similar course. If the cicatricial changes results in distortion of a free tissue margin such as the eyelid (ectropion) or the lip (eclabium), surgical correction is often necessary.

Another complication resulting from flap contraction is the *trapdoor deformity (pin cushioning)*. Although the cause of this condition remains an enigma, several surgical techniques have proven useful in minimizing this complication. First, the flap, donor site, and defect should be widely undermined so that the postoperative tension on the flap approximates the preoperative skin tension. Second, the flap should be meticulously defatted and thinned so that the flap tissue is slightly thinner than the defect. Third, the flap should be sutured with careful eversion of the edges so that the center of the flap is slightly sunken beneath the defect tissue plane and the epidermal edges are perfectly approximated. Once trapdoor deformity has occurred, surgical revision is often necessary. As with other complications, trapdoor deformity is easier to prevent than to fix (Fig. 27).

CONCLUSION

A thorough understanding of flap design and tissue movement is an absolute prerequisite to performing flap surgery.

It is important to master the skills of basic surgical principles, which are commonly used in primary excisional surgery, before undertaking flap reconstructive surgery. The same basic surgical principles used in simple primary closure are also applied in even the most complex flap reconstruction. With knowledge, skillful technique, and experience the surgeon can confidently approach a wide variety of surgical defects with flap reconstruction.

SUGGESTED READING LIST

1. Baker SR, Swanson NA. Local flaps in facial reconstruction. St. Louis: CV Mosby, 1995.
2. Bennett RG. Fundamentals of cutaneous surgery. St. Louis: CV Mosby, 1988.
3. Brodland DG. Fundamentals of flap and graft wound closure in cutaneous surgery. Cutis 1994;53:192.
4. Burget GC, Menick FJ. Aesthetic reconstruction of the nose. St. Louis: CV Mosby, 1994.
5. Dzubow LM. Facial flaps: biomechanics and regional application. Norwalk, CT: Appleton & Lange, 1990.
6. Fazio MJ, Zitelli JA. Principles of reconstruction following excision of nonmelanoma skin cancer. In: Moy RL, Telfer NR, guest eds. Clin Dermatol 1995;13:601.
7. Fewkes JL, Cheney ML, Pollack SV. Illustrated atlas of cutaneous surgery. New York: Gower, 1991.
8. Jackson IT. Local flaps in head and neck reconstruction. St. Louis: CV Mosby, 1985.
9. Lask GP, Moy RL. Principles and techniques of cutaneous surgery. New York: McGraw-Hill, 1996.
10. Moy RL. Atlas of cutaneous facial flaps and grafts: a differential diagnosis of wound closure. Philadelphia: Lea & Febiger, 1990.
11. Salasche SJ, Bernstein G, Senkarik M. Surgical anatomy of the skin. Norwalk, CT: Appleton & Lange, 1988.
12. Skouge JW. Upper-lip repair: the subcutaneous island pedicle flap. J Dermatol Surg Oncol 1990;16:63.
13. Summers BK, Siegle RJ. Facial cutaneous reconstructive surgery: facial flaps. J Am Acad Dermatol 1993;29:917.
14. Summers BK, Siegle RJ. Facial cutaneous reconstructive surgery: general aesthetic principles. J Am Acad Dermatol 1993;29:669.
15. Zitelli JA. The bilobed flap for nasal reconstruction. Arch Dermatol 1989;125:957.
16. Zitelli JA. Tips for wound closure: pearls for minimizing dog-ears and applications of periosteal sutures. Dermatol Clin 1989;7:123.
17. Zitelli JA, Moy RL. Buried vertical mattress suture. J Dermatol Surg Oncol 1989;15:17.
18. Zitelli JA. The nasolabial flap as a single-stage procedure. Arch Dermatol 1990;126:1445.
19. Zitelli JA. Tips for better ellipse. J Am Acad Dermatol 1990;22:101.
20. Zitelli JA, Brodland DG. A regional approach to reconstruction of the lip. J Dermatol Surg Oncol 1991;17:143.
21. Zitelli JA, Fazio MJ. Reconstruction of the nose with local flaps. J Dermatol Surg Oncol 1991;17:184.

Textbook of Dermatologic Surgery, edited by John L. Ratz.
Lippincott–Raven Publishers, Philadelphia © 1998.

CHAPTER 17

Facelift Surgery

Thomas Alt

HISTORY

Facelift surgery is a very satisfying procedure for the dermatologic surgeon. Although the public may perceive that only plastic surgeons perform this surgery, logic and history show that it is easily within the domain of the dermatologic surgeon. First, it is self-evident that most of the facial flap procedures are performed by dermatologists. Second, facelift surgery, developed after World War I, was first reported in a comprehensive treatise by Madame Noel, a Parisian dermatologist, in 1926 and later expanded in 1928. Although Passot published the first paper on facelift in 1919, his comments were essentially a resume of Noel's procedure, since he had studied under her direction. Not to be outdone, Joseph published a paper in 1921 stating that he had performed a facelift operation in 1912. Gamesmanship was prevalent even in the early 20th century when, in 1931, Lexer published a paper stating that he was the first to perform such a procedure in 1906. Additional surgeons from around

the world but principally from the United States began reporting the benefits of these early facelift procedures, including Bames of Los Angeles, Bettman of Portland, Booth of Seattle, Bourguet and Lagarde of Paris, Hunt of New York, Miller of Chicago, and Stein of Vienna. Since that time, hundreds of surgeons have written on the technique, effects, and complications of facelift surgery.

PREOPERATIVE PLANNING

Definition of Purpose

Although laypersons believe that a facelift will improve the forehead rhytides, glabellar frown, eyelids, periorbital areas, deep nasolabial folds, jowling, accentuated marionette lines, and excessive skin and fat of the anterior cervical region, the facelift—better termed *cervicofacial rhytidectomy*—is limited in its benefits to the lower third of the face. The two principal mechanisms of the procedure result in reinforcement of the underlying muscular and fascial structures and remove excess skin of the lower third of the face.

Thomas Alt: Alt Cosmetic Surgery Center, 4920 Lincoln Drive, Minneapolis MN 55436.

Removal of wrinkles or rhytides is not a goal of the procedure; as a consequence, a patient may be disappointed if this is not outlined by the surgeon at the initial evaluation.

The potential benefits of a cervicofacial rhytidectomy are as follows:

1. Improvement of mandibular jowling that is the result of excess fat and/or the descent of skin secondary to the loss of elasticity.
2. Removal of excess fat of the anterior cervical region.
3. Improved definition of the cervicomental angle.
4. Improvement of any existing platysmal banding.
5. Redraping of the angles of the mouth to diminish or delete the marionette lines.

It is advisable to outline and discuss these five aspects with the patient at the time of the initial consultation.

Consultation

At the initial consultation the author prefers to open the discussion by asking, "What do you *want* a facelift to do for you?" or, using a slightly different approach, "What do you *think* a facelift will do for you?" After the patient responds, he or she is placed in front of a mirror with overhead illumination providing oblique light, which accentuates the contours of the face. Patients are then asked to describe and point out their personal needs. The author firmly believes that it is not the surgeon's responsibility to tell the patients what their needs are but rather to first understand the patient's needs and desires and then responsibly comment on the ability and inability of the procedure to achieve these goals. It is important for the surgeon to emphasize the limited nature of the cervicofacial rhytidectomy with its minimal effect on the upper half of the nasolabial folds and lack of any effect on the forehead, brow, or eyelids. Although the procedure usually ends in improvement of the marionette lines, there is no improvement of the perioral or periorbital rhytides.

Patients who have moderate elastotic changes in whom bony structures are prominent with a well-defined cervicomental angle are ideal candidates. By contrast, individuals with a severe loss of elasticity or extensive actinic damage and those with an ill-defined anterior area of neck resulting from a low hyoid bone cannot expect to have as dramatic a result as the ideal patient. Platysmal banding, when obvious, may be difficult or impossible to eliminate and usually is the first defect to return as the aging process continues following the surgery. A wise surgeon will consider including all of these aspects in the consultation.

Facial implants of the chin and malar areas, lipotransfer or facial liposuction, facial chemical peeling, upper and lower lid blepharoplasty, elevation of the eyebrow using procedures such as the direct brow lift, midforehead lift, the pretricheal lift, or the coronal lift can also be discussed at the initial consultation so that the patient recognizes that multiple procedures are available for rejuvenation that may be necessary. The physician becomes a responsible consultant by using a thorough discussion of the advantages and disadvantages of each procedure. By allowing patients to understand and evaluate their own needs in an educated sense, the surgeon can participate with patients in guiding them to a decision that best meets their personal needs. During these discussions the surgeon becomes aware of a patient's realistic or unrealistic expectations. Every surgeon performing cosmetic surgery should also be aware of the patterns of neurotic and psychotic responses from a prospective cosmetic surgical patient. The reading and understanding of Wright's studies on this subject is advised.

The history of the patient can be critical in the decision to proceed with surgery. Both the physical and psychological health should be evaluated before a patient is accepted for surgery. Patients in the American Society of Anesthesiologists (ASA) class 1 or class 2 are usually appropriate candidates for surgery. ASA class 1 candidates are in excellent health; ASA class 2 candidates are in good health with minor systemic disease under good control, such as hypertension. This information can usually be obtained by a history form completed by the patient before the consultation. Questioning of the patient's regular physician can further assist in the acceptance or rejection of the candidate. Occasionally, because patients are so motivated to have this surgery performed, they withhold important information because they fear denial of the surgery if their present health status is exposed. This situation is usually eliminated if the patient's regular physician performs the preoperative history and physical examination necessary for the procedure. It is also important to carefully evaluate the psychological status of patients with specific questions as to the patient's present and past well-being included in the preoperative history form.

When accepting a patient, age is not necessarily an eliminating factor. Many experienced cosmetic surgeons performing cervicofacial rhytidectomy have been consulted by patients in their mid to late 30s who will definitely benefit from the procedure even though the changes will be subtle.

Studies have evaluated that younger patients will appreciate their surgery more than older patients. Also, patients should not be denied surgery solely on the basis of age. Although the benefits of this procedure diminish with advancing age, the procedure has been performed on a number of patients in their 70s and 80s who enjoy very good health and anticipate enjoying the rewards of this surgery for years to come.

Explanation of Procedure

During the physical examination the anterior cervical region should be palpated to determine the amount of lax skin and the underlying adipose tissue. The fat present in the submental area is usually greater than that found on the lower anterior cervical region. The thickness of the fat should be progressively palpated in the midline from the mentum to the sternum. The minimum thickness is usually found at an area approximately 4 cm superior to the sternum. This thickness can be considered normal for the patient and therefore becomes the goal for the surgeon to create uniformly over the anterior neck and submental area. The patient should grimace, which contracts the platysmal muscle and shows any significant bands. These bands should be shown to the patient and an explanation made to outline the difficulty of permanent improvement in this banding. It is important that a preoperative picture be included in the photographic series demonstrating that these bands existed before surgery. The cervicomental angle should be evaluated and discussed with the patient, since many individuals have a low-lying hyoid bone that increases the cervicomental angle, resulting in a less pleasing profile. The surgeon cannot change this physical characteristic with cervicofacial rhytidectomy. The jowls are palpated to determine the amount of underlying fat, which should be compared with the amount present in the central cheek. An evaluation of the angles of the mouth with the usually concomitant marionette lines should be pointed out to the patient, and emphasis should be made that they can expect little improvement to the superior portion of the nasolabial folds. Injection of fat into the marionette lines can often be helpful, along with the upward lift that occurs during rhytidectomy.

The preauricular tuft of hair, the tragal contour, and the lobule of the external ear are very important areas, since they are obvious and can be significantly changed in appearance, contour, and position with the various methods of rhytidectomy. The method used by the author conserves the major portion of the hair in the preauricular tuft, a topic that is emphasized to the prospective patient. Most patients are unaware that the vast majority of surgeons move this tuft superiorly and posteriorly and therefore eliminate the normal appearance of the sideburn. Many patients request hair transplantation, stating that after a rhytidectomy had been performed elsewhere, their hair ceased growing in this area. It was not that their hair ceased growing; it was that it had been moved out of this region and non–hair-bearing skin, which was originally at a lower position, replaced the preauricular tuft.

The tragus is the second most commonly deformed area following a poorly planned rhytidectomy. It may be the most difficult area to recontour. The ideal incision is placed at the juncture of the tragal crest and the external auditory canal, a position that hides the incision and often makes the scar virtually impossible to see. If the skin flap is placed under tension at closure, the resulting scar contracture causes the tragus to advance anteriorly, opening the orifice of the external auditory canal and creating an abnormal-appearing ear. If the tragus is projected at an angle greater than 45 degrees from the surface of the adjacent cheek in the preauricular

area, the author occasionally opts to place the scar in a pretragal position rather than a posttragal position. It is difficult to drape the skin over the tragus and prevent tragal advancement anteriorly when the normal position already lies in a more anterior position than is usually seen.

The lobule of the ear is also another common deformity where poorly planned facelift surgery is readily apparent. My incision and redraping of the skin prevent the anterior and inferior displacement of the lobule that occurs during the subsequent normal contraction phase of the maturing sheet of scar. The method used to prevent this is discussed in detail later. The incision should be placed at the juncture of the lobule and the cheek skin rather than 3 to 5 mm anterior and inferior to the lobule, which is an incision commonly used by our colleagues in plastic surgery. The incisions that eliminate the preauricular tuft of hair, alter the normal tragal contour, and displace the normal position of the lobule should be discussed with patients before surgery, since virtually none are sophisticated enough to know the alternatives to facelift incisions and their resultant postoperative appearance.

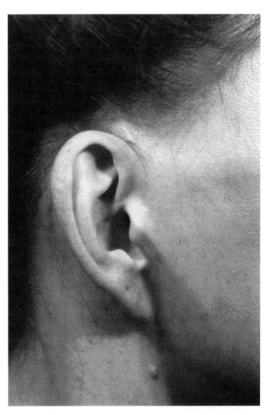

FIG. 1. Several abnormalities that result from poor planning are evident. The entire sideburn has been eliminated by placing a vertical incision in the temple area and elevating the sideburn in a superoposterior manner. There is an anteroinferior displacement of the lobule resulting from improper positioning and a disregard for the fact that all scars contract. An obvious ridge present from the crest of the tragus anteriorly at a 45-degree angle is a third defect. This results from excessive tension being placed on the flap.

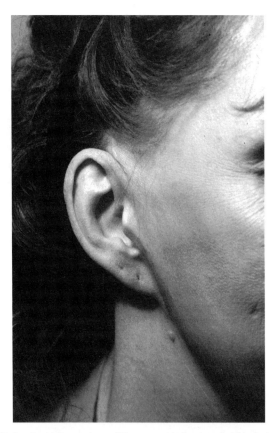

FIG. 2. An oblique view of the same patient as in Fig. 1 shows the deformed lobule that resulted from scar contracture creating an elf or pixie ear appearance. The total absence of the sideburn is quite apparent, and the elevation of skin between the crest of the tragus and lower cheek is obvious.

The postauricular incision that is carried into the hairline rather than below the hairline is described to the patient, outlining the advantage of scar camouflage when compared with the incision placed inferior to the hairline. Counter to this advantage of scar camouflage, an incision that enters the hairline entails the disadvantage that a step in the hairline is created as the flap in this area is rotated superiorly and posteriorly. The major pull that removes excess skin from the jowl and anterior cervical region must be in this direction. Some surgeons claim that they can maintain the hairline by advancing the skin superiorly and anteriorly, thus removing a wedge of hair-bearing skin without creating a step. There appears to be no logic or good results with this maneuver, since the advancement of the skin flap in the cervicomental region and jowl is severely limited because this method would produce anterior advancement rather than posterior advancement of the flap. Although these surgeons may preserve the straight line along the postauricular hairline, they diminish the removal of skin, which results in less tightening of the jowl and anterior cervical skin—the main purpose of the operation. It seems unreasonable to sacrifice an improved appearance in these two major anatomic areas that are readily seen, to produce a better result in an area that is normally

covered by scalp hair. Using the methods outlined here, even hair as short as 1 inch can cover this step.

Explanation of Cervicofacial Rhytidectomy

As outlined earlier, it is advantageous for the surgeon to clearly explain the surgical procedure to provide a basis for informed consent. This includes placing a patient in front of the mirror and showing the proposed incision lines and those used by other surgeons. Since patients are usually unaware of these options and their disadvantages, it helpful to discuss the following: disadvantages that can result in the diminution or elimination of the preauricular tuft of hair (Figs. 1–3), a vertical incision anterior to the external ear (Figs. 3 and 8), incisions that result in the formation of an elf or pixie ear, which creates a downward and anterior displacement of the lobule (Figs. 1–3), and postauricular incisions that are inferior to the hairline (Figs. 4–8). The decision to create a pretragal or posttragal incision is best made after this discussion. After the advantages and disadvantages of these two options have been discussed, the selected incision sites should be noted in the chart.

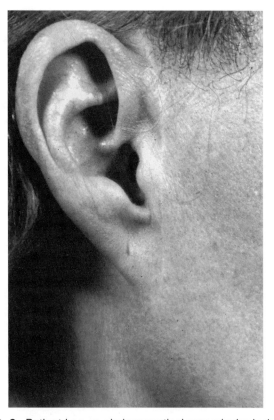

FIG. 3. Patient has an obvious vertical preauricular incision that did not follow the curvature of the external ear. The sideburn is also absent as a result of a vertical incision in the temporal area that advanced the flap superoposteriorly without regard to preservation of the temporal tuft of hair. This also represents an extreme example of the inferior displacement of the lobule creating an elf ear or pixie ear.

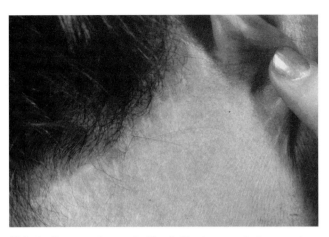

FIG. 4. Same patient as in Fig. 3. She has an obvious postauricular scar that is inferior to the hairline rather than hidden in the hair as the author recommends. Because of this scar, the patient must style her hair down and around her shoulders.

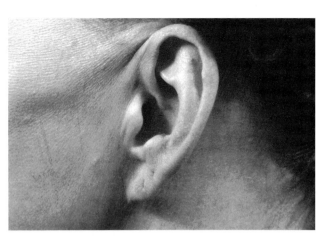

FIG. 7. Same patient as in Figs. 1 and 2. There is an obvious postauricular scar at the inferior border of the occipital hairline. The elf ear deformity is less severe than that shown in Figs. 1 and 2. There is a large, conspicuous band of elevated skin from the superior border of the auricle extending down to the area of the zygoma. The temporal hair tuft has been elevated with elimination of the sideburn.

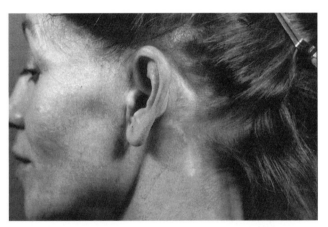

FIG. 5. A very wide postauricular scar placed below the hairline. The scar extends below the occipital hair and eliminates the possibility of the patient styling her hair upward.

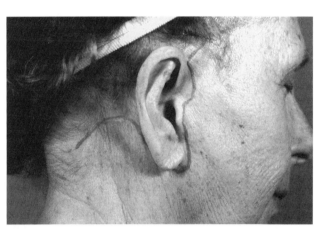

FIG. 8. Absence of the sideburn, anterior displacement of the tragus, an obvious scar that is 5 mm below the lobule, and a postauricular scar that is below the hairline.

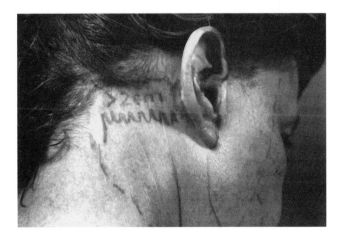

FIG. 6. A very wide retroauricular horizontal scar with a posterior limb angling 90 degrees in the vertical position. In this case adequate support was not provided, resulting in the sutures coming untied on the first postoperative day. Marking shows the extent of the scar, which at many points is wider than 2 cm.

TABLE 17-1. *Postoperative facelift instructions*

Follow these instructions during your postoperative facelift recovery period:

1. Patients should be at bed rest for the remainder of the day of surgery. When up to the bathroom you should have assistance. This is because when you stand up, dizziness and fainting spells may occur. The chance of this greatly diminishes after 24 hours. Sometimes dizziness and weakness may occur following surgery which will subside in a few days.
2. To reduce swelling, elevate the head on two to three pillows for approximately 2 weeks following surgery.
3. The turban applied at the time of your surgery should not be adjusted. Talking and visitors are discouraged the first 48 hours. We suggest using a notepad and pencil to communicate the first 2 days.
4. A chinstrap will replace the turban dressing on the third day. It is to be worn continuously, except to wash, shower, or shampoo, until the 14th day. Beginning the third week wear the chinstrap all hours when at home, awake or asleep, through the third month.
5. You will experience a tight or heavy feeling of the face. Very little discomfort will accompany this surgery. *Do not take aspirin, aspirin products, or ibuprofen.* To alleviate your discomfort, either Double-Strength Tylenol or the pain medication prescribed for you may be taken.
6. To avoid bleeding and excess swelling, limit motion of the face. Do not bend the head forward, backward, or sideways. Avoid gum and foods that are hard to chew for 2 weeks.
7. Avoid anything that could result in hitting or bumping your face. Do not hold or lift children. We advise sleeping on your back for 30 nights. *Do not roll over on your face.* A recliner at a 45-degree angle may be used.
8. Do not turn your head or stretch your neck for 2 weeks. Move your head and shoulders as one section. This is to avoid stretching the healing incisions.
9. No alcohol should be consumed for 1 week before and 1 week following surgery to avoid bleeding.
10. Do not wear clothing that must be pulled over your head.
11. There will be swelling following your surgery. This is normal. Discoloration is normal and usually subsides within 2 or 3 weeks.
12. You may experience some numbness or tingling in the area. This is usually temporary.
13. Should bleeding occur, go to bed, elevate the head, and apply pressure to that area. Call immediately.
14. If you feel warm, take your temperature. A temperature of 100 degrees or less is normal. Any persistent fever over 100 degrees should be reported.
15. You may shower and shampoo any time after the large dressing has been removed, usually the third day.
16. You may wear your eyeglasses after the bandages have been removed. Contact lenses may be worn the day after surgery. If you have had eyelid surgery, do not wear contact lenses for 7 days.
17. Once your bandages have been removed, use full-strength hydrogen peroxide on a Q-Tip to clean over your suture lines 2 or 3 times daily. A generous amount of Polysporin should be applied to the suture line in front and back of the ear after each peroxide treatment while the sutures are in. Apply a small strip of Saran Wrap to each suture line on top of the Polysporin.
18. Do not bend or lift for 2 weeks to avoid bleeding.
19. Do not tweeze eyebrows for 1 week. Do not visit a hair salon for 2 weeks, and do not have a permanent for 3 weeks following surgery.
20. Do not wash your face for the first week following surgery to avoid bleeding. When showering and shampooing, let the soap and water stream from your scalp over your face for cleansing. Pat the face dry, do not rub it dry. *After the first week* wash your face twice a day with your fingertips and a mild soap using an upward motion.
21. Your sutures and clips will be removed beginning 5 to 7 days after your surgery. All clips will be removed by 14 days.
22. Do not smoke for 2 weeks before and 2 weeks after our surgery. Some studies claim that smoking can increase serious complications 12 times. One cigarette can significantly decrease blood flow up to 20 hours. Do not use a nicotine patch or Nicorette gum.
23. Do not drive for 2 weeks. It is necessary to make arrangements ahead of time for someone to drive you to the office for your postoperative visits. These visits usually include the first 3 days after surgery and usually 2 days the next week depending on your progress.
24. The average patient returns to work in 2 or 3 weeks. This will vary with your job.
25. Athletic activities and exercise should be delayed for 4 weeks. Slow walks may be taken after 4 days.
26. Restoril 15 mg will be prescribed to be taken at bedtime for sleep, if needed.
27. A laxative may be used to avoid straining.
28. Your scars will appear a deep pink following suture and/or clip removal and will diminish with the passage of time. In most cases this process takes months.
29. It is normal to have some depression. Divert your attention by reading a good book, watching television or taking a nice ride in the car.
30. All postoperative appointments should be scheduled in advance with the office.

Office private line: 000-0000
Thomas H. Alt, M.D.: 000-0000
Dr. Alt's Pager No. is: 000-0000. Call this number; then enter your number and the # sign.
Surgical Fellow: _____
Home Phone No.: _____
Pager No.: _____

TABLE 17-2. *Preoperative instructions for facelift*

Name: _____

Date: _____

Your facelift has been scheduled for _____ .

Please arrive at the office at _____

The fee for this procedure is $_____: $_____ for surgery and $_____ for anesthesia. Full payment is to be made 2 weeks before the surgery. Because we must preplan our nurses and operating room schedule, your surgical fee must be received by that time. We hope you understand that if this payment is not received we will have to remove your name from our schedule. If, during the 2-week period before your surgery, you should decide to cancel your surgery, a prorata amount of your prepaid surgical fee will be refunded, based on our ability to fill the time with another surgery and materials fee.

PLEASE NOTE THE INSTRUCTIONS BELOW TO BE FOLLOWED BEFORE YOUR SURGERY:

- Do not wear clothing that must be pulled over the head.
- Shampoo your scalp with Phisoderm for 10 minutes on the evening before and the morning of your surgery. Following the use of Phisoderm, you may use a hair conditioner.
- Cleanse your face for 5 minutes twice daily with Phisoderm for at least 1 day before your surgery.
- Have a good night's rest. NOTHING BY MOUTH AFTER MIDNIGHT.
- For out-of-town patients, make arrangements to stay in town for a period of 7 days.
- If preoperative pictures have not been taken, please call our office immediately for an appointment to have them taken.

AVOID THE FOLLOWING:

- Aspirin, aspirin-containing products, and ibuprofen: do not take for 7 days before surgery.
- Vitamin E: do not take for 14 days before surgery.
- Alcohol, mood-altering drugs or substances: do not use for 2 days before surgery. Prescription drugs administered under the care of your physician and reported on the history form you completed at the time of consultation may be taken unless you were instructed otherwise.
- A prescription for Mephyton is enclosed. This medication controls bleeding during surgery. Take 1 tablet four times daily for 5 days, taking the last tablet the evening before surgery. If you prefer a vitamin K injection at no charge, in place of Mephyton, please make arrangements with our office to have it administered 1 to 3 days before your surgery.
- Cephalexin, the antibiotic prescribed for you, should be started 1 full day before surgery and continued for a total of 5 days. Take one capsule three times a day. Omit on the morning of surgery. A prescription is enclosed.

ITEMS TO BE PURCHASED:

The following items should be purchased before surgery:

- Phisoderm: for scalp and facial washings before surgery.
- Saran Wrap: to cover suture lines following surgery.
- Two tubes of Polysporin ointment: to be used on suture lines.
- Q-Tips: to cleanse and apply Polysporin ointment to suture lines.
- Hydrogen peroxide: to cleanse suture lines.
- Cotton balls: to wash your face following surgery.
- Neutrogena soap: to cleanse face following surgery.

FOLLOWING YOUR SURGERY:

- You must have a RESPONSIBLE ADULT, friend or relative, 21 years or older, drive you home following surgery and remain with you for the first 24 hours after surgery. We will not allow you to ride home in a taxi following surgery.
- Arrange for a driver to transport you to the office for your postoperative visits, as you WILL NOT be allowed to drive for 2 weeks. Your first visits will be at 24 hours and 48 hours following surgery.

It is also worthwhile to point out that, although lifting of the skin with the surgeon's fingers does not definitively predict an end result, the tension placed on the skin by the surgeon is considerably less than that which is applied by the patient when he or she attempts to visualize a postoperative result. Patients usually apply excessive malar pressure, which usually eliminates most of the nasolabial fold but also causes gross distortion of the inferolateral aspect of the periorbital tissues. This should be demonstrated to patients so that they recognize that there is a considerable distortion of the periorbital area. This is the time for the surgeon to reemphasize the facelift's limited improvement of the nasolabial fold.

An evaluation of the platysmal bands and cervical and

submental fat should be made, and cervical liposuction should be considered. At this phase it would be appropriate to discuss other ancillary and alternative procedures mentioned earlier. Surgical goals and expected results of the cervicofacial rhytidectomy and other ancillary treatment should be summarized.

The postoperative course and patient responsibility during this important phase should be understood by the patient before making a decision to proceed with surgery. The need and extent of postoperative dressings, visits, and restrictions are outlined. The side effects and complications that may occur are discussed in detail. The postoperative instructions are given to patients so that they may carefully review them before making a final decision (Table 17-1). An informed patient usually complies with the surgeon's written and verbal instructions after surgery, and no surprises occur for the patient if the surgeon is thorough in this important preoperative discussion. Most patients understand that a minimum of several weeks is required before the edema and ecchymosis resolve sufficiently. Although many patients could return to work at the end of 2 weeks, the author advises patients to remain off for 3 weeks. Preoperative instructions are sent after a surgical date is confirmed (Table 17-2).

Preoperative Physical and Laboratory Evaluation

Most patients prefer to be unconscious during the surgery. Intravenous sedation or general anesthesia are the most common methods used. Both of these methods require evaluation of the patient's health and an appropriate laboratory evaluation. Patients are instructed to obtain a physical examination performed by their personal physician comparable to that which is used for same-day surgery. A letter outlining the parameters of this physical examination is provided to the patients so that the examining physician can provide the necessary services. The preoperative laboratory tests are also outlined in this letter (Table 17-3).

The preoperative history may show areas that require special evaluation. These should be outlined for the conduct of the preoperative physical examination, and the laboratory evaluation may vary because of this. The author recognizes that laboratory evaluation varies among surgeons.

The physical examination (Table 17-4) and laboratory tests should be performed 7 to 14 days before the surgery so that results are present in the surgeon's office with sufficient time for the surgeon to evaluate results, order additional laboratory evaluation, or delay or decline surgery in individuals with abnormal physical or laboratory findings.

Preoperative Medications

Options concerning the use of preoperative medications vary among surgeons. Most use systemic antibiotic therapy with erythromycin or cephalexin 24 hours before surgery and 48 to 72 hours after surgery. These doses given orally

are supplemented by an intravenous push during surgery. Vitamin K therapy in the form of Mephyton (Santos Nutrition Corporation, Clinical Products Division, Minneapolis, MN) is also used by some surgeons, as is vitamin C (ascorbic acid) for improved wound healing. There is no definitive answer regarding the use of these preoperative and postoperative medications, although the surgeon should remember that patients hold the physician to a higher standard of performance when elective cosmetic procedures are performed.

TABLE 17-3. *Laboratory tests for facelift*

You must be fasting for 8 hours before having these tests performed:
1. Complete blood cell count with differential.
2. Platelet count.
3. Prothrombin time.
4. Partial thromboplastin time.
5. SMA 12: to include sodium and potassium.
6. Human immunodeficiency virus test.
7. Hepatitis B surface antigen.
8. Urinalysis.
9. Urine pregnancy test (even for those who are using contraceptive techniques).

If you are over 40 years of age, provide the following which have been done within the past 24 months:
11. Chest x-ray
12. Electrocardiogram (EKG).

TABLE 17-4. *History and physical examination for facelift*

Please have a history and physical examination performed by your physician. The physician should then send the results and the blood test results to our office at least 2 weeks before your surgery date.

Past and present history

Physical examination
Head and neck:

Breasts:

Chest and lungs:

Heart:

Abdomen:

Extremities:

Other:
Summary of positive findings:

Please note any changes in health which may contraindicate the safe use of anesthesia (i.e., present medications, bleeding, upper respiratory tract infection, allergies, fever, etc.) and notify our office immediately. Thank you.

Preoperative Photography

Preoperative photographs are obligatory not only for medicolegal purposes but also for preoperative and postoperative evaluation (see Chapter 8). Virtually every patient wants to and should review his or her improvement following surgery. The patient attains a normal appearance with resolution of ecchymosis and very little residual edema at the end of the third week. This is an excellent time to review the preoperative photographs to show the subsequent improvement. Adequate preoperative photographs provide this medium. It is advisable to obtain a series of preoperative photographs 2 weeks before the surgery if the film is being forwarded to a distant laboratory such as Kodalux when using Kodak film. If the photographs are inadequate upon return or if the developed film does not return, the surgeon is aware of this prior to surgery and must repeat these essential photographs. Twenty-one views are used by the author to photographically document the preoperative status. These views are described and shown in Figs. 9–29.

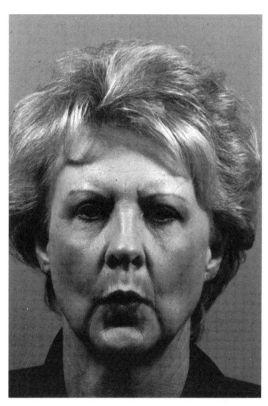

FIG. 10. At 4 feet, frontal view, vertical position, with lips pursed.

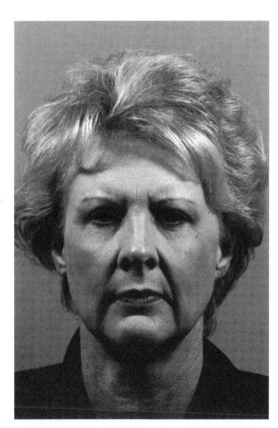

FIG. 9. Preoperative photographs in 21 poses are taken with the patient in a neutral position. Two photo floodlamps are used employing 250-watt tungsten bulbs of 3200 Kelvin temperature on movable stands. A 35-mm camera with a 100-mm macro lens is used. Kodak Ektachrome tungsten film of ISO 160 is color balanced for use with these photo floodlamps. This view is taken at 4 feet, frontal view, vertical position of the camera body.

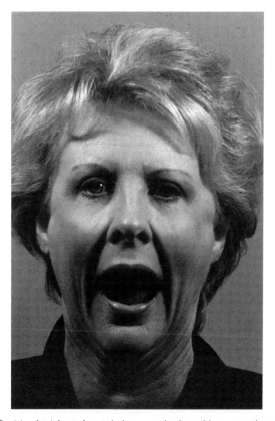

FIG. 11. At 4 feet, frontal view, vertical position, mouth open to evaluate function of the facial mimetic muscles.

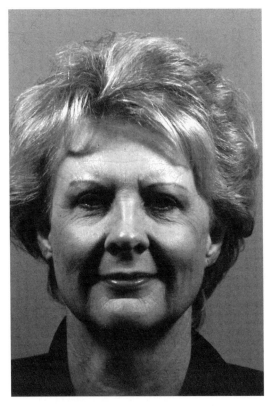

FIG. 12. At 4 feet, frontal view, vertical position, with patient smiling.

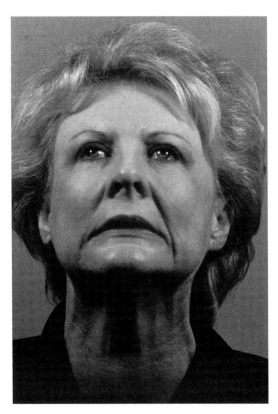

FIG. 14. At 4 feet, frontal view, head tipped back, vertical position, patient grimacing with platysma contracted.

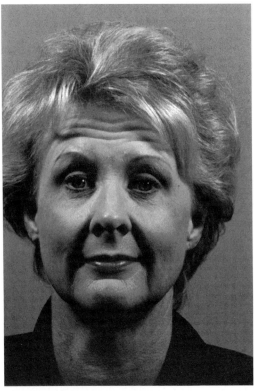

FIG. 13. At 4 feet, frontal view, vertical position, frontalis muscle contracted with eyebrows elevated.

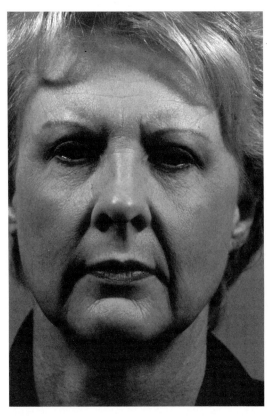

FIG. 15. At 3 feet, frontal view, vertical position.

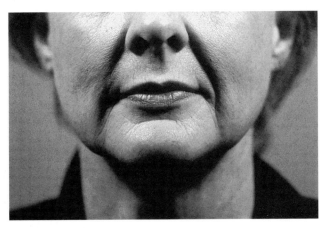

FIG. 16. At 2½ feet, frontal view, horizontal position, from the tip of the nose including the chin and neck.

The patient is placed in a neutral position using the Frankfort plane, which is a horizontal line from the superior border of the auditory meatus to the inferior border of the infraorbital rim. When this line is level, flexion or extension of the head and neck is eliminated. Jewelry and earrings should be removed, and photographic floodlights are used instead of a camera-mounted flash, since the former show the subtle contouring and wrinkling of the face that is the reason the patient is requesting improvement. In addition, the oblique light of a photographic floodlamp has the further advantage of being moved from position to position to accentuate the shadows created by these contour defects. A camera employing an attached photoflash produces flat light that may completely eliminate most or all of the shadows created by contour changes and wrinkling.

Occasionally a patient is unable to have the photographs completed until the day of surgery. We obtain two series of preoperative photographs using two different cameras on two different rolls of films. One roll is sent to Kodalux. The second roll is sent locally so that the processing may be completed in 24 hours and available during the early days of

FIG. 18. At 4 feet, left oblique view, vertical position.

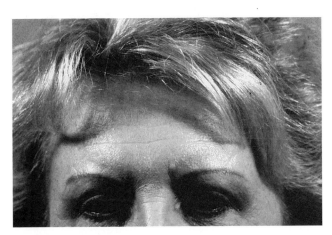

FIG. 17. At 2½ feet, frontal view, horizontal position, from top of forehead to middle of nose.

FIG. 19. At 3 feet, left oblique view, vertical position.

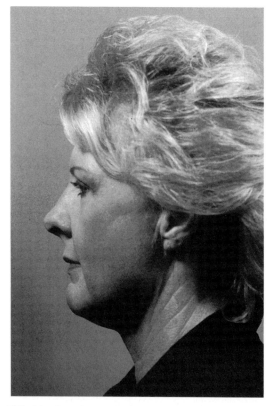

FIG. 20. At 4 feet, left lateral view, vertical position.

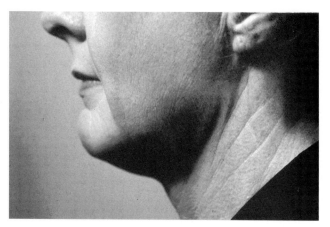

FIG. 22. At 2½ feet, left lateral view, horizontal position from tip of nose including chin and neck.

the postoperative phase. This virtually eliminates two major mishaps that the author has experienced during his 25 years of performing facelift surgery. These include the malfunction of a camera, which will not be apparent until after the photographs return from processing. The other is the remote possibility that film will be lost or destroyed during processing. By using two cameras, two different rolls of film, and two different processing laboratories, both of these possibilities are eliminated.

FIG. 21. At 3 feet, left lateral view, vertical position.

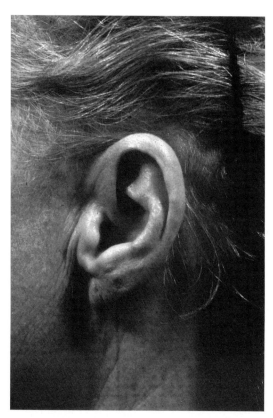

FIG. 23. At 2 feet, left lateral view, vertical position showing ear.

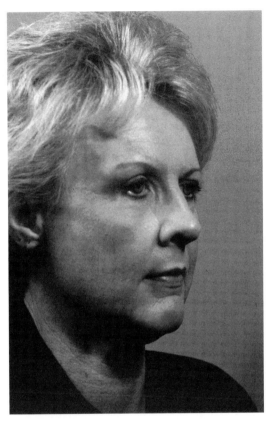

FIG. 24. At 4 feet, right oblique view, vertical position.

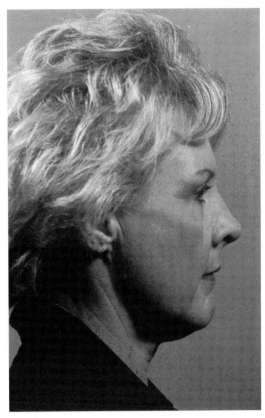

FIG. 26. At 4 feet, right lateral view, vertical position.

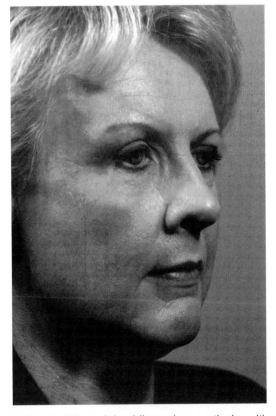

FIG. 25. At 3 feet, right oblique view, vertical position.

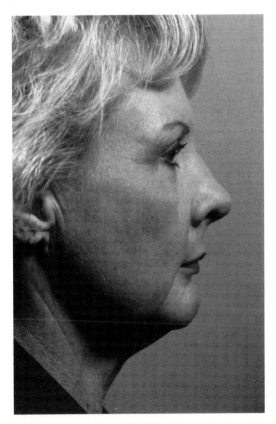

FIG. 27. At 3 feet, right lateral view, vertical position.

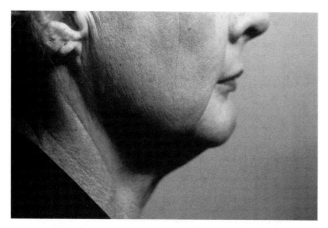

FIG. 28. At 2½ feet, right lateral view, horizontal position from tip of nose including chin and neck.

If an anatomic peculiarity or asymmetry is noted during the initial consultation or the photographic session, this should be discussed with the patient and carefully documented both in writing and photographically. The necessity for obtaining adequate preoperative photographs cannot be emphasized enough. Although each of us looks at our face in a mirror many times during the day, no one can accurately and completely describe his or her facial contour without error. Patients do not note subtle and sometimes even marked

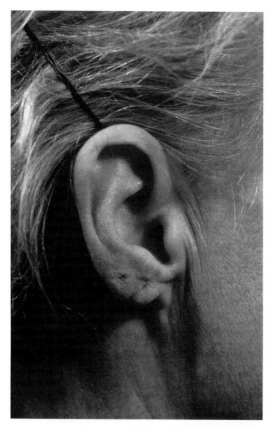

FIG. 29. At 2 feet, right lateral view, vertical position showing ear.

changes in their anatomy but readily find them after the surgery because they will be looking intently at the changes that appear during their postoperative phase. Peculiar anatomic shapes and asymmetry are often noted by the patient after surgery with the claim that they were the result of the surgery. Since the surgery does not affect the underlying structure that causes most of these contour asymmetries, the surgeon's only line of defense is adequate preoperative photographs; even then, some patients only reluctantly accept this evidence. A case in point is a patient who claimed that one side of her face ''was caved in and the other side pushed out during the surgery.'' Although her stated objective during the consultation was to improve her jowls and anterior cervical region, she focused primarily on this midface, bony contour asymmetry, which created a conflict. Not having recognized this asymmetry during the consultation or the photographic session, the author explained to the patient before evaluating the photographs that the subtle differences were the result of the underlying bony structure, which had not been altered by the surgery. She vehemently denied that these changes were present before surgery. Even after being shown the preoperative pictures, she was unwilling to accept this photographic evidence, her retort being, ''You altered the preoperative pictures.'' Of course, it was impossible to have done this, and when presented with the fact that the author would have had to know what type of postoperative defect would occur in order to be able to alter her photographs before surgery, the patient was unable to contemplate the situation rationally. Only after her edema and ecchymosis resolved and she evaluated her final results did she accept the fact that these contour differences were present before surgery. Only then was she happy and appreciative of the surgical improvement. If the preoperative photographs had not been present, this case could conceivably have led to litigation.

Preoperative Preparation

Patients are instructed to wash their face and shampoo their hair on the night before surgery, as outlined in the preoperative instructions (Table 17-2). All medication regimens are started as instructed per prescription. All cosmetics, particularly eyeliner, should be thoroughly removed. The patient should arrive without jewelry and in appropriate clothing, such as a blouse or shirt that buttons, so that the clothing need not be put on or taken off over the large, bulky postoperative head dressing. Money, jewelry, and articles of value should be left at home, and the patient should take no tranquilizers or mood-altering substances before reading and completing the preoperative consent form. If the patient wishes to have some hypnotic for the evening before surgery, the preoperative consent form and the interim history should be signed at least 1 day before the surgery to avoid any legal claim that the patient did not possess his or her full faculties at the time of signing the consent. The author uses an interim

TABLE 17-5. *Interim medical history*

Please answer the following questions and explain any YES responses:

YES	NO	
_____	_____	Have you had any recent change in your general health? Explain.
_____	_____	Have you had any recent localized infection? Explain.
_____	_____	Do you have any known drug allergies? Explain.

Have you recently had any of the following:

_____	_____	Diagnosed medical condition
_____	_____	High blood pressure
_____	_____	Diabetes
_____	_____	Heart condition
_____	_____	Sugar in urine
_____	_____	Accutane treatment for acne? Explain.
_____	_____	Are you taking any medications at the present time? (Please include those medications prescribed for you by Dr. Alt.) If so, please list:

_____

Address and phone number where you may be reached after surgery:

_____

_____

_____

Date: _____   _____

Signature

history to ensure that there are no changes in medications or the patient's physical status as compared with the first history obtained in the original consultation (Table 17-5). The results of laboratory and physical examinations should be in the surgeon's office no later than several days before the surgery and should again be reviewed with the anesthesiologist or anesthetist. Any final questions are reviewed with the patient and family at this time.

Operative Method

There are numerous methods to perform the facelift, with hundreds of variations in the incisions. Flap techniques include the miniflap, which undermines only several centimeters of skin and does not alter the underlying fascia; the short flap, which undermines 5 to 7 cm along the mandibular body, usually combined with plication (a folding over) or imbrication (a undermining, cutting, and tacking of the fascia); and the long flap, which may be extended to an area near the oral commissures. The recent subperiosteal approach and deep-plane facelift are just a few of the options. The content of this chapter is not designed to address all or even the

major types mentioned. The purpose is to provide the reader with an effective, logical method in which excellent, reliable results can be expected. The reader should review the surgical literature and compare other methods with this technique.

Webster was the first to advocate the short flap technique that is the basis of the author's method. The following method describes the technique used and modified by the author over the past 23 years. This method has been shown to provide safety with effective, long-lasting results.

TECHNIQUE

Plication Versus Imbrication of Superficial Musculoaponeurotic System

Aufricht was the first to report, in 1961, on the use of buried suspensory sutures. A major contribution was the identification of the superficial musculoaponeurotic system (SMAS) described by Mitz and Peyronie. They postulated that the SMAS was responsible for the long-term beneficial effects of the suspension sutures. There are two methods in which the SMAS may be advanced. Plication is the term used when the SMAS is folded upon itself and fixed by buried sutures. Imbrication is the term used when the SMAS is undermined and advanced over the underlying tissues, the excess being trimmed and the remaining edge fixed with buried sutures. Webster reported that imbrication has no advantage over plication. Since imbrication requires more time and is more likely to cause postoperative bleeding and nerve damage, it is sensible for the surgeon to use plication. Plication of the SMAS provides marked improvement in long-term effects. In studies in which only one side of the face received SMAS plication Webster showed in an evaluation performed more than 10 years later that the improvement was more evident on the side receiving the SMAS suspension. Improvement of platysmal banding, preservation of the cervicomental angle, and improvement of the jowl on the plicated side were evident.

Marking

Begin by placing the patient in a clean surgical gown. Prepare the face, neck, and shoulders with Technicare Surgical Scrub (Care-Tech Laboratory, St. Louis, MO) for a minimum of 3 minutes. Using gloves, a ruler, and a gentian violet marking pen, all of which are sterile, I outline the extent of undermining, the area of cervical liposuction, and the incision lines, (Figs. 30–35).

I mark the distance of undermining by measuring 5 cm from the lobule of the ear to the middle portion of the body of the mandible and a second segment of 7 to 8 cm from the lobule to the midportion of the sternocleidomastoid muscle (Figs. 30 and 31). The anterior extent of the undermining over the zygomatic process is two thirds of the distance of a line measured from the anterior border of the pinna to the

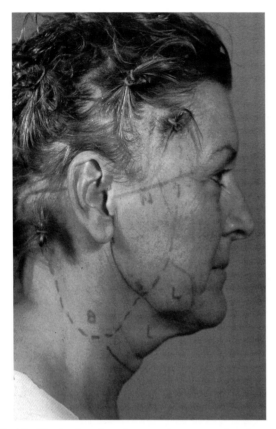

FIG. 30. The broken line denotes the extent of undermining measured from the inferior border of the lobule to the mandibular body, which is 5 cm. The inferior border of the cervical flap is measured from the inferior border of the lobule to the midbelly of the sternocleidomastoid muscle and measures 8 cm in this patient. The solid line from the inferior portion of the lateral cervical flap to the thyroid cartilage at the midline denotes the inferior limit of the anterior cervical liposuction.

lateral aspect of the orbital rim (Fig. 30). These three points are connected by a curved line from the sternocleidomastoid muscle to the mandibular body and onto the zygomatic arch (Fig. 30). From this point and superiorly the flap follows a vertical line from the zygomatic arch to a point level with the temporal peak of the scalp hair (Fig. 30). The posterior portion of the flap is limited by a curved line running from the middle portion of the sternocleidomastoid to the posterior extent of the horizontal retroauricular incision (Figs. 30 and 31).

I begin the incision line with a 2- to 3-cm horizontal segment at the level of the temporal peak (Fig. 30). The incision turns 90 degrees at the posterior extent and becomes vertical through the temporal hair to include the posterior half or two thirds of the temporal hair (Figs. 32 and 33). The incision curves posteriorly to encompass all of the hair at its inferior border and then traverses posteriorly and superiorly at a 45-degree angle. It then curves approximately 165 degrees and continues parallel to the anterior border of the pinna (Fig.

33). When the incision reaches the superior border of the tragus, a 90-degree angle is made and the incision progresses posteriorly for several millimeters until the posterior border of the crest of the tragus is reached (Fig. 34). A second 90-degree angle is made, allowing the incision to traverse inferiorly at the posterior border of the crest of the tragus so that the incision line will be hidden. At the inferior border of the tragus, it makes a 90-degree angle anteriorly until the anterior border at the superior portion of the lobule is reached. The incision then takes another 90-degree turn and travels inferiorly in the crease of the lobule. The incision curves around the inferior border of the lobule and remains in the crease created by the posterior border of the lobule and the cervical skin. At the point where the incision meets the superior portion of the lobule it displaces 3 to 5 mm onto the pinna until it reaches a level 1 cm above the superior border of the external auditory meatus (Fig. 35). The incision then makes a 45-degree turn and travels inferiorly and posteriorly to the base of the postauricular sulcus. The incision turns 90 degrees at the base of the sulcus to create a V at

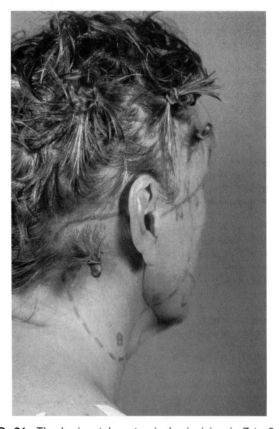

FIG. 31. The horizontal postauricular incision is 7 to 8 cm and is placed 1 cm above the level of the external auditory meatus. At the extreme posterior portion the incision curves downward at a 90-degree angle to allow correction of the dog ear effect after the flap has been rotated. A solid line drawn along the inferior border of the mandibular body denotes the superior limitation of the cervical liposuction.

the sulcus. Extend this posterior limb to equal the distance of the anterior limb. Make a 135-degree angle to allow the incision to traverse posteriorly in the horizontal plane for 6 to 8 cm, depending on the size of the patient (Figs. 30 and 31). At the posterior portion of the horizontal incision the marking is curved with the incision ending in a vertical position, creating a 90-degree angle until the extent of incision is approximately 2 cm below the level of the horizontal limb (Fig. 31).

A line of caution is drawn from the inferior border of the tragus to the lateral aspect of the eyebrow to denote the approximate course of the temporal branch of the facial nerve (Figs. 30 and 33). Draw a second line at the inferior border of the mandibular ramus to delineate the superior aspect of the intended cervical liposuction (Fig. 31). Removal of fat superior to this line creates a ridge when the flap is advanced superiorly and posteriorly, as it is redraped. Draw a third line from the inferior portion of the proposed

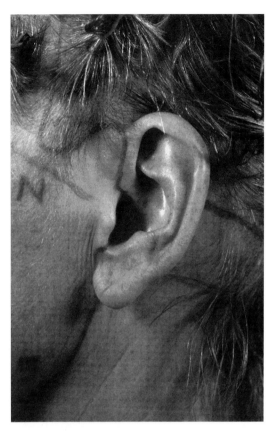

FIG. 33. The inferior portion of the temporal incision curves around the inferior border of the sideburn and traverses posterosuperiorly over the glabrous skin for approximately 2 cm. It then curves downward and follows the anterior border of the pinna. The hair has been combed and secured with rubber binders to eliminate an obstruction of the operative site. The solid line *(N)* is the approximate course of the temporal branch of the facial nerve.

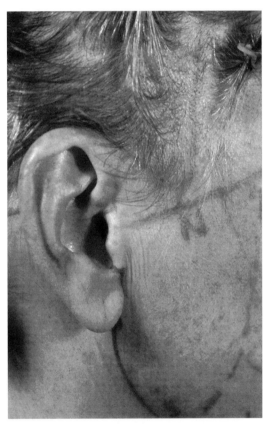

FIG. 32. The superior horizontal portion of the temporal incision is level to the temporal peak of the scalp hair and is 2 to 3 cm. It is evident superoposterior to the rubber binder holding the hair away from the incision site. The vertical incision is placed at the midpoint or at the frontal third of the temporal tuft of hair that constitutes the sideburn. Undermining is extended anteriorly from the vertical incision to a point that is two thirds of the distance from the anterior border of the pinna to the lateral portion of the orbital rim (see Fig. 30).

flap over the belly of the sternocleidomastoid to the thyroid cartilage or to the inferior border of the anterior cervical skin where the subcutaneous fat attains its thinnest measurement (Figs. 30 and 31). This represents the inferior extent of anterior cervical liposuction.

Trim the hair of the temporal tuft to a width of 1 cm along the incision lines. Fix the hair using rubber binders to avoid obstruction of the surgical site (Figs. 32–34). On the horizontal postauricular incision, trim the hair slightly below and to 1 cm above the incision line (Figs. 31 and 35). Photographs of the preoperative markings are taken and the patient is accompanied to the operative suite, where an intravenous line containing lactated Ringer's solution is inserted for the administration of preoperative, intraoperative, and postoperative medications. Cover the entire upper half and headrest of the surgical table with sterile drapes. Place full-body draping over the patient from the neck downward. Position a nasal cannula that has been gas-sterilized. Anchor it with sterile tape to the nose to provide a continuous flow of nasal oxygen during the procedure.

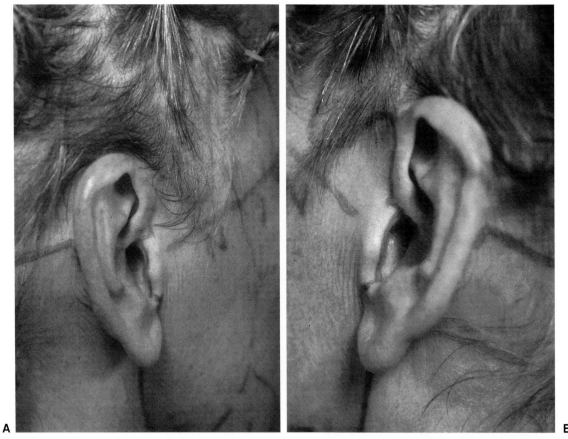

A   B

FIG. 34. The preauricular incision begins as it courses caudally along the anterior border of the pinna of the ear. The vertical incision is then converted to a short horizontal segment by a right-angle turn at the superior border of the tragus. A distance of approximately 5 mm is traversed; then a second right-angle turn is made as the incision reaches the posterior border of the crest of the tragus. The resulting vertical incision follows the posterior border of the tragal crest until it reaches the inferior portion of the tragus, where a third right-angle turn is made. This inferior horizontal incision passes anteriorly until it reaches the anterior border of the lobule, a distance of 3 to 4 mm. A fourth right-angle turn is made as the incision becomes vertical in the crease made by the cheek skin and the lobule. The tragal incision employs four right-angle turns to decrease or eliminate scar contracture. This is similar to performing a W-plasty.

Optional Pretragal Incision

There are two conditions in which the pretragal incision is appropriate. First, men usually obtain better postoperative results with the pretragal approach because when the posttragal incision is used, the whisker-bearing skin advances onto the anterior portion of the helix and tragus. Male skin is thicker than that of females and is more difficult to redrape over the subtle contours of the tragal area. In addition, whisker hair would grow on the tragus requiring either daily shaving or removal by electrolysis. The pretragal incision in males is placed approximately 1 cm anterior to the helix and traverses vertically through the depression anterior to the tragus. It then passes in the crease of the anterior border of the lobule (Fig. 36).

The second condition favoring the pretragal incision is in women with a protruding tragus that is angled greater than

45 degrees from the plane of the adjacent cheek. When the tragus protrudes at such an angle, redraping of the preauricular skin over the tragus is difficult.

Intravenous Sedation

A facelift can be performed using local anesthesia, intravenous sedation, or general anesthesia. Local anesthesia can be supplemented with oral or intramuscular sedatives. Most patients prefer to be heavily sedated or unconscious during the procedure. Although general anesthesia provides this unconscious state, there is a slightly increased risk and the endotracheal tube is an inconvenience in the operative site. Consider the safety, effectiveness, ease of use, and decreased likelihood of postoperative nausea provided by intravenous sedation. Generally, patients recover more rapidly and have less nausea with intravenous sedation than with general anesthesia. The initial administration of 1 to 2 mg of midazolam hydrochloride (Versed, Roche Dermatologics, a division of Hoffmann–LaRoche Inc., Nutley, NJ) and 50 μg of fentanyl citrate (Sublimaze, Janssen Pharmaceutica Inc., Piscataway, NJ) achieves sedation. The purpose is to maintain sedation so that the patient does not experience the discomfort associated with the administration of the local anesthetic or any subsequent part of the surgical procedure. At the completion of the local anesthesia, the level of sedation may be decreased, since discomfort should be absent. This level is increased before the infiltration of the second side with the local anesthetic. Many patients experience retrograde amnesia and do not recall any of the surgical events, even though they sometimes talk during the procedure. Since the diaphragm or accessory muscles of the thoracic cage are not paralyzed with this form of intravenous sedation, it is not necessary to assist the patient's breathing with an endotracheal tube or anesthesia machine. The patient's condition is monitored by the anesthesiologist or anesthetist using a pulse oximeter, an automatic or manual blood pressure cuff, and a cardiac monitor. An emergency cart is available on which there are graduated endotracheal tubes, and a standard anesthesia machine and a cardiac defibrillator are in the room (Fig. 37).

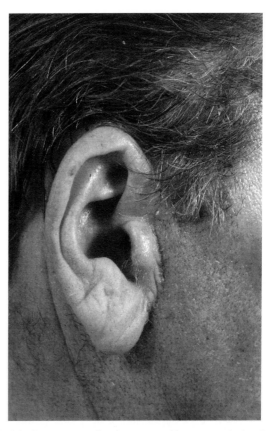

FIG. 36. In a man or in a woman with an anteriorly placed tragus the incision is placed in the pretragal position. It begins 1 cm anterior to the helix and travels in the crease adjacent to the tragus and into the lobular crease. Male patient is shown 14 days after rhytidectomy.

Local Anesthesia

Local anesthesia is infiltrated using lidocaine (Xylocaine) with epinephrine (Astra Pharmaceutical Products, Inc., Westboro, MA) into the areas of proposed liposuction and flap creation. Two strengths are employed. A 1% solution of lidocaine (10 mg/ml) with epinephrine 1:100,000 buffered with 8.4% sodium bicarbonate using a 10:1 dilution is administered with a 10-ml control syringe through a 25-gauge 1½-inch needle to the proposed incision sites (Fig. 38). Anesthetize all remaining areas using 0.5% lidocaine (5 mg/ml) with epinephrine 1:200,000 in a 10-ml control syringe with a 22-gauge 3½-inch spinal needle (Fig. 39).

Because the cervical liposuction is the first procedure to be performed, initially infiltrate the anesthesia into the anterior cervical region. Infiltrate the 1% lidocaine solution into a limited area to allow a small submental incision to be performed at the midline. Through this incision introduce the spinal needle and administer 0.5% lidocaine with epinephrine over the anterior cervical region. Make additional injections of 1% lidocaine with epinephrine at incision sites in the retrolobular areas. Complete infiltration using the 0.5% lidocaine with epinephrine solution over the areas of

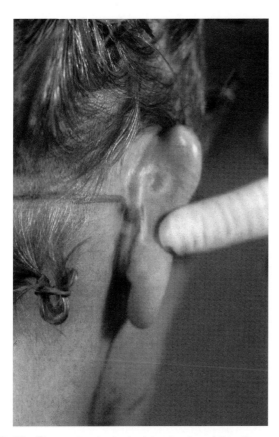

FIG. 35. The postauricular incision is placed 3 to 5 mm onto the posterior surface of the cartilaginous external ear. A V-shaped incision is placed with the inferior point crossing the postauricular sulcus to eliminate a bridging scar when normal contraction occurs.

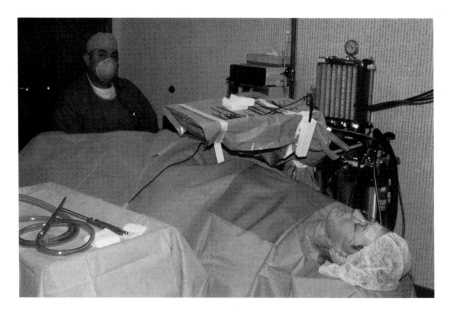

FIG. 37. During the operative procedure the patient is monitored with a pulse oximeter, an automatic or manual blood pressure cuff, and an electrocardiogram. Intravenous sedation is used in combination with local anesthesia. A sterilized nasal cannula is used to continuously deliver oxygen. An emergency cart with endotracheal tubes and appropriate medications, an anesthesia machine, and a cardiac defibrillator are in the room.

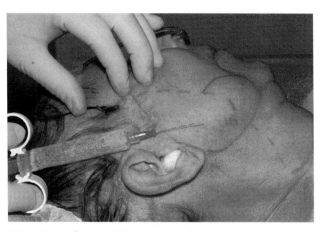

FIG. 38. A 1½-inch, 25-gauge needle placed on a 10-ml control syringe is used for the infiltration of all incision lines. Syringes are labeled with the concentration of lidocaine.

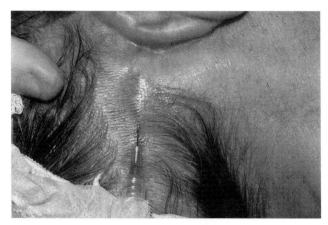

FIG. 40. The incision lines are infiltrated with 1% lidocaine (10 mg/ml) with epinephrine 1:100,000.

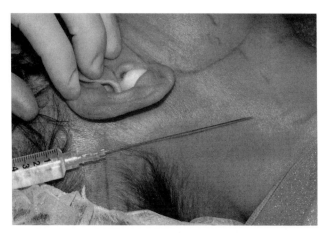

FIG. 39. A 22-gauge, 3½-inch spinal needle placed on a 10-ml control syringe is used to infiltrate the flaps and the liposuction sites. Anesthetic consists of 0.5% lidocaine (5 mg/ml) with epinephrine 1:200,000.

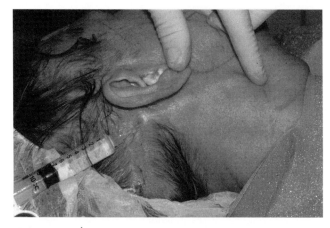

FIG. 41. A 3½-inch, 22-gauge spinal needle is quite effective in allowing dispersion of anesthetic over a large field. The needle is introduced in the hairline of the postauricular area and the temporal region to avoid puncture wounds in the flap skin. A third entry site is the submental incision used for liposuction.

anticipated liposuction. Infiltrate the lines of incision using the 1% lidocaine solution (Fig. 40). Use 0.5% lidocaine in the postauricular and lateral cervical areas where the flaps in the mandibular, preauricular, and temporal areas will be created (Fig. 41). Because the entire anterior cervical region is suctioned initially, administer anesthetic to both right and left sides. Because there is a significant time delay from the creation of the first flap on the right side to the creation of the second flap on the left side, administer anesthetic only to the flaps of the right side, and in the same sequence in which the surgery will be performed. When nearing the completion of surgery on the right side, infiltrate anesthetic into the left side. Liposuction of the anterior cervical region does not commence until 20 minutes have elapsed to allow for maximum vasoconstriction.

Cervical Liposuction

I use a 15-cm-long, flat spatula cannula of 4-mm diameter with a single orifice to initially suction the anterior cervical region (Figs. 42 and 43). Employ full negative pressure from a standard liposuction machine. Initially direct the orifice of the cannula away from the skin surface. When the liposuction nears its completion, turn the cannula 90 degrees and with the index finger and thumb hold the skin gently over the orifice of the cannula (Fig. 43). Retain a small amount of fat on the skin flap to allow the skin to properly redrape. If the liposuction is too aggressive, the dermis can be damaged, creating fibrosis, postoperative skin contracture, and a flap that is firmly fixed to the underlying platysma. After the superficial fat is removed, use the larger, 6-mm spatula cannula to remove any remaining fat from the platysma (Figs. 42, 44, and 45).

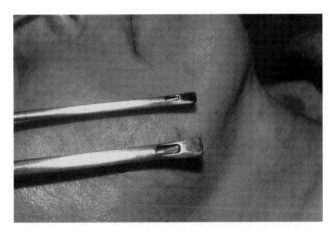

FIG. 42. To facilitate the liposuction of the anterior cervical area, two cannulas of 15-cm length are employed. This special type of cannula is called a spatula because of its flat tip. In this case, cannulas are in 4- and 6-mm sizes. Because of its smaller size, the 4-mm cannula readily passes through the fibrous tissue and fat. The larger, 6-mm cannula is introduced secondarily to remove any additional fat that remains on the platysma.

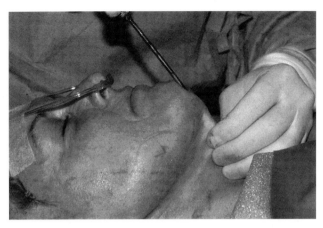

FIG. 43. To remove submental fat, a 4-mm spatula cannula is introduced through the submental incision with the orifice facing away from the skin. When there is excessive fat, this cannula is used over the entire anterior cervical region.

A single submental incision is adequate if only a small amount of submental fat is to be removed. If subcutaneous fat is present over the entire cervical region, make incisions in the postauricular area at the level of the lobule. Thick fibrous tissue anterior and inferior to the lobular incision is difficult to penetrate using the blunt dissection of the liposuction cannula and can be accomplished more readily with Ragnell scissors (Fig. 45). Following the use of a 4-mm spatula, a larger, 6-mm spatula with a single orifice is introduced both anteriorly and laterally to remove any remaining fat from the platysma (Fig. 46).

When fat in the jowl area requires liposuction, use a very small cannula, preferably a 3-mm size with one small orifice. If a standard suction machine is used at the full negative pressure of 27 to 28 inches of mercury, the small orifice is obligatory to eliminate excessive extraction of fat. Use of a larger cannula or one with multiple ports may lead to excessive extraction and result in ridging. This is difficult to cor-

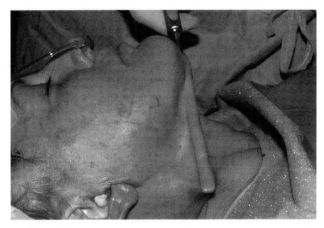

FIG. 44. The 4-mm cannula is replaced with a 6-mm spatula to remove any remaining fat that is present over the platysma. Suction extends to the anterior border of the sternocleidomastoid muscle.

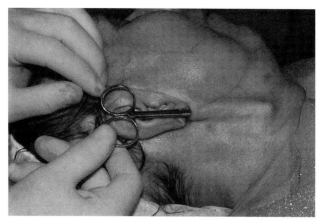

FIG. 45. A short incision is made posterior to the lobule made to allow introduction of the 4- and 6-mm cannulas. Because of the fibrous nature of the tissues overlying the mastoid area, small Ragnell dissecting scissors are necessary to open a tunnel for the 4-mm cannula.

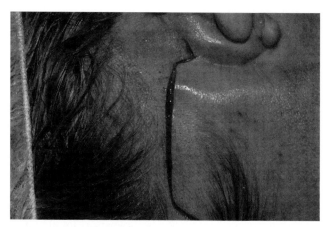

FIG. 47. The horizontal segment of the retroauricular incision is placed approximately 1 cm superior to the level of the superior aspect of the external auditory meatus. It travels posteriorly 7 to 8 cm, where it makes a curved, 90-degree angle and travels inferiorly approximately 2 cm. This 90-degree turn allows for correction of the dog ear that results from the rotation of the flap.

rect even with lipotransfer. Usually liposuction of the jowl is performed after the preauricular flap has been created and the plication completed. The use of syringe-assisted liposuction is an alternative approach.

Flap Creation

Postauricular Flap

I begin the postauricular incision by making a horizontal cut at a level 1 cm above the external auditory canal. Carry the incision posteriorly for 7 to 8 cm, and curve downward until it reaches a vertical position approximately 2 cm below the horizontal segment (Fig. 47). Make the incision perpendicular to the skin, not parallel to the hair follicles, to provide for an increased number of hairs that can potentially grow through the resulting scar. Make the incision through the

subcutaneous fat that is below the hair follicles but above the fascial plane of the occipitalis and temporoparietalis muscles. Cauterize small arterioles in this area before developing the retroauricular flap to avoid significant bleeding.

I use a No. 15 blade to make an incision along the infero-posterior border of the lobule. When it reaches the cartilaginous portion of the ear, proceed superiorly from the sulcus 3 to 5 mm onto the posterior of the auricle to a level 1 cm superior to the external auditory meatus (Fig. 48). Cut the skin in a V fashion over the sulcus with the apex of the V resting in the sulcus. This broken-line closure minimizes the likelihood of a scar contracture leading to an elevated band

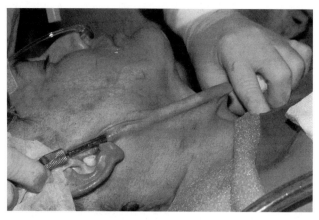

FIG. 46. The 4-mm spatula cannula (15 cm long) can be easily introduced and will reach the midline. Then the 6-mm spatula is introduced to remove the remaining fat from the platysma.

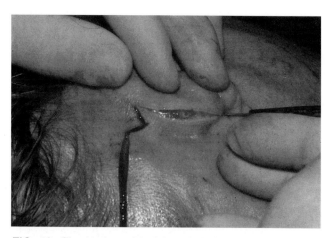

FIG. 48. The V-shaped incision placed in the postauricular sulcus diminishes the likelihood of an elevated band of scar that occurs if a straight line incision passes over this depression. The vertical portion of the retroauricular incision is placed 3 to 5 mm anterior to the postauricular sulcus. When the incision reaches the superior portion of the lobule, it is placed in the postauricular sulcus.

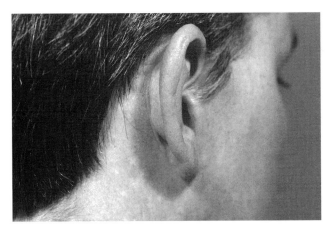

FIG. 49. If a broken-line incision is used to cross the retroauricular sulcus, a contracted, elevated scar is not produced, resulting in a natural-appearing postauricular sulcus. Patient has undergone a facelift using this technique. Her scar is imperceptible.

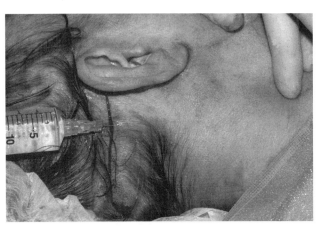

FIG. 51. Thirty cubic centimeters of normal saline may be infiltrated over the postauricular flap to provide hydrodissection. Attention should be focused on the mastoid process and the belly of the sternocleidomastoid muscle over which more of the saline is placed. The mastoid area is fibrotic, and important nerve structures traverse the body of the sternocleidomastoid muscle.

across this concave surface as normal healing proceeds (Fig. 49). Make a small scratch on the inferior portion of the lobule to identify its location when it is later attached to the redraped skin (Fig. 50). Hydrodissection using 30 cc of normal saline instilled with a 25 gauge spinal needle over the area of the retroauricular flap, and in particular to that region of the flap overlying the mastoid area and the sternocleidomastoid muscle, will facilitate rapid dissection (Fig. 51). An additional benefit is that the hydrodissection protects the great auricular nerve as it lies on the belly of the sternocleidomastoid muscle by separating the fascial plane from the overlying dermis. The use of chilled dilute lidocaine with epinephrine is preferred by Asken, since the decreased temperature increases vasoconstriction.

Have an assistant hold the skin under tension by applying digital pressure at the inferior extent of the flap; then grasp

the cut edge with forceps and undermine the flap using a 7-inch Gorney straight facelift scissors or 7½-inch Gorney-Freeman straight facelift scissors. Create the first 1 to 2 cm of flap using sharp dissection by opening and closing the jaws of the scissors. Once this is accomplished, quickly complete the flap by opening the scissors partially and advancing the scissors in the subcutaneous fatty plane to the inferior extent of the proposed undermining (Fig. 52). The jaws of the scissors may have to be opened and closed at the distal extent of the flap, since mere advancement of the open scissors to this level is generally not possible. Rapidly elevate

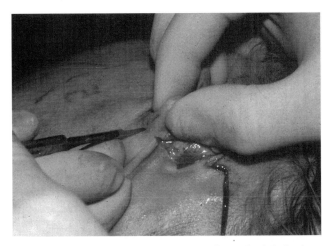

FIG. 50. A small scratch incision is made on the inferior border of the lobule so that this location may be identified during the final repositioning of the lobule when the incision lines are sutured.

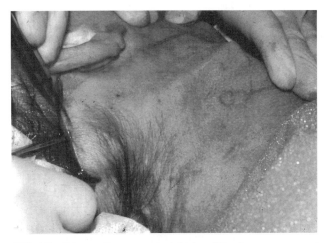

FIG. 52. Gorney-Freeman straight facelift scissors are used for the sharp dissection of the postauricular and lateral cervical flaps. This dissection must be below the level of the hair follicles but can proceed rapidly when proper tension is placed at the inferior border of the flap by the surgical assistant. The scissor tips are held approximately 1½ cm apart while they are advanced. The jaws are closed to cut tissue only when the scissors cannot be advanced further.

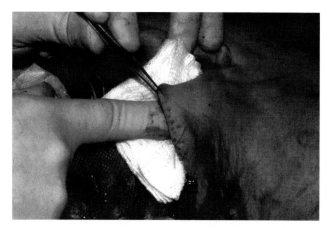

FIG. 53. Three sterile gauze pads are placed under the post-auricular flap to provide for tamponade, which promotes coagulation in this area while the preauricular and temporal flaps are being created. Cautery is not performed in this area until the flap is rotated for final positioning and suturing.

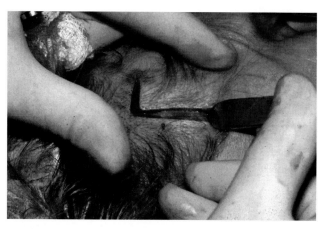

FIG. 55. A No. 15 or a No. 10 blade is used for the vertical incision in the temporal area, which is carried to the level of the underlying fascia. This incision is cut parallel to the hair shafts. The incision is enlarged by using the back of the scalpel handle to facilitate carrying the incision to the underlying fascia. The hair follicles are apparent and easily identifiable.

the flap and strive to complete the procedure in less than 2 minutes. Over the sternocleidomastoid muscle care must be taken to avoid the great auricular nerve that lies superficial to the belly of this muscle where it is posterior and parallel to the external jugular vein. Infiltration of additional saline to assist in dissection is particularly advantageous to the surgeon. Bleeding in the area of the retroauricular flap is usually temporary, and a tamponade of three gauze pads placed in the site facilitates coagulation while the preauricular flap is constructed (Fig. 53).

Temporal Flap

Begin to create the temporal flap by placing a horizontal incision in the temporal hair (Fig. 54). Make the horizontal

or anterior segment perpendicular to the skin so that the greatest number of hair follicles are preserved in the superior retained skin. This means that the blade will be cutting across some of the hair shafts. The incision then makes a right angle, and proceeds inferiorly through the middle or anterior third of the preauricular tuft of hair. This preserves half or two thirds of the sideburn. If the hair follicles grow inferiorly and posteriorly in this area, make the incision parallel to the shaft to retain follicles. If the hair grows inferiorly and anteriorly, make the incision perpendicular to the skin to retain the greatest number of follicles. Make this incision with either a No. 15 or a No. 10 blade. Carry the incision to the fatty layer, where the end of the blade handle is used to separate the tissue down to the superficial temporal fascia (Fig. 55). At the inferior portion of the temporal tuft of hair, use a No. 15 blade to make a curved incision at the bottom

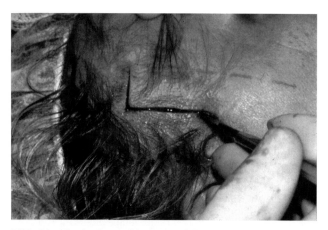

FIG. 54. The horizontal incision of the temporal flap is made at the level of the temporal peak in the scalp hair. (This segment is in the vertical position in this photograph because the patient is supine.) Its length is between 2 and 3 cm and is perpendicular to the skin rather than parallel to the hairs so that more hair follicles are incorporated in the remaining skin, thereby allowing more hairs to grow through the scar.

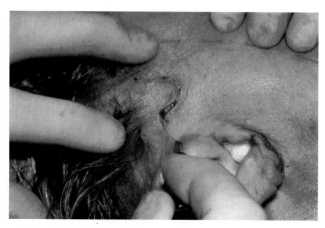

FIG. 56. The incision at the inferior pole of the sideburn curves posterosuperiorly to incorporate the glabrous skin of the superior preauricular area, then curves downward to parallel the anterior border of the helix.

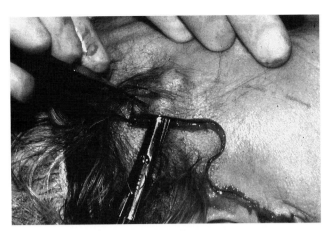

FIG. 57. The anterior temporal flap is grasped with a forceps and undermined with either blunt dissection using the back of a blade handle or with curved Matarasso facelift scissors with blunt tips as shown. The initial undermining is made beneath the hair follicles and then becomes more superficial in the non–hair-bearing skin to avoid the temporal nerve.

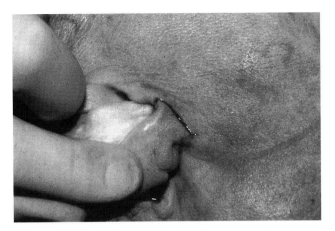

FIG. 58. The preauricular incision is begun in the crease where the cheek skin meets the lobule. It is carried superiorly along the anterior border of the lobule, where it makes a 90-angle posteriorly at the base of the tragus.

of the sideburn or at an area where the hair becomes sparse. The incision then closely follows the posterior edge of the temporal tuft, creating a small flap of preauricular skin. The incision makes a 135-degree curved turn and reaches the anterior portion of the auricle (Fig. 56).

Undermining begins at the superior portion of the temporal skin. Raise the corner of the flap, and identify the hair follicles. Use a 7-inch curved Matarasso facelift scissors with blunt tips (A. B. Stille-Werner, Stockholm, Sweden; distributor is Baxter V. Mueller, Deerfield, IL) for elevation (Fig. 57). This dissection is deep to the hair follicles until the anterior border of the temporal hair is reached, whereupon dissection becomes superficial to avoid the temporal branch of the facial nerve. Continue elevation of the flap with either sharp dissection using Matarasso scissors or with blunt dissection using the handle of the Bard-Parker scalpel. Continue the flap anteriorly for a total distance of 2.5 to 3 cm. Accidental incision of the temporal vein frequently occurs. Cauterize this vein with caution to avoid any permanent damage to the temporal nerve. There is usually no additional bleeding with the exception of small vessels on the skin edges.

Preauricular Flap

Create the preauricular flap by beginning an incision on the anterior border of the lobule, and proceed superiorly to the area anterior and horizontal to the inferior portion of the calebra cavum (Fig. 58). Make a right angle, and proceed posteriorly in a horizontal fashion immediately inferior to the tragus for 3 to 4 mm until the incision reaches the concha. Make the superior incision on the anterior border of the helix. Cut a second right angle at the superior border of the tragus and continue posteriorly for 5 mm (Fig. 59). The incision then makes a third right angle and follows inferiorly in the vertical direction along the posterior border of the crest of

the tragus (Fig. 60). Do not place the incision too far posteriorly, to avoid the necessity of draping the skin over the entire crest of the tragus. At the inferior border of the tragus pass the incision anteriorly after another right angle has been made in the horizontal plane. Carry the incision 3 to 4 mm anteriorly until it reaches the lobular incision. Extend the undermining superior to the tragus to meet the undermining that has been completed in the temporal flap. Additional undermining inferior to the tragus extends over the mandibular body to meet the undermining that has previously been completed in the postauricular and lateral cervical regions (Fig. 61).

A thick flap is preferable in the preauricular and jowl areas, since the flap is longer than that in the temporal regions and therefore has a more tenuous blood supply. A thin flap in these areas has two disadvantages. First, undermining

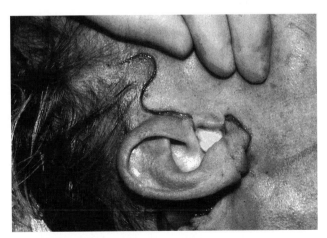

FIG. 59. The second portion of the preauricular incision is made superior to the tragus, where it follows the anterior border of the helix. At the inferior point of this incision a 90-degree angle is made as the incision runs posteriorly approximately 5 mm at the superior border of the tragus.

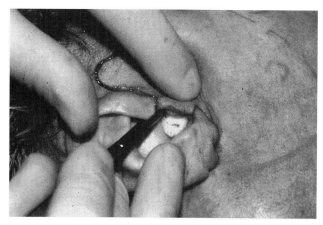

FIG. 60. An incision is made on the posterior portion of the tragal crest connecting the inferior and superior incisions described earlier. This completes the tragal incision, which creates a broken-line closure incorporating four right-angle turns. This closure discourages the development of elevated bands of scar that may occur with normal scar contracture.

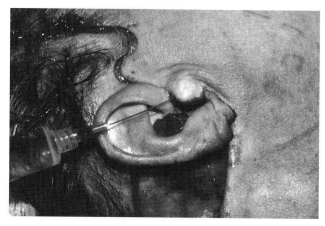

FIG. 62. This leaves the skin attached to the tragus as the only tissue that is not elevated. Saline is injected in the area to provide hydrodissection.

can damage the dermal capillary plexus, which provides perfusion to the flap. Second, a thin flap draped over the parotid fascia from which the fat has been suctioned is semitransparent, giving the skin an unnatural color. Since the facial nerve is embedded in the parotid gland in the preauricular area, undermining can be placed at a deeper level than that at the temporal region where the temporal branch becomes superficial. Skin in the area of the postauricular flap is thicker and lends itself naturally to adequate undermining. Undermining of the temporal and preauricular flaps is accomplished with a long, curved scissors such as 7-inch Matarasso facelift scissors (Stille) or Ragnell scissors; both have broad, blunt tips to avoid cutting through the surface of the skin. I use straight scissors for the retroauricular and lateral cervical flap, since the skin in these areas is thicker and has less curves.

The preauricular flap undermines quite easily, and undermining is usually accompanied by very little bleeding. Begin

the superior portion of the preauricular flap from the temporal site and complete the procedure as far inferiorly as possible. Raise the lower portion through the surgical incision anterior to the lobule. Once the flap is completed, the only portion remaining is the skin attached to the tragus. Again, use hydrodissection over the tragus to elevate the skin off the cartilage (Fig. 62). Use 6-inch Ragnell scissors to create this flap, paying attention to avoid injury to the cartilage, which could result in chondritis (Fig. 63). This completes the undermining of the entire flap, including the postauricular, temporal, and preauricular portions (Fig. 64). With experience, skill, and a trained assistant the creation of the incisions and elevation of the three areas of the flap complex usually require 8 to 12 minutes, depending on the amount of bleeding encountered.

Facial Liposuction

A fatty layer of tissue exists over the cheek from the zygoma to the mandibular body. Since plication folds the

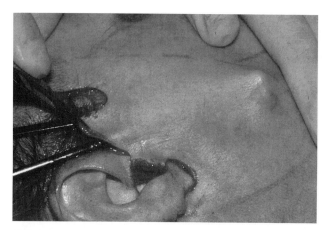

FIG. 61. With tension applied to the flap, undermining is completed in the preauricular area, which connects the previously constructed temporal and cervical flaps.

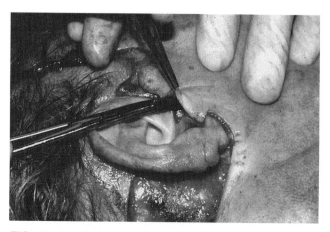

FIG. 63. The flap is created over the tragus using Ragnell scissors. It is important to avoid injury to the tragal cartilage, which may result in persistent chondritis.

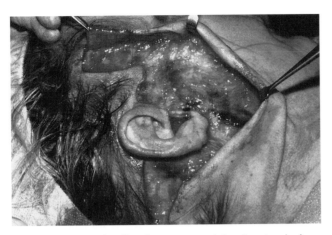

FIG. 64. The entire flap is now complete. It extends from the temporal region through the preauricular area over the mandibular region and the lateral cervical area and into the postauricular region.

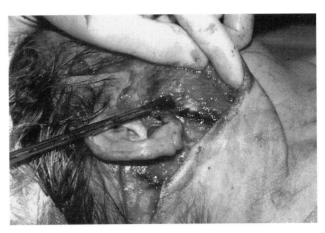

FIG. 66. The cannula is directed over the parotid area, the region of the mandibular angle, and posterior third of the body to remove any fat from the superficial musculoaponeurotic system (SMAS).

parotid fascia upon itself, thoroughly remove this fat. Before the introduction of liposuction, sharp dissection was used to remove this fat. This was more difficult and increased the likelihood of injury to the parotid fascia and parotid gland. Liposuction makes this extraction of fat rapid and safe with a No. 6 flat spatula cannula with a large orifice using a standard liposuction machine (Figs. 65–67). At this time, complete coagulation of any bleeding vessels. Coagulation of these vessels during the elevation of the flaps increases the duration of the procedure, since bleeding recurs with liposuction of the fat.

Remove the pretragal fat with sharp scissors to create a depression (Fig. 67). This reconstructs the normal contour after the skin has been redraped. A significant amount of fat is removed beyond what is harvested by liposuction (Fig. 68). Establish hemostasis (Fig. 69).

Remove the three gauze pads that were previously placed

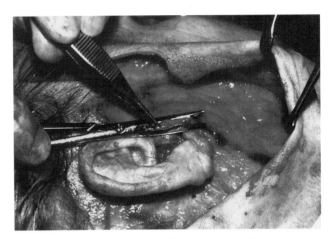

FIG. 67. To create a depression anterior to the tragus, remaining fat and fibrous tissue are removed with Ragnell scissors. The incision should not be carried through the parotid fascia.

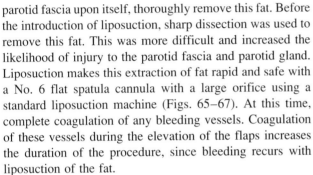

FIG. 65. A 15-cm, No. 6 spatula cannula is used to remove fat from the preauricular and mandibular areas that are to be plicated. There is usually little fat over the sternocleidomastoid muscle, postauricular area, or temporal region.

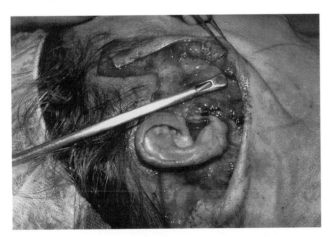

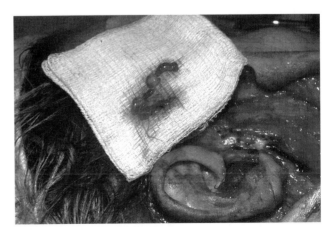

FIG. 68. Removal of fibrous tissue and fat overlying the parotid fascia provides a more normal final contour in the pretragal area.

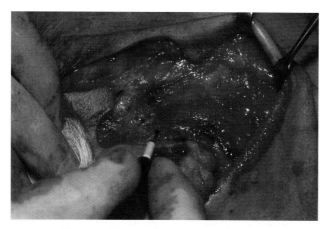

FIG. 69. Hemostasis is performed using electrocautery. All areas of the flap and underlying tissues are carefully examined to ensure complete hemostasis. Clots that may have occurred are easily removed using the No. 6 spatula cannula before electrocautery.

in the postauricular flap, and use dry gauze or cannula suction to remove any blood that may have accumulated. Hemostasis of this area must be absolute, since this is the most likely area for a postoperative hematoma to occur. The most common areas are in the distal end of the flap over the sternocleidomastoid muscle and in the posterior cervical triangle. Particularly important in this lateral cervical region is to infiltrate the epinephrine-containing anesthetic several centimeters beyond the planned extent of the undermining, since the area is difficult to access and often develops bleeding during the operative procedure.

Plication of the Superficial Musculoaponeurotic System

Plication or imbrication of the SMAS significantly improves the long-term results in rhytidectomy surgery. Since the results of plication vs. imbrication show no significant difference, the former method is preferable because it requires less time, results in less injury and bleeding, and has fewer potential complications. A strong braided synthetic permanent suture (Ethibond 2.0; Ethicon Inc., Johnson & Johnson Co., Somerville, NJ) is used for plication. An alternative absorbable suture that retains its tensile strength for 6 weeks is 2.0 polydioxanone (PDS, Ethicon). Although most surgeons who plicate or imbricate the SMAS use only one or two buried sutures to elevate the jowl and anterior cervical region, the placement of 12 to 15 buried sutures along the anterior border of the sternocleidomastoid muscle and extending upward from the lobule of the ear anterior to the preauricular incision and into the temporal area is preferable. This distributes the tension on the SMAS evenly, which avoids a depression at the site of each buried suture that occurs when only several sutures are used. Four key sutures are placed during plication. Their direction is as follows:

1. From the inferior border of the tragus toward the mentum
2. From the superior border of the tragus toward the oral commissure
3. From the juncture of the horizontal and vertical incisions of the temporal flap toward the lateral portion of the orbital rim
4. From the mastoid process toward the cervicomental angle

These key sutures correspondingly elevate the jowl, the angle of the mouth, the lateral portion of the eyebrow, and the cervicomental angle. The proper laying of each knot is critical. Each knot contains three throws, with the exception of the key suture between the mastoid and cervicomental angle, where four throws are used, since this is the most critical suture and it is where the greatest amount of tension is applied. There is a significant difference between the proper and improper tying of these knots. Surgeons often lay multiple half-hitches rather than alternating the laying of each loop in the fashion of the square knot. A half-hitch is an unstable knot that can come undone, regardless of the number of throws tied. A properly laid knot provides stability and will not come undone.

Place the first plication suture at a point slightly anterior to the inferior border of the tragus, and direct it to a point approximately 5 cm inferior and anterior in the direction of the mentum (Figs. 70 and 71). With this first plication suture, a large amount of tissue is folded upon itself, providing support to the SMAS and eliminating the laxity in the jowl area. At the completion of cinching the first loop, use a smooth jaw needle holder to hold the knot until the second loop can be tied (Fig. 72). Carefully bury all knots to avoid spontaneous postoperative extrusion.

Place the second plication suture between the superior border of the tragus and the angle of the mouth (Fig. 73). The distance this suture travels is considerably less and probably will provide for less than 2 cm of tightening. Place the

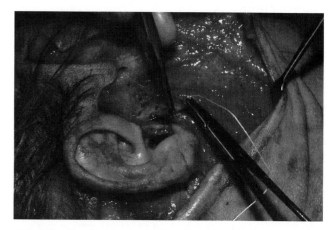

FIG. 70. The first key suture of the plication is placed with its posterior bite at a level slightly anterior to the inferior border of the tragus.

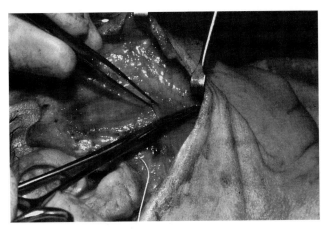

FIG. 71. The distal bite of the first key suture of plication is taken approximately 3 to 5 cm inferoanterior in the direction of the mentum. This distance varies depending on the laxity of the underlying tissues.

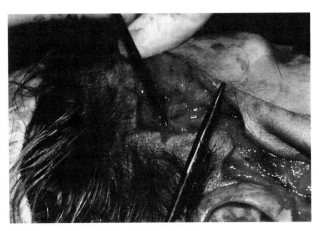

FIG. 74. The third key suture is placed high in the temporal region adjacent to the horizontal incision. This suture is directed anteroinferiorly toward the lateral orbital rim. Elevation of 2 to 3 cm is usually possible. Care should be taken to prevent deep bites with the needle to avoid injury of the temporal nerve.

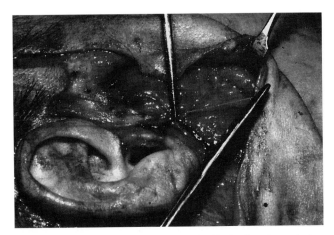

FIG. 72. A simple square knot is tied with the first throw being stabilized with a smooth-jawed clamp. Second and third throws are made, with the surgeon being sure to tie in the fashion of a square knot, not a half-hitch.

third key suture high in the temporal region anterior to the vertical skin incision. Place the distal portion of the suture in the temporal fascia superior to the lateral orbital rim (Fig. 74). This elevates the lateral portion of the eyebrow and the malar area. Cut the sutures on the knot so that fraying of the braided suture is minimized, thus decreasing the likelihood of postoperative infection. Laschal suture scissors facilitate the rapid, automatic cutting of these sutures (Fig. 75).

Place the fourth and most important key suture into the fibrous tissue immediately inferior to the mastoid process at the origin of the sternocleidomastoid muscle (Figs. 76 and 77). Depending on the laxity of the tissues, a very large amount of tissue (frequently up to 5 cm in length) is drawn tight. Direct the anterior bite of the suture toward the cervicomental angle (Fig. 78). It is this suture upon which the greatest amount of pressure is placed. Four throws are tied rather

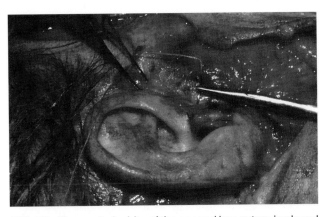

FIG. 73. The posterior bite of the second key suture is placed anterior to the superior border of the tragus and is directed toward the angle of the mouth. The anteroinferior bite is much shorter than the first key suture and encompasses only about 2 cm before the draw-down of the knot.

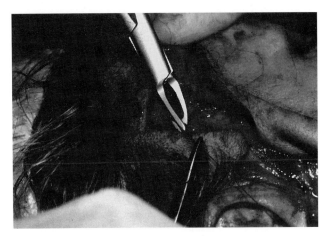

FIG. 75. All sutures are cut on the knot using the Laschal scissors, which automatically performs the cut at this level.

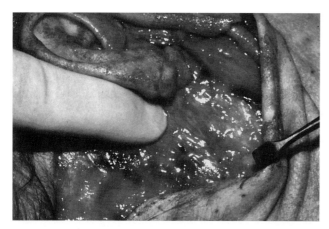

FIG. 76. The fourth and most important key suture is placed on the anterior border of the mastoid bone where it connects with the thick fibrous tissue of the origin of the sternocleidomastoid muscle. This can be easily identified by means of palpation.

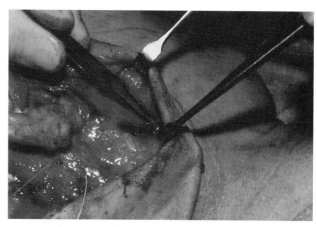

FIG. 78. Using two Senn retractors, the flap is elevated and the inferior portion of the fourth key suture is directed toward the cervicomental angle. Depending on the laxity of the tissues, the length of this bite may be up to 6 cm.

than three, which are used in other key sutures, or two, which are used in the remaining, less critical sutures. Maintain pressure on the first loop of each of these knots using a small needle holder with smooth jaws clamped on the initial throw after it is tightened. Remove the clamp as the second loop is cinched down (Fig. 79). The fourth key suture frequently remains exposed for a small distance superficial to the sternocleidomastoid and platysma at the completion of the tie. Sutures placed superior and inferior to the fourth key suture distribute the tension. Then remove and replace the fourth key suture with a new suture that can be buried with either less or no suture exposed. Pull this area tightly so that a groove passing between the mastoid process and the cervicomental angle is formed. This groove persists and is present even after redraping of the skin, which may cause concern in the physician and patient. With subsequent relaxation of the tissues and a decrease in the postoperative edema this

groove always resolves, leaving a well-defined cervicomental angle.

Place additional sutures inferior to the mastoid process with their posterior bites being in the anterior border of the sternocleidomastoid muscle. These sutures usually tighten the tissues 2 cm in the superior portion and decrease to approximately 1 cm in the inferior portion of the lateral cervical area. Bunching of the tissue occurs if the bite is too long in this inferior portion. This creates an obvious bulge postoperatively that must be corrected before skin redraping (Fig. 80). The use of multiple sutures not only gives support to the anterior cervical region but also progressively distributes the tension on the underlying tissues so that unnecessary bulges will not be apparent. In this area take care to avoid

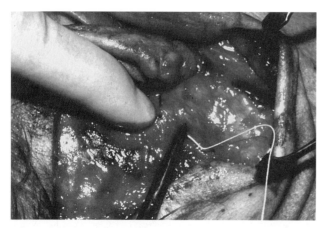

FIG. 77. A deep bite is taken with the needle into the fibrous tissue of the origin of the sternocleidomastoid muscle. This provides stable, long-term support for elevation of the cervicomental angle.

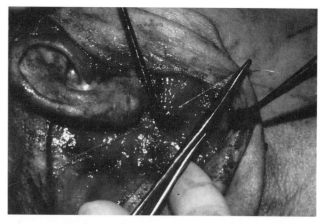

FIG. 79. The fourth key suture is tied under considerable tension and therefore must be held securely with a smooth-jawed clamp after the first throw is cinched down. A surgeon's knot is used rather than a square knot for this suture, since it is the most important key suture. A total of four throws are used in this knot, in contrast to the two or three loops that are used in other knots. All knots are buried to decrease the likelihood of postoperative extrusion.

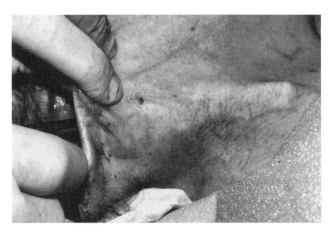

FIG. 80. After all the plication sutures are completed and the flap is advanced and redraped, a small bulge may be present over the inferior plicating suture. This can be corrected by removing and resuturing this inferior pole or, as an alternative, by undermining more inferiorly over the sternocleidomastoid muscle.

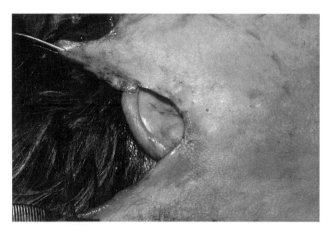

FIG. 81. After the suspension of the SMAS with plication sutures, moderate tension is placed on the flap edge that is advanced superoposteriorly. Even with limited tension, there is a considerable amount of excess skin resulting from the resuspension of the underlying SMAS and the advancement of redundant cervicomental skin.

suturing the great auricular nerve that is present on the anterior border of the sternocleidomastoid muscle. If this inadvertently occurs, the lower third of the external ear will be hypoesthetic, a side effect that is usually temporary, lasting only several months.

Place additional, accessory sutures between the key sutures to provide support and to avoid depressions that alternate with elevations when too few sutures are used. Determine proper placement of these sutures by grasping the SMAS with a forceps and placing tension on it to see whether any movement upward and posteriorly is possible. If the SMAS moves sufficiently, a suture should be placed at that site. Place sutures adjacent to the vertical incision in the temporal area. In the preauricular area place sutures approximately 1 cm anterior to the incision line.

Redraping of the Skin Flap

After the plication sutures have been placed, redrape the skin (Fig. 81). Since the long-term support of the SMAS and underlying muscular tissues is the most important aspect of the rhytidectomy procedure, it is important to understand that only limited tension is placed on the skin. Place moderate tension on the flap in the postauricular and temporal areas to provide for a well-defined cervicomental angle and elevation of the lateral portion of the eyebrow. Place only minimal tension on the area superior and inferior to the tragus, and place no tension on the flap in the area of the tragus.

Temporarily reattach the preauricular skin at the region between the crus and the temporal hair tuft (Fig. 82). Advance the flap posteriorly and superiorly under minimal tension at approximately a 70-degree angle. Use a No. 15 blade to make an incision into the flap, and place a staple to secure the flap (Figs. 82 and 83). The flap is usually advanced 2 to 3 cm in the preauricular area.

Postauricular Flap

Focus attention now on the postauricular area, and advance the flap at approximately a 60-degree angle from the horizontal position (Fig. 84). Advance the portion of the flap that was originally at the inferior border of the lobule to a point either at or slightly below the level of the horizontal postauricular incision, yielding approximately 4 to 6 cm of advancement (Figs. 85 and 86). Place a temporary staple 1 cm posterior to the postauricular sulcus. The incisions into the flap can be safely made by advancing the flap under moderate tension. Place a No. 15 blade on the skin at the level of the horizontal retroauricular incision line, which can be viewed by slightly elevating the flap so that the indentation made by the blade can be seen in its relationship to the horizontal incision.

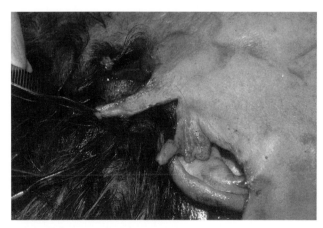

FIG. 82. Under minimal tension the flap in the preauricular area is redraped using a directional pull that is approximately 70 degrees from horizontal. An incision is made through the excess skin, which in this case is 3 cm.

FIG. 83. A temporary staple is placed through the skin flap and the glabrous skin immediately superoanterior to the top of the external ear.

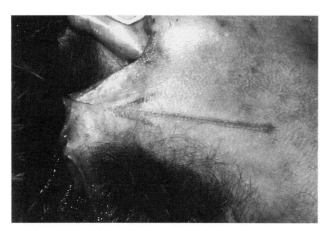

FIG. 84. The postauricular flap is advanced superoposteriorly in a direction approximately 60 degrees from horizontal. More tension is placed on this segment of the flap, since it is necessary to redrape the skin of the cervicomental angle and jowl area.

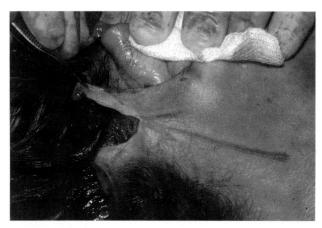

FIG. 85. The excess skin of the flap is excised to the level of the horizontal retroauricular incision. The point of the first incision is placed approximately 1 cm posterior to the postauricular sulcus.

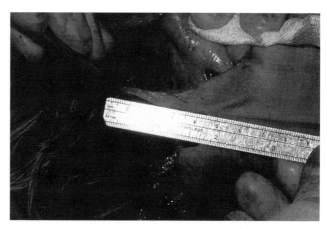

FIG. 86. Although this is the area of greatest tension on the entire flap complex, the surgeon must remember that this represents the longest segment of the flap, and the skin is the thinnest of the flap complex. Only moderate tension should be placed on the flap during its advancement. Excess skin in this area is usually between 5 and 6 cm. Patient in this case has 5 cm of excess skin.

This is the most important part of the advancement and should not be so great as to create undue tension, since this is the longest segment of the flap. Use reduced tension when the patient is a known smoker. A significant number of surgeons refuse to perform facelift surgery on smokers.

Working in a posterior direction, place additional portions of the retroauricular flap under tension and advance the flap superiorly. Cut segments of skin 2 cm in width using the method described earlier (Figs. 87 and 88). Advance the middle section of the retroauricular flap superiorly, without any posterior displacement, to improve the alignment of the newly created retroauricular hairline. In the posterior third of the flap, advancement is superior and anterior. Some surgeons create an anterior and superior pull along the entire

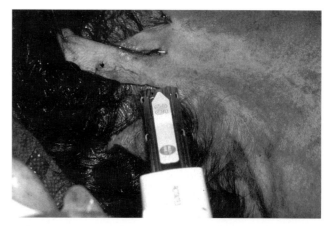

FIG. 87. Additional segments of the postauricular flap are advanced superiorly without any posterior displacement. This improves the appearance of the occipital hairline by decreasing the step formation that occurs with advancement of the flap. Small segments of skin approximately 2 cm wide are incised and stapled to the horizontal postauricular incision.

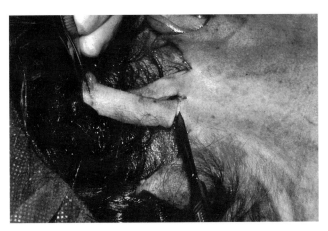

FIG. 88. The 2-cm wide strips of excess skin are cut between the staples.

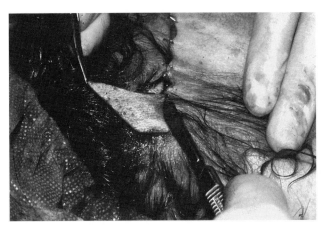

FIG. 90. The flap is elevated, and the excess skin is removed by incising a straight line from the last staple in the middle portion of the flap to the inferior extension of the postauricular incision. This makes both the superior and inferior limbs equal.

segment of the posterior incision in an attempt to approximate the preoperative hairline. This eliminates any significant posterior movement of the flap, which is essential to obtain maximum improvement of the cervicomental angle. This also creates an excess amount of skin in the area of the lobule and does not create sufficient tension on the flap in the region of the cervicomental angle. If this possibility is discussed in detail at the initial consultation, patients universally prefer to improve the cervicomental angle at the expense of a slight step in the postauricular hairline. If the retroauricular horizontal incision is placed 1 cm above the level of the external auditory canal, this step is inconsequential because of this high placement; the incision is not visible, even in patients who wear very short hair.

Hand suture the glabrous skin from the postauricular sulcus to the hair-bearing skin using a running locked suture of 6.0 black nylon on a P-3 needle (Ethicon). This avoids scarring from the use of staples. Use staples only in areas

of hair-bearing skin. The 90-degree inferior curve at the posterior end of the retroauricular incision assists significantly in eliminating a dog ear when the posterior segment of the flap is constructed (see Figs. 30 and 31). In the posterior third of this closure the remaining segment of skin on the flap is usually longer than the remaining retroauricular incision line. It is often necessary to undermine both the posterior segment of the flap and the hair-bearing skin superior to the retroauricular incision to eliminate any creases or ridges that developed during flap rotation (Fig. 89). By creating a straight line excision on the excess skin, from the last staple at the farthest point of the juncture of the middle third and posterior third to the farthest point of the incision as it curves downward, these lengths are equalized, eliminating the dog ear (Figs. 90 and 91). In contrast to the initial incision in the retroauricular area that was made perpendicular to the skin, the excess that is removed from the flap is beveled in

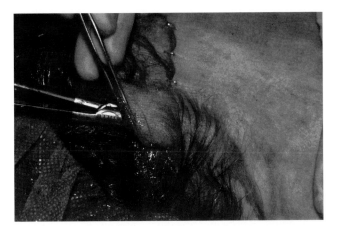

FIG. 89. The remaining posterior limb of the flap is longer than the remaining length of the retroauricular incision. This creates a dog ear that must be corrected. It is often necessary to undermine both the flap and the hair-bearing skin under the retroauricular incision to eliminate any ridges that have developed during flap rotation.

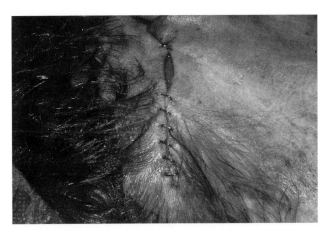

FIG. 91. The incision on the flap is made parallel to the hair follicles. The hair-bearing area of the flap is closed with surgical staples. The glabrous skin is closed by hand using 6.0 black nylon employing a running locked suture.

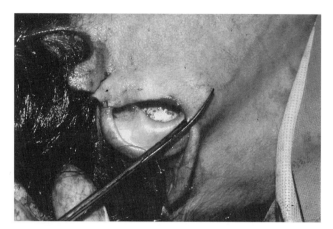

FIG. 92. The excess skin between the temporal area and the retroauricular area covers the external ear. An incision is begun where the helix joins the lobule with 6-inch, curved Peck-Joseph scissors. The incision is made slightly anterior and parallel to the posterior border of the auricle. The incision is extended to 0.5 cm short of the attachment of the lobule.

an upward angle parallel to the growth of the hair. This preserves as many follicles as possible.

The stabilization of the flap in the supraauricular and retroauricular areas has been completed. The next area to be addressed is the lobule. The anterior portion and lower half of the external ear are covered when advancing the flap (Fig. 92). Using 6-inch curved Peck-Joseph scissors (Snowden–Pencer, Inc., Tucker, GA), place the instrument parallel to the posterior border of the external ear and cut an incision 0.5 cm short of the attachment of the lobule. Deliver the lobule through this incision, the length of which is carefully extended with the scissors until the lobule is snugly elevated by the flap without creating any redundant skin at the juncture of the flap with the inferior attachment of the lobule (Fig. 93). Displace the lobule superiorly and posteriorly from

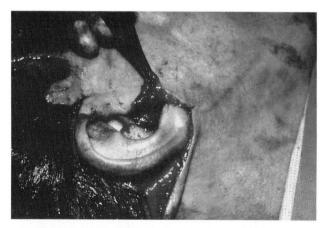

FIG. 93. The lobule is delivered through the incision, where its position will be superior to its desired final placement. The incision is lengthened anteriorly without any inferior component until the lobule is snugly elevated by the flap without creating redundant skin at the juncture of the lobule and the flap.

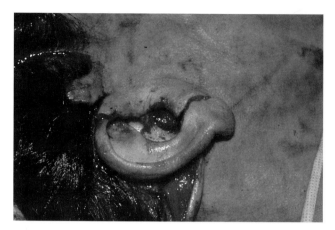

FIG. 94. The position of the lobule at the completion of the surgery should be superoposterior to its natural position because contraction of the flap will draw the lobule anteriorly and inferiorly during normal healing.

its natural position (Fig. 94). Do not cut the flap so that the lobule will lie in its natural position because after surgery, when the plane of scar normally contracts, the flap will move anteriorly and inferiorly, causing a similar advancement of the lobule. Almost universally, surgeons fail to recognize this important aspect of normal wound healing and complete the procedure by placing the lobule in its normal position. With the contracture of the flap, the lobule is pulled downward and forward, causing a spread of the scar and elongation of the lobule and creating an elf or pixie ear (Figs. 1–4). Poor planning results in this defect, which is grossly obvious from the anterior and lateral positions and can quickly lead to the identification of a patient who has undergone a poorly planned rhytidectomy. This defect is often combined with a poorly planned retroauricular incision placed below the hairline, which is also obvious.

Advance the remaining anterior portion of the postauricular flap under minimal tension. The flap is very thin here, so use caution to avoid increased tension that occurs after surgery with expected edema, which can lead to ischemia (Fig. 95).

Temporal Flap

Redirect attention to the temporal flap, and remove and readjust, if necessary, the initial temporary staple. The additional tension placed on the postauricular flap pulls this flap downward; therefore place only a minimal amount of tension on the flap when the initial incision is made for the temporary staple. Since this is a short flap with excellent blood supply, this additional pressure should not cause any embarrassment of blood flow.

Trim some of the excess skin in the temporal flap to allow better assessment. This does not represent the final trimming (Fig. 96). Complete the excision of the superior portion of the temporal flap by rounding the flap between its horizontal

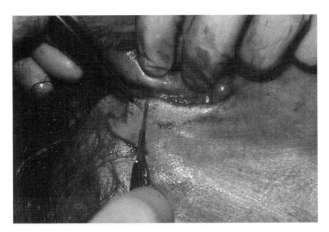

FIG. 95. The remaining portion of the postauricular flap is placed under minimal tension and excised. The non–hair-bearing skin that abuts to the horizontal retroauricular incision is closed by hand using 6.0 black nylon with a running locked suture.

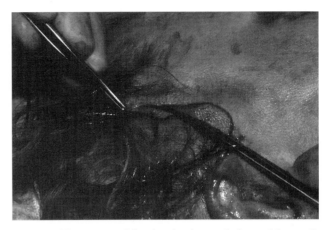

FIG. 97. The temporal flap is raised superiorly, and the vertical and horizontal limbs that were cut at a right angle are trimmed in the shape of a curve. This allows the flap to be moved superiorly or inferiorly without creating a dog ear.

and vertical segments rather than by cutting a right angle to correspond to these two segments (Fig. 97). By rounding this edge, this flap can be adjusted so that it can be rotated either superiorly or inferiorly without creating a dog ear (Fig. 98). The skin edge should be beveled if necessary, so that the incision is parallel to the hair growth. This is particularly important in patients with low hair density. The vector of pull on the flap is mostly superior, with only a small amount of posterior displacement. This preserves the greatest amount of hair-bearing temporal skin of the sideburn. Staple the horizontal and vertical segments of the flap in the hair-bearing area beginning at the anterior portion of the horizontal segment (Fig. 99). Limit skin excision so that the vertical incision can be closed under minimal tension to avoid a spread of the scar. Inappropriate beveling of the edge cuts off follicles if the hair grows in an anterior or inferior direction. This gives the appearance of a spread scar, since loss

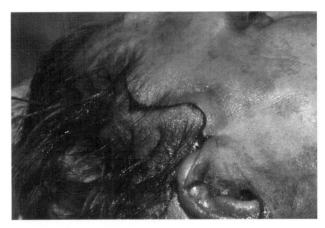

FIG. 98. Trimming creates a curve on the temporal flap edge that is to be reattached to the right angle created by the initial vertical and horizontal incisions.

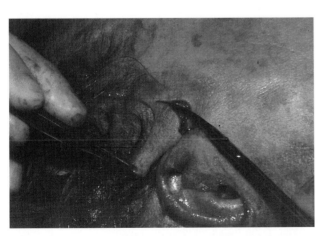

FIG. 96. A major portion of the excess skin of the temporal area is excised to provide better vision during the final trimming in this area. Care should be taken not to excise too much skin initially.

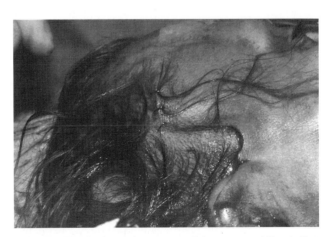

FIG. 99. The horizontal segment of the temporal flap is first stapled at the anterior portion to avoid a dog ear in the temporal peak of hair.

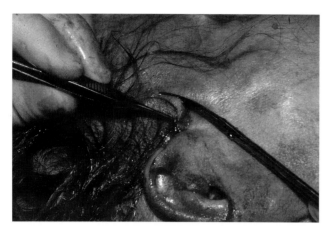

FIG. 100. The remaining small amount of excess skin on the lower portion of the temporal flap is trimmed using 6-inch, curved Peck-Joseph scissors.

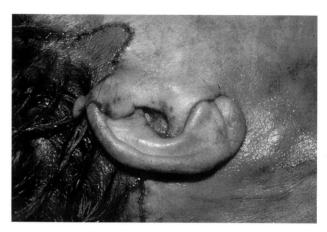

FIG. 102. The excess preauricular skin is draped over the tragal and pretragal area. The flap has been smoothed into the pretragal depression and is not pulled taut over the tragus.

of follicles creates a non–hair-bearing segment of skin, particularly in patients who have sparse hair in the temporal tuft.

Final trimming of the inferior portion of the temporal flap is done with 6-inch curved Peck-Joseph scissors (Fig. 100). Place very little tension on this segment as it traverses onto the newly constructed anterior border of the temporal hair tuft and as it curves around the inferior portion of that tuft (Fig. 101). These areas should abut without tension so that the spread of the postoperative scar is minimized. The edges are closed with a running locked suture of 6.0 black nylon. When a small amount of skin is inadvertently removed and the skin edges do not abut, buried sutures may be placed to advance the flap superiorly and posteriorly. An alternative solution is to undermine the sideburn and advance it anteriorly until the two flaps meet without tension. Then perform a layered closure with deep absorbable sutures and cutaneous nonabsorbable sutures.

Preauricular Flap

The remaining skin between the sideburn and the lobule will be trimmed, to form the preauricular flap (Fig. 102). An upward-angled incision is made to a point several millimeters inferior to the tragus (Fig. 103). Flatten the flap over the preauricular area with the finger, and trim the remaining excess anterior to the lobule (Fig. 104). The flap should abut perfectly with the lobule (Fig. 105). Trim some of the excess skin of the remaining flap to allow better vision (Fig. 106). Aggressively remove fat from the skin over and anterior to the tragus as is done in a full-thickness skin graft (Fig. 107). This provides a thin flap that can follow the contour of the tragus. An interrupted absorbable suture attaches the flap at the inferior pole of the tragus (Fig. 108).

The untrimmed flap that remains overlying the tragus should be trimmed only minimally or not at all. Excess skin

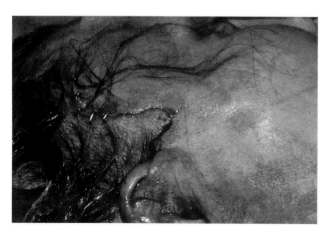

FIG. 101. No tension should be placed on this portion of the flap, and it should abut perfectly to the temporal tuft of hair in the sideburn so that no spread scar appears after surgery. The incision is closed using a running locked suture of 6.0 black nylon.

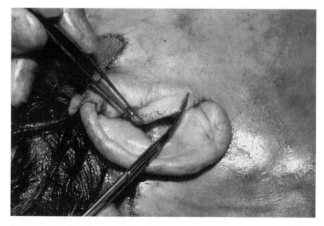

FIG. 103. An upward-angled incision is made to the inferior border of the tragus. If tension is applied to the flap during the cutting of this incision, the cut should not be carried to the anterior border of the lobule. The flap should be redraped into the pretragal depression to accurately measure the length of this final cut.

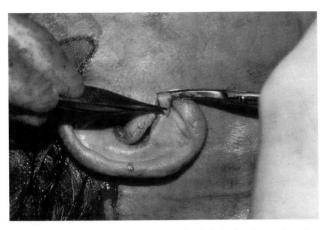

FIG. 104. Excess skin anterior to the lobule is trimmed under no tension. The flap should abut perfectly to the lobule.

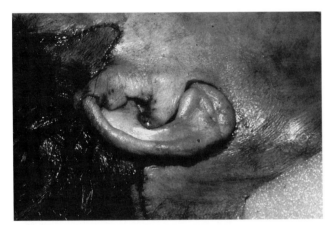

FIG. 105. The lobule should fit into the trimmed flap and abut without any gap on the junction. No tension is placed on the flap over the entire preauricular site to minimize displacement of the lobule and tragus anteroinferiorly with scar maturation.

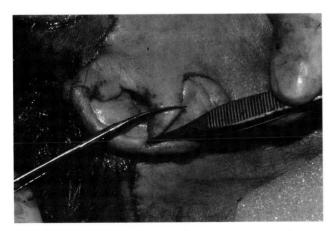

FIG. 106. Excess portions of the flap are excised to allow for improved vision. A considerable amount of excess skin must remain for the final trimming.

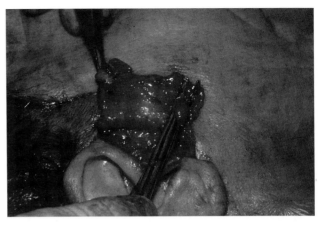

FIG. 107. The preauricular flap is raised and excess fat is aggressively removed using Ragnell scissors. This trimming allows the flap to conform to the contours of the pretragal depression and the tragal crest.

must be sufficient to accommodate for two factors. There is a normal depression anterior to the tragus so that when proper redraping occurs, the skin edge moves anteriorly. If the flap has been trimmed before the skin is redraped into the depression, there will be a gap between the remaining skin on the posterior portion of the tragus and the newly created flap. Complete the redraping and fixation of the flap in the pretragal depression by smoothing the skin into this depression and placing three to five interrupted sutures of 5.0 chromic through the skin and into the underlying parotid fascia (Fig. 109). Leave 1 or 2 mm of skin between each of these sutures to allow for adequate capillary filling of the tragal segment. Remove these sutures on the fifth postoperative day; they may be removed earlier if the flap overlying the tragus appears ischemic. The second factor for providing excess skin on the tragal flap is that normal postoperative scar con-

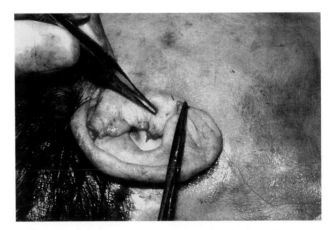

FIG. 108. A suture of 6.0 chromic catgut is placed through the anterior right-angle incision at the superior portion of the lobule and is attached to the right-angle cut made into the preauricular flap. This is a single interrupted suture. The anterior portion of the lobule is closed using a running lock suture of 6.0 black nylon.

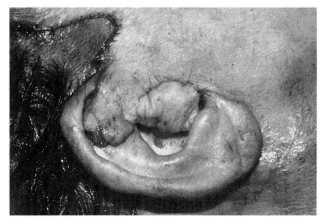

FIG. 109. Three to five interrupted sutures of 5.0 chromic catgut are used to anchor the flap into the pretragal depression. Despite these sutures, the tragal flap obtains sufficient perfusion. These sutures are removed on the fifth postoperative day.

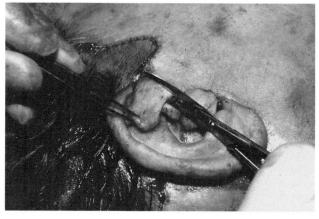

FIG. 111. The excess skin above the tragus undergoes a preliminary trimming with curved Peck-Joseph scissors. The skin is smoothed into the depression anterior to the external ear.

tracture rotates the tragus anteriorly if the skin is draped snugly. This anterior displacement of the tragus alters the appearance of the external auditory meatus and tragus, providing another telltale sign of a poorly executed rhytidectomy.

Make a downward-angled incision through the remaining superior portion of the flap to a position slightly superior to the tragus until the anterior border of the crus is reached (Fig. 110). Superior to this, make a vertical incision parallel to the anterior border of the external ear to remove a major portion but not all of the excess skin (Fig. 111). Smooth the skin below the sideburn, and make the final trimming (Fig. 112). Close the skin edges using a running locked suture of 6.0 nylon (Fig. 113).

Inspect the flap over the tragus and remove fat a second time, if necessary (Fig. 114). This flap should be very thin to accommodate the contouring necessary over the tragal

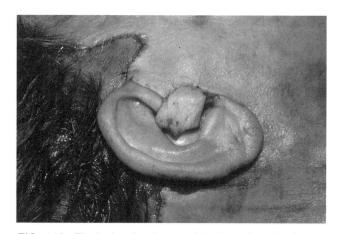

FIG. 112. Final trimming is completed to allow the flap to abut to the external ear without any gaping or tension.

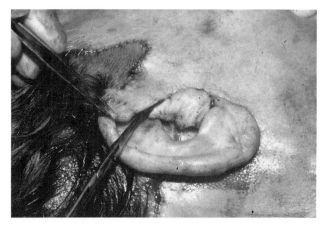

FIG. 110. An angled incision is made anteroinferiorly to the superior portion of the tragus. The incision is not made in a horizontal fashion, since this may remove too much skin at the superior pole of the tragus.

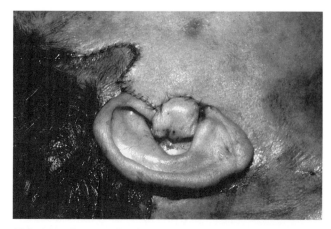

FIG. 113. Segment is closed using a running lock suture of 6.0 black nylon.

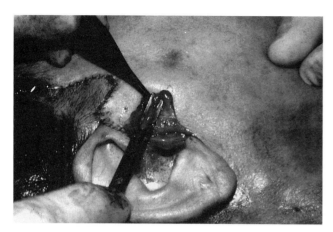

FIG. 114. Second defatting of the tragal flap is accomplished when indicated.

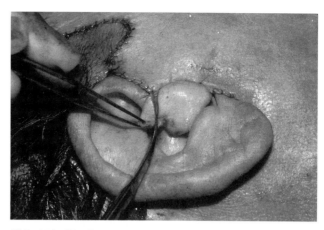

FIG. 116. The flap is draped over the tragus and excess skin of the superior portion is trimmed, creating a right-angle cut that lies horizontal to the superior pole of the tragus.

crest (Fig. 115). Trim the superior portion of the tragal flap to create a right-angle cut that lies horizontal to the superior pole of the tragus (Fig. 116). Trim the posterior portion of the flap so that 1 to 2 mm of excess skin remains when the flap is draped over the crest of the tragus (Fig. 117). This excess skin always contracts, leaving an attractive and cosmetically acceptable tragal contour (Fig. 118). The initial incision that was placed slightly posterior to the crest of the tragus camouflages the scar better than an incision and a suture line that are placed on the crest of the tragus. Since these sutures can be difficult to remove, employ several interrupted absorbable sutures of 6.0 catgut over the posterior border of the tragus (Fig. 119).

Lobule

Identify the inferior portion of the lobule by finding the scratch made at the onset of the surgical procedure. Place an anchoring suture of 6.0 chromic gut in this location (Fig. 120). Place the lobule in a position that is vertical to the

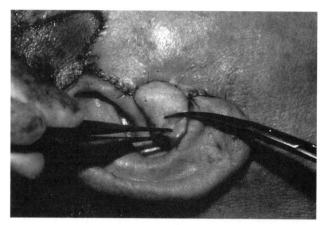

FIG. 117. The excess on the posterior border of the tragal flap is trimmed, leaving a generous portion of skin. This remaining excess skin should be 1 to 2 mm and appears bulky at the time of final closure.

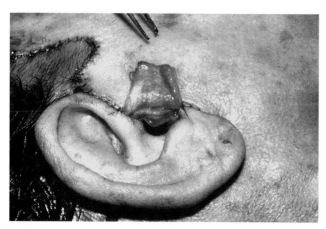

FIG. 115. This flap should be very thin to accommodate the contouring that is necessary over the tragal crest.

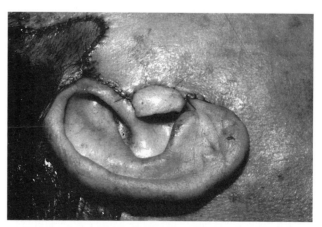

FIG. 118. The excess skin that remains on the tragal flap contracts during normal scar maturation and fits snugly over the tragal crest. If no excess skin is present at closure, the scar contracture causes anterior displacement of the tragus.

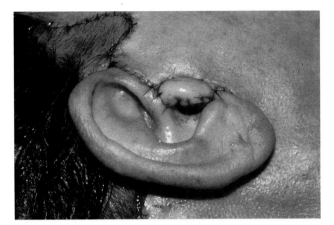

FIG. 119. The incision along the tragal crest is closed with interrupted sutures of absorbable 6.0 chromic catgut. Sutures at this location are difficult to remove after surgery; therefore the absorbable suture is preferable.

external ear rather than its natural position, which is slightly anterior. The lobule migrates anteriorly and inferiorly with normal scar contraction. Close the incisions anterior to the lobule using a running locked suture of 6.0 black nylon on a P-3 needle (Ethicon). Suture the incision line superior to the tragus using a running locked suture of 6.0 black nylon.

The appearance of both the tragus and the lobule should be slightly abnormal at the conclusion of the procedure (Fig. 119). Subsequent scar contracture will provide an excellent final result. If the external ear looks perfect at the conclusion of the surgery, the scar contracture will create an imperfect final result.

Postauricular Sulcus

Complete the flap closure by suturing the vertical portion of the retroauricular portion of the skin flap to the postauricu-

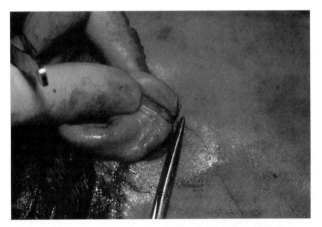

FIG. 120. The inferior portion of the lobule is identified by the scratch made at the beginning of the surgery. An absorbable 6.0 chromic catgut suture anchors the inferior portion of the lobule to the skin flap. The lobule must be compressed and displaced superoposteriorly to allow for inferoanterior migration resulting from scar maturation.

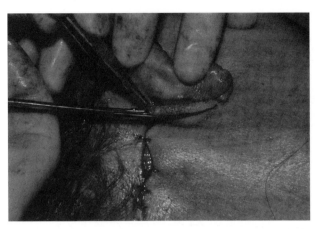

FIG. 121. The excess skin of the flap over the postauricular sulcus is placed under moderate tension. It should fold into the postauricular sulcus and reach onto the posterior portion of the external ear to easily reach the incision line.

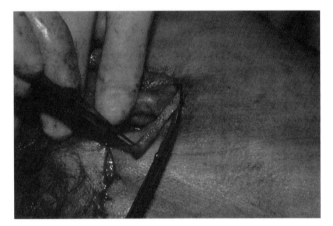

FIG. 122. Only a small strip of excess skin must be excised from the flap. In some instances no skin excision is necessary, except to freshen the edge in preparation for final closure.

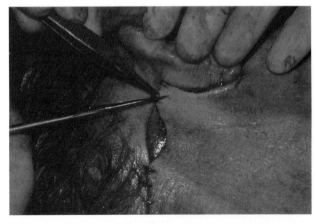

FIG. 123. A V-shaped excision is made into the postauricular flap corresponding to the segment of skin that was created at the postauricular sulcus during the initial incision.

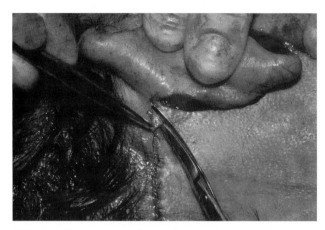

FIG. 124. Under usual circumstances the second leg of the V-shaped excision is completed. When the flap is under tension because of a shortened anterior-to-posterior distance, a simple vertical incision replaces the V-shaped incision and allows the superior portion of the flap to advance anteriorly, decreasing some of this tension.

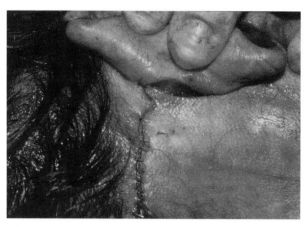

FIG. 126. The horizontal segment of the retroauricular incision is closed using a running locked suture of 6.0 black nylon. When the external ear is advanced anteriorly, there is a small gap of approximately 2 cm from the horizontal retroauricular incision along the postauricular sulcus. This opening is not sutured and allows an orifice for delivery of pooled blood or clots that may occur during the postoperative period.

lar sulcus. Since the advancement of this portion of the post-auricular flap has been primarily superior in direction, there is little or no excess skin to trim. If there is excess skin, excise it (Figs. 121 and 122).

Trim a small V in the flap at the juncture of the horizontal and vertical incisions (Figs. 123 and 124). This creates a broken-line closure of the postauricular incision, which decreases the likelihood of scar contraction over the retroauricular sulcus. Close the three points of the V excision using 6.0 chromic catgut (Fig. 125). A 1- to 2-cm length of flap is left unsutured at the superior portion of the vertical incision as it attaches to the external ear (Fig. 126) to provide an inconspicuous opening that is used to evacuate any intraoperative or postoperative bleeding. Evacuate fresh blood or clots through this opening either by using a small liposuction cannula or by gently applying pressure on the flap to direct

the blood through this opening. Close the inferior portion of the postauricular sulcus with absorbable suture (Fig. 127).

In addition to this postauricular opening, the submental incision may be left unsutured to provide for an avenue of drainage. Some surgeons use a Jackson-Pratt drain during the first 24 to 48 hours. These drains may not be necessary, since very little blood or serum should accumulate postoperatively if cautery has been sufficient. Since this flap is limited in length, there is considerably less likelihood of postoperative bleeding. Suction drains add cost and introduce a foreign body into the surgical site that can be a nidus of infection.

Fifteen to 20 minutes before completing the closure of the first side, administer anesthetic to the left side. The au-

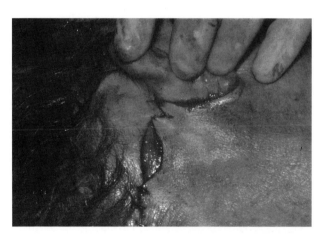

FIG. 125. The three points of the incision are closed using absorbable 6.0 chromic catgut suture. If staples or nonabsorbable sutures are used here and in the postauricular sulcus, they become buried by postoperative edema.

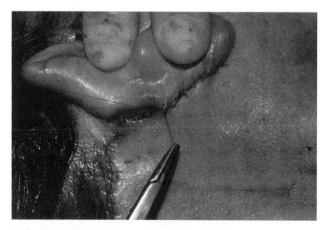

FIG. 127. The inferior portion of the postauricular sulcus is closed using a running locked suture of 6.0 chromic catgut. These sutures degrade spontaneously with the regular postoperative cleansing with hydrogen peroxide and application of an antibiotic ointment.

thor prefers to administer the anesthetic before the final trimming and suturing of the preauricular flap on the first side.

POSTOPERATIVE MANAGEMENT

Postoperative Dressing

At the conclusion of the surgery, the face is gently cleansed and any excess blood is expressed through the opening that remains in the postauricular sulcus. A bulky compression dressing is placed over the cheek and neck areas. This consists of sterile, absorbent 12-inch cotton batting (Red Cross Cotton, USP, Johnson & Johnson, Skillman, NJ) that immobilize Telfa strips (Kendall Company Hospital Products, Boston, MA) and Polysporin ointment (Burroughs Wellcome Co. Research Triangle Parks, NC) covering the lines of incision (Fig. 128). Special attention is given to the external ear with additional cotton being placed into the sulcus to provide support of the underlying cartilage. If this is not done, the pressure dressing may temporarily collapse the cartilage and cause considerable postoperative discomfort. The cotton batting is secured by three rolls of sterilized 3.5-inch Kerlix (Kendall Healthcare Products Co., Mansfield, MA). This is covered by three rolls of 4-inch Coban

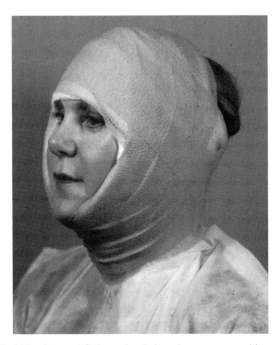

FIG. 129. Several Coban elastic bandages are used for moderate compression. It is impossible to apply adequate compression over the lower cervical regions, which leads to ecchymosis occurring in these dependent sites. This dressing is removed at the end of the first postoperative day and is reapplied for a second 24-hour period.

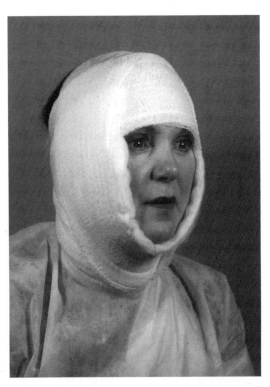

FIG. 128. A large compression dressing is used during the first 48 hours. It consists of sterile cotton batting and Kerlix to provide an absorbent medium. The incision sites are covered with Polysporin ointment and Telfa. The cartilage of the external ear is supported with cotton batting in the postauricular sulcus to prevent distortion, which can cause considerable discomfort.

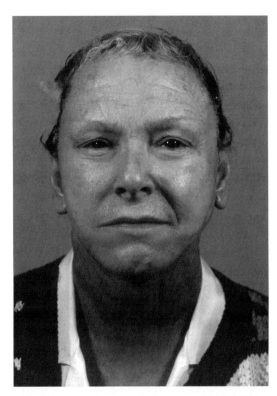

FIG. 130. The face is expected to have some distortion and a tight appearance after the large dressing is removed on the first postoperative day. Removal of the dressing allows for the flaps to be carefully examined, nerve function evaluated, and bleeding identified.

bandage (3M Medical Surgical Division, St. Paul, MN), which is applied using light to moderate pressure. The dressing is carried onto the anterior cervical region as far as possible (Fig. 129). If pressure is too tight over the hyoid bone, a 1-inch vertical midline incision may be placed through the dressing. The dressing is usually not capable of applying sufficient pressure to the inferior border of the undermined area in the lateral cervical region. As a result, ecchymosis usually forms in this area and in the inferior portion of the anterior cervical region if the latter has undergone liposuction. The patient is instructed not to talk and to ingest only a liquid diet to diminish motion of the head and neck. Liquids are easily administered with the use of a straw or a squeeze bottle. The use of a pen and writing pad diminishes the necessity for the patient to converse after surgery. This dressing does not obstruct the view of the eyebrows or the mouth and allows the surgeon to evaluate the function of the temporal and marginal mandibular nerves, which may develop temporary paralysis as a result of infiltration anesthesia. Although the flaps may not be directly viewed, palpation through the anterior and posterior portions of this dressing allows the surgeon to evaluate the possibility of any postoperative clot formation.

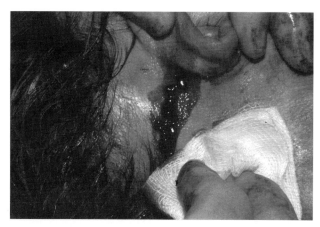

FIG. 132. The 2-cm orifice that has remained patent can be used at the conclusion of surgery and during postoperative visits to express any clots that have occurred. Occasionally, it is necessary to introduce a sterile curved hemostat to disrupt the cohesions that have occurred during the first 24 hours of healing. A 4- or 6-mm spatula cannula can also be introduced through this orifice.

On the following morning the dressing is removed, and the patient is fully examined (Figs. 130–138). Any blood found in the posterior flap is expressed through the opening in the retroauricular sulcus (Fig. 132). This is usually not necessary, since it is uncommon for a patient to bleed with this procedure. A similar dressing is reapplied for the second 24-hour period to limit motion and provide a moderate amount of compression. Since patients usually experience only minimal discomfort, this bulky dressing is advisable because it is a reminder to the patient to remain inactive. On the second postoperative day the patient is again reexamined, and the large dressing is replaced by a facial support garment (Foundations Too Contour, Dallas, TX) that the patient wears continuously for the following 12 days (Figs. 139 and 140).

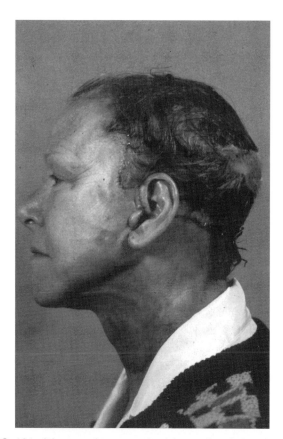

FIG. 131. It is normal to expect bruising and ecchymosis over all areas of undermining. Since the preauricular flap is short, very little ecchymosis is present. Bruising is more evident over the anterior cervical, lateral cervical, and postauricular flaps, as seen in this patient who has undergone extensive cervical liposuction.

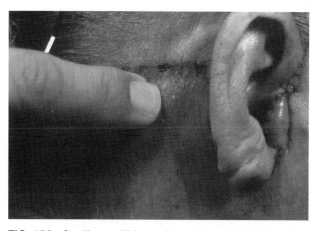

FIG. 133. Capillary refill is crucial to the viability of the flaps. The adequacy of vascular flow can be established by placing light digital pressure on the flap. Removing the pressure shows a blanched area. The rapidity of refill denotes the adequacy of perfusion.

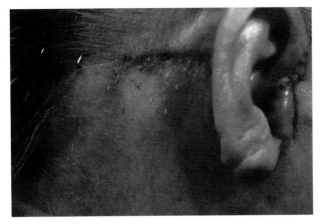

FIG. 134. Hyperemia and pustule formation are present on the fifth postoperative day, which represents venous congestion in a flap under increased tension. Arterial supply is adequate, but venous outflow is decreased. This usually does not lead to tissue necrosis.

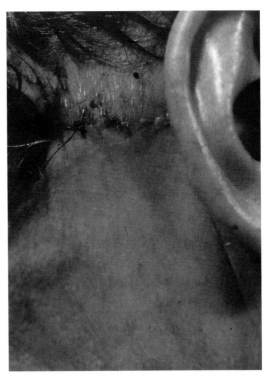

FIG. 136. Following removal of the offending staple, tension on the flap is decreased and the blanching quickly subsides, showing that the capillary flow is now adequate.

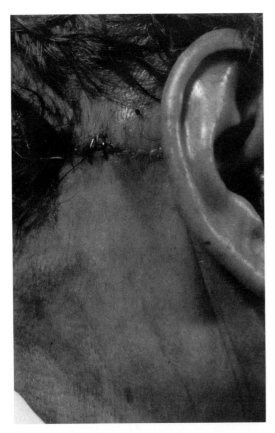

FIG. 135. Occasionally, a staple applies excessive pressure to the postauricular flap. The most anterior staple in this patient has created a triangular area of blanching in the flap.

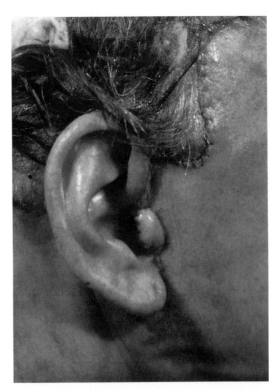

FIG. 137. At the first postoperative visit the tragal flap appears edematous but should have normal skin color. Capillary refill is not always evident in this flap. If normal skin color is present, the surgeon should not be alarmed.

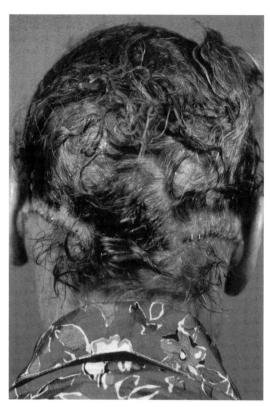

FIG. 138. The posterior extensions of the postauricular flaps are in the hair-bearing area of the scalp and are quite thick. Ischemia of this flap would be most unlikely.

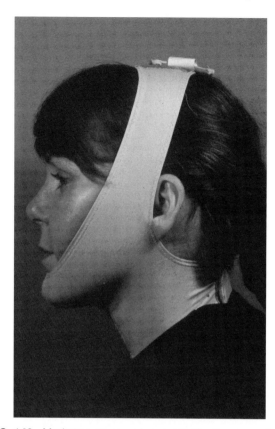

FIG. 140. Moderate pressure is provided by the support garment to the undermined areas of the anterior and lateral cervical regions, the cervicomental angle, and the preauricular and temporal regions.

Postoperative Instructions

During the immediate postoperative phase the patient is advised to have very limited activity, preferably confined to bed rest, a liquid or soft diet, elevation of the head and chest on two pillows for the first 2 days, continuation of the preoperative antibiotics, and an analgesic or hypnotic for the relief of discomfort. A responsible adult is required to attend the patient for the first 24 hours so that if there is a need for assistance or advice, transfer to the surgeon's office or hospital can be readily accomplished. A list of the postoperative instructions are provided in Table 17-1.

Mild to moderate discomfort occurs primarily over the mastoid process and the sternocleidomastoid muscle where the plicating sutures have been anchored. A mild analgesic such as acetaminophen (Tylenol, McNeil Consumers Products Company, Division of McNeil-PPC, Inc., Fort Washington, PA) with Codeine 0.5 grain or plain acetaminophen (Tylenol) is administered. Since patients experience some mild discomfort and must wear the large dressing and keep the head elevated, most have some difficulty in sleeping. During the first 4 to 5 days a mild hypnotic such as temazepam (Restoril, Sandoz Pharmaceuticals, East Hanover, NJ) is prescribed. Prescriptions for analgesics and hypnotics are not refilled to emphasize to the patient that minimal activity

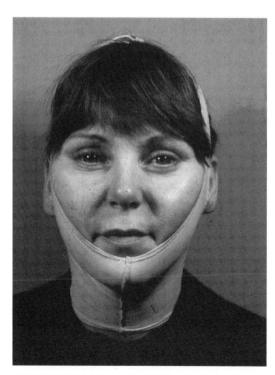

FIG. 139. An elastic garment providing facial support is used continuously from the 3rd to the 14th postoperative day. After this period the patient is encouraged to use this support garment when at home for the following 3 months.

is important. A complaint of pain by the patient occurring after the fourth day is usually the result of overactivity. Most patients are up and about on the second postoperative day and can enjoy limited activity.

There is little likelihood of postoperative bleeding after the first 48 hours, and activity may be liberalized to allow the patient to take short walks without raising the heart rate. Any additional exercise is strictly prohibited during the first 2 weeks. The patient is seen daily for the first 2 postoperative days for dressing changes and evaluation. On the fifth day the patient returns for removal of the sutures in the areas that are visible i.e., the temporal hair tuft, the pretragal tacking sutures, and the preauricular area. On the seventh day half of the staples are removed, along with all the remaining nonabsorbable sutures. Absorbable chromic sutures in the postauricular sulcus and on the posterior portion of the tragus are difficult to remove and absorb spontaneously if cleansed with hydrogen peroxide and kept moist with Polysporin ointment. Patients are instructed to remain in the local vicinity for the first 5 days so that medical attention is prompt if any need should arise.

Patients are allowed to travel and have limited activity the second week. This allows them a sedentary week away from work and physical activity. They are asked to avoid bending and straining, which eliminates some activities normally occurring with housework. They are instructed not to drive during the first 2 weeks so that they avoid excessive motion of the head and neck. The patient is permitted to drive on the 14th postoperative day, at which time all remaining staples are removed.

It is usual for edema and ecchymosis to occur in areas of cervical liposuction and flap creation (Figs. 130 and 131). Ecchymosis is increased in the anterior cervical region if the patient had a considerable amount of fat suctioned. The anterior cervical area, particularly the inferior portion, is difficult to secure a compression dressing. A similar situation occurs in the inferior portion of the lateral cervical flap, which lies over the middle and inferior portions of the sternocleidomastoid muscle. The cervicomental angle has temporary distortion as a result of the plicating sutures. The same is true of the mandibular outline and the preauricular area. The face appears drawn and tight during the first week, this tightness gradually diminishes over the next 2 weeks. After 3 weeks the patient appears normal to friends and casual observers. The patient and surgeon can appreciate a subtle tightness that persists for another 2 to 3 weeks. Most patients have no change in their appearance after 3 months, meaning this will be their ultimate appearance, since almost all of their edema has subsided.

Hypoesthesia always occurs over areas of flap creation and regions that have undergone liposuction. Normal sensation returns in 2 to 4 months in areas of the liposuction. However, areas that have been undermined by sharp dissection will probably have permanently altered sensation, although most patients are unaware of this subtle change.

Although some surgeons allow their patients to return to work and normal activity at 1 week, a 2- to 3-week delay is recommended.

Postoperative Visits

The patient is seen the morning following the surgery, preferably in the early morning so that if any corrective procedures are necessary, time is available. The patient is initially asked how the evening was, and questions concerning nausea and vomiting are posed. Vomiting or coughing increases the likelihood of postoperative bleeding. The large pressure dressing is removed and the surgical sites are examined carefully, both visually and digitally with a sterile gloved hand. The evaluation primarily focuses on four areas: postoperative bleeding, potential skin slough, nerve damage, and integrity of the suture lines.

Postoperative Bleeding

It is normal to expect edema and ecchymosis with contour distortion (Figs. 130 and 131). Bruising and ecchymosis are more apparent over the cervical flaps and postauricular area. All flaps should be palpated to determine whether any bleeding has occurred. If a moderate amount of bleeding has occurred, a fluid level will be noticeable. Marked bleeding causes considerable distortion of the flaps and will be readily apparent. A hematoma can be expressed easily through the orifice that has been left in the postauricular sulcus (Fig. 132). This is accomplished either with the hand or by rolling a 3 × 3 sterile gauze into a cigar shape and rolling it along the flap until the clot is expressed. If the orifice does not readily open, a curved or straight hemostat may be introduced to eliminate the adherence. An alternative method is to introduce a 4- or 6-mm spatula cannula and use liposuction, either machine-assisted or with syringe assistance.

Potential Skin Slough

The most likely area for poor capillary flow is in the postauricular flap. Capillary flow is evaluated by placing a finger on the flap to apply moderate pressure (Fig. 133). When the pressure is released, a blanched area is present (Fig. 134). The rapidity with which the blanched area is filled by capillary blood flow determines the adequacy of the blood supply to the flap. Occasionally, a staple applies too much pressure on the flap and a blanched area is present immediately below the staple (Fig. 135). After removing the staple, there will be an improvement in the capillary flow with a decrease in the triangular blanched area where the staple has applied tension (Fig. 136). If the flap continues to have poor blood flow, consideration for the use of vasodilators should be made. In rare instances a hyperbaric chamber, if available, can be used. Blood flow to the tragal area is also evaluated. Despite the three to five pretragal interrupted sutures, this flap usually has excellent blood flow. Even in instances where capillary return is not readily apparent the author has not removed the pretragal sutures if the skin has adequate color (Fig. 137). The postauricular flaps in the hair-bearing area of the scalp are relatively short and have excellent blood supply. Therefore they are not susceptible to ischemia (Fig. 138).

Nerve Damage

The most susceptible nerve to intraoperative damage is the marginal mandibular nerve because liposuction of the neck is now so common. The function can be tested by having the patient open the mouth. If a deficit is present, the area affected does not draw down because the perioral depressors are paralyzed. Smiling and puckering of the mouth show only minimal changes if this nerve has been affected. The temporal nerve is less likely to be affected, and damage is readily apparent by the patient's inability to raise an eyebrow. One side may be weak or completely paralyzed. The great auricular nerve provides sensation to the earlobe and lower third of the external ear. These areas are not uncommonly hypoesthetic and occasionally are anesthetic. This usually results from traction on the great auricular nerve as it traverses the sternocleidomastoid muscle. The plication sutures can apply traction to the nerve, which causes a temporary deficit. It is uncommon to sever this nerve, but this can happen with aggressive liposuction or sharp dissection that violates the fascia of the sternocleidomastoid muscle. If the spinal accessory nerve is affected, this is evident because the patient is unable to raise the shoulder. This would be a very uncommon event with the type of approach discussed.

Integrity of the Suture Line

All the staples and sutures are carefully examined to ensure that there has been no loss of integrity. Staples and sutures can be added or deleted as needed.

The large dressing is again reapplied using moderate to light tension. Adequate cotton batting is placed behind the external ear to avoid buckling of the cartilage, which causes considerable discomfort. Patients usually complain of discomfort over the mastoid area. This is a result of the plication sutures that draw the cervicomental angle up and backward toward the mastoid process. This discomfort usually decreases significantly during the second postoperative day.

Patients are sent home with a responsible adult and are asked to return in 24 hours, at which time the large dressing is removed and the surgical sites are cleaned and reexamined. At this point a chin strap is used continuously for the next 12 days (Figs. 139 and 140). Activity is somewhat increased but remains limited through the end of the first week. During the second week the patient is allowed to travel out of town after all the nylon sutures and half of the staples

have been removed on the seventh day. The pretragal and preauricular sutures and nylon sutures of the temporal tuft and lobule are removed on the fifth postoperative day. On the fourteenth day all the remaining staples are removed; the patient is instructed to wear the chin strap while at home but is allowed to discontinue its use when he or she is in public places. Makeup may be worn after the second week.

ADVERSE SEQUELAE AND COMPLICATIONS

Adverse Sequelae

Edema, ecchymosis, hypoesthesia, and contour distortion are expected changes following a rhytidectomy. All of these changes should resolve spontaneously with the exception of the subtle hypoesthesia, which will persist for a long time in areas where a flap has been created using sharp dissection.

Complications

Bleeding and Hematoma

Bleeding is the most common postoperative complication but is usually minor. The most common areas for this to occur are in the inferior portion of the lateral cervical flap and the retroauricular area overlying the mastoid bone. In these areas most blood loss amounts to less than 10 ml, and blood is readily expressed through the retroauricular opening by applying gentle pressure with the hand. If the blood has clotted or large amounts have accumulated, extraction through the retroauricular opening using a 4-mm liposuction cannula either on a syringe or machine-assisted, or by employing a transcutaneous approach using a 16-gauge needle on a 5- or 10-ml syringe is quite effective (Fig. 132). If bleeding has occurred that is impossible to reach from the postauricular opening, several sutures may be cut in the temporal or preauricular flap or the submental incision may be reopened to allow introduction of the cannula. It is rare, following the expression of liquid blood or clot, that bleeding will recur. Removal of all sutures with subsequent takedown of the flap to allow additional cautery is very rare but may be necessary in some patients. The author recalls only two patients over the past 20 years who have required such a maneuver. After evacuation of blood, another compression dressing is applied and the patient reexamined the following day. Early postoperative bleeding usually results from vasodilation following the cessation of the epinephrine effect on the vascular tree. It may also be the result of overactivity by the patient (Fig. 141).

Late bleeding that occurs after 48 hours may be caused by factors such as vomiting, overexertion, and the consumption of alcohol or bending and lifting. Any activity that results in a Valsalva maneuver is likely to initiate postoperative bleeding. The evacuation of any palpable clot is important so that a period of weeks of induration and distortion that

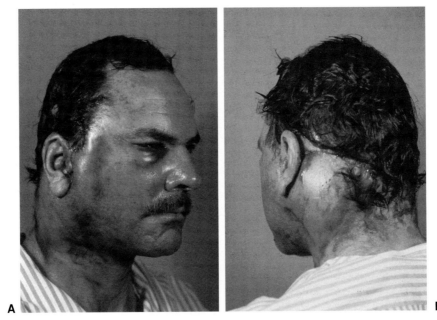

FIG. 141. (**A**) A 48-year-old man seen 24 hours after surgery with very large bilateral hematomas of the undermined areas. The anterior cervical region is not involved, since no liposuction was performed there. Through the postauricular sulcus a cannula was introduced using a Gomco machine at a pressure of 10 inches of mercury. Three hundred millimeters of dark-red blood was removed, and a second pressure dressing was applied. (**B**) At 24 hours showing a very large hematoma on the left flap. The area continued to ooze, and daily evacuation of the clot using digital pressure or needle evacuation was required. At 2 weeks, no further bleeding occurred. The patient had excellent skin perfusion, despite the fact that he had been a lifelong smoker. He had discontinued cigarettes 3 weeks before the surgery.

normally occur during organization of the clot is avoided. These organizing clots can also be treated with ultrasound or a small amount of triamcinolone acetonide diluted to 2.5 mg/ml (Aristocort, Fujisawa USA, Inc., Deerfield, IL).

Nerve Damage

Nerve damage is the most feared complication of facelift surgery. Although uncommon, it can lead to permanent disability and deformity. In the procedure explained in this chapter there are four nerves that are susceptible to damage. They are the marginal mandibular nerve, the temporal branch of the facial nerve, the great auricular nerve, and the lesser occipital nerve. Other nerves that can be damaged when more extensive undermining is employed are the zygomatic and buccal branches of the facial nerve and the spinal accessory nerve.

The marginal mandibular nerve is probably the most susceptible to damage since the advent of liposuction. This motor dysfunction varies in duration but usually resolves in less than 6 months. Since only blunt dissection is used during liposuction, the patient can be assured that this defect will be temporary. The marginal mandibular nerve exits from the parotid gland near the angle of the jaw and overlies the masseter muscle. Along the mandibular ramus it is covered by subcutaneous fat and the platysma muscle and is therefore

usually spared any operative injury. Since the platysma muscle is highly variable and may be very thin or totally absent in some patients, this complication must be expected in a small percentage of patients (Fig. 142).

The temporal branch of the facial nerve travels an area that is centered over a line from the inferior border of the tragus to the lateral aspect of the eyebrow (Figs. 30 and 33). Careful undermining of the temporal flap should occur in this area. The undermining should be immediately below the hair follicles of the temporal hair tuft and then raised to a superficial level as the dissection advances anteriorly. The temporal branch is at its greatest risk as it crosses the zygomatic arch. The approximate location of the nerve can be identified by drawing a line from 0.5 cm below the tragus to a point 1.5 to 2.0 cm above the lateral aspect of the eyebrow. As an alternative, the area of greatest vulnerability occurs between a superior line that connects the superior border of the tragus to the most superior wrinkle on the forehead and an inferior line from the superior border of the ear lobe to the lateral aspect of the eyebrow.

The frontalis muscle is innervated by the temporal nerve which, when injured, prevents elevation of the eyebrow and affects normal animation of the forehead (Fig. 143). The downward displacement of an eyebrow and the absence of wrinkling on one side of the forehead are clinical signs of frontalis muscle paralysis. It is common for this nerve to be paralyzed during the infiltration of the operative anesthetic.

When lidocaine is combined with epinephrine, this temporary paralysis may last for 6 to 8 hours. Although normal function may not be observed at the time of discharge, an intact nerve resumes normal function that is apparent on the following morning. The perioral muscles, which are innervated by the marginal mandibular nerve, can also develop temporary paralysis from anesthetic infiltration.

The great auricular nerve can be injured as it traverses along the anterior border of the sternocleidomastoid muscle. Because of its superficial location, dissection must proceed carefully along the anterior border of the middle third of this muscle. Another cause of injury to this nerve is the placement of plicating sutures into the anterior border of the muscle during elevation of the platysma. This latter injury usually results in only temporary anesthesia, and full recovery of the nerve can be expected. Cautery is usually not necessary in this area and therefore is not the usual cause of damage. The great auricular nerve exists from the posterior border of the middle portion of the sternocleidomastoid muscle and courses anteriorly and superiorly on the body of this muscle toward the external ear. Its location underneath the fascia of the muscle provides some protection unless the fascia is interrupted during dissection. The nerve can also be identified by its parallel and posterior position to the external jugular vein. The great auricular nerve provides sensory per-

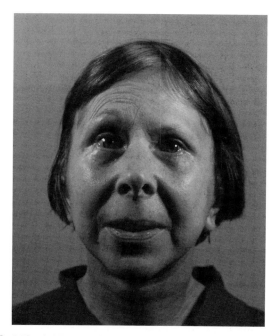

FIG. 143. A 67-year-old woman who was examined 24 hours after a rhytidectomy. There is weakness in the frontalis muscle on the left side. This can result from edema, manipulation, cautery, or traction to the temporal nerve from the plication sutures, causing a temporary paralysis of the muscle. It is unusual for this nerve to be severed; therefore return of function is usually present in 3 to 6 months.

ception for the skin of the inferior third of the external ear, lateral neck, angle of the jaw, and the postauricular region. Its function can be tested by lightly touching the earlobe to evaluate sensory response.

The lesser occipital nerve also exits from the posterior border of the sternocleidomastoid muscle, which it then parallels as it advances superiorly to innervate the neck and the scalp skin posterior to the external ear. Damage to this nerve is uncommon.

The zygomatic branch of the facial nerve can be injured if sharp dissection is extended over the zygomatic arch. The buccal branches of the facial nerve may also be damaged if dissection is extended to the oral commissure. The above-described rhytidectomy method does not create a flap that extends into either of these two regions, so injury to these two nerves should not occur.

The spinal accessory nerve may also suffer injury during facelift surgery. This motor nerve is found in the posterior cervical triangle where it exits the middle position of the posterior border of the sternocleidomastoid muscle and passes inferiorly and posteriorly to enter the trapezius muscle. If the nerve is damaged in this triangle, a resulting weakness of the trapezius muscle leading to chronic aching of the shoulder, paresthesia of the arm, shoulder drop, and an inability to abduct the shoulder to more than 80 degrees occurs. This symptom becomes evident as a flaring of the wing of the scapula.

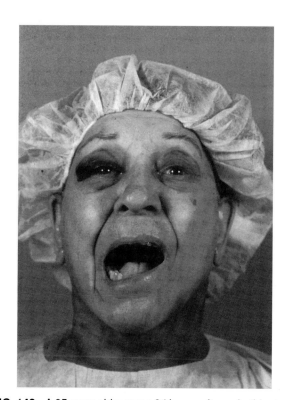

FIG. 142. A 65-year-old woman 24 hours after a rhytidectomy and extensive anterior cervical liposuction. A weakness of the perioral depressor muscles is evident on her left side. This results from liposuction over the left marginal mandibular nerve. This patient had improvement within 1 week. A delay in improvement of 3 to 6 months is not unusual.

Infection

With the use of proper sterile technique and the use of preoperative, intraoperative, and postoperative antibiotics this complication is exceedingly rare.

Skin Necrosis

Necrosis of the skin flap is rare. Some surgeons believe that smokers are at high risk for this complication because of impaired vascular flow. The greatest length of the flap is in the retroauricular site where the vertical and horizontal incisions meet in the postauricular sulcus. This skin is thin and placed under significant tension to improve the cervicomental angle. It is in this area that the flap is most susceptible to postoperative ischemia and subsequent scarring (Fig. 144). If capillary filling is absent in this area, the sutures in the horizontal incision should be removed to decrease tension on the flap. Although a spread horizontal scar may result from removal of these sutures, this defect is considerably easier to correct than a linear vertical scar that has its origin at the horizontal incision line and extends inferiorly behind the external ear. Even with scar revision, a long vertical and visible scar remains.

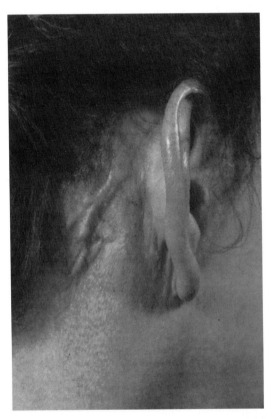

FIG. 144. Postoperative ischemia resulting in full-thickness skin slough is most commonly found in smokers, as is evident in this patient. Hypertrophic scarring may result, which can be treated with topical and intralesional steroid injections or Silastic gel sheeting.

A full-thickness skin slough in the preauricular area is extremely rare but disastrous when it occurs. This can result from excessive tension placed on the anterior flap, overzealous thinning of the flap resulting in damage of the dermal capillary plexus, application of icepacks directly to the skin, and unrecognized postoperative hematoma placing excessive tension on the flap. Using the method described, in the author's experience this complication has never occurred. If the size of the scarred area is moderate to large, correction of this defect is close to impossible. When the scar is small and adjacent to the preauricular incision, tissue expanders may help to remove the scar. The author does not perform a chemical peel on the flap or adjacent tissues because edema may apply additional pressure on the flap.

Alopecia

Alopecia results when undermining of the flap is superficial to the hair follicles. This may occur in either the temporal area or the retroauricular region. Hair follicles are readily visualized when the flap is raised, so this should be an uncommon complication. The much more common absence of hair in the temporal tuft occurs when surgeons extend the vertical preauricular incision superiorly into the temporal area without preserving any of the temporal tuft of hair. In the author's experience this is the most common method used by other surgeons performing rhytidectomy. Since the author's method eliminates this cosmetic alternation, it is highly recommended. A third cause of alopecia can result from anagen effluvium caused by a compromise of the vascular supply. This should be only temporary in duration.

Abnormal Scarring

Hypertrophic scars can occur, particularly in areas where the flap is placed under increased tension such as the horizontal retroauricular incision. Since this area is usually covered by hair, an elevated or spread scar does not create a serious cosmetic defect. By avoiding tension in the preauricular and lower temporal regions, the likelihood of hypertrophic scarring is decreased and the occurrence of spread scar is unlikely. An elevated band of scar tissue can occur where the incision has passed across the postauricular sulcus (Fig. 145). The author's method as described in this chapter diminishes the likelihood of this scarring.

Contour Irregularities

Multiple depressions and irregular contouring can result from placing too few plication sutures. A sufficient number of these sutures must be present over the preauricular area to create only minimal elevations and depressions. Liposuction using a large-caliber cannula over the cheek and jowl can cause permanent ridging (Figs. 146–147). This can be

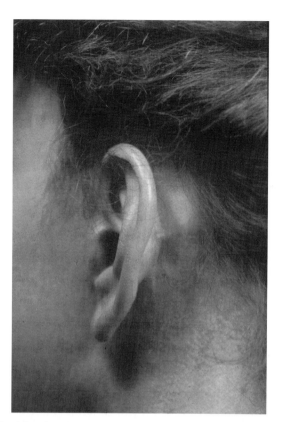

FIG. 145. An elevated band of scar can occur where the retroauricular incision passes across the sulcus. This occurs because any straight-line scar as it passes across a concavity contracts and can form an elevated defect. To diminish this likelihood, the incision should be constructed in a V shape (see Figs. 36, 48, 49, and 124–126).

avoided by using a cannula of 3-mm size or less with only one port. Suctioning should be limited to small amounts, usually less than 1 ml, using the syringe-assisted technique. Lipotransfer should be used in an attempt to improve these ridges, although results can be limited (Fig. 147B).

Intractable Pain

Pain of long duration is very uncommon and usually subsides in 6 months. Only two cases were reported by Rees, despite his extensive experience. These patients were judged to be disappointed with their cosmetic results, although the surgeon evaluated them as excellent. No anatomic reason for the discomfort was found. Conway also had a similar case and suggested that either trauma or surgical resection of the branches of the cervical sensory nerves was the probable cause. These nerves theoretically may be severed as they exit from the posterior border of the sternocleidomastoid muscle.

Suture Extrusion

Rarely the permanent sutures that are buried for the plication extrude. The author has had two such cases over the

past 20 years. A 57-year-old man sought medical attention with crusted keratotic lesions in the right preauricular area (Fig. 148). The visit was 25 months after his rhytidectomy. The patient stated that he had noted inflammatory papules 3 months earlier, which continued to increase in size. He presumed these were malignant lesions and was fearful; consequently, he delayed medical examination. Because the keratotic crusts were linear and in the area where the plicating sutures were placed, a presumptive diagnosis of inflammatory response secondary to extrusion of the permanently buried sutures was made. Further examination showed that the buried Ethibond sutures were found at the base of each of these inflammatory keratotic lesions. The suture material was removed by simply cutting through the knot. Polysporin antibiotic ointment was applied, and no perceptible scarring developed; the patient has not had any more extrusion of sutures during the ensuing 5 years. The second patient was a 54-year-old woman who had an inflammatory papule 26 months after surgery. There was no associated keratotic le-

FIG. 146. Using large cannulas for liposuction of the jowl and cheek can result in permanent linear defects. When liposuction of the face was first introduced, the use of a large-bore cannula was recommended. A 6-mm spatula cannula with a single large orifice was used in this patient. Lipotransfer helped but did not resolve the defect. A blunt 3-mm cannula with one small orifice is now used. These defects occur more commonly in older patients or when excessive loss of elasticity is present.

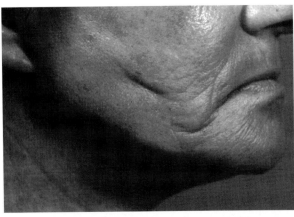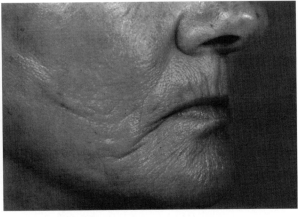

A   B

FIG. 147. (**A**) This 60-year-old woman has moderately severe actinic degeneration. Seven months after rhytidectomy a continuing linear defect is evident in the cheek area, resulting from liposuction performed with a 6-mm spatula cannula with one large orifice. The patient subsequently underwent three sessions of lipotransfer with satisfactory improvement. (**B**) Seven months later, the patient had undergone two sessions of lipotransfer with excellent results. She received a third session of lipotransfer after this picture was taken, which resolved the defect.

sion present. She also healed without a scar after the suture was removed.

Contact Dermatitis

Contact dermatitis can be either irritant or allergic. Many patients complain of dry, irritated, scaling skin, which results from their use of Phisoderm for 3 days as a facial and scalp preparation before the surgery (Table 17-2). Allergic contact dermatitis can result from use of topical antibiotics, particularly those containing Neomycin, or chromic sutures (Fig.

149). The differentiation between topical antibiotic allergy vs. a chromate allergy is that the former is present along the entire suture line, whereas the latter is not seen where nylon or other synthetic nonabsorbable sutures are used.

POSTOPERATIVE RESULTS

The following figures are of patients in whom the rhytidectomy procedure described in this chapter has been performed by the author. The results of the pretragal and posttragal incisions are shown (Figs. 150–154).The step created in the postauricular hairline and the retroauricular incisions in patients who wear very short hair is also demonstrated (Figs. 151,153C).

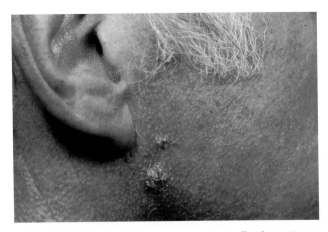

FIG. 148. Extrusion of buried permanent plication sutures occurs very rarely. Patient presented with three crusted keratotic inflammatory lesions of the right preauricular area 25 months after rhytidectomy. The diagnosis of foreign body reaction secondary to extrusion of permanent buried sutures was made. Removal of the crust confirmed the diagnosis with the 2.0 Ethibond sutures found at the base of each lesion. These areas healed without any perceptible scar.

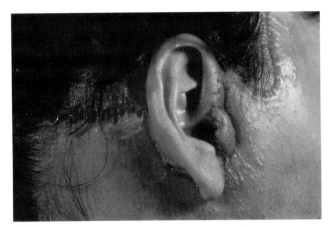

FIG. 149. Contact dermatitis of either the irritant or allergic type can occur. In this patient an allergy to Polysporin ointment developed. Allergy to chromic catgut suture may also occur.

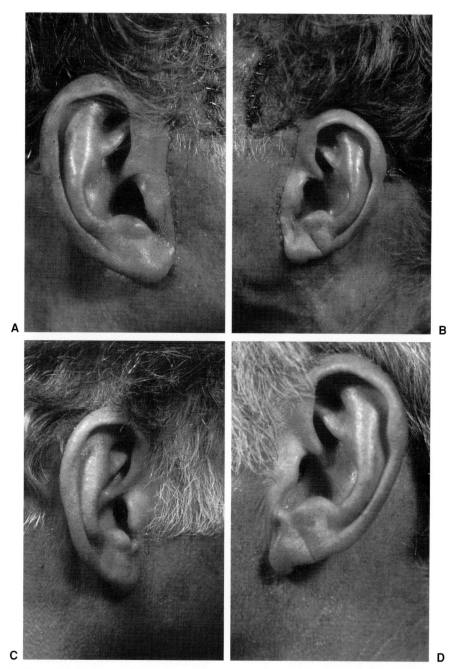

FIG. 150. (A and B) The preauricular incision in males is begun approximately 1 cm anterior to the helix and is carried vertically in the depression anterior to the tragus. It then follows the crease along the anterior border of the lobule. **(C)** Same patient 6 weeks after rhytidectomy. **(D)** Same patient 17 months after rhytidectomy.

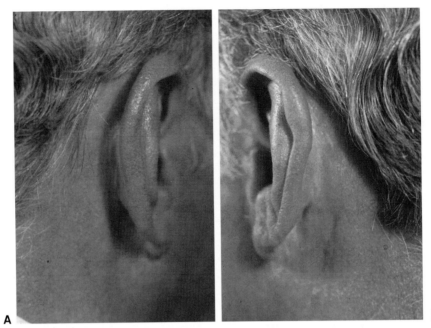

FIG. 151. Same patient as in Fig. 150, 17 months after rhytidectomy. Absence of an elevated banded scar in the postauricular sulcus, the ability to easily camouflage the step in the retroauricular incision, and the difficulty in identifying the horizontal retroauricular incision as it passes across the glabrous skin from the scalp hair to the retroauricular sulcus are evident.

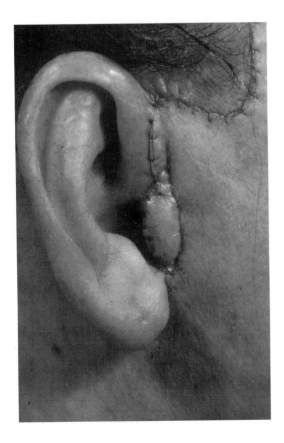

FIG. 152. One day after rhytidectomy, three interrupted pretragal sutures, two interrupted sutures anterior to the helix, the temporary posterior and superior displacement of the lobule, and the retained tuft of temporal hair are evident.

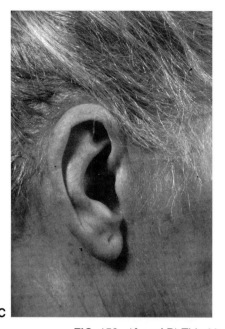 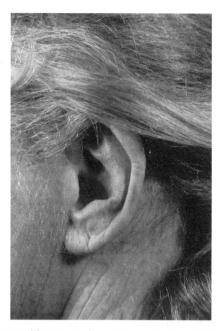 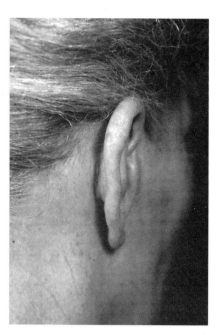

A–C

FIG. 153. (**A and B**) This 63-year-old woman shows the typical result following the technique described earlier employing the posttragal incision. (**C**) Absence of any significant step in the postauricular hairline.

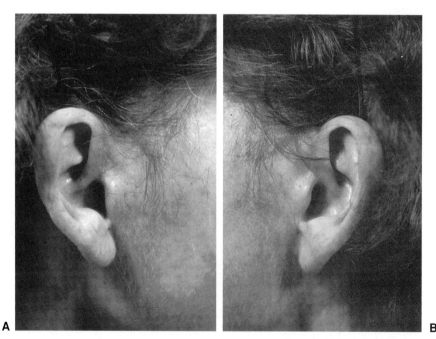

A   B

FIG. 154. This 72-year-old woman has undergone the previously described rhytidectomy technique using the posttragal incision. Normal appearance of the tragus and the absence of lobular distortion are evident.

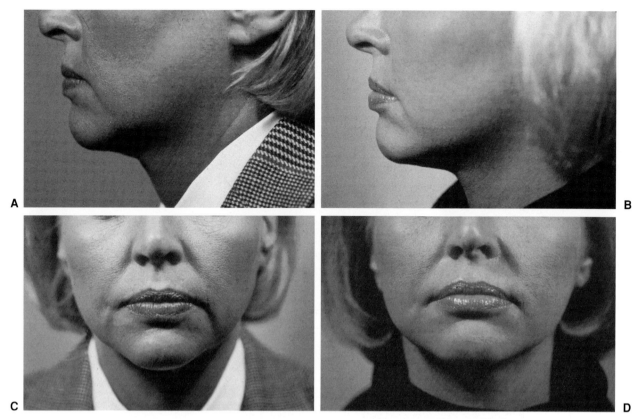

FIG. 155. (**A and C**) Forty-one-year-old patient has only minor jowling and marionette lines. (**B and D**) Postoperative results show complete elimination of the jowling with significant improvement of the marionette lines.

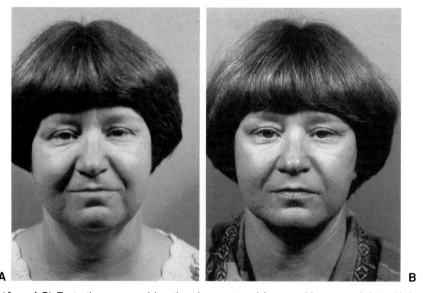

FIG. 156. (**A and C**) Forty-three-year-old patient has a round face and is overweight, with jowling and excess cervical skin and fat. On her 4-month postoperative pictures there is little improvement on the frontal view; however, the lateral view shows definitive improvement of the excess submental fat and skin, yielding an improved cervicomental angle (**B and D**).

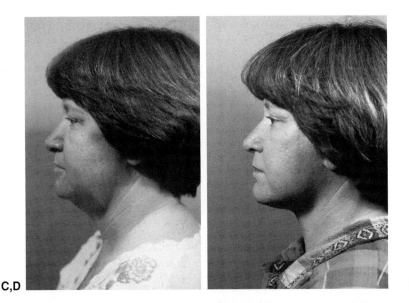

C,D

FIG. 156. *Continued.*

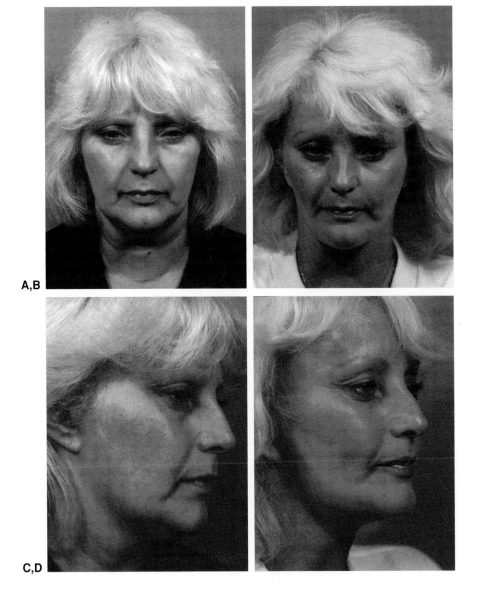

A,B

C,D

FIG. 157. (**A and C**) Forty-six-year-old patient has excessive jowling, marionette lines, and excessive anterior cervical fat and skin. (**B and D**) Three-month postoperative pictures show marked improvement of jowling, with reestablishment of a pleasing cervicomental angle. There is only modest improvement in marionette lines.

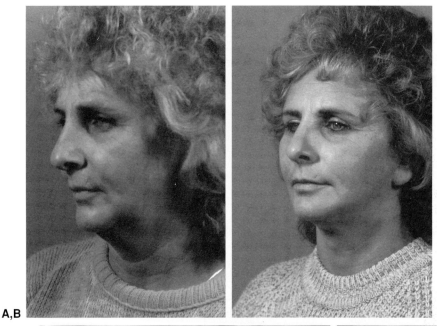

A,B

FIG. 158. (**A and C**) Forty-eight-year-old patient is overweight with modest jowling and significant excess anterior cervical fat and skin. Her postoperative pictures were taken at 1 year and 10 months (**B and D.**) They show marked improvement of cervicomental angle and almost complete obliteration of jowling. Despite these significant improvements, this patient was unhappy with her results.

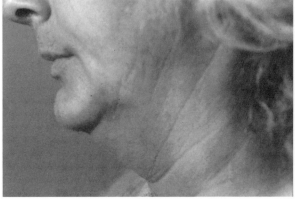
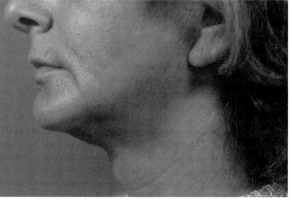

C,D

A,B

FIG. 159. (**A and C**) Fifty-year-old patient has excellent skeletal anatomy with only minimal jowling and subtle excess submental fat and anterior cervical skin. (**B and D**) Three-month postoperative pictures show no significant change in marionette lines, but an improved cervicomental angle and obliteration of the subtle jowling are evident.

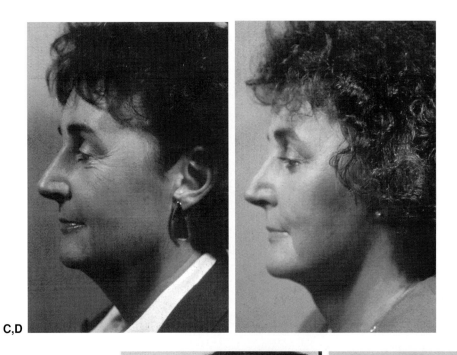

C,D

FIG. 159. *Continued.*

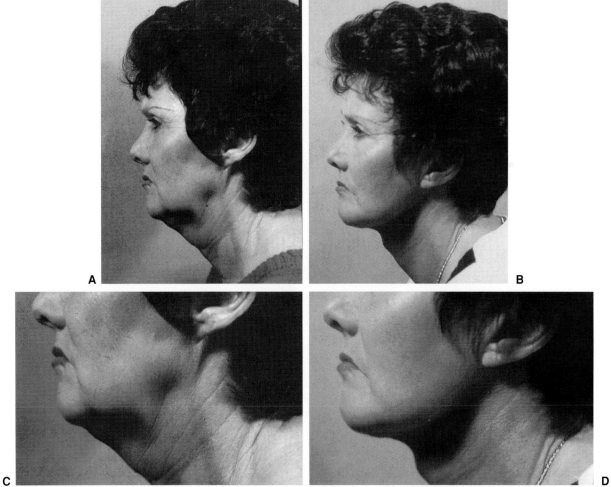

A

B

C

D

FIG. 160. (**A and C**) Fifty-two-year-old patient had marked marionette lines, excessive jowling, and significant anterior cervical fat and skin. (**B and D**) Her 4-month postoperative pictures show a dramatic improvement with complete eradication of jowling and remarkable improvement of the cervicomental angle. Marionette lines were significantly improved, which eliminated her angry look.

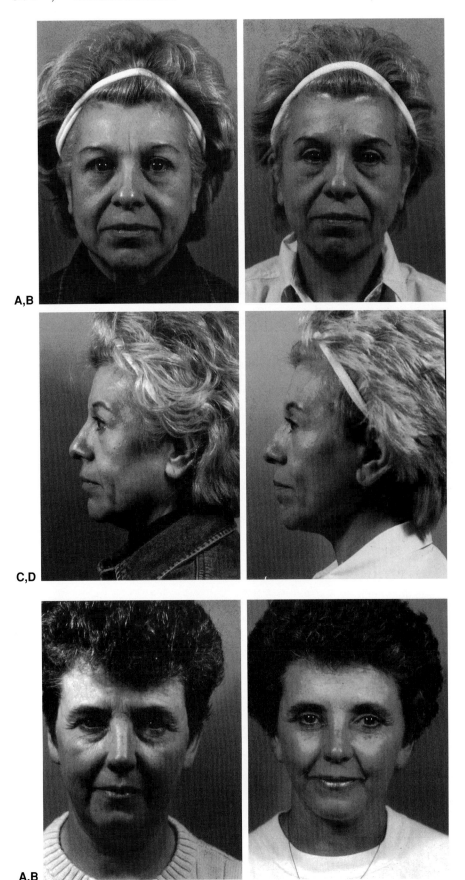

A,B

C,D

A,B

FIG. 161. (**A and C**) Fifty-four-year-old patient had deep nasolabial folds, subtle marionette lines, significant jowling, a modest amount of submental fat, and excess anterior cervical skin. (**B and D**) Eight-month postoperative photos show no change in nasolabial folds, modest improvement in marionette lines, and complete eradication of jowling with elimination of submental fat and skin, resulting in an improved cervicomental angle.

FIG. 162. (**A and C**) Fifty-six-year-old patient shows moderate marionette lines, excessive jowling, and significant excess anterior cervical skin and fat. (**B and D**) Postoperative photos at 14½ months show complete eradication of the jowling, with improvement of marionette lines and significant improvement of cervico-mental angle.

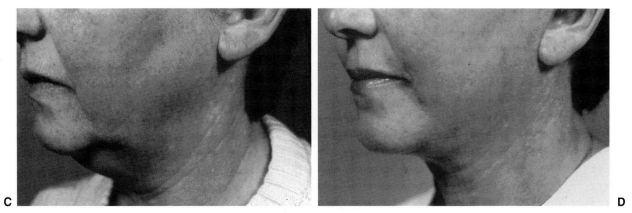

FIG. 162. *Continued.*

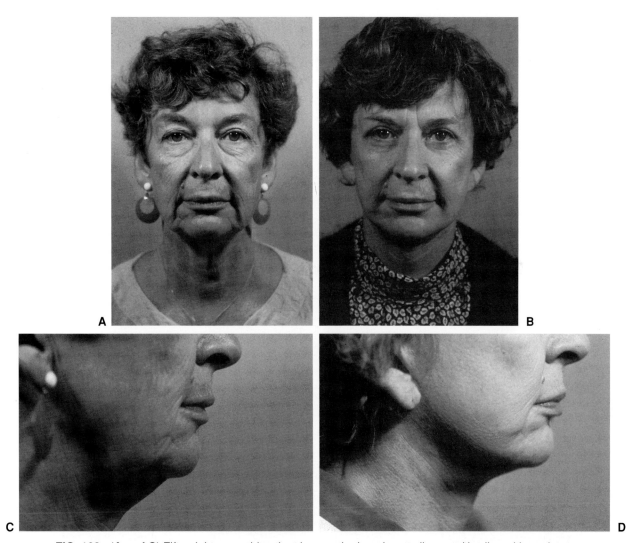

FIG. 163. (**A and C**) Fifty-eight-year-old patient has marked marionette lines and jowling with moderate excess anterior cervical skin and modest submental fat. (**B and D**) Three-month postoperative photographs show marked improvement of jowling and marionette lines with complete elimination of excess anterior cervical skin. The presence of earrings distracts from the preoperative photographs. All jewelry should be removed before photographic documentation.

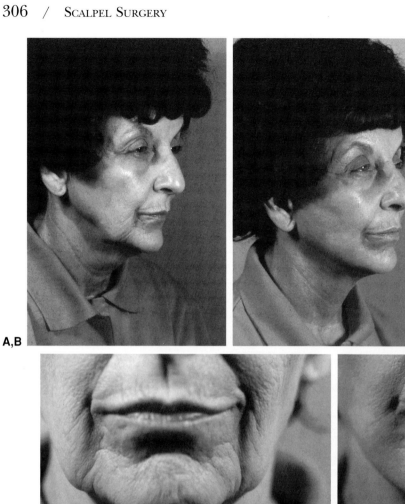

A,B

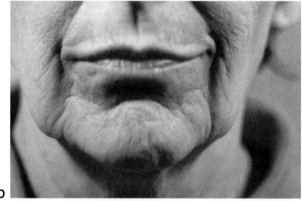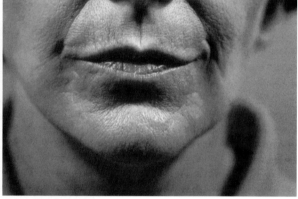

C,D

FIG. 164. (**A and C**) Sixty-four-year-old patient has considerable jowling with very deep marionette lines extending to the mandibular ramus, and modest anterior cervical skin. (**B and C**) Three-month postoperative photographs show complete elimination of the jowling, marionette lines, and excess anterior cervical skin.

A,B

FIG. 165. (**A and C**) Sixty-eight-year-old patient shows very deep nasolabial folds and deep marionette lines leading to the mandibular ramus but no significant submental fat or excess anterior cervical skin. (**B and D**) Three-month postoperative photos show modest improvement of nasolabial folds and marionette lines with complete eradication of jowling. The excellent contour of her tragus and lobule is evident.

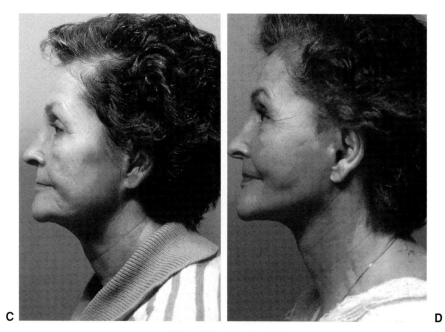

FIG. 165. *Continued.*

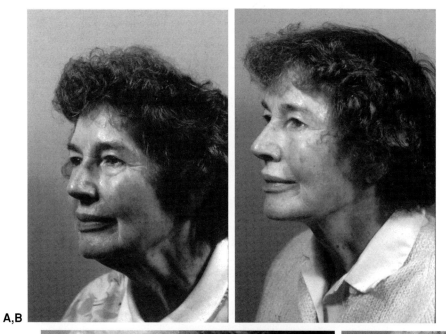

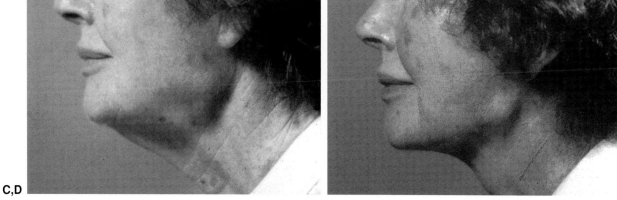

FIG. 166. (**A and C**) Seventy-two-year-old patient had moderate marionette lines and jowling with significant excess anterior cervical skin and visible platysmal banding. (**B and D**) Fifteen-month postoperative photos show complete obliteration of her jowling and excess anterior cervical skin. The platysmal bands are improved because of the plicating sutures. The postoperative photos of this patient's posttragal incision line are shown in Fig. 154.

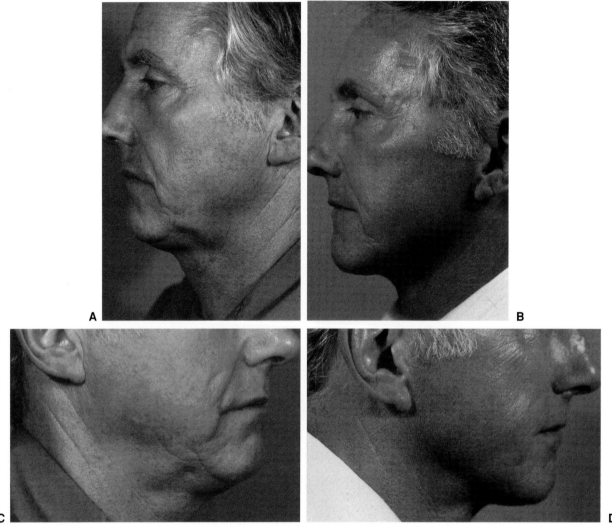

FIG. 167. (A and C) Fifty-seven-year-old male has moderate nasolabial folds, marionette lines, and jowling with only modest submental fat and anterior cervical skin. Seventeen-month postoperative photos show significant improvement of the marionette lines with complete elimination of the jowling and excess submental fat and anterior cervical skin. This patient had subsequent spontaneous extrusion of buried nonabsorbable sutures (see Fig. 148).

SUGGESTED READING LIST

1. Asken S. The facelift-cervicofacial rhytidectomy. In: Coleman WP, Hanke CW, Alt T, Asken S, eds. Cosmetic surgery of the skin: principles and techniques. Philadelphia: BC Decker, 1991:335.
2. Aufricht G. Surgery for excessive skin of the face. In: Wallace AB, ed. Transactions of the Second Congress of the International Society of Plastic Surgeons. Baltimore: Williams & Wilkins, 1971.
3. Bames HO. Truth and fallacies of face peeling and face lifting, M J Rec 1927;126:86.
4. Bettman AG. Plastic and cosmetic surgery of the face. Northwest Med 1920;19:205.
5. Booth FA. Cosmetic surgery of face, neck and breast. Northwest Med 1922;21:170.
6. Bourguet J. La disparition chirurgicale des rides et plis du visage. Bull Acad Med Paris 1919;82:183.
7. Conway H. Factors underlying prolonged pain following rhytidectomy. In: Transactions of the Fourth International Congress of Plastic and Reconstructive Surgery. Amsterdam: Excerpta Medica Foundation, 1969, 1120.
8. Hunt HL. Plastic surgery of the head, face and neck. Philadelphia: Lea & Febiger, 1926.
9. Joseph J. Plastic operation on protruding cheek. Dtsch Med Wochenschr 1921;47:287.
10. Lagarde M. Cirurgie estetique du visage. Cron Med Lima 1921;38: 321.
11. Lewis CM. Should face lifts be performed before the age of 40? Aesthet Plast Surg 1985;9:47.
12. Lexer E. Die Gesamte Wiederherstellungs-Chirurgie. Leipzig: Johann Ambrosius Barth, 1931 (vols 1 and 2).
13. Miller CC. Cosmetic surgery. 2nd ed. Chicago: Oak Printing and Publishing, 1908.
14. Mitz D, Peyronie M. The superficial musculo-aponeurotic system (SMAS) in the carotid and cheek area. Plast Reconstr Surg 1976;58: 80.
15. Noel A. La chirurgie esthetique: son role social. Paris: Masson & Cie, 1926.
16. Noel A. La chirurgie esthetique. Thiron & A Cie: Clermont (Oise), 1928.
17. Passot R. La chirurgie esthetique des rides du visage. Presse Med 1919; 27:258.

18. Pitanguy I, Ramos AS. The frontal branch of the facial nerve: the importance of its variations in face lifting. Plast Reconstr Surg 1966; 38:352.

19. Rees TD. Facelift. In: Rees TD, Wood-Smith eds. Cosmetic facial surgery. Philadelphia: WB Saunders, 1973:134.

20. Salasche SJ, Bernstein G, Senkarik M. Surgical anatomy of the skin. Norwalk, CN: Appleton & Lange, 1988.

21. Stein RO. New methods in cosmetic face lifting (face tightening), Wein Klin Wochenschr 1927;4:83 (Ger.)

22. Webster RC, Beeson WH, McCollough EG. In: Beeson WH, McCollough EG, eds. Facelift in aesthetic surgery of the aging face. St. Louis: CV Mosby, 1986:78.

23. Webster RC, Hamdan US, Smith RC. The considered and considerate facelift. Part I. Conservative underminding, role of limited redraping, and choice of direction of pull. Am J Cosmet Surg 1985;2(3): 1.

24. Webster RC, Hamdan US, Smith RC. The considered and considerate facelift. Part II. SMAS plication vs. imbrication, theory of SMAS anatomy and dynamics, and conservation of platysma. Am J Cosmet Surg 1985;2(4):65.

25. Webster R, Davidson T, White M. Conservative facelifta surgery. Arch Laryngol 1976;102:657.

26. Webster R, Smith R, Smith K. Facelift. Part I. Extent of undermining of skin flaps. Head Neck Surg 1983;5(6):525.

27. Webster R, Smith R, Smith K. Facelift. Part II. Etiology of platysmal cords and its relationship to treatment. Head Neck Surg 1983;6(1):590.

28. Webster R, Smith R, Smith K. Facelift. Part III. Plication of the superficial musculaoponeurotic system. Head Neck Surg 1983;6(2):696.

29. Webster R, Smith R, Smith K. Facelift. Part IV. Use of superficial musculoaponeurotic system suspending sutures. Head Neck Surg 1984; 6(3):780.

30. Webster R, Smith R, Smith K. The facelift. Part V. Suspending sutures for platysma cords. Head Neck Surg 1984;6(4):870.

31. Wright MR. Psychological evaluation of a cosmetic surgical patient. In: Coleman WP, Hanke CW, Alt TH, Asken S, eds. Cosmetic surgery of the skin: principles and techniques. Philadelphia: BC Decker, 1991: 373.

Textbook of Dermatologic Surgery, edited by John L. Ratz.
Lippincott–Raven Publishers, Philadelphia © 1998.

CHAPTER 18

Blepharoplasty

Paul S. Collins

HISTORY

Techniques to remove upper eyelid skin have indubitably been in existence for over 1000 years. The technique was used to help improve vision obstructed by excess ptotic lid tissue. MacKenzie and Dupuytren described eyelid surgery in the 1830s, and Miller in 1907 described the cosmetic removal of "folds, bags, and wrinkles of the skin above the eyes. . . ." Castanares in the early 1960s refined the traditional procedure based on anatomic findings, and his procedure has continued to be refined by a number of surgeons. The transconjunctival approach to periorbital fat was described by Bourguet in 1928. Recently there has been a resurgence in the transconjunctival procedure in younger patients with minimal excess skin desiring improvement. Older patients with moderate amounts of excess skin can also obtain good results. Transconjunctival blepharoplasty has the advantage of not producing a cutaneous wound that can require weeks before it becomes inconspicuous. However, it is not free of complications such as ectropion, entropion, and diplopia. Laser blepharoplasty, a recent development, is touted by some surgeons as causing minimal bleeding and bruising, which decrease healing time (see chapter 23 for section on CO_2 Laser Transconjunctival Blepharoplasty.). This chapter deals with the traditional blepharoplasty procedure.

Paul S. Collins: Department of Dermatology, Stanford Medical School, Stanford, California 94305.

EXPECTED CHANGES AND DURATION OF CHANGES

The eyes are a main focal point on the face, and any improvement in their appearance can cause a dramatic improvement. The human eye can be beautified by removing redundant tissue, which alters the slitlike appearance, thus enlarging the appearance of the eyes. The "tired look," especially noticeable when lower-lid fat pads protrude and produce a tired, sleepless, and aged appearance, can be improved, thus adding to a youthful appearance. Hooding, the cause of the "sad-eye" look, can also be eliminated by removal of bulky lateral upper lid tissue.

The duration of change of the upper eyelid depends on stability of the brow and the frontalis muscle. With aging, ptosis becomes more prominent as forehead tissue sinks further over the orbital rim into the orbital socket, compromising the previous upper lid surgery. The upper medial and the lower lateral fat pads are frequently overlooked during surgery and become overtly protuberant with time.

PREOPERATIVE PLANNING

Medical and ophthalmic conditions can adversely affect the success of this operation, so a thorough medical history, including allergies and medications, should be reviewed to ensure that there will be no undue risks to the proposed surgery. The patient should be in good general health or have stable systemic disease, for example, atherosclerotic cardiovascular disease with stable angina. Patients with severe systemic disease (active hepatitis) or an unstable disease (congestive heart failure, myocardial infarction within the past 6 months, or psychiatric problems) should not undergo the procedure. Uncontrolled hypertension, coagulation disorders, and severe atherosclerotic disease can increase the risk of bleeding and the threat of retrobulbar hematoma. Diabetes mellitus is associated with postoperative infection and poor wound healing. Smoking exacerbates local edema and is also associated with poor wound healing. In addition, smoking can increase the patient's blood pressure and pulse rate, augmenting bleeding tendencies.

Blepharoplasty surgery has its limitations. Rhytides in the orbital region, either laterally (''crow's feet'') or from the inferior eyelid region, are not corrected by blepharoplasty. While there can be some improvement of the inferior eyelid rhytides, the lateral rhytides will remain unchanged. The procedure also does not correct hyperpigmentation (dark circles under the eyes), nor does it eliminate chronic edema or festoons, a common patient expectation. Lower lid laxity and ectropion require additional procedures other than a standard blepharoplasty for their correction.

Recognition of factors that reduce or compromise the surgical results is vital. Avoidance of surgery is prudent if a compromising factor is present. Patients legally blind in one eye may be considered poor candidates. A surgical complication in the ''good'' eye can result in disastrous total blindness. Scar tissue from a previous surgery can compromise healing and may lead to excess bleeding, but most important, it weakens the integrity of the lower eyelid. Weakened lower lid structures are susceptible to ectropion. Exophthalmus, familial or hyperthyroid, limits improvement or can lead to lid closure complications. Mild facial and eyelid asymmetry is fairly common. Previously frank eyelid asymmetry, obscured by the aging, fat protrusions, and ptotic skin, can be unmasked by the surgery. The final appearance can be incorrectly attributed to poor surgical technique. The presence of deep-seated eyes, the ''cadaverous'' or ''sunken-eye'' appearance, will be exaggerated after surgery.

A thorough preoperative ophthalmologic examination is recommended, for it will reveal the presence of potential problems. Thyroid disease is associated with ophthalmopathy. Hyperthyroidism produces exophthalmus; hypothyroidism produces edema (myxedema) with thickening of the eyelid skin, causing drooping and bagginess. Even the euthyroid patient can have ophthalmic disease such as scleral show, chemosis, persistent eyelid edema, lagophthalmos, or proptosis. Allergies can cause recurrent and permanent periorbital edema and blepharochalasis. Stress, including surgical stress, can aggravate multiple sclerosis, and ocular multiple sclerosis can decrease or cause loss of visual acuity. Similar complications can occur with unrecognized or poorly controlled glaucoma. Keratoconjunctivitis sicca, associated with Sjögren's disease, produces the ''dry-eye'' syndrome. In this case conservative surgery can minimize aggravation of dry-eye symptoms. The presence of previously unknown lenticular opacities or retinal disease should be recognized during the ophthalmologic examination.

Medications that potentiate bleeding must be discontinued before surgery. The most common medications causing excess surgical bleeding are aspirin and aspirin-containing medications. Since patients are not typically knowledgeable about the aspirin-containing medications, a good resource for the patient and physician is the local pharmacist, who can usually provide a list of aspirin-containing medications. Ask about all medications, including over-the-counter drugs. The patient should be advised not to take any new medication before the surgery without notifying the physician's office. A list of medications that can produce excessive bleeding should be given to the patient. Other drugs can also adversely affect bleeding. These include alcohol, which also has a synergistic effect with aspirin, and vitamin E.

Hypertensive patients taking a nonselective β-adrenergic blocker such as propranolol can be adversely affected. Cardiac blood vessels have only β-receptors, whereas peripheral vessels have both β-receptors and α-receptors. Epinephrine in the presence of propranolol can paradoxically produce a marked hypertensive episode followed quickly by reflex bradycardia. This combination can result in cardiac arrest. Selective β-blockers, however, do not cause this drug interaction with epinephrine. Studies indicate that arrhythmias do not occur with epinephrine doses of 5 µg/ml (1:200,000 epinephrine) or less. Usually the volume of anesthetic with epinephrine that is used in blepharoplasty is small and not of consequence, even in the presence of nonselective β-adrenergic blocker. Care should be taken when several procedures are performed simultaneously, thus increasing the total dose of epinephrine. Remember that sudden cessation of propranolol can produce a rebound adrenergic excess and increased angina. Dilute concentrations of epinephrine (1:800,000) have been shown to provide adequate cutaneous hemostasis.

EXAMINATION OF THE EYELIDS AND PERIORBITAL REGION

A general orbital examination should be performed. Attention should be placed on symmetry of the bony orbit, eyelids, and eyes. Considerable asymmetry can be camouflaged by presence of redundant skin and/or periorbital fat and should be noted before surgery. For instance, the orbital rim may be prominent, especially laterally, and may encroach on the globe and eyelids. This restricts the ability to create a distinct upper eyelid crease. The eye sockets can vary in size or position. Sunken sockets, rendering a cadaverous appearance, are difficult to surgically correct. Surgery can even exaggerate anatomic variations. Eyelid edema, festoons, and lateral eyelid rhytides should be recorded, since they will not be corrected by the surgery. Look for blemishes, tumors, or other cutaneous abnormalities of the skin such as xanthelasma, milia, syringoma, and hyperpigmentation, and make note of them. Some of the conditions can be corrected before, during, or after the blepharoplasty.

Horizontal rhytides of the forehead suggest the presence of a brow ptosis. Creases above the brow are caused by frontalis muscle contraction, which elevates the eyebrow. The greater the brow ptosis, the deeper and more numerous the forehead rhytides. The action of the frontalis muscles can be assessed by having the patient direct the eyes forward. Massage the patient's forehead downward to relax the muscles. The contribution of the brow impingement into the orbital region can then be correctly assessed.

The conjunctiva and sclera should be clear and without evidence of inflammation or abnormalities. Check the patient's eyesight on gross examination. In the preoperative ophthalmic consultation, these areas will be evaluated in greater detail, and the physician will report the presence of any retinal disease or glaucoma.

Upper Eyelid Examination

The fullness of the upper eyelids is directly influenced by the brow. A major portion of upper eyelid ptosis may be entirely due to a ptotic brow impinging into the orbital socket. Unless the brow is lifted, ptosis will recur after blepharoplasty. Removal of the eyelid tissue allows the ptotic brow tissue to fall even further into the orbital socket, and it may be impossible to correct the ptotic brow after blepharoplasty. There may be inadequate orbital tissue remaining to lift the brow without producing lagophthalmos.

The upper lid should be examined for symmetry. Examine for levator muscle dehiscence with subsequent lid ptosis. The lid normally covers approximately 1 mm of the upper cornea with the eyes in the primary position. Deviation greater than 1 ml may suggest levator muscle malfunction. In addition, one can measure the vertical eyelid fissure opening. This is the distance from the lower eyelid margin to the upper eyelid margin at its greatest dimension. The greatest height of the eyelid fissure generally occurs on the nasal edge of the pupil. Normal vertical eyelid fissure for men is 7 to 10 mm and for women, 8 to 12 mm. Any deviation from normal requires further evaluation of levator muscle function. The standard blepharoplasty does not correct ptosis attributable to levator malfunction.

The presence of bulging medial and middle fat pads is to be noted. The lateral upper eyelid region may bulge as a result of a protruding orbital lobe of the lacrimal gland or occasionally because of the presence of a lateral fat pad. Lacrimal gland ptosis is corrected by retacking, not excision. Differentiation of lacrimal from adipose tissue is usually simple. Adipose tissue responds to electrocoagulation by retraction, unlike lacrimal gland tissue. Examine for lateral hooding. Correction requires extension of the upper eyelid excision onto the temporal skin. Sometimes the lateral upper eyelid tissue is heavy and thickened, lending to the exaggerated hooded appearance. Awareness enables the surgeon to carefully trim the subcutaneous tissue in this region, thus lending to a more satisfying cosmetic result. The temple incision heals more slowly and with more significant and prolonged erythema than the orbital excision. Upper eyelid skin tumors, such as xanthelasma or seborrheic keratosis, may require prior treatment.

Lower Eyelid Examination

The presence of scleral show, lid laxity, ectropion or entropion, pigmentation, fat protrusions, orbicularis oculi muscle hypertrophy, eyelid edema, and festoons or malar pouches should be recorded in detail. Lower eyelid hyperpigmentation responds to a chemical peel with either trichloroacetic acid or phenol. Orbital rim pouches, palpebral bags, malar pouch, or festoons may be the result of chronic pockets of edema resulting in fibrosis and recurrent edema. They cannot be corrected by blepharoplasty. Scleral show (vertical retraction of lower eyelids) may be present. It is commonly caused by a previous lower eyelid blepharoplasty.

Lower eyelid malposition is a serious complication of blepharoplasty; thus the integrity of the lower eyelid must be carefully evaluated before surgery. Eyelid laxity is usually the result of the lateral and/or medial canthal tendon stretching, as opposed to actual tarsal lengthening. The differential forces between the anterior (skin and orbicularis muscle) and posterior lamella (tarsus and eyelid retractors) determine whether an ectropion or entropion will occur. Horizontal lid laxity is evaluated by pulling the lower eyelid in a horizontal direction. Normal excursion is less than 8 mm (Fig. 1A and B). Abnormal excursion is a function of a redundant, stretched lower eyelid. Gentle flicking of the lower eyelid downward should result in a brisk ''snaps back'' of the lid to its original position against the globe. This should occur without a blink reflex. If blinking is necessary for the eyelid to obtain its normal position, laxity is present. These valuable, simple tests assess the function of the lower eyelid and help avoid complications.

Orbicularis oculi muscle hypertrophy of the lower eyelid is more prominent in younger patients. The ''muscle roll'' of the orbicularis oculi muscle is accentuated by face animation. However, it is a normal variant, and the patient must understand that blepharoplasty will not eliminate the roll. Careful trimming of the muscle without concomitant excision of the overlying skin can improve, but not necessarily eliminate, the extent of prominence.

ANATOMY OF THE EYE

The upper eyelid is divided into an orbital (preseptal) and a tarsal portion (Fig. 2). The orbital portion lies between the orbital rim and the superior border of the tarsus with the tarsal portion of the eyelid overlying the tarsal plate. The upper eyelid crease, or the superior palpebral fold, is located 8 to 11 mm above the eyelid margin and is formed by the attachment of the levator aponeurosis. Superior to the eyelid crease is the septal portion of the eyelid, which is composed

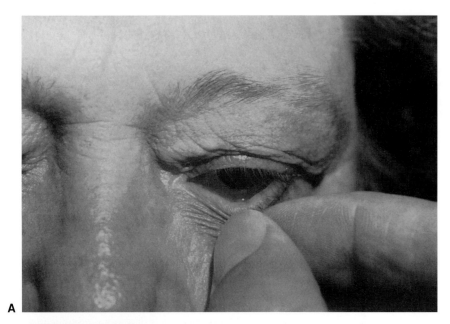

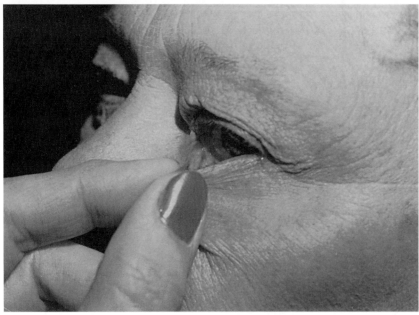

FIG. 1. (A and B) Examination for lower lid laxity. Normal excursion less than 8 mm.

of six major layers: orbicularis muscle, orbital septum, orbital fat, levator aponeurosis, Múller's muscle, and conjunctiva. The lower lid tarsus (4 to 5 mm at the central lid) is smaller than the upper lid tarsus (8 to 10 mm at the central lid).

ANESTHESIA

Local anesthesia in most cases is sufficient to perform blepharoplasty. Administer subcutaneously approximately 2 ml of a 2% lidocaine (Xylocaine) solution with 1:100,000 epinephrine via a 30-gauge needle. However, to ensure the patient's comfort, additional analgesia and sedation may be warranted. Mild sedation can be achieved by administering

sublingual diazepam, 10 to 20 mg, 30 minutes before local anesthesia. Intramuscular meperidine, 25 to 50 mg, and promethazine hydrochloride, 50 mg, along with intravenous diazepam, titrated slowly in increments of 2.5 mg to a total of 10 to 15 mg gives additional anesthesia for anxious patients without subjecting them to undue respiratory risk. Intravenous diazepam should be given slowly; subsequently the patient should be attended to at all times. Midazolam in titrated doses of 1 mg is also very effective but carries a greater risk of respiratory depression if administered too quickly or when given in conjunction with narcotics. Use of a pulse oximeter ensures that somnolent patients are not in respiratory distress.

It is not necessary to start an intravenous fluid line, as this is a relatively short operation with minimal risk of insen-

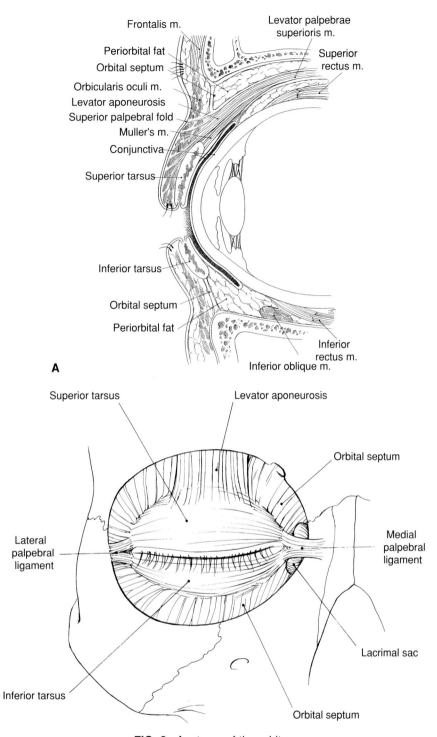

Frontalis m.

Levator palpebrae superioris m.

Periorbital fat

Orbital septum

Superior rectus m.

Orbicularis oculi m.

Levator aponeurosis

Superior palpebral fold

Muller's m.

Conjunctiva

Superior tarsus

Inferior tarsus

Orbital septum

Periorbital fat

Inferior rectus m.

Inferior oblique m.

A

Superior tarsus

Levator aponeurosis

Orbital septum

Lateral palpebral ligament

Medial palpebral ligament

Lacrimal sac

Inferior tarsus

Orbital septum

B

FIG. 2. Anatomy of the orbit.

sible fluid loss and dehydration. To minimize postoperative edema and enhance recovery time, 250 to 500 ml Ringer's solution containing 250 to 375 mg methylprednisolone (Solu-Medrol) is administered.

There is a choice of cleansing and antibacterial agents that are used to prepare the periorbital region. Ocular exposure to chlorhexidine (Hibiclens) can cause marked pain with severe conjunctival and corneal epithelial inflam-

mation. The corneal toxicity can progress to loss of corneal endothelial cells, corneal edema, and ultimately, corneal opacification. This may not be recognized when general anesthesia is administered. With a normal pain response in an alert patient, ocular exposure to chorhexidine immediately causes pain and blurred vision. Accidental exposure is treated with copious irrigation. Ophthalmic consultation may be prudent.

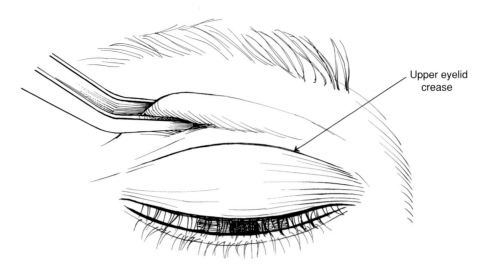

FIG. 3. Technique for measurement of upper eyelid skin laxity.

UPPER EYELID PROCEDURE

Crucial to an aesthetic upper lid blepharoplasty is a determination of the quantity of skin to be excised. This determination must be made before infiltration of the local anesthetic. An important landmark in an aesthetically pleasing upper eyelid blepharoplasty is the eyelid crease or supratarsal fold. A well-formed eyelid crease masks many imperfections. The upper-lid tarsal plate varies in width from 7 to 12 mm. The upper eyelid crease marks the transition and marks the superior edge where the levator aponeurosis attaches to the tarsal plate. The location of this crease is important, since it usually indicates where the inferior edge of the upper eyelid incision should be placed. A superiorly placed incision creating a higher eyelid crease may be more desirable in women.

The quantity of upper-eyelid redundant tissue to be removed can be estimated by careful observation (Fig. 3). Fine, redundant, crinkled skin can be observed above the eyelid crease within the superior palpebral fold. It is this fine, crinkled skin that is excessive and requires removal. Place the superior incision line where the fine skin meets the heavier skin of the orbit. To verify the incision line, grasp the upper lid tissue with plain forceps with the lower border established above the tarsal edge or eyelid crease. Increasing quantities of tissue are grasped until pinching of the skin barely pulls open the eyelid. Mark the tissue to establish the superior border of the incision. This is the maximal quantity of upper lid skin that can be removed safely. A conservative excisional blepharoplasty dictates less tissue removal. The widest portion of ellipse should be located just lateral to the pupil (Fig. 4).

An obtrusive sign of aging is the lateral hooding of the

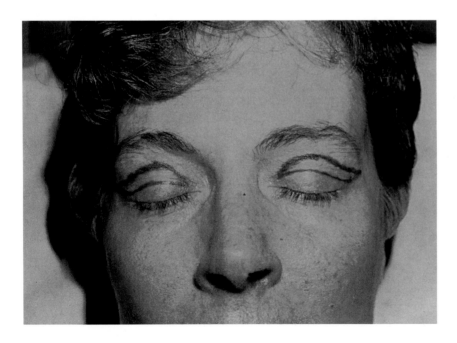

FIG. 4. Ink marking of incision lines for upper lid incision.

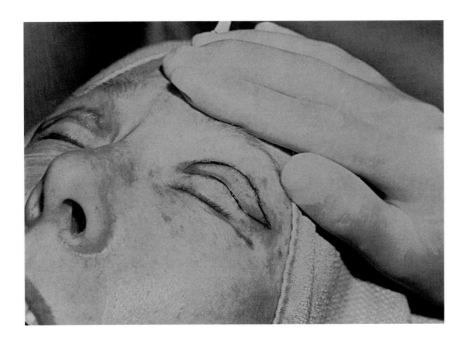

FIG. 5. Initial incision for upper lid surgery.

upper eyelids. Extending the lateral incision beyond the orbital rim onto the temporal facial skin can correct hooding that is not associated with brow ptosis. When hooding is not present, it is not necessary to extend the incision this far laterally. Do not place the incision low into a natural lateral crease. The incision must be higher, producing a horizontal rather than a S-shaped line. An incision placed too low pulls the lateral eyebrow and supraorbital skin downward. Furthermore, an incision too close to the lateral canthus interferes with lymphatic drainage and results in persistent upper eyelid edema. The more superior the final lateral incision closure, the greater the support expected from above it, and the more hooding eliminated. Healing required for the tem-

poral facial extension contrasts sharply with the minimal time required for healing of the eyelid skin. The lateral incision line may remain erythematous for weeks to months. The lateral eyelid is now free of hooding and wrinkling and is demarcated by a defined lateral eyelid sulcus. To aid in the creation of the eyelid rim sulcus, remove muscle from the center of lateral aspect of the incision.

The medial (nasal) incision markings should be rounded. This allows the skin to fall naturally into the defect created when the underlying fat pad and muscle are removed. End the incision before it reaches the nasal tissue to prevent the risk of webbing. Remove the skin and underlying muscle with small Metzenbaum scissors. Using a fine-tooth forceps,

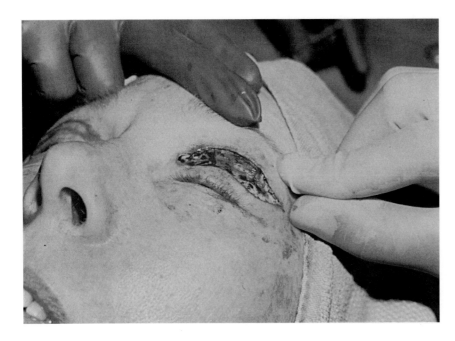

FIG. 6. Exposure of upper-lid fat pads after excision of skin, septum, and muscle.

any additional underlying muscularis in the middle of the incision is tented up and a narrow strip of orbicularis oculi muscle is removed. The amount of orbicularis muscle removed is 5 to 8 mm wide, but leave a 1- to 2-mm border above the superior edge of the tarsal plate (Fig. 5). This minimizes accidental injury to the underlying levator where it attaches to the tarsal plate. With removal of the orbicularis muscle, the underlying septum and the enclosed fat are now exposed (Fig. 6). Removal of a strip of the orbicularis muscle allows the skin to adhere to the underlying levator aponeurosis. This improves definition of the supratarsal sulcus and the lid crease, forming a natural-appearing eyelid. The male eyelid does not require the same quantity of skin and muscle tissue removal as the female eyelid. Overzealous removal

can feminize a male eye. Elderly patients may require only sufficient removal of eyelid tissue to eliminate obstruction of the upper and lateral visual fields. Achieve careful hemostasis before proceeding to fat removal.

Removal of the muscle exposes orbital fat and attenuated orbital septum and allows them to extrude through the opening in the muscle. Placing pressure on the eyelid bulges the septum forward and delineates the underlying fat. The upper lid has two fat compartments, the medial and the middle. Occasionally, a lateral fat pad is seen in the area of the superior lacrimal gland. Lacrimal gland tissue is identified as being paler and does not desiccate and shrink with electrocoagulation. A bulky lateral eyelid temporal region can be improved by excision of the subcutaneous muscle and fascia.

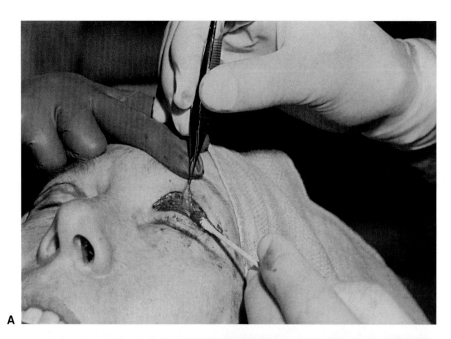

A

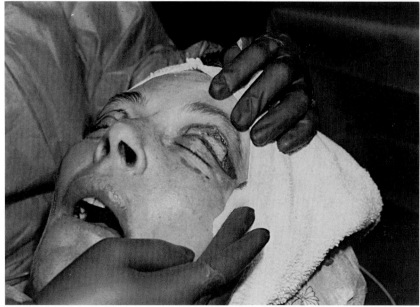

B

FIG. 7. Removal of upper-eyelid fat pad. **(A)** Grasping the fat lobule and gently separating it from the surrounding tissue with a cotton Q-tip. **(B)** The fat lobule, separated and loose, ready for removal.

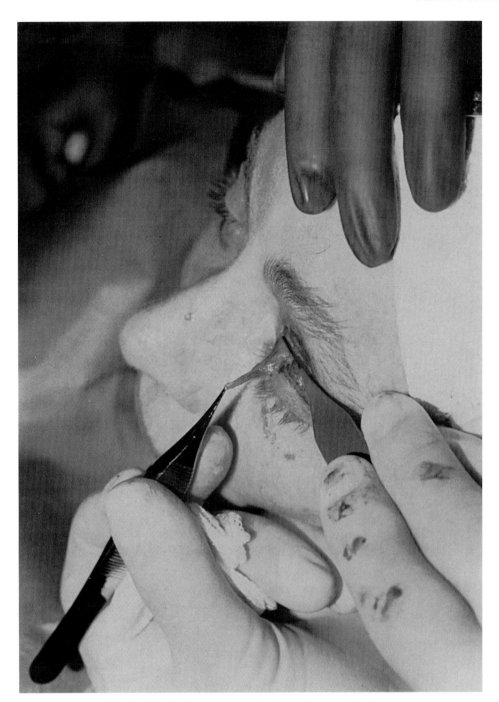

FIG. 8. Bipolar forceps cauterization at base of fat lobule.

Reduction in the fullness of the lateral orbital temporal skin lends to the cosmetic result.

Separate the orbital septum with blunt scissors to expose the middle fat lobules, and gently tease out the excess fat. Separate the fat from the surrounding tissue with the use of forceps and a cotton-tipped applicator (Fig. 7). Light pressure on the globe raises the fat pads upward, facilitating their removal. Using the bipolar forceps, the base of the fat lobule is crushed and then cauterized (Fig. 8). Excise the excess fat with scissors just superior to the line of cauterization.

Excessive removal of fat is to be avoided. Remember that errors of omission are correctable; errors of commission may not be. Now focus your attention on the medial fat lobules. The medial fat lobule often has a cap of membranous tissue that prevents forward movement. Gentle pressure on the globe causes the pad to protrude for easier identification. The membranous cap must be opened for the fat to extrude forward. The medial fat lobule is typically more whitish than the centrally located one. Examine the lateral upper eyelid compartment for fullness. Occasionally, there is a lateral

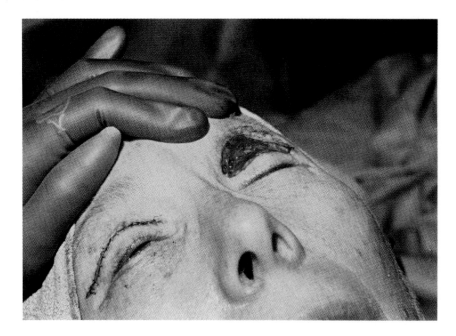

FIG. 9. Examination for uniform fat pad removal and hemostasis.

upper-eyelid fat pad. Distinguish this from the lacrimal gland, which has a similar appearance. Fat lobules, when touched with electrocautery, desiccate and shrink; the lacrimal gland tissue does not.

Examine the entire lid to ensure adequate, even fat removal, and ensure that complete hemostasis is obtained (Fig. 9).Although most bleeding is due to violation of the orbicularis muscle, complete hemostasis of the fat is mandatory. Neither the septum nor the orbicularis muscle is sutured closed. Begin your skin closure medially with either 6-0 or 7-0 silk (if no known allergy exists), interlocking the suture. Occasionally, over the middle of the incision an interrupted suture may be required to ensure complete apposition of the wound (Fig. 10). The conjunctival sac is now cleansed of all blood and debris with sterile eye-irrigating solution. An antibiotic ointment is placed within the sac, and a damp gauze sponge is placed over the eye (without pressure or taping) to absorb blood and to keep the wound moist, which promotes healing. It is not unusual to observe lagophthalmos of several millimeters on completion of the procedure. This is due to tissue edema from the local anesthetic and surgical trauma, not a result of excess tissue resection. The lagophthalmos disappears within several hours.

LOWER EYELID PROCEDURE

Draw a line from the puncta in a lateral direction to just beyond the lateral orbital rim. This line is placed within

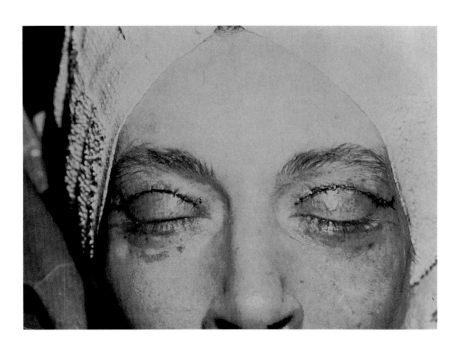

FIG. 10. Interlocking sutures of 6-0 or 7-0 silk in place.

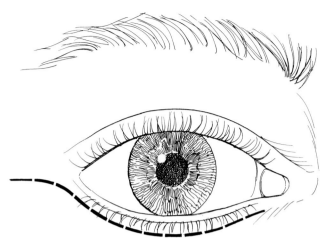

FIG. 11. Placement of lower lid incision.

the first natural skin crease below the eyelid margin. Locate the incision line approximately 2 to 3 mm below the eyelid margin. The lateral lower eyelid incision should arch upward before it reaches the lateral palpebral angle (Fig. 11). This places the incision higher on the orbital rim. Initially this makes the incision line obvious; however, the incision is in the eyelid area where dark eye-shadow makeup can be used for camouflage. The final scar also will not amplify an existing lateral orbital crease. The incision should not have a sharp vertical angulate, which can produce pouching at the angle of the eye.

Begin the scalpel incision superficially through the skin below the eyelid. Laterally the incision should extend deeper and lateral to the orbital rim to incise the underlying muscle (Fig. 12). This allows access into the correct tissue plane, which is below the orbital muscle and above the orbital septum. The tissue is raised laterally with forceps, and the subor-

bicularis muscle plane is located by tissue separation with blunt scissors. The skin-muscle flap is separated from the lower eyelid orbital septum by gently opening the scissor blades (Fig. 13). Curved scissors are used to complete the incision under the eyelid, separating the skin muscle flap from the lid margin. Place a suture through the lower lid margin and pull the lid up over the globe, exposing the underlying tissue while protecting the globe from injury (Fig. 14). Continue blunt dissection caudally to the infraorbital rim, completely elevating the skin-muscle flap. The flap can now be held down with the assistance of a dull multiprong retractor (Fig. 15).

Gently pressing on the globe pushes the fat forward so that it bulges out against the orbital septum (Fig. 16). The fat is then visually obvious, and this aids in further dissection. The orbital septum is opened, and the fat gently teased out (Fig. 17). Use blunt or fine-tooth forceps and a cotton-tipped applicator to gently separate the fat from the surrounding tissue. This technique minimizes trauma and bleeding. Once the fat is separated, inject it with a minute quantity of anesthetic (Fig. 18A). Coagulation of the lower-lid fat pads is often uncomfortable unless the fat is anesthetized. The base of the fat is cauterized with the bipolar forceps (Fig. 18B), and the cauterized stump is partially cut with scissors. Then recauterize the remaining portion of the stump with the bipolar coagulating forceps. This ensures that the blood vessels at the base of the fat are properly coagulated and will not bleed. Excise the fat completely.

The lower eyelid has three fat compartments: medial, middle, and lateral (Fig. 19). The middle pad is typically the most prominent and the most accessible. The medial fat compartment is not readily accessible if the incision is not extended far enough medially. Extending the incision aids discovery and removal of the medial fat pad. The lateral

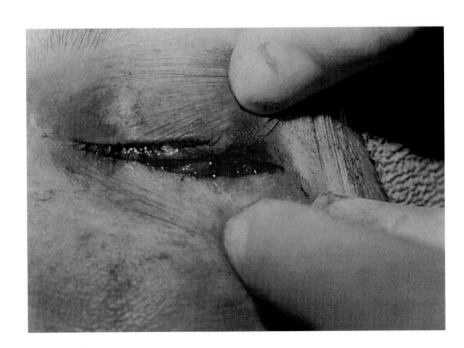

FIG. 12. Lateral lower-lid orbit incision. Deeper lateral extension is evident.

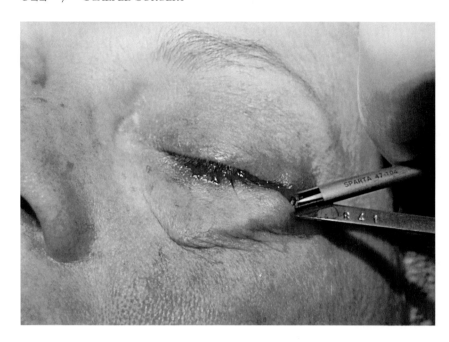

FIG. 13. Scissor separation of skin-muscle flap from lower eyelid septum.

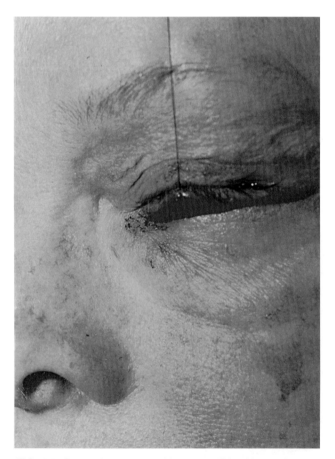

FIG. 14. Retraction suture of lower eyelid, with tension applied upward to protect the globe.

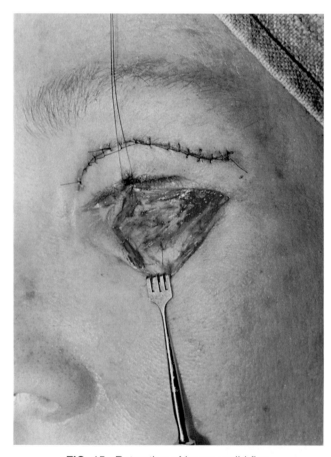

FIG. 15. Retraction of lower eyelid flap.

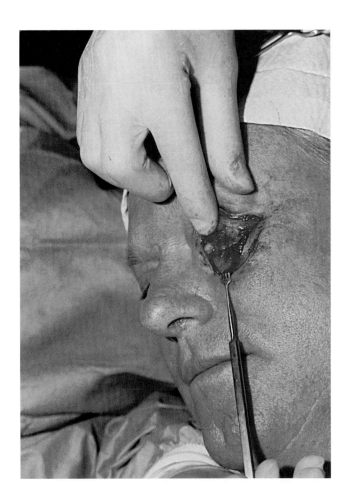

FIG. 16. Gentle pressure on globe allows lower medial fat pad to protrude.

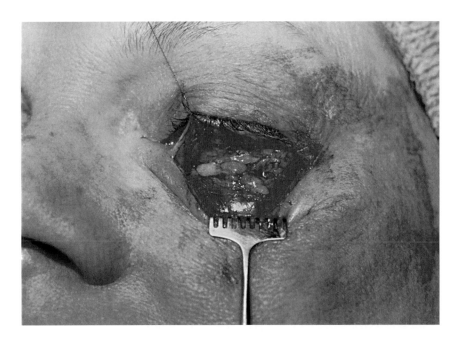

FIG. 17. Exposure of lower-eyelid fat pads.

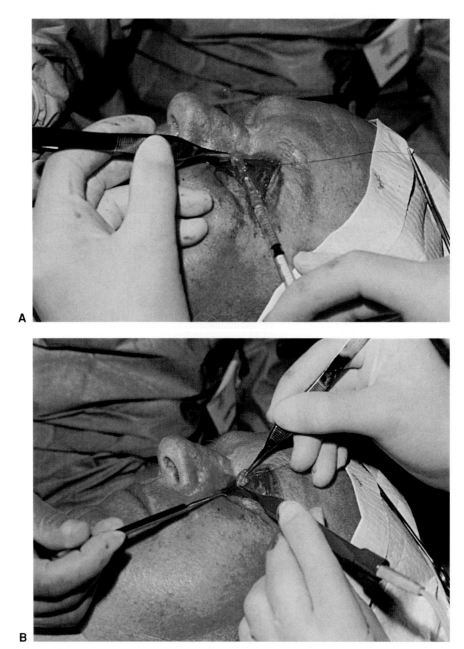

FIG. 18. (A and B) Exposure of lower-lid fat pad, reinjection at its base with local anesthetic, and cauterization of its base.

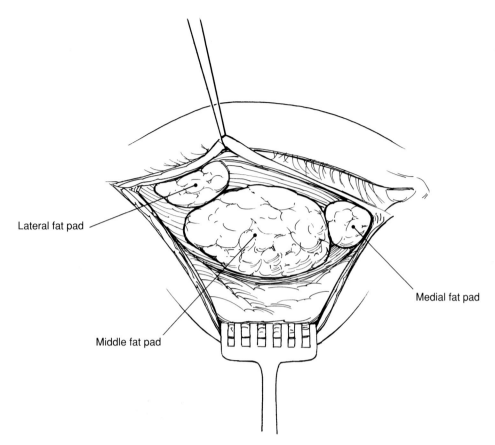

Lateral fat pad

Medial fat pad

Middle fat pad

FIG. 19. Anatomy of lower eyelid. Lower-eyelid fat compartments. The lateral fat pad is in a superior plane to the medial and middle fat pads.

compartment is located lateral and superior to the middle fat. Its superior position places it at a different level from the other two fat compartments and is the reason why the lateral compartment is often overlooked during surgery. Note the superficial vascular tissue that overlies this lateral fat compartment. In exposing the lateral fat, brisk bleeding often results. Complete hemostasis is mandatory to prevent persistent oozing or subsequent hemorrhage and hematoma. The quantity of fat removal from each side may differ because the amount of intraorbital fat is not related to body habitus, and right and left orbits in the same patient can demonstrate unequal amounts of fat.

Remove the fat, as previously described, and on completion of fat removal carefully examine the operative site for bleeding. The suture is then released, and the lid flap allowed to settle back onto the lower eyelid site. The skin-muscle flap is smoothed over the surgical site with the aid of a wet sponge, and the presence of any unusual protrusions is noted. A bulge implies the presence of excess fat, which requires additional removal. Another method of determining the presence of fat excess is by placing gentle pressure on the globe, which magnifies the orbital fat that is present. It is more common and easier to remove excessive fat from the upper eyelid than from the lower eyelid. The reason is that the eyeball settles downward when the patient stands up, producing a deeper upper eyelid sulcus.

Pull the skin muscle flap in a superior and lateral direction. (Fig. 20). With the flap draped lateral to the eye, trim off its excess. Inferior to the eye, minimal skin resection is performed to avoid unnecessary tension and the possibility of lower lid eversion. To accurately measure the quantity of flap to be resected, the patient should look superiorly toward the top of his or her head. With the patient's eyes focused in this direction, the surgeon can correctly determine the excess lower lid skin needed for removal. Most of the excess skin falls into the depression thus produced, reducing or even eliminating excess lower lid skin required for removal. This is especially likely to occur in a patient with marked fat protrusions. The skin falls into the cavity created by the removal of the bulging fat, thus reducing the excess skin. It is wiser to err on the side of excess skin remaining (often improved with a chemical peel) than to deal with an ectropion resulting from excessive skin removal.

Next, the skin-muscle flap lateral to the eye is split down to the approximate line of the original lower lid excision. The split extends to the orbital bone (Fig. 21), and the excess skin of the lateral portion of the split flap is removed (Fig. 22). Attention is then turned to the lateral bony orbital ridge. In the area of the excised flap, open a small pocket (using sharp scissors) through deep tissue to expose the underlying periosteum of the orbital bone. This pocket is made at a point superior to the line of excision, enabling the tissue to

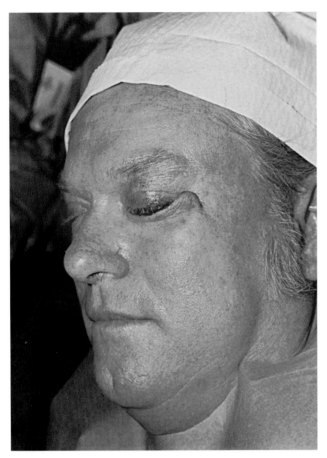

FIG. 20. Measurement of skin-muscle fat pad for excision.

be supported in an upward and outward direction (Fig. 23A). The suturing minimizes sagging, the risk of ectropion, and formation of the "round eye." A 6-0 permanent suture is used to attach the muscle of the skin-muscle flap to the lateral orbital bone periosteum (Fig. 23B). The suture is buried within this pocket (Fig. 24). Placement of the buried suture is critical. It must pull the skin flap in a superior and lateral direction without puckering the surface. Attachment to the periosteum anchors the suture securely, maintaining the flap position and preventing its drift inferiorly.

With several interrupted sutures, secure the position of the lateral eyelid skin. A running 6-0 silk, loosely sutured, closes the lower eyelid (Fig. 25). Wet sponges are applied without pressure or tape, supplying moisture to the wound while absorbing blood oozing from the superficial tissues.

POSTOPERATIVE MANAGEMENT

Absolute rest is mandatory for the first 24 to 48 hours. The risk of retrobulbar hematoma and blindness is greatest within the first few hours. The head is elevated during the first 48 hours to minimize periorbital edema. The patient should avoid all activity that involves straining or that can elevate the blood pressure. This helps minimize both edema and bruising and in turn shortens recovery. A responsible individual should be present to provide for all patient needs during this period. During this period patients may experience soreness, but pain, especially of the eyeball, requires immediate investigation, since it is a symptom of retrobulbar hemorrhaging. Acetaminophen (Tylenol) is usually adequate for the soreness, although most patients appreciate a mild narcotic such as acetaminophen with codeine phosphate (Tylenol with Codeine) or propoxyphene hydrocholoride (Darvocet) during the first postoperative night.

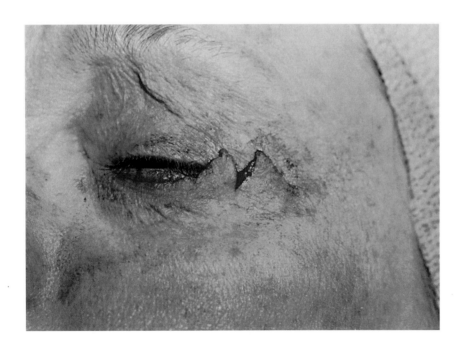

FIG. 21. Vertical incision of flap to a level at the original lower lid excision.

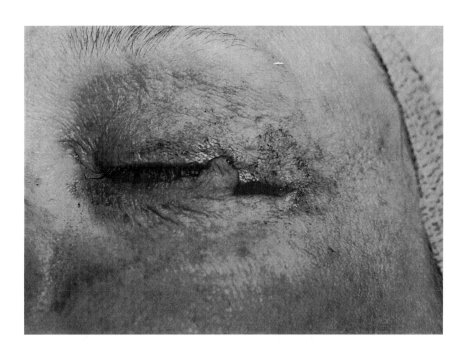

FIG. 22. Trimmed portion of laterally split flap.

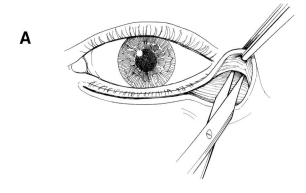

A

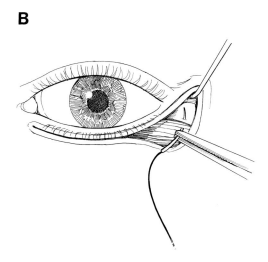

B

FIG. 23. (A and B) Identifying and securing the obicularis muscle to orbital periosteum. Create a pocket through the tissues to expose the periosteum of the orbital bone. The pocket is superior to the excision line. Suturing here allows the flap to be pulled up and outward.

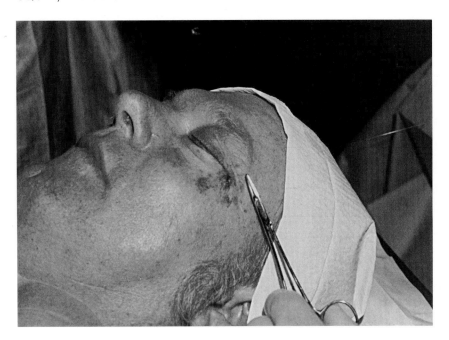

FIG. 24. Final position of periosteal, tacked skin flap. Flap should be suspended in an upward and outward direction.

Cool, wet gauze sponges are applied to the orbital region to absorb oozing of blood and facilitate healing. They should be placed on the eyes without pressure or taping. Some patients use a bag of frozen peas to help minimize swelling. An ophthalmic antibiotic ointment (erythromycin ophthalmic ointment) is applied to the conjunctiva to prevent corneal abrasions while the patient is sleeping. Lagophthalmos is common during the first several days after the surgery, and the exposed cornea can be injured if not protected with ointment. This short-lived lagophthalmos is due to temporary muscle weakness resulting from the anesthetic and surgical trauma. Sutures are removed on the third or fourth postoperative day. The incidence of sutures tracks and milia formation increases if the sutures remain longer.

Patient activity should be limited for the next 5 to 7 days. During this time the patient may be up but should avoid all bending, straining, and physical exertion. After 1 week the patient may return to normal activities, and after 2 weeks of normal healing the patient may partake in strenuous activities (aerobics, lifting, running). Resuming full, strenuous activities prematurely can exacerbate periorbital edema and delay full recovery. A conservative approach to activities based on the patient's individual recovery limits surgical sequelae and complications (Fig. 26A and B)

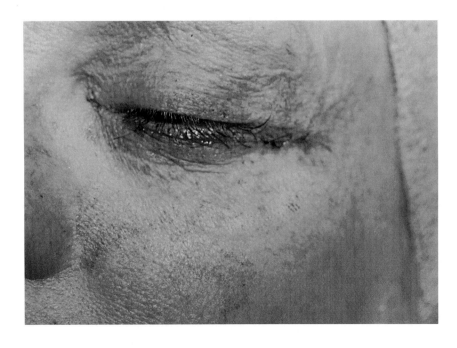

FIG. 25. Final appearance of sutured lower lid.

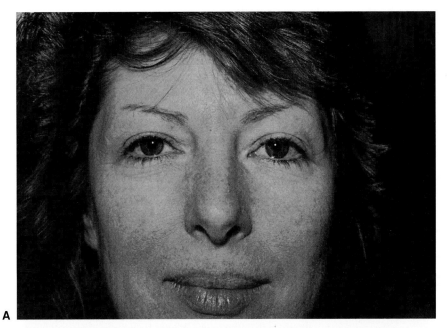

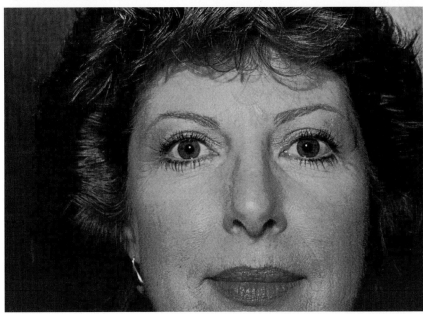

FIG. 26. Postoperative appearance after lower and upper lid blepharoplasty **(A)** without and **(B)** with makeup.

ADVERSE SEQUELAE

Adverse sequelae are normal occurrences after surgery. Normally they are little more than the annoying injuries expected from surgery. They may, however, require care to prevent progression to complications. Some of these sequelae can be disturbing to the patient who is uneducated in such normally expected events. Bleeding from the suture line is typical for the first few hours, and cool, wet compresses soothe the wound and absorb the leakage, minimizing edema, ecchymoses, and bruising. The ensuing bruising is expected and reaches its zenith between the second and fourth days. It resolves sufficiently within 2 weeks to be unobtrusive. Many patients have only a greenish-yellow hue

over their cheeks after the first week. Some discomfort and soreness are normal for the first few days. Acetaminophen or a non–aspirin-containing codeine compound is adequate for comfort. Pain is unusual and must be investigated, since eye pain is a sign of retrobulbar hematoma.

Blurring of vision and dryness of the eyes are common. They are due to surgical "widening of the eyes" with exposure to the elements. The blink reflex and corneal tear film are inadequate until the eyes readjust with an increased blinking periodicity. The precorneal tear film is normally quite unstable. It relies both on effective eyelid closure and on an adequate blink rate to remain protective. If blinking is prevented or markedly decreased in frequency, observable areas of desiccation can appear on the corneal surface. These can predispose to more corneal desiccation and eventually result in epithelial damage. Lagophthalmos attributable to muscle trauma and local anesthetics compounds this problem. Blinking the eyes several times rapidly when either visual blurring or grittiness (dryness) is experienced restores the tear film and reeducates the blinking reflex to a new periodicity. Ophthalmic antibiotic ointment is applied into the conjunctival sac for lubrication before sleeping during the first week. This prevents corneal dryness during sleep, when the blink reflex is diminished and lid closure is defective. This dryness resolves within weeks when a new frequency of blink reflex is established. Reading is difficult during the first few days because of a dry tear film and the ophthalmic antibiotic ointment applied to the conjunctiva sac.

Epiphora (excessive tearing) can be present in the immediate postoperative period. Most tears are lost through evaporation, and the remainder drained through the lacrimal system. After surgery the lower puncta and canaliculi may be obstructed by edema and inflammation, resulting in excessive tearing that is transient.

Edema can be generalized facial edema or localized edema of the lower eyelids and cheeks. During sleep the orbital socket is in a dependent position; thus edema is usually worse on awakening. The edema can be severe enough to close the eyes or it can also be localized, asymmetric, and exasperatingly slow to resolve. Edema of the lower lid can cling along the incision line, be asymmetric, and remain for weeks or, rarely, for months. A portion of the entire lower lid can be involved and be significantly dissimilar to the other lower lid for months. Blepharoplasty can also induce malar edema that can persist for weeks to months. The patient may perceive its presence as permanent: reassurance is necessary. Since the edema usually spontaneously resolves, any treatment should be delayed for several months. The extent and severity of edema are related to excessive electrocoagulation and skin-muscle flap dissection. Edema is more common with a lower lid belpharoplasty.

Premature treatment of an edematous area can result in too rapid a correction. This will render other normally healing areas more noticeably edematous and asymmetric and result in additional patient complaints. Uncommonly, the swellings can last for months and be very distressing. Swelling may be caused by a small hematoma that resolves with residual fibrosis. Injection of a dilute corticosteroid (triamcinolone [Kenalog R 10] diluted to a 10% solution) into the site of edema hastens resolution. Extreme care should be taken to limit the strength of the solution and the interval between injections to avoid unnecessary and permanent subcutaneous atrophy.

Several frightening events can occur postoperatively. The conjunctiva of one or both eyes may become suffused with bright red blood. This resolves without complication within 1 to 2 weeks without residual. Chemosis, excessive edema of the ocular conjunctiva with actual bulging of the tissue over the lower lid, may persist for several weeks. It may be due to irritation from residual debris such as from gauze or a cotton-tipped applicator. Antibiotic ophthalmic ointment in conjunction with cortisporin ophthalmic ointment applied three times daily hastens resolution.

COMPLICATIONS

Complications can be classified as minor or major. Minor complications resolve without inordinate morbidity or permanent impairment, but major complications are usually associated with considerable patient morbidity and can result in permanent impairment. Anesthetic complications are not discussed but can also be a source of major complications.

Minor Complications

Suture removal on the third or fourth day can occasionally lead to partial dehiscence. Dehiscence may be caused by the presence of a small wound hematoma, excessive tension laterally, or trauma. Treatment is simple. The dehiscence is closed with Steri-Strips, or the wound is allowed to granulate. Milia formation is common and more likely if sutures are not removed within 4 days. Milia be simply expressed by incision with a No. 11 blade.

Carelessly left debris, coagulated blood, and thread strands from sponges and cotton-tipped applicators can irritate the conjunctiva. This can cause hypertrophic changes laterally within the sac. Thorough cleansing of all debris during and after surgery is preventive. Conjunctival irritation responds to the application of a topical ophthalmic antibiotic and corticosteroid.

Surgical omissions are not uncommon in this exacting surgical procedure. A millimeter or two of difference in the upper lid can be noticeable to the discerning patient. Correction should be delayed until upper lid edema has resolved. Incomplete fat removal or a missed fat pad is commonly seen with upper- and lower-lid medial pads and the lateral lower-lid pad. A wide stab wound over the offending fat pad leaves a small, inconspicuous scar. The fat pad should be carefully marked before anesthetic infiltration, which can obscure the offending bulging fat.

Major Complications

Retrobulbar Hematoma and Blindness

The most serious complication of blepharoplasty, blindness, is rare. Whatever the cause, the ultimate event leading to permanently impaired vision is ischemia. Pressure from the ensuing hematoma causes progressive ischemia of the optic nerve and vessels. The incidence is higher with surgery of the lower lid, but the complication has also been reported with isolated upper lid surgery. Retrobulbar hematoma is the feature that is common to most cases of visual loss.

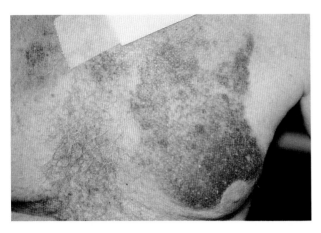 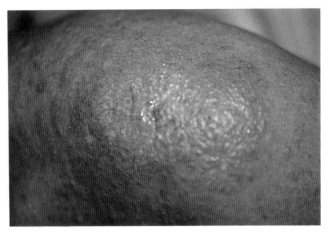

COLOR PLATE 1. (Left) Postoperative ecchymosis of the chest attributable to aspirin use. (See Fig. 1 on p. 61.) **(Right)** Contact dermatitis from topical antibiotic. (See Fig. 13 on p. 70.)

 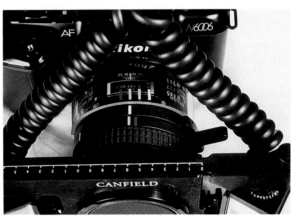

COLOR PLATE 2. The color coding of the photographic system for dermatologists makes it easy to determine which views to take. (See Figs. 22B and 22C on p. 91.)

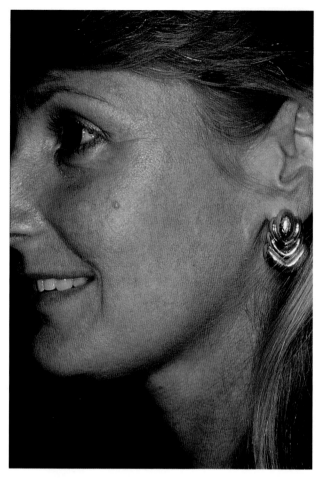

COLOR PLATE 3. Diffuse small-diameter telangiectases of the face. (See Fig. 1 on p. 350.)

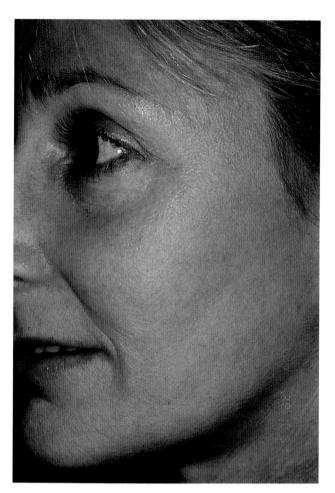

COLOR PLATE 4. Postoperative view after three treatments with the Photoderm filtered, flashlamp-pumped light source at an energy of 30 J/cm^2, filter of 515 nanometers and pulse width of 3.5 msec. (See Fig. 2 on p. 351.)

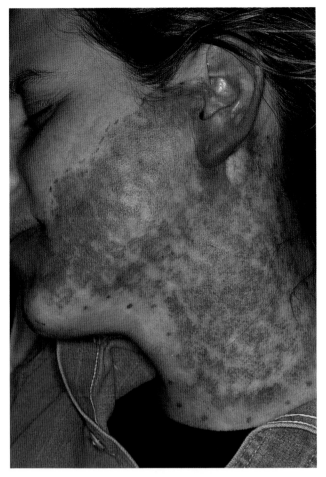

COLOR PLATE 5. Purpura over treated area following treatment with pulsed-dye laser (PDL). (See Fig. 3 on p. 351.)

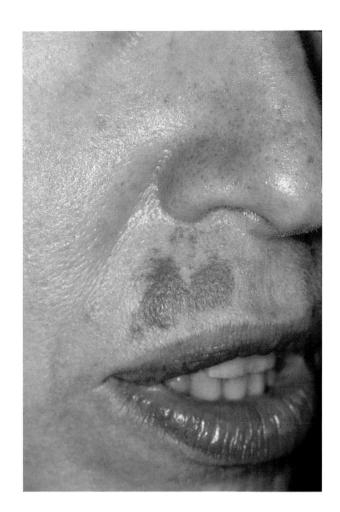

COLOR PLATE 6. Port wine stain of the upper lip. (See Fig. 4 on p. 353.)

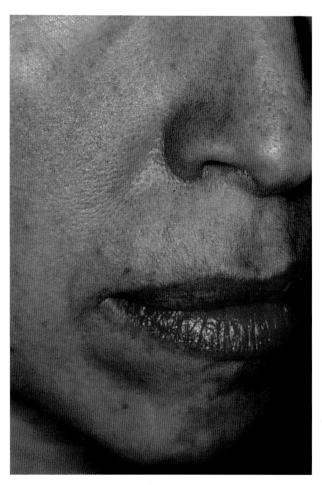

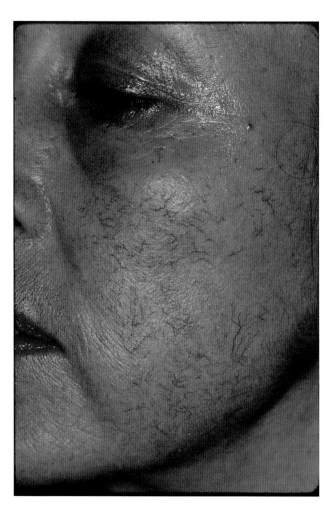

COLOR PLATE 7. Postoperative view after PDL photocoagulation of an upper-lip port wine stain. Five treatments were required at an energy of 7.25 J/cm^2 and a spot size of 5.0 mm. (See Fig. 5 on p. 354.)

COLOR PLATE 8. Diffuse, medium diameter telangiectases of the cheeks. (See Fig. 6 on p. 354.)

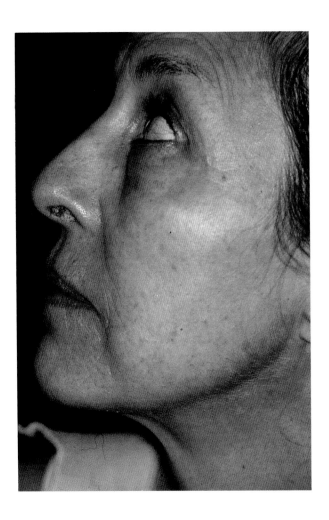

COLOR PLATE 9. Postoperative view after two treatments with the PDL using an elliptic spot size at 6.75 J/cm^2. (See Fig. 7 on p. 355.)

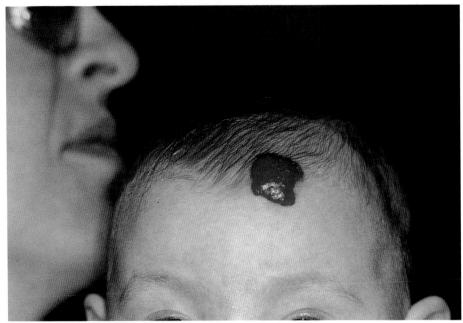

COLOR PLATE 10. Four-month-old child with a superficial but thick hemangioma. (See Fig. 8 on p. 355.)

COLOR PLATE 11. Postoperative photograph of the same child as in Color Plate 10 at eight months of age after four treatments with the PDL using a 5-mm spot size at 8 J/cm^2. (See Fig. 9 on p. 355.)

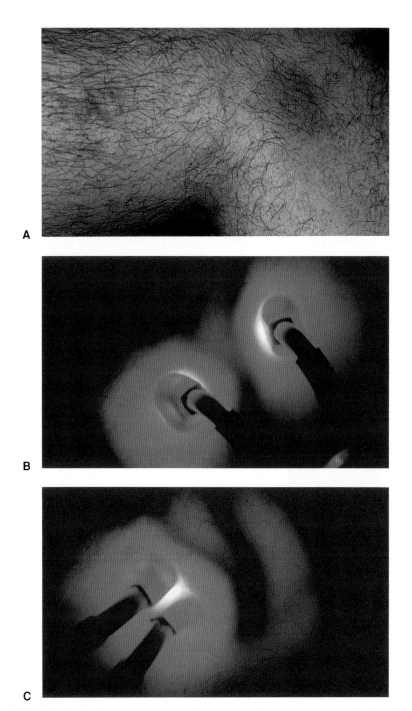

COLOR PLATE 12A–C. A. Normal view of medial aspect of leg at knee level. Varicosities are difficult to see. **B.** Venoscope transillumination shows varicosity as a black shadow. **C.** When skin is elevated by pinching and transillumination is provided from the side, more detail is visible. The reticular varicosity is looping back on itself. (See Figs. 7A–C on p. 589.)

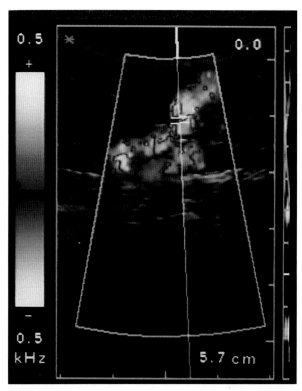

COLOR PLATE 13. Duplex ultrasound of the insufficient DPP. (See Fig. 27B on p. 605.)

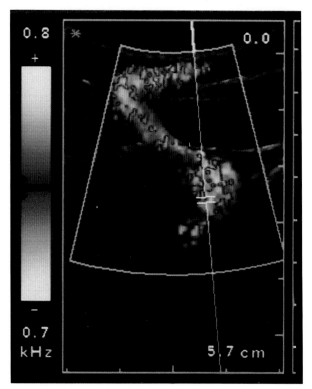

COLOR PLATE 14. Duplex ultrasound image of the Hach profound perforating vein varicosis. (See Fig. 41C on p. 613.)

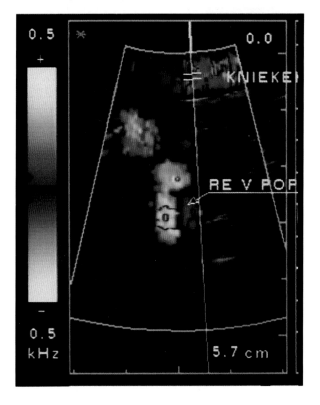

COLOR PLATE 15. Duplex ultrasound image of the PPV varicosis clinical picture. (See Fig. 42B1 on p. 613.)

Needle injection trauma, rough handling of the intraorbital fat, blood vessel spasm from trauma or vasopressor agents (epinephrine injected into a blood vessel), and exacerbating factors such as uncontrolled hypertension and coagulation disorders caused by medications have also been sited as the causes of retrobulbar hematoma.

The appearance of proptosis, eye pain, and/or visual disturbances is evidence of increased pressure and a developing retrobulbar hematoma. Immediate decompression of the orbital septum by removal of sutures, a reopening of the wound, and pinpoint coagulation of any bleeders is paramount. This halts further progression of symptoms and prevents visual loss. Delay in doing this can be disastrous. Ophthalmic consultation is imperative if symptoms are not immediately ameliorated or if there is progression of visual symptoms. The patient's head should be elevated, and some authors advocate the use of steroids to minimize edema.

The most important factor in preventing retrobulbar hemorrhage and blindness, besides the elimination of medical causes, is the careful handling of intraorbital fat. Most cases of retrobulbar hematoma rarely lead to blindness. Bleeding with the threat of retrobulbar hematoma has its highest incidence within the first few hours after the surgery. The surgeon must be within instant communication range of and in close proximity to the surgical operatory to prevent this potential disaster. Postoperatively the incidence of this severe complication exponentially decreases after several hours.

Ectropion and Lid Retraction

Ectropion can be temporary or permanent, and its severity ranges from mild lower lid retraction to frank ectropion with marked, symptomatic, lower lid retraction. Causes include failure to correct a preexisting eyelid laxity, excessive lower lid skin removal, and anatomic factors such as proptosis and exophthalmus. The most common cause of ectropion following lower lid blepharoplasty is an inadequate preoperative evaluation. Failure to recognize preoperative problems can result in a permanent ectropion requiring further surgical intervention.

There are remediable causes of ectropion that can spontaneously resolve. These include wound edema, dystonic orbicularis oculi muscle function (from the anesthetic and muscle trauma), scar contracture, adhesions of the orbital septum, and hematoma. Good postoperative wound care, massage of the lower eyelid, supporting the lower eyelid by taping, and injection of intralesional steroids into the site of edema and scar often alleviate or markedly improve the lid laxity. Ectropion that has not improved within 6 months requires repair. Persistent ectropion requires either a lid-shortening procedure (lateral lid tendon laxity) or a skin graft (excessive skin removal). Ectropion attributable to medial tendon laxity is a more difficult problem, usually requiring the assistance of an ophthalmic plastic surgeon.

Ptosis

Ptosis can be due to edema and the anesthetic effects on the ocular muscle. It is common in the first few postoperative hours. Temporary ptosis can rarely persist for several days and be quite worrisome. Unrecognized preoperative ptosis attributable to levator aponeurosis dehiscence is a serious problem. Ptsosis can also be the direct result of careless surgery. Patients who use contact lenses are predisposed to levator aponeurosis dehiscence. Minimal dehiscence can progress as a result of edema, hematoma, or excess cautery to frank ptosis. Repair of the dehiscent levator is difficult.

Lagophthalmos

Skin excisions from the upper eyelids can be quite generous without producing lagophthalmos. Excessive skin removal, usually in an attempt to achieve the perfect blepharoplasty, can result in lagophthalmos. Permanent lagophthalmos is uncommon and can lead to corneal drying and ulceration. Treatment requires replacement of the upper lid skin via grafting. Temporary lagophthalmos is not unusual in the first 12 hours as a result of tissue edema and the anesthetic.

CONCLUSION

Classical blepharoplasty of the upper and lower lids are two markedly different procedures. Whereas upper lid blepharoplasty failure is usually due to errors of inadequate tissue removal, either from the lid itself or the brow, the lower lid blepharoplasty is fraught with complications of excessive tissue removal.

The physician must differentiate redundancy of the upper lid from that due to brow ptosis. Failure to properly evaluate both upper lid and brow in conjunction will result in inadequate and possibly uncorrectable results. Performing upper lid surgery in the face of a ptotic brow will result in the ptotic brow sagging lower onto the lid. The compromised upper visual fields are exacerbated, and correction may not be possible because too little of the upper eyelid remains to lift the brow without a complicating lid lag and corneal exposure. The only solution would be the placement of skin grafts to increase the volume of the upper lids. This is not an easy solution as there is no donor tissue readily available that is of comparable thinness to eyelid skin.

It is too easy for the insouciant surgeon to remove excessive skin from the lower lid while the patient is in a recumbent position and the eyes resting in an inferior direction. It is wiser to err by removing inadequate tissue. Of course, if the surgeon failed to notice lid lag or excessive lid excursion prior to the procedure, even this precaution may not prevent ectropion. A simple lid wedge excision will usually correct an ectropion that is based on lateral canthal relaxation. Medial canthal relaxation is more difficult to correct and, when present, the author does not perform blepharoplasty, instead referring these patients to another specialist.

Lastly, a good preoperative examination of the eyelids, brows, and visual eyesight, as well as a search for evidence of thyroid disease, will delineate practically all the complicating problems associated with blepharoplasty. All that remains is to perform the surgical procedure and eliminate the precise quantity of excessive fat and skin present, a task that can be daunting even to the most skilled of surgeons.

SUGGESTED READING LIST

1. Adams B, Feurstein S. Complications of blepharoplasty. Ear Nose Throat J 1986;5:11.
2. Asken S. Cosmetic eyelid surgery: blepharoplasty. In: Coleman WP et al., eds. Cosmetic surgery of the skin. Philadelphia: DC Decker, 1991:335.
3. Doxanas MT, Anderson RL. Blepharoplasty: key anatomical concepts. Facial Plast Surg 1984;1(4):259.
4. Foster CA, Aston SJ. Propranolol-epinephrine interaction: a potential disaster. Plast Reconstr Surg 1983;72:74.
5. Gradinger GP. Preoperative considerations in blepharoplasty. In: Kaye BL, Gradinger GP, eds. Symposium on problems and complications in aesthetic plastic surgery of the face. Vol. 23. St Louis, MO: Mosby, 1984:195.
6. Mahaffey PJ, Wallace AF. Blindness following cosmetic blepharoplasty: a review. Br J Plast Surg 1986;39:213.
7. McGraw BL, Adamson PA. Postblepharoplasty ectropion. Arch Otolaryngol Head Neck Surg 1991;117:852.
8. McKinney P, Zukowski ML. The value of tear film breakup and Schrimer's tests in preoperative blepharoplasty evaluation. Plast Reconstr Surg 1989;84:572.
9. Mladick RA. The muscle-suspension lower blepharoplasty. Plast Reconstr Surg 1979;64:171.
10. Owsley JQ. Resection of the prominent lateral fat pad during upper lid blepharoplasty. Plast Reconstr Surg 1980;65:4.
11. Pastorek N. New ideas in upper blepharoplasty. Facial Plast Surg 1984; 1(4):268.
12. Rees TD. Prevention of ectropion by horizontal shortening of the lower lid during blepharoplasty. Ann Plast Surg 1983;11(1):17.
13. Shagets FW, Shore JW. The management of eyelid laxity during lower eyelid blepharoplasty. Arch Otolaryngol Head Neck Surg 1986;112:729.
14. Small RG. Extended lower eyelid blepharoplasty. Arch Ophthalmol 1981;99:1402.
15. Wolfley DE, Guibor P. Preoperative evaluation of the blepharoplasty patient. Facial Plast Surg 1984;1(4):284.
16. Zide BM. Anatomy of the eyelids. Clin Plast Surg 1981;8(4):623.

SECTION III

Laser Surgery

Textbook of Dermatologic Surgery, edited by John L. Ratz.
Lippincott–Raven Publishers, Philadelphia © 1998.

CHAPTER 19

Introduction to Laser Surgery

George J. Hruza

Lasers have become an essential tool for dermatologic surgeons. Conditions that until very recently could not be successfully treated with an acceptable risk-benefit ratio can now be easily treated in the office setting by using one of an ever-expanding array of lasers. Lasers have become the treatment of choice for port wine stains, other vascular skin lesions, benign pigmented lesions, tattoos, actinic cheilitis, scars, unwanted hair, and fine to moderate rhytides. Additional indications are rapidly being added as laser technology and our understanding of laser tissue interaction advance.

HISTORY

The theoretical concept of laser light production was first proposed by Albert Einstein in 1916. It took almost 40 years for technology to catch up with theory in the development of an ammonia gas maser (microwave amplification by stimulated emission of radiation) by Townes and Gordon in 1954. The first functional laser (light amplification by stimulated emission of radiation) system was a ruby laser developed by Maiman in 1960. The first laser to be used in humans was a ruby laser studied by Leon Goldman, a dermatologist,

in the early 1960s. He tested the laser on normal skin and on benign and malignant lesions. He made many insightful observations on specific laser effects on epidermal skin components. The most encouraging results were obtained in the treatment of tattoos with the pulsed ruby laser. The tattoos faded with minimal risk of scarring. However, while the Q-switched ruby laser has been used for treatment of tattoos in Scotland since the early 1980s, it has been approved for tattoo treatment in the United States only since 1990.

Lasers became widely used in dermatology in the 1970s with the development of the carbon dioxide (CO_2) and argon lasers. Carbon dioxide laser light with a wavelength of 10,600 nm was useful for nonspecific tissue vaporization and bloodless excision because of its strong absorption by water, but the results were less than optimal because of extensive, unwanted peripheral thermal coagulation that increased the risk of scarring. Argon laser light with wavelengths of 488 and 514 nm was used for the treatment of vascular lesions because of its relatively strong hemoglobin absorption, but the results were also limited by unwanted peripheral thermal coagulation, with 4% to 15% incidence of scarring reported in the treatment of port wine stains.

The breakthrough for lasers in dermatology came in the early 1980s with the proposal by Anderson and Parrish of the theory of selective photothermolysis. This theory states that selective tissue injury can be produced by laser light of the appropriate wavelength and pulse duration. A yellow-

George J. Hruza: Departments of Medicine (Dermatology Surgery), Otolaryngology, and Surgery, Washington University School of Medicine, St. Louis, MO 63110.

light, pulsed-dye laser was developed for the treatment of port wine stains based on the selective photothermolysis model. This was the first laser to be developed with a specific indication in mind rather than building a laser first and then trying it out on various lesions until a practical use is found, as was the case with the ruby, argon, and CO_2 lasers. Selective photothermolysis has increased our understanding of laser light–tissue interactions and has resulted in the development of numerous additional lasers, as well as the revival of the Q-switched ruby laser, for the selective treatment of vascular lesions, pigmented lesions, tattoos, unwanted hair, rhytides, and scars. Lasers in dermatology have developed from being a relatively nonselective ''blowtorch'' to a precise surgical instrument that can selectively destroy cells and even intracellular structures while preserving the surrounding tissue.

LASER LIGHT PROPERTIES

''*Light amplification by stimulated emission of radiation*'' describes the mechanism by which a laser produces tremendously bright light and is made possible by quantum mechanics of matter. Atoms are composed of a nucleus with electrons orbiting around it. The electrons are usually in an orbit as close as possible to the nucleus, which is their ''resting'' or ground state. If an electron absorbs a photon of light, it moves into a higher, more energetic orbit that matches the energy absorbed from the photon. This more energetic or ''excited'' state is relatively unstable, and the electron falls back down spontaneously to its resting state orbit while emitting a photon of light with the same energy that it had originally absorbed, thus maintaining energy conservation. This process represents spontaneous emission of radiation and is seen in fluorescence and phosphorescence phenomena.

Stimulated emission of radiation occurs when an electron already in an excited state absorbs a photon of light and emits *two* photons of light while returning to the resting-state orbit. The emitted photons match the absorbed photon in wavelength, phase, and direction. The electron was originally raised to an excited state by pumping energy into the laser cavity. The energy for emission of the two photons comes from the difference in energy between the excited and resting states of the electron plus the energy of the photon that the electron just absorbed. This maintains energy conservation while doubling the number of photons in the laser cavity. This process is repeated many times in the laser cavity to create a very bright laser beam. Normally the population of electrons is such that most of the electrons reside in the resting state. When the majority of electrons in the laser cavity are raised to higher orbits by absorbing energy, the population is said to be inverted. The process of stimulated emission does not produce a very efficient or even noticeable amplification unless a population inversion occurs.

Stimulated emission of radiation creates light that not only is very bright but also has several unique properties. The most important for selective lesion treatment is laser light *monochromaticity*. All of the light is of a single, discrete wavelength or, more precisely, the light is of a narrow wavelength band in a gaussian distribution around the characteristic wavelength of the laser. The wavelength is determined solely by the laser medium, such as a ruby rod, that is present in the optical cavity (Fig. 1). Some lasers have more than one characteristic wavelength, such as the argon laser with wavelengths of 488 and 514 nm. This occurs because when an electron is returning to a resting state from an excited state, it may release photons (energy) in individual steps as it drops to intermediate excited states before returning completely back down to the resting state.

Laser light is *temporally and spatially coherent* (Fig. 2). That is, the light waves are in phase both in time and space. Light can be thought of as sinusoidal waves of energy. These waves are perfectly aligned in laser light so that each peak exactly matches both in time and space and each trough likewise matches up with every trough. Coherence is similar to that of soldiers marching in a parade. They are lined up in perfect rows and marching in the same direction for spatial coherence, and they step forward with the same foot at any

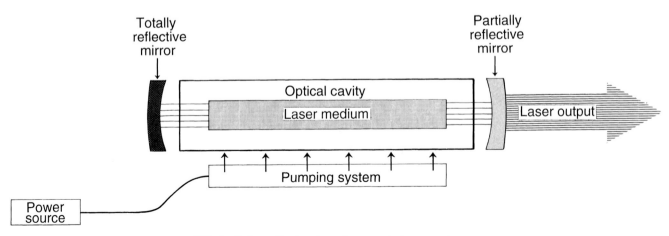

FIG. 1. Schematic drawing of a generic laser system.

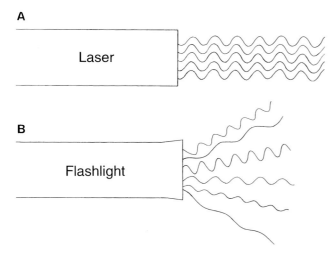

FIG. 2. Comparison of **(A)** spacially and temporally coherent, collimated and monochromatic laser light with **(B)** incoherent and divergent white light from a normal light source.

given time for temporal coherence. This property is important for beam handling, shaping, focusing, and coupling into optical fibers.

Laser light waves are *collimated* or exactly parallel with each other (Fig. 3). This is a direct result of temporal and spatial coherence. This highly ordered pattern of light allows the beam to be propagated across long distances along optical fibers without beam spreading or loss of energy. A collimated laser beam has the same spot size, no matter how far away or close to the skin one holds the laser handpiece. Thus the effect on tissue does not change, whether the handpiece is near or far from the skin. This property has been exploited in one of the CO_2 lasers used for skin resurfacing, in which a collimated laser handpiece is used to reduce operator error. as an alternative, the beam can be focused into a small spot, as seen with the CO_2 laser when it is used as a light scalpel for bloodless cutting. Most lasers use a focusing lens in the handpiece (Fig. 3). This means that the spot size varies de-

pending on how far away from or close to the skin one holds the handpiece. For example, with most CO_2 lasers the laser beam is focused when the handpiece touches the skin. Once the handpiece is moved away from the skin, the spot size enlarges, reducing the energy fluence, and the tissue is vaporized or coagulated rather than cut. The CO_2 laser is operated distal to the focal point. The Q-switched lasers are operated proximal to the focal point of the laser beam because of the very large power densities that would occur at the focal point with resultant plasma formation and loss of energy. As the handpiece is moved away from the skin, the spot size decreases, which can cause greater tissue damage as a result of the much higher energy fluences that develop.

Laser light is *extremely bright*, exceeding that of any natural light source. This is important to successfully perform coagulation, vaporization, or ablation. Lasers have been developed throughout most of the electromagnetic spectrum ranging from infrared through the visible, ultraviolet (UV) and x-ray regions. For dermatologic applications lasers in the visible and infrared wavelength range are used.

LASERS

All lasers consist of the following basic elements: the lasing medium (gain medium), optical cavity (optical resonator), and pumping system (Fig. 1). The lasing medium supplies the electrons needed for stimulated emission of radiation. It is this laser component that gives laser light its characteristic wavelength and for which the laser is named. The lasing medium can be gaseous (e.g., argon, CO_2, He-Ne, copper vapor, copper bromide, excimer, or krypton), liquid (e.g., tunable dye), solid (e.g., alexandrite, erbium : yttrium-aluminum-garnet [Er : YAG], neodynium : yttrium-aluminum-garnet [Nd : YAG], ruby or diode [GaAs]), or free electrons.

The pumping system provides energy to the lasing medium. The energy is supplied by an electrical, chemical, or

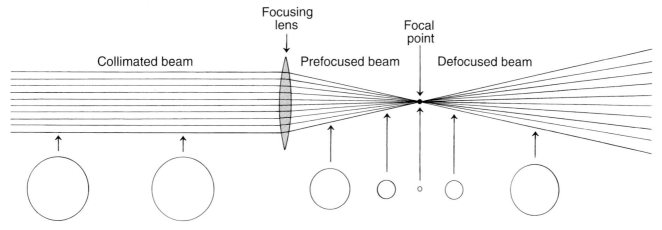

FIG. 3. Collimated laser beam with identical spot sizes alongits length. After focusing with a lens in the laser handpiece, various spot sizes can be obtained before (prefocused) and past (defocused) the focal point with the smallest spot size achieved at the focal point.

optical source. This energy is converted into laser light by stimulated emission of radiation by the lasing medium. The lasing medium is enclosed in the laser cavity, which is a resonant cavity consisting of two parallel, opposing mirrors, one of which is only partially reflective. Once energy has been supplied to the lasing medium, laser light is created by photons of light traveling back and forth between the parallel mirrors, being augmented by many cycles of stimulated emission until sufficient light is present in the laser cavity to allow a clinically useful laser beam to exit through the partially reflective mirror.

The light then travels through the delivery system, which consists of either a fiberoptic cable or an articulated arm with multiple mirrors. In general, a fiberoptic cable is preferred, since it is much lighter and less awkward to use than an articulated arm. Also, a fiberoptic cable allows the laser treatment room to be distant from the actual laser because very little energy is lost as light travels down the cable. Some lasers, including the CO_2, Q-switched ruby, and Q-switched Nd:YAG lasers, use articulated arms because laser light from these lasers has so much energy that most fiberoptic cables would melt or shatter. Articulated arms tend to be heavier and more prone to misalignment than fiberoptic cables.

At the end of the fiber or articulated arm is the laser handpiece. It usually contains lenses to focus the laser beam to the desired spot size (Fig. 3). However, some lasers, including the copper bromide laser, are used without a focusing handpiece. The end of the fiber nearly touches the lesion being treated. A collimated handpiece as used with the UltraPulse CO_2 laser also omits a lens to allow the unaltered collimated beam through to the skin (Fig. 3). As an alternative, a scanner can be placed at the end of the fiber. The scanner can move the beam across a predetermined area with a specific speed so that each portion of the skin is irradiated for a limited period. Both parameters can be programmed into the handpiece based on the desired clinical end point. Scanning devices have been mostly used with lasers, such as the argon, tunable dye, copper vapor, copper bromide, krypton, potassium titanyl phosphate (KTP), and CO_2 lasers, that have continuous energy output.

Different lasers are distinguished not only by their wavelength and lasing medium, but also by their pulse duration (Fig. 4). Continuous-wave lasers, such as the conventional CO_2, argon, tunable dye, Nd:YAG, and krypton lasers, start lasing as the foot pedal is depressed and continue to lase until it is released. In addition, the laser light can be shuttered with a mechanical shutter that is open for a set time ranging from 0.02 to 1 second or more with an off-time in a similar range with power outputs in the 1- to 100-W range. Another group of lasers, including superpulse CO_2, copper vapor, copper bromide, and KTP lasers, operate by generating a rapid train of short pulses. These pulses are so close together that the skin sees them as continuous irradiation because there is inadequate time for the skin to cool off between individual pulses. These quasicontinuous-wave lasers inter-

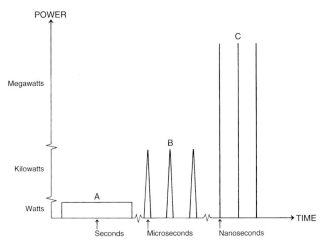

FIG. 4. Main laser types, including **(A)** continuous-wave, **(B)** pulsed, and **(C)** Q-switched lasers.

act clinically with skin in the same way as continuous-wave lasers.

Pulsed lasers, including the flashlamp-pumped, pulsed-dye laser, generate laser energy as individual pulses controlled with the foot pedal or hand switch. The rate of these pulses is slow enough that individual pulses can be applied to the tissue without causing additive heating. The pulse durations range from 0.5 to 1.5 milliseconds with high peak pulse power in the kilowatt range. Even shorter pulses can be achieved by releasing all the energy in one conventional pulse all at once. This method is called Q-switching. An electrooptic switch is placed in the laser cavity. While the switch is turned on, the laser light cannot get through the switch because of polarizers at right angles to each other. When the Q-switch is turned off, the polarizers become parallel and all of the light stored in the laser cavity is released in a very brief, 5- to 100-nanosecond, extremely high peak-power, megawatt to gigawatt laser pulse. The Q-switch compresses all the energy from a conventional pulse into one thousandth of the time, resulting in a much greater rate of energy delivery. Available Q-switched lasers include alexandrite, ruby, and Nd:YAG lasers. The very high peak-power pulses of these lasers can fragment subcellular particles such as melanosomes and tattoo ink because of the extremely high temperature gradients achieved (Table 19-1).

SKIN OPTICS

The optics of skin are constantly changing with changes in pigmentation, hydration, age, body site, and genetic background. However, a simplified model of skin optics has been developed. Light can interact with skin in the following main ways: reflection, transmission, absorption, and scattering (Fig. 5). Approximately 4% to 7% of incident light is reflected from the stratum corneum air interface without any clinical effect. Very little light can be transmitted through the full thickness of the epidermis and dermis, since even

TABLE 19-1. *Lasers used in clinical dermatology*

Wavelength (nm)	Laser	Indications
488; 514 (blue-green)	Argon (continuous)	Telangiectases, thick PWS in adults; epidermal pigmented lesions
504–690 (green-yellow-red)	Argon-pumped tunable dye (continuous)	Telangiectases, thick PWS in adults; epidermal pigmented lesions; photodynamic therapy
510 (green)	Flashlamp-pumped dye (short-pulsed)	Epidermal pigmented lesions; red tattoos
511 (green)	Copper vapor/bromide (quasicontinuous)	Epidermal pigmented lesions
521; 531 (green)	Krypton (continuous)	Epidermal pigmented lesions
532 (green)	KTP (quasicontinuous)	Telangiectases, thick PWS in adults; epidermal pigmented lesions
532 (green)	Frequency-doubled Q-switched Nd:YAG (pulsed)	Epidermal pigmented lesions; red tattoos
568 (yellow)	Krypton (continuous)	Telangiectases, thick PWS in adults
578 (yellow)	Copper vapor/bromide (qausicontinuous)	Telangiectases, thick PWS in adults
585 (yellow)	Flashlamp-pump dye (long-pulsed)	Flat PWS, PWS in children, telangiectases, warts, hypertrophic scars
694 (red)	Q-switched ruby (pulsed)	Epidermal and dermal pigmented lesions; blue, black, and green tattoos
694 (red)	Normal mode ruby (pulsed)	Unwanted hair
755 (infrared)	Normal mode Alexandrite (pulsed)	Unwanted hair
755 (infrared)	Q-switched alexandrite (pulsed)	Epidermal and dermal pigmented lesions; blue, black, and green tattoos
1064 (infrared)	Q-switched Nd:YAG (pulsed)	Dermal pigmented lesions; blue and black tattoos
1064 (infrared)	Nd:YAG (continuous)	Deep coagulation of tissue
2940 (infrared)	Normal mode Er:YAG (pulsed)	Skin resurfacing of rhytides and scars
10600 (infrared)	Carbon dioxide (continuous; superpulse; ultrapulse; flash-scanner)	Coagulation, vaporization and cutting of tissue; skin resurfacing of rhytides, scars

PWS, port wine stain; Nd:YAG, neodymium:yttrium-aluminum-garnet.

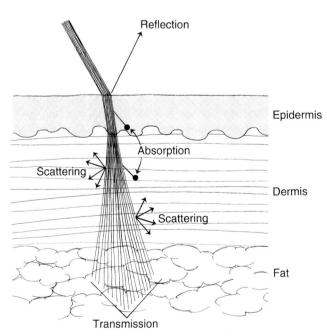

FIG. 5. Laser light–tissue interaction consists of reflection, absorption, scattering, and transmission.

the most penetrating wavelengths penetrate only to a depth of about 2 mm.

Absorption

The two most significant light interactions with skin are light scattering and absorption (Fig. 6). The first law of photobiology, the Grotthus-Draper law, states that light absorption is required for effect in tissue. If there is no absorption of light, no effect or damage can be observed. This is the basis for selective tissue effects achieved with lasers. When a photon of light is absorbed by an absorbing molecule or chromophore, all of the photon's energy is transferred to that molecule with resultant clinical effects. Laser light is selectively absorbed by the target tissue chromophore while minimal absorption by competing surrounding chromophores occurs. This allows for the selective destruction of the target chromophore while protecting the surrounding tissue from damage.

Common chromophores in skin include proteins and nucleic acids that absorb in the ultraviolet B (UVB) and ultraviolet C (UVC) regions. Melanin absorbs strongly in the UVC, UVB, and ultraviolet A (UVA) regions and throughout the visible region with decreasing absorption into the near-infrared region. This is consistent with its protective function against sunlight. Water is the dominant chromophore in the mid- and far-infrared regions. The most important dermal

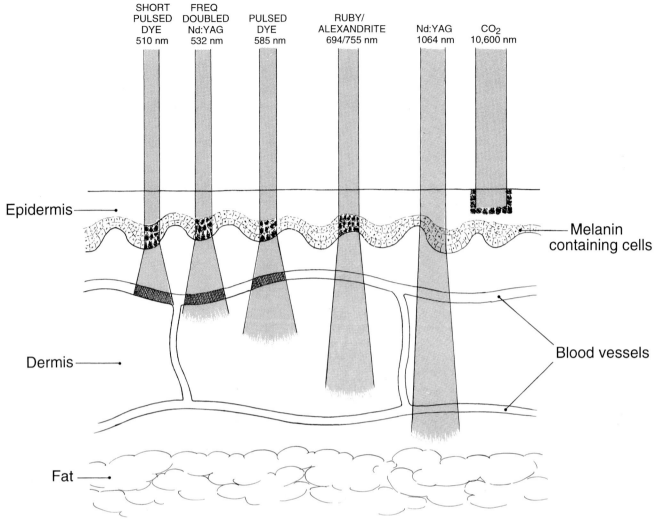

FIG. 6. Laser light depth of penetration generally increases with increasing wavelength except where the light is absorbed by strongly absorbing chromophores.

chromophores are oxyhemoglobins and deoxyhemoglobins with absorption peaks in the UVA, blue (400 nm), green (541 nm), and yellow (577 nm) wavelengths. Exogenous chromophores include tattoo ink, psoralen, hematoporphyrin derivative, and indocyanine green dye. These can then be photoactivated to achieve a desired clinical effect or photodisrupted in the case of tattoo ink to fade a tattoo.

Scattering

Light scattering in the epidermis is minimal with most scattering occurring in the dermis as a result of the presence of collagen. Scattering occurs when the direction of photon travel is changed on light interaction with an object. Different types of scattering occur depending on the size of the object. For objects that are much smaller than the wavelength of light, Rayleigh scattering occurs. This is relatively weak scattering that is approximately equal in all directions (forward, backward, and laterally) and varies inversely with the fourth power of the wavelength. For example, the molecular scattering of sunlight gives the sky its blue color. When the particle size approximately matches that of the incident-light wavelength, much stronger, more forward-directed scattering occurs that varies inversely with the wavelength. Bluish cigarette smoke is an example of this type of scattering. For objects that are much greater than the incident-light wavelength, a highly forward-directed scattering that is essentially independent of wavelength occurs. White clouds are a common example of large-particle scattering. Within the dermis all three types of scattering occur, but the predominant form of scattering is by collagen, which is approximately the size of the incident-light wavelength in the visible and near-infrared ranges. This accounts for the Tindall effect in skin, in which black particles appear bluish because of the greater scattering of blue light by collagen. backward scattering by the dermis allows greater energy fluence to be found in the superficial dermis than what is present in the incident-light beam. This effect can be seen with a conventional Nd:YAG laser: the dermis can be massively thermally coagulated before any changes are visible at the surface.

Penetration of Light Into Skin

Light is attenuated gradually by scattering and absorption. The penetration depth generally refers to the depth at which 1/e (37%) of the incident-light intensity remains. The magnitude of scattering decreases with increasing wavelength (Fig. 6). Therefore at short wavelengths of 300 to 400 nm, light penetration into the skin is limited by strong scattering of the beam with penetration of less than 0.1 mm. At longer wavelengths of 600 to 1200 nm in the red and near-infrared regions, scattering as well as absorption by endogenous chromophores is weak, allowing light to penetrate up to 2 mm into the dermis. This optical window is an ideal wavelength range for treatment of dermal lesions, especially when exogenous chromophores are present. This optical window has been used in the treatment of dermal pigmented lesions such as nevus of Ota and tattoos with the Q-switched ruby laser at 694 nm, Q-switched alexandrite laser at 755 nm, and Q-switched Nd:YAG laser at 1064 nm. Photodynamic therapy of tumors is also performed with red laser light to maximize depth of penetration.

LASER-TISSUE INTERACTION

As far as the skin is concerned, what happens in the laser cavity is irrelevant. Any clinical effect depends only on the properties of the light entering the skin and the presence of chromophores and scattering objects in the skin. Knowing these properties of laser light, predictions of clinical effect can be made. With an understanding of laser tissue interaction, one can select appropriate laser(s) for the lesion to be treated. Also, with the great recent advances of laser technology, lasers can be and have been built to emit light with very specific properties to solve specific clinical problems.

When a photon of laser light is absorbed by a chromophore, electronic or vibrational excitation of the chromophore occurs. The energy carried by a photon is inversely proportional to its wavelength, according to Planck's law. Therefore the more energetic UV- and visible-light photons can promote electrons to higher, more reactive orbits that may achieve photochemical effects. However, most energy carried by UV, visible, and infrared light is converted into heat. Therefore thermal effects predominate after laser irradiation. These can be manifested as directly photothermal effects or as photomechanical effects that result from extremely rapid thermal expansion occurring with short pulse laser light absorption.

Energy Fluence

To achieve clinical change in a lesion, a certain amount of energy has to be absorbed by the lesion. The delivered "dose" is measured by the energy (joules [J]) delivered per unit area (cm^2) and is called the energy fluence(J/cm^2). As the energy fluence increases, the clinical effect, such as tissue coagulation, increases as well. Energy fluence is equal to the laser power output (watts) times the pulse duration (seconds) divided by the effective spot size (cm^2). For pulsed-dye lasers that are operated to achieve selective lesion destruction through selective photothermolysis, the energy fluences used for clinical effect are strikingly similar, with a range of 3 to 10 J/cm^2. For less selective continuous or quasicontinuous-wave lasers such as the copper vapor laser the therapeutic range is greater than 15 J/cm^2 because of additional heating of the surrounding tissue. Energy fluence is generally used when referring to pulsed-dye lasers or robotically scanned, continuous-wave lasers, since it is easily calculated for each pulse or exposure.

Irradiance

The irradiance is the rate of energy delivery per unit area to an object. The shorter the pulse duration of a laser, the higher the irradiance must be to deliver sufficient energy for clinical effect. Very high irradiance achieves much faster heating of an object than lower irradiance. This has clinical implications. Low irradiances slowly heat the tissue, resulting in coagulation, whereas faster heating using higher irradiances can achieve tissue vaporization. At the extremely high irradiances in megawatts to gigawatts per cm^2 that are achieved with Q-switched lasers, the heating is so rapid that the target shatters or explodes. This photomechanical or photoacoustic injury is caused by rapid thermal expansion, high-pressure waves, and local vaporization. Irradiance is independent of pulse duration. Therefore it is usually used when referring to continuous-wave lasers such as the CO_2 laser, since there is no fixed pulse duration. Irradiance is easily calculated from the laser power output and known spot size. Irradiance (W/cm^2) equals the laser power output (watts) divided by the spot size (cm^2)

Selective Photothermolysis

The theory of selective photothermolysis states that selective heating is achieved by preferential light absorption and heat production in the target chromophore when the pulse duration is equal to or shorter than the thermal relaxation time of the target (Fig. 7). When a target chromophore absorbs laser energy, it is heated relative to its surroundings. The chromophore then gradually gives up this heat to the surrounding tissue via radiation, conduction (diffusion), and convection (transport away by blood) until it has reached equilibrium. The smaller the object, the faster it cools. The time it takes an object to cool by 63% is called the thermal relaxation time. The thermal relaxation time varies with the square of the object's diameter. Therefore the thermal relaxation time of small objects such as melanosomes is much

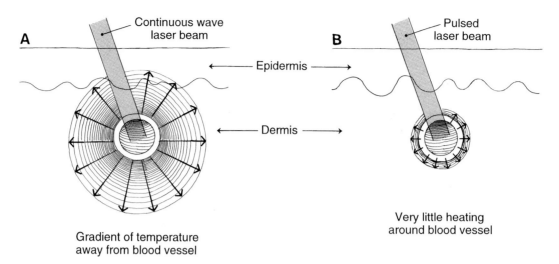

FIG. 7. (A) A continuous-wave laser beam will beabsorbed in the blood vessel, but plenty of time will be available for heat to diffuse to the surrounding structure, causing nonspecific thermal damage. **(B)** A pulsed-dye laser beam with a pulse shorter than the blood vessel's thermal relaxation time will be absorbed in the blood vessel, and before significant heat diffusion has occurred to the surroundings the pulse will end, thus achieving selective photothermolysis.

shorter than that of larger objects such as small blood vessels. In general, the thermal relaxation time in seconds is approximately equal to the square of the object size in millimeters. Therefore a 10^{-3}-mm melanosome cools in $(10^{-3})^2$ seconds, which is 1 microsecond.

If a chromophore is heated by a laser pulse longer than its thermal relaxation time, there will be plenty of time for heat diffusion to the surrounding tissue to occur with resultant thermal damage to the surrounding tissue (Fig. 7A). The chromophore and the surrounding tissue get hot together. For example, argon laser light is absorbed by oxyhemoglobin, but because the pulse duration is far longer than the thermal relaxation time of the target blood vessel, heat diffusion and resultant destruction of surrounding structures occur, with potential risk of scarring. If the laser pulse is shorter than the thermal relaxation time, the heat is confined to the target with very little heat diffusion into the surrounding tissue (Fig. 7B). The target is hot relative to the surrounding tissue. Thus the target can be selectively destroyed without associated collateral damage. For example, pulsed-dye laser light with a pulse duration of approximately 0.5 milliseconds is absorbed by oxyhemoglobin and the destruction is confined to the target vessel because the pulse is shorter than the thermal relaxation time of the blood vessel. This dramatically reduces the risk of scarring.

By knowing the wavelength and pulse duration of a given laser, one can predict useful clinical indications for the laser. For example, the Q-switched ruby laser has a wavelength of 694 nm and pulse duration of 20 nanoseconds. At 694 nm the most prominent endogenous chromophore is melanin. The thermal relaxation time of 1-mm melanosomes is approximately 1 microsecond. At 694 nm, toos, rhytids, low absorption and low scattering in the dermis allow light to penetrate relatively deeply into the dermis. Therefore the

ruby laser would be expected to remove both epidermal and dermal pigmented lesions with minimal risk of scarring. Indeed, this has been found to be the case. Lasers that can selectively remove or fade vascular lesions, benign pigmented lesions, unwanted hair, and tattoos have been developed based on the theory of selective photothermolysis.

Vaporization

The most abundant chromophore in skin is water. Therefore, to efficiently remove layers of skin or to cut into skin, the laser wavelength is chosen to target water. Water absorption peaks are present throughout the mid- to far-infrared regions. The two commercially available lasers that target water are the Er:YAG laser at 2,940 nm and theCO₂ laser at 10,600 nm. The Er:YAG laser has been used for superficial lesion vaporization in Europe and is now being used in the United States for removal of scars and rhytides. The CO_2 laser has been used for skin vaporization and cutting since the 1970s. The main advantage of the laser over cold steel surgery is the relatively hemostatic cutting that can be achieved because of the peripheral zone of thermal coagulation around the incision site caused by heat diffusion from the incision. This thermal damage zone, which can be as thick as 1 mm, has also been a limiting factor because of delayed healing and risk of scarring in the treated areas. For hemostatic tissue removal without increased risk of scarring, a 50-μm thermal zone of damage is ideal. Less thermal damage increases bleeding, and more thermal damage increases the risk of scarring.

Carbon dioxide laser light is absorbed within 20 to 50 μm of skin because of its very strong absorption by water. Therefore all the incident energy is absorbed within the epidermis on the first pass. To achieve tissue vaporization, 4 to 5 J/cm^2 must be delivered to the tissue. The thermal relaxation time of the 20- to 50-μm heated layer of epidermis is calculated to be approximately 1 millisecond. A conventional continuous-wave CO_2 laser deposits energy into the tissue at a relatively slow rate, requiring more than 50 milliseconds to deliver enough energy to achieve vaporization. Therefore there is time for much of the heat to diffuse to the surrounding tissue with resultant thermal coagulation up to 1 mm away from the impact site. In addition, once vaporization starts, there is a buildup of desiccated tissue at the surface that cannot be further vaporized. This tissue heats up and develops charring with additional energy deposition, and this energy further heats the surrounding tissue via diffusion. This is similar to barbecuing a steak. Initially the meat cooks, but once the surface has been desiccated, it begins to develop charring (carbonization). Therefore, to minimize peripheral thermal damage, the laser energy should be delivered very quickly (at high irradiance) to achieve complete vaporization rapidly or even explosively. This rapidly vaporized tissue would remove most of the incident energy in the laser plume and leave behind very little residual thermal damage. The rate of vaporization has to be faster than the 1-millisecond thermal relaxation time of the 20- to 50-μm tissue absorption layer.

Recently two new CO_2 laser technologies have been developed that deposit at least 5 J/cm^2 in less than 1 millisecond into tissue with exact operator control. One system relies on a very high peak-power, 1-millisecond laser pulse to deliver the energy. The other system scans a focusedCO_2 laser beam in a spiral pattern around the field so that any given spot along its path is irradiated for less than 1 millisecond. The very high irradiance achieved by focusing the beam to a small spot size delivers sufficient energy for complete vaporization. These new lasers have revived interest in the CO_2 laser by using selective photothermolysisto resurface skin for the removal of rhytides and scars.

Er:YAG laser light at 2,940 nm is completely absorbed in less than 2 μm of tissue because the absorption coefficient of water at 2,940 nm is 10 times greater than at 10,600 nm. Also, the laser has pulse durations of less than 1 millisecond in the conventional mode and less than 1 microsecond in the Q-switched mode. Therefore the Er:YAG achieves even more precise tissue vaporization with even less residual thermal damage than the CO_2 laser.

Controlled tissue ablation does not require water as the chromophore. Studies have demonstrated very precise tissue ablation with short UV-light, argon fluoride (ArF) excimer lasers that rely on proteins and nucleic acids as the chromophore. The ArF laser at 193 nm has been used to remove individual layers of stratum corneum without collateral damage. However, the ablation is so clean that the laser cuts are not hemostatic, with bleeding evident as soon as the papillary dermis is entered. In addition, there is concern regarding the potential carcinogenicity and/or mutagenicity of UV-light lasers, which may limit their development for dermatologic

surgery. However, these lasers are being successfully used for ophthalmologic surgery.

Photomechanical Effects

High peak-power, short-pulse lasers generate extremely rapid heating of the target chromophore ranging from 300,000°C/sec for the flashlamp-pumped, pulsed-dye laser at 585 nm to 10,000,000,000°C/sec for the Q-switched ruby laser. These temperature gradients cause supersonic, photoacoustic, high-pressure shock waves and rapid thermal expansion and cavitation (sudden expansion and collapse of a steam bubble), which result in photomechanical tissue, cell, and/or organelle disruption. In the case of the pulsed-dye laser, this causes disruption of blood vessel walls with extravasation of erythrocytes and resultant purpura, which is an unwanted side effect of treatment.

On the other hand, photomechanical disruption of the target chromophore in the selective photothermolysis laser treatment of tattoos and benign dermal pigmented lesions with Q-switched lasers may be the major therapeutic mechanism. The tattoo ink particles or melanosomes are shattered or exploded by the extremely rapid heating. This kills the macrophages or nevus cells containing the tattoo ink particles or melanosomes, respectively. What happens to the cellular and particle debris is unclear, but it is thought to be gradually removed by activated macrophages to the lymphatic system.

Photochemical Effects

Photodynamic therapy is based on the use of an exogenously administered photosensitizing drug (dye) that is selectively taken up by pathologic tissue and subsequently irradiated by a specific wavelength of light. The combination of drug, light, and oxygen causes a photochemical reaction to occur in the tissue. This generally results in target tissue necrosis, which is thought to be mediated by singlet oxygen formation acting on lesional vasculature as well as on tumor cells directly. Singlet oxygen oxidizes cell membranes and other sites, resulting in cell death. The major photosensitizer used for photodynamic therapy has been porfimer sodium (Photofrin), a partially purified mixture of photoactive porphyrins. Although laser light is not necessary to activate the drug, most studies have used deeply penetrating red laser light. The laser's high energy output of the appropriate wavelength minimizes exposure time and permits treatment of deep tumors through fiberoptic delivery systems. Selective destruction of nonmelanoma skin cancer has been achieved with porfimer sodium and red, continuous-wave laser light at 630 nm (tunable dye laser). The main drawback of photodynamic therapy has been the month-long period of UV- and visible-light skin photosensitivity. New, second-generation photosensitizing drugs with photosensitivity lasting only a few days are now being studied for the treatment of nonmelanoma skin cancer, psoriasis, and vascular lesions.

Spot Size

The area of skin that is irradiated by an individual laser pulse is the spot size. It varies by how far away from or close to the skin surface the focal point of the laser beam is located. Most lasers come with several spot sizes available. When targeting epidermal lesions or for tissue ablation, spot size is relatively unimportant, as long as different spot sizes have equal energy fluences and irradiances. However, for pulsed lasers operating to produce selective photothermolysis of dermal targets such as melanin, blood vessels, hair follicles, and tattoo inks, the spot size can have a significant effect on therapeutic efficacy. Because of lateral scattering by collagen in the dermis, laser light loses energy fluence and lateral scattering increases with smaller spot sizes. Because of backward scattering in the dermis, laser light becomes more concentrated (increased energy fluence) in the upper dermis and backward scattering decreases with smaller spot sizes. Forward scattering is also decreased with small spot sizes. The combination of increased lateral scattering, decreased backward scattering, and decreased forward scattering with small spot sizes results in reduced energy fluence in the upper dermis, as well as reduced laser light depth of penetration. Clinically, larger spot sizes of any given energy fluence are more effective than smaller spot sizes for dermal lesions. With the flashlamp-pumped, pulsed-dye laser, much lower energy fluences are needed to treat vascular lesions with 7- to 10-mm spot sizes than those with small 2- to 3-mm spot sizes. For targeting of dermal lesions with visible and near-infrared light lasers, the spot size should be at least 3 to 5 mm or larger for optimal depth of penetration and efficacy.

The effective spot size also depends on the laser beam intensity profile. The ideal laser beam would deliver the light with an energy fluence that is equal in the center and periphery of the spot. In this manner all parts of the lesion being treated would receive the same amount of energy for an even clinical response. No currently available lasers achieve this ideal. Instead, almost all lasers produce a Gaussian beam profile. In a Gaussian distribution the center of the beam has greater energy fluence than the edges. Therefore, to achieve uniform energy delivery to a lesion, the circular laser spots have to be overlapped to a varying degree depending on the specific laser being used. Failure to adequately overlap may result in a reticulated pattern. This is often seen in the treatment of port wine stains or poikiloderma of Civatte with the flashlamp-pumped, pulsed-dye laser. Usually this reticulated pattern can be eliminated with additional treatments by centering the second treatment spots on the reticulations with the remaining blood vessels.

LASER SAFETY

Lasers have associated with them certain very specific safety concerns. For the safety of the patients, operators, and staff, these concerns have to be addressed in a formal manner. Hospitals that use lasers have a laser safety officer who develops and enforces safety and credentialing rules for laser use. If a laser is used in an office setting, adherence to safety protocols developed by the American National Standards Institute (ANSI Z-136.3) is expected. The major safety hazard of lasers includes, first and foremost, eye injury. Additional hazards include fire, electric shock, and biohazards from laser plume.

Eye Injury

Laser-caused eye injury is estimated to occur one or two times per week in the United States. Lasers are placed in one of four categories according to how dangerous they are to the eyes (Table 19-2). Class I includes diagnostic and supermarket-checkout lasers that do not emit hazardous radiation; warning signs are not necessary. Class II lasers are visible lasers with power of <1 mW, such as the helium-neon aiming laser. These lasers do not have enough power to injure the eye accidentally but may cause retinal damage after prolonged, direct exposure that is longer than the blinking reflex of approximately 0.25 seconds. A caution label is required. Class IIIa includes lasers used for outdoor surveying and new diode aiming lasers with a power range of 1 to 5 mW. They may cause eye injury in less than 0.25 seconds if focused directly onto the eye. Class IIIb comprises lasers with a power range of 5 to 500 mW that are hazardous to the eye if the eye is exposed directly or through specular (mirrorlike) reflection of the beam, and a "danger" label is required. Lasers with power outputs greater than 500 mW are classified as class IV. All lasers used in dermatologic surgery fall into this category. These lasers pose skin and

TABLE 19-2. *Laser categories*

Class	Power (mW)	Type	Eye injury danger
I		Diagnostic; supermarket checkout	None
II	<1	He-Ne aiming beam	>0.25-sec direct eye exposure
IIIa	1–5	Diode aiming beam; outdoor surveying	<0.25-sec direct eye exposure
IIIb	5–500	Infrared coagulator	Direct exposure or specular reflection
IV	>500	All dermatologic lasers	Scattered or diffuse reflection

TABLE 19-3. *Laser eye injury damage sites*

Wavelength (nm)	Radiation type	Eye injury damage site
<180	Gamma, x-ray	Nonspecific ocular damage
180–280	Ultraviolet C	Cornea
280–320	Ultraviolet B	Cornea
320–400	Ultraviolet A	Lens
400–700	Visible	Retina, choroid
780–1,400	Near infrared	Lens, vitreous, retina
1,400–1,000,000	Middle and far infrared	Cornea

fire hazards, as well as eye hazards. Even scattered or diffuse reflection of the laser beam is hazardous to the eye. Specific labeling is required. Even a single pulse with any of these lasers directed at the unprotected eye causes immediate, irreversible damage. Even reflected class IV laser light may be harmful to the eye.

Ocular damage sites are based on the chromophore that will absorb laser energy at the specific laser wavelength (Table 19-3). Gamma rays and x-rays cause nonspecific ocular damage. Ultraviolet C, UVB, and mid- to far-infrared region light will be absorbed by the cornea with resultant corneal damage. Ultraviolet A laser light damages the lens of the eye. Visible light is absorbed by melanin in the retina and hemoglobin in the choroid with resulting thermal coagulation of those structures. The intensity of the laser light is increased by as much as a factor of 100,000 at the level of the retina because of focusing to a 10- to 20-μm spot by the cornea and lens, resulting in greater retinal injury. Near-infrared laser light damages the lens and vitreous as well as the retina.

The best protection against laser eye injury is for all persons in the operating room to wear proper protective eyewear with side shields. Laser protective eyewear is wavelength specific, but laser safety glasses for different wavelengths may have very similar lens colors. Therefore it is important to check the label on the glasses to make sure that the specific safety glasses being used are appropriate for the laser wavelength being used. The patient should also wear laser safety glasses, opaque goggles, or wet gauze eye-patch pads secured with tape. If an area on the eyelid is to be treated, stainless steel eye shields should be placed between the cornea and eyelids.

The effectiveness of laser safety glasses is determined by the optical density (OD) of the glasses for the specific laser wavelength. The optical density is the $\log_{10}$ of beam attenuation across the protective eyewear. In other words, the higher the OD of the glasses, the greater the filtration of laser light provided by the glasses. For example, glasses with an OD of 6 transmit only one millionth of the incident laser light through to the eye. The eyewear should protect against the maximum irradiance of the laser with an OD of at least 5.

The area around the laser handpiece in which the laser beam is hazardous is called the nominal hazard zone. Most lasers are used with a focusing lens in the handpiece. Therefore the beam diverges relatively quickly so that it may be much less harmful a few feet away from the handpiece, resulting in a small nominal hazard zone. However, a new collimated handpiece used with a skin resurfacing CO_2 laser does not diverge. Therefore it is just as dangerous several feet away as at the handpiece exit point, which results in a very large nominal hazard zone.

Skin Injury

Inadvertent pulsed laser irradiation of normal skin of the operator or patient may be painful, but otherwise there is minimal associated morbidity. On the other hand, irradiation with a continuous-wave laser such as the CO_2 laser can cause a significant second- or even third-degree burn that may heal with a scar.

There are several commonsense, standard precautions to protect the skin and eyes. All personnel and patient wear appropriate laser safety glasses or goggles. The handpiece should never be looked into, even with safety glasses, when the laser is turned on. Jewelry and other reflective objects should be removed from the surgical field. Some surgeons use anodized or ebonized surgical instruments to reduce the risk of specular laser light reflections. The laser operating room doors should be kept closed and laser warning signs prominently displayed outside the door. An extra pair of safety glasses should be placed outside the laser room door to facilitate safe entry. The laser should be armed only when in use. Whenever lasing is stopped, the laser should be returned to the standby position and the operator should remove his or her foot from the foot pedal. By keeping the number of persons in the operating room to a minimum, accidents are less likely to occur.

Fire Hazards

Laser light has more than enough energy to ignite flammable materials close to the beam. This is especially true for continuous-wave lasers such as the argon and CO_2, but fires have been reported even with pulsed lasers such as the flashlamp-pumped, pulsed-dye laser. The greatest risk of fire occurs when oxygen is present in the laser treatment field. Since most laser procedures are performed with the patient under local or no anesthesia, flowing oxygen is usually not a problem. When general anesthesia is used, the anesthesia apparatus, including all connections, should be carefully secured to prevent oxygen leaks into the laser surgery field. The endotracheal tube should be made of metal or wrapped in aluminum foil or wet towels to prevent laser beam perforation of the tube. Endotracheal tube fires ignited by CO_2 lasers have resulted in severe tracheobronchial burns with fatal outcome. Nasal oxygen prongs have no place in a laser treatment field.

A number of precautions can be taken to minimize the risk of fire. All makeup should be removed from the treatment site, and any hair in the area should be shaved if the lesion is under the hair. As an alternative, the hair can be kept moist with water or saline during treatment. Flammable preparation agents such as acetone and alcohol should be avoided whenever possible. If alcohol is used, it should be allowed to dry completely before lasing is begun. Only wet or moist gauze should be used in the treatment area. When using a continuous-wave surgical laser such as the CO_2 laser, wet towels must be placed around the surgical field to protect surrounding areas from inadvertent irradiation. If the perianal area is being treated, a wet rectal tampon has to be placed inside the anal canal to protect against a methane gas explosion.

Extremely high voltages are stored in the laser often, even when it has been turned off. Therefore the laser should be opened only by properly trained personnel. All medical lasers are required to have safety interlocks that prevent the laser from operating if the laser container is open. The laser room should have a fire extinguisher and easy access to water. Dye lasers contain dyes that may be flammable and are toxic to humans. When changing dye kits, extreme caution should be exercised.

Laser Plume Hazards

When vaporizing tissue with a CO_2 laser, a significant amount of plume is generated. This plume contains steam and dozens of highly carcinogenic compounds including acrolein, benzene, formaldehyde, and polycyclic hydrocarbons, as well as incompletely burned components of tissue. The carcinogens present in laser plume are similar to those in cigarette smoke. Vaporization of 1 g of tissue generates as much mutagenic smoke as is present in three to six cigarettes. The plume contains particles in the 0.5- to 5-μm range that are easily aspirated into lung alveoli where they settle. Animal studies have demonstrated the development of significant pulmonary disease in rats breathing unfiltered laser plume.

The main concern centers on the cellular debris. This debris has been found to contain intact human and infective bovine papilloma virus when tissue infected with those viruses was vaporized with a CO_2 laser. Even more chilling is the recovery of live, albeit somewhat damaged, human immunodeficiency virus type 1 (HIV-1) from laser plume after in vitro vaporizing of HIV-1–infected tissue culture. Effective smoke evacuation is the best defense against potentially infectious agents. The smoke evacuator should be kept within 1 cm of the laser impact site. If the smoke evacuator is moved 2 cm away, smoke evacuation efficiency drops by up to 50%. The smoke evacuator has to be a high-efficiency unit that filters particles less than 0.1 μm in diameter. Closely fitting laser masks that filter particles as small as 0.1 μm in diameter are worn by all personnel in the laser

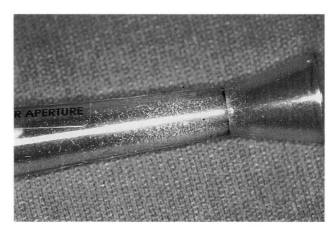

FIG. 8. Q-switched laser–generated debris including tissue fragments, intact cells, and cellular elements captured on a plastic cone during tattoo treatment.

room, with the realization that some potentially contaminated air will find its way around the edges of the mask and into the operator's lungs. Masks have been designed as a barrier to protect the patient from the physician rather than the other way around. What the infectious risk of laser plume might be has not been determined. To date, there have been no cases of HIV transmission from a patient to a physician through laser plume. Human papilloma virus also appears to be very difficult to transmit via laser plume, with no increased incidence of verrucae reported in physicians using the CO_2 laser for the treatment of warts. A smoke evacuator should be used with any laser that generates appreciable plume. This includes the CO_2 laser when used for any indication and the flashlamp-pumped, pulsed-dye laser when used for the treatment of verrucae.

At high-energy fluences, Q-switched lasers, including the alexandrite, ruby, and Nd:YAG lasers, eject skin debris from the impact site at supersonic speeds (Fig. 8). The debris contains cells that have been determined to be viable. Because of the high speed of the particles, smoke evacuators are ineffective in removing them. To protect the laser operator, all of the Q-switched lasers come with various plastic cones to catch the ejected debris. As an alternative, the debris can be captured by lasing through a clear dressing such as Vigilon. The dressing catches all the debris. In addition, the operator should wear surgical gloves and a 0.1-μm laser mask.

To eliminate the risk of cross-contamination, the handpiece should be changed or disinfected after laser surgery in each patient.

CONCLUSION

Dermatologic laser surgery is a rapidly evolving field with new lasers and new indications being developed almost daily, while older lasers are rapidly becoming obsolete. With an understanding of laser tissue interactions, especially of the theory of selective photothermolysis, the clinician can keep new developments in perspective and critically assess the various claims and counterclaims presented by the various laser manufacturers.

Currently lasers in dermatology are used for the effective treatment of vascular lesions, benign pigmented lesions, tattoos, rhytides, scars, small benign neoplasms, verrucae, unwanted hair, and hypertrophic scars (Table 19-1). In the near future, lasers may be perfected for the treatment of lower-extremity telangiectasias. Photodynamic therapy may provide a nonsurgical alternative for the treatment of nonmelanoma skin cancer, as well as inflammatory conditions such as psoriasis and acne. With the exception of ophthalmology, lasers are not in extensive clinical diagnostic use. The confocal laser scanning microscope uses laser light to visualize cellular and subcellular detail *in vivo* with great clarity and may be used in the near future to obtain a "light biopsy" of skin without surgical removal of tissue.

As has happened with computers, advances in laser technology, especially the development of solid-state diode lasers, should significantly reduce the cost of owning a laser. Within a few years lasers may become as prevalent in dermatologists' offices as electrosurgical units are today.

SUGGESTED READING LIST

1. Anderson RR. Laser tissue interactions in dermatology. In: Lasers in cutaneous and aesthetic surgery. Arndt KA, Dover JS, eds. Philadelphia: Lippincott–Raven, 1997:25.
2. Anderson RR, Jaenicke KF, Parrish JA. Mechanisms of selective vascular changes caused by dye lasers. Lasers Surg Med 1983;3:211.
3. Anderson RR, Levins PC, Grevelink JM. Lasers in dermatology. In: Fitzpatrick TB, Eisen AZ, Wolff K, Freedberg IM, Austen KF, eds. Dermatology in general medicine, 4th ed. New York City: McGraw-Hill, 1993:1755.
4. Anderson RR, Margolis RJ, Watanabe S, Flotte T, Hruza GJ, Dover JS. Selective photothermolysis of cutaneous pigmentation by Q-switched Nd:YAG laser pulses at 1064, 532, and 355 nm. J Invest Dermatol 1989;93:28.
5. Anderson RR, Parrish JA. Microvasculature can be selectively damaged using dye lasers: a basic theory and experimental evidence in human skin. Lasers Surg Med 1981;1:263.
6. Anderson RR, Parrish JA. Optical properties of human skin. In: Regan JD, Parrish JA, eds. The science of photomedicine. New York City: Plenum, 1982:147.
7. Anderson RR, Parrish JA. The optics of human skin. J Invest Dermatol 1981;77:13.
8. Anderson RR, Parrish RR. Selective photothermolysis: precise microsurgery by selective absorption of pulsed radiation. Science 1983;220:524.
9. Apfelberg DB, Maser MR, Lash H. Extended clinical use of the argon laser for cutaneous lesions. Arch Dermatol 1979;115:719.
10. Arndt KA, Noe JM, Northam DBC. Laser therapy: basic concepts and nomenclature. J Am Acad Dermatol 1981;5:649.
11. Arndt KA. Argon laser therapy of small cutaneous vascular lesions. Arch Dermatol 1982;118:220.
12. Baggish MS, Baltoyannis P, Sze E. Protection of the rat lung from the harmful effects of laser smoke. Lasers Surg Med 1988;8:248.
13. Baggish MS, Elbakry M. The effects of laser smoke on the lungs of rats. Am J Obstet Gynecol 1987;156:1260.
14. Baggish MS, Poiesz BJ, Joret D, Williamson P, Refai A. Presence of human immunodeficiency virus DNA in laser smoke. Lasers Surg Med 1991;11:197.
15. Byer RL. Diode lasers: pumped solid-state lasers. Science 1988;239:742.
16. Dover JS, Arndt KA, Geronemus RG. Illustrated cutaneous laser surgery: a practical guide. Norwalk, CT: Appleton & Lange, 1990.
17. Dover JS, Margolis RJ, Polla LL, et al. Pigmented guinea pigskin irradiated with Q-switched ruby laser pulses: morphologic and histologic findings. Arch Dermatol 1989;125:43.
18. Einstein A. Zur quantentheorie der strahlung. Physik Z 1917;18:121.
19. Epstein RH, Brummett RRJ, Lask GD. Incendiary potential of the flashlamp-pumped, 585-nm tunable dye laser. Anesth Analg 1990;71:171.
20. Fitzpatrick RE, Ruiz EJ, Goldman MP. The depth of thermal necrosis using the CO$_2$ laser: a comparison of the super pulsed mode and conventional mode. J Dermatol Surg Oncol 1991;17:340.
21. Garden JM, Geronemus RG. Dermatologic laser surgery. J Dermatol Surg Oncol 1990;16:156.
22. Garden JM, O'Banion K, Shelnitz LS, et al. Papillomavirus in the vapor of carbon dioxide laser-treated verrucae. JAMA 1988;259:1199.
23. Goldman L, Blaney DJ, Kindel DJ, et al. Effect of the laser beam on the skin: preliminary report. J Invest Dermatol 1963;40:121.
24. Goldman L, Blaney DJ, Kindel DJ, Richfield D, Franke EK. Pathology of the effect of the laser beam on the skin. Nature 1963;197:912.
25. Goldman L, Michaelson SM, Rockwell RJ, Sliney DH, Tengroth BM, Wolbarsht ML. Nonionizing radiation protection: optical radiation, with particular reference to lasers. WHO Reg Publ EurSer 1988;25:49.
26. Goldman L, Rockwell RJ, Meyer R, Otten R, Wilson RG, Kitzmiller KW. Laser treatment of tattoos: a preliminary survey of three year's clinical experience. JAMA 1967;201:841.
27. Goldman L, Rockwell RJ, Meyer R, Otten R. Investigative studies with the laser in the treatment of basal cell epitheliomas. South Med J 1968;61:735.
28. Goldman MP, Fitzpatrick RE. Cutaneous laser surgery: the art and science of selective photothermolysis. St. Louis, MO: Mosby, 1993.
29. Green HA, Burd EE, Nishioka NS, Compton CC. Skin graft take and healing following 193-nm excimer, continuous-wave carbon dioxide (CO$_2$), pulsed CO$_2$, or pulsedholmium:YAG laser ablation of the graft bed. Arch Dermatol 1993;129:979.
30. Greenwald J, Rosen S, Anderson RR, et al. Comparative histological studies of the tunable dye (at 577 nm) laser and argon laser: the specific vascular effects of the dye laser. J Invest Dermatol 1981;77:305.
31. Hruza GJ, Dover JS, Flotte TJ, Goetschkes M, Watanabe S, Anderson RR. Q-switched ruby laser irradiation of normal human skin: histologic and ultrastructural findings. Arch Dermatol 1991;127:1799.
32. Hruza GJ, Geronemus RG, Dover JS, Arndt KA. Lasers indermatology: 1993. Arch Dermatol 1993;129:1026.
33. Itzkan I, Drake EH. History of lasers in medicine. In: Lasers in cutaneous and aesthetic surgery. Arndt KA, Dover JS, Olbright SM, eds. Philadelphia: Lippincott–Raven, 1997:3.
34. Kamat BR, Carney JM, Arndt KA, Stern RS, Rosen S. Cutaneous tissue repair following CO$_2$ laser irradiation. J Invest Dermatol 1986;87:268.
35. Kawana S, Segawa A. Confocal laser scanning microscopic and immunoelectronmicroscopic study on the anatomical distribution of fibrillar IgA deposits in dermatitis herpetiformis. Arch Dermatol 1993;129:456.
36. Kennedy JC, Pottier RH, Pross DC. Photodynamic therapy with endogenous protoporphyrin IX: basic principles and present clinical experience. J Photochem Photobiol B 1990;6:143.
37. Lanzafame RJ, Naim JO, Rogers DW, Hinshaw JR. Comparison of continuous-wave, chop-wave, and super pulse laser wounds. Lasers Surg Med 1988;8:119.
38. Lui H, Anderson RR. Photodynamic therapy in dermatology: shedding a different light on skin disease. Arch Dermatol 1992;128:1631.
39. Maiman TH. Stimulated optical radiation in ruby. Nature 1960;187:493.
40. Margolis RJ, Dover JS, Polla LL, et al. Visible action spectrum for melanin-specific selective photothermolysis. Lasers Surg Med 1989;9:389.
41. Matthews J, Newsom SW, Walker NP. Aerobiology of irradiation with the carbon dioxide laser. J Hosp Infect Dis 1985;6:230.
42. McKenzie AL. How far does thermal damage extend beneath the surface of CO$_2$ laser incisions? Phys Med Biol 1983;28:905.
43. Murphy GF, Shepard RS, Paul BS, Menkes A, Anderson RR, Parrish JA. Organelle-specific injury to melanin-containing cells in human skin by pulsed laser irradiation. Lagb Invest 1983;49:680.
44. Nezhat C, Winer WK, Nezhat F, Nezhat C, Forrest D, Reeves

WG.Smoke from laser surgery: is there a health hazard? Lasers SurgMed 1987;7:376.

45. Parrish JA, Anderson RR, Harrist T, Paul B, Murphy GF. Selective thermal effects with pulsed irradiation from lasers: from organ to organelle. J Invest Dermatol 1983;80(suppl):75.

46. Polanyi TG. Physics of surgery with lasers. Clin ChestMed 1985;6:179.

47. Polla LL, Margolis RJ, Dover JS, et al. Melanosomes are a primary target of Q-switched ruby laser irradiation in guinea pig skin. J Invest Dermatol 1987;89:281.

48. Reid WH, McLeod PJ, Ritchie A, Ferguson-Pell M. Q-switched ruby laser treatment of black tattoos. Br J Plast Surg 1983;36:455.

49. Sawchuck WS, Felton RP. Infectious potential of aerosolized particles. Arch Dermatol 1989;125:1089.

50. Sawchuck WS, Weber PJ, Lowy DR, Dzubow LM. Infectious human papillomavirus in the vapor of warts treated with carbon dioxide laser or electrocoagulation. J Am Acad Dermatol1989;21:41.

51. Sliney DH, Trokel SL. Medical lasers and their safe use. New York: Springer-Verlag, 1993.

52. Sliney DH. Laser tissue interactions. Clin Chest Med 1985;6:203.

53. Smith JP, Moss CE, Bryant CJ, Fleeger AK. Evaluation of a smoke evacuator used for laser surgery. Laser Surg Med 1989;9:276.

54. Starr JC, Kilmer SL, Wheeland RG. Analysis of the carbon dioxide laser plume for simian immunodeficiency virus. J Dermatol Surg Oncol 1992;18:297.

55. Tan OT, Carney JM, Margolis R, et al. Histologic responses of portwine stains treated by argon, carbon dioxide, and tunable dye lasers: a preliminary report. Arch Dermatol 1986;122:1016.

56. Tan OT, Sherwood K, Gilchrest BA. Treatment of children with portwine stains using the flashlamp-pulsed tunable dye laser. N Engl J Med 1989;320:416.

57. Taylor CR, Gange RW, Dover JS, et al. Treatment of tattoos by Q-switched ruby laser: a dose-response study. Arch Dermatol 1990;126:893.

58. Tomita Y, Mihashi S, Nagata K, et al. Mutagenicity of smoke condensates induced by CO_2 laser irradiation and electrocauterization. Mutat Res 1981;89:145.

59. Touquet VLR, Carruth JAS. Review of the argon laser treatment of port wine stains with the argon laser: Lasers Surg Med 1984;4:191.

60. Walker NP, Matthews J, Newsom SW. Possible hazards from irradiation with the carbon dioxide laser. Lasers Surg Med 1986;6:84.

61. Walsh J, Morelli J, Parrish JA. Laser-tissue interactions and their clinical applications. Curr Probl Dermatol 1986;15:94.

62. Walsh JJ, Flotte TJ, Anderson RR, Deutsch TF. Pulsed CO_2 laser tissue ablation: effect of tissue type and pulse duration on thermal damage. Lasers Surg Med 1988;8:108.

63. Watanabe S, Anderson RR, Brorson S, Dalickas G, Fujimoto JG, Flotte TJ. Comparative studies of femtosecond to microsecond laser pulses on selective pigmented cell injury in skin. Photochem Photobiol 1991;53:757.

64. Watanabe S, Flotte TJ, McAuliffe DJ, Jacques SL. Putative photoacoustic damage in skin induced by pulsed ArF excimer laser. J Invest Dermatol 1988;90:761.

65. Wenig BL, Stenson KA, Wenig BM. Effects of plume produced by the Nd:YAG laser and electrocautery on the respiratory system. Lasers Surg Med 1993;13:242.

66. Wheeland RG, Walker NP. Lasers: 25 years later. Int J Dermatol 1986;25:209.

67. Wheeland RG. Clinical uses of lasers in dermatology. Lasers Surg Med 1995;16:2.

68. Wyman A, Duffy S, Sweetland HM, Sharp F, Rogers K. Preliminary evaluation of a new high-power diode laser. Lasers Surg Med 1992;12:506.

Textbook of Dermatologic Surgery, edited by John L. Ratz.
Lippincott–Raven Publishers, Philadelphia © 1998.

CHAPTER 20

Pulsed Light Sources for Vascular Lesions

Heidi A. Waldorf, Arielle N.B. Kauvar, and Roy G. Geronemus

HISTORY

A major advance in the treatment of cutaneous vascular lesions came in 1986 with U.S. Food and Drug Administration (FDA) approval of the flashlamp-pumped, pulsed-dye laser (PDL), the first laser to be based on the theory of selective photothermolysis. The wavelength of the PDL was initially set at 577 nm, the absorption maximum of oxyhemoglobin. This has since been increased to 585 nm, which provides greater depth of dermal penetration with similar vascular selectivity. Compared with the blue-green wavelengths emitted by the argon laser, this yellow-light laser minimizes absorptive interference by melanin. The longer, yellow wavelengths penetrate the skin more deeply than the shorter, blue-green wavelengths of the argon laser. The PDL pulse duration of 450 seconds is shorter than the 1- to 5-milliseconds thermal relaxation time of superficial blood vessels. Unlike continuous-wave lasers, each PDL pulse ends before heat can diffuse to adjacent structures. Damage is thereby isolated to the targeted blood vessels, sparing the surrounding tissue.

Originally studied on port wine stains, histologic evaluation confirmed the theoretical benefits of the PDL over continuous-wave lasers. Papillary and upper reticular dermal vessels reveal agglutination of erythrocytes and vessel wall degeneration to a depth of 1.2 mm. Fine granulation tissue replaces the damaged vessels after 1 week. Specimens taken at 1 month show a normal-appearing dermis and epidermis with fine capillaries and normal adnexal structures without fibrosis. On clinical examination these changes correlate with a 5- to 14-day period of posttreatment purpura with partial or complete vessel clearance without scarring at 1 month.

The efficacy and safety of the PDL have been proven for a variety of vascular lesions (Table 20-1). Scarring occurs in less than 0.1% of patients, and pigmentary changes are also rare and temporary. Infants as young as several days of age are now routinely given treatment for port wine stains and hemangiomas. In all age-groups, port wine stains show approximately 75% clearance after two or three treatment sessions. Complete clearing can be achieved in over 90% of patients with repetitive treatments. The rate and final degree of clearance depend on anatomic location of the lesion: unilateral port wine stains involving the central face and port wine stains of the extremities respond at the slowest rate. The PDL is also used to treat hemangiomas but has been most beneficial for superficial lesions.

Other vascular lesions have had similar success. Over 70% of spider telangiectasias of the face in children and 93% in adults clear after one PDL treatment. Patients with diffuse facial telangiectasias as a component of rosacea, actinic damage, and long-term corticosteroid therapy may require multiple treatment sessions but can achieve excellent cosmetic results. Indeed, there is some evidence to suggest that even the inflammatory component of rosacea is decreased following PDL treatment of telangiectasias. In addition, the incidence of flushing induced by vasodilation of

Heidi A. Waldorf: Department of Dermatology, Mount Sinai Medical Center, New York, New York; and Waldorf Dermatology and Laser Associates, Nanuet, New York 10954.

Arielle N.B. Kauvar: Department of Dermatology, New York University Medical Center; and the Laser Surgery Center of New York, New York, New York 10016.

Roy G. Geronemus: Department of Dermatology, New York University Medical Center; and the Laser Surgery Center of New York, 317 E 34th St, New York, New York 10016.

TABLE 20-1. *Cutaneous lesions responsive to the flashlamp-pumped pulsed-dye laser*

Vascular
Angiomas
Hemangiomas
Port wine stains
Pyogenic granuloma
Telangiectasias
    Actinic damage
    Poikiloderma of Civatte
    Rosacea
    Flushing
    Rothmund–Thomson syndrome
    Chronic corticosteroids (topical or systemic)
    Postsclerotherapy telangiectatic matting
    Postrhinoplasty red nose
    Surgical wounds under tension
Venous lake
Other
Erythematous/hypertrophic scars
Warts

telangiectatic vessels is reduced. Thicker vascular lesions such as pyogenic granulomas and venous lakes have also been treated with the PDL. Most recently, hypertrophic scars and recalcitrant warts have been successfully treated with the PDL, although the exact mechanism is unknown.

Clinical research on the PDL is ongoing. The PDLs currently available have several handpieces that deliver beams ranging from 2 to 10 mm in diameter. The spot size selected can now be tailored to the type of lesion to be treated. For example, for a large port wine stain, a larger spot size both increases the effective energy delivered and speeds treatment, since a larger surface area is covered with each laser pulse. Smaller spot sizes reduce purpura and may be more appropriate for small, isolated telangiectasias. An experimental handpiece currently under study produces an elliptic beam designed to optimize the treatment of linear vessels. Modifications in pulse duration may aid in targeting larger-caliber, thicker-walled venules such as those of the lower extremities. These vessels may require pulse durations of 1 to 10 milliseconds to be sufficiently damaged. Such long-pulse PDLs are currently undergoing clinical trials. Devices designed to cool the skin before each laser pulse may reduce epidermal damage caused by the PDL and allow the use of higher fluences.

A new, pulsed light source, the Photoderm VL, produces a noncoherent beam that includes a wide spectrum of wavelengths (500 to 1100 nm). The inclusion of longer wavelengths theoretically should provide deeper penetration to the target vessels and improved absorption by the deoxyhemoglobin that predominates in venules. Preliminary results for port wine stains, telangiectasias, and leg veins are promising; however, further clinical evaluations are required to determine the role of this device in the therapeutic armamentarium for the treatment of vascular disorders. The Photoderm device allows for treatment without significant darken-

ing or purpura of the treated area in most instances (Figs. 1 and 2). As with PDL treatment of vascular disorders, darker skinned individuals are more prone to pigmentary change after Photoderm treatment. This light source can be used with a variety of different parameters including wavelengths, pulse width, energy fluence, number of pulses, and interval between pulses. The specific parameters to be used will vary depending on the diameter of the blood vessel, anatomic location, and skin type.

PREOPERATIVE PLANNING

An important part of planning PDL treatment of any lesion is to prepare the patient for the resultant purpura. The lesions appear gray immediately after treatment and gradually turn deep purple or black over the next several hours. This purpura lasts 5 to 14 days depending on the spot size and energy fluence used. It takes several days before patients are able to cover the treated area effectively with cosmetics. Patients often prefer to plan treatments around weekends, holidays, or vacations. Another strategy is to limit each treatment to small areas that can be more easily covered with a bandage. Patients can be shown photographs of the purpura (Fig. 3).

FIG. 1. Diffuse, small-diameter telangiectases of the face. (See Color Plate 3.)

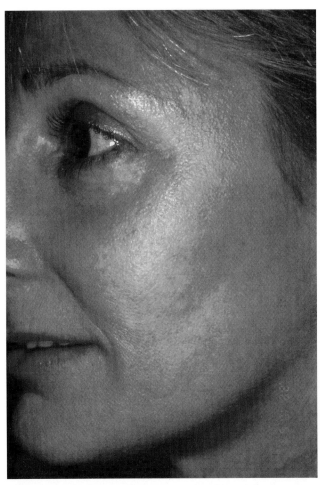

FIG. 2. Postoperative view after three treatments with the Photoderm filtered, flashlamp-pumped light source at an energy of 30 J/cm², filter of 515 nm, and pulse width of 3.5 milliseconds. (See Color Plate 4.)

In addition, we recommend that patients undergo a small test site (2 to 3 cm in diameter) before undergoing treatment of a larger area, so they can plan future treatments accordingly.

Patients should also have realistic expectations about the number of treatments required for a given lesion. Although many individual telangiectasias are cleared with one PDL treatment, some patients may require additional sessions, particularly if electrosurgery has previously failed. When treating diffuse vessel involvement, as in erythrotelangiectatic rosacea or port wine stains, patients must be advised that the area will appear latticelike between the initial treatments as a result of the vessels remaining between adjacent, nonoverlapping pulses.

TECHNIQUE

Preparation

Preparation must include reducing the risk of fire. Before laser treatment, remove all makeup on or around the treatment site with a nonflammable cleanser. Avoid using isopropyl alcohol, acetone, or other flammable preparatory solutions on the treatment site or the laser handpiece. If these substances must be used, follow with a thorough saline rinse and allow the area to dry completely before beginning laser treatment. Use water, saline, or a water-based lubricant to moisten any potentially combustible materials that remain in the field, including gauze and drapes. In particular, keep hair in or adjacent to the treatment site moist, or consider shaving.

All staff should wear wavelength-specific safety goggles. The eye protection used for the patient depends on the location of the lesion to be treated. For lesions on the eyelids, use a metal ocular shield for the affected side. Coat the inside of the shield with an ophthalmologic antibiotic ointment. After anesthetizing the eye with an ophthalmologic anesthetic drop, slide the shield under the lids. To decrease the risk of corneal abrasion after the shield is removed, patch this eye for 3 hours. The contralateral eye may be covered with wet gauze or a solid metal shield during PDL treatment. For lesions elsewhere, the eyes may be covered with wet gauze, opaque goggles, or wavelength-specific safety goggles.

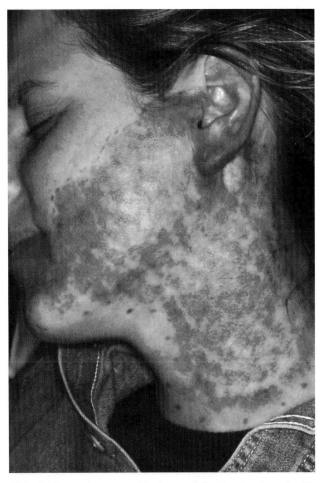

FIG. 3. Purpura over treated area following treatment with pulsed-dye laser (PDL). (See Color Plate 5.)

Anesthesia

The need for anesthesia with the PDL depends on the size and location of the lesion to be treated and the age and pain tolerance of the patient. Each PDL pulse causes a sharp, stinging pain that is often compared with the sensation of the snap of a rubber band accompanied by the feeling of heat. Because the discomfort is short-lived, even a young child can usually tolerate the few pulses required to ablate an isolated spider telangiectasia. Larger surface areas can also often be treated without anesthesia in young infants and many adults. Use the patient's response to a PDL test treatment to guide the use of anesthesia for subsequent sessions.

The issue of anesthesia most commonly arises for young children with port wine stains but may also be applicable for some adults. Patients over 6 months of age can be given an eutectic mixture of local anesthetic (EMLA) cream topically and/or anesthesia with 2% lidocaine without epinephrine, either by local infiltration or regional nerve block. Outline in ink the vascular lesion to be treated before applying topical or local anesthesia because of vasoconstriction induced by the anesthetic agent.

The safe use of the PDL depends on immobilizing the patient to avoid excessive overlapping of laser pulses and to prevent the accidental displacement of protective eyewear. For young children and some adults with port wine stains involving multiple dermatomes, this may require general anesthesia. Nonflammable inhalational agents, intramuscular ketamine, or intravenous propofol may be helpful. General anesthesia should be administered by an experienced anesthesiologist in an environment with up-to-date monitoring and emergency equipment.

Because of the risk of combustion when the PDL is used in the presence of oxygen, use the PDL in room air whenever possible. However, some patients do require the use of supplemental oxygen because of the length of treatment, patient medical requirements, or restrictions applied by the anesthesia team. In these cases take precautions to reduce the risk of oxygen pooling and leakage. Avoid the use of nasal cannula and face masks. Endotracheal intubation may be considered but adds to the morbidity and invasiveness of an otherwise relatively brief, uncomplicated laser procedure. An alternative to endotracheal intubation is the laryngeal mask airway. Insert this device into the patient's pharynx after anesthesia is induced. Then inflate the cuff of mask to form a low-pressure seal around the larynx to limit oxygen leakage. With any form of intubation, oxygen leakage is more likely to occur if used with positive-pressure ventilation. To confirm that the airway has been sealed, test the oxygen concentration at the mouth with an oxygen analyzer or capnograph. However, the laser surgeon and anesthesiologist must be aware that leaks can occur during treatment if a cuff becomes dislodged. All masks, cannulas, and airways should be made of clear or translucent materials because colored masks and airway materials can ignite with the PDL.

Laser Protocol

The location and morphologic features of the lesion being treated determine the initial parameters for the PDL and the interval time between treatment sessions (Table 20-2). In general, treat infants and children with lower fluences than for adults. Lesions on the face can tolerate higher fluences than those on the neck and chest. The fluence must also be modified based on skin pigmentation. Because melanin interferes with absorption of the dye laser pulses, energy delivery is reduced in more highly pigmented skin. However, if higher fluences are used, the resultant epidermal temperature change can induce epidermal blistering. In darkly pigmented patients the laser treatment dosages must be kept very low, often subtherapeutic, to avoid damage to the epidermis and prevent the possibility of scarring. The hyperpigmentation sometimes induced by PDL treatment can also interfere with therapy, and additional laser treatments should be deferred for a given site until the pigmentation has resolved.

Use the clinical response to a test pulse as a gauge for the appropriate PDL parameters. Suitable laser settings should produce purpura without excessive edema, crusting, blistering, or other epidermal change. Lower the expected degree of vessel clearance when using a larger spot size. Test one or several fluences and spot sizes simultaneously.

TABLE 20-2. *Recommended pulsed-dye laser treatment parameters for select cutaneous lesions**

Lesion	Energy fluence (J/cm^2)/ spot size (mm)	Treatment interval (weeks)
Port wine stain		
Child	5.75–7.75/>5 4.5–5.0/10	4–6
Adult	6.50–8.0/>5 5.0/10	4–6
Telangiectasia		
Facial telangiectasia	7.0–8.0/2	4
	6.0–7.5/5	4
Poikiloderma (neck)	5.0–7.0/>5 4–4.5/10	4
Postsclerotherapy Matting (legs)	6.5–8.0/>5	10–12†
Hemangiomas		
Proliferative phase	5.0–7.0/>5 5/10	2–3
Involution phase	5.0–7.0/>5 5/10	4–8
Hypertrophic scars	6.0–7.5/>5	4–8
Warts	7.0–9.0/>5	4

* Parameters should be modified for lesion location, skin pigmentation, and individual response to treatment as described in the text. When larger spot sizes are used, the fluence should begin at the lower range.

† Retreatment may be resumed earlier if postinflammatory hyperpigmentation is resolved.

Port Wine Stains

The PDL is the treatment of choice for port wine stains (Figs. 3–5). The entire lesion may be treated in one session, or it can be subdivided into smaller areas for each treatment. Any given site should be treated no more frequently than every 4 weeks. Although some authors advocate overlapping spots by 10% to 33%, using nonoverlapping pulses reduces the risk of epidermal change. Use a fluence of 5.75 to 7.75 J/cm^2 with a 5- or 7-mm diameter beam for children. For adults whose port wine stains may involve larger vessels, higher fluences of 6.5 to 8 J/cm^2 are often needed. An average improvement of 50% is seen after one PDL treatment with an additional 10% clearance with each subsequent session. The response of resistant port wine stains can be improved by increasing the spot size. Port wine stains with hypertrophic scarring or skin texture changes from past treatment with continuous-wave lasers or irradiation may require increasing the laser fluence used by 0.5 to 1 J/cm^2. Vaporize nodular lesions within the port wine stain with a continuous-wave vascular laser, a carbon dioxide laser, or electrosurgery at the time of PDL treatment.

Telangiectasia

The PDL is useful for a variety of telangiectatic lesions (Fig. 6). Spider telangiectasias generally clear after one or two PDL treatments using fluences of 6.0 to 7.5 J/cm^2 with a 5-mm spot size. Reserve higher fluences for older children, adults, or subsequent treatment of resistant vessels. In lesions smaller than the spot size used, apply one pulse to the central punctum of the spider lesion. The lesion should become purpuric immediately and should no longer blanch with pressure. If the lesion still blanches, fire a second superimposed pulse. Treat radiating vessels not covered by the initial pulse with subsequent pulses with 0% to 10% overlap. Smaller spot sizes have the advantage of reduced purpura, but to be effective, use higher fluences of 8.5 to 10 J/cm^2.

Other forms of facial telangiectasias respond well to the PDL but are more likely to require more than one treatment session. Narrow, linear vessels such as those frequently found around the nasal ala respond well to treatment using an elliptic spot size at 6.5 to 6.75 J/cm^2. Larger, blue vessels respond less well than smaller, red vessels as a result of a longer thermal relaxation time and a higher ratio of deoxygenated to oxygenated hemoglobin in the former. Vessels larger than 1 mm in diameter may respond better to a continuous-wave vascular laser like the tunable dye or copper vapor lasers. Clearance of large areas of fine, interlacing vessels on the face such as found in rosacea and certain genetic syndromes is best achieved using nonoverlapping pulses of a larger spot size (5 or 7 mm) with a fluence of 6 to 7.5 J/cm^2 or a 10-mm spot at 4.5 to 5 J/cm^2.

Treatment of nonfacial telangiectasias requires special attention to the lesion site. The photodistributed reticulated

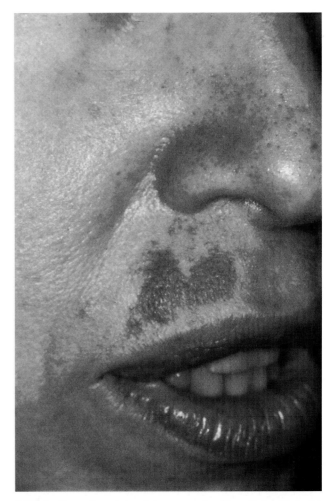

FIG. 4. Port wine stain of the upper lip. (See Color Plate 6.)

telangiectasia of the cheeks, neck, and upper chest of poikiloderma of Civatte is effectively cleared at fluences of 6.5 to 7 J/cm^2 with a 5-mm spot size after an average of four treatment sessions. Because the neck and chest are particularly susceptible to adverse side effects, it is important to evaluate a test treatment at a low energy level before treating a large area. For fair-skinned whites, test a fluence of 5 to 6 J/cm^2 with a 7-mm spot or 4 to 4.5 J/cm^2 with a 10-mm spot. Generalized essential telangiectasia, a progressive disorder characterized by netlike, noninflamed, dilated vessels, particularly on the lower extremities, has been treated similarly.

Laser treatment of leg telangiectasias has posed a more difficult challenge. Early attempts to treat lower-extremity telangiectasias with the PDL were disappointing with less improvement and more and longer lasting hypopigmentation and hyperpigmentation than is seen after treatment of other sites. More recent attempts to define the usefulness of the PDL for leg telangiectasias have had more success. Many red telangiectasias less than 0.6 mm in diameter, including postsclerotherapy telangiectatic matting, are responsive to fluences of 6.5 to 8 J/cm^2 using a 5- or 7-mm spot. PDL therapy is most effective if associated varicose and reticular feeding vessels are treated first. Hyperpigmentation for up to 12 weeks following treatment is common but not predictable.

Hemangiomas

The treatment of hemangiomas with the PDL has produced some controversy between pediatricians and laser surgeons. It is well known that after a proliferative phase, hemangiomas spontaneously involute; however, this process can take many years and be both psychologically and functionally devastating for a child. Excessive growth can lead to soft tissue deformities requiring surgical correction. The therapeutic goal of early intervention during the proliferative phase is to eliminate or retard the growth of the superficial component before it has the opportunity to expand. By minimizing growth, ulceration, bleeding, and obstruction of vital organs may be lessened or avoided. Subsequently, PDL

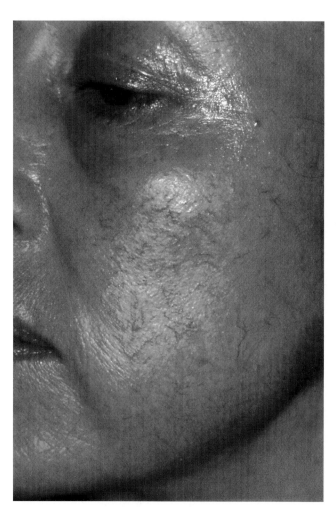

FIG. 6. Diffuse, medium-diameter telangiectases of the cheeks. (See Color Plate 8.)

treatment may hasten resolution of involuting lesions. Although the deepest portion of a cavernous or mixed hemangioma is beyond the approximate 1.5-mm depth of PDL penetration, as the superficial component is cleared, deeper vessels might be reached with successive treatments. For proliferating hemangiomas use a fluence of 5 to 7J/cm^2 every 2 to 3 weeks until the parents report that new growth has stopped or the lesion appears silver-gray, signifying the start of involution. Once involution has begun, prolong the treatment interval to 1 to 2 months. Compressing the hemangioma with a glass slide during laser treatment may help target the deeper vessels. Ninety percent of superficial lesions clear completely. Rapidly proliferating hemangiomas and those obstructing vital organs require prompt attention and referral to an experienced physician for intralesional or systemic steroids, interferon, or surgery (Figs. 8 and 9).

Scars and Striae

The treatment of scars has been advanced by the PDL. Treat scar telangiectasias as well as persistent background

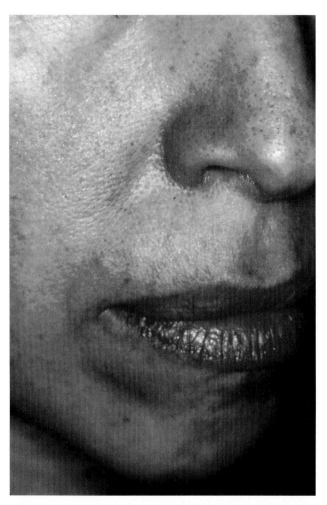

FIG. 5. Postoperative view after PDL photocoagulation of an upper-lip port wine stain. Five treatments were required at an energy of 7.25 J/cm^2 and a spot size of 5.0 mm. (See Color Plate 7.)

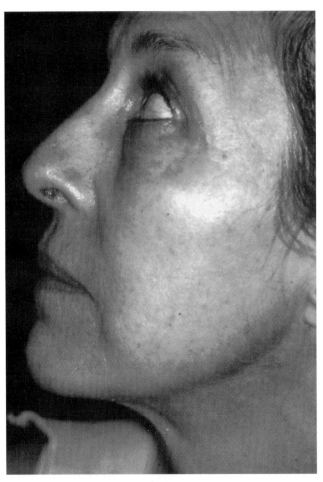

FIG. 7. Postoperative view after two treatments with the PDL using an elliptic spot size at 6.75 J/cm². (See Color Plate 9.)

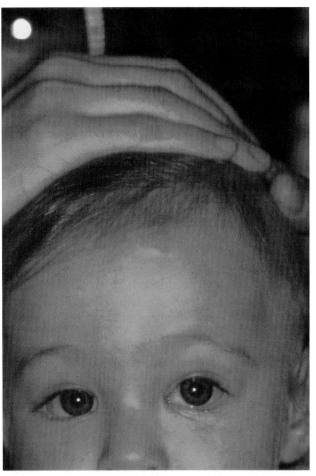

FIG. 9. Postoperative view of same child as in Fig. 8 at 8 months of age after four treatments with the PDL using a 5-mm spot size at 8 J/cm². (See Color Plate 11.)

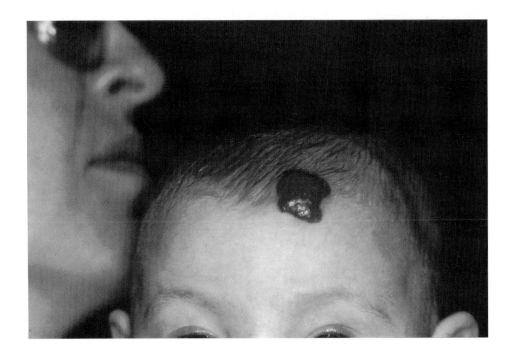

FIG. 8. (A) Four-month-old child with a superficial but thick hemangioma. (See Color Plate 10.)

erythema as described earlier for telangiectasias. An advantage of the PDL for hypertrophic scars and keloids is the observed flattening and softening of the scar first reported in an study of median sternotomy scars. The origin of this effect is unknown but has been postulated to be a consequence of reduced perfusion, a shift in collagen synthesis, or possibly a result of decreasing endothelial-directed collagen synthesis. Use a large spot size at 6 to 7.5 J/cm² and a treatment interval of 4 to 8 weeks. The PDL treatment may be combined with the use of intralesional steroids and topical silicone dressings for a synergistic effect. The PDL has also been used to improve the texture of stretch marks at low fluences of 4 to 4.5 J/cm² with the 10-mm spot size.

Warts

The PDL has recently been approved by the FDA for the treatment of warts. In a recent multicenter trial complete resolution of warts was achieved in 93% of patients after an average of two to three PDL treatments. To treat hyperkeratotic warts, pare each wart to reveal bleeding points. Achieve hemostasis with aluminum chloride. Then fire 3 or 4 superimposed, repetitive pulses using a 5- or 7-mm-diameter beam at 7 to 9 J/cm² to each wart and its peripheral border. The presumed mechanism is vascular-specific injury inflicted on the wart's predominantly dermal blood supply. If no response is seen after approximately three treatments, complete resolution is unlikely. Warts of immune-compromised patients do not respond to the PDL.

POSTOPERATIVE MANAGEMENT

Although no dressing is necessary, immediately after PDL treatment of a vascular lesion or scar apply a cool hydrogel dressing to decrease discomfort. As an alternative, some physicians prefer to apply an antibiotic ointment. Patients are instructed that they can wash the area gently. If there is any crusting or blister formation, an antibiotic ointment and nonstick dressing should be changed twice daily until resolution. If there is no epidermal change, the patient can begin to use cosmetics on the day of treatment.

Following the treatment of warts with the PDL, cleanse the area with povidone-iodine solution and allow it to dry before applying a nonstick dressing. The patient should change this dressing twice daily. Ointments are avoided to prevent a moist environment conductive to spread of the papilloma virus.

ADVERSE SEQUELAE AND COMPLICATIONS

As described, the PDL is effective for a variety of lesions with minimal incidence of adverse sequelae. The major disadvantage of the technique is the transient purpura that lasts up to 2 weeks and may be difficult to camouflage in the initial days after treatment. During this period the most common epidermal changes are crusting and scaling, which occur after 4% and 12% of treatments, respectively. Blistering is seen in less than 1% of cases. A spongiotic dermatitis has also been reported after multiple treatments with the PDL. When dermatitis or blistering are seen in and around the treated area, a contact dermatitis caused by the antibiotic ointment or dressing should be suspected.

Pigmentation changes are infrequent. In a retrospective study by Levine and Geronemus of 500 patients with cutaneous vascular lesions treated with the PDL, transient hyperpigmentation and hypopigmentation were seen in 1% and 2.6% of patients, respectively. Pigmentation changes generally resolve in several months. They are more frequent in darkly pigmented or tan skin and on the lower extremities.

Scarring is rare. In the study just mentioned the incidence of atrophic scarring was less than 0.1%. The use of overlapping pulses increases this risk. Biopsies of double-pulsed areas reveal nonspecific thermal damage to the superficial dermis and epidermis. Hypertrophic scarring was not seen in this study and had been reported with the PDL only once. This can be compared with the risk of hypertrophic scarring with the argon laser, which has been reported to be as high as 40%. Using the lowest effective fluences and minimizing pulse overlapping reduce the risk of complications with the PDL.

Infection following PDL treatment is also highly unusual. Bacterial impetigo following epidermal disruption can be avoided with proper wound care. Herpes simplex infection of a treated area has been reported anecdotally but is not a standard risk. PDL treatment should be deferred in patients with an active herpes lesion. Partial-thickness burns have been reported during the use of the PDL in the presence of supplemental oxygen by us and others. No permanent scarring has occurred to date.

SUGGESTED READING LIST

1. Alster TS. Improvement of erythematous and hypertrophic scars by the 585-nm pulsed dye laser. Ann Plast Surg 1994;32:186.
2. American national standard for the safe use of lasers. Orlando, FL: Laser Institute of America, February 1993.
3. Anderson RR, Parrish JA. Microvasculature can be selectively damaged using dye lasers: a basic theory and experimental evidence in human skin. Lasers Surg Med 1981;1:263.
4. Anderson RR, Parrish JA. Selective photothermolysis: precise microsurgery by selective absorption of pulsed radiation. Science 1983;220:524.
5. Ashinoff R, Geronemus RG. Capillary hemangiomas and treatment with the flashlamp-pulsed dye laser. Arch Dermatol 1991;127:202.
6. Ashinoff R, Geronemus RG. Flashlamp-pumped pulsed dye laser for port-wine stains in infancy: earliest versus later treatment. J Am Acad Dermatol 1991;24:467.
7. Ashinoff R, Geronemus RG. Treatment of port-wine stain in a black patient with the pulsed dye laser. J Dermatol Surg Oncol 1992;18:147.
8. Association of Operating Room Nurses. Standards and recommended practices. Denver, CO: The Association, 1994.
9. Broska P, Martinho E, Goodman M. Comparisons of the argon tunable dye laser with the flashlamp pulsed dye laser in treatment of facial telangiectasia. J Dermatol Surg Oncol 1994;20:749.
10. Diericky C, Goldman MP, Fitzpatrick RE. Laser treatment of erythema-

tous/hypertrophic and pigmented scars in 26 patients. Plast Reconstr Surg 1995;95:84.

11. Dover JS, Arndt KA, Geronemus RG, et al. Understanding lasers. In: Illustrated cutaneous laser surgery: a practitioner's guide. Norwalk, CT: Appleton & Lange, 1990:1.

12. Epstein RH, Brummett RR, Lask GP. Incendiary potential of the flash-lamp pumped 585 nm tunable dye laser. Anesth Analg 1990;71:171.

13. Epstein RH, Halmi BH. Oxygen leakage around the laryngeal mask airway during laser treatment of port-wine stains in children. Anesth Analg 1994;78:486.

14. Epstein RH, Halmi B, Lask GP. Anesthesia for cutaneous laser therapy. Clin Dermatol 1995;13:21.

15. Garbin GS, et al. The laryngeal mask as an airway during laser treatment of port wine stains. Anesthesiology 1991;75:A953.

16. Garden JM, Bakus AD, Paller AS. Treatment of cutaneous hemangiomas by the flashlamp-pumped pulsed dye laser: prospective analysis. J Pediatr 1992;120:550.

17. Garden JM, Kauvar AN, Bakus AD, Waldorf HA, Geronemus RG. Pulsed dye laser treatment of superficial leg veins. Lasers Surg Med 1995;(suppl 7):57.

18. Garden JM, Polla LL, Tan OT. The treatment of port-wine stains by the pulsed dye laser. Arch Dermatol 1988;124:889.

19. Garden JM, Tan OT, Kerschmann R, et al. Effect of dye laser pulse duration on selective cutaneous vascular injury. J Invest Dermatol 1986;87:653.

20. Geronemus RG. Poikiloderma of Civatte. Arch Dermatol 1990;126:547 (letter).

21. Geronemus R. Treatment of spider telangiectasias in children using the flashlamp-pulsed dye laser. Pediatr Dermatol 1991;8:61.

22. Geronemus RG, Ashinoff R. The medical necessity of evaluation and treatment of port-wine stains. J Dermatol Surg Oncol 1991;17:76.

23. Goldman MP, Bennett RG. Treatment of telangiectasia: are view. J Am Acad Dermatol 1987;17:167.

24. Goldman MP, Fitzpatrick RE. Pulsed-dye laser treatment of leg telangiectasia: with and without simultaneous sclerotherapy. J Dermatol Surg Oncol 1990;16:338.

25. Goldman MP, Fitzpatrick RE. Treatment of cutaneous vascular lesions. In: Goldman MP, Fitzpatrick RE, eds. Cutaneous laser surgery: the art and science of selective photothermolysis. St. Louis, MO: Mosby, 1994:19.

26. Goldman MP, Weiss RA, Brody HJ, Coeman WP, Fitzpatrick RE. Treatment of facial telangiectasia with sclerotherapy, laser surgery, and/or electrodesiccation: a review. J Dermatol Surg Oncol 1993;19:889.

27. Gonzalez E, Gange RW, Momtaz K. Treatment of telangiectasias and other benign vascular lesions with the 577-nm pulsed dye laser. J Am Acad Dermatol 1992;27:220.

28. Greenwald J, Rosen S, Anderson RR, et al. Comparative histological studies of the tunable dye (at 577 nm) laser and argon laser: the specific vascular effects of the dye laser. J Invest Dermatol 1981;77:305.

29. Hermens JM, Bennett MJ, Hirshman CA. Anesthesia for laser surgery. Anesth Analg 1983;62:218.

30. Hruza GJ, Geronemus RG, Dover JS, Arndt KA. Lasers in dermatology: 1993. Arch Dermatol 1993;129:1026.

31. Kauvar AB, Geronemus RG. Repetitive treatments of persistent port-wine stains with the pulsed dye laser is beneficial in most patients. Lasers Surg Med 1994;14(suppl 6):47.

32. Kauvar AN, Waldorf HA, Geronemus RG. Effect of 7 mm vs. 5 mm spot size on pulsed dye laser treatment of port-wine stains and hemangiomas. Lasers Surg Med 1995;(suppl 7):56.

33. Levine VJ, Geronemus RG. Adverse effects associated with the 577- and 585-nanometer pulsed dye laser in the treatment of cutaneous vascular lesions: a study of 500 patients. J Am Acad Dermatol 1995;32:613.

34. Lowe NJ, Behr KL, Fitzpatrick R, Goldman M, Ruiz-Esparza J. Flashlamp pumped dye laser for rosacea-associated telangiectasia and erythema. J Dermatol Surg Oncol 1991;17:522.

35. Lowe NJ, Burgess P, Borden H. Flashlamp dye laser fire during general anesthesia oxygenation: case report. J Clin Laser Med Surg 1990.

36. Mulikan JB, Yound AE. Vascular birthmarks: hemangiomas and malformations. Philadelphia: WB Saunders, 1988.

37. Nelson JS, Milner TE, Anvari B, et al. Dynamic epidermal cooling during pulsed laser treatment of port-wine stain: a new methodology with preliminary clinical evaluation. Arch Dermatol 1995;131:695.

38. Noe JM, Finley J, Rosen S, Arndt KA. Postrhinoplasty red nose: differential diagnosis and treatment by laser. Plast Reconstr Surg 1981;67:661.

39. Potozkin JR, Geronemus RG. Treatment of the poikilodermatous component of the Rothmund-Thomson syndrome with the flash lamp-pumped pulsed dye laser: a case report. Pediatr Dermatol 1991;8:162.

40. Rabinowitz LG, Esterly NB. Special symposium: anesthesia and/or sedation for pulsed dye laser therapy. Pediatr Dermatol 1992;9:132.

41. Renfro LR, Geronemus RG, Kauvar AB. Anatomical differences of port-wine stains located on the trunk and extremities in response to treatment with the pulsed dye laser. Lasers Surg Med 1994;14(suppl 6):47.

42. Reyes BA, Geronemus RG. Treatment of port-wine stains during childhood with the flashlamp-pumped dye laser. J Am Acad Dermatol 1990;23:1142.

43. Sherwood KA, Tan OT. The treatment of capillary hemangiomas with the flashlamp-pumped pulsed dye laser. J Am Acad Dermatol 1990;22:136.

44. Sosis MB. Operating room safety during laser surgery. In: Medical laser safety reference guide. Orlando, FL: Laser Institute of America, November 1990, p. 124.

45. Tan OT, Sherwood K, Gilchrest BA. Treatment of children with port-wine stains using the flashlamp-pumped pulsed dye laser. N Engl J Med 1989;320:416.

46. Waldorf HA, Alster TS, Kauvar AN, McMillan K, Geronemus RG, Nelson S. Effect of dynamic cooling on 585-nm pulsed dye laser treatment of port-wine stain birthmarks. Derm Surg 1997;23:657.

47. Waldorf HA, Kauvar AN, Geronemus RG, Leffell DJ. Remote fire with the pulsed dye laser: risk and prevention. J Am Acad Dermatol 1996;34:503.

48. Waldorf HA, Lask G, Geronemus R. Laser treatment of telangiectasias. In: Alster T, Apfelberg D, eds. Cosmetic laser surgery. New York: Wiley-Liss and Sons, 1996:93.

Textbook of Dermatologic Surgery, edited by John L. Ratz.
Lippincott–Raven Publishers, Philadelphia © 1998.

CHAPTER 21

Continuous-Wave Lasers and Automated Scanners

Brooke A. Jackson, Elizabeth McBurney, David H. McDaniel, and Jeffrey Steven Dover

HISTORY

Continuous-wave (CW) visible-light lasers have been used since the early 1970s in the treatment of benign vascular lesions. The argon laser was the mainstay of cutaneous laser surgery for the treatment of port wine stains and facial telangiectasias for almost 20 years. Other CW and quasi-CW lasers such as the CW dye, copper vapor, and krypton lasers were added to the visible-light laser armamentarium over the years. A major breakthrough for treatment of vascular lesions came in the late 1980s with the development of the pulsed-dye laser. While pulsed lasers have become the treatment of choice for port wine stains, especially immature lesions, visible-light CW lasers remain valuable tools for the treatment of ectatic vessels because of the absence of purpura in the healing phase.

Brooke A. Jackson: Derm Surgery Associates, 7515 Main St., Suite 240, Houston, TX 77030.

Elizabeth McBurney: Department of Dermatology, Tulane University Medical Center, New Orleans, LA.

David H. McDaniel: Department of Dermatology and Plastic Surgery, Eastern Virginia Medical School, Norfolk, VA 23507.

Jeffrey Steven Dover: Division of Dermatology, Beth Israel Deaconess Hospital, Boston, MA, 02215.

GENERAL CONSIDERATIONS

Continuous wave lasers and pulse train lasers in the visible spectrum used in the treatment of cutaneous vascular and pigmented disorders include three CW lasers—the argon laser with principal wavelengths of 488 and 514 nm, the CW argon pumped-dye laser (most often used at 577 to 585 nm or 514 nm), and the krypton laser with wavelengths of 520 and 568 nm—and two pulse train lasers: the copper vapor laser (used at 511 nm for pigmented lesions and 578 nm for vascular lesions) and the potassium titanyl phosphate (KTP) laser, which emits radiation at 532 nm. Robotic optical scanners and automated, robotized handpieces may be used with all of these lasers to achieve more precise target destruction and minimize scarring.

The wavelengths at which visible-light CW lasers operate are effective for cutaneous therapy because they are absorbed by the two major cutaneous chromophores, hemoglobin and melanin. These lasers are useful in the treatment of cutaneous vascular lesions such as port wine stains, hemangiomas, telangiectasias, spider nevi, cherry angiomas and venous malformations. They are also useful in the treatment of epidermal pigmented lesions such as benign lentigines and benign junctional nevi.

The wavelengths of the CW dye (577 to 585 nm), the copper vapor (578 nm), and the krypton (568 nm) lasers coincide with the beta absorption peak of oxyhemoglobin (577 nm), providing excellent absorption in blood vessels. Although the emission spectrum of the argon and KTP lasers does not coincide with absorption peaks of hemoglobin (488, 514, and 532 nm), the chromophore absorbs sufficient light at these wavelengths to result in somewhat selective tissue damage causing thrombosis and obliteration of vessels. Surrounding tissue, however, may be damaged from heat diffusion from the target chromophore. Spatial confinement of thermal damage is essential to localize vascular damage without collateral damage. Despite slightly heightened hemoglobin absorption, tissue adjacent to the vessels may be damaged with all these devices because the dwell time of the laser is frequently greater than the thermal relaxation time. Robotic scanners that operate in a 1- to 10-milliseconds range theoretically resolve this problem.

Laser light emitted by the visible-light CW lasers is also absorbed by melanin. The depth of penetration of CW laser light into skin is approximately 1 mm. The depth of penetration is determined by the wave length, spot size, and degree of pigmentation. Epidermal melanin in more darkly complected individuals absorbs more laser light and decreases transmission to dermal vessels. Although ideal for the treatment of epidermal lesions such as lentigines, the short penetration depth limits their ability to target dermal pigmented lesions such as nevus of Ota. For the same reason that CW lasers produce nonspecific thermal damage of vascular targets, they also induce nonspecific thermal damage when used in treatment of pigmented disorders, thus limiting the treatment precision and increasing nonspecific damage.

ARGON LASER

The argon laser was one of the first lasers to be widely used in clinical practice. Continuous wave medical argon lasers are capable of producing 1 to 20 W of power and emit blue-green light at six wavelengths in the visible spectrum between 488 and 514 nm. Most argon lasers operate at only a few watts of power and primarily use either 514 nm (green) or combine 488- and 514-nm (blue-green) wavelengths. Combined 488- and 514-nm wavelengths are used in the treatment of vascular lesions, whereas 514-nm light is selected for treatment of pigmented lesions. The laser energy emitted from the argon laser is delivered through an optical fiber to which handpieces of various spot sizes and with different focusing optics can be placed for delivery to the tissue target. Exposure time is controlled by a mechanical shutter or a robotic scanner.

CONTINUOUS-WAVE DYE LASER

The CW dye laser, otherwise known as the tunable dye laser, uses organic yellow rhodamine dye that is pumped by an argon laser to produce an adjustable band of wavelengths of yellow light ranging from 488 to 638 nm. The CW dye laser is most often used between 577 and 590 nm for the treatment of vascular lesions in an effort to maximize hemoglobin absorption. It is usually used at shorter or longer wavelengths when treating pigmented lesions in an effort to avoid competing absorption by the beta absorption peak of oxyhemoglobin. This light energy can either be delivered as a continuous wave or be shuttered mechanically or electronically. Handpieces of various spot sizes are coupled to a fiberoptic and can be used freehand to trace individual vessels or attached to a robotized scanning device to treat larger areas.

KRYPTON LASER

The krypton laser uses a benign gas medium to produce light at several wavelengths, including 488 and 514 nm (blue and green), 514 nm (green), 568 nm (yellow) and 630 nm (red). The variety of wavelengths that can be delivered by this laser allows a range of treatment modalities for vascular or melanocytic lesions. The 568-nm wavelength is chosen for vascular lesions, whereas 514 nm is used for the treatment of pigmented lesions. This light is delivered through a fiberoptic coupled to a handpiece or through an automated scanner.

COPPER VAPOR LASER

The copper vapor laser produces both yellow and green light at wavelengths of 578 and 511 nm, respectively. The wavelength of 578 nm is used to treat vascular lesions, and 511 nm to treat pigmented lesions. Laser energy produced by heating elemental copper or copper bromide within the optical cavity of the laser is released as a train of 20- to 40-nanosecond pulses at a frequency of 10 to 15 kHz. This laser is referred to as a "quasicontinuous" laser because the frequency of emission of short pulse in the train is so high that it is recognized by the skin as a continuous wave of laser energy. The term "CW wave lasers" is used in the remainder of this chapter to refer to both CW and quasi-CW lasers. Like the argon laser, the copper vapor laser may be used either freehand from a handpiece coupled to a fiberoptic to trace individual vessels and pigmented areas or with an automated scanning device.

POTASSIUM TITANYL PHOSPHATE KTP LASER

The KTP laser is a frequency-doubled Nd:YAG laser that produces green light at 532 nm. The infrared light of the Nd:YAG laser at 1064 nm is passed through a KTP crystal, which then doubles its frequency and halves its wavelength to 532 nm. Because the 532-nm wavelength closely approximates the 542-nm absorption peak of oxyhemoglobin, the KTP laser is a useful tool in the treatment of vascular lesions. Three new KTP lasers that operate in the pulsed mode have recently been developed. Early clinical data demonstrate highly specific thermal damage restricted to cutaneous blood vessels.

AUTOMATED SCANNING DEVICES

Automated scanning devices can be attached to the end of the fiberoptic delivery system which convert the CW laser beam into a scanned, shuttered beam in an effort to reproduce the biologic effect of a pulsed laser. Thus automated scanning devices allow delivery of equivalent, reproducible laser treatments while minimizing untoward effects of CW lasers. Pulses of equivalent laser energy are delivered in varied, preprogrammed patterns and spot sizes to minimize thermal injury and scarring from CW lasers.

Several automated handpieces and robotic scanners are currently available. The Hexascan is the most commonly used robotic scanning device. It places uniform spots of laser irradiation in a hexagonal pattern up to 13 mm in diameter in such a way that no two adjacent areas are irradiated sequentially. The pulse duration is adjustable from 30 to 990 milliseconds. The original Mark I model is the one described in the literature and references. However, a Mark II model is now available that achieves shorter pulse durations. This is accomplished by using a smaller spot size. Pulses of energy are placed 2 mm apart at 50-millisecond intervals in nonadjacent spots. The final pattern is closely packed and resembles racked billiard balls. These devices reduce the tedium involved with individually tracing each vessel with the freehand method and provide faster treatment by covering larger lesional areas.

One limitation of the early versions of automated scanners was the inability to produce durations of exposure as long as 1 millisecond, which approximates the thermal relaxation time of 100-μm blood vessels. First generation scanners powered by low output CW lasers produced pulse durations longer than 30 milliseconds, too long to selectively damage cutaneous blood vessels. Newer-generation scanners have the capability of producing 1- to 10-millisecond exposures, which will theoretically improve treatment outcomes. Early animal and human study data support this potential (personal communication, C. Dierickx, MD, April 1996). One disadvantage of the scanners is the appearance of skip areas within the grid pattern. This is due to the gaussian curve of laser light deliverance. The edges of the grids can be difficult to overlap, and freehand tracing may be required to fill in the skip areas or a waffle iron–like pattern may result.

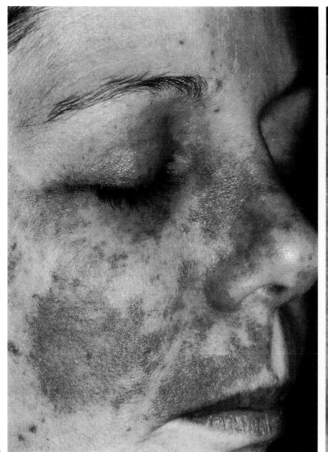 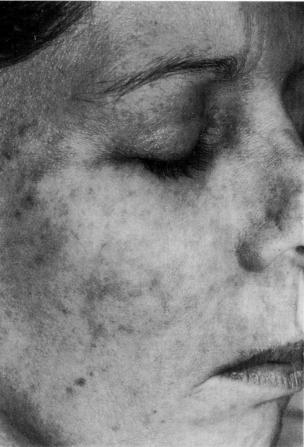

A
B

FIG. 1. (A) Congenital vascular capillary anomaly, port wine stain type. **(B)** One year after treatment (after five treatments at 8- to 12-week intervals): 585 nm, continuous-wave (CW) dye laser, Hexascan I, 22 J/cm², 130 milliseconds, 13-mm field size.

TREATMENT OF VASCULAR LESIONS

The following detailed discussion refers in general to the technique used for the treatment of port wine stains with CW visible-light lasers. The treatment of other vascular lesions and pigmented lesions is similar to that for port wine stains and is discussed in an abbreviated manner.

Preoperative Planning

Patient Selection

In selecting a patient for laser treatment the following criteria should be considered, to maximize treatment results.

Skin Type

Epidermal pigment in darkly complected patients absorbs laser light, allowing less penetration to the intended vascular target. Patients with skin types I and II respond best. Post-treatment hypopigmentation and hyperpigmentation are also more common in individuals with skin types III–VI.

Color

Flat or raised, deep red to purple port wine stains respond best. Some hypertrophic port wine stains in adults may improve even though they have been unresponsive to the pulsed dye laser. Immature port wine stains (light

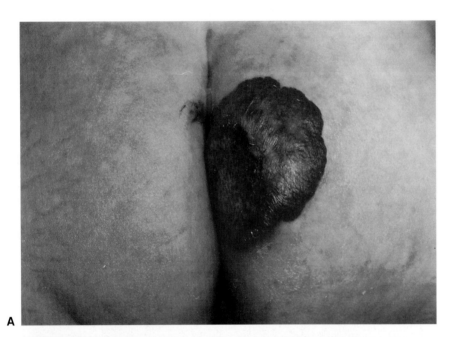

A

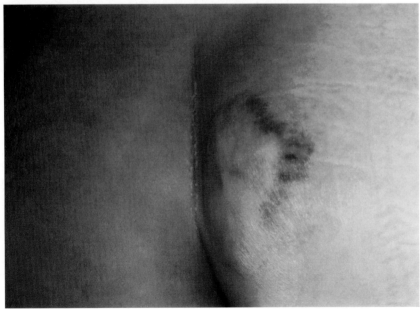

B

FIG. 2. (A) Hemangioma on right-side of buttocks in 3-month-old infant girl before treatment. (B) Six months after two treatments: 514 nm, argon laser, Hexascan I, 10 J/cm², 130 milliseconds, 13-mm field size.

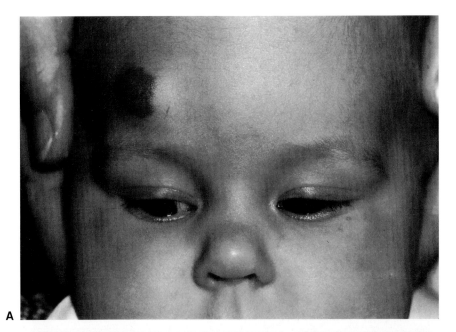

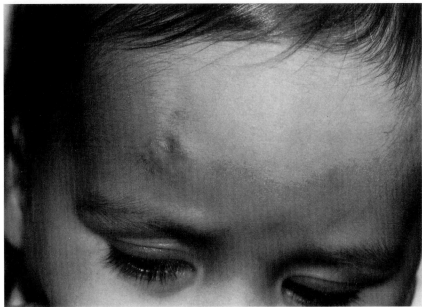

FIG. 3. (A) Cavernous hemangioma on right side of forehead in 4-month-old girl before treatment. **(B)** Four months after treatment (four sessions): 585 nm, CW dye laser, 1-mm spot, 0.6 to 0.8 W (focused and defocused), freehand painting technique.

pink, flat lesions) respond less well, mostly because the amount of absolute lightening is less, although the amount of relative lightening may be the same. The risk of scarring in immature port wine stains ranges from 1% to as high as 25% using the freehand technique, depending on the experience of the operator. This rate is thought to be significantly lower using robotized scanners. Given the success of the 585-nm, flashlamp-pumped, pulsed-dye laser in the treatment of immature port wine stains and the very low risk-benefit ratio, this pulsed-dye laser is the treatment of choice in children. Continuous-wave lasers have been used successfully in this age-group, and when used with a robotized scanner and in experienced hands, the risk of

scarring may be as low as that of the pulsed-dye laser, although this has not been demonstrated in a therapeutic trial.

Location

Port wine stains of the head and neck respond best (Fig. 1). Certain facial port wine stains, such as those of the upper lip, side of the nose, and neck, have a higher risk of healing with hypertrophic scarring as do port wine stains of the trunk and limbs. Lesions on the distal extremities respond less well than those situated on the proximal extremities.

Test Area

Although not an absolute predictor of final outcome, treatment of a test site in an inconspicuous area is an important indication of outcome in patients with port wine stains before CW visible-light laser treatment. Mark a 1- to 3-cm lesional area, and photograph it before treatment. The site is anesthetized using 1% lidocaine without epinephrine. Topical anesthetics such as eutectic mixture of local anesthetics (EMLA) cream or 30% lidocaine cream are not as effective but may be sufficient in some individuals. Hold the handpiece perpendicular and approximately 2 cm from the skin. Move the handpiece either in a continuous back-and-forth motion or in an enlarging concentric motion, avoiding overlap. Treated areas turn whitish/gray as a result of thermal coagulation of protein. Place noncollimated handpieces and robotic scanners directly on the skin so that their guide or foot plate gently touches the skin. Vessel disappearance with little or no graying is the desired end point.

The treated areas form a scab that may last up to 10 days or 2 weeks. Postoperative wound care consists of cleansing twice daily with mild soap and water and application of a topical antibiotic ointment with or without biologic dressing until the scab has resolved. Care should be taken not to lift or remove the scab, since this may induce scar formation. Sun avoidance and broad-spectrum sunscreen use are encouraged. Makeup may be applied once the scab has resolved.

The test site is evaluated 2 to 4 months after treatment. Pursuing further treatment is based on the degree of lightening, textural improvement, presence of pigmentary alteration, and presence of textural change of scarring.

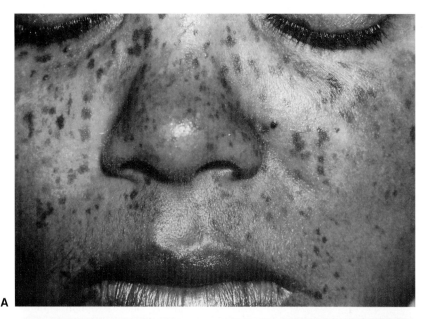

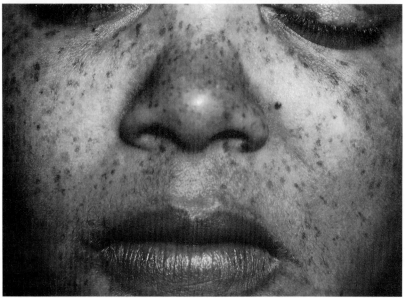

FIG. 4. **(A)** Benign facial lentigines in 36-year-old woman before treatment. **(B)** Five months after two treatments: 514 nm, argon laser, Hexascan I, 10 J/cm², 34 milliseconds, 3- to 5-mm field size. (Residual lesions were not evident.)

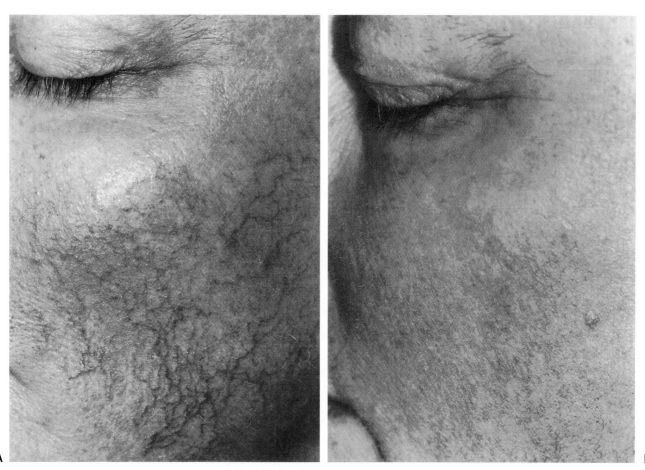

FIG. 5. (A) Rosacea-related facial telangiectasia in 54-year-old woman before treatment. **(B)** Fifteen months after treatment with vessel tracing technique: 585 nm, CW dye laser, 0.1-mm spot, 0.3 W (total of five treatment or touchup sessions).

Technique

Many techniques for using CW visible-light lasers to treat port wine stains have been devised. The freehand technique is commonly used. Move the handpiece in a continuous back-and-forth motion over the area to be treated. Treat nodular blebs of the port wine stain with higher power than the surrounding macular areas. Carry out procedures with the patient under local anesthesia using lidocaine with or without epinephrine. Topical EMLA does not usually provide sufficient anesthesia. The stripe technique—treating alternating rows of skin—and polka-dot method—treating 1- to 2-mm spots of skin while leaving areas of untreated skin between—are two methods of treatment thought to decrease potential scarring; however, neither method has proved to decrease the incidence of scarring, and patients are often dissatisfied with alternating areas of treated and untreated skin.

Adverse Sequelae

Complications after CW visible-light laser treatment include hypertrophic and atrophic scarring, as well as permanent hypopigmentation, depigmentation, and hyperpigmentation. The incidence of hypertrophic scarring ranges from 1% to 26% with the use of the freehand technique and in experienced hands may be considerably lower with the use of the robotized scanner. Factors contributing to this wide range include operator experience and treatment parameters. Although the risk of scarring on the upper lip and lateral nose is higher than for other areas of the face, this risk is even higher on nonfacial skin. Poor postoperative wound care with superficial infection and patient manipulation of crusting have the potential to cause scarring as well.

Other Vascular Lesions

Capillary Hemangiomas

Consider laser treatment of capillary hemangiomas for lesions in a rapid-growth phase, lesions causing functional problems of vital organs that are subject to repeated trauma, ulcerated hemangiomas, lesions causing a high level of parental anxiety, and lesions in a school-age child that have shown no sign of resolution.

If laser therapy is considered, the 585-nm, flash lamp-pumped pulsed-dye laser is the first line of therapy in superficial hemangiomas because of its low risk-benefit

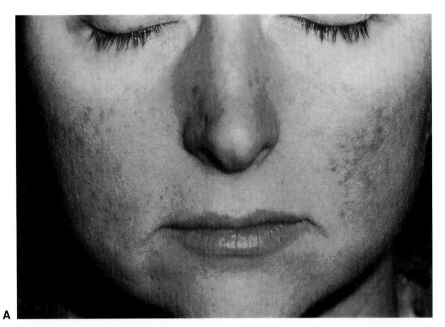

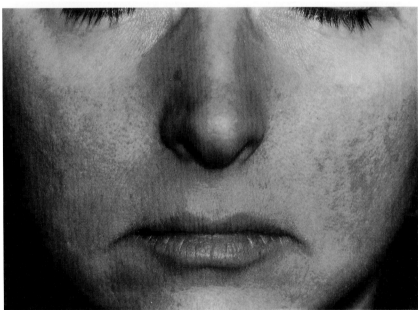

FIG. 6. (A) Rosacea-related telangiectasia in 37-year-old man before treatment. **(B)** One year after two treatments: 585 nm, CW dye laser, Hexascan I, 22 J/cm², 72 milliseconds, 13-mm field size.

ratio. Consider CW lasers in children whose hemangiomas have failed treatment with the 585-nm pulsed-dye laser or in whom there is a deeper vascular component, or in hemangiomas with thickness greater than 2 mm above the skin surface (Figs. 2 and 3). Although both the argon laser with 1-mm depth of penetration and the CW Nd:YAG laser with a depth of penetration of 2 to 8 mm may be more effective in treating lesions with a deeper component, they are not without risk of scarring. Use of a robotized scanning device may be of more benefit than either alone. Although it is desirable to use short dwell times to minimize undesired nonspecific thermal damage for other vascular disorders, selection of longer dwell times may be useful in recalcitrant hemangiomas.

Telangiectasia

Telangiectasias of the face (Figs. 4–6), trunk, and upper extremity are effectively treated with the CW visible-light lasers using the continuous method to "heat seal" the vessel. Hold the handpiece like a pen perpendicular to the surface of the skin. The rate of tracing and power settings are determined by the point at which the vessel seals or "disappears" without whitening. Anesthesia is not usually necessary; however, certain areas such as the tip and sides of the nose are sensitive, and in certain patients the pain threshold is relatively low. Application of EMLA cream for 1 or 2 hours under occlusion before treatment is helpful in these situations.

Choose the laser spot size to approximate the diameter of

the vessels to be treated. Choose the smallest effective spot size to minimize thermal damage and potential scarring. Use power settings of 0.1 to 0.3 W for vessels less than 0.1 to 0.3 mm in diameter. Trace vessels with a focused beam while the power output is slowly increased until the threshold for heat sealing is achieved. Power of 0.2 to 0.5 W may be needed to treat vessels up to 0.5 mm in diameter, and 0.6 to 0.8 W may be needed to treat vessels up to 1 mm in diameter. Exercise caution at these high power settings when treating nasal alar rim vessels to avoid overtreating, which can result in atrophic grooves or scars.

Reactive erythema that develops as the treatment progresses makes distinction between treated and untreated areas difficult and, along with discomfort, is often the limiting factor for an individual treatment session.

A linear crust often forms over the treated vessels within a day and lasts from a few days up to 2 weeks. Occasionally, edema may be observed. Advise the patient to cleanse the area twice daily with mild soap and water followed by application of a topical antibacterial ointment. Makeup may be worn after the crusting resolves. Sun avoidance and use of broad-spectrum ultraviolet A and B sunscreens are encouraged during wound healing and for up to 6 weeks in an effort to prevent hyperpigmentation, particularly over the malar eminence. Multiple, sequential laser treatments may be required for larger vessels.

Linear hyperpigmentation is a common side effect. This can be minimized by treating vessels less than 0.2 mm in diameter with the lowest effective power, using a spot size only slightly larger than the size of the vessel being treated,

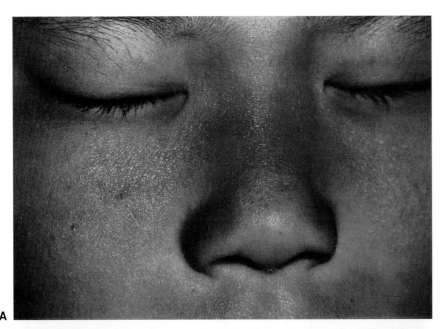

A

B

FIG. 7. (A) Spider angioma on right cheek in 9-year-old girl before treatment. **(B)** Six weeks after single treatment: CW dye laser, 585 nm, Hexascan I, 22 J/cm², 80 milliseconds.

and by sun avoidance during the healing phase. Although rare, atrophic scarring may also occur. Other side effects include hypopigmentation and linear, depressed scarring.

Vessels of the nasal alae and large-caliber blue facial vessels are the most difficult to clear. Results of CW visible-light laser treatment of the lower-extremity vessels have been disappointing. The best results are seen with vessels less than 0.1 mm in diameter. Recurrence and persistent hyperpigmentation are the most frequent adverse side effects.

Spider Nevi

Treatment of spider nevi with CW visible-light lasers yields consistently good results (Fig. 7). Treat the central feeder vessels to opalescence with a 0.5- or 1.0-mm spot size, and trace the surrounding vessels with a spot size equal to their diameter. Another option for treatment incorporates 585-nm pulsed-dye laser treatment of the entire lesion followed by CW visible-light laser treatment of residual flow in the central vessel. In high-flow lesions the central vessel may be compressed with a glass slide to reduce the flow. Treatment proceeds through the glass slide.

Recurrences are frequent only with high-flow lesions. The CW visible-light lasers are the choice over the pulsed-dye laser for high-flow lesions because they can generate higher tissue energy. Overzealous treatment of the central vessel in an effort to prevent recurrence can result in a scar.

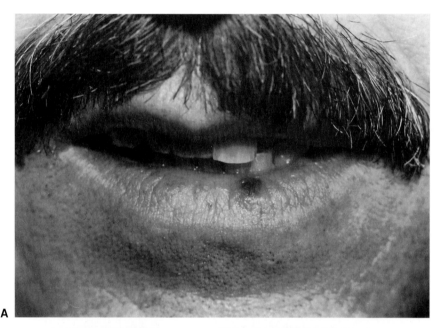

A

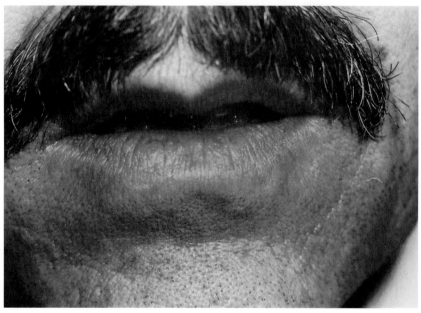

B

FIG. 8. (A) Venous lake on lower lip in 53-year-old man before treatment. **(B)** Four weeks after single treatment: 585 nm, CW dye laser, 1.0-mm spot, (focused and defocused), 0.6 W, freehand painting technique.

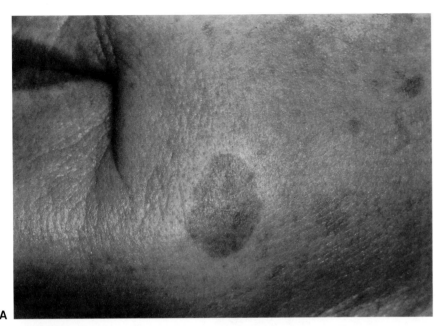

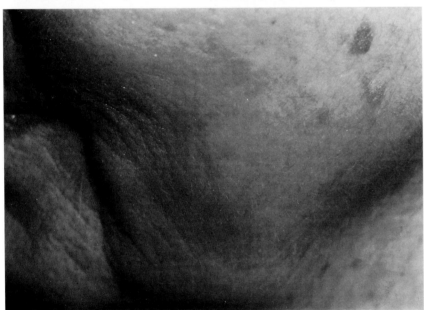

FIG. 9. (A) Benign solar lentigo in 65-year-old man before treatment. **(B)** Three weeks after treatment: 514 nm, argon laser, Hexascan I, 10 J/cm^2, 53 milliseconds, 13-mm field size.

Angiokeratomas and Cherry Angiomas

Both angiokeratomas and cherry angiomas respond well to freehand CW laser treatment. Use a 1-mm handpiece and 0.8 W power to irradiate the lesion until flattening but before whitening occurs.

Venous Lakes

The superficial location of the venous lakes allows for good penetration of the laser beam. Compress the lesion with a glass slide to its reduced size; then perform treatment through the glass slide. Opalescence is the desired end point. Most small lesions require only one treatment (Fig. 8); how-

ever, larger lesions may require a second treatment at monthly intervals. Care should be taken not to overtreat larger lesions in a single treatment session, since atrophic scarring and hypopigmentation may result.

COMPARATIVE EFFICACY OF CONTINUOUS-WAVE LASERS IN THE TREATMENT OF VASCULAR LESIONS

In general, there is little difference in the effectiveness of the various visible-light lasers when used freehand in the treatment of vascular lesions. Theoretically, lasers that emit nearest to the absorption peaks of hemoglobin absorption should produce the best results. This, however, has not been borne out by clinical results. The argon laser emitting at 488 and 514 nm is comparably effective to the CW dye laser at 577 nm for the treatment of facial telangiectasias. This may be accounted for by more vessel wall damage produced by argon laser light because of less selective hemoglobin absorption. There is a suggestion that the copper vapor laser produces less scarring and less posttreatment hyperpigmentation than the argon laser because of more selective vascular injury related to the laser's pulse duration.

Scanners increase the reproducibility of results and also increase the safety margin of CW lasers in the treatment of vascular lesions. It appears that, when scanned, the copper vapor laser produces more selective vessel destruction, which may result in better clinical outcomes. The power output (watts) of the laser attached to the scanner may be of greater importance than the wavelength, since the dwell time achievable is affected by the power input. Laser/scanner combinations vary, but the one that produces shorter dwell times may yield better clinical results. Despite the improvement in results in the treatment of port wine stains with scanned CW visible-light lasers, two controlled studies have conclusively demonstrated that the pulsed-dye laser achieves more lightening with less pigmentary changes than either the scanned CW dye laser or the scanned copper vapor laser. The new, larger spot sizes for the pulsed-dye lasers have improved results and speed up treatment of port wine stains, thus diminishing the role of CW laser for this disorder.

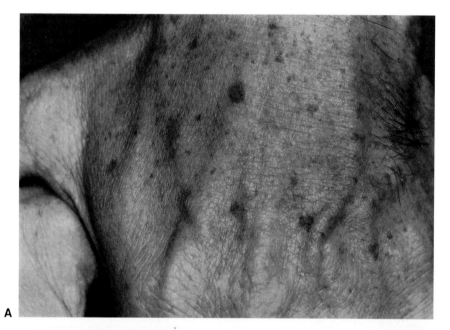

A

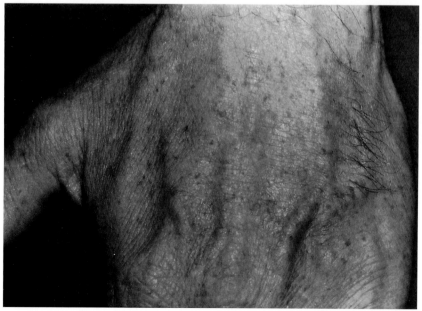

B

FIG. 10. **(A)** Benign solar lentigines on dorsal surface of hands in 55-year-old man before treatment. **(B)** Five weeks after single treatment: 514 nm, argon laser, Hexascan I, 16 J/cm², 55 milliseconds, 5-mm field size.

TREATMENT OF PIGMENTED LESIONS

Continuous-wave visible-light lasers (511, 514, and 532 nm) are useful in treating many benign lentigines and some benign pigmented lesions of the epidermis and dermoepidermal junction. Proper diagnosis of cutaneous melanocytic disorders is required before selecting and treating this modality. Continuous-wave visible-light lasers have limited depth of penetration and thus have no role in the treatment of dermal pigmented lesions. Continuous-wave lasers in combination with robotized scanning devices have been successful in treating a wide range of melanocytic disorders.

Epidermal Pigmented Lesions

Continuous-wave lasers are effective in the treatment of a variety of superficial pigmented lesions such as lentigines (Figs. 9 and 10). Local anesthesia is not required for treatment of these lesions.

Using the freehand technique, treat the lesion with a slightly defocused beam until it appears opalescent. A crust will form over the treated area within 1 to 2 days and will last up to 2 weeks. Advise the patient to cleanse the area twice daily with mild soap and water followed by application of a topical antibiotic ointment. A nonadherent dressing may be applied to larger treated areas.

Encourage sun avoidance for the treated areas. These CW lasers may also be used in combination with robotized scanning devices, which should be used in the 30- to 50-millisecond range.

TREATMENT TECHNIQUE WITH AUTOMATED SCANNING DEVICES

It is advisable to treat a test area in an inconspicuous location on the patient. Treatment description with the Hexascan is provided as an example of scanned CW laser treatment. Attach the Hexascan to the argon laser to deliver 514 nm (green) light at 10 to 12 J/cm^2. Use laser power of 2.0 to 2.2 W with pulse widths of 30 to 50 microseconds. Use lower fluences of 8 to 10 J/cm^2 for more darkly complected patients. Choose a scan size to approximate the size of the lesion or test area to be treated. Hold the scanner perpendicular to the skin and do not move it until the scan cycle is complete. although maximal fading or disappearance of the lesion occurs after 4 weeks, some lesions may require several treatments, which should be given at 4- to 6-week intervals.

Side effects include hypopigmentation, hyperpigmentation, and atrophic and hypertrophic scarring. Irregular placement of scanned fields can result in the appearance of geometric patterns and can be avoided with minimal overlap.

Controversy surrounds treatment of melanocytic nevi with CW lasers. The treatment of benign melanocytic nevi such as junctional nevi is a reasonable option if performed by knowledgeable and skilled physicians.

Although CW lasers are capable of treating a variety of benign pigmented lesions, they are not necessarily better than standard therapies. A recent comparative study evaluated liquid nitrogen cryotherapy, low fluence CO_2 laser, and a scanned argon laser beam—three commonly used modalities—in the treatment of lentigines. Liquid nitrogen was found to be superior to the other modalities in the degree of lightening achieved. Short-pulsed lasers, such as the Q-switched ruby laser, may be more effective.

Lentigo Maligna

The recurrence rate after argon laser treatment of lentigo maligna has been reported to be as high as 50%. Therefore CW lasers should be considered only as a treatment of last resort in poor surgical candidates in whom long-term follow-up is ensured.

Dermal Pigmented Lesions

Dermal pigmented lesions are not suited for treatment with CW visible-light lasers for two reasons. The penetration depth of these lasers is relatively shallow and spatial heat confinement cannot be assured results in nonspecific thermal damage. Although tattoos and nevi of Ota have been successfully treated with CW lasers, the final result is obtained by virtual replacement of the lesion with scar tissue. Short-pulsed lasers such as the Q-switched ruby, Nd:YAG, or alexandrite are the lasers of choice for dermal pigmented lesions.

COMPARATIVE EFFICACY OF CONTINUOUS-WAVE LASERS IN THE TREATMENT OF PIGMENTED LESIONS

There are no studies comparing the efficacy of the various CW visible-light lasers in the treatment of pigmented lesions. It is generally believed, however, that there is no sizable difference in outcome among these different lasers.

SUGGESTED READING LIST

1. Anderson R, Parrish J. Selective photothermolysis: precise microsurgery by selective absorption of pulsed radiation. Science 1983;220:524.
2. Apfelberg DB, Bailin PL, Rosenberg H. Preliminary investigation of KTP/532 laser light in the treatment of hemangiomas and tattoos. Lasers Surg Med 1986;6:38.
3. Apfelberg DP, Smith T, Maser MR, et al. Dot or pontillistic method for improvement in results of hypertrophic scarring in the argon laser treatment of port wine hemangiomas. Lasers Surg Med 1987;6:552.
4. Arndt KA. Argon laser therapy of small cutaneous vascular lesions. Arch Dermatol 1982;118:220.
5. Arndt KA. Argon laser treatment of lentigo maligna. J Am Acad Dermatol 1984;10:953.
6. Dierickx CC, Farinelli WA, Flotte T, Anderson RR. Effect of long-pulsed 532-nm Nd:YAG laser on port wine stains. Lasers Surg Med 1996; suppl 8:33.

7. Dinehart S, Waner M, Flock S. The copper vapor laser for treatment of cutaneous vascular and pigmented lesions. J Dermatol Surg Oncol 1993;19:370.

8. Dixon JA, Rotering RH, Heuther SE. Patients' evaluation of argon laser therapy of port wine stains, decorative tattoos and essential telangiectasia. Lasers Surg Med 1984;4:181.

9. Dixon JA, Heuther S, Rotering R. Hypertrophic scarring in argon laser treatment of port wine stains. Plast Reconstr Surg 1984;73:771.

10. Dover JS, Arndt KA, Geronemus RG, Olbricht SM, Noe JM, Stern RS. Illustrated cutaneous laser surgery: a practitioner's guide. Norwalk, CT: Appleton & Lange, 1990:73.

11. Dover JS, Geronemus R, Stern RS, O'Hare D, Arndt KA. Dye laser treatment of port wine stains: comparison of the continuous wave dye laser with a robotized scanning device and the pulsed-dye laser. J Am Acad Dermatol 1995;32(1):237.

12. Hruza GJ, Geronemus RG, Dover JS, Arndt KA. Lasers in dermatology: 1993. Arch Dermatol 1993;129:1026 (editorial).

13. Landthaler M, Haina D, Brunner R, et al. Neodymium YAG laser therapy for vascular lesions. J Am Acad Dermatol 1986;14:107.

14. McBurney E. Clinical usefulness of the argon laser for the 1990s. J Dermatol Surg Oncol 1993:19:358.

15. McDaniel DH, Mordon S. Hexascan: a new robotized scanning laser handpiece. Cutis 1990;45:300.

16. McDaniel DH. Clinical usefulness of the Hexascan: treatment of cutaneous vascular and melanocytic disorders. J Dermatol Surg Oncol 1993; 19:312.

17. McDaniel DH, Apfelberg DB. Options for laser selection in the treatment of cutaneous vascular and pigmented disorders and tattoos. Operative Techniques Plast Reconstr Surg 1994;1(3):181.

18. Mordon S, Rotteleur G, Brunetaud JM, Apfelberg DB. Rationale for automated scanners in laser treatment of port wine stains. Lasers Surg Med 1993;13:113.

19. Neuman RA, Leonhartsberger H, Bohler-Sommereggev K, Knobler R, Kokoschka EM, Honigsmann H. Results and tissue healing after copper vapor laser treatment of port wine stains and facial telangiectasia. Br J Dermatol 1993;128:306.

20. Neumann RA, Leonhartsberg H, Bohler-Sommeregger K, Knobler R,Kokoschka EM, Honigsmann H. Results and tissue healing after copper vapor laser (578 nm) treatment of port wine stains and facial telangiectasias. Br J Dermatol 1993;128:306.

21. Neumann RA, Knobler RM, Leonhartsberg H, Geghart W. Comparative histochemistry of port wine stains after copper vapor laser (578 nm) and argon laser treatment. J Invest Dermatol 1992;99:160.

22. Noe JM, Barsky SH, Geer DE, et al. Port wine stains and the response to argon laser therapy: successful treatment and the predictive role of color, age and biopsy. Plast Reconstr Surg 1980;65:130.

23. Pickering JW, Walker PHB, Halewyn CN. Copper vapor laser treatment of port wine stains and other vascular malformations. Br J Plast Surg 1990;43:273.

24. Rotteleur G, Mordon S, Buys B, et al. Robotized scanning laser handpiece for the treatment of port wine stains and other angiodysplasias. Lasers Surg Med 1988;8:283.

25. Sheehan-Dare RA, Cotterill JA. Copper vapor laser treatment of port wine stains: clinical evaluation and comparison with conventional argon laser therapy. Br J Dermatol 1993;128(5):546.

26. Sheehan-Dare RA, Cotterill JA. Copper vapor laser (578 nm) and flashlamp-pumped tunable dye laser (578 nm) treatment of port wine stains: results of a comparative study using test sites. Br J Dermatol 1994;130(4):478.

27. Sheibner A, Wheeland RG. Argon pumped tunable dye laser therapy for facial port wine stain hemangiomas in adults: a new technique using small spot size and minimal power. J Dermatol Surg Oncol 1989;15:277.

28. Stern RS, Dover JS, Levin JA, Arndt KA. Laser therapy versuscryo therapy of lentigines: a comparative trial. J Am Acad Dermatol 1994; 30:985-987.

29. Touquet VLR, Carruth JAS. Review of treatment of port wine stains with the argon laser. Lasers Surg Med 1984;4:191.

30. Yanar A, Fukada O, Soyano S, et al. Argon laser therapy of port wine stains: effects and limitations. Plast Reconstr Surg 1985;75:520.

Textbook of Dermatologic Surgery, edited by John L. Ratz.
Lippincott–Raven Publishers, Philadelphia © 1998.

CHAPTER **22**

Q-Switched Laser Treatment of Tattoos and Pigmented Lesions

Suzanne Linsmeier Kilmer and Brian D. Zelickson

HISTORY

Before the advent of laser technology, most cutaneous pigmented lesions and tattoos were removed by surgical excision, abrasive techniques, cryosurgery, or chemical peels. Although epidermal pigmented lesions can frequently be treated using superficial techniques, violation of the dermis to treat deeper pigmented lesions often leaves an equally undesirable scar.

The first research involving medical lasers, pioneered by Leon Goldman in the early 1960s, suggested that laser surgery on dermal pigmentation could be performed with little scarring. He explored normal-mode and Q-switched ruby laser (QSRL) light as a potential treatment modality for nevi and tattoos. Although results were promising, technical difficulties kept this particular laser from further exploration until its resurgence 20 years later. Soon to follow the initial ruby laser studies were those on continuous-wave carbon dioxide (CO_2) and argon lasers. The CO_2 laser (10,600 nm) has a wavelength well absorbed by water; thus cutaneous pigment is removed by nonselectively destroying skin. The blue-green light of the continuous-wave argon laser (488 to 514 nm), although more selective for melanin, has a relatively long exposure time that allows heat to dissipate into the surrounding tissue, causing nonselective thermal injury and scarring.

In 1981, Anderson and Parrish studied this phenomenon and described the principle of selective photothermolysis, now employed in the development of most currently used lasers. Selective photothermolysis describes the process of selectively destroying a target through heat generated by light. By definition, the laser light must be a wavelength preferentially absorbed by the target (and, it is hoped, ignored by surrounding chromophores), and the exposure time must be limited so that the heat generated by the laser-tissue interaction is confined to the target itself. Sufficient energy must be delivered to cause the desired effect. Rapid-pulsed lasers were produced to create these ultrashort bursts of light for treatment of pigment-containing lesions. Current Q-switched lasers have pulse durations as short as 5 ns, wavelengths well absorbed by melanin and many tattoo inks, and very high peak powers.

With the use of the appropriate wavelength, these lasers are able to selectively destroy or alter endogenous (melanin, hemoglobin, hemosiderin) and exogenous (tattoo ink, graphite, asphalt) pigments. Figure 1 illustrates the absorption patterns of melanin and hemoglobin and includes all the lasers discussed here. Longer wavelengths have less affinity for melanin; however, they penetrate more deeply into the skin.

Suzanne Linsmeier Kilmer: Laser and Skin Surgery Center of Northern California, 87 Scripps Drive, Suite 202, Sacramento, CA 95825, Department of Dermatology, University of California Davis, School of Medicine.
Brian D. Zelickson: Department of Dermatology, University of Minnesota, 825 Nicollett Mall, Medical Arts Building 1002, Minneapolis, MN, 55402.

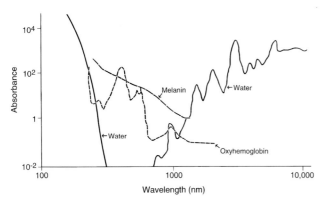

FIG. 1. This graph illustrates the absorption patterns of melanin and hemoglobin and includes the wavelengths of all lasers discussed in this chapter.

Tattoo ink color has a dramatic effect on the ability of a particular wavelength to remove the ink particles. Ink absorption spectra help to predict the most appropriate wavelength. Red ink is best treated by green light and, conversely, green ink is best treated by red light. Absorption for black ink is fairly constant throughout the visible to near-infrared spectrum; it responds equally well to red and near-infrared laser light, but less well to green light, probably because of its more limited depth of penetration.

As will be discussed further, differences in wavelength and pulse duration, which are currently set by the laser manufacturers, have clinical relevance. To perform laser surgery for the removal of cutaneous pigment, the surgeon must have a working knowledge of all pulsed lasers currently available for the procedure (Table 1). At the present time, no single pulsed laser can optimally remove all pigmented lesions. The following is a discussion of the benefits and limitations of each laser system.

LASER TYPES

Q-Switched Ruby Laser (694 nm)

The QSRL has a wavelength of 694.3 nm and a pulse width of 28 to 40 ns. Current models employ a mirrored, articulated arm with a variable spot size of 5 or 6.5 mm and a repetition rate of up to 1 Hz (pulses/sec). With strong melanin absorption and good depth of penetration, the QSRL is very effective in the treatment of cutaneous pigmented lesions, both the more superficial epidermal lesions and deeper, dermal lesions. As effective as other Q-switched lasers for removing black ink, it is one of the better lasers for removing green and blue inks, but relatively ineffective for red or yellow inks. Its strong melanin absorption must be kept in mind when treating tattoos because transient hypopigmentation is frequent and may take months to resolve. More rarely, small areas of depigmentation can occur (reported at a rate of 1% to 5% of cases). Consequently, this laser is not the best system for treating tattoos in darker-skinned patients.

When selecting the energy level for the QSRL, we look for immediate tissue whitening with minimal to no bleeding (Fig. 2). The required energy density varies depending on the spot size used and the amount and color of pigment in the skin. The 6.5-mm spot size is recommended for most lesions with an initial fluence of 4.0 to 6.0 J/cm^2.

Q-Switched ND:YAG Laser (1064 and 532 nm)

In an effort to treat tattoos without interference by melanin absorption and its aforementioned complications, the Q-switched neodynium:yttrium, aluminum, garnet (QS-Nd:YAG) laser was developed. This laser system has two wavelengths, 1064 and 532 nm, and a pulse duration of 5 to 10 ns that is delivered via a mirrored, articulated arm. Current models have spot sizes of 1.5 to 4 mm and can operate at up to 10 Hz. Advantages of this laser include dual wavelengths, reliability, and portability.

The 1064-nm wavelength is most effective for treating black tattoos and less effective at removing blue and green pigment. The longer wavelength has only moderate absorption by melanin; however, it has the deepest penetration. This wavelength is the least efficacious for epidermal pigment but successfully lightens deeper benign lesions such as nevus of Ota and dark tattoo ink.

Used at the 532-nm wavelength, this laser is the most effective for removing red pigment, which can frequently be cleared with four treatments or less. Absorbed well by melanin and hemoglobin, it is also effective for treating epidermal pigmented lesions as well as some vascular lesions.

TABLE 22-1. *Wavelength, spot size, and pulse rate*

Laser type	Wavelength (nm)	Spot size (mm)	Pulse repetition rate (Hertz)
Q-switched ruby	694.3	5, 6.5	0.5, 1
Alexandrite	755	2, 3, 4	1, 5, 10, 15
Q-switched Nd:YAG	1,064/532	1.5, 2, 3	1, 5, 10
Pulsed dye (green)	510	3, 5	1
CO$_2$	10,600	0.1–3	semicontinuous, pulsed

Nd:YAG, neodynium:yttrium-aluminum-garnet.

FIG. 2. Professional tattoo halfway through treatment with the Q-switched ruby laser, showing the immediate postoperative tissue whitening.

Purpura is usually present for 7 to 10 days after treatment, as a result of hemoglobin absorption.

When using the 1064-nm wavelength, start with a 3-mm spot size (or 4 mm if available and fluence is sufficient) and 5 to 6 J/cm². Fig. 3A and B shows an amateur tattoo before and after treatments with the QS-Nd:YAG laser. The clinical end point is whitening of the skin with occasional pinpoint bleeding; higher fluences result in greater bleeding. With the 532-nm wavelength, fluences of 2 to 4 J/cm² are best for treating red, orange, or purple tattoos and epidermal pigmented lesions. The clinical end point with this setting is whitening of the skin with minimal to no bleeding.

Because of the short pulse duration, this laser has the greatest amount of tissue splatter, which can be minimized with use of larger spot sizes. Recent studies have shown that larger spot sizes and lower fluences are as effective at removing tattoo pigment with less side effects than smaller spot sizes and higher energy levels. In addition, models with a square beam, rather than a gaussian beam profile, deliver light more evenly with less epidermal damage.

Q-Switched Alexandrite Laser (755 nm)

The alexandrite laser has a wavelength of 755 nm, a pulse duration of 50 to 100 ns, and a spot size of 2 to 4 mm, delivered via a fiberoptic or mirrored, articulated arm at a repetition rate of up to 15 Hz. The longer pulse duration of this laser is associated with the least amount of tissue splatter and allows for the use of a fiberoptic delivery system. The fiberoptic cable evens out the laser energy to help create a more even beam profile with fewer hot spots. Newer developments to the older alexandrite laser systems should greatly improve their reliability and efficacy.

This laser, similar to the QSRL, is effective at removing black, blue, and most green inks and less proficient at removing red or yellow inks (Fig. 4A and B). Similarly, it treats superficial pigmented lesions such as solar lentigines, as well as deeper lesions such as nevus of Ota. When using this laser, look for a clinical end point of mild tissue whitening. Depending on the spot size, a starting fluence of 5.0 to 6.5 J/cm² is usually employed.

Pigmented Lesion Dye Laser (510 nm)

The 510-nm, 300-nanosecond pulse width, 3- to 5-mm spot size, and 1-Hz pulsed-dye laser is used to remove epidermal pigmented lesions, such as solar lentigines, café-au-lait macules, and red tattoo ink. Choose an energy level of 5.0 to 6.0 J/cm² for treating tattoos and 4.0 to 5.0 J/cm² for epidermal pigmented lesions. The desired tissue reaction is whitening of the skin with minimal to no bleeding. Similar to the 532-nm wavelength, purpura is produced that usually resolves within 1 to 2 weeks.

Pulsed Carbon Dioxide Lasers (10,600 nm)

Several pulsed or scanned CO_2 lasers are now available. These lasers ablate tissue containing water similar to the continuous-wave CO^2 lasers, yet they have very short, controlled tissue exposure times. Therefore the tissue destruction can be well controlled with little collateral thermal damage. Although these lasers nonselectively destroy skin containing melanin and tattoo ink, they may be helpful in resistant tattoos by removing the epidermis immediately before Q-switched laser treatment.

GENERAL PRINCIPLES FOR TREATMENT OF TATOOS

In general, tattoos placed with either a professional or homemade tattoo gun contain more ink and therefore usually require more treatment sessions. Densely pigmented, decorative tattoos with a variety of colored, metallic pigments (e.g., cadmium, mercury, cobalt, and copper) may be particularly difficult to remove, requiring more than 10 treatment ses-

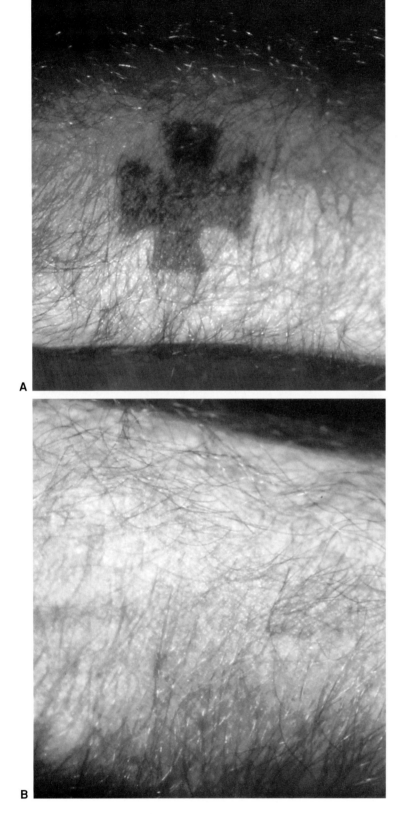

FIG. 3. Amateur tattoo (**A**) before and (**B**) after five treatments with 1064-nm.

FIG. 4. Professional tattoo **(A)** before and **(B)** immediately after treatment with the alexandrite laser. When using this laser, the desired clinical end point is mild tissue whitening.

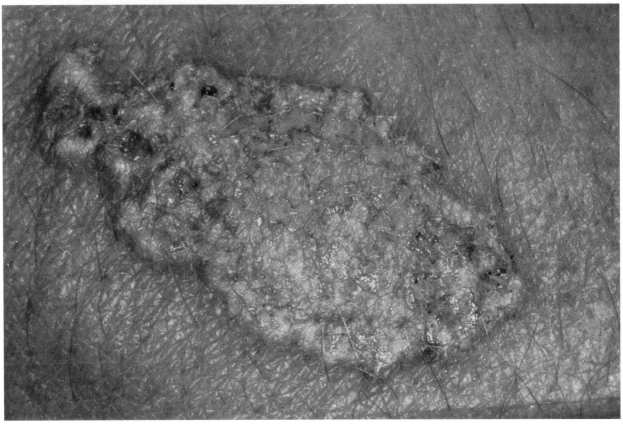

sions in some cases. Amateur tattoos, on the other hand, are typically less dense and made up of carbon-based India ink that responds more readily to Q-switched laser treatment. As noted earlier, the ability of a particular wavelength to remove colored ink particles can be predicted by the ink's absorption spectra. Red-containing inks are best treated by the 532- or 510-nm wavelengths (green light); conversely, green-containing inks are best treated by the QSRL or Q-switched alexandrite (red light) lasers. Black ink responds well to all three Q-switched lasers systems. For darker-skinned patients the 1064-nm wavelength suffers less interference by melanin, allowing deeper penetration of the light to the targeted ink and less damage to the melanin-containing keratinocytes and melanocytes, thereby reducing potential pigmentary problems. Appropriate wavelength selection allows the most efficacious treatment with the least side effects.

There is still much to be learned about actual tattoo pigment removal. Once ink is implanted into the dermis, ink particles are engulfed by residing macrophages. These cells cannot remove or break down the particle, so it remains a "permanent" part of the cell. Most likely, Q-switched laser pulses fracture the ink into smaller, more manageably sized particles. Some of the resulting fragments are eliminated transepidermally, but the majority are either taken away by scavenger cells to the local lymph nodes or picked up again by resident macrophage cells.

There are few relative contraindications to laser tattoo removal. The most serious complication from pulsed laser tattoo removal has been the occurrence of a systemic allergic reaction developing after tattoo treatment with the ultrashort-pulsed lasers. Unlike previous destructive methods for tattoo removal, the ink is not removed from the body, but rather mobilized, potentially triggering an allergic response. Systemic allergic reactions are more prevalent in patients exhibiting a localized allergic reaction at the tattoo site. Therefore, if a patient exhibits a cutaneous reaction within the tattoo, Q-switched laser treatment is not advised. Pulsed CO_2 lasers do not seem to trigger this reaction because of their absorption characteristics and may be helpful to enhance transepidermal elimination of the ink when cutaneous allergy is a concern.

A second possible complication is the development of immediate pigment darkening after pulsed laser treatment. Most often seen in red, white, and flesh-toned tattoos and cosmetic tattoos, the blackened tattoo pigment (Fig. 5) cannot always be removed with successive laser treatments.

Because of the expense of these lasers, it is rare for every laser surgeon to have access and experience with each type of laser. To provide an unbiased view of laser tattoo removal, we sent a questionnaire to 11 physicians with extensive experience in laser tattoo removal. On average, the physicians found that 65% (0% to 100%) of professional and 90% (75% to 100%) of amateur tattoos can be effectively cleared in 9 (6 to 13) and 5 (4 to 8) treatments, respectively. The energy density used ranged from 4.0 to 8.0 J/cm² using the largest

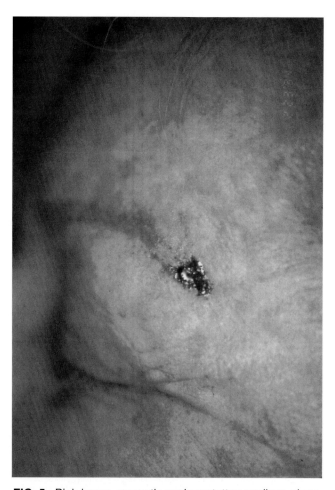

FIG. 5. Pink-brown cosmetic eyebrow tattoo eyeliner, showing pigment darkening immediately after treatment of the left side. This area was immediately retreated (bleeding area is evident) and the tattoo cleared after eight treatments with the Q-switched Nd:YAG laser.

spot sizes available. On average, 60% of patients receiving treatment needed topical anesthesia, such as EMLA (eutectic mixture of lidocaine and prilocaine) cream, and 5% to 30% needed intralesional anesthesia. The treatment interval used was from 6 to more than 8 weeks. Complications including textural change, hyperpigmentation, and hypopigmentation occurred but were uncommon.

GENERAL PRINCIPLES FOR TREATMENT OF BENIGN PIGMENTED LESIONS

Melanin, the targeted chromophore when treating benign pigmented lesions, is found primarily in keratinocytes, melanocytes, and in the case of postinflammatory hyperpigmentation, melanophages. Although pulsed lasers destroy melanosome granules, they may not destroy all the cells in which the granules are found. In particular, melanocytes with a low concentration of melanin, such as the deeper ones in melanocytic nevi, may survive laser treatment. This is im-

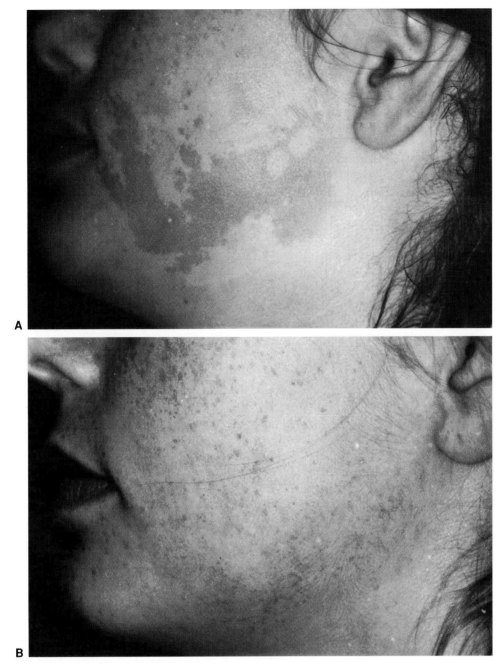

FIG. 6. (A) Café-au-lait macule (CALM) of the left cheek after test treatment with the QS-Nd:YAG laser at 532 nm. **(B)** Same lesion 3 months after 2 treatments.

portant when deciding which lesions are amenable to laser treatment.

In general, superficial pigmented lesions are better removed with the green and red wavelengths (510, 532, 694, and 755 nm), whereas lesions with deeper pigment respond better to the longer, red to near-infrared wavelengths (694, 755, and 1064 nm), since the energy can penetrate to the depth of the pigment. Benign epidermal pigmented lesions in which few active melanocytes are present and keratinocytes carry most of the pigment, such as lentigines and ephilids, respond well. They often require only a single treatment,

and the lesions rarely recur. Lesions with many active melanocytes, such as café-au-lait macules (Fig. 6A and B), some nevi, and melasma, have a variable response to laser treatment.

Café-au-lait macules (CALM) usually take 2 to 4 (or more) treatments and may recur. It is believed that the entire lesions must be cleared, removing the entire reservoir of melanocytes triggering the café-au-lait macules. Much work still needs to be done to understand the underlying biology of these lesions. Similar to café-au-lait macules are Becker's nevi, although they tend to require more treatment sessions and recur more often. These lesions are also prone to hyperpigmentation.

Melasma is particularly difficult to treat, especially if the hormonal drive to pigment is still present. Its predominence in darker-skinned individuals makes postinflammatory hyperpigmentation with the Q-switched laser treatment a frequent and frustrating problem. Test sites are recommended, since patients may look worse after Q-switched laser treatment.

Melanocytic lesions are also variable in their response. Superficial pigment may be easy to treat; however, the underlying melanocytes may prove difficult to eradicate. In addition, in lesions with the potential to undergo malignant transformation, as in congenital nevi, it is not known whether laser treatment will decrease this tendency by decreasing the melanocytic load or increase it by irritating the melanocytes. Furthermore, if a potentially malignant lesion is lightened with laser treatment, it may be difficult to watch for signs of malignant degeneration. A biopsy may be prudent to confirm diagnosis (i.e., lentigo vs. lentigo maligna), and dysplastic nevi or malignant lesions should not be routinely treated with these lasers.

Interestingly, nevus of Ota, with melanocytes located in the deep dermis, can usually be cleared with Q-switched laser treatment (Fig. 7A and B), whereas congenital nevi, with superficial and deep nevus cells, generally have a poorer response. In the Asian countries, all three Q-switched laser systems have been widely used to successfully treat nevus of Ota with excellent results noted after 4 to 10 treatment sessions. Other melanocytic nevi are not as well studied, and there is great variability among nevus type, size, location, depth, and potential for malignant transformation; further study is needed before recommendations can be made. Treatment of nevocellular nevi is very controversial; studies are underway to further elucidate the impact of high-energy laser light on melanocytes.

The risk of scarring from laser treatment is minimal; however, postinflammatory hyperpigmentation from Q-switched laser treatment in patients with darker skin types is not uncommon (Fig. 8). Instruct the patient to stay out of the sun and use hydroquinone cream before and after treatment to enhance the penetration of the laser light and help prevent postinflammatory hyperpigmentation. Testing sites with all available, potentially useful wavelengths is recommended

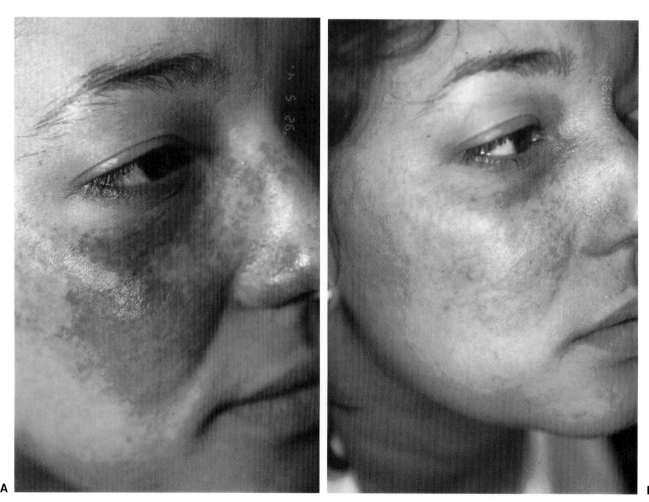

A   **B**

FIG. 7. (A) Nevus of Ota before and after test treatment with the QS-Nd:YAG laser at 1064 nm. **(B)** Same lesion after two treatments.

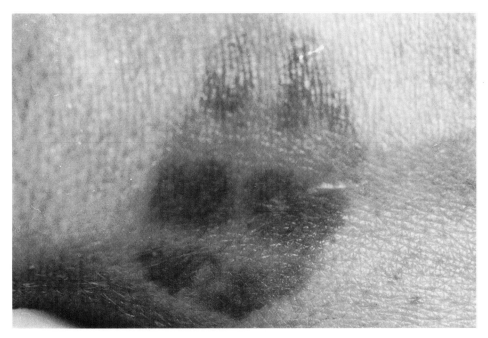

FIG. 8. Café-au-lait macule of the dorsal surface of hand showing postinflammatory hyperpigmentation 3 months after test treatments with the Q-switched ruby laser.

for café-au-lait macules, melasma, Becker's nevi, and postinflammatory hyperpigmentation to help predict potential treatment benefits and side effects.

PROCEDURE

Preoperative Planning

Treatment of tattoos and benign pigmented lesions with the previously discussed lasers is relatively uncomplicated, so an extensive patient evaluation is unnecessary. However, as with all cutaneous surgical procedures, there are several guidelines that one should follow before performing the procedure.

A general history of current medical conditions and medications, allergies, and past surgeries, including bleeding tendencies and wound healing, should be obtained. If the patient has a history of recurrent herpes simplex in or near the treatment area, prescribe a course of acyclovir or a similar antiviral, starting 1 to 2 days before each treatment. For patients with a tendency to hyperpigmentation, prescribe a hydroquinone to be used twice daily at least 1 week before each treatment session.

The patient should be educated in all aspects of the procedure. This is probably the most important part of the preoperative planning. Many patients are ill informed and thus have unrealistic expectations about laser treatment. It is very helpful to show patients photographs of similar lesions before treatment, and final results. In doing so, it is important that they see your average results, not just your best results.

Patients should be informed of all of the costs involved

in the procedure. This is best put in writing, for the treatment can easily take several months to a year to complete. Charging a fee for each visit rather than a global fee is recommended, since it is difficult to predict how many treatments will be needed to achieve the desired response.

Photographs should be obtained before each treatment. Fading of the treated lesion is gradual, and patients may not remember the original lesion's darkness. In addition, scarring is not uncommon with tattoo placement and may become more noticeable once the ink is removed; photodocumentation is helpful.

Tattoos

Emphasize that not all tattoos can be removed completely and successful tattoo removal or lightening may take many treatment sessions at 6-week intervals. Amateur tattoos usually clear in 4 to 6 treatments, whereas professional tattoos usually require 8 to 12 treatments to clear. Black ink is relatively easy to remove, whereas colored inks tend to be more difficult, especially if the optimal wavelength is not used. Some pigments (red, white, and flesh-toned inks, especially those used for cosmetic tattooing), may turn brown, black, or gray after laser treatment and then may be very difficult to remove. Ask about any itchy rashes in the area of the tattoo; allergic reactions may be intermittent.

Benign Pigmented Lesion Treatments

For benign pigmented lesions the patients must be informed that not all lesions can be removed completely.

Pulsed laser treatment removes only the pigment within the lesion and may not remove all the cells that produce the pigment. Therefore the lesion may recur, even if it appears clear after treatment. Successful removal or lightening can take several treatments. Lentigines and ephilids usually take one or two treatments to obtain optimal clearing. Wait 1 month between each treatment. Nevus of Ota may take four to eight treatments to obtain optimal clearing. Wait 6 months between each treatment. Melasma, café-au-lait lesions, and postinflammatory hyperpigmentation tend to have a variable response to laser treatment and may recur after clearing.

Treatment

Q-switched laser treatments are a relatively easy in-office procedure, often performed without any anesthesia. If anesthesia is needed, topical EMLA cream or 40% lidocaine in an acid mantle base applied 2 hours before the procedure can be used to greatly diminish the discomfort. For quicker or more complete anesthesia, 1% lidocaine (with or without epinephrine) can be used for local or regional block. Other than for young children, oral sedation or general anesthesia is rarely needed.

When using pulsed lasers, one must be concerned about ocular injury and exposure to infection. Ultrashort pulse durations elicit a significant amount of tissue splatter. Use universal precautions with every patient, including protective clothing, goggles, masks, and laser cone containment devices. Treatment may be performed through a clear protective dressing (Vigilon or nonsterile equivalent) for extra precaution. Correct protective eyewear must be worn by all individuals in the room. Laser-protective eye shields should be used when treating periorbital lesions.

The laser handpiece should be held perpendicular to the area to be treated, and pulses delivered with a 10% overlap until the entire lesion is treated. When a cone containment device is used, hold it flush with the skin surface. The desired laser-tissue interaction should include immediate, bright whitening of the impacted tissue and possibly minor pinpoint bleeding. Use the largest spot size that elicits brisk whitening. If epidermal debris is significant, lower the fluence. Higher fluences may be needed for subsequent treatment sessions when less of the targeted chromophore remains and it is deeper in the skin.

When treating a tattoo with colors that may darken, deliver a single pulse; then look for immediate darkening. Wait for the whitening to clear to best visualize the treated area. If darkening does not occur, proceed with treatment. If it does, re-treat that same test site area to be sure the ink can be lightened before proceeding. Again, discuss other treatment options.

After treatment, apply antibiotic ointment and nonstick dressing. If a Vigilon dressing is used, it can be left in place as the bandage or removed as needed. Instruct the patient in basic wound care, including sun avoidance. Have the patient leave the dressing on and keep the wound dry for 24 hours. The patient should then gently cleanse the wound with a mild soap and water and apply an antibiotic ointment and nonstick dressing until the wound has reepithelialized. If any hyperpigmentation is noted, start hydroquinone therapy twice daily until it resolves.

CONCLUSION

All the lasers presented in this chapter can effectively remove many benign cutaneous pigmented lesions and tattoos with minimal scarring. Although these lasers remove superficial epidermal pigment by disrupting melanosomes, they do not directly target melanocytes. Therefore, some lesions such as café-au-lait macules and melasma have a variable response to treatment with frequent recurrences. Dysplastic and malignant lesions should not be treated with the current pulsed lasers. Not all tattoos can be completely cleared, and several wavelengths are usually needed to optimally treat multicolored tattoos.

The major advantage of these lasers for removing benign cutaneous pigmented lesions and tattoos is the very low risk of scarring. As a trained laser surgeon, it is important not only to inform patients of the great advantages of these pulsed lasers, but also to teach them of their limitations, including the need for multiple treatments, minimal to incomplete responses, and the possibility of pigmentary and textural changes. Research continues in an effort to perfect laser removal of tattoos and cutaneous pigmented lesions.

SUGGESTED READING LIST

1. Anderson RR, Geronemus R, Kilmer SL, Farinelli W, Fitzpatrick RE. Cosmetic tattoo ink darkening: a complication of Q-switched and pulsed-laser treatment. Arch Dermatol 1993;129(8):1010.
2. Anderson RR, Margolis RJ, Watenabe S, Flotte T, Hruza GJ, Dover JS. Selective photothermolysis of cutaneous pigmentation by Q-switched Nd:YAG laser pulses at 1064, 532, and 355 nm. J Invest Dermatol 1989;93(1):28.
3. Anderson RR, Parrish JA. Selective photothermolysis: precise microsurgery by selective absorption of pulsed radiation. Science 1983; 220(4596):524.
4. Ashinoff R, Geronemus RG. Q-switched ruby laser treatment of labial lentigos. J Am Acad Dermatol 1992;27(5, part 2):809.
5. Ashinoff R, Geronemus RG. Rapid response of traumatic and medical tattoos to treatment with the Q-switched ruby laser. Plast Reconstr Surg 1993;91(5):841.
6. Dover JS, Margolis RJ, Polla LL, et al. Pigmented guinea pig skin irradiated with Q-switched ruby laser pulses: morphologic and histologic findings. Arch Dermatol 1989;125(1):43.
7. Fitzpatrick RE. Laser therapy for benign pigmented cutaneous lesions. West J Med 1992;156(2):194.
8. Fitzpatrick RE, Goldman MP. Tattoo removal using the alexandrite laser. Arch Dermatol 1994;130(12):1508.
9. Fitzpatrick RE, Goldman MP, Dierickx C. Laser ablation of facial cosmetic tattoos. Aesth Plast Surg 1994;18(1):91.
10. Fitzpatrick RE, Goldman MP, Ruiz-Esparza J. Laser treatment of benign pigmented epidermal lesions using a 300-nsecond pulse and 510-nm wavelength. J Dermatol Surg Oncol 1993;19(4):341.
11. Fitzpatrick RE, Goldman MP, Ruiz-Esparza J. Use of the alexandrite laser (755 nm, 100 nsec) for tattoo pigment removal in an animal model. J Am Acad Dermatol 1993;28(5, part 1):745.

12. Geronemus RG. Q-switched ruby laser therapy of nevus of Ota. Arch Dermatol 1992;128(12):1618.

13. Goldberg DJ. Benign pigmented lesions of the skin: treatment with the Q-switched ruby laser. J Dermatol Surg Oncol 1993;19(4):376.

14. Goldberg DJ, Nychay SG. Q-switched ruby laser treatment of nevus of Ota. J Dermatol Surg Oncol 1992;18(9):817.

15. Goldman L, Hornby P, Meyer R. Radiation from a Q-switched ruby laser with a total output of 10 megawatts on a tattoo of a man. J Invest Dermatol 1965; 44:69.

16. Goldman L, Ingelman JM, Richfield DF. Impact of the laser in nevi and melanomas. Arch Dermatol 1964;90:71.

17. Goldman L, Rockwell RJ, Meyer R, Otten R, Wilson RG, Kitzmiller KW. Laser treatment of tattoos: a preliminary survey of three year's clinical experience. JAMA 1967;201(11):841.

18. Grekin RC, Shelton RM, Geisse JK, Frieden I. 510-nm pigmented lesion dye laser: its characteristics and clinical uses. J Dermatol Surg Oncol 1993;19(4):380.

19. Hruza GJ, Dover JS, Flotte TJ, Goetschkes M, Watanabe S, Anderson RR. Q-switched ruby laser irradiation of normal human skin: histologic and ultrastructural findings. Arch Dermatol 1991;127(12):1799.

20. Kilmer SL, Anderson RR. Clinical use of the Q-switched ruby and the Q-switched Nd:YAG (1064 nm and 532 nm) lasers for treatment of tattoos. J Dermatol Surg Oncol 1993;19(4):330.

21. Kilmer SL, Casparian JC, Wimberly J, Anderson RR. Hazards of Q-switched lasers. Lasers Surg Med Suppl 1993;5:56.

22. Kilmer SL, Lee MS, Grevelink JM, Flotte TJ, Anderson RR. The Q-switched Nd:YAG laser effectively treats tattoos: a controlled, dose-response study. Arch Dermatol 1993;129(8):971.

23. Kilmer SL, Wheeland RG, Goldberg DJ, Anderson RR. Treatment of epidermal pigmented lesions with the frequency-doubled Q-switched Nd:YAG laser: a controlled, single-impact, dose-response, multicenter trial. Arch Dermatol 1994;130(12):1515.

24. Lowe NJ, Luftman D, Sawcer D. Q-switched ruby laser: further observations on treatment of professional tattoos. J Dermatol Surg Oncol 1994;20(5):307.

25. Lowe NJ, Wieder JM, Sawcer D, Burrows P, Chalet M. Nevus of Ota: treatment with high-energy fluences of the Q-switched ruby laser. J Am Acad Dermatol 1993;29(6):997.

26. Murphy GF, Shepard RS, Paul BS, et al. Organelle-specific injury to melanin-containing cells in human skin by pulsed laser irradiation. Lab Invest 1987;49:680.

27. Polla LL, Margolis RJ, Dover JS, et al. Melanosomes are a primary target of Q-switched ruby laser irradiation in guinea pig skin. J Invest Dermatol 1987;89:281.

28. Reid WH, McLeod PJ, Ritchie A, Ferguson-Pell M. Q-switched ruby laser treatment of black tattoos. Br J Plast Surg 1983;36:455.

29. Sherwood KA, Murray S, Kurban AK, Tan OT. Effect of wavelength on cutaneous pigment using pulsed irradiation. J Invest Dermatol 1989; 92: 717.

30. Stern RS, Dover JS, Levin JA, Arndt KA. Laser therapy versus cryotherapy of lentigines: a comparative trial. J Am Acad Dermatol 1994; 30(6):985.

31. Tan OT, Morelli JG, Kurban AK. Pulsed-dye laser treatment of benign cutaneous pigmented lesions. Lasers Surg Med 1992;12(5):538.

32. Taylor CR, Grange RW, Dover JS, et al. Treatment of tattoos by Q-switched ruby laser. Arch Dermatol 1990;126:893.

33. Watenabe S, Flotte TJ, Margolis R, et al. The effect of pulse duration on selective pigment cell injury by dye lasers. J Invest Dermatol 1987; 88:523.

34. Watts MT, Downes RN, Collin JR, Walker NP. The use of Q-switched Nd:Yag laser for removal of permanent eyeliner tattoo. Ophthalmic Plast Reconstr Surg 1992;8(4):292.

35. Zelickson BD, Mehregan DA, Zarrin AA, Coles C, Hartwig P, Olson S, Leaf-Davis J. Clinical,histologic, and ultrastructural evaluation of tattoos treated with three laser systems. Lasers Surg Med 1994; 15:364.

Textbook of Dermatologic Surgery, edited by John L. Ratz.
Lippincott–Raven Publishers, Philadelphia © 1998.

CHAPTER 23

Carbon Dioxide Laser Applications

John Louis Ratz, Mitchel P. Goldman, Richard E. Fitzpatrick,
and Laurence M. David

Part I   Conventional Carbon Dioxide Laser Procedures

HISTORY

The carbon dioxide (CO_2) laser was once called the workhorse of lasers in dermatology. Although it was one of the first lasers developed, work with this laser was sporadic at first. Then in the mid- to late 1970s, reports began appearing in the dermatologic literature attesting to its effectiveness, first, as an ablation tool, and shortly thereafter as a precision cutting instrument with capabilities of cutting finely enough for use in Mohs' surgery (see Chapter 25) and blepharoplasty (see Chapter 18). Numerous applications were reported for this laser, and its use became widespread—thus the designation, workhorse.

However, the reported good results of work with this laser are often user- or technique-dependent, and these techniques are not always easily mastered. It is a situation somewhat analogous to someone trying to paint a picture with Michelangelo's brush—proper equipment, but perhaps something lacking in technique.

John Louis Ratz: Louisiana State University School of Medicine, 1452 Tulane Avenue, New Orleans, LA 70112.

Mitchel P. Goldman: University of California, San Diego, Dermatology Associates of San Diego County, Inc., 850 Prospect Street, La Jolla, CA 92037.

Richard E. Fitzpatrick: Department of Dermatology and Medicine, University of California at San Diego, Dermatology Associates of San Diego County, Inc., 850 Prospect Street, La Jolla, CA 92037.

Laurence M. David: Institute of Laser Cosmetic Surgery, 415 Pier Avenue, Hermosa Beach, CA 90254.

This chapter attempts to teach proper technique for both ablative and incisional procedures. The first section deals with conventional CO_2 laser procedures and the second with some of the newer developments of this laser that make it much more user friendly. Although resurfacing techniques were first performed with conventional CO_2 lasers, the advent of newer, soft-touch delivery systems has made the more technique-dependent resurfacing procedures with conventional CO_2 lasers obsolete and unnecessarily risky procedures, as long as technology is available to simplify them in a safe and effective way.

PREOPERATIVE CONSIDERATIONS

Several attributes of CO_2 laser surgery must be considered, regardless of the type of CO_2 laser being used and the type of procedure being performed. These can be summarized as planning, safety, settings, and spot size.

Planning

Although it may seem unnecessary to some practitioners. preoperative planning is essential. At some point it becomes second nature to most surgeons. Determine the type of procedure to be performed (ablative vs. incisional). Select the appropriate anesthesia (and sedation, if necessary). Make the patient aware of what to expect postoperatively with regard to pain, restriction of activities, and wound care, as well as anticipated duration of these inconveniences. Ensure that all equipment is in proper working order and that all necessary instrumentation is available (including smoke evacuation equipment, appropriate surgical instruments, electrocautery for backup if needed for hemostasis, accessible water supply, and appropriate safety equipment and supplies). Make certain that postoperative dressing material is at hand.

Safety

Laser safety is extremely important. It is the surgeon's responsibility to ensure the safety of the patient, surgical staff, and any observers, with laser both in and out of hand. Appropriate warning signs should be placed at all access points. A designated laser operator should be positioned at the laser control panel to make necessary adjustments and to put the laser in the standby mode when appropriate. Laser safety equipment should include proper smoke evacuation equipment, as well as laser-approved surgical masks, protective eyewear for all including the patient, accessible water supply, and wet draping where necessary. The use of dulled, blackened, or ebonized equipment should be considered relative to the nature of the procedure and the experience of the laser surgeon.

Setting

Appropriate settings vary from surgeon to surgeon. Settings given for procedures in this chapter should be considered representative. However, knowing how to make the appropriate adjustments and in which parameters require an understanding of the basic science of laser operation, as well as familiarity with the laser equipment being used. Changes in power being delivered to a target can be adjusted by actually adjusting the laser output or by changing the impact spot size. There is literally a multitude of combinations of maneuvers that can be performed to make an anticipated change in the power being delivered to the target tissue. Learning how to make such changes, and what changes to make, is best accomplished under the watchful eye of an experienced preceptor.

Spot Size

Although spot size is a setting, it warrants separate comments. Handpieces are available that allow for delivery of a variety of spot sizes. Perhaps the most common are those that allow for delivery of impact spots of 1.0 mm and 0.2 mm. Understand that the impact spot imprinted on the handpiece is only for that handpiece and only when it is held at the focal distance that is appropriate for the lens in that handpiece. This is usually accomplished safely, accurately, and successfully with the use of the stylus of appropriate length that can be fitted to the end of the bore of the handpiece. *The beam exiting from a CO_2 laser is not parallel but divergent,* and withdrawing the handpiece from the appropriate focal distance increases the size of the impact spot. (Moving the handpiece closer than the focal length has a similar effect, as well as the added effect of overshoot.) Although this can be a very effective way of performing ablative procedures, it does require skill and experience and is best learned under the watchful eye of a preceptor. On the other hand, incisional procedures are less forgiving and require the handpiece to be held at the appropriate distance for reasonable, safe, and char-free cutting. Handpieces are available with cutting spot sizes of 0.1 mm. The most common incisional handpieces, however, have 0.2-mm spot sizes. Although it may seem a minor difference, consider that *the power required to cut with a 0.2-mm impact spot in the same manner as with a 0.1-mm spot is higher by a factor of four than with the 0.1-mm spot.* In other words, because the 0.2-mm spot size is double that of the 0.1-mm spot, the energy necessary for an equivalent cut is four times greater than for the 0.1-mm spot.

TECHNIQUE

Incision

Appropriately prepare, drape, and anesthetize the patient. (Remember that alcohol is flammable and when ignited, its flame may not be visible. It is probably not an appropriate preparatory agent.) Draw the intended incision or excision with a surgical marking pen (Fig. 1). Make sure the laser is set appropriately and that the preoperative considerations have been reviewed. Drape the immediate surgical field with wet sterile sponges or towels. They do not need to be excessively wet to be effective. Have the assistant turn on the smoke evacuation system and bring it to the field prepared to remove vapor when the laser is operating. Have the laser operator turn the laser into the ready or on position. Reasonable starting parameters should be 5 to 10 W for a 0.1-mm spot or 10 to 20 W for a 0.2-mm spot (the exact settings depend on the nature of the procedure and experience). Take a sterile tongue depressor and, away from the surgical field, impact on the tongue depressor to test for size and depth and to make certain the laser is operating properly. Use a stylus to gauge the appropriate distance at which the handpiece should be held from the target. Make an incision along the tongue depressor as a final check of power, spot, distance, alignment of aiming and working beams, and hand stability. Move onto the surgical field and, if necessary, have the assistants apply tension to the field. Check for the brightness of the aiming beam, and adjust it appropriately. With the laser properly aligned, place the handpiece at the appropriate focal distance from the target tissue and place the aiming beam on or slightly inside the proposed incision line. Angle the handpiece along the line of incision, but do not angle it

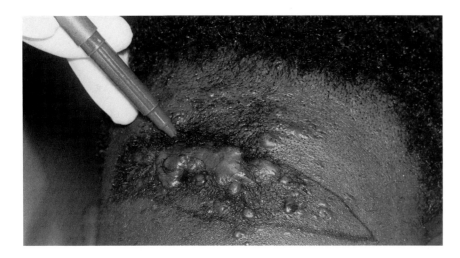

FIG. 1. Draw the intended excision with a surgical marker.

to the right or left of the line of incision unless the cut is to be beveled. Begin by making only a brief impact (controlled by the foot pedal) on the target area. Check for incisional width, depth, and angle of entry. Make adjustments at this time, and retest inside the excisional field. If all settings and angles are appropriate, begin with the initial incisional pass (Fig. 2). Move smoothly and steadily at a hand speed that provides the appropriate depth without an excess buildup of char.

After completing the first incisional pass, assess the wound. Direct the assistants to apply appropriate tension on the wound, and make any necessary adjustments in parameters. At this point, depending on the nature of the procedure, and if the initial laser pass is of acceptable depth, it would be appropriate to increase the power output to the laser for maximum efficiency. This could mean increases to 40 or 50 W or higher, regardless of spot size. (The appropriate adjustment here is highly dependent on skill, experience,

and level of comfort.) Continue with the next laser pass, and direct the assistants to keep blood or melted fat from the field. Accomplish this with cotton-tipped applicators or gauze sponges. Should oozing or bleeding occur, direct the assistants to apply pressure with a cotton-tipped applicator and slowly, but with continued downward pressure, role the applicator off the bleeding focus. Immediately withdraw the handpiece several inches from the site, and with the aiming beam pinpointing the target, vaporize to achieve hemostasis. Repeat if necessary, and make adjustments in the laser-target distance to maximize the hemostatic effect of the laser. Remember that the CO_2 laser does not penetrate liquid. If the field is not dry and/or actions are not quick enough, attempts at hemostasis will be futile. If all attempts at laser hemostasis fail, of if there is an arteriole bleed, suspend the laser procedure and achieve hemostasis in the conventional manner with electrocautery and/or ligature.

Repeat the incisional passes until the desired depth of

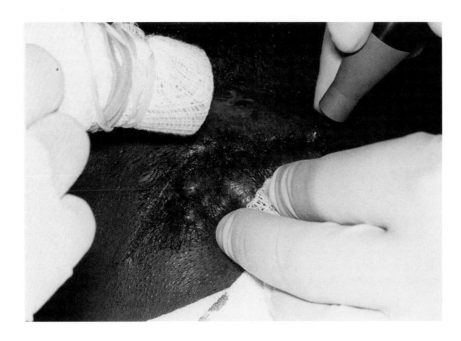

FIG. 2. Carefully begin the initial excisional pass.

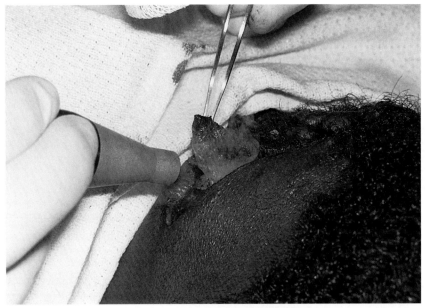

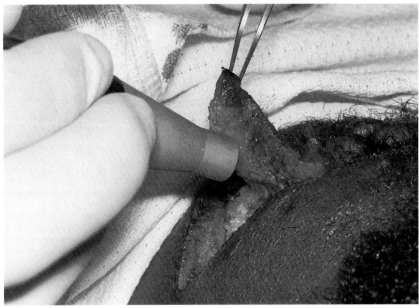

FIG. 3. Complete the excision by pulling the specimen **(A)** up and **(B)** away firmly yet gently while **(C)** cutting at the base of the tissue in steady, smooth horizontal movements.

penetration is reached. With wet drapes brought into the immediate outside borders of the incision, grasp the near end of the tissue being excised with a toothed forceps. (As an alternative, a towel clamp works extremely well for large specimens.) Pull upward and out, gently but firmly, and apply the laser near the base of the specimen in a continuous and smooth horizontal movement (Fig. 3). Direct the assistants to maintain a dry field after each pass to maximize the effective cutting of the laser. Affect hemostasis where necessary by either defocusing the laser, as mentioned earlier, or by conventional methods. When performing this portion of the procedure, it is important to remember that only deeper tissue or a wet barrier will prevent the laser from overshooting the intended target and impacting on skin or tissue outside the surgical field. *Always make sure that there*

is a wet backdrop for the laser to impact on when excising tissue. Continue with the horizontal excisional passes until the end of the specimen is near. At this point take a little extra care to avoid overshooting. Relax the upward and backward pressure on the specimen, and hold it in such a way that it is clear of the field but not held so firmly as to jerk from the field when finally released by the laser. Too much tension on the specimen results in jerk and greatly increases the probability of damage caused by overshooting. Not enough elevation of the specimen obscures the target and makes the final cuts more difficult and time-consuming than necessary.

Make the final cuts carefully, and remove the specimen from the field. As before, achieve any further hemostasis, if necessary, and check the field carefully for any unintended damage (Fig. 4).

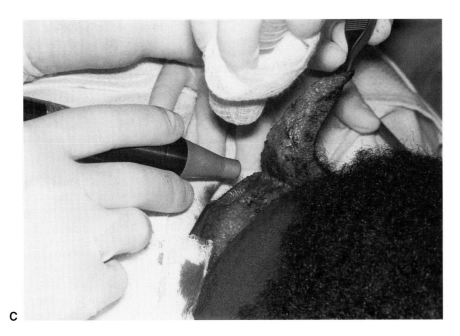

C

FIG. 3. *Continued*

If the intent is to close the wound and to undermine, these procedures can be accomplished with the laser as well. Simply grasp the wound edge with a toothed forceps or skin hook and gently elevate. Place the aiming beam at the appropriate level for undermining, and proceed with the same horizontal motions used for excision. Continue with this same maneuver for all adjacent tissue until all surrounding tissue has been appropriately undermined. Achieve hemostasis as before.

Closure can proceed in standard fashion (Fig. 5). The only difference with laser-cut wounds is that maximum tensile strength is achieved somewhat later than for scalpel-cut wounds. Suture duration might be affected by this but is technique and location specific. Have the patient return at the usual time for suture removal; then decide whether to remove the sutures based on observation of the wound.

Ablation

Follow the usual procedure for preparation and anesthesia. (Review the earlier discussion of incision.) Make certain that all safety measures are in place, that protective eyewear is in use by all present, that the assistants are ready, and that the smoke evacuation system is on and in working order. Ablation parameters are quite varied and depend on experi-

FIG. 4. Achieve hemostasis by defocusing or, if necessary, with electrocautery.

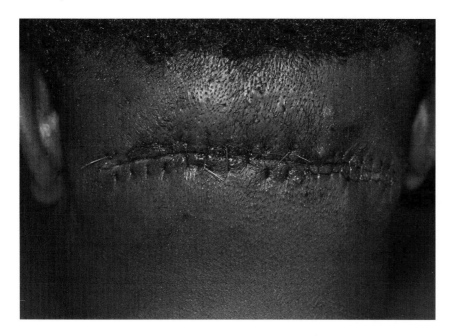

FIG. 5. Closure, if desired, can be completed in conventional fashion.

ence and skill as well as the type of ablative procedure being performed. Generally, however, a check of power and spot size, as mentioned earlier for incision, should be performed in this situation as well. Off the field and with the parameters set, impact on a tongue blade to ensure alignment of the aiming beam with the CO_2 beam. Spot size during most ablative procedures varies somewhat during the procedure, but it is important to develop a good "feel" for the kind of impact to be delivered with the laser being used, unlike incisional procedures, in which the distance from laser to target is critical and must be at the focal length of the lens. The possible exceptions to this are for the handpieces that are self-adjusting for spot size and also for the procedures for which the spot size for the lens being used is acceptable

for the procedure being performed. For example, the 1.0 mm handpiece produces a 1.0 mm spot at focality, which could be a reasonable impact for some ablative procedures.

Once alignment and spot size are confirmed with the tongue blade, move to the target tissue. Target an area inside the field to be ablated, and briefly impact to reconfirm the chosen parameters on tissue and to check for appropriate level of anesthesia. Be ready to begin the ablative procedure.

Representatives procedures are discussed next.

Warts

With the laser set at a power output of 10 W and with the handpiece held at a distance that will result in an impact

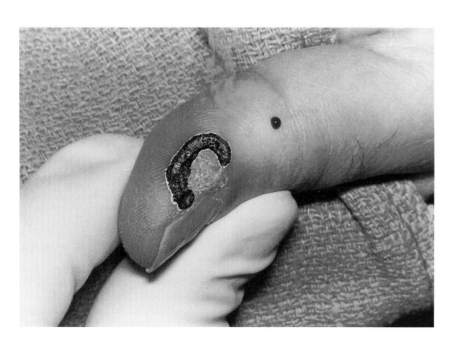

FIG. 6. Begin vaporization by treating the entire perimeter of the wart. Halfway completed process is shown.

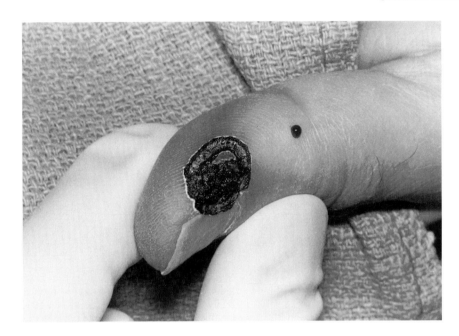

FIG. 7. Continue to vaporize the entire surface of the lesion.

spot of 3 to 4 mm, begin with a short impact in the center of the lesion. Repeat this with a continuous burst, and move to the peripheral margin of the wart. Make a continuous vaporization onto the normal tissue immediately adjacent to the wart, and continue to vaporize the entire perimeter (Fig. 6). Once this has been completed, vaporize the entire surface of the wart in similar fashion (Fig. 7). Stop when the surface has been totally treated. With a cotton-tipped applicator or gauze sponge moistened with hydrogen peroxide, clean off the resulting char. Bring the laser handpiece back to the field, and aim once again just outside the peripheral border of the wart onto normal tissue. Sharpen the focus to deliver an impact spot of 1 to 2 mm, and vaporize the entire perimeter in continuous fashion. When this perimeter vaporization is complete, withdraw the handpiece to a distance at which an impact of 3 to 4 mm will once again be delivered, and vaporize the surface of the wart in continuous fashion. Once again, vigorously cleanse the resulting char from the target tissue. If the wart does not detach at this point, repeat this step as often as necessary until the wart detaches from its moorings. The main maneuver allowing for detachment of the wart is vaporizing through the epithelium peripherally allowing for complete separation in normal tissue. When vaporization is performed properly, the entire surface portion of the wart detaches, exposing bleeding wart tissue directly underneath (Fig. 8). This bleeding can be controlled by direct pressure from a moist, but not wet, cotton-tipped applicator or gauze sponge. With gentle downward pressure, slowly expose the

FIG. 8. The entire surface portion of the wart detaches, revealing a bleeding base.

FIG. 9. Apply downward pressure and slowly expose bleeding areas to vaporization until all bleeding areas have been treated and bleeding has stopped.

bleeding surface, and carefully vaporize with an impact spot of 3 to 4 mm (Fig. 9). Cleanse vigorously with hydrogen peroxide and repeat the vaporize-cleanse cycle until the bleeding is stable and the wound created appears reasonably uniform. Once the wart has detached and bleeding has been controlled, it may be useful to trim the small margin of surrounding normal but separated epithelium with curved Iris or similar scissors (Fig. 10).

In vaporizing wart tissue, several visual clues are used as guidance. These are subtle and may require a keen eye for proper identification. When vaporized, wart tissue seems to bubble or splatter. On the other hand, normal tissue has a tendency to contract or shrink. Normal tissue does not usually bleed when vaporized, except perhaps at the very margins of the wound. Any irregularities in the wound surface could be wart tissue. To verify this, if necessary, take a curette and gently scrape the areas in question. Wart tissue produces fine, pinpoint bleeding; normal tissue generally does not. In addition, if working on fingers or toes, the experienced eye is able to detect dermatoglycins. These are normal structures. If they are interrupted or irregular, it generally means that additional wart tissue is present.

If additional foci of wart tissue can be identified, vaporize these foci, as performed for the surface of the wart at the beginning of this procedure. Cleanse as before and repeat the vaporize-cleanse cycle until there is no further clinical evidence of wart tissue (Fig. 11).

A word of caution is appropriate here. If the wart invades

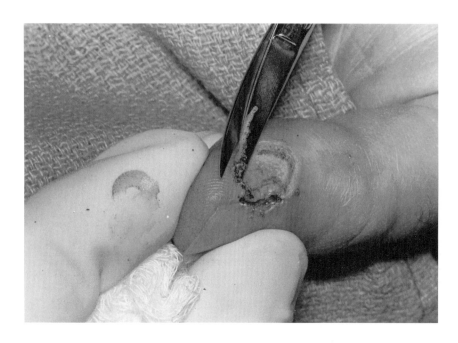

FIG. 10. Trim away excess perimeter epithelium.

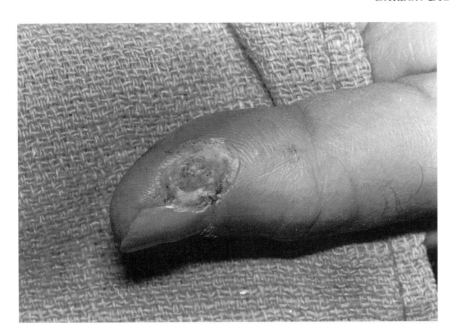

FIG. 11. Continue treatment until there are no further clinical signs of wart tissue.

deeply enough, penetration focally into subcutaneous fat might occur. When this happens, fine, small, almost white, fingerlike projections herniate into the field. These have a very characteristic appearance and should not be mistaken for wart tissue. Also of note are periungual and subungual warts. Simply consider the nail as epithelium, and vaporize away the appropriate tissue for complete exposure. It is not unusual for larger portions of the nail then originally considered to be vaporized away while tracing wart tissue as it invades subungually.

Similar Ablative Procedures

The procedure outline earlier, with its attendant parameters, can be used for ablation of a multitude of cutaneous problems . The list includes but is not limited to tattoos (see Chapter 22), seborrheic keratoses, superficial basal cell carcinoma, squamous cell carcinoma *in situ,* adenoma sebaceum, trichoepitheliomas, neurofibromas, dermatofibromas, lentigines, and dystrophic or onychomycotic nails. Each entity targeted for ablation differs in the visual clues that are present during the procedure, but virtually all are easily distinguishable from normal tissue. Several entities such as dermatosis papulosa nigra, syringomas, and milia can be ablated at slightly different parameters for which topical or local anesthesia is not usually necessary. The ablative procedure is similar to that already described except for the parameters; that is, ablate, cleanse with hydrogen peroxide, and repeat the ablate-cleanse cycle until the pathologic entity is no longer apparent. The parameters used for these entities are the same as for the procedure that follows for the treatment of ''ice-pick'' scars. The visual clues, however, are different, as is the progression of the procedure.

''Ice-Pick'' Scars

Clean and drape the area appropriately, and ensure that all safety measures have been employed and that the smoke evacuation system is on and functioning properly. Local anesthesia is optional, and its use depends on patient tolerance. Ablation at the parameters for this procedure make it more annoying than painful, and many patients prefer to forego the needle stick of local anesthesia. Set the laser at an output of 2 W and, assuming the laser being used has an adjustable pulse, set the pulse duration for 0.02 seconds. The pulse should be set at a comfortable repeat rate and may be increased as a ''feel'' is developed for the procedure.

It is probably reasonable to begin with a rate of 1 Hz and increase to 5 or 10 Hz as desired. The spot size initially should be less than 1 mm and depends on the size of the target area. This should be tested as before on a tongue depressor off the field of confirmation. Move the handpiece to the field, and aim for the edge of the ice-pick scar where it meets the normal skin surface. Begin with a single pulse to confirm the settings on skin, and make any necessary adjustments. Proceed by moving slowly but steadily along the outside rim of the scar (Fig. 12). Once the entire outside rim has been treated, cleanse the area, if necessary, with a cotton-tipped applicator moistened with hydrogen peroxide. Focus the beam slightly to deliver a slightly larger impact, and re-treat the same area as before (Fig. 13). This results in a larger but shallower impact and begins a beveling of the area. When the procedure has been completed around the scar rim, cleanse the area if necessary. Defocus further, and begin treating the rim as before, but now begin moving the impact spot in a spiral or looping fashion to broaden the target area and further minimize thermal damage to the area. Cleanse the area if necessary, and repeat the spiraling abla-

FIG. 12. (A) Line drawing and **(B)** clinical appearance of the vaporization process. Begin vaporization by moving steadily along the outside rim of the scar.

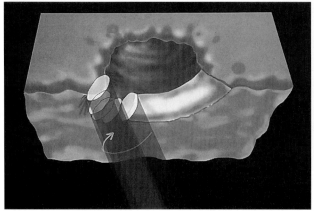

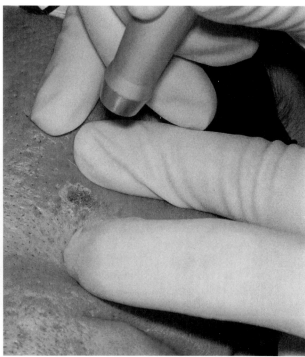

A   B

tion, increasing the spot size slightly by defocusing with each new pass. This results in moving over the base of the scar as well as onto normal tissue beyond the original scar rim and creates a beveled, saucerized ablation wound (Figs. 14 and 15). (Note that for dematosis papulosa nigra, milia, syringomas, and the like, ablate only the target tissue and do not move beyond onto normal skin.)

POSTOPERATIVE MANAGEMENT

Postoperative management is straightforward. For incisional wounds that have been closed, suture removal should be completed at approximately the same time as for scalpel-created wounds but possibly slightly later. Reasonable guidelines would be 6 to 7 days for facial locations, 8 to 10

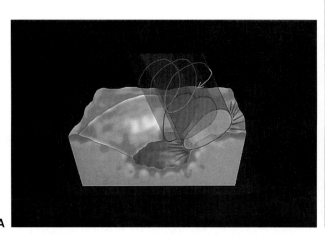

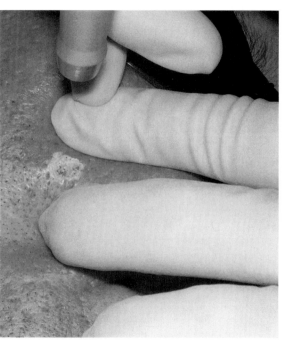

A   B

FIG. 13. (A) Line drawing and **(B)** clinical appearance of re-treating. Defocus the beam and re-treat the same area, delivering a larger but shallower impact.

FIG. 14. (A) Line drawing and (B) clinical appearance of ablation wound. By continually defocusing and vaporizing the scars, a large saucerization is created that may extend onto other treatment sites, resulting in a large, confluent wound.

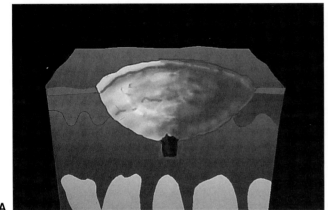

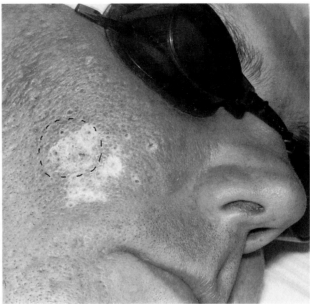

A

B

days for torso and extremities, and 10 to 14 days for the scalp. Wound care before suture removal should be the same as for other closed wounds and should include cleansing the wound at least once daily.

For incisional wounds and ablation wounds, rigorous wound care negates the need for antibiotic prophylaxis and results in rapid healing with early reepithelialization. An example of appropriate wound care instructions is provided in Fig. 16.

ADVERSE SEQUELAE AND COMPLICATIONS

Most adverse sequelae and complications are no different from those of other surgical wounds. However, several situations may be unique to CO_2 laser–created wounds. Delayed maximal tensile strength of these laser wounds has already been mentioned, and closure and timing of suture removal should take this into account. With experience comes better prediction of appropriate timing for suture removal. In the interim consider placing only interrupted sutures or backing

any running closure with a few spaced, interrupted sutures. The patient should return at the time that is normal for suture removal. The wound should be examined for strength and integrity. If sutures are ready for removal, remove them; if not, have the patient return at another appropriate time.

Wounds allowed to heal by second intention may also have slightly delayed healing when compared with similar nonlaser wounds. This should not be cause for concern, but the patient should be aware of a possibly extended healing time. When the wounds are reepithelialized, they have a tendency to be quite pink. This erythema can be persistent for many months and resolves spontaneously. However, faster resolution can be obtained by treating the wound with a flash-pumped dye laser or argon-pumped dye laser.

In some locations keloid removal, as well as ablative procedures, can result in erythematous hypertrophic scarring. This type of result can respond nicely to treatment with either the flash-pumped or argon-pumped dye lasers and/or the application of silicone sheeting.

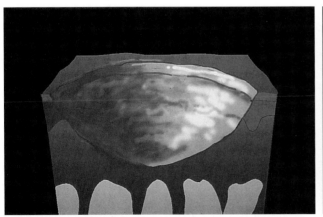

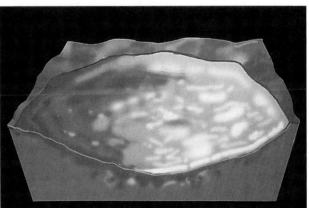

A

B

FIG. 15. (A,B) The technique for the treatment of "ice-pick" or craterform scars.

CO₂ LASER POSTOPERATIVE INSTRUCTIONS

1. Keep the treatment site dry for 24 hours following treatment.

2. After 24 hours, remove the dressing. The dressing may be soaked in hydrogen peroxide to loosen it if it sticks to the wound.

3. Clean the wound with hydrogen peroxide at least once per day. Peroxide is best applied with a cotton tipped swab (Q-tip) saturated with the solution and rubbed (do not be too gentle) over the area to remove any residual ointment or debris. Do not allow a scab or thick crust to form.

4. After cleaning the wound, roll a clean, dry cotton swab over the area.

5. Apply **POLYSPORIN** ointment liberally.

6. Cover the wound with a clean dressing. Vigilon or Telfa pads will prevent the dressing from adhering to the wound. Be sure to apply the Telfa with the shiny side against the wound. The wound will heal faster if it is kept clean and moist with the ointment and covered with a bandage or dressing.

7. If you have any discomfort, acetaminophen (Tylenol) is usually best for controlling the pain. Do not take aspirin, aspirin-containing medications or Ibuprofen (Motrin, Advil, Nuprin) for one week.

8. Do not use any cosmetic or cover-ups on this treatment site until the skin has totally healed.

If you have any questions or problems, please call the office at 842-3940 or call 842-3000 to page the dermatology resident on call.

FIG. 16. Appropriate wound care instructions.

Part II   CO₂ Laser Transconjunctival Blepharoplasty

HISTORY

Use of the CO_2 laser in performing blepharoplasties was first reported by Baker et al. in 1984. This was followed by a paired comparison of laser versus conventional blepharoplasties by David and Sanders in 1987. They showed quite convincingly that there is a significantly lower incidence of ecchymosis and edema following laser blepharoplasty than with cold steel and electrocautery, and the recovery period is shorter as well. The subject of blepharoplasty has already been discussed in Chapter 18. However, laser blepharoplasty and transconjunctival blepharoplasty were not covered in that chapter. The reader should be aware that the carbon dioxide laser can be used instead of scalpel and cautery in performing both conventional upper and lower lid blepharoplasties. However, because the transconjunctival approach affords a lower incidence of ectropion and scleral show than conventional lower lid blepharoplasty, and because the CO_2 laser reduces ecchymosis and edema postoperatively, the use of the CO_2 in performing transconjunctival lower lid blepharoplasty results in the combined benefits of both the laser procedure and the transconjunctival approach.

PREOPERATIVE PLANNING

The reader is asked to review the sections on preoperative planning, eyelid examination, and anatomy of the eye discussed in Chapter 18, before proceeding with material in this discussion.

Transconjunctival lower lid CO_2 laser blepharoplasty requires a Continuous Wave (CW) carbon dioxide laser that is fitted with a handpiece capable of delivering a spot size of 0.2 mm or smaller at its focal point. A 0.1 mm spot is highly recommended. Smoke evacuation will be necessary and surgical equipment should include a Desmares retractor and a Jaeger plate. The Jaeger plate is available in both methacrylate and stainless steel varieties, but the stainless are less cumbersome and much easier to use. Toothed forceps, such as an Adsons, should be available as should sterile normal saline and cotton-tipped applicators. Electrocautery should also be available and ready to use should unexpectedly brisk bleeding occur. Iced compresses should be on hand for immediate postoperative use.

Two surgical assistants will need to be present for the procedure; one to retract the lower lid and serve as assistant and one to handle the smoke evacuator and control the laser for ready and standby operation. Prior to the procedure, both assistants need to understand their responsibilities and be comfortable with them.

It will be necessary to have both topical and local anesthesia on hand as well as a sedating medication such as Valium. The patients can be given either oral or sublingual Valium prior to their being brought to the office or 10 mg can be administered intravenously just prior to the delivery of anesthesia. For topical anesthesia, either tetracaine, proparacaine hydrochloride 0.05%, or other similar topical anesthetic which is approved for ophthalmic use can be utilized. Local anesthesia can be 1% to 2% Lidocaine with epinephrine $1:100,000$ or $1:200,000$. If anesthesia of longer duration is desired, Marcaine 0.75% can be mixed with an equal amount of Lidocaine. Before beginning the procedure, examine the patient while he or she is in the sitting position so that you can refamiliarize yourself with the extent of periorbital fat in each of the lower lid compartments. You should have a ''feel'' for the amount of fat which will need to be removed. In this way you are more likely to remove exactly the correct amount of fat from each compartment. Removal of too little fat can be dealt with in a second procedure but removal of too much fat is not very easily resolved.

TECHNIQUE

Once the patient has been reevaluated, have the patient lie in the supine position with his or her head resting comfortably on a pillow with the head tilted back slightly. Prepare the patient for electrocautery by placing the grounding plate or pad properly and clasping the cautery pencil in a readily accessible location. Drape the patient's head with a sterile towel. Pull the upper lid of one eye gently upward and instruct the patient to look down. Introduce one to two drops of topical anesthesia directly to the globe, and release the upper lid. Blot excess fluid with a sterile sponge. Repeat this procedure for the second eye as well. Although there will be little or no contact with any skin surface, it is wise to prep the periorbital area with a nonflammable surgical scrub such as chlorhexidene gluconate. Do this carefully and avoid direct contact with the eye. If sedation is needed and the patient has not been given oral or sublingual sedation, administer 10 mg Valium intravenously at this time. When sedation has been achieved, working from behind the head

of the surgical table, position the table and the patient's head in such a way that you will have direct and comfortable access to the conjunctival cul de sac. Identify the infraorbital foramen and mark its location. Retract the lower eyelid with the Desmares retractor and identify the cul de sac. Introduce the 1 inch, 30 gauge needle of your anesthetic syringe into the conjunctival cul de sac and toward the infraorbital foramen. You should feel the bone of the infraorbital ridge and can guide the syringe to the foramen by using your mark. Administer approximately 1.0 cc of anesthesia in the foraminal area. Administer $\frac{1}{2}$ to 1.0 cc medially and the same amount laterally. Repeat this procedure for the second eye. Wait 15 to 20 minutes to obtain the full benefit of the epinephrine and to allow proper time for your anesthetic block to take.

Set the laser to 10 watts and assure yourself that the proper handpiece is in place by doing a test impact on a tongue blade. Have one assistant retract the lower lid with the Desmares retractor and have the other deploy the smoke evacuator. Take the Jaeger plate in your non-dominant hand and direct the patient to open the eye and look upward. Gently place the Jaeger plate on the globe. This will prevent the upper lid from interrupting the procedure. Beginning nasally in the conjunctival cul de sac, and, with the laser handpiece in your dominant hand, make your first impact in one short pulse. This will assure anesthesia and positioning. After making any necessary adjustments, begin your incision on or near your initial impact site and proceed laterally with your incision. The incision should be slightly curved, conforming to the curvature of the globe. Reposition your assistant's Desmares retractor if you have not identified the periorbital fat pad, and reincise at the same location. It occasionally takes several passes to reach the fat pads. Once you have reached the fat pads, identify the lateral, middle, and nasal or lateral components. The fat in the middle compartment will be the most plentiful and most accessible. It will be identified by its position and typically yellow fat appearance. The fat of the nasal and lateral compartments are not as easily accessible and have a more stringy and pale appearance.

With your non-dominant hand still on the Jaeger plate, place firm but gentle pressure downward (toward the posterior orbit). This will force the fat out of its compartment and into full view (Fig. 17). If this does not occur, try gently teasing the fat outwards with the toothed Addsons forceps. Once the fat is exposed, have your assistant place a cotton tipped applicator, wet with sterile normal saline, behind the fat but in front of the Desmares retractor. Incise the base of the fat which is lying against the cotton tipped applicator (Fig. 18). Readjust the positioning of the retractor, applicator and fat until you have detached the fat. Place the fat on a sterile sponge. It is a good idea to place this sponge on the cheek of the side you are working on so that you can readily assess the amount of fat which has been removed and com-

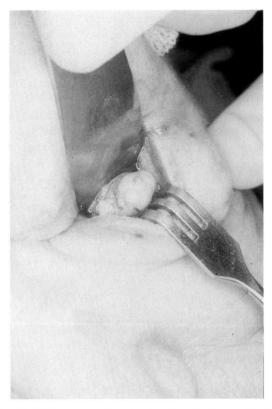

FIG. 17. With your assistant retracting the lower lid with a Desmares retractor and following your incision in the inferior cul de sac, place firm but gentle pressure on the Jaeger plate. This will force the fat out of its compartment and into full view.

pare it to the amount you predicted would be removed. Should you incur any bleeding during the procedure, simply defocus the laser, have your assistant roll a dry cotton-tipped applicator over the bleeding site and immediately impact on this area with the defocused laser. If this fails after several attempts, feel free to use electrocoagulation. Continue on with your fat removal until you have removed the desired amount of fat. Apply a small amount of ophthalmic antibiotic to the conjunctival area and remove the retractor and the plate. Allow the patient to close that eye, or assist the patient by manually closing that eyelid.

Repeat the above procedure for the opposite eye. It is helpful to keep the first eye's fat in its cheek position as a readily available reference to the amount of fat removed from that eye.

Once the procedure is completed for both sides and if an upper lid blepharoplasty has already been done or is not going to be done, place iced compresses over both eyes and make certain the patient is in a comfortable position. If an upper lid blepharoplasty is to be done, complete that procedure and then position the iced compresses. To minimize any edema, administer 1.0 cc (6 mg) of Celestone intramuscularly. Maintain the patient in the supine position with the

compresses in place for about 30 minutes. Reevaluate the patient at that time. And, if all is well, allow the patient to be driven home, there to rest in a reclining position for the remainder of the day. Pain medication is usually unnecessary.

POSTOPERATIVE CONSIDERATIONS

Immediately after blepharoplasty, regardless of how it is accomplished, the patient may experience diplopia. This is transient and should resolve spontaneously. Other common, but transient, complaints include dryness or just the opposite, epiphora. A burning sensation is encountered occasionally. This can be due to an irritating substance coming into contact with the eye such as the surgical prep or the antibiotic ointment being used. However, it can also be due to corneal or bulbar conjunctival damage done during the surgery. Since the procedure is basically painless as is the postoperative course, any complaints of pain of any kind should require ophthalmologic evaluation. The physician (and patient) is well-served who has the common sense to have an ophthalmological colleague available on short notice for such problems. (See Postoperative Management in Chapter 18.)

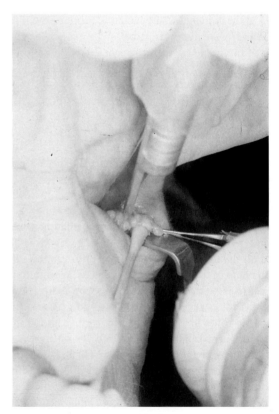

FIG. 18. Once the fat is exposed, have your assistant place a cotton-tipped applicator, wet with sterile normal saline, behind the fat but in front of the Desmares retractor.

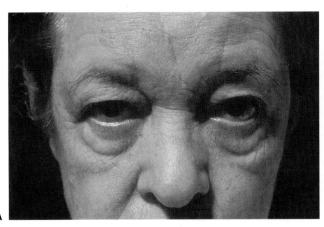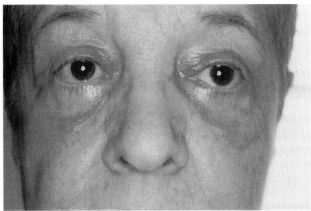

A

B

FIG. 19. (A) Pre and (B) one-month postoperative photos of a patient who has had only CO_2 laser transconjunctival lower lid blepharoplasty and no excess skin removal. Note the "snap back" effect of the excess tissue. Upper lids were done with the CO_2 laser.

The patient who has had blepharoplasty surgery should be evaluated on the very next day, then as needed or in one week, and again at one month. There are numerous ophthalmic preparations which are combination steroid/antibacterial preparations. Any one of these can be used two to three times daily for minor irritation.

To a physician who is experienced in laser excisional surgery and also in blepharoplasty, complications of this procedure are rare. The procedure can be completed in twenty minutes or less and the patient may be ready for normal activity after as little as 24 hours, with little if anything in the way of ecchymosis or edema.

CONCLUSION

CO_2 laser blepharoplasty has many advantages over the same procedures done conventionally. Some will argue that the transconjunctival procedure has a disadvantage in that any excess skin which needs to be removed would require a second procedure to do so. The response from many laser surgeons would be that most patients undergoing lower lid blepharoplasty will not need excess skin removed as any excess will "snap back" in a month or so (Figs. 19, 20). The safest practice is probably to do the transconjunctival procedure first and inform your patient about the possible need to come back for the removal of excess skin at a later date for a minor charge, such as a surgical tray charge. Most patients will be happy at the prospect of minimizing the risk of ectropion and scleral show as well as a visible suture line, by having a single safe and quick procedure done with the smallest chance of a second procedure which would be done only if needed.

The transconjunctival CO_2 laser blepharoplasty is safe. It can be completed in only 20 minutes or less, decreases the incidence of ectropion and scleral show, and minimizes the ecchymosis and edema postoperatively. The incision site requires no suturing and generally closes in three to five days.

The procedure is essentially painless and there are few if any postoperative sequelae. Patients can be back to normal activity in as little as 24 hours, and there is only a minimal change that they may need a second procedure to remove excess skin; if only the same could be said for other procedures performed by the dermatologic surgeon.

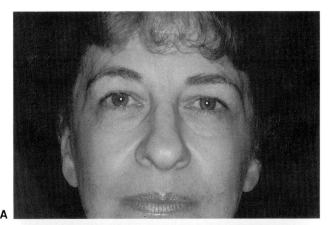

A

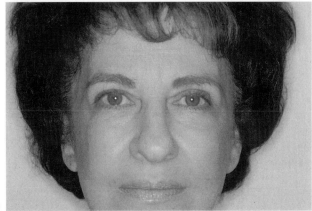

B

FIG. 20. Another (A) pre and (B) one month postoperative photo of a patient who had CO_2 laser lower lid transconjunctival and CO_2 laser upper lid blepharoplasty.

Part III   Pulsed Carbon Dioxide Laser Resurfacing of Photoaged Facial Skin

As previously described, the CO_2 laser is capable of producing relatively specific vaporization of cutaneous lesions. However, most CO_2 lasers can achieve this specificity only through meticulous technique by the surgeon. At times, total lesional specificity is not necessary, as in destruction of skin cancers and certain benign lesions such as warts with resultant fibrosis and hemostasis. A new role for the CO_2 laser has been to rejuvenate the skin. In this application, control of residual thermal damage is critical to achieve clinical improvement without risk for adverse healing. Achieving this degree of heat control requires a high-energy pulsed CO_2 laser. Therefore, with this procedure, the laser is used to produce highly specific vaporization of the photodamaged epidermis and epidermal lesions (seborrheic keratoses, solar lentigo, actinic keratoses). In addition, subsequent passes with the CO_2 laser result in contraction of dermal collagen through specific thermal effects. This section discusses the use of the CO_2 laser for facial rejuvenation.

Techniques for rejuvenation of sun-damaged, aging skin have expanded and progressed over the past decade in conjunction with increased understanding of the histopathologic and physiologic changes of chronologic aging and photoaging. Cosmetic surgical procedures for rejuvenation of the skin surface concentrate on destruction or removal of the outer, damaged skin layers and their subsequent replacement by newly formed collagen and epidermis. Chemical peels (see Chapter 29) and dermabrasion (see Chapter 28) have been the mainstays of therapy for treatment of cutaneous photoaging. Although dramatic results can be achieved with these procedures, each carries significant disadvantages and risks. Variable results arise because of the difficulty in achieving a specific, predictable depth of tissue removal with these modalities. To avoid hypopigmentation, persistent erythema, and scarring that may accompany deep dermal tissue removal, superficial resurfacing may be performed, resulting frequently in insufficient cosmetic improvement. In addition, dermabrasion continues to lose favor because of technical difficulties, as well as the potential for contamination with blood-borne pathogens. Therefore poor predictability of results, as well as the risk of poor healing, continues to be associated with both chemical peeling and dermabrasion.

The potential advantages of pulsed laser cutaneous resurfacing relate to the precise control of tissue vaporization, minimization of residual thermal damage, dermal heating, and achievement of hemostasis. These advantages are achieved by single-pulse vaporization of tissue using a high-energy microsecond-domain pulsed CO_2 laser. The CO_2 wavelength (10,600 nm) is efficiently absorbed in water, resulting in an optical penetration depth of only 30 μ. As previously discussed, intracellular water is the laser's target, and upon absorption, heat transfer results in instantaneous heating to more than 100°C with vaporization and cellular ablation. If this energy is delivered continuously, the tissue becomes progressively desiccated and accumulates heat because of loss of its water target, reaching temperatures of up to 600°C. This results in diffusion of heat to several hundred microns below the level of vaporization. This layer of thermal necrosis interferes with wound healing and may result in significant scarring. To avoid this scenario, the laser energy must be delivered rapidly, in less time than it takes the tissue to cool (estimated to be 1 millisecond or less). However, if the individual pulses do not deliver adequate energy to vaporize tissue, multiple pulses become necessary and complicate the situation because of heat diffusion between pulses. Ideally the tissue should be vaporized in a single pulse, since this dissipates heat away from the treated tissue and does not allow significant heat diffusion to occur below the level of vaporization. The degree of clinical improvement achieved in treating perioral and periorbital wrinkles using a high-energy, pulsed CO_2 laser in a blinded, retrospective review of graded pretreatment and posttreatment photographs showed a highly reproducible 50% decrease in the extent of wrinkling with all patients, regardless of treatment location.

PREOPERATIVE PREPARATION

The skin is prepared preoperatively at least 2 weeks before CO_2 laser resurfacing. One recommended regimen is tretinoin cream 0.025% every night at bedtime, a broad-spectrum sunscreen every morning, and for Fitzpatrick skin type III, 4% hydroquinone solution twice daily. Having patients apply Cellex-C (a topical vitamin C preparation) every morning as well appears to lead to decreased erythema and faster reepithelialization. On the day of the procedure, begin a regimen of an oral, gram-positive antibacterial agent and antiviral agent, valacyclovir (500 mg by mouth three times daily) or famacyclovir (250 mg). Cleanse the entire facial skin with a nonflammable detergent solution like Septisol and thoroughly rinse with normal saline.

Before treating local areas such as the perioral or periorbital area some patients receive oral diazepam (5 to 10 mg),

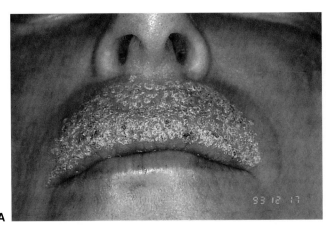 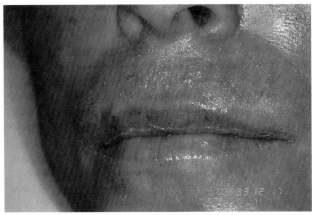

A   B

FIG. 21. (A) Single-impact CO_2 laser vaporization leaves a char-free residue of thermally denatured proteinaceous debris resulting from vaporization of intracellular water. **(B)** This surface debris is debrided by vigorously scrubbing with saline-saturated gauze before making an additional laser pass. This not only removes desiccated, nonvaporizing debris, but also rehydrates the underlying tissue layer. It is important to follow this by dry gauze wipe to remove excess saline from the tissue surface, to avoid blocking the beam by absorption in the saline layer on the tissue surface.

intramuscular meperidine hydrochloride, promethazine hydrochloride (25 to 50 mg of each), or an intravenous bolus of midazolam hydrochloride, 2.5 mg, before induction of anesthesia as a ring block with or without maxillary and/or mandibular nerve blocks with 1% lidocaine with epinephrine 1:200,000. When performing full-face resurfacing, intravenous sedation using propofol and midazolam is administered with appropriate monitoring by an anesthesiologist.

TECHNIQUE

Apply the laser treatment to the skin with the goal of single-pulse vaporization. Cover the treatment area with confluent single pulses with 10% to 30% overlap using a 3-mm collimated beam. A layer of nonvaporized, thermally denatured, proteinaceous debris resulting from this first pass is debrided with saline-saturated gauze pads or cotton-tipped applicators by rubbing vigorously (Fig. 21). Perform additional passes in the same manner, confined predominantly to

visibly photodamaged tissue (viewed under telescopes with 2.7× magnification). If the photodamaged area demonstrates confluent papular elastosis or wrinkle lines positioned less than 3 mm apart, re-treat the entire involved area. If photodamage is scattered and distinct wrinkle lines sparsely positioned, treat the elevated elastotic papules and elevated "shoulders" of wrinkle lines to level and smooth the irregular surface contours (Fig. 22). Perform additional passes as necessary to achieve as flat and smooth a surface texture as possible (perioral: one to five passes, average = 3; periorbital: one to four passes, average = 2). Each subsequent pass after the first covers progressively less surface area.

Other factors to consider when deciding how many passes to perform consist of tissue color and contraction. When the first layer is removed, the epidermis/dermis appears pink; further vaporization produces a change in tissue color to gray and then yellow or chamois. These color changes may denote thermal changes in skin. Continued vaporization results in a dark tan to light brown appearance, which denotes increasing thermal injury to the dermis. This tissue sloughs during the next

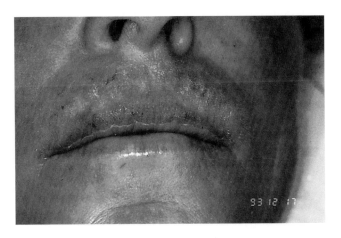

FIG. 22. Additional laser passes beyond removal of the epidermal layer are directed at photodamaged tissue with the goal of achieving a level, smooth surface. Isolated wrinkle lines are treated by concentrating on the elevated shoulders of the wrinkles. Tissue coagulation is visible as yellow-white streaks against a background of erythema from papillary dermal capillaries.

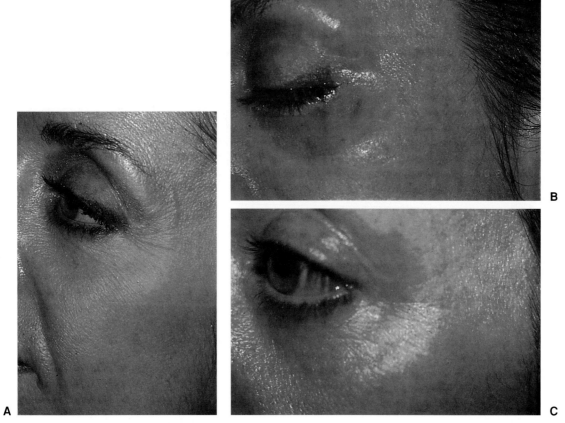

FIG. 23. When the entire face is not treated, the regional wrinkle lines are ablated in their full length; the peripheral zone is then treated with single, concentric layers of 1 to 1.5 cm of decreasing pulse energy (350 to 200 mJ per pulse) to feather the treated area into nontreated skin. **(A)** Preoperative appearance. **(B)** Immediate postoperative appearance after two passes of 350 mJ, 2 W, and feathering of the periphery with a single pass of 200 mJ, 4 W. **(C)** Eight weeks after surgery.

1 to 2 weeks, and it is difficult to judge the depth of this tissue damage. Avoid continued vaporization to prevent deep thermal damage. Discontinue further laser treatment when the yellow or chamois color is apparent. In addition, tissue contraction is obvious with vaporization. A maximal amount of tissue contraction occurs with the second or third pass. Areas of thin skin (periorbital) contract to a larger extent than areas of thicker skin (forehead). Do not proceed with further vaporization when tissue contraction no longer occurs, except to selectively vaporize specific lesions (keratoses).

Employ pulse energies of 500 mJ for the first pass. Perform subsequent passes at 500 to 350 me depending on the area being treated. Periorbital areas are generally best treated at lower energy fluence to avoid deep vaporization. Power settings of 1 to 4 W, resulting in pulse frequencies of 4 to 8 Hz, are generally recommended, since frequencies above 8 Hz are too fast to allow for precise placement of laser impacts. When treating local areas, use a feathering technique at the periphery of each treatment area, decreasing the pulse energy by 100 mJ with each peripheral pass to a minimum of 200 to 300 mJ in one or two concentric zones while also gradually decreasing the density of applied laser pulses (Fig. 23).

In an effort to produce more reproducible and evenly spaced laser impacts a computer pattern generator is available. This tool emits laser fluence at 300 mJ through a 2.25-mm-diameter spot in various patterns of various sizes and various densities in a rapid (333 Hz) manner (Fig. 24). A specific pattern may be chosen to match the lesion or area treated. This device allows delivery of individual laser pulses in a concise, safe, and rapid manner. Use of this accessory not only speeds the procedure time significantly, but also improves the safety profile by virtue of its precise application of single pulses for tissue vaporization.

Use of rectangular or square patterns to cover the treated area in a uniform, confluent manner is recommended (Fig. 25). Patterns 3 and 5 seem to be most useful and are most commonly used at their largest size (7 or 8) with densities of 3 to 5 to produce relatively confluent vaporization. When making second or third passes, it is sometimes useful to decrease the density (1 to 3) to separate the laser impact sites and provide another degree of safety in avoidance of

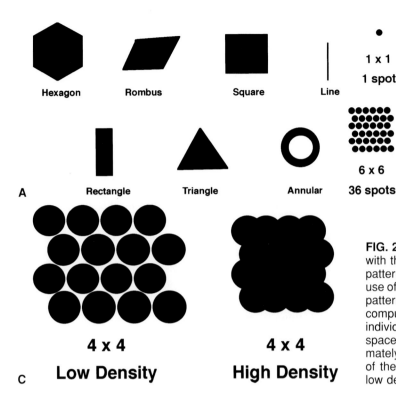

FIG. 24. **(A)** Seven different patterns are available for use with the Coherent UltraPulse CO_2 laser with the computer pattern generator. **(B)** Nine different sizes are available with use of the Coherent UltraPulse CO_2 laser with the computer pattern generator. **(C)** The Coherent UltraPulse CO2 laser computer pattern generator allows control of the density of individual impacts from a low density, which represents 10% space between spots, to a high density (shown) of approximately 40% overlapping of spots. With high density the size of the generated pattern is significantly smaller than with low density.

thermal injury. In addition, the pulse energy may be decreased in thin dermal areas such as the eyelids and periorbital tissue.

POSTOPERATIVE CARE

Wound care following treatment should be directed toward gentle debridement of serous exudate and necrotic tissue by frequent soaking (four times a day or more) with tap water containing acetic acid (white vinegar, 1 teaspoon per cup of water) and maintenance of a moist tissue surface with continuous application of a nonsensitizing ointment such as petroleum. The combined polymyxin B sulfate–bacitracin zinc and mupirocin are sensitizing to many patients. Some occlusive dressings such as hydrogels can be difficult to apply, and once placed on the treated skin, stay in place. There is a need for the manufacturers of such occlusive dressings to develop a mask that can be easily applied.

Preoperative topical medications are restarted 3 to 4 weeks after surgery and continued for a minimum of 3 (hydroquinone) to 6 months (tretinoin, sunscreen, Cellex-C) postoperatively. If areas of itching or a sensation of tightness is noted, alclometasone dipropionate 0.05% ointment is applied twice daily (for 1 to 2 weeks). Postinflammatory hyperpigmentation is treated with retinoic acid cream 0.025% every night

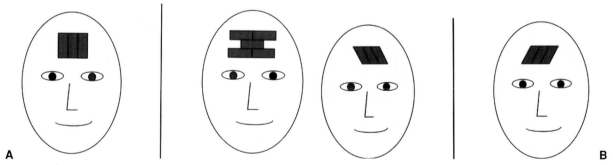

FIG. 25. **(A)** The 5 rectangular pattern can be used to resurface the face. The first pass with the rectangular pattern is in a vertical orientation. The second pass in this pattern is placed horizontally after wiping the skin of surface debris. **(B)** The third layer is vaporized using an obliquely oriented pattern after first wiping the surface of any debris. If a fourth pass is necessary, a reverse oblique orientation is used.

at bedtime, 4% hydroquinone solution twice daily, or 2% kojic acid solution, or a combination of these.

COMPLICATIONS

Except for temporary erythema and blotchy pigmentation, there are few complications with this procedure. Rarely, patients with a history of cystic acne have an acne flare as a result of occlusion that occurs from the white petrolatum ointment. This is easily treated with tetracycline, comedonal expression, and, rarely, intralesional injection of triamcinolone 2.5 mg/ml.

Patients with no history of prior lesions of herpes simplex have developed acute onset of typical perioral herpetic lesions postoperatively, and there is at least one report of a patient who had pain and patchy erythema in a dermatomal distribution typical of herpes zoster in the facial nerve distribution. These patients did not take prophylactic valacyclovir. An additional patient developed facial herpes simplex 1 day after discontinuing valacyclovir 5 days after surgery. All of these patients completely healed without any scarring or adverse sequelae when treated with acyclovir or valacyclovir.

In some patients after full-face or perioral laser resurfacing an unusual, generalized pustulopapular eruption develops over the face 4 to 8 days after surgery, causing sensations of burning pain with delayed wound healing (Fig. 26). This may be due to a yeast wound infection and can be successfully treated with ketoconazole 200 mg every day or itraconazole 200 mg every day for 2–5 days. Postoperative infection with *Staphylococcus aureus* and *Pseudomonas aeruginosa* has also been seen. These infections clear without adverse sequelae with appropriate antibiotic treatment.

Two factors that are present in all of these postoperative complications are delayed wound healing and new-onset facial pain. Therefore the surgeon must carefully evaluate patients with pain after surgery. A KOH scraping is recommended for any nonhealing lesions, which should also be cultured for bacteria as well as herpes simplex virus. Patients should be immediately started on antibacterial and antiviral agents pending culture results. An anticandidal oral agent should be given if budding yeasts are evident on KOH examination. A preoperative history should determine whether patients are at any increased risk for postoperative infections.

CONCLUSION

Photoaged skin has been found to have an atrophic epidermis with atypical keratinocytes at an increased number and altered distribution of melanocytes. This abnormal epidermis overlies a distinctively altered dermis characterized by decreased amounts and alterations of collagen and a marked increase in elastotic material. This elastotic material does not manifest the normal structure or physiologic properties of cross-linked elastic fibers. In addition, there is a decrease in number and size of the dermal capillaries. These histopathologic abnormalities create the clinical features that are identified clinically as photoaging or dermatoheliosis: wrinkles; papular elastosis; yellow, pallid color; and uneven pigmentation. Removal of this layer of the photodamaged epidermis and dermis, which may measure 100 to 500 μm or more in thickness, results in immediate clinical improvement, as well as the potential for delayed improvement that occurs through increased collagen type I deposition and collagen remodeling. These events occur whether the treatment mechanism is caustic (chemical peels), mechanical (dermabrasion), or thermal (laser vaporization). However, the microsecond-domain, pulsed CO_2 laser achieves these goals with greater precision and control.

When the results are evaluated by subgroup and by location, there is a striking uniformity in the degree of improvement—45% to 50%. As for clinical expectations of improvement after laser resurfacing, it appears that patients with mild wrinkling may expect nearly complete wrinkle clearing, and patients with moderate to severe photodamage can expect 50% improvement. Although complete removal of moderate and severe wrinkling may not be easily achieved, the degree of improvement is very significant and no patients remain relatively unresponsive, not even those with severe wrinkling (Figs. 27, 28, and 29).

An additional reason exists for the improved clinical re-

FIG. 26. Beefy-red appearance of *Candida albicans* infection 7 days after laser resurfacing. Erythematous satellite papular lesions are evident.

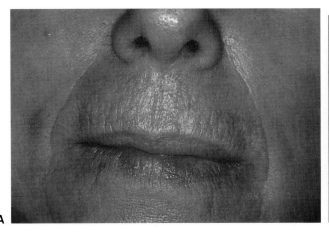
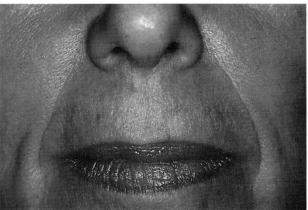

FIG. 27. (A) Clinical appearance before treatment of a 62-year-old woman demonstrating grade 3 wrinkling of the upper lip. **(B)** Four months after laser resurfacing.

sults, beyond that of improved precision and control in targeting wrinkle lines. When the CO_2 laser interacts with tissue, there are three different and distinct zones of tissue alteration correlating to the degree of tissue heating. The zone of direct interaction results in vaporization of intracellular water and tissue ablation. Underlying this zone is a layer of irreversible thermal damage and denaturation resulting in tissue necrosis, and below this layer is a zone of reversible thermal damage. It is in this zone of reversible thermal damage that collagen shrinkage takes place. It is likely that it is the repair of this layer during the healing phase that accounts for tightening of sagging skin and improvement of creases and explains the longer-than-expected duration of erythema that is observed. The tightened collagen helix may contract the tissue so that an altered tissue scaffold exists during the period of new collagen synthesis, resulting in permanently tightened skin.

Heat-induced collagen shrinkage was first reported for corneal reshaping approximately 100 years ago. Type I collagen fibrils shrink rapidly at temperatures of 55°C to 60°C to as much as one third of their original length. Since it is known that tissue necrosis occurs at temperatures greater than 70°C, this tissue shrinkage phenomenon can be accomplished without fear of tissue necrosis and scarring, if the tissue temperatures can be controlled in a predictable manner. Studies on rat skin have shown this heat-induced collagen shrinkage to occur in three phases: denaturation of the triple helix, unwinding of the helix, and hydrolysis of collagen cross-links resulting in relaxation as the temperature increases further. Although the changes that are seen on clinical examination are stable and persistent for at least the 3 years or more of clinical observation by the authors, it is not known whether the thermally altered collagen persists indefinitely in its new form or acts as a matrix for new collagen formation that recapitulates its shortened overall structure. Further studies are needed to better understand the observed skin shrinkage phenomenon created by these microsecond-domain, high-energy CO_2 laser pulses.

The safety and precision of this procedure are based on single-pulse tissue vaporization. The use of high powers re-

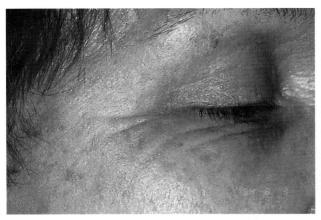
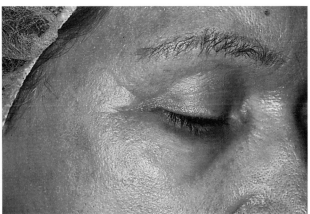

FIG. 28. (A) Clinical appearance of periorbital wrinkling in a 55-year-old patient with grade 3 wrinkling. **(B)** Six months following resurfacing.

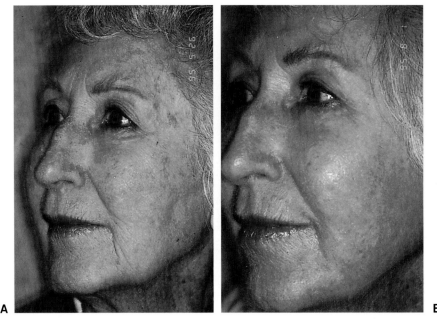

FIG. 29. (A) Clinical appearance of extensive dermatoheliotic changes including solar lentigines, actinic keratosis, and multiple scars from skin cancer surgery in a 72-year-old woman. **(B)** Following resurfacing.

sulting in rapid pulse delivery or moving the handpiece too slowly results in multiple pulses impacting the same tissue site and overrides the advantages given by the specific pulse parameters. In this situation the tissue is progressively desiccated and heated by subsequent pulses, resulting in an increasing zone of thermal necrosis that may interfere with wound healing and result in scarring.

With attention to proper treatment protocol (as well as observation of laser-tissue interaction to detect signs of tissue thermal damage) and appropriate postoperative wound care, resurfacing of photoaged facial skin using a very-high-energy, microsecond-domain, pulsed CO_2 laser is a safe and precise procedure with predictable results. Further study and enhancement of this procedure are under way.

SUGGESTED READING LIST

1. Allain JC, Lous LE, Cohen-Solal L, Bagin S, Maroteaux P. Isometric tensions developed during the hydrothermal swelling of rat skin. Connect Tissue Res 1980;7:127.
2. Bailin PL, Ratz JL, Levine HL. Removal of tattoos by CO_2 laser. J Dermatol Surg Oncol 1980;6:977.
3. Bailin PL, Ratz JL, Wheeland RG, eds. Dermatologic clinics. Pennsylvania: WB Saunders, 1987.
3a. Baker S, Muenzler WS, Small RG, Leonard JE. Carbon dioxide laser blepharoplasty. Ophthalmology 1984;91:238–243.
4. Baker TJ, Gordon HL, Mosienko P, Seckinger DL. Long-term histological study of skin after chemical face peeling. Plast Reconstr Surg 1974; 53:522.
5. Behin F, Feuerstein SS, Marovitz WF. Comparative histological study of mini pig skin after chemical peel and dermabrasion. Arch Otolaryngol 1977;103:271.
6. Benedetto AV, Griffin TD, Bendetto EA, Humenink HM. Dermabrasion: therapy and prophylaxis of the photoaged face. J Am Acad Dermatol 1992;27:439.
7. Bolgnia JL. Aging skin. Am J Med 1995;98(suppl 1A):99S.
8. Braverman IM, Fonferko BA. Studies in cutaneous aging. Part I. The elastic fiber network. J Invest Dermatol 1982;78:434.
9. Braverman IM, Fonferko BA. Studies in cutaneous aging. Part II. The microvasculature. J Invest Dermatol 1982;78:444.
9a. David LM, Saunders G. CO_2 laser blepharoplasty: A comparison to cold steel and electrocautery. Journ Dermatol Surg 1987;13(2):110–114.
10. Finley EM, Ratz JL. Treatment of hidradenitis suppurativa with carbon dioxide laser excision and second intention healing. J Am Acad Dermatol 1996;34:465.
11. Fitzpatrick RE, Goldman MP. Advances in carbon dioxide laser surgery. Clin Dermatol 1995;13:35.
12. Fitzpatrick RE, Goldman MP. CO_2 Laser Surgery. In: Goldman MP, Fitzpatrick RE, eds. Cutaneous laser surgery: the art and science of selective photothermolysis. St. Louis, MO: Mosby, 1994.
13. Fitzpatrick RE, Goldman MP, Ruiz-Exparza J. Laser treatment of benign pigmented epidermal lesions using a 300-nsecond pulse and 510-nm wavelength. J Dermatol Surg Oncol 1993;19:341.
14. Fitzpatrick RE, Goldman MP, Satur NM, Tope WD. Ultra pulsed CO_2 laser resurfacing of photoaged facial skin. Arch Dermatol 1996;132:395.
15. Fitzpatrick RE, Tope WD, Satur NM, Goldman MP. Pulsed CO_2 laser, trichloracetic acid, Baker–Gordon phenol, and dermabrasion: a comparative clinical and histological study of cutaneous resurfacing in a porcine model. Arch Dermatol 1996;132:469.
16. Gilchrest BA. Skin aging and photoaging: an overview. J Am Acad Dermatol 1989;21:610.
17. Green HA, Burd E, Mishioka NS, et al. Middermal wound healing: a comparison between dermatomal excision and pulsed carbon dioxide laser ablation. Arch Dermatol 1992;128:639.
18. Hall RR. The healing of tissues incised by a carbon-dioxide laser. Br J Surg 1971;58:222.
19. Kantor GR, Ratz JL, Wheeland RG: Treatment of acne keloidalis nuchae with the carbon dioxide laser. J Am Acad Dermatol 1986;14(2, part 1):263.
20. Kligman AM, Baker TJ, Gordon HL. Long-term histologic follow-up: phenol face peels. Plast Reconstr Surg 1985;75:652.
21. Kurban RS, Bhawan J. Histologic changes in skin associated with aging. J Dermatol Surg Oncol 1990;16:908.
22. Lask, GP, editor. Clinics in dermatology: cutaneous laser therapy. New York: Elsevier Science, 1995;13:1.
23. Mandy SH. Tretinoin in the preoperative and postoperative management of dermabrasion. J Am Acad Dermatol 1986;15:878.
24. McBurney EI. Carbon dioxide laser surgery of dermatologic lesions. South Med J 1978;7:189.

25. Montagna W, Kirchner S, Carlisle K. Histology of sun-damaged skin. J Am Acad Dermatol 1989;21:907.
26. Nelson BR, Fader DJ, Gillard M, et al. Pilot histologic and ultrastructural study of the effects of medium-depth chemical facial peels on dermal collagen in patients with actinically damaged skin. J Am Acad Dermatol 1995;32:472.
27. Nelson BR, Majmudar G, Griffiths EM, et al. Clinical improvement following dermabrasion of photoaged skin correlates with synthesis of collagen I. Arch Dermatol 1994;130:1136.
28. Polanyi TG. Laser physics. Otolaryngol Clin North Am 1983;16:753.
29. Rainoldi R, Candiani P, Virgilis G, et al. Connective tissue regeneration after CO_2 laser therapy. Int Surg 1983;68:167.
30. Ratz JL: Carbon dioxide laser as an excision tool. Monografias de Dermatologia. 1992;5(1):23.
31. Ratz JL: CO_2 laser for the treatment of balanitis xerotica obliterans. J Am Acad Dermatol 1994;10(5):925.
32. Ratz JL: Laser applications in dermatology. In: Dixon JA, ed. Surgical application of lasers. 2nd ed. Chicago: Yearbook Medical, 1987.
33. Ratz JL. Laser physics. Clin Dermatol 1995;13(1):11.
34. Ratz JL, ed. Lasers in cutaneous medicine and surgery. Chicago: Yearbook Medical, 1986.
35. Ratz JL, Bailin PL: CO_2 laser. In: Roenigk RK, Roenigk HH Jr, eds. Dermatologic surgery: principles and practice. 2nd ed. New York: Marcel Dekker, 1995.
36. Ratz JL, Bailin PL, Levine HL. CO_2 laser treatment of portwine stains: a preliminary report. J Dermatol Surg Oncol 1982;8:12.
37. Ratz JL, Bailin PL, Wheeland RG: CO_2 laser treatment of epidermal nevi. J Dermatol Surg Oncol 1986;12:567.
38. Ratz JL, McGillis ST: CO_2 laser treatment of acne scarring. Am J Cosmetic Surg 1992;9(2):181.
39. Smith L. Histopathologic characteristics and ultrastructure of aging skin. Cutis 1989;43:414.
40. Spira M, Dahl C, Freeman R, Gerow FJ, Hardy SB. Chemosurgery: a histological study. Plast Reconstr Surg 1970;45:247.
41. Stringer AR, Shaw EL, Kaufmann HE, et al. Themokeratoplasty. Trans Am Acad Opthalmol Otolaryngol 1973;77:441.
42. Stringer H, Parr J. Shrinkage temperature of eye collagen. Nature 1964;204:1307.
43. Tans LJ. Experimentelle untersuchungen iber entstehung von astigmatisumus durch nicht: perforirende Corneawunden. Graefes Arch Opthalmol 1898;45:117.
44. Thompson VM, Seiler T, Durrie DS, Cavanaugh TB. Holmium: YAG laser thermokeratoplasty for hyperopia and astigmatism: an overview. Refract Corneal Surg 1993;9(suppl):S134.
45. Warren R, Gartstein V, Kligman AM, et al. Sunlight and facial skin: a histologic and quantitative study. J Am Acad Dermatol 1991;25:751.
46. West MD. The cellular and molecular biology of skin aging. Arch Dermatol 1994;130:87.

Textbook of Dermatologic Surgery, edited by John L. Ratz.
Lippincott–Raven Publishers, Philadelphia © 1998.

CHAPTER 24

Future Considerations in Laser Surgery

Joop M. Grevelink

HISTORY

The rapidly evolving field of cutaneous laser surgery is not unlike the computer world with its monthly updates and constant explosion of new technology. Cutaneous lasers have been around since the early 1960s. However, in the last 12 years progress and expansion in their use through research has been exponential, mainly as a result of the emergence of the concept of "selective photothermolysis" coined by Anderson and Parrish. Selective photothermolysis has been applied in the evolution of lasers in surgery. Concomitantly, industrial lasers are being converted into medical lasers at increasing rates. Political and economic factors have also influenced the future of lasers. The end of the Cold War has allowed for previously classified military laser technology to be released for civilian uses. Although National Institutes of Health funding has diminished in the early 1990s, there is now a keen interest from institutional and private investors in technology issues, capitalizing the existing and startup laser companies and bringing new medical laser applications to fruition. From a regulatory standpoint, the Medical Devices Branch of the Food and Drug Administration, in the past sometimes maligned for its slow bureaucratic maneuvering, presently appears to operate quite efficiently. This augmented efficiency decreases the hurdle for new devices to come to market in an expedient fashion. Laser companies

are thus able to spend more resources on research and development.

NEW OR IMPROVED THERAPEUTIC LASER TOOLS IN EXISTING APPLICATIONS

Carbon Dioxide Lasers

The rebirth of the carbon dioxide (CO_2) laser has energized the laser industry. Once the old workhorse of cutaneous lasers, it is now refined by the advent of high-energy, short-pulsed lasers or clever scanners attached to the existing laser itself. Applications of this revitalized system now also include the treatment of photoaged skin, removal of rhytides, and acne scarring. The new CO_2 lasers may effective lyreplace conventional techniques such as dermabrasion and deep chemical peeling.

Further innovations of current cutaneous laser systems will allow even more precise ablation or destruction without excessive thermal damage. Although our understanding of wound healing after thermal effects is still in its infancy, it appears that wounds created by the excimer and erbium:yttrium, aluminum and garnet (Er:YAG) lasers heal in similar fashion to surgical scalpel wounds. The exact parameters of these lasers are still in development; however, a general framework of criteria exists for their use. To minimize altered dermal stromal tissue (i.e., thermally induced collagen and elastin denaturation) with resultant scarring and unwanted pigmentary changes, certain skin structures must re-

Joop M. Grevelink: Dermatology Laser Center, Massachusetts General Hospital, Boston, MA.

main intact to allow for repopulation with melanocytes and keratinocytes. Parts of the follicular and the appendageal apparatus will function as a reservoir for reseeding. Dangers to avoid are extensive ablation and heat deposition. These would reach into the deeper layers of the reticular dermis with irreparable effects. However, some thermal damage is necessary to induce the tissue shrinkage that is thought to be partially responsible for the clinical improvement observed. Since improvement is observed more than 6 to 8 months after treatment, the role of collagen reformation and remodeling after laser abrasion is actively studied as well.

Pulsed Er:YAG lasers are being explored as precise ablative tools. These lasers can ablate tissue at a depth of 10 to 30 μm, practically without any residual thermal necrosis. Like excimer lasers, ablative photodecomposition might be the mechanism of action. Excess laser energy is said to be expelled in the very tissue fragments it produces. Ablative photodecomposition, however, theoretically results in limited hemostasis, since thermal effects are minimal. In addition, collagen shrinkage by heat deposition might not contribute to the elimination of surface irregularities. Clinical studies are presently underway to investigate and optimize the parameters for this laser.

The titanium:sapphire laser is a solid-state system that employs titanium doped aluminum oxide(Al_2O_3) as a laser medium. It is operated at a wavelength of 800 nm with peak intensities of 10 terawatts (10^{12} watts) and with very short pulses of 120 femtoseconds (10^{-15} seconds) induration. Similar to the pulsed Er:YAG laser, it has the capacity to precisely ablate tissue without creating thermal injury by ablative photodecomposition. As a result, a "plasma" is created that forms as high-energy photons from the laser break molecular bonds. Production of photoacoustic shock waves and cavitation bubbles incites this reaction. The laser light is transmitted by fiberoptics and delivered using synthetic sapphire tips in a contact mode to incise or vaporize soft tissue. Seeming advantages of the titanium:sapphire laser are its flexibility and the ensuing decrease in harm to surrounding tissue. Using this system can produce precise ablation of epidermis by controlling the number and energy of pulses delivered. Nonthermal, collateral damage is minimal and ranges from 0 to 30 μm.

Other advances include emergent technology called chirp-pulse amplification. This modality is able to create subpicosecond pulses that are too short to transfer significant energy to surrounding material, thus minimizing collateral damage. In addition, a decreased sensitivity to tissue type might be seen with these devices, allowing surgeons to microsculpt different forms of tissue in an expedient and safe manner. Increasing the surgeon's capacity to accurately control and direct the laser light source while limiting the amount of injury to the affected area appears to be the ultimate goal for progress in the field of laser surgery.

The combination of high-energy, short-pulsed lasers with scanners might prove beneficial in the future. For example, the Ultrapulse laser with computer-assisted pattern generator (CPG) (Coherent Medical Group, Palo Alto, CA) can lay down variable patterns on the skin by quickly pasting together the 3.0-mm-diameter spots into larger areas. It is even possible to condense and expand patterns by overlapping and not overlapping individual laser impact spots for faster or deeper ablation. Similarly, the high-energy, pulse-doublet waveform of the SurgiPulse XJ (Sharplan Lasers, Allendale, NJ) is suited for adaptation to a scanner. Other systems under active investigation include the Tru-Pulse (Tissue Technologies, Inc., Albuquerque, NM) and the Luxar NovaPulse laser (Bothell, WA). These two CO_2 lasers are medium- to high-energy systems with or without scanners attached. Although very difficult to predict at present, the Tru-Pulse appears promising mainly because it maintains a relatively short pulse duration at 60 microseconds, minimizing thermal injury. However, it is not clear at this time whether larger pulse widths are required to obtain the desired amount of collagen remodeling.

Diode Lasers

Diode lasers are semiconductor lasers that emit energy at 805 nm in a continuous or pulsed fashion. Currently they are available as both surgical desiccators and coagulators in their relatively low-powered, direct-output variants. Their applicability to dermatologic laser surgery lies in the potential to produce precise noncontact laser-tissue interaction much like a continuous-wave (CW) Nd:YAG laser at 1064 nm can.

Diode-pumped solid-state lasers are high-powered (systems producing over 1000 W are currently commercially available), usually in an array that pumps other lasers such as the Nd:YAG. These diode lasers hold great promise when they are affordable in the clinical setting. Their extremely compact construction and reliability should prove advantageous to surgeons. Thus, when fully developed, they should be small, high-powered, very reliable, and inexpensive.

Solid-State Dye Technology

Revolutions in solid-state dye technology involve a class of dye-impregnated polymers that lase at specific visible wavelengths. These advances are now suitable for incorporation into cutaneous laser systems. One of the expected benefits is the versatility, since one can easily change wavelengths by "swapping" dye rods. Other advantageous characteristics include low maintenance, decreased environmental sensitivity, and high-powered capability when compared with liquid-dye technology that is present in the current generation of pulsed-dye lasers. The use of solid-dye technology is beneficial, since a number of different wavelengths can be easily obtained. This adaptability leads to a twofold value for the laser surgeon. First, solid-state dye lasers may be used for treatment of a wide variety of different dermal pigments or inks. Second, these lasers may be helpful in the treatment of resistant vascular lesions, using deeper penetrating wavelengths.

Optical parametric oscillators (OPOs) represent an additional technologic advance affecting solid-state laser devices. Their incorporation into these systems alters wavelength and intensity using recently developed, excellent-quality nonlinear crystals. When pumped with a Nd:YAG laser, a module converts the 1064-nm output of the Nd:YAG laser to various wavelengths, depending on the nonlinear crystals used. Essentially, short, fixed-wavelength pulses are converted to longer, tunable, narrow line-width, high-brightness radiation ranging in wavelengths from ultaviolet through mid-infrared.

Raman shifting is another technique to alter the wavelength of lasers. This can be achieved with a Raman shifting device attached to almost any laser. Current research appears promising. The flexibility in variant wavelength access through advances in dye technology, OPOs, and Raman shifting should prove to further shape the use of lasers in dermatologic surgery.

The use of nonlaser light sources is a recently explored technologic innovation. Although underpowered when compared with regular laser light sources, nonlaser light sources like flashlamps and flashlamp-pumped fluorescent emitters can be used with appropriate fluences and pulse duration to achieve a biologic effect on tissue. These light sources are mainly advocated for the treatment of vascular lesions.

To create versatility in clinical applications, laser manufacturers have moved to build multiple lasers in one compact box. Earlier systems were quite cumbersome, but new arrangements and technology afford the treating physician multiple choices for varying conditions at the touch of a button. A disadvantage of this concept is evident in the increased expense of these bundled systems that results from the additive cost of the multiple lasers.

NEW CLINICAL APPLICATIONS

Applications of the advances in laser technology discussed earlier are continually being researched and implemented into clinical practice. Not one aspect of cutaneous disease or the cutaneous integument should be excluded from possible laser or laser-assisted therapy.

Vascular Lesions

After the initial excitement surrounding the successful treatment of vascular lesions such as port wine stains and hemangiomas, resistant lesions of this nature have been targeted. In addition, for pigmented lesions a number of tattoo inks appear to be partially or nonresponsive to laser treatment. Side effects such as hyperpigmentation, hypopigmentation, or depigmentation are not uncommonly seen with these laser treatments. The quest for conditions that are treatable with lasers is ongoing. In recent years the pulsed-dye laser has been used for almost any condition or disease that appears to have increased vascularity associated with it.

The anatomy of vascular lesions like port wine stains is such that only the most superficial portion can be safely treated by the existing nonscarring lasers like the pulsed-dye laser. Pushing more energy into the tissue to photocoagulate deeper layers containing these ectatic microvessels can easily lead to excess thermal energy outside the targeted vessels. This almost inevitably results in unwanted events such as scarring and permanent pigmentary changes.

Varying treatment modalities are currently used to mimimize impairment to surrounding tissues and to optimize positive results. Changing the circumference of the applied laser beam has been shown to improve therapeutic outcome. Larger spot sizes, which presumably increase the photon-photon interaction in the dermis, give enhanced results. With the pulsed-dye laser, there has been an evolution from 3.0- to 10.0-mm spot sizes.

By cooling the overlying epidermis, one can effectively reduce the thermal energy deposited in the superficial layers, while the deeper layers (containing the thus far untreated vessels) receive the bulk of the energy needed to attain sufficient and safe photocoagulation. Dynamic cooling is a technique in which, in a time- and volume-controlled fashion, cryogens are administered to cool the skin to exactly measured temperatures.

In yet another approach, multiple pulses in rapid succession are administered to photocoagulate blood vessels, while still respecting the thermal relaxation time to reduce unwanted heat spillage to surrounding dermal stromal tissue.

Robotic smart-scanners that will identify the presence and diameter of treatable blood vessels in the skin will guide laser treatment in the future in the most efficient way. These devices will avoid treatment of unwanted areas and enhance selectivity and effectiveness.

Psoriasis, Verruca, Scars, and Striae

The complex developments in laser technology have led to a broad range of conditions now treatable with laser. The treatment of psoriasis with its increased vessels in the dermal papillae is based on the increased absorption of yellow light at 585 nm as emitted by the pulsed-dye laser. The treatment of verruca vulgaris is based on a similar principle. Simple thermal effects might contribute to the success rates observed in the literature; nonetheless, the pulsed-dye laser at 585 nm appears to be at least partially or temporarily effective in treating these stubborn conditions. Ongoing research will undoubtedly lead to further refinement and elucidation of the mechanisms involved.

Pulsed-dye laser treatment of scars and striae is still in its infancy, but very encouraging results are seen in the treatment of early hypertrophic, acne, and burn scars. Again, the mechanism of the response to the pulsed-dye laser treatment has not yet been explained. Multifactorial reasons are often postulated, including thermal effects, mast cell degranulation surrounding blood vessels, and increased collagenase production.

Varying treatment modalities are currently used to minimize impairment to surrounding tissues and to optimize results.

Hair Removal and Hair Growth

Hair removal by laser is currently creating the greatest flurry of excitement in the field of dermatologic laser surgery. Multiple systems using lasers have been devised to remove excess and unwanted hair in a relatively painless and (semi) permanent fashion when compared with the present technique of electrolysis. One system uses a carbonic suspension that is applied to the skin and trickles down the hair shaft. A Q-switched Nd:YAG laser at 1064 nm is then used to bring photons to the site of the hair follicle. The enhanced absorption by combining the suspension and laser light allows for relatively selective destruction of the hair follicle. In a similar fashion, but without any adjuvant agent, the long-pulse ruby laser (1 millisecond, 80 J/cm^2) appears to be able to produce similar results when removing hair. Another method uses photodynamic therapy with 20% delta–amino levulinic acid applied to the skin, followed by 630-nm, low-dose laser light.

By contrast, hair growth is an arena of great interest and development. In hair transplantation, laser is being used to create round or slit recipient sites in an expedient fashion by using flashscanner-enhanced CO$_2$ lasers or high-energy pulsed lasers. This reduces bleeding greatly, thus diminishing operative time. The laser is especially useful for micrografts (one-hair and dual-hair grafts), and graft survival appears to be equal to that of conventional transplantation techniques.

Stimulating hair growth and/or inhibiting the miniaturization of hairs to effectively restore a healthy anagen hair cycle may be feasible by using lasers. Either by biostimulation through low-powered lasers or by combining photodynamic therapy and lasers for this problem interesting, new treatment modalities might be provided.

Biostimulation

The use of lasers in biostimulation continues to be controversial. Certainly, a scientific basis for the operation of low-energy lasers with regard to medical applications is still being sought. However, through well-designed, double-blind trials, a new role might be found for the low-powered lasers. Stimulating hair growth is one area of interest, as stated earlier. Similarly, there appears to be evidence for melanogenesis at low-dose ruby laser radiation, which might be applicable for diseases like vitiligo. Future research will address these speculations.

Laser Welding

Laser welding involves the employment of a laser system to thermally weld skin incisions together by creating a protein coagulum. Prior investigations have been focused on laser welding of small blood vessels such as coronary arteries. Laser welding is still in an active research phase for future standardization. In laser welding of skin incisions, tensile strengths equivalent to that seen in conventional methods of repair are not yet attainable but with further study should be achievable.

Newest Clinical Applications

New areas of research focus on common diseases like acne vulgaris. Laser treatment is targeted toward the inflamed sebaceous gland. Although often deep-seated, these glands can be reached by photons through enhancing the selectivity of the selected laser by application or ingestion of photothermal sensitizers.

In liposuction, the subcutaneous removal of adipose tissue, the laser may play role by enhancing hemostasis, thus diminishing bleeding from the subcutaneous vessels during the procedure.

NEW OR IMPROVED DIAGNOSTIC LASER TOOLS

Clinicians are in need of new ways to look at skin. Traditional methods such as magnification with loupes or the light microscope give us details of only the very surface of the skin. New diagnostic tools are being developed to enhance our vision all the way into the dermis in a noninvasive fashion. By examining tissue by these spectroscopic methods and applying the laser to map out structures, biopsies of tissue in certain circumstances may not be necessary in the future. Two promising methods are discussed.

Optical Coherent Tomography

This optical analog of ultrasound detects backward scatter of light in biologic structures. Similar to ultrasound imaging, light of a laser is used to generate two-dimensional, cross-sectional images of dermal layers. Spatial resolution is approximately 10 to 20 μm, which is an order of magnitude better than with computerized tomography or magnetic resonance imaging. Quite suited for use in examining skin tissue, the relatively shallow depth (several millimeters) of the scattered light can be a limiting factor when thick tissue must be evaluated. Superluminescent, low-coherence diodes (around 1300 nm) are used as the source of light that is first directed into a compact fiber interferometer and then onto the tissue sample for examination. The back-scattered light is collected and computer processed to yield two-dimensional maps of the skin.

Confocal Laser Scanning Microscopy

A tightly focused, rapidly scanning laser beam optically transects skin tissue. As with optical coherent tomography, structures in the epidermis and superficial dermis can easily be visualized. Marked detail of melanocytes, the basal cell layer, and the papillary dermis can be observed. Studies are under way to obtain reference maps to delineate normal from abnormal tissue. Both techniques appear very promising and will add to the armamentarium of skin specialists.

CONCLUSION

To accurately predict the future is an impossible task. Some of the treatments or devices mentioned in this chapter will never be used in human skin applications. However, this chapter is written at a time when, as never before, cosmetic laser therapy and cosmoceuticals are being heavily promoted by physicians and industry. Driven by decreasing reimbursements for medical dermatology, considerable resources are dedicated to the development and capturing of the cosmetic marketplace. These financial resources should and will be used to further research in the relatively young field of laser medicine.

SUGGESTED READING LIST

1. Alster RS. Improvement of erythematous and hypertrophic scars by the 585-nm flashlamp-pumped pulsed-dye laser. Ann Plast Surg 1994; 32:186.
2. Alster TS, McMeekin TO. Improvement of keloid sternotomy scars with 585-nm flashlamp-pumped pulsed-dye laser. Lancet 1995;345: 1198.
3. Alster TS, West TB. Resurfacing of atrophic facial acne scars with a high-energy, pulsed carbon dioxide laser. Dermatol Surg 1996;22:151.
4. Anderson RR, Parrish JA. Selective photothermolysis: precise microsurgery by selective absorption of pulsed radiation. Science 1983;220: 524.
5. Baker P. Laser applications: preparing for the Golden Age. Photonics Spectra 1995;29:86.
6. Biophotonics Research: Optical coherence tomography: an imaging method with great promise. Biophotonics Int 1995;2:58.
7. Dierickx CC, Farinelli WA, Anderson RR. Multiple-pulse photocoagulation of port wine stain blood vessels (PWS) with a 585-nm pulsed-dye Laser. Lasers Surg Med Suppl 1995;7:56.
8. Frederickson KS, White WE, Wheeland RG, Slaughter DR. Precise ablation of skin with reduced collateral damage using the femtosecond-pulsed, terawatt titanium-sapphire Laser. Arch Dermatol 1993;129:989.
9. Grevelink JM, Brennick JB. Hair transplantation facilitated by flash-scanner-enhanced carbon dioxide laser. Operat Techn Otolaryngol Head Neck Surg 1994; 5:278.
10. Grossman MC, Rajadhyaksha M, Esterowitz D, Webb R, Anderson RR. Live confocal scanning laser microscopy of human skin. LasersSurg Med Suppl 1995;7:49.
11. Izatt JA, Hee MR, Fujimoto JG. Optical coherence tomography form-icron-resolution anatomical imaging in biological tissue. Lasers Surg Med Suppl 1995;7:1.
12. Jaffe BH, Walsh JT. Water flux from partial-thickness skin wounds: comparative study of the effects of Er:YAG and Ho:YA Glasers. Lasers Surg Med 1996;18:1.
13. Kauvar ANB, McDaniel DH, Geronemus RG. Pulsed-dye laser treatment of warts. Arch Fam Med 1995;4:1035.
14. Milner TE, Anvari B, Si M, et al. "Dynamic cooling" for spatial confinement of laser-induced thermal damage in collagen. Lasers Surg Med Suppl 1995;7:57.
15. Moretti MM. An eye for tomorrow's applications spells success in medical lasers. Photonics Spectra 1994;28:82.
16. Spicer MS, Goldberg DJ. Lasers in dermatology. J Am Acad Dermatol 1996;34:1.
17. Unger WP. Laser hair transplantation. Part I. J Dermatol Surg Oncol 1994;20:515.
18. Unger WP. Laser hair transplantation. Part II. J Dermatol Surg Oncol 1995;21:759.
19. Wheeland RG. Clinical uses of lasers in dermatology. Lasers Surg Med 1995;16:17.
20. Zelickson BD, Cook A. Pulsed-dye laser therapy on psoriasis: effects of pulse width on disease regression. Lasers Surg Med Suppl 1995;7: 58.

SECTION IV

Special Procedures

Textbook of Dermatologic Surgery, edited by John L. Ratz.
Lippincott–Raven Publishers, Philadelphia © 1998.

CHAPTER 25

Mohs Micrographic Surgery

Eric M. Finley and John Louis Ratz

Mohs micrographic surgery is used to treat cutaneous neoplasia, most often basal cell carcinoma and squamous cell carcinoma of the skin. The modality has been available for more than 50 years and is a way in which cutaneous carcinoma may be excised with histologic control of 100% of the surgical margin. Because the extent of the carcinoma is traced until clear on histologic examination, uninvolved normal tissue may be spared from excision, facilitating easier reconstruction. The recurrence rates from this procedure are quite low, and Mohs surgery has become the treatment of choice for all recurrent lesions. An added advantage is that the procedure is safe, and virtually all cases can be conducted in the outpatient setting under local anesthesia.

HISTORY

Mohs micrographic surgery bears the name of Frederic Mohs, who developed the procedure. The original article by Mohs in 1941 presented 440 patients with cutaneous malignancies treated with "chemosurgery," as he described it. After 8 years of laboratory investigation and 4 years of clinical data collection, some of which he began as a medical student, Mohs developed a way of *in situ* fixation of tissue with zinc chloride paste. To treat a tumor with chemosurgery, the paste was applied to the patient's tumor. The area was excised 24 hours later, a detailed map was made, and the tissue was examined histologically. The process was repeated until a tumor-free plane was achieved. Disadvantages of this technique included pain associated with the zinc chloride fixation and the time commitment required for each stage of surgery. This chemosurgery technique later became known as Mohs micrographic surgery fixed-tissue technique.

In 1953 Mohs began using a modified procedure to avoid the irritation of the eye associated with the application of zinc chloride paste. This was the "fresh-tissue technique." In this technique local anesthesia was used to infiltrate the area, tissue was obtained surgically, and the tissue was processed for frozen sections. This modification did not gain wide acceptance until 1970, when Tromovitch and Stegman presented 75 cases treated with the fresh-tissue technique at the annual meeting of the American College of Chemosurgery, followed by a 1974 publication in which 85 patients with 102 basal cell carcinomas were treated in the same manner. Since the mid-1970s, the fresh-tissue technique has virtually replaced the fixed-tissue technique.

INDICATIONS

The strongest indication for Mohs surgery, as outlined in the literature, is recurrent basal cell and squamous cell carcinomas; however, basal cell and squamous cell primary (previously untreated) carcinomas with indistinct clinical margins or in high-risk locations should be treated with Mohs surgery as well. High-risk locations include areas on and around the eyes, nose, and ears because lesions in these areas tend to be deeply invasive. The underlying theory is that embryonic fusion planes offer a path of minimal resistance through which the tumors dissect. The scalp is another area where basal cell carcinomas may behave aggressively, invading along the periosteal plane. Mohs surgery should be used for basal cell carcinomas in this area as well.

Eric M. Finley: Dermatologic Surgery, Department of Dermatology, Keesler Medical Center, Keesler Air Force Base, MS, 39534-2519.

John Louis Ratz: Louisiana State University School of Medicine, 1452 Tulane Avenue, New Orleans, LA 70112.

Any tumor with a diameter greater than 2 cm should be removed with Mohs surgery. Histologically aggressive basal cell carcinomas are yet another indication for this procedure. Histologically aggressive subtypes of basal cell carcinoma include morpheaform (sclerotic), metatypical (basosquamous, keratinizing), adenoidal, superficial (multicentric), or any type classified as "infiltrating." Mohs surgery is especially useful in tumors exhibiting perineural, periappendageal, or perivascular invasion. Tumors in locations where conservation of tissue is a high priority should be treated with Mohs surgery, such as tumors located on the eyelid, genitalia, external auditory meatus, nostril, fingers, or toes. Tumors reported with positive margins after conventional excisions, basal cell carcinomas occurring or recurring in irradiated skin, and radiation-induced basal cell and squamous cell carcinomas should all be treated with Mohs surgery.

Mohs micrographic surgery is most commonly used for basal cell and squamous cell carcinomas, but other lesions have been treated with this technique, such as squamous cell carcinoma *in situ,* dermatofibrosarcoma protuberans, verrucous carcinoma, keratoacanthoma, extramammary Paget's disease, sebaceous carcinoma, and microcystic adnexal carcinoma. Merkel cell carcinoma has been treated with Mohs surgery by 30% of the members of the American College of Mohs Micrographic Surgery and Cutaneous Oncology. Melanoma has been treated with Mohs micrographic surgery for nearly 30 years. Generally, treatment with Mohs surgery has been confined to clinical stage I thin melanoma. Mohs published reports in the 1950s on the fixed-tissue technique being used to treat melanoma. Zitelli et al. have reported extensively on the fresh-tissue technique being used to remove invasive and *in situ* malignant melanomas. Their reported survival rates and local recurrence rates compare favorably with the results obtained with wide excision. McGillis et al. reported that 15% of the members of the Mohs college use Mohs surgery to treat melanoma and 38% use it to treat lentigo maligna. Debate currently exists regarding whether frozen sections can be reliably interpreted for melanocytic lesions. These data show that the treatment of melanoma with Mohs surgery is controversial and is not performed by a majority of Mohs surgeons.

Case reports also exist of using Mohs surgery to treat malignant fibrous histiocytoma, eccrine adenocarcinoma, adenoid cystic carcinoma, leiomyosarcoma, and angiosarcoma with mixed results.

PREOPERATIVE PLANNING

Mohs micrographic surgery is a very-low-risk outpatient surgical procedure that is performed with the patient under local anesthesia, but proper preoperative evaluation is imperative. Preoperative evaluation consists of a thorough history and physical examination. Give special consideration to patients with hypertension, heart disease, diabetes, connective tissue disorders, or bleeding disorders or those who are taking anticoagulants. Although none of these conditions is a contraindication to Mohs surgery, they could alter the operative plan. Patients with hypertension or heart disease may require more dilute concentrations of epinephrine in the local anesthesia. Patients with diabetes or connective tissue disorders may pose problems with healing, and those with bleeding disorders or those who are taking anticoagulants require meticulous attention to hemostasis. During the history, explore risk factors for the development of cutaneous carcinoma. Previous exposure to sunlight, ionizing radiation, and inorganic arsenic predisposes patients to basal cell and squamous cell carcinomas. Hydrocarbon exposure, burn scars, chronic ulcers, chronic sinus tract disease, psoralen ultraviolet A–range exposure, and immunosuppression increase the risk of squamous cell carcinomas. Also, consider heritable syndromes that predispose the patient to cutaneous carcinomas.

Before surgery, document prior treatment of the presenting carcinoma to more accurately counsel the patient on cure rates and repair options. Some Mohs surgeons suggest that very aggressive and recurrent tumors be allowed to heal by second intention, with repairs being performed only after a recurrence-free interval of 6 months to 2 years.

Assess the patient's smoking history preoperatively to ascertain if a flap might be compromised. Record allergies and medications. Although true allergy to local anesthesia is rare, if an allergy history is elicited, the surgical plan is obviouslyaltered. A patient profile medical history database is shown in Fig. 1.

Perform a thorough physical examination by examining, measuring, and photographing the carcinoma, as well as assessing the lymphatic drainage. Give careful consideration to the surface anatomy and deeper structures that might be encountered during the procedure. Examine the integument for other lesions suspected of carcinoma. Order preoperative laboratory examinations or subspecialty consultations only as dictated by the history and physical examination on a case-by-case basis. It is prudent to order chest x-rays in all patients with squamous cell carcinoma and basosquamous carcinoma of the skin to disclose possible metastatic disease.

Explain the risks, benefits, alternatives, complications, reasonable expectations (including the extent of the anticipated defect), and anticipated repair options. Advise the patient to avoid alcohol 3 days before the procedure and nonprescription, nonsteroidal antiinflammatory agents for 1 week before the procedure. If the patient is taking prescribed aspirin, antiinflammatory medications, or warfarin (Coumadin) as part of a treatment regimen, continue the medication and carefully achieve hemostasis with electrocoagulation. Recommend that the patient take all prescribed medications the morning of the procedure and eat a light breakfast.

To lessen anxiety and ensure that the patient will have transportation home in the event that a dressing obscures vision, a friend or relative should accompany the patient on the day of the procedure.

PATIENT PROFILE
SECTION OF DERMATOLOGIC SURGERY
OCHSNER CLINIC

DATE:_____   REFERRED BY:_____

NAME: _____   AGE: ____ CLINIC #:_____

NATURE OF PROBLEM: _____

_____

GENERAL HEALTH: NOW OR IN THE PAST:

____ High Blood Pressure ____ Diabetes ____ Heart Disease ____ Bleeding Problems

____ Skin Cancer ____ Other Cancer ____ Phlebitis ____ Connective Tissue Disease

____ X-Ray Therapy ____ Other Major Problem(s) or HIV Risk Factors (Transfusion,

Homo or Bisexual Activity, H/O Unusual Infections) _____

_____

_____

MEDICATIONS: _____

ALLERGIES: _____

SMOKING HISTORY: _____

PROBLEMS WITH PAST SURGERIES OR HEALING: _____

MEDICATIONS NECESSARY BEFORE SURGERY: _____

SIGNIFICANT FAMILY HISTORY: _____

_____

_____

_____

FIG. 1. Patient profile form for medical database.

Do not perform Mohs micrographic surgery in patients who are poor surgical candidates. In addition, avoid this procedure in patients who are allergic to local anesthesia. If the patient has a pacemaker, obtain cardiology clearance before using electrocoagulation. If using electrosurgical devices in a patient with a pacemaker, apply the current in such a way that the pacemaker is not in the circuit from active to indifferent electrodes. Apply the current in short bursts only. In selected patients, using a carbon dioxide (CO_2) laser in the defocused mode to obtain hemostasis may be beneficial.

Address patient anxiety in each Mohs surgery case. Patients are often apprehensive about procedures being conducted on the face or are anxious because the full extent of the tumor is unknown. Occasionally, anxiety is so great that it seems to override the effects of the local anesthesia. Treat preoperative anxiety with diazepam 10 mg sublingually before anesthetizing the area. If anxiety is extreme and is evident before the morning of the procedure, instruct the patient to take diazepam 10 mg orally the night before the procedure and repeat this dosage the morning of the procedure, 1 to 2 hours before the scheduled arrival time.

Many patients harbor an intense fear of needles. To reduce the anxiety associated with anesthetizing the operative site, apply ice to the area to be infiltrated for 5 to 10 minutes, and inject the anesthesia slowly through a 30-gauge needle. Advance the needle through previously anesthetized areas only.

Take special precautions when operating around the eye. Surgical lights can be bright, and patients frequently find them annoying. Tape gauze pads into place to protect the eyes from this light and from accidental injury. If a tumor is on the eyelid margin, place a methylmethacrylate eye shield directly over the globe after applying topical eye anesthesia (such as tetracaine).

TECHNIQUE

Conventional surgical excision involves vertical incisions made perpendicular to the cutaneous surface. Histologic examination is usually conducted by "breadloafing" the fusiform specimen. However, this type of processing examines only 0.1% of the actual pathologic margin. Fig. 2 illustrates the difference between conventional pathologic examination and Mohs histologic examination.

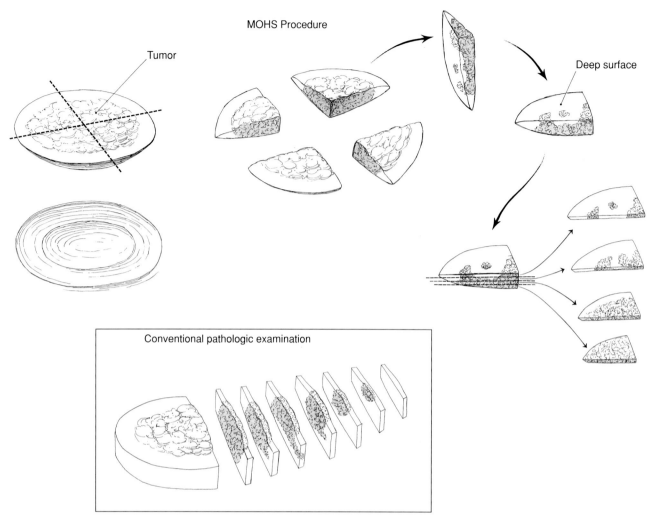

MOHS Procedure

Tumor

Deep surface

Conventional pathologic examination

FIG. 2. Conventional histologic examination vs. horizontal sectioning of Mohs micrographic surgery.

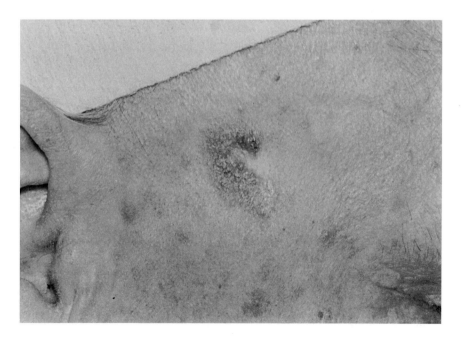

FIG. 3. Recurrent basal cell carcinoma of the right preauricular area.

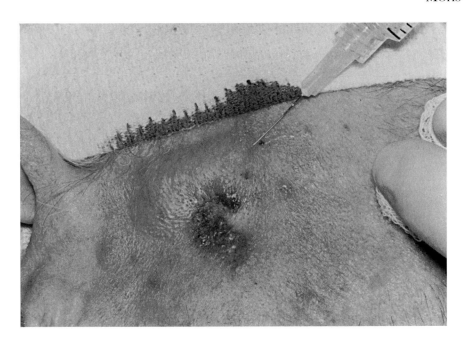

FIG. 4. Intradermal and subcutaneous infiltration of local anesthesia.

Begin the procedure by examining the tumor carefully; prepare the skin with povidone-iodine (Betadine) or chlorhexidine, and anesthetize the area with local anesthetic (Fig. 3 and 4). Use 1% lidocaine with epinephrine 1:100,000, buffered with 8.4% sodium bicarbonate 10:1. In patients with cardiac problems or hypertension, add 1% lidocaine 1:1 with 1% lidocaine with epinephrine 1:100,000 to deliver an epinephrine concentration of 1:200,000 (occasionally, a more dilute solution of epinephrine of 1:400,000 maybe necessary). Cover the operative field with sterile drapes or towels.

Figure 5 is a schematic diagram of the various steps involved in the Mohs surgery technique. Debulk the lesion with a curette or scalpel (Fig. 6). Using curettage with electrodesiccation to establish the extent of a tumor before the first stage of Mohs surgery is often beneficial. Incise the tissue by beveling the scalpel blade at a 45-degree angle. Keep a 1- to 3-mm margin around the curettage defect, and mark the orientation of the tissue by scoring the specimen and the wound edge with the scalpel (Figs. 7A and B and 8). Continue to increase the beveling of the scalpel until horizontal cutting is achieved at the deep margin of the specimen (Figs. 9A–F and 10A–C). Grip the tissue lightly with forceps, and carefully preserve proper orientation of the specimen. Place the excised tissue on a blotter card and compress with a gauze sponge (Figs. 11 and 12). Obtain hemostasis with spot electrocoagulation. Measure the wound, record the dimensions, place Gelfoam in the wound, and apply a temporary dressing. Draw and label a surgical map, and section the specimen (Fig. 13 and 14). Figure 15 shows tissue edges being dyed: use merbromin (Mercurochrome) to dye an edge red and map this with a solid line, use laundry bluing agent to mark an edge blue and map this as a broken line, and use India ink if necessary to dye an edge black and map

this with a wavy line. Place the pieces on a saline-moistened gauze pad in a Petri dish with the epidermal-edge margin pointed down (Fig. 16). Present the specimen to the histotechnician, who inverts the tissue, compresses it with a forceps handle, and embeds the tissue in optimum cutting temperature (OCT) compound on a cryostat chuck (Figs. 17 and 18). The technician uses a heat extractor to flatten the specimen into the OCT (Fig. 19). The technician then uses a cryostat to make 4- to 7-μm frozen sections beginning from the deep aspect of the horizontally sectioned tissue obtained (Fig. 20A and B). The sections are placed sequentially on a glass slide beginning opposite the frosted end of the slide (Fig. 21), dried, stained with hematoxylin and eosin or toluidine blue (Fig. 22), and examined histologically by the Mohs surgeon (Fig. 23A and B). Plot areas that are positive for residual carcinoma on the map that has already been prepared (Fig. 24). For each positive region repeat the process until a tumor-free plane has been achieved (Figs. 25 and 26). Once a tumor-free plane has been achieved, the wound may be allowed to heal by second intention or immediate reconstruction may be performed (Fig. 27).

Not infrequently, tumors are large and irregularly shaped, yielding a specimen with one or more acute angles following removal by Mohs surgery (Fig. 28). Such acute angles are technically difficult to process; as a result, the lateral edge of epidermis may be lost and absent on the completed slides. Score and divide such tissue so that all acute angles are bisected (Fig. 28, inset).

Occasionally, the first stage of Mohs surgery yields a specimen that must be divided into multiple pieces for adequate processing. In such cases, cut the specimen into pieces small enough for appropriate placement on a glass microscope slide (Fig. 29). Pieces without a lateral skin edgecan be marked with three or four different colors (Figs. 30 and 31).

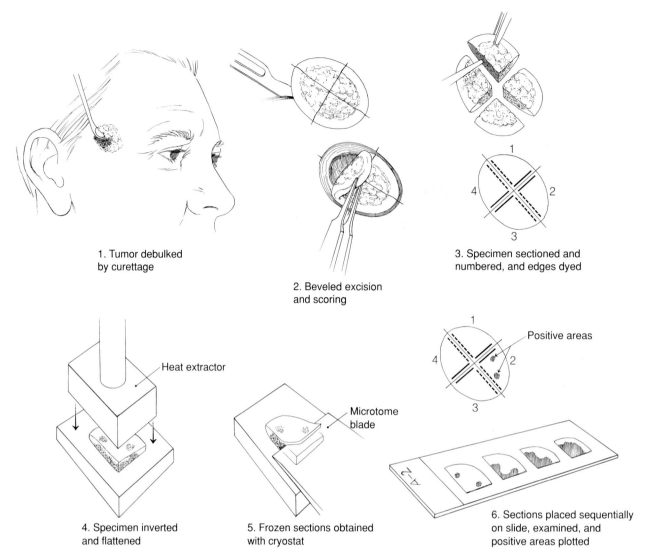

1. Tumor debulked by curettage

2. Beveled excision and scoring

3. Specimen sectioned and numbered, and edges dyed

Heat extractor

4. Specimen inverted and flattened

Microtome blade

5. Frozen sections obtained with cryostat

Positive areas

6. Sections placed sequentially on slide, examined, and positive areas plotted

FIG. 5. Schematic representation of the steps used in Mohs micrographic surgery.

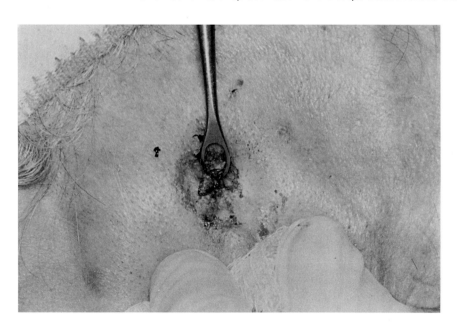

FIG. 6. Debulking the tumor with a curette.

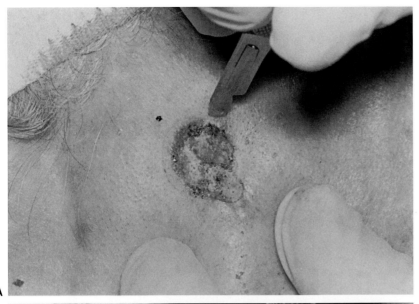

A

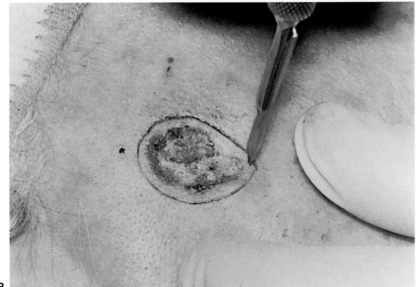

B

FIG. 7. (**A and B**) Incision around the defect including a 1- to 3-mm margin of clinically normal skin.

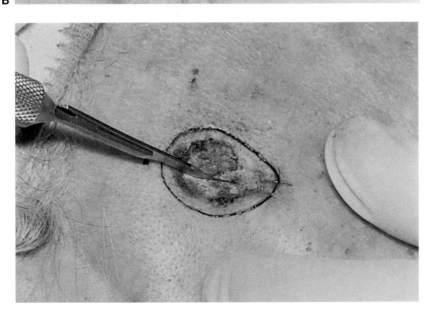

FIG. 8. Scoring the specimen to maintain orientation.

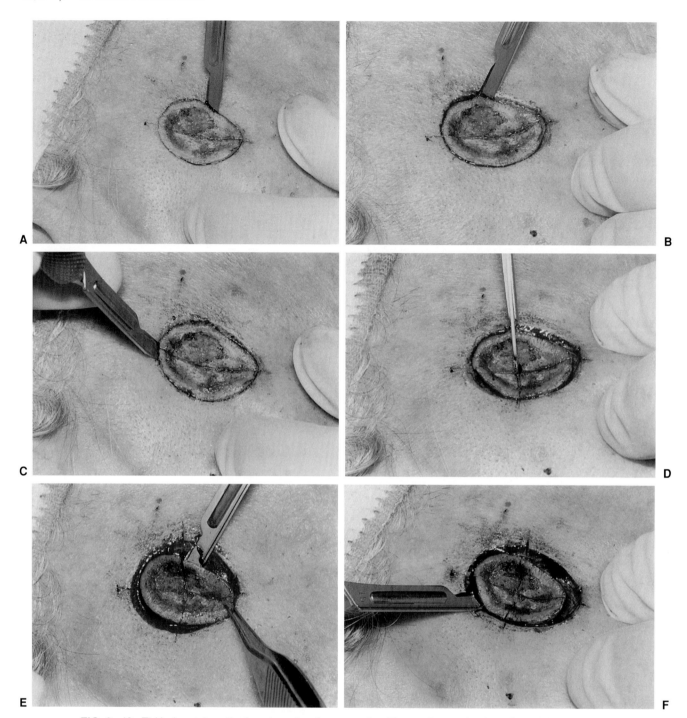

FIG. 9. (**A–F**) Horizontal sectioning along the deep margin with ever-increasing beveling of the scalpel. Scoring across the specimen in several directions aids in tissue orientation.

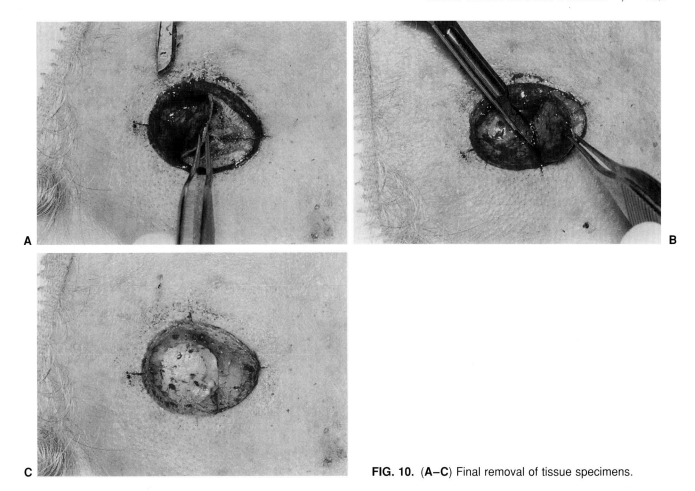

FIG. 10. (A–C) Final removal of tissue specimens.

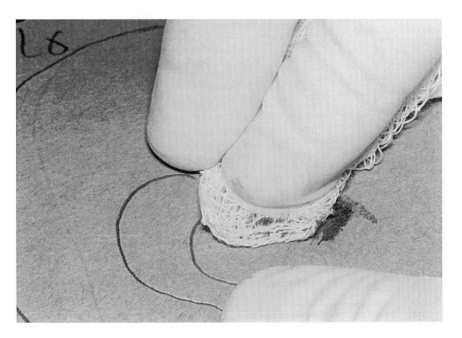

FIG. 11. Specimen compressed on blotter card to achieve maximum flattening of horizontally excised specimen.

FIG. 12. Specimen oriented on labeled blotter card.

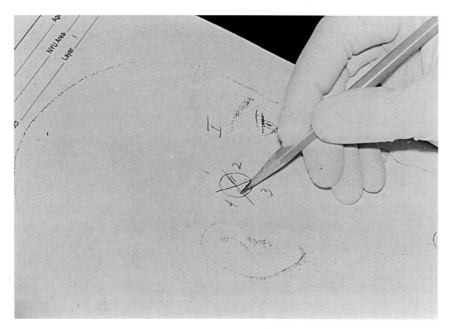

FIG. 13. Mohs surgical map; solid lines represent red-dyed margins; broken lines represent blue-dyed margins.

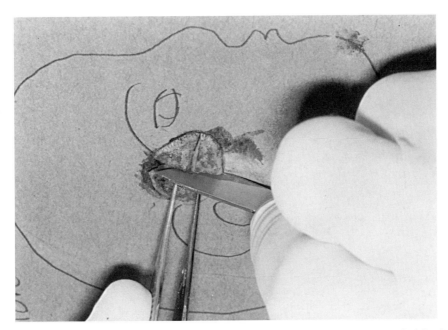

FIG. 14. Specimen sectioned into pieces small enough to be processed by the histotechnician by cutting along the score marks.

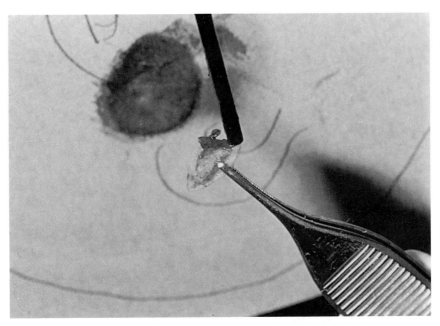

FIG. 15. Pieces carefully dyed with merbromin (Mercurochrome) and laundry bluing agent.

FIG. 16. Dyed pieces placed on saline-moistened gauze in a Petri dish for transport to the histology laboratory.

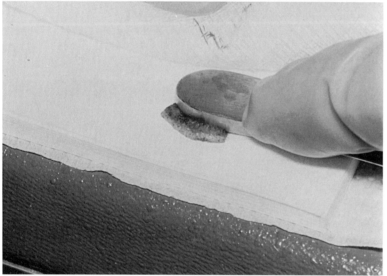

FIG. 17. Specimen inverted and compressed again.

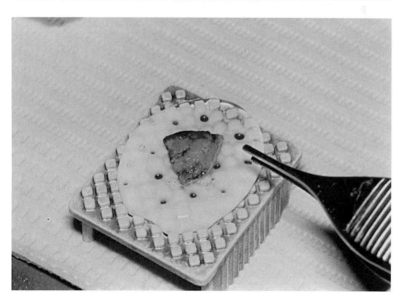

FIG. 18. Specimen placed in optimum cutting temperature compound on a cryostat chuck.

FIG. 19. Heat extractor used to compress the specimen into the optimum cutting temperature compound.

A

B

FIG. 20. (A and B) Four- to seven-micrometer sections made beginning with the underside of the specimen.

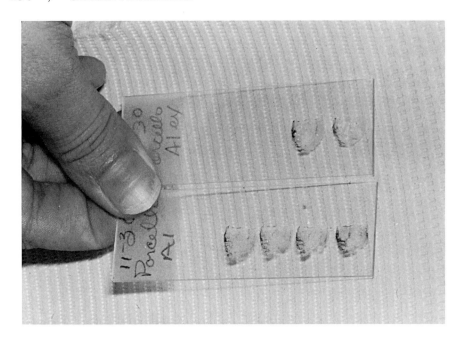

FIG. 21. Sectioned specimen on glass slide with first sections obtained placed opposite frosted end.

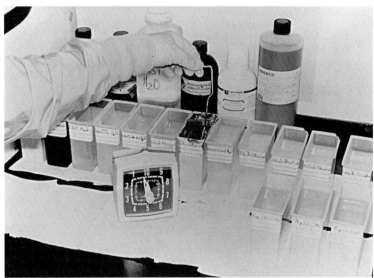

FIG. 22. Section specimen being stained with hematoxylin and eosin.

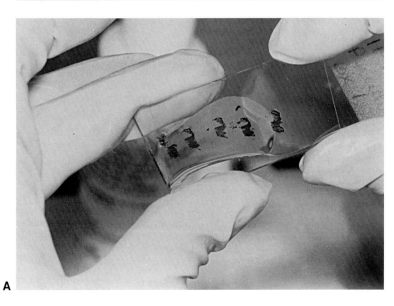

FIG. 23. (**A**) Coverslip being placed over stained specimens before examination by Mohs surgeon and (**B**) completed slides.

A

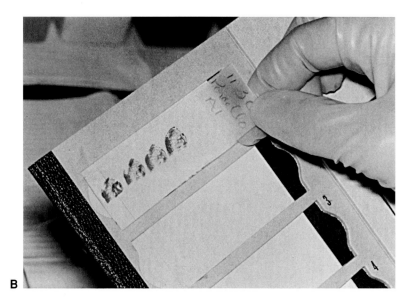

B

FIG. 23. *Continued.*

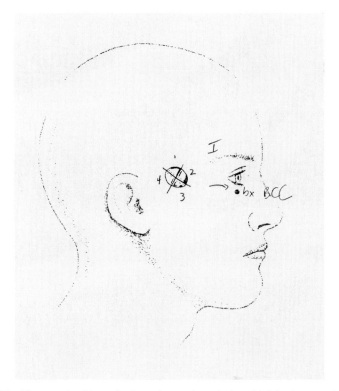

FIG. 24. Map marked in red where tumor is noted on histologic examination.

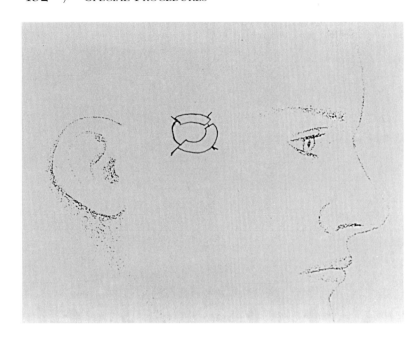

FIG. 25. Map of planned second stage of Mohs surgery.

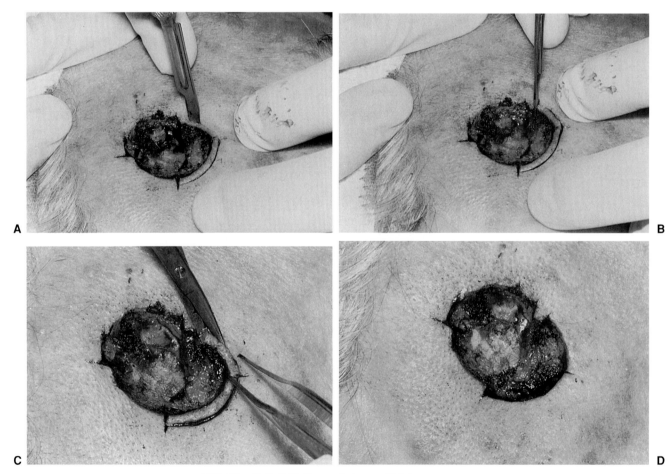

FIG. 26. (**A,B,C,D**) Second stage of Mohs surgery.

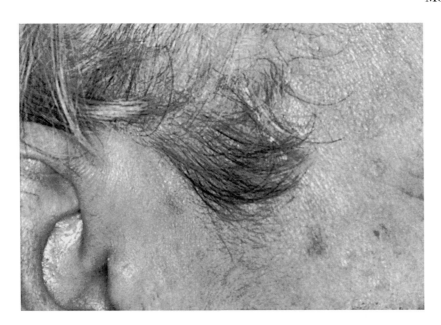

FIG. 27. Scar 2 months after procedure with second-intention healing.

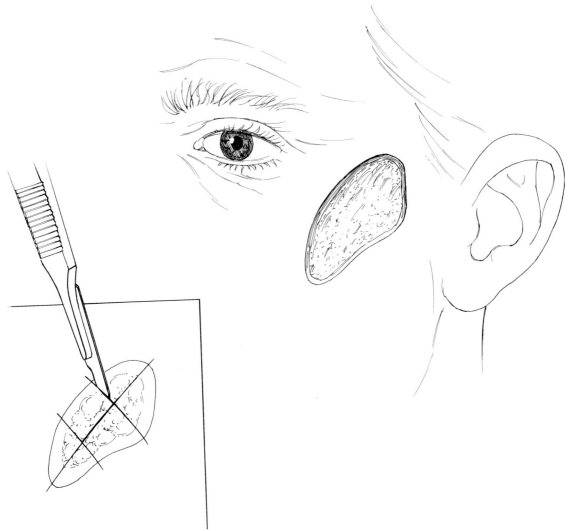

FIG. 28. Schematic of Mohs surgical defect of left preauricular region. (**Inset**) Schematic representation of score marks made on the tissue for optimal processing.

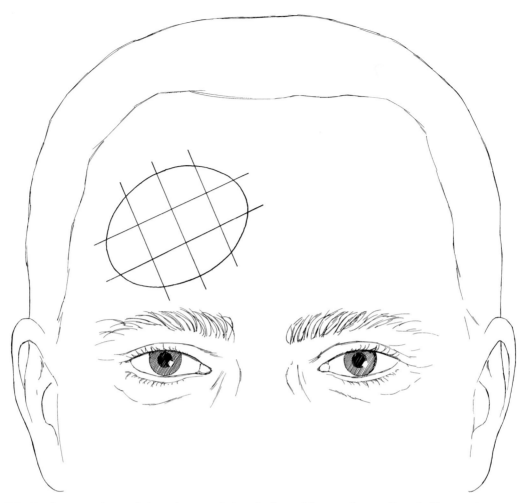

FIG. 29. Score marks made in such a way that each piece of the specimen will easily fit on a microscope slide.

Control bleeding with electrocoagulation. Epinephrine in the local anesthetic is quite effective in causing vasoconstriction; however, large superficial arterioles are encountered occasionally and significant hemorrhage ensues. Ligate these vessels with absorbable suture. Because the distribution of the superficial temporal artery might be prone to significant hemorrhage, ligate this vessel if it is sacrificed during the procedure.

POSTOPERATIVE MANAGEMENT

Postoperative management in the Mohs surgery patient depends largely on whether the wound is repaired or allowed to heal by second intention. If the wound is left to heal by second intention, dress it with antibiotic ointment and oxidized cellulose or hemostatic gauze, and cover it with a nonadherent pad (Telfa) and tape, a self-adherent wrap, or stretch bandage. Have the patient cleanse the wounds once or twice daily with 3% hydrogen peroxide and apply antibiotic ointment and Telfa. Usually 4 to 6 weeks of wound care is required until healing is complete.

Dress repaired wounds with antibiotic ointment and Telfa, and keep them covered for 24 hours. After the initial 24 hours, direct the patient to leave the wounds uncovered, but to clean the suture line with hydrogen peroxide and apply a film of antibiotic ointment. Treat primary closures and flaps in this manner. Dress grafts with a bolster dressing, and leave it in place for 1 week until suture removal.

Postoperative pain from Mohs surgery is usually minimal. Wounds left to heal by second intention are often pain free. Generally, pain is associated with repairs in areas of movement. Acetaminophen 1 g orally every 6 hours can generally control the pain adequately. Patients who have greater pain or a lower pain threshold can require narcotic analgesics.

When cartilaginous structures are exposed during the procedure, chondritis can ensue. It can also occur when perichondrium is removed or electrocoagulation is used adjacent to cartilaginous structures. To prevent chondritis when lesions on the ear or nasal ala are removed and healing will

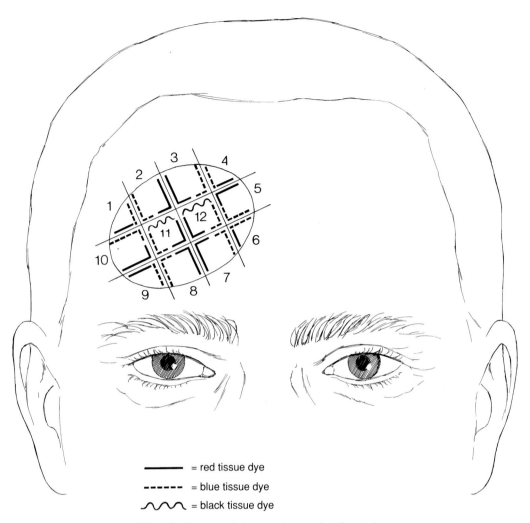

——— = red tissue dye

------ = blue tissue dye

〜〜〜 = black tissue dye

FIG. 30. Dyeing of tissue edges using three dyes.

be by second intention, give the patient a short course of an antibiotic (such as erythromycin).

ADVERSE SEQUELAE

Although Mohs micrographic surgery is a low-risk outpatient procedure, one adverse sequela is scarring. Scarring depends largely on the wound size, depth, and location. Another factor affecting the nature of the scarring is whether the wound is repaired or left to heal by second intention. Concave areas of the head and neck generally heal well by second intention, giving rise to very acceptable scars. Convex areas, on the other hand, can give rise to unacceptable scars when allowed to heal by second intention. Once reepithelialized, wounds allowed to heal by second intention are slightly erythematous and edematous. This improves with time and can appear nearly normal in texture and color as soon as 6 months after surgery. If healing by second intention yields an undesirable outcome, delayed reconstruction can

be performed and is often a smaller procedure than would have been required if immediate repair had been undertaken.

Mohs surgery defects on the free margins of some structures can result in deforming scars when allowed to heal by second intention. To prevent retraction of these anatomic structures, repair defects on the margins of the eyelids, lips, or nasal alae. If the defects are too large or intimidating, consult an oculoplastic or plastic surgeon. Occasionally, lesions can be large, deeply invasive, or in difficult locations, which may necessitate a multidisciplinary approach. When applicable, consult freely otolaryngologists, plastic surgeons, ophthalmologists, or neurosurgeons to ensure extirpation of problematic tumors with the highest standard of care.

When using a multidisciplinary approach for an extensive tumor, it may be necessary to consider general anesthesia. Patient comfort issues must be weighed against the danger of prolonged anesthesia. Whether to use general anesthesia for time-consuming Mohs surgery is not an easy issue to resolve, and each case must be evaluated individually.

Very infrequently, tumors invade into bone. To appreciate

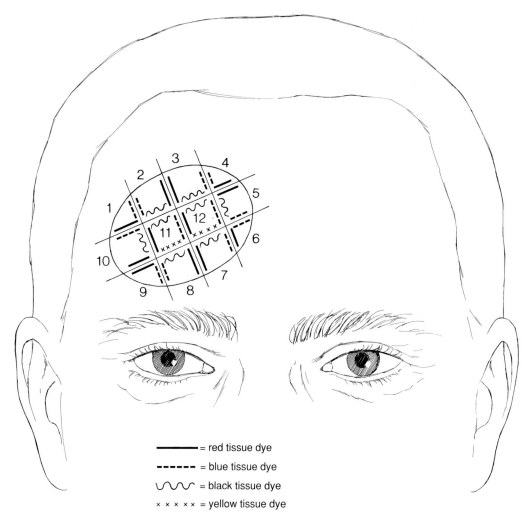

——— = red tissue dye

- - - - - = blue tissue dye

∿∿∿ = black tissue dye

× × × × × = yellow tissue dye

FIG. 31. Dyeing of tissue edges using four dyes.

the extent of the tumor, imaging these tumors preoperatively with computed axial tomography or magnetic resonance imaging may be necessary. Approach these tumors carefully, and include bone chisels on the operative tray for removing the diseased bone. In these instances, if necessary, the fixed-tissue technique (with zinc chloride paste) can be used to remove bone containing tumor. Obtain the appropriate consultations for assistance in these difficult cases.

Although most wounds left to heal by second intention do so in 4 to 6 weeks, patients do not describe any adverse effects other than modest inconvenience from the daily dressing changes.

COMPLICATIONS

Nerve damage may complicate Mohs micrographic surgery procedures. Sensation may be disrupted in the area of surgery, and postoperative anesthesia, dysesthesia, and paresthesia are not uncommon, especially when a flap is used to repair the defect. The damage is rarely long-lasting, and

any sensory deficits normally correct themselves in a few months. Motor nerves are not likely to be injured during Mohs surgery unless the tumors are very large, are recurrent, or have perineural involvement. Be aware of the areas of the head and neck that have superficial motor nerves—the mandibular edge immediately anterior to the masseter muscle (marginal mandibular branch of the facial nerve), the temple immediately superior to the zygomatic arch (temporal branch of the facial nerve), and Erb's point on the posterior cervical triangle of the neck (the spinal accessory nerve). When operating in these areas, infiltrate with generous amounts of local anesthesia to "balloon out" the skin and subcutaneous structures, thus lessening the risk of transecting the nerve in the early stages of Mohs surgery. When operating in areas where nerve damage can occur, before the operation inform the patient of the risk posed to the nerve and the deficit that might result, as well as the procedure that could be required to correct the deficit.

Although postoperative bleeding and potential hematoma formation are risks of any cutaneous surgical procedure, they are not very likely to occur with Mohs technique. However, before performing the procedure inform all patients that these complications might result from the planned procedure. Because patients often panic when these complications occur postoperatively, give them a well-written explanation sheet with steps to follow in the event of bleeding or hematoma formation. In a Mohs defect allowed to heal by second intention, bleeding, although rare, is usually caused when the patient allows the wound to desiccate and fissure. Keeping the wound covered with antibacterial ointment and a dressing lessens the likelihood of bleeding.

Although ecchymoses, secondary bacterial infection, edema, seroma formation, necrosis, and dehiscence may occur in association with the repair of a Mohs surgery defect, these complications are no more likely to occur in Mohs surgery than in any other type of cutaneous surgery. To avoid these complications, use meticulous surgical technique, apply sterile compression dressings, and instruct the patient in diligent postoperative wound care.

The competent Mohs surgeon should be prepared in the event of emergency during the procedure. Although very rare, anaphylaxis to local anesthetics or medications given for anxiety could occur. Arrhythmias in patients with histories of cardiac disease could possibly lead to cardiac arrest. Mechanisms should be in place for handling such emergencies. Access to a cardiac monitor with defibrillator and a code cart is recommended. The American College of Mohs Micrographic Surgery and Cutaneous Oncology requires American Cardiac Life Support certification for all fellows in accredited Mohs micrographic surgery fellowships.

Be alert for one particular complication of Mohs surgery. When a deep surgical defect exists on the nasal ala and the support structures have been lost, repair of the defect is recommended. If allowed to heal by second intention, the ala can function in a ball-valve manner and collapse during inspiration. The problem may not be apparent during the day and may cause problems only during sleep. The patient often complains of not being able to breathe without applying lateral traction to the ipsilateral cheek. Suggest reconstruction of the ala, and make the appropriate referrals if this complication occurs.

RECURRENCE RATES

Recurrence rates for Mohs surgery in the treatment of primary basal cell carcinoma are lower than for any other treatment modality currently available for this neoplasm. The 5-year recurrence rate for Mohs surgery is 1% compared with a 5-year recurrence rate of 10.1% for surgical excision, a 7.7% rate for curettage and electrodesiccation, an 8.7% rate for radiation therapy, and a 7.5% rate for cryotherapy. In a large study from the Cleveland Clinic, Roenigk et al. reported 4-year cure rates for primary basal cell carcinoma of 98.6%. In that study the cure rate for traditional methods when Mohs surgery was not indicated was 97.1%.

The 5-year recurrence rate for recurrent basal cell carcinoma treated with Mohs surgery is 5.6%. Various authors report 5-year cure rates of 96% to 97% for recurrent basal cell carcinomas. The 4-year cure rate as reported by Roenigk et al. for recurrent tumors treated with Mohs surgery was 95.8%, whereas the cure rate for non-Mohs modalities was 84.5%. Rowe et al. reported that the 5-year recurrence rate for surgical excision to treat recurrent basal cell carcinomas is 17.4%; for curettage and electrodesiccation, 40%; and for radiation therapy, 9.8%. Five-year recurrence rates have not been reported for cryotherapy used to treat recurrent basal cell carcinomas, but the rate is 13% for a follow-up period of less than 5 years.

The cure rate for squamous cell carcinoma has been reported to be 96% to 99%. The literature also stated that primary squamous cell carcinoma, recurrent squamous cell carcinoma, squamous cell carcinoma with perineural involvement, squamous cell carcinoma with a diameter greater than 2 cm, and poorly differentiated squamous cell carcinoma all had significantly lower recurrence rates when Mohs surgery treatment was used vs. non-Mohs treatments. Roenigk & Roenigk reported cure rates of 92% to 99% forsquamous cell carcinoma. One significant observation is that the recurrence rate increases as the grade of the squamous cell carcinoma being treated increases.

SUGGESTED READING LIST

1. Bailin PL, Ratz JL, Wheeland RG. Mohs micrographic surgery technique. In: Roenigk RK, Roenigk HH, eds. Dermatologic surgery: principles and practice. New York: Marcel Dekker, 1989:833.
2. Cottel WI, Bailin PL, Albom MJ, et al. Essentials of Mohs micrographic surgery. J Dermatol Surg Oncol 1988;14:11.
3. Dinehart SM, Pollack SV. Mohs micrographic surgery for skin cancer. Cancer Treat Rev 1989;16:257.
4. Hruza GJ. Mohs micrographic surgery. Otolaryngol Clin North Am 1990;23:845.
5. Kwa RE, Campana K, Moy RL. Biology of cutaneous squamous cell carcinoma. J Am Acad Dermatol 1992;26:1.
6. McGillis ST, Wheeland RG, Sebben JE. Current issues in the performance of Mohs micrographic surgery. J Dermatol Surg Oncol 1991;17:681.
7. Miller SJ. Biology of basal cell carcinoma. Part I. J Am Acad Dermatol 1991;24:1.
8. Mohs FE. Chemosurgery: microscopically controlled method of cancer excision. Arch Surg 1941;42:279.
9. Mohs FE. Mohs micrographic surgery: a historical perspective. Dermatol Clin 1989;7:609.
10. Phelan JT. The use of the Mohs chemosurgery technic in the treatment of basal cell carcinoma. Ann Surg 1968;168:1023.
11. Rapini RP. Pitfalls of Mohs micrographic surgery. J Am Acad Dermatol 1990;22:681 (review).
12. Robins P, Albom MJ. Mohs surgery: fresh tissue technique. J Dermatol Surg 1975;1:37.
13. Robinson JK. Mohs micrographic surgery. Clin Plast Surg 1993;20:149 (review).
14. Roenigk RK, Ratz JL, Bailin PL, Wheeland RG. Trends in the presentation and treatment of basal cell carcinomas. J Dermatol Surg Oncol 1986;12:860.
15. Roenigk RK, Roenigk HH Jr. Current surgical management ofskin cancer in dermatology. J Dermatol Surg Oncol 1990;16:136 (review).
16. Rowe DE, Carroll RJ, Day CL Jr. Long-term recurrence rates in previously untreated (primary) basal cell carcinoma: implications for patient follow-up. J Dermatol Surg Oncol 1989;15:315 (review).

17. Rowe DE, Carroll RJ, Day CL Jr. Mohs surgery is the treatment of choice for recurrent (previously treated) basal cell carcinoma. J Dermatol Surg Oncol 1989;15:424.

18. Swanson NA. Mohs surgery. Technique, indications, applications, and the future. Arch Dermatol 1983;119:761 (review).

19. Tromovitch TA, Stegeman SJ. Microscopically controlled excision of skin tumors. Chemotherapy (Mohs): fresh tissue technique. Arch Dermatol 1974;110:231.

20. Tromovitch TA, Stegeman SJ. Microscopic-controlled excision of cuta-neous tumors: chemosurgery, fresh tissue technique. Cancer 1978;41: 653.

21. Zitelli JA. Wound healing by secondary intention: a cosmetic appraisal. J Am Acad Dermatol 1983;9:407.

22. Zitelli JA, Mohs FE, Larson P, Snow S. Mohs micrographic surgery for melanoma. Dermatol Clin 1989;7:833 (review).

23. Zitelli JA, Moy RL, Abell E. The reliability of frozen sections in the evaluation of surgical margins for melanoma. J Am Acad Dermatol 1991;24:102.

Textbook of Dermatologic Surgery, edited by John L. Ratz.
Lippincott–Raven Publishers, Philadelphia © 1998.

CHAPTER 26

Cryosurgery

Gloria F. Graham

HISTORY

The first known use of cryotherapy was among the Egyptians, who, as early as 2500 BC, used cold in the treatment of injuries and inflammation. Hippocrates (460-370 BC), the father of medicine, wrote about the use of cold in relief of pain from injury and illness. In 1661, Bartholinus, a Dane, described the use of ice, snow, and other forms of cold as an anesthetic in the perineal area for certain operations. Baron Dominique Jean Lorrey, a surgeon in Napoleon's historic retreat from Moscow, used cold as an aid in amputation procedures. There was no hemorrhage if the part had been covered with snow or ice, and the cold had a sedatory effect on the brain and nervous system. Later, a London physician, James Arnott, used cold for the treatment of neuralgia and as palliation in terminally ill cancer patients. With his use of a brine solution, he was able to lower temperatures to $-24°C$.

Modern cryosurgery was made possible when Linde, in 1895, developed a method to make large quantities of liquid air and oxygen commercially. The development of the Dewar in 1898 was another significant contribution.

In 1899, White, a New York dermatologist, became the first cryosurgeon when he dipped a cotton-tipped applicator into liquified air and successfully treated warts, nevi, precancerous lesions, and some skin cancers. In 1907, Whitehouse, another New York dermatologist, developed a spray method using a laboratory wash bottle. Later, Zacarian used this idea when he developed the Kryospray and the C21 unit.

In 1907, Pusey was the first dermatologist in the United States to use carbon dioxide (CO_2) for treatment of acne and nevi. Around 1948, Allington introduced the use of liquid nitrogen. Torre, in 1967, used a spray of liquid nitrogen based on instruments developed by Cooper, a neurosurgeon.

Torre and Zacarian both pioneered in the work of freezing for the treatment of skin malignancies, and numerous other cryosurgeons have published their results in the treatment of benign and malignant skin lesions.

PREOPERATIVE PLANNING

Freezing may be performed in a number of ways. Cryogens, including dry-ice slush, the Kidde apparatus, liquid nitrogen applied with a cotton swab (Fig. 1), nitrous oxide, and liquid nitrogen instruments (some large units and some handheld) are a few of the methods. The smaller, handheld units that use liquid nitrogen are most popular in the United States, although for certain lesions nitrous oxide is quite acceptable and is widely used in France. The Verruca-Freeze is convenient for treating warts in children and for treating lesions in elderly patients.

Some of the available units are shown in Fig. 3. The cryogens and their specific temperatures are presented in Table 26-1. Various spray tips are available with sizes starting from 1 to 2 mm. Also available are cones for restricting spray (Fig. 4) and miniprobes of 1 to 3 mm and larger. A "door-knob" probe may be used for treatment of hemangiomas when compression of the blood from the lesion is needed (Fig. 5). Although spray and probe are equally effective if used appropriately, some cryogens seem to prefer the probe, and others prefer the spray. The most frequently used cryo-

Gloria F. Graham: Graham's Dermatology Services, PA, 3604 Medical Park Court, Morehead City, NC 28557.

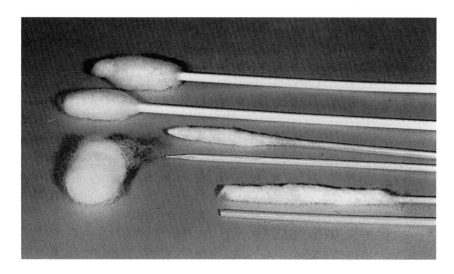

FIG. 1. Cotton swabs for use in treatment of benign lesions. (Courtesy of Delasco Dermatologic Lab & Supply.)

gen is liquid nitrogen, which, at $-195.8°C$, has the lowest temperature and is the most effective cryogen in treatment of skin cancer.

DIPSTICK METHOD

A disadvantage of the dipstick is the possible viral contamination of the liquid nitrogen when the swab is reintroduced into the liquid nitrogen container after treating warts or other infected lesions. The other disadvantages are lack of control and adequate spread of freeze, problems of dripping, limitations in depth of freezing, and the necessity of dipping the cotton swab into the liquid nitrogen. When this technique is used, it is preferable to pour a small amount of liquid nitrogen into a steel container (Fig. 6) and then dip the cotton swabs into the smaller container. Thus the large Dewar of

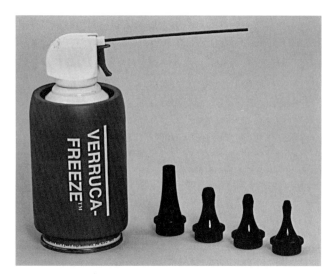

FIG. 2. Verruca-Freeze, which is useful for nursing home consultations. Kit comes with restrictive cones. (Photographs courtesy of CryoSurgery, Inc.)

liquid nitrogen is not contaminated. Liquid nitrogen is usually stored in Dewars of 20 to 32 L (Fig. 7).

Many conditions can be treated with cryosurgery. A list of benign precancerous and cancerous lesions, which is included in the *Guidelines of Care for Cryosurgery,* is provided in Table 26-2). If malignancies are to be treated, use of thermocouple needles is recommended until significant experience has been gained (Fig. 8). These are rarely needed in the treatment of benign lesions but are useful in precancerous lesions such as lentigo maligna.

PATIENT SELECTION

Dermatologists have a wide variety of treatment options available, including excision, shave excision, electrodesiccation, laser, chemical therapy, and cryosurgery. The selection may depend on the patients and their expectations, skin types, and general health. Some patients make better candidates for freezing (e.g., patients receiving anticoagulants, those who might be anticipated to have poor wound healing, and those with fair skin).

A patient with multiple, large lesions is usually a good candidate for freezing, but patients with multiple, small, 1- 2-mm lesions may be tested with electrodesiccation. Freezing is a safe and useful method for treatment of warts (Fig. 9), molluscum contagiosum (Fig. 10), and Kaposi's sarcoma in patients with human immunodeficiency virus infection. For nursing home patients, freezing is often the treatment

TABLE 26-1. *Cryogens and their temperatures*

Cryogens	Boiling point STP (°C)
Freon 114	+3.8
Freon 12	−27.8
Freon 22	−40.8
Carbon dioxide (solid)	−78.5
Nitrous oxide (liquid)	−89.5
Liquid nitrogen	−195.8

STP, standard temperature and pressure

A-C

FIG. 3. (A) The smaller Brymill 30 cryosurgical unit, which holds 30 ml of liquid nitrogen. The static holding time is 24 hours. **(B)** Large Brymill unit, the CryAc, which holds 2 L of liquid nitrogen. **(C)** The Cryo-Surg liquid nitrogen spray unit by Frigitronics.

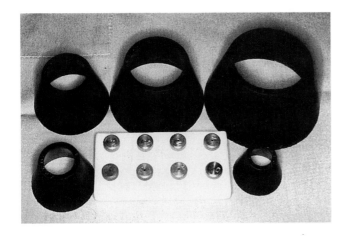

FIG. 4. Various sizes of cones and spray tips. Cones are used for restriction of spray. The tips that are used on Brymill CryAc units vary the size of the spray. *A* tip for lesions 1 cm or larger. *B* tip for lesions 0.5 to 1.0 cm. *C* tip for lesions less than 0.5 cm.

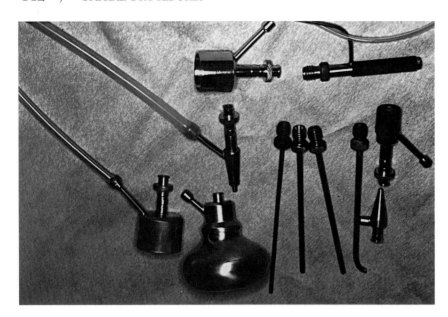

FIG. 5. Various probes and spray tips available for use with different cryosurgery units, which include the "doorknob" spray tip for use in hemangiomas.

FIG. 6. The Asepticator by Delasco. This unit helps prevent contamination of the liquid nitrogen. (Photograph courtesy of Delasco Labs.)

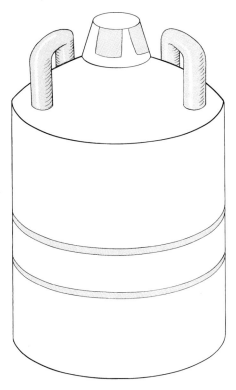

FIG. 7. Liquid nitrogen is stored in 20 to 32 liter Dewars.

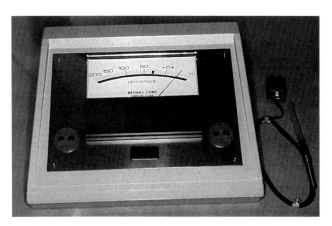

FIG. 8. Brymill pyrometer and thermocouple needle, which are used for monitoring depth of freeze in the treatment of malignancies.

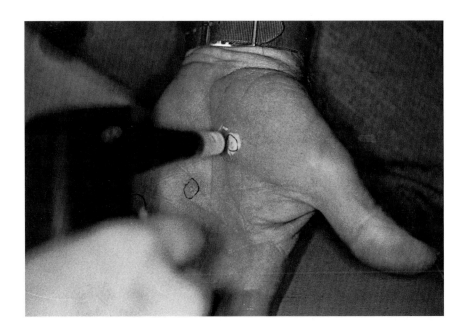

FIG. 9. Wart being treated with the Cryo-Surg.

TABLE 26-2. *Lesions that may be treated with cryosurgery*

Benign lesions	Precancerous lesions or tumors of uncertain behavior	Malignant lesions	Miscellaneous
Acne vulgaris, cystic	Actinic cheilitis	Basal cell carcinoma	Although cryosurgery is not widely used, small plaques of psoriasis, lichen simplex chronicus, and hypertrophic lichen planus may be eradicated by full-thickness epidermal freezing (10–15 seconds of spray with liquid nitrogen). However, superficial freezing may irritate and produce a Koebner response and is not generally recommended for these inflammatory conditions.
Angiolymphoid hyperplasia	Actinic keratoses	Bowen's disease	
Angiokeratoma: Fordyce and solitary type	Keratoacanthoma	(carcinoma *in situ*)	
Angioma, cherry and spider	Lentigo maligna	Kaposi's sarcoma	
Chondrodermatitis nodularis chronicus helicis	Leukoplakia	Metastatic melanoma	
Dermatofibroma	Other (bowenoid papulosis)	(palliative only)	
Disseminated superficial actinic porokeratosis		Squamous cell carcinoma	
Granuloma faciale		Actinic keratosis with	
Granuloma fissuratum		squamous cell	
Hemangioma, strawberry and cavernous		carcinoma	
Hidradenitis suppurativa		Adenoid squamous cell	
Keloid		carcinoma	
Leishmaniasis		De novo squamous cell	
Lentigines, lentigo simplex, solar lentigo		carcinoma	
Lichen planus, hypertrophic form		Other	
Lichen sclerosus et atrophicus			
Lichen simplex chronicus			
Lymphocytoma cutis			
Molluscum contagiosum			
Mucocele			
Myxoid cyst			
Nevi including epidermal type			
Porokeratosis of Mibelli			
Porokeratosis plantaris discreta			
Prurigo nodularis			
Psoriatic plaques			
Pyogenic granuloma			
Rosacea			
Sebaceous hyperplasia			
Seborrheic keratosis			
Steatocystoma multiplex			
Syringoma			
Trichiasis			
Venous lake			
Verrucae (condyloma acuminatum, periungual verruca, verruca plana, verruca palmaris et plantaris, verruca vulgaris)			
Other			

From Drake LA, Ceilley RI, Cornelison RL, et al: *J Am Acad Dermatol.* 1994;31:648–653.

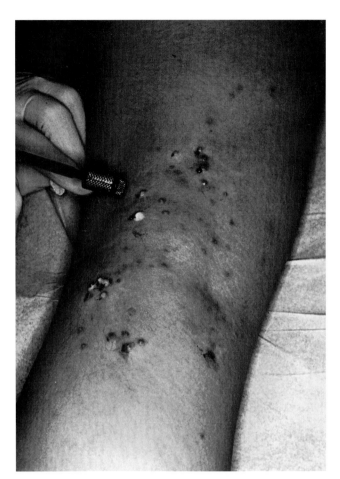

FIG. 10. *C* tip on CryAc is being used to treat tiny molluscum contagiosum on the leg.

of choice because the unit can be carried to the nursing home and treatment performed with ease. There are few complications, and minimal wound care is required.

Treatment of choice may depend on skin type and location of the lesion. For example, a lesion on the pinna of the ear responds well to freezing (Fig. 11), whereas a lesion treated on the nose of a well-tanned or dark-skinned patient (Fig. 12) may not yield the best cosmetic result because of decrease in pigmentation.

Therefore the choice in method may depend on location, skin color, size and number of lesions, response to previous therapy, and condition of underlying and surrounding skin. Those who have had prior radiation therapy respond well to freezing, whereas freezing should be avoided in a patient with severe arteriosclerosis in the lower leg. The cost-effectiveness of freezing may be a significant reason for using this technique, since the cost-benefit ratio is often higher with cryosurgery than with many other procedures.

TECHNIQUE

In selecting the preferable technique of cryosurgery for a particular lesion, consider the following (Table 26-3):

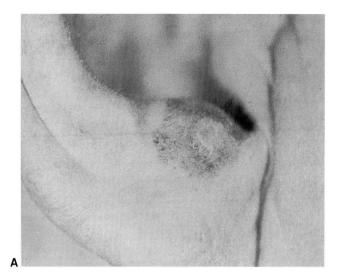

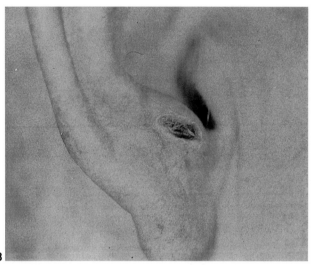

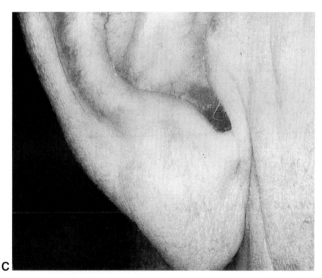

FIG. 11. (A) Lentigo maligna involving the right ear. **(B)** Eschar following freezing of lentigo maligna. **(C)** Complete clearing of lentigo maligna following cryosurgery.

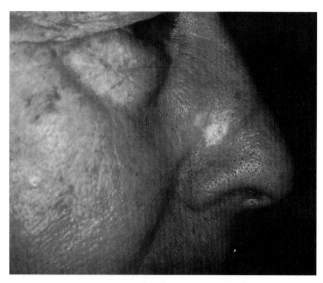

FIG. 12. Hypopigmented scar after cryosurgery following treatment of basal cell carcinoma.

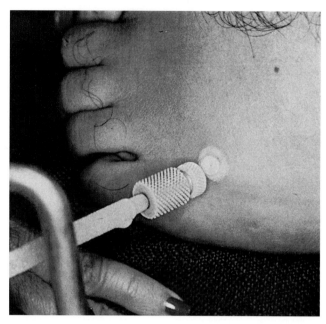

FIG. 13. Verruca on the foot being treated with Liquid Nitrogen spray. Two-millimeter margin of freeze around the wart is evident.

1. Type of lesion
2. Time of treatment
3. Target or depth
4. Use of spray or probe
5. Number of cycles (e.g., one or two cycles)
6. Use of thermocouples

NONMALIGNANT LESIONS

Freeze the lesion until a 1- 2-mm zone of normal tissue has been frozen (Fig. 13). An intermittent spray of the cryogen can be used. In some locations, such as the commissure of the eye or when treating a vascular lesion such as a cherry

angioma or a small, deep dermatofibroma, a small probe tip may be preferred to a spray tip (Fig. 14).

For all lesions, give special consideration to treatment time (Table 26-4). For a premalignant lesion such as actinic keratosis, use a freeze time of 8 to 12 seconds. For hypertrophic actinic keratosis, 20 seconds of freezing time is usually required, and for a cutaneous horn, 30 seconds or longer. Debulking of the horn before freezing is preferable (Fig. 15). Outline the lesions with a marking pencil before freezing, since the margins are obscured once freezing begins (Fig. 16). With many lesions, such as seborrheic keratoses, a cryo-

TABLE 26-3. *Treatment Chart: T table*

Type	Treatment	Tip	Time (sec)	Target (mm)	Technique	Thermo-couple	Turnout
Hypertrophic actinic keratosis	* ✔Choice Alternate Adjunct	B	F = 20–30 T = 30 40	2	✔Cryospray Cryoprobe 1 Cryocycle	No	Excellent to good
Seborrheic keratosis	Choice ✔Alternate ✔Adjunct	B	F = 8–15 T = 15–30	2.5	✔Cryospray Cryoprobe 1 Cryocycle	No	Good
Dermatofibroma	✔Choice ✔Alternate ✔Adjunct (with shave)	B or probe	F = 20–30 T = 30–40	3–4	✔Cryospray ✔Cryoprobe 1 Cryocycle	No	Good
Basal cell carcinoma (BCC)	✔Choice ✔Alternate ✔Adjunct (with shave or curettage)	>1 cm = A <1 cm = B (for small, deep BCC on nose, use probe)	F = 60–120 T = 60–180	3–4	✔Cryospray ✔Cryoprobe 2–3 Cryocycles	Yes	Good
Lentigo maligna	✔Choice Alternate Adjunct	A or B	F = 60–120 T = 90–120	3–4	✔Cryospray ✔Cryoprobe 2–3 Cryocycles	Yes	Good to fair (hypopigmentation)

Using Brymill CryAc, intermittent spray.
* Check (✔) indicates treatment of choice, alternate or adjunct.

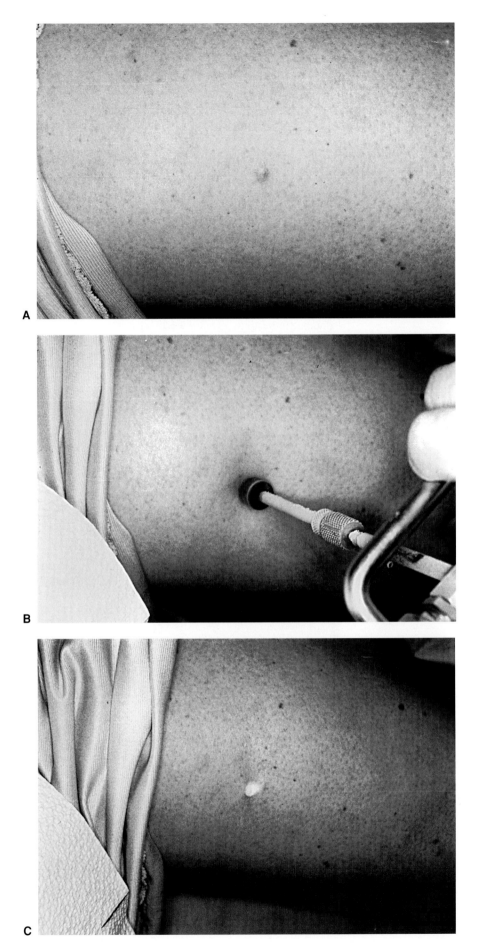

FIG. 14. (A) Dermatofibroma on the thigh. **(B)** Treatment of dermatofibroma with probe. **(C)** The frozen site with a 2-mm border around the lesion is evident.

447

TABLE 26-4. *Comparison to freeze times for benign and malignant lesions and range of expected cosmetic results*

Lesion	Freeze time (sec)	Range of expected cosmetic results
Acne scarring	10	Good to fair
Actinic keratoses	5–10	Excellent to good
Chondrodermatitis	30	Good to fair
Granuloma faciale	30	Good to fair
Hemangioma	60 +	Good to fair
Hypertrophic scarring	20	Good to fair
Keloidal scarring	30	Good to fair
Keratoacanthoma	30	Excellent to good
Lentigines	10	Excellent to good
Lentigo maligna	60–120	Excellent to good
Morphea type of BCC*	90–120	Good to fair
Nevi	10	Good to fair
Nodular BCC*	60–90	Excellent to good
Sebaceous hyperplasia	5–10	Excellent to good
Seborrheic keratoses	10	Good to fair
Superficial BCC*	60	Excellent to good

Using intermittent spray.
* Basal cell carcinoma.

pattern develops that shows specifically where the lesion is, so marking is unnecessary (Fig. 17).

MALIGNANT LESIONS

When treating malignant lesions, use a thermocouple needle positioned under the base of the tumor, especially until significant experience with freezing has been aquired. Mark the margin of the lesion before inserting the thermocouple needle (Figs. 16 and 18). Freeze the tumor with an intermittent spray until a zone of 5 mm of frozen tissue is reached around the tumor (Fig. 16). A freeze time of around 60 seconds for a 0.5- to 1.0-cm lesion is customary. For deeper, more aggressive skin malignancies, such as a morpheaform basal cell carcinoma, longer freeze time using a double freeze-thaw cycle is necessary. Allow the lesion to thaw and repeat the freeze. Recording the freeze and thaw times in the patient's record is prudent.

To prepare the lesion for freezing, it is frequently best to debulk it by tangentially removing the lesion with a razor

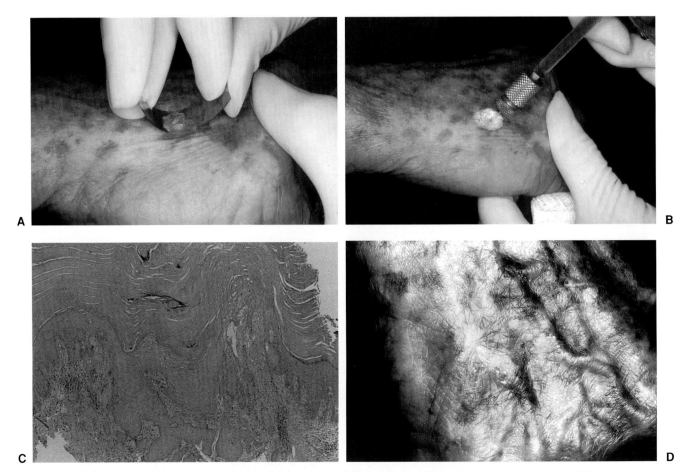

FIG. 15. (A) Shave excision of an actinic keratosis with squamous cell carcinoma on the dorsum of the right hand. **(B)** After the shave, the area is treated with liquid nitrogen spray using a *B* tip on the CryAc unit. **(C)** Note the depth of the excision and the presence of an actinic keratosis. This was a squamous cell carcinoma arising from actinic keratosis. **(D)** Three months later, the area is well healed.

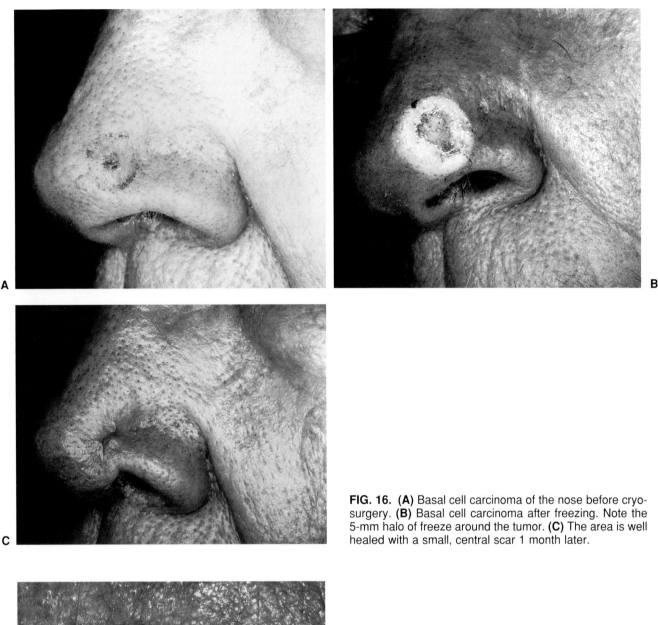

FIG. 16. (A) Basal cell carcinoma of the nose before cryo-surgery. **(B)** Basal cell carcinoma after freezing. Note the 5-mm halo of freeze around the tumor. **(C)** The area is well healed with a small, central scar 1 month later.

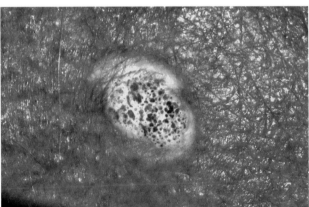

FIG. 17. Seborrheic keratosis treated with freezing shows the typical cryopattern.

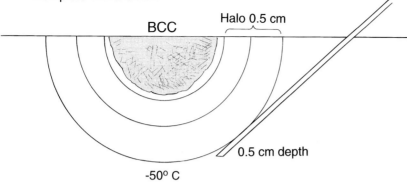

F.T 45-60 sec.
Halo T.T. 60 sec.
Complete T.T. 2-5 min.

BCC

Halo 0.5 cm

0.5 cm depth

-50° C

FIG. 18. Thermocouple needle positioned under the base of the tumor. Halo of freezing around tumor should be 5 mm, and freezing carried out to −50°C. Freeze time ranges from 45 to 60 seconds per cycle. A double freeze-thaw cycle is performed for deeper lesions.

blade (Fig. 19), curetting the base, and freezing using a double freeze-thaw cycle (Fig. 20). Freeze until the thermocouple needle reaches −50°C to −55°C. Freeze time may be 60 to 90 seconds. Allow the lesion to thaw. Thaw time for the halo will be around 60 to 90 seconds; the entire lesion may take up to 5 minutes to thaw. Apply Monsel's solution or aluminum chloride for hemostasis.

To treat extensive lesions, freeze in stages over several months rather than have a thick eschar, which may require up to 3 months to separate and heal completely (Fig. 21).

Take care to avoid loss of eyebrow or scalp hair when possible (Fig. 22). This is uncommon in the treatment of benign lesions but happens more frequently in the treatment of malignancies. Cryosurgery is especially effective for freezing lesions overlying cartilage, such as the pinna of the ear (Fig. 23A–C) and the postauricular sulcus (Fig. 23D). Protect the external auditory canal with a cotton pledget or

with your hand; protect the nares with a tongue blade and the eye with a Jagher retractor.

POSTOPERATIVE MANAGEMENT

The patient is instructed to wash the lesion with soap and water, one ot two times daily. When possible, the lesion should not be dressed with gauze, since this sometimes removes the eschar prematurely and results in a less than satisfactory cosmetic result. The lesion may be covered, however, when the patient is going out in public. If the original eschar becomes very hard, an ointment such as Polysporin® may be used to soften it. If the eschar becomes detached or infection results, removal may be required. Although infrequent, if this occurs, a dressing such as Duoderm may be applied to the wound.

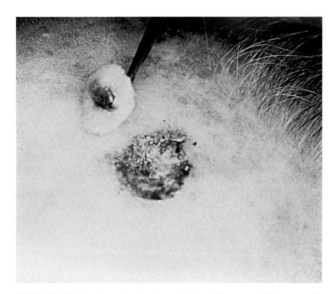

FIG. 19. Technique for treatment of malignancy. Shave excision using a razor blade.

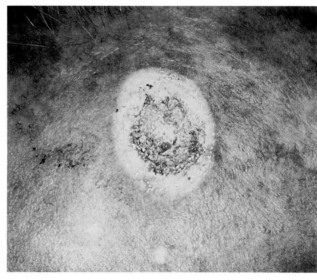

FIG. 20. Area of tumor is frozen with 5-mm border of normal skin frozen around it.

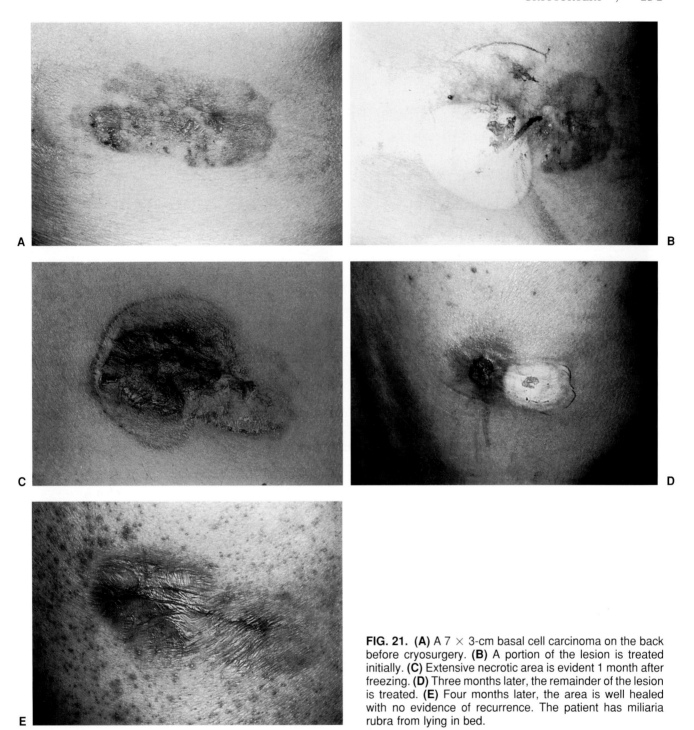

FIG. 21. **(A)** A 7 × 3-cm basal cell carcinoma on the back before cryosurgery. **(B)** A portion of the lesion is treated initially. **(C)** Extensive necrotic area is evident 1 month after freezing. **(D)** Three months later, the remainder of the lesion is treated. **(E)** Four months later, the area is well healed with no evidence of recurrence. The patient has miliaria rubra from lying in bed.

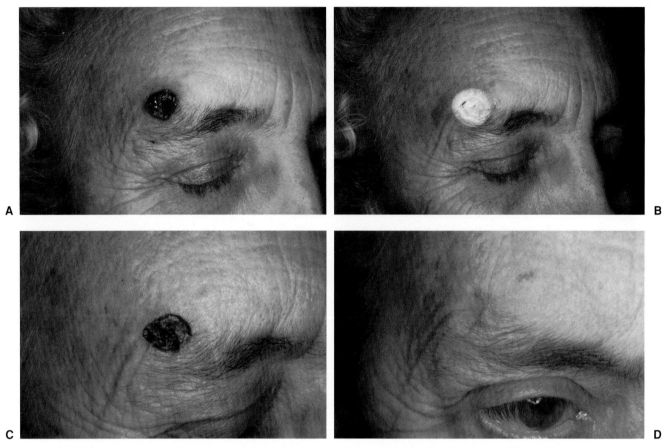

FIG. 22. **(A)** A 1.2-cm basal cell carcinoma of the right forehead, extending into the eyebrow. **(B)** Basal cell carcinoma treated with cryosurgery. The ice ball extends into the eyebrow area. **(C)** Eschar 3 weeks after cryosurgery. **(D)** Linear scar 5 months after cryosurgery. There is minimal loss of eyebrows following the procedure.

FIG. 23. **(A)** A basal cell carcinoma inside the left concha of the ear. **(B)** Cotton pledget is evident inside the auricular canal during freezing.

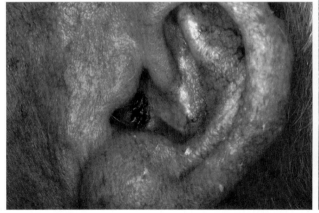

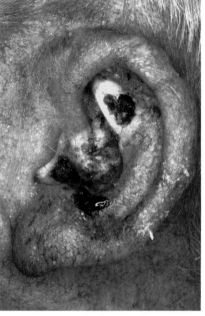

FIG. 23. *Continued.* **(C)** Two months later, there is a glistening erythematous response and no evidence of recurrent tumor. **(D)** Exudative reaction at the site of cryosurgery for adenoid squamous cell carcinoma 5 days after treatment.

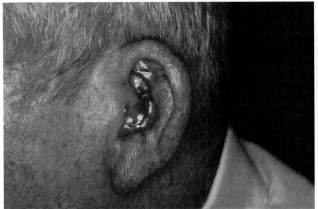

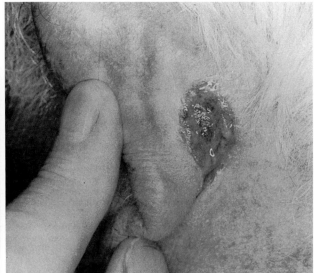

C

D

ADVERSE SEQUELAE

Edema, vesicles, bullae, weeping (Fig. 23D), and eschar formation (Fig. 24) as a result of the inflammatory reaction from freezing can be expected. When treating malignancies, systemic steroids may be given to prevent some of the edema, especially in the periorbital area. Relief of pain on the fingers and the soles of the feet after treatment of warts may require analgesics such as aspirin for 24 to 48 hours. Caution the patient with regard to headaches when freezing tumors of the scalp, forehead, or temple. Periorbital edema often results when treating these tumors as well. Although bleeding following freezing is uncommon, it may occur, especially in patients receiving anticoagulants or aspirin.

COMPLICATIONS

Nitrogen gas insufflation is a rare complication and is due to escape of liquid nitrogen into the perilesional skin,

producing crepitance. The gas may be expelled from the tissue simply by applying pressure to the involved site. If a biopsy specimen is obtained before spraying the area, application of a cone to the surrounding skin prevents insufflation of gas (Fig. 25).

When using a probe, prechill it before application to a mucous membrane to prevent adherence of the probe to the mucosa. Attachment to the mucosa may pull it away when removing the probe (Fig. 26). Application of lubricating (K-Y) jelly may also help prevent adherence of the probe.

Although rare, syncopal episodes following freezing of warts on the fingers or soles of the feet may occur. Patients should be monitored for a few minutes after treatment so they do not faint just as they reach the front desk.

Although uncommon following freezing, damage to underlying nerves or infection may result. A temporary neuropathy may exist for 3 to 6 months and in some patients for over a year. If infection results, treatment with topical antibiotic ointment or a systemic antibiotic is indicated.

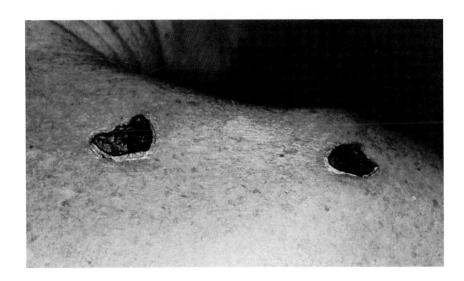

FIG. 24. Dry eschars 2 months after treatment of two large basal cell carcinomas on the back. Large lesions may require up to 3 months for healing.

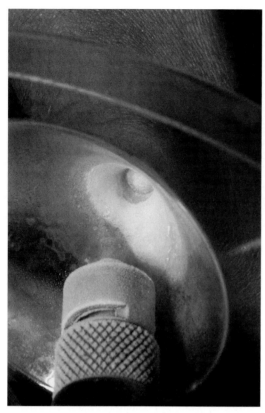

FIG. 25. A plastic cone presses down the edges of the lesion to prevent insufflation of gas into surrounding skin.

Necrosis of cartilage is not common, although it can occur on the helix of the ear, especially if through-and-through freezing of the pinna is performed.

Freeze times of over 20 seconds may produce alopecia in hair-bearing areas. If freezing a thick seborrheic keratosis on the scalp, precede freezing with curettage to lessen the freeze time and help prevent this complication. When treating malignancies, alopecia is much more common.

Although atrophy of the skin may develop following freezing, it is not a usual occurrence. Monitoring to avoid overfreezing may help prevent this occurrence. A thicker, sebaceous type of skin is more prone to show thinning as a result of destruction of the hair follicles.

Hypertrophic scarring may occur in a linear fashion similar to excision and suturing, especially on the nose and upper lip. Regression with time is hastened by pressure, topical steroids, and dressing such as Epiguard (Fig. 27). Freezing may produce hyperpigmentation on the lower legs and at the periphery of seborrheic keratoses and lentigines. Topical steroids, retinoids, glycolic acids, and other bleaching agents may be helpful before and after treatment to reduce the incidence of this pigmentation change.

The usual change following freezing is hypopigmentation as a result of sensitivity of the pigment cells, which are destroyed at $-4°C$. Repigmentation may result if freezing has been brief, but freezing of 30 to 60 seconds routinely results in some decrease in pigment (Figs. 28–30). Although much hypopigmentation is temporary, the patient should be forewarned that hypopigmentation may at times be permanent.

Ectropion, or notching of the eyelid margin, although rare,

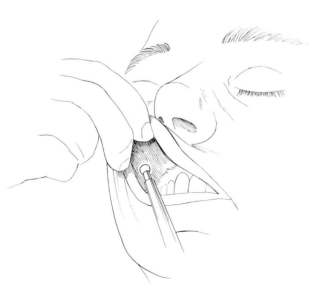

FIG. 26. Probe tips should be prechilled before application to a mucous membrane to prevent adherence of the probe to the mucosa.

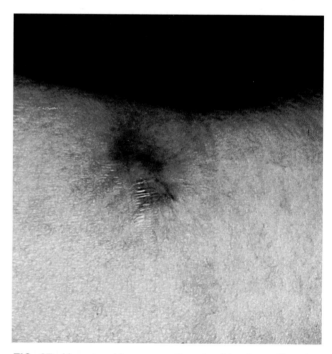

FIG. 27. Hypertrophic scar on the shoulder 2 months after treatment of basal cell carcinoma.

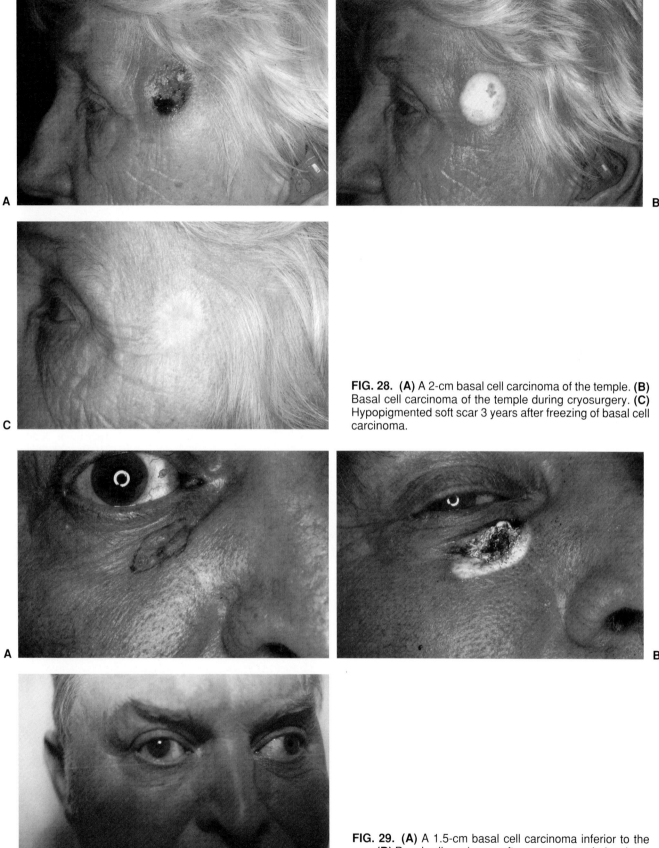

FIG. 28. (A) A 2-cm basal cell carcinoma of the temple. **(B)** Basal cell carcinoma of the temple during cryosurgery. **(C)** Hypopigmented soft scar 3 years after freezing of basal cell carcinoma.

FIG. 29. (A) A 1.5-cm basal cell carcinoma inferior to the eye. **(B)** Basal cell carcinoma after cryosurgery during thaw. **(C)** Area well healed. Hypopigmented scar 5 months after cryosurgery.

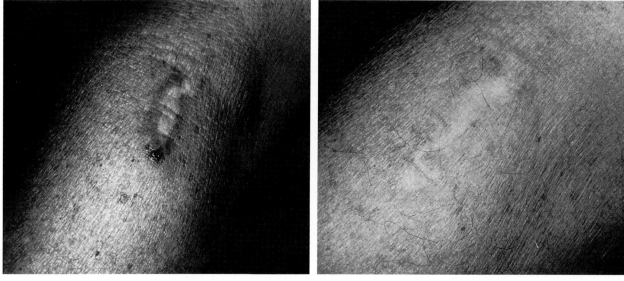

FIG. 30. (A) Linear area of prurigo nodularis. **(B)** Hypopigmentation following freezing of prurigo nodularis. The lesion of prurigo nodularis has cleared 1 month after cryosurgery.

may occur, as well as notching of the ala of the nose and the helix of the ear. Avoidance of overfreezing by careful monitoring lessens these occurrences.

CONCLUSION

Cryosurgery is a versatile, safe technique that is often used for treatment of a wide range of benign, premalignant, and malignant skin lesions. Attention to proper patient selection, treatment techniques, and freezing times produces the best cosmetic results. Use of thermocouple monitoring, especially when one is learning cryosurgery, yields high cure rates when treating malignancies and helps avert certain complications.

Because cryosurgery is an economical and time-efficient treatment, it is well suited for the busy dermatology practice in this era of managed care. Physicians well trained in cryosurgery are able to manage many more skin tumors with fewer complications, higher cure rate, and lower cost. In contrast to lasers, one cryosurgical instrument is far less expensive and may be used to treat a wider array of lesions. Many lesions can be treated without local anesthesia, which is another cost- and time-saving benefit.

With the increasing concern about spread of viral diseases to physicians and staff, cryosurgery offers a safe alternative to laser and excisional surgery. Better training in the proper use of freezing will allow safer, more effective treatment of patients.

SUGGESTED READING LIST

1. Allington HD. Liquid nitrogen in the treatment of skin disease. California Med 1950;72:153.
2. Castro-Ron G. Cryosurgery of angiomas and birth defects. In: Zacarian SA, ed. Cryosurgery for skin cancer and cutaneous disorders. St. Louis, MO: Mosby, 1985:77.
3. Chiarello SE. Cryopeeling. J Dermatol Surg Oncol 1992;18:329.
4. Dachow-Siwiec E. Treatment of cryosurgery in the premalignant and benign lesions of skin. In: Breitbart E, Dachow-Siwiec E, eds. Clinics in dermatology: advances in cryosurgery. Vol 8. New York: Elsevier, 1990:75.
5. Elton RF. Complications of cutaneous cryosurgery. J Am Acad Dermatol 1983;8:513.
6. Gage AA, Kuflik EG. Cryosurgical equipment. In: Cryosurgical treatment for skin cancer. New York: Igaku-Shoin, 1990:53.
7. Graham GF. Cryotherapy in the treatment of acne. In: Epstein E, Epstein E Jr, eds. Skin surgery. 5th ed. Springfield, IL: Charles C Thomas, 1982:680.
8. Graham GF, Clark LC. Statistical analysis in cryosurgery of skin cancer. In: Breitbart E, Dachow-Siwiec E, eds. Clinics in dermatology: advances in cryosurgery. Vol 8. New York: Elsevier, 1990:101.
9. Graham GF. Cryosurgery. Clin Plast Surg 1993;20:131.
10. Graham G. Cryosurgery for benign, premalignant, and malignant lesions. In: Wheeland RG, ed. Cutaneous surgery. 1st ed. Philadelphia: WB Saunders, 1994:835.
11. Holt P. Cryotherapy for skin cancer: results over a 5-year period using liquid nitrogen spray cryotherapy. Br J Dermatol 1988;119:231.
12. Kuflik EG, Gage AA. The five-year cure rate achieved by cryosurgery for skin cancer. J Am Acad Dermatol 1991;24:1002.
13. Kuflik EG. Cryosurgery updated. J Am Acad Dermatol 1994;31:925.
14. Lubritz RR, Smolewski SA. Cryosurgery cure rate of actinic keratoses. J Am Acad Dermatol 1982;7:631.
15. Lubritz RR. Cryosurgical approach to benign and precancerous tumors of the skin. In: Zacarian SA, ed. Cryosurgery for skin cancer and cutaneous disorders. St. Louis, MO: Mosby, 1985:45.
16. Spiller WF, Spiller RF. Cryosurgery in dermatology office practice. South Med J 1975;68:157.
17. Torre D. Cryosurgery of basal cell carcinoma. J Am Acad Dermatol 1986;15:917.
18. Zacarian SA. Cryosurgery of cutaneous carcinomas: an 18-year study of 3022 patients with 4228 carcinomas. J Am Acad Dermatol 1983;9:947.
19. Zacarian SA. Cryosurgery in the treatment of skin cancer. In: Friedman RJ, Riegel DS, Kopf AW, et al., eds. Cancer of the skin. Philadelphia: WB Saunders, 1991:451.

Textbook of Dermatologic Surgery, edited by John L. Ratz.
Lippincott–Raven Publishers, Philadelphia © 1998.

CHAPTER 27

Electrosurgery

Jack E. Sebben

HISTORY

Medical practitioners have used heat for tissue destruction for centuries. However, the use of electrically generated heat destruction did not occur until the mid 19th century when electrical physics advanced to a level of practical application. Claude Paquelin developed the use of electrocautery in 1875. This new modality was similar to the old form of hot cautery except that it generated heat electrically. The real beginnings for modern electrosurgery were the recognition and development of high-frequency alternating current. In 1891, d'Arsonval developed the circuitry for generation of high-frequency electricity. He found that high-frequency currents above 10,000 Hz could pass through the body without pain or muscle contraction.

In 1893, Oudin designed a resonated circuit with a balance between capacitive resistance and inductive resistance. This allowed a maximum amount of current flow by minimizing the amount of circuit resistance. Oudin used the resonated gap generator to destroy various skin lesions. A very small electrode maximized the destructive effect of high-frequency current. In 1908, Walter de Keating-Hart noted that high-frequency current could spark from the electrode to the tissue in long sparks resembling lightning (fulgur). He used these long sparks to destroy skin cancers and therefore developed the modality of electrofulguration. In 1911, William Clark used very high voltage and low amperage for monopolar

tissue destruction. Current applied directly to tissue produced marked desiccation in the area of electrical contact. Clark identified the modality as electrodesiccation.

The role of electricity in surgery changed when a neurosurgeon, Harvey Cushing, became fascinated with the possible uses of electrosurgery for neurologic and vascular tumors. Cushing was aware that the Harvard physicist, William Bovie, was experimenting with electrosurgical equipment. The academic medical community had not accepted Bovie's equipment. Once the renowned Cushing enlisted Bovie and his equipment for assistance in the operating room, electrosurgery entered the realm of acceptable medical practice. Bovie, with the production help of George Liebel of the Liebel–Flasheim Company, developed a new electrosurgical unit capable of producing high-frequency currents that were useful for superficial desiccation, tissue coagulation, and cutting. Modern electrosurgical generators use solid-state circuits to produce more reliable and precise currents than Bovie's original machine, but the treatment modalities remain much the same.

PREOPERATIVE PLANNING

Since electrosurgery is a tool that is used with many forms of surgery, preoperative planning centers primarily on the specific surgical procedure. However, some considerations are specific to electrosurgery.

The surgeon must consider the risks of hypertrophic scarring. Special precautions are necessary for patients prone to hypertrophic scarring or keloids. Similar attention

Jack E. Sebben: University of California, Davis, Department of Dermatology, Sacramento, CA 95816.

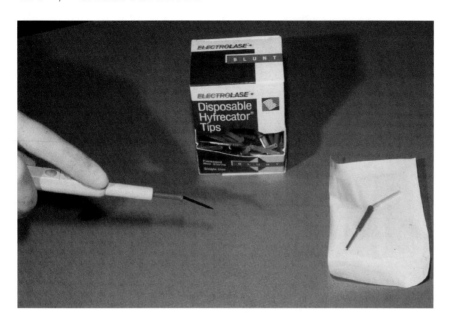

FIG. 1. Disposable electrodes are most popular for superficial electrodesiccation and coagulation procedures. They are available either sterile or nonsterile. The nonsterile electrodes are economical and are fine for most superficial treatments.

is necessary for scar-prone regions such as the presternum, deltoid areas, hands, and feet. One should always use minimal power settings when performing electrosurgery in these areas.

Cardiac pacemakers are now relatively immune to interference from electrosurgery. The surgeon should identify these pacemaker patients and use appropriate precautions, which include proper grounding and avoidance of high-amperage outputs, particularly with cutting current procedures.

The surgeon must select the appropriate electrosurgical equipment for the operative procedure. The first item to consider is the electrosurgical generator. A wide variety of generators is available. Physicians should choose a unit that best serves their needs. Most dermatologists rarely use cutting

current. A physician who never uses this modality would be better served by choosing a simpler, less expensive unit that only delivers current for electrofulguration, electrode siccation, and very light electrocoagulation. Instruments with only these capabilities often have a higher voltage and lower amperage than the more complex units and therefore are more useful for superficial treatments. The larger units with higher outputs and cutting current capability sometimes do not function as well for very light electrofulguration and electrodesiccation.

Treatment electrodes for high-frequency electro surgery, like generators, come in many shapes and sizes. For most electrosurgical procedures in dermatology, a few electrodes are popular. The tissue response varies greatly depending on the type of electrode used. Thus the dermatologist must

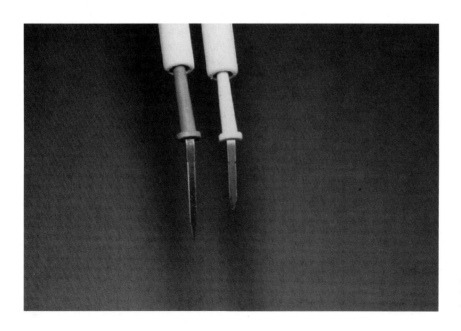

FIG. 2. The slightly blunt disposable electrode *(left)* works best for most desiccation procedures. The very sharp electrode *(right)* tends to produce a slight cutting quality at the tip.

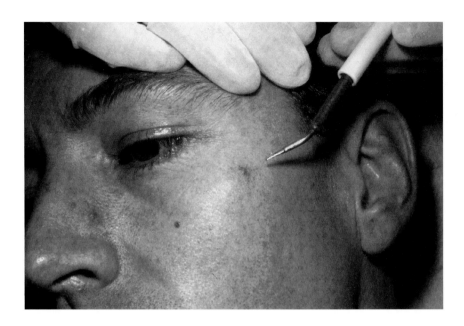

FIG. 3. Spider angiomas are sometimes difficult to treat because of the dilated central feeding vessels.

be familiar with the characteristics and tissue responses of the common electrodes.

The portion of an electrode that fits into the handle is usually a metal shaft $\frac{3}{32}$ of an inch in diameter. The standardization of electrode size allows interchangeability among brands. Several accessory manufacturers supply wide selections of electrodes for various electrosurgical units. Disposable electrodes are most popular today (Fig. 1).

For common superficial electrodesiccation, slightly pointed electrodes seem to produce the best effect (Fig. 2). Sharp disposable or needle electrodes focus energy so precisely that they are less efficient for broad electrode siccation. Less sharp electrodes are useful for applying compression to small vascular lesions during the administration of desiccation current (Figs. 3–5). On the other hand, cut-

tingcurrent electrodes enter the tissue, making the power density a prime consideration. To minimize adjacent tissue damage, cutting current electrodes should be as small as possible, preferably a fine wire.

TECHNIQUE

The most common method of electrosurgery is the application of very-high-frequency, high-voltage electrical current with a monoterminal electrode and without the use of a dispersive electrode. Most of the following discussion applies to this technique. Some equipment or procedures require the use of a dispersive electrode. The principles discussed in this chapter are the same, whether or not a dispersive electrode is necessary.

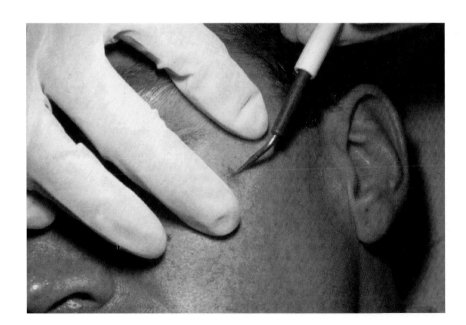

FIG. 4. A blunt electrode can compress the blood out of the central vessel before coagulation.

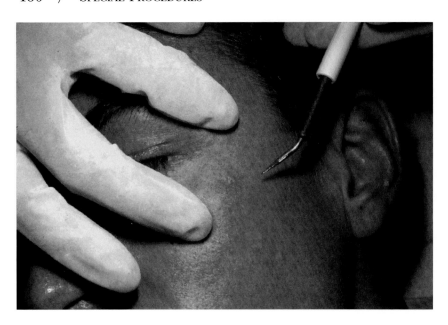

FIG. 5. Medium- to low-level current applied to the compressed vessel seals it in a fraction of a second.

Electrosurgical Modalities

Direct-Current Surgical Galvanism

Few physicians have the equipment available for the production of the direct galvanic current. Galvanic current can remove very small superficial lesions. It has been used for nail matrix destruction. Galvanic surgery has very few useful applications in everyday practice.

The most common use of galvanic current is in electrolysis. Electrolysis is a time-consuming procedure and is often referred to a technician trained in epilation. When the physician wishes to ablate an occasional hair follicle, the use of equipment with an option of high-frequency epilation or thermolysis is more convenient.

Electrofulguration

The difference between electrofulguration and electrodesiccation is largely a matter of electrode position. In electrofulguration the treatment electrode does not contact the patient. There is a very small distance across which the high-frequency current must arc to achieve tissue action. The action on the tissue is essentially that of light electrodesiccation. The advantage of electrofulguration is that there is sufficient power to stop bleeding but less damage to the tissue than with direct contact electrodesiccation. It also may produce less scarring than with electrodesiccation.

High-amperage electrosurgical generators used primarily for coagulation do not produce sufficient voltage to deliver electrofulguration current. Some units have a secondary coil added to the circuit to boost the current to a voltage level sufficient to bridge the air gap. Cutaneous lesions treated by this technique usually heal rapidly because there is very little thermal damage.

The arc need only span a very small distance. A common error in the application of fulguration is to turn the electrosurgical machine to a very high setting so that a large, visible spark arcs across a great distance. The large amount of current applied can produce excessive tissue damage, charring, and carbonization. Electrofulguration offers no advantage at high power settings (Fig. 6).

Electrodesiccation

Dermatologists most commonly use electrodesiccation. The treatment electrode contacts the tissue, resulting in dehydration and coagulation. There is usually a combination of electrodesiccation and electrofulguration because the treatment electrode is not always in complete tissue contact and some degree of arcing occurs. When using minimal power settings, most of the damage is epidermal and there is minimal risk of scarring. However, at high power settings there is coagulation of the deeper tissues and potential scarring. The term ''electrodesiccation'' usually refers to any form of monoterminal (one treatment electrode) high-frequency electrosurgical treatment on the skin surface.

Electrocoagulation

As with fulguration and desiccation, there is a vague distinction between electrodesiccation and electrocoagulation. Coagulation occurs with most desiccation. Electrocoagulation refers to wider and deeper destruction. Electrocoagulation usually requires either a biterminal electrode (two treatment electrodes, as with bipolar electrodes) or a monoterminal treatment electrode combined with a dispersive electrode. A dispersive electrode permits the use of a lower voltage with accompanying higher amperage, produc-

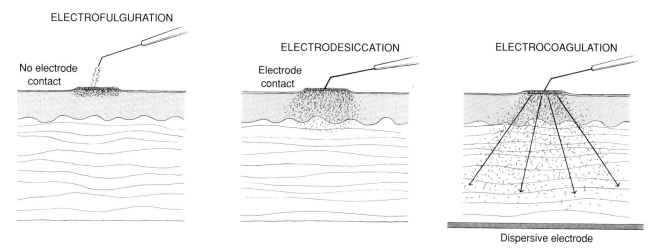

FIG. 6. High-frequency electrosurgery varies with electrodeposition and the amount of current delivered.

ing greater tissue effect. The clamping of a bleeding point or blood vessel with an energized clamp constitutes electrocoagulation (Fig. 7).

Electrocautery

"Cautery" in common usage usually indicates any form of electrosurgery (particularly electrodesiccation). However, true cautery is from a heat-producing electrode without the transfer of electrical current. High-frequency equipment has largely replaced cautery today. Electrodesiccation can produce essentially the same results, but electrocautery can cause greater tissue damage and slower healing. It may be useful for treating patients who must avoid high-frequency current. One advantage of electrocautery is that it works on nonconductive tissues. High-frequency electrical current does not conduct to exposed cartilage, bone, or nails, but electrocautery produces its effect in these tissues quite well.

Electrocautery can also work in a bloody surgical field. A red-hot wire electrode produces the tissue action. A test cut on a cotton sponge helps determine the appropriate power level for electrocautery (Fig. 8).

Cutting Current

Use cutting current whenever the surgeon wishes to excise a lesion in a relatively bloodless manner. Excisional procedures are often faster than with scalpel surgery. However, there can be greater tissue damage and slower healing with cutting current. Wounds that have been created with cutting current can often be closed primarily, but the wound takes longer to achieve satisfactory tensile strength. Use this technique only be on wounds that are to be closed if the cutting current is applied judiciously and with considerable skill. Excessive energy levels or a very slow cutting speed can produce overcoagulation and poor healing.

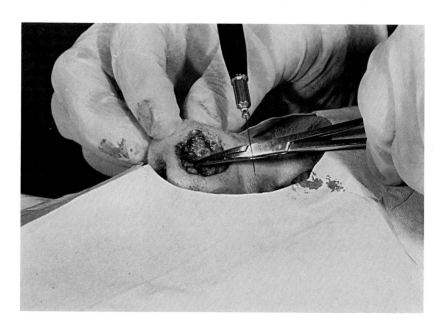

FIG. 7. When clamping bleeding vessels, make sure only a small amount of tissue is grasped with the forceps. By contacting minimal tissue, only a small amount of current is required. In this example, a sterile needle electrode in contact with a hemostat conducts coagulation current to the tissue.

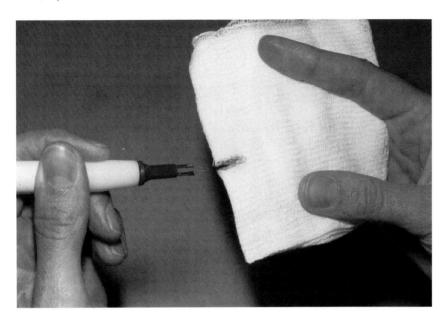

FIG. 8. A hot cautery electrode is properly adjusted when it is red-hot and cuts through cotton gauze with no resistance.

Power Control to Minimize Tissue Damage

To avoid excessive tissue damage and subsequent scarring, adjust the power level to be as low as possible to achieve the desired effect. A coin or another metal object provides a useful test for power level adjustment for electrodesiccation (Fig. 9). For all but the smallest lesions, combine routine electrosurgery with other cutting instruments. If a large lesion is simply burned off with electrodesiccation or electrocoagulation, the depth of destruction is not easily monitored. It is preferable to remove the bulk of the lesion by means of a superficial excision with either scalpel or scissors. Treat the remaining base electrosurgically. In addition to providing precise, visible control over the depth of the destruction, provide a specimen for histologic analysis.

Hemostasis

Apply electrical current to a dry surgical field. If there is a barrier of blood, the electrical current is conducted through the blood and distributed over a wider area of tissue. The coagulation effect is diminished or prevented through dispersion. The fluid barrier can sometimes be overcome by selecting extremely high power levels when attempting to perform coagulation in a very bloody field, but avoid high power outputs whenever possible. Stretching or pinching the surrounding skin controls most bleeding in superficial wounds, thus allowing coagulation in a relatively dry field (Fig. 10). Extensive current applied to bloody areas results in excessive tissue damage. Even if hemostasis is achieved, there will be a large mass of coagulated and carbonized tissue, which may

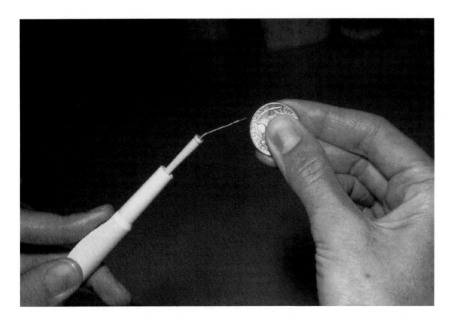

FIG. 9. Adjust the power level of electrodesiccation current to the point where a small spark occurs at the contact point of a handheld coin or another grounded metallic object.

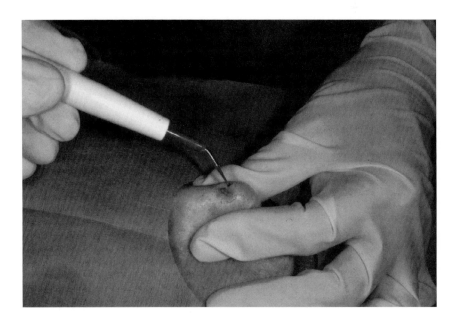

FIG. 10. Coagulation current should be applied to a bloodless wound. Bleeding is controlled by pinching or lateral traction.

slough and cause delayed bleeding. Properly applied coagulation should leave only white or light tan desiccated tissue (Fig. 11).

Whenever possible, wait 5 to 10 minutes after the infiltration of epinephrine-containing anesthetic to allow the epinephrine to produce the maximum amount of vasoconstriction. There will be a smaller amount of bleeding and less electrocoagulation will be necessary. However, in common clinical practice, electrosurgery is used for brief procedures such as simple shave excisions and biopsies. It is often not convenient to wait for the maximal epinephrine effect to occur.

Special Techniques for Cutting Current

Cutting current is most effective when the power density to the tissue is high. Keep the area of activity very small to achieve maximum power density with a minimal amount of current. The power density value increases as the radius of the curvature on the electrode decreases. A fine wire is actually a cylinder with a very small radius. As the current approaches the needlelike tip of the wire, the added curvature of the tip approximates a portion of a sphere, resulting in increased electrical activity at the distal end of the wire. Since flattened electrodes and loop electrodes require increased electrical energy to produce the same degree of cutting as a wire, there is increased heat production in the surrounding tissue. The heat from a large electrode produces more tissue destruction and poor wound healing (Fig. 12). For debulking procedures such as rhinophyma excisions, use a fine wire loop to remove tissue efficiently and quickly (Figs. 13–17).

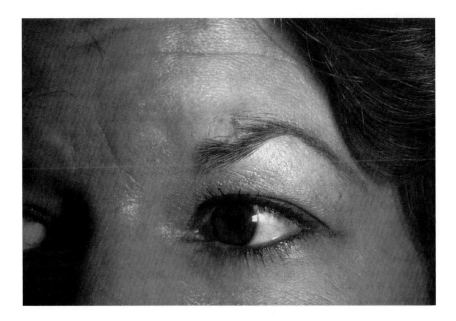

FIG. 11. Charred tissue should not be present on desiccated shave biopsy sites. Nevus shave excision site at the upper edge of the eyebrow shows the desired light-tan color of mild desiccation.

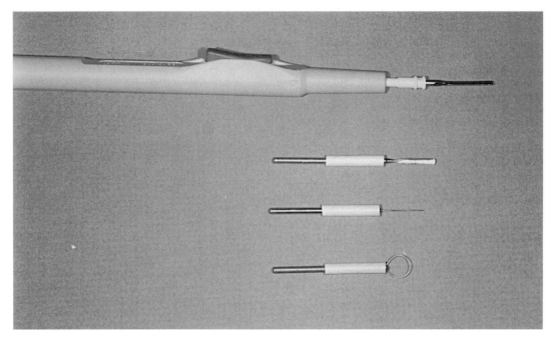

FIG. 12. Of the popular cutting current electrodes illustrated, only the fine, straight wire electrode is recommended because it is easiest to manipulate, requires the lowest power settings, and produces the least tissue damage. A switching handle is shown. Many surgeons prefer foot switch power control because the surgeon's fingers are free for optimal electrode manipulation.

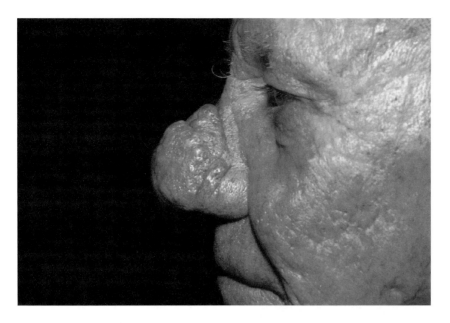

FIG. 13. Preoperative view of a patient with moderate rhinophyma.

Cutting current is monoterminal because there is a single treatment electrode. However, because of the relatively large amounts of current applied to the patient, there must be a dispersive electrode to handle this higher current flow.

Cutting should be at a brisk speed. Keep motion at a rate that incises the tissue adequately without a cooked or charred appearance. A very slow rate of cutting achieves a better level of hemostasis but produces a wider band of tissue damage, resulting in slower and poorer wound healing. An optimal rate of electrode movement is 5 to 10 mm per second.

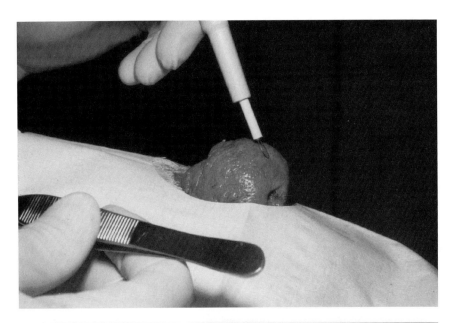

FIG. 14. A wire loop electrode removes the hyperplastic sebaceous tissue with cutting current.

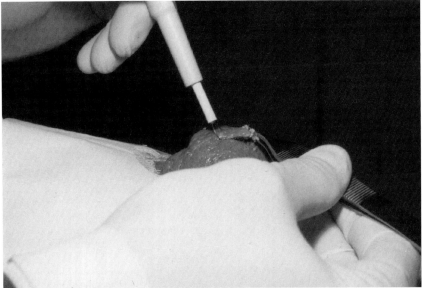

FIG. 15. The loop quickly cuts away strips of tissue.

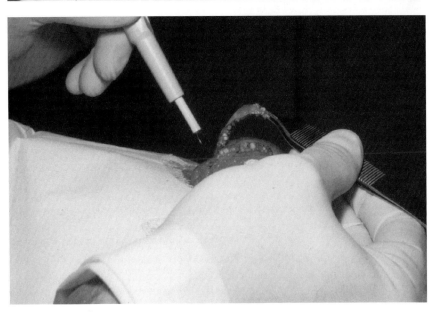

FIG. 16. The bloodless field provides excellent visualization of the contouring excisions.

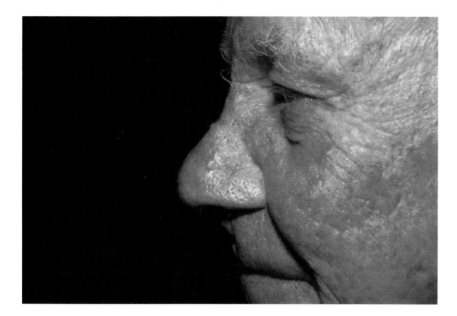

FIG. 17. Five months after rhinophyma treatment.

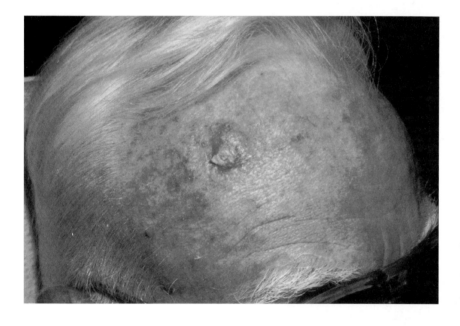

FIG. 18. Preoperative view of squamous cell carcinoma on the forehead. For removal by cutting current, the surgeon should wait at least 5 minutes after anesthetic infiltration for the hemostatic effect of epinephrine. Also, the cutting current is conducted into the tissue more effectively after the anesthetic has diffused through the tissue.

Practice is necessary to produce satisfactory incisions with a cutting current electrode. The normal tissue resistance encountered with a scalpel is not present when using cutting current. It is more difficult to cut smooth, straight, and curved lines. The lack of tissue resistance also allows the electrode to fall deeply into the tissues with potential damage to underlying structures. For tumor excisions, a straight, wire electrode cuts through tissue with greater precision than blade electrodes (Figs. 18–22).

If the power level is set too low, there will be either a failure to cut or a moderate amount of resistance, which keeps the cutting rate quite slow. If the power is too high, there will be exaggerated arcing of the current with excessive smoke production and tissue charring. The power level set-

tings on any instrument are relative and must be adjusted for each procedure. It is best to slowly increase the power level until a satisfactory speed or cutting is achieved without resistance. Pedunculated growths and large skin tags provide excellent material for testing the cutting capabilities of electrosurgical equipment (Fig. 23).

POSTOPERATIVE MANAGEMENT

Most superficial electrosurgical wounds heal very well secondarily with basic wound care principles that apply to most cutaneous surgical wounds. Many surgeons close cutting current wounds. The wounds do not develop tensile

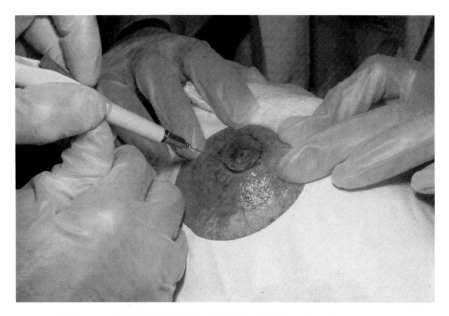

FIG. 19. The surgeon performs the initial cutting current incision using a needle electrode, moving at a brisk, steady pace. The fine, wirelike electrode is omnidirectional and provides precise control of the cut. Activation of power before tissue contact produces a superior cut.

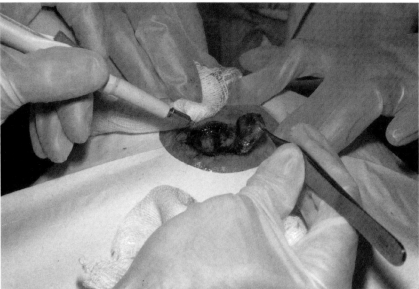

FIG. 20. The electrode undercuts the specimen with very little resistance.

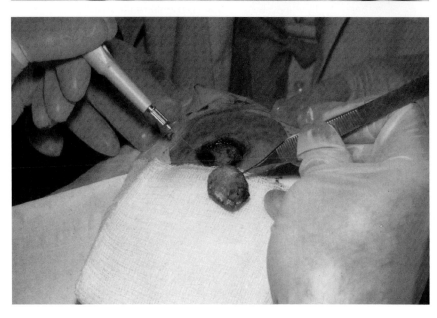

FIG. 21. The needle electrode spot-coagulates individual, persistent bleeders after the initial cutting current incision.

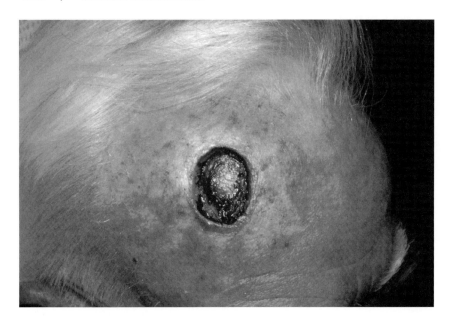

FIG. 22. The final defect may be either closed primarily or left open to heal by secondary intention.

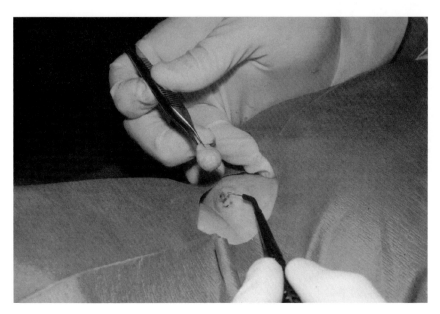

FIG. 23. Fine wire electrodes provide effortless and bloodless cutting current removal of pedunculated growths. Such lesions are excellent for gaining familiarity with cutting current incisions.

strength as rapidly as scalpel wounds. However, they do quite well if good cutting current technique is used so that minimal tissue damage occurs along the lines of incision. The electrosurgically incised wounds that are sutured are weaker for the first 21 days. However, after 21 days, the tensile strength is the same as for scalpel wounds. Closure of an electrosurgically incised wound is best reserved for surgeons experienced and skilled in the use of cutting current.

ADVERSE SEQUELAE AND COMPLICATIONS

Excessive Damage

The greatest hazard of electrosurgery is associated with treatment technique and involves excessive destruction of tissue. Excessive application of electrodesiccation or electrocoagulation current can produce tissue destruction extending far beyond the actual treatment site. As a result, slow healing and tissue necrosis can lead to an unsightly or hypertrophic scar. When treating superficial lesions, such as shave biopsy sites, the electrosurgical current applied is usually referred to as electrodesiccation, which is really a very superficial form of electrocoagulation. The electrical current should stop the bleeding, and the treatment sites should appear slightly pink to pale white but should not have large areas of charred, black, coagulated tissue. A large, charred mass of tissue is quite friable and may dislodge later, resulting in delayed bleeding. Bleeding points are sometimes clamped with forceps or hemostats and then electrocoagulated. Care should be exercised in clamping only a very small amount of tissue, primarily the bleeding vessel only. If a large mass

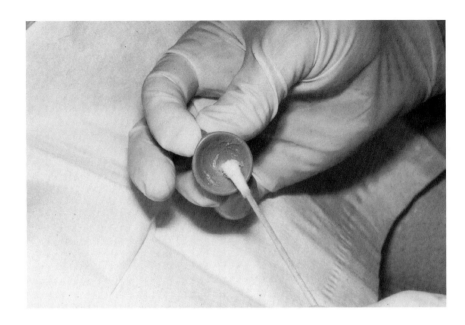

FIG. 24. For electrosurgical procedures on the eyelids, corneal shields provide excellent eye protection. Select the appropriate size of metal or plastic shield, and coat the back with antibiotic ointment.

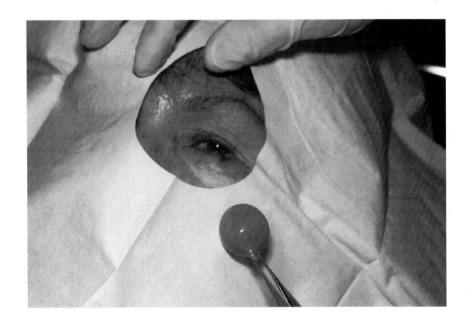

FIG. 25. Place two drops of ophthalmic anesthetic in eye before insertion of shield.

of tissue is clamped, there will be extensive tissue destruction that may lead to tissue breakdown and postoperative bleeding. In addition, a sutured surgical wound is quite intolerant of large amounts of necrotic tissue.

The surgeon must take special care to avoid electrosurgical damage to adjacent areas. When working near the eyes, special shields protect corneas (Fig 24–28).

Histologic Alteration

If heavy coagulation is applied to tissue that is to be excised and submitted for pathologic study, the electrosurgical destruction may obscure the histologic landmarks. Histologic destruction may be particularly troublesome when the pathologist is attempting to interpret adequate surgical margins around a narrowly excised malignant tumor. Obliteration of histologic features can result from heavy coagulation used to control bleeding. Also, cutting current used in tumor removal can produce a broad band of histologic destruction.

Electrical Shock and Burns

The risk of significant shock is quite minimal. All modern medical electrical devices should have an adequate three-pronged grounding plug. Most units are designed so that treatment circuit is isolated from the power circuit. In the event of an electrical malfunction within the unit, the exces-

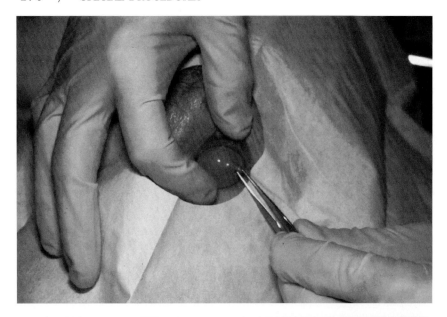

FIG. 26. Carefully insert the shield while retracting the upper eyelid.

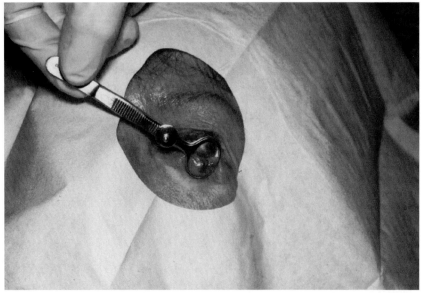

FIG. 27. A chalazion clamp provides additional protection and stabilization for eyelid procedures.

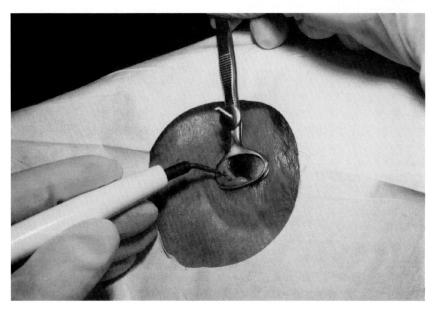

FIG. 28. Take care to not apply electrical current directly to the metal clamp. However, there is minimal risk because any brief current conducted to the metal clamp is harmlessly dispersed over the large contact area.

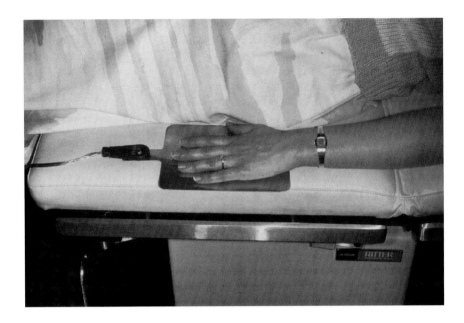

FIG. 29. The hand provides adequate surface contact on a dispersive electrode. However, the patient is actively involved and must remember to maintain contact. The leg or calf provides a more reliable surface contact.

sive current should be diverted to the electrical ground. The patient should not be connected to an earthed ground. If there is an electrical malfunction, the aberrant electrical current could find the path of least resistance to the earth through the patient and into the grounded examination table.

The most common form of shock that a patient may experience occurs during simple electrodesiccation. If the patient has a very small area of skin contact with a grounded examination table, there can be an arcing of electrical current. A shock is noticed, but this is usually not destructive and is not a significant hazard.

A dispersive electrode plate minimizes these problems. However, most high-voltage generators used for light electrodesiccation do not need dispersion. Cutting current machines and heavy coagulators always need a dispersive electrode. Care should be taken to make sure that there are several centimeters of skin contact with a dispersive electrode. A small contact area may produce an electrode burn (Fig. 29).

Cardiac Pacemaker Interference

Modern cardiac pacemakers are very well shielded and provide excellent rejection of any external electrical interference. The risk of damage to a cardiac pacemaker from elec-

trosurgery is negligible. The only theoretical risk with electrosurgery is the abnormal interpretation of impulses by the pacemaker sensor. Most cardiac pacemakers are of the demand type. When the pacemaker senses normal electrical activity, the pacemaker fails to provide stimulus to the heart. In the absence of intrinsic pacing, a demand pacemaker takes over control of the heart. It is during this control that the pacer can misinterpret electrosurgical energy as cardiac electrical activity. If the pacemaker confuses these impulses with cardiac activity, the pacemaker stops supplying impulses to the heart. However, once the extraneous impulses cease, the pacemaker resumes control of the cardiac activity. Thus, if electrosurgical treatments are applied briefly, there should be no more than a brief pause in cardiac activity, much like that of a premature ventricular contraction. Electrosurgical bursts should be less than 5 seconds in pacemaker patients.

Contamination Risks

A high-frequency electrode tip generates no heat. It has been shown that infection can be transferred on such electrodes. It has now become standard practice either to resterilize treatment electrodes or to use disposable electrodes for the treatment of minor lesions in the office setting.

Another significant contamination potential in the office

FIG. 30. To minimize cross-contamination, the operator should always use a disposable or sterilized electrode and also a disposable protective cover for the handle.

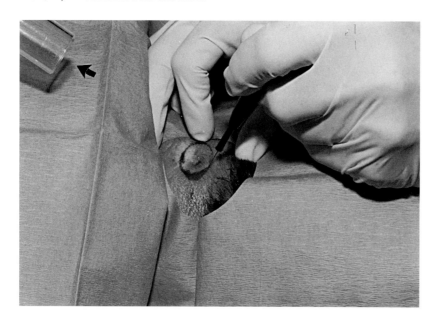

FIG. 31. Cutting current procedures and large lesion destruction produce much smoke and odor. A smoke evacuator near the surgery site keeps the environment more pleasing. Evacuation also minimizes the risk of infected smoke particle inhalation.

setting is from the handling of electrosurgical pencils and cords. Even though the electrode may be changed, the handle may be subject to contamination. A variety of disposable covers is now available, which may be slipped over the treatment handle, minimizing the risk of transfer of organisms through these structures (Fig. 30).

Studies have shown that electrosurgical smoke can carry viable viruses within the particulate matter of the smoke. Smoke evacuation devices are now being used for many forms of electrosurgery (Fig. 31). In addition, the administration of high-frequency electrosurgical current to tissue produces immediate vaporization of fluids with an aerosolization of tissue fluids and blood. The microdroplets may be dispersed a great distance and possibly be inhaled by nearby medical personnel. With present concerns about hepatitis B exposure, as well as human immunodeficiency virus, the prudent physician should consider wearing a mask and eye protection for any electrosurgical procedure.

SUGGESTED READING LIST

1. Bennett RG. Fundamentals of cutaneous surgery. St. Louis, MO: Mosby, 1988:553.
2. Bennett RG, Kraffert CA. Bacterial transference during electrodesiccation and electrocoagulation. Arch Dermatol 1990;126:751.
3. Burdick, KH. Electrosurgical apparatus and their application in dermatology. Springfield, IL: Charles C Thomas, 1966.
4. Elliott JA Jr. Electrosurgery: its use in dermatology, with a review of its development and technologic aspects. Arch Dermatol 1966;94:340.
5. Goldwyn RM. Bovie: The man and the machine. Ann Plast Surg 1979; 2:135.
6. Pierce JA. Electrosurgery. New York: Wiley Medical, 1986.
7. Pollack SJ. Electrosurgery of the skin. New York: Churchill Livingstone, 1991.
8. Sebben JE. Cutaneous electrosurgery. Chicago: Year Book Medical, 1989.
9. Sebben JE. Electrosurgery and cardiac pacemakers. J Am Acad Dermatol 1983;9:457.
10. Sebben JE. Principles of electrosurgery: high-frequency modalities. J Dermatol Surg Oncol 1988;14:367.
11. Sebben JE. The hazards of electrosurgery. J Am Acad Dermatol 1987; 16:869.
12. Watson AB, Loughman J. The surgical diathermy: principles of operation and safe use. Anaesth Intens Care 1978;6:310.

Textbook of Dermatologic Surgery, edited by John L. Ratz.
Lippincott–Raven Publishers, Philadelphia © 1998.

CHAPTER 28

Dermabrasion

R. Steven Padilla and John M. Yarborough, Jr.

HISTORY

The term *dermabrasion* is of recent vintage. Today it is used to describe a procedure in which skin, particularly the epidermis, is removed in variable amounts. This procedure also removes some depths of the supporting connective tissue. The means by which this is accomplished is primarily mechanical and can be with the use of sandpaper, diamond fraises, or a revolving wire brush.

The technique was used in ancient times by Egyptians to remove blemishes and smooth the skin. At that time they used pumice and alabaster as the abrading tools. Modern advances in dermabrasion began in 1905 with the German physician Kromayer. He was the first physician to formulate a method of skin abrasion. His early writings described its use for postacne scarring, and his innovations in the technique included the use of carbon dioxide "snow" to firm and anesthetize the skin, the development of skin punches, and the concept of power-driven instruments.

In 1928 Shie reported the use of dental drills to remove tattoos, and in 1935 Janson described the use of a stiff-bristle brush to abrade tattoos. The use of common sandpaper was introduced by the American plastic surgeon Iverson in 1947.

Iverson also used this technique to remove a facial tattoo induced by gun powder, and in 1953 he reported on the technique to treat postacne scarring.

The greatest advances in the technique are attributable to an American dermatologist, Abner Kurtin. He, along with Noel Robbins, developed and produced the instruments of today, which include the modified power-driven instruments and skin refrigerants to aid in dermabrasion. Robbins founded the Robbins Instrument Company and eventually produced and marketed wire brushes and diamond fraises.

Although the indications for the use of dermabrasion have expanded, the basic technique as developed by Kurtin remains essentially unchanged.

PREOPERATIVE PLANNING

One of the key, if not the major, predictor of successful dermabrasion is proper patient selection. Since this is a cosmetic surgical procedure, a prospective consultation session is essential. At this time, a thorough history, review of systems, and pertinent physical examination should be performed. A major portion of the session should entail an explanation of the risks, complications, and potential alternative procedures available to the patient. At this visit an assessment is made of the patient's candidacy and consequent realistic expectation of the outcome. Assuming a particular level of skill as a physician and dermabrasion surgeon, coupled with knowledge of the technique, the real

R. Steven Padilla: Department of Dermatology, University of New Mexico School of Medicine, 4775 Indian School Road NE, Suite 100, Albuquerque, NM 87110.

John M. Yarborough, Jr.: Tulane University Medical School, New Orleans, LA 70115.

outcome should be matched as closely as possible to the patient's expectation. If these parameters are matched with care, a favorable outcome for the patient and physician can be achieved.

CONSULTATION AND PATIENT EVALUATION

The consultation appointment should be scheduled in a comfortable atmosphere with adequate time allotted to address all the patient's concerns. The session usually begins with the patient's request for evaluation and information on the specific procedure. An initial history should be taken and specific questions asked to determine whether there are any contraindications to the procedure. There are major and minor contraindications to dermabrasion, and they should be considered carefully (Table 1). Historical information about the patient's tendency to form scar, inability to tan or form irregular pigmentation (hyperpigmentation and hypopigmentation), and specific history of herpes simplex infections should be sought. Ask specific questions about underlying illnesses such as connective tissue disorders, cold intolerance, or Raynaud's phenomenon. An individual with a history of Raynaud's disease or cryoglobulinemia may not be a candidate for dermabrasion if a refrigerant is used to chill the patient's skin. Medication usage should be reviewed carefully, specifically for drugs that may inhibit healing, extend bleeding time, or alter the patient's mental status.

PHYSICAL EXAMINATION

The relevant physical examination should be undertaken to determine the type of defect or the condition for which the patient desires the dermabrasion. Careful attention should be placed on the type and location of the disease. Dermabrasion has been used for numerous conditions including those listed in Table 2. Dermabrasion is most often used to improve cosmesis by correction or remodeling of facial scarring. Scars should be evaluated for their suitability for treatment by dermabrasion. Scars such as deep, ice pick–type scars may not be modified appreciably by dermabrasion alone. Evaluate the scars for the degree of response to a middermal skin planing. If there are wide furrows or deep, ice pick–type scars, multiple procedures may be necessary for maximal

TABLE 28-1. *Dermabrasion contraindications*

Burns
  Deep thermal
  Chemical
Congenital ectodermal defect
History of keloids
History of hypertrophic scars (relative)
Radiodermatitis (severe)
Pyoderma
Psychosis
Viral infections (active or those that can be reactivated)

TABLE 28-2. *Conditions treated with dermabrasion*

Acne rosacea
Actinically damaged skin
Active acne
Adenoma sebaceum
Angiofibromas of tuberous sclerosis
Basal cell carcinomas (superficial type)
Blast tattoos (gunpowder)
Chloasma
Chronic radiation dermatitis (mild)
Congenital pigmented nevi
Darier's disease
Dermatitis papillaris capillitii
Early operative scars
Facial wrinkle lines
Favre–Racouchot syndrome
Fox–Fordyce disease
Freckles
Hair transplantation (elevated recipient sites)
Hemangiomas
Hypertrophic scars
Keratoacanthomas
Lentigines
Lichen amyloidosis
Lichenified dermatoses
Linear epidermal nevus
Discoid lupus erythematosus
Mibelli's porokeratosis
Multiple pigmented nevi
Multiple seborrheic keratoses
Multiple trichoepitheliomas
Neurotic excoriations
Postacne scars
Pseudofolliculitis barbae
Rhinophyma
Scleromyxedema
Smallpox or chickenpox scars
Striae distensae
Syringomas
Syrinocystadenoma papilliferum
Tattoos (decorative and traumatic)
Telangiectasia
Traumatic scars
Verrucous nevus
Vitiligo
Xanthelasma
Xeroderma pigmentosum

improvement. Careful evaluation of the patient's potential for dyspigmentation should be noted.

PATIENT DISCUSSION AND INFORMED CONSENT

At this time the physician should explain to the patient the realistic potential for correction of the skin defect by dermabrasion. This is also part of the preoperative preparation. All of the risks, complications, general costs, and alternative procedures and what is expected of the patient during and after the procedure should be explained. Given the anatomic site and disease being treated, a realistic appraisal of the possible complications, the most common being dyspigmentation, infection, and scarring, should be explained. An opportunity should be given to the patient to ask questions. Answer them honestly and frankly. Explain to the patient the probable or realistic expectations from the physician's perspective that one would have for a favorable outcome. Describe the procedures that will occur during surgery to reassure the patient and to alleviate anxiety associated with the unknown. If all has gone well during this session and you agree that the patient is a candidate for the procedure, a signed informed-consent form should be executed by both parties and the procedure scheduled. It may be useful to have the patient take the written informed-consent form home to reread so that the patient can have a more thorough understanding of the procedure, and to permit the patient to think of additional questions. At this same time, give the patient written office materials describing the technique and the postoperative course and management. It is important to remember that a physician performing a cosmetic surgical procedure is held to a higher standard of ensuring informed consent than a physician performing other types of procedures.

DERMABRASION TEST SPOTS

Many surgeons find that a test spot close to the area of the desired dermabrasion can be quite helpful in exposing the patient to the planned procedure (Fig. 1). This allows them to experience in limited fashion the procedure and outcome. It is important to note that the result of the test spot may not be predictive of the overall outcome. A test-spot dermabrasion is considered a very conservative approach before engaging in the full dermabrasion procedure and may be valuable to both the patient and the physician. One's clinical judgment as to whether this is a necessary preoperative procedure is essential. Usually a 1-cm area is abraded under a local anesthetic in an area representative of the condition but that at the same time is somewhat obscured by normal anatomy if further treatment is not desired.

EQUIPMENT

The standard equipment includes a dermabrator and a choice of planing tips that includes diamond fraises, serrated wheels and wire brushes, cryogenic spray, and the standard surgical tray. (Figs. 2–4).

The choice of dermabrator is operator dependent, and various machines have been developed over the years. A major consideration in choosing a particular piece of equipment is the physician's level of comfort with its use and the desired rotational speed and/or torque needed to perform the procedure. Most machines are electrically powered, but some are driven by compressed nitrogen gas. Compressed-gas units are capable of generating greater torque and higher rotational

FIG. 1. Test spot, right posterior ear. Note color and texture of abraded area.

speed. The need to constantly replenish and store nitrogen gas cylinders has been a drawback to their wide use. Currently the electrically powered units are the most convenient and feasible to use. For years, a cable-driven unit was the standard machine, but since the early 1980s, smaller electrically powered, handheld machines have been developed. The cable-driven unit is a motor attached to a cable with the dermabrator tip inserted into the handpiece. This machine is capable of generating rotational speeds in the range of 800 to 1,200 rpm. This unit is used less now because of its

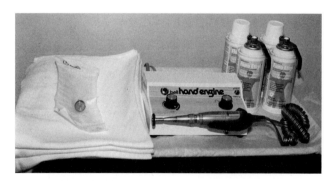

FIG. 2. Standard dermabrasion equipment tray.

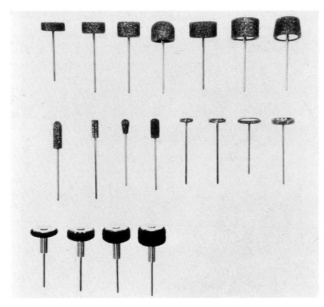

FIG. 3. Planning devices: the wheel, fraise, and wire brush.

potential for frictional burnout of the cable and the distressing, high-pitched noise, which can be upsetting to the patient and surgeon at the time of the procedure.

One of the most common and useful, smaller handheld machines is the Bell international unit (Fig. 2). The electrical abraded cord is attached to a comfortable handheld unit; the abrading tool is placed in the unit's tip. The handpiece is easily maneuverable, and the speed of the rotating tip can be controlled by graduated pressure applied to a foot switch. The abrader speeds generated from this machine range from 400 to 33,000 rpm. One shortcoming of this unit is less torque, but this does not appear to be a serious drawback to carrying out the procedure.

Abrading Tools

The choices of end pieces or cutting tools are the diamond fraise, the serrated wheel, and the wire brush (Fig. 3). Most often, the diamond fraise is the tool of choice but, again, the specific tool is operator dependent.

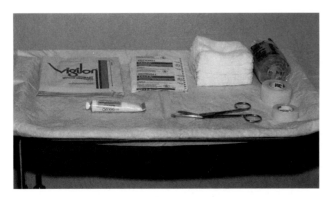

FIG. 4. Postdermabrasion bandage tray.

Diamond Fraise

The fraises are usually stainless steel wheels with industrial-grade diamonds bonded to them. They are graded according to barrel width, shape, and coarseness of the diamonds. The choice of the fraise depends on the anatomic site, the skin and scar contour, the area treated, and the depth of the abrasion desired. In general, the more course or rough the diamond surface and the faster the cutting speed, the greater the penetration into tissues. For a beginning surgeon, a greater margin of safety is given by the use of a wide-barrel fraise with a fine grade of diamonds.

Wire Wheel

The wire brush is probably the second most commonly used cutting tool and was the most widely used tip in the early development of the technique. The brush itself is made of stainless steel wire; bristles may be slightly angulated or straight. They also tend to disseminate particulate matter, blood, and tissue over the operating field. More care must be exerted when using a wire brush because of the potential for more rapid and deeper tissue planing. Greater injury obviously contributes to greater tissue damage and a greater potential for a complication.

Serrated Wheel

The serrated wheel is a circular wheel having on its surface small spikes. The spikes are more widely spaced on a barrel-type tip than the bristles on a wire brush and therefore create a greater likelihood of tissue gouging. This particular tip is not used as often today, and its use is recommended for a surgeon with a higher level of skill because it has greater potential for tissue damage and is difficult to control.

CARE OF EQUIPMENT

Regular maintenance of equipment is essential. The machine should be checked periodically to ensure that there are no breaks in the electrical cords and that the moving parts are regularly lubricated. All of the equipment should be thoroughly cleaned and sterilized. Before sterilization the fraises, brushes, or wheels should be cleaned manually with a wire brush to ensure the removal of all particulate matter. The instruments can be packaged individually or in surgical trays, depending on the surgeon's needs.

TECHNIQUE

Preoperative Preparation

Before undertaking the procedure, consider several alternatives that may enhance the overall surgical outcome. Retinoid acid 0.05% cream has been used in pretreatment of facial skin to shorten the time of reepithelization and possibly to reduce the incidence of postoperative milia formation and hyperpigmentation. Preoperative punch grafting, punch elevation, or excision of prominent punctate scars before dermabrasion appears to enhance the overall cosmetic appearance. Consideration should be given to these latter techniques for deep pock marks, sinus tracts, or irregular, deep scarring. Postoperative injection of finely furrowed or gradually sloping scars with injectable collagen can also be helpful in improving the overall outcome of the procedure.

Preoperative Medication and Local Anesthetic

Consciousness-altering drugs may be used with a local anesthetic to decrease patient anxiety and aid in pain reduction. Before their use, reevaluate the patient's current medications. Ask about prescription and nonprescription items as well as illicit drug usage. Many drugs have an effect not only on the patient's mental state, but also on respiratory and cardiovascular status. Use of consciousness-altering drugs requires close clinical observation. Pulse oximetry monitors blood oxygenation, and cardiac behavior is visualized by electrocardiography. With rare exception, unconsciousness is unnecessary and patient cooperation is desirable during the procedure.

The choice of anesthetic is a personal one. The procedure is usually performed with the patient under light sedation in an outpatient setting. A mild hypnotic agent can be prescribed the night before. Oral dimenhydrinate (Dramamine) in a dose of 100 to 200 mg before retiring ensures a good night's rest. On the day of the procedure the patient may be given an oral dose of the same agent or 100 mg of secobarbital sodium (Seconal). An intramuscular injection of meperidine hydrochloride (50 to 100 mg) is also useful and preferred by many surgeons. Before beginning the procedure an intravenous drip may be started with 5% dextrose and water. Maintain the line throughout the procedure to allow for the administration of additional medications at the beginning of the procedure, which may include diazepam (5 mg) or meperidine (50 mg). Both may be given as an intravenous bullous injection to provide additional sedation. In addition the intravenous line allow for venous access in the event thata reversing agent is needed to counteract the effects of meperidine hydrochloride. Shorter-acting injectable imidazole medications are becoming more frequently used, since their margin of safety is greater and they appear to have greater anxiolytic effects. Some surgeons prefer intramuscular over intravenous administration. Atavan (lorazepam) is a drug often used. The goals of these medications are pain relief and anxiety reduction.

At the beginning of the procedure some surgeons perform a regional facial nerve block with 1% lidocaine either plain or with epinephrine (1:200,000), but it is not essential. Newer techniques such as tumescent anesthesia, which entails the infiltration of saline fluid containing dilute lidocaine, bicarbonate, and epinephrine, are also now being used. Tumescent anesthesia provides excellent local anesthesia and sometimes obviates need for use of cryogenic agents except when rigid skin is necessary for the wire brush technique. The disadvantage of tumescent anesthesia is the obliteration of cutaneous typography that is essential to ensure proper abrading of scars.

Preoperative antibiotics are not generally necessary. Prophylactic antiviral agents have been shown to be effective in preventing recurrences of facial herpes simplex. Acyclovir, Valacyclovir and Famvir have been effectively used to prevent recurrent herpes simplex in the dosage of 1 g per day for 10 days beginning 3 days before surgery.

Surgical Technique

After sedation and local anesthesia, the patient is placed in a comfortable, mobile position. The area to be abraded is positioned to be easily accessible to the surgeon and assistant. Whether the surgeon and assistant stand or are seated is determined by the anatomic site being abraded. For facial scar dermabrasion the surgeon often stands because standing allows for easier maneuverability of the operator. An armboard may be used for dermabrasion of an extremity; in this case the operator could easily be seated.

A standard sterile surgical tray should be within easy reach of the surgeon and assistant. It usually includes the refrigerant, sterile 4 × 4 gauze pads, a gauze wrap, gentian violet, cotton-tip swab sticks, epinephrine, and the antibiotic ointment of choice to be used to cover the site before bandaging.

Before facial dermabrasion, prechill the patient's skin by the direct application of ice packs for 30 minutes before the procedure (Fig. 5). Prechilling enhances the effectiveness of the local cryospray anesthesia that is later administered. In the case of a facial dermabrasion, some surgeons begin by painting the patient's face with gentian violet. If gentian violet is used, the area painted should extend slightly into the hairline and approximately 1 cm below the jaw line. This

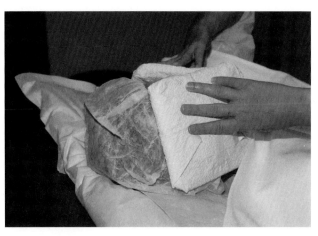

FIG. 5. Predermabrasion face ice-pack.

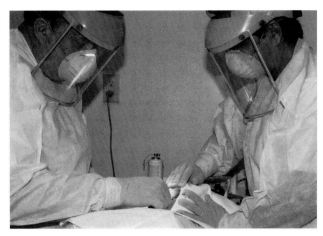

FIG. 6. Operative attire: face mask, face protector, and gloves.

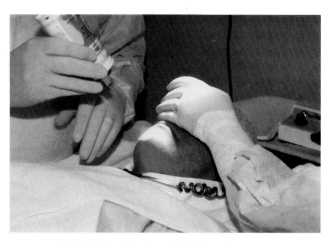

FIG. 7. Application of refrigerant spray.

mask gives the operator a map of the area to be abraded and acts as a gauge to the effectiveness of the dermabrasion. Cover the patient's eyes with gauze and goggles; apply sterile ointment to the intervening skin to ensure a good seal. This enhances eye protection. The depth of penetration is gauged by observation of the underlying tissues. The papillary dermis depth can be recognized as very fine collagenous fibrils with pinpoint bleeding, whereas the deeper reticular dermis reveals coarser collagen fibers.

The correct operating attire should be fitted to the surgeon and the assistant (Fig. 6). This usually consists of rubber gloves, gown, and a plastic facial mask. It is helpful for the assistant to wear cotton gloves over the rubber gloves. This allows for a better grip of the patient's skin and adds protection from the freezing agent.

A facial dermabrasion usually begins with the surgeon standing to the side of the patient that is most comfortable to the surgeon, allowing for a full range of motion of the dominant hand.

One should plan to perform the dermabrasion in subunits. Plan areas that are to be abraded in 2-inch squares; in addition, it may be helpful to border this area with gauze or cotton towels, but this is not essential. Three-point tension is placed on the skin by the operator and the assistant, and the topical refrigerant sprayed onto the site for 20 to 30 seconds until the skin is firm to touch and covered by white frost (Fig. 7). Care should be taken not to freeze the skin too deeply, particularly over bony prominences such as the mandible, zygomatic arch, chin, and forehead. Extensive, deep freezing has been associated with postoperative scarring.

When the skin is frozen to the desired firmness, the area is abraded (Fig. 8). The motion is up and down or circular with the fraise but unidirectionally with the brush, away from vital structures such as the eye. Abrasion depth is determined by the depth of the scar, but in general the surgeon does not go deeper than the midreticular dermis (Fig. 9). How aggressively and deeply one abrades is determined by the

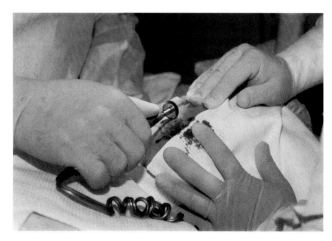

FIG. 8. Skin abrasion with wire brush. Note the grasp of the instrument and the perpendicular direction of movement of the wire brush.

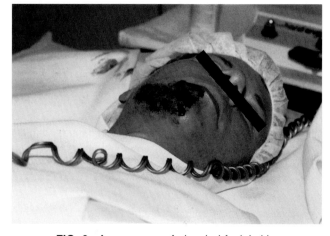

FIG. 9. Appearance of abraded facial skin.

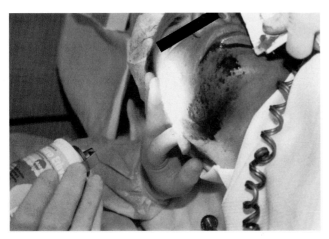

FIG. 10. Application of refrigerant to adjacent area of skin to be abraded.

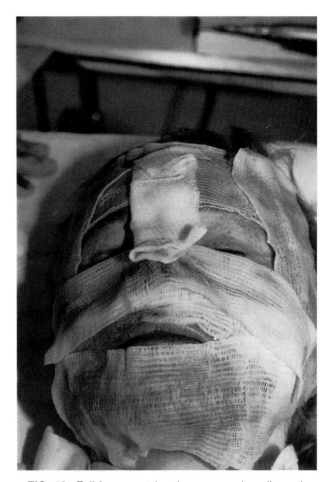

FIG. 12. Full-face, postabrasion gauze adrenalin soak.

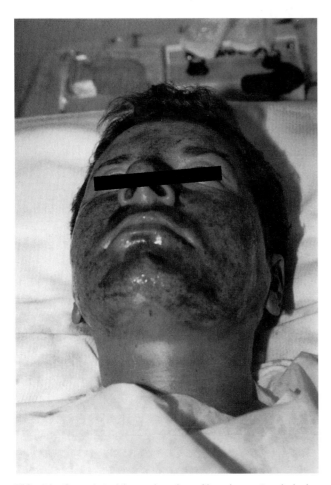

FIG. 11. Completed face abrasion. Abrasion extends below the jaw line.

surgeon's level of skill and experience, but in general it is best to be conservative to avoid complications such as scarring.

After a section is abraded, cover it with gauze or a cotton towel. In moving to the next area, take care not to refreeze the adjacent skin edge because this will create more tissue damage and potential for scarring (Figs. 10 and 11). Pressure is applied to the previous area to aid in hemostasis. If necessary, gauze pledgets soaked in epinephrine 1 : 100,000 can be used to control bleeding and to relieve postoperative stinging (Fig. 12).

The most popular freezing agents used now are Frigiderm and Fluorethel. Ethylene chloride was popular in years past, but because of its flammable nature and explosive properties, it is rarely used today. These newer agents cool skin to approximately $-40°C$ to $-42°C$ in about 25 seconds. Cryogens that freeze the skin to a lower temperature of $-60°C$ are associated with more tissue necrosis and potential for scarring. Conduct the dermabrasion in an orderly fashion of freezing and planing. A logical order is to begin to work from the forehead, then move to the temples and cheeks followed by the mandibular area, nose, and periorbital and perioral regions. After the complete procedure is performed a reabrasion of deeper scars or areas of persistent gentian violet can be performed. More selective or precise abrasion can be performed with a smaller or diamond-tipped fraise.

Dermabrasion can also be used to revise or camouflage scars from traumatic or surgical injury. The procedure is performed in a similar fashion, not necessarily with a local freezing agent, but with just a local anesthetic. This is quite effective in camouflaging scars when performed within the first 6 to 8 weeks of repair of initial injury.

Postoperative Management

Postoperative management begins with the application of the bandage and instructions to the patient about the cleansing technique. Review the use of the topical agents and the precautions and expected outcomes of the procedure. Emphasize the need to keep follow-up appointments. The instructions should be given orally and in written form. This is also an ideal opportunity for further instructions to the patient by the nurse, who could demonstrate application of the bandages and discuss use of pain medications or the reinstitution of previously prescribed medications. Give the patient opportunity to ask questions about what to expect and the materials needed during this healing phase.

For a face dermabrasion a full-face dressing is usually

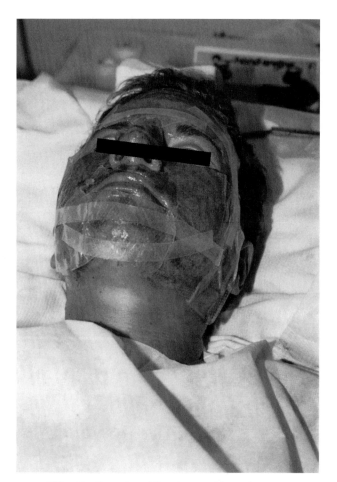

FIG. 14. Completed first layer of face dressing.

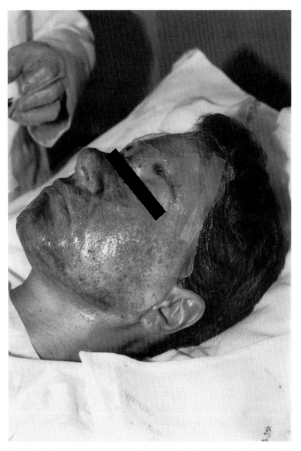

FIG. 13. Bandage application: beginning application of biologic dressing after topical antibiotic layer.

applied to the entire abraded surface. Having achieved hemostasis, a layer of antibiotic ointment is applied. Next, a precisely cut, synthetic, nonstick surgical dressing such as polyethylene oxide (Telfa) petroleum jelly type of gauze or a biologic dressing is applied (Figs. 13 and 14). This is followed by layers of gauze squares and finally a gauze wrap to keep the dressing in place (Fig. 15). The wound usually exudes serosanguinous material for several days after surgery, and it is important to apply highly absorbent dressing materials. The patient may be given prescriptions for pain, swelling, or sleep and instructed to return home in the company of a friend or relative if sedating agents have been used. In addition, the patient should be instructed to sleep with their head at a 45- to 60-degree angle to help decrease postoperative swelling. The patient should be instructed to return to the surgeon's office the following day for a dressing change. At this time, the bulky, absorbent dressing need not be reapplied. The newer biologic dressings may be applied and are easier to use; they appear to decrease pain and promote accelerated wound healing. Thereafter, the patient can clean and reapply the dressing once or twice daily. Topical cleansing can be done with normal saline or a solution of water and very dilute hydrogen peroxide (1 to 2 drops per ounce of water) followed by the reapplication of the antibi-

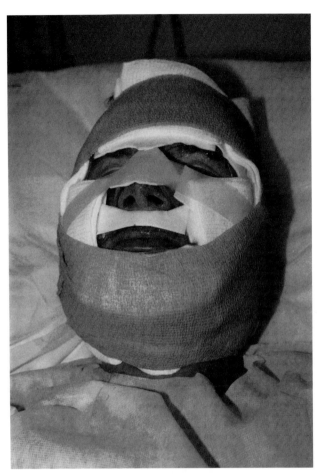

FIG. 15. Full-face dressing with second layer of gauze for absorption and final Coban layer for stability and mild compression.

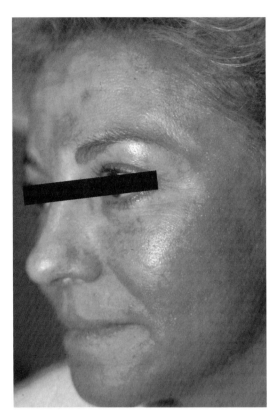

FIG. 16. Postoperative facial milia.

otic ointment or emollient. The patient should be seen in 5 days or sooner if necessary. It is always important to reassure the patient that he or she can call you at any time with questions. It is also nice to have your nurse call in a day or two following the procedure to see how the patient is doing. Depending on the depth of the abrasion, reepithelialization usually occurs within 5 to 15 days. For 3 months after surgery the patient must avoid excessive sun exposure. After reepithelialization, sunscreens should be used routinely. This may help circumvent hyperpigmentation.

Persistent splotchy erythema can be considered prodromal to cicatrization. Early application of a topical corticosteroid-impregnated tape can reduce the erythema and circumvent scarring. Reassuring your patient at all stages of the procedure is important.

Adverse Sequelae and Complications

A complication or untoward event after dermabrasion is an uncommon problem. However, given the desired outcome of improving cosmesis, the relative risk-benefit ratio if a complication occurs is greater. These events may be defined

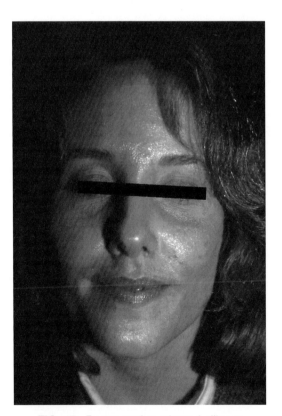

FIG. 17. Postoperative rebound oiliness.

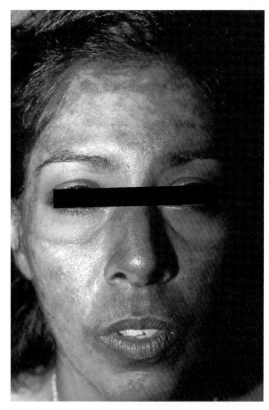

FIG. 18. Postoperative hyperpigmentation.

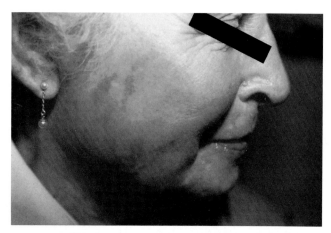

FIG. 20. Splotchy erythema, prodrome to scar.

as any condition or state which makes the postoperative course or event more complex or severe or works against or opposes the ultimate desired effect (Figs. 16–24). Common untoward effects are listed in Table 3. Careful attention to patient evaluation, their expectations, and the technical aspects of the procedure helps to limit complications. For example, the elimination of the patient as a candidate for the procedure in view of a history of hypertrophic scarring or taking an inappropriate oral medication that would lead to a complication is paramount.

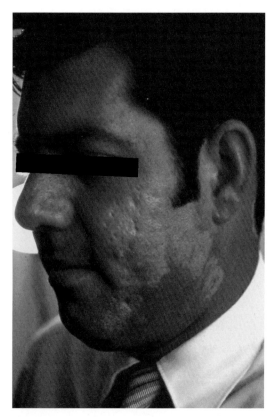

FIG. 19. Postoperative, persistent splotchy erythema and hypopigmentation.

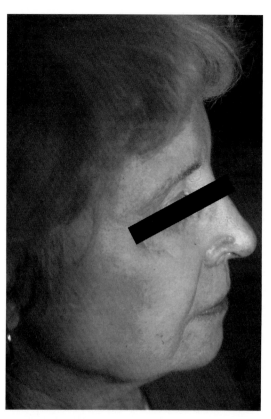

FIG. 21. Scar resolution after application of Cordran tape plus intralesional steroids.

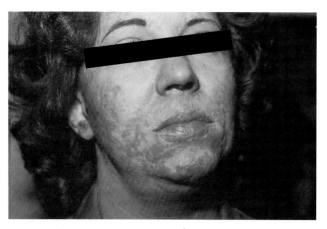

FIG. 24. Koebner phenomenon after scar planing of discoid lupus erythematosis.

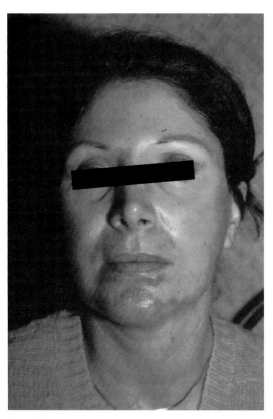

FIG. 22. Postoperative hypertrophic scar on chin.

Milia, which are common sequelae, usually resolve with use of tretinoin or a mild abrading pad such as a Buff Puff. Hyperpigmentation, which is predictable in patients of intermediate color, may be corrected by propitious use of hydroquinones, but hypopigmentation often is permanent. Hypertrophic scarring usually can be avoided by meticulous attention to depth of planing and extent of freeze, particularly over areas of bony prominence. Potential for scarring in areas of persistent splotchy erythema may be averted by early application of a topical corticosteroid–impregnated tape. If scars are already apparent, intralesional corticosteroid injections may be necessary. The avoidance of viral infections such as herpes simplex reactivation can be enhanced by attention to the history and prophylactic use of acyclovir. Bacterial infections, which are rare, require appropriate topical and systemic antibiotics. Any unusual or per-

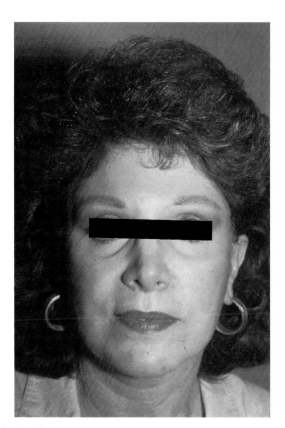

FIG. 23. Scar resolution after Cordran tape application plus intralesional steroids.

TABLE 28-3. *Untoward reactions after dermabrasion*

I. Sequence
  A. Milia
  B. Rebound oiliness
  C. Acneiform eruption
  D. Edema
II. Complications
  A. Pigmentary
    1. Hyperpigmentation
    2. Hypopigmentation
  B. Cicatricial
    1. Hypertrophic
      a. Deep dermal cold injury
      b. Drug induced (isotretinoin)
    2. Atrophic
      a. Deep dermal to subcutaneous abrasion
  C. Infections
    1. Viral
    2. Bacterial
    3. Fungal
  D. Reactive
    1. Persistent erythema
    2. Koebnerization
III. Unrealistic expectations

sistent deviation from the normal course of healing warrants intense evaluation.

SUGGESTED READING LIST

1. Agrawal K, Veliath AJ, Mishra S, Panda KN. Xeroderma pigmentosum: resurfacing versus dermabrasion. Br J Plast Surg 1992;45:311.
2. Alt TH, Coleman WP III, Hanke CW, Yarborough JM. Dermabrasion. In: Coleman WP III, Hanke CW, Alt TH, Asken S, eds. Cosmetic surgery of the skin. Philadelphia: BC Decker, 1991;147.
3. Benedetto AV, Griffin TD, Benedetto EA, Humeniuk HM. Dermabrasion: therapy and prophylaxis of the photoaged face. J Am Acad Dermatol 1992;27:439.
4. Coleman WP. A visit to the office of Dr. John Yarborough. J Dermatol Surg Oncol 1994;20:332.
5. Coleman WP. Dermabrasion and hypertrophic scars. Int J Dermatol 1991;30:629.
6. Coleman WP, Klein JA. Use of the tumescent technique for scalp surgery, dermabrasion, and soft tissue reconstruction. J Dermatol Surg Oncol 1992;18:130.
7. Drake DB, Morgan RF, Cooper PH. Shave excision and dermabrasion for facial angiofibroma in tuberous sclerosis. Ann Plast Surg 1992;28:377.
8. Drake LA, Ceilley RI, Cornelison RL, et al. Guidelines of care for dermabrasion. J Am Acad Dermatol 1994;31:654.
9. Dwyer CM, Kerr RE, Knight SL, Walker E. Pseudomelanoma after dermabrasion. J Am Acad Dermatol 1993;28:263.
10. Fulton JE. The prevention and management of postdermabrasion complications. J Dermatol Surg Oncol 1991;17:431.
11. Goodman G. Dermabrasion using tumescent anesthesia. Dermatol Surg Oncol 1994;20:802.
12. Grimes PE, Hunt SG. Considerations for cosmetic surgery in the black population. Clin Plast Surg 1993;20:27.
13. Gross DJ. Spot dermabrasion. J Dermatol Surg Oncol 1994;20:699 (letter to the editor).
14. Hamm H, Metze D, Brocker EB. Hailey-Hailey disease. Arch Dermatol 1994;130:1143.
15. Harris DR, Noodleman FR. Combining manual dermasanding with low-strength trichloroacetic acid to improve antinically injured skin. J Dermatol Surg Oncol 1994;20:436.
16. Iverson PC. Surgical removal of traumatic tattoos of the face. Plast Reconstr Surg 1947;2:427.
17. Janson P. Eine einfache Methode der Entfernung von Tatowierungen. Dermatol Wochenschr 1935;101:894.
18. Kahn AM, Cohen MJ, Kaplan L, Highton A. Vitiligo: treatment by dermabrasion and epithelial sheet grafting. J Am Acad Dermatol 1993;28:773.
19. Katz BE, MacFarlane DF. Atypical facial scarring after isotretinoin therapy in a patient with previous dermabrasion. J Am Acad Dermatol 1994;30:852.
20. Katz BE, Oca AGS. A controlled study of the effectiveness of spot dermabrasion (''scarabrasion'') on the appearance of surgical scars. J Am Acad Dermatol 1991;24:462.
21. Kirtschig G, Gieler U, Happle R. Treatment of Hailey-Hailey disease by dermabrasion. J Am Acad Dermatol 1993;28:784.
22. Kromayer E. Rotationinstrumente: Ein neues technisches Verfahren in der dermatilogischen Kleinchirurgie. Dermatol Z 1905;12:26.
23. Kurtin A. Corrective surgical planning of skin. Arch Dermatol Syph 1953;68:389.
24. Lusthaus S, Benmeir P, Neuman A, et al. The use of sandpaper in chemical peeling combined with dermabrasion of the face. Ann Plast Surg 1993;31:281.
25. Mancuso A, Farber GA. The abraded punch graft for pitted facial scars. J Dermatol Surg Oncol 1991;17:32.
26. Reserved.
27. Nelson BR, Majmudar G, Griffiths CEM, et al. Arch Dermatol 1994;130:1136.
28. O'Connell JB. EMLA cream in dermabrasion. Plast Reconstr Surg 1994;1310 (letter).
29. Raab B. A new hydrophilic copolymer membrane for dermabrasion. J Dermatol Surg Oncol 1991;170:323.
30. Robbins N. Dr. Abner Kurtin: father of ambulatory dermabrasion. J Dermatol Surg Oncol 1988;14(4):425.
31. Stein RO. Therapeutische Technizismen. Arch Dermatol Syph 1928;155:304.
32. Tezuka T, Saheki M, Kusuda S, Umemoto K. Treatment of nonhairy melanocytic macules by dermabrasion and topical application of 5% hydroquinone monobenzyl ether cream. J Am Acad Dermatol 1993;28:771.
33. Weber PJ, Wulc AE. The use of a contained breathing apparatus to isolate the operator and assistant for aerosolizing procedures including dermabrasion and laser surgery. Ann Plast Surg 1992;29:182.
34. Yarborough JM. Ablation of facial scars by programmed dermabrasion. J Dermatol Surg Oncol 1988; 14:292.
35. Yarborough JM. Dermabrasion by wire brush. J Dermatol Surg Oncol 1987;13:10.
36. Yarborough JM. Preoperative evaluation of the patient for dermabrasion. J Dermatol Surg Oncol 1987; 13:652.

Textbook of Dermatologic Surgery, edited by John L. Ratz.
Lippincott–Raven Publishers, Philadelphia © 1998.

CHAPTER **29**

Chemical Peels

Mark G. Rubin

HISTORY

The concept of chemical peeling of the skin is an old one. There is ample evidence of this type of therapy being used as long ago as the time of the ancient Romans. Since that time, interest in peeling has waxed and waned. Starting in the late 1800s, there was another resurgence of interest in peeling. At that time several authors wrote of their experience with the use of caustic agents for skin peeling.

In the current generation of physicians the fathers of modern chemical peeling are Baker and Gordon, who pioneered chemical peeling with phenol in 1961. Since that time, there has been a general trend toward less aggressive types of peels including trichloroacetic acid (TCA) and, more recently, alpha hydroxy acids (AHAs). The field of chemical peeling and facial rejuvenation continues to evolve. The widespread acceptance of skin care programs, both before and after peeling, has given physicians the ability to achieve better, long-lasting results from peels. However, increased patient interest in lighter peels such as Jessner's solution and glycolic acid has made it more difficult for physicians to master all the peeling agents currently available.

Mark G. Rubin: Lasky Clinic, Beverly Hills, CA 90212.

The purpose of this chapter is to describe peeling techniques with four popular peeling agents. Although there are certainly other peeling agents available, the four agents described in this chapter offer the ability to perform all levels of chemical peeling (Fig. 1).

Chemical peels are classified according to their depth of penetration. Basically, chemical peels are divided into the following levels:

Superficial: Intraepidermal peels
Medium: Peel extends into the papillary dermis
Deep: Peel extends into the reticular dermis

GLYCOLIC ACID

Formula

Currently there are many different types of glycolic acid solutions on the market. Some use free acid; others use partially neutralized acid (which also contains the salt of the acid).

As a general rule, these are all aqueous solutions made

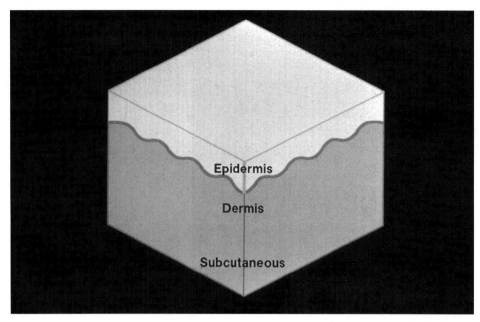

FIG. 1. The levels of chemical peels are classified according to their depth of penetration.

from glycolic acid, water, and in the partially neutralized solution, sodium hydroxide or ammonium hydroxide.

History

Glycolic acid is one of the group of AHAs. Currently it is the AHA most commonly used as a peeling agent. Its use in peeling was first described by Van Scott and Yu in the 1980s. Since then, glycolic acid has grown to be one of the most popular (if not the most popular) peeling agents in the United States and abroad.

Glycolic acid is generally used as a superficial peeling agent. Since it is a fairly new peeling agent, all physicians are not in agreement as to its best use. The debate continues over what is the most effective way to use glycolic acid peels and includes the following:

1. The efficacy of free acid versus partially neutralized acid solutions
2. How often the peels should be repeated
3. What time interval should be allowed between peels
4. How many glycolic acid peels should be performed for maximum benefit
5. What concentrations of glycolic acid solutions should be used

Since the answers to these questions have not been agreed on, presented here is 6 years of experience with them.

Preoperative Planning

Glycolic acid peels are very superficial, intraepidermal peels. They appear best suited for the treatment of rough-textured skin, comedones, and superficial dyschromias. However, unlike other superficial peeling agents, glycolic acid appears to have a more pronounced stimulatory effect on the induction of dermal collagen and glycosaminoglycans, which may lead to tightening of the skin. Therefore in certain patients these peels have the ability to improve superficial wrinkling attributable to papillary dermal elastosis and atrophy. This affect appears to be quite variable from patient to patient. (Fig. 2).

Because of the superficial level of this peel, a singular glycolic acid peel usually gives only subtle improvement. Most patients must undergo several of these peels to achieve their best benefits. Two of these peels, separated by 3 to 4 weeks, followed by reevaluation of the patient's need for more glycolic acid peels versus a more aggressive therapy, is the preferred approach to treatment.

Like all other patients receiving peels, those undergoing glycolic acid peeling seem to do best if the skin has been primed for at least 2 weeks before the peel. However, since many patients undergo glycolic acid peeling to improve very superficial problems with their skin, occasionally the priming regimen for some patients may improve them to such a degree that they do not feel the need to undergo the peel.

The first step in performing a glycolic acid peel is to select the appropriate peeling agent. A partially neutralized 70% solution is preferred. The 70% free acid solutions have a faster penetration with an increased ability to create focal areas of epidermolysis and necrosis, so these solutions are avoided, except in patients who have very "tough" skin (i.e., those who can tolerate a 70% partially neutralized solution for over 8 to 10 minutes without showing erythema). In patients with sensitive skin, still recommended is the use of 70% partially neutralized solution. Plan on leaving it on

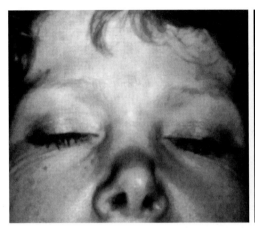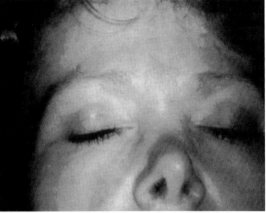

FIG. 2. (A) A woman with fine wrinkles below the eyes. **(B)** The same woman 2 months after a 2-minute, 70% free glycolic acid peel and 10% glycolic acid gel applied twice a day. (From Rubin MG. Manual of chemical peels: superficial and medium depth. Philadelphia: JB Lippincott, 1995.)

the skin for only a short time (approximately 1 minute). Some practitioners prefer to perform the first peel with 30% or 50% free acid. However, the pH of these acids is still quite low (below 2), and these are more reactive than the partially neutralized 70% solution. Therefore the partially neutralized 70% solution is the safest solution initially.

Technique

Gently cleanse the skin with a degreasing agent such as soap and water, alcohol, or a 5% to 10% glycolic acid solution. Acetone scrubs are rarely used, since they are more aggressive as a degreasing routine and they can remove the stratum corneum, causing the glycolic peel to penetrate deeply, thereby increasing the risk of an accidental dermal wound.

Gently apply the glycolic acid solution to the skin with a sable hair brush, large cotton-tipped applicators, or a gauze square. Rubbing the acid into the skin does not seem to appreciably increase the penetration of the acid (as it does with some other peeling agents). Overlapping areas of acid application also have no effect on increasing the penetration of the acid.

Rapidly apply the acid to the entire area to be peeled. The entire face can usually be treated within 15 to 20 seconds. Speed is important, since the longer the acid remains on the skin, the deeper it penetrates. If the acid is applied to the face very slowly, certain areas of the face will be in contact with the acid for longer periods, leading to deeper penetration of the peeling agent in these areas. Normally a timer is started when the peel is applied, to note how long the acid was left in place. This is helpful is gauging the length of time the acid should be left in place in subsequent peels.

When the skin begins to show areas of blotchy erythema, neutralize the peel (Fig. 3). This is the end point of a superficial glycolic acid peel, whether it takes 1 minute or 10 minutes. Neutralization can be accomplished with any solution

or lotion containing a base. A 10% sodium bicarbonate solution is one of the more frequently used agents. The peel can be washed off with water, but this is not as effective in stopping the peel as the use of a true neutralizer with a higher pH.

If the peel is not neutralized when blotchy erythema is noted, the next clinical signs are areas of pronounced erythema, followed by epidermolysis (showing as a gray-white

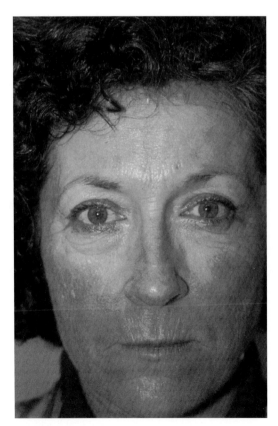

FIG. 3. Diffuse, blotchy erythema signaling the end point of a glycolic acid peel.

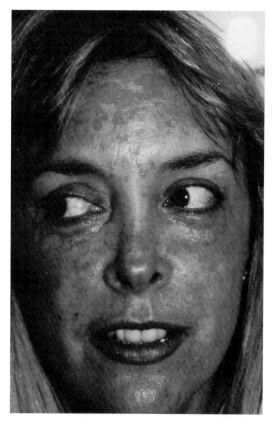

FIG. 4. Epidermolysis and vesiculation resulting from a 3-minute glycolic acid peel performed with 70% free acid.

patch) or vesiculation (Fig. 4). During this time frame the patient feels tingling or stinging, but it is normally fairly mild and never requires sedation or analgesics.

Another important point to keep in mind with glycolic acid peeling is that the acid reacts quite differently with different patients (Fig.5). In some patients erythema develops 1 minute after the acid is applied, whereas in other patients it may be 10 to 15 minutes before any erythema is observed. Therefore watch the patient closely during the peel, and be ready to rapidly neutralize the peel.

Postoperative Management

The majority of patients undergoing glycolic acid peels have mild erythema for 30 to 60 minutes after the peel and then their appearance is normal. It is unusual to see erythema persist for 24 to 48 hours. In addition, anything other than very mild exfoliation (seen as dryness or flaking) is distinctly uncommon. However, if the acid was left in place long enough to create epidermolysis, those areas initially heal with mild crusting.

During the healing phase of 1 to 2 days the patient should avoid the use of all potentially irritating products, including those containing AHAs, retinoic acid, astringents, and facial scrubs. They should wash gently with a mild cleanser such as Cetaphil, Neutrogena, or Dove and apply a bland moisturizer as often as needed. As soon as the skin feels normal, they can resume the use of the home regimen of products.

It is important to counsel the patient undergoing this level of peel that they should not expect to look like they had a peel. This procedure is often called the ''lunch-time peel'' because a patient can have it performed during a lunch break and then return to work in 1 to 2 hours looking normal.

If the patient accidentally had overpeeling and areas of necrosis and crusting develop, the patient should be treated with topical antibiotic ointments and followed closely by the physician until healing is complete.

Complications

Significant complications from glycolic acid peels are extremely rare, since the peel is so superficial. There have been only a few cases of scars developing from glycolic acid peels, and they seem to be due to the failure to terminate

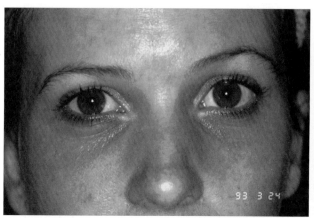

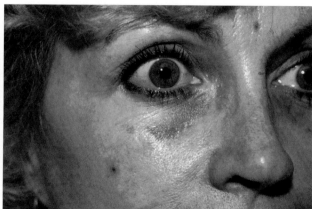

FIG. 5. (A) Pronounced erythema under the eyes 90 seconds after the application of 70% free glycolic acid. **(B)** Vesiculation and erosion under the eyes 3 minutes after the application of 70% free glycolic acid.

the peel at the appropriate times, leading to a deeper peel than intended. If areas of crusting develop after a glycolic acid peel, those areas must be aggressively treated with topical antibiotics. If they fail to resolve rapidly, oral antibiotics and topical compresses with saline or dilute acetic acid are indicated.

The more common complications are quite mild and include erythema lasting from days to a few weeks, increased skin sensitivity lasting a few weeks, and acne flare-ups (presumably a result of comedolytic effect of the peeling agent).

As with any peeling agent capable of causing inflammation in the skin, an occasional patient may have a flare-up of herpes labialis. However, the incidence of herpes flare-ups is less with this type of peel than with more aggressive ones. Similarly, the incidence of postinflammatory hyperpigmentation is much less with glycolic acid peels because of the low levels of inflammation they induce.

JESSNER'S PEEL

Formula

Salicylic acid (14 g)
Resorcinol (14 g)
Lactic acid (85%, 14 g)
Ethanol (QSAD, 100 ML)

History

Jessner's peel, formulated by Max Jessner, is a superficial peel that has enjoyed popularity for many years among both physicians and lay practitioners of peeling. Because of the superficial penetration of this peeling agent, it has an excellent safety record. It is often used to peel nonfacial areas where inadvertent deep peels can create serious complications. When this peel is used on an appropriate peel candidate it can give impressive results. However, because of its superficial level, this peel is often repeated several times to achieve the best results.

Preoperative Planning

Jessner's peel is an intraepidermal peel. Therefore it should only be used in the treatment of intraepidermal problems. The use of this peel in the treatment of dermal defects creates disappointing results. As with any skin peel, the patient's skin should be primed for at least 2 weeks before this peel. This rule is not as important when performing more superficial peels as it is in medium-depth peeling, but in general, patients undergoing Jessner's peel achieve better results if their skin has been primed.

Technique

Gently cleanse the skin with a cleanser such as soap, alcohol, or acetone. Since this is meant to be a superficial peel, there is no need to perform an aggressive scrub to clean the skin. The goal is to remove oil, dirt, and debris, not to scrub off the stratum corneum.

Apply Jessner's solution, most commonly, with a sable hairbrush (Fig. 6). Any type of applicator is appropriate; however, it is important to realize that rubbing the solution into the skin with a gauze sponge creates a deeper penetration of the solution than if it is painted onto the skin with a sable hairbrush.

After the solution is applied to the skin and allowed to

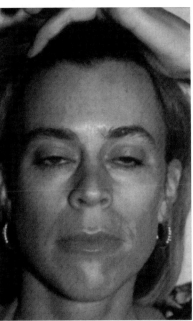

FIG. 6. (A) A woman 10 minutes after two coats of Jessner's solution were applied with a sable hairbrush on the patient's right side and rubbed into the skin with a 2 × 2 gauze on the left side. (B) The same patient 2 days later. The areas of erythema and hypopigmentation are more pronounced on the patient's left side in the infraorbital and chin area (the side to which the acid was applied with a gauze sponge). This is evidence of the increased depth of wounding achieve by rubbing the acid into the skin. (From Rubin MG. Manual of chemical peels: superficial and medium depth. Philadelphia: JB Lippincott, 1995.)

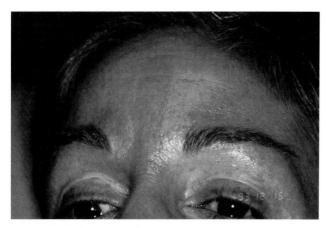

FIG. 7. Dull, white film is evident on the forehead after application of Jessner's solution. Note how easily the film has been removed from the central forehead with a damp cotton ball.

dry for 4 to 5 minutes, it leaves a dull, white film on the skin (Fig. 7). The depth of the peel can be increased by continuing to apply additional coats of the solution every 4 to 5 minutes. As the peel continues to penetrate more deeply with each successive application of the solution, the skin becomes increasingly more erythematous. If additional coats of the solution are applied, the skin begins to show scattered, whitish areas of "frosting." This is believed to be due to the coagulation of protein in the skin. Even at this depth of penetration, Jessner's peel is still only intraepidermal and is relatively free of complications. Jessner's peel of any level creates mild stinging and burning, which can easily be tolerated by patients without the use of analgesics. A few words of encouragement, as well as the use of a handheld fan, are sufficient for the patient's comfort.

Postoperative Management

Jessner's peel creates a darkening of the skin with associated tightening. This generally occurs for 1 to 3 days; then the skin exfoliates for an additional 1 to 4 days. A light or superficial Jessner's peel flakes lightly, whereas the deeper Jessner's peel shows some peeling of the skin similar to that seen with a sunburn.

During the healing phase of these peels the patient is instructed to apply bland emollients as often as needed to keep the skin supple and comfortable. No astringents, scrubs, AHAs, or retinoic acid are allowed during the peeling phase because the skin can be quite sensitive during this time. Most patients can continue a fairly normal business and social life during these peels, and often they can wear makeup over their peeling skin to help allow them to be less self-conscious of their appearance.

Complications

Since Jessner's peel is a superficial peel, complications are uncommon. Occasionally, some patients complain of

persistent erythema lasting several weeks after their peel, but this is self-limited and quite rare.

In certain patients the erythema induced by Jessner's peel may be sufficient to induce postinflammatory hyperpigmentation. Therefore in patients predisposed to this condition it is extremely important to resume the use of bleaching agents and sunscreen immediately after the patient has healed from the peel. Also, remember that since this peel creates inflammation, it may trigger an outbreak of herpes labialis. Therefore patients with a history of herpes labialis should be treated prophylactically with acyclovir 400 mg three times daily.

It has been stated in the literature that the resorcinol in Jessner's peel can create systemic toxicity and that it has a high rate of contact allergy. However, the incidence of contact allergy to resorcinol appears to be less than 0.1%. In addition, the toxicity of resorcinol is only seen in peels using concentrations of resorcinol three times greater than that used in Jessner's solution.

The limiting factor in the use of Jessner's peels appears to be the absorption of salicylic acid. If Jessner's peel is applied to a large surface area at one time (i.e., the face, throat, and arms) it is possible to induce salicylism as a result of the absorption of salicylic acid. Therefore it is prudent to limit the size of the area peeled with Jessner's solution to avoid salicylism.

TRICHLOROACETIC ACID

Formula

Trichloroacetic acid solutions are made using weight-to-volume (w/v) measurements (e.g., a 30% TCA solution is made with 30 g of U.S. Pharmacopeia TCA crystals to which is added distilled water until the total volume equals 100 ml). If 30 g of TCA is added to 100 ml of water, the solution created is 26% w/v.

History

Trichloroacetic acid has been in use as a chemical peeling agent since the early part of this century. However, its efficacy and histologic impact on the skin were not well described until the 1960s. Since that time, TCA peeling has become increasingly popular. Its popularity is based on the following facts: TCA has no systemic toxicity or reports of allergic reaction, TCA solutions are stable for long periods, and several studies have shown the histologic effects of different concentrations of TCA.

Preoperative Planning

Trichloroacetic acid peels can be superficial, medium-depth, or deep. At this time, most physicians agree that deep peeling with TCA is generally a riskier procedure than deep peeling with phenol. Evidence suggests that TCA in concentrations of 50% or higher inherently creates more scarring than do other peeling agents used to create a wound of similar depth. For this reason, TCA is most commonly used for superficial and medium-depth peels. In clinical practice this means that abnormalities in the epidermis and papillary dermis should be amenable to TCA peeling.

As with all patients undergoing skin peeling, the skin must be primed for at least 2 weeks before the peel. The goals of priming are to prepare the skin so that the peeling solution is absorbed uniformly and to stimulate the skin to heal faster from the wound of the peel. Both retinoic acid and AHAs have been shown to thin and compact the stratum corneum, thereby enhancing the penetration of the peeling agent. However, at this time, only retinoic acid has been studied for its ability to speed reepithelialization. It is not known whether AHAs can speed healing as well; therefore for superficial peels with TCA use either tretinoin every night at bedtime or an AHA 8% to 15% product twice daily. If performing a medium-depth peel, tretinoin (Retin-A) is recommended, since the increased speed of reepithelialization for these peels can be very helpful.

The other products routinely used to prime the skin are kojic acid or hydroquinone (both tyrosinase inhibitors). The use of either of these agents in a 2% to 4% concentration mixed with 6% to 10% AHA for at least 2 weeks before the peel appears to decrease the risk of postinflammatory hyperpigmentation. These products are recommended in all patients undergoing superficial or medium-depth TCA peels who have any problems with dyschromia.

Technique

Ask the patient to come to the office without makeup on the day of the peel. Clean the skin with 70% isopropyl alcohol followed by a 10% glycolic acid solution. Apply the solutions with a cotton ball so that the skin is degreased, not aggressively scrubbed.

After the skin has been cleaned, have the patient lie down on an examination table with the head elevated about 45 degrees. Give the patient a facial tissue to dab any tears that may form during the peel and a handheld fan to use to help alleviate any stinging or burning that may occur with the application of the acid. The stinging associated with superficial and medium-depth peels is usually mild enough that analgesics are not needed.

Apply the acid to the skin with a brush, cotton-tipped applicator, or 2×2 gauze. A gauze square that has been folded into quarters is recommended because it allows the TCA to be rubbed into the skin, thereby enhancing its penetration. Apply the acid in the midline of the forehead and proceed to both temples and to the nose. At that time, stop the application to allow the patient's stinging to stop. This is the opportunity to observe the skin changes and frost de-

veloping in the area just peeled. Begin the second stage of application under the left eye starting 2 to 3 mm below the lid margin, then covering the entire left cheek and perioral area. Stop and watch the frost develop. After allowing the patient to rest, begin the third stage below the right eye and extend across the entire right cheek (Fig. 8).

As previously stated, it is imperative to determine the depth of the peel required for appropriate treatment in the patient before performing the peel. Once a decision has been made about depth, a judgment must be made about when that level of a peel has been achieved. With TCA the depth of the peel seems to correlate well with the intensity of the frost observed on the skin.

The types of frost created by superficial or medium-depth TCA peels can be classified into the following levels:

1. Irregular, light frost giving the skin a wispy appearance. This is a superficial, intraepidermal peel (Fig. 9).
2. The skin shows a uniform white color with a strong pink-red background color. This is a superficial peel extending to approximately the dermal-epidermal junction (Fig. 10).
3. The skin shows a solid, intense white frost with no pink or red background. This is a peel that extends into the papillary dermis (Fig. 11).

These levels of frost are guidelines and can vary from patient to patient. However, they do define a general pattern that helps to delineate the depth of the chemical peel created.

Once the appropriate frost has been achieved, rinse the patient's face with room-temperature water to remove any excess acid remaining on the skin. This does not "neutralize" the TCA; it dilutes any remaining reservoir of acid to prevent a deepening of the peel.

As a general rule, nonfacial peels should be limited to epidermal wounds (level 2 or less). Papillary dermal peels on the neck, chest, and hands have a high incidence of scarring and abnormal textural changes.

In general, TCA in concentrations of 10% to 30% is used as an intraepidermal peeling agent and in concentrations of 35% to 45% is a papillary dermal peeling agent. The actual depth of penetration of the peeling agent is affected by several variables other than the concentration of the acid. These include the type and thickness of the skin, intensity of the skin priming, how much acid is applied to the skin, and how aggressively the acid is rubbed into the skin.

Postoperative Management

The postoperative healing phase of a TCA peel can vary tremendously depending on the depth of the peel created (i.e., superficial, medium, or deep). However, the goal of postoperative management in all levels of TCA peeling is to keep the skin moist and to try to avoid accelerating the natural peeling process by washing vigorously or picking at the skin.

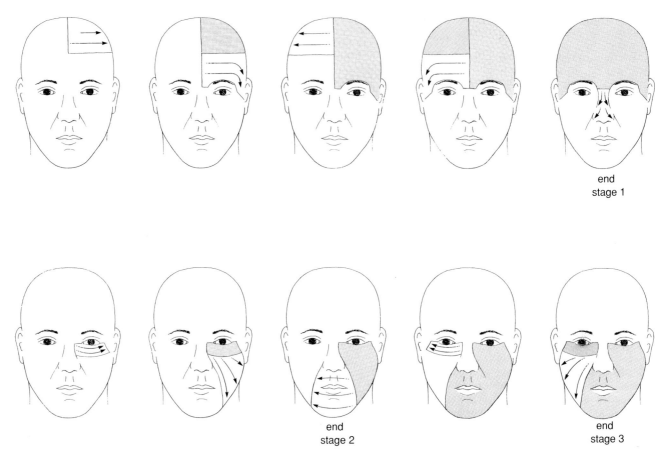

FIG. 8. Diagram of the three stages used in the application of a trichloroacetic acid (TCA) peel to the face. (Modified from Rubin MG. Manual of chemical peels: superficial and medium depth. Philadelphia: JB Lippincott, 1995.)

Superficial TCA peels are by definition intraepidermal and result in an appearance quite similar to that of Jessner's peel. Patients have mild erythema and darkening of the peeling skin but have no crusting or weeping and minimal or no edema. These patients must keep the peeling skin moist with bland emollient creams and avoid scrubs, astringents, and products containing potentially irritating ingredients like AHAs and tretinoin.

Medium-depth TCA peels are wounds extending into the papillary dermis. This level of peel commonly creates several days of mild to do moderate edema (more in the morning and decreasing during the day). In addition, these patients typically have a significant amount of erythema and darkening of the peeling skin. This skin tightens over a 2- to 4-day period and begins peeling first in areas of greatest skin movement (i.e., the perioral and periorbital areas). Over a 3- to 9-day period the skin peels off in an outward direction. During this time the skin looks a great deal like a sunburn, but the patient has no discomfort. Itching or increased sensitivity is common during this time but can be minimized by keeping the skin moist.

Dermal peels require more intensive postoperative care, since they have a higher incidence of complications than

superficial peels. These peels heal best with the use of ointment-based products, since emollients are unable to sufficiently hydrate the peeling skin. The ointment can be petrolatum, a topical antibiotic (avoid those containing neomycin), or 1% hydrocortisone. In addition, many physicians have the patient take a broad-spectrum oral antibiotic during the entire course of the peel in an effort to decrease bacterial colonization of the peeling skin.

When the skin has finished peeling, it is extremely important to restart the patient on their skin care regimen, including sunscreens, AHA and/or tretinoin, and a bleaching agent (if needed). These products can usually be restarted within 48 hours after the skin has reepithelialized. However, it is important to realize that these products should be restarted one at a time to decrease their ability to irritate the newly exposed skin.

With deep TCA peels, the face normally swells a great deal for 3 to 4 days. The peeled skin darkens significantly and at times obscures the underlying erythema. On occasion, during the first few days, the skin may be so edematous that it weeps. In that situation compresses applied three to four times daily with dilute acetic acid or 3% hydrogen peroxide can be helpful in decreasing the weeping. Hydration with

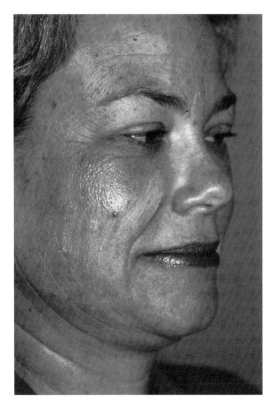

FIG. 9. Level-1 peel (an intraepidermal peel).

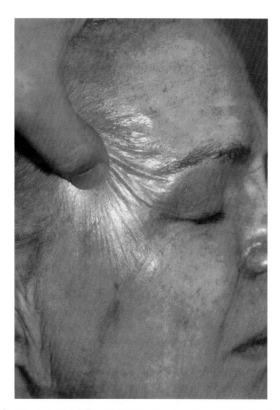

FIG. 10. Level-2 TCA peel showing a uniform white frost with a prominent pink background still visible through the frost. (The entire face had not been peeled at the time of this photograph.)

ointment is very important with these peels to decrease patient discomfort and to minimize the possibility of the peeling skin developing fissures. Hydrocortisone ointment (1%) can be used to decrease the inflammation associated with this level of peel; however, many physicians prefer to use a topical antibiotic ointment.

Complications

Because TCA peels are generally not used to create deep dermal wounds, they have significantly less risk of scarring, persistent erythema, or permanent hypopigmentation than phenol peels. However, the rate of occurrence of herpes labialis seems to be similar to that seen with deep peels. (It is prudent to pretreat all patients with a history of herpes labialis with acyclovir capsules, 400 mg three times per day, until the skin has reepithelialized, starting the evening before the peel).

The most common complication of freshening peels is dyschromia, particularly hyperpigmentation. ''Fanatical'' use of tretinoin, AHAs, hydroquinone, kojic acid, broad-spectrum sunscreens, and sun avoidance before and after the peel can help reduce the risk of postinflammatory hyperpigmentation. Equally important is the avoidance of unnecessary inflammation during the peel, as is often created by premature peeling (Fig. 12).

Patients taking birth control pills or receiving supplemental hormone therapy appear to be at greater risk of

development of hyperpigmentation. If a patient is willing to discontinue the use of these products for 3 to 4 weeks before the peel, this may decrease the chances of hyperpigmentation.

Other complications to be aware of include the following.

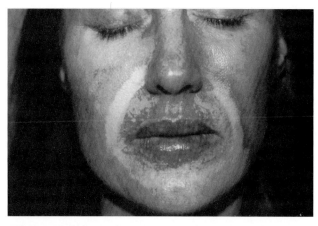

FIG. 11. A patient with a level-1 TCA peel on the upper lip, a level-2 peel on the right cheek, and a level-3 peel in the nasolabial area.

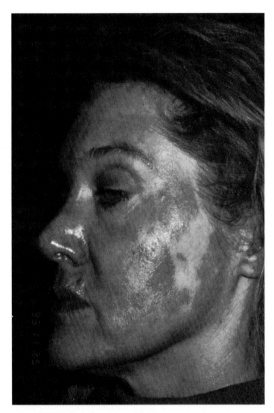

FIG. 12. A woman 5 days after a level-3 TCA peel. The sharply demarcated areas of bright erythema correspond to the areas that peeled prematurely.

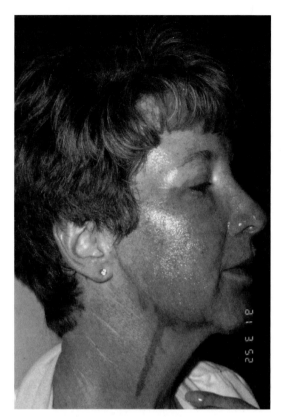

FIG. 13. A patient 2 days after a level-3 TCA peel. During the peel a tear ran down her cheek and carried acid onto her neck, where it created a linear area of peeling.

Accidental Tearing During the Peel

A tear running down the cheeks dilutes the peeling solution and leaves a linear streak where the peel is more superficial. In addition, if it runs down onto the neck, it can create an inadvertent area of peeling there. Therefore it is very important to blot tears that form during the peel with a tissue or cotton-tipped applicator before they run down the cheek (Fig. 13).

Infection

Light and medium-depth peels normally do not create crusts. Any area of crusting is a potential area of infection. Bacterial infections with *Staphylococcus* and *Streptococcus* species are the most common, with occasional rare cases of infection with *Pseudomonas* organisms (Fig. 14). With the use of prophylactic antibiotics the infection rate is quite low. Crusted areas may be due to herpes simplex, *Candida* organisms, or even a contact dermatitis to a topical medication. It is prudent to culture these areas as soon as possible and then institute appropriate oral and topical treatments. Areas of infection are more prone to scarring and postinflammatory hyperpigmentation, so it is imperative to treat all infections aggressively.

Scarring

Scarring is an unusual complication of medium-depth peels because they do not create deep dermal wounds. Most scarring occurs in areas of maximal tissue movement (i.e., the jaw line and the upper lip). Usually the formation of hypertrophic scarring is preceded by areas of persistent erythema, which may not appear until several weeks after a peel. Failure to intervene at this point may allow these areas to progress into full-blown hypertrophic scars.

Areas of persistent erythema should be aggressively treated with either potent fluorinated topical steroids, a steroid-impregnated tape (Cordran), or silastic sheeting. If hypertrophic scarring has developed, the use of intralesion triamcinolone acetonide (2 to 40 mg/ml) repeated every 2 to 4 weeks helps hasten the resolution of the scar. In addition, the use of silastic sheeting over a several-month period can help reduce the scarring (Fig. 15).

Hypopigmentation

It is very uncommon for a medium-depth peel to create permanent hypopigmentation (Fig. 16). However, if the peel is deep enough to damage melanin in the hair follicle, it is possible for the patient to have permanent hypopigmenta-

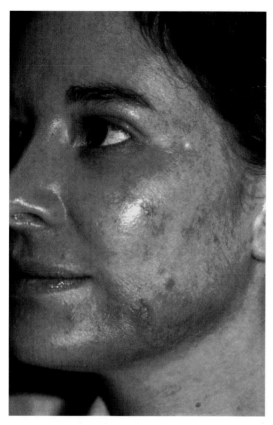

FIG. 14. An early infection with *Staphylococcus aureus* along the jaw line 7 days after a level-3 peel.

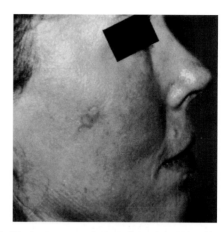

FIG. 15. Typical, somewhat stellate, hypertrophic scar in a patient who underwent a level-3 TCA peel several months after completing a course of isotretinoin (Accutane). (From Rubin MG. Manual of chemical peels: superficial and medium depth. Philadelphia: JB Lippincott, 1995.)

tion. Remember that transient hypopigmentation is normal for 6 to 8 weeks after most medium-depth peels.

Others

Unlike deep peels, light and medium-depth peels do not normally cause persistent hypersensitivity and flushing of the skin, changes in facial telangiectasias, or miliaformation.

PHENOL

History

Phenol, or carbolic acid, is the peeling agent most commonly used to perform a deep peel. It has been used by physicians and lay practitioners of peeling throughout this century for the treatment of wrinkles and scars. In the early 1960s, Baker and Gordon published their results with the use of a modified phenol peel. Since that time, phenol peeling has become a well-accepted treatment modality among the medical profession.

Preoperative Planning

There are several different phenol peel formulas currently in use. These can be divided into either pure phenol or a

diluted mixture of phenol containing surfactants and epidermal irritants. Pure phenol is 88% phenol, and paradoxically it creates a more superficial peel than the more dilute formulas containing 50% to 70% phenol. It is believed that this is due to the higher-strength phenol formulas creating coagulation of surface protein, which functions as a barrier to further penetration of the acid.

The effects of phenol on the skin are similar to those of other chemical peeling agents with a few exceptions. Phenol appears to be able to stimulate more pronounced collagen growth as a response to the peel, leading to tighter skin and a more impressive clinical result. Also, it damages the ability of melanocytes to function normally, thereby leading to some degree of permanent hypopigmentation in areas that have been peeled. Phenol is absorbed through the skin, creating the risk of systemic toxicity. There have been numerous reports documenting the occurrence of cardiac arrhythmias associated with phenol peels.

Phenol peels are used to create deep peels extending into

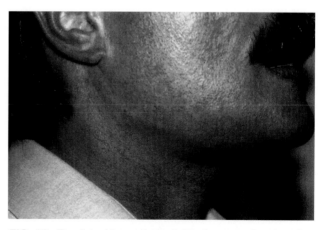

FIG. 16. Persistent hypopigmentation in a man 2 years after a deep, reticular dermal TCA peel.

the reticular dermis. Therefore they are useful for treating marked wrinkling, extensive photodamage, and premalignant lesions. They can also be useful in treating some forms of dyschromia that fail to respond to more conservative therapy.

Because of the potential for pigmentation change with phenol peeling, the patients must be thoroughly counseled in regard to the possibility of permanent lightening of the peeled skin. This is obviously a more significant problem for patients with darker skin types or patients with heavy freckling on the face, neck, and chest, where a line of demarcation would be quite obvious. Because of its depth of penetration and its tendency to create hypopigmentation, phenol is generally used only for facial peeling. The use of phenol in nonfacial areas rarely gives good cosmetic results and carries a high risk of scarring.

In view of the systemic toxicity associated with phenol, patients with underlying cardiac or renal disease must be identified and excluded.

Technique

Priming the skin does not appear to be as important with phenol peeling as with other peeling agents because before a phenol peel the skin is usually scrubbed aggressively with gauze dipped in acetone. This degreases the skin and removes the stratum corneum completely, allowing for an even penetration of the peeling agent.

After the skin has been scrubbed, place the patient in a sitting position and mark the jaw line with a surgical pen. The peel is extended just past this line so that any line of demarcation is hidden by the shadow of the mandible. Once the patient's jaw line has been marked, start an intravenous (IV) line. The IV line is useful because it allows the easy and rapid administration of analgesics and medications to treat cardiac arrythmias and it allows the infusion of 1 to 2 L of fluids during the peel to speed the excretion of phenol by the kidneys.

Phenol peels are quite uncomfortable for the patient, and some form of analgesic is needed. Various practitioners recommend nerve blocks; IV midazolam (Versed), fentanyl (Sublimaze), diazepam (Valium), meperidine (Demerol), or the like; or even general anesthesia (which may actually decrease the incidence of cardiac arrythmias). Decide which form of analgesic is preferred. However, no matter which is used, it is mandatory that the patient have cardiac monitoring if he or she is undergoing full-face peeling with phenol.

Apply the phenol solution to the skin using one or two cotton-tipped applicators that are wrung dry. Rub the solution into the skin until a solid white frost develops. It is imperative to extend the phenol solution into the hairline and eyebrows to prevent unpeeled areas with obvious color differences. Usually the face is divided into five or six units that are each peeled separately and then left for 10 to 15 minutes before applying phenol to the next area. Do this to decrease the toxicity of the phenol by allowing the body time to excrete part of the previously applied phenol before applying an additional amount.

After the phenol has been applied to all sections of the face, decide whether the peel should be "taped." Occluding a phenol peel increases its depth and hence its antiwrinkle ability. Occlusion with petrolatum is sufficient for many patients; however, for areas of deep wrinkling, the application of waterproof tape gives an enhanced occlusive effect. Be sure that the tape has adhered to all areas to which it has been applied; otherwise, a "skip area" of more superficial peeling will be evident postoperatively.

Postoperative Management

The aftercare of a phenol peel varies tremendously from physician to physician. Most patients leave the doctor's office with oral pain medication containing a narcotic, and frequently they have also had an injection of a short-acting corticosteroid such as betamethasone (Celestone) to decrease swelling.

If the peel has not been taped, aftercare of the peel consists of washing the face several times a day with a gentle cleanser and then applying a topical antibiotic ointment such as polymyxin B sulfate (Bacitracin), or mupirocin (Bactroban). This routine is continued until the skin has reepithelialized.

Patients who have had their face taped will return to the office 48 hours after treatment for removal of the tape. This procedure can be performed with or without anesthesia but is generally much less painful if the face was shaved before the peel to remove the vellus hairs. Once the tape mask has been removed, the face appears raw and weeps heavily. Drying the skin with a hair dryer (set on cool) permits easier application of the antibiotic ointment.

During the 8 to 12 days of healing time the skin may feel warm, stingy, or itchy. The use of oral antihistamines and nonsteroidal antiinflammatory drugs can help a great deal, as well as the application of 1% hydrocortisone ointment. Once the skin has reepithelialized, daily use of broad-spectrum sunscreens is mandatory, as well as attempting to avoid sun exposure.

Complications

The deeper the peel, the greater the risk of complications. Therefore phenol peeling has a higher incidence of complications, although most are transient.

The list of complications previously discussed for TCA pertains to phenol peeling as well. However, phenol peelings carry a greater risk of hypopigmentation, persistent erythema and sensitivity of the skin, milia formation, atrophy, and scarring.

CONCLUSION

The information presented in this chapter should serve as an overview of chemical peeling. Although the formulas and their application to the skin are an important part of chemical peeling, they are only one part. The preoperative evaluation of the skin to decide exactly what type of peel the patient needs is probably the most important step in the entire peeling process. Selection of an inappropriate peeling agent for a patient ensures a suboptimal result. Obviously, poor preoperative or postoperative skin treatments also lead to an inferior result.

The goal of this chapter is to stress all aspects of the peeling process. By thinking about each of these steps with each patient who is examined and treated, the art of chemical peeling becomes second nature.

SUGGESTED READING LIST

Basic Peel Information

1. Ayres S III. Superficial chemosurgery in treating aging skin. Arch Dermatol 1962;85:125.
2. Baker TJ, Gordon HL. Chemical face peeling and dermabrasion. Surg Clin North Am 1971;51:387.
3. Collins PS, Farber GA, Wilhelmus SM et al. Superficial repetitive chemosurgery of the hands. J. Dermatol Surg Oncol 1985:11(Oct)22–24.
4. Epstein E, Epstein E Jr. Skin surgery. 6th ed. Philadelphia: WB Saunders, 1987:412.
5. Matarasso S, Salman S, Glogau R and Rogers G. The role of chemical peeling in the treatment of photodamaged skin. J Dermatol Surg Oncol1990;16:945.
6. Peikert JM. Exploring the efficacy of degreasing agents in the TCA peel. Cosmet Dermatol 1994;7:5:31.
7. Rubin M. Manual of chemical peels. Philadelphia: JB Lippincott, 1995.
8. Rubin M. Trichloroacetic acid and other nonphenol peels. Clin Plast Surg 1992;19:525.
9. Stegman S, Tromovitch TA. Cosmetic dermatologic surgery.: Year Book Medical, 1984:27.

Alpha Hydroxy Acids

10. Elson M. The utilization of glycolic acid in photoaging. Cosmet Dermatol 1992;5:12.
11. Kligman A. Results of a pilot study evaluating the compatibility of topical tretinoin in combination with glycolic acid. Cosmet Dermatol 1993;6(10):28.
12. Moy LS. A comparison of depths of wounding of different peeling agents. Presented at the Update on Alpha Hydroxy Acid Symposium. San Diego, CA: June 1993.
13. Van Scott EJ. The unfolding therapeutic uses of the alpha hydroxy acids. Mediguide Dermatol 1988;3:1.
14. Van Scott EJ, Yu RJ. Alpha hydroxy acids: procedures for use in clinical practice. Cutis 1989;43:222.
15. Van Scott EJ, Yu RJ. Hyperkeratinization, corneosyte cohesion and alpha hydroxy acids. J Am Acad Dermatol 1984;11:867.

Trichloracetic Acid

16. Brodland D, Roenigk R. Trichloroacetic acid chemex foliation (chemical peel) for extensive premalignant actinic damage of the face and scalp. Mayo Clin Proc 1988;63:887.
17. Brody H, Hailey C. Medium-depth chemical peeling of the skin: a variation of superficial chemosurgery. J Dermatol Surg Oncol 1986; 12:1268.
18. Resnik SS. Chemical peeling with trichloroacetic acid. J Dermatol Surg Oncol 1986;10:549.
19. Resnik SS, Lewis LA. The cosmetic uses of trichloroacetic acid peeling in dermatology. South Med J 1973;66:225.
20. Resnik SS, Lewis LA, Cohen BH. Trichloroacetic acid peeling. Cutis 1976;17:127.
21. Stegman S. Medium-depth chemical peeling: digging beneath the surface. J Dermatol Surg Oncol 1986;12:1245.

Textbook of Dermatologic Surgery, edited by John L. Ratz.
Lippincott–Raven Publishers, Philadelphia © 1998.

CHAPTER 30

Hair Replacement

Walter P. Unger, Dow B. Stough, Francisco J. Jimenez,
Marc Avram, and Richard E. Fitzpatrick

Part 1: Male Pattern Baldness

HISTORY

The first publication on the surgical correction of alopecia by autotransplantation of hair was contained in a doctoral

Walter P. Unger: Department of Dermatology, University of Toronto, 111 Avenue Road, Suite 800, Toronto, Canada M5R3J8.
Dow B. Stough: Department of Dermatology, University of Arkansas for Medical Sciences, Little Rock, AK 72205.
Francisco J. Jimenez: Department of Dermatology, Stough Clinic, Suite 304, 1 Mercy Lane, Hot Springs, AK 71913.
Marc Avram: Cornell University, 927 Fifth Avenue, New York, NY 10021.
Richard E. Fitzpatrick: Dermatology Associates of San Diego Co., Inc., 9834 Genesee, Suite 480, La Jolla, CA 92037.

thesis written by Diefenbach at Wurzburg in 1823. Diefenbach was careful to credit his teacher Karl Unger for originating the concept, which he successfully used. Although hair-bearing autografts in the form of flaps and relatively large free grafts were sporadically reported on after that date, it was not until Norman Orentreich's 1959 report on the successful use of 4-mm, round grafts for the treatment of male pattern baldness (MPB) that widespread utilization of this form of treatment for MPB began. Thousands of publications have now been written on the subject, which continues to evolve into varied and more refined procedures. This relatively short chapter is adequate only to describe the distilled

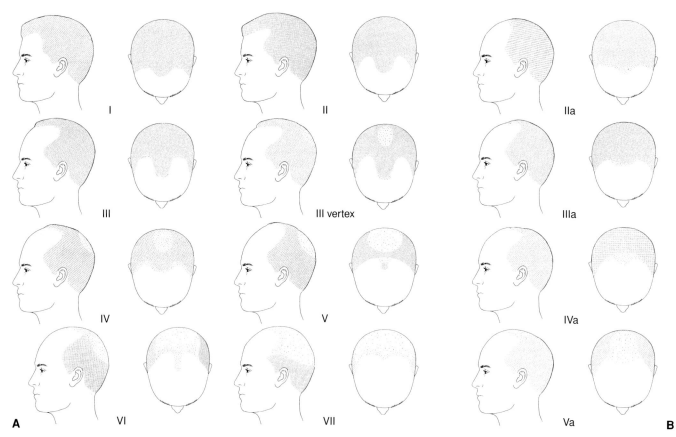

FIG. 1. (A) Norwood classification of most common types of male pattern baldness (MPB). **(B)** Norwood classification for type A variant of MPB. (From Stough, Dowling B. *Hair transplantation.* New York: McGraw-Hill, 1995.)

views of the specific authors represented here. A more complete description of options and, more important, *reasons* for them, is recommended and can be found in sources listed in the Suggested Reading List. In particular, the 830-page, 1995 edition of my textbook, *Hair Transplantation,* should be carefully reviewed by anyone interested in working in this field. All subjects referred to below are described in detail in that text.

PREOPERATIVE PLANNING

Long-Term Considerations

Any plan for the surgical treatment of MPB must begin with the recognition that MPB is a progressive disorder (Tables 30-1 and 30-2; Fig. 1A and B). Planning should take into consideration present as well as future areas of involve-

TABLE 30-1. *Incidence of male pattern baldness in 1,000 men by type and age*

Type	Age (years)						
	18–29	30–39	40–49	50–59	60–69	70–79	80
Type I	110 (60%)	60 (36%)	55 (33%)	45 (28%)	29 (19%)	18 (17%)	12 (16%)
Type II	52 (28%)	43 (26%)	38 (22%)	32 (20%)	24 (16%)	20 (19%)	11 (14%)
Type III	14 (6%)	30 (18%)	37 (20%)	34 (23%)	22 (15%)	16 (16%)	12 (16%)
		(3V)*	(15V)*	(15V)*	(10V)*	(7V)*	(8V)*
Type IV	4 (3%)	16 (10%)	15 (10%)	21 (9%)	17 (12%)	13 (13%)	9 (12%)
Type V	3 (2%)	10 (6%)	13 (8%)	15 (10%)	22 (15%)	13 (13%)	9 (12%)
Type VI	2 (1%)	4 (3%)	7 (4%)	10 (7%)	19 (13%)	11 (11%)	10 (13%)
Type VII	0	2 (1%)	5 (3%)	4 (3%)	16 (10%)	11 (11%)	14 (17%)
Total	185 (100%)	165 (100%)	165 (100%)	156 (100%)	149 (100%)	102 (100%)	77 (100%)

* Numbers in parentheses under Type III represent Type III Vertex individuals.

(Reprinted with permission from Dr. O'Tar Norwood, from *Hair Transplant Surgery,* Charles C. Thomas, 1984.)

TABLE 30-2. *Age and degree of MPB*

Type	65–69[a] (%)	70–74[b] (%)	75–79[c] (%)	80+[d] (%)
		Age (yr)		
I	2 (3.6)	5 (6.2)	4 (5.5)	2 (1.7)
II	9 (16.4)	7 (8.6)	7 (9.6)	12 (10.1)
III	4 (7.3)	15 (18.5)	18 (24.7)	11 (9.2)
IV	10 (18.2)	16 (19.8)	8 (11.0)	10 (8.4)
V	6 (10.9)	7 (8.6)	10 (13.7)	16 (13.4)
VI	13 (23.6)	19 (23.5)	16 (21.9)	37 (31.1)
VII	11 (20.0)	12 (14.8)	10 (13.7)	31 (26.1)
Total	55 (100)	81 (100)	73 (100)	119 (100)

[a] If one excludes types I and II, 33 of remaining 4 (75%) have types III–VI.

[b] If one excluded types I and II, 57 of remaining 69 (82.6%) have types III–VI.

[c] If one excludes types I and II, 52 of remaining 62 (83.9%) have types III–VI.

[d] If one excludes types I and II, 74 of remaining 105 (70.5%) have types III–VI.

(Incidence of various types of MPB in 328 men aged 65 years and older. Reprinted with permission from Unger, W., *Hair Transplantation,* 3rd Ed, Marcel Dekker Inc., 1995.)

ment. The superior border of the "permanent" fringe hair, nearly always runs inferiorly as one moves posteriorly from the hairline (Fig. 2A and B). Therefore the approach should include grafting into areas that are still hair-bearing but can reasonably be expected to lose hair in the future (Fig. 3A–D). This will make a constant and frustrating "chasing" of an enlarging alopecic area less likely. The "price" to be paid for this long-term planning is that a smaller proportion of the currently clearly thinning areas can be transplanted. Patients will initially be more impressed with the treatment of a larger proportion of the more obvious areas of thinning (short-term planning), but in the long-run the disadvantages of such an approach will become evident. Lack of long-term planning is the most common reason why patients are seen for "correction" of transplanting performed elsewhere.

Perfect prognostication of the degree of alopecia any given patient will develop is impossible, so a reserve of what is expected to be permanent hair-bearing donor areas should always be maintained. When dealing with younger patients, either limit the size of the area to be treated or leave some areas that are judged to eventually lose hair for excision rather than grafting (Fig. 3D), or employ only micrografts and minigrafts that will allow natural-looking results with less donor tissue (see below).

Choice of Hairline

The beginning and end of the hairline chosen must be the *eventual* or ultimate anterosuperior-most temporal points. The midline point of the hairline should then be located so that when the hairline is viewed laterally, it will run more or less horizontally. This midline point can be moved more

superiorly, thereby decreasing the length of the area of MPB to be treated, by creating and accentuating a bell shape to the hairline or by raising the anterosuperior-most temporal points with alopecia reduction (AR) or reductions (ARs) (Fig. 4). Utilizing either of these options will allow for a higher midline hairline point without affecting its cosmetically advantageous horizontal orientation.

Alopecia Reduction

This topic is more fully discussed below, but a few comments on its role in planning are warranted here:

1. Use AR or plan to use AR in the future, whenever the goal is maximum coverage (Fig. 3D).
2. Use a pattern of AR that does not leave a scar in an area that you are not planning to transplant later. Not only does this avoid permanently noticeable scars, but if the patient is one of the few who develop a wider than normal scar, this can be easily corrected with hair-bearing grafts.
3. Unless using scalp extension, as described by Frechet to achieve a rapid elimination of all alopecic areas and planning to correct the "slot" defect that results from this objective with Frechet's three-flap "slot correction" operation, do not aim for excision of all of the alopecic area. This will result in an abnormal hair direction at the midline, which has been referred to as the "parting of the Red Sea" effect. For many patients a reasonable goal is to decrease the width of alopecia to approximately 5 to 6 cm. This remaining area can be transplanted with grafts that produce a gradual change of hair direction from left to right or vice versa.
4. The wider the area of alopecia eventually removed, the sparser the hair in the permanent fringe will become, since it is stretched over a larger surface area. Remember also that fringe hair will gradually become sparser with age; this should be factored into the objectives for AR. Despite arguments to the contrary, this is the *only* negative consequence of AR that is not *completely* avoidable or easily treated; therefore it warrants serious consideration. Two or three modified major ARs rarely have a significantly negative impact on rim hair density. Anything more aggressive warrants more thought.
5. When surgical technique is good, "stretch-back," or loss of some of the gain obtained, is minimal in the vast majority of patients. In Nordstrom's study on 13 patients there was a 30% to 52% loss of the original gain, depending on the patient and how many previous ARs had been performed. But Nordstrom has admitted to closing under considerable tension in order to maximize the original results. Unger's study on 56 patients, whose excisions were closed with minimal tension, reported *no* stretch-back in 55% and less than 3 mm loss of gain in another 43% of the patients treated. Hitzig has reported on 40 AR patients, 50% of whom had no stretch-

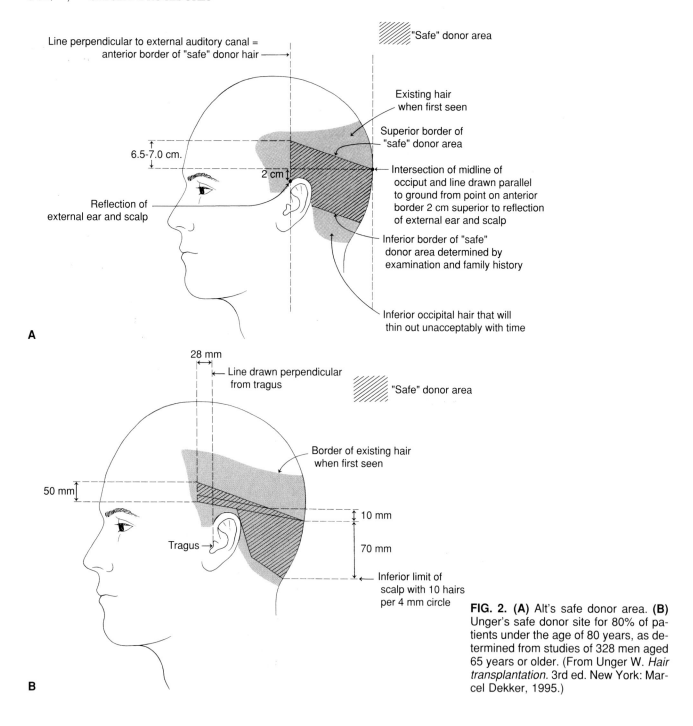

Line perpendicular to external auditory canal = anterior border of "safe" donor hair

▨▨▨ "Safe" donor area

Existing hair when first seen

Superior border of "safe" donor area

6.5–7.0 cm.

2 cm

Intersection of midline of occiput and line drawn parallel to ground from point on anterior border 2 cm superior to reflection of external ear and scalp

Reflection of external ear and scalp

Inferior border of "safe" donor area determined by examination and family history

Inferior occipital hair that will thin out unacceptably with time

A

28 mm

Line drawn perpendicular from tragus

▨▨▨ "Safe" donor area

Border of existing hair when first seen

50 mm

10 mm

Tragus

70 mm

Inferior limit of scalp with 10 hairs per 4 mm circle

B

FIG. 2. (A) Alt's safe donor area. **(B)** Unger's safe donor site for 80% of patients under the age of 80 years, as determined from studies of 328 men aged 65 years or older. (From Unger W. *Hair transplantation.* 3rd ed. New York: Marcel Dekker, 1995.)

FIG. 3. (A) In many patients with less than complete alopecia, a triangular corner area is present, with some hairs still within it, that will eventually be lost. Such a triangular area is marked. It should be transplanted along with the obviously bald areas more anteriorly, to avoid constantly "chasing" a receding line. **(B)** Slit grafts have been prepared in areas of obvious vertex thinning, as well as to the left side ("part side") and in less obvious thinning areas revealed by wetting the hair. Nearly 50% of the sites are in such still–hair-bearing areas. No grafts were transplanted into the comparable area on the right side that has been left for one or more future alopecia reductions (ARs). One such AR was also performed 3 months before this first hair transplant session to the vertex. **(C)** Six months later. Hair has grown, and area left for AR was excised 4 weeks before this photo was taken. **(D)** Schematic drawing with general planning of transplanting (hair) density and incorporation of AR into planning.

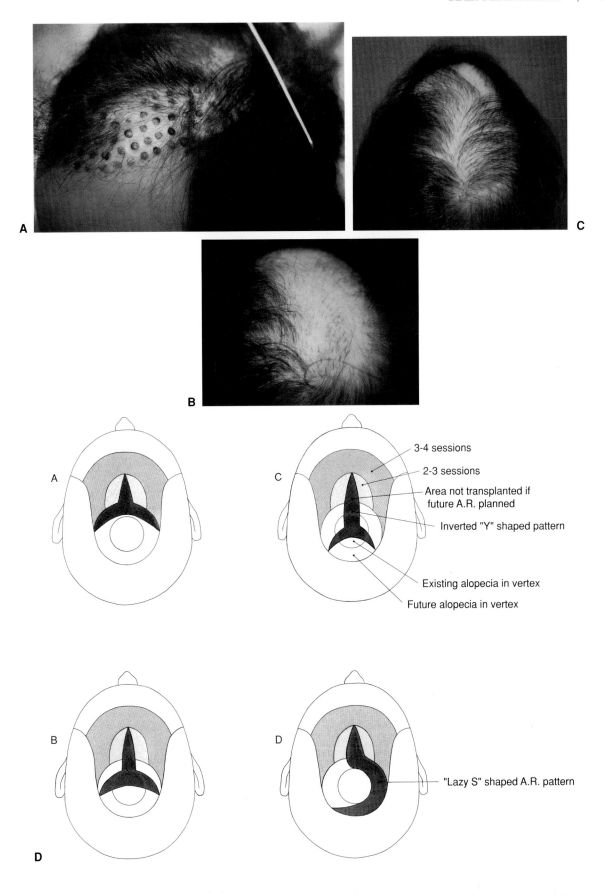

3-4 sessions

2-3 sessions

Area not transplanted if
future A.R. planned

Inverted "Y" shaped pattern

Existing alopecia in vertex

Future alopecia in vertex

"Lazy S" shaped A.R. pattern

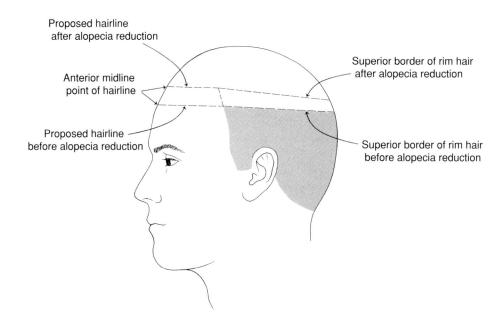

Proposed hairline
after alopecia reduction

Anterior midline
point of hairline

Proposed hairline
before alopecia reduction

Superior border of rim hair
after alopecia reduction

Superior border of rim hair
before alopecia reduction

FIG. 4. AR raises the anterosuperior points of the temporal area—the starting and ending points of the new hairline—so that the most anterior midline point of the hairline can also be placed more superiorly, while still maintaining a hairline that runs more or less parallel to the ground when viewed laterally.

back and another 25% of whom had less than 10% stretch-back. For some reason, Nordstrom's study of 13 patients has inappropriately received far more attention than these substantially larger ones.

6. AR is a very useful tool for the treatment of MPB that has extended beyond its originally estimated borders.

Graft Type

For this discussion, graft types are defined as follows:

1. "Standard" grafts are obtained by sectioning 3.5- to 3.75-mm-wide strips of donor tissue into rectangles that contain 18 to 30 hairs and that completely fill holes punched out with 3.25- to 3.5-mm round trephines.
2. "Micrografts" are one to two hair grafts obtained by sectioning strips of donor tissue 2 mm wide. They are placed into holes prepared with a 16-gauge needle.
3. "Minigrafts" are grafts containing three or four or, less commonly, five to six hairs. They are obtained by sectioning strips of donor tissue 1.5 to 2 mm wide. If they are placed into slits made with a scalpel blade, they are referred to as "slit" grafts. If they are placed into holes made with a round trephine, they are referred to as "round minigrafts."
4. "Small" minigrafts, whether they are round minigrafts or slit grafts, contain three to four hairs.
5. "Large" minigrafts, whether they are round minigrafts or slit grafts, contain five to six hairs.

Micrografts and minigrafts are used whenever the ultimate hair density objective is less than maximum density. They should virtually always be used in the hairline zone and

posterior half of larger areas of MPB (Fig. 5A–E). Obviously, the younger the patient, the less certain the eventual size of the area of MPB (and donor area), and often the wise decision would be to aim for less density with the attendant utilization of less donor tissue.

If you choose to use minigrafting, the following suggestions apply:

1. For whites, unless donor hair is white, salt-and-pepper colored, blonde, or *light brown* and the consequent contrast between hair and scalp color is minimal, nearly always use micrografts, *small* slit grafts, and *small* round minigrafts.
2. For Asians with high-caliber hair you should virtually always use micrografts, *small* slit grafts, and *small* round minigrafts.
3. For blacks or those with naturally curly hair, use micrografts and small or large minigrafts.
4. The finer the hair texture or the lighter the hair color, the more acceptable large minigrafts become.
5. However, in general, when using minigrafts in whites and all Asians, it is advantageous to use micrografts and slit grafts instead of round minigrafts for the initial session(s) (see below). After transplants from the first session(s) have grown in, it is often useful to scatter some round minigrafts between the grafts transplanted in the previous session(s), thus producing more density but minimizing any noticeable temporary clumpiness. Be prepared to use *all* types of grafts, depending on patient characteristics and objectives. In general, small slit grafts are superior to small round minigrafts in producing light coverage with minimal clumpiness, because of their linear shape. The less ideal the hair and skin characteristics, the more true this statement. For example, picture a pale-skinned individual with a small

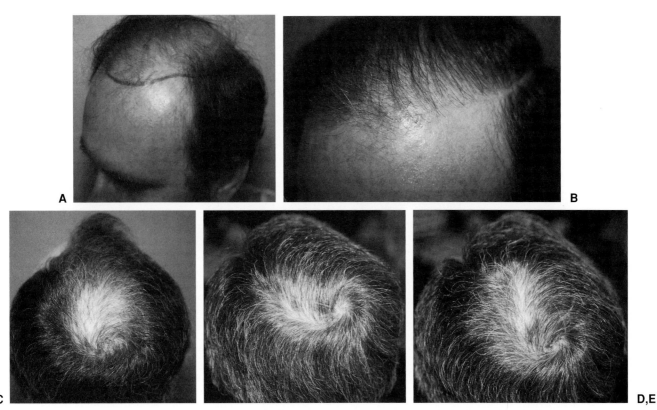

FIG. 5. **(A)** Patient C.A. before treatment. Patient wanted to undergo only one operation and was only looking for enough permanent hair that he would "not be shiny bald" at any time. Because his hair was quite fine, this objective was achievable. **(B)** Nine months after a single session of 60 micrografts and 325 slit grafts. **(C)** The vertex of this patient had been essentially bald. The photo was taken 4 months after an initial session of 350 slit grafts. **(D)** Six months after the third session of slit grafts (total of 1120 slit grafts). Note that the part-side lateral border of the vertex has not been transplanted densely. This is created whether or not dense coverage of the rest of the vertex is planned. The superior border of rim hair adjacent to the vertex will gradually thin out as the patient ages. Ideally, adjacent vertex hair should never be denser than its neighboring rim hair, especially on the part side. **(E)** Photo taken at the same time as Fig. 5 **(D),** but with the hair parted through the midline of the transplanted area. Note the very even distribution of hair and the absence of clumpiness that can be achieved when an area is transplanted with all slit grafts.

group of black, coarse hairs in a small circle and another patient with similar characteristics whose transplanted hairs are dispersed single file in a short line. The latter will obviously look less clumpy. Avoid "compression" of dark, coarse hair into unsightly dense lines in these patients by using grafts with no more than three to four hairs. The possibility of compression can be further minimized by removing the epidermis of the grafts before they are inserted into the slits, thereby facilitating the alignment of the hairs into a single-file row.

Small slit grafts produce a greater increase in hair density than small round minigrafts, if *working in an area that still contains some of its original hair* (Fig. 6A–C). Making round recipient sites of any size removes some of the original hair, so the ultimate gain in hair is the *difference* between what is removed and what is added. On the other hand, scalpel incisions for slit grafts can be made *between* existing hairs without causing permanent injury to them. Thus the

increase in hair will not be decreased by any concomitant loss of hair, and the net increase in hair density will be equal to *all* the transplanted hair. On the other hand, *in alopecic recipient sites* greater hair density can be produced with round minigrafts in the short run, as well as the long run. This is because bald skin is being removed at the same time as hair is being added--something that does not happen with slit grafts. In younger patients with early MPB the following apply:

1. They usually prefer the greater initial hair density produced by slit grafts.
2. They can have small round minigrafts added to the transplanted area when more of the original hair has been lost, thus balancing the disadvantage, eventually, of less density with slit grafts.
3. They may not object to somewhat less hair density when they are older and have lost all of their original hair.
4. They just *may* have enough donor hair available to have

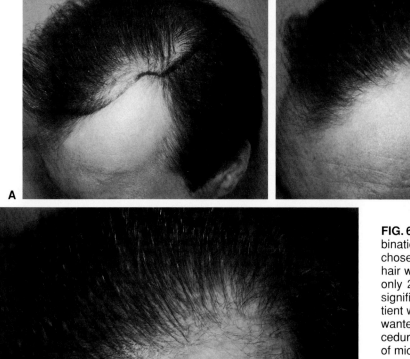

FIG. 6. (A) Patient before transplanting. A combination of only micrografts and slit grafts was chosen for treatment because (1) the temporal hair was relatively sparse and, with the patient only 20 years-old, could be anticipated to get significantly sparser over his lifetime; (2) the patient was not looking for dense hair; and (3) he wanted minimal hair loss as a result of the procedure. (B) Six months after a single session of micrografts and 325 slit grafts. Further treatments will keep pace with the loss; ultimately, a total of three sessions should be sufficient to produce approximately the density shown above, when only transplanted hair remains in the frontal third of the area of MPB. (C) Close-up photo of the hairline taken at the same time as Fig. 6 (B).

additional sessions of slit grafts that will produce hair density equal to or greater than that achieved with round grafts, although at the cost of using more donor tissue.

Sessions of all micrografts should be used only if hair density objectives are quite low (Fig. 7A and B). They are the least efficient way of producing substantial hair density. On the other hand, micrografts produce the least clumped effect of any graft types. A word of caution: All-micrograft sessions and coarse hair are not as advantageous a combination as it may first seem. Hair becomes finer-textured as it becomes sparser during the balding process. Thus hair density and texture must be appropriate for each other if a natural appearance is to be produced. Low-density, coarse hair will not look natural until enough sessions have been carried out to produce hair density appropriate to the texture of hair used. Always use the finest hair available for micrografts, and if fine hair is not present, be aware that natural-looking results will require repeated sessions.

"Megasessions" of thousands of grafts in a single sitting and "dense packing" have been suggested as a means of accomplishing more in less time. Sessions of 8 hours or longer are necessary and may be medically unwise for some individuals. There are also questions as to whether hair survival is as good as it is with standard-sized sessions. One individual who had a "megasession" with "dense packing" carried out and who 6 months later estimated that only half of the hair was growing had worked for one of the originators of the megasession/dense packing technique and was aware of friends of his who had similar procedures carried out. He contacted them and found that their experience was similar to his. It is unlikely that all patients undergoing megasessions and dense packing will have such poor results, but it is not clear how to distinguish between those who would have successful results and those who would not. In dealing with a limited resource—permanent hair—until the incidence of poor regrowth is clarified, it is wise to avoid megasessions and dense packing.

TECHNIQUE

Preparation

Ask the patients to abstain from drugs and substances that could result in excessive bleeding. Alcohol should be

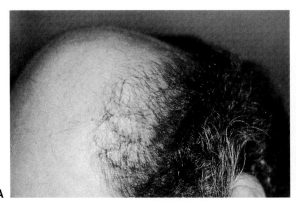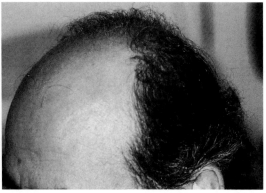

FIG. 7. (A) Fifty-seven-year-old patient with type VI MPB that was clearly destined to evolve to type VII had an unusual request. He wanted to preserve what was left of his temporary fringe hair and raise it to a level where he would look like he had type V MPB. Because superior fringe hair normally only has low to moderate density and because all micrograft sessions will produce the required density in two or at most three sessions (in addition to producing the least noticeable temporary and incremental increase in hair), it was decided to proceed that way. **(B)** Five months after the second transplant session and 10 months after the first. (After seeing the results in the fringe area, the patient changed his mind and decided to produce a band of hair from the left temple to the right temple so as to break up the broad expanse of baldness. The author refers to this pattern as "a bridge over troubled waters.")

avoided for 1 week preoperatively, and vitamin E or acetylsalicylic acid preparations for 3 weeks preoperatively. Vitamin K, 5 mg three times daily, can be given for 1 week before any session, if more than average bleeding is anticipated. It is harmless and may be helpful. Ask the patient about *any* medication routinely taken, in case it should not be combined with drugs used during surgery. For example, monoamine oxidase inhibitors have been reported as causing fatal reactions when combined with some local anesthetics. Consider preceding medical conditions when the operative plan is being made. Screen patients for human immunodeficiency virus (HIV). Screening should also be undertaken for hepatitis B (unless *all* staff are hepatitis B antibody positive) and hepatitis C.

Hair should be washed with a chlorhexidine gluconate soap wash (for example, Hibitane) the night before and morning of surgery. Cefadroxil (Duricef), 2 g, is given 2 hours before surgery and again 6 hours later, unless it is not tolerated or there is an allergy to penicillin or cefadroxil, in which case erythromycin or trimethoprim-sulfamethoxazole (Septra Ds) can be used instead.

Administer diazepam (Valium), 20 mg orally, 30 minutes before surgery, to minimize anxiety and the possibility of anesthetic toxicity. Oral meperidine hydrochloride (Demerol), 50 mg, or oxycodone (Percocet) can be added to the diazepam for patients with low pain thresholds or more than average nervousness. Unless there is a contraindication, you should inject 2 ml of methyl prednisolone acetate 40 mg/ml (Depo-Medrol) intramuscularly just before beginning surgery, to minimize postoperative edema. A single such dose has never been associated with aseptic necrosis in joints—one of the most feared complications of systemic corticosteroids—and there is no evidence that it has any other negative effects.

Anesthesia

Prepare a tumescent anesthetic solution for the donor area by adding 19 ml of 2% lidocaine with 1:100,000 epinephrine and 1 ml of 1:1000 epinephrine to a 100-ml intravenous (IV) bag of saline. In addition, buffer 10 ml of 1% lidocaine with 1:100,000 epinephrine and 10 ml of 2% lidocaine with 1:100,000 epinephrine with the addition of sodium bicarbonate to produce mixtures containing 5.2 mEq/L of sodium bicarbonate. Injections of buffered solutions are far less painful than stock 1% and 2% lidocaine.*

Use a 30-gauge needle and the buffered 1% lidocaine solution to produce a line of anesthesia inferior to the proposed donor areas. Produce four or five wheals approximately 3 cm apart from each other along that line; wait 60 to 90 seconds, and then complete the field block by injecting through the already anesthetized sites. Thus the number of injections is minimized, and the pain of each injection is also minor because of the buffering of the anesthetic. After the field block is in place, inject 50 to 100 ml of the tumescent solution superior to that block through an 18-gauge, 3.5-inch spinal needle. Introduce the needle at approximately the midpoint of the donor area, and advance it just beyond the limits of the donor area in one direction. Slowly withdraw the needle concomitant with infiltration of the solution. It should then be advanced in the opposite direction through the same point of entry, far enough to completely prepare the entire donor site. Once again, slowly withdraw it as the solution is injected. The donor area should be quite turgid

---

*For example, for 10 ml of a buffered 1% solution, add 0.1 ml of 1:1000 epinephrine and 5 ml of 2% lidocaine without epinephrine to 5 ml of a solution made as follows: add 0.4 ml of 1:1000 epinephrine to 5 ml of 2% lidocaine without epinephrine and 0.52 ml of sodium bicarbonate (1 mEq/ ml) (Abbott Laboratories, Abbott Park, IL).

at the completion of infiltration. You can use an automated "Klein pump" to inject the solution without any hand strain if you prefer. You may need to reinforce occasional "hot spots" with 2% lidocaine with 1:100,000 epinephrine in some patients, but large amounts of tumescent solution always minimize bleeding and provide excellent anesthesia for most individuals.

Once the donor area has been harvested and sutured, prepare the recipient area by beginning with a field block produced in the same manner as that described above for the donor area, but using a buffered 2% lidocaine solution instead of a 1% solution. This field block should be approximately 2 cm anterolateral to the recipient area borders. Up to 10 ml of *unbuffered* 2% lidocaine with 1:100,000 epinephrine should be used to produce a second field block superior to the first. Buffering of the anesthetic solution, while producing less pain on injection, causes more bleeding by accelerating the denaturing of epinephrine in the solution. Hence the need for an unbuffered field block superior to the first, in any area where incisions will actually be made. Then 10 ml of 1:50,000 epinephrine should be infiltrated *superficially* in small amounts and in many spots into the rest of the recipient area to minimize bleeding during surgery. Premixed and self-administered nitrous oxide 50% and oxygen 50% can be safely used for patients who need it to further minimize the pain of injections.

Use a field block of bupivacaine (Marcaine) 0.5% in the donor area before the patient leaves the office, to prolong anesthesia at that site. Ketorolac tromethamine (Toradol), 30 to 60 mg, can also be administered intramuscularly at the end of the procedure. It will eliminate virtually all pain in most patients for 6 to 8 hours postoperatively. It should not be used in patients with a history of asthma or ulcers. A single dose of Toradol has never been reported as causing acute glomerulonephritis—one of its most serious potential complications.

Be familiar with maximum-dose schedules, and be prepared to manage anesthetic toxicity or allergy with oxygen and an appropriate "crash cart."

Donor Area

The importance of improvements in donor area harvesting in the last 5 to 10 years cannot be overstated. What is possible to accomplish with hair transplantation has been revolutionized. Conceptually one attempts to excise an appropriately sized area of the donor area, and section it into the desired number and types of grafts. Employ two donor zones in most patients, one inferiorly in the occipital area and the other more superiorly that extends from the midline into the parietal area and as far anteriorly as a line drawn perpendicularly from the tragus (Figs. 2B and 8A and B). Take the former from an area that is judged to be permanently hairbearing but that contains relatively fine hair which is ideal for use in the hairline zone. Remember that hair in the inferior occipital area will also become sparser with aging;

choice of inferior donor zones should take this into account. The superior donor zone should contain hair that is coarser and can be used to produce greater density posterior to the hairline zone. If the hair texture in the entire donor area is relatively similar, especially if it is fine or light colored, use a single *elliptic* donor zone instead of two. Before excision, clip the hair in the donor zones to approximately a 2-mm length and apply a povidone-iodine (Betadine) solution. If the patient is allergic to iodine, use chlorhexidine (Hibiclens) instead.

In a study that included 328 men aged 65 years or older, "acceptable" donor sites were defined as areas containing eight hairs or more per 4-mm-diameter circle. The widest inferior-to-superior measurements of zones containing this hair density were recorded in temporal, parietal, and midline occipital areas. In individuals with type I and II alopecia the height of the donor area was arbitrarily limited to that of the individual with the greatest height in type III MPB. Using data obtained in this study, a donor area that is "safe" for 80% of the patients under the age of 80 years was established (Fig. 2B). In the occipital region, that area was found to be 70 mm high; in the parietal region, approximately 80 mm high; and in the temporal region, approximately 50 mm high.

Use No. 10 Persona Plus blades in a four or more bladed scalpel handle. The blades should be inserted at the midline end of the proposed donor area and drawn smoothly across its full length. Use a No. 15 scalpel blade to produce a triangular tapering of both ends. Incisions should be made into the midsubcutaneous tissue, and the blades should always be angled at the angle of existing hair. Lift one end of the donor tissue with a small-toothed forceps, and use small, curved scissors to separate the tissue from its underlying bed. Use a hyfercator set at unipolar delivery and "80" to cauterize any vessels that are bleeding excessively. The fumes produced during electrocautery of blood vessels contain benzenes, aldehydes, hydrocarbons, carcinogenic carbonized particles, *virus*, and even bacteria. Always vacuum the fumes with an efficient smoke evacuator system.

Generally no undermining is necessary; however, if there is any indication of tension on closure, undermine at least one of the flaps. The less cautery and undermining, the less postoperative pain there will be. Therefore both should be employed as little as possible. Use 2-0 Supramid on a CL20 needle and running continuous suturing to close the wound. Remove sutures in 7 to 10 days, at which time both donor and recipient areas can also be assessed. Employ a self-dissolving suture, such as Vicryl 2-0, if it is awkward for the patient to return for suture removal (Fig. 9A–E).

Set the blades 1.5 mm to 2.5 mm apart on the multibladed scalpel that will be used to harvest the inferior donor zone. The most superior border of the superior donor zone should be contralateral and approximately 44 mm superior to the inferior border of the inferior donor zone, if only micrografts and minigrafts are being used (Fig. 8A), or approximately 50.75 mm superior to it if a combination of micrografts, minigrafts, and standard grafts is being used (Fig. 8B). It is

Strip Harvesting

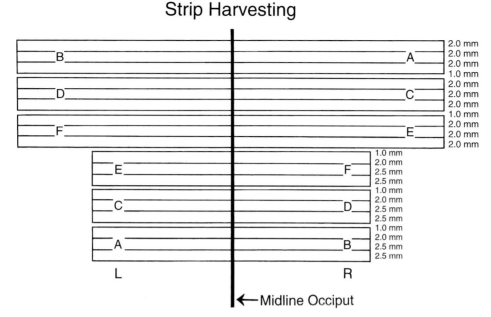

A   Total = 44 mm

Combination Standard Round Grafts
and Minigraft Harvesting

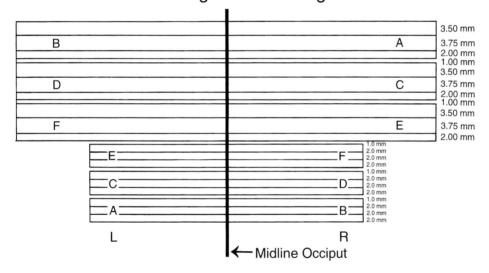

B   Total = 50.75 mm

FIG. 8. **(A)** Zones A, B, C, D, E, and F represent donor zones for sessions 1, 2, 3, 4, 5, and 6 with the width of strips taken as shown to the right side of the schematic drawing. (The 1-mm spaces shown between donor sites used in different sessions represent scar line from previous sessions). A total of only 44 mm of donor tissue will be required for six sessions, each yielding approximately 200 micrografts and 350 to 400 minigrafts. The inferior donor zones are used for micrografts in areas where finer hair is preferable, for example, the hairline and the center of the whorl of the vertex. **(B)** Only a total of 50.75 mm of donor tissue is necessary to produce grafts for six sessions, each of which consists of approximately 200 to 250 minigrafts, 200 micrografts, and 50 to 60 standard round grafts. Standard round grafts are taken from the superior donor zones. The 2-mm gaps between each of the superior donor rows are used to produce micrografts and additional minigrafts. The 1-mm space shown between the adjacent sessions represents scar tissue. It is reexcised during each subsequent harvesting.

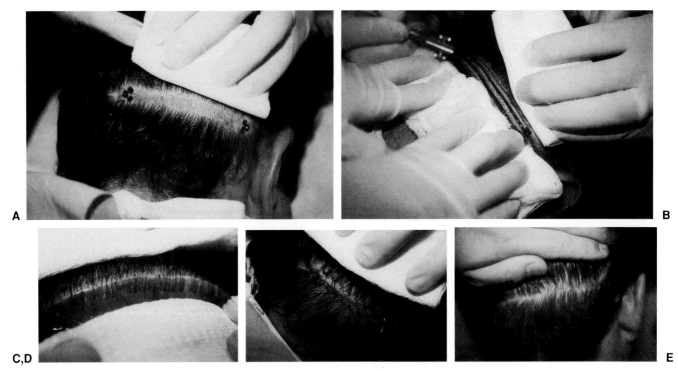

FIG. 9. (A) Three holes were produced with a 4- to 4.5-mm trephine on either end of the proposed harvest, to produce the shape of a triangle and thus the tapering of the end of the strips. The round grafts are removed, and the bridges between them cut. As an alternative, a No. 15 scalpel blade can be used to produce a tapering of the strip after the incisions have been made by the multiple-bladed scalpel. **(B)** The donor zone is infiltrated with normal saline to produce maximum tissue turgor and a triple- or quadruple-bladed knife is inserted at its medial or lateral end. It is drawn evenly across the donor zone, with care being taken to angle the blades in the direction of hair at that site and to go deep enough to include hair matrices. **(C)** Note how well one is able to match the angle of adjacent hair with scalpel incisions. **(D)** The strip is carefully lifted from its bed using small scissors or a No. 15 scalpel blade. Larger blood vessels are cauterized and a CL 20 Supramid suture is used to close the defect. Undermining of the wound edges or galeal sutures are used only if there will be any tension at the suture line. **(E)** Six months later, a fine scar line denotes the donor site. It will be reexcised as part of future donor harvests.

important to also note that the strip widths shown in Fig. 8A and B are those used in most but not all patients. They should be increased slightly if the donor hair density is lower than average or decreased slightly if it is higher than average. Both of the preceding harvesting patterns allow for six sessions to be carried out using a donor zone substantially smaller than 70 mm high and thus fall well within the "safe" donor area described earlier. Note that during subsequent sessions, any scar tissue left from previous ones should be excised at the same time as the new harvesting so that only one or two scars will ultimately be left—no matter how many sessions are carried out. The remarkable efficiency of the described total excision technique (TET) allows one to obtain all the grafts necessary for six sessions from an area as small as 44 to 50.75 mm wide, traversing the parietooccipital area from approximately the left ear to the right ear. Each session will typically yield 200 or more micrografts, and either 350 to 400 minigrafts or 200 to 250 minigrafts, and 50 to 60 standard round grafts.

Recipient Area

In my mind, I try to divide the anterior half of the recipient area into two zones: (1) the hairline zone, which is approximately 2.5 cm wide, and (2) the main body of the recipient area.

Use small slit grafts in the hairline zone during the first session. Scatter 120–200 or more micrografts anterior to the slit zone area, as well as within it. Prepare recipient sites with a Beaver ES miniblade while micrograft recipient sites are prepared with a 16- or 18-gauge needle. There is no need to employ dilators, although, if you or your technicians are relative novices, you may find them useful. After 4 or more months have elapsed, place a similar session of slit grafts and micrografts between those transplanted during the first session. In addition, as noted earlier, for greater density in the hairline zone, small round minigrafts should be scattered here and there between the slit grafts. At this point, the hair growing from the first session will help to camouflage any slight

FIG. 10. If the hair within any of the previously transplanted grafts is accidentally too coarse or dense, a small round punch should be used to excise it. It is then replaced with one containing fine and/or less dense hair. Shown is a single session of micrografting and slit grafting into an essentially alopecic area. A black line has been drawn to point out one disturbingly dense, coarse-haired graft that will be repositioned during this session. Try to picture how much more natural this result would look without that graft.

clumpiness the round minigrafts might have otherwise produced. If the hair within any of the previously transplanted grafts is accidentally too coarse or dense, use a small round punch to excise that graft, which is then replaced with one containing finer and/or less dense hair (Fig. 10). Four or more months later, a third session, similar to the second, should be conducted to complete the hairline zone. You may use shorter intervals between sessions if your patient is completely alopecic when treatment begins, although, as described above, the

longer intervals will allow adjustments to be made on following sessions according to what is seen growing from previous ones. Intervals of longer than 4 months between sessions can be employed, especially if a reasonable amount of hair is still present in the recipient area.

It is important to note that, although ultimately looking for a random, and therefore natural-looking distribution of hair in this hairline zone, *a very "organized disorganization" produces a better short-term and long-term appearance.* During the first session, place grafts approximately 3 mm apart from each other on the same line, as well as being 1 mm anterior or posterior to their neighbors. This produces the most even distribution of hair in that zone while not creating a straight line (Fig. 11). During the second session, place the grafts approximately midway between those of the first session, again "juggling" them slightly anterior or posterior to their neighbors. During the third session, use a similar approach. Thus a very even distribution of hair over the entire surface will be created, without, for example, some grafts being closer to the neighboring graft on the left side than to the neighboring graft on the right side. At the same time, the careful juggling of grafts slightly anterior or posterior to adjacent grafts produces a random, natural-looking distribution of hair. Two other parameters are important: (1) Follow the direction of the original hair in that area and (2) mimic the angle at which the hair originally exited the scalp.

Thus the cutting of each slit should satisfy the following parameters: (1) they are 3 mm apart, (2) they are 1 mm anterior or posterior to their neighbor, (3) they are directed in the direction of the original hair in that area, and (4) the

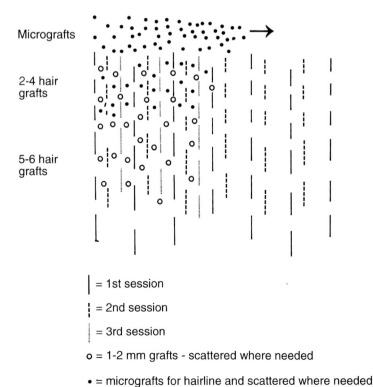

Micrografts

2-4 hair grafts

5-6 hair grafts

| = 1st session

¦ = 2nd session

⋮ = 3rd session

o = 1-2 mm grafts - scattered where needed

• = micrografts for hairline and scattered where needed

FIG. 11. During the first session grafts should be placed approximately 3 mm apart from each other in the same line, as well as being 1 mm anterior or posterior to their neighbors. This produces the most even distribution of hair in that zone, while not creating a straight line. The second and third sessions are distributed as shown in a similarly organized fashion. Micrografts and 1- to 2-mm round grafts should be scattered here and there between the slit grafts during second and third sessions in this area.

angle at which they exit the scalp mimics that of the original hair in that area. Micrografts and round minigrafts (if you are using them) should be scattered *randomly* between the carefully spaced slit grafts but should follow their direction and angle.

As indicated earlier, similar types of grafts and distribution of grafts will probably be used in 90% or more of your patients for the *entire* recipient area. If you are treating the entire anterior or posterior half of the area of MPB with minigrafts, you will require approximately 200 micrografts and 350 to 400 minigrafts per session. In female patients, only slit grafts, micrografts, and round minigrafts should be employed. The vertex area of MPB should similarly be treated only with slit grafts, micrografts, and small round minigrafts. However, in 5% to 10% of male patients, posterior to the hairline zone you may want to switch to an organized pattern of standard-sized grafts (see below). In such cases, each session will usually require 200 or more micrografts, 150 to 250 slit grafts, and either 100 to 120 2-mm grafts or 50 to 60 standard grafts or a combination of both.

When the objective is the greatest density possible, the recipient area superior to the hairline zone should be treated with standard grafts with or without a preceding zone of small round grafts. The latter should be employed when the hair is particularly dense, coarse, or dark but should be spaced similarly to that described below for standard grafts (Figs. 12 and 13). Generally, twice the number of round minigrafts will be required, when they are used instead of standard grafts in any given area.

Just as an organized disorganization is used in the zone treated with slit grafts, in that treated with round grafts use an organized disorganization pattern of standard graft distribution during each session. Any given area of alopecia can be solidly filled with either three or four sessions of standard grafts (Fig. 14). (The four-stage filling pattern is most commonly used.) In practice, very few areas should, in fact, be solidly filled, but it is important for you to maintain the option to do so in four or fewer sessions. The interval used between sessions of standard grafts should be similar to that employed for slit grafts. Waiting for 4 months or more between sessions will allow you to see hair growth in the previously transplanted grafts before trying to fill the spaces between them. The distribution of hair over the surface of previously transplanted grafts may not be even; therefore larger grafts may be required to overlap previously transplanted ones if solid filling is the objective (Fig. 15). During the first session, grafts should be put into what will be rows 1, 3, 5, 7, and so on, and should be spaced exactly one graft apart as shown in Fig. 16.

In the second session, if the area is completely alopecic (or nearly so) and an interval of less than 4 months is being

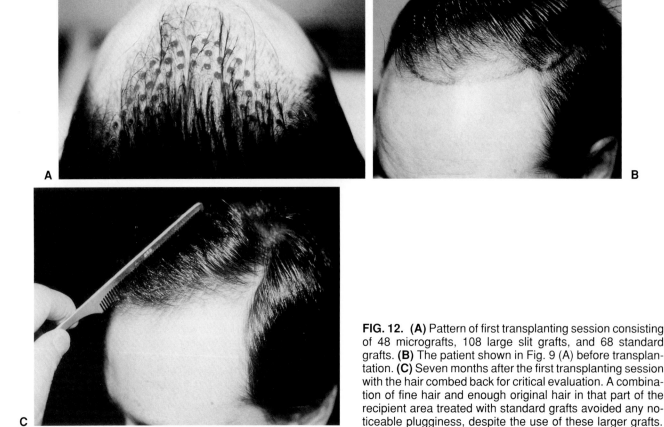

FIG. 12. (A) Pattern of first transplanting session consisting of 48 micrografts, 108 large slit grafts, and 68 standard grafts. **(B)** The patient shown in Fig. 9 (A) before transplantation. **(C)** Seven months after the first transplanting session with the hair combed back for critical evaluation. A combination of fine hair and enough original hair in that part of the recipient area treated with standard grafts avoided any noticeable plugginess, despite the use of these larger grafts.

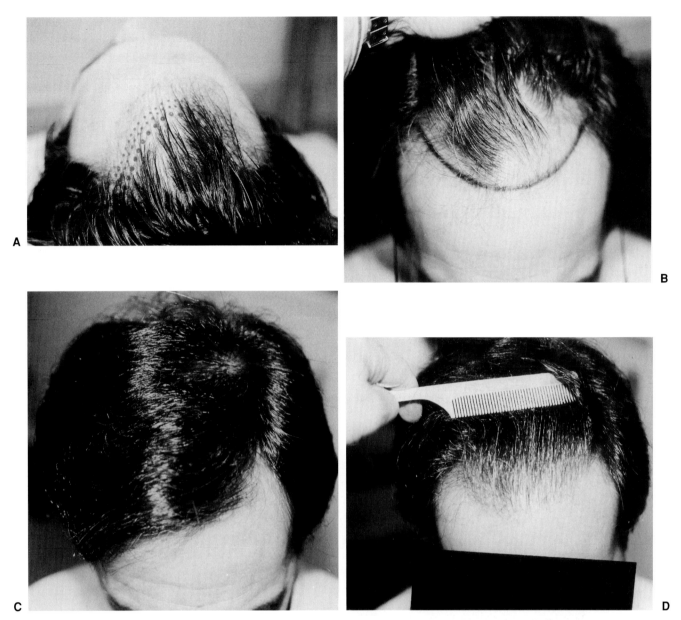

FIG. 13. (A) Pattern frequently used if a combination of all graft types is being employed. **(B)** Before transplanting (same patient as shown in Fig. 13 (A)). **(C)** One year after a first session consisting of 60 micrografts, 162 large slit grafts, 22 standard grafts, and 100 2-mm grafts. **(D)** Photo taken at the same time as Fig. 13 (B) but with the hair combed straight back for critical evaluation. Note the minimal amount of noticeable plugginess, despite such a combination of grafts.

used, grafts should be placed on alternate rows, that is, rows 2, 4, 6, 8, and so on. The following parameters must be satisfied:

1. Grafts should be put one graft apart on the same row.
2. They should be offset from the grafts in the row anterior to them, that is, neither directly behind the spaces in the anterior row nor directly behind the grafts in that row.
3. They should touch the grafts in the row just anterior as well as posterior to them.

To satisfy these three parameters, grafts of at least two different sizes will be necessary because the lengths of rows change as you move from the anterior-most to the posterior-most row. If the spacing used during the first session is fairly accurate, usually the use of 3.25- and 3.5-mm recipient site punches (for 3.5- and 3.75-mm-wide grafts, respectively) allows for the three parameters to be satisfied (Fig. 17).

On the third session the grafts must completely fill the spaces left between adjacent clumps of hair growing in grafts transplanted during the first session. This will usually require recipient site punches 3.0 to 3.5 mm in diameter (Fig. 18). Usually, trimmed 3.5-mm-wide grafts can be placed into the 3-mm holes, 3.75-mm grafts can be placed into those made with 3.25-mm punches, and 4.0-mm-wide grafts can be

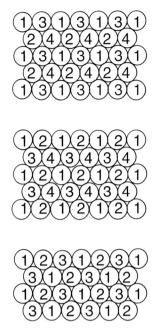

FIG. 14. Any area of alopecia can be solidly filled in one of three different ways. **(Top)** The method shown is the usual four-stage approach. **(Middle)** Still–hair-bearing areas are treated as shown. **(Bottom)** The approach shown is the three-stage filling described by the Orentreichs. (Ann NY Acad Sci 1959;463:83.)

placed into those made with 3.5-mm punches. The grafts on this third session should also touch those transplanted during the second session, that is, on alternate rows. It can be seen that the *size* of the graft used in the spaces on the third session depends on the distance between adjacent clumps of hair on the same row; their *position* depends on them touching the grafts of the alternate rows (second session). One of the results of trying to accomplish the above is that not only are grafts of different sizes used, but they must also be placed slightly anterior to or posterior to those grafts already present on rows 1, 3, 5, 7, and so on, producing a more "juggled" and natural anterior line of round grafts. The "peninsula" between the arms of the round grafted U-shaped area is often left untransplanted, leaving room for future ARs that might excise this site, but slit grafts and/or round minigrafts should be used in any areas that will not be removed with AR. The treatment of this area should be similar to that described earlier for the hairline zone.

During the fourth session, use whatever size of punch is required to completely excise the remaining hairless spaces. If the space requires a 4-mm punch to completely remove it, generally a 4.25-mm-wide graft should be placed into that hole. If the space is irregular, for example, keyhole shaped, two different sizes of punch should be employed to produce holes almost touching or slightly overlapping each other. Two grafts of varying sizes may be used, or a larger graft can be trimmed with small scissors to fit the irregular shape.

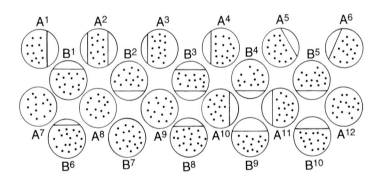

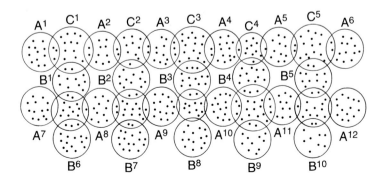

FIG. 15. The surgeon has waited until hair in the first two sessions has grown in **(upper section).** Hairless portions of preceding grafts are clearly evident, and, as shown in lower section, larger grafts can be used, as between A1 and A2, A3 and A4, and A5 and A6. When hair growth has extended to the edge of previous grafts, because of allowance for slight overlapping, smaller grafts can be used, as between A4 and A5, A9 and A10 **(lower section),** and so on. Use of same-sized grafts in these sites would have removed some of the hair previously transplanted.

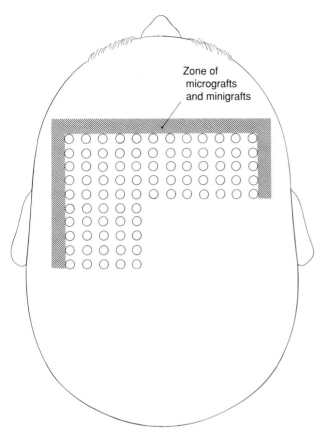

FIG. 16. During the first session, grafts should be put into what will be rows 1, 3, 5, 7, and so on and should be spaced exactly one graft apart as shown. A zone of micrografting and minigrafting is used anterior to them.

The intent should be to solidly fill any area that has been treated with standard grafts, to produce maximum density, and also, just as important, to avoid any potentially noticeable "plugginess" when the hair is wet or windblown. It is very important to emphasize, however, that less than solid filling is *far* less cosmetically problematic when standard grafts are being used posterior to a hairline zone of micrografts and minigrafts than it was in the past when standard grafts were being used to create a hairline.

The peninsula between the arms of the "U" should be treated with slit and round minigrafts, again leaving room for one or more future ARs in many patients. In addition, if the patient intends to transplant the crown, you can start transplanting this area at the same time as the fourth session is being carried out in the anterior half of the area of MPB, for example, as a "ledge" of slit grafts on the part side more posteriorly (or bilaterally). A third session to the transplanted peninsula will usually be done after the last AR is completed in this area and frequently can be carried out while transplanting in the vertex area. As an alternative, if AR is carried out between the second and third sessions and/or the third and fourth sessions, or if you have no intention to transplant

more posteriorly at any time, you can treat the entire area of the peninsula between the arms of the "U" during the third or fourth session, or both (Fig. 19). A fifth, smaller session of transplanting to this area may be necessary to produce acceptable coverage.

Anticipating the size of spaces being left is extremely important. During each session, before standard round recipient sites are prepared, always consider how the remaining hairless site can be totally filled with the balance of the basic four sessions. This is relatively easy in the first two sessions but must be especially carefully estimated at the time of the third session.

As indicated earlier, carry out round minigrafting in most areas other than the hairline zone and "peninsula" area on the basis of the above principles aimed at producing solid filling of those sites.

The amount of tissue infiltration with local anesthetic and saline and the angling of the punch are important variables. A more acute angle will produce a larger hole, as will more anesthetic or saline infiltration. A smaller recipient site hole will result in a tighter fit for the graft. Therefore it is wise

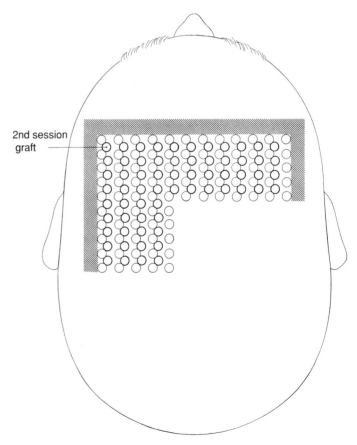

FIG. 17. In the second session, grafts are placed in alternate rows; that is, rows 2, 4, 6, 8, and so on. Three parameters must be satisfied: they should be one graft apart on the same row, they should be offset, and they should touch the grafts in the row just anterior as well as posterior to them.

FIG. 18. On the third session the grafts must completely fill the space left between adjacent grafts of the first session. This will usually require recipient site punches from 3 to 3.5 mm in diameter. Therefore the size of the graft used in the spaces on the third session depends on the distance between adjacent clumps of hair on the same row. Their position, however, depends on them touching the grafts placed during the second session, that is, on alternate rows. Therefore, not only will grafts be different sizes, but they are also placed slightly anterior to or posterior to those grafts already present in rows 1, 3, 5, 7, and so on, to touch the grafts in rows 2, 4, 6, 8, and so on. This produces a more juggled and natural-looking demarcation between the hairline zone and the denser area posterior to it. (This photo shows a patient treated more than 15 years ago, who therefore lacks a hairline zone of minigrafts anterior to the standard grafts.)

to punch out the first recipient site with a 3.0-mm punch and to try a graft in that hole initially to see whether it fits well or if the fit is too tight. If the fit is too snug, drill out the same hole with a 3.25-mm punch and insert another test graft. If the hole is still too small, drill the same site with a 3.5-mm punch, and so on, *until the optimum donor area/ recipient area ratio is determined for that particular individual with your particular technique. In the anterior two to four rows,* virtually always use a 3.5-mm recipient site punch for grafts obtained from 3.75-mm to 4.0 mm wide strips. A 3.25-mm recipient site punch should be employed for grafts obtained from 3.5-mm to 3.75 mm wide strips.

Other factors, including the ratio of the potential recipient area to the potential donor area and hair characteristics, should also affect the donor-recipient graft differential. The less ideal the recipient area/donor area ratio, the more use you should make of 3.5-mm recipient site punches for all rows behind row 1 on the *nonpart side* to conserve grafts. The more ideal the hair texture, density, wave, caliber, and color, the more use you can make of 3.5-mm recipient punches on *both part and nonpart sides.* This, once again, will conserve grafts while having only slightly negative but still acceptable cosmetic effects.

The diamond-shaped bare spaces left between round recipient sites becomes larger as the grafts become larger, (Fig. 20) so more allowance for overlapping (to remove these spaces) becomes necessary when larger round sites are used and, conversely, less overlapping is necessary with the use of progressively smaller round grafts. The more overlapping, the larger the potential loss of previously transplanted hair becomes. Therefore it is conceivable that if overlapping is used to avoid the empty spaces, there may less less hair than if smaller grafts were used. Thus it is best if such spaces are treated with micrografts or excised with small round punches at the time of the third and fourth sessions. An alternative approach is to not allow for overlapping or concomitant minigrafting and micrografting and to use a fifth and possibly a sixth "filler" session to transplant the diamond-shaped spaces. In this approach, however, extra sessions (and time) are required. Note that offsetting the grafts converts the diamond-shaped areas into smaller triangular spaces and should always be used, regardless of the round recipient site size employed (Fig. 21).

FIG. 19. If there is no intention to carry out AR or to transplant more posteriorly at any time, the entire area of the peninsula between the arms of the U shape can be treated during both the third and fourth sessions, with a combination of slit and/ or small round grafts.

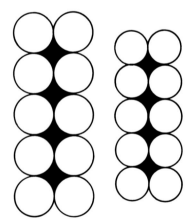

FIG. 20. Diamond-shaped bare spaces left between larger round grafts become larger, so that more allowance for overlapping becomes necessary when larger grafts are used. The drawing shows smaller and larger grafts, with respectively smaller and larger diamond-shaped bare areas (in black) between them.

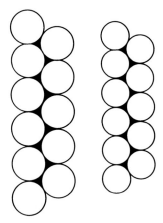

FIG. 21. Off-setting of grafts converts the larger diamond-shaped areas shown in Fig. 20 to smaller, triangular spaces. Off-setting should always be used, regardless of the graft size employed.

As noted earlier, for slit grafting, make an attempt to follow the original hair direction and angle whenever possible. The usual direction of hair growth in the anterior scalp and crown is shown in Fig. 22A and B. Some physicians prefer to change the angle of growth to one that may be more acute than originally, to produce a "shingling" effect whereby the hairs in adjacent grafts overlap each other and produce a denser, less tufted appearance. However, very acute angling of recipient grafts is difficult to deal with, especially when trying to completely fill the spaces between round grafts. In addition, of course, a change in hair angle from that originally present is impossible in any area where hair is still growing without injuring adjacent follicles and causing more marked thinning of hair growth at that site than would occur if angling were the same. It is worthwhile to note that micrografting and slit grafting are far less likely to damage existing hair than round minigrafting and standard grafting, if the direction or angle of transplantation is incorrect or is intentionally different.

A problem arises when transplanting into a hair-bearing area where sharp changes of hair direction are present. The two most frequent sites where this occurs are the center of the whorl of the crown in some individuals and the anterior 2 to 3 cm of the hairline in a very small number of patients. In this latter group, hair usually grows in one direction in the anterior 2.5 to 3 cm and posterior to that point might grow at quite a different angle. Transplanting into the anterior 2.5 to 3 cm should be performed in a direction parallel to the bulk of the hair more posteriorly rather than in the direction of the more limited amount of anterior zone hair. Direct crown hair to produce a gradual whorl at its origin (Fig. 22A), notwithstanding the original direction of hair being very disorganized. Gross direction changes cannot be mimicked even with slit grafting. The other alternative is to use only micrografts; in that case four or more sessions will often be necessary to produce adequate density, but it is frequently the best course to follow at the center of the whorl of the vertex.

If a significant amount of hair is left in recipient areas with sharply differing hair directions at the time transplanting commences, an obvious conflict of interest results. In the first place, "early" transplanting is being done to thicken the thinning area; therefore as little damage as possible should be done to existing hairs. On the other hand, long-term goals may require that the direction of the transplanted hair be different than that of some of the original hairs at that site. Therefore, transplanting in such individuals should generally consist of micrografting and slit grafting and is usually not recommended until there is at least a moderate amount of hair loss present (unless, as noted above, only micrografts are used in the areas of conflicting hair direction).

The need for consistent direction and angling of recipient sites cannot be overemphasized. Slight changes in the angle or direction in which a recipient site is prepared, especially for round recipient sites, can result in injury to or excision of adjacent previously transplanted hair matrices—and the creation of new small areas of alopecia (Fig. 23).

Tissue turgor is as important in the recipient area as it is in the donor area, if injury to hair adjacent to the recipient sites being prepared during any given session is to be minimized. Just as in the donor area, significant amounts of saline may be necessary for this purpose.

For black patients, nearly always use a combination

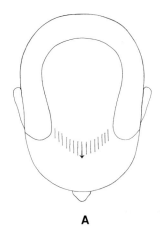

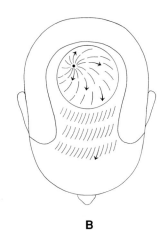

A   B

FIG. 22. (A) A variant of the usual direction of hair growth. (Direction of hair adjacent to temporal hair usually mimics that of the temporal hair.) **(B)** The usual direction of hair growth in the crown and anterior scalp is shown. In the latter area, hair points anteriorly and to the right on the left side of the scalp, gradually changing to point more and more to the right as one moves to the right side of the midline (or vice versa).

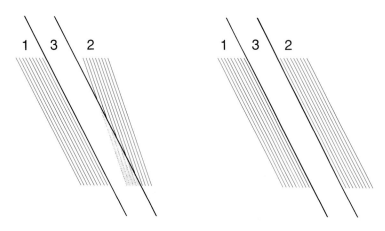

FIG. 23. (Left) Second round graft (2) was incorrectly angled more steeply than first graft. If one attempts to prepare a recipient site for the third graft (3) at the same angle as the first graft, injury to follicles in the second graft cannot be avoided. **(Right)** First and second grafts have been angled similarly. The site for the third graft can be made without any injury to adjacent follicles. The necessity of "consistent angling" also exists in the third dimension, which is not possible to show here, that is, in relation to grafts anterior and posterior to it.

of micrografts and minigrafts for the hairline zone and round recipient sites of various sizes posterior to the hairline zone. For all other races the use of this combination of graft types is optional.

An Ultrapulse CO_2 laser can be employed to make recipient sites for slit grafts or for round grafts while a Sharplan CO_2 laser should be used only for round grafts. Both produce recipient sites with less bleeding and probably less edema and postoperative pain. The use of a laser to produce round holes does not result in superior cosmetic results but is associated with less bleeding and eliminates the need to remove tissue from the hole. The chance that some tissue may be left behind to cause epidermal cysts is thus eliminated, and the time consumed in removing recipient site plugs is also saved. When slits are made with a laser, tissue is ablated. Thus the density and absence of compression of round grafting sites are combined with the cosmetically superior, linear shape of a slit graft.

Remarkably natural-looking results are possible with only one session (Fig. 24A–D) that surpass the naturalness of slit grafts or round grafting while achieving the density of the latter. On the other hand, there is usually additional early crusting over the grafts and a delay of 2 to 6 weeks before hair growth begins, as compared with when a laser is not employed. The exact parameters that should be used in laser transplantation have not yet been established, but it is likely that lasers will play an increasingly important role in hair transplantation.

Graft Preparation and Insertion

After removing the strips of tissue from the donor area, carefully separate them from each other and lay them out on a moistened tongue-depressor. Orientate the strips so that a clear view of hair follicles is possible. Using a small jeweler's forceps and Personna superstainless shaper blades, carefully section the strips into pieces containing the desired number of hairs (Fig. 25). Keep the strip constantly moist, and after separating the sections from the strip place them immediately into a Petri dish with a 4×4 gauze that has

been at least half-filled with a saline solution. No spicules of hairs that do not include their matrices should be left on the grafts, since these only act as foreign bodies in the recipient area. Although hair can regenerate from only the upper half of the hair follicle—specifically, the hair "bulge" just inferior to the entry of the sebaceous gland into the hair follicle—hair growth from such partial follicles is sporadic at best, while annoying, persistent foreign body reactions in the recipient area are more certain.

Only approximately 2 mm of subcutaneous tissue should be left below the level of the deepest hair bulbs. The rest of the subcutaneous tissue should be sectioned off the grafts as part of the cleaning process. Leave a little extra subcutaneous tissue beneath each graft rather than taking off too much, since the former may result in injury to hair matrices. If the hair is particularly coarse or dark, remove the epidermal portion of each slit graft by slicing off the top of the graft at approximately a 45-degree angle to the skin surface. This will allow the hair to align itself in more of a single file and will minimize the possibility of "compression" of hair into unsightly dense, dark, or coarse lines. It is not necessary or advisable to remove the epidermis of round grafts of any size.

Gently ease the prepared grafts into the recipient sites using small serrated forceps or jeweler's forceps. Do not grasp grafts by their follicular end. This averts damaging the hair matrices. As mentioned earlier, for a relative novice it may be useful to use dilators, which are available from most suppliers for hair transplant surgeons. These are inserted for at least 5 minutes before the placement of grafts and are removed immediately before their insertion. Apply steady pressure to control any bleeding in the area and to ensure that the grafts are flush with the surrounding skin. Be careful to avoid "burying" the grafts beneath the level of the skin. It is better to leave a graft protruding *slightly* above the level of the surrounding skin than below it, since inclusion cysts may result from the latter. Occasionally, standard grafts will not sit flush with the surrounding skin, despite prolonged manipulation and pressure. In such individuals, apply an ethyl cyanoacrylate glue (Loctite 15494) in two or three small droplets to the edge of the graft.

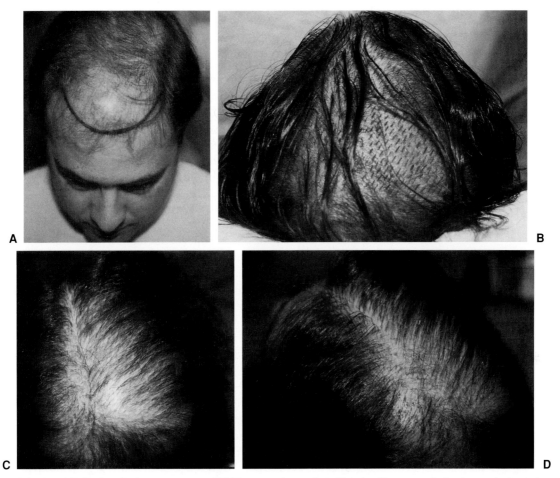

FIG. 24. (A) Patient before treatment. **(B)** Two sessions of grafting had been carried out anteriorly and are shown growing. In addition, 110 laser slit sites are evident on the right side of the area between the arms of the transplanted "U." A comparable number of conventionally produced slit graft sites are present on the left side of the peninsula. **(C)** Results at 9 months of this single session of grafts into the peninsula between the arms of the "U." Very even and natural distribution of hair on the laser-treated side is evident. The patient and his wife were both certain that no transplanting had been carried out in that area until they were shown the "before" pictures. They then asked that all future transplanting be carried out with a laser. **(D)** A different view of the results shown in Fig. 24 (C), which demonstrates the more stringy, less even distribution of hair on the conventionally treated side on the left as compared with the laser-treated side on the right. Remarkably natural-looking results are possible with only one laser session. These results have passed the naturalness of conventionally treated slit grafts or round grafts while achieving the density of the latter.

It cannot be overemphasized that grafts must be kept moist at all times during the procedure. In addition, it may be useful to segregate them into groups that contain, for example, fine hair, coarse hair, gray hair, and so on. They should be further segregated according to the number of hairs they contain. Thus, when looking for the ideal graft for any particular recipient site, it is readily available.

Bandaging

Use a small overnight dressing postoperatively. It need not cover the ears (Fig. 26). Its purpose is primarily to keep the grafts in place and to prevent their accidentally being knocked out of position during the first postoperative night.

It will also absorb any small amount of serosanguinous exudate that might develop.

The dressing consists of Bacitracin ointment applied to both recipient and donor areas, followed by Telfa sheets on the recipient area only. Place 4 × 4-inch gauze pieces on top of the Telfa and directly on top of the donor area. Cotton batting behind and in front of the ears will prevent undue pressure on them. Take care that they are lying flat against the head rather than being accidentally bent forward. Two Kerlix bandages should be used to hold everything in place. While the first is encircling the head, the second is passed from front to back and back to front. Each pass of the encircling Kerlix bandage anchors in place the one being passed back and forth.

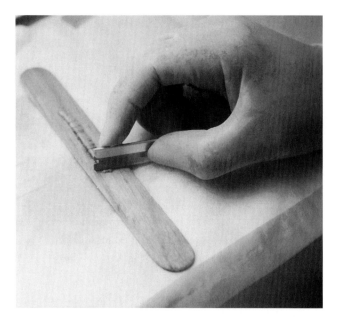

FIG. 25. A slit graft is sliced off a strip of donor tissue. A one-to two-hair micrograft will be sectioned off this graft.

If there is no more than the usual amount of bleeding during the course of transplanting, patients may leave without a bandage. Use a hairdryer set on cool to dry any minor exudation around the grafts, which creates a firmer adhesion between them and their recipient sites. Have the patients remain in the office for 1 to several hours after surgery to confirm that no bleeding will occur. Whether or not a bandage is used, the patient should ideally return the next day to confirm that the grafts are still positioned properly, as well as to carefully cleanse away any blood clots that may have developed overnight with hydrogen peroxide–soaked gauze

FIG. 26. Stegman-Tromovitch bandage.

and cotton tipped swab sticks. Properly trained assistants should then carefully wash, style, and dry the patient's hair.

POSTOPERATIVE COURSE

Supply your patients with three strengths of analgesic. Acetaminophen tablets with 30 mg of codeine (Tylenol-3), oxycodone, and meperidine hydrochloride, 50 mg, to be used as required. Most patients do not use anything more than the Tylenol-3 tablets and then only for the first night. Intramuscular ketorolac tromethamine, 30 to 60 mg, is extremely effective in eliminating all postoperative pain for 6 to 8 hours in virtually all patients.

A small amount of postoperative crusting will occur. Most of this is removed during the first cleansing and washing. Instruct the patients to use Baciguent ointment or any other sterile moisturizing ointment three times daily until all of the crusting ceases. Shedding of the crusts can also be expedited if the patient is asked to wash the hair twice daily, after soaking the donor and recipient areas for 15 minutes.

As noted earlier, use 2 ml of methyl prednisolone acetate 40 mg/ml in a single intramuscular injection 30 minutes before surgery (unless it is contraindicated), to minimize edema. A variable amount of postoperative swelling can be expected, so warn the patient that in a small number of cases the edema may be sufficient to cause echymoses around the eyes, which will last for a week to 10 days.

The transplanted grafts will shed their hair in 2 to 6 weeks, although occasionally some will retain their hair without an initial effluvium. New hair growth usually begins 10 to 20 weeks after surgery, but in general occurs somewhat earlier in micrografts and minigrafts than in standard round grafts. Not all grafts begin growing hair at the same time, nor do all hairs in an individual graft grow simultaneously. Patients should be told that, although hair growth begins at approximately 3 months, it will be 6 months from the day of surgery before they have a fairly good idea of how much hair they are going to obtain. It will be 9 months after surgery before the *ultimate* cosmetic effect of any given session can be clearly perceived. Give your patients a 2% to 3% solution of minoxidil to use twice daily for 5 to 6 weeks postoperatively. It often accelerates regrowth of hair.

Because of the type of donor harvesting that is employed today and the numerous incisions that are made in the recipient area, some postoperative hypoesthesia of the scalp can be expected to occur in nearly everyone. This is usually temporary but may persist for as long as 18 months. In rare cases there may be a permanent decreased sensitivity of a small area of the scalp. Forewarn your patients.

The incidence of ingrown hairs during the healing period has increased substantially since we started extensive use of slit grafts. Hairs on the periphery of grafts that are compressed in narrow scalpel incisions can quite easily accidentally grow into the adjacent tissue. It is most likely to occur approximately 2 to 3 months after surgery, when new growth is commencing.

Complications

True infection in the recipient area occurs in fewer than 0.1% of patients. It usually consists of papules or papulopustules and often cannot be clinically distinguished from an ingrown hair or foreign body reaction. However, cultures grow pathogens. In the donor area, infection around sutures occurs slightly more often. Usually, it is quite mild and resolves quickly after the sutures are removed. Whenever infection is suspected, a sample of the exudate should be taken for culture and sensitivity testing, and the patient should be started on a regimen of topical as well as systemic antibiotics. Hot saline compresses on the area three times daily should also be used.

Grafts may be slightly elevated ("cobblestoning") or slightly depressed. Cobblestoning can be treated with light electrodesiccation; depressed grafts should be excised and replaced with grafts that lie flush with the skin.

Epidermal cysts result from accidentally leaving small pieces of skin in a minigraft recipient hole or "piggy-backing" one graft on top of another, or from grafts slipping beneath the skin surface. Such lesions should be incised and their contents expressed. A small, curved forceps with teeth is a useful instrument in retrieving material, including balls of hair, from within these epidermal cysts.

Postoperative bleeding is a rare complication of hair transplanting and is easily handled by a suture through the offending site.

Keloids and hypertrophic scars are extremely unusual complications of transplanting, occurring in less than 0.1% of patients. A careful family history and a test graft in those who are suspected of being prone to keloid formation (for example, blacks or Asians) is very helpful in avoiding this problem. Seventy-five percent of keloids occur in black patients, and a test graft should be made on all blacks before transplanting a large area.

"Hyperfibrotic healing" has been reported in a small number of patients. These individuals develop thick, firm skin in the recipient area. There is a distinct ridge at the junction of the forehead and that area. Biopsy findings in one of these patients revealed a perifollicular and focal chronic inflammatory infiltrate in the dermis and, more significantly, ectopic hair shafts devoid of follicular tissue in the subcutaneous tissue. Marked fibrosis was present both in the dermis and in subcutaneous tissue. The findings suggest accidental trapping of hair shafts or debris in the recipient area incisions at the time of surgery and, perhaps, inadequate graft preparation before insertion.

There have been isolated reports of patients in whom virtually no hair grows in transplanted grafts, for no apparent reason. Such patients have been labeled as having the "X factor."

Arteriovenous fistulas occur in approximately 1 in 5000 surgeries. They become evident as pulsating nodules and may develop in either the recipient or donor areas as the result of an accidental joining of a small severed vein and arteriole. If left alone, they usually resolve spontaneously in 3 to 6 months. As an alternative, the lesion may be eliminated by tying off the afferent and efferent vessels. The nodular or cystic component is excised concomitantly.

A single case of osteomyelitis secondary to hair transplanting has been reported in the literature. This is a complication that should never have occurred and will never occur if infection is promptly treated.

Other complications can occur and include telogen effluvium; chronic follicullitis; accelerated hair loss; temporary curly, lusterless hair; indented "grooves" in the recipient area; and wound dehiscence. These are either temporary, minor, or rare sequelae of hair transplanting and should be viewed from that perspective.

Part 2: Minigrafting and Micrografting

HISTORY OF TREATMENT OF ANDROGENETIC ALOPECIA

Throughout the 1960s and 1970s grafts were harvested with 4- to 5-mm trephines and transplanted to areas of alopecia. Graft survival was good, but the cosmetic result was unacceptable to many patients. In the 1980s innovations in instrumentation and technique transformed the ability of a surgeon to create natural transplants on a more consistent basis. Surgeons cut the standard 4- to 5-mm grafts into halves or quarters, producing smaller grafts that were inserted into smaller holes or slit incisions. This produced less "plugginess" and thus a more natural result.

In the 1990s surgeons moved toward harvesting donor grafts by scalpel excision rather than by trephine punch biopsies. Multiple-bladed knives have gained widespread acceptance. They allow for excision of several narrow strips, resulting in a maximum yield of grafts while preserving future donor graft sites. Others have abandoned the hand-engine harvesting method in favor of single-bladed harvesting of the donor areas. Recently, laser technology has entered the field of hair transplantation. It is used for creating recipient sites, but time will clarify its real role and utility.

PREOPERATIVE PLANNING

The majority of poor results seen in hair transplantation are not medical complications (e.g., infection, cyst, hematoma), but poor cosmetic outcomes. The goal in hair restoration is to create a positive, visible appearance change that looks natural and undetectable. A proper screening of candidates during the consultation will define an appropriate patient for surgery and increase the likelihood of success. The foundation for a successful transplantation is created in the consult room.

Candidate Selection

What qualifies a patient as a good or bad candidate for hair transplantation is a compilation of the following factors: (1) patient expectations, (2) the donor supply, (3) the degree of alopecia, (4) the hair quality, (5) the skin type, and (6) the age of the patient.

Individuals with a severe grade of baldness (Norwood types V to VII) will generally be satisfied with a diffuse thinning appearance created by hair transplantation. In these patients the goal is to frame the face. Facial framing will return the center of the attention to the face and away from the bald scalp. On the other end of the spectrum is the individual presenting with minimal hair loss (Norwood types II to III) who desires higher density and correction of temporal recessions. Unless realistic expectations are present, surgery in these patients should be postponed until a more defined pattern of alopecia develops. As alopecia progresses, the net loss of nontransplanted hair will exceed the transplanted hair and the net density gain will not significantly increase. After a few years, the patient may look balder than before the hair transplantation as a result of continued hair loss. The above scenario underscores the need to require the specific goals and expectations of the patient. It is vital that the patient and surgeon have similar long-term goals.

Regardless of the technique used, donor density must be adequate to achieve coverage that is acceptable to the patient. In general, the older the patient, the better the candidate. Androgenetic alopecia is a lifelong process. It will always be easier to obtain good surgical results and a satisfied patient over the short and long term in an individual who has advanced patterns of hair loss. Patients in their late teens and early twenties comprise a high-risk group in regard to predicting future hair loss. With few exceptions, rarely is a patient younger than 25 years a candidate for transplantation.

The following hair and skin features are important in the selection process and planning: (1) contrast between skin color and hair color, (2) texture or caliber of the hair, and (3) curliness of hair. Curly hair is better for transplantation than straight hair because it covers more area of bald skin. The contrast between the color of skin and the color of hair is also very important. Individuals with black hair and pale skin are more challenging candidates for transplantation, since they often will appear to have a "transplanted look." This occurs because the black transplanted hairs stand out against a white scalp. Better candidates are those with salt-and-pepper colored, gray, blonde, red, or light brown hair because there is less contrast with the skin. However, it is

TABLE 30-3. *Length of the donor strip required according to the number and size of mini-micrografts transplanted per session*

Desired number of grafts	Required length of 4 mm wide strip			
	Single	1.00 mm	1.25 mm	1.5 mm
50	1.25 cm	2 cm	3 cm	4 cm
100	2.50 cm	4 cm	6 cm	8 cm
150	3.75 cm	6 cm	9 cm	12 cm
200	5 cm	8 cm	12 cm	16 cm

[a] Strip taken with triple bladed knife, and 2 mm spacers.
[b] These measurements are for patients with average donor density (18–22 hairs in a 4 mm circle).
[c] Adjustment Factor: Reduce 10% of total length if hair density is >22. Increase 10% if hair density is <18.

possible to obtain good results in those with a high degree of contrast between their skin color and hair color if only on to four hair grafts are used. Larger autografts should be avoided in this subset, since they tend to produce a strikingly pluggy appearance.

Evaluation of the Density in the Donor Area

To ensure that the correct number of grafts are obtained, the amount of donor scalp to be harvested must be determined. Table 30-3 aids in estimating the donor strip length, depending on the desired number of grafts and hair density. The data in Table 30-3 assume a triple-bladed knife with 2-mm spacers. For example, to transplant 100 single hair grafts and 250 1-mm hair grafts, the size of the strip to be excised will be 12 cm long and 4 mm wide (assuming average hair density). This allows harvesting of the appropriate number of grafts for each session and minimizes any "wasted" grafts.

Another factor to consider is hair density, which for standardization purposes is the number of hairs present within a 4-mm-diameter circle. The average hair density of men presenting themselves for hair transplantation surgery is 18 to 22 hairs per 12.5 mm^2 (area of 4-mm circle). The length of the strip must be increased or decreased for patients with

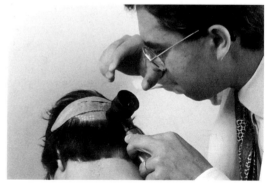

FIG. 27. Hair density of the donor area is estimated with an epiluminescent skin surface microscope.

below- or above-average density, respectively, according to the adjustment factor listed in Table 30-3. The hair density of the patient can be objectively measured before beginning a transplantation. A variety of methods have been developed for this purpose, including a modified epiluminescent skin surface microscope that provides magnification ×10 and strong illumination of a 4-mm-wide field (Fig. 27). The majority of hair in the donor area emerges in bundles of two, three, or four hairs. Casual inspection with the naked eye will often overlook this fact; therefore, if magnification is not used, a patient's hair density is often underestimated.

Hairline Design

A poorly designed hairline is a common reason for a poor result in hair transplantation. The following discussion should serve as a general guideline. Individual facial features, hair characteristics, age, and goals of patients will alter the hairline design in many cases.

Three points should be drawn: A, B, and C (Fig. 28). Point A is midline and represents the hairline starting point. This point varies with facial features but generally begins 8 to 11 cm above the midglabellar area. Point B indicates the start of temporal recess. Point C is the highest area of the temporo-parietal fringe at which the new grafted hairline will meet the temporal hairline. When viewed from the front, this point falls very close to a line drawn vertically from the outer canthus. It is important to note that points A, B, and C should be connected in a horizontal plane. Although the hairline can be drawn as a symmetric, oval line, in practice the single hair grafts on the hairline are placed in a deliberately irregular pattern. The goal is strict avoidance of building a wall, with emphasis on building a zone (the ''feathering zone''), a transition zone that mimics the natural hairline.

The progressive, relentless nature of alopecia mandates that hairlines be placed in a position that anticipates future hair loss. Thus all rules and guidelines must be flexible enough to accommodate the expected changes as alopecia progresses. Family history of alopecia is a factor to consider in the final pattern of hair loss, but it does not significantly alter the design of the frontal hairline in each patient.

In drawing a hairline in a young male patient who wants his hairline lowered and his temporal recessions filled, the patient must be reminded that 10 or 20 years from now, when future balding occurs, a low hairline without temporal recessions will look unnatural. In general it is better to design a high, narrow hairline, leaving the normal temporal recessions intact. A low hairline is difficult to raise. It is the obligation of the surgeon to place the hairline in the optimal place for each patient and resist frequent patient requests for low hairlines.

Size and Number of Grafts per Session (see Chapter 30, Part 1)

A micrograft contains one or two hairs. A minigraft refers to a graft that is less than 2 mm in diameter. To be more precise, always mention the number of hairs contained in it or the recipient hole diameter (for example, ''1-mm minigraft'' or ''four-hair minigraft''). Any graft of 2 mm or larger is known as a standard graft. The number and size of grafts transplanted per session are estimated at the beginning of each session. This is one of the most difficult aspects for the beginner because there are no recipes to follow on this issue. In general, this will be influenced by a variety of factors, including the pattern and extent of alopecia, the quality of hair, and the experience and skill of the surgical team. However, for any given patient, different experienced hair transplant surgeons may have various criteria for the number and size of grafts per session. Thus transplantation is part art and part science.

Regarding the size of the grafts, one to three hair grafts are employed in the majority of patients. The single hair grafts are implanted into slits and positioned in the frontal hairline, creating a transition zone 1 to 2 cm wide. Behind this zone, we place the grafts containing two and three hairs in 1-mm holes. Only in patients with excellent match of hair to skin color do we advise 1.25-mm minigrafts containing three to four hairs.

The number of grafts inserted into a bald area is limited. In a 1 × 1-cm² bald area we can make approximately seven 1-mm holes for grafts containing two and three hairs, and 11 recipient sites for single hair grafts. Therefore the number of grafts per session should be dictated by the need of each patient (the degree of alopecia) and by the skills and speed of the technical personnel available to dissect and plant the grafts.

There is a trend to move to the megasessions, that is, transplanting a large number of grafts per session (1000 to 2000). Increased procedure time and fatigue of the patient and personal are problems that arise when those numbers are reached. Large grafts sessions do not directly correlate with better results or thicker hair. Whether to perform one 2000-grafts session or four 500-graft sessions is irrelevant, as long as the final product is a hair transplant that looks natural and undetectable in both the short and long term. The number of grafts transplanted and number of sessions performed vary with each patient.

Instructions and Medications

The night before and the morning of the procedure, the patient shampoos his hair with chlorhexidine gluconate (Hibiclens). A first-generation cephalosporin, cephradine 500 mg (Velosef), is taken 1 hour before surgery, and 10 mg of diazepam (Valium) is taken 40 minutes before arriving at the clinic.

OPERATIVE TECHNIQUE

Excision of the Donor Site

The length of the donor area varies according to the number of grafts required (Table 30-3). Mark and trim the area

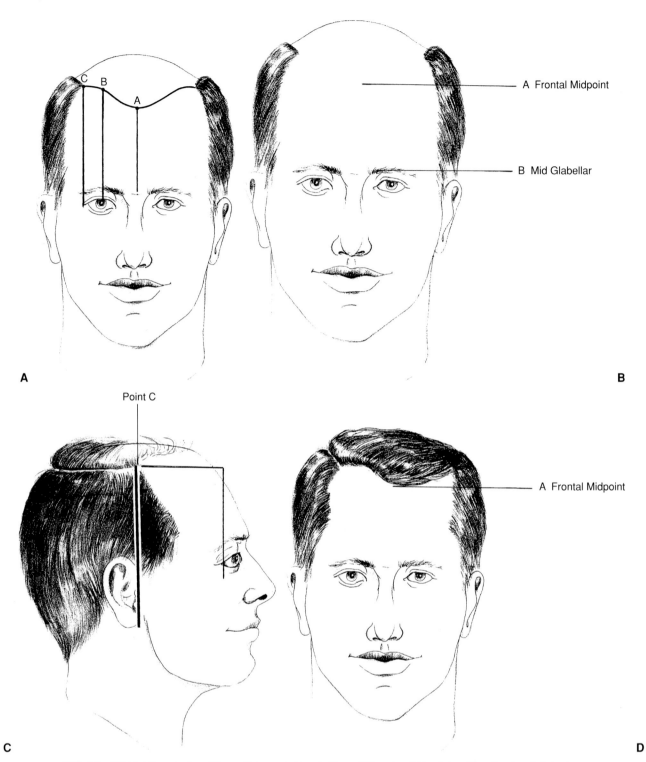

FIG. 28. (A) Hairline design. These three points—A, B, and C—should be joined in a horizontal design. **(B)** Point A is midline and represents the hairline starting point. This point varies with facial features but generally begins between 8 and 11 cm above the midglabellar area. **(C)** Point C is the highest area of the temporal fringe, at which the new grafted hairline will meet the temporal hairline. When viewed from the front, this point falls very close to a vertical line from the outer canthus. **(D)** The hairline is initially drawn in a symmetric oval line, but deliberate indentions are placed in the areas of the temporal recess.

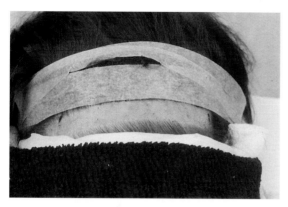

FIG. 29. The occipital donor area is trimmed, and the length of the donor strip is marked according to the number of grafts required to harvest.

FIG. 31. The orientation of the blades must be maintained parallel to the hair shafts to avoid hair transection.

with a moustache trimmer (Fig. 29). Place the patient on his stomach on the operating table with the head on a prone pillow. Clean the donor area with alcohol followed by an injection of 10 to 20 ml of lidocaine 0.5% with epinephrine 1:200,000. Immediately before excision, infiltrate the dermis with 10 to 20 ml of saline to obtain dermal turgor.

Excise a long strip of hair-bearing scalp from the occipital area. Achieve this by a conventional scalpel or a multiple-bladed knife, such as a straight triple-bladed knife with 2-mm spacers (Fig. 30), thereby obtaining two long strips, each 2 ml wide. Hold the knife parallel to the patient's hair follicles, but never perpendicular to the skin, since this would result in a significant degree of hair shaft transection (Figs. 31 and 32). The depth of insertion should be approximately 7 mm into the scalp, enough to reach a depth of 1 to 2 mm below the terminus of the hair follicles (Fig. 33). Deeper incisions result in a greater frequency of transection of the occipital arteries. Contour the ends of the strips with a single surgical scalpel blade to produce an elliptic pattern. Use sharp scissors to section the strips from their base, taking care to preserve the hair follicles (Fig. 34). Immediately place the strips into a Petri dish with cold saline at 4°C. Have the technicians start the dissection of the grafts immediately.

After excising the donor strips, carefully inspect the wound and coagulate or suture the bleeding vessels as needed (Fig. 35). Close the wound using staples (3M 25DS) (Fig. 36), which seem to be preferred by patients over sutures and heal more rapidly. Apply polysporin ointment, and place a temporary pressure bandage over the donor area.

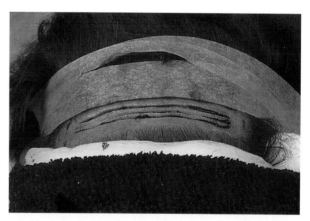

FIG. 32. Intraoperative view showing two 2-mm strips immediately after the incisions.

FIG. 33. Good donor strips with minimal hair transection. The fat below the hair bulbs is trimmed away before starting the graft dissection.

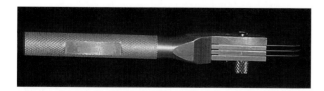

FIG. 30. A triple-bladed knife is used to excise the donor strips.

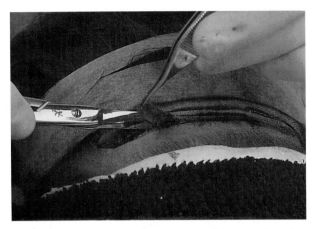

FIG. 34. The strips are released from their base at the subcutaneous level using sharp scissors.

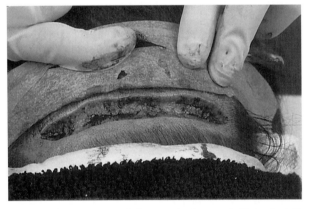

FIG. 35. Appearance of the surgical wound. Note that the depth of the wound is above the galea.

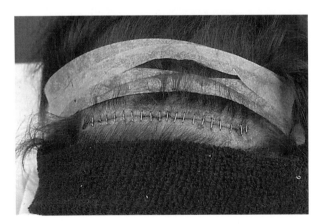

FIG. 36. Closure is achieved with staples.

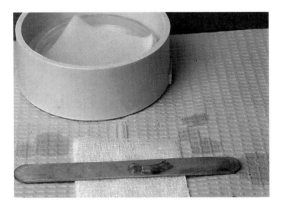

FIG. 37. A small portion (1 to 2 cm) of the strip is placed on a wet tongue-depressor blade and is dissected with a No. 10 Personna blade and jeweler's forceps. Petri dish is placed into an ice container that maintains the grafts at a cold temperature of 3°C.

Graft Preparation

The transplantation of hundreds of micrografts is a time-consuming procedure that requires team effort, with the hair transplant surgeon acting as coordinator of this team. The role the technicians play in the graft preparation is crucial. To a great extent, the survival of the grafts depends on how carefully they are handled. Mechanical trauma can occur during graft preparation or during graft placement.

Maintain all donor hair in chilled isotonic saline at 4°C. Have the technicians separate the strips from each other and begin sectioning follicles from the end of the strips. Specifically, place a small (1-cm) segment of the strip on a wet tongue-depressor blade and section it using a No. 10 surgical blade (Personna Plus) (Fig. 37). Employ a fine jeweler's forceps to hold the hair grafts. It is important to hold them gently, avoiding compression of the hair bulbs. It is easier to section the grafts based on the number of hairs rather than on their size. The single hair grafts are separated from the two or three hair grafts (Fig. 38). An expert technician will be able to cut between 200 to 300 grafts per hour. To achieve

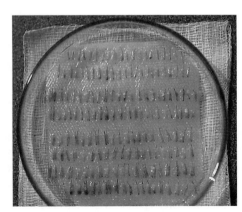

FIG. 38. One, two, and three hair grafts dissected on a Petri dish.

this level of expertise, a technician needs several months of supervised training.

Preparation of the Recipient Sites

While the assistants prepare the grafts, administer the anesthetic for the recipient area to the patient. Nitrous oxide is helpful in reducing pain from local anesthetic infiltration of the recipient area. Perform a bilateral supraorbital nerve block using 1 to 2 ml of 0.5% lidocaine with 1:200,000 epinephrine on each site. This approach will partially anesthetize a great portion of the frontal and anterior midhalf of the scalp, a region quite sensitive to needle sticks. Following the nerve block, infiltrate the recipient scalp locally, using 10 ml of 0.5% lidocaine with 1:200,000 epinephrine and 10 ml of 0.25% bupivacaine with 1:200,000 epinephrine. With this approach, patients will achieve complete anesthesia for the duration of the procedure.

Fifteen to 30 minutes before making the graft sites, infiltrate subcutaneously a mixture of 12 ml of saline and 0.1 ml of epinephrine 1:1000 to reduce bleeding.

Slits Versus Holes

Holes offer a theoretical advantage over slits because bald skin is removed and replaced by skin that contains hair. This advantage, however, has never been demonstrated in practice. Slits can be packed more closely than holes; therefore the number of grafts per recipient area (density) will be superior with slits. However, slits can cause compression when using grafts containing more than two hairs.

The combination of slits for single hair grafts and holes for two to four hair grafts is one approach. Hair transplant trephines and a hand-engine are used to make 1-mm holes for the two to three hair grafts, and 1.25-mm holes for three to four hair grafts. Slit incisions are used only for the single hair grafts and in areas where it is important to preserve

FIG. 40. Instruments to create single hair recipient sites. **(Left to right)** Accuhair needle, 18-gauge No-Kor needle, and microspear point SP90 miniblade.

existing hair. The sequence begins with drilling the holes from posterior to anterior. It is important to position the patient on his back so the bleeding will drain posteriorly and will not obstruct visualization. Periodically, clean the operative field by spraying a mixture of half hydrogen peroxide 3% and half water.

For the hair to grow in a natural direction, angle both the holes and the slits with a mediocentral orientation (i.e., pointing toward the nose; Fig. 39). It is important that, when the hair transplant punch is angled, care is taken not to transect adjacent hair follicles. The appropriate angle of recipient sites allows easy grooming in the future.

To make the slits for single hair recipient sites use either a No. 18 gauge No-Kor needle, a No. 61 Beaver blade, a microspear point SP90 blade, or a No. 17 gauge Accuhair needle (Fig. 40). The requirement for graft depth is approximately 5 to 7 mm deep. The Accuhair needle is 7 mm long and cannot penetrate deeper, thus providing precise depth control. These slits are distributed randomly along the frontal hairline (Fig. 41). No attempt is made to produce a distinct, sharply demarcated hairline (Figs. 42 and 43). Dilators are not used, since the single hair grafts can be easily placed into these slit incisions.

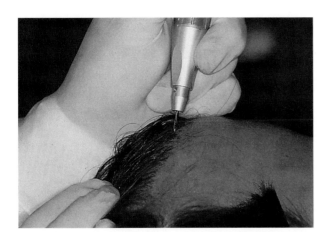

FIG. 39. A motor-driven punch is used to create the recipient sites. The anteriomedial angulation of the hair transplant punch is evident.

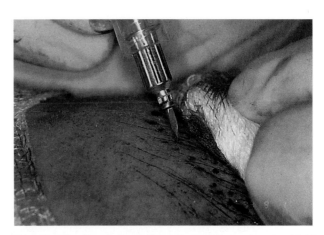

FIG. 41. The Accuhair needle make slits 7 mm deep and 1.25 mm long that are adequate for one or two hair micrografts.

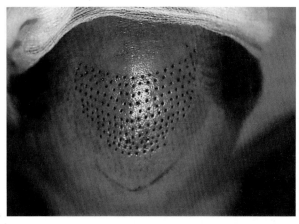
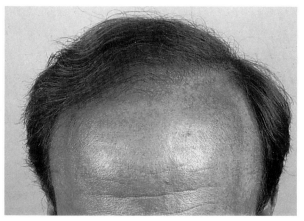

FIG. 42. (A) Thirty-seven-year-old patient with Norwood type VI androgenetic alopecia showing the distribution of the recipient sites: 1.25-mm holes for three to four hair minigrafts, and slits for single hair grafts (in the anterior hairline). **(B)** Two years later, after five sessions. A total of 555 single hair grafts, 474 1-mm minigrafts, and 634 1.25-mm minigrafts have been transplanted.

Insertion of the Grafts

Once the recipient sites are made, two technicians begin graft placement. With a jeweler's forceps (Fig. 44), pull the grafts down into the hole or slit. With the other hand, use a moistened piece of gauze to hold the graft in place when it is released by the forceps. This technique requires expertise and meticulous care to avoid mechanical trauma to the follicles.

POSTOPERATIVE MANAGEMENT

Postoperative Dressing

After completing the transplant session, visually inspect the recipient and donor sites to confirm secure graft placement and adequate hemostasis. A postoperative pressure dressing is applied over the donor and recipient areas. It will remain overnight and will be removed the following morning. The postoperative dressing involves the application of polysporin-coated Telfa pads over the donor and recipient areas. Reston foam is then placed over the Telfa pad in the donor area (Fig. 45). In the frontal region, gauze is placed over the Telfa pad and Micropore tape secures the dressing (Fig. 46). A sagittal strip of tape is placed over the entire scalp, preventing contact of tape with hair by using gauze. Using a roll of Kling, the dressing is secured by encircling the scalp from the mid forehead to below the nuchal ridge and traversing the scalp from side to side and from back to front (Fig. 47). The final step involves stretching a length of 6-inch stockinette bandage over the gauze bandage (Fig. 48).

Postoperative Medications and Wound Care Instructions

The following medications are given to the patient: oxycodone (Percocet), one to two tablets every 4 to 6 hours as

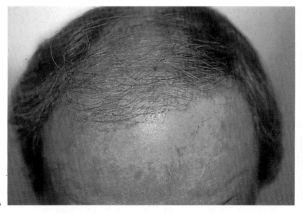
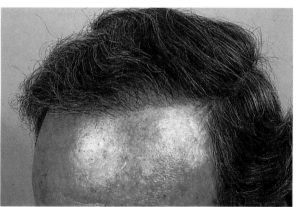

FIG. 43. (A) Sixty-two-year-old patient with Norwood type V androgenetic alopecia. **(B)** After transplanting a total of 1533 grafts in six sessions (465 single hair grafts, 259 1-mm minigrafts, and 809 1.25-mm minigrafts).

FIG. 44. Insertion of a two-hair minigraft with a jeweler's forceps.

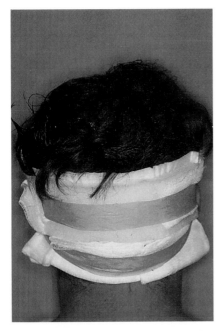

FIG. 45. Donor site is covered with Telfa pad and Reston foam, which is secured with tape.

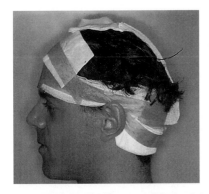

FIG. 46. Telfa pads coated with an antibiotic ointment (Polysporin) are secured over the recipient site.

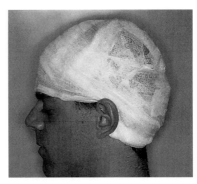

FIG. 47. A roll of Kling gauze is used to wrap the entire scalp and is secured with tape.

needed; cephradine, a single 500-mg dose 2 hours after surgery; 10 mg of diazepam before sleep if needed; and prednisone, 20 mg twice a day for 5 days.

Review with the patient the common side effects that can occur after a hair transplant (edema, pain, bleeding, telogen effluvium). Edema is usually minimal; when experienced, the patient is instructed to sleep with the head elevated on two or three pillows. Prednisone helps to reduce the postoperative edema. Discomfort may be experienced during 24 to 48 hours and is controlled with analgesics. In case of bleeding the patient is instructed to apply constant pressure for 20 minutes. Telogen effluvium or shock hair loss is a common phenomenon in which the grafted hairs go into telogen and fall out several weeks after the procedure. We reassure the patient that this is an expected phenomenon and that the hair will start to regrow 2 to 4 months after the procedure.

The dressing will be removed by the patient the morning after surgery. Before shampooing with a mild shampoo, the patient will clean the areas with half-strength hydrogen peroxide. We instruct the patient to apply polysporin to the graft sites after the shampooing using a cotton swab every day for 4 to 5 days. Wounds heal faster in a moist environment. Crust will form over the transplant sites and will naturally fall off within 2 weeks. The surgical staples in the donor area will be removed 7 days after the procedure.

The patient will not need to be seen until the next session, which will be after 4 months.

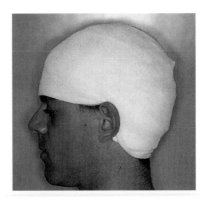

FIG. 48. Stockinette bandage over the gauze bandage.

TABLE 30-4. Complications

Complications with Total Micro and Minigrafting	
Unavoidable:	Avoidable:
Infection	Poor hairline design
Cyst formation	Poor harvesting techniques
Curling of	Poor graft sectioning
transplanted	Improper graft placement
hair	Improper candidate selection
Wide scars	Detectable surgical scars
	Lack of anticipation of future hair loss.

COMPLICATIONS AND ADVERSE SEQUELAE

Table 30-4 lists the complications that can occur after the procedure. Avoidable complications are those that can be minimized with careful preoperative planning and operative technique.

Bleeding is the result of transecting the vessel in the supragaleal plexus and can be avoided if the incision is made to a certain depth (5 to 6 mm) and adequate hemostasis is obtained. We have seen fewer problems with widening of the scars with the use of staples as opposed to sutures. The excision of strips of small width (less than 1 cm) minimizes scar widening.

Infection is a very rare event in hair transplantation. Cyst formation is more common and is due to reaction to a foreign body or inclusion of epidermal fragments below the skin surface.

Poor hair growth can occur as a result of technical problems such as trauma to the grafts, excessive handling of the grafts, and drying of the grafts. In theory, a dense packing of minigrafts and micrografts could affect the vascular supply and subsequently affect hair growth. However, no studies have proven or disproven this theory.

Part 3: Alopecia Reduction

HISTORY

The first published description of scalp reduction techniques was a report by Blanchard and Blanchard in 1977 describing serial paramedian fusiform excisions of bald scalp up to 3 cm in width in 100 patients. As many as six procedures separated by 4 to 6 weeks were performed. Unger and Unger reported a series of 60 patients in 1978 in whom excisions of 2 to 4 cm in width and 15 to 20 cm in length were performed using six different patterns of excision. They calculated that the excision of 40 cm^2 of bald skin eliminated the need for 180 to 360 hair transplant plugs of 3.5-mm diameter. In 1980 the Bosley group reported their experience with a series of 749 scalp reduction procedures. Since that time many alternative methods, modifications, and refinements have been reported.

A midline incision has been used most commonly in scalp reduction procedures, but modifications that have been reported include the following:

1. Paramedian pattern
2. Mercedes pattern
3. Y-plasty and its modifications
4. M-plastics
5. U-shaped patterns
6. Mini-reductions
7. S-, J-, and C-shaped lateral patterns
8. Zig-zag patterns
9. Large flaps such as the Marzola, Brandy, and Juri flaps and Frechet's three-flap slot correction
10. Unger's modified major scalp reduction
11. Use of parallel galeatomies

12. Use of adjuvant tissue stretching devices such as volumetric tissue expander; intraoperative scalp extension with externally applied devices such as the Miami STAR; towel clips and the Sure-Closure device; and delayed scalp extension with the Frechet extender

Among these refinements, the most significant changes in technique have been Brandy's "scalp lift" and Frechet's scalp extender and triple-flap procedure. Although Brandy's scalp-lift technique is more surgically aggressive than what many patients or physicians desire, it is the first alopecia reduction procedure to consistently and predictively allow complete excision of alopecic scalp in patients with extensive hair loss, by using the stretch provided by neck skin. Frechet's scalp extender, on the other hand, has allowed this degree of reduction to be performed without undermining into the neck tissue. Both of these procedures have created a new problem by virtue of their success: the midline scar with extension posteriorly. The Frechet triple-flap procedure has been shown to successfully correct this problem.

Each of these many scalp reduction procedures has its advantages and disadvantages. There has not been one procedure that has clearly come to be recognized as the procedure of choice.

The ideal procedure should be:

1. Effective (remove as much bald skin as needed)
2. Aesthetic (no prominent disfiguring scar, does not distort natural hair direction)
3. Lasting (not inducing secondary expansion of bald skin by "stretch-back")
4. Simple (no need for accessory devices other than cut-

ting, undermining, and suturing or simple intraoperative devices)

5. Safe (no significant adverse result)
6. Fast (not time-consuming operatively)
7. Permissive (does not interfere with further corrective measures, such as micrografts or minigrafts)
8. Cost-effective (relative cost is consistent with current procedures)

During the 1980s there were a large number of scalp reductions performed by hair restoration surgeons, but in the 1990s the numbers of procedures performed are decreasing. The primary reasons for this relative disenchantment with these procedures are (1)the success of micrografting and minigrafting and (2) problems with the scalp reduction procedures. The three problems that have resulted in disillusionment with the procedure are (1) disfiguring scars that are difficult to hide with grafts, (2) the change in hair direction

that occurs with successful scalp reduction pulling the two sides together and leaving a midline scar with hair projecting away from the scar in opposite directions on each side, and (3) that many patients do not have enough donor hair to permit satisfactory coverage by grafts even after maximal reduction of alopecia by surgical excision.

PREOPERATIVE PLANNING

Patient Selection

The choice of patients who will benefit from the procedure has been made more difficult by the success of micrografting and minigrafting. There are basically four types of patients who will benefit significantly from alopecia reduction as noted by Unger:

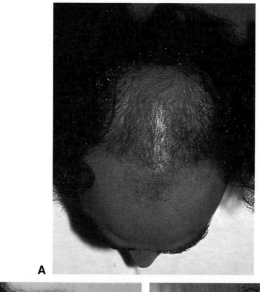

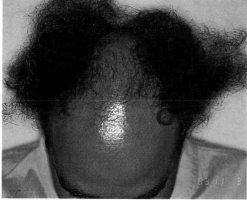

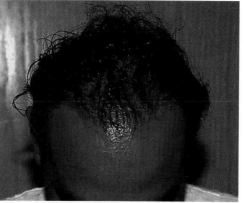

FIG. 49. (A) Preoperative evaluation of extent of alopecia in a patient desiring coverage that is as dense as possible. **(B)** Reduction of alopecic skin is accomplished by serial surgical excisions using a U-shaped pattern. **(C)** Hair transplantation is then used to establish frontal hairline and to fill in areas remaining after scalp reduction.

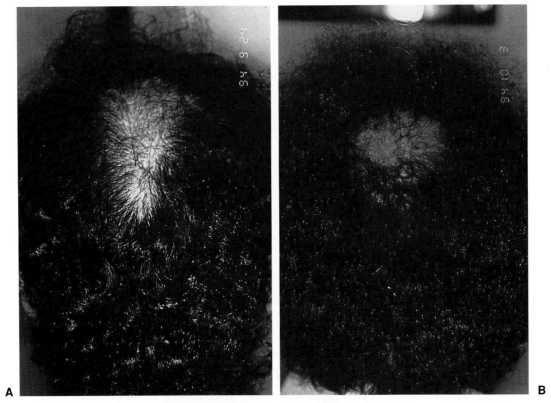

FIG. 50. (A) Following serial scalp reductions, a midline posterior slot deformity is visible. **(B)** This is corrected using Frechet's triple-flap procedure.

1. Patients whose goal is complete and maximum coverage. This is the only group for whom alopecia reduction should be used to its maximum extent and the use of Frechet's three-flap slot correction operation becomes a necessity (Figs. 49 and 50).

2. The patient with male pattern baldness who has had prior grafting (usually with large grafts) and then has had extension of alopecia beyond the originally estimated borders resulting in a halo of lost hair around the transplanted area (Fig. 51).

3. The patient with types IV to VI alopecia who desires dense overall coverage (Fig. 52). These patients will benefit from limited (one or two sessions) but not maximal reduction. Avoidance of change in hair direction is critical in these patients.

4. The burn patient (Fig. 53) or traumatically scarred patient, as well as the patient with medical conditions such as localized morphea, nevus sebaceous of Jadassohn, discoid lupus erythematosus, pseudopelade, aplasia cutis congenita, or traction alopecia.

The philosophy on how to use alopecia reduction in the correction of male pattern baldness is addressed well by Marritt and Dzubow, in their position paper published in the *Journal of Dermatologic Surgery* in 1995. There are two basic concepts presented that must be taken into consideration when planning alopecia correction. First, male pattern alopecia extends further and is more progressive than anyone ever realized before the advent of surgical correction of alopecia and its focused study as a result of these procedures. Second, it must be realized that any corrective procedure for alopecia is a redistribution procedure of existing hair. Every procedure that is performed has some downside, so the proper choice of procedures must take these facts into consideration, along with other possible adverse sequelae.

The original problem of alopecia reduction was that of stretch-back of the scar and the fact that bald tissue, not hair-bearing skin, was being stretched. These problems were solved by using more extensive surgeries, especially scalp lifting as developed by Brandy or the modified major scalp reduction as reported by Unger. As an alternative or in addition, stretching devices have been used to stretch the nonbald skin to finally enable the junction of hair-bearing skin from both sides of the scalp to come together in the middle portion of the scalp (Fig. 54). However, these successes created new problems of misdirected hair (Fig. 55), severely decreased donor density, elevation of the inferior aspect of the posterior hairline (Fig. 56), and detectable surgical scars. The solution to these new problems is to avoid complete excision of the bald scalp and use alopecia reduction to only partially reduce the baldness and hence enable the use of micrografts and minigrafts to completely but thinly cover the remaining bald area if necessary (Fig. 57). In general, in these patients the

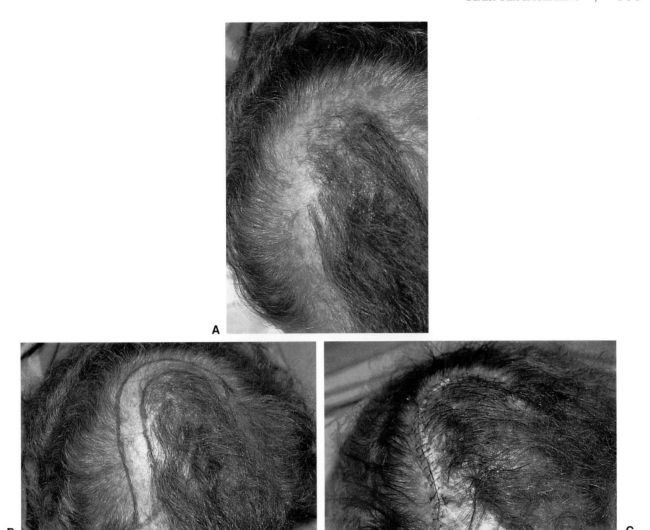

FIG. 51. (A) Progression of male pattern alopecia following hair transplantation years previously has resulted in a halo of bald skin around the grafted area. **(B)** This zone of bald tissue may be excised in two sessions of unilateral J-shaped excisions. **(C)** Completion of this scalp reduction unites the previously grafted skin with the stable hair remaining below the halo of balding scalp.

original width of bald scalp is 10 to 15 cm. This degree of alopecia can be improved by using one or two U-shaped alopecia reductions, as described by Unger's modified major alopecia reduction procedure, or by using two or four paramedian excisions.

It is a mistake to excise areas of thinning hair with the assumption that the remaining hair is going to be lost over time anyway. In reality, it may take many years before the hair is lost, and excising useful hair robs the patient of those years that the hair would have been there. Instead, it is much wiser to use micrografting between the existing hairs in this area of thinning. Use alopecia reduction only in areas of virtually complete alopecia. Proper patient selection is probably the key element to having a satisfied patient. There are many dissatisfied patients who have been subjected to repeated alopecia reduction resulting in visible scarring without reaching the goal of coverage desired.

Choice of Procedure

In general, the most common scalp reduction performed throughout the country is a midline sagittal ellipse. It is the easiest procedure to perform and has the least risk of significant bleeding because of its distance from major vessels. The midline linear approach makes it easy to use intraoperative volumetric tissue expansion, intraoperative tissue extension, or presuturing of the excision areas 12 to 24 hours before the procedure. Other modifications such as the Mercedes Benz incision, the lazy-S incision, a J-shaped incision, M-plasties, or Y-plasties are easily incorporated into this approach. However, the first disadvantage of these midline patterns is that the scar is *always* visible and it may be more difficult to cover. Second, because of the design of these midline incisions, the amount of tissue actually removed with each procedure is limited to about 40 cm^2. Third, the

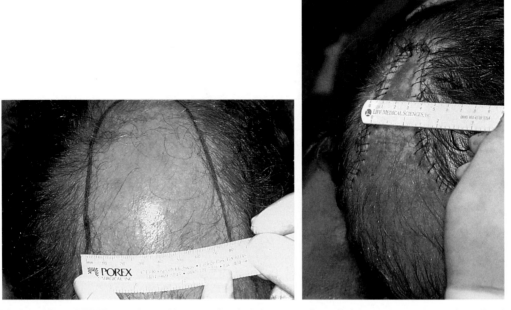

FIG. 52. (A and B) The patient with extensive hair loss may benefit from one or two scalp reduction sessions before hair transplantation, as the area to be transplanted is reduced and the level of residual hair is raised to a higher level.

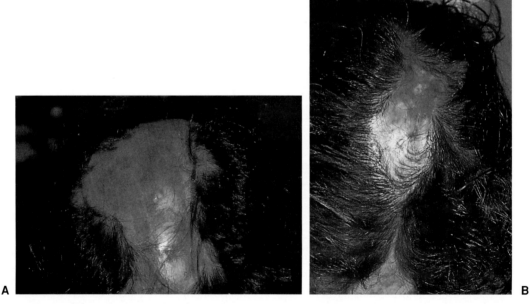

FIG. 53. (A) Patient with extensive scarring of the scalp secondary to a severe burn. **(B)** Reduction of the area of scar tissue is successfully achieved with a single procedure. Repeated procedures may almost completely eliminate the residual scar tissue. Usually at least one session of hair transplantation into the final excisional scar is desirable.

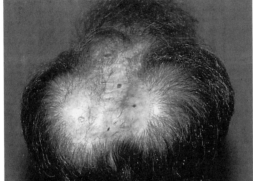

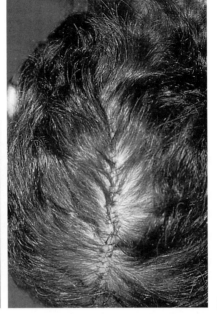

A   B

FIG. 54. (A) Tissue expansion using indwelling expanders bilaterally with gradual inflation results in significant stretching of the hair-bearing tissue laterally. **(B)** Excision of the alopecic tissue following deflation and removal of the tissue expanders results in complete elimination of the bald tissue, suturing the hair-bearing tissue together.

maximum stretch on any wound is on the tissue immediately adjacent to the point of closure. With this midline approach, this means that the maximum tissue stretch will be on bald skin, not hair-bearing skin. Fourth, the tissue stress vectors are all directly perpendicular to the incision line (Fig. 58). This fact, as well as the limitations of undermining with this approach, contribute to a higher incidence of stretch-back.

The use of a U-shaped pattern is preferable to the midline approach for several reasons. First, it distributes the stretch of tissue onto the hair-bearing skin, not the bald skin, as the incision is placed at the juncture of hair-bearing skin and bald skin. Second, this approach allows excision of more

bald skin, as the length of the excision is much greater than that of a linear sagittal excision. In a midline approach, approximately 40 cm^2 is excised vs. approximately 60 cm^2 using a U-shaped excision (Fig. 59). Third, the stress vectors are distributed circumferentially in varying direction so that there is much less risk of tissue stretch-back and greater ease of closure. Fourth, it is much easier to perform the undermining that is necessary and to visualize the areas being undermined down to the periphery of the wound. The undermining is a critical factor in allowing movement of

FIG. 55. The successful elimination of bald scalp by serial scalp reduction results in the undesirable effects of a midline scar with hair directed in opposite directions on each side of the scar.

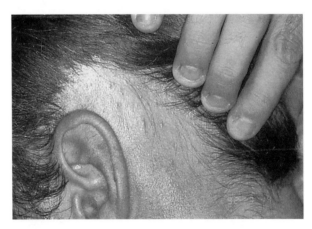

FIG. 56. When extensive undermining is performed into the neck tissue (with ligation of the occipital arteries), complete excision of bald scalp is often accomplished. However, it must be realized that since much of the tissue stretch occurs in the neck tissue, the posterior-inferior hairline will be elevated by that stretch.

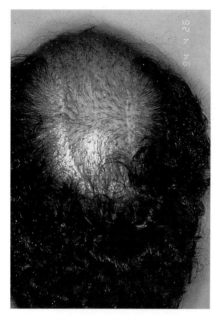

FIG. 57. Once scalp reduction is completed, an island of remaining tissue allows creation of a normal-appearing swirl of hair, as required for the normal change in direction of hair that occurs at the crown.

the tissue and removal of larger amounts of bald skin with avoidance of stretch-back. Fifth, it is easier to conceal the scar because it is at the edge of the hair-bearing skin and not in the center of the hair loss area.

Timing of Reductions

In general, it is best to perform scalp reduction before hair transplantation so that the scars resulting from scalp reduction can be easily covered by hair transplantation and also so that the proper ratio of scalp reduction to hair donor supply can be determined. Some authors promote hair transplantation as the initial procedure in order to harvest skin that has not been stretched by reductions and therefore has higher hair density. However, the occipital skin is rarely stretched significantly, and even if it has been, this is a very minor factor when using micrografts and minigrafts. If a scalp reduction procedure is being performed following hair transplantation, it is best to wait 6 weeks or longer from the last hair transplant procedure before beginning the scalp reduction to allow more complete wound healing. As far as timing of the intervals between scalp reductions, unless a Frechet extender is being used, (in which case the second procedure must follow the first by 30 days), it is best to wait at least 12 weeks between procedures to allow adequate and complete healing of the scalp.

Preparation of the Patient

Gradual stretching of the scalp tissue can be performed manually by the patient starting 1 month before the procedure, as advocated by Nicholas Brandy. This gradual stretching does result in increased looseness of the scalp and improves the ease with which the scalp reduction surgery can be performed but depends on the patient consistently stretching the scalp for 10 minutes three times a day. This stretching is performed by manually pulling on the scalp, using the hair to grasp the tissue. To actually perform this requires a great deal of discipline, since the stretching procedure is not only uncomfortable to perform, but also tedious.

Beginning 3 days before the procedure, the patient should shampoo the scalp for 5 minutes a day using either Hibiclens

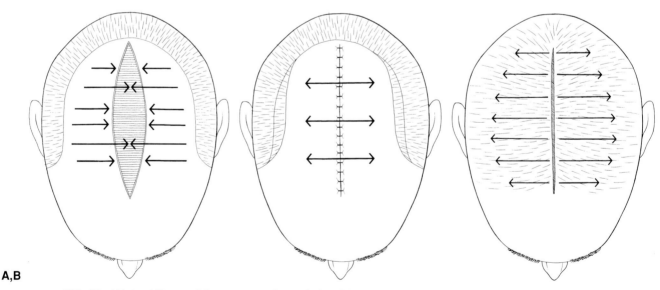

A,B   **C**

FIG. 58. **(A)** A midline excision removes the majority of its tissue in its central area and in closure puts the maximum stretch on the immediately adjacent bald tissue. **(B)** The stress vectors of the linear midline excision are all directly perpendicular to the line of closure and are maximal centrally. **(C)** This approach results in a visible midline scar, with hair direction in opposite directions on either side of the scar.

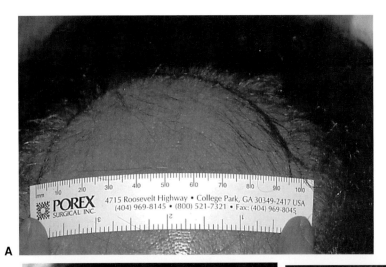

FIG. 59. (A–C) The U-shaped excision allows the removal of a larger amount of tissue in a single procedure because of the length of the curving excision, combined with its geometric efficiency.

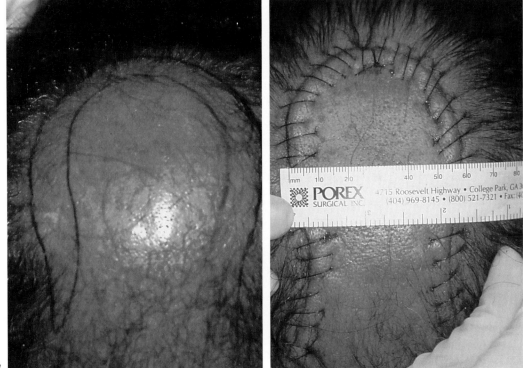

or pHisohex. Beginning 5 days before surgery, the patient takes Mephyton (vitamin K) 5 mg daily. The patient is also instructed to abstain from alcohol for 2 weeks before surgery, as well as aspirin, ibuprofen, and cough and cold medications. On the morning of surgery, he should begin erythromycin or cephalexin (Keflex) in a divided daily dose equaling 1 g; this should be continued for 5 days after surgery. Beginning the morning of surgery he also begin a regimen of prednisone, 20 mg three times a day for 5 days.

It is best to perform a preoperative examination 1 to 2 weeks before the surgery. At this time, blood work is obtained that includes prothrombin time, partial thromboplastin time, complete blood cell count; human immunodeficiency virus (HIV) and hepatitis antigen testing; and SMA-20. During this preoperative visit photographs are taken and financial matters are concluded. By performing these procedures 2 weeks before surgery, unsuspected medical problems and clotting disorders can be discovered and financial discussions can be finalized. The preoperative photographs may be checked before surgery to determine that they have been performed properly as well (see Chapter 8). It also requires the patient to make a commitment to the surgery at that point rather than the night before surgery and therefore cuts down on last-minute cancellations because of "second thoughts."

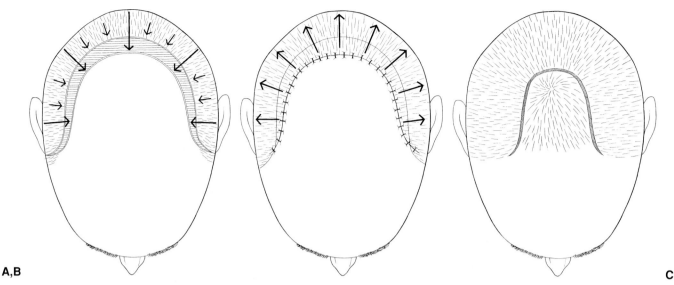

A,B

C

FIG. 60. (A) The U-shaped pattern places the excision of bald skin at the juncture of the hair-bearing tissue with the bald tissue. This places the stretch of tissue into the area of residual hair as this tissue is moved to close the wound. **(B)** Once the wound is closed, the stress vectors are noted to be directed in various directions around the excision, eliminating the unidirectional pull of a linear excision. **(C)** The resultant scar is more easily concealed, as it is located at the juncture with hair-bearing tissue and also allows re-creation of the directional changes of hair at the crown.

TECHNIQUE

Perform the surgery on an outpatient basis, in the office, surgical suite, or an outpatient surgery clinic. In general, this procedure is performed with local anesthesia and oral or intramuscular (IM) sedation. Although it can be performed with intravenous (IV) sedation or general anesthesia, this degree of sedation may be a disadvantage to the surgeon because of loss of cooperation of the patient and the fact that changes in position may be necessary during the procedure. There are patients, however, who cannot tolerate the procedure psychologically or cannot tolerate the pain and discomfort of the multiple lidocaine (Xylocaine) injections necessary for local anesthesia and therefore require IV sedation. In these cases, IV sedation using a nurse anesthetist or anesthesiologist is necessary.

The patient arrives at the office 45 minutes to 1 hour before the scheduled procedure. At this time, he removes his shirt, and his scalp is washed using Hibiclens soap. He is given a surgical gown and then, while resting either in a comfortable chair or on the surgical table, is given 5 to 10 mg of diazepam orally and 25 to 50 mg of meperidine (Demerol) and promethazine (Phenergan) IM; the dose depends on body weight, as well as sensitivities to sedative medications. At this time, mark the lines and pattern of the reduction on the scalp using a gentian violet pen (Fig. 60). The next step is achieving local anesthesia. It is useful to perform a supraorbital nerve block, as the anesthesia induced by this nerve block extends significantly posteriorly and covers the entire top of the scalp (Fig. 61). This nerve block is achieved by locating the supraorbital notch and compressing

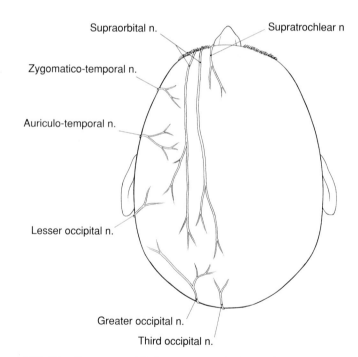

FIG. 61. The supraorbital nerves supply the majority of the tissue of the front and top of the scalp, extending in a significant manner posteriorly. Blocking these nerves is extremely beneficial in achieving anesthesia necessary for scalp reduction.

this tissue with the index finger of the left hand, while injecting lidocaine/bupivacaine (Marcaine) with a 30-gauge needle approaching from above the eyebrow. Insert the needle at a 45-degree angle down to the periosteum immediately below the left fingertip. By approaching from a superior angle, the potential of inadvertently inserting the needle into the nerve foramen and injuring the nerve is completely avoided. Use a mixture of 0.5% bupivacaine and 1% lidocaine, the lidocaine having epinephrine 1:100,000 and bupivacaine having no epinephrine. Inject approximately 0.5 ml at the supraorbital notch and another 0.5 ml at the supratrochlear notch; another 1 ml is infiltrated along the superior border of the eyebrow. This is performed bilaterally. Using the same solution, the planned incision site is infiltrated directly for an area of approximately 1.5 to 2 cm on each side of the incision line. Next, inject a mixture containing 2% lidocaine with epinephrine 1:100,000 mixed with normal saline in a 10-ml syringe, using 2.5 ml of lidocaine and 7.5 ml of saline and a 21-gauge needle, into the area that will be undermined. Starting about 1.5 cm from the planned incision line and proceeding laterally, inject this solution into the immediate periosteal vicinity covering the remainder of the lateral and posterior scalp.

PATTERNS OF SCALP REDUCTION

Sagittal midline ellipse, as mentioned, has been the most popular excision used. The principal advantage of this pattern is that it is the safest and technically the easiest pattern to perform. There also is no resultant postoperative anesthesia or hypoesthesia of the scalp, and there is little danger of significant bleeding from a major vessel. However, additional disadvantages other than those previously discussed include that it removes little tissue at the anterior and posterior ends of the excision, since the tissue removed by the excision is predominantly in the midportion of the scalp. By modifying this sagittal midline ellipse to a Y-shaped pattern or a Mercedes Benz pattern, greater tissue excision at the posterior aspect becomes possible with some resultant lifting of the posterior hairline. In addition, a linear midline excision without this modification has a tendency to lengthen the posterior aspect of the excision because of "dog-ear" formation. There are also Z-plasty techniques which may increase the amount of tissue excised, as well as better camouflage of the scar and, it is hoped, avoid some of the problems of change in hair direction.

The second group of patterns commonly used includes the lateral patterns. Perform these patterns unilaterally, and place the scar at the periphery of the bald area at the juncture with hair-bearing skin. These patterns include S-, J- and C-shaped configurations, as described by Alt and Norwood. These patterns are more useful primarily because the stretch is then diverted to the hair-bearing tissue instead of the bald tissue, and it is easier to hide the resultant scar because of its proximity to hair-bearing tissue. However, since only one side is treated at a time, two procedures are required to remove tissue symmetrically.

The third group is the U-shaped patterns. Place the open end of the U anteriorly; the U follows the hairline around the crown, as previously described. This pattern is most useful, and Martin Unger has written an excellent report describing his use of this pattern as the "modified major scalp reduction." This approach was developed as a result of the desire to remove larger areas of alopecic skin than those allowed by standard reductions and to take advantage of placing the scar adjacent to the hair-bearing tissue, resulting in stretching the hair-bearing tissue instead of the bald tissue. A continuous change in the direction of stretch vectors also allows better healing without as much tension on the wound.

SURGICAL PROCEDURE

Perform the surgery in an aseptic manner; drape the patient accordingly. The use of a CO_2 laser in scalp reduction is very beneficial because of better control of bleeding. The laser coagulates and seals all vessels in the incision smaller than 0.5 mm in diameter. Although scalp reduction procedures have successfully been performed with superpulsed as well as continuous-wave CO_2 lasers, it is much more advantageous to use the UltraPulse CO_2 laser because of the control provided over residual thermal damage. Using this laser with a focused beam, a 200-μm spot size, a 500 mJ/pulse, and a power setting of 15 watts, it is important to keep the spot moving continuously across the tissue while making the incision. Initially cut about halfway through the dermis; then have the wound spread open by assistants (Fig. 62). Once to this level, it may be advantageous to increase the lateral heat damage to give better thermal coagulation of vessels while going into the subcutaneous tissue. Accomplish this by backing the handpiece away from the tissue slightly so that the spot size is larger. Also, increase the power so that the delivery of pulses comes more rapidly, which results in multiple pulses impacting the same target tissue. Slowing down the hand motion across the tissue accomplishes the same result. This procedure should be performed by an experienced laser surgeon, with attention being paid to laser tissue interaction, so that there is no excessive lateral thermal damage that may interfere with wound healing. However, whether the laser or a scalpel is used, the procedure is the same except for the frequency of electrocautery required. Electrocautery will always be required, even with the laser, since there are vessels too large for the laser to coagulate.

The anterior aspect of the U-shaped incision initially was carried down into the hairline parallel to the anterior temporal hairline. However, this anterior scar sometimes tends to be visible, and extending the anterior margin into this temporal hairline offers minimal advantage. Perform the incision on the anterior aspect of the scalp without extending inferiorly into the temporal scalp (Fig. 63). Start this cuta-

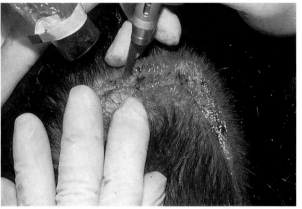

A   B

FIG. 62. (A) Using the Coherent UltraPulse CO_2 laser as an incisional instrument results in a relatively bloodless surgical field. **(B)** As the incision proceeds deeper in the tissue, larger vessels may be encountered that may require electrocoagulation for control of bleeding. However, the lateral thermal effects achieved by defocusing the laser may be adequate for many vessels.

neous incision on one side, and continue all the way around to the opposite side. Since this incision should be made through the galea to the periosteum, some relatively large vessels will be encountered. Clamp these vessels using a curved hemostat, and cauterize each after accumulating 8 to 10 vessels of this type. Once this incision has been made all the way around the posterior scalp and hemostasis has been achieved, use 7-inch, curved Metzenbaum scissors to dissect into the relatively avascular space that is between the periosteum and underneath the galea (Fig. 64). To achieve this initial undermining, insert the Metzenbaum scissors, open the scissors, and spread the tissue. The initial area that is undermined is approximately 5 to 6 cm. Once this has been achieved, use the fingers as much as possible for further dissection. However, in the parietal and occipital regions, use 11-inch, curved Metzenbaum scissors to continue the dissection to just above the nuchal ridge on each side and down to the ears laterally. When doing this, take care to avoid injury to the occipital artery and nerve, as well as the temporal artery. Although the pattern of the incision allows good visibility, especially when using a retractor such as the

Unger scalp retractor, it should be realized that because of the curve of the skull the inferior aspect of this dissection may have to be performed blindly. If this results in significant bleeding, it may be necessary to make a lateral incision in this lower area in order to have visual access to bleeding vessels.

Once undermining is complete, meticulously perform hemostasis of the undermined area using electrocautery. Because of the hemostasis provided by the use of the laser as a surgical tool, relaxing galeatomies may be performed, making a series of parallel incisions placed about 1.5 cm apart in the lateral aspects of the scalp bilaterally, increasing the amount of stretch of this tissue (Fig. 65). This is not advisable when using a scalpel as an incisional instrument because of the excessive bleeding and increased risk of hematoma that may occur. Once these steps have been accomplished, stretch the tissue medially and anteriorly over the bald scalp to give an indication of the amount of bald tissue that may be removed. Achieve this estimation either by mak-

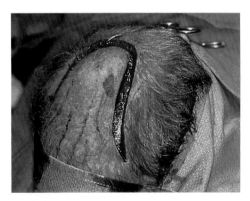

FIG. 63. Extend the U-shaped excision anteriorly to anterior temporal area, but do not extend inferiorly, since this may result in a visible scar.

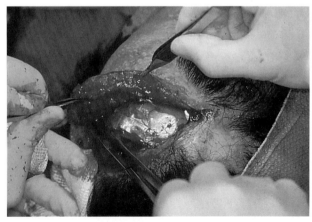

FIG. 64. Undermine the scalp in the relatively avascular tissue of the subgaleal space.

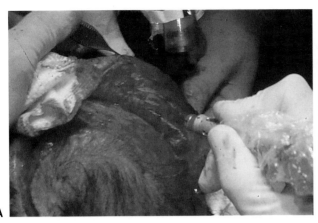

A   B

FIG. 65. (A and B) Use of the Coherent UltraPulse CO_2 laser with a defocused beam allows creation of relaxing galeotomies, increasing the stretch of the scalp tissue, without causing risk of bleeding because of the thermal effects of the laser.

ing an imprint on the scalp from the blood present on the subcutaneous tissue or, as an alternative, by making a series of small parallel incisions in the tissue being stretched starting at about 1 cm from the tissue border and extending to about 3 cm, placed at about 5-mm intervals so that the surgeon can visualize through the flap extended over the bald tissue precisely how much tissue to be excised. Using a scalpel, a puncture can be made through this small incision point to the bald scalp to mark the excision line. A third alternative is to use a D'Assumpeau rhytidoplasty marker to determine the amount of redundant tissue to be excised.

It is best to perform this excision of bald tissue one side at a time. In case the amount that can be removed has been overestimated, adjustments can be made on the contralateral side.

If a Frechet scalp extender is to be placed, create the tunnel for this underneath the remaining island of bald scalp (Fig. 66). In this situation, continue the complete removal of bald tissue throughout the distance of the U shape so that one side may be apposed to the other. If there is no adjuvant tissue-stretching procedure to be performed, excise one side and suture before performing contralateral excision. However, in most cases, always perform a secondary intraoperative tissue-stretching procedure. Insert tissue expanders at this stage or use a Sure-Closure device. These procedures are performed before excision of any bald tissue (Fig. 67).

When placing tissue expanders, perform this bilaterally underneath the hair-bearing tissue (Fig. 68). The tissue expanders are generally 200 cc in size. Once the tissue expander has been placed, suture the tissue loosely using running 0-0 polydioxanone (PDS) sutures or staples, being careful not to injure the tissue expanders. Perform a series of three maximal inflations of the tissue expander for 3 minutes followed by 3 minutes of rest to stretch the tissue. Once tissue expansion has been achieved and the amount of tissue to be excised marked, excise one side of the incision of this tissue and place three subcutaneous, interrupted 2-0 galeal sutures: one anterior, one midparietal, and one lateraoccipital. Place 2-0 Vicryl sutures between these points. Ideally, at this time, use running 2-0 Prolene suture to close the wound continu-

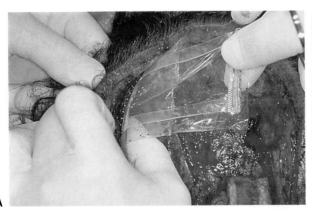

A   B

FIG. 66. (A) Placement of the Frechet tissue extender requires elevation of the central flap when a U-shaped excision is used. **(B)** Hook the extender into the contralateral tissue using a specialized instrument; then lay back the central flap into position over the tissue extender.

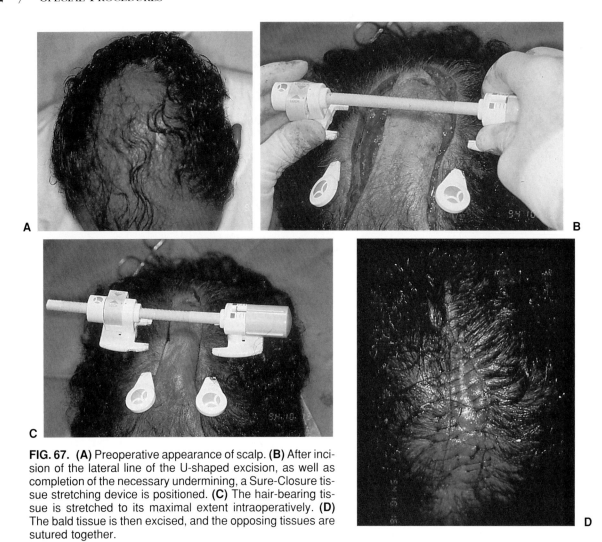

FIG. 67. **(A)** Preoperative appearance of scalp. **(B)** After incision of the lateral line of the U-shaped excision, as well as completion of the necessary undermining, a Sure-Closure tissue stretching device is positioned. **(C)** The hair-bearing tissue is stretched to its maximal extent intraoperatively. **(D)** The bald tissue is then excised, and the opposing tissues are sutured together.

ously back to the midpoint of the occipital area. Then, move to the contralateral side of the head, since the amount of tissue to be excised can be determined much more precisely because the opposite side has already been sutured. The same procedure is followed until complete closure of the wound is achieved.

As an alternative, use the Sure-Closure device on one side of the incision, excise the tissue, and repeat the process on the opposite side. These adjunctive procedures for tissue expansion add another 40 to 45 minutes to the scalp reduction procedure.

Once suturing is finished, clean the scalp with hydrogen peroxide and apply Polysporin ointment. Place Telfa dressings over the wound itself and then, using Kling gauze, wrap the scalp with 4 × 4-inch gauze placed over the Telfa, as well as inferior to the incision sites (over the hair bearing-portions of the skin). Follow this with application of Elastoplast elastic dressing to form a turbanlike bandage. No drains are placed.

COMPLICATIONS AND MANAGEMENT

Complications are rare but include postoperative bleeding and hematoma, seroma, infection, removal of excessive scalp tissue with inability to completely close the wound, and injuries to nerves.

Postoperative bleeding and hematoma are rarely encountered if attention is paid to good surgical technique and controlling bleeding intraoperatively. The fact that the wound is almost always closed under tension results in pressure hemostasis. In addition, the turbanlike bandage adequately applies additional pressure. Should postoperative swelling and bleeding be noted, the possibility of a hematoma must be explored. If a hematoma is discovered, it is best to open the wound, evacuate the hematoma, and eliminate the bleeding vessel or vessels by electrocautery or by tying them off.

Infection is very rare and usually related to a foreign body reaction (i.e., a suture or tissue extender). If there are signs of infection, cultures must be obtained and, if necessary, any

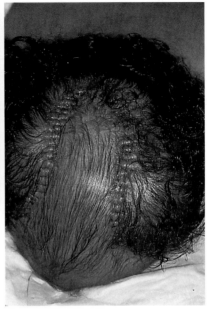

FIG. 68. (A) When tissue expanders are used intraoperatively, they may be placed bilaterally or repositioned during the surgery for serial inflation. **(B)** During this inflation stage the overlying tissue must be sutured, to allow inflation of the tissue expanders and stretching of the hair-bearing skin.

foreign material removed. Seromas are generally related to the presence of tissue extenders. These may be drained by needle aspiration and cultured, and intralesional triamainolone acetonide (Kenalog) 10 mg/ml injected into the seroma.

When excessive bald scalp tissue is excised, preventing wound closure, one of the following procedures may be performed:

1. Relaxing incisions parallel to the closure line may be placed to allow further tissue stretch.
2. A portion of the excised scalp tissue may be used as a full-thickness skin graft to fill the closure defect.
3. The area may be allowed to granulate in and heal by secondary intention.

Generally options 1 or 2 is preferable, since option 3 is time-consuming and cosmetically undesirable. A second corrective procedure will generally be necessary to remove the excessive scar tissue resulting from any of these options. If additional scalp reductions are to be performed, the scar tissue is simple excised as part of the next scalp reduction procedure.

Trauma to sensory nerves may result in areas of anesthesia of the scalp. This occurs in the posterior scalp when the occipital nerves are cut, as occipital arteries are tied in the Brandy procedure. This is a permanent sensory loss, and patients should be advised of this before surgery. Other small areas of sensory loss are related to trauma or cutting of more peripheral nerve branches and tend to recover very slowly over a period of a few years.

CONCLUSION

The opinions expressed by the authors of this chapter have been formulated as a result of their personal experiences. This is only natural, but because our experiences have been different our advice will also vary. Thus, for example, though we would both agree that the older the patient the better, I have less hesitation in recommending early intervention than does Dr. Stough. I also like to employ a larger variety of grafts for different purposes than does Dr. Stough, and Dr. Fitzpatrick and I more readily incorporate alopecia reduction into our operative plan than he does. I prefer tumescent anesthesia in the donor area, while Dr. Stough does not use it. The reader may therefore be left somewhat confused—though needlessly so. We have each sorted out what works best in our hands and what we personally are comfortable with, given our experiences and observations. Our patients are probably equally happy with their results. ''Many roads lead to Rome'' is often quoted, but far less frequently believed. Use only that advice given here with which you are comfortable. The passage of time and further experience will lead you to your own personal ''road.''

What is beyond doubt is the extraordinary improvement in hair restoration surgery that has occurred over the last decade. In particular, the perfecting of minigrafting, total excision techniques in the donor area, and alopecia reduction have profoundly affected what we can hope to do for our patients. Those of you who are relatively new to this field are extremely fortunate to have entered it at this time because you and your patients have been spared many problems.

I am still astonished at the pace of continuing evolution in this area. For those of you who have some experience in hair restoration surgery, if you have changed nothing in your technique since the previous year, you have started down the slope of obsolescence. Hopefully, this chapter will give you something to think about and will help you to avoid that fate.

Conclusion by Walter P. Unger

SUGGESTED READING LIST

Part 1

1. Alt T. The Donor Site. In: Unger W, Nordstrom R, eds. Hair transplantation. 2nd ed. New York: Marcel Dekker, 1988.
2. Frechet P. Scalp extension. In: Unger W. Hair transplantation. 3rd ed. New York: Marcel Dekker, 1995.
3. Hitzig GC, Saddick NS. A new technique for curvilinear scalp reduction. J Dermatol Surg Oncol 1989;15:1108.
4. Marritt E, Dzubow L. A redefinition of male pattern baldness and its treatment implications. Dermatol Surg 1995;21:123.
5. Marritt E, Dzubow L. The isolated forelock. Dermatol Surg 1995;21:523.
6. Nordstrom R. Stretchback in scalp reductions for male pattern baldness. Plast Reconstr Surg 1984;73:422.
7. Norwood OT. In: Norwood OT, Schiell R, eds. Hair transplant surgery. 2nd ed. Springfield, IL: Charles C Thomas, 1984.
8. Rassman W. Megasessions: dense packing. Hair Transplant Forum 1994;4(3):5.
9. Stough, Dowling B. Hair transplantation. New York: McGraw-Hill, 1995.
10. Unger M. Improved scalp reduction results with prolonged acute tissue expansion (pate). J Am Acad Cosmet Surg 1995;12(3):231.
11. Unger MG. Alopecia reduction and stretchback. Clin Dermatol 1992;10:345.
12. Unger W. Hair transplantation. 3rd ed. New York: Marcel Dekker, 1995.
13. Unger W. Laser hair transplantation. Part II. J Dermatol Surg Oncol 1995;21:759.
14. Unger W. What's new in hair replacement surgery. Dermatol Clin 1996;14(4):783.
15. Unger W, David L. Laser hair transplantation. J Dermatol Surg Oncol 1994;20:515.

Part 2

1. Brandy DA. A new instrument for the expedient production of minigrafts. J Dermatol Surg Oncol 1992;18:487.
2. Brandy, D, Meshkin M. Utilization of No-Kor needles for slit micrografting. J Dermatol Surg Oncol 1994;20:3369.
3. Jimenez F, Avram M, Stough DB. The Yeh needle: a solid needle for single hair recipient sites. J Am Acad Dermatol 1995;32:1041.
4. Lucas MWG. The use of minigrafts in hair transplantation surgery. J Dermatol Surg Oncol 1988;14:1389.
5. Marritt E. Single hair transplantation for hairline refinement: a practical solution. J Dermatol Surg Oncol 1984;10:962.
6. Maritt E, Dzubow L. The isolated frontal forelock. Dermatol Surg 1995;21:523.
7. Marritt E, Konior RJ. Patient selection, candidacy and treatment plan for hair replacement surgery. Facial Plast Surg Clin North Am 1994;2:39.
8. Nordstrom REA. "Micrografts" for the improvement of the frontal hairline after hair transplantation. Aesthet Plast Surg 1981;97:5.
9. Norwood OT. Patient selection, hair transsplant design, and hairstyle. J Dermatol Surg Oncol 1992;18:386.
10. Norwood OT, Taylor B. Hairline design and placement. J Dermatol Surg Oncol 1991;17;510.
11. Okuda S. Clinical and experimental studies of trnasplantation of living hairs. Jpn J Dermatol Urol 1939;46:135.
12. Orentreich N. Autografts in alopecias and other selected dermatological conditions. Ann NY Acad Sci 1959;463:83.
13. Rassman WR, Pomerzntz MA. The art and science of minigrafting. Int J Aesthet Restorative Surg 1993;1:27.
14. Sadick NS, Militana CJ. Use of nitrous oxide in hair transplantation surgery. J Dermatol Surg Oncol 1994;20;186.
15. Stough DB. Hair replacement: medical and surgical. St. Louis: Mosby, 1995 (in press).
16. Stough DB IV. Hair transplantation by the feathering zone technique: new tools for the nineties. Am J Cosmet Surg 1992;21:243.
17. Stough DB, Nelson BR, Stough DB. Incisional slit grafting. J Dermatol Surg Oncol 1991;17:53.
18. Stough D, Jimenez F, Avram M. Hair: Don't stop thinking about tomorrow—it'll soon be here. Dermatol Surg 1995;21:415.
19. Uebel CO. Micrografts and minigrafts; a new approach for baldness surgery. Ann Plast Surg 1991;27:476.
20. Unger WR, ed. Hair transplantation, 2nd ed. New York: Marcel Dekker, 1987:333

Part 3

1. Alt TH. Advantages of the paramedian scalp reduction. J Dermatol Surg Oncol 1988;14(3):257.
2. Alt TH. Aids to scalp reduction surgery. J Dermatol Surg Oncol 1988;14(3):309.
3. Alt TH. Scalp reduction as an adjunct to hair transplantation: a review of relevant literature and presentation of an improved technique. J Dermatol Surg Oncol 1980;6(12):1011.
4. Bell ML. Role of scalp reduction in the treatment of male pattern baldness. Plastic Reconstr Surg 1982;69(2):272.
5. Blanchard G, Blanchard B. Obliteration of alopecia by hair-lifting: a new concept and technique. J National Med Assoc 1977;69(9):639.
6. Bosley LL, Hope CR, Montroy RE. Male pattern reduction (MPR) for surgical reduction of male pattern baldness. Curr Therapeutic Res 1979;25(2):281.
7. Bosley LL, Hope CR, Montroy RE, Straub PM. Reduction of male pattern baldness in multiple stages: a retrospective study. J Dermatol Surg Oncol 1980;6(6):498.
8. Brandy DA. A new surgical approach for the treatment of extensive baldness. Am J Cosmet Surg 1986;3(4):19.
9. Brandy DA. Pitfalls and pearls of extensive scalp-lifting. Am J Cosmet Surg 1987;4(3):217.
10. Brandy DA. The bilateral occipito-parietal flap. J Dermatol Surg Oncol 1986;12(10):1062.
11. Brandy DA. The Brandy bitemporal flap. Am J Cosmet Surg 1986;3(2):11.
12. Brandy DA. The effectiveness of occipital artery ligations as a priming procedure for extensive scalp-lifting. J Dermatol Surg Oncol 1991;17:946.
13. Brandy DA. The principles of scalp extension. Am J Cosmet Surg 1994;11(4):245.
14. Earles RM. Hair transplantation, scalp reduction, and flap rotation in black men. J Dermatol Surg Oncol 1986;12(1):87.
15. Frechet P. A new method for correction of the vertical scar observed following scalp reduction for extensive alopecia. J Dermatol Surg Oncol 1990;16(7):640.
16. Frechet P. Scalp extension. J Dermatol Surg Oncol 1993;19:616.
17. Kabaker SS, Kridel RWH, Krugman ME, Swenson RW. Tissue expansion in the treatment of alopecia. Arch Otolaryngol Head Neck Surg 1986;112:720.
18. Marritt E, Dzubow L. A redefinition of male pattern baldness and its treatment implications: a position paper. Dermatol Surg 1995;21:123.
19. Marritt E, Dzubow L. The isolated frontal forelock. Dermatol Surg 1995;21:523.
20. Nelson BR, Stough DB, Gillard M, Stough DB, Johnson TM. The paramedian scalp reduction with posterior Z-plasty: a technique to minimize the "slot" defect. J Dermatol Surg Oncol 1992;18:990.
21. Nordström REA. Scalp kinetics in multiple excisions for correction of male pattern baldness. J Dermatol Surg Oncol 1984;10(12):991.
22. Nordström REA. "Stretch-back" in scalp reductions for male pattern baldness. Plast Reconstr Surg 1984;3:422.
23. Norwood OT. Scalp reduction in the treatment of androgenic alopecia. Dermatol Clin 1987;5(3):531.
24. Norwood OT, Shiell RC, Morrison ID. Complications of scalp reductions. J Dermatol Surg Oncol 1983;9(10):828.
25. Pierce HE. Possible use of the Radovan tissue expander in hair replacement surgery. J Dermatol Surg Oncol 1985;11(4):413.
26. Roenigk HH Jr. 70 scalp reduction. Dermatologic surgery: principles and practice. 1989;55:1025.
27. Unger MG. Postoperative necrosis following bilateral lateral scalp reduction. J Dermatol Surg Oncol 1988;14(5):541.
28. Unger MG. Scalp reduction. Clin Dermatol 1992;10:345.
29. Unger MG. Scalp reductions. Facial Plast Surg 1985;2(3):253.
30. Unger MG. The modified major scalp reduction. J Dermatol Surg Oncol 1988;14(1):80.
31. Unger MG, Unger WP. Management of alopecia of the scalp by a

combination of excisions and transplantations. J Dermatol Surg Oncol 1978;4(9):670.

APPENDIX

Surgical Products for Hair Transplantation

I. Sterile surgical tray for excising donor strip
  A. Multiple bladeholder with straight, 2-mm spacers (Van Sickle Co., Tiemann, Byron)
  B. Personna Plus No. 10
  C. No. 3 scalpel handle
  D. One pair specialized strip scissors (Van Sickle Co.)
  E. Three small hemostats, Micro-Mosquito 4¾-inch
  F. Adson's forceps with teeth
  G. Needle holder
  H. Staples, 3M Precise DS-25 (3M Medical Division)
  I. Staple remover
  J. Petri dishes with gauze and chilled saline at 4°C

II. Surgical tray for cutting grafts
  A. Jeweler's forceps (Van Sickle microdilator forceps, Snowden Pencer microvascular jeweler's forceps)
  B. No. 3 scalpel handle with No. 10 blade, plastic cutting board, 13 × 10-inch; tongue-depressor blade; Petri dish with chilled saline
  C. Nu-Gauze, 3 × 3-inch, for base of Petri dish (Johnson & Johnson)

III. Surgical tray for preparing recipient site
  A. Hand-engine, Model 25D (Robbins, Bell)
  B. AEU-12 Electrimax (Aseptico)
  C. Exelna II mobile unit, No. 403601 (Bell)
  D. Hair transplant punches, 1.0, 1.25, and 1.5 mm (Tiemann, Robbins Benn Instrument Co.)
  E. Instruments for single hair recipient site. From left to right:
    1. Beaver No. 61 blade (Swann-Morton, Ltd.)
    2. Yeh needle (Accu-Derm, Inc.)
    3. No-Kor, 18-gauge (Becton-Dickinson)
    4. Standard 18-gauge needle

IV. Tray for graft implantation
  A. Jeweler's forceps
  B. Petri dish

V. Syringes
  A. Lidocaine 0.5% with 1:200,000 epinephrine, one or two 10-ml syringes for donor site, and two 10-ml syringes for recipient site
  B. Saline, 20 ml for donor site
  C. Saline (12 ml) containing 0.1 ml epinephrine 1:000 (1:120,000 total epinephrine concentrate) for recipient site

VI. Other supplies
  A. Prone pillow (Robbins)
  B. Moustache trimmer (Whal, Inc.)
  C. Hydrogen peroxide 3% (1:1 mixture of H_2O_2 and water is placed in a spray bottle for dampening the scalp during the surgical procedure)
  D. Adhesive tape remover (Detachol [Ferndale Laboratories, Inc.])
  E. Postoperative dressings
    1. Telfa nonadhesive dressing (Kendall 3 × 8-inch)
    2. Tape (Micropore, 1-inch [3M Inc.])
    3. Reston foam (20 × 30 cm [3M Inc.])
    4. Tubular stockinette dressing, cotton blend, 6-inch (De Busk, Inc.)
    5. Conforming gauze bandage (Kling) (3 × 131-inch [Johnson & Johnson])
    6. Gauze sponges (4 × 4-inch)
    7. Emergency kit (Bayan International Co.)
    8. Pulse oximeter (Nelcor, Inc.)

Textbook of Dermatologic Surgery, edited by John L. Ratz.
Lippincott–Raven Publishers, Philadelphia © 1998.

CHAPTER 31

Liposuction

Rhoda S. Narins

HISTORY

Tremendous strides have been made in liposuction since it first began in the early to mid-1970s. Yves Illouz, Pierre Fournier of Paris, and Giorgio Fisher of Rome in the clinic of Illouz in Paris are three of the originators of liposuction. Illouz made liposuction possible by designing a blunt rather than a sharp cannula and using a "wet" technique infiltrating hypotonic saline solution into the fatty tissue before surgery. These advances markedly diminished the bleeding that occurred with previous procedures, making the extraction of fat safe. Illouz also popularized liposuction at various medical meetings.

The second important advance in liposuction occurred in 1986 with the development of the tumescent technique of local anesthesia by Jeffrey A. Klein, a dermatologic surgeon.

Rhoda S. Narins: Department of Dermatology, New York University Medical Center, 550 First Avenue, New York, New York, 10016.

This technique allowed the surgeon to perform liposuction using local anesthesia alone. In addition to the development of the tumescent solution, other advances have been made, including the use of a pressure pump or electric pumps (Figs. 1 and 2) to deliver the anesthesia, as well as a better understanding of the pharmacology of lidocaine (Xylocaine) injected into third spaces. Other developments that have occurred over the years have been decreasing cannula size (Fig. 3), the availability of multiple cannula designs (Fig. 4), the use of a criss-cross cannula approach for the removal of fat, the ability to make smaller incisions, and different postoperative care regimens. The development of tiny cannulas led to less rippling and added the technique of "liposculpture" to that of liposuction. Disposable instruments, tubing, and canisters, as well as viral filters, have been developed to comply with Occupational Safety and Health Administration (OSHA) standards (Figs. 5 and 6). For some people, excisions of lax skin may be necessary, along with liposuction, to obtain the best results. Ongoing studies include the treatment of obesity, confluential reduction, and volume reduc-

FIG. 1. Pressure bag for delivery of anesthetic solution.

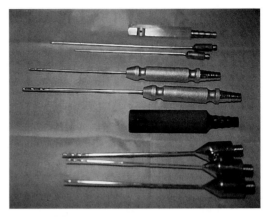

FIG. 4. Multiple cannula designs.

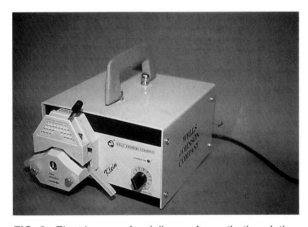

FIG. 2. Electric pump for delivery of anesthetic solution.

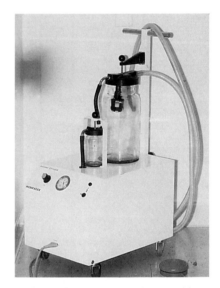

FIG. 5. French liposuction machine.

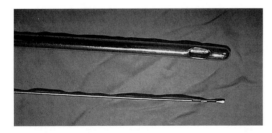

FIG. 3. Comparison of original Illouz No. 10 cannula with new Klein 12-gauge cannula.

FIG. 6. New liposuction machine with disposable canisters, tubing, and viral filter.

tion. Liposuction is among the safest and most common cosmetic surgical procedures performed today. Many advances have been and are being made by dermatologic surgeons.

PREOPERATIVE PLANNING: CONSULTATION

The most important part of any cosmetic procedure is the consultation. The physician can determine whether the patient is a good candidate for the procedure and has realistic expectations of what can be achieved. It is important to know what the patient desires and expects. The physical examination is performed concentrating on the localization of fat and the skin turgor. The procedure is discussed with the patient at this time, including the benefits that can be achieved along with the possible complications and risks.

A Polaroid photograph is also taken and used when discussing the expected result. A medical history, including illnesses, medication, history of bleeding, previous surgeries, and allergies, is also taken at this time. Photographs of other patients who have undergone the surgery are shown and discussed.

If the patient decides to proceed with the procedure, blood pressure is taken and urine and blood tests are performed, including complete blood cell count, SMAC, prothrombin time, and partial thromboplastin time and tests for hepatitis C surface antibody, hepatitis B surface antigen, and human immunodeficiency virus. All medical problems are evaluated individually, and any patient taking systemic medication or with abnormal blood test results or history of illness should be evaluated by the family physician before the procedure. Preoperative and postoperative instructions are reviewed with the patient, and the postoperative course is discussed. An antibiotic regimen may be prescribed to be started the day before the surgery. The patient should be warned to discontinue all aspirin, aspirin-containing compounds, and nonsteroidal antiinflammatory drugs 2 weeks before surgery. Patients are advised to wear comfortable clothing and have a friend or relative accompany them home. Patients are also advised to bring towels and large plastic garbage bags to sit on for the ride home, since there will be some drainage from the treated areas. Provision is made for postoperative compression, including garments or tape, or both. Patients must be told that liposuction this is not a procedure to correct striae, spider veins, skin tightness, or cellulite but that it is a contouring procedure. Any deformities and unusual prominence of anatomic bony structures must be discussed with the patient at this time. Most patients are extremely realistic about the results that can be achieved. There are those patients who can expect a perfect contour, but in most patients liposuction surgery gives extremely gratifying but not perfect results with very little scarring or morbidity. Patients are happy to look better in clothing and have a nicer contour.

PREOPERATIVE PROCEDURE: DAY OF SURGERY

When the patient comes in on the morning of surgery, vital signs and weight are measured. Weight is measured to calculate the total amounts of lidocaine and preoperative sedation that are safe to use. Follow-up of patients is helpful to determine whether there is weight gain or weight loss in the future so that the postoperative results can be evaluated. The patient must sign the consent form before any sedation is given. Polaroid and 35-mm photographs (see Chapter 8) are taken, which are used in the operating room and then kept in the patient chart so that the patient can be evaluated at 6-month intervals. Usually four views are taken: 90 degrees on the right side, 90 degrees on the left side, and back and front views. A matte-colored background is helpful. It is important to have a routine so that preoperative and postoperative photographs are comparable. The patient's body is marked while the patient is in a standing position and then in various other positions, to see how the fat falls (Fig. 7). Areas to avoid should be marked by writing "avoid," and areas of large fat depositions should be marked with an X. All possible incision marks are drawn at this time and shown to the patient. These marks are made using an indelible marker. Following this, preoperative sedation can be given.

SURGICAL PROCEDURE

Liposuction surgery involves the introduction of blunt cannulas of varying lengths and designs through small incisions in the skin. These allow removal of adipose tissue, sparing neurovascular septae while leaving connective tissue bridges between overlying and deeper elements. A series of tunnels fan out radially and criss-cross under the skin from each incision point.

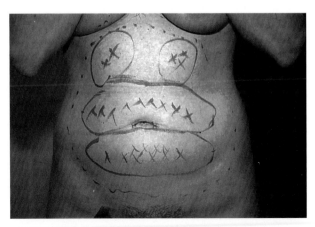

FIG. 7. Preoperative marking of patient.

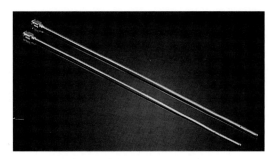

FIG. 8. "Showerhead" infiltrators.

ANESTHESIA

Equipment

For tumescent anesthesia, it is necessary to have bags of tumescent solution, a No. 11 blade for incisions, spinal needles, infiltrators (Fig. 8) through which to inject the solution, and syringes with 30-gauge, ½-inch needles to inject the incision sites. If a pressure cuff around the bag of anesthetic solution is being used for delivery of the anesthetic solution, a pressure cuff (Fig. 1) is needed, as well as intravenous tubing and extension tubing. If electric pump infiltrators are being used, special tubing, as well as the electric infiltrator (Fig. 2), is required.

Anesthetic Solution

The anesthetic solution is composed of various percentages of lidocaine. The formulas for 0.05% and 0.1% lidocaine solutions can be found in Tables 31-1 and 31-2. Solutions for small treatment areas are made up in smaller bags (Table 31-3). In addition, some anesthesiologists make up 0.075% solutions. The solutions contain normal saline as a diluent with lidocaine for anesthesia, epinephrine to decrease absorption of the anesthetic as well as decrease bleeding, bicarbonate to decrease the pain of the anesthetic and possibly prevent infection, and triamcinolone acetonide, which may decrease postoperative swelling. The total amount of anesthetic should be calculated based on the patient's weight. A safe amount is 35 to 50 mg of lidocaine per kilogram of body weight. When the number of bags must be maximized because of the number of areas being treated or the size of the patient, it is possible to use more of the 0.05%

TABLE 31-1. *Tumescent Liposuction Solution .05%*

1000 cc	Normal Saline	.9%
50 cc	Lidocaine	1%
1 cc	Epinephrine	1/1000
12.5 cc	Bicarbonate	8.4%
1 cc	Triamcinolone acetonide (optional)	10 mg/cc
Total: 400 mg lidocaine = .05% 1/1 million epinephrine		

TABLE 31-2. *Tumescent Liposuction Solution .1%*

1000 cc	Normal Saline	.9%
50 cc	Lidocaine	2%
1 cc	Epinephrine	1/1000
12.5 cc	Bicarbonate	8.4%
1 cc	Triamcinolone acetonide (optional)	10 mg/cc
Total: 1000 mg lidocaine = .1% 1/1 million epinephrine		

solution and less of the 0.1% solution. If only small areas are being treated, the entire procedure can usually be performed with the 0.1% lidocaine solution.

Delivery of Anesthetic Solution

Deliver the anesthesia in three stages. The first stage is the injection of the incision sites with a 0.1% lidocaine, epinephrine, and bicarbonate solution using a syringe attached to a 30-gauge, ½-inch needle. The second stage is to inject slowly and radially through the incision areas using the tumescent solution and a spinal needle. This gives painless preliminary anesthesia. The third stage is the tumescent technique. Inject the tumescent solution into the subcutaneous tissue using an infiltrator (Fig. 8) inserted through a small incision area made with a No. 11 blade through the incision site. Inject most of the tumescent solution deeply through tunnels radiating from the incision site. Try to criss-cross the tunnels using more than one incision site, injecting some of the solution superficially as well. It is important not to raise a peau d'orange in the skin, since this changes landmarks during surgery.

Benefits of Tumescent Anesthesia

Tumescent anesthesia enables liposuction to be performed with no risk from general anesthesia or intravenous sedation. Patients feel much better after surgery. In addition, there is virtually no blood loss, and no need for transfusions (Fig. 9). The anesthetic effect of the solution lasts for a long time, making the surgery basically pain free. In past cases, there has been no need for fluid replacement, and patients can turn themselves to the exact position necessary for easy removal of any pocket of fat.

TABLE 31-3. *Tumescent Solution for Smaller Areas*

250 cc	Normal Saline	.9%
25 cc	Lidocaine	1%
¼ cc	Epinephrine	1/1000
4 cc	Bicarbonate	8.4%
Total: 250 mg lidocaine = .1% 1/1 million epinephrine		

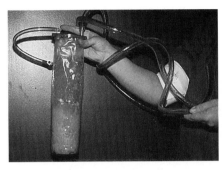

FIG. 9. Fat in disposable canister. Lack of blood is evident.

EQUIPMENT

Cannulas

Many new cannulas are now available. It is important to use a blunt, less aggressive cannula with the opening further away from the tip when first beginning liposuction surgery. With experience, more aggressive cannulas can be used in sharper tips such as the Lamprey, Cobra, Accelerator, Pinto, or Cook, as well as the Narins, screw designs. For training purposes, hands-on experience allows manipulation of the instruments. The original Illouz cannulas were blunt and were as large as 10 mm (Fig. 3), which now looks enormous. With these larger cannulas it was important to stay deep in the fatty tissue to avoid the result of rippling. With smaller cannulas finer adjustments can be obtained, since they can be used closer to the surface of the skin to perform "liposculpture." Multiple cannulas are usually used in every patient. Depending on the area being treated, several other cannulas may be used as well. A single handle with interchangeable tips for most procedures may be advantageous.

Aspiration Pump and Tubing

There are many manufacturers of aspiration pumps that develop negative air pressure approaching 30″, for example, the Wells Johnson pump (Fig. 2). Disposable canisters or canisters with disposable bags, disposable tubing, and viral filters comply with OSHA regulations (Fig. 6). Small canisters for small areas are used during treatment of lipoma, knees, or upper neck alone.

Pulse Oximeter

A pulse oximeter is a useful adjunct to measure oxygen saturation in the bloodstream, since lidocaine toxicity is related to decreased oxygen. Patients are awake with the tu-

mescent technique, and the surgeon can just tell them to take a deep breath if the oxygen level decreases.

Disposable Syringe Technique

Pierre Fournier developed a syringe technique with disposable syringes and cannulas that require no pump or tubing (Fig. 10). This technique has been used on patients with hepatitis C. Many liters of fat have been removed from the patient without any problem. This technique may be more cumbersome than using a machine, but it is a less expensive method of liposuction that certainly works; in addition, it is good to have this technique available in the office as a backup procedure in the event that a usual liposuction machine malfunctions.

PREOPERATIVE PREPARATION

Encourage the patient to go to the bathroom before the procedure; otherwise, he or she will be uncomfortable during the surgery because of the large amount of fluid injected. After taking the patient to the operating room, prepare the areas to be treated with povidone-iodine (Betadine) and place the patient onto the operating table in sterile fashion. Prepare the patient for surgery with the usual sterile precautions and setup. After the patient is prepared for surgery, inject the anesthetic. After the anesthetic is injected, wait 15 to 30 minutes; during this time, repeat preparation of the patient with povidone-iodine and redrape. This wait ensures minimal bleeding and maximum anesthesia.

SURGICAL TECHNIQUE

Perform liposuction in the deeper areas first, in a radial, criss-cross fashion using the Klein 12-gauge cannula, and

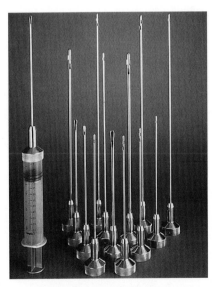

FIG. 10. Disposable syringes and cannulas for syringe technique.

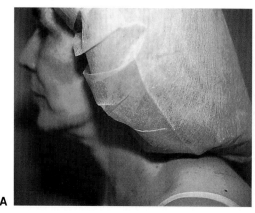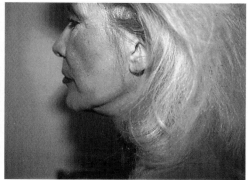

FIG. 11. Neck **(A)** before and **(B)** after surgery.

follow that with the workhorse cannula (e.g., the Lamprey 4-mm). With the non–cannula-grasping hand guide the cannula to those areas from which adipose tissue is to be removed. The movement is used at varying depths to accomplish the liposculpturing process. Use the larger cannulas more deeply, and use the smaller cannulas both deeply and superficially. Limits are determined by the preoperative markings, the surgeon's estimate of how much fat should be removed from a particular area, visual observation of the quality of the aspirant, and assessment of the amount of blood loss occurring and the looseness of the skin. It is good to leave a small layer of fat under the surface of the skin so that the area is smooth after surgery. Preservation of vascular septae is important to preclude cavity formation with the attendant risks of hematoma, seroma, infection, or postoperative deformity. Never allow a windshield wiper–like, sweeping movement in any part of the body except the submental area. (Even there, its use is a subject of controversy.) Liposuction is a debulking procedure, but the subsequent fibrous tissues that form afterward also retract the skin. During the procedure palpate the area so that possible residual masses of fat are noted and removed. The major aspirations should be along vertical lines where possible, again using

the criss-cross technique. before the use of tumescent anesthesia, the safe amount of fat to be removed was generally considered to be under 2000 cc. However, with the use of large volumes of anesthetic fluid, many surgeons remove between 2000 and 4000 cc of fat; the average amount of fat removed at one time is 2500 cc. Not suturing the incision sites allows the fluid to drain after surgery. If a surgeon is going to suture any of the sites, suturing should not be performed until after the procedure is finished; this allows the most drainage to occur during surgery.

SURGICAL TREATMENT OF SPECIFIC BODY AREAS

Head and Neck

The neck is probably the easiest area in which to perform liposuction surgery. Skin retraction is excellent here. Fatty deposits range from submental accumulations to a tremendous double chin that involves most of the neck from ear to ear. The superficial fat in the neck lies between the skin and the platysma and can easily be removed with liposuction.

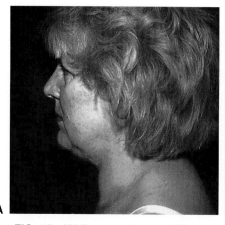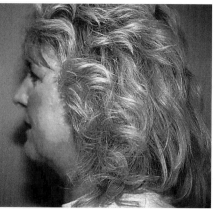

FIG. 12. (A) Preoperative and **(B)** postoperastive views of the neck (one incision).

FIG. 13. (A) Preoperative and (B) postoperative views of the neck (three incisions).

A clean, sharp angle of the jaw line gives a very youthful appearance (Fig. 11). When the fat is limited to the submental region, one small incision in the submental crease is all that is needed (Fig. 12). If there is a large accumulation of fat, three incisions, one in the submental region and then one behind each ear, are needed to remove all of the fat (Fig. 13). Through these incisions liposuction of the jowls can also be performed (Fig. 14). The neck is one area where a surgeon sometimes turns the cannula over with the hole facing toward the surface of the skin to remove as much fat as possible. Usually the amount of aspirate from the neck is quite small, ranging from 10 to 100 cc, yet the result may be astonishingly great. This is an easy procedure for the patient, and with tumescent anesthesia there is usually no postoperative bruising. Patients can remove the dressing 2 or 3 days after surgery.

Caveats

Liposuction alone will not take care of platysmal bands. In addition, while obliteration of the anterior cervicomandibular angle may be due to fat, it is sometimes due to muscle

or a high hyoid bone (Fig. 15). These are familial traits and limit the success of liposuction. In some patients, the skin is so lax that retraction is limited. In these patients a neck lift should be considered; if the patient does not wish that, an excision in the submental crease may be performed at the same time as liposuction. This can give excellent results, considering the low morbidity of the procedure. The submental excision is made easier because the undermining has already been accomplished during the preceding liposuction.

When wrapping the neck, tape the area for 2 days and have the patient wear a chin guard at night. Separate the initial pieces of tape by 1 cm in the center of the neck so that there is less chance of vertical folds (Fig. 16). These folds, if they occur, are temporary.

Occasionally there is some temporary trauma to the cervical mandibular branch of the facial nerve, but there has never been a report of permanent damage, although there has been a case in which partial paralysis lasted for 2 months.

Occasionally the area may get very hard after surgery. This is also temporary, but if it is bothersome to the patient, inject dilute triamcinolone acetonide (1 mg/cc) intralesionally.

Liposuction of the face, of course, is routinely used as an

FIG. 14. (A) Preoperative and (B) postoperative views of neck and jowls.

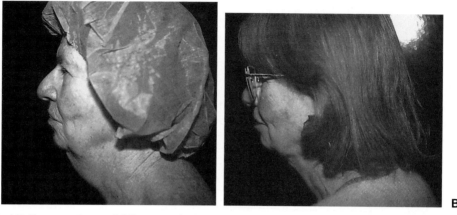

FIG. 15. (A) Preoperative and **(B)** postoperative views of neck with prominent anterior hyoid bone.

adjunct to rhytidectomy and in fact has made the procedure much easier to perform. Liposuction of the face should be performed very carefully by an experienced operator with very small cannulas. Although the lateral cheeks respond well, liposuction in the nasolabial fold may yield a flat, unattractive look.

Arms

Many women accumulate fat in the upper arms as a result of heredity and/or obesity. It is important to perform the liposuction in this area before the skin gets so loose that liposuction results in unsightly, hanging skin. In the usual patient with moderately good skin turgor excellent results can be achieved (Fig. 17) through one to four incisions above the elbow and one incision in the posterior axillary line. Postoperative wrapping is easily accomplished with support stocking, which gives even pressure over the area.

Pseudogynecomastia

Tumescent liposuction is a wonderful technique for psuedogynecomastia because it gives a tremendous improve-

ment without scarring and without loss of time from work (Figs. 18 and 19). Patients can go about their business the next day wearing a binder that no one can see.

This is one of the more difficult areas in which to perform liposuction because of the amount of fibrous tissue present. In fact, generally liposuction in men is more difficult because they have more fibrous tissue. Make the first incision in the axilla, where it is not visible. Turn the cannula upside down so that as much breast tissue as possible is scraped out with

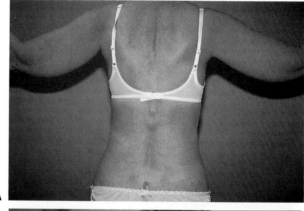

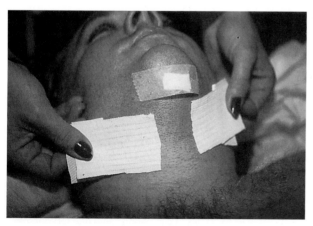

FIG. 16. Postoperative taping of neck.

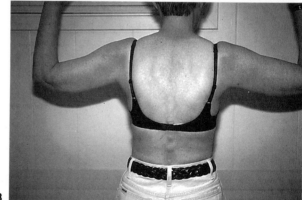

FIG. 17. (A) Preoperative and **(B)** postoperative views of arms.

a very aggressive cannula. Use the cannula with the openings facing the skin in the infraareolar and periareolar areas only. This is an area in which as much fat as possible needs to be removed and we want the skin to retract as much as possible. Routinely send the material removed for biopsy.

"Buffalo Hump"

The "dowager deformity buffalo hump" lends itself easily to liposuction surgery (Fig. 20). One or two tiny incisions allow the operator to criss-cross the area and easily remove this very soft fat, which does not recur.

Flanks

The flanks are the most common area for accumulation of fat in men as they get older. This area responds well to liposuction surgery (Fig. 21). Many patients who request this procedure are in excellent physical condition and yet have an unsightly protrusion that hangs over their waistband. Fibrosis and retraction occur in this area with significant contour improvement. The back is a very fibrous area, which necessitates the use of aggressive and smaller cannulas, and is often treated with the flanks in men and with the waist and hips in women. Because these areas are so fibrous, multiple small incisions are sometimes needed. The Klein 10- and 12-gauge cannulas are very well suited for this area.

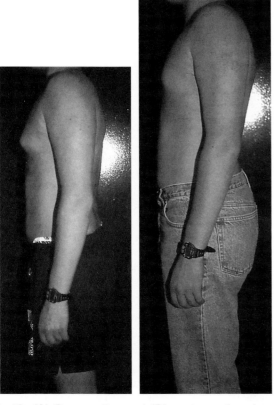

FIG. 18. (A) Preoperative and **(B)** postoperative views of gynecomastia.

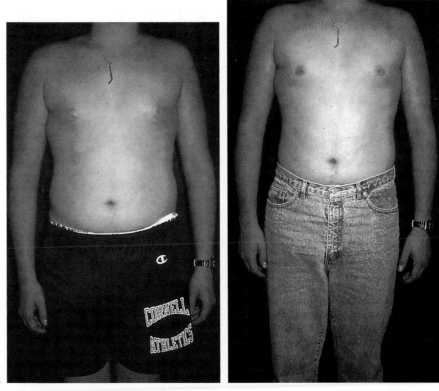

FIG. 19. (A) Preoperative and **(B)** postoperative views of gynecomastia.

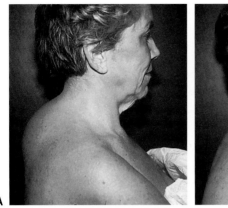
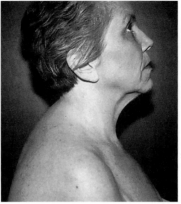

FIG. 20. (A) Preoperative and **(B)** postoperative views of "buffalo hump."

Abdomen

The abdomen is one of the most common areas for liposuction and is the area where women accumulate fat as they get older. The fat is soft and easy to remove (Figs. 22 and 23) and can be divided into two general regions—the upper abdomen above the umbilicus and the lower abdomen from just above the umbilicus to the pubic area. The upper abdomen is the more difficult area to treat because it is more fibrous and the skin does not retract as well; it can be approached through an incision above the umbilicus or from either side. It is probably best not to use the same incision that is used for the lower abdomen in women with a definite waistband, to avoid breaking the waistbands that hold in the waistline (Figs. 24 and 25). After the tumescent anesthetic is injected, use straight 1% lidocaine and epinephrine around the umbilicus to give more complete anesthesia in this area. The incisions for the lower abdomen can be in the two lateral umbilical lines and one on either side of the lower abdomen, just below the protrusion in the pubic line. For patients with larger abdomens and when hips are being treated, make two suprapubic incisions and one incision on either side of the abdomen. As previously mentioned, use three to five incisions in this area; as an alternative, a grid pattern with multi-

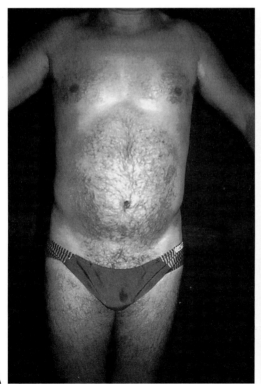
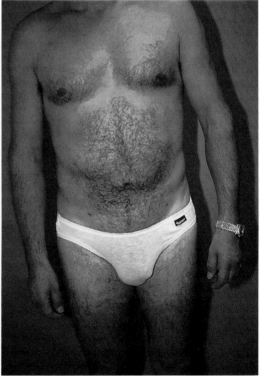

FIG. 21. (A) Preoperative and **(B)** postoperative views of abdomen and flanks.

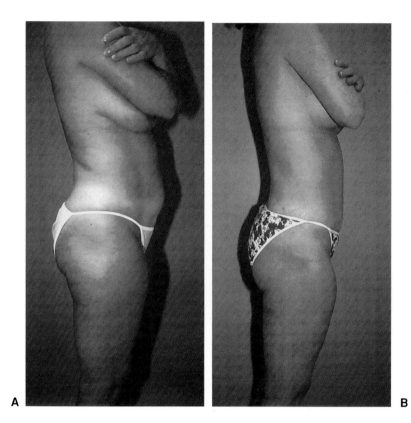

FIG. 22. (A) Preoperative and **(B)** postoperative views of abdomen.

A
B

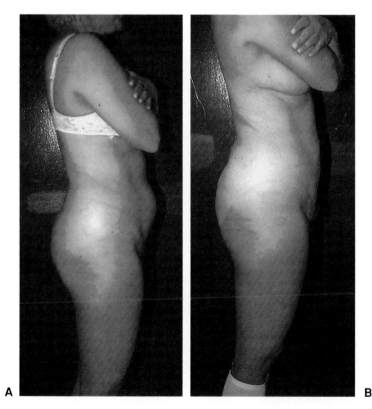

FIG. 23. (A) Preoperative and **(B)** postoperative views of abdomen.

A
B

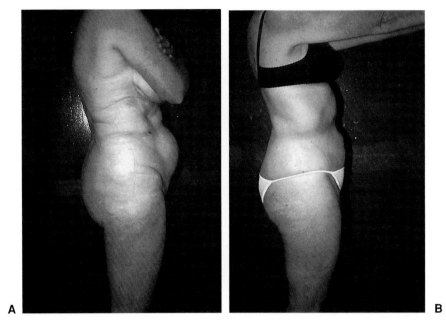

FIG. 24. (A) Preoperative and **(B)** postoperative views of abdomen with waistband intact.

ple tiny incision areas can also be used. Gear incisions to the areas that are to be treated. It is important in this area to perform the deep liposuction first, followed by use of smaller cannulas more superficially. Tumescence of fat in women is usually easy to accomplish, and the fat easy to remove surgically. It is amazing how even an abdominal apron will pull back after surgery (Fig. 26).

When the skin is so lax after pregnancy that it is tissue-paper thin, in addition to performing liposuction surgery, perform a suprapubic excision of skin immediately following liposuction to give a nicer result. Again, this excision is made easier because the liposuction undermines the tissue before the excision.

A very small number of people do not benefit from liposuction and would be better served with an open lipectomy and repair of the rectus abdominous muscle. The "beer belly" fat that occurs in men lies behind the muscle and thus cannot be removed but generally responds well to diet and exercise. It is important to rule out the presence of a ventral hernia before surgery.

Pubic Area

Both men and women may have deposits of fat in the mons pubis. At the same time that abdominal liposcution is

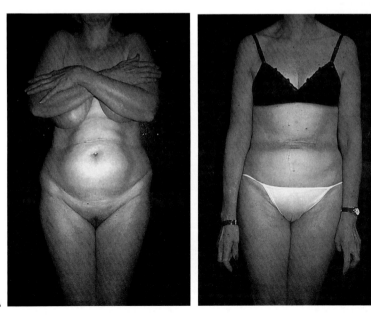

FIG. 25. (A) Preoperative and **(B)** postoperative views of abdomen with waistband intact.

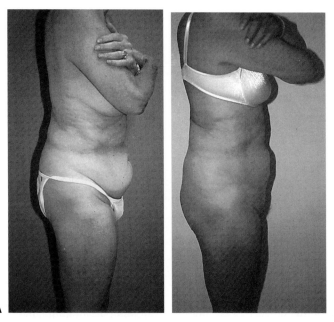

FIG. 26. (A) Preoperative and (B) postoperative views of abdomen with small apron.

performed, a small amount of fat from the pubic area can be removed. Warn patients that they can have marked swelling and ecchymosis in this area.

Lateral Thighs (''Saddle Bags''), Hips, and Buttocks

Lateral thighs are the most common area for which women request liposuction (Figs. 27–29). Often the hips may be involved in a ''violin deformity.'' Using two incisions, both the hip and lateral thigh can be treated (Fig. 30). One incision is made below the hip and above the lateral thigh protrusion, and one just under the buttock to criss-cross horizontally over the lateral thigh protrusion and give a more even result.

Most of the surgery should be performed vertically if possible. If, when the patient on examination faces away from you and tightens the buttocks, the lateral thighs diminish in size, it is necessary to treat the buttocks area at the same time (Figs. 31 and 32).

Surgery in the buttocks area is done through the infragluteal incision used for the lateral thighs, and occasionally an additional infragluteal incision more medially to criss-cross over this area. The lateral thigh area, as well as the hip, generally has good skin turgor and responds easily to liposuction with excellent results. Patients often ask about cellulite in this area. Although the fibrous septae around the cellulite are sometimes broken and the patient may look better, it

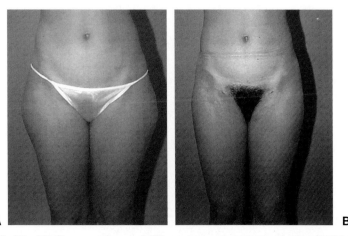

FIG. 27. (A) Preoperative and (B) postoperative views of lateral thighs.

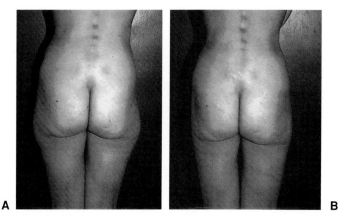

FIG. 28. (A) Preoperative and **(B)** postoperative views of lateral thighs.

is best to tell the patient there will probably be no change. Adipose deposits in the lateral thigh and buttock areas can occur even in thin women, are usually inherited, and can be evident at an early age.

Some patients have very deep trochanteric depressions, which can be filled in with fat transplantation at the same time that liposuction of the lateral thigh, hips, and buttocks is performed.

Do not come too close to the surface of the lower buttock so that the skin does not become loose in this area. Under the buttock in the upper posterior thigh is the "banana roll." Great care should be taken not to remove too much fat in this area so that the buttock does not sag.

Inner Thighs

The inner thighs are one of the more difficult areas to treat because the skin is often thin and there is a limit to how much fat can be removed without leaving some sagging. Explain this to the patient at the consultation. Generally the fat is easy to remove through two incisions, one in the ante-

rior groin area and one in the medial posterior infragluteal fold. With the patient on her side remove the fat by criss-crossing over the area. It is very important to mark this region before surgery, indicating the greatest deposit of fat, because landmarks can be misleading during surgery. Do not make an incision in the midthigh area because it often leaves an indentation. If the patient has very loose skin in this area and not much fat, suggest to the patient a thigh lift with liposuction followed by excision of skin with a subsequent surgical scar in the medial groin.

Circumferential Thigh Reduction

Perform circumferential thigh reduction through multiple incisions above the knee going around the entire thigh. Use long cannulas in this area. Generally perform these reductions serially because they are much more difficult to perform than liposuction of the lateral thigh, knee, or inner thigh, since there is much more fibrous tissue and, often, large protuberant muscles.

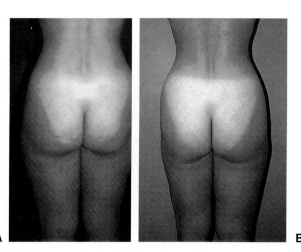

FIG. 29. (A) Preoperative and **(B)** postoperative views of lateral thighs.

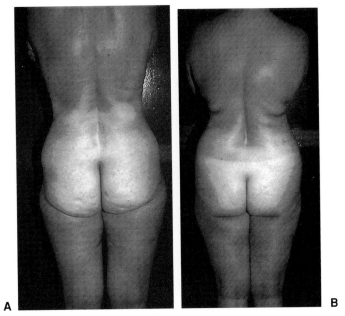

FIG. 30. (A) Preoperative and **(B)** postoperative views of "violin deformity."

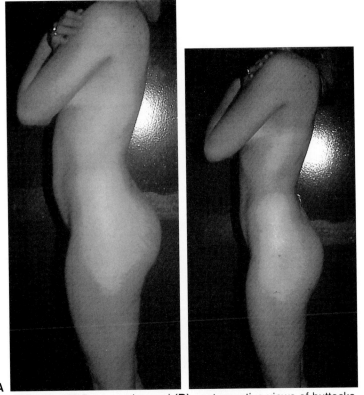

FIG. 31. (A) Preoperative and **(B)** postoperative views of buttocks.

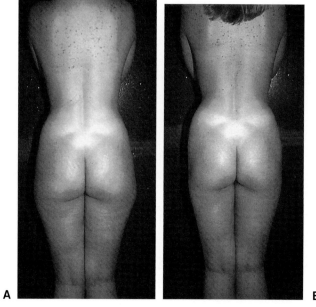

FIG. 32. (A) Preoperative and **(B)** postoperative views of buttocks.

Knees

Knees are easy to treat, and surgery often can be performed through one tiny incision per knee. Use small cannulas, and be careful not to do too much work and leave the area depressed. The upper medial part of the calf can be treated as well, to give a better, shapelier contour.

Calves and Ankles

With the advent of the smaller Klein cannulas liposuction surgery for calves and ankles has become easier. With the small cannulas multiple tiny incisions can be made, and the fat carefully sculpted from these areas.

Lipomas

The removal of even massive lipomas can be accomplished through very small incisions (Fig. 33). However, the fibrous stroma is very difficult to remove, and the liposuction cannulas are used to remove the fat and separate the lipoma from the surrounding tissue. After this has been accomplished, squeeze out the remaining tissue through the tiny opening. It is very satisfying when the last bit of fibrous stroma lipoma pops out. Tape this area with a pressure dressing.

FAT TRANSPLANTATION

Fat transplantation into trochanteric depressions or areas of facial scars or folds is performed at the same time as

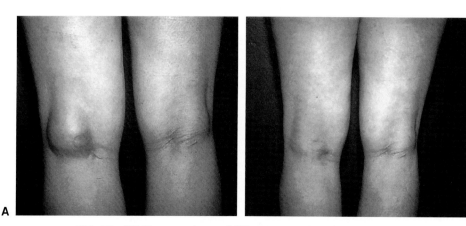

FIG. 33. (A) Preoperative and **(B)** postoperative views of lipoma.

liposuction using a collector to collect 150 to 200 cc of fat during the procedure. After the injection, flash-freeze the remaining fat in liquid nitrogen and store in the freezer for later use. With this technique the long-term success of fat transplantation is markedly improved.

POSTOPERATIVE MANAGEMENT

Immediate Postoperative Care

Immediately after surgery the patient is washed, and ice packs are applied to the treated area. The patient is advised that the treated areas will drain for 24 to 72 hours. Generally, the tighter the skin turgor, the less drainage there will be. Sanitary napkins can be used over the incision sites, and towels with plastic bags underneath can be used to sit and sleep on. Patients should also bring towels and a large plastic bag to cover the seat of the car when going home after surgery. Patients are routinely given 2 cc of intramuscular betamethasone (Celestone) immediately after surgery, and a regimen of phylactic antibiotics is continued. Antibiotic therapy is started 1 day before surgery and continued for 5 days after surgery.

Postoperative Care

Not only does the compression dressing redrape the skin, but it also is useful in preventing hematoma and seroma formation. The patient also feels less discomfort because the skin is stabilized. In addition to the tape, garments are also used. Compression with tape dressings is very important in certain areas (e.g., on lateral thighs to redrape the skin, as well as on the abdomen). A dressing is important in the upper neck area for 2 to 3 days. After 2 to 3 days remove all the tape compression dressings. A dressing is sometimes reapplied for another 3 days on the lateral thighs and abdomen if the skin is loose. Once the tape is removed, garments are worn 24 hours a day for 1 to 3 weeks, depending on the patient's skin turgor and the size of the area that was treated. The patient may be advised to wear the garment for an additional week or two at night, again depending on the looseness of the skin. Once the tape is removed, the patient can shower daily. Within 1 to 3 days the patient can return to work, and patients can resume light-intensity, nonjarring exercise as soon as they feel up to it. Light-intensity exercise means nonjarring activities such as walking, riding Stairmaster types of exercise bicycles, and the like. If large areas have been treated, especially in patients with loose skin, patients are not allowed to return to jarring activities such as aerobic exercises, tennis, or jogging for 3 to 4 weeks. Patients are routinely called on the night of surgery to check on how they are doing, and patients have the doctor's and nurse's phone numbers in case they have any problems. Patients are advised to watch their caloric intake, especially their intake of fat, and to begin a regular exercise program.

Follow-up Care

If there are no problems, patients are seen 2 days, 1 week, 1 month, 3 months, and 6 months after surgery. At the 3- and 6-month visits photographs are taken so that the patient and the physician can follow the improvement. It is always amazing that patients who have lived with deformities for most of their lives cannot remember them 1 month later. When the photographs are taken, it is important that the patient be weighed so that the surgeon can compare the weight with that before the procedure.

COMPLICATIONS

Complications with tumescent liposuction are rare. The usual postoperative sequelae include dysesthesia, ecchymosis that may last 2 to 3 weeks, and occasional soreness. There have been a few reports of seroma, infection, and hematoma, but these are remarkably uncommon. There have been no deaths related to tumescent liposuction surgery performed without general or intravenous anesthesia. Other uncommon complications include waviness, dimpling, hypopigmentation, and the like.

The end results of liposuction are generally excellent.

CONCLUSION

Liposuction has become the most popular cosmetic surgical procedure performed today because it is extremely safe and patients are very gratified with the results. The tumescent technique of anesthesia developed by dermatologic surgeons has made this procedure even safer and easier to perform. Many areas of the body are amenable to treatment by liposuction and often multiple areas can be done at the same time. However, some procedures must be divided into two or more sessions because of the need to stay within the published safety limits for lidocaine and fluid.

Liposuction is a contouring procedure—not a treatment for weight loss or obesity. It is very important to choose a realistic patient who is a good candidate for this surgery. The advent of smaller cannulas requiring smaller incisions, the increased experience of many surgeons, the proliferation of hands-on, live surgery and didactic lecture courses, enabling new surgeons to learn to do this procedure, as well as the work in external and internal ultrasonic techniques, make liposuction a procedure which is continually improving and continually expanding its parameters.

SUGGESTED READING LIST

1. Special liposuction issue. Am J Cosmet Surg 1986;1.
2. Asken, SA. Manual of Liposuction surgery and autologous fat transplantation under local anesthesia. 2nd ed. Irvine, CA: Keith C. Terry & Associates, 1986.
3. Coleman WP III. The history of dermatologic liposuction. Dermatol Clin 1990;8:381.

4. Committee on Guidelines of Care. Guidelines of care for liposuction. J Am Acad Dermatol 1991;24:489.

5. Cook W Jr. Preoperative consultation and evaluation. Lectures at ASDS, 1996.

6. Cook W Jr. Regional liposuction: face/neck and arms. Lectures at ASDS, 1996.

7. Cook W Jr. Technical aspects of liposuction. Lectures at ASDS, 1996.

8. Courtiss EH, Chouair RJ, Donelan MB. Large-volume suction lipectomy: an analysis of 108 patients. Plast Reconstr Surg 1992;89:1068.

9. Dillerud E. Suction lipoplasty: a report on complications, undesired results, and patient satisfaction based on 3511 procedures. Plast Reconstr Surg 1991;88:239.

10. Elam M, Fournier P. Liposuction: the Franco-American experience. Beverly Hills, CA: Medical Aesthetics, Inc., 1986.

11. Field L, Narins R. Liposuction surgery. In: Epstein E, Epstein E Jr. Skin surgery. 6th ed. Philadelphia: WB Saunders, 1987:370.

12. Field LM. The dermatologic surgeon and liposculpturing. In: Fournier PF, ed. Liposculpture: the syringe technique. Paris: Arnette Blackwell, 1991:265.

13. Field LM. Liposuction surgery: a review. J Dermatol Surg Oncol 1984; 10:530.

14. Fischer A, Fischer G. Revised techniques for cellulitis fat reduction in riding breeches deformity. Bull Int Acad Cosmet Surg 1977;2:40.

15. Fournier P. Body sculpturing through syringe lipo-extractions and autologous fat re-injection. Solana Beach, CA: Samuel Rolf International, 1988.

16. Fournier P, Otteni F. Lipodissection in body sculpturing: the dry procedure. Plast Reconstr Surg 1983;72:598.

17. Fournier PF. Liposculpture: the syringe technique. Paris: Arnette Blackwell, 1991:163.

18. Hanke CW. Liposuction under local anesthesia. J Dermatol Surg Oncol 1989;15:12 (editorial).

19. Hanke C, Bernstein G, Bullock S. Safety of tumescent liposuction in 15,336 patients. New York: Elsevier Science, 1995.

20. Hetter G. Lipoplasty: the theory and practice of blunt suction lipectomy. Boston/Toronto: Little, Brown, 1984.

21. Illouz Y. Body contouring by lipolysis: a 5-year experience with over 3000 cases. Plast Reconstr Surg 1983;72:591.

22. Klein JA. Anesthesia for liposuction in dermatologic surgery. J Dermatol Surg Oncol 1988;14:1124.

23. Klein JA. Peak plasma lidocaine levels are diminished and delayed twelve hours by tumescent technique for liposuction, permitting maximum safe lidocaine doses of 35 mg/kg. J Dermatol Surg Oncol 1990.

24. Klein JA. Tumescent liposuction: totally by local anesthesia. In: Lask GP, Moy RI, eds. Principles and practice of dermatological surgery. New York: McGraw-Hill, 1993.

25. Klein JA. The tumescent technique: anesthesia and modified liposuction technique. Dermatol Clin 1990;8:425.

26. Klein JA. Tumescent technique for regional anesthesia permits lidocaine doses of 35 mg/kg for lipsosuction. J Dermatol Surg Oncol 1990; 16:248–63.

27. Klein JA. Tumescent liposuction and improved postoperative care using tumescent liposuction garments. Dermatol Clin 1995;13:329.

28. Klein JA. Tumescent technique chronicles. Elsevier Science, 1995.

29. Klein JA. Tumescent technique for local anesthesia improves safety in large-volume liposuction. Am Acad Cosmet Surg 1992.

30. Klein JA. The tumescent technique for liposuction surgery. Am J Surg 1987;4:263.

31. Lillis PJ. Liposuction surgery under local anesthesia: limited blood loss and minimal lidocaine absorption. J Dermatol Surg Oncol 1988;14: 1145.

32. Lillis PJ, Coleman WP III, eds. Liposuction. Dermatol Clin 1990;8: 439.

33. Lillis PJ, Coleman WP III. Liposuction for treatment of axillary hyperhidrosis. Dermatol Clin 1990;8:479.

34. McKay W, Morris R, Mushlin P. Sodium bicarbonate attenuates pain on skin infiltration with lidocaine with or without epinephrine. Anesth Analg 1987;66:572.

35. Narins RS. Liposuction and anesthesia. Dermatol Clin 1990;8:421.

36. Narins RS. Liposuction of the face and neck. In Elson ML, ed. Evaluation and treatment of the aging face. 1984.

37. Newman J, Dolsky R. Liposuction surgery: history and development. J Dermatol Surg Oncol 1984;10:467.

38. Stegman S, Tromovitch T. Liposuction. In: Cosmetic dermatologic surgery. Chicago: Year Book Medical, 1983:216.

39. Teimourian B. Suction lipectomy and body sculpturing. St. Louis: CV Mosby, 1987.

Textbook of Dermatologic Surgery, edited by John L. Ratz.
Lippincott–Raven Publishers, Philadelphia © 1998.

CHAPTER 32

Soft Tissue Augmentation

William P. Coleman III

HISTORY

Even dating back to ancient times, physicians have sought methods for correcting soft tissue defects. They quickly discovered that autologous materials (e.g., bone, cartilage, dermis, fat) became viable implants, whereas nonbiologic materials (metal, plastic, and so forth) often relocated or extruded after implantation.

In the latter part of the 19th century, en bloc transplantation of fat was performed successfully. Physicians reported a success rate of approximately 50%. However, this technique relied on an incision in both the donor and recipient sites, effectively trading one defect for another.

There was a great deal of interest in dermal grafting in the 1930s. Physicians harvested skin from an inobtrusive donor site and removed epidermis from the graft. They then placed the remaining dermis in subcutaneous pockets to correct contour defects. Although moderately successful, this procedure resulted in an unacceptable rate of cyst formation and deforming fibrosis.

In the postwar years liquid silicone became quite popular for tissue augmentation. Physicians soon discovered that, when used in a microdroplet approach, predictable results could be obtained. However, large-volume implantations of silicone often resulted in migration of the material, fibrosis, and scarring. Injection of large volumes of silicone for breast implantation caused public fury when it became clear that many patients were severely deformed using this approach. Injections of small aliquots at a time, however, proved to be successful. Studies demonstrated that the silicone provoked an inflammatory response and subsequent deposition of collagen around each droplet. This decreased the tendency for migration of the material. Physicians reported excellent long-term augmentation of dermis defects using the microdroplet silicone approach.

The U.S. Food and Drug Administration (FDA) intervened, claiming that there were no adequate studies of liquid silicone and that it was potentially dangerous to humans. Also, there was no system for preventing its misuse. Dow Corning, the manufacturer of silicone, initially planned to submit an application for FDA approval of their compound. However, the company subsequently changed its course, deciding that continued production of medical-grade silicone was not financially rewarding enough to recoup the expense of FDA drug trials. For years after this, physicians around the United States continued to use medical-grade silicone, but gradually the FDA took a harder stance against this practice, eventually raiding physicians' offices and threatening

William P. Coleman III: Department of Dermatology, Tulane University School of Medicine, 4425 Conlin Street, Metairie, LA 70006.

them with violation of federal law. Although most dermatologists clearly support the use of medical-grade silicone, the FDA's attitude has made its use impossible at this time.

In the late 1970s the Collagen Corporation developed Zyderm collagen. This substance is made from cow (bovine) collagen, which is processed and purified into a sterile, nonviscous implant suitable for dermal augmentation in humans. Collagen has been used widely since its approval by the FDA in 1981. Its major disadvantage is that some patients develop allergic sensitization to Zyderm implantation. Almost 3% of the population is allergic to this material, but most of these individuals can be identified by appropriate skin testing. The current standard of care is to perform double testing consisting of a first test followed, if the result is negative, by a second test 2 to 4 weeks later. Implantation of Zyderm collagen should not be attempted until the physician verifies that the skin test results are negative. Most physicians wait at least 2 weeks after a second negative skin test before beginning treatment.

The Collagen Corporation has subsequently obtained approval for Zyderm II and Zyplast collagen. These materials appear to provide longer-lasting results than the original Zyderm. However, both are more viscous; Zyderm II is 65 mg/ml of bovine collagen, and Zyderm I is 35 mg/ml. Zyplast is treated with gluteraldehyde to increase collagen cross-linking.

In 1985 Fibrel was approved by the FDA for dermal augmentation. This material is harvested from porcine dermis. Fibrel is a gelatin powder to which E-aminocaproic acid is added. Once mixed with plasma, it becomes a gelatin matrix. In the dermis this stimulates collagen formation. Fibrel appears to sensitize humans far less frequently than does Zyderm. Skin testing, however, is also recommended before its use. Fibrel involves more complex preparation: it must be mixed with the patient's own plasma before injection. This extra step of handling blood products has limited its popularity. However, Fibrel remains an excellent modality for augmentation of distensible scars.

The development of liposuction in the late 1970s provided physicians with another source of tissue for augmentation. French physicians began injecting aspirated fat in the early 1980s. As opposed to the cruder 19th-century technique of en bloc harvesting, fat could now be obtained using a needle and syringe. Fat proved to be a convenient source of autologous tissue for subcutaneous defects, but it was too viscous for injection into the dermis.

The notion of autologous collagen processed from aspirated fat first appeared in the late 1980s. Aspirated fat was processed by mixing it with sterile distilled water and then freezing it, leading to rupture of the fat cells. This left a liquid fraction of intracellular triglycerides and a solid fraction of ruptured lipocytes. This autologous material could be injected through a smaller-gauge needle than pure fat and was suitable for dermal augmentation. Autologous collagen has gradually become more popular for augmentation of dermal

defects, especially in patients who are allergic to Zyderm collagen.

Recently two new devices have been proposed for soft tissue augmentation. Gore-Tex (expanded polytetrafluorethylene) has been used in cardiac surgery for years. This material can be folded into narrow ribbons and passed through a trocar through the length of a wrinkle. The ends of the ribbons are then cut off. This buried substance may give good augmentation for years. However, in some patients surface irregularities develop, or the Gore-Tex may migrate. There is no FDA approval for this substance, and its use is not supported by the manufacturer for this indication.

Hylan gel is also being used experimentally for soft tissue augmentation. This substance is derived from hyaluronan polymer. The FDA has approved this material for cataract and retinal surgery but not for soft tissue augmentation. Further experimentation will determine its place as a dermal filler.

PREOPERATIVE PLANNING

Patient Evaluation

A patient coming to to a physician for evaluation to rectify a soft tissue defect usually has poorly conceived notions about what can and cannot be accomplished. The physician must evaluate the defect and choose among the various modalities available for tissue augmentation. In some cases a variety of techniques is feasible, each with its own advantages and disadvantages.

The physician must first determine the cause of the defect. Most soft tissue depressions are the result of trauma, disease, or aging. Sometimes there is a combination of one or more of these factors at work. If trauma is the cause, the patient can usually tell the physician when the accident occurred, the circumstances surrounding the injury, and what medical care has been given to the injured tissue. Very often, early or intermediate intervention by other physicians has altered the healing of the defect for better or worse. The examining physician must document this history to determine the likelihood of success using filler agents. He or she should also determine whether the patient has hired an attorney and who is responsible for the cost of repairing the defect.

Iatrogenic lipodystrophy as a result of injection of corticosteroids often improves spontaneously, but this can take several years. The physician considering soft tissue augmentation should be certain that the atrophy is permanent before proceeding to augment it. This is especially true if a malpractice suit is alleged by the patient.

If disease is the causative factor, the patient may or may not have a good grasp of the chronology of the problem. In many cases the patient consults the physician not only for improvement of the defect but also to determine its cause. The physician may decide that a biopsy of the problem area is indicated to determine etiologic factors. The physician must also decide whether the disease process is still active. Generally it is best to wait for the disease process to stabilize before attempting to fill in the defect. Scleroderma is one of the main causes of subcutaneous atrophy. If the scleroderma is still active, it is inadvisable to attempt to augment a defect that is likely to worsen. Idiopathic lipodystrophy should be managed in the same manner.

Appropriate Patients

Many patients seek soft tissue augmentation for correction of tissue that has degenerated because of aging. This can vary from minor wrinkles and furrows to massive lose of subcutaneous tissue in older individuals. Often the patients consult the physician about improving their appearance without even considering soft tissue augmentation. Many aging individuals automatically think that a face lift will correct the problem. Face lifting involves relocation, tightening, and subtraction of tissue. The classic face lift is primarily indicated for correction of jowls and drooping necks. Face lifting does not correct atrophic nasolabial furrows, or subcutaneous atrophy of the chin. Face lifting also does not usually correct wrinkles in lines of expression. It also does not help hollow cheeks and may cause this problem to worsen. These problems, however, can all be improved by soft tissue augmentation. Dermal fillers are quite useful for softening expression lines. Younger patients with early signs of aging are also interested in procedures to correct minor soft tissue defects. Dermal fillers are quite valuable in these individuals and can be used with minimal expense and risk.

Size of Defect

The size of the soft tissue defect is also an important factor. Larger defects are usually best filled using fat. Smaller defects are better corrected using the simpler techniques of Zyderm collagen or Fibrel. The size of the defect does not correlate with the chances of improvement. Often, larger subcutaneous defects can be dramatically improved by microlipoinjection. Smaller wrinkles or scars may improve only slightly when dermal fillers are used. In general, larger defects require more involved techniques. Prepackaged fillers such as Zyderm gollagen or Fibrel are convenient but expensive per milliliter.

Location of Defect

The location of the defect may determine the preferable type of soft tissue augmentation. Defects of the extremities are less well vascularized than those of the face. Soft tissue augmentation is less successful in these areas. Extremely mobile parts of the body are usually less successful sites for soft tissue augmentation. Constant movement of the augmented tissue breaks it down more rapidly, requiring more frequent touch-up procedures. For example, the atrophic skin of the dorsum of the hand can readily be improved in appearance by microlipoinjection. This provides immediate dramatic rejuvenation. However, because the hand is so mobile, the benefits are short-lasting. Often, most of the augmentation has disappeared within a few months. In contrast, augmentation of subcutaneous defects of the malar area may last for years.

Type of Defect

The type of defect is important to the physicians' planning. Is the tissue in and around the problem area supple, or is it bound down? Is there extensive fibrosis or scarring? Does the floor of the defect have viable dermis and epidermis, or has it been replaced by scar? The physician must take into account all these factors in planning for the proper mode of correction. Generally, scarred, bound-down defects are harder to augment. The filler substances also survive less well in these because of decreased vascularization. Bound-down defects such as acne "ice-pick scars" are often best excised rather than augmented, since they are so difficult to expand.

PROPER MATERIAL

Zyderm Collagen

Since its approval for human use in 1981, Zyderm collagen has become the most widely used substance for soft tissue augmentation. It is available as Zyderm I and II and Zyplast. This product is conveniently prepackaged in 1-ml or 0.5-ml treatment syringes. The physician can usually inject this material through a 30-gauge needle.

Although convenient to use, Zyderm collagen is expensive. Many patients may not be able to afford Zyderm collagen for correction of large defects. However, for small wrinkles and furrows, Zyderm collagen is probably the ideal treatment option. Initial erythema may appear as a result of treatment but usually resolves within 1 day.

Fibrel

Fibrel is conveniently packaged. It is designed to be mixed with the patient's plasma. This process is time-consuming and exposes the physician or technician to contact with human blood. Recently some physicians have been substituting normal saline or lidocaine for the plasma. Initial clinical reports indicate that the Fibrel works just as well without the addition of plasma. If this impression is verified, Fibrel may attract broader use. Fibrel is primarily useful for augmenting soft scars such as those resulting from acne. Fibrel has also received FDA approval for augmentation of wrinkles. However, it has never been used widely for this purpose. Most physician prefer Zyderm collagen over Fibrel for use in wrinkles.

Fat

Almost all individuals have excess fat that can easily be harvested for use as a filler. Since the fat must be obtained from the patient before a defect can be corrected, this technique is more complex than ready-to-use fillers such as Zyderm collagen and Fibrel. However, fat is available in large quantities. Therefore it is more economical for use in larger augmentations. Fat transplantation works best for filling subcutaneous defects and appears to survive well when injected into subcutaneous tissue. A larger-gauge needle (16-gauge or larger) must be used to inject the fat, resulting in more bruising and erythema after surgery than with Fibrel or Zyderm Collagen.

Autologous Collagen

Autologous collagen is prepared from harvested fat. Consequently, this technique is more complex than ready-to-use dermal fillers such as Zyderm collagen and Fibrel. However, autologous collagen does not have the potential for allergic sensitivity, as do these foreign animal tissues. Many patients with deep wrinkles caused by aging can benefit from subcutaneous as well as dermal augmentation. Autologous collagen is particularly appropriate for these individuals. First, the physician injects fat into the subcutaneous layer. Then, after preparing some of the fat into autologous collagen, the physician can instill a second layer within the dermis. This layering approach gives better results than augmentation of only the dermis or only the fatty layer.

CONSULTATION WITH THE PATIENT

After properly evaluating the defect the physician can recommend various options for soft tissue augmentation. In some cases the physician may inform the patient that a variety of different methods could be used for the particular problem. the physician can then describe the advantages and disadvantages of each and make the final decision in concert with the patient's wishes.

The physician should also discuss the anticipated longevity of the various methods of soft tissue augmentation. Since silicone is no longer available to physicians in the United States, no method can be expected to last indefinitely. In most cases the augmentation begins to diminish within the first postoperative year, regardless of the filler substance. Some patients are not comfortable with this lack of permanancy and do not choose to undergo soft tissue augmentation. Most, however, recognize that medicine is an inexact science and that a permanent method has not yet been found.

As part of the informed-consent process the physician should explain to the patient the usual procedure involved in the chosen method of soft tissue augmentation. The details of anesthesia, sedation, and operative and postoperative pain are also discussed. The physician should also give the patient an idea of average recovery after the augmentation and how soon the patient will be able to feel comfortable in social and work situations. If the physician anticipates the need for further treatments, he or she should outline a typical schedule of touch-up treatments. The physician should also openly discuss the costs of the initial and touch-up treatments and should review options the patient might have other than soft tissue augmentation.

Before treatment the physician should take photographs of the defect undergoing treatment (see Chapter 8). These are a permanent part of the medical record and may be valuable in the future when both the patient and physician forget the exact appearance of the preoperative defect.

The physician should personally review the operative consents with the patient, once again going over the complications and alternatives to treatment. Naturally, this process should be completed before the patient receives any sedatives or other agents that might impair judgment.

TECHNIQUE

Zyderm Collagen

Augmentation with Zyderm collagen is a straightforward procedure. First, select the appropriate type of collagen. Most physicians prefer Zyderm I for augmentation of shallow wrinkles such as those found near the canthi. Zyderm II is the ideal choice for augmentation of the glabellar folds. Localized skin necrosis occasionally occurs when the thicker Zyplast is used in this area. Deeper wrinkles such as the nasolabial furrows respond best to augmentation with Zyplast. Often, Zyderm I or II is used to overlay the Zyplast in a two-level augmentation.

All Zyderm collagen products contain Xylocaine (lidocaine). Most physicians do not anesthetize the skin before injecting these materials. These collagen products pass easily through a 30-gauge needle and therefore produce only minimal pain on injection. However, some physicians prefer to use nerve blocks or topical anesthesia such as EMLA (eutectie mixture of prilocaine and Xylocaine; Astra USA Inc., Westboro, MA) before augmentation. Field-block anesthesia may distort the defect and make it more difficult to judge the adequacy of the augmentation. Nerve blocks work well in locations where they are feasible, such as the upper lip. EMLA applications 30 to 90 minutes before augmentation provide partial anesthesia.

Allow the refrigerated collagen product to warm up to at least room temperature before injection. Some physicians ask their patients to hold the syringes tightly in their palms for 5 minutes before treatment. Inject the collagen material at the proper depth depending on the product chosen (Fig.

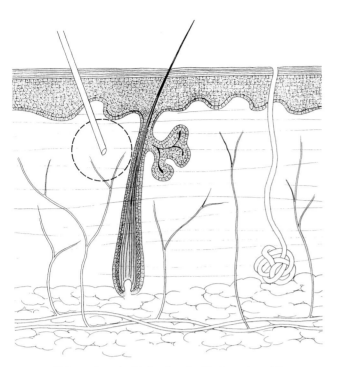

FIG. 1. Level of injection for Zyderm I and II.

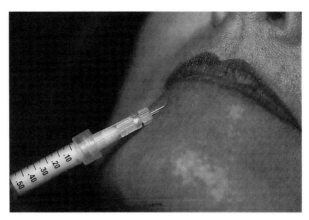

FIG. 3. The needle is angled at 10 to 15 degrees when injecting Zyderm 1 (Copyright William P. Coleman III, MD.)

1). Instill Zyderm I into the superficial dermis. Injection should produce a visible wheal (Fig. 2). Place Zyderm II high in the dermis and Zyplast in the lower dermis. Any material injected into the subcutaneous tissue is rapidly absorbed. Stabilize the skin between two fingers of the nondominant hand while injecting. Inject Zyderm I at an acute angle (10 to 15 degrees) (Fig. 3). Angle the needle less for Zyderm II and even less for Zyplast augmentation. Recently

the Collagen Corporation has received FDA approval for the use of the adjustable-depth gauge (ADG) needle (Fig. 4). The needle features an adjustable hub that can be rotated to reveal increasing lengths of the needle. After dialing in a short needle exposure, the tip's depth in a superficial plane can more easily be maintained (Fig. 5). This approach works well with Zyderm I augmentation and reduces the need for an acute angle of injection. Initial physician response has been positive, and most physicians believe that the ADG device enhances their injection technique.

Inject the Zyderm collagen through multiple punctures. Normally, small beads of collagen are visible through the skin immediately after injection. This is especially true after superficial augmentation with Zyderm I. Digitally massage these small beads immediately after injection. This usually smooths them out to provide an even fill of the defect. Strive for slight overcorrection, especially with Zyderm I or II. This usually rapidly flattens out over the next 24 to 48 hours. Overcorrection with Zyplast may result in temporary "beading" or lumpiness. Although this resolves spontaneously within several weeks, it can be distressing to the patient.

Bruising may occur in some patients after Zyderm aug-

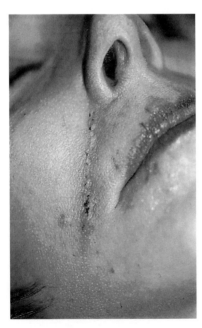

FIG. 2. Injection of Zyderm I should produce a visible wheal. (Copyright William P. Coleman III, MD.)

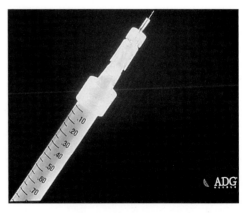

FIG. 4. The adjustable-depth gauge (ADG) needle with an adjustable hub. (Copyright William P. Coleman III, MD.)

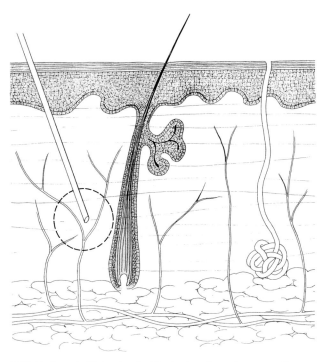

FIG. 5. Level of injection for Zyplast and autologous collagen.

FIG. 7. The custom undermining needle for Fibrel. (Copyright William P. Coleman III, MD.)

mentation. Immediate iceing after injection of the material helps to minimize this result. However, some patients have a propensity to bruise. Advise these patients to avoid aspirin, alcohol, and other blood thinners for at least 1 week before Zyderm augmentation. Although collagen rapidly becomes a viable implant in the dermis, during the first few hours after injection it may be pushed out of the defect if there is excessive facial animation. Patients should attempt to maintain a ''stone face'' for the first few hours after Zyderm collagen implantation.

All patients require touch-up treatments with Zyderm collagen. Properly warn patients of this. Generally, 2 to 4 weeks after the first treatment with collagen is an ideal time for the physician and patient to reevaluate the augmentation and add additional collagen if needed (Fig. 6). Once patients

are successfully augmented they usually require touch-up treatments every 6 to 12 months. This interval appears to lengthen in patients who have had repeated replacement therapy. Generation of host collagen around the injected animal collagen may contribute to the increasing longevity of these treatments. Some patients are quite observant and return for retreatment at the first signs of loss of the augmentation. Others wait until the effect has completely faded before returning for retreatment. This variation in patient perception probably explains the continuing debate over how long Zyderm collagen replacement lasts.

Fibrel

Fibrel cannot be injected through a needle with as small of a gauge as Zyderm collagen. Generally, a 25-gauge needle is required. Consequently, augmentation with this material is more painful and usually requires local anesthesia. Since Fibrel is primarily used for augmenting scars, the technique of injection differs from that of Zyderm collagen. A special needle is supplied with the Fibrel packaging. This device has a spadelike tip and can be used to undermine the base of scars and allow more material to be injected (Fig. 7).

Employ field-block anesthesia, taking care not to distort the contours of the defect. Two percent lidocaine used in small quantities is preferable (see Fig. 8). After the anesthetic takes effect, use the custom needle to loosen the inferior portion of the scar from the underlying subcutaneous tissue.

FIG. 6. (A) Fine lines of the outer canthus before treatment. **(B)** Three months after treatment with Zyderm I, the lines are largely filed in. (Copyright William P. Coleman III, MD.)

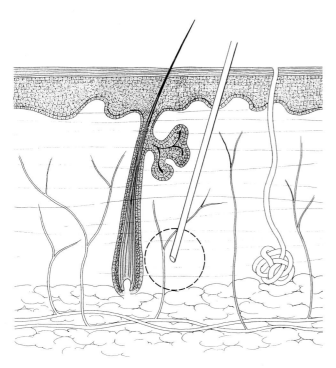

FIG. 8. Level of injection for Fibrel.

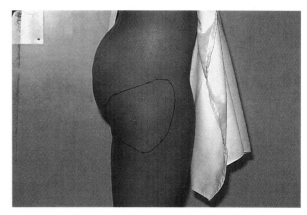

FIG. 9. Donor site is premarked with the patient standing. (Copyright William P. Coleman III, MD.)

This creates a pocket into which Fibrel is instilled. Inject additional gelatin matrix into the residual dermis of the scar.

Fibrel is supplied in a package containing all the elements needed for preparation. Combine the powder with plasma to activate the fibrin in the material. Squirt the mixture back and forth between two syringes until it is thoroughly blended. Inject the foamy yellow product into the scar. Overcorrection is recommended. Subsequent secondary augmentations 2 to 4 weeks after the initial treatment may be required.

Fibrel appears to have a longevity of 9 to 15 months when used in acne scars. Patients may return for touch-up treatments when they perceive that the augmentation has subsided. Fibrel appears to provide poorer clinical results than Zyderm collagen when used for wrinkles. Although there is some softening, the benefit is not as complete using Fibrel.

Fat Transplantation

Fat transplantation requires surgical manipulation of a donor as well as a recipient site. Therefore it is less convenient to use than prepackaged materials such as Zyderm collagen and Fibrel. Obtain the fat from any site where there is excess. There are no convincing studies proving that one donor site is preferable to others. Along with the patient, choose a site of a localized adiposity. Although removing a small quantity of fat does not dramatically change the patient's contour, it often provides minor visible improvement. In some cases fat transplantation is combined with liposuction. In this situation, save some of the aspirated fat for reinjection and discard the rest.

Because fat can only be injected through larger-gauge needles (16-gauge or larger), anesthetize both the donor and recipient sites. Although stock solutions of 1% or 2% lidocaine can be used, tumescent anesthesia is recommended in the donor area. Inject large quantities of dilute lidocaine and epinephrine (0.1% lidocaine, 1 : 1,000,000 epinephrine). For the typical case of fat transplantation, inject about 100 ml of this solution into the intended donor site. Premark the donor contours with the patient standing, before installation of the anesthetic (Fig. 9).

The recipient area also requires local or nerve-block anesthesia. Inject enough material to deaden the tissues without distorting the contours of the defect. There is, inevitably, some swelling from the injection of field-block anesthetic. Mentally ''subtract'' this swelling while augmenting the defect.

After the skin over the donor site begins to blanch (indicating vasoconstriction) begin to harvest the fat. Attach a 10-ml syringe to a minicannula of 14-gauge diameter (Fig. 10). Using a No. 11 blade, make a small puncture in the skin on the perimeter of the marked donor site. Push the cannula through the skin into subcutaneous tissue (Fig. 11). Holding the plunger out, move the tip of the cannula to and fro in the subcutaneous layer. Fat should immediately begin to fill the chamber of the syringe (Fig. 12). The puncture wound must be small to avoid loss of pressure. If the cannula is pulled out too far, pressure is lost. The physician uses the nondominant hand to squeeze the fat around the tip of the

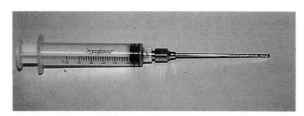

FIG. 10. A 10-ml syringe with a 14-gauge minicannula attached. (Copyright William P. Coleman III, MD.)

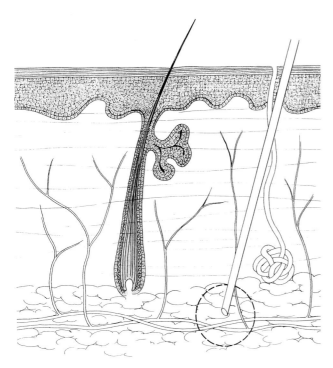

FIG. 11. Level of injection for fat.

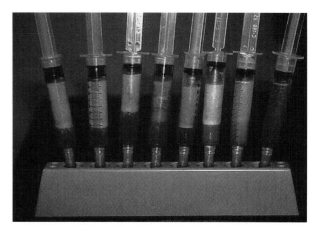

FIG. 13. Gravity allows separation of the fat from the infranate of blood and injectate. (Copyright William P. Coleman III, MD.)

cannula. A tunneling approach rather than ''a windshield-wiper'' method of harvesting allows the donor area to contract evenly without dimples or depressions.

After obtaining enough fat for the augmentation, including any additional material anticipated for touch-up procedures, place a pressure dressing over the donor site. Usually multiple syringes of fat are harvested. As each is filled, the assistant caps the tip and places it upright in a test-tube rack. Gravity allows separation of the supernate fat and an infranate of injectate and tissue fluid (Fig. 13). Usually there is very little blood in the fat if the tumescent anesthetic approach has been employed. Once the fat has sufficiently separated, injection can begin. There is no need to wash the fat or prepare it in any fashion. Washing the fat with saline

was originally recommended by surgeons who did not use the tumescent anesthetic approach and were concerned that the large amount of blood in the aspirate would decrease the survival of the injected fat. However, washing exposes the fat to unneeded trauma, which may itself impair its viability.

Inject the fat into the subcutaneous defect with a moderate degree of overcorrection. Extreme overcorrection may take several days to resolve and lengthen the patient's convalescence. A 16-gauge needle is ideal for injection. Larger needles may leave permanent puncture marks. Smaller needles may rupture fat cells and decrease overall survival. Custom-made, blunt, 16-gauge needles are available from a variety of manufacturers. Sharp needles increase the potential for lacerating blood vessels.

Penetrate the skin with a sharp 16-gauge needle. Advance the blunt needle into the subcutaneous tissue, pushing it the full length of the defect before injecting. Inject in a retrograde manner, laying down thin ribbons of fat while pulling the needle back through the defect (Fig. 14). When augmenting a large subcutaneous defect such as that seen with lipo-

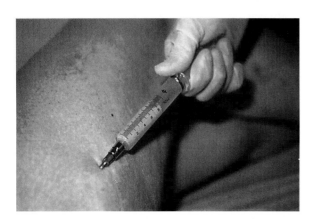

FIG. 12. Removal of fat from the donor site. (Copyright William P. Coleman III, MD.)

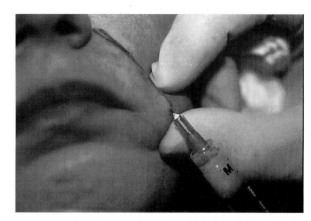

FIG. 14. Injecting fat into the subcutaneous layer to augment the marked defect. (Copyright William P. Coleman III, MD.)

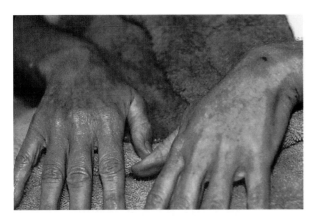

FIG. 15. The left hand has been augmented with transplanted fat. The right has not been treated yet. (Copyright William P. Coleman III, MD.)

dystrophy, it may be preferable to distribute the ribbons of fat from several different injection sites. Injection of boli of fat probably results in poorer viability of the cells. Immediately after injection the fat is quite pliable and can be sculpted into the desired contour (Fig. 15). Milk excess fat out of the injection puncture.

Patients should expect some swelling after fat transplantation in both the donor and recipient sites. Often the donor site is slightly painful; the recipient site is usually not. Tumescent anesthetic fluid may drain from the donor site for up to 24 hours. The potential for swelling can be reduced if rapid-acting injectable corticosteroids are administered to the patient after surgery. However, some swelling and bruising usually occur and may take 2 to 3 days to resolve.

Store excess fat in a freezer for use in subsequent touch-up procedures. Some physicians have successfully stored fat for up to 1 year and used it with good results. However, long-term storage of fat may be associated with increased potential for growth of bacteria. Careful labeling of each patient's tissue is critical to avoid confusion.

Most patients undergoing fat transplantation require a touch-up procedure 2 to 4 weeks after the initial treatment. After this procedure, contours typically remain stabile for 1 year or more (Fig. 16). When the augmentation begins to subside, transplant more fat into the area or it will gradually return to its original state.

Autologous Collagen

The term "autologous collagen" is probably a misnomer. Lipocytic dermal augmentation has been suggested as a more appropriate term to describe this technique. In reality, very little collagen is injected using this technique. However, the injected material provokes an inflammatory response, resulting in the deposition of new collagen produced in the recipient site. Autologous collagen is a natural companion to fat transplantation. Many physicians perform the two procedures simultaneously. This allows augmentation of the subcutaneous layer using fat and augmentation of the dermis using autologous collagen.

Obtain fat for processing into autologous collagen using the same techniques as with fat transplantation. The syringes containing aspirated fat stand in test-tube racks until gravity separates the pure fat from the infranate. Expel the tissue fluid and injectate, and add sterile water to the fat. Using a

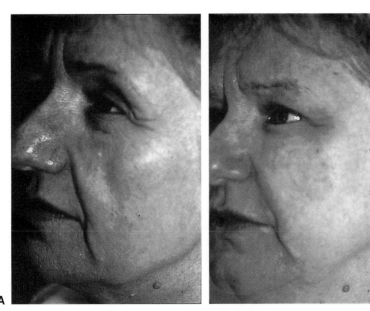

FIG. 16. (A) Idiopathic lipodystrophy of the left side of the cheek before fat transplantation. **(B)** One year after augmentation the corrected contours are still improved. (Copyright William P. Coleman III, MD.)

FIG. 17. A bi-luer lock device for mixing the autologous collagen. (Copyright William P. Coleman III, MD.)

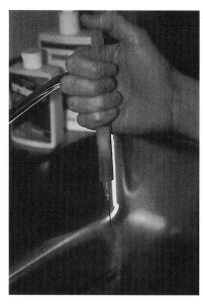

FIG. 19. Autologous collagen preparation. The frozen fat-distilled water emulsion is thawed, and the infranate is expelled. (Copyright William P. Coleman III, MD.)

bi-luer lock adapter, squirt the mixture back and forth between two 10-ml syringes (Fig. 17). Transfer the mixture to 3-ml syringes, and centrifuge at 1000 rpm. Take care to not overfill the small syringes so that with plungers out they fit into a standard centrifuge (Fig. 18). Tightly cap the bottom of the syringes so that fat is not lost during centrifugation. Place the small syringes upright again to allow gravity to separate the fatty portion from a clear infranate, which contains triglycerides and excess water. Then place the syringes in liquid nitrogen for rapid freezing. If the patient is treated at the same time that the fat is harvested, allow the frozen emulsion to slowly thaw at this point. If the material is to be stored for later use, place the frozen syringes in a freezer.

Whether the material is used immediately or stored, thaw the frozen emulsion first. Place the syringes in an upright position, and allow gravity to separate the material into a yellow viscous supernate and a clear infranate comprised of triglycerides (Fig. 19). Expel the infranate, leaving a fraction composed of ruptured lipocytes. The small syringes can then be centrifuged again to separate additional amounts of triglycerides. Next, attach two syringes to a bi-luer lock adaptor and squirt the material back and forth between the two syringes until it flows smoothly. The autologous collagen is now ready for injection. If allowed to stand too long, it will harden and be more difficult to inject.

Inject autologous collagen in a similar fashion to Zyplast. The fat of most patients cannot be broken down enough to allow injection through a 30-gauge needle; generally a 23- or 25-gauge needle is required (Fig. 32-5). Therefore the patient must be anesthetized before augmentation. If field-block anesthesia is employed, be certain not to distort the contours of the defect. Using a small syringe, inject the autologous material into the dermis, raising a slight wheal (Fig. 20). The implant is pliable and can be massaged into a smooth contour immediately after injection. Initial erythema usually fades within 48 hours (Fig. 21).

In many cases, when correcting deep folds, physicians

FIG. 18. Small syringes that are half-filled can fit into most centrifuges. (Copyright William P. Coleman III, MD.)

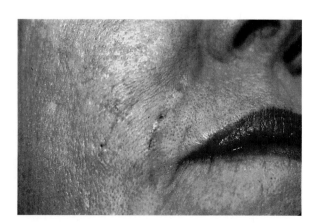

FIG. 20. Visible wheals after injection of autologous collagen indicate dermal placement of the material. (Copyright William P. Coleman III, MD.)

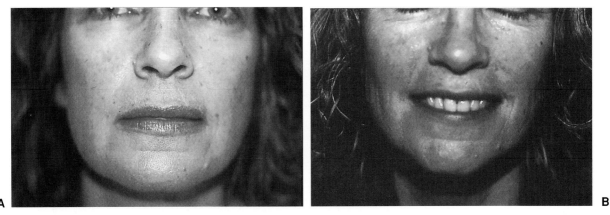

FIG. 21. (A) Preoperative augmentation of the nasolabial furrows. **(B)** One month after lipolytic dermal augmentation the contours are improved. (Copyright William P. Coleman III, MD.)

perform augmentation using fat in the subcutaneous tissue and autologous collagen in the dermis in a two-layered approach (Fig. 22). Typically the physician injects the fat first and then overlays it with lipocytic dermal augmentation. Available volume of donor fat is usually not a problem, and the physician can generously augment large areas of subcutaneous atrophy or deep folds using this approach. Freeze extra autologous material to be reinjected in a subsequent touch-up session 2 to 4 weeks later. Multiple freezing and thawing cycles are not recommended, since this increases the potential for bacterial contamination. If periodic touch-up treatments are chosen, store autologous collagen in small, separate syringes that can be thawed individually as needed. Again, the longer this material is stored, the greater the potential for bacterial contamination. Carefully

label all stored material with the patient's name and date extracted to avoid mix-ups.

POSTOPERATIVE MANAGEMENT

Very little postoperative management is required for patients who have undergone soft tissue augmentation. Patients are urged to keep the augmented areas immobile for several hours after treatment. Ice packing for 10 minutes of every hour helps to minimize bruising and discomfort. With microlipoinjection and lipocytic dermal augmentation there may be mild discomfort in the donor site. This usually persists for 24 to 48 hours and does not require analgesia.

The prudent physician sees the patient in a follow-up visit

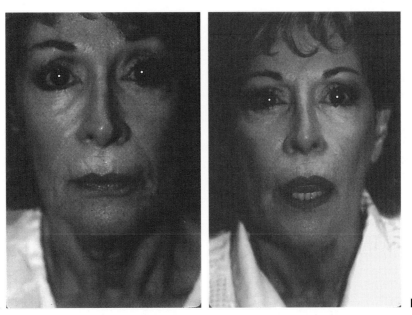

FIG. 22. (A) Before two-layered transplantation of fat and autologous collagen to the perioral area. **(B)** Nine months later there is excellent improvement of the contours. (Copyright William P. Coleman III, MD.)

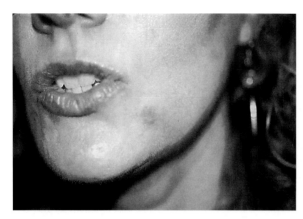

FIG. 23. Delayed hypersensitivity reaction to Zyderm after two negative skin test results. (Copyright William P. Coleman III, MD.)

several days after the augmentation to check for the adequacy of treatment, as well as to detect any potential complications. Patients are urged to see the physician again when the correction begins to fade.

COMPLICATIONS

Although soft tissue augmentation is a relatively safe procedure, the potential for complications does exist. Most of these complications are trivial and quickly respond to physician intervention. However, permanent complications rarely occur. The most devastating of these is blindness. There have been rare reports of blindness after injection of both Zyderm collagen and fat. These occurred when the material was used to augment defects above the eye. This has also been reported with the use of other particulate matter near the eye and is assumed to be due to arterial injection leading to thrombus formation in the retinal artery. The physician should take care to avoid intravascular injections of these materials. Augmentation of the glabellar folds is most safely performed with the needle directed away from the eye, injecting in an inferior to superior direction.

Allergic reactions to Zyderm collagen products have been reported in about 1% of patients who had previous negative results of skin testing (Fig. 23). In some cases this delayed sensitivity develops in a gradual fashion, revealing itself only when the skin is overheated during exercise or showering. Subsequent repeat injections of collagen may lead to long-lasting hypersensitivity reactions. In other cases the allergic sensitivity appears rapidly within a few days after injection and is persistent. Administration of intralesional steroids helps to minimize the erythema and swelling of such reactions. However, this therapy is only palliative, and it may be months or years before the collagen is absorbed and the reaction fades. Double skin testing at least 2 weeks apart before treatment helps to minimize the potential for this complication. However, a small percentage of patients become sensitive to collagen only after multiple exposures.

Local necrosis of augmented skin occurs rarely with Zyderm collagen. This has been reported in acne scars and glabellar wrinkles. Zyplast appears to be the cause in most cases. Therefore it is recommended that Zyderm I or II be used to augment these types of defects. The viscosity of the Zyplast probably occludes local circulation, causing the necrosis. If recognized early, it can be treated in some cases. After injection there is an immediate blanch (vasoconstriction) and there is pain around the augmentation site, suggesting vascular compromise. Immediate application of heat and massage and possibly nitroglycerin paste may help to dilate vessels and reverse the problem. If the necrosis does occur, it progresses to a bruise, then to crusting and ulceration. It can be treated as any skin wound with topical antibiotics and occlusive dressings (hydrogel). Most cases of skin necrosis heal well and sometimes even scar slightly and permanently fill in the defect that was augmented. However, some cases can be quite extensive and result in permanent scars.

Even more rare are cystic reactions to the implanted collagen (less than 0.001%). These are usually delayed painful reactions characterized by fluctuant erythema. These are similar to foreign body abcesses and are best treated with small-needle drainage and intralesional steroid therapy.

Most subcutaneous augmentation results in mild bruising and erythema. This result is seen far less with Zyderm collagen products than with Fibrel or fat. The size of the needle used to implant the material is probably the cause. Patients with bruising tendencies should be carefully screened for use of aspirin, alcohol, and other blood thinners. An occasional patient may have a clotting abnormality and may require hematologic consultation.

Beading of the overlying skin occurs after soft tissue augmentation but usually resolves within 24 hours. In some cases this beading may persist for several weeks. It usually resolves spontaneously, however, although it may be annoying to both patients and physicians. Overcorrection may take longer to resolve. If this occurs with augmentation of wrinkles, subsequent touch-up treatment of the contralateral side helps to even out this problem. The overcorrection, of course, dissipates with time. If a subcutaneous defect is overcorrected with microlipoinjection, it may be possible to milk excess fat out, even several weeks after the augmentation. As an alternative, intralesional steroids injected into the transplanted fat help to diminish the overcorrection.

Bacterial infection is quite rare with all forms of soft tissue augmentation. This probably occurs more with fat transplantation than with Zyderm collagen or Fibrel. Careful preoperative cleansing with a germicidal preparation prevents this in most cases. However, pain or erythema in an augmented site beginning 24 to 72 hours after surgery suggests incipient infection. Prompt treatment with oral antibiotics almost always prevents further progression of the infection.

Viral infections may occur after soft tissue augmentation. Recurrent herpes simplex may be activated by injection through the "trigger" zone. The characteristic vesicular appearance makes the diagnosis straightforward. Early treatment with acyclovir usually provides rapid resolution of the problem. Untreated, however, herpes simplex in augmentation sites may result in permanent scarring.

CONCLUSION

Soft tissue augmentation is a valuable tool in correcting contour defects of many varieties. The key to successful soft tissue augmentation lies in choosing the most appropriate material for each patient's specific defect. This begins with careful evaluation of the cutaneous depression and a consideration of its cause (aging, photodamage, or disease). The nature of the defect will then determine the choice of material for augmentation. In some cases, several materials may be appropriate.

After the physician makes clinical decisions about the appropriate approaches to soft tissue augmentation, the patient must be properly educated as to the nature of the procedure, the potential benefits, the likely recovery, and the possibility of complications. Once patients understand these parameters, they can make informed decisions as to whether or not to proceed. The final satisfaction with the clinical results will depend upon the limitations of the material chosen as well as the techniques employed. As with all surgical endeavors, a range of responses to therapy can be anticipated. Typically soft tissue augmentation is a satisfying procedure for both patients and physicians alike.

SUGGESTED READING LIST

1. Afifi AK et al. Partial (localized) lipodystrophy. J Am Acad Dermatol 1985;12:199.
2. Bartynski J, Marion MS, Wang TD. Histopathologic evaluation of adipose autografts in a rabbit ear model. Otolaryngol Head Neck Surg 1990;120:314.
3. Billings E, May JW. Historical review and present status of free fat graft autografts in plastic and reconstructive surgery. Plast Reconstr Surg 1989;83:368.
4. Campbell GL, Laudslager N, Newman J. The effect of mechanical stress on adipocyte morphology and metabolism. Am J Cosmet Surg 1987;4:89.
5. Chajchin A, Benzaques I. Fat grafting injection for soft tissue augmentation. Plast Reconstr Surg 1989;84:921.
6. Coleman WP, Lawrence N, Sherman RN, Reed RJ, Pinski KS. Autologous collagen? Lipocytic dermal augmentation: a histopathologic study. J Dermatol Surg Oncol 1993;19:1032.
7. DeLustro F, Fries J, Kang A et al. Immunity to injectable collagen and autoimmune disease: a summary of current understanding. J Dermatol Surg Oncol 1988;14(suppl 1):57.
8. Elson ML. Clinical assessment of Zyplast implant: a year of experience for soft tissue contour correction. J Am Acad Dermatol 1988;18:707.
9. Elson ML. The role of skin testing in the use of collagen injectable materials. J Dermatol Surg Oncol 1989;15:301.
10. Fournier PF. Facial recontouring with fat grafting. Dermatol Clin 1990;8:523.
11. Fournier PF. Collagen autologue. In: Liposculpture ma technique. Paris: Arnette, 1989:277.
12. Glogau RG. Microlipoinjection. Arch Dermatol 1988;124:1340.
13. Hochberg M. The cosmetic surgical procedures and connective tissue disease: the Cleopatra syndrome revisited. Ann Intern Med 1993;118:981.
14. Illouz Y. The fat cell ''graft'': a new technique to fill depressions. Plast Reconstr Surg 1986;78:122.
15. Lauber JS, Abrams H, Coleman WP III. Application of the tumescent technique to hand augmentation. J Dermatol Surg Oncol 1990;16:369.
16. Lever WF, Lever GS. Tumors of fibrous tissue. In: Histopathology of the skin. 7th ed. Philadelphia: J.B. Lippincott, 1990.
17. Millikan LE. Long-term safety and efficacy with Fibrel in the treatment of cutaneous scars: results of a multicenter study. J Dermatol Surg Oncol 1989;15:837.
18. Moscona R, Ullman Y, Har-Shai Y, Hirshowitz B. Free fat injections for the correction of hemifacial atrophy. Plast Reconstr Surg 1989;84:501.
19. Nguyen A, Pasyk KA, Brewer TN et al. Comparative study of survival of autologous adipose tissue taken and transplanted by different techniques. Plast Reconstr Surg 1990;85:378.
20. Orentrich D, Orentrich N. Injectable fluid silicone. In: Roenigk RK, Roenigk HH, eds. Dermatologic surgery. New York: Marcel Dekker, 1988.
21. Peer LA. Loss of weight and volume in human fat grafts. Plast Reconstr Surg 1950;5:217.
22. Peer LA: The neglected ''fat free graft'': its behavior and clinical use. Am J Surg 1956;92:40.
23. Pinksi KS, Roenigk HH. Autologous fat transplantation: long-term follow-up. J Dermatol Surg Oncol 1992;18:179.
24. Sergott TJ, Limoli JP, Baldwin CM, Laub DR. Human adjuvant disease: possible autoimmune disease after silicone implantation—a review of the literature, case studies, and speculation for the future. Plast Reconstr Surg 1988;78:104.
25. Skouge JW. Autologous fat transplantation in facial surgery. In: Coleman WP, Hanke CW, Asken S, Alt T, eds. Cosmetic surgery of the skin. Philadelphia: B.C. Decker, 1991:239.
26. Skouge JW, Canning DA, Jefs RD. Long-term survival of perivesical fat harvested and injection by microlipoinjection techniques in a rabbit model. Presented at the 16th Annual American Society for Dermatologic Surgery Meeting. Fort Lauderdale, FL, March 1989.
27. Stegman SJ, Tromovitch TA. Implantation of collagen for depressed scars. J Dermatol Surg Oncol 1980;6:450.
28. Stegman SJ. A comparative histologic study of the effects of three peeling agents and dermabrasion on normal and sun-damaged skin. Aesthet Plast Surg 1982;6:123.
29. Telmourian B. Blindness following fat injections. Plast Reconstr Surg 1988;82(2):361 (letter to the editor).
30. Webster RC, Fuleihan NS, Hamdan US, et al. Injectable silicone: report of 17,000 facial treatments since 1962. Am J Cosmet Surg 1986;3:41.
31. Zocchi M. Methode de production de collagene autologue par traitement du tissu graisseaux. J Med Esthet Chir Dermatol 1990;17(66)105.

Textbook of Dermatologic Surgery, edited by John L. Ratz.
Lippincott–Raven Publishers, Philadelphia © 1998.

CHAPTER 33

Phlebology

Robert A. Weiss, Mitchel P. Goldman, and Alina A. M. Fratila

33.1   Sclerotherapy Treatment of Varicose and Telangiectatic Leg Veins

Robert A. Weiss and Mitchel P. Goldman

HISTORY

Sclerotherapy treatment was first performed by a Swiss physician on the vein of a bull in the 1600s with the use of

Robert A. Weiss.: Department of Dermatology, Johns Hopkins University School of Medicine, Dermatology Associates, 54 Scott Adam Road, Hunt Valley MD 21030.

Mitchel P. Goldman: University of California, San Diego, Dermatology Associates of San Diego County Inc., 850 Prospect Street, La Jolla, CA 92037.

Alina A.M. Fratila: Department of Allergy and Phlebology, Facharztin fur Haut und Geschlechtskrankheiten Bonn, Germany.

a reed. With the invention of the hypodermic syringe in the 1800s, sclerotherapy treatment was performed on humans. However, the lack of sterile, safe solutions resulted in poor and even fatal results. A resurgence in treatment occurred at the turn of this century when it was observed that treatment of syphilis with various pyrogenic agents resulted in sclerosis of veins. However, excellent results were not achieved until the 1930s, when better solutions were developed and a more rational treatment approach, combining optimal concentrations of solution given to feeding veins before distal veins followed by posttreatment compression, was popularized.

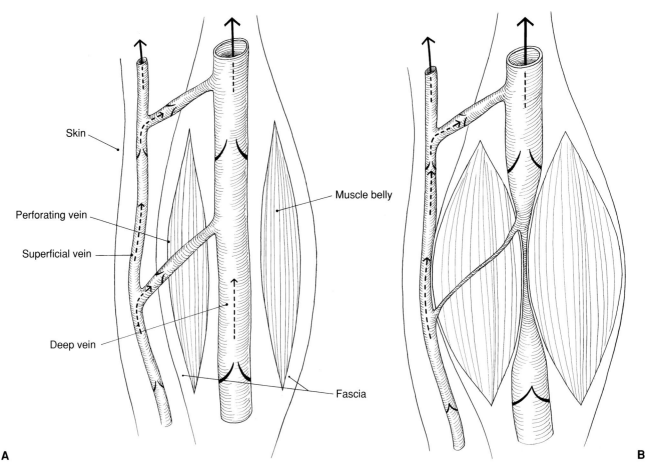

FIG. 1. Schematic representation of venous flow. **(A)** Muscle relaxation. The deep venous system dilates with muscle relaxation, causing negative pressure, which draws blood from the superficial venous system through perforators. During this phase there is movement of blood toward the deep compartment through both competent and incompetent perforators. **(B)** Muscle contraction. The deep venous system is compressed, generating high pressures, and blood is propelled proximally with great force through deep veins.

The earliest reported use of sclerotherapy for telangiectasia in the presence of occlusion of the deep venous circulation appeared in 1934 in the United States. Before the 1970s, dermatologists had been recommending only cosmetic camouflage for telangiectasias. In the early 1970s and 1980s, sclerotherapy was reported for the treatment of telangiectatic leg veins in a large group of patients by Tretbar, Shields, and Jansen; Alderman; and Goldman and Duffy.

Varicose and telangiectatic leg veins commonly occur in men and women, increasing in frequency with age. The pathophysiology is complex with the most common cause being venous wall weakness or defective venous valves. These defects result in reverse flow with calf muscle pump and gravitational (or hydrostatic) pressure causing distention and pain (Fig. 1). Some discussion of their etiology is necessary before explaining the preoperative and operative procedures.

When varicosities arise directly from reflux at the junctions of the saphenous system with the deep system or major perforating veins, they are called truncal varicosities. Smaller, nontruncal varicose veins include minor varicosities arising from incompetent perforating veins not directly

related to the saphenous system; reticular varicosities are seen as blue veins just below the dermis. Telangiectasia usually arise from a ''feeding'' reticular vein but may have a direct connection to deeper veins or, at times, appear unassociated with other veins.

When beginning treatment, an accurate and logical diagnosis of reflux sites is necessary to separate patients who may be treated by surgery, sclerotherapy, or external compression, or a combination of these (Table 33-1). Sclerotherapy is a well-accepted technique for treating varicose veins, blue reticular veins (minor varicose veins), and telangiectatic veins. Sclerotherapy involves direct injection of a small quantity of a sclerosing solution into an abnormally enlarged vein with immediate application of compression to maintain contact of the solution with the endothelium. Within seconds to minutes, the solution disrupts the endothelium and penetrates further into the vessel wall, causing vessel wall destruction. Red blood cells remaining in the vessel lumen form an intravascular coagulum. Within weeks to months, depending on the degree of vessel wall destruction at the time of sclerotherapy, the treated vein either recannu-

TABLE 33-1. *Treatment of varicose veins and telangiectasia*

Location	Therapy
Incompetent saphenofemoral or saphenopopliteal junction	Ligation and short stripping
Incompetent perforators	Sclerotherapy or ligation/phlebectomy
Incompetent nontruncal or recurrent varicosities	Sclerotherapy of phlebectomy
Incompetent reticular veins with or without associated telangiectasia	Sclerotherapy and/or phlebectomy
Telangiectasia	Sclerotherapy or photosclerosis

All categories included graduated compression as part of treatment. Larger vessels must be eliminated before smaller ones may be treated.

lates (although possibly with a smaller diameter) or undergoes full-thickness sclerosis with subsequent total disappearance. Sigg, Orbach, Fegan, Goldman, and others emphasize the importance of combining compression with injection. The "compression" technique markedly improves the results of sclerotherapy with results comparing favorably to surgery for nontruncal varicose veins.

PREOPERATIVE PLANNING

Complete physical examination of the lower extremities allows diagnosis of common patterns of varicosities and telangiectases that subsequently directs noninvasive diagnostic examination before treatment (Fig. 2). Patients with scattered, isolated, asymptomatic telangiectasias 1 mm or less in diameter with no obvious associated venulectasias (reticular or blue) or varicose veins and a negative history of symptoms require no further diagnostic testing.

When varicosities of any size extend into the groin or popliteal fossa, when varicosities larger than 3 mm stretch along the leg, or if large groups of symptomatic telangiectasias in association with a venulectasia or reticular vein are seen, further evaluation by noninvasive examination is indicated. Continuous-wave Doppler ultrasound locates the source of reflux and guides selection of entry points for treatment with sclerotherapy. In minutes, a physician can assess the superficial venous system using an 8-MHz Doppler transducer, including competence of the saphenofemoral junction (SFJ) and lesser saphenopopliteal junction (SPJ) bilaterally; points of reflux through suspected incompetent perforating veins in the calf, thigh, and ankle; and venous outflow from the femoral vein with reflux in the deep veins at the ankles. Accuracy for Doppler diagnosis ranges from 49% to 96%.

Photoplethysmography (PPG) or light reflection rheography is required for diagnosis of functional deep venous system disease. This helps determine whether treatment of the superficial venous system is beneficial and, even more important, safe. Doppler detects valvular incompetence, whereas PPG measures the total physiologic impact of valvular incompetence.

Doppler Examination

Continuous-wave Doppler ultrasound emits a continuous beam of ultrasound waves that detect red blood cells moving within the targeted vein or artery. Optimal frequencies for examining superficial vessels are 8 to 10 MHz; deeper vessels require a lower frequency of 4 to 5 MHz. A probe angle of 30 to 45 degrees relative to blood flow yields the most consistent waveform height, since flow velocity waveform relates to the probe angle.

It is important to remember that the venous system is a series of wide channels experiencing slow flow, unlike the high-pressure contractile pipes of the arterial system. Venous flow is generated by muscle contractions occurring at irregular intervals. At rest, spontaneous flow signals are difficult to hear by Doppler ultrasound. Exceptions are large veins in the groin communicating with abdominal veins, which are influenced by excursions of the diaphragm (spontaneous (S) sounds). To generate or augment an audible signal of flow, a maneuver such as manual compression of the calf to simulate muscle contraction must be performed by the examiner (augmented (A) sound). When compression is released, gravitational hydrostatic pressure causes reverse flow to cease within 0.5 to 1.5 seconds when valves are competent, but a long flow sound is audible when valves are incompetent

With the patient standing or sitting up and with a 4- to 5-MHz transducer in a warm room, begin the examination in the medial groin at the inguinal ligament by locating the femoral arterial signal. Moving the transducer slightly medially over the common femoral vein, normal respiratory excursions of venous flow are heard. Distal manual thigh compression with the hand not holding the transducer briefly enhances the signal. The patient is requested to perform Valsalva's maneuver. A long reflux sound is indicative of femoral venous reflux, which can be confirmed with duplex ultrasound examination.

After examining the common femoral vein, move the transducer approximately 4 cm distally with light pressure, to listen below the saphenofemoral junction. While performing a short series of thigh compressions to generate venous flow signals, move the transducer from side to side, to locate the greater saphenous vein (GSV)—a 7- to 8-Mhz probe is useful. Gentle external compression and release of the thigh *distal* to the transducer should lead to transient increases in signal frequency (amplitude) followed by rapid cessation of the signal as competent valves snap shut. When valvular insufficiency at the SFJ is present, initial increase in flow is followed by a prolonged backflow signal.

During Valsalva's maneuver, a continuous, pronounced reflux signal is a reliable sign of valvular insufficiency.

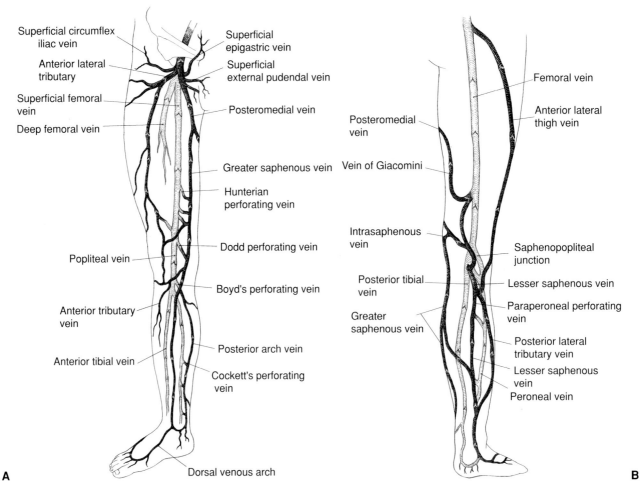

FIG. 2. Anatomy of the superficial venous system. **(A)** The long or greater saphenous vein originates on the medial aspect of the foot at the confluence of the dorsal venous arch. It receives tributaries from the deep foot veins as it courses upward, just anterior to the medial malleolus. Below the ankle the valves of the tributary veins point outward, allowing flow from the deep to the superficial system. Above the medial malleolus, the valves of the perforating veins point inward, allowing emptying only. The greater saphenous vein continues up the anteromedial aspect of the thigh, receiving tributaries from the posterior arch vein and anterior tributary vein. Just before the greater saphenous vein joins the femoral vein it receives important tributary veins such as the lateral and medial femoral cutaneous (tributary) branches, the superficial iliac circumflex vein, the superficial epigastric vein, and the pudendal vein. Varicose veins in the groin may arise from any of these tributaries, particularly from the pudendal. **(B)** The lesser saphenous vein receives tributaries from deep veins from the lateral aspect of the dorsal venous arch of the foot. Other tributaries arise from medial and lateral aspects of the calf with a posterolateral tributary vein most commonly seen. The lesser saphenous vein most commonly terminates in the popliteal vein at or slightly above the popliteal fossa, but may penetrate the deep fascia at any point upward from the midcalf. Occasionally, branches may continue up the posterior aspect of the thigh to join one of the tributaries to the greater saphenous vein (vein of Giacomini). (**A** and **B** adapted from Goldman MP. Sclerotherapy: treatment of varicose and telangiectatic leg veins. 2nd ed. St. Louis: Mosby, 1995 pp. 12,13.)

However, mild and brief reflux can be found in 15% of normal individuals. The generally agreed upon duration of backflow signal considered abnormal is greater than 1 second. An equivocal result may require a duplex ultrasound examination for a definitive answer. When varicosities are seen on the upper thigh but Valsalva's maneuver is negative for reflux at the SFJ, compression and release maneuvers are repeated to identify sources of reflux. On the extreme upper thigh incompetent communications may exist, causing varicosities of iliac, pudendal, pelvic, or epigastric veins. Commonly, incompetent hunterian perforating veins causing varicosities in the midthigh are demonstrated by distal compression and release. For superficial varicosities originating in the lower third of the thigh, Dodd's perforating veins may be found. Common sites of perforating veins are shown in Fig. 2.

Popliteal Fossa and Knee

The popliteal fossa can be a difficult region to evaluate. Many superficial veins traversing the popliteal space may reveal reflux during distal compression and release. The patient is examined while standing with the leg slightly flexed with weight supported on the opposite leg. The probe is positioned at the upper portion of the popliteal space just lateral to the midline. Constant pulsation of the popliteal artery can be heard. The popliteal vein usually lies deep to the artery. Listening for reflux during distal compression and release will be accompanied by background arterial pulsation. If reflex is heard with the 4 to 5 MHz transducer, then deep reflux is probably present. By moving slightly distally, many venous sounds may be heard since gastrocnemius veins, posterior tibial veins, and peroneal veins all converge within a relatively short distance.

At about midportion of the popliteal space, switching to an 8-MHz probe, a similar sequence of external compression and release can be performed for the lesser saphenous vein (LSV) beginning at its junction with the popliteal vein. Light compression of the calf distal to the Doppler probe is the best method to demonstrate reflux. Valsalva's maneuver is less reliable in this area, since proximal valves are often competent. Because the LSV runs a course down the center of the calf, reflux within it should usually be audible for several centimeters below the SPJ. Only theoretically can this be distinguished from deep reflux. Occasionally, the LSV extends far proximally before terminating into the deep system. The LSV occasionally terminates in the greater saphenous vein (GSV) on the middle to upper medial thigh through the vein of Giacomini. Distally, the LSV can be followed to its origin just posterior to the lateral malleolus. On the anteromedial aspect of the leg the important site to examine by Doppler is Boyd's perforator group. Located medial to the tibia several centimeters below the knee, this is the *most common site for spontaneous appearance of primary varicose veins.* This region must be investigated for reflux by distal compression and release.

Ankle

The deep veins at the ankle are actually quite close to the surface, often communicate with the posterior arch vein, and can be heard with an 8-MHz probe (legs dependent). Strict adherence to anatomic landmarks should differentiate these from superficial veins. Reflux within the deep system at the ankle is important in evaluating patients with venous ulceration. The posterior tibial veins lie just posterior to the medial malleolus and surround the posterior tibial artery. Arterial pulsatile sounds are identified; then distal compression is applied to the foot, or proximal compression to the calf, to identify flow and reflux in these deep veins.

Perforating veins at the ankle of greatest concern are Cockett's perforators and the retromalleolar and inframalleolar perforators. These perforating veins are in communication with the posterior arch vein. Varicosities on the medial ankle can often be traced to reflux in Cockett's perforators. The deep purple ''corona phlebectasia'' on the dorsal foot can often be traced to reflux in the inframalleolar perforators.

Photoplethysmography

The term ''plethysmography'' describes a number of techniques used to measure volume changes. These are particularly useful to measure the entire venous volume of the leg or selected parts of the venous system. A plethysmograph consists of a mechanism to sense displacement and a modifying unit (transducer) that translates changes from a displacement-sensing device into another form of energy, which is then recorded. Photoplethysmography (PPG) requires a light-emitting diode and a receiving diode to measures changes in blood volume in the subcutaneous venous plexus. These volume changes reflect regional venous volume changes rather than volume changes of the entire leg. Photoplethysmography permits quantification of the physiologic significance of Doppler findings, whereas venous Doppler ultrasound is used to detect exact sites of valvular incompetence. Photoplethysmography allows differentiation between superficial and deep venous insufficiency and has the additional advantage of independence from examiner experience, unlike Doppler ultrasound examination.

With PPG a single photoelectric light source illuminates a small area of skin, and an adjacent photoelectric sensor measures the reflectance of light. Near-infrared (940 nm) wavelength is suited for optimal measurement of skin blood content because epidermal absorption at this wavelength is limited to 15% of emitted light. Recent advances have led to greater reliability with digital PPG,[*] in which a dedicated microprocessor standardizes the signal received by the photoelectric sensor. This arrangement leads to a reproducible, standardized baseline, regardless of skin thickness or pigmentation, allowing quantitative rather than qualitative venous pump measurements. An additional advantage is the ability to follow improvements in venous function after treatment.

For PPG examination, the patient sits relaxed with the knees bent at a 110- to 120-degree angle. By convention, a small probe containing light-emitting and sensing diodes is taped to the medial aspect of the lower leg about 8 to 10 cm (four finger widths) above the medial malleolus. After resting the leg for several minutes to establish a constant baseline, the patient produces dorsiflexion of the foot 8 to 10 times, activating the calf muscle pump and effecting drainage of the venous system. As the skin venous plexus empties, it causes increased reflectance of light. A tracing is made of the changes in reflected light from the

---

[*] D-PPG, ELCAT GmbH, Schiesstattstrasse 29, D82515 Wolfratshausen, Germany.

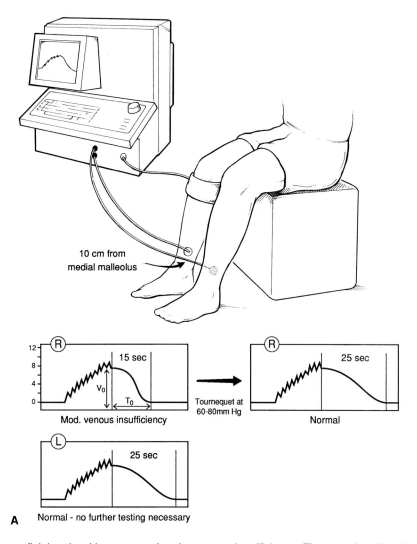

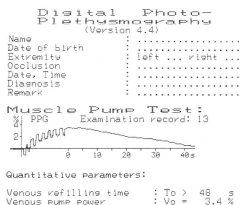

Digital Photo-
Plethysmography
(Version 4.4)
Name   : ....
Date of birth   : ....
Extremity   : left ... right ...
Occlusion   : ....
Date, Time   : ....
Diagnosis   : ....
Remark   : ....

Muscle Pump Test:

PPG   Examination record: 13

Quantitative parameters:

Venous refilling time   : To > 48   s
Venous pump power   : Vo =   3.4 %

FIG. 3. Photoplethysmography (PPG). **(A)** Diagram. By convention the sending and receiving diode is taped to the medial leg 10 cm or four finger widths above the medial malleolus. The patient pumps the foot by flexion at the ankle 8 to 10 times. The tracing produced shows the changes in reflection of near-infrared light of the dermal capillary plexus. For digital PPG the total height of the curve (Vo) indicates quantitative muscle pump power. The time to return to baseline from the peak is the refill time (To). Refill time of less than 25 seconds is abnormal and indicates venous insufficiency. One must then search by physical examination and/or continuous-wave Doppler to find the anatomic cause of venous insufficiency. Repeating an abnormal test with a tourniquet compressing the superficial varicosities allows one to predict the results of elimination of the superficial varicosities. In this case venous insufficiency is eliminated by repeating the PPG on the right leg with a below-knee tourniquet. In this case the PPG reverts back to normal, indicating that the superficial varicosities are causing the venous insufficiency. These varicosities should respond well to treatment. (From Goldman MP, Weiss RA, Bergan JJ: Diagnosis and treatment of varicose veins: a review. J Am Acad Dermatol 1994;31:402.) **(B)** Tracing produced by D-PPG (ELCAT Gbmh, Wolfrathausen, Germany).

skin under the probe (Fig. 3). After the calf muscle pumping ceases, blood refills the skin plexus, which absorbs increasing amounts of light as venules fill. A direct relationship is assumed between filling of deep leg veins and filling of veins measured in the skin. Excellent correlation of vessel surface filling time (PPG refill time) with direct invasive pressure refill time has been shown. The PPG tracing returns to its initial resting value as the calf venous system refills. A refill time shorter than 25 seconds indicates venous valvular insufficiency. Longer refill times indicate normal venous valve function.

When the initial test is abnormal, (a refill time less than 25 seconds), the test is repeated with a tourniquet at 80 to 100 mm Hg placed 1 inch above the knee. The refill time should return to normal if the source of reflux is the superficial system above the knee. When the PPG refill time remains less than 25 seconds with the above-knee tourniquet, the test is repeated with a tourniquet below the knee. Repeat-

ing the PPG with a below-knee tourniquet is especially indicated if varicosities are observed near calf or ankle perforating veins. The refill time should normalize if reflux is from the superficial system. A PPG examination result that does not normalize by application of tourniquets requires further investigation before treatment is initiated.

The PPG may give abnormal readings when ankle joint mobility is reduced or when arterial occlusive disease prevents normal inflow to the skin. Present uses of PPG include forecasting outcome of elimination of varicosities, measurement of functional pumping of the deep venous system of the calf, and evaluating the treatment results.

Duplex Ultrasound

The ultimate in noninvasive examination of the venous system is duplex ultrasound, which allows direct visualization of the veins and identification of flow through venous valves. An image is created by an array of Doppler transducers, which are switched on and off sequentially. This is combined with a method to obtain an echo-pulse of a Doppler signal. The echo-pulse is recorded as a dot that is located on the X and Y axes and is brighter in proportion to the intensity of the reflected signal (Z axis). This creates a two-dimensional ultrasound image. The Doppler velocity recording allows an image produced by reflection from moving red blood cells to be seen so that blood vessels and flow are shown. Duplex scanning combines echo-pulse with Doppler velocity recording. Color units have circuitry to indicate flow from the transducer in red and toward the transducer in blue (Fig. 4).

Duplex scanners are found in fully equipped vascular laboratories, but laboratory personnel must be instructed in the examination of the superficial venous system. This must include an assessment of the SFJ and the SPJ, often with the patient standing. A complete duplex ultrasound examination also maps superficial and deep veins with precise identification of sources of venous reflux. Once the evaluation of the patient is complete, the presence and source of significant venous reflux should have been identified. If the patient has significant saphenofemoral reflux, treatment may include surgical control of that reflux before sclerotherapy. Experienced European or Canadian phlebologists may attempt to sclerose the SFJ. They have reported a 93% short-term success rate with strong sclerosing solutions not available in the United States. However, we believe that saphenous vein insufficiency from an incompetent SFJ is best managed by surgery.

Sclerosing Solutions

Hypertonic Saline

Although approved by the U.S. Food and Drug Administration (FDA) only for use as an abortifacient, the most commonly employed solution among dermatologists in the United States at present is hypertonic saline (HS) at a concentration of 23.4%. The advantage of HS is its theoretical total lack of allergenicity when unadulterated. Hypertonic saline has been commonly used in various concentrations from 10% to 30%, with the addition of heparin, procaine, or lidocaine. With claims of pain reduction with procaine or lidocaine unproven, HS is used either unadulterated or diluted to 11.7% with sterile water for smaller telangiectasias. A high success rate with HS in the treatment of telangiectasias is expected.

Some patients abandon HS, despite the low risk of allergic reactions, after experiencing burning pain or muscle cramping immediately following injection. Because hypertonic solutions affect all cells in the path of the osmotic gradient, nerve endings in the vessel adventitia or the underlying muscle may be stimulated, causing a burning pain or cramping sensation lasting from seconds to minutes; the duration is rarely longer than 5 minutes. With hypertonic solutions, damage of tissue adjacent to injection sites may easily occur. *Large ulcers may be produced by extravasation at the injection site, particularly when injecting very close to the skin surface.* Intradermal injection of 0.1 ml HS in rabbit skin produces necrosis. Immediate intense pain on extravasation warns against further injection at the site. Meticulous technique with absolutely minimal extravasation is necessary for safe use of HS.

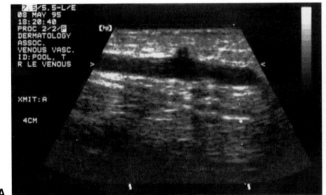
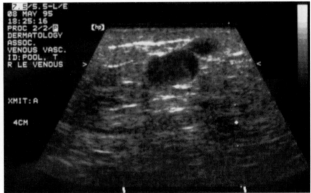

FIG. 4. Duplex examination of varicose vein. For proper understanding of three-dimensional configuration, varicosities should be viewed in both transverse and longitudinal views. **(A)** Longitudinal view of the greater saphenous vein (GSV) in the region of Boyd's perforator near a superficial varicosity (see Fig. 7). The bulge through the superficial fascia is evident, which then takes a sharp turn away from the longitudinal axis of the GSV. **(B)** When viewed in the transverse direction, a large saccular dilation of the GSV in the region of the perforating vein is seen. Being trapped between two fascial layers, the GSV expands more readily laterally than superiorly and inferiorly. A useless, floppy valve leaflet is seen on the lower wall of the dilation floating in the GSV. A superficial varicose vein heads towards the surface as it bulges like a balloon above the superficial fascia. Because varicose veins are tortuous, moving the transducer up and down and side to side is often necessary to follow the varicose vein in its entirety.

Hypertonic Dextrose with Hypertonic Saline[**]

Sclerodex is a mixture of dextrose 250 mg/ml, sodium chloride 100 mg/ml, propylene glycol 100 mg/ml, and phenethyl alcohol 8 mg/ml. Sclerodex is a relatively weak sclerosant recommended for treatment of telangiectasia, with a total volume of injection not to exceed 10 ml per visit with 0.1 to 1 ml per injection site. Sclerodex has been used predominantly in Canada and is reported to result in less discomfort than HS, although a slight burning sensation occurs. The lower concentration of saline combined with the nonionic dextrose causes a hypertonic injury without the intense nerve-end stimulation of pure HS. Use of Sclerodex has resulted in fewer complications than HS but a similar incidence of pigmentation as compared with polidocanol (POL) and sodium tetradecyl sulfate (STS). The advantage of decreased pain on injection is slightly offset by the potential increased allergenicity of the phenethyl alcohol component of Sclerodex, with one case reported of allergic reactions. Use in the United States must await FDA approval, although this solution is easily compounded by local pharmacies.

Polidocanol

Although polidocanol,[†] a urethane compound, was originally developed as an anesthetic, it was found to have the property of sclerosing small-diameter vessels after intradermal injection. Polidocanol contains hydroxypolyethoxydodecane dissolved in distilled water with 5% ethanol as a stabilizer. First used as a sclerosing agent in the late 1960s in Germany, POL is popular worldwide because of painless injection and the extremely rare incidence of cutaneous necrosis with intradermal injection. However, POL is *not* approved by the FDA.

In the rabbit ear dorsal vein model, 1% POL is equivalent to 0.5% STS and 23.4% HS. By extrapolating from several clinical studies, when used on human telangiectasia 0.5% POL appears to be equivalent to 11.7% HS and 0.1% to 0.2% STS. Allergic reactions occur rarely.

Sodium Tetradecyl Sulfate

Sodium tetradecyl sulfate (Sotradecol)[‡] is a long-chain fatty acid salt with strong detergent properties and is a very effective sclerosing agent approved by the FDA. Although popular with vascular surgeons since the 1960s and first described for use in telangiectasias in the 1970s, STS has been unpopular with dermatologists until recently. This is probably because of the relatively high incidence of post-

sclerosis pigmentation reported with use of a 1% STS concentration and the possibility of cutaneous necrosis even in the absence of recognized extravasation. Cutaneous necrosis is concentration dependent with a relative low risk at concentrations less than 0.3%. Intradermal injection of 0.5% STS (0.1 ml) into rabbit skin leads to dermal and epidermal necrosis. Although noted to cause allergic reactions such as generalized urticaria, bronchospasm, anaphylactic shock, and even death, the actual incidence of allergic reactions is extremely low and not significantly different from POL. Fegan reported 15 of 16,000 cases of rash or urticaria, but no anaphylactic reactions. Fegan's positive experience with such large numbers of patients indicates that STS is a relatively safe sclerosing solution.

Using 0.1% to 0.25% concentration for telangiectasias up to 1 mm in diameter, 0.2% to 0.5% for reticular veins or small varicosities (1 to 3 mm), and 0.5% to 3% for larger varicosities or at major sites of valvular reflux is recommended. The maximum recommended dosage per treatment session is 10 ml of 3% solution.

Sodium Morrhuate

Sodium morrhuate[§] is a 5% solution of the salts of saturated and unsaturated fatty acids in cod-liver oil. Approximately 10% of its fatty acid composition is unknown, and use by dermatologic surgeons is limited by reports of fatalities resulting from anaphylaxis.

Although sodium morrhuate is approved by the FDA for the sclerosis of varicose veins, use in treatment of telangiectasias is not recommended because of the caustic qualities with an increased potential for cutaneous necrosis compared with other available solutions.

Chemical Irritants

The chemical irritants including polyiodinated iodine (very strong) and chromated glycerine (very weak) are believed to have a direct toxic effect on endothelium with injury confined primarily around the injection site. After injection of polyiodinated iodine, the endothelium is destroyed within seconds. This occurs within millimeters of the site of injection because of rapid inactivation from serum proteins. The subendothelial layers are exposed after endothelial fibrin is rapidly deposited. At the sites of endothelial destruction the chemical can penetrate further and diffuse into deeper layers of the vessel wall, causing further destruction. A recent preliminary study indicates that no activation of blood coagulation occurs with sodium iodide, indicating little risk for propagation of a thrombus. The chemical irritants may yet turn out to be the most specific sclerosing agents, targeting injury to the site of injection by quick inactivation by blood proteins accompanied by minimal thrombus forma-

---

[**] Sclerodex, Omega Laboratories Ltd., Montreal, Canada.

[†] Aethoxysklerol, Chemische Fabrik Kreussler & Co., Wiesbaden-Biebrich, Germany; Aetoxisclerol, Laboratories Pharmaceutiques Dexe, Nanterre, France; Sclerovein, Resinag AG, Zurich, Switzerland.

[‡] Sotradecol, Wyeth-Ayerst Laboratories, Philadelphia, PA.; STD injection, STD Pharmaceuticals, United Kingdom; Thromboject, Omega Labs, Montreal, Canada.

[§] Scleromate, Palisades Pharmaceuticals, Inc., Tenafly, NJ.

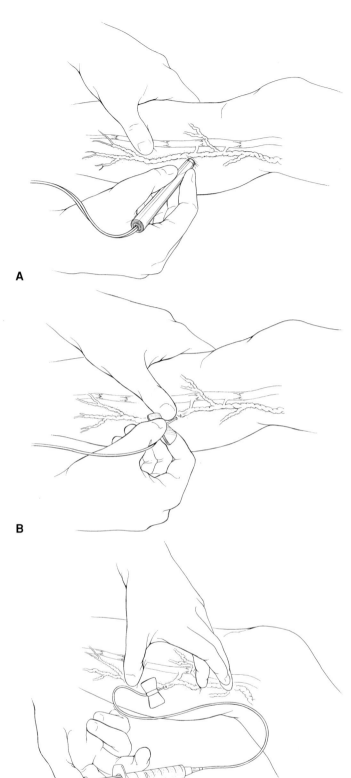

A

B

C

FIG. 5. Sclerotherapy treatment of large veins with butterfly needle. **(A)** Localization of an incompetent perforating vein through use of Doppler ultrasound. **(B)** Cannulation of the incompetent communicating vein with a 26-gauge butterfly needle. **(C)** The leg is elevated 45 degrees, and 0.5 to 1 ml of sclerosant is placed in the now emptied communicating vein under minimal pressure. A finger is placed distal to the

TABLE 33-2. *Principles of varicose vein sclerotherapy*

- Larger veins are treated before smaller veins.
- Proceed from most proximal veins distally.
- Reflux points are determined initially and treated specifically.
- Vein must be emptied of blood by various maneuvers before injection.
- Direct finger pressure in a spreading and compressing motion following injection.
- Entire varicosity is treated at one session.
- Apply immediate and adequate compression.

tion and deep diffusion into the vessel wall. Use of the chemical irritants is presently prohibited in the United States by lack of FDA approval, although these compounds can be prepared in sterile form for injection with approved chemicals (e.g., iodine, glycerine).

TECHNIQUE

Although sclerotherapy treatment has been used for all types of varicose and telangiectatic leg veins, its main advantage over surgical treatment is in treating nontruncal varicose veins less than 6 mm in diameter, reticular veins, and telangiectasia (Table 33-2). Truncal veins (those associated with the GSV and veins larger than 6 mm in diameter) are better treated with surgical techniques such as ambulatory phlebectomy as described in Part 2.

Treatment of Large Varicose Veins

The technique presently used most widely is that of Fegan with minor modifications. Sit the patient at the end of the examining table with the treated leg dependent. Cannulate a bulging varicosity with a needle, butterfly needle, or angiocatheter held or taped in place. Before injection, elevate the leg and support it above cardiac level for 1 to 2 minutes to allow drainage of blood. Draw a small amount of blood back from the syringe to ensure that the needle remains in the varicosity lumen. Inject approximately 0.5 to 1 ml of the sclerosing solution, and apply finger pressure several centimeters above and below the injection point to confine the action. Maintain finger pressure for 30 to 60 seconds followed by the immediate application of compression with a foam pad. Immediately secure the pad by foam-elastic tape or a relatively inelastic, wrap-around bandage to maintain compression. Fegan's method is particularly effective for incompetent perforators. Fascial defects through which perforators course may be palpated and serve as the site of needle entry (Fig. 5).

injection site to feel for extravasation of solution, which would indicate improper placement of the needle. (**A–C** Adapted from Goldman MP. Sclerotherapy treatment of varicose and spider leg veins. In: Bergan JJ, Kistner RL, eds. Atlas of venous surgery. Philadelphia: WB Saunders, 1992;50–51.)

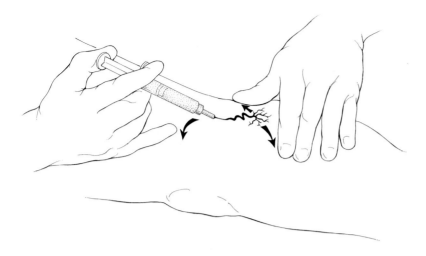

FIG. 6. Position of hands for sclerotherapy. Finer control is obtained by a three-point stretch on the skin. The nondominant hand is used to stretch the injection site in two directions with the fifth finger of the dominant hand used to produce a third point of stretch away from the injection site. This technique also leads to easier cannulation of the telangiectasia. (From Goldman MP. Sclerotherapy: treatment of varicose and telangiectatic leg veins. 2nd ed. St. Louis: Mosby, 1995, p 415.)

As an alternative, multiple injections along the course of a varicosity independent of the perforators is also effective. Make injections every 4 to 6 cm until the entire varix is sclerosed. Injection in a proximal to distal manner minimizes postinjection spasm of distal varices (Fig. 6).

A widely used variation of Fegan's technique is the marking of varicosities with the patient standing; needle insertion occurs with the patient recumbent. This minimizes movement of the leg and the inserted needle. To limit possible displacement of the inserted needle but improve likelihood of cannulation, the needle may be inserted with the patient in slight reverse Trendelenburg's position on a power-operated table and then the table moved hydraulically to place the patient in a venous pressure-neutral or reverse Trendelenburg's position. Immediately after injection, elevate the leg and apply compression. Direct finger pressure in a spreading and compressing motion outward both proximal and distal to the injection site is often very useful, not only to spread the sclerosing solution laterally but to promote contact with greater endothelial surface area while propelling blood out of the vessel.

Rapid, immediate, and adequate compression following injection of sclerosant is very important. For increased compression, bunches of cotton balls may be substituted for foam pads, although the use of foam pads (STD-E pads, STD Pharmaceuticals, Hereford, United Kingdom) probably allows for the strongest, most complete and pressure point–free local compression over injection sites. Graduated compression hose (30 to 40 mm Hg) are usually worn immediately following treatment. Stretch these over local compression at the treatment sites. During treatment of large varicosities (>5 mm in diameter) patients wear two stockings, one on top of the other, while standing and remove the outer stocking when recumbent. This technique provides a doubling of compression pressure. As an alternative, apply a relatively nonelastic bandage to provide graduated compression. Patients may shower after taping a plastic bag over the compression bandage or stocking.

Although some physicians minimize the importance of compression, several theoretical and practical considerations affirm its necessity. Compression limits flow of blood back into the varicosity, thus decreasing thrombus formation and the tendency for recanalization. In addition, with less thrombus formation there is less thrombophlebitic reaction and less postsclerosis pigmentation. Compression has been shown to improve the effectiveness of treatment of both small and large varicosities. Use of graduated compression hose also permits the patient complete mobility following treatment and enhances muscle pump function. This rapidly dilutes and removes any sclerosing solution that inadvertently enters the deep system.

The optimal duration of compression is still debated. Based on histopathologic examination of multiple veins evaluated at various times after sclerotherapy, Fegan recommended 6 weeks of compression, but 3 to 5 days of compression has been suggested as adequate. A trial comparing compression for 1, 3, and 6 weeks concluded that 3 weeks of compression was optimal, and most phlebologists have patients wear compression hose of 30 to 40 mm Hg for 2 to 6 weeks.

Immediate ambulation following treatment is believed to cause rapid dilution of sclerosing solution, which prevents high concentrations of sclerosing solution from maintaining content within deep veins. Walking may also lessen risks of deep venous thrombosis (DVT) by avoiding stagnation of blood flow. In conjunction with graduated compression, ambulation also causes the muscle pump of the calf to reduce venous hypertension in superficial veins by decreasing venous volume.

Treatment of Reticular Veins

Treatment of reticular veins is very similar to large varicose veins, although the concentration, strength, and volume of sclerosing solution is decreased. Treat subdermic reticular

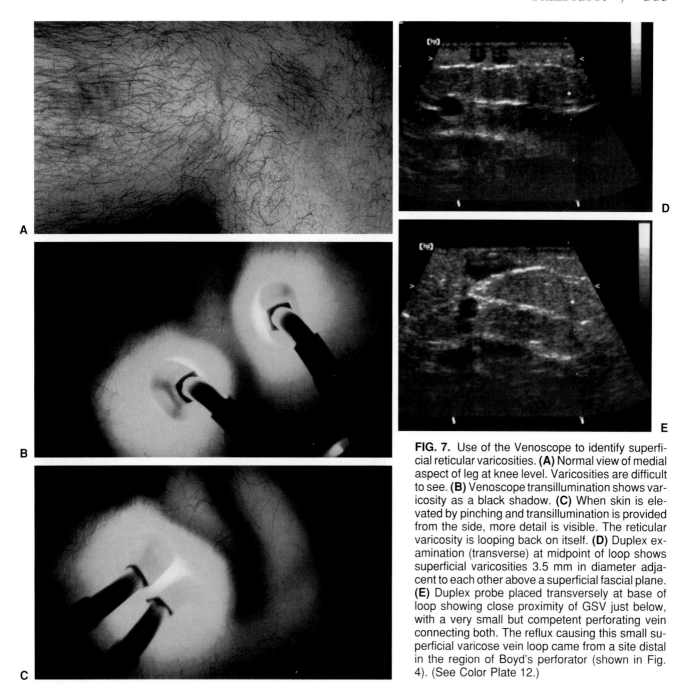

FIG. 7. Use of the Venoscope to identify superficial reticular varicosities. **(A)** Normal view of medial aspect of leg at knee level. Varicosities are difficult to see. **(B)** Venoscope transillumination shows varicosity as a black shadow. **(C)** When skin is elevated by pinching and transillumination is provided from the side, more detail is visible. The reticular varicosity is looping back on itself. **(D)** Duplex examination (transverse) at midpoint of loop shows superficial varicosities 3.5 mm in diameter adjacent to each other above a superficial fascial plane. **(E)** Duplex probe placed transversely at base of loop showing close proximity of GSV just below, with a very small but competent perforating vein connecting both. The reflux causing this small superficial varicose vein loop came from a site distal in the region of Boyd's perforator (shown in Fig. 4). (See Color Plate 12.)

veins only after all sources of reflux have been treated by sclerotherapy and/or surgery. Doppler ultrasound may also be used as a guide to demonstrate reflux in the reticular veins and to locate those that require treatment. In a darkened room the Venoscope can help locate reticular veins that are difficult to visualize (Fig. 7).

With the patient recumbent, insert the 3-ml syringe with a 27- to 30-gauge needle into the reticular vein; since this vein is usually superficial and visibly blue, it usually does not require marking by pen. Avoid strong overhead lighting, since it may wash out the appearance of veins, making their identification difficult. When the sensation of piercing the vein is felt, gently pull back the plunger until blood is seen beginning to back up into the transparent hub. This is possible even with a 30-gauge needle, although a 27-gauge needle is commonly employed. Usually, inject no more than 0.5 ml of sclerosing solution per injection site and, often, considerably less. The most commonly used sclerosing solution is STS in concentrations of 0.2% to 0.5% or POL 0.75% to 1%. Treatment of reticular veins greatly reduces the recurrence rate of telangiectasias associated with them, as well as reducing postsclerotherapy pigmentation and telangiectatic matting.

Treatment of Telangiectasia

Place the patient in either the prone or supine position, preferably on a hydraulic table allowing easy access to groups of telangiectasias anywhere on the leg. Cleanse the area with cotton balls heavily saturated with 70% isopropyl alcohol. This allows better visualization of the vessels by increasing light transmission through otherwise reflective white scale on the epidermal surface. Place a 30-gauge needle, bent to an angle of 30 to 45 degrees with the bevel up, on the skin so that the needle is parallel to the skin surface. Fill a 3-ml syringe with 2 ml of solution; hold the syringe between the index and middle fingers while the fourth and fifth finger support the syringe against the leg in a fixed position facilitating accurate penetration of the vessel. Use the nondominant hand to stretch the skin around the needle in a three-point manner (Fig. 8). The thumb may also offer additional support for the needle. Move the firmly supported needle quickly through the skin with a second, slower movement into the vessel lumen while maintaining gentle pressure on the syringe plunger. When the vessel is cannulated, the red blood cells clear and the flow of solution into the vessel can be seen, as well a decrease in pressure. Magnifying lenses on the order of $\times 2$ to $\times 3$ are recommended for visualizing cannulation of the smallest telangiectasias.

This technique requires a gentle, precise touch to appreciate the subtle sensation of piercing the telangiectasia. If cannulation is difficult, minimal withdrawal of the needle may occasionally allow easy flow of sclerosing solution. A very sharp needle is critical for this fine touch; needles are changed as often as necessary to minimize tearing the vessel, as well as pain. The use of 32- to 33-gauge needles is not advised because they dull rather quickly, are very expensive, and are not stiff enough to penetrate the skin without veering off course.

Injection of a tiny bolus of air (<0.05 cc) may be helpful to establish that the needle is within the vein, as slight clearing 1 to 3 mm ahead of the needle can be seen. The air-bolus technique is particularly useful when injecting hypertonic solutions, since these sclerosing agents may produce pain, punctate pigmentation, and ulceraton with even slight extravasation of solution.

Perform the injection *very slowly* using a small amount of sclerosant (0.1 to 0.5 ml or less) and with minimal or no pressure on a 3 -ml syringe to maintain filling of the veins for 10 to 15 seconds. Often, this may produce spasm of the vessel, which potentiates closure before application of compression. In addition, vessel spasm prevents or minimizes bleeding from the pierced vessel. Rapid flushing of the vessels with large volumes of sclerosant is not necessary for successful sclerotherapy and is absolutely contraindicated for any varicosity. Rapid infiltration of sclerosing solution may allow the sclerosing solution to enter the deep venous system rapidly in an undiluted state, resulting in a risk of DVT. Particularly when using a hypertonic solution, stop the injection of sclerosant when blanching in a radius of 2 cm has occurred or when 15 seconds has passed, thus minimizing the cramping and burning. When using painless detergent sclerosants such as STS and POL, small volumes minimize side effects such as telangiectatic matting. Occasionally, no blanching occurs at the injection site and the sclerosing solution flows easily through the telangiectasia or can even be seen flowing through adjacent telangiectasias or reticular veins several centimeters away from the injection site. In this case, stop the injection after 0.5 ml of sclerosant has been injected, and apply immediate manual compression. As a general rule, inject no more than 0.5 ml into any single site. At each session, clearly note all sites treated in anatomic diagrams with vein diameter, location, presence of reflux, and concentration and volume of sclerosant clearly indicated.

By minimizing volume, pressure, and duration of injection, not only is pain minimized, but the risks of extravasation are minimized as well. Multiple areas (e.g., at least 10 2- to 4-cm areas of varicosities on one thigh) can be treated with as little as 2 to 3 ml of sclerosant. To minimize skin necrosis, avoid extravasation. If resistance to the easy injection of sclerosant or the beginning of any bleb at the injection site is noted, stop the injection immediately. Keep an eye on the injection site at all times in order to notice the bleb at the moment of its occurrence. Perhaps, keep a syringe of 5 to 10 ml of normal saline and an ampule of hyaluronidase 300 IU nearby to flush and dilute any areas of extravasation that may develop.

POSTOPERATIVE MANAGEMENT

Immediately after injection, gently massage the treated area. This may help to reduce pain and muscle cramping that are common with injection of hypertonic solutions and hasten the spread of the sclerosant through the vessels. Any vessel larger than approximately 0.5 mm in diameter or, more important, of any size that protrudes above the surface of the skin benefits from compression. For these larger telangiectasia and varicose veins, secure cotton balls or foam pads over the injection sites by paper tape or Micropore.‖ Subsequently, maintain any additional graduated compression by graduated compression support hose or specially applied bandages for 3 days to 2 weeks, depending on the size and type of vessel treated. Recommendations vary, but one cannot be faulted with recommending compression for all patients. Seventy-two hours of compression for all patients with a 30- to 40-mm Hg graduated compression stocking is recommended. When reticular veins are treated, 1 week of compression is recommended, and 2 weeks of compression are recommended when treating larger varicose veins. Encourage patients to walk and not restrict their activi-

---

‖ 3M—Medical-Surgical Division, St. Paul, MN.

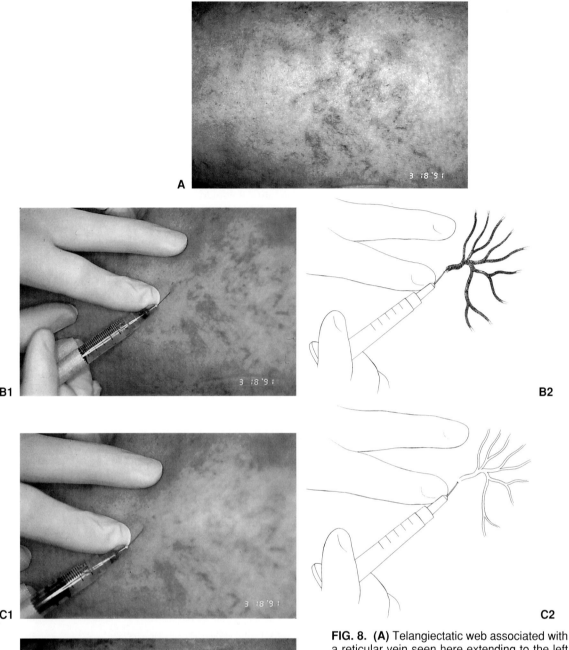

FIG. 8. (A) Telangiectatic web associated with a reticular vein seen here extending to the left side, which in this case is the distal portion of the lateral thigh. **(B)** Proper injection technique consists of injecting the reticular vein near the source of reflux (not shown) and then following with an injection in the largest vein near the initial branch point of the telangiectatic web. The nondominant hand is used to stretch the skin tightly to facilitate cannulation of the reticular vein. The nondominant hand also may serve a support function for the needle hub. Approximately 0.5 ml of 0.2% sodium tetradecyl sulfate is injected. **(C)** As the injection proceeds, the majority of the telangiectatic web blanches as

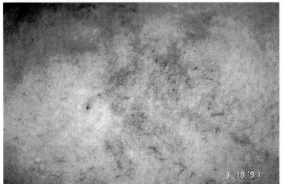

venous blood is replaced by the clear sclerosing solution. The goal of an injection is to fill this telangiectatic network as completely as possible and then stop the injection. The solution is held in place for 10 to 15 seconds without additional pressure. **(D)** After 5 to 10 minutes an irritant reaction is visible. This is evident in a blurring of the vascular margins with very little surrounding inflammation. This is the correct end-point. Vessels that exhibit no reaction are unlikely to improve, while excessive swelling or inflammation of adjacent capillaries is likely to cause hyperpigmentation or telangiectatic matting.

ties, with the exceptions of heavy weight-lifting with the legs and exercise that produces Valsalva's pressure. Allowing 4 to 8 weeks between treatments helps minimize the total number of treatments, since treated vessels should be given adequate time to resolve before retreatment.

ADVERSE SEQUELAE AND COMPLICATIONS

Postsclerotherapy Hyperpigmentation

Postsclerosis pigmentation is defined as the appearance of increased visible pigmentation along the course of a treated vein of any size. This pigmentation may be the result of sclerotherapy but may also be preexisting overlying a varicosity to be treated; in this case, pretreatment photographs are invaluable. Perivascular hemosiderin deposition, not increased melanin production, causes postsclerosis pigmentation. The incidence of pigmentation is variable and has been reported to depend on both the dilution and type of sclerosing agent, as well as the diameter of the treated vessel, with smaller vessels having decreased frequency. The incidence in the treatment of telangiectasias has been reported to be from 11% to 30%. Use of 1% STS for treatment of telangiectasias causes a nearly 80% incidence of pigmentation, whereas with 0.1% STS incidence of pigmentation can be lowered to 11%, comparable to 0.5% with POL and 23.4% with HS. The incidence of pigmentation may be reduced in varicose veins by expressing the liquefied coagulum or intravascular hematoma that may accumulate 1 to 4 weeks after sclerotherapy.

Spontaneous resolution of pigmentation occurs in 70% to 99% of cases within 6 months with rare persistence for more than a year. Attempts to hasten resolution of pigmentation have been mostly unsuccessful, since the pigment is dermal hemosiderin, not epidermal melanin. Bleaching agents, exfoliants such as trichloroacetic acid or phenol, and cryotherapy have achieved limited success, since these do not interact with hemosiderin. Various lasers including the copper vapor laser; the flashlamp pumped-dye laser at 510 nm; and the Q-switched alexandrite, ruby, and Nd:YAG lasers have been found to effectively treat this common adverse sequella in 30% to 50% of patients.

Telangiectatic Matting

Telangiectatic matting (TM) is defined as the appearance of groups of new, fine (<0.2 mm in diameter) telangiectasias surrounding a previously treated area in a blushlike manner. A recent published retrospective analysis of over 2000 patients reported an incidence of 16% in patients treated with HS and POL. Resolution usually occurs spontaneously within a 3- to 12-month period with a spontaneous resolution rate of 70% to 80% within the first 6 months. Only 10% of patients with TM require repeat treatment of the area.

Telangiectatic matting may also occur as a result of trauma

to the leg, in association with pregnancy or hormonal therapy, or in scars around previous sites of surgical stripping or ligation. Sclerotherapy-induced TM may be caused by excessive sclerosing solution concentrations or volumes, excessive hydrostatic pressure of injection, or improper compression.

Predisposing factors include predilection for certain areas of the leg such as the thigh and a number of epidemiologic factors related to individual susceptibility; these include obesity and hormonal therapy with estrogen. The only successful treatment of TM to date has been with the pulsed-dye 585-nm laser and the Photoderm VL® (Energy Systems Corporation, Wayland, MA), although temporary hyperpigmentation usually occurs following laser therapy (not Photoderm®). In most cases further treatment is not necessary, since TM resolves spontaneously.

Cutaneous Necrosis and Ulceration

Avoiding the complication of necrosis is most dependent on the skill of the physician; however, cutaneous ulceration may occur with *any* sclerosing solution even with most skilled technique, since injection into an arteriole feeding the telangiectasia may be unavoidable. Extravasation is minimized by stopping further injection at the first sign of a bleb, the slightest resistance to injection, or when the patient notices a sudden increase in pain.

Unavoidably, a tiny amount of sclerosing solution may be left along the needle tract as the needle is withdrawn. Sclerosing solution may also leak out into the skin through the small puncture sites of vessel cannulation. Inadvertent puncture through the entire vessel may result in small perforations on the back wall of the treated vein through which more solution may leak. When the treated vein has a particularly fragile, thin wall, sclerosant may cause rapid full-thickness injury leading to rupture with perivascular accumulation. In addition, injection may inadvertently occur into a small arteriole associated with a "spider" telangiectasia with resultant necrosis and ulceration.

When the dermatologic surgeon recognizes that extravasation has occurred, the risk for necrosis can be minimized by injecting normal saline containing hyaluronidase 300 IU in a ratio of 10:1 into the extravasation site. Spasm or injection into a feeding arteriole is usually evident in immediate blanching of the injected site. Pain is usually noted unless POL is used as the sclerosing solution (since it is an anesthetic agent). Performing extensive massage as quickly as possible minimizes prolonged blanching of the area and reverses vessel spasm. As an alternative or in addition, topical nitroglycerine paste massaged immediately into the extravasation or arteriolar injection site appears to prevent or minimize the development of necrosis.

Superficial Thrombophlebitis

Superficial thrombophlebitis is most commonly mistaken for the normal nodular fibrosis that occurs with proper sclerotherapy, termed "endosclerosis" by Fegan. After sclerotherapy of larger varicosities (4 to 8 mm in diameter), a *nontender,* nonpigmented, nonerythematous fibrotic cord may be palpable along the course of the vein and persist for months. Superficial thrombophlebitis is characterized on clinical examination by a very tender, indurated, linear erythematous swelling. Incidence is quite variable and is estimated at 1% to 0.01% following sclerotherapy. A liquefied coagulum usually accompanies the presence of superficial thrombophlebitis and should be evacuated. Treatment also consists of leg elevation and/or compression and regular administration of aspirin or other nonsteroidal antiinflammatory drugs. Extension of superficial thrombophlebitis into the deep venous system is extremely rare but may occur through the saphenofemoral or saphenopopliteal junctions.

Pulmonary Embolism

Pulmonary emboli occur from either extension of a superficial thrombus into the deep venous system or from direct damage to deep veins from sclerosing solution. Evidence of superficial or deep thrombosis or should be treated promptly by anticoagulation. The incidence of pulmonary embolism has been associated with injection of large quantities of sclerosant at a single site. The incidence is extremely low with less than 1 in 40,000 patients treated.

Exogenous hormonal therapy may increase the risk of DVT and pulmonary embolism. Compression followed by immediate ambulation and adherence to the principle of ad-ministering no more than 0.5 to 1 ml of sclerosing solution per injection site is thought to minimize the risks of DVT and subsequent emboli. In addition, since thrombus formation usually occurs 6 to 8 hours after a traumatic event to the venous system (sclerotherapy) and there is a relative stasis of blood flow while sleeping, wearing graduated compression stockings during the first 24 hours after sclerotherapy may help prevent this complication.

Arterial Injection

This dreaded medical emergency is extremely rare. Warning signs include immediate, intense pain far beyond the normal discomfort at the initiation of injection. Continuous intense burning pain with immediate, bone-white cutaneous blanching over a large area is the usual initial sign. Progression to a sharply demarcated cyanosis within minutes confirms arterial injection and must be recognized immediately. Emergency treatment involves immediate application of ice, attempts to flush the inadvertently injected artery with heparin, injection of 3% procaine to inactivate STS, and emergency consultation with a vascular surgeon for intravenous anticoagulation therapy. Rarely, arterial injection may not be accompanied by the usual signs of immediately intense pain and discoloration. Arterial injection may lead to necrosis of skin, subcutaneous tissue, and muscle. Although the dermatologic surgeon must be able to recognize and treat complications arising from sclerotherapy, the incidence of severe adverse sequelae is very rare.

33.2   Surgical Treatment of Primary Varicosis

Alina A.M. Fratila

HISTORY

It was not until the end of the 16th century, when Fabricius von Acquapendente discovered the venous valves, that varicose veins were correctly diagnosed as being diseased parts of the venous circulation. Before that and until the end of the 18th century, varicosities were treated as a local disease and cauterized. In the 17th century, the Italian surgeon Tomasso Rima first recognized the importance of venous reflux at the saphenofemoral junction (SFJ) as a causative factor in the pathogenesis of varicosities of the greater saphenous vein (GSV). Although ligation of the GSV at the SFJ was performed during this period, the procedure was abandoned because of the high mortality rate. Crossectomy (flush ligation of the SFJ or the saphenopopliteal junction [SPJ]) with stripping of the GSV was first successfully accomplished in 1891 in Bonn by a German surgeon named Trendelenburg.

The development of asepsis by Lister at the same time certainly contributed to the favorable outcome. Because of the development of sclerotherapy (see previous section) between World Wars I and II, surgical treatment of varicose veins "took a back seat" until shortly after World War II with the increasing use of the Babcock stripper, developed in 1907 by the surgeon after whom it is named. Since Robert Müller, a Swiss dermatologist, introduced the operative technique of ambulatory phlebectomy in the mid-1950s, treatment of varicose veins has been widely performed as an in-office outpatient procedure.

PREOPERATIVE PLANNING

Regardless of the symptoms and clinical aspects of varicose veins and the experience of the phlebologist, the phlebologic examinations should be performed in the sequence

TABLE 33-3. *Noninvasive phlebological investigation*

Specific history
Complete clinical examination
Continuous-wave Doppler ultrasound examination of the superficial and deep venous system

No valvular incompetence ... Valvular incompetence

Photoplethysmyography (PPG)

Normal to ... Briefer than 25 seconds to

No venous insufficiency ... Venous insufficiency is not present at the examined area ... Venous insufficiency

PPG with tourniquet

To normalized or improved ... To does not improve

Superficial venous insufficiency ... Deep venous insufficiency
Color duplex ultrasound if invasive therapy is required ... Insufficient perforating veins
Insufficient pumping ability

detailed in Table 33-3. The significance of these examinations according to the type of varicosis is depicted in Table 33-4.

If the surgical treatment of varicose veins is performed in an outpatient surgery clinic, patients must be carefully evaluated with regard to their general state of health. Patients with serious medical problems, such as elderly patients with cardiac diseases, postthrombotic syndrome, and severe recurrent varicosis, may be treated in an inpatient facility equipped to deal with unforeseen complications.

Relative contraindications for crossectomy, stripping, and phlebectomy are listed in Table 33-5. After a recent deep vein thrombosis, allow several months to pass before reevaluation for surgery. Thrombophlebitis with severely inflamed areas is a temporary contraindication. If it is localized, the operation will bring relief of pain and other symptoms. A special form of thrombophlebitis is the ascending phlebitis of the GSV. The progression of thrombus does not always stop at the SFJ. Often the thrombus may develop farther on, moving into the common femoral vein (CFV). Pulmonary embolism—an often fatal complication—may develop. A patient having ascending phlebitis of the GSV must be seen daily. Begin treatment with anticoagulants and compression bandages. If the condition worsens, be prepared to perform emergency crossectomy as a final solution.

Pregnancy is also a relative contraindication, since many varicose veins return to normal shortly after delivery of the fetus. Diabetics, obese women, or those with severe edema may have wounds that will not heal, so unsightly dehiscence scars always result. The usual contraindications for the performance of general surgery (e.g., suppurative infections, acute skin inflammation or erysipelas, severe skin eczema, purulent leg ulcers) apply to varicose vein surgery as well.

Absolute contraindications for surgery of the primary varicosis are listed in Table 33-6. Sometimes a varicose vein is actually a naturally developed compensatory bypass for

TABLE 33-4. *Significance of phlebologic investigations according to the type of varicosis*

	Clinical examination	Continuous-wave Doppler	Photoplethysmyography	Duplex	Phlebography
Telangiectasia					
Asymptomatic	+	+			
Symptomatic	+	+	+		
Incompetent reticular veins	+	+ +	+		
Side-branch varicosis	+	+ +	+	+ +	
Insufficient perforating vein	+	+	+	+ +	(+)
Complete truncal varicosis	+	+ +	+	+ +	
Incomplete truncal varicosis	+	+ +	+	+ +	(+)
Recurrent varicosis	+	+	+	+ +	+ +
Deep venous insufficiency	+	+ +	+	+	(+)

(+) = This examination offers additional information but should only be performed if diagnosis is still unclear.
  + = This examination reveals only partial information.
+ + = This examination offers best diagnostic information.

TABLE 33-5. *Relative contraindications for surgery of varicose veins*

- Recent deep vein thrombosis
- Very severe thrombophlebitis
- Pregnancy
- Obesity
- Marked edema
- Diabetes
- Contraindications for general surgery

a deep venous obstruction. If this condition is diagnosed in a patient with postthrombotic syndrome or chronic venous insufficiency (CVI), surgery should not be performed. If arterial occlusive disease or lymphedema is moderate, patients may be surgically treated, but conservatively, perhaps using only crossectomy or crossectomy with limited stripping. Exceptionally thin men can have prominent veins with normal valves or tubular venectasia. Such patients do not require surgery. Surgery is recommended for truncal varicosis or large varicose veins that cause signs and symptoms of CVI, if secondary popliteal and femoral vein insufficiency develops or the patient develops a complication such as thrombophlebitis. It is inadvisable to operate prophylactically on Stage I or II varicosis of the GSV, according to Hach (Fig. 9), especially in female patients or in patients without symptoms. Aside from the risk of complications as with any surgical treatment, telangiectasia may occur after stripping. Those patients should return for an examination every year. If the varicosis has progressed to Stage III, symptoms are present, and an abnormal polyplethmyographic finding is demonstrated, surgery is the correct choice.

An informed consent form must be read and signed by the patient and the surgeon. The patient should understand that primary varicosis is a multifactorial disease with a familial predisposition and a chronic developmental history. For this reason, recurrence is to be anticipated. A truncal varicosis will not recur if the operation is performed properly, but a double GSV, if overlooked, may become insufficient if connection to the deep venous system develops (pudendal veins, perforating veins, and so forth). Scarring is minimized if minisurgical techniques are used, but prolonged, dark red discoloration may be seen. Particularly the female patient

TABLE 33-6. *Absolute contraindications for surgery of varicose veins*

- Severe arterial occlusive disease
- Bedridden patient
- Severe lymphedema
- Congestion arthrodesis syndrome
- Coagulopathy
- Elderly patient with asymptomatic varicose veins
- Cardiovascular insufficiency with To briefer than 25 seconds in photoplethysmography, nonimprovable with tourniquets
- Tubular venectasia

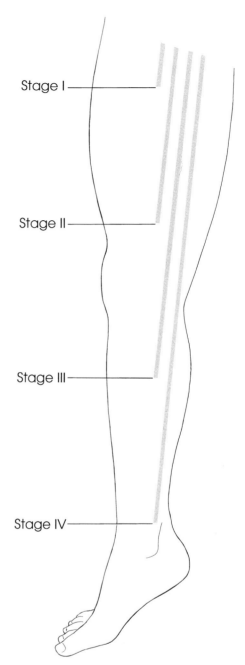

FIG. 9. According to Hach, the distal point of insufficiency (DPI) defines the four stages of greater saphenous vein (GSV) varicosis.

must understand and accept that telangiectasia may occur postoperatively.

Ideally, the patient should understand that his or her condition should be treated before signs and symptoms of CVI occur.

The patient should be in the office 1 hour before surgery so that the surgeon can mark the varicose veins preoperatively. Marking is guided by clinical examination (all visible varicose veins), palpation, continuous-wave Doppler ultrasound examination, and duplex ultrasound examination (see Chapter 33, Part 1).

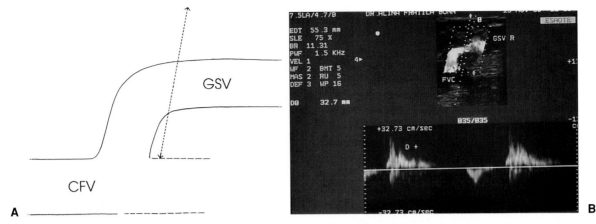

FIG. 10. Longitudinal section of the groin. The depth of the SFJ measures 32.7 mm.

Continuous-Wave Doppler Ultrasound Examination

The Doppler examination is used to determine the following extremely important information for the surgical treatment:

1. The proximal point of insufficiency (PPI) (i.e., whether it is the cross[*] of the GSV, or distally located in an insufficient Dodd's perforating vein [DPV] , or the "cross" of the lesser saphenous vein [LSV]).
2. The vein that is presenting valvular insufficiency (GSV or LSV) (i.e., does valvular damage affect the entire vein or only part of it and the distal point of insufficiency [DPI]?).
3. Whether there are incompetent tributaries.
4. Whether there are other transfascial communications besides the cross of the GSV or LSV (e.g., Hunter's perforating veins, DPV, Boyd's perforating vein [BPV], or May's perforating vein [MPV])? Other insufficient perforating veins (e.g., Cockett's perforating veins [CPV], lateral perforating vein, or Hach profound perforating vein [HPPV]).
5. Atypical reflux. For example, is Valsalva's maneuver or calf decompression negative for reflux at the SFJ but positive further down on the thigh? This may indicate an insufficient perforating vein or a communicator causing varicosities of iliac, pelvic, pudendal, or epigastric veins. An intersaphenous anastomosis (IA) may even exist.
6. Is the deep venous system normal or dilated? Are there pathologic refluxes?

Since the examined veins cannot be visualized by continuous-wave Doppler ultrasound, diagnostic pitfalls may occur in anatomically difficult regions. The popliteal fossa is a classic example of this type of region.

---

[*] The cross represents the last 3 to 4 cm of the greater saphenous vein found as a curved entrance into the common femoral vein.

Duplex Ultrasound Examination

In preoperative exploration of primary varicosis, duplex ultrasound has become the method of choice in the examination and exact localization of the SFJ, the SPJ, the perforating veins, and the reflux pathway. Not only can valve insufficiency be visualized, but also the truncal diameter and the depth of the SFJ (Fig. 10) and SPJ (Fig. 11) can be measured. In ambiguous cases of GSV insufficiency with normal valves and no reflux at the SFJ, as well as no perforators (e.g., DPV) or tributaries (e.g., a medial accessory saphenous vein [MASV]) entering the GSV farther down, duplex ultrasound may reveal the pudendal artery crossing the CFV just below the cross of the GSV, thereby giving the GSV real support. This situation is almost always confirmed intraoperatively. Complete (11%) or partial (15%) duplication of the GSV, as well as tributaries on both sides of the saphenous trunk or perforating veins such as DPV and BPV entering the GSV, can be visualized.

Ascending Pressure Phlebography and Varicography

If there is any discrepancy between the results of the noninvasive investigations described above and therapeutic consequences are involved, varicography should then be performed (Table 32-7).

The surgeon should work together with a radiologist specialized in phlebology. Knowledge of the anatomy of the venous system and an understanding of the reflux pathways are essential (Fig. 12). Without this additional expertise, vital clues to conditions that may not be obvious will remain undiagnosed.

If only an isolated side-branch varicosis is present and transfascial communication (the insufficient perforating vein) cannot be detected accurately, a varicography is recommended. Unlike the ascending pressure phlebography, whereby contrast medium is injected into a vein located on the dorsal aspect of the foot and a tourniquet is placed above

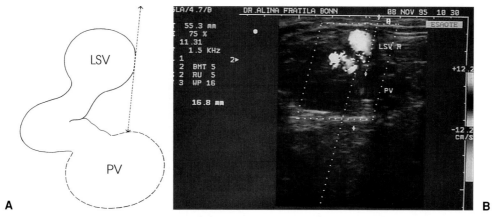

FIG. 11. Transverse section of the popliteal fossa. The depth of the saphenopopliteal junction (SPJ) is 16.8 mm.

the malleolus, a varicography examination involves the injection of contrast medium into the insufficient side branch itself, thereby making visualization of the transfascial communication possible.

On the day of surgery, ask the patient to shave the hair in the groin, shower, and avoid the application of any skin creams or lotions to the operative area. Makeup, nail polish, contact lenses, dentures or partial dentures, and all jewelry must be removed.

With a water-resistant indelible marker (felt-tip pen) (Edding 3000) the veins should be marked. Mark only the insufficient veins and perforators with the patient standing. Use different marks for thick and thin varices. Mark the exact location of the SFJ or the level and type of the SPJ, the PPI for incomplete varicosis types, all the reflux pathways (e.g. the insufficient trunk of the GSV or LSV, the insufficient side branches, communicating and perforating veins), and the DPI.

Instrumentation

Include the following standard instruments on the surgical table: three (for the GSV) or two (for the LSV) Parker or Roux retractors, one Langenbeck retractor for the LSV, one cardiovascular dressing forceps, one toothed and one non-toothed forceps, one Metzenbaum dissecting scissors, a Mixter forceps, one nontoothed and one toothed strong hemo-

---

TABLE 33-7. *Suggested indications for phlebography*

- Advanced stages of primary varicosis with complex reflux pathway
- Recurrent primary varicosis
- PPI can not be detected accurately
- Unclear reflux pathway in the case of incomplete varicosis especially of the GSV
- Suspected deep vein insufficiency which cannot be ruled out by other noninvasive methods
- Suspected anomalies of the venous system

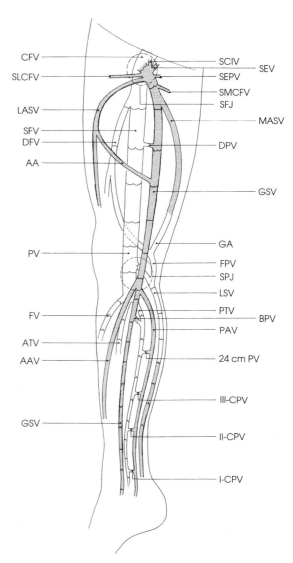

FIG. 12. Superficial and deep veins of the leg.

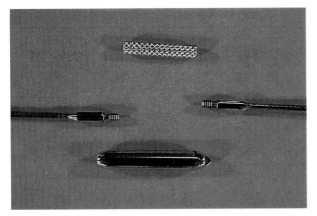

FIG. 13. Fischer stripper without the conical end tip, with torpedo connecting piece above and dolphin piece below.

static forceps, two Kocher hemostatic forceps, a regular needle holder, one No. 11 scalpel blade with holder, a holder for microblades (special, very small, sharply pointed blades), several straight and curved Halstead mosquito forceps, one pair of operating scissors, one long (for the GSV) or one short (for the LSV) Fischer stripper (Fig. 13),

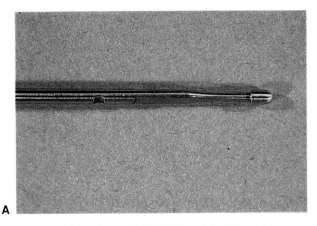

A

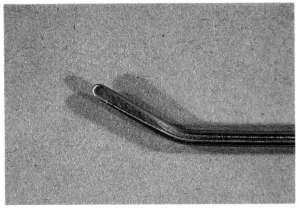

B

FIG. 14. perforation invagination Oesch (PIN) stripper. **(A)** Proximal end, with a very small head followed by a flattened neck and a notch. **(B)** Distal curved end, which can perforate the vein.

TABLE 33-8. *Klein anesthetic solution for tumescent technique (safe dose is 35 mg/kg)*

Lidocaine	500 mg (50 ml of 1% lidocaine solution)
Epinephrine	1 mg (1 ml of 1:1000 solution of epinephrine)
Sodium bicarbonate	12.5 mEq (12.5 ml of an 8.4% NaH_2CO_3 solution)
Normal saline	500 to 1000 ml of 0.9% NaCl solution

and one Oesch[**] 30-cm long perforation invagination Oesch (PIN) stripper for the LSV (Fig. 14A and B). Minisurgical phlebectomy may be performed using various phlebectomy hooks: Muller[†](Fig. 15), Ramelet[‡] (Fig. 16), Oesch[‡] (Fig. 17), Varaday[§], Dortu, or the Millet phlebectomy hooks.

Operate with the patient under general anesthesia without premedication if the patient is very obese, if there is a severe or a recurrent varicosis, at the patient's request, or if operating with the Löfqvist tourniquet[||]. Otherwise, local infiltration with preoperative analgesia under respiratory and cardiac monitoring is preferred. Administer local anesthetic 10 ml 1% lidocaine with 1:100,000 epinephrine in the groin and tumescent solution described by Klein for the rest of the veins (Table 33-8). The tumescent technique was developed for use in liposuction surgery, but the advantages when used in phlebectomy include diminished cardiotoxicity and lessened risk of organized hematomas and thrombophlebitis. Also, the stripping maneuver and phlebectomy are more easily performed because venous connections to surrounding tissue are altered by the anesthetic solution. Another advantage for the patient is the prolonged anesthetic effect, which lasts for a minimum of 12 hours postoperatively.

TECHNIQUE

Depending on the type of the primary varicosis (Table 33-9), perform the following surgical steps:

1. Perform flush ligation and division of the originating reflux point (crossectomy of the GSV or LSV for complete varicosis and dissection of the insufficient transfascial communication for incomplete varicosis).
2. Use the Löfqvist tourniquet to minimize postoperative hematomas resulting from the removal of very promi-

** Venosan GmbH 78628 Rottweil, Germany.
† The Muller hook exists in four models, which can be distinguished by the number on the handle.
‡ The Ramelet hook exists in two models, a fine and a thicker one.
‡ The Oesch hook exists in three models, which can be distinguished by the number of notches on the handle. The standard instrument is hook No. 2. No. 3 has a finer tip and is used for small veins or for highly cosmetic demands. All three hooks are available for right- and left-handed surgeons.
§ The Varady hooks offer one end as a phlebextractor and the other as a phlebodissector (Aesculap AG, Tuttlingen, Germany, and San Francisco, CA).
|| Boazul AB, Box 444, 64127 Katrineholm, Sweden.

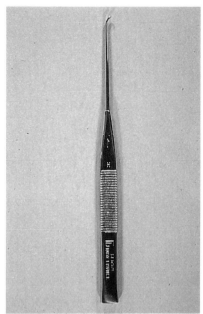

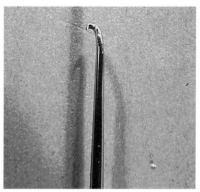

FIG. 15. Phlebectomy hook by Muller **(A)** with detail **(B).**

nent varicose veins of the GSV system when operating under general anesthesia.

3. Dissect the hemodynamically relevant insufficient perforating veins.
4. Perform minisurgical phlebectomy of the insufficient side branches (tributaries) after crossectomy but before stripping of the GSV or LSV.
5. Strip the insufficient and dilated trunk of the GSV or LSV from the originating reflex point down to its most distal point.

To avoid damage to the saphenous nerve and the lymph vessels, perform stripping of the GSV just beyond BPV only (groin-to-knee downward, inside-out stripping). In cases where the valves in the distal saphenous vein are incompetent and the vein is very meandering or prominent, strip down to the ankles. To avoid damage to the sural nerve, limited downward, inside-out stripping is recommended for the LSV as well. Limited stripping of the GSV can be performed on an outpatient basis and offers the best long-term results. When using the cryoprobe to perform the upward, invaginated stripping of the GSV, there is no need for a second distal incision to expose the vein trunk. The vein will stick on the probe and will tear. Because the cryoprobe is a rigid, stainless steel rod, it can only be used if the GSV is not meandering. There is a high recurrence rate following simple ligation and division of the GSV, but this can be an

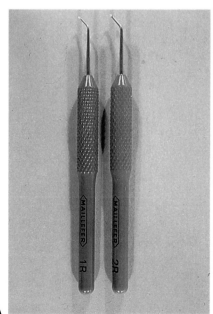

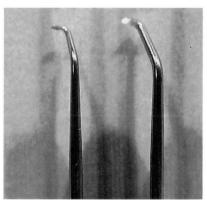

FIG. 16. Phlebectomy hooks by Ramelet **(A)** with detail **(B).**

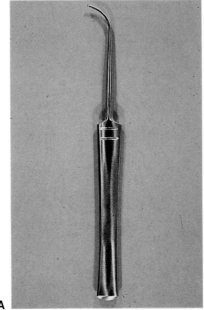

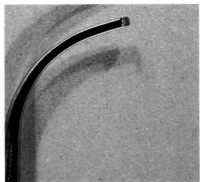

FIG. 17. Phlebectomy hook by Oesch **(A)** with detail **(B).**

alternative procedure in patients with with lymphedema or arterial occlusive disease. However, crossectomy alone followed immediately by catheter sclerotherapy can be an alternative procedure in elderly patients.

Crossectomy of the Greater Saphenous Vein

For crossectomy of the GSV, place the patient supine in Trendelenburg's position. The hip and the knee are flexed

TABLE 33-9. *Type of primary varicosis*

Complete varicosis of the greater saphenous vein (GSV)
Incomplete varicosis of the GSV
  Perforating type
    With deep venous insufficiency
    Without deep venous insufficiency
  Side-branch type
    Inguinal infravalvular type
    Inguinal supravalvular type
  Dorsal type
  Pudendal type
Combined truncal and perforating varicosis of the GSV
Combined truncal and side-branch varicosis of the GSV
Pudendal varicosis
Complete varicosis of the lesser saphenous vein
  With deep venous insufficiency
  Without deep venous insufficiency
Incomplete varicosis of the lesser saphenous vein
  Peforating type
  Caused GSV insufficiency
Perforating varicosis
  Hach profound perforating vein varicosis
  Popliteal perforating vein varicosis
Side-branch varicosis
  Transfascial type
  Extrafascial type
Reticular varicosis
Telangiectasia

and the limb externally rotated; use a towel to support the knee if necessary (Fig. 19). This positioning allows optimal exposure of the groin and makes possible the ligation of the MASV entering the GSV at a distance of several centimeters further down. Make the groin incision at the level of the SFJ as determined by duplex ultrasound, which normally lies in the fold or about 2 cm higher. If the SFJ is very superficial, the incision can be short, but even long incisions heal with good cosmetic results. Carefully perform blunt dissection of fatty tissue parallel to the long axis of the leg to minimize damage to the lymphatic vessels. Carefully split the superfi-

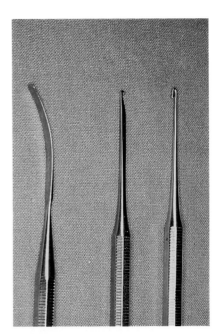

FIG. 18. Phlebectomy hooks by Varady, detail.

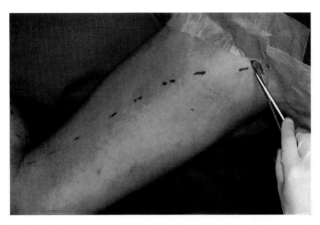

FIG. 19. For crossectomy of the GSV, the patient lies with an externally rotated limb. The hip and the knee are also flexed.

cial and deep fascia. Identify the GSV by its bluish color, and dissect it periadventitially to minimize intraoperative bleeding. Do not cut the GSV at this point, but secure and elevate it (Fig. 20). Isolate the vein up to the SFJ, and ligate and divide all the tributaries (Fig. 21). Expose the upper, lateral, and medial aspects of the CFV to see and ligate the deep external pudendal veins or veins directly entering the CFV. Use nonresorbable suture material for the ligation of the deep external pudendal veins without dividing the veins, a so-called selective suture. Use nonresorbable suture material for the flush ligation of the SFJ as well, although resorbable sutures may also be used. Ligate the GSV with a double suture with one of the sutures being transfixed (Fig. 22). Avoid leaving a stump or creating a stricture at the site of the SFJ. If the pudendal artery crosses the GSV anteriorly, it may be divided, but this is not recommended for female

patients with a history of cesarean sections. Necrosis of the vulva has been described in such cases. Introduce the Fischer stripper into the vein from the proximal to the distal point of insufficiency. The stripper will not advance further when the distal point of insufficiency has been reached because of obstruction by a normally healthy valve. Below BPV, make a 2- to 3-mm incision in the relaxed skin tension lines exactly over the end of the stripper, and hook only the GSV with a mosquito clamp. Ligate the GSV distally, although this is not mandatory. Tie the proximal end of the vein around and below the small head of the stripper with a trailing (guiding) thread, which should be more than twice the length of the vein segment to be stripped. As a result of the distal end of the stripper being pulled, the vein will start to invaginate. Facilitate the beginning of the invagination by holding the vein with two forceps. Place a Löfqvist tourniquet on the thigh at this point. (When operating with the patient under general anesthesia and with the Löfqvist tourniquet, it is suggested that crossectomy be performed with short stripping only and that the side-branches be removed by minisurgical phlebectomy using tumescent anesthesia and phlebectomy hooks as a second procedure some days later. The minisurgical phlebectomy is a very meticulous technique and can take a lot of time to complete. This will unnecessarily prolong the general anesthesia and the use of the tourniquet as well, which may be a limiting factor anyway.) Strip the GSV downward, inside-out from the groin to knee (Fig. 23). Avoid tearing the GSV during invaginated stripping by avulsing big anchoring tributaries with phlebectomy hooks. Sometimes the anterior or posterior arch veins (AAVs or PAVs) do not tear but come out with the GSV (Fig. 24). If, despite all these precautions, the GSV tears, ligate the long, guiding thread to the Fischer stripper with the dolphin head (Fig. 13) and reintroduce the stripper in an antegrade fashion through the distal end of the

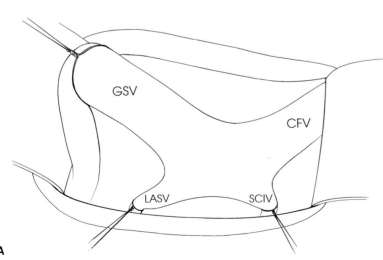

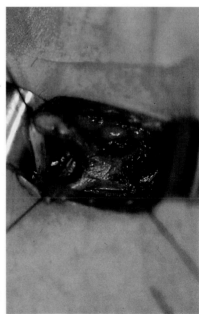

A

FIG. 20. The GSV secured and raised on a thread; tributaries are ligated as well.

B

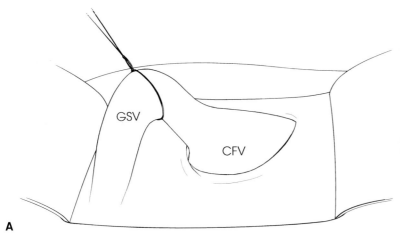

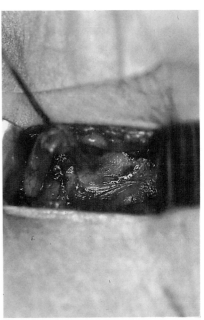

FIG. 21. After dividing the tributaries, the saphenofemoral junction (SFJ) is clearly visible.

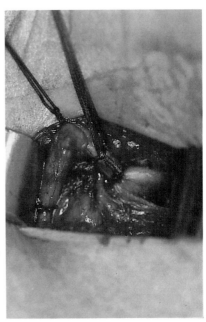

FIG. 22. The GSV is ligated with a double suture, one of which is transfixed.

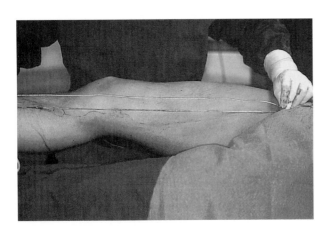

FIG. 23. The GSV stripped inside-out from the groin to below the knee. Above the vein is the stripper by Fischer.

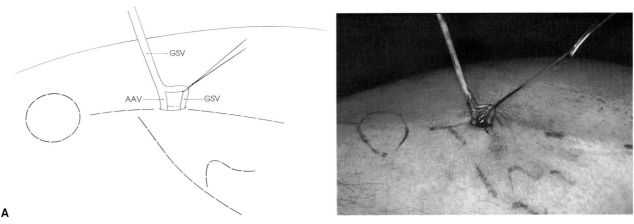

FIG. 24. The GSV coming out with the anterior arch vein.

GSV. An antegrade inside-out stripping of the distal part of the GSV will complete the stripping maneuver. If indicated, perform endoscopic selective dissection of the perforating veins through the exit point of the stripper (a larger distal incision is then necessary). Prevention of hematomas by compression bandages is the rationale for performing the stripping maneuver at the end of the operation.

According to the type of primary varicosis (Table 33-10), there are some slight modifications of the operating technique. The location of the PPI defines whether the varicosis is complete or incomplete. In case of complete varico-

sis of the GSV (Fig. 25), the PPI is in the groin at the SFJ. In incomplete varicosis of the GSV, the PPI represents the point where the transfascial communicating vein enters the GSV and is located more distally (i.e., in the middle of the upper thigh if there is a DPV causing the insufficiency of the GSV or below the knee if there is an insufficient BPV). The DPI defines the stage of the varicosis, and Hach divided varicosis into the following stages:

Stage 1 is the insufficiency of the SFJ.
In stage 2 the DPI is located 10 cm above the knee.

TABLE 33-10. *Surgical treatment of primary varicosis according to type of varicosis*

1. Complete varicosis of the GSV: Crossectomy of SFJ and limited invaginated stripping
2. Incomplete varicosis of the GSV
    Perforating type
        With deep venous insufficiency: Ligation of DPV and limited stripping of GSV
        Without deep venous insufficiency: Ligation and limited stripping or sclerotherapy
    Side-branch type
        Inguinal infravalvular type: Crossectomy of the SFJ, phlebectomy of AA, and limited stripping of GSV
        Inguinal supravalvular type: Ligation of LASV, phlebectomy of AA, and limited stripping of GSV
    Dorsal type: "Crossectomy" of the SPJ; phlebectomy of FPV, GA, and MASV, and limited stripping of the GSV
    Pudendal type: Phlebectomy of pudendal vein and limited stripping of the GSV
3. Combined truncal and perforating varicosis of the GSV: Crossectomy of the SFJ, phlebectomy of AA, and limited stripping of GSV
5. Pudendal varicosis: Phlebectomy or sclerotherapy
6. Complete varicosis of the LSV
        With deep venous insufficiency: "Crossectomy" of the SPJ and limited stripping of LSV
        Without deep venous insufficiency: "Crossectomy" of the SPJ and limited stripping or sclerotherapy
7. Incomplete varicosis of the LSV
    Perforating type: Ligation of MPV and limited stripping of LSV
    Caused by GSV insufficiency: Crossectomy of the SFJ, limited stripping of GSV, phlebectomy of the IA, and limited stripping of LSV
8. Perforating varicosis
    Hach profound perforating vein varicosis: Ligation, phlebectomy or sclerotherapy
    Popliteal perforating vein varicosis: Ligation, phlebectomy, or sclerotherapy
9. Side-branch varicosis
    Transfacial type: Ligation of perforator, phlebectomy, or sclerotherapy
    Extrafascial type: Phlebectomy or sclerotherapy
10. Reticular varicosis: Phlebectomy or sclerotherapy
11. Telangiectasia: Sclerotherapy or photosclerosis

Abbreviations are expanded in Chapter 33, Appendix.

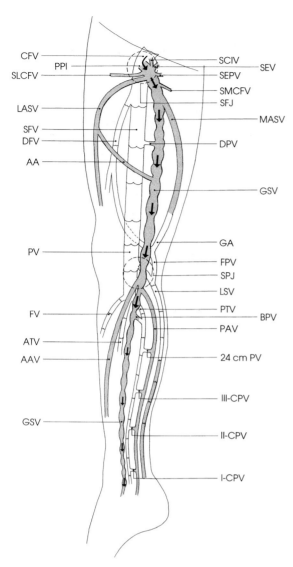

FIG. 25. Complete varicosis of the GSV: diagram.

In stage 3 the DPI is located 10 cm below the knee
In stage 4 the DPI is located in the ankle region (Fig. 9).
Table 33-10 gives the steps for the operating procedure according to the type of varicosis.

In case of a complete varicosis of the GSV, perform crossectomy with groin-to-knee downward, inside-out stripping (Fig. 25). By performing this so-called limited invaginated stripping (short stripping/partial saphenectomy), the rate of saphenous nerve injury compared with the Babcock stripping technique can be reduced significantly. In incomplete varicosis of the GSV, first ligate the transfascial communication. If there is an insufficient DPV or a Hunter's insufficient perforating vein with DVI and reflux from the external iliac vein into the femoral vein (Fig. 26), perform subfascial dissection of the perforating vein and stripping of the insufficient part of the GSV from the PPI below BPV. If there is no reflux and no deep venous insuffi-

ciency, perform subfascial dissection or sclerotherapy. The PPI, in case of incomplete GSV of the so-called perforating type, can be well visualized by color duplex ultrasound (Fig. 27). In incomplete GSV varicosis of the so-called side-branch type, there is an insufficient lateral accessory saphenous vein (LASV) representing the transfascial communication in the groin and an accessory anastomosis (AA) connecting the LASV with the trunk of the GSV. The LASV may enter the cross of the GSV distally to the last valve, the so-called infravalvular type (Fig. 28). In this case, perform crossectomy of the SFJ. If the LASV enters the cross of the GSV proximally to the last valve or directly into the CFV (Fig. 29A and B), only dissection of the LASV is necessary. The level where the AA enters the GSV represents the PPI and usually is located very high on the thigh. If the proximal segment of the GSV down to the PPI is very short (e.g., 10 cm), strip the whole

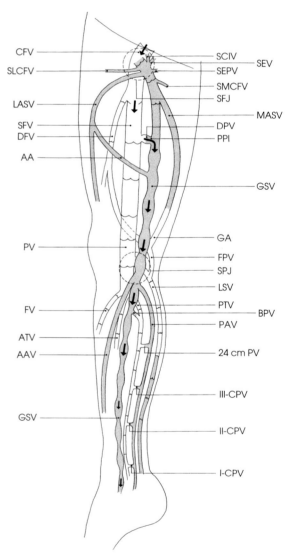

FIG. 26. Incomplete varicosis of the GSV, perforating type, with deep reflux diagram.

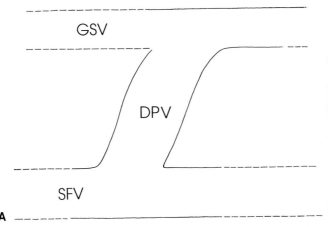

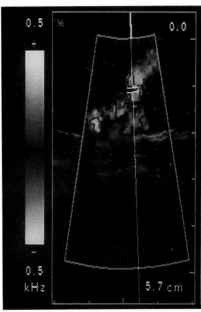

FIG. 27. Dulplex ultrasound of the insufficient DPV. See Fig. 26 for diagram. (See Color Plate 13.)

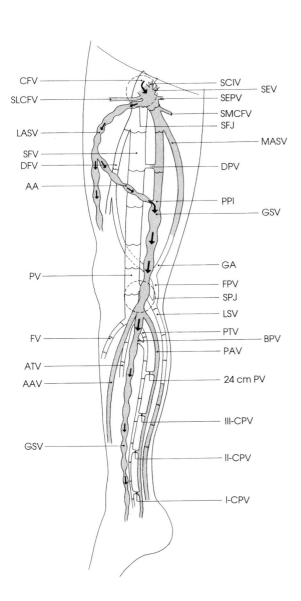

FIG. 28. Incomplete varicosis of the GSV, side-branch type, inguinal infravalvular type.

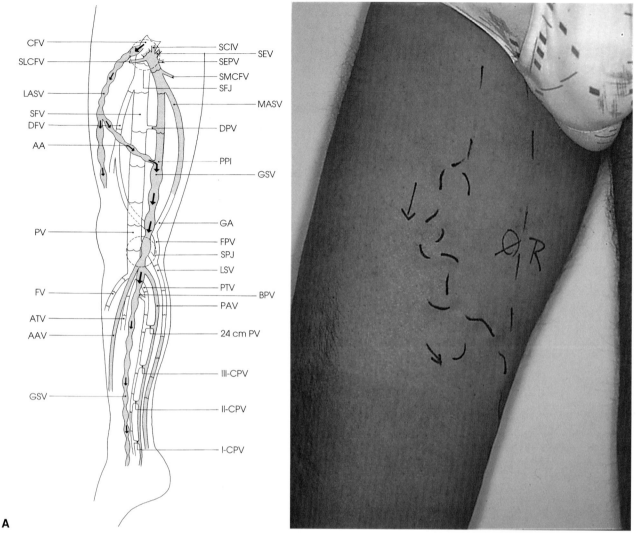

FIG. 29. Incomplete varicosis of the GSV, side-branch type, inguinal supravalvular type: diagram **(A)** and clinical picture **(B).**

GSV from groin to knee together with phlebectomy of the LASV and the AA after having performed the crossectomy. However seldom, a thrombosis in the remaining saphenous stump may develop. With a very good color duplex sonography unit and some experience, it can easily be determined whether the LASV enters the cross of the GSV distally (Fig. 30) or proximally to the last valve. This aspect is more important for the side-branch varicosis of the LASV than for the incomplete GSV varicosis of the so-called side-branch type, because crossectomy will avert major recurrences. In case of incomplete GSV varicosis of the so-called dorsal type, there is a hemodynamically efficient anastomosis, the Giacomini anastomosis (GA) between the femoropopliteal vein (FPV) as a side branch of the LSV and the MASV as a side branch of the GSV. The reflux pathway usually begins in the insufficient popliteal vein, continues through the insufficient cross of the LSV, then via the FPV, GA, and MASV into the GSV (Fig. 31). The correct treatment in this case is

to first undertake "crossectomy" of the SPJ followed by phlebectomy of the insufficient veins (i.e., FPV, GA, MASV) and then downward, inside-out stripping of the GSV beginning at the PPI and extending below BPV. The incomplete GSV varicosis of the so-called pudendal type is very rare (Fig. 32A and B). The reflux comes via the insufficient internal pudendal vein from the internal iliac vein and follows the plexus ovaricus/spermaticus and external pudendal vein. Perform phlebectomy of the external pudendal vein followed by stripping of the GSV from the PPI in the middle of the thigh below the knee. Combined main and perforating varicosis of the GSV is often diagnosed (Fig. 33A and B). The combination requires GSV crossectomy, as well as the dissection of transfascial communication (e.g., DPV) followed by limited downward, invaginated stripping of the GSV. By ligating the transfascial communication, intraoperative bleeding and postoperative hematoma resulting from laceration of the large DPV are avoided. The pudendal vari-

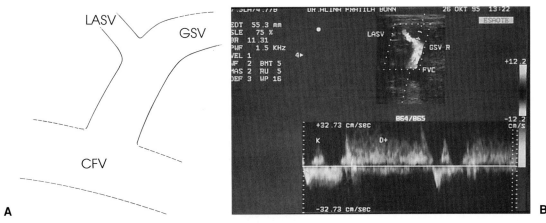

A   B

FIG. 30. Duplex ultrasound of the SFJ: lateral accessory saphenous vein (LASV) enters the cross of the GSV 2 cm before SFJ.

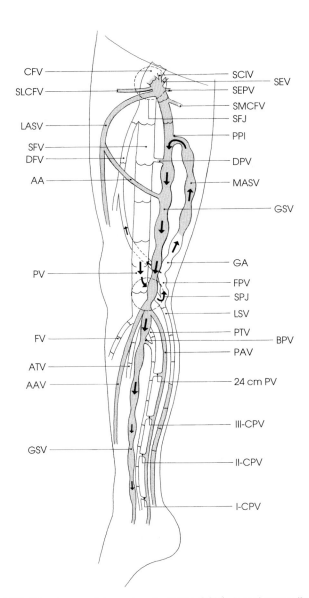

FIG. 31. Incomplete varicosis of the GSV, dorsal type: diagram.

cosis as an isolated varicosis running on either the inner or dorsal aspect of the thigh is another possible but rare type of varicosis that is usually seen in female patients. In this case, perform either phlebectomy or sclerotherapy.

Lesser Saphenous Vein Ligation and PIN Stripping

In contrast to SFJ, there are many types of SPJ, so duplex ultrasound examination is mandatory preoperatively. In the popliteal fossa, a duplex ultrasound examination allows exact differentiation between the popliteal vein (PV), the LSV, the FPV, and the gastrocnemius veins (Fig. 34) and also visualizes the direction from which the LSV enters the PV. Start the examination at the proximal end of the popliteal fossa in transversal sections. The LSV usually comes into view on the lateral side of the PV (Fig. 11). Gastrocnemius veins will appear on either side of the PV. It is important to determine and mark the level of the incision in the popliteal fossa immediately before surgery. Because there is much variability for the location of the vein entrance if a real ''crossectomy'' of the LSV is being performed, it is important to know exactly the level of the entrance of the LSV into the PV. For operating on the LSV, have the patient lie face down on the operating table with the dorsum of the foot elevated on a pillow so that the knee is flexed at least 30 degrees. In this position the fascia in the popliteal fossa will be relaxed. Especially for the LSV, the preferred anesthesia is local anesthesia because a heavy patient does not have to be turned after intubation. In addition, the patient may give warning by reacting during coagulation or ligation of a nerve. Have the patient climb onto the operating table, thereby facilitating disinfection by active lifting of the leg. With the 27-gauge, 40-mm-long needle, infiltrate the skin and the fascia in the popliteal fossa. After bending the needle twice and starting from the previously placed depot, anesthetize the skin overlying the varicose veins. *The saphenous vein itself is not anesthetized.* The incision in the popliteal fossa is horizontal within relaxed skin tension lines. The

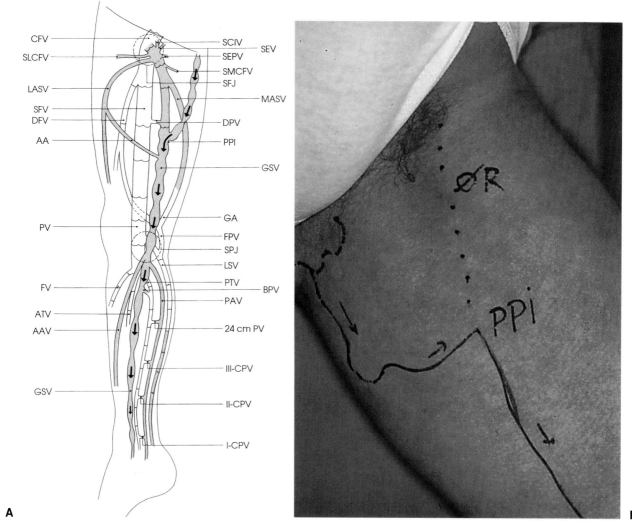

FIG. 32. Incomplete varicosis of the GSV, pudendal type: diagram **(A)** and clinical picture **(B)**.

fascia, however, is cut in a longitudinal direction. This allows a prolongation of the incision if preparation up to the SPJ is necessary higher than previously planned. Secure the LSV with a suture and elevate it. Then isolate the vein up to the SPJ, and ligate and divide all the tributaries. The term ''cross'' is not very appropriate for the LSV because it has no real cross as in the case of the GSV. The question regarding the LSV ligation is whether this ligation should be performed at the SPJ or just subfascially. The high-level ligation of the LSV (i.e., at the SPJ) has the advantages of a low recurrence rate and good functional results. On the other hand, the operation is more invasive and dangerous, there is more risk of PV thrombosis, and the incision in the popliteal fossa is bigger and cosmetically less attractive. By completing the ligation of the LSV only immediately under the fascia, there is a high recurrence rate (Fig. 35). The results of the subfascial ligation are cosmetically excellent, and there is almost no postoperative risk. Since the recurrence rate of the LSV is generally more than 30%, a nonaggressive surgical procedure that is safe for an outpatient is clearly preferred

by many surgeons. The question of whether to ligate the gastrocnemius veins has not yet been definitely answered. Whenever possible, place the ligation directly at the SPJ, especially if there is a deep venous insufficiency simultaneously, if the LSV is of large caliber, or if the patient is being operated on for recurrence varicosis. Be very careful not to traumatize the PV by pulling or compression.

A very valuable invention for the atraumatic downward, inside-out limited stripping of the LSV is the PIN stripper (Fig. 14). The vein wall is blindly perforated with the tip of the PIN stripper at a point determined by external finger pressure. Pull the tip of the instrument out through a stab incision in the skin. This instrument allows minute incisions wherever the stripper is withdrawn, and the risk of damaging the suralis nerve is minimal. Oesch's PIN stripper is a flexible, fine (less than 2 mm), stainless steel rod with one curved end that can perforate the vein and get under the skin where a stab incision can be made (Fig. 14B). The other end has a slim part with a hole where the suture ligature is placed, a flat part that is used for clamping and guiding the stripper,

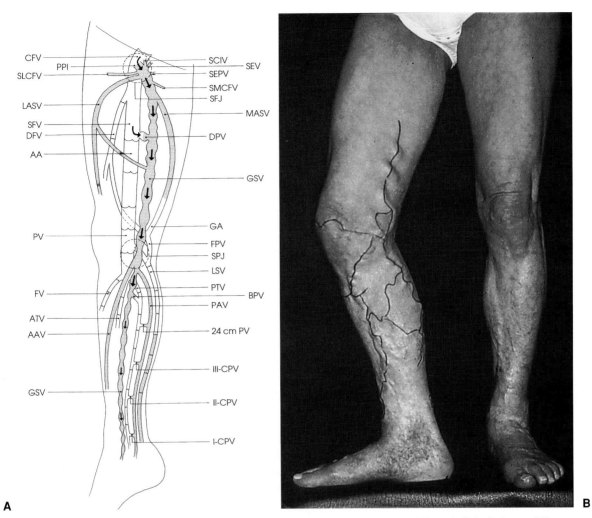

FIG. 33. Combined main and perforating varicosis of the GSV: diagram **(A)** and clinical picture **(B)**.

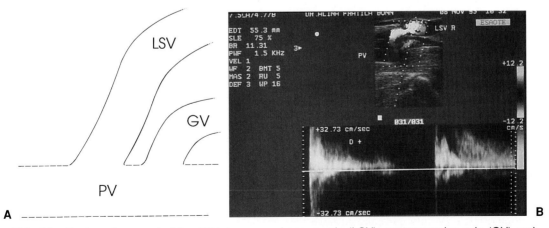

FIG. 34. Duplex ultrasound of the SPJ: lesser saphenous vein (LSV), gastrocnemius vein (GV) and popliteal vein (PV) are visible.

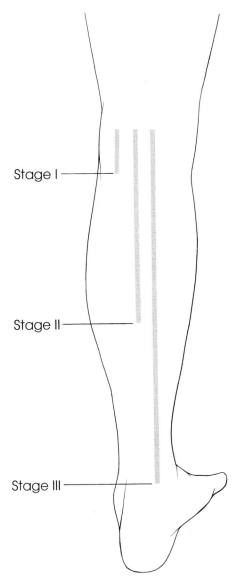

Stage I

Stage II

Stage III

FIG. 35. According to Hach, the DPI defines the three stages of LSV varicosis.

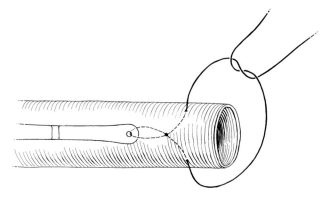

FIG. 37. PIN stripper with thread tied around its head and the two arms of the floating knot being transfixed through opposing vein walls.

and a notch placed just below the flattened neck to indicate the position of the curved end (Fig. 14A). The PIN stripper comes in two sizes: 47.5 cm for the GSV and 30 cm for the LSV. Introduce the PIN stripper into the vein with the angulated end first. Distally to the presumed end-point of stripping, position the index finger below the pointed tip, and firmly press down the LSV. Force the tip of the PIN stripper to perforate through the vein wall until it distends the skin (Fig. 36A and B). Here, make a stab incision, and pass the stripper through the skin without the need to dissect and directly visualize the vein. Tie a thread through the small hole of the upper end of the PIN stripper (only the new version of the PIN stripper has a hole), make a floating knot (Fig. 37), and leave the thread twice as long as the intended vein segment to be stripped. Contrary to other stripping devices, do not tie the vein directly onto the stripper head. Pull the PIN stripper down until it disappears completely inside the vein. First pass the two arms of the floating knot around two clamps that anchor the vein; then tie firmly in front of and behind the clamps. The two ends of the thread may also be transfixed through the opposing vein walls with the help of a bare needle. Take care to catch only the vein and not the stripper as well. As the PIN stripper is slowly pulled down, the vein invaginates automatically and the upper end

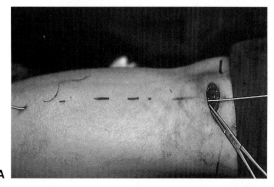

A

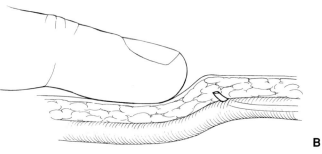

B

FIG. 36. Oesch PIN stripper perforating the skin distally on the calf. Clinical picture **(A).** PIN stripper perforating the anterior vein wall: diagram **(B).**

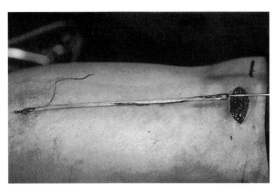

FIG. 38. The invaginated LSV has the long thread inside.

appears in the distal stab incision. As long as no big tributaries are torn, the patient feels no pain. Now, tear out the point where the vein was perforated. The invaginated LSV has the long thread inside (Fig. 38). The upper part of the thread lies in the bed of the removed vein. If the vein should rupture, it will serve as a guideline to facilitate retrieval with

a phlebectomy hook. Twist the distal segment of the LSV until breaking; then pull out without any ligatures. Leave open the skin incision to drain the hematoma. Before stripping the LSV, perform phlebectomy of all the side branches. Suture the fascia in the popliteal fossa with 0-0 Vicryl. Close the skin incision by interrupted, buried resorbable mattress stitches, and apply the compressive bandage. The phlebectomy wounds may be protected with an Op-site dressing. There are no stitches at all to be removed.

As with the varicosis of the GSV, the localization of the PPI defines whether the varicosis of the LSV is complete or incomplete. In case of a complete varicosis of the LSV without deep venous insufficiency, sclerotherapy can be performed as an individual treatment alternative to the surgical treatment. If there is a deep venous insufficiency (Fig. 39A and B), the surgical treatment is preferred. Except for complete varicosis of the LSV, "crossectomy" of the SPJ is unnecessary. If MPV is causing the incomplete varicosis of the LSV of the so-called perforating type, dissect the perforating vein, followed by phlebectomy or limited strip-

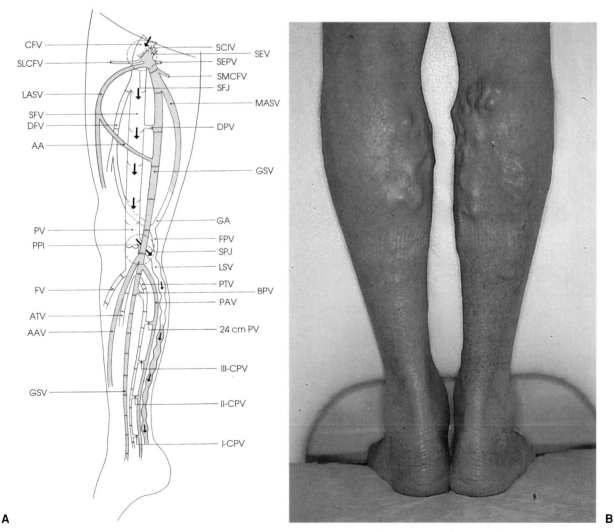

FIG. 39. Complete varicosis of the LSV with deep reflux diagram **(A)** and clinical picture **(B)**.

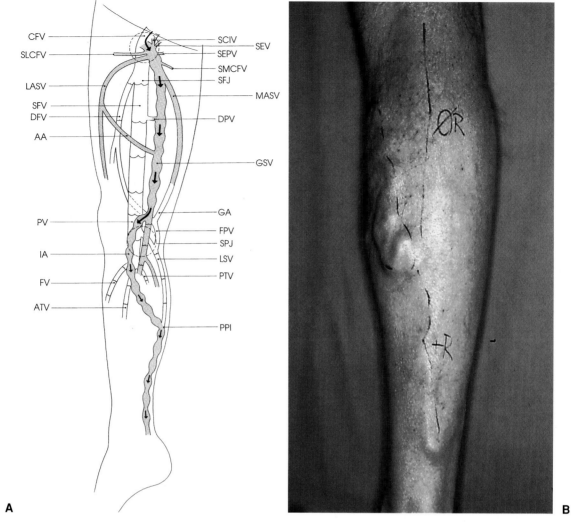

FIG. 40. Incomplete varicosis of the LSV, caused by GSV insufficiency: diagram **(A)** and clinical picture **(B)**.

ping of the LSV. Alternative sclerotherapy can be performed as well.

In case of incomplete varicosis of the LSV caused by GSV insufficiency (Fig. 40A and B) with the pathway of reflux being an IA, crossectomy of the SFJ with limited stripping of the GSV down to the DPI followed by phlebectomy of the IA and the insufficient part of the LSV is the therapy of choice.

Perforating Varicosis

The isolated perforating varicosis is quite often seen, and some types are very well defined, such as HPPV and popliteal perforating vein (PPV) varicosis. With a color duplex ultrasound examination, it is possible to simultaneously visualize the flux and reflux of blood flow during compression and decompression of the calf. This can be observed in the

perforating veins and tributaries, as well as in deep and superficial veins. Rabe proposed the following types of insufficient perforating veins:

1. Primary perforating vein insufficiency. The insufficient perforating veins may be connected to the GSV or LSV systems, but there are many exceptions. Insufficient perforating veins can also be the transfascial communication of a side-branch varicosis like the HPPV varicosis (Fig. 41A and B) or the PPV varicosis (Fig. 42A and B). The following main groups of perforating veins may play an important role in varicose pathology: DPV, Hunter's perforating veins, BPV, Sherman's perforating vein, CPV, HPPV, PPV, MPV, and lateral perforating vein.
2. Secondary perforating vein insufficiency in primary varicosis with or without deep venous reflux (e.g., CPV). If the primary varicosis is not operated on in time, sec-

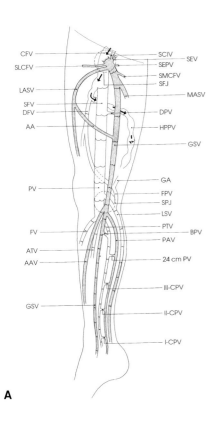

A

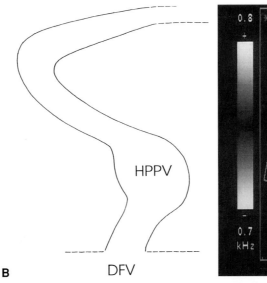

B

HPPV

DFV

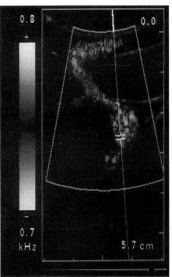

C

FIG. 41. Hach profound perforating vein varicosis: diagram **(A)** and duplex ultrasound image **(B)**. (See Color Plate 14.)

ondary popliteal and femoral vein insufficiency with all the symptoms of CVI and secondary perforating vein insufficiency occurs.

3. Secondary perforating vein insufficiency in the post-thrombotic syndrome. According to this classification of perforating vein insufficiency, dissection of the insufficient perforating vein is not always necessary. The increased venous pressure present in primary varicosis

probably causes the secondary perforating vein insufficiency. If the deep venous system is still normal and there is no "blow-out" after operating on the insufficient GSV, the insufficient perforating vein usually normalizes. In this situation, neither epifascial dissection nor subfascial endoscopy is recommended. On the other hand, if deep venous reflux is also present, the dissection of the insufficient perforating vein (epifascial dissection

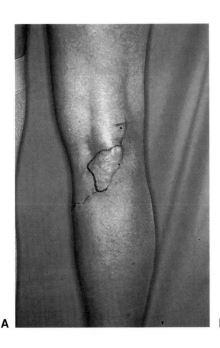

A

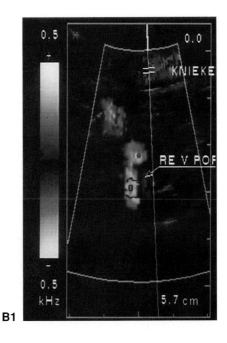

B1

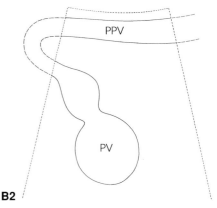

B2

FIG. 42. Popliteal perforating vein (PPV) varicosis: clinical picture **(A)** and duplex ultrasound image **(B)**. (See Color Plate 15.)

TABLE 33-11. *Treatment modalities of the perforating vein insufficiency (PVI)*

	Sclerotherapy	Epifascial/subfascial dissection	Subfascial endoscopy
Primary PVI			
Small caliber and no reflux	(+)	+	−
Big caliber ± deep reflux	−	+	−
Secondary PVI in primary varicosis			
With deep venous reflux ± blow out	(+)	+	+
No deep venous reflux, no blow out	−	−	−
Secondary PVI	−	+	+

+ = Treatment of choice.
(+) = Can be performed.
− = Unnecessary or not recommended.

or subfascial endoscopy) is advisable (Table 33-11). Perform epifascial dissection of an insufficient perforating vein by using 2- to 3-mm incisions as in the phlebectomy technique (Muller, Oesch, Ramelet, or Varady) or employing slightly longer incisions as with the ringhook method of Feuerstein. Put the perforating vein under torsion until it breaks. To prevent bleeding, apply digital pressure immediately. Primary perforating vein insufficiency can be treated using sclerotherapy if the perforator is of a small caliber or if there is no reflux present in the tributaries' deep veins. Otherwise, dissection of the perforating vein followed by phlebectomy of the superficial tributaries is the alternative treatment for perforating veins of a large caliber or those in which deep reflux is present.

Side-Branch Varicosis

Isolated side-branch varicosis is more often of the transfascial type than of the extrafascial type. The transfascial type represents an isolated perforating varicosis without connection to the GSV or LSV. Varicosis of the LASV ascending from the lateral aspect of the calf, passing the knee into the thigh, and entering the CFV is a typical situation of side-branch varicosis of the transfascial type. Phlebectomy of the side branch with dissection of the transfascial communication can be performed, as well as sclerotherapy. The varicose pudendal veins are avulsed by phlebectomy at as high a level as possible and ruptured proximally by twisting, a maneuver that stops the bleeding. For treatment of the extrafascial type of side-branch varicosis, phlebectomy or sclerotherapy may be performed.

Minisurgical Phlebectomy

Minisurgical phlebectomy (also known as hook phlebectomy) is an alternative procedure to sclerotherapy. Unlike sclerotherapy, hook phlebectomy may be performed with very pleasing results on the dorsal aspect of the foot, around the ankle, in the popliteal fossa, or over the anterior aspect of the knee. Pinpoint all the veins to be removed by minisurgical phlebectomy preoperatively directly over the vein. During the surgery the patient is prone with slightly elevated legs to prevent bleeding. As a local anesthetic, use tumescent anesthesia with Klein solution. First, perform the ligation of the transfascial communication. If there is a complete insufficiency of the GSV, perform the crossectomy first. By performing this ligation first, bleeding and possible mobilization of thrombus in the deep venous system are avoided. If both crossectomy and stripping have to be performed, perform the minisurgical phlebectomy after crossectomy but before stripping. In this way, compression bandages can be applied immediately after stripping. Then perform the phlebectomy beginning from the dorsal aspect of the foot and continuing up toward the thigh. Place the very small 1- to 2-mm incisions vertically to the limb quite close to the marked varices or between the pinpoints. Only in the popliteal fossa or on the anterior aspect of the knee are the stab incisions oriented horizontally. Because the subcutaneous layer on the dorsal aspect of the foot is very thin, it is recommended that a skin fold be pulled up to make the incision. The size of

FIG. 43. Minute incision using the tip of the No. 11 blade.

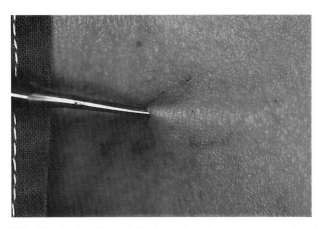

FIG. 44. Using the phlebodissector, the veins are isolated in both directions.

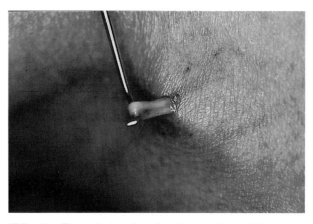

FIG. 46. The vein is gripped and teased out with a hook.

the incision depends on the size of the varicose vein, the thickness of the vein wall, and its adherence to surrounding tissue (Fig. 43). Avoid trauma to the edges of the incision and laceration to the skin. It is better to lengthen an incision if it is inadequate. The veins over the tibia or on the anterior aspect of the knee are very difficult to hook because they are firmly embedded in the subcutaneous tissue. Here the Varady phlebodissector is very helpful to dissect the vein from the surrounding tissue (Fig. 44). Make one incision at a time, and place the next one at the most distant point where the vein, kept under traction, is palpable as a hard cord through the skin (Fig. 45). Throughout the procedure, the veins are first isolated in both directions using the Varady phlebodissector. With the Muller, Ramelet, or Oesch phlebectomy hooks, mobilize the vein. The vein can be identified as a rolling string when pushing the tip of the hook against your finger. With the help of the Varady phlebextractor or another hook, grip and tease the vein out (Fig. 46). Make sure that the hooked white structure is a vein, since nerves and veins may be difficult to distinguish from each other. When operating with the patient under local anesthesia,

grasping a sensory nerve will cause pain or an "electric shock" sensation. Divide the exteriorized vein loop, and avulse both ends separately. Seize the veins with clamps. and slowly pull them out with a linear traction or a gentle "to-and-fro" rocking movement, or even twist them on the grasping clamp. These movements will detach the vein from the perivenous tissue and exteriorize additional lengths of the varicose veins. With the help of the other hand, pull the skin over the vein to facilitate further detachment of the vein. Place the next stab incision where the palpatory cordlike vein is felt, and hook the counterpart of the vein. For large varicose veins, use 14-cm hemostatic forceps because they grasp better, do not break the vein, and permit a stronger traction. It is possible to remove very long segments with a single incision, but normally the veins will break after a few centimeters (Fig. 47). Using the No. 3 Oesch hook or the Ramelet fine hook, which have the finest tips, phlebectomy is possible through an incision made with a 1.2-mm injection needle. In hook phlebectomy, close the veins by external depression and make no ligatures. Leave open the stab incisions. Cover with sterile absorbent pads or Op-site dressing. Apply a firm compressive bandage on the leg.

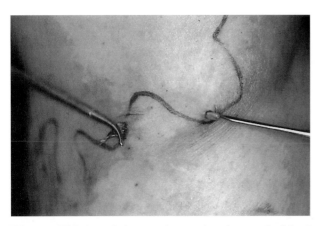

FIG. 45. With the vein kept under traction, the next incision is placed at the most distant point where the vein is still palpable.

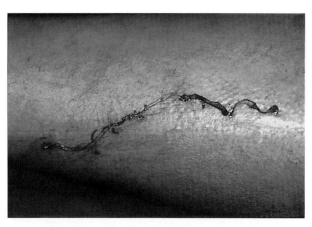

FIG. 47. Vein segments after phlebectomy.

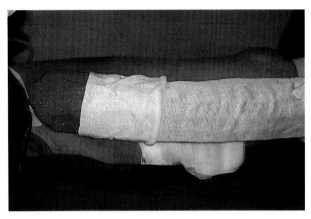

FIG. 48. Compression pads made of foam rubber for additional compression of the tunnel remaining after the stripping of the GSV.

TABLE 33-12. *Adverse sequelae and complications*

Injury to the common femoral vein
Injury to the common femoral artery
Injury to the saphenous or sural nerves
Bleeding, hematoma, ecchymosis
Infections
Lymphocele
Persisting edema
Thrombophlebitis
Telangiectatic matting
Hypertrophic and pigmented scars

POSTOPERATIVE MANAGEMENT

After stripping the GSV, a small towel is rolled from the knee up to the groin over the remaining space to press out any residual blood through the groin incision. The space is compressed until the compression bandage is completed. However, this is not necessary if operating with the Löfqvist tourniquet. After crossectomy and stripping of the GSV, a compression bandage up to the groin should be applied with additional compression pads (made of foam rubber with oblique edges) for the tunnel remaining after the stripping of the GSV (Fig. 48). The bandage used must have a short, two-way stretch capability offering a high pressure when the patient is upright or standing. Depending on the length of a leg, usually one 8-cm bandage, two 10-cm bandages, and a 12-cm-wide bandage are used. The Löfqvist tourniquet is now rolled off over the compression bandage. The incision in the groin is closed with buried sutures with 5-0 Vicryl, and a big gauze pad is placed over the groin incision. The compression bandage is secured with a 10-cm-wide adhesive elastic bandage (Tricoplast) applied in spiral, overlapping loops from the medial aspect of the thigh around the anterior, lateral, and posterior aspect of the thigh over the last 20 cm of the thigh, crossed over the groin, and finished over the iliac crest (Fig. 49). The patient can now leave the operating room. Even when operating on outpatients, prophylaxis against thrombosis is recommended for 1 to 5 days depending on the patient. The compression bandage is followed after 1 week by class 2 (30 mm Hg) compression stockings for a further period of at least 3 weeks.

ADVERSE SEQUELAE AND COMPLICATIONS

During or after surgery the following complications may occur: injury to the common femoral vein and artery, injury to the saphenous or sural nerves, and bleeding, which mostly appears immediately following surgery (Table 33-12). The patient is asked to walk for 10 minutes in the clinic and is observed for at least 1 hour after surgery. If bleeding does occur, an additional compressive bandage is applied on top of the already existing one. Significant hematoma formation is unusual, but ecchymosis is almost always present. Locally enhanced compression and lymphatic drainage will speed reabsorption of hematoma. Large hematomas, however, should be evacuated. Tumescent anesthesia and liposuction cannulas can be used to aspirate the hematomas (Fig. 50). Local infiltra-

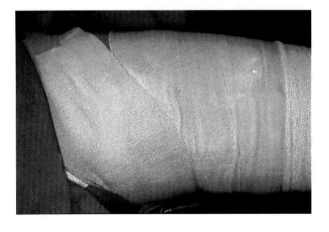

FIG. 49. Compression bandages complete with an additional adhesive elastic bandage.

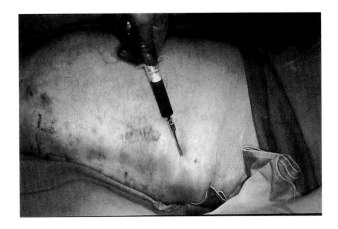

FIG. 50. Extensive hematomas caused by unallowed removal of the compressive bandages on the same day as the operation. The blood is aspirated with liposuction canulas.

tion anesthetic close to the head of the fibula may reach the fibularis nerve (the motor branch of the external sciatic-popliteal nerve) causing ''foot drop'' and creating ambulatory problems. Permanent nerve injury can occur if a nerve is hooked out and avulsed. Infections are rare because the incisions and the tissue trauma are minimal, hematoma is limited, and the compression bandages all have an antiinflammatory effect. In day-surgery clinics there are no drug-resistant, hospital-acquired infections. Lymphocele, a very rare complication, usually develops on the anteriolateral aspect of the lower leg. Horizontal incisions or avulsion of a lymphatic vessel by hook phlebectomy is the cause of this lymphocele. Evacuation by needle aspiration and local compression is the appropriate treatment. Persistent edema is seen only after aggressive surgery with multiple, big, and horizontal incisions.

Superficial thrombophlebitis may occur in residual side branches and must be treated with local compression and antiinflammatory drugs. The stab incisions after phlebectomy may persist as dark red scars for months after surgery. The real cause of telangiectatic matting has not yet been fully explained, but aggressive phlebectomy and stripping, as well as inflammation and neovascularization in scar tissue, seem to play a causative role. Stretch blisters occasionally occur next to the compression pads or under Steri-Strip and may leave a prolonged discoloration of the skin. They should only be punctured and covered with petrolatum gauze.

The latest diagnostic tools enable the phlebologist to make an accurate diagnosis and develop a treatment plan that will optimally combine surgery, sclerotherapy, and compression therapy to obtain the best functional and cosmetic results,

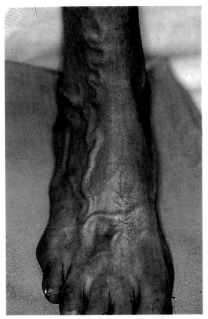
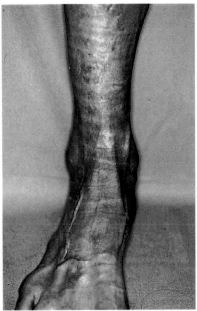

A   **B**

FIG. 51. Varicose veins on the dorsal aspect of the foot (**A**). Postoperative result 2 days after minisurgical phlebectomy and compressive bandages (**B**).

as well as minimize recurrences, morbidity, complications, and scarring. The combination of crossectomy and limited invaginated stripping of the GSV/LSV with minisurgical phlebectomy of the side branches results in a minimal complication rate and an excellent cosmetic result. PIN stripping is recommended in the stripping of the LSV and the partial resection of the GSV. The most elegant and atraumatic method for removal of varicose veins other than the saphenous veins is hook phlebectomy (Fig. 51A and B).

ACKNOWLEDGMENTS

I would like to thank Mr. D. Thompson, Dr. M. P. Goldman, Dr. P. Campion, and Mrs. L. Ault for their help in editing the manuscript, and Mr. J. Dunst for the outstanding diagrams.

SUGGESTED READING LIST

PART 1

1. Bodian EL. Techniques of sclerotherapy for sunburst venous blemishes. J Dermatol Surg Oncol 1985;11:696.
2. Duffy DM. Small vessel sclerotherapy: an overview. Adv Deermatol 1988;3:221.
3. Engel A, Johnson ML, Haynes SG. Health effects of sunlight exposure in the United States: results from the first national health and nutrition examination survey, 1971–1974. Arch Dermatol 1988;124:72.
4. Fegan WG. Continuous compression technique of injecting varicose veins. Lancet 1963;2:109.
5. Fegan WG. Varicose veins: compression sclerotherapy. London: William Heinemann Medical Books, 1967.
6. Fronek A. Noninvasive diagnostics in vascular disease. New York: McGraw-Hill, 1989.
7. Goldman MP. Sclerotherapy of superficial venules and telangiectasias of the lower extremities. Dermatol Clin 1987;5:369.
8. Goldman MP. Compression in the treatment of leg telangiectasia: theoretical considerations. J Dermatol Surg Oncol 1989;15:184.
9. Goldman MP. Postsclerotherapy hyperpigmentation: treatment with a flashlamp-excited pulsed-dye laser. J Dermatol Surg Oncol 1992;18:417.
10. Goldman MP. Sclerotherapy: Sclerotherapy: treatment of varicose and telangiectatic leg veins. 2nd ed. St. Louis: Mosby, 1995.
11. Goldman MP, Beaudoing D, Marley W, Lopez L, Butie A. Compression in the treatment of leg telangiectasia: a preliminary report. J Dermatol Surg Oncol 1990;16:322.
12. Goldman MP, Bennett RG. Treatment of telangiectasia: a review. J Am Acad Dermatol 1987;17:167.
13. Goldman MP, Fitzpatrick RE. Pulsed-dye laser treatment of leg telangiectasia: with and without simultaneous sclerotherapy. J Dermatol Surg Oncol 1990;16:338.
14. Goldman MP, Kaplan RP, Duffy DM. Postsclerotherapy hyperpigmentation: a histologic evaluation. J Dermatol Surg Oncol 1987;13:547.
15. Goldman MP, Kaplan RP, Oki LN, et al. Extravascular effects of sclerosants in rabbit skin: a clinical and histologic examination. J Dermatol Surg Oncol 1986;12:1085.
16. Goldman MP, Weiss RA, Bergan JJ. Diagnosis and treatment of varicose veins: a review. J Am Acad Dermatol 1994;31:393.
17. Henry MEF, Corless C. The incidence of varicose veins in Ireland. Phlebology 1989;4:133.
18. Hobbs JT. The treatment of varicose veins: a random trial of injection/compression versus surgery. Br J Surg 1968;55:777.
19. Hobbs JT. Surgery and sclerotherapy in the treatment of varicose veins: a random trial. Arch Surg 1974;109:793.
20. Hobbs JT. Compression sclerotherapy in venous insufficiency. Acta Chir Scand Suppl 1988;544:75.
21. Neglen P. Treatment of varicosities of saphenous origin: comparison of ligation, selective excision, and sclerotherapy. In: Bergan JJ, Goldman MP, eds. Varicose veins and telangiectasias: diagnosis and treatment. St. Louis: Quality Medical, 1993;148.
22. Orbach EJ. A new approach to the sclerotherapy of varicose veins. Angiology 1950;1:302.
23. Sigg K. The treatment of varicosities and accompanying complications. Angiology 1952;3:355.
24. Somjen GM, Ziegenbein R, Johnston AH, Royle JP. Anatomical examination of leg telangiectases with duplex scanning. J Dermatol Surg Oncol 1993;19:940.
25. Thibault P, Bray A, Wlodarczyk J, Lewis W. Cosmetic leg veins: evaluation using duplex venous imaging. J Dermatol Surg Oncol 1990;16:612.
26. Weiss RA. Evaluation of the venous system by Doppler ultrasound and photoplethysmography or light reflection rheography before sclerotherapy. Semin Dermatol 1993;12:78.
27. Weiss RA, Weiss MA. Resolution of pain associated with varicose andtelangiectatic leg veins after compression sclerotherapy. J Dermatol Surg Oncol 1990;16:333.
28. Weiss RA, Weiss MA. Painful telangiectasias: diagnosis and treatment. In: Bergan JJ, Goldman MP, eds. Varicose veins and telangiectasias: diagnosis and treatment. St. Louis: Quality Medical, 1993;389.
29. Weiss RA, Weiss MA. Doppler ultrasound findings in reticular veins of the thigh subdermic lateral venous system and implications for sclerotherapy. J Dermatol Surg Oncol 1993;19:947.
30. Weiss RA, Weiss MA, Goldman MP. Physicians' negative perception of sclerotherapy for venous disorders: review of a 7-year experience with modern sclerotherapy. South Med J 1992;85:1101.
31. Widmer LK. Peripheral venous disorders: prevalence and sociomedical importance of observations in 4529 apparently healthy persons. Basle Study. III. Bern, Stuttgart, Vienna: Hans Huber Publishers, 1978.

PART 2

1. Albanese AR, Albanese AM, Albanese EF. Lateral subdermic varicose vein system of the legs: its surgical treatment by the chiseling tube method. Vasc Surg 1969;3:81.
2. Bergan JJ. Surgical procedures for varicose veins: axial stripping and stab avulsion. In: Atlas of venous surgery. Bergan JJ, Kistner RL, eds. Philadelphia: WB Saunders, 1992:61.
3. Bishop CC, Jarrett PEM. Outpatient varicose vein surgery under local anaesthesia. Br J Surg 198;73:821.
4. Conrad P. Groin-to-knee downward stripping of the long saphenous vein. Phlébologie 1992;7:20.
5. Corbett CR, Njayakumar K. Cleanup varicose vein surgery: use of a tourniquet. Ann R Coll Surg Engl 1989;71:57.
6. Corbett CR, Runcie JJ, Lea Thomas M, et al. Reasons to strip the long saphenous vein. Phlébologie 1988;41:766.
7. Dieudonne G. Les saphenectomies par invagination sur fil sous anesthésie locale. Phlébologie 1988;41:309.
8. Dodd H. The varicose tributaries of the superficial femoral vein passing into Hunter's canal. Postgrad Med 1959;35:18.
9. Dortu J, Dortu J-A. Les veines honteuses externes. Phlébologie 1990;43:329.
10. Fawer R, Dettling A, Weihs D, et al. Effect of menstrual cycle, oral contraception, and pregnancy on forearm blood flow, venous distensibility, and clotting factors. Eur J Clin Pharmacol 1978;13:251.
11. Fischer R. Die Resultate der Strippingoperation bei der Vena saphena parva. Vasa 1987;16:349.
12. Fischer R. Die chirurgische Behandlung der Varizen. Grundlagen und heutiger Stand. Praxis 1990;79:155.
13. Fischer R. Eine neue Generation der Varizenchirurgie? Vasa 1991;20:311.
14. Fischer R, Füllemann HJ, Alder W. Zum phlebologischen Dogma der Prädilektionsstellen der Cockett schen Venae perforantes. Phlébologie 1987;16:184.
15. Fischer, R, Sattler G. Die Indikation zur subfaszialen Endoskopie der Cockett schen Vene perforantes. Phlébologie 1994;23:174.
16. Fratila A, Rabe E. The differentiated surgical treatment of primary varicosis. Semin Dermatol 1993;12:102.
17. Fratila A, Rabe E, Kreysel HW. Percutaneous minisurgical phlebectomy. Semin Dermatol 1993;12:117.
18. Goldman MP. Schlerotherapy: treatment of varicose and telangiectatic leg veins. 2nd ed. St. Louis: Mosby, 1995.

19. Goldman MP, Weiss RA, Bergan JJ. Diagnosis and treatment of varicose veins: a review. J Am Acad Dermatol 1994;31:393.

20. Goren G, Yellin AE. Primary varicose veins: topographic and hemodynamic correlations. J Cardiovasc Surg 1990;31:672.

21. Goren G, Yellin AE. Minimally invasive surgery for primary varicose veins: limited invaginated axial stripping and tributary (hook) stab avulsion. Ann Vasc Surg 1995;9:401.

22. Greenhalgh RM. Vascular surgical techniques. Philadelphia: WB Saunders, 1989.

23. Grundersen J, Hauge M. Hereditary factors in venous insufficiency. Angiology 1969;20:346.

24. Hach W. Spezielle Diagnostik der primaren Varikose. Gräfelfing: Demeter, 1982.

25. Hach W. Phlebographie der Bein- und Beckenvenen. Konstanz: Schnetztor, 1985.

26. Hach W. Primäre Varikose, Moderne Aspekte der chirurgischen Therapie. Dt Ärztebl 1988;85(43):2075.

27. Hauer G. Diagnostik und chrirurgische Therapie der Varikosis. Herz 1989;14(5):274.

28. Hauser M, Brunner U. Neue pathophysiologische und funktionelle Gesichtspunkte zur Insuffizienz der Vena saphena parva: Vorläufige Mitteilung. Vasa 1993;22:338.

29. Hobbs JT. The treatment of varicose veins: a random trial of injection/compression versus surgery. Br J Surg 1968;55:777.

30. Hobbs JT. Surgery and sclerotherapy in the treatment of varicose veins: a random trial. Arch Surg 1974;109:793.

31. Hübner K. Ambulante Therapie der Stammvarikose mittels Krossektomie und Sklerotherapie. Phlébologie 1991;20:85.

32. Kluess HG, Fratila A, Rabe E, Kreysel HW. Sanierung des Ulcus cruris venosum durch die paratibiale Fasziotomie. In: Mahrle G, et al., eds. Fortschritte der operativen und onkologischen Dermatologie. Band 8. Berlin, Heidelberg, New York: Springer, 1994;219.

33. Lea Thomas M, Chan O: Anatomical variations of the short saphenous vein: a phlebographic study. Vasa 1988;17:51.

34. MacFarlin R, Godwin RJ, Barabas AP. Are varicose veins and coronary artery bypass surgery compatible? Lancet 1985;1:859.

35. Marin ML, Veith FJ, Panetta TF, et al. Saphenous vein biopsy: a predictor of vein graft failure. J Vasc Surg 1993;18:407.

36. May R, Nissl R. Die Phlebographie der unteren Extremitäten. Stuttgart: Georg Thieme, 1973.

37. McMullin GM, Coleridge-Smith PD, Scurr JH. Objective assessment of high ligation without stripping the long saphenous vein. Br J Surg 1991;78:1139.

38. Munn SR, Morton JB, MacBeth Waag, et al.. To strip or not to strip the long saphenous vein? A varicose vein trial. Br J Surg 1981;68:426.

39. Neglen P. Treatment of varicosities of saphenous origin: comparison of ligation, selective excision, and sclerotherapy. In: Bergan JJ, Goldman MP, eds. Varicose veins and telangiectasias: diagnosis and management. St. Louis: Quality Medical, 1993;148.

40. Oesch A. PIN stripping. Phlébologie (in press).

41. Partsch H. Primäre Varikose der Vena saphena magna und parva. In: Kriessmann A, Bollinger A, Keller HM, eds. Praxis der Doppler-Sonographie. Stuttgart: Thieme, 1990;109.

42. Rabe E, Fratila A. Doppler-sonography, duplex- and photoplethysmography in chronic venous diseases. Personal Communication, ISDS Budapest 1995.

42. Rabe E, Fratila A, Kluess H, Kreysel HW. Color-duplex investigations of insufficient perforating veins at the lower leg. In: Raymond-Martimbeau P, Prescott R, Zummo M, eds. Phlébologie. Paris: John Libbey Eurotext, 1992:574.

44. Rabe E, Fratila A, Stranzenbach W, Kreysel HW. Die pudendale Varicosis. Phlébologie. 1991;20:222.

45. Rabe E, Fratila A, Stranzenbach W, et al. Wertigkeit der farbkodierten Duplex-Sonographie in der Diagnostik der chronischen venösen Insuffizienz. Phlébologie 1992;21:130.

46. Rabe E, Gallenkemper G, Kluess H, Kreysel HW. Duplex-scanning of the direction of the saphenopopliteal junction. Phlébologie 1995; 10(suppl 1):245.

47. Ramelet A-A. Müller phlebectomy: a new phlebectomy hook. J Dermatol Surg Oncol 1991;17:814.

48. Ramelet A-A. Die Behandlung der Besenreiservarizen: Indikationen der Phlebektomie nach Müller. Phlébologie. 1993;22:163.

49. Ramelet A-A, Monti M. Phlébologie. Paris, Milan: Masson, 1994.

50. Ricci S, Georgiev M, Goldmann MP. Ambulatory phlebectomy: practical guide for treating varicose veins. St. Louis: Mosby, 1995.

51. Ruckley CV. Surgical management of venous disease. London: Wolfe Medical, 1988.

52. Sarin S, Scurr JH, Coleridge-Smith PD. Assessment of stripping the long saphenous vein in the treatment of primary varicose veins. Br J Surg 1992;79:889.

53. Sattler G, Mössler K, Hagedorn M. Endoscopic perforating vein dissection and paratibial fasciotomy for the treatment of the venous ulcer. In: Raymond-Martimbeau P, Prescott R, Zummo M, eds. Phlébologie. Paris. John Libbey Eurotext, 1992;1089.

54. Sattler G, Mösler K, Hagedorn M. Prophylaxe und Therapie des Ulcus cruris: endoskopische Perforansvenendiszision und antegrade paratibiale Fasziotomie. In: Mahrle G, et al., eds. Fortschritte der operativen und onkologischen Dermatologie, Band 8. Berlin, Heidelberg, New York: Springer, 1994:225.

55. Schadeck M. Duplex and Phlebology. Napoli: Gnocchi, 1994

56. Schultz-Ehrenburg U, Hübner HJ. Reflux diagnostik mit Doppler Ultraschall. Stuttgart: Schattauer, 1987.

57. Sheppard M. The incidence, diagnosis and management of saphenopopliteal incompetence. Phlébologie 1986;1:23.

58. Shouler PJ, Runchman PC. Varicose veins: optimum compression after surgery and sclerotherapy. Ann R Coll Surg Engl 1989;71:402.

59. Sommoggy St v, Dörrler J, Maurer PC. Chirurgische Therapie der Varikosis. Chir Praxis 1991;43:507.

60. Staubesand J, Stemmer R. Etudes anatomiques sur la constance des perforantes de Cockett. Phlébologie 1987;40:599.

61. Stemmer R. Die Varizenverödung. St. Gallen: Ganzoni and Cie, 1988.

62. Stemmer R. Postoperative Kompressionstherapie in der Venenchirurgie. Med Welt 1989;40:59.

63. Thompson H. The surgical anatomy of the superficial and perforating veins of the lower limb. Ann R Coll Surg Engl 1979;61:198.

64. Trempe J. Long-term results of sclerotherapy and surgical treatment of the short saphenous vein. J Dermatol Surg Oncol 1991;17:597.

65. van der Stricht J. Saphénectomy par invagination sur fil. Press Med 1963;71:1081.

66. van der Stricht J. La saphène externe, son passé, son avenir. Phlébologie 1993;46:539.

67. van Limborgh J. L anatomie du système veineux de l'extremité inférieure en relation avec la pathologie variqueuse. Folia Angiol 1961; 8:240.

68. van Limborgh J, Banga DA, Meijerink CJH, Luigies JHH. Démonstration d un modèle anatomique des veines de l extrémité inférieure. Phlébologie 1961;14:175.

69. Vanscheidt W, Partsch H. Diagnostic procedures. In: Westerhof W, ed. Leg ulcers: diagnosis and treatment. Amsterdam: Elsevier, 1993: 65.

70. Weiss RA. Evaluation of the venous system by Doppler ultrasound and photoplethysmography or light reflection rheography before sclerotherapy. Semin Dermatol 1993;12:78.

71. Weiss RA. Vascular studies of the legs for venous or arterial disease. Dermatol Clin 1994;12:175.

72. Weiss RA, Weiss MA. Painful telngiectasias: diagnosis and treatment. In: Bergan JJ, Goldman MP, eds. Varicose veins and telangiectasias: diagnosis and treatment. St. Louis: Quality Medical, 1993;389.

73. Wuppermann T. Varizen, Ulcus cruris und Thrombose. Berlin: Springer, 1986.

APPENDIX

Abbreviations

AA—Accessory anastomosis

AAV—Anterior arch vein

ATV—Anterior tibial veins

BPV—Boyd's perforating vein

CFV—Common femoral vein

CPV—Cockett's perforating veins

CVI—Chronic vein insufficiency

DPI—Distal point of insufficiency

DPV–Dodd's perforating veins
FPV–Femoropopliteal vein
GA–Giacomini anastomosis
GSV–Greater saphenous vein
HPPV–Hach profound perforating vein
IA–Intersaphenous anastomosis
LASV–Lateral accessory saphenous vein
LSV–Lesser saphenous vein

MASV–Medial accessory saphenous vein
MPV–May's perforating vein
PAV–Posterior arch vein
PPI–Proximal point of insufficiency
PPV–Popliteal perforating vein
PV–Popliteal vein
SFJ–Saphenofemoral junction
SPJ–Saphenopopliteal junction

Textbook of Dermatologic Surgery, edited by John L. Ratz.
Lippincott–Raven Publishers, Philadelphia © 1998.

CHAPTER 34

Nail Surgery

Deborah F. MacFarlane and Richard K. Scher

HISTORY

Until recently, the possibility of surgical correction of nail deformities had been limited. Over the past decade, however, the application of plastic and hand surgery techniques has allowed the practice of nail surgery to expand greatly. Approximately 5% to 10% of all new patient visits to cutaneous surgeons are for nail problems, and it behooves the dermatologist to be familiar with this type of surgery.

The objectives of nail surgery are primarily fourfold:

1. Pain relief
2. Treatment of infection
3. Correction of anatomic deformity
4. Exposure of subungual conditions for biopsy, anatomic delineation, or excision

Deborah F. MacFarlane.: Department of Dermatology, Oklahoma University Health Sciences, 619 Northeast 13th St, Oklahoma City, OK 73104.

Richard K. Scher: Department of Dermatology, Columbia University, 25 Sutton Place, South, New York, NY 10022.

PREOPERATIVE PLANNING

Patient Evaluation and Consent

A complete history should be taken and a physical examination performed preoperatively. The medical history should include details of illness causing nail dysfunction, previous surgical procedures, current medications, and drug allergies. Monoamine oxidase inhibitors, β-blockers, or phenothiazines may affect anesthesia; aspirin or anticoagulants may prolong bleeding; systemic or topical steroids may delay healing. Antitetanus immunization status should be ascertained. An accurate preoperative diagnosis and patient evaluation are necessary. Peripheral vascular disease, diabetes mellitus, and moderately severe distal interphalangeal arthritis increase the morbidity for surgical manipulation of the nail unit. Preoperative evaluation may require laboratory tests, including complete blood cell count with platelets, prothrombin time, partial thromboplastin time, serum electrolyte levels, and renal function.

The objectives and possible side effects of the surgical procedure, as well as photography (**see Chapter 8**), when performed, should be discussed in detail with the patient before surgery.

Instrumentation

- A Freer septum elevator or dental spatula may beused to separate the nail plate from the underlying nail bed and the overlying proximal nail fold.
- A nail splitter is useful for partial longitudinal nail avulsion and is designed so that the lower blade has a smooth anvil-like surface that glides atraumatically along the nail bed, while the upper surface, resembling a scissors, cuts through the nail plate.
- Nail nippers: Dual action (bone rongeur).
- Punch biopsies (disposable).
- Skin hooks.
- Tourniquet: A Penrose drain (⅜ inch) secured with a hemostat at the finger base provides a safe tourniquet for the critical 15 minutes most operations take. The tourniquet should be released every 10 minutes. As an alternative, a strip of rubber cut from a glove can be wrapped around the digit in question in an exsanguinating manner, and its edges rolled to form a band. Many nail procedures, however, may be performed easily even without a tournquet.

Radiographs

Preoperative radiographic studies should be obtained when the condition may possibly involve the bony structure of the phalanx.

Positioning and Preparation of Patient

To avoid a possible vasovagal response, patients should be placed in a reclining or supine position. The limb or digit in question should be cleansed well and a sterile field used during the surgical procedure.

Sedation and Anesthesia

Preoperative sedation may be given the evening before and repeated 2 hours before surgery. In many cases, no sedation is required.

The use of a 30-gauge needle and slow infusion of the anesthetic agent minimizes pain. Five to 10 minutes should be allowed for the anesthesia to take full effect. A 1% to 2% solution of lidocaine provides excellent anesthesia. Because of the possibility of unexplained local ischemia, it is advisable that epinephrine-free anesthetic be used. Bupivacaine (Marcaine) and 1% prilocaine (Citanest) provide longer-acting anesthesia of 1 to 2 hours, and carbocaine is useful in patients allergic to lidocaine.

Traditionally, anesthesia of the nail unit has been achieved by the use of distal or proximal digital nerve block.

Distal Digital Nerve Block

A distal digital nerve block is useful for procedures on the nail fold or matrix and anesthetizes the terminal transverse and descending branch of the digital nerve. The anesthetic is injected 3 mm proximal to the junction of the proximal and lateral nail folds. Additional increments of 0.5 ml of 1% lidocaine at 5-ml intervals across the nail fold may be needed for complete anesthesia.

Proximal Digital Nerve Block

The proximal digital nerve block anesthetizes the dorsal and ventral digital sensory nerves near the base of the digit. Anesthesia is introduced below the dermis, beginning midway between the dorsal and ventral aspects of the digit and injecting radially from the dorsal to the palmar aspect of the digit. Dorsal and palmar digital nerves on the medial and lateral aspects of the digit are anesthetized by injecting approximately 1 ml of anesthetic into each side of the digit.

Perionychial Nerve Block

In this method, the first injection is placed at the junction of the proximal and lateral nail folds, proceeds across the proximal nail fold to the contralateral side, and then extends distally along the lateral nail folds bilaterally. An additional amount of anesthesia may be injected into the distal tip of the digit to ensure complete anesthesia (Fig. 1).

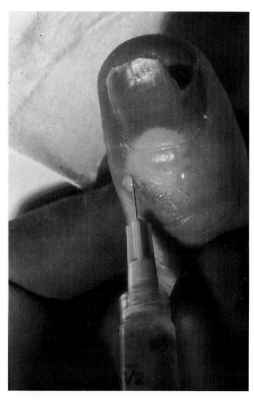

FIG. 1. Local perionychial block anesthesia.

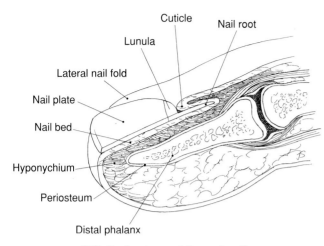

FIG. 2. Anatomy of the nail unit.

Cuticle
Nail root
Lunula
Lateral nail fold
Nail plate
Nail bed
Hyponychium
Periosteum
Distal phalanx

Antibiotics

Preoperative antibiotics should be used if active infection is present and may be given the evening before surgery.

ANATOMY

It is essential that the surgeon be familiar with the anatomy of the nail. The various anatomic parts of the nail unit include the following (Fig. 2):

Nail plate: An oblong, keratin plate that sits in the nail folds, bordered by them laterally and proximally, and is adherent to the underlying nail matrix and bed.

Perionychium: Consists of the soft tissue surrounding the nail plate and includes the proximal and lateral nail.

Nail bed: The soft tissue beneath the nail plate from the lunula to the hyponychium. It is adherent to the nail plate and has no granular layer or subcutaneous fat.

Nail matrix: The germinative epithelium responsible for the nail plate that is found deep beneath the cuticle and separated from the distal phalanx by only a few millimeters. This structure also has no granular layer or subcutaneous fat. The lunula is the distal matrix visible from the nail surface.

Hyponychium: Has a granular layer, like normal skin, and begins at the point of separation between the nail plate and nail bed and terminates at the distal nail groove.

Blood Supply

The blood supply to the nails is derived from two arches, proximal and distal, that originate in turn from digital arteriesin the pulp space below the distal phalanx. A branch of the digital artery also runs dorsally over the distal interphalangeal joint to anastamose with the proximal arch.

Venous drainage is by the combination of veins on either side of the nail plate lying within the proximal nail fold. Long, thin-walled vessels are found beneath the hyponychium, and rupture of these allows blood to fill the longitudinal channels of the nail bed, resulting in splinter hemorrhages.

Nerve Supply

The nerve supply of the nail unit parallels that of the blood supply.

Physiology of Nail Plate Growth

The proximal matrix produces the dorsal nail plate, while the distal matrix produces the ventral nail plate.

TECHNIQUE

Nail Avulsion

The purpose of nail plate avulsion is to expose the nail bed and matrix in order to perform a matricectomy or bed or matrix biopsy and to treat onychomycosis, chronic mucocutaneous candidiasis, or ingrown nails (Fig. 3). Avulsion is not curative for onychodystrophy attributable to matrix

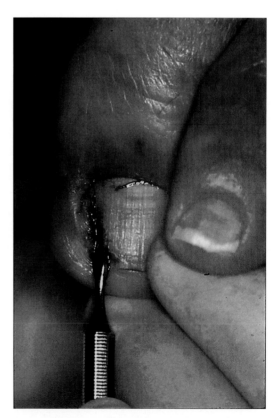

FIG. 3. Longitudinal strip avulsion of nail plate for recalcitrant ingrown toenail.

disease, ingrown toenails, or large nail bed defects. Repeated nail avulsion may, in fact, cause thickening and overcurvature of the nails, as well as impaction of the plate against the digit. Avulsion of the nail plate may be partial or total. In partial avulsion, longitudinal strips of nail plate are removed from underlying structures, as in the treatment of ingrown toenails. In total nail avulsion, the entire nail plate is removed. The nail plate must be separated from two points of attachment—the nail bed and the proximal nail fold.

In the usual distal approach, introduce the Freer elevator under the free edge of the nail plate and push proximally. Resistance is felt until the matrix area is reached, where the resistance is weaker. It is important not to push the elevator into the proximal nail groove, causing injury. Insert the elevator in a longitudinal manner until the nail plate is detached. Grasp the nail plate with a hemostat and remove with a circular motion.

Use the more difficult proximal approach when a cleavage plane cannot be found at the distal free edge or is obscured by a disease process such as distal subungual onychomycosis. Use the Freer elevator to loosen the proximal nail fold and to flip around the edge of the plate into the cleavage plane between the plate and the matrix. Insert the septum elevator in a ''backward'' direction so that it conforms to the curve of the nail bed after it is turned and directed distally. Then advance the elevator until it reaches the distal free edge. Gradually free the nail plate and remove with a hemostat.

Nail Matrix Exploration

To expose the nail matrix and proximal nail fold fully, make two full-thickness incisions laterally and proximally from a point where the lateral and proximal nail folds meet. To protect underlying structures, insert the Freer elevator into the proximal nail groove. Then retract the flap with either skin hooks or forceps to fully expose the matrix. Once surgery is completed, use sutures or Steri-Strips to fashion the flap back in place.

Biopsy of the Nail Unit

Nail unit biopsy may be needed to diagnose dermatosis, a chronic mycotic infection, or a tumor. A nail biopsy may also be curative for some of the tumors of the nail unit.

Nail Matrix

The indications for nail matrix biopsy are longitudinal hyperpigmented streaks in the nail plate, full-length nail plate deformities, and tumors of the matrix (Fig. 5). Small tumors can be removed with a 3-mm punch if the biopsy does not involve the proximal matrix, in which case a permanently split nail may result. Following anesthesia, expose the matrix by reflection of the proximal nail fold. To prevent permanent defects on the surface plate, avoid the most proximal matrix

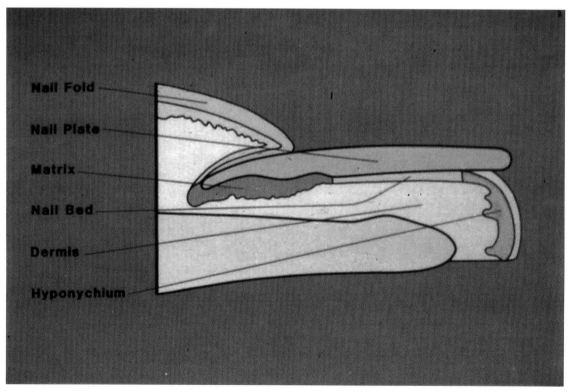

FIG. 4. Appearance of the nail matrix.

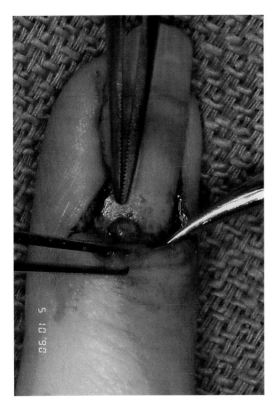

FIG. 5. Punch biopsy of nail matrix for melanonychia striata.

when possible (Fig. 4). To accurately position the biopsy, mark the proximal nail fold in line with the lesion. Following anesthesia, reflect the proximal nail fold to expose the entire matrix. For primary closure use a fine absorbable suture such as 5.0 polyglycolic acid or 6.0 surgical gut, plain type A. Repair the proximal nail fold with sutures or sterile Steri-Strips.

Nail Bed

Perform nail bed biopsy with or without avulsion of the nail plate. To avoid nail avulsion, make a sharp 3-mm punch through the nail until periosteum is met and the specimen recovered using Iris or Gradle scissors (Fig. 6). In the two-

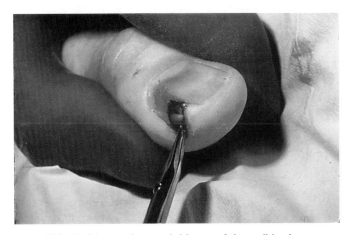

FIG. 6. Diagnostic punch biopsy of the nail bed.

punch technique, make a larger punch through the nail plate and a small punch through the nail bed, which makes it easier to collect the specimen. Use oxidized cellulose or aluminum chloride for hemostasis. To allow better visualization or to perform a larger nail bed biopsy, avulse the nail first. For small lesions use the punch technique; make an elliptical excision for larger lesions. Orient the ellipse longitudinally, and do not exceed 3 mm in width. Care is taken to avoid the matrix. Skewer the specimen with a 3-mm punch needle with the tip bent to provide a handle, which prevents specimen crushing and facilitates orientation by the laboratory.

En Bloc Nail Unit Biopsy

A biopsy of the entire nail unit, known as an ''en bloc'' or ''longitudinal resection,''is the removal of a tissue wedge that includes the nail fold, matrix, bed, and hyponychium. As well as providing a diagnosis for diseases such as lichen planus and Darier's disease, this technique can be used to diagnose and treat neoplastic processes and ingrown toenails. Essentially, make two parallel incisions from the proximal nail fold to the finger tip using a sterile, No. 15 scalpel. To prevent severe scarring, gently slide the blade tip over the bony phalanx. The distance between the incisions should not exceed 3 mm. Dissect the specimen with a pair of curved Iris scissors. Sutures may disturb the normal nail shape and are therefore unnecessary. An alternative is to avulse the nail, excise the specimen, undermine the edges, and primarily close the proximal nail fold, matrix, and hyponychium with fine sutures.

Matricectomy

Partial matricectomy is destruction of that part of the nail matrix responsible for causing disease and is used for the treatment of the ingrown toenail and pincer nail syndrome.

Use total matricectomy in extensive cases of onychomycosis, onychogryphosis, and other chronic, painful, or distorted nail growth conditions.

In a chemical matricectomy, anesthetize the digit, apply an exsanguinating tourniquet, and make a full-length, full-thickness split in the nail plate approximately 2 to 3 ml from the affected lateral nail fold. Ablate the matrix by firmly pressing cotton swabs saturated with phenol onto it for approximately 30 seconds. Dilute the phenol by flooding with isopropyl alcohol, and repeat these two steps. Repeat these two steps. Use Gelfoam pads to stop any significant bleeding. Apply a bulky dressing, and instruct the patient to keep the affected site elevated. The area should be cleansed daily with hydrogen peroxide followed by the application of an antibiotic ointment (Fig. 7).

In a total permanent matricectomy apply phenol to the entire matrix, including that beneath the proximal nail fold, and to both lateral nail horns.

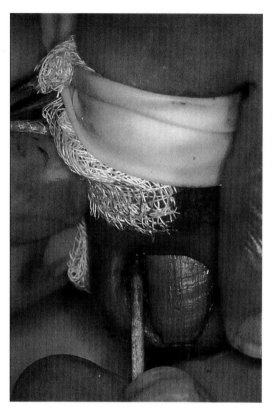

FIG. 7. Localized phenolization of the nail matrix.

Paronychial Surgery

The paronychial area includes the proximal and lateral nail folds. Diseases affecting this region that may require surgery include infections, inflammatory conditions, and benign and malignant tumors.

Incisional Biopsy

The incisional biopsy is most commonly used when diagnostic tissue is required from the proximal or lateral nail fold (Fig. 8).

An incisional biopsy of the proximal nail fold parallels the skin tension lines. Place the incision as far away as possible from the distal interphalangeal joint to avoid lacerating the tendon of extensor digitorum communis, which inserts onto the proximal dorsal portion of the terminal phalanx (Fig. 9). Make the incision down to periosteum, and close the lesion primarily with a nonreactive nylon suture to be removed in approximately 7 days. Divide the specimen and send portions for hematoxylin-eosin and periodic acid–Schiff staining, culture, and immunofluorescence.

Biopsy of the lateral nail fold should be performed in a longitudinal direction and down to periosteum. Closure is as described earlier. If the lesion extends into the lateral nailgroove or onto the nail bed, it will be necessary to remove the nail plate and obtain biopsy specimens from those areas.

Excisional Biopsy

En Bloc Excision of Proximal Nail Fold

Excisional biopsy of the proximal nail fold is especially useful in the treatment of myxoid cysts (Fig. 10). These dome-shaped, mucin-filled cysts compress the nail matrix and cause various dystrophies. Following local anesthesia, antiseptic preparation, and tourniquet application, insert a Freer septum elevator into the proximal nail groove and slide it below with the aid of a scalpel to avoid the chance of cutting too deeply into the nail matrix or the proximal extensor tendon. Hemostasis is with electrodesiccation or the use of Gelfoam. Instruct the patient to cleanse the wound twice daily with dilute hydrogen peroxide, apply an antibiotic ointment, and place a clean, bulky dressing. The proximal nail fold will be restored by secondary intention approximately 2 to 5 mm proximal to the original nail fold.

Lateral Nail Folds

Excisional surgery of the lateral nail fold is often used to remove the hypertrophic tissue attributable to chronically ingrown toenails. Cut the ingrowing area of the nail plate longitudinally from the free nail edge to the nail plate be-

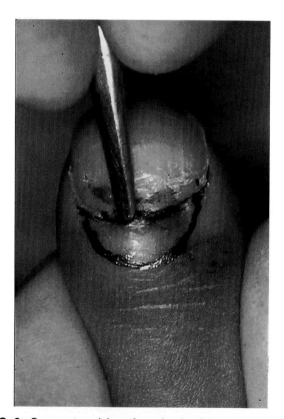

FIG. 8. Crescent excision of proximal nail fold for diagnosis of collagen vascular disorder.

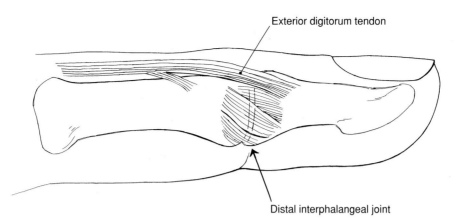

Exterior digitorum tendon

Distal interphalangeal joint

FIG. 9. Insertion of extensor digitorum communis tendon to distal interphalangeal joint.

neath the proximal nail fold and then remove. Make a longitudinal incision beginning 3 mm distal to the nail bed and extending proximally to a point on the nail fold 10 mm above the cuticle. Extend the next incision from the proximal nail fold through the lateral nail fold, and intersect the origin of the first incision. Extend all incisions down to periosteum. The excised tissue should include part of the nail bed, nail groove, proximal nail fold, and lateral nail wall. Suture the intact lateral nail fold to the nail plate with 4.0 nylon sutures.

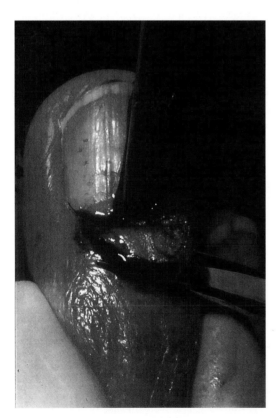

FIG. 10. Excision of proximal nail fold to remove myxoid cyst.

Nail Plate Debridement

Chemical Technique

Use chemical or nonsurgical destruction of the nail plate in the treatment of symptomatic, dystrophic nails in patients in whom poor wound healing or postoperative infection may occur, or in those who refuse nail avulsion. Use chemicals also to expose the underlying normal nail unit to therapeutic agents in the treatment of onychomycosis or hypertrophic, psoriatic nails. The most commonly known agent is urea ointment, which contains 40% urea, 5% beeswax, 20% lanolin, 25% petrolatum, and a 10% silica gel and has a shelf life of 4 months. Urea acts to soften the dystrophic nail plate and leave the normal nail intact. A salicylic acid and urea mixture is useful in the destruction of painful, dystrophic nails.

It is important to protect the surrounding skin and keep the paste on the nail. One technique is to fold a sheet of adhesive felt in half, cut a hole out for the nail plate, and apply the felt to the skin surrounding the nail plate. Apply a waterproof, hypoallergenic tape over the paste, and keep the area dry for several days. Then remove the dressing and paste and debride the nail. Following clinical debridement, treat onychomycotic nails with twice-daily applications of topical antifungal agents. Treat psoriatic nail beds with topical steroids or calcipotriol, or both.

Mechanical Technique

Use the mechanical technique as a palliative for symptomatic onychauxis, onychogryphosis, or any other hypertrophic nail dystrophy. Double-action nippers cause less pain in cutting extremely thickened nails. Carefully use a dermabrasion hand engine, a hand drill, or an air-powered drill to sand the surfaces of very thick nails. It is advisable that both physician and patient protect themselves from the nail dust by wearing masks or protective goggles. Use of a variable-speed drill prevents both the generation of thermal energy and possible injury to the matrix or nail bed and the pain caused by a high-speed drill.

Treatment of Acute Injuries

Subungual Hematoma

Subungual hematomas result from blunt injury to the vascular nail bed. The subungual collection of blood produces pressure on the periosteum, often causing intense pain. Decompress hematomas with greater than 25% nail involvement. Direct a heated needle, paper clip, or electrocautery in a perpendicular fashion to the nail over the hematoma and apply slow, steady pressure. Upon removal of the trephine, evacuate the hematoma for immediate pain relief. Make radiographs when subungual hematoma involves more than 50% of the nail; explore the nail bed if a fracture is evident. In such cases, after appropriate anesthesia, avulse the nail and repair lacerations larger than 2 to 3 mm with fine absorbable sutures. Suture the avulsed nail plate to the lateral nail folds. Administer systemic antibiotics and tetanus prophylaxis following trephination over a fractured distal phalanx or after possibly contaminated crush injuries.

Lacerations

Simple Lacerations

Superficial lacerations of the nail bed or lateral nail folds heal after application of the edges with tape or sutures. Repair lacerations larger than 3 mm. Avulse the nail plate proximal to the laceration, and close the nail plate with 5.0 or 6.0 absorbable, interrupted nylon sutures.

Complex Lacerations

Involvement of the proximal nail fold and germinal matrix can occur with complex lacerations and nail dystrophies, and deformities can occur following such injuries. Remove the nail plate for inspection of the matrix. Restore the matrix using 5.0 or 6.0 absorbable sutures and the proximal nail fold with 5.0 nylon sutures.

Treatment of Benign Tumors

Verrucae

Electrosurgical Treatment

Most warts respond to cryotherapy. Periungual and subungual verrucae, however, tend to be very destructive and often require surgical intervention. Following local anesthesia and removal of as much nail plate as is needed for visualization, apply saline-soaked gauze the affected digit and leave on for 5 to 10 minutes so that moisture hydrates the lesion and

thereby facilitates tissue vaporization. Apply the electrosurgery tip to the verruca until the tissue "bubbles." Use a curet to remove the dead tissue, and attend to any capillary bleeding with light electrodesiccation, aluminum chloride, or application of Gelfoam pads. Healing by secondary intention without scarring occurs in 3 to 4 weeks.

Carbon Dioxide Laser Treatment (see Chapter 23)

Using local anesthesia, vaporize the verruca with a carbon dioxide laser. Treat subungual warts by vaporizing through the nail plate directly and continuing until the involved area is destroyed. It is important to avoid thermal damage to the underlying bony phalanx and surrounding soft tissue.

Mucous Cysts

Mucous cysts are dome-shaped, translucent nodules that compress the nail matrix and cause various dystrophies. Those over the distal interphalangeal joint may be connected to the underlying joint space. Those located at the proximal nail fold may be due to overproduction of hyaluronic acid by local fibroblasts. If intralesional corticosteroids or cryotherapy fails, en bloc excision of the proximal nail fold including the cyst has been successful, as previously detailed.

Glomus Tumor

Approximately 75% of glomus tumors occur in the hand, often in the subungual region. On clinical examination, they appear as a small, blue-red spot seen through the nail plate and are extremely painful on compression or cold exposure. Remove small tumors by making a small hole through the nail plate over the tumor; incise the affected nail bed and enucleate the lesion from its capsule. With larger tumors, remove the nail, incise and elevate the matrix, excise the tumor, and reapproximate the matrix.

Pyogenic Granuloma and Fibroadenoma

Less frequently found benign tumors of the nail include pyogenic granuloma and fibroadenoma. The former may occur following minor trauma with implantation dermal and epidermal elements into subcutaneous tissue and is best excised. A variety of fibroadenomas may occur in the periungual-subungual area and may be locally resected with nail bed reconstruction.

Treatment of Malignant Tumors: Mohs Surgery

Bowen's disease and invasive squamous cell carcinoma of the nail unit usually do not metastasize. Once a radiograph has ruled out bone involvement, use Mohs' tissue-sparing surgery instead of amputation. Use the fresh-tissue technique, which eliminates the use of a zinc paste (see Chapter 25).

POSTOPERATIVE MANAGEMENT

Instructions

Preprinted instructions educate patients in basic home care and provide information on how to obtain aid, should problems occur after office hours. To reduce edema and pain, patients should be instructed to elevate the affected digit and extremity for 48 hours postoperatively. Oral acetaminophen, codeine, and nonsteroidal antiinflammatories may be used for pain control.

Dressings

To secure hemostasis, gelatin sponges (Gelfoam) or collagen matrix sponges (Instat or Helistat) are effective. Iodoform gauze strips packed beneath the nail folds also stop bleeding. Since Monsel's solution may cause a tattoo effect that can affect future histopathologic features of the site, it should be avoided. Minor surgical procedures such as a punch biopsy of the nail unit require merely wound cleansing with dilute hydrogen peroxide, application of an antibiotic ointment, and a simple adhesive dressing that can be changed daily until there is no further exudation from the wound. This minimizes the collection of serosanguinous bacterial growth medium.

More extensive procedures can be treated with the application of antibiotic ointment and covered with a Telfa dressing. This in turn may be secured by the longitudinal placement of paper tape. Circumferential wrapping of the digit may act as a constricting band and must therefore be avoided. Several layers of X-span tubing or Surgitube are then applied and secured with paper tape. Use of an orthopedic Reese or Zimmer boot provides additional protection or immobilization if necessary.

Antibiotics

Following possibly contaminated crush injuries or trephination over a fractured distal phalanx, both systemic antibiotics and tetanus prophylaxis are advised. Most nail surgery, however, does not necessitate systemic antibiotic use.

ADVERSE SEQUELAE AND COMPLICATIONS

Acute Complications

Bleeding

In simple procedures such as nail avulsion or biopsy, hemostasis can be controlled by the use of a Penrose drain as a tourniquet or the application of pressure to the lateral digital arteries. An exsanguinating tourniquet can be made with a surgical glove: cut across the rubber on the involved finger, and roll the glove down the finger. Oxidized cellulose (Gelfoam) or aluminum chloride may also be used for hemostasis.

Infection

When infection is present, the organism should be cultured and treated with antibiotics and antiseptic soaks. Postoperative surgical infection has significant morbidity in the distal phalanx, including felon, compartmental cellulitis, lymphangitis, and osteomyelitis.

Necrosis

Necrosis can occur when sutures are placed too tightly and are not removed at the appropriate time.

Chronic Complications

Disfigurement

If crush injuries are not adequately repaired, small pieces of subungual tissue may grow independently, causing nail horns or spicules that require removal. Nail deformities may occur following the evacuation of subungual hematoma by drilling the nail plate and by the rough removal of the nail to expose the bed. Polyglactin 910 (Vicryl) sutures used for nail bed repair may, if too large, dissolve very slowly and affect new nail growth, causing onycholysis and nail ridging.

Miscellaneous Complications

Reflex sympathetic dystrophy has occurred following the biopsy of a nail bed.

SUGGESTED READING LIST

1. Albom MJ: Squamous cell carcinoma of the finger and nail bed: a review of the literature and treatment by Mohs surgical technique. J Dermatol Surg Oncol 1975;1:43.
2. Baran R, Haneke E. Surgery of the nail. In: Epstein E, Epstein E Jr, eds. Skin surgery. 6th ed. Philadelphia: WB Saunders, 1987.
3. Clark RE, Tope WD. Nail surgery. In: Wheeland RG. Cutaneous surgery. Philadelphia: WB Saunders, 1994.
4. Herndon JH, Myers SR, Akelman E. In Scher RK, Daniel CR. Nails: therapy, diagnosis, surgery. 2nd ed. Philadelphia: WB Saunders, 1997 pp. 350–362.
5. McBurney EI, Rosen DA: Carbon dioxide laser treatment of verrucae vulgaris. J Dermatol Surg Oncol 1984;10:45.
6. Miller PK, Roenigk RK: Diagnostic and therapeutic nail surgery. J Dermatol Surg Oncol 1991;17:674.
7. Mohs FE: Chemosurgery in cancer, gangrene and infections. Charles C. Thomas: Springfield, IL, 1978:131.
8. Monheit GD. Nail surgery. Dermatol Clin 1985;3(3):521.
9. Salasche SJ. Myxoid cysts of the proximal nail fold: a surgical approach. J Dermatol Surg Oncol 1984;10:35.

10. Salasche SJ, Peters V. Tips on nail surgery. Cutis 1984;35:428.
11. Salasche SJ. Surgery. In Scher RK, Daniel CR. Nails: therapy, diagnosis, surgery. 2nd ed. Philadelphia: WB Saunders, 1997, pp. 326–349.
12. Scher RK. Biopsy of the matrix of the nail. J Dermatol Surg Oncol 1980;6:19.
13. Scher RK. Longitudinal resection of nails for purposes of biopsy and treatment. J Dermatol Surg Oncol 1980;6:805.
14. Scher RK. Nail surgery. Clin Dermatol 1987;5:135.
15. Scher RK. Punch biopsies of the nail: a simple valuable procedure. J Dermatol Surg Oncol 1978;4:528.
16. Scher RK. Surgery of the nails. In Epstein E, Epstein E Jr, eds. Techniques in skin surgery. Philadelphia: Lea & Febiger, 1979.
17. Scher RK. Surgical avulsion of nail plates by a proximal to distal technique. J Dermatol Surg Oncol 1981;7:296.
18. Seigle RJ, Harkness JJ, Swanson NA. The phenol alcohol technique for permanent matricectomy. Arch Dermatol 1984;120:348.
19. Seigle RJ, Swanson NA. Nail surgery: a review. J Dermatol Surg Oncol 1982;8:659.
20. Tom D, Scher R. Melanonychia striata in longitudinum. Am J Dermatopathol 1985;7:161.

SUBJECT INDEX